1981 Edition
Bud Hastin's

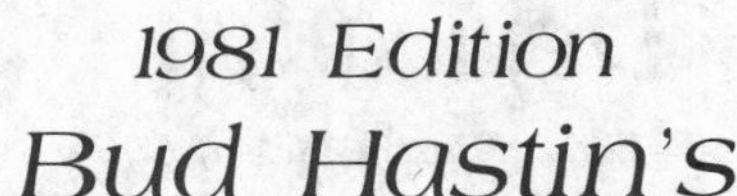

AVON BOTTLE ENCYCLOPEDIA™

The Official Avon Collector's Guide 8th Edition

Written, photographed and researched by
Bud & Vickie Hastin

Bud & Vickie Hastin are in no way responsible for buying, selling or trading Avon bottles at the prices quoted in this guide book. It is published only as a guide and prices vary from state to state as much as 50%. Most prices quoted are top prices in mint condition and it is not uncommon for prices to be quoted differently, usually being lower. Bud Hastin does not solicit Avon bottles to buy or sell.

The 1981 Bud Hastin's Avon Bottle Encyclopedia$_{TM}$ is recognized by the National Association of Avon Clubs as the only official and most complete collector's guide in print.

Dedication

This book is dedicated to my father, Wilbur Hastin, Sr., of Butler, MO. It was through his efforts that I became a bottle collector myself, many years ago, and his encouragement to always strive to do and be the best at everything in life has led me to where and what I am today.

It was through his love and encouragement, to me as a child, to do my best (and believe me it took a lot of years to sink in), that now gives me the patience and drive to make this Avon Encyclopedia the best book possible on Avon collecting.

I love you Dad. I hope all sons can say they had a Dad as good as you!

ACKNOWLEDGEMENTS AND CREDITS

Bud Hastin personally thanks all the Avon collectors across the nation who have permitted him to photograph their collections to update this book. Much credit goes to all the following people for their assistance and help, be it big or small. For without them there would never have been an Avon Encyclopedia.

Jo Olsen, MI
James Hackney, IL
Ruth Hershberger, Canada
Dick Kovac, CA
Gene Boyd, CA
Darlene Faulkner, CA
Maynard Watson, CA
Bud & Rosilund Hoover, OR
Gerardo Diaz, TX
Sara June Lloyd, CA
James Puckett, GA
Velva Faulkner, CA
George Gaspar, IL
Ray Potter, IL
Whitey Collins, TX
Alice Brown, NJ
Ed Bea, Sr., NJ
Mary Rose Brown, OK
Garnett Harter, IN
Jerry Graham, IA
Grace Powers, GA
Del Fultz, AR
Joan Beckler, CA
Eleanor Hutchinson, MO
Renee Streisant, NY
Marcella Latoof, NJ
Ron and Mary Tyson, CA
Bob Rix, AR
Dick & Beverly Pardini, CA
Dwight & Vera Young, KA
Beverly Bonfert, CA
Elmo Bennett, CA
Nola Murdock, CA
Opal Fry, AR
Florence Lewis, OR
Ray & Ralphi Lintz, CA
Barbara Spann, CA
Dee Schneider, CA
Bob Rudolph, CA
Troy Walker, IL
Bob & Marge Augerson, CA
Leonard Talys, PA
Phyllis Smalley, OH
Donna Kott, CA
Gene Arthur, MO
Vera Shaw, WA
Robert Hardy, OH
Lola Schlining, IN
Jill Fox, CA
Daisy Gularte, CA
Mrs. Johnie Kennedy, TX
Bessie Varney, KY
Tom Smith, CA
Mike & Linda Stone, CA
Eleanor Kamie, CA
Teresa Eubanks, CA
Mrs. Lyal Witchey, OH
Ray Cobb, CA
Hazel Boseck, CA
Connie Clark, MO
Cindy Rood, CA
Tally Jones, CA
Frances Holley, CA
Della La Galt, CA
Genevieve Lewis, CA
Edna Holland, CA
Gene Boyd, CA
Forrest Fichthorn, WA
Doyle & Faye Darch, CA
Georgina Ross, CA
Mr. & Mrs. Sam Anderson, MO
Beatrice Underwood, CA
Shirley Mae Onstot, CA
Lucille Saira, CA
May Dudra, CA
Aline Hoffman, CA
Margie & Bill Hoffman, CA
Mike Sinks, IL
Carl & Veona Fisher, IA
Ann Cinquepalmi, IL
June Ladd, IN
Jenny & Jim Stanley, OH.
Vivian Riley, IL
Shirley Fairbanks, MN

Bud & Vickie Hastin

Bud Hastin was born April 24, 1939, in Butler, Missouri, to Wilbur and Velma Hastin.

He grew up in Butler, where he graduated from Butler High School in 1957. He then spent three years in the United States Air Force. Bud went into the Auto Glass business in 1964 and sold Mobile Auto Glass of Kansas City in 1971, to devote full time to preparing Avon Guides for the collector. Bud met his wife Vickie in 1975 when they immediately became a good working team and have been working together as a team since.

Bud says his father is responsible for getting him interested in the bottle hobby when someone gave him some fancy cut glass bottles and Bud liked them so much that he started collecting.

The Avon hobby as a whole, covers a tremendous volume of material. Avon collectables include bottles, tin containers, plastic containers, jars, soaps, samples, candles, jewelry, plates, trays, needlecraft, prizes, catalogs, magazine advertisements, Outlooks, and many more. There is far too much to collect for the average person to work on all catagories.

No. 1 Rule of Avon Collecting: "Set a goal for your hobby and collect only what you want to collect. You rule the hobby, it doesn't rule you. Decide what part of the overall hobby appeals to you, set your goal and work hard toward that goal. Ask yourself some questions. How much room do I have? How much can I spend each month? What do I enjoy most about Avon Collecting? Base your goal on the answers.

Since 1969 Bud has sold over 500,000 copies of his Avon Collectors book. This book is the 13th book on Avon collecting by Bud Hastin. The first, being sold in 1969, was the Avon Collectors Guide, Vol. I, then followed the 1970 Avon Collectors Guide Vol. II, the 1971 Avon Encyclopedia, the 1971 Avon Collectors Guide for Beginners, the 1972 Avon Encyclopedia, the 1972 Avon Beginners Guide, the 1974 Avon Encyclopedia, and the Avon Encyclopedia special hardbound edition for collectors. Only 1,000 were printed and each was signed by Bud.

The 1976-77 Avon Encyclopedia – There were 500 hardbound copies of the 1976 Avon Encyclopedia. The 1979 Avon Encyclopedia – There were 350 special hardbound collectors editions on 1979 Encyclopedia.

Many people are starting to collect the older Avon books published by Bud.

Bud and Vickie traveled the world gathering information on Avon collecting. From these

1969

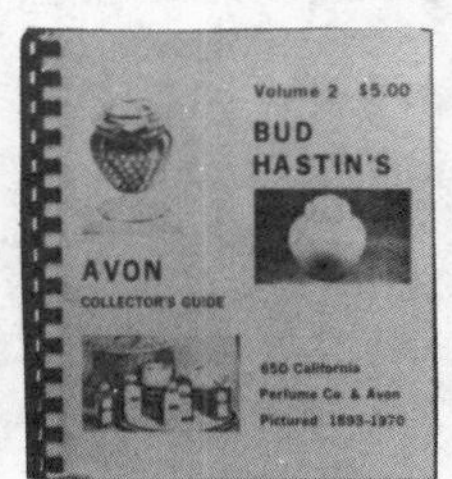

1970

1971

1971

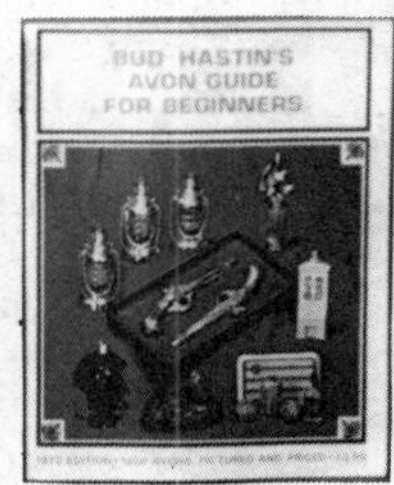

1972

1972

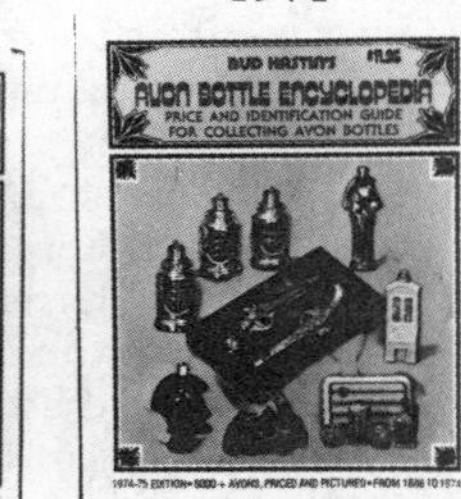

1974

1976

1979

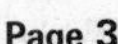

travels they have added a Foreign Avon section to this book.

Bud's personal views on Avon collecting are: "I think the Avon collecting hobby is the best hobby around today. It is one of the few hobbies that you will probably never find all of them and that's what collecting is all about, the challenge to find something you don't have. The thrill is finding a high priced Avon bottle in a flea market or garage sale for a low price. You see very few Avon collections the same and this always makes the challenge greater to find the one that your friend has. Avon collecting is one of the biggest hobbies in the U.S. I wonder how many of the old and rare C.P.C. and Avon bottles are lying around in sombodies attics and cellars just waiting to be discovered by some informed collector? Garage sales, rummage sales, etc. are the gold fields and it is almost as big a thrill to find a $100.00 C.P.C. as it was for the treasure hunters of old to find gold. Avon collecting is for all ages, both young and old. It's a hobby for the entire family."

NATIONAL ASSOCIATION OF AVON CLUBS

Bud is Chairman of the Board of the National Association of Avon Clubs, and was the founder of the National Organization in 1971. The N.A.A.C. is not a club, but an organization to help promote Avon collecting in the United States. The N.A.A.C. is run by an elected board of Directors. The N.A.A.C. is ready to help anyone start a new Avon collectors club in your area. For information on starting a new Avon Club, write to N.A.A.C. in care of Bud Hastin and we will see that all N.A.A.C. material is sent to you. At present there are 150 active Avon Clubs in the N.A.A.C. A National Convention is held each year along with a National Bottle Show. Each year it is held in a different section of the U.S. The N.A.A.C. is a non-profit organization and financed by the sale of the N.A.A.C. club bottle each year. See the N.A.A.C. section of this book for N.A.A.C. Club Bottles. These club bottles are very limited editions and have skyrocketed in price after they are released. Profits from the sale of the club bottles are used to send a delegate from the member clubs to the National Convention each year.

HELPFUL HINTS & MEANING OF TERMS

The 1981 Avon Encyclopedia has been compiled by Bud and Vickie Hastin. To best understand this book and its contents, please read this before starting through the book.

All items from 1929 to 1980 will give the first year and the last year date that the items were sold by the Avon Company. Dates will read, for instance, 1930 - 36. This means this item was introduced sometime in 1930 and was discontinued for the last time in 1936. Dates like 1970-71 mean the item sold in both years, but is very possible it sold for less than one year selling time. An item dated for three years like 1958 - 60 means it sold in all three years, but could have only been on the market for a period of about two years total time. All items dated 1886 to 1928 mean the first and last year sold. All dates from 1929 to 1980 with only one year given means this item was sold during that one year only and usually for a very short period. These items are usually considered a short-issue and hard to find.

O.S.P. means Original Selling Price. This is the full value price Avon puts on an item. It does not represent a special selling price which is from 20% to 50% off the O.S.P. The O.S.P. is given on all items in this book. **S.S.P.** means Special Selling Price (reduced in price). The O.S.P. or S.S.P. price may vary as Avon may have put a different special selling price each time it was offered and the O.S.P, may have been changed from the time it was introduced to the time it was taken off the market because of rising cost to make the product. Prices quoted are just to give you an idea of what the item sold for from Avon.

C.M.V. means Current Market Value that most collectors are willing to pay for that particular item. Many items priced in this book are priced both item only and item in box. Items in the original box need not be full. The collectors price is for an empty bottle. If it is current and full, and in the box, then you can expect to pay full retail price or the special selling price that Avon sells this item for. Only after Avon stops selling the item and it has been placed on the annual discontinued list Avon prints each year of items that will not be offered for sale again on its original design, will Avon be considered as a Collectors item and the value could start to increase.

B.O. means bottle only (mint), no box. **M.B.** means mint and boxed in perfect condition.

All Avon tubes priced in this book are for full mint condition tubes. If a tooth paste tube or other type tube has been used then it would not be mint. Tubes and soaps are the only items in this book that have to be full to be mint condition. Most all other items are priced empty unless otherwise stated. In most cases all older items will bring as much empty as they would full.

This book has been compiled from original CPC and Avon Catalogs, Original California Perfume Company catalogs used in the 1981 Avon Encyclopedia have been copied completely and all items pictured in these original catalogs are pictured in the book. The CPC was used from the years 1896 through 1929. From 1916 to 1929 the CPC sales catalogs were black leather type covers. 1916 to 1920 these books were hard bound. 1921 to 1929 the same size books were soft cover bound. January, 1929, was the introduction of Avon Products with the Avon name first appearing on a number of CPC Products.

The CPC sales catalogs 1896 to 1906 were smaller booklet type with soft covers measuring 6 5/8" x 4 3/4". The 1908 booklet is also a soft booklet measuring 4 1/8" x 8". The 1915 booklet is the last of the small sales catalogs before the large black books in color were issued in 1916. The 1915 book is dated and measures 4" x 7 1/8". 1930 through 1935 the Avon sales catalogs had CPC/Avon Products in them in a 6 3/4" x 10" dark blue soft cover book. 1936 through 1957 the sales catalogs are the same size only with a green cover.

An entire set of Avon sales catalogs from 1930 to 1980 were used to compile the Avon Encyclopedia. Almost a complete set of Avon Sales Outlooks from 1905 to 1980 were also used. Special Christmas sales catalogs from 1934 to 1980 were also used showing many special sets sold only at Christmas time each year. Some of the CPC and Avon catalogs and Outlooks were borrowed, so we would like to complete our own file on these original books and catalogs. If you have any of the old catalogs both regular or special sales catalogs or Outlooks, write to Bud Hastin, P.O. Box 8400, Ft. Lauderdale, FL 33310, as I am always trying to buy these books to help keep you, the collector, up to date on the true facts about your hobby. I only want catalogs 1947 or older.

GRADING CONDITIONS OF AVONS

People have asked me **WHAT A BOTTLE IS WORTH WITHOUT A LABEL.** If it is an old bottle where the label is the main thing that identifies the bottle and it is missing, then it's worth whatever you can get, which is usually not too much. If it is a newer figural bottle, then it will usually take a few dollars off the price.

MINT CONDITION means items must be in new condition as originally sold, with all labels bright and correct, and cap and/or stopper. Items need not be full or boxed, but will bring a higher price in most cases if they are in the box. All items in the book are priced empty in mint condition only with right cap and all labels. Bottles with no cap or label are of little or no value.

GRADING EXAMPLES

1969-73 Gold Cadillac. . . Chipped paint, deduct 50% from CMV

1966-67 Casey's Lantern. Chipped paint, broken bail ears, deduct 70% from CMV

1971 French Telephone . . Gold chip on handle, deduct 10-40% CMV, label off handle, deduct 40% CMV

1961-63 Cotillion Cologne .Cap turning grey,deduct 25-50% CMV, lettering faint

1947-56 Golden Promise Cologne . . . . Letters or printing gone, deduct 20-80% CMV. Gold off cap, deduct 20-40% CMV

1948-50 Quaintance Perfume . . Letters gone on printing, deduct 20-80% CMV

1963 Topaze Perfume Oil for Bath . . . . . Letters fading on printing, deduct 30-50% CMV

1958 "Old 99" Soap . . . . Chip on soap, deduct 40% CMV. Box torn, deduct 10-50% CMV

1961-62 Avon Slugger. . Crack in handle, deduct 20-60% CMV

1896-1908 French Perfume. . Torn or damaged label, deduct 10-50% CMV

CPC bottles may have the same shape but with different labels. Be sure to check labels and boxes to get the right date on your bottles.

All items are dated in this book from actual old Avon catalogs I have in my possession. Most of the CPC items in this book dated 1896 are probably some of the original 1886 to 1896 items. They did not change the bottles for many years in the early days of CPC. 1896 was the first year a CPC catalog was printed.

TO BUY AND SELL AVONS. Garage sales, flea markets antique shops, bottle shops are the best places to buy and sell Avon bottles locally. To sell Avons in your own town, place a small ad in you local paper and say Avon bottles for sale with your address or phone number. Have a garage sale and put Avon bottles on your sign. People will come to you. If you have no luck locally, then **Bud Hastin's National Avon Club magazine, The Avon Times, is the number one spot in the U.S. to sell those extra Avons.** The National Avon Club is the largest in the world and Avon ads get the best result anywhere. Write Bud Hastin, P.O. Box 8400, Ft. Lauderdale, FL 33310, for a sample copy of this club magazine. Send 20c in stamps to cover postage.

IF A SET HAS THE BOTTLE MISSING, look up the individual bottle in this book to determine the price to deduct.

There are several reasons for pricing all items empty. After Shave bottles are known to explode in sunlight or heat. Full bottles sitting on glass shelves increase the chance of the shelves breaking. After a few years, the contents become spoiled or unsafe to skin and dangerous in the hands of children. I feel if you buy the item new, use the contents and you will still have the pretty bottles.

Several people ask about **INSURANCE ON BOTTLE COLLECTIONS.** Bottle insurance is available through your home owners policy. Check with your local agent.

EVERY ITEM IN THIS BOOK IS GLASS UNLESS OTHERWISE STATED. Bottles will differ in color shades due to various dates in manufacture. It is difficult to get exactly the same color each time. Unless a bottle comes out in a completely different color, it will be of the same value.

THE SILVER METAL SALT & PEPPER SHAKERS WITH AVON PAT. DATE 1927 - 1928, is not Avon Cosmetic Co. items. **THE AVON NAME WAS NOT USED UNTIL 1929.** The name Avon has been used by several companies and still is. Only the name Avon Products Incorporated is copyrighted.

IF YOU ARE AN AVON SALESLADY, AND WOULD LIKE TO SELL THIS BOOK TO YOUR CUSTOMERS, see volume prices in back of book or write Bud Hastin, P.O. Box 8400, Ft. Lauderdale, FL 33310.

I WILL BUY ANY CALIFORNIA PERFUME COMPANY SALES CATALOG, 1929 or older in good condition. I will buy any different, complete Avon salesbook for 1947 or earlier. Please write to me before you send them.

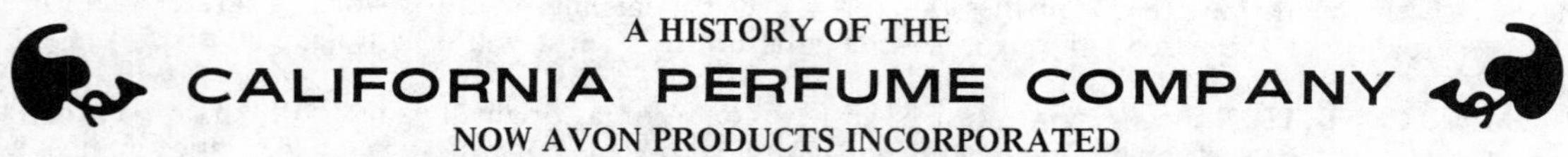

A HISTORY OF THE CALIFORNIA PERFUME COMPANY
NOW AVON PRODUCTS INCORPORATED
WRITTEN BY THE FOUNDER D.H. McCONNELL, SR., IN 1903

To give you a sketch or history of the birth and growth of the *California Perfume Company is, in a measure, like writing an autobiography. Our lives have become so identical and so interwoven that it seems almost impossible to separate us, even in history. I will ask, you therefore, to pardon whatever personal reference I may make of myself in describing to you how the California Perfume Company has become the largest of its kind, not only in the United States, but I believe, in the entire world.

In 1878, when but a mere lad, I left my father's farm located near Oswego City, New York State. Here I spent my boyhood days, and through hard work and proper training developed a good, strong, hardy, rugged constitution. When I started out in the world "to make my fortune", I had this positive advantage over many who were less favored.

My first experience in the business world was as a book agent. I took this up during my school vacation, and developed quite a faculty for talking, which I have since learned is quite essential, and has stood me well in hand many times.

My success in canvassing was such as to invite me into the same field the following year, and after two years hard work in the canvass, I was promoted from local canvasser to that of General Traveling Agent. As General Agent I traveled in nearly every state east of the Rocky Mountains; this gave me a valuable knowledge regarding the country. And my experience, both as canvasser and as General Agent, gave me a good insight into human nature.

It is uninteresting to you to follow me through the different work from Chicago to New York and from New York to Atlanta, Georgia, and back to Chicago, and finally, back to New York. During all these years I represented in different ways the same publishing company with which I originally started as a canvasser;

canvassing, appointing and drilling agents; starting and drilling General Agents, and corresponding with both after they once entered the field. My work as a canvasser and on the road taught me not to enter right into the everyday work of the canvasser and advise and encourage, so as to obtain the best results. If I learned to be anything, I learned to be practical.

The book business was not congenial to me, although I was, in every sense, successful in it, but there were many things that were not pleasant.

On my return from Chicago, I purchased the entire business from my employer and managed it myself for sometime. During this time the one thing I learned successfully was how to sell goods to the consumer.

My ambition was to manufacture a line of goods that would be consumed, used up, and to sell it through canvassing agents, direct from the factory to the consumer.

The starting of the perfume business was the result of most careful and thorough investigation, guided by the experience of several years successful operation in the book business. That is, in selling goods direct to the consumer or purchaser. I learned during this time that the proper and most advantageous way of selling goods was to be able to submit the goods themselves to the people. In investigating this matter nearly every line of business was gone over, and it seemed to me, then, as it has since been proved, that the perfume business in its different branches afforded the very best possible opportunity to build up a permanent and well-established trade. Having once decided that the perfume business was the business, the question naturally presented itself, "By what name are these perfumes to be known: by what name is this company to be called?" The gentleman who took me from the farm as a boy became in the past years, not only my employer but my personal friend, and after buying him out he moved to California, and while there wrote me glowing accounts of the country, and to him belongs the idea of the name California, as associated with this business.

I started the perfume business in a space scarcely larger than an ordinary kitchen pantry. At first I manufactured but five odors: Violet, White Rose, Heliotrope, Lily-of-the-Valley and Hyacinth. I did much experimental work in making these odors, and the selling price to the first batch of perfumes I made did not cover one-half the actual cost of the goods, but experience is a great teacher, and I applied myself to the task of making perfumes with the same vim and energy that I had in selling books, and after a short time, I fancied that I could produce as fine an odor as some of the old and tried perfumes. At least my perfumes pleased my customers; they were the natural perfumes of the flower, made in the most natural way and by the process employed by the large French perfumers.

Continued on next page . . .

Avon Calling

The phrase "Avon Calling" rings 'round the world as the signature of a firm devoted to the manufacture and sales of high quality cosmetic and toiletry items for all members of the family.

From its start in 1886, as the California Perfume Company, Avon has grown steadily, expanding its operation throughout the world. Today fourteen manufacturing laboratories and twenty five distribution branches, all using the most modern and efficient equipment and all staffed by well trained and experienced employees, produce a vast variety of ever changing, imaginative products.

The Avon Representative, focal point of the company, employs the oldest method of distribution in the world . . . direct-to-the-home selling. This means she brings the latest news in beauty and grooming, the finest products, and the most personal kind of service directly to her customers in their homes.

Avon's growth from a one room laboratory in downtown New York to the current world-wide network of manufacturing laboratories and distribution branches is a success story based on quality . . . quality of product, quality of service, quality of relationships with people.

Avon is the world's largest manufacturere and distributor of cosmetics, fragrances and costume jewelry. Its products are sold by more than 1,200,000 active Representatives to customers in the home in the United States and 30 other countries. Plus their products are sold in almost every country of the world.

I soon found it necessary to increase the odors, and to add to the line other articles for the toilet. Among those first put out were: Shampoo Cream, Witch Hazel Cream, Almond Cream Balm, Tooth Paste, which afterwards was made in the Tooth Tablet, Toilet Waters, etc.

As the business increased the laboratory must, of necessity grow, so that at the end of two years I was occupying one entire floor in this building for manufacturing purposes alone.

It is perhaps unfair to note the progress of one side of the business without carrying with it the natural development on the other.

My ambition was to manufacture a line of goods superior to any other, to be moneyed value into the good themselves, and just enough money in the package to make them respectable, and as stated above, take these goods through canvassing agents direct from the laboratory to the consumer.

Mrs. P. F. E. Albee
First CPC Avon Representative

While in the book business I had in my employ, as *General Traveling Agent, a Mrs. P.F.E. Albee, of Winchester, N.H. Mrs. Albee was one of the most successful General Agents I had in the book work, and it was in her hands I placed the first sample case, or outfit, in the perfume business. Mrs. Albee was the only General Agent employed for the first six months of the business. During that time she secured a number of good workers, some of whom are with us today. It is, therefore, only befitting that we give her the honorary title of Mother of the California Perfume Company. For the system that we now use for distributing our goods is the system that was put in practical operation by Mrs. Albee.

As the business grew, through the work of our agents, we were forced from time to time to increase our laboratory space, and in 1895 we built our own laboratory in Suffern, New York, 32 miles out on the main line of the Erie Railroad. This building has been enlarged and remodeled three different times, until today we have a building 120 feet long, main building 50 feet wide and the wing 30 feet, all three stories and basement giving us four working floors, each floor having 4,800 square feet of floor space, or a total floor capacity of 17,200 feet. This building is equiped with the best possible machinery, the latest devices for bottling goods and son on, until I feel we can truthfully say that there is not a plant of our kind in the country so large and so well fitted for our business, as the laboratory of the California Perfume Company.

As well directed efforts and hard work must eventually win their way to the front, so the manufacturing end of the California Perfume Company grew out of my hands; that is to say, I found that it was almost impossible for me to manufacture, to give the personal attention to both manufacturing and correspondence which the merits of each required. Therefore, in 1896, I secured the services of the best perfumer I could find, a gnetleman who had been in the perfume business himself for 25 years and had the reputation in New York and vicinity for making the finest perfumes on the American market. In order to secure his services I was obliged to buy out his business and close up his laboratory, and he now has full charge of the manufacturing of every ounce of goods that we put out.

My object in locating the laboratory at Suffern was that as Suffern is my home I can give much more personal attention and supervision to the affairs of the laboratory than if it was located in New York. So that every day in the year, unless when I am out on one of my trips, visiting agents and general agents, I am at the laboratory every morning, and spend an hour with our chemist, going over his work and see that every ounce of goods, every package in every department is made and put up in the best possible shape.

Contrast, if you please, the appearance of our office today with that of when Mrs. Albee first started out with the California Perfume Company's goods. Then, I had one stenographer, and I myself filled the position of correspondent, cashier, bookkeeper, shipping clerk and office boy, and manufacturing chemist. Today we have on our weekly payroll over 125 employees. Mrs. Albee for the first six months was the only general agent on the road. Today we have 48 general agents traveling over this country and selecting and drilling agents for this work. The first six months we had perhaps 100 agents in the field, today we have over 10,000 good, honest, industrious and energetic Depot Managers. All of you have your own customers, so that it is difficult to accurately estimate today the vast number of families that are using our goods. If each of you have 100 customers, or sell goods to only one different families, we are supplying goods to at least one million families in the United States. This will give you an idea of the magnitude of our business. The growth of the California Perfume Company only emphasizes what energy and fair dealings with everyone can accomplish. We propose first to be fair and our customers – your customers – by giving them the very best goods that can be made for the money. We propose to be fair and just, even liberal, with you who form the bone and sinew of our business.

Avon Representatives in the early days of the California Perfume Company were called Agents or Depot Managers.

A BRIEF NARRATIVE OF THE ROMANCE, EARLY STRUGGLES AND SUCCESS TO DATE OF

Mr. & Mrs. D. H. McConnell

Miss Lucy Hays and David H. McConnell were introduced to each other by mutual friends, when Mr. McConnell was in Chicago on business. They fell in love and were quietly married at the home of Miss Hays' sister. Mr. McConnell brought his bride back east with him.

Even then, Mr. McConnell was developing a plan of business that would better serve the customer and give profitable employment to many women. There was no guaranteed merchandise then, and he saw many untrained women left on their own resources with families to support with no means of earning money.

At this time, Mr. and Mrs. McConnel were living in Brooklyn. He opened a combined office, laboratory and shipping room in down town New York. Mrs. McConnel spent much time with him, helping him in many ways. From the first the business grew.

They both preferred living in the country, and a friend told them of the beautiful little town of Suffern.

They located a house they liked and bought it. They also bought a building for the first factory, and moved to Suffern.

Meantime, three children were born; Edna, Doris, and David, Jr. The children have all grown up now and have homes and children of their own. The factory is many times larger, a modern, up-to-date plant. Edna married a brillant young engineer and chemist, Mr. W. Van Allen Clark. Some years ago, Mr. McConnell persuaded him to come in with him, and he is now Vice President in charge of the factory. They live in Suffern. Doris lives in Connecticut with her family, not far from Suffern. David, Jr. and his family also live in Suffern, and he is now Executive Vice President of the company.

This very briefly covers the 51 years of married life of our President and his wife, and the growth of the company. They are more than usually interwoven, as you see. They both know many of the Representatives, Supervisors and employees. Their success is your success, your success is theirs. They are heart and mind with you, and always have been. That is why the Committee knows that the success of this campaign you yourselves have planned ,and will carry out to a glorious conclusion will so please them. Your loyalty, and interest, and good work will mean more to them than anything else possibly could.

AVON MISCELLANEA

EARLY DAYS

In June, 1886, the California Perfume Company was incorporated and started selling "The Little Dot" perfume set, which contained three bottles of perfume. The company's name suggest a likely California beginning, but it has no such meaning; the manufacturing, shipping, and office work in the beginning was done at 126 Chambers St, New York City. The name followed a suggestion made by a friend of Mr. McConnel's who had just visited California and returned to New York greatly enthused over the gorgeous flowers he had seen there. Since only perfumes were being sold, he suggested that the name of the company be "The California Perfume Company".

A LARGE LINE

By 1915 we had a large line. Our products were well and favorably known among our customers, but were not known to the public at large. No advertising was done. The customers told their friends about these splendid products and the CPC Representatives' service. From the beginning all products were sold under the CPC trademark. All were offered to customers by Representatives (our products have never been sold through stores) and, always the products were unconditionally guaranteed. This was most unusual in the early days.

THE PANAMA PACIFIC EXPOSITION

We were invited to exhibit at the Panama Pacific Exposition in San Francisco in 1914 - 1915. This was a World's Fair, and prizes were given for the best articles exhibited in various classifications. Our entire line of perfumes, toilet articles and household products was entered in competition with like products from all over the world, and were awarded the Gold Medal, both for the quality of the products, and the beauty of the packages. This Gold Medal appeared on all packages until it was replaced by the seal that is recognized and followed throughout the world as a consumer's guide to the highest quality of merchandise – The Good Housekeeping Seal of Approval.

NEW NAMES – NEW PACKAGES

Through the years, our chemist were following every avenue of research, improving products wherever possible, and discovering new ones that in every way measured up to the standards of the first ones. Manufacturing methods were improved to the point that every product was the sum of perfection as to blending and handling. Then in 1929, the chemist suggested an entirely new line of cosmetics. They had it ready, the managers agreed, and the Avon line was presented to Representatives and customers. The household line was named "Perfection" and given its own trademark.

GOOD HOUSEKEEPING'S SEAL OF APPROVAL

In 1931 the first group of Avon Cosmetics were approved by Good Houskeeping, and from that time on, other groups were sent, tested, approved, and the Seal added to our packages. By 1936, our 50th Anniversary year, Good Housekeeping completed their tests and approved all Avon and Perfection products which came within their scope. All products added since that time bear the Seal of Approval.

A NEW POLICY – NATIONAL ADVERTISING

Steadily increasing business over a period of 50 years without any advertising was a remarkable record, but with the celebration of a Golden Jubilee we changed our policy and began to advertise. All during 1936 and1937, our advertisements appeared in Good Housekeeping. They are appearing now, telling the public that Avon products are unconditionally guaranteed and that our Representatives will give the Avon service. We tell readers how convenient shopping the "Avon Way" is for them.

A Calendar of Avon Years

1886
David McConnell starts the California Perfume Company, at the age of 28, in a room in downtown Manahttan. He and his wife, Lucy, create and manufacture the first product — the Little Dot Perfume Set. It is sold by the first Representative, Mrs. P.F.E. Albee, who recruits others to sell at the same time.

1894
Mr. McConnell expands to six floors in the Manhattan building.

1896
The first catalog is issued on November 2. Text only (no pictures).

1897
The first laboratory is built, a three story wooden structure in Suffern.

1902
10,000 Representatives are now selling the company's products.

1903
The first branch is opened in Kansas City, Missouri.

1905
The first Outlook is published, with news and selling tips for Representatives.

1906
The first company advertisement appears. The product: Roses perfume. The magazine: Good Housekeeping.

1912
Over 5,000,000 products are sold during this hear.

1914
A Canadian office is opened in Montreal.

1915
The company wins the Panama-Pacific International Exposition gold medal for quality and packaging.

1920
Sales reach the $1,000,000 mark.

1928
A line of new products, called "Avon" is introduced. It includes a toothbrush, cleaner and talc.

1932
Three week selling campaigns begin in August. Up to this time, Representatives have been asked to send in orders every month. As a result of the change, sales increase by over 70% during America's bleak Depression years. The first Specials also appear with products sold at less than regular prices.

1935
The company sponsors a national radio program, called "Friends", a twice weekly show of music and chatter.

1936
An important step is taken to reach customers in urban and suburban areas. Site of this experiment is the Midwest, where several cities - Kansas City, Wichita and Oklahoma City- are divided into Territories. Each Territory is to be covered by a Representative with a Manager in charge. Later, after the war, this is to become the universal Avon sales structure.

1937
The home office moves to 30 Rockefeller Plaza in New York City. David McConnell dies at age 79.

1939
On October 6, the California Perfume Company changes its name to Avon Products, Inc.

1942-45
The company joins the war effort, with over 50% of the Suffern plant converted to production for the Armed Forces. Among the items manufactured are insect repellent, pharmaceuticals, paratrooper kits and gas mask canisters.

1949
Avon now has 2,500 employees. 1,175 shareholders, 65,000 Representatives and $25 million in sales. The company has facilities in New York City, Suffern, Kansas City, Middletown, Chicago and Pasadena.

1951
The Atlanta distribution branch opens.

1952
The Newark distribution branch opens.

1954
On TV advertising, the "Ding-Dong, Avon Calling" bell is heard for the first time. Avon goes international with its entry into Puerto Rico and Venezuela.

1955
Sales brochures are introduced to support campaign selling.

1956
The Morton Grove shipping facilities open.

1959
Monrovia shipping and warehousing facilities open.

1960
The Rye branch opens.

1964
On April 2, the New York Stock Exchange starts trading Avon stock. The "advance call-back" brochure selling plan is adopted, with Representatives leaving mini-brochures at customers homes, then returning for the orders.

1965
The Springdale laboratory/distribution facilities open. A new research and development laboratory is completed in Suffern.

1968
Two week selling is introduced in the U.S. The first car decanter appears, launching our most successful decanter series.

1970
The Glenview distribution branch opens.

1971
Jewelry is first introduced in the U.S.

1972
Avon moves into new world headquarters at 9 West 57th Street in New York City. Sales top the billion-dollar mark.

AVON PRODUCTS, INC.,

9 WEST 57th STREET
NEW YORK, N.Y. 10019

1886 CPC FACTORY

1980 Avon World Headquarters (50 stories)
9 West 57th St., New York, NY

AND IN . . .

■● Suffern, NY ● Middletown, NY ●★ Morton Grove, IL ●★ Pasadena, CA ●★ Springdale, OH ★ Atlanta, GA ★ Kansas City, MO ★ Newark, DE ★ Rye, NY ★ 1914 Canada ★ 1954 Puerto Rico, Venezuela ★ 1958 Mexico ★ 1959 Germany, Brazil, United Kingdom ★ 1963 Australia, Belgium ★ 1966 France, Italy, Spain ★ 1969 Japan ★ 1970 Argentina ★ 1971 Sweden ★ 1972 Netherlands ★ 1975 Guatemala ★ 1976 Hong Kong ★ 1977 Paraguay, Malaysia, Chile ★ 1978 Thailand, New Zealand, Philippines, Ivory Coast ★ 1979 El Salvador, Uruguay, Liberia, Senegal.
NOTE: ■ National Research Laboratory ● Manufacturing Laboratories ★ Sales and Distribution Branches

1974-76 CORD '37
7 oz. yellow painted with yellow plastic cap & black plastic top. Came in Tai Winds or Wild Country After Shave. S.S.P. $7.00 CMV $7.00 MB $5.00 BO

COLLECTORS:
ALL CONTAINERS ARE PRICED EMPTY
BO means Bottle Only —empty
CMV means Current Market Value Mint
SSP means Special Selling Price
OSP means Original Selling Price
See Page 5 for Grading Examples on Mint Condition.

MEN'S DECANTERS

1975-76 TRIUMPH-TR 3 '56
2 oz. blue-green glass with plastic cap. Came with Spicy or Wild Country After Shave. OSP $4.00 CMV $3.00 BO $5.00 MB

1976 - '68 PORSCHE DECANTER
2 oz. amber glass with amber plastic cap. Holds Wild Country or Spicy After Shave. OSP $3.00 CMV $3.00 BO $5.00 MB

1971-73 STATION WAGON
6 oz. green glass car with tan plastic top. Came in Wild Country or Tai Winds After Shave. O.S.P. $6.00 C.M.V. $5.00 M.B. $6.00

1971-72 STANLEY STEAMER
5 oz. blue glass bottle with black plastic seats & tire cap. Came in Wild Country or Windjammer After Shave. O.S.P. $5.00 C.M.V. $4.00 M.B. $5.00

1973-74 HAYNES APPERSON 1902
4.5 oz. green glass with green plastic front over cap. Has silver tiller-steering rod. Holds Avon Blend 7 or Tai Winds After Shave. SSP $5.00 CMV $5.00 MB $3.00 BO

1972-74 MAXWELL '23 DECANTER
6 oz. green glass with beige plastic top & trunk over cap. Came in Deep Woods or Tribute Cologne or After Shave. SSP $5.00 CMV $5.00 - $7.00 MB

1972-75 ROLLS ROYCE
6 oz. beige painted glass with dark brown & silver plastic parts. Came in Deep Woods or Tai Winds After Shave. S.S.P. $7.00 CMV $6.00 BO $8.00 MB

1972-73 REO DEPOT WAGON
5" long - 5 oz. amber glass with black plastic top & cap. Holds Tai Winds & Oland After Shave Lotion. O.S.P. $6.00 CMV $4.50 MB $7.00

1974-75 BUGATTI 27
6.5 oz. black glass with chrome colored plastic trim. Came with Wild Country or Deep Woods Cologne or After Shave. OSP $6.00 CMV $10.00 - $12.00 MB

1979-80 CEMENT MIXER DECANTER
3 piece bottle. Front section is dark amber glass. Comes in Wild Country or Everest After Shave. Center plastic section connects to 6 oz. pale yellow plastic rear section bottle. Holds talc. Has stick on decals. SSP $11.99 CMV $10.00 MB

1968-70 STERLING SIX
7 oz. Came in 4 different shades of amber glass, black tire cap, rough top roof. Came in Spicy, Tribute, Leather After Shave. OSP $4.00 CMV $3.00 BO MB $5.00
Smooth top in very light amber glass. Test bottle. C.M.V. $45.00

1973-74 STERLING SIX
7 oz. green glass with white tire cap. Came in Wild Country or Tai Winds After Shave. SSP $4.00 CMV $4.00 BO $6.00 MB

1970-72 PACKARD ROADSTER
6 oz. lt. amber glass & matching plastic rumble seat cap. Came in Oland & Leather Cologne. 6½" long. O.S.P. $6.00 C.M.V. $4.00 M.B. $6.00

Pricing Current Market Value

All pricing in this book for *CMV* has been set by several qualified Avon bottle dealers and collectors across the United States. The prices reflected are what the item is actually selling for in their respective areas. While many items have increased in value some have been lowered; only slightly. This in no way reflects a fall out in the market of Avon collecting. It is stronger today than ever and we are trying to reflect the approximate true collector's value; or what a collector will actually pay for the item in Mint condition. *All items are priced empty* unless otherwise stated. On the pricing of new Avon products dated 1978 to 1980, the *CMV* is usually the same as the *Special Selling Price* Avon sold it for, or it is priced a little under the *SSP*. The future *CMV* on these products may very well fall somewhat in future issues of this book to reflect the true collector's value. Remember, the price paid to the Avon Representative is not a collector's price, but a new product price. You are paying for the contents. After you use the product, the price usually goes down and it becomes a used item. After you buy the item from Avon it is a used item. It takes some time for the item to become scarce on the collector's market before you see a true collector's price.

WHAT IS C.M.V.?

Current market value — Definition: A willing buyer and a willing seller with neither under duress to make the transaction.

What makes an Avon valuable? Shape, color, unusual design, scarcity and how well it will display:

a. Too big — takes too much room
b. Too small — gets lost in collection
c. Odd shapes — doesn't fit shelves, also takes too much room

Condition: Refer to coin collectors. Mint means perfect condition, unused, exceptional and undamaged. Mint means *Mint*, commands top dollar: *(See page 5 for grading examples of Mint items)*

a. Boxes were made to protect the container, keeping it clean and brilliant. Boxes advertise the product and instruct the user — Boxes tell a story. When you say original condition, that was with a box. Boxes (especially men's) were usually thrown away immediately. A good clean, crisp box will help make the item bring a premium.
b. Grading and condition become even more important for an item with a CMV over $25.00.
c. Example: 1966-67 Tall Pony Post. In my opinion CMV on bottle only is too high but the box is probably the hardest to find of the modern figurals. Box should have a CMV of $10.00.

Sets — The bug-a-boo of Avon grading!!! Many sets have a premium value because they display so well. They are packaged in unusual ways and are much harder to find with perfect box and superior contents. I agree with the statement: Poor box — Poor set, subtract 50% to 75% of listed value.

a. Accuracy and Authenticity — example, at the next major Avon sale you attend, check the most abused set in Avon collecting. 1948 or 46-47 Color Cluster Sets. Wrong year of lipstick, rouge or nail polish used. Not matched, wrong filler. Correct and Mint (all articles) this set should command a $20.00 premium.

A mint box is at least twice as hard to obtain as the mint bottle that came in it. As good as Avon is in packaging — order 10 items of the same thing and only 4 will be truly mint boxes and containers. That is: creased or crushed box, corner of label not securely glued. If the first half of this letter sounds like my ideas — they are not!!! You, the Avon Collector, have made these statements facts.

1975-76 - '51 STUDEBAKER
2 oz. blue glass with blue plastic parts. Holds Avon Spicy or Wild Country. OSP $2.50 CMV $2.50 BO $4.00 MB

1975 CORVETTE STINGRAY '65
2 oz. green glass with green plastic cap. Holds Wild Country, Deep Woods or Avon Spicy After Shave. O.S.P. $3.00 CMV $3.00 BO $5.00 MB

1975-76 BIG RIG
3.5 blue glass cab with 6 oz. white & blue plastic trailer. Cab holds After Shave, Trailer holds Talc in Wild Country or Deep Woods. OSP $10.00 CMV $10.00 MB $7.00 BO

1972-75 SURE WINNER RACING CAR
5.5 oz. blue glass with blue cap. Came in Sure Winner Bracing Lotion. O.S.P. $5.00 C.M.V. $5.00 MB $3.00 BO

1973-76 JAGUAR CAR DECANTER
5 oz. jade green glass with green plastic trunk over cap. Holds Deep Woods or Wild Country After Shave. S.S.P. $5.00 CMV $5.00 MB $3.00 BO

1975-76 VOLKSWAGEN BUS DECANTER
5 oz. red painted glass with silver gray motorcycle plastic closure. Set of 4 "decorate-it-yourself" labels come with each decanter. Came with Tai Winds After Shave or Sure Winner Bracing Lotion. O.S.P. $5.00 CMV $5.00 BO $6.00 MB

1974-76 THE THOMAS FLYER 1908
6 oz. white painted glass with red & blue plastic parts with white tire cap on back. Came in Wild Country or Oland After Shave. OSP $6.00 CMV $4.00 BO $6.00 MB

1974-75 FERRARI '53
2 oz. dark amber glass with plastic closure. Came in Wild Country After Shave or Avon Protein Hair Lotion for Men. O.S.P. $3.00 CMV $3.00 BO $4.00 MB

1974-75 THUNDERBIRD '55
2 oz. blue glass with blue plastic closure. Came in Wild Country or Deep Woods After Shave. O.S.P. $3.00 C.M.V. $3.00 BO $4.00 MB

1975-77 PIERCE ARROW '33
5 oz. dark blue sprayed glass with beige plastic cap. Came in Wild Country or Deep Woods After Shave. O.S.P. $6.00 C.M.V. $5.00 BO $6.00 MB

1974-75 STOCK CAR RACER
5 oz. blue glass with blue plastic cap. Holds Wild Country After Shave or Electric Pre-Shave Lotion. O.S.P. $6.00 C.M.V. $6.00 $5.00 BO $6.00 MB

1970-72 ELECTRIC CHARGER
5 oz. black glass with red trunk cap and red side decals. Came in Spicy, Leather or Wild Country After Shave. O.S.P. $4.00 C.M.V. $3.00 BO $4.00 MB

1970-77 STAGE COACH
5 oz. dark amber glass with gold cap. Came in Wild Country, Tai Winds or Oland After Shave. OSP $5.00 CMV $3.00 BO $5.00 MB

1969-73 GOLD CADILLAC
6 oz. gold paint over clear glass, gold cap. Came in Excalibur, Leather & Wild Country After Shave. OSP $5.00 CMV $6.00 BO mint $9.00 MB

1970-72 SILVER DUESENBERG
6 oz. silver paint over clear glass. Came in Oland & Wild Country After Shave. O.S.P. $6.00 CMV $6.00 BO mint $9.00 MB

1969-71 STRAIGHT 8
5 oz. dark green glass with black trunk cap. No. 8 on hood. Came in Wild Country, Windjammer & Island Lime After Shave. OSP $3.50 CMV $4.00 MB $2.00 BO

1973-75 STRAIGHT 8
5 oz. green glass. Came in Wild Country & Island Lime After Shave. O.S.P. $3.50 CMV $2.00 BO $4.00 MB

1971-73 DUNE BUGGY
5 oz. blue glass, silver motor cap. Came in Spicy After Shave, Liquid Hair Lotion & Sports Rally Bracing Lotion. O.S.P. $5.00 C.M.V. $3.00 M.B. $5.00

1969-70 TOURING T
6½" long, 6 oz. black glass with black plastic top & tire cap. Came in Excalibur or Tribute After Shave. O.S.P. $6.00 CMV $5.00 BO $7.00 MB

1969 TOURING T TEST BOTTLE
Dark amber glass factory test bottle. Also came in clear glass. C.M.V. $75.00 clear, $100.00 amber. Not shown.

1972-74 MODEL A
4 oz. yellow painted over clear glass, yellow cap. Holds Wild Country or Leather After Shave. S.S.P. $4.00 CMV $3.00 BO $4.50 MB

1973-74 BLUE VOLKSWAGEN
4 oz. lt. blue painted with plastic cap. Holds Oland or Windjammer After Shave. SSP $3.00 CMV $5.00 BO $7.00 MB

1970-72 BLACK VOLKSWAGEN
4 oz. black glass with black plastic cap. Holds Wild Country After Shave or Electric Pre-Shave Lotion. S.S.P. $2.00 CMV $3.00 MB $2.00 BO

1972 RED VOLKSWAGEN
4 oz. painted red with red plastic cap. Came in Oland or Wild Country After Shave or Sports Rally Bracing Lotion. SSP $3.00 CMV $5.00 BO $7.00 MB

1972-74 THE CAMPER
5 oz. green glass truck with After Shave. 4 oz. Talc in beige plastic camper. Came in Deep Woods or Oland. S.S.P. $8.00 CMV $8.00 MB $6.00 BO

1973-75 THE HARVESTER DECANTER
5.5 oz. amber glass with amber plastic front. Holds Wild Country After Shave or Protein Hair Lotion for Men. O.S.P. $5.00 C.M.V. $5.00 BO $7.00 MB

1975-76 '55 CHEVY
5 oz. sprayed green glass with white plastic parts. Holds Wild Country or Electric Pre-Shave Lotion. SSP $5.00 CMV $4.00 BO $6.00 MB

1974-77 STUTZ BEARCAT 1914
6 oz. red painted with black plastic seats and cap. Came in Oland or Blend 7 After Shave. SSP $6.00 CMV $6.00 MB $5.00 BO

1974-75 1936 MG DECANTER
5 oz. red painted with red plastic cap & white plastic top. Came in Avon Blend 7, Tai Winds or Wild Country After Shave. SSP $4.00 CMV $4.00 BO $5.00 MB

1973 COUNTRY VENDOR DECANTER
5 oz. brown glass with brown plastic top, has picture of fruits & vegetables on side. Holds Wild Country or Avon Spicy After Shave. SSP $7.00 CMV $8.00 MB $6.00 BO

1972-73 MINI-BIKE
4 oz. lt. amber glass coated over clear glass with lt. amber plastic wheel & silver handle bars with yellow grips. Came in Wild Country After Shave, Sure Winner Bracing Lotion, or Protein Hair Lotion for men. SSP $5.00 CMV $5.00 MB $3.00 BO

1973-74 ROAD RUNNER DECANTER
5.5 oz. blue glass with blue plastic front wheel, silver handle bars with black grips. Holds Sure Winner Bracing Lotion or Wild Country After Shave. S.S.P. $6.00 CMV $6.00 MB $4.00 BO

1971-72 SUPER CYCLE AFTER SHAVE
4 oz. gray glass regular issue. Came in Wild Country, Island Lime or Sports Rally Bracing Lotion. Clear test bottle center & factory reject in black glass with a purple tint. Regular issue SSP $5.00, CMV $5.00. Clear test bottle CMV $35.00. Black glass $15.00. 1974-75 issued in blue glass. Came in Wild Country & Spicy After Shave. S.S.P. $5.00 CMV $5.00 MB $4.00 BO

1975 FIRE FIGHTER 1910 DECANTER
6 oz. red painted over glass with red plastic back. Came in Wild Country or Tai Winds After Shave. O.S.P. $6.00 C.MV. $6.00 MB $4.00 BO

1971-72 GENERAL 4-4-0
5½ oz. dark blue glass & cap. Came in Tai Winds or Wild Country After Shave. O.S.P. $7.50 C.M.V. $5.00 M.B. $7.50

1972-75 AVON OPEN GOLF CART
5½" long, green glass bottle with green plastic front end, red plastic golf bags. Holds 5 oz. Wild Country or Windjammer After Have. Came in light or darker green glass. OSP $6.00 CMV $5.00 MB $4.00 BO

1974-75 SNOWMOBIL
4 oz. blue glass with yellow plastic front and black runners. Came in Oland or Windjammer After Shave. S.S.P. $6.00 CMV $4.00 BO $6.00 MB

1970-71 COVERED WAGON
6 oz. 4½" long. Dark amber glass bottom, white painted top & gold cap. Came in Spicy & Wild Country After Shave. O.S.P. $5.00 CMV $4.00 MB $5.00

1971-72 SIDE WHEELER
5 oz. dark amber glass, black plastic stacks, silver or gold cap. Came in Wild Country & Spicy After Shave. O.S.P. $6.00 C.M.V. $2.00 MB $4.00 Reissued 1976 in Tai Winds same CMV

1974-75 ARMY JEEP
4 oz. olive drab green with plastic closure. Came with Wild Country or Avon Spice After Shave. OSP $5.00 CMV $5.00 BO $6.00 MB

1974-76 GOLDEN ROCKET 0-2-2
6 oz. smokey gold over clear glass with gold plastic cap. Came in Tai Winds or Wild Country After Shave. O.S.P. $7.00 CMV $7.00 MB $6.00 BO. Factory Reject from factory is indented sides and gold coated. CMV $20.00

1973-75 ATLANTIC 4-4-2 DECANTER
5 oz. silver over clear glass with silver plastic parts. Holds Deep Woods or Leather After Shave or Cologne. SSP $8.00 CMV $8.00 MB $6.00 BO

1971-72 FIRST VOLUNTEER
6 oz. gold coated over clear glass. Oland or Tai Winds Cologne. O.S.P. $8.50 C.M.V. $7.00 M.B. $8.50

1976-77 CANNONBALL EXPRESS 4-6-0
3.25 oz. black glass, black cap. Came in Deep Woods or Wild Country Cologne or After Shave. SSP $5.99 CMV $4.00 BO $6.00 MB

1973-75 BIG MACK
6 oz. green glass with beige bed. Holds Oland or Windjammer After Shave. SSP $5.00 CMV $6.00 MB $4.00 BO

1978-79 1973 FORD RANGER PICK-UP
5 oz. blue paint over clear glass, blue plastic bed cap. Stick on decals. Came in Wild Country or Deep Woods. S.S.P. $6.99 CMV $4.00 BO $5.00 MB

1976-77 '36 FORD
5 oz. orange paint over clear glass. Plastic stick on hub caps & grill. Came in Tai Winds or Oland. S.S.P. $5.99 CMV $4.00 BO $5.00 MB

1978 TOURING T SILVER
6 oz. silver plated over clear glass. May, 1978 on bottom. Came in Deep Woods or Everest. SSP $8.99 CMV $5.00 BO $7.00 MB
PHOTO COMP. Used by Avon. 1 of a kind. Never sold! Solid lucite. CMV $200.00 with Avon letter.

LEFT 1977-79 EXTRA SPECIAL MALE
3 oz. blue glass, dark blue cap & white plastic roof. Separate American eagle and red striped stick on decals. Came in Deep Woods or Everest After Shave. SSP $4.44 CMV $3.50 MB $2.50 BO
RIGHT 1976-78 '64 MUSTANG
2 oz. size blue glass & blue tail cap. Came in Spicy or Tai Winds. S.S.P. $2.99 CMV $2.00 BO $3.00 MB

1976-77 '31 GREYHOUND BUS
5 oz. blue painted over clear glass. Blue plastic front cap. White plastic roof will pop off. Came in Avon Spicy or Everest. S.S.P. $5.99 CMV $4.00 BO $5.00 MB

1979 MODEL T CAR FRESHENER
3" high light yellow wax pomander comes in green and yellow box with green hang up rope. S.S.P. $1.99, C.M.V. $1.99 M.B.

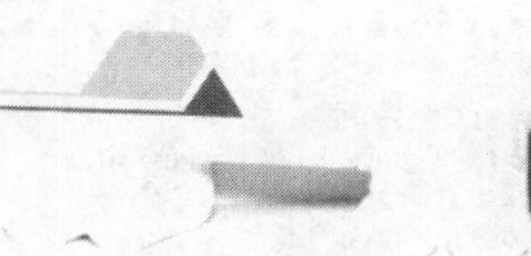

1977-79 HIGHWAY KING
4 oz. green glass bottle with white plastic center connection piece & rear section is 6.5 oz. white plastic talc. bottle. Came in Wild Country or Everest. OSP $12.50 CMV $7.00 MB $5.00 BO

1976 '48 CHRYSLER TOWN & COUNTRY
4.25 oz. off red painted over clear glass. Beige plastic top, Came in Everest or Wild Country. S.S.P. $5.99 C.M.V. $5.00 BO $6.00 MB

1974-75 CABLE CAR AFTER SHAVE DECANTER
4oz. green painted over clear glass has plastic green & white top. Came in Wild Country or Avon Leather. S.S.P. $7.00 CMV $6.00 BO $8.00 MB

1978 STERLING SIX SILVER
7 oz. silver plated over clear glass. Came in Tai Winds or Deep Woods After Shave. May 1978 on bottom. S.S.P. $8.99 CMV $5.00 BO $7.00 MB
PHOTO COMP. Used by Avon. 1 of a kind with letter from Avon. Was not sold. CMV $200.00 with Avon letter.

1977-78 1926 CHECKER CAB
5 oz. yellow painted over clear glass. Black plastic trunk cap & top. Stick on decal hub caps, bumper & checker design. Came in Everest or Wild Country. SSP $6.99 CMV $5.00 BO $6.00 MB

1977-79 VIKING DISCOVERER
4 oz. blue green glass & matching plastic cap. Red & white metal sail. Black plastic sail post. Came in Wild Country or Everest. S.S.P. $9.99 C.M.V. $7.00 MB $6.00 BO

1979 - 80 BUICK 53 SKYLARK
4 oz. emerald green glass and cap. Stick on decals. Came in Clint or Everest After Shave. S.S.P. $9.99, C.M.V. $9.99 M.B.

1979 - 80 VAN TASTIC DECANTER
5 oz. burgundy color glass. Stick on decals. Comes in Wild Country or Everest After Shave. S.S.P. $6.99, C.M.V. $6.99 M.B.

1978 STANLEY STEAMER (Silver)
5 oz. silver paint over clear glass. Came in Tai Winds or Deep Woods after shave. S.S.P. $8.99, C.M.V. $8.99 M.B.

1978-79 WINNEBAGO MOTOR HOME
5 oz. white painted over clear glass. Stick on trim decals. Holds Wild Country or Deep Woods After Shave. S.S.P. $6.99, C.M.V. $6.99.

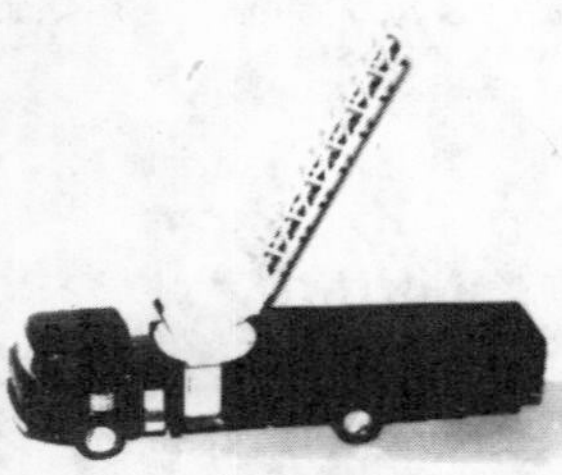

1978-79 RED SENTINEL
"FIRE TRUCK"
4 piece decanter. Engine is 3½ oz. clear glass painted red. Holds Wild Country or Deep Woods After Shave. Plastic hook and ladder center section and 6 oz. rear red plastic section holds talc. Comes with stick on decals. S.S.P. $11.99, C.M.V. $11.99 M.B.

1978-79 TRAIN 1876
CENTENNIAL EXPRESS DECANTER
5.5 oz. dark green glass with stick on trim decals. Holds Wild Country or Everest After Shave. S.S.P. $5.99, C.M.V. $5.99 M.B.

1978 GOODYEAR BLIMP DECANTER
2 oz. silver gray paint over clear glass, blue letters. Came in Everest or Wild Country After Shave. S.S.P. $5.99 CMV $5.00 MB $4.00 BO

1970-72 SPIRIT OF ST. LOUIS
6 oz. silver paint over clear glass. Came in Windjammer & Excalibur After Shave. 7½" long. O.S.P. $8.50 C.M.V. $6.00 M.B. $8.50

1973-74 COLLECTOR'S PIPE DECANTER
3 oz. brown glass with black stem. Holds Deep Woods or Windjammer After Shave or Cologne. S.S.P. Cologne $4.00 C.M.V. $4.00 M.B. S.S.P. After Shave $300 CMV $5.00 MB $3.00 BO

1971-72 PIPE FULL DECANTER
2 oz. brown glass with black stem. Holds Spicy, Oland, Tai Winds or Excalibur After Shave. SSP $2.00 CMV $3.00 MB $2.00 BO

1972-74 PIPE FULL DECANTER
2 oz. lt. green glass with brown plastic stem. Holds Tai Winds or Spicy After Shave. SSP $2.00 CMV $2.00 BO $3.00 MB

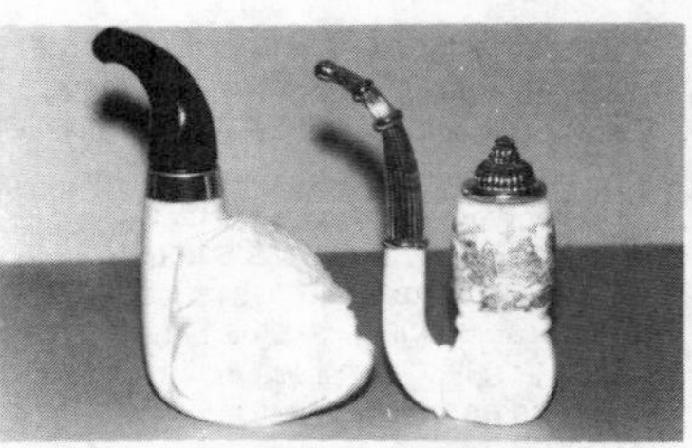

1972-73 BULL DOG PIPE DECANTER
6 oz. cream colored milk glass with black stem. Came in Wild Country or Oland After Shave or Cologne. S.S.P. After Shave $4.00 CMV $4.00 BO $5.00 MB

1973-74 DUTCH PIPE
2 oz. white milk glass, blue design, silver handle & cap. Came in Tribute Cologne or Tai Winds Cologne. S.S.P. $7.00 C.M.V. $7.00 B.O. $9.00 M.B.

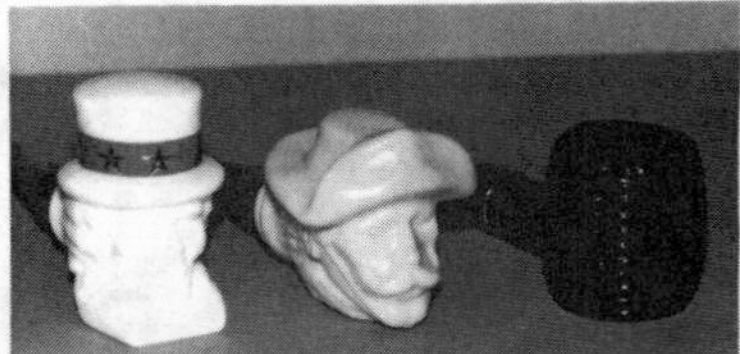

1975-76 UNCLE SAM PIPE
3 oz. white opal glass with blue band & blue plastic stem. Holds Wild Country or Deep Woods After Shave. O.S.P. $5.00 CMV $5.00 MB $4.00 BO

1975-76 PONY EXPRESS RIDER PIPE DECANTER
3 oz. white milk glass with black plastic stem. Holds Wild Country or Tai Winds Cologne. OSP $5.00 CMV $5.00 MB $4.00 BO

1974-75 CORNCOB PIPE DECANTER
3 oz. amber glass with black plastic stem. Holds Wild Country or Avon Spicy. OSP $3.00, CMV $3.00 BO, $4.00 MB

1974-75 AMERICAN EAGLE PIPE
5 oz. dark amber glass with gold plastic top & black handle. Holds Wild Country or Tai Winds Cologne. O.S.P. $5.00 C.M.V. $5.00 MB $3.00 BO

1974-75 CALABASH PIPE DECANTER
3 oz. yellow gold sprayed glass with yellow gold plastic cap & black plastic stand. Holds Wild Country or Deep Woods After Shave. OSP $8.00 CMV $8.00 $6.00 BO

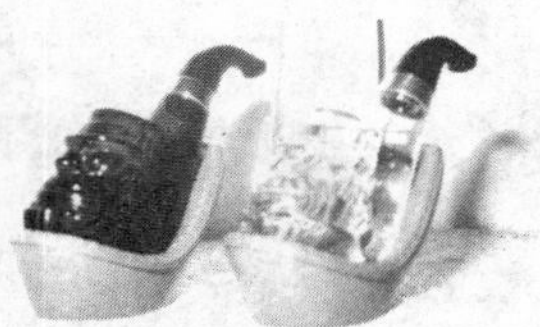

1967 PIPE DREAM
6 oz. dark amber glass, black cap, tan plastic base. Came in Spicy, Tribute & Leather After Shave. O.S.P. $5.00 C.M.V. $12.50 BO $17.50 MB

1967 PIPE DREAM CLEAR TEST BOTTLE
6 oz. clear glass factory test bottle. C.M.V. $250.00

1976 BLOOD HOUND PIPE DECANTER
5 oz. lt. tan paint over clear glass, brown & silver cap. Came in Wild Country or Deep Woods After Shave. O.S.P. $7.00 C.M.V. $5.00 MB $4.00 BO

1976 CHIEF PONTIAC CAR ORNAMENT CLASSIC
4 oz. black ribbed glass with silver Indian Came in Tai Winds or Deep Woods After Shave. OSP $8.00 CMV $4.00 BO $5.00 MB

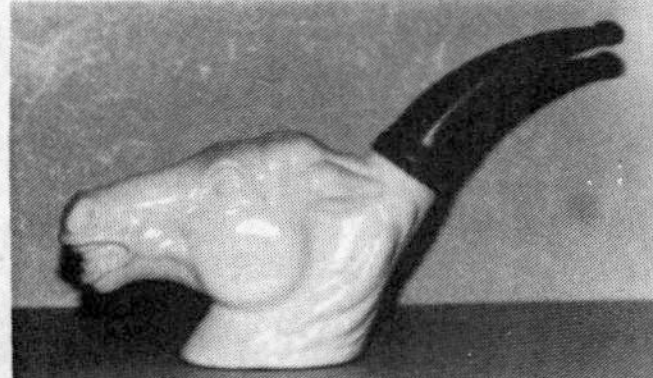

1976-77 WILD MUSTANG PIPE DECANTER
3 oz. white glass. Holds Wild Country or Deep Woods Cologne. SSP $5.00 CMV $5.00 MB

1979-80 LUCKY HORSESHOE SOAP DISH & SOAP
Brown box holds amber glass horseshoe soap dish & soap. SSP $7.99 CMV $7.99 MB

1979-80 PERPETUAL CALENDAR CONTAINER & SOAP
Yellow box holds Avon tin can calendar & white bar of soap. Bottom of can says Made in England for Avon. SSP $7.99 CMV $7.99 MB

1979-80 FARMERS ALMANAC THERMOMETER & SOAPS
Box holds tin top with plastic bottom with 2 bars of Farmers Almanac soap. Comes with copy of Avon 1980 Farmers Almanac. SSP $8.99 MB complete CMV Farmers Almanac only $1.00

1979-80 DUTCH BOY HEAVY DUTY POWDER HAND CLEANER
12 oz. blue & white paper sides. Yellow plastic top, gray bottom. No box. SSP $3.99 CMV $3.00 mint

1979-80 BATH BREW DECANTER
4 oz. dark amber glass, gold cap. Brown box. Holds Wild Country Bubble Bath. SSP $3.99 CMV $3.99 MB

1980 LOVER BOY AFTER SHAVE
3 oz. clear glass. Red letters & cap. Red box. SSP $3.49 CMV $3.00 MB

1980 LOVER BOY SCRATCH 'N SNIFF CARDS
Pad of 20 cards for samples. CMV 50c pad.

1980 WILSON STEPPING OUT FOOT POWDER
5 oz. yellow & red. SSP $1.99 CMV $1.00 mint

1979-80 WILSON CARE DEEPLY LIP BALM
Yellow & red. 3" high. CMV 50c

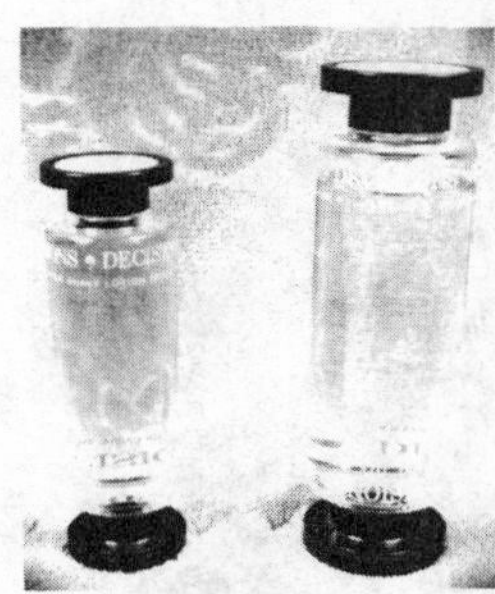

FOREIGN DECISIONS
Smaller than American Decisions. C.M.V. $30.00 B.O. M.B. $35.00

1965 DECISIONS
8 oz. red painted labels, black caps with red centers that say Panic Buttons. Came in After Shave Lotion, Spicy. O.S.P. $2.50 CMV $25.00 MB $15.00 BO

1978-79 WEEKEND DECISION MAKER DECANTER
3 oz. green and white painted over clear glass. Green top. Holds Wild Country or Tai Winds After Shave. S.S.P. $5.99, C.M.V. $5.99 M.B.

1978-79 THERMOS PLAID BRAND DECANTER
3 oz. white milk glass. Red cap and plaid design. Holds Wild Country After Shave or Sweet Honesty Body Splash. S.S.P. $3.66, C.M.V. $3.66 M.B.

1978-79 DOMINO DECANTER
1.5 oz. black glass with white spots. Holds Everest or Tai Winds After Shave. S.S.P. $3.99, C.M.V. $3.99 M.B.

1979-80 SUPER SLEUTH MAGNIFIER
10" long. Bottom is dark amber glass and top is real magnifying glass. Came in Wild Country or Everest After Shave. S.S.P. $7.99, C.M.V. $7.99 M.B.

1979-80 COUNTRY LANTERN
4 oz. clear glass painted red. Red wire handle. Holds Wild Country or Deep Woods After Shave. S.S.P. $5.99, C.M.V. $5.99 M.B.

1979-80 GENTLEMAN'S TALC
3.75 oz. green can. Holds Clint, Trazarra or Wild Country Talc. S.S.P. $3.99, C.M.V. $2.00 mint, no box.

1979-80 ON TAP MUG DECANTER
4 oz. clear glass with white plastic top. Holds Wild Country or Deep Woods After Shave. S.S.P. $5.99, C.M.V. $5.99 M.B.

1979 PAUL REVERE BELL DECANTER
4 oz. clear glass painted gold. Brown and silver handle. 1979 stamped in bottom. Holds Clint After Shave or Sweet Honesty Body Splash. S.S.P. $7.99, C.M.V. $7.99 M.B.

1978-79 LITTLE BROWN JUG DECANTER
Brown glass, tan plastic cap. Beige painted sides. Holds 2 oz. Deep Woods or Tai Winds After Shave. S.S.P. $2.99, C.M.V. $2.99 M.B.

1978-79 BABY BASSETT DECANTER
1.25 oz. amber glass and matching plastic head. Holds Topaze or Sweet Honesty cologne. S.S.P. $2.99, C.M.V. $2.99 M.B.

1978-79 QUAKER STATE POWDERED HAND CLEANER
12 oz. cardboard sides and gold plastic top and bottom. Holds heavy duty powdered hand cleaner. S.S.P. $2.99, C.M.V. $2.99, can without box.

1969 AVON CLASSICS
6 oz. each OSP $3.50 Leather in clear & dark amber glass. Wind-Jammer in blue & clear glass. Wild Country in light & dark amber glass & clear glass. Tribute After Shave in clear glass, light & dark amber glass. All bottle caps & labels must match in color, gold or silver. CMV $5.00 BO each $8.00 MB

1967-68 FIRST EDITION
6 oz. gold cap. Came in Bay Rum CMV $9.00 BO $12.00 MB. Wild Country & Leather After Shave. OSP $3.50 CMV $5.00 BO $8.00 MB

1973 SUPER SHAVER
4 oz. blue glass with gray plastic top, holds Sure Winner Bracing Lotion or Avon Spicy After Shave. SSP $3.00 CMV $4.00 MB $3.00 BO

1973 BOTTLED BY AVON
5 oz. clear glass with silver lift off cap, holds Oland or Windjammer After Shave. S.S.P. $3.00 CMV $4.00 MB $3.00 BO

1966-67 ALPINE FLASK
8 oz. 8¾" high, brown glass, gold cap & neck chain. Came in Spicy, Original, Blue Blazer & Leather After Shave. O.S.P. $4.00 CMV $60.00 MB $45.00 BO

1965-66 ROYAL ORB
8 oz. round bottle, gold cap, red felt around neck. Came in Spicy & Original After Shave. Red letters painted on bottle common issue. O.S.P. $3.50 C.M.V. $16.50. M.B. $25.00. White letter Orb C.M.V. $75.00

1970 CAPTAINS PRIDE
6 oz. bottle with ship decal, tan cap & blue neck label. Sits on black plastic stand. Came in Oland & Windjammer After Shave. O.S.P. $5.00 CMV $4.00 BO $6.00 MB

1972-73 BIG WHISTLE
4 oz. blue glass with silver cap. Came in Tai Winds or Spicy After Shave or Electric Pre-Shave Lotion, S.S.P. $3.50 CMV $4.50 MB $3.50 BO

1969 FUTURA
5 oz. 7½" high, silver paint over clear glass, silver cap. Came in Excalibur & Wild Country Cologne. O.S.P. $7.00 C.M.V. $12.50 M.B. $10.00 BO

1971 WORLDS GREATEST DAD DECANTER
4 oz. clear glass, red cap. Came in Spicy or Tribute After Shave or Electric Pre-Shave Lotion. OSP $3.50 CMV $2.50 MB $1.50 BO

1966-67 CASEY'S LANTERN
10 oz. gold paint on clear glass bottle, gold caps. Came in Leather After Shave in red window, Tribute in amber window & Island Lime in green window. O.S.P. ea. $6.00 C.M.V. amber & green $55.00 M.B. Red $45.00 M.B. Bottles only $5.00 less each mint.

1973-74 AUTO LANTERN
Shiny gold with amber windows. Left bottle holds 5 oz. Oland or Deep Woods After Shave. Right base holds 1.25 oz. Oland or Deep Woods Talc. S.S.P. $12.00 CMV $10.00 MB $8.00 BO

1975-76 CAPTAIN'S LANTERN 1864 DECANTER
7 oz. black glass with black plastic cap & gold ring. Came in Wild Country or Oland After Shave. OSP $5.00 CMV $5.00 MB $4.00 BO

1974-75 WHALE OIL LANTERN DECANTER
5 oz. green glass with silver toned plastic top & base. Holds Wild Country, Oland or Tai Winds. OSP $4.00 CMV $4.00 MB $3.00 BO

1978 SMOOTH GOING OIL CAN
1.5 oz. silver plated over clear glass. Came in Deep Woods or Everest After Shave. SSP $3.99 CMV $3.00 MB $2.00 BO

1978-79 "HAMMER" ON THE MARK DECANTER
8½" long dark amber glass with silver top holds 2.5 oz. of Everest or Wild Country After Shave. S.S.P. $4.99, C.M.V. $4.99 M.B.

1978-79 ON THE LEVEL DECANTER
3 oz. silver coated over clear glass holds Everest or Deep Woods After Shave. S.S.P. $3.99, C.M.V. $3.99 M.B.

LEFT 1977-79 BREAKER 19
2 oz. black glass with black & silver plastic cap. Wild Country or Sweet Honesty. S.S.P. $3.99 C.M.V. $3.00 MB $2.00

RIGHT 1977-79 COLEMAN LANTERN
5 oz. green painted over clear glass. Green cap, silver bail handle. Came in Wild Country or Deep Woods. SSP $5.99 CMV $4.00 BO $5.00 MB

LEFT 1977-78 JUKE BOX
4.5 oz. amber glass, silver top. Came in Sweet Honesty or Wild Country. Came with Decals. SSP $4.99 CMV $5.00 MB $4.00 BO

RIGHT 1975-76 AVON ON THE AIR DECANTER
3 oz. black glass with silver plastic stand. Holds Wild Country, Deep Woods, or Spicy After Shave. O.S.P. $4.00 C.M.V.$4.00 MB $3.00 BO

1972 PIANO DECANTER
4" high, 4 oz. dark amber glass piano with white music stack cap. Holds Tai Winds or Tribute After Shave Lotion. O.S.P. $4.00 C.M.V. $4.00 M.B. $5.00

1971-72 FIELDER'S CHOICE
5 oz. dark amber glass, black cap. Came in Sports Rally Bracing Lotion, Liquid Hair Trainer or Wild Country After Shave. O.S.P. $4.00 C.M.V. $2.50 M.B. $4.00

1975-76 STAR SIGNS DECANTER
4 oz. black glass with gold cap. Came in Sweet Honesty Cologne or Wild Country After Shave. Came blank with choice of one of 12 Zodiac signs sticker to apply. OSP $3.50 CMV $3.50 MB each $2.50 BO

1975-76 SPARK PLUG DECANTER
1.5 oz. white milk glass with gray cap. Holds Wild Country, Tai Winds or Avon Spicy After Shave. O.S.P. $2.00 C.M.V. $2.00 MB $1.50 BO

1975-76 STOP! DECANTER
5 oz. red plastic with white plastic base. Holds Wild Country After Shave or Sweet Honesty After Bath Freshner. O.S.P. $3.00 C.M.V. $3.00

1974-75 STOP 'N GO
4 oz. green glass with green cap. Holds Wild Country or Avon Spicy After Shave. OSP $4.00 CMV $4.00 MB $3.00 BO

1968-69 TOWN PUMP
8" high black glass bottle with gold cap & plastic shoe horn. Holds 6 oz. of Leather, Windjammer, Wild Country. O.S.P. $5.00 CMV $3.00 BO $4.00 MB

1970 ANGLER
5 oz. 4½" high blue glass with silver reel cap & trim. Came in Windjammer & Wild Country After Shave. O.S.P. $5.00 C.M.V. $5.00 M.B. $6.50

1973 EIGHT BALL DECANTER
3 oz. black glass with black cap & white 8. Came in Spicy After Shave, Avon Protein Lotion for men or Electric Pre-Shave Lotion. SSP $2.00 CMV $4.00 MB $3.00 BO

1970-72 LIBERTY DOLLAR
6 oz. Silver paint over clear glass, silver cap with eagle. 6" high. Came in Oland & Tribute After Shave. O.S.P. $5.00 C.M.V. $4.00 M.B. $5.00. Same bottle only gold. Rare $40.00 M.B.

1971-72 TWENTY DOLLAR GOLD PIECE
6 oz. gold paint over clear glass. Gold cap. Came in Windjammer After Shave & Electric Pre-Shave Lotion. O.S.P. $5.00 C.M.V. $4.00 B.O., $6.00 M.B.

1971-72 BUFFALO NICKEL
5 oz. nickel plated over clear glass with matching cap. Came in Spicy, Wild Country After Shave or Liquid Hair Lotion. SSP $4.00 CMV $5.00 MB $4.00 BO

1970-72 INDIAN HEAD PENNY
4 oz. 4" high. Bronze paint & cap over clear glass. Came in Bravo, Tribute, Exacalibur After Shave. OSP $4.00 CMV $4.00 MB $3.00 BO

1963 CLOSE HARMONY (BARBER BOTTLE)
8 oz. white glass bottle, gold painted letters & neck band. White cap with tip. Came in Spicy & Original After Shave. O.S.P. $2.25 Vigorate & After Shower Cologne O.S.P. $2.50 CMV without tip. With tip $15.00 MB $30.00

1966-67 DOLLAR'S 'N' SCENTS
8 oz. white glass bottle with green dollar painted on. Silver cap. Came in Spicy After Shave. Red rubber band around bottle. OSP $2.50 CMV $28.00 MB $16.00 BO

1966-67 TOP DOLLAR SOAP ON ROPE
White 1886 dollar soap. O.S.P. $1.75 CMV $37.50 MB $25.00 soap only, mint.

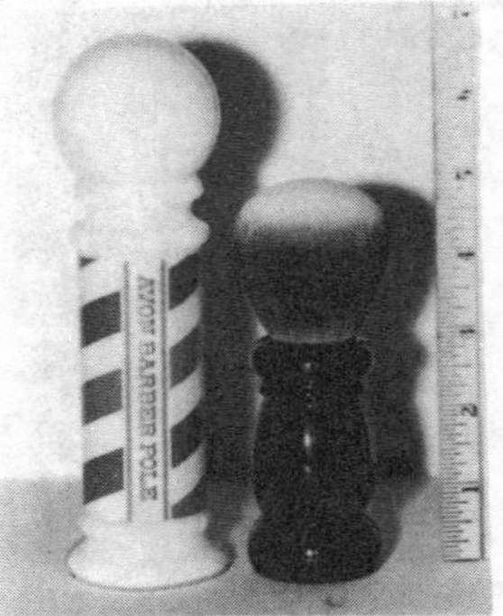

1974-75 BARBER POLE
3 oz. white milk glass with red & blue paper striped label & white plastic cap. Holds Avon Protein Hair/Scalp Conditioner or Wild Country After Shave. O.S.P. $3.00 CMV $3.00 MB $2.00 BO

1976 BARBER SHOP BRUSH
1.5 oz. brown glass with black & white plastic brush cap. Came in Tai Winds or Wild Country Cologne. O.S.P. $4.00 CMV $3.00 MB $2.00 BO

1971-72 LIBERTY BELL
5 oz. lt. amber glass coated over clear glass, brown cap. Came in Tribute or Oland After Shave or Cologne. OSP $5.00 CMV $5.00 MB $4.00 BO

1976 LIBERTY BELL
5 oz. sprayed bronze with bronze cap. Came in Oland or Deep Woods After Shave. OSP $5.00 CMV $5.00 MB $4.00 BO

1970-71 ITS A BLAST
5 oz. 8½" high, gold paint over clear glass, black rubber horn on cap. Came in Oland & Windjammer After Shave. O.S.P. $7.00 CMV $4.00 BO $5.00 MB

1969-70 MAN'S WORLD
Brown plastic stand holds 6 oz. globe. Gold paint over clear glass, gold cap. Came in Bravo, Windjammer & Tribute After Shave. 4" high. O.S.P. $5.00 C.M.V. $6.00 M.B. $7.00

1974-75 AFTER SHAVE ON TAP
5 oz. dark amber glass with gold plastic spigot cap. Holds Wild Country or Oland After Shave. O.S.P. $3.00 C.M.V. $4.00 MB $3.00 BO

1976 AFTER SHAVE ON TAP
5 oz. amber glass, red spigot cap. Holds Spicy or Wild Country. O.S.P. $4.00 CMV $4.00 MB $3.00 BO

1974-76 TRIPLE CROWN DECANTER
4 oz. brown glass with red plastic cap. Holds Avon Spicy After Shave or Avon Protein Hair/ Scalp Conditioner. O.S.P. $3.00 C.M.V. $3.00 MB $2.00 BO

1975-76 NO PARKING
6 oz. red painted glass with red cap. Came in Wild Country After Shave or Electric Pre-Shave. OSP $4.00 CMV $3.00 MB $2.00 BO

1975-76 FIRE ALARM BOX
4 oz. red painted glass with black cap. Came in Avon Spicy After Shave, Avon Protein Hair Lotion or Electric Pre-Shave. O.S.P. $3.00 CMV $3.00 MB $2.00 BO

1970-71 PAID STAMP
5" high, dark amber glass with black cap & red rubber paid stamp on bottom. Holds 4 oz. of Spicy or Windjammer After Shave. OSP $4.00 CMV $3.00 BO $5.00 MB

1969-71 SWINGER GOLF BAG
5 oz. black glass, red & silver clubs. Came in Wild Country & Bravo After Shave. O.S.P. $5.00 CMV $3.00 BO $5.00 MB

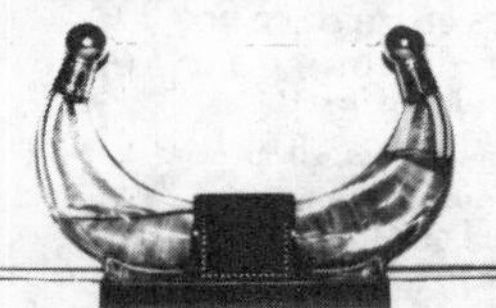

1967 WESTERN CHOICE (STEER HORNS)
Brown plastic base with red center. Holds 2 - 3 oz. bottles with silver caps. Came in Wild Country & Leather After Shave. OSP $6.00 CMV $15.00 BO $25.00 MB

1967 WESTERN CHOICE (STEER HORNS) "MANAGERS"
Managers received the steer horns in a special box with Avon embossed all over the box. Was used to show at meetings on introduction of Steer Horns. Rare in this box. CMV $35.00 MB as shown

1967-68 GAVEL
5 oz. dark amber glass with brown plastic handle. 8" long. Came in Island Lime, Original & Spicy. O.S.P. $4.00 C.M.V. $8.00 BO $12.00 MB

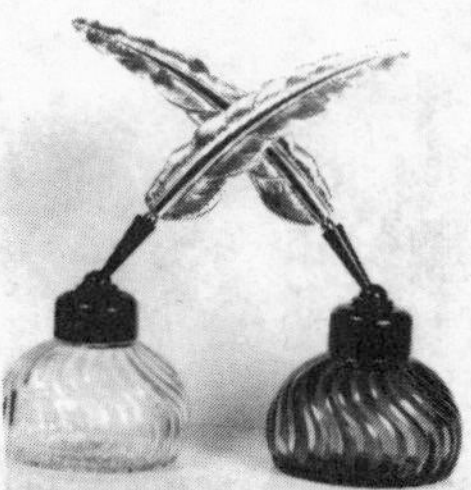

1969-70 INKWELL
6 oz. amber with purple tint, black cap with gold or silver pen. Came in Windjammer & Spicy After Shave. O.S.P. $6.00 C.M.V. $4.00 BO $6.00 MB

1969 INKWELL TEST BOTTLE
Clear glass factory test bottle. C.M.V. $60.00

1970-71 FIRST CLASS MALE
4½" high. 4 oz. blue glass with red cap. Came in Bravo or Wild Country After Shave or Liquid Hair Lotion. O.S.P. $3.00 C.M.V. $4.00 M.B. $4.50

1970 FIRST CLASS MALE TEST BOTTLE
Clear glass factory test bottle. C.M.V. $6.00

1971-72 FOREIGN FIRST CLASS MALE
From Canada. Clear glass bottle painted red with red cap. Remove paint & is same as factory test bottle C.M.V. $7.00 M.B. $8.00

1970-71 POT BELLY STOVE
5" high, 5 oz. black glass bottle with black cap. Came in Bravo or Excalibur After Shave. OSP $4.00 CMV $3.00 BO $4.00 MB

LEFT 1969 FOREIGN OLD BARREL
6 oz. brown & silver with brown cap. $22.00 BO, $25.00 MB

RIGHT 1965-67 BAY RUM KEG
8 oz. brown & silver paint over clear glass bottle. OSP $2.50, CMV $14.00 BO, $20.00 MB

1968 KEG DECANTER-EUROPE
Not shown. Same shape as Bay Rum Keg. 180 cc size. Brown & silver painted over clear glass. Brown cap, silver label. Holds after shave. Comes in keg decanter box. Bottle is smaller than U.S. Bay Rum Keg. Rare. CMV $30.00 MB $25.00 BO

1974-75 ELECTRIC GUITAR DECANTER
6 oz. brown glass with silver plastic handle. Came in Avon Sure Winner Bracing Lotion or Wild Country After Shave. S.S.P. $4.00 CMV $4.00 MB $3.00 BO

1975 TOTEM POLE DECANTER
6 oz. dark amber glass with plastic cap. Holds Wild Country, Deep Woods or Avon Spicy After Shave. O.S.P. $5.00 CMV $4.00 MB $3.00 BO

1968-70 DAYLIGHT SHAVING TIME
6 oz. gold paint over clear glass. Came in Wild Country, Windjammer, Bravo & Leather After Shave. OSP $5.00 CMV $4.00 BO $5.00 MB

DAYLIGHT SHAVING TIME-FOREIGN
Gold clock. 150 cc size. CMV $20.00 MB $25.00

1968-69 SCIMITAR
10" long, 6 oz. Gold paint with red windows over clear glass, gold cap. Came in Tribute & Windjammer After Shave Lotion. O.S.P. $6.00 C.M.V. $16.00 M.B. $22.00.

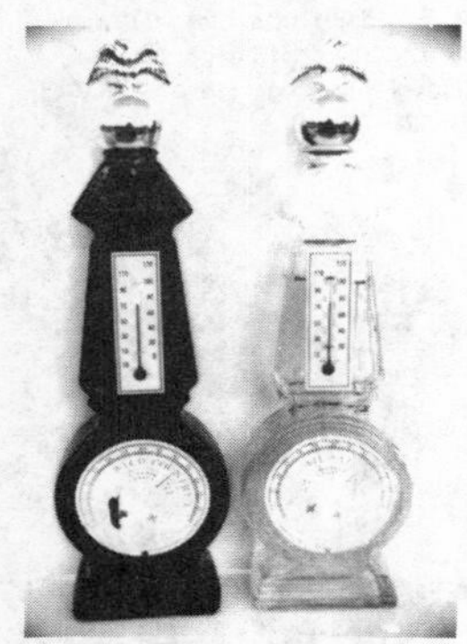

1969-71 WEATHER-OR-NOT
5 oz. dark amber glass, regular issue on left, gold cap. Came in Leather & Oland, Tribute, Wild Country & Spicy After Shave. OSP $5.00. There are 5 different Thermometers starting with 20 below, 10 below, 0, 10 above & 20 above. All same price. CMV $4.00 BO, $6.00 MB
1969 WEATHER-OR-NOT CLEAR TEST BOTTLE
5 oz. gold cap, clear glass. CMV $75.00

1972-75 INDIAN CHIEFTAIN
4 oz. brown glass with gold cap. Came in Avon Spicy After Shave or Avon Protein Hair Lotion for Men. O.S.P. $2.50 C.M.V. $3.00 M.B.
1974-75 INDIAN TEPEE DECANTER
4 oz. amber glass with brown plastic cap. Holds Wild Country or Avon Spicy. OSP $3.00, CMV $3.00 MB, $2.00 BO

LEFT 1976-77 BIG BOLT
2 oz. silver plated over clear glass. Silver cap. Came in Deep Woods or Wild Country. S.S.P. $2.99 C.M.V. $2.00M.B.
CENTER 1976-78 DURACELL SUPER CHARGE
1½ oz. black glass with bronze & silver cap. Came in Spicy or Everest. S.S.P. $1.99 C.M.V. $1.50 M.B.
RIGHT 1977 RIGHT CONNECTION "FUSE"
1.5 oz. clear glass, with gold & brown cap. Came in Oland or Wild Country. S.S.P. $2.99 C.M.V. $2.00 M.B.

LEFT 1977-78 JUST A TWIST
2 oz. silver plated over clear glass. Came in Sweet Honesty or Deep Woods S.S.P. $3.99 C.M.V. $3.00 M.B.
RIGHT HARD HAT 1977-78
4 oz. yellow paint over clear glass. Yellow plastic base. Came with seven decals. Came in Everest or Deep Woods. SSP $4.99 CMV $4.00 MB $3.00 BO

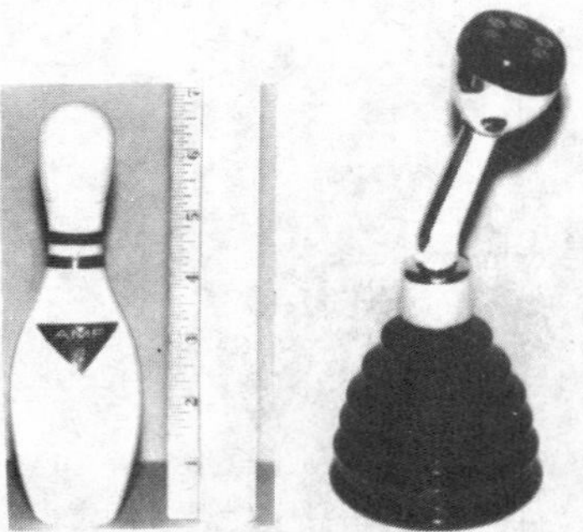

1978-79 STRIKE DECANTER
4 oz. white milk glass, white cap. Red painted on AMF designs. Came in Sweet Honesty or Wild Country. SSP $3.66 CMV $2.50 MB $1.50 BO
1978 SUPER SHIFT
4 oz. black glass bottle with silver & black shifter cap. Came in Sure Winner Bracing Lotion or Everest Cologne. 7" high. SSP $5.99 CMV $5.00 MB $4.00 BO

1976-78 MOTOCROSS HELMET
6 oz. white plastic bottle with stick on decals, bule plastic face gard cap. Came in Wild Country or Avon Protein Hair Lotion for men. S.S.P. $3.99 CMV $3.00 MB $2.00 BO

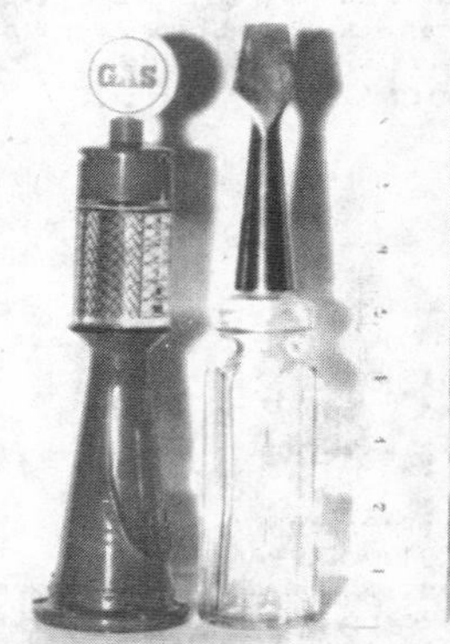

LEFT 1976-77 REMEMBER WHEN GAS PUMP
4 oz. red painted over clear glass. Red & white plastic cap. Came in Deep Woods or Wild Country. S.S.P. $5.99 CMV $5.00 MB $4.00 BO
RIGHT 1976 ONE GOOD TURN "SCREWDRIVER"
4 oz. clear glass, silver cap. Came in Tai Winds or Avon Spicy. S.S.P. $3.99 CMV $4.00 MB $3.00 BO

LEFT 1977-80 NBA DECANTER
Came with your choice of individual NBA team labels. Came in Wild Country or Sure Winner Bracing Lotion. 6 oz. dark amber glass. Silver top. SSP $6.99 CMV $6.00 MB $5.00 BO
RIGHT 1976-77 NFL DECANTER
Came with choice of NFL team emblem out of 28 member clubs of the National Football League. Came in Wild Country or Sure Winner Bracing Lotion. 6 oz. black glass with silver top. SSP $5.99 CMV $5.00 MB $4.00 BO

LEFT 1976-79 ARCTIC KING
5 oz. blue glass bottle, silver bear cap. Came in Everest only. S.S.P. $5.99 CMV $4.00 MB $3.00 BO

RIGHT 1976-78 BOLD EAGLE
3 oz. gold plated over clear glass, gold top. Came in Tai Winds or Wild Country. SSP $7.99 CMV $6.00 MB $5.00 BO

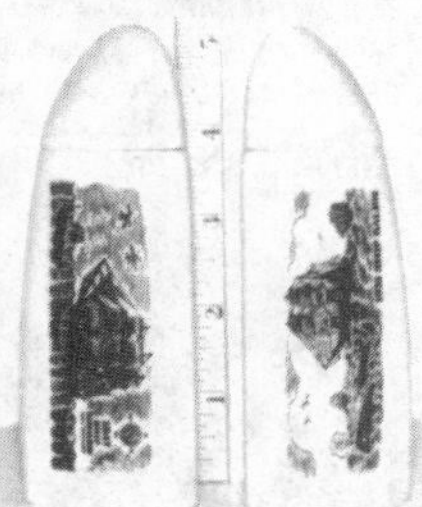

1973 WHALE ORGANIZER BOTTLES
3 oz. ivory milk glass with dark blue design. Holds After Shave & Cologne in Deep Woods or Avon Blend 7. Sold only in Whale Organizer. C.M.V. $5.00 each.

1971-72 WESTERN SADDLE
5 oz. brown glass with brown cap, sets on beige fence. Came in Wild Country or Avon Leather After Shave. S.S.P. $6.00 C.M.V. $6.00 M.B.

LEFT 1977-78 FIRM GRIP
1.5 oz. silver plated over clear glass. Came in Wild Country or Everest. S.S.P. $3.99 C.M.V. $3.00 M.B.

RIGHT 1977-78 WEATHER VANE
4 oz. red painted over clear glass. Silver top with black horse weather vane Came in Wild Country or Deep Woods. S.S.P. $4.99 C.M.V. $4.00 M.B.

LEFT 1968 STEIN - SILVER
6 oz. silver paint over clear glass, silver cap. Came in Spicy, Windjammer & Tribute After Shave. O.S.P. $4.50 CMV $4.00. In box $7.00

RIGHT 1965-66 STEIN - SILVER
8 oz. silver paint over clear glass, silver cap. Came in Tribute. O.S.P. $4.00 Spicy O.S.P. $3.50. Blue Blazer & 4A After Shave O.S.P. $3.75 ea. C.M.V. $5.00 BO $8.00 MB

1972 HUNTER'S STEIN
8 oz. nickle plated over clear glass, has gray & black plastic bottle inside. Holds Deep Woods or Wild Country After Shave. SSP $9.00 CMV $12.00 MB CMV plastic bottle only $2.00, stein only $8.00

1974-76 IRON HORSE SHAVING MUG
White milk glass mug holds 7 oz. plastic bottle with gold cap. Came in Avon Blend 7, Deep Woods or Avon Leather After Shave. SSP $6.00 CMV $6.00 MB $2.00 BO $3.00 mug only

1978-79 GET THE MESSAGE DECANTER
3 oz. black glass base with silver & black plastic top. Came in Clint or Sweet Honesty. SSP $5.99 CMV $4.00 MB $3.00 BO

1978-80 NO CAUSE FOR ALARM DECANTER
4 oz. silver plated over clear glass. Silver plastic top. Came in Deep Woods, or Tai Winds. SSP $7.99 CMV $6.50 MB $5.50 BO

LEFT 1976-80 GOOD SHOT
2 oz. plastic bottle, gold cap. Red bottle in Wild Country or Brisk Spice After Shave & yellow bottle in Deep Woods or Cool Sage After Shave. SSP $2.99 CMV $2.00 MB $1.00 BO

RIGHT 1977-78 WILD WEST "BULLIT"
1.5 oz. bronze plated over clear glass. Silver top. Wild Country or Everest. SSP $2.50 CMV $2.00 MB $1.00 BO

LEFT 1977-78 MIXED DOUBLES TENNIS BALL
3 oz. light green flock over clear glass. Green cap base. Came in Sweet Honesty Body Splash or Avon Spicy. S.S.P. $3.99 CMV $3.00 MB $2.00 BO

RIGHT 1977 SURE CATCH
1 oz. white milk glass, with red cap, yellow tassel, black eyes. Came in Spicy or Wild Country. S.S.P. $3.99 CMV $3.00 MB $2.00 BO

1979-80 CAR CLASSICS CERAMIC STEIN
9" high ceramic stein made in Brazil & numbered on the bottom. Comes with 8 oz. plastic bottle of Trazarra Cologne. SSP $32.99 CMV $30.00 MB

1978-80 SPORTING STEIN DECANTER
9" tall, ceramic stein marked on bottom "Made in Brazil for Avon Products 1978" Came with choice of 8 oz. Trazarra or Wild Country Cologne with gold cap in red plastic bottle. Each stein is numbered on the bottom. SSP $26.99 CMV $25.00 MB with bottle.

1977-79 TALL SHIPS STEIN
Ceramic stein, pewter handle & lid. Came with 8 oz red plastic bottle of Clint or brown plastic of Wild Country cologne for men. Silver cap. Each stein was hand made in Brazil and numbered on the bottom. O.S.P.$24.99 CMV $20.00 MB $15.00 stein only

1976-79 COLLECTORS STEIN
Hand made ceramic blue stein. Made in Brazil and numbered on bottom. Came with 8 oz. plastic bottle of Everest or Wild Country. S.S.P. $24.99 CMV $20.00 MB $15.00 stein only

1972-73 AMERICAN SCHOONER DECANTER
4.5 oz. blue glass with blue plastic end over cap. Some are blue painted over clear glass. Came in Oland or Spicy After Shave. S.S.P. $5.00 CMV $5.00 MB $4.00 BO

CHESS PIECE DECANTER
(THE OPPOSING SET)
3 oz. silver over glass with amber plastic tops. OSP $3.00 CMV $3.00 MB $2.00 BO
1975-78 SMART MOVE II
Came in Wild Country After Shave, Avon Protein Hair Lotion or Avon Protein Hair/Scalp Conditioner for men.
1975-78 THE KING II
Came in Avon Spicy After Shave or Avon Protein Hair Lotion.
1975-78 THE QUEEN II
Came in Avon Spicy After Shave or Avon Protein Hair/Scalp Conditioner.
1975-78 THE ROOK II
Came in Wild Country After Shave or Protein Hair Lotion for men.
1975-78 THE BISHOP II
Came in Avon Spicy After Shave or Avon Protein Hair Lotion for men. CMV $5.00 MB $4.00 BO
1975-78 THE PAWN II
Came in Avon Spicy After Shave or Avon Protein Hair/Scalp Conditioner for men.
Pieces needed for one side are 2 Smart Moves, 1 King, 1 Queen, 2 Rooks, 2 Bishops, 8 Pawns.

1970-72 WASHINGTON BOTTLE
5½" high, 4 oz. bottle with gold eagle cap. Holds Spicy or Tribute After Shave. O.S.P. $3.50 CMV $3.00 MB $2.00 BO
1971-72 LINCOLN BOTTLE
5½" high, 4 oz. bottle with gold eagle cap. Holds Wild Country or Leather After Shave. OSP $3.50 CMV $3.00 MB $2.00 BO

1973 AVON CALLING 1905 DECANTER
7 oz. brown glass with brown plastic top, has gold bell & black plastic receiver. Holds 7 oz. After Shave & .75 oz. Talc. Came in Wild Country or Avon Spicy. S.S.P. $9.00 CMV $8.00 MB $6.00 BO
1969-70 AVON CALLING FOR MEN
8½" high, 6 oz. gold paint over clear glass, gold cap, black mouth piece, black plastic ear piece. Holds 1¼ oz. Talc. Came in Wild Country & Leather Cologne. O.S.P. $8.00 C.M.V. $10.00 M.B. $12.00

CHESS PIECE DECANTER
(THE ORIGINAL SET)
3 oz. dark amber glass with silver toned tops.
1971-72 SMART MOVE
Came in Tribute & Oland Cologne. O.S.P. $4.00 C.M.V. $8.00
1973-78 Smart Move came in Wild Country After Shave or Protein Hair/Scalp Conditioner. O.S.P. $4.00 C.M.V. $4.00 M.B.
1972-73 THE KING
Came in Tai Winds or Oland After Shave. O.S.P. $4.00 C.M.V. $8.00 M.B.
1973-78 The King came in Wild Country or Oland. O.S.P. $4.00 C.M.V. $4.00 M.B.
1973-74 THE QUEEN
Came in Tai Winds or Oland After Shave. O.S.P. $4.00 C.M.V. $7.00 M.B.
1974-78 The Queen came in Wild Country or Deep Woods After Shave. O.S.P. $4.00 C.M.V. $4.00 M.B.
1973-74 THE ROOK
Came in Oland & Spicy After Shave. O.S.P. $4.00 C.M.V. $7.00 M.B.
1974-78 The Rook came in Wild Country or Avon Spicy After Shave. O.S.P. $4.00 C.M.V. $4.00 M.B.
1974-78 THE BISHOP
Came in Wild Country, Avon Blend 7 or Avon Protein Hair Lotion for men. O.S.P. $4.00 C.M.V. $4.00 M.B.
1974-78 THE PAWN
Came in Wild Country or Electric Pre-Shave Lotion. O.S.P. $4.00 CMV $4.00 BO $5.00 MB
Pieces needed for one side are: 2 Smart Moves, 1 King, 1 Queen, 2 Rooks, 2 Bishops, 8 Pawns.

1968-69 OPENING PLAY
6 oz. each, 4" high. Gold caps, white plastic face guards. Came in Sports Rally Bracing Lotion, Spicy & Wild Country After Shave. O.S.P. ea. $4.00 Shiny gold over blue glass was issued one campaign only, on last campaign Open Play was sold. C.M.V. shiny gold $25.00. In box $30.00. Dull gold over blue glass with blue stripe C.M.V. $10.00 $12.00 M.B. Dull gold over blue glass, no stripe C.M.V. $14.00. In box $16.00

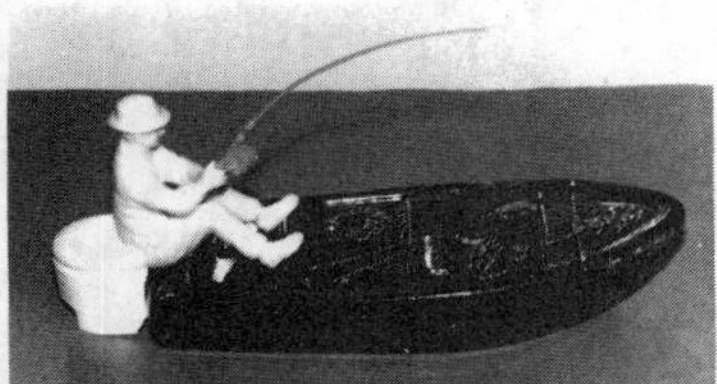

1973-74 GONE FISHING DECANTER
5 oz. lt. blue boat with white plastic man, yellow fishing rod. Came in Tai Winds or Spicy. SSP $6.00, CMV $7.00 MB, $5.00 BO.

1967 TRIBUTE SILVER WARRIOR
6" high, 6 oz. silver & blue paint over clear glass, silver cap. Came in Tribute After Shave. OSP $4.50 CMV $12.50 BO mint $18.00 M.B. All blue glass $30.00 mint
1971-73 TRIBUTE RIBBED WARRIOR
6" high, 6 oz. clear ribbed glass, silver cap. Came in Tribute Cologne. O.S.P. $4.00 C.M.V. $4.00 $5.00 M.B.
FOREIGN RIBBED WARRIOR
Same as U.S. except nose & chin is rounded off & U.S. is more pointed. Foreign label on bottom. C.M.V. $14.00 on foreign. M.B. $18.00
1968-71 TRIBUTE FROSTED WARRIOR
6" high, 6 oz. frosted glass, silver cap. Came in Tribute Cologne. O.S.P. $4.00 C.M.V. $3.00 BO $5.00 MB

1974-76 PRESIDENT WASHINGTON DECANTER
6 oz. white spray over clear glass, white plastic head. Holds Wild Country or Tai Winds After Shave. (1976 came in Deep Woods or Tai Winds After Shave). O.S.P. $6.00 CMV $6.00 BO $7.00 MB
1973 PRESIDENT LINCOLN DECANTER
6 oz. white spray over clear glass, white plastic head. Holds Wild Country or Tai Winds After Shave. O.S.P. $5.00 C.M.V. $9.00 BO $12.00 MB
1974-76 BENJAMIN FRANKLIN DECANTER
6 oz. white spray over clear glass, white plastic head. Holds Wild Country or Tai Winds After Shave. O.S.P. $6.00 C.M.V. $6.00 BO $7.00 MB

LEFT 1975-76 THEODORE ROOSEVELT
6 oz. white paint over clear glass. Came in Wild Country or Tai Winds After Shave. OSP $9.00 CMV $6.00 BO $7.00 MB
RIGHT 1977-78 THOMAS JEFFERSON
5 oz. white paint over clear glass. White head cap. Came in Wild Country or Everest. After Shave. S.S.P. $7.99 CMV $6.00 BO $7.00 MB

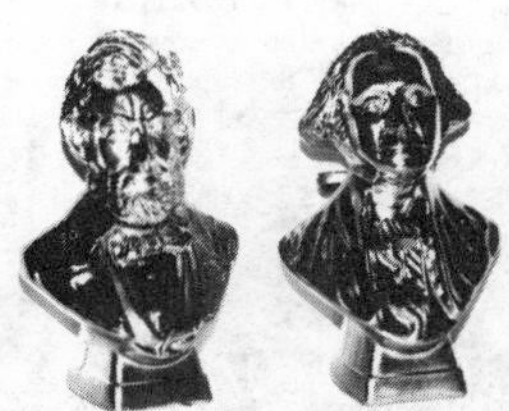

1979 PRESIDENT LINCOLN BRONZE DECANTER
6 oz. bronze tone over clear glass. Dated 1979 on bottom. Holds Wild Country or Tai Winds After Shave. S.S.P. $10.99, C.M.V. $10.99 M.B.
1979 PRESIDENT WASHINGTON BRONZE DECANTER
6 oz. bronze tone over clear glass. Dated 1979 on bottom. Holds Wild Country or Tai Winds After Shave. S.S.P. $10.99, C.M.V. $10.99 M.B.

1973-74 SURE WINNER BASEBALL DECANTER
White ball with dark blue lettering, dark blue base contains Liquid Hair Trainer. SSP $2.00 CMV $3.50 MB $2.00 BO
1970 Only - FIRST DOWN
5 oz. brown glass, white plastic base. Came in Wild Country or Sports Rally Bracing Lotion. O.S.P. $4.00 C.M.V. $5.00 M.B.
1973-74 FIRST DOWN
5 oz. brown glass, white base. Came in Deep Woods & Sure Winner Bracing Lotion. S.S.P. $3.00 C.M.V. $4.00 M.B.

1973-74 MARINE BINOCULARS DECANTER
Black over clear glass with gold caps. One side holds 4 oz. Tai Winds or Tribute Cologne, other side holds 4 oz. Tai Winds or Tribute After Shave. S.S.P. $8.00 CMV $8.00 MB $6.00 BO

1973-75 PASS PLAY DECANTER
5 oz. blue glass with white soft plastic top over cap. Came in Sure Winner Bracing Lotion or Wild Country After Shave. OSP $5.00 CMV $6.00 BO $7.00 MB
1975-76 PERFECT DRIVE DECANTER
4 oz. green glass with white plastic top over cap. Holds Avon Spicy After Shave or Avon Protein Hair/Scalp Conditioner. OSP $6.00 CMV $6.00 BO $7.00 MB

1976-77 CAPITOL DECANTER
4.5 oz. white milk glass with white cap & gold tip. Came in Spicy or Wild Country After Shave. O.S.P. $4.00 C.M.V. $4.00 MB $3.00 BO

1970-72 CAPITOL DECANTER
5 oz. lt. amber glass, gold cap. Came in Leather & Tribute After Shave. O.S.P. $5.00 CMV $4.00 MB $5.00

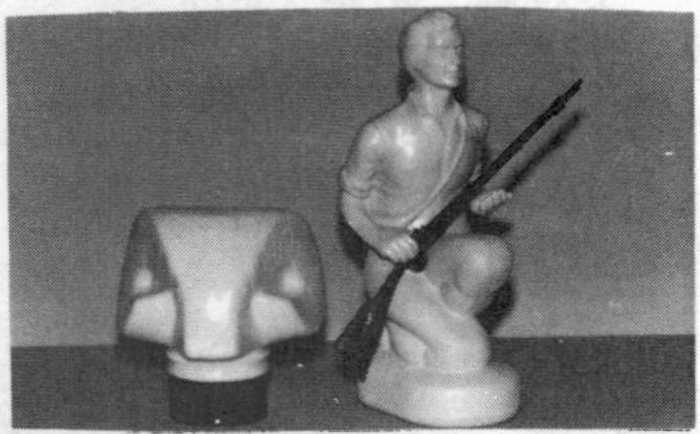

1975-76 RAM'S HEAD DECANTER
5 oz. white opal glass on brown plastic base. Holds Wild Country or Avon Blend 7 After Shave. OSP $5.00 CMV $4.00 MB $3.00 BO

1975-76 MINUTEMAN DECANTER
4 oz. white opal glass with plastic top. Holds Wild Country or Tai Winds After Shave. OSP $7.00 CMV $7.00 BO $8.00 MB

1974-76 SUPER SHOE DECANTER
6 oz. white plastic shoe with blue plastic toe section cap. Holds Sure Winner Liquid Hair Trainer or Sure Winner Bracing Lotion. OSP $3.00 CMV $3.00 MB $2.00 BO

1974-75 JUST FOR KICKS DECANTER
7 oz. black & white plastic shoe with black plastic cap. Holds Avon Spicy or Avon Sure Winner Bracing Lotion. O.S.P. $4.00 CMV $3.00 MB $2.00 BO

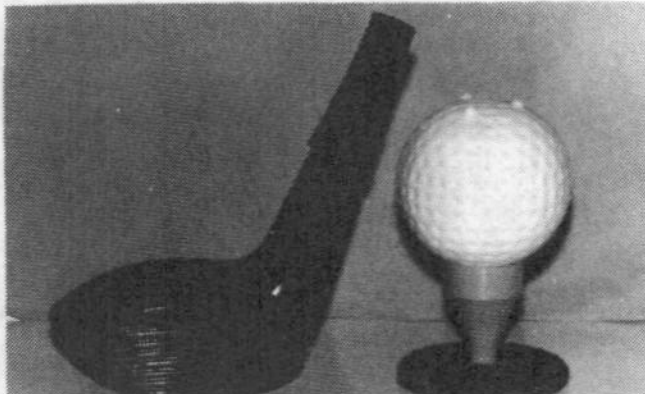

1973-75 LONG DRIVE DECANTER
4 oz. brown glass with black cap. Holds Deep Woods After Shave or Electric Pre-Shave Lotion. SSP $4.00 CMV $4.00 MB $3.00 BO

1973-75 TEE-OFF DECANTER
3 oz. white golf ball on a yellow tee & fits into a green plastic green. Holds Protein Hair Lotion for Men, Avon Spicy After Shave or Electric Pre-Shave Lotion. SSP $3.00 CMV $4.00 MB $3.00 BO

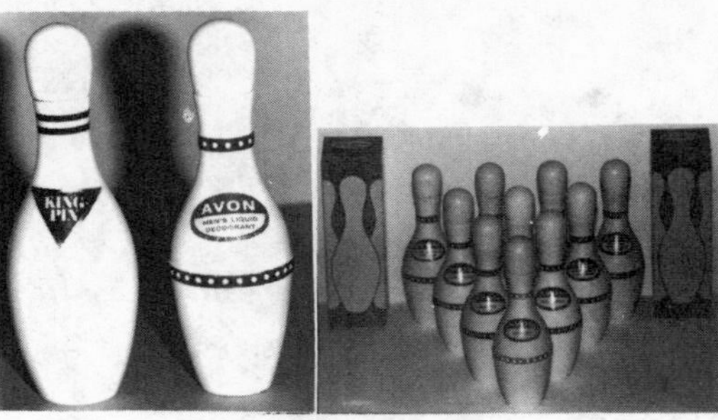

1969-70 KING PIN
4 oz. 6½" high. White glass & cap, red label. Came in Wild Country & Bravo After Shave. OSP $3.00 CMV $3.00 MB $2.00 BO

1960-62 BOWLING PIN
4 oz. white plastic trimmed in red. Came in Vigorate, Liquid Deodorant, Hand Guard, Hair Trainer, After Shaving Lotion, After Shower for Men, Liquid Hair Lotion, Shampoo, Cream Hair Lotion & Electric Pre-Shave. O.S.P. $1.19 CMV 10 different. $16.00 each BO $19.00 MB Vigorate $20.00 BO $24.00 MB

1965-66 BOOT "SILVER TOP"
8 oz. amber glass, silver cap with hook on cap. Came in Leather All Purpose Lotion for Men. O.S.P. $5.00 C.M.V. $6.50 $10.00 in box.

1966-71 BOOT "GOLD TOP"
8 oz. amber glass with hook on cap. Came in Leather All Purpose Cologne for Men. O.S.P. $5.00 C.M.V. $3.00 M.B. $4.00 Gold top boot with no hook on cap is 1971-72 with Leather Cologne. O.S.P. $5.00 C.M.V. $2.00

1967-70 BOOT SPRAY COLOGNE
3 oz. tan plastic coated with black cap. Came in Leather All Purpose Cologne in early issues. C.M.V. $6.00 M.B. & Leather Cologne Spray in later issues. O.S.P. $4.00 C.M.V. $3.50 M.B. $4.00

1972-73 BIG GAME RHINO
4 oz. green glass with green plastic head over cap. Came in Spicy or Tai Winds After Shave. S.S.P. $4.00 C.M.V. $4.00 BO $5.00 MB

1972-73 BLACKSMITH'S ANVIL DECANTER
4 oz. black glass with silver cap. Came in Deep Woods or Avon Leather After Shave. SSP $4.00 CMV $4.00 MB $3.00 BO

1969-70 WISE CHOICE OWL
4 oz. silver top, lt. amber bottom. Came in Excalibur or Leather After Shave. OSP $4.00 CMV $4.00 MB $6.00

1972-73 RADIO
5" high, dark amber glass with gold cap & paper dial on front. Holds 5 oz. liquid Hair Lotion, Wild Country or Spicy After Shave. OSP $4.00 CMV $4.00 MB $5.00

1973-75 WESTERN BOOT
5 oz. dark amber glass bottle, silver cap & clamp on spurs. Came in Wild Country or Leather. SSP $4.00 CMV $4.00 MB $3.00 BO Light green glass boot, test bottle. CMV $35.00

1975-76 REVOLUTIONARY CANNON
2 oz. bronze spray over glass with plastic cap. Holds Avon Spicy or Avon Blend 7 After Shave. OSP $4.00 CMV $3.00 MB $2.00 BO

1973-74 HOMESTEAD DECANTER
4 oz. brown glass with gray plastic chimney over cap. Holds Wild Country After Shave or Electric Pre-Shave. O.S.P. $3.00 CMV $3.00 MB $2.00 BO

1966 DEFENDER CANNON
6 oz. 9½" long, amber glass, brown plastic stand, gold caps & gold center band, small paper label. Came in Leather, Island Lime & Tribute After Shave. O.S.P. $5.00 C.M.V. $20.00 in box, $15.00 bottle & stand.

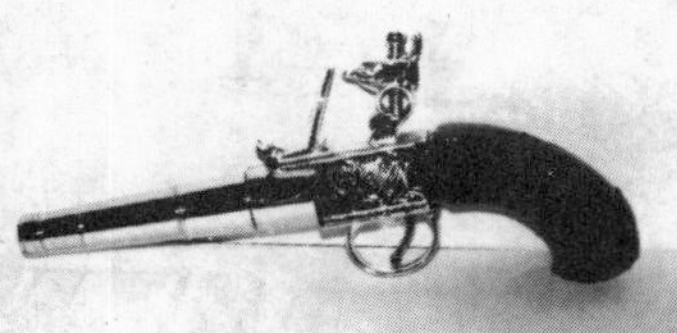

1978-79 THOMAS JEFFERSON HAND GUN DECANTER
10" long 2.5 oz. dark amber glass with gold and silver plastic cap. Holds Deep Woods or Everest cologne. S.S.P. $9.99, C.M.V. $9.99 M.B.

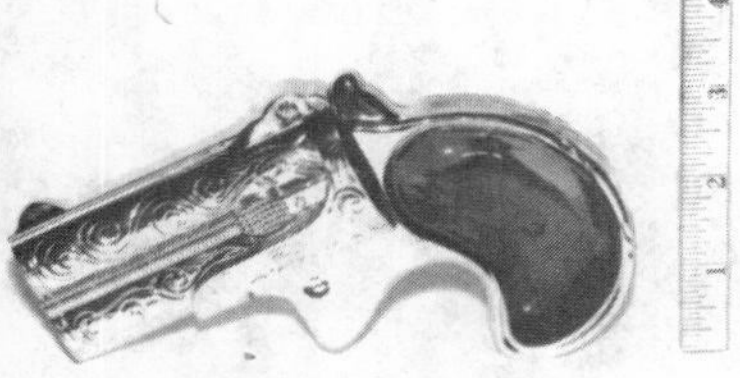

1977 DERRINGER
2 oz. gold plated over amber glass. Came in Deep Woods or Wild Country. SSP $6.66 CMV $5.00 MB $4.00 BO

1976-77 PEPPERBOX PISTOL 1850
3 oz. silver plated over clear glass barrel bottle with gold and brown plastic handle cap. Came in Everest or Tai Winds. SSP $7.77 CMV $6.50 MB $5.50 BO

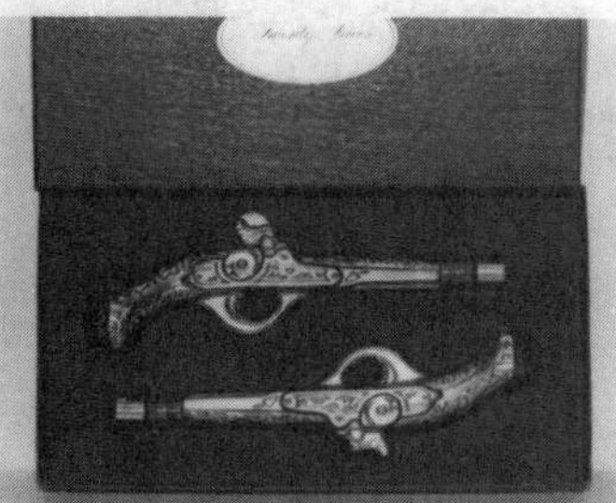

1967-69 TWENTY PACES
3 oz. each, 10" long. Gold paint over clear glass, gold cap. Red paper labels on end of barrel. Came in All Purpose Cologne, Wild Country & Leather After Shave. O.S.P. $11.95 CMV brown box lined with red $40.00. Black lined box $115.00. Blue lined box $150.00. Very rare gun with raised sight did not break off in glass mold. Shown in top half of picture. CMV $100.00. Raised sight gun only.

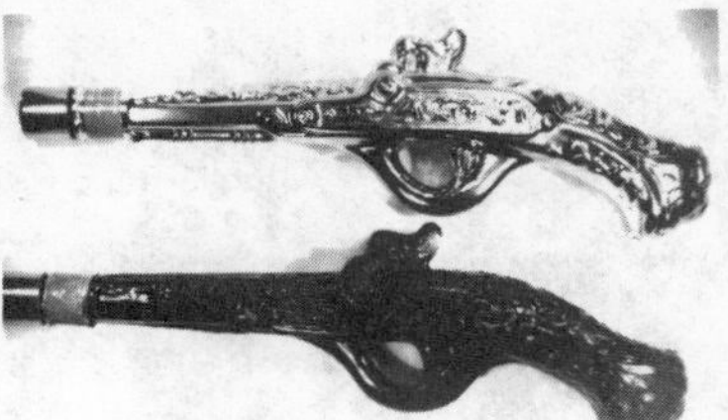

1967-69 TWENTY PACES
3 oz. gold paint over clear glass, gold cap. Came in All Purpose Cologne, Wild Country & Leather After Shave. Came in sets of 2. CMV $10.00 each.

1967 TWENTY PACES FACTORY TEST BOTTLE
3 oz. dark amber glass. Never filled or sold. C.M.V. $85.00

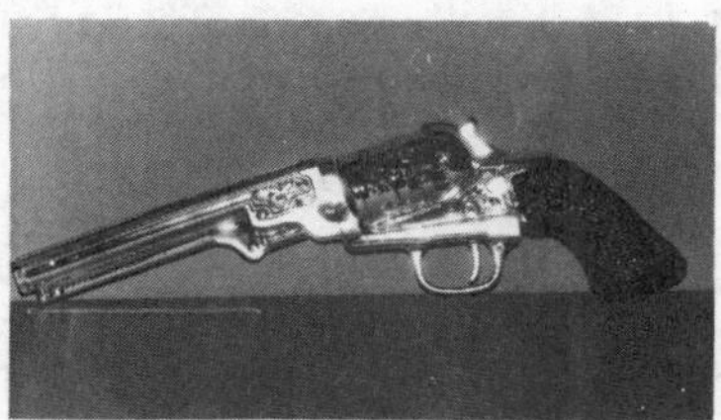

1975-76 COLT REVOLVER (1851)
3 oz. amber glass with silver plastic barrel. Holds Wild Country or Deep Woods After Shave. OSP $9.00 CMV $9.00 MB $8.00 BO

1973-74 DUELING PISTOL 1760
4 oz. brown glass with silver clamp on parts, silver cap. Holds Deep Woods or Tai Winds After Shave. S.S.P. $8.00 CMV $7.00 MB $6.00 BO

1975 DUELING PISTOL II
Same as above but black glass & gold plastic parts. Came in Wild Country or Tai Winds. SSP $8.00 CMV $8.00 BO $9.00 MB

1976 BLUNDERBUSS PISTOL 1780
12½" long, 5.5 oz. dark amber glass, gold cap & plastic trigger. O.S.P. $12.00 CMV $9.00 MB $8.00 BO

1979-80 GAS PUMP - REMEMBER WHEN DECANTER
4 oz. clear glass painted yellow, white top, yellow cap. Came in Light Musk or Cool Sage. SSP $6.99 CMV $6.99 MB

1979-80 VOLCANIC REPEATING PISTOL DECANTER
2 oz. silver coated over clear glass. Silver & pearl plastic handle. Holds Wild Country or Brisk Spice Cologne. SSP $10.99 CMV $10.99

1971-72 AMERICAN EAGLE
6" high, dark amber glass with gold eagle head. Holds 5 oz. Oland or Windjammer After Shave. O.S.P. $5.00 C.M.V. $4.00 M.B. $5.00
1973-75 Eagle is black glass with dark gold head. CMV $5.00 BO $6.00 MB

1964-65 CAPTAINS CHOICE
8 oz. green glass with green paper label, gold cap. Came in Spicy & Original After Shave Lotion, Electric Pre-Shave Lotion, Spicy After Shower Cologne for Men & Vigorate After Shave Lotion. O.S.P. $2.50 C.M.V. $7.00 - $10.00 in box.

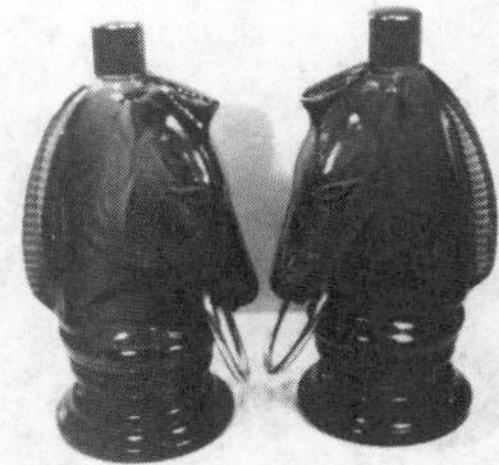

1968-69 SHORT PONY DECANTER
Right - 4 oz. green glass, gold cap. Came in Wild Country, Windjammer, Spicy or Electric Pre-Shave. O.S.P. $3.50 C.M.V. $2.00 BO $3.00 MB

FOREIGN SHORT PONY DECANTER
Gold cap. greenish amber color. $7.00
Bright green from Germany M.B. $15.00

1966 VIKING HORN
7 oz. dark amber glass with gold cap & decoration. Came in Spicy, Blue Blazer & original After Shave. O.S.P. $5.00 CMV $12.00 BO $17.50 MB

1971-72 PONY EXPRESS
5 oz. brown glass with copper colored man on cap. Came in Avon Leather or Wild Country After Shave. S.S.P. $4.00 CMV $6.00 MB $4.00 BO

1971-72 BUCKING BRONCO
6 oz. dark amber glass horse with bronze plastic cowboy cap. O.S.P. $6.00 C.M.V. $3.00 M.B. $6.00

1971 DUCK AFTER SHAVE
3 oz. glass bottles with gold caps & ducks painted on sides. Came in Collector's Organizer Set only in Tai Winds & Wild Country After Shave. C.M.V. $3.00 ea.

1973-74 PONY POST MINIATURE
1.5 oz. clear glass with gold cap & ring. Holds Oland or Spicy After Shave. O.S.P. $3.00 CMV $2.00 BO $3.00 MB

1972-73 PONY POST
5 oz. bronze paint over clear glass with bronze cap & nose ring. Holds Tai Winds or Leather After Shave. O.S.P. $5.00 CMV $3.00 BO $4.00 MB

1966-67 PONY POST "TALL"
8 oz. green glass with gold cap & nose ring. Holds Island Lime, Tribute or Leather After Shave. O.S.P. $4.00 CMV $12.00 MB $5.00 BO

1974-75 ALASKAN MOOSE
8 oz. amber glass with cream colored plastic antlers. Holds Deep Woods or Wild Country After Shave. O.S.P. $7.00 CMV $7.00 BO $9.00 MB

1973-74 TEN-POINT BUCK DECANTER
6 oz. redish brown glass with redish brown plastic head & gold antlers. Holds Wild Country or Leather After Shave. O.S.P. $7.00 CMV $7.00 MB $5.00 BO

1974-76 WILD TURKEY
6 oz. amber glass with silver & red plastic head. Holds Wild Country or Deep Woods After Shave. OSP $5.00 CMV $5.00 BO $6.00 MB

1973-75 QUAIL DECANTER
5.5 oz. brown glass, gold cap. Came in Avon Blend 7, Deep Woods or Wild Country After Shave. OSP $6.00 CMV $5.00 MB $4.00 BO

1967-68 MALLARD DUCK
6 oz. green glass, silver head. Came in Spicy, Tribute, Blue Blazer, Windjammer After Shave. OSP $5.00 CMV $6.00 BO $10.00 MB

1974-76 MALLARD-IN-FLIGHT
5 oz. amber glass with green plastic head. Holds Wild Country or Tai Winds Cologne or After Shave. OSP $6.00 CMV $7.00 MB $6.00 BO

RIGHT 1972 SEA TROPHY
5.5 oz. lt. blue with plastic blue head over cap. Came in Wild Country or Windjammer After Shave. S.S.P. $5.00 C.M.V. $7.00 B.O. $9.00 M.B.

LEFT 1973-74 RAINBOW TROUT DECANTER
over cap. Holds Deep Woods or Tai Winds SSP $5.00 CMV $5.00 MB $4.00 BO

1975 SPORT OF KINGS DECANTER
5 oz. amber glass with plastic head. Holds Wild Country, Avon Spicy or Avon Leather After Shave. O.S.P. $5.00 C.MV. $4.00 MB $3.00 BO

1975-76 THE AMERICAN BUFFALO
5 oz. amber glass with amber plastic head & ivory colored horns. Holds Wild Country or Deep Woods After Shave. O.S.P. $6.00 CMV $6.00 MB $5.00 BO

1972-74 PHEASANT DECANTER
5 oz. brown glass with green plastic head. Holds Oland or Leather After Shave. OSP $6.00 CMV $6.00 MB $4.00 BO

1973-74 CANADA GOOSE DECANTER
5 oz. brown glass with black plastic head. Holds Deep Woods or Wild Country After Shave or Cologne. O.S.P. After Shave $6.00 CMV $6.00 BO $8.00 MB

HOW TO INVEST

RULES FOR COLLECTING

"The hunger to find a tin toy for $30.00, rather than a good night's sleep drives a painter to wake up at three in the morning in his Brooklyn home. He's rushing to Rennger's flea market in Pennsylvania by the time the rosy fingers of dawn peek over the tents." Does this sound familiar? Of course it does, if you're an Avon collector. How many foolish things have you ever done while seeking that hoped-for bargain or very much sought after item? People are doing this kind of thing in every part of America — and they are doing it for almost anything you could name; be it a tin toy or a campaign button. In today's market, anything is collectible if it has aesthetic vitality, if it's pleasing to the eye and to the senses. However, we are interested in Avon and California Perfume . . . and Avon collecting is now a big collecting field. For the new collectors and to refresh seasoned collectors — we've found collecting, like other investments, has rules to follow for the best results:

- If you don't like an item, don't buy it no matter how much of a bargain it seems to be. The only good investments are those that are enjoyed.
- The old goes up in value, or at least retains its resale value. New items take longer to increase in value and stay around longer. Of course, we all know, there are more collectors today.
- Buy it when you see it; Avons don't stay put . . . some don't have a very long shelf life.
- If you don't know your dealers, be sure you know your Avons. Fakes can be convincing (don't we all know that!).
- It is acceptable to haggle - it cannot hurt to ask if there is a lower price. Often in a booth or flea market there will be a better price available - don't be timid.
- Start small and learn the market. Browse, study the guides and learn all you can before you start buying.
- Measure your space - don't be the collector who buys a lot of items only to bring them home with no place to put them (ha, ha).
- Don't change your item in any way - don't paint it, add lettering etc. . . . this may destroy the value.

The above rules are good ones to keep in mind - the advice I've found most helpful is to have FUN while collecting . . . whether it be at a flea market, garage sale or convention.

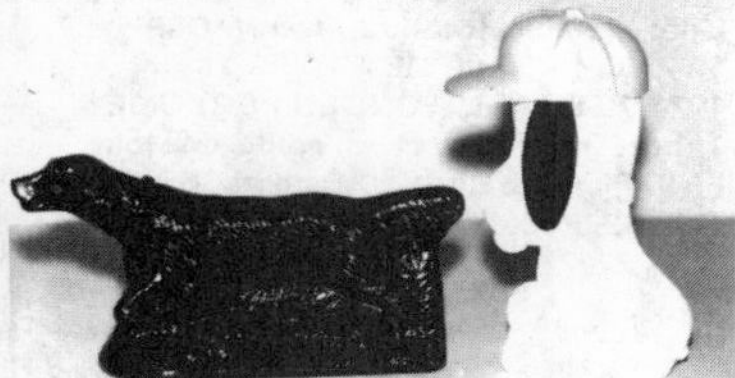

1973-74 AT POINT DECANTER
5 oz. redish brown glass with redish brown plastic head. SSP $4.00, CMV $4.00 MB, $2.00 BO

1969-71 SNOOPY SURPRISE
5 oz. - 5½" high. White glass with blue or yellow hat & black ears. Came in Wild Country, Excalibur After Shave & Sports Rally Bracing Lotion. OSP $4.00, CMV $3.00 MB, $4.00

1972-73 OLD FAITHFUL
5 oz. brown glass with brown plastic head & gold keg. Holds Wild Country or Spicy After Shave. SSP $5.00 CMV $5.00 BO $7.00 MB Smaller German St. Bernard on right (silver barrel) CMV $10.00

1975-77 NOBLE PRINCE DECANTER
4 oz. brown glass with brown plastic head Holds Wild Country After Shave or Electric Pre-Shave Lotion. O.S.P. $3.25 CMV $4.00 MB $3.00 BO

1973-75 CLASSIC LION
8 oz. green glass with green plastic head. Holds Wild Country, Tribute After Shave or Deep Woods Emollient After Shave. OSP $6.00 CMV $5.00 MB $4.00 BO

1975-76 LONGHORN STEER
5 oz. dark amber glass with amber plastic head, ivory colored horns. Holds Wild Country or Tai Winds After Shave. O.S.P. $6.00 C.M.V. $6.00 M.B.

1977 MAJESTIC ELEPHANT
5.5 oz. gray painted over clear glass. Gray head cap. Came in Wild Country or Deep Woods. S.S.P. $8.99 CMV $6.00 MB $5.00 BO

1976-77 WILDERNESS CLASSIC
6 oz. silver plated over clear glass. Silver plastic head. Came in Sweet Honesty or Deep Woods. S.S.P. $8.99 CMV $10.00 MB $8.00 BO

LEFT 1977-79 FAITHFUL LADDIE
4 oz. light amber glass & amber head cap. Came in Wild Country or Deep Woods. SSP $4.99 CMV $4.00 MB $3.00 BO
RIGHT 1977 KODIAK BEAR
6 oz. dark amber glass & head. Came in Wild Country or Deep Woods. SSP $4.99 CMV $4.00 MB $3.00 BO

1977-80 DESK CADDY
Brown cork holder, silver top made in Spain. Holds 4 oz. clear glass bottle of Clint Cologne, red letters, silver cap or Wild Country. SSP $8.99 CMV $6.50 MB

LEFT 1977-78 GIFT COLOGNE FOR MEN
2 oz. clear glass bottle, dark blue cap. Came in Wild Country, Deep Woods, Clint or Everest cologne. O.S.P. $3.00 CMV $1.00 MB 50c BO
RIGHT 1977-78 LOCKER TIME
6 oz. green plastic bottle, yellow cap. Came in Sweet Honesty Body Splash or Wild Country. Came with 13 stick on decals. SSP $3.99 CMV $2.00 MB $1.00 BO

WOMEN'S DECANTERS

ALL CONTAINERS PRICED EMPTY

1972-73 DREAM GARDEN
½ oz. pink frosted glass with gold cap. Came in Moonwind, Bird of Paradise, Charisma Elusive or Unforgettable perfume oil. O.S.P. $5.00 CMV $15.00 MB $8.00 BO
1973 SNOW MAN PETITE PERFUME
.25 oz. textured glass with pink eyes, mouth & scarf. Gold cap. Came in Cotillion, Bird of Paradise, Field Flowers. O.S.P. $4.00 CMV $5.00 BO $6.00 MB
1974-76 PRECIOUS SWAN PERFUME DECANTER
1/8 oz. frosted glass with gold cap. Came in Field Flowers, Bird of Paradise or Charisma OSP $4.00 CMV $3.00 BO $4.00 MB

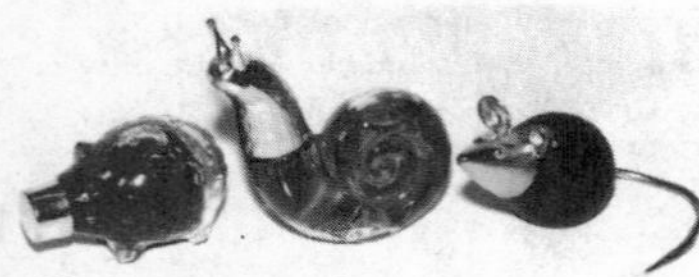

1972 PETITE PIGLET
2" long embossed clear glass with gold cap. Holds ¼oz. perfume in Field Flowers, Bird of Paradise, Elusive & Charisma. O.S.P. $5.00 CMV $6.00 BO $7.00 MB
1968-69 SNAIL PERFUME
¼ oz. gold cap, clear glass. Came in Charisma, Brocade, Regence, Unforgettable, Rapture & Occur!. OSP $6.25 CMV $13.50 MB $7.00 BO
1970 PERFUME PETITE MOUSE
Frosted glass with gold head and tail, holds ¼ oz. perfume in Elusive, Charisma, Brocade, Regence. O.S.P. $7.50 Unforgettable, Rapture & Occur. O.S.P. $6.25 C.M.V. $17.50 MB $12.00 BO

1975-76 PRECIOUS TURTLE
.66 oz. gold jar with plastic lid. Came in Patchword, or Roses, Roses Cream Sachet. OSP $4.00 CMV $4.00 MB $3.00 BO
1971-73 TREASURE TURTLE
1 oz. brown glass turtle with gold head. Holds Field Flowers, Hana Gasa, Bird of Paradise, Elusive, Charisma, Brocade, Unforgettable, Rapture, Occur!, Somewhere, Topaze, Cotillion, Here's My Heart and Persian Wood. O.S.P. $3.50 C.M.V. $4.00 MB $3.00 BO

1974-76 ONE DRAM PERFUME
Clear glass with gold cap. Came in Bird of Paradise, Charisma or Field Flowers. O.S.P. $3.75 Sonnet, Moonwind or Imperial Garden. OSP $4.25 CMV $3.50 MB $2.00 BO
1974-75 STRAWBERRY FAIR PERFUME
1/8 oz. red glass, silver cap. Came in Moonwind, Charisma or Sonnet. O.S.P. $4.00 CMV $4.00 MB $3.00 BO

1967 CHRISTMAS ORNAMENTS
Round 4 oz. bubble bath. Came in gold, silver, red, green. Silver caps. O.S.P. $1.75 CMV $9.00 each MB $7.00 each BO mint

1973-74 PRECIOUS SLIPPER
.25oz. frosted glass bottle with gold cap. Came in Sonnet or Moonwind. O.S.P. $4.00 CMV $6.00 MB $5.00 BO
1969-70 LOVE BIRD PERFUME
¼ oz. frosted bird with silver cap. 2½" long. Came in Charisma, Elusive, Brocade, Regence, Unforgettable, Rapture, Occur! OSP $6.25 CMV $9.00 MB $5.00 BO
1972-73 SMALL WONDER PERFUME
1/8 oz. frosted glass with gold cap. Holds Field Flowers, Bird of Paradise, Charisma OSP $2.50 CMV $6.00 MB $4.00 BO

1975 SEWING NOTIONS
1 oz. pink and white glass with silver cap. Holds Sweet Honesty, To A Wild Rose or Cotillion. OSP $3.00 CMV $3.00 MB $2.00 BO
1975 CRYSTALIER COLOGNE DECANTER
2 oz. clear glass. Filled with Field Flowers, Bird of Paradise or Roses, Roses Cologne. OSP $4.00 CMV $4.00 MB $3.00 BO
1975-77 BABY OWL
1 oz. clear glass, gold cap. Holds Sweet Honesty or Occur Cologne. O.S.P. $2.00 CMV $2.00 BO $3.00 MB
1975-76 PERT PENGUIN
1 oz. clear glass, gold cap. Holds Field Flowers or Cotillion Cologne. O.S.P. $2.00 CMV $2.00 BO $3.00 MB

AVON

MAZE GAME

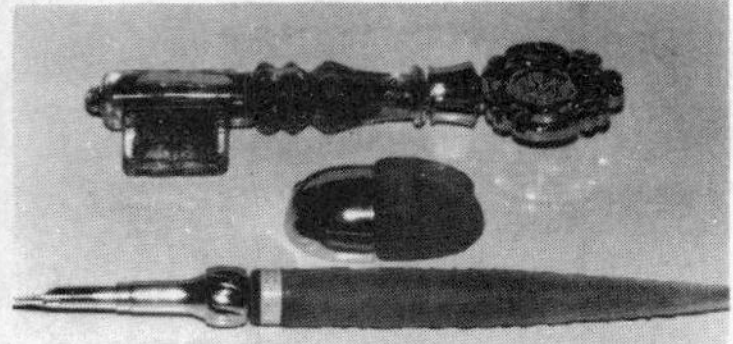

1967 KEY NOTE PERFUME
¼ oz. glass key with gold plastic cap. 4A design on cap. Came in Here's My Heart, To A Wild Rose. OSP $5.00. Somewhere Topaze, Cotillion OSP $5.50. Unforgettable, Rapture, Occur! OSP $6.50 CMV $20.00 in box $10.00 key only.

1975-76 LADY BUG PERFUME DECANTER
1/8 oz. frosted glass, gold cap. Came in Sonnet, Moonwind or Patchwork. O.S.P. $4.00 CMV $3.00 BO $4.00 MB

1971-72 SCENT WITH LOVE
¼ oz. frosted glass with gold pen cap, white and gold label around bottle. Came in Field Flowers, Moonwind, Bird of Paradise, Charisma, Elusive, Moonwind. OSP $6.00 CMV $12.50 MB $7.00 BO

1974-79 YULE TREE
3 oz. green glass with green plastic top and gold star. Came in Sonnet, Moonwind or Field Flowers cologne. O.S.P. $4.00 C.M.V. $3.00 BO $4.00 MB

1975 TOUCH OF CHRISTMAS
1 oz. green glass with red cap. Holds Unforgetable or Imperial Garden. O.S.P. $2.50 CMV $3.00 MB, $2.00 BO. Reissued 1979 in Zany & Here's My Heart. Same CMV

1975 CRYSTALTREE COLOGNE DECANTER
3 oz. clear glass with gold plastic star cap. Holds Moonwind or Sonnet. O.S.P. $6.00 CMV $5.00 MB $4.00 BO

1972-74 COLOGNE ROYALE
1 oz. clear glass, gold cap. Came in Field Flowers, Roses, Roses, Bird of Paradise, Sonnet, Charisma, Unforgettable, Somewhere. SSP $1.75 CMV $3.00 MB $2.00 BO

1973-74 COURTING CARRIAGE
1 oz. clear glass, gold cap. Came in Moonwind, Sonnet, Field Flowers or Flower Talk. SSP $2.00 CMV $3.00 MB $2.00 BO

1972-74 PINEAPPLE PETITE COLOGNE
1 oz. clear glass, gold cap. Came in Roses, Roses, Charisma, Elusive, Brocade or Regence. SSP $2.00 CMV $3.00 MB $2.00 BO

LEFT 1974-75 HEAVENLY ANGEL COLOGNE
2 oz. clear glass with white top. Holds Occur!, Unforgettable, Somewhere, Here's My Heart, or Sweet Honesty cologne. OSP $4.00 CMV $4.00 MB $3.00 BO

RIGHT 1968-69 GOLDEN ANGEL BATH OIL
4 oz. Gold bottle, gold paper wings. Gold & white cap. O.S.P. $3.50 C.M.V. $7.00 M.B. $4.00 BO Mint

1970-71 CHRISTMAS ORNAMENT BUBBLE BATH
5 oz. Christmas ornament with bubble bath in red, orange or green plastic bottles with silver caps. O.S.P. $2.50 C.M.V. $5.00 M.B. $3.00 BO

1968-69 CHRISTMAS SPARKLERS
4 oz. Bubble bath. Came in gold, green, blue & red with gold caps. 2 sides of bottle are indented. OSP $2.50 CMV $7.00 MB $5.00 BO mint.

1968 CHRISTMAS SPARKLER-PURPLE
4 oz. painted purple over clear glass, gold cap. OSP $2.50 CMV $22.50 Mint. Sold only on West Coast area.

1969-70 CHRISTMAS COLOGNE
3 oz. ea. Unforgettable is silver & pink, Occur! is gold & blue. Somewhere is silver & green. Topaze is bronze & yellow. O.S.P. $3.50 C.M.V. Somewhere or Topaze $9.00 M.B. Unforgettable or Occur! $7.00 M.B. $2.00 less no box.

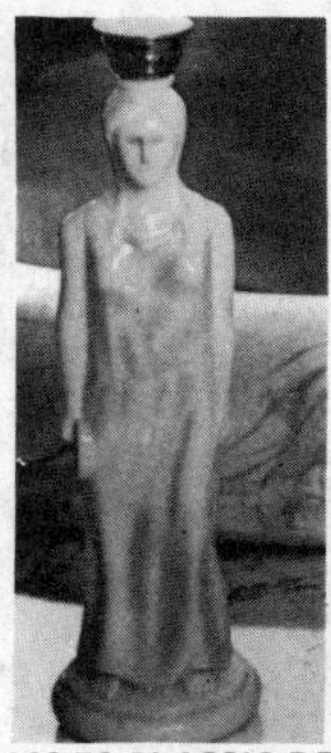

1969-70 CLASSIC DECANTER
8 oz. white glass bottle with gold cap. 11" high, filled with Skin-So-Soft bath oil. S.S.P. $5.00 C.M.V. $7.00 in box. $5.00 bottle only.

1971-72 SEA MAIDEN SKIN-SO-SOFT
6 oz. gold cap, clear glass, 10" high. SSP $5.00 CMV $7.00 MB $5.00 BO

1967-68 ICICLE PERFUME
1 dram, gold cap. Came in Here's My Heart, To A wild Rose, O.S.P. $2.50, Somewhere, Topaz, Cotillion, O.S.P. $2.75, Unforgettable, Rapture, Occur. O.S.P. $3.25 Regence, O.S.P. $3.75, with gold neck label. C.M.V. $5.00 in box. $4.00 bottle only.

1968-70 CHRISTMAS TREES
4 oz. Bubble bath. Came in red, green, gold & silver painted over clear glass. O.S.P. $2.50 CMV $7.00 MB $5.00 BO Mint

AN OPEN LETTER TO ALL AVON REPS.

Do you want to increase the number of Avon collectors in the world? This would greatly increase your sales, too, you know! Try to find out your customer's various interests and those of her children and husband, too! For example:

Mrs. Smith loves animals - bring every animal decanter to her attention as they appear on the market. Sell her the first one and she'll likely buy more, or all, that come! Mr. Smith is a sports fan! Point out what a smart collection he could have on a neat shelf in his den. Young Johnny would love the majestic elephant, or that dinosaur decanter and teenager Sue really "digs" the "Fried Egg" or "Hamburger" compacts.

All these people have a good chance of ending up being a collector! So what does that really mean? Well it means that your collectables will maintain their value and the market will grow steadily. Avon Reps. will have good steady sales. Collectors will have a wider and wider circle of ever growing and interested folk to swap and shop with.

Show your own collection to friends, help to stir the interest of others. Believe me, it will pay off in the end!!

Most important of all, don't forget to carry a copy of the Avon Encyclopedia to show your customers. Show them the color pages on "How collectors display their Avons." By showing this book to your customers, you can help create new collectors and you will profit 10 fold, as collectors will buy many more Avon products from you. Be sure to point out information on the Bud Hastin Avon Club which they can enjoy right from their own living room. Tell them about the free advertising to over 4000 members to buy, sell or trade Avons. Remember, if you help educate your customers on Avon Collecting you will profit greatly in bigger future sales.

1974-75 18th CENTURY CLASSIC FIGURINE YOUNG BOY
4 oz. white sprayed glass with white plastic head. Choice of Sonnet or Moonwind cologne or foaming bath oil. O.S.P. $5.00 CMV $7.00 BO $9.00 MB
1974-75 18th CENTURY CLASSIC FIGURINE YOUNG GIRL
4 oz. white sprayed glass with white plastic head. Choice of Sonnet or Moonwind cologne or foaming bath oil. O.S.P. $5.00 CMV $5.00 BO $7.00 MB

1975-77 FLY-A-BALLOON
3 oz. glass sprayed blue with light blue top & red plastic balloon. Holds Moonwind or Bird of Paradise cologne. OSP $7.00 CMV $7.00 BO $8.00 MB
1975-77 SKIP-A-ROPE
4 oz. yellow sprayed glass with yellow plastic top and white plastic rope. Holds Sweet Honesty, Bird of Paradise or Roses, Roses cologne. O.S.P. $7.00 C.M.V. $7.00 BO $8.00 MB

1973 MY PET & JENNIFER FIGURINES
LEFT - MY PET Green & brown, white kitten, ceramic figurine. 1973 embossed in ceramic & printed on box.
RIGHT - JENNIFER Pastel turquoise dress & hat, ceramic figurine. 1973 embossed in ceramic & printed on box. Both issued from Springdale, Ohio, branch only. Some came with flowers in center of hat & some with flowers on the right side of hat. Same CMV. OSP $9.99 CMV - My Pet $35.00 CMV - Jennifer $45.00

1976-77 LIBRARY LAMP DECANTER
4 oz. gold plated base over clear glass, gold cap. Came in Topaze & Charisma cologne. OSP $9.00 CMV $5.00 BO $6.00 MB
1976-79 BRIDAL MOMENTS
5 oz. white paint over clear glass. White plastic top. Came in Sweet Honesty or Unforgettable cologne. O.S.P. $9.00 CMV $7.00 MB $6.00 BO

1970 BOW TIE PERFUME
1/8 oz. clear glass. Shape of bow with gold cap. Came in Pink Slipper Soap in Charisma & Cotillion. CMV $4.00 mint

1972-73 VICTORIAN LADY
5 oz. white milk glass, white plastic cap. Came in Bird of Paradise, Unforgettable, Occur!, Charisma Foaming Bath Oil. SSP $4.00 CMV $5.00 BO $7.00 MB

LEFT TO RIGHT

1974-75 PRETTY GIRL PINK
6 oz. glass sprayed pink base with light pink top. Holds Unforgettable, Topaze or Occur! Cologne. OSP $4.00 CMV $7.00 BO $9.00 MB

1972-73 LITTLE GIRL BLUE
3 oz. blue painted glass with blue plastic cap. Came in Brocade, Unforgettable, Somewhere or Cotillion. S.S.P. $4.00 C.M.V. $7.00 BO $9.00 MB

1973-74 LITTLE KATE
3 oz. pastel orange painted glass with orange plastic hat over cap. Came in Bird of Paradise, Charisma, Unforgettable. S.S.P. $4.00 CMV $7.00 BO $9.00 MB

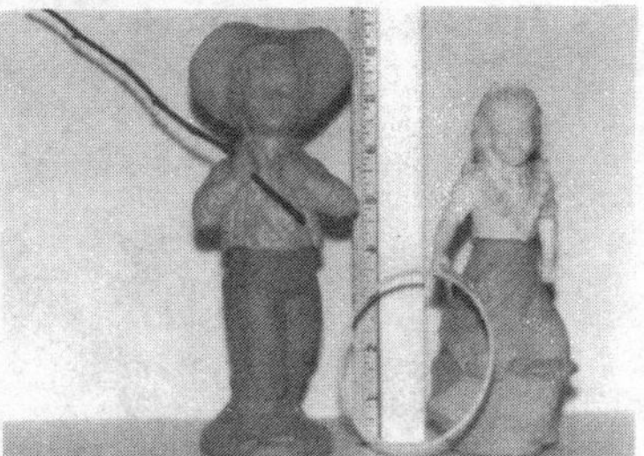

1976-78 CATCH-A-FISH DECANTER
3 oz. dark tan, painted over clear glass, light tan plastic top, yellow hat & brown plastic removable pole. Came in Field Flowers or Sonnet cologne. O.S.P.$9.50 CMV $7.00 BO $8.00 MB

1977-78 ROLL-A-HOOP DECANTER
3.75 oz. dull pink painted over clear glass base. light pink plastic top, white plastic hoop. Came in Field Flowers or Cotillion cologne. O.S.P. $10.00 CMV $7.00 BO $8.00 MB

LEFT 1976-78 AMERICAN BELL
4 oz. yellow dull paint over clear glass, yellow cap. Came in Cotillion or Sonnet cologne. SSP $5.99 CMV $6.00 MB $5.00 BO

RIGHT 1976-78 LITTLE BO PEEP DECANTER
2 oz. white dull paint over white milk glass base, white plastic top & cane. Came in Sweet Honesty or Unforgettable cologne. SSP $4.99 CMV $5.00 MB $4.00 BO

LEFT TO RIGHT

1971-72 FASHION FIGURINE COLOGNE
4 oz. white plastic top & white painted bottom, over clear glass. Later issue light blue, 6" high. Came in Field Flowers, Elusive, Bird of Paradise, Brocade. S.S.P. $4.00 CMV $9.00 BO $12.00 MB

1973-74 VICTORIAN FASHION FIGURINE
4 oz. light green (some call it blue or aqua) painted over clear glass base with green plastic top. Came in Charisma, Field Flowers, Bird of Paradise Cologne. S.S.P. $4.00 C.M.V. $25.00 BO $27.50 MB

1972 ELIZABETHAN FASHION FIGURINE
4 oz. pink painted glass bottom over clear glass with pink plastic top. 6" high. Came in Moonwind, Charisma, Field Flowers & Bird of Paradise Cologne. SSP $5.00 CMV $16.00 BO $20.00 MB Also came pink painted over white milk glass. Remove cap to see difference. CMV $15.00

LEFT 1978-80 LITTLE MISS MUFFET DECANTER
2 oz. white painted over milk glass. Came in Sweet Honesty or Topaze. OSP $7.00 CMV $5.00 MB $4.00 BO

RIGHT 1978-79 CHURCH MOUSE BRIDE DECANTER
Plastic top with separate white veil. Came in Delicate Daisies cologne. Base is white dull paint over milk glass. O.S.P. $6.00 CMV $5.00 MB $4.00 BO

1978 CHURCH MOUSE COMP.
Solid plaster painted white, plaster head, cloth veil. Used to photograph for Avon Catalog. 1 of a kind letter from Avon. Rare. Was never sold by Avon. CMV $275.00 with Avon letter.

1975 GARDEN GIRL COLOGNE
4 oz. sprayed frosted glass with yellow plastic top. Holds Sweet Honesty, Somewhere, Cotillion or To A Wild Rose. OSP $3.50 CMV $7.00 BO $9.00 MB

1973-74 FLOWER MAIDEN COLOGNE DECANTER
4 oz. yellow skirt painted over clear glass with white plastic top. Came in Unforgettable, Somewhere, Topaze, Cotillion. SSP $5.00 CMV $7.00 MB $5.00 BO

1974 DEAR FRIENDS COLOGNE DECANTER
4 oz. pink painted with light pink plastic top. Came in Field Flowers, Bird of Paradise or Roses, Roses Cologne. S.S.P. $4.00 CMV $12.00 MB $10.00 BO

1976 BETSY ROSS DECANTER
4 oz. white painted over clear glass. Came in Sonnet or Topaze Cologne. Sold 2 campaigns only. S.S.P. $6.99 OSP $10.00 CMV $6.00 MB $5.00 BO Also came white painted over white milk glass. Remove cap to see color of bottle. C.M.V. $20.00 M.B. The regular issue Betsy Ross bottle was one of the all time biggest sellers in Avons history.

1976-77 MAGIC PUMPKIN COACH
1 oz. clear glass, gold cap. Comes in Bird of Paradise or Occur! Cologne. O.S.P. $5.00 CMV $3.00 MB $2.00 BO

LEFT 1977 SONG OF SPRING
1 oz. frosted glass with frosted plastic bird bath top. Blue plastic bird attachment. Came in Sweet Honesty or Topaze. OSP $6.00 CMV $4.00 MB $3.00 BO

RIGHT 1977-78 FELINA FLUFFLES
2 oz. blue paint over clear glass, white plastic top, blue ribbon on head. Pink cheeks. Came in Pink & Pretty Cologne. O.S.P. $6.00 C.M.V. $4.00 M.B.

1975 SCOTTISH LASS
4 oz. blue with red, green & blue plaid skirt, blue plastic top. Holds Sweet Honesty, Bird of Paradise, Roses, Roses or Cotillion Cologne. OSP $5.00 CMV $6.00 BO $8.00 MB
1975-76 SPANISH SENORITA
4 oz. red base with white designs and pink plastic top. Holds Moonwind, To A Wild Rose or Topaze cologne. O.S.P. $5.00 CMV $10.00 BO $12.00 MB
1972-74 ROARING TWENTIES FASHION FIGURINE
3 oz. purple painted over clear glass with plastic purple top. Came in Unforgettable, Topaze, Somewhere, Cotillion. S.S.P. $4.00 CMV $8.00 BO $10.00 MB

LEFT 1977-79 DUTCH MAID
4 oz. blue painted base over clear glass, flower design & blue plastic top. Came in Sonnet or Moonwind cologne. OSP $7.50 CMV $6.00 MB $5.00 BO
CENTER 1977-79 MARY MARY COLOGNE DECANTER
2 oz. frosted white over milk glass & white plastic top. Came in Sweet Honesty or Topaze. O.S.P. $7.00 CMV $5.00 MB $4.00 BO
RIGHT 1977-78 SKATERS WALTZ-RED
4 oz. red flock on clear glass & pink plastic tip. Came in Moonwind or Charisma cologne. O.S.P. $8.50 C.M.V. $6.50 M.B.

1976 SILVER DOVE ORNAMENT COLOGNE DECANTER
1/2 oz. bottle with gold or silver cap. Came in silver metal bird holder marked Christmas '76 on both sides & Avon on inside. Came in Bird of Paradise or Occur! cologne. S.S.P. $4.99 CMV $4.00 MB $3.00 no box

LEFT TO RIGHT
1973-74 DUTCH GIRL FIGURINE COLOGNE
3 oz. blue painted with light blue plastic top. Came in Unforgettable, Topaze or Somewhere. SSP $5.00 CMV $8.00 BO $11.00 MB
1974 GAY NINETIES COLOGNE
3 oz. orange sprayed bottle with white top and orange hat. Holds Unforgettable, Topaze or Somewhere. O.S.P. $4.00 C.M.V. $10.00 BO $13.00 MB
1974 SWEET DREAMS COLOGNE
3 oz. sprayed white bottom with blue top. Holds Pink & Pretty or Sweet Honesty cologne. OSP $4.00 CMV $10.00 BO $13.00 MB

1973-74 REGENCY CANDLESTICK COLOGNE
4 oz. clear glass. Came in Bird of Paradise, Charisma, Elusive or Roses, Roses. S.S.P. $7.00 CMV $5.00 MB $4.00 BO

1971-72 PARLOR LAMP
2 sections. Gold cap over 3 oz. cologne top section in light amber iridescent glass. Yellow frosted glass bottom with talc 6½" high. Holds Bird of Paradise, Elusive, Charisma, Regence or Moonwind. OSP $7.00 CMV $10.00 MB $8.00 BO
1970-71 COURTING LAMP COLOGNE
5 oz. blue glass base with white milk glass shade & blue velvet ribbon. Holds Elusive, Brocade, Charisma, Hana Gasa or Regence. OSP $6.00 CMV $11.00 MB $9.00 BO

1971-72 VICTORIAN PITCHER & BOWL
6 oz. turquoise glass pitcher with Skin-So-Soft bath oil & turquoise glass bowl with Avon on bottom. Some bowls have double Avon stamp on bottom. O.S.P. $7.50 CMV $11.00 MB $9.00 no box $12.00 with double stamp on bottom.
1972-73 VICTORIAN PITCHER & BOWL
Same as above only came in Moonwind, Field Flowers Foaming Bath Oil. S.S.P. $7.00 CMV $8.00 no box $11.00 MB
1972-74 VICTORIAN POWDER SACHET
1.5 oz. turquoise glass jar & lid. Came in Moonwind, Field Flowers. S.S.P. $5.00 CMV $6.00 MB $5.00 BO
1972-73 VICTORIAN DISH & SOAP
Turquoise glass dish with white soap. S.S.P. $4.00 CMV $8.00 MB Dish only $3.00

1975-76 COLOGNE & CANDLELIGHT
2 oz. clear glass with gold cap and clear plastic collar. Holds Imperial Gardens, Roses, Roses or Charisma. OSP $3.00 CMV $2.00 MB $1.00 BO
1970-71 CANDLESTICK COLOGNE
4 oz. Red glass bottle, gold cap. Holds Elusive, Charisma, Brocade, Regence, Bird of Paradise. OSP $6.00 CMV $5.00 MB $3.00 BO Also came in smoked red glass. Appears much darker than red glass issue. It looks smokey red. CMV $12.00 MB

1966 CANDLESTICK COLOGNE
3 oz. silver coated over clear glass. Silver cap. Came in Occur, Rapture, Unforgettable OSP $3.75 CMV $9.00 Mint $14.00 MB

1977-78 BATH GARDEN HANGING PLANTER
Light green glass planter, green hanging rope. Came with 6 1 oz. packets of mineral spring bath crystals.
O.S.P. $12.00 C.M.V. $9.00 M.B. complete. $4.00 Hanging planter only.

1978 VICTORIANA SOAP DISH
Blue marbleized glass - white soap. May 1978 on bottom.
SSP $5.99 CMV $6.00 MB

1978 VICTORIANA PITCHER & BOWL
Blue marbleized glass bowl and 6 oz. pitcher. Holds bubble bath. May 1978 on bottom. SSP $9.99 CMV $8.00 MB $6.00 no box

1976-77 OPALIQUE CANDLESTICK COLOGNE
5 oz. swirl glass & cap. Came in Charisma or Sweet Honesty. S.S.P. $8.99.
CMV $5.00 MB $4.00 BO

1970-71 CRYSTALLITE COLOGNE
Clear glass bottle with gold cap holds 4 oz. of cologne in Unforgettable, Rapture, Occur, Somewhere, Topaze & Cotillion.
OSP $5.50 CMV $4.00 MB $3.00 BO

1972-75 CANDLESTICK COLOGNE
5 oz. silver painted over clear glass with silver cap. Came in Moonwind, Field Flowers, Bird of Paradise, Roses, Roses.
SSP $6.00 CMV $4.00 MB $3.00 BO
1975 came only in Imperial Garden, Moonwind or Sonnet. CMV $4.00 MB $3.00 BO

1974-75 PARISIAN GARDEN PERFUME
.33 oz. white milk glass with gold cap. Came in Sonnet, Moonwind, or Charisma Perfume.
OSP $5.00 CMV $5.00 MB $4.00 BO

1974-75 EVENING GLOW PERFUME DECANTER
.33 oz. white milk glass with green flowers white and gold plastic cap. Came in Moonwind, Sonnet, or Charisma. O.S.P. $6.00 CMV $5.00 BO $6.00 MB

1971-74 FRAGRANCE SPLENDOR
4½" high clear glass bottle with gold cap & frosted plastic handle. Holds perfume oil in Bird of Paradise, Elusive, Occur! Charisma or Unforgettable. O.S.P. $5.00 C.M.V. $5.00 MB $4.00 BO

1974-76 MING BLUE LAMP
5 oz. blue glass lamp, white plastic shade with gold tip. Holds Charisma, Bird of Paradise or Field Flowers, foaming bath oil.
OSP $6.00 CMV $6.00 MB $5.00 BO

1975-76 CHARMLIGHT DECANTER
.88 oz. cream sachet in white shade and 2 oz. cologne in pink base. Holds Imperial Garden, Sonnet or Moonwind. O.S.P. $7.00 CMV $7.00 MB $6.00 BO

LEFT 1976-77 COUNTRY CHARM DECANTER
4.8 oz. white milk glass, yellow stove window. Green & white plastic top. Came in Field Flowers or Sonnet.
SSP $6.99 CMV $7.00 MB $6.00 BO

1973-74 HURRICANE LAMP COLOGNE DECANTER
6 oz. white milk glass bottom with clear glass shade, gold cap. Holds Roses, Roses, Field Flowers. Bird of Paradise or Charisma Cologne. SSP $8.00 CMV $11.00 MB $9.00 BO

1972-74 TIFFANY LAMP COLOGNE
5 oz. brown glass base with pink shade, pink and orange flowers, green leaves on lavender background. Came in Sonnet, Moonwind, Field Flowers, Roses, Roses. S.S.P. $7.00 CMV $9.00 MB $8.00 BO. Also came in pink and yellow flowers on shade, also all white flowers. CMV $11.00 MB

1973-76 HEARTH LAMP COLOGNE DECANTER
8 oz. black glass with gold handle, has daisies around neck with yellow & white shade. Holds Roses, Roses, Bird of Paradise or Elusive. S.S.P. $8.00 C.M.V. $8.00 MB $7.00 BO

1973-74 CHIMNEY LAMP COLOGNE MIST DECANTER
2 oz. clear glass bottom with white plastic shade with pink flowers. Holds Patchwork, Sonnet or Moonwind. S.S.P. $4.00 C.M.V. $6.00 MB $5.00 BO

1975-76 CRYSTALSONG
4 oz. red glass with frosted bow and handle. Holds Timeless or Sonnet. O.S.P. $6.00 C.M.V. $4.00 M.B.

1974-75 CHRISTMAS BELLS COLOGNE
1 oz. red painted glass with gold cap. Came in Topaze, Occur!, Cotillion or To A Wild Rose. OSP $2.25 CMV $2.00 BO $3.00 MB

LEFT TO RIGHT

1968-69 FRAGRANCE BELL COLOGNE
1 oz. Gold handle. Bell actually rings. Came in Charisma, Brocade, Regence, Unforgettable, Rapture, Occur, Somewhere, Topaze, Cotillion, Here's My Heart & To A Wild Rose. OSP $2.00 CMV $4.00 MB $3.00 BO

1965-66 FRAGRANCE BELL COLOGNE
4 oz. clear glass, plastic handle, neck tag. Came in Rapture, Occur, O.S.P. $5.00 Somewhere, Topaze, Cotillion O.S.P. $4.00 Here's My Heart, To A Wild Rose, Wishing, O.S.P. $3.50 C.M.V. Bell with tag $15.00 $20.00 M.B.

1973-74 HOBNAIL BELL COLOGNE DECANTER
2 oz. white milk glass with gold handle & gold bell underneath. Holds Unforgettable, Topaze, Here's My Heart, To A Wild Rose or Sweet Honesty. S.S.P. $4.00 C.M.V. $4.00 MB $3.00 BO

1971-73 BATH URN
5 oz. white glass & cap with gold top plate. Foaming bath oil in Elusive & Charisma or bath foam in Lemon Velvet & Silk & Honey. 6" high. SSP $4.00 CMV $3.00 MB $2.00 BO

1971-74 KOFFEE KLATCH
5 oz. yellow paint over clear glass pot with gold top. Foaming Bath Oil in Field Flowers, Honeysuckle, or Lilac. Also Lemon Velvet Bath Foam. SSP $5.00 CMV $5.00 MB $4.00 BO

1970-72 LEISURE HOURS
5 oz. white milk glass bottle contains foaming bath oil. Gold cap. O.S.P. $4.00 C.M.V. $4.00 $5.00 M.B.

1974 LEISURE HOURS MINIATURE
1.5 oz. white milk glass bottle gold cap. Holds Field Flowers, Bird of Paradise or Charisma cologne. O.S.P. $3.00 C.M.V. $3.00 $4.00 M.B.

LEFT 1977-78 FUNBURGER LIP GLOSS
Came in Frostlight Rose & Frostlight Coral lip gloss. Brown plastic. OSP $4.50 CMV $1.50 BO $2.50 MB

CENTER 1976 CHRISTMAS SURPRISE DECANTER
1 oz. green glass boot came in Sweet Honesty, Moonwind, Charisma or Topaze cologne. Red cap or silver cap. SSP 99c CMV $2.00 MB $1.00 BO

RIGHT 1977 ORIENTAL PEONY VASE DECANTER
1.5 oz. red paint over clear glass with gold design. Came in Sweet Honesty or Moonwind. OSP $6.00 CMV $4.00 MB $3.00 BO

1975 ORIENTAL EGG – CHINESE PHEASANT
Upside down label mistake made at factory. Upside down bottle only CMV $18.00

1978-79 SCENTIMENTS COLOGNE DECANTER
2 oz. clear glass. Game with pink card on front to write your own message. Came in Sweet Honesty, or Here's My Heart cologne. SSP $4.99 CMV $4.00 MB $2.00 BO

1978-79 GOLDEN BAMBOO VASE
1 oz. yellow painted over clear glass, black cap base. Came in Moonwind or Sweet Honesty cologne. S.S.P. $3.99 CMV $3.00 $2.00 BO

LEFT 1978 ROSEPOINT BELL DECANTER
4 oz. clear glass, clear plastic top. Came in Charisma or Roses Roses cologne. OSP $8.50 CMV $6.00 MB $5.00 BO

RIGHT 1976-77 HOSPITALITY BELL COLOGNE DECANTER
Silver top. 3.75 oz. blue glass bottom. Came in Moonwind or Roses Roses cologne. Avon 1976 stamped in bottom. OSP $8.00 CMV $6.00 MB $5.00 BO

1975 ORIENTAL EGG CHINESE PHEASANT (Left)
1 oz. white opal glass, black plastic base. Came in Imperial Gardens, Charisma & Bird of Paradise Cologne. O.S.P. $6.50 CMV $10.00 MB $8.00 BO

1974-75 ORIENTAL EGG PEACH ORCHARD DECANTER (right)
1 oz. white opal glass with green marbleized plastic base. Came in Imperial Garden, Sonnet or Moonwind perfume concentre'. SSP $5.99 CMV $7.00 MB $6.00 BO

1975-76 ORIENTAL EGG DELICATE BLOSSOMS (center)
1 oz. light blue opal glass with blue green plastic base. Came in Patchwork, Sonnet, & Charisma cologne. O.S.P. $7.50 CMV $7.00 MB $6.00 BO

1974-80 BUTTERFLY FANTASY PORCELAIN TREASURE EGG
5½" long white porcelain multicolored butterfly decals. Sold empty. 1974 stamped on bottom. Sold 1974-75 then was reissued 1978. The 1978 issue has a 1974 "R" for reissue on bottom and the big butterfly on top is much lighter than the 1974 issue. O.S.P. $12.00 C.M.V. $25.00 M.B for 1974 issue. C.M.V. $15.00 M.B. for 1974 "R" issue. 1979-80 issue has "R" 1979 on bottom. CMV $15.00 MB Also came with bottom label upside down or backwards. Add $6.00 CMV

1974 BUTTER CUP CANDLE STICK COLOGNE
6 oz. white milk glass, yellow & white flowers. Holds Moonwind, Sonnet or Imperial Gardens cologne. O.S.P. $7.00 1st issue has yellow band around neck. C.M.V. $9.00 M.B. Later issue was plain with no band on neck and yellow or brown decals. CMV $7.00 MB $2.00 less no box

1974 BUTTERCUP FLOWER HOLDER PERFUMED SKIN SOFTENER
5 oz. milk glass with plastic white top. Holds Moonwind, Imperial Garden or Sonnet. OSP $5.00 CMV $5.00 MB $3.00 BO

1974 BUTTERCUP SALT SHAKER CREAM SACHET
1.5 oz. white milk glass with yellow & white flowers, yellow plastic cap. Came in Moonwind, Sonnet or Imperial Garden. O.S.P. $2.50 CMV $3.00 MB $2.00 BO

1963-64 BATH URN (CRUET)
8 oz. white glass top & bottle. Perfume bath oil in Somewhere, Topaze, Cotillion. O.S.P. $3.75 ea.
Here's My Heart, Persian Wood, To A Wild Rose, O.S.P. $3.50 ea. C.M.V. $15.00 in box. $10.00 bottle with label.
Right - **FOREIGN BATH URN**
180cc size, clear glass. Smaller than American bath urn. C.M.V. $20.00

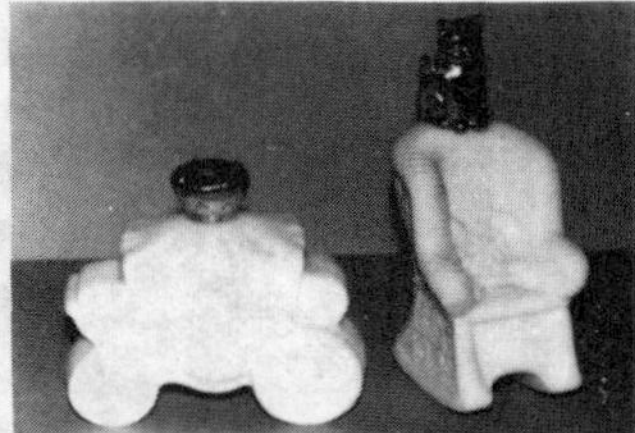

1972-73 ROYAL COACH
5 oz. white milk glass, gold cap. Holds Moonwind, Bird of Paradise, Charisma & Field Flowers foaming bath oil. O.S.P. $5.00 CMV $5.00 MB $4.00 BO

1971-73 SITTING PRETTY COLOGNE
4 oz. white milk glass with gold cat cap. Came in Topaze, Rapture, Cotillion, Somewhere & Persian Wood. O.S.P. $5.00 CMV $7.00 MB $5.00 BO

1972-73 ENCHANTED HOURS
5 oz. blue glass bottle with gold cap. Came in Roses, Roses, Charisma, Unforgettable or Somewhere Cologne. S.S.P. $5.00 C.M.V. $7.00 MB $5.00 BO

1973-74 BEAUTIFUL AWAKENING
3 oz. gold painted over clear glass front paper clock face, gold cap. Came in Elusive, Roses, Roses, Topaze. S.S.P. $5.00 C.M.V. $4.00 BO $6.00 MB

1967 BATH SEASONS
3 oz. Foaming bath oil. Each is white glass & top with orange design in Honeysuckle, green in Lily of the Valley. CMV $7.00 BO $9.00 MB each. Lavender in Lilac, yellow in Jasmine. Matching ribbons on each OSP $2.50 each. CMV $6.00 BO each, $8.00 MB

1968-70 SALT SHAKERS
3 oz. pink ribbon, pink flowers. Yellow ribbon & flowers in Hawaiian White Ginger, Honeysuckle & Lilac bath oil. OSP $2.50 CMV $5.00 MB ea., $4.00 BO

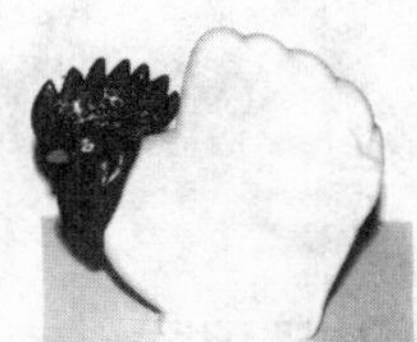

1973-75 COUNTRY KITCHEN DECANTER
6 oz. white milk glass with red plastic head. Holds moisturized hand lotion. S.S.P. $5.00 C.M.V. $5.00 MB $4.00 BO

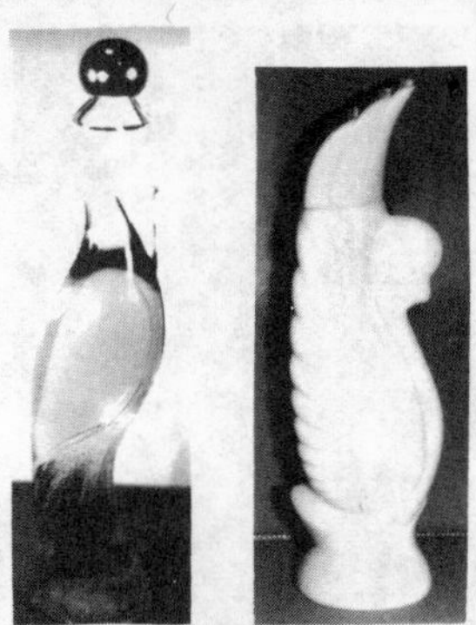

1971-72 FLAMINGO DECANTER
5 oz. Clear bird shaped bottle with gold cap. 10" tall. Came in Bird of Paradise, Elusive, Charisma, Brocade, S.S.P. $4.50 C.M.V. $5.00 MB $4.00 BO

1972-76 SWAN LAKE COLOGNE
8" high, 3 oz. white glass bottle with white cap. Came in Bird of Paradise, Charisma & Elusive. O.S.P. $5.00 Moonwind S.S.P. $5.00 CMV $4.00 MB, $3.00 BO

1971 DUTCH TREAT DEMI-CUPS
3 oz. White glass filed with Cream Lotion in Honeysuckle, yellow cap. Blue Lotus, blue cap. Hawiian White Ginger, pink cap. OSP $3.50 CMV $6.00, $4.00 BO. Also each came with white caps.

1968-70 BLUE DEMI-CUP BATH OIL
3 oz. white glass, blue cap & design, some came with gold top with blue lid. Came in Brocade, Topaze, Unforgettable. O.S.P. $3.50 CMV $7.00 MB $5.00 BO

1969-70 DEMI-CUP BATH OIL
3 oz. white milk glass, Charisma has red cap & design. Regence has green cap & design. OSP $3.50 CMV $7.00 MB $5.00 BO

1969 TO A WILD ROSE DEMI-CUP
3 oz. white glass, red rose, pink cap. 6½" high. Contains Foaming Bath Oil. O.S.P. $3.50 CMV $8.00 MB $6.00 BO

1971-73 FRAGRANCE HOURS COLOGNE
6 oz. ivory glass grandfathers clock, gold cap. Bird of Paradise, Field Flowers, Charisma or Elusive. S.S.P. $5.00 C.M.V. $5.00 MB $4.00 BO

1970 EIFFEL TOWER COLOGNE
3 oz. 9'' high, clear glass with gold cap. Came in Occur, Rapture, Somewhere Topaze, Cotillion & Unforgettable. S.S.P. $4.00 CMV $7.00 MB $5.00 BO

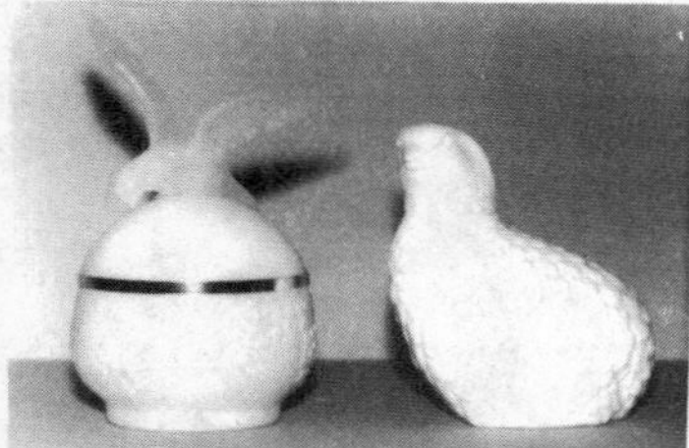

1975 FLIGHT TO BEAUTY
5 oz. glass jar with white frosted top. Holds Rich Moisture or Vita-Moist Cream or SSS Skin Softener. O.S.P. $5.00 C.M.V. $4.00 MB $3.00 BO

1973-75 PARTRIDGE COLOGNE DECANTER
5 oz. white milk glass with white plastic lid. Came in Unforgettable, Topaze, Occur!, Somewhere. OSP $5.00 CMV $4.00 MB $3.00 BO

1972-74 SWEET SHOPPE PIN CUSHION CREAM SACHET DECANTER
1 oz. white milk glass bottom with white plastic back with hot pink pin cushion seat. Came in Sonnet, Moonwind, Field Flowers, Roses, Roses, Bird of Paradise, Charisma. SSP $4.00 CMV $5.00 MB $4.00 BO

1969-70 FRAGRANCE TOUCH
3 oz. white milk glass. Cologne came in Elusive, Charisma, Brocade, Regence. OSP $5.00 CMV $4.00 MB $3.00 BO

1973-75 VENETIAN PITCHER COLOGNE MIST
3 oz. blue plastic coated bottle with silver plastic top. Came in Imperial Garden, Patchword, Sonnet or Moonwind, S.S.P. $6.00 CMV $5.00 MB $3.00 BO

1972-75 COMPOTE COLOGNE DECANTER
5 oz. white milk glass bottle, gold cap. Came in Moonwind, Field Flowers, Elusive, Brocade. SSP $5.00 CMV $4.00 MB $3.00 BO

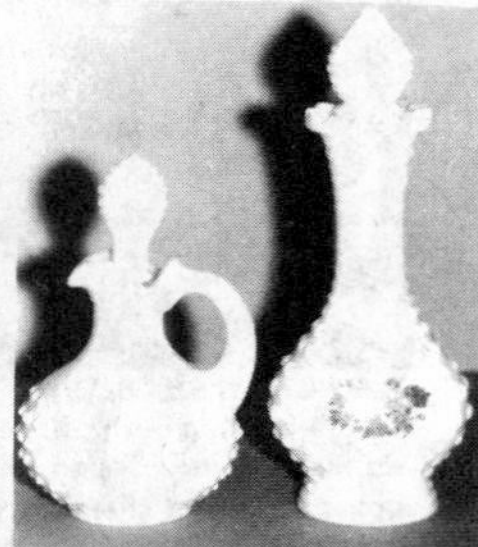

1972-73 VICTORIAN MANOR COLOGNE DECANTER
5 oz. white painted over clear glass with pink plaster roof. Holds Roses, Roses, Bird of Paradise, Unforgettable, Cotillion. S.S.P. $5.00 CMV $8.00 MB $7.00 BO

1972-74 HOBNAIL DECANTER FOAMING BATH OIL
5 oz. white opal glass, came in Moonwind, Elusive, Roses, Roses, Bath Foam, Lemon Velvet Bath Foam. S.S.P. $6.00 C.M.V. $6.00 MB $4.00 BO

1973-74 HOBNAIL BUD VASE
4 oz. white milk glass with red & yellow roses. Holds Charisma, Topaze, Roses, Roses Cologne. SSP $6.00 CMV $5.00 MB $4.00 BO. Also came 4.75 oz. size.

1972-76 GRECIAN PITCHER
6½'' high, 5 oz. white glass bottle & white stopper holds skin-so-soft. S.S.P. $5.00 CMV $5.00 MB $4.00 BO

1971-76 CORNUCOPIA SKIN-SO-SOFT
6 oz. white glass, gold cap, 5½'' high. SSP $5.00 CMV $4.00 MB $3.00 BO

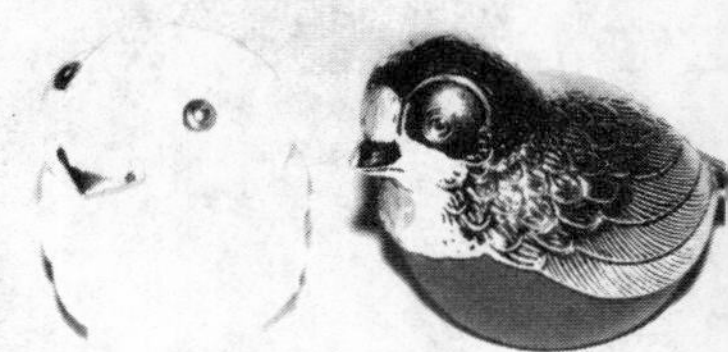

1973-74 SNOW BIRD CREAM SACHET
1.5 oz. white milk glass, white plastic cap. Came in Patchwork, Moonwind, Sonnet Cream Sachet. O.S.P. $2.50 C.M.V. $3.00 MB $2.00 BO

1974-75 ROBIN RED-BREAST COLOGNE DECANTER
2 oz. red frosted glass with silver plastic top. Holds Charisma, Roses, Roses, Bird of Paradise. OSP $4.00 CMV $4.00 MB $3.00 BO

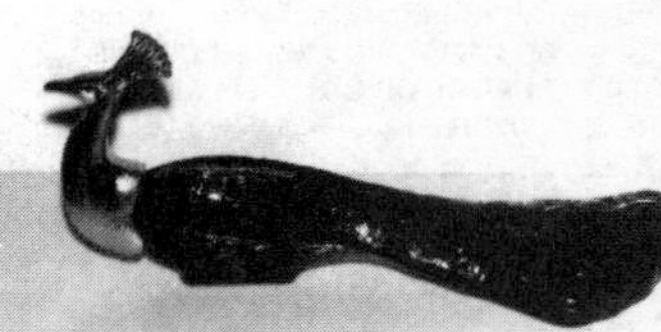

1973-74 REGAL PEACOCK
4 oz. blue glass with gold cap. Came in Patchwork, Sonnet or Moonwind. S.S.P. $6.00 CMV $9.00 MB $7.00 BO

1973-75 CRYSTAL FACETS COLOGNE GELEE
3 oz. clear glass. Choice of Roses, Roses or Field Flowers. O.S.P. $4.00 C.M.V. $4.00 MB $3.00 BO

1974-76 OWL FANCY COLOGNE GELEE
4 oz. clear glass top. Came in Raining Violets or Roses, Roses. S.S.P. $4.00 CMV $4.00 MB $3.00 BO

1971-72 ROYAL SWAN COLOGNE
1 oz. white glass, gold crown cap. Came in Elusive, Charisma, Bird of Paradise, Topaze, Unforgettable, Cotillion. S.S.P. $3.00 CMV $5.00 MB $3.00 BO

1974 ROYAL SWAN COLOGNE
1 oz. blue glass with gold crown cap. Came in Unforgettable, Topaze, Cotillion, Here's My Heart. SSP $2.50 CMV $6.00 MB $5.00 BO

1971-72 SONG BIRD COLOGNE
1.5 oz. clear glass with gold base cap. Came in Unforgettable, Topaze, Occur!, Here's My Heart & Cotillion. O.S.P. $3.00 CMV $5.00 MB $4.00 BO

1975-76 BIRD OF HAPPINESS COLOGNE
1.5 oz. light blue glass gold cap. Holds Charisma, Topaze, Occur! or Unforgettable cologne. OSP $3.00 CMV $5.00 MB $4.00 BO

1974-76 PERFUME CONCENTRE
1 oz. clear glass with gold cap. Came in Imperial Garden, Moonwind or Sonnet, Charisma or Bird of Paradise. S.S.P. $4.00 CMV $4.00 $2.00 BO

1974-75 UNICORN COLOGNE DECANTER
2 oz. clear glass with gold cap. Came in Field Flowers, Charisma, Bird of Paradise or Brocade. SSP $4.00 CMV $4.00 MB $3.00 BO

1975-76 GOOD LUCK ELEPHANT
1.5 oz. frosted glass gold cap. Holds Sonnet, Imperial Garden or Patchwork Cologne. OSP $3.00 CMV $3.00 MB $2.00 BO

1974-75 SWISS MOUSE
3 oz. frosted glass, gold cap. Holds Roses, Roses, Field Flowers or Bird of Paradise Cologne. OSP $4.00 CMV $4.00 MB $3.00 BO

1974-75 TEATIME POWDER SACHET
1.25 oz. frosted white with gold cap. Holds Moonwind, Sonnet or Roses, Roses. OSP $4.00 CMV $4.00 MB $3.00 BO

1975-76 SCENT WITH LOVE
.66 oz. gold toned glass base with amber plastic top that is a stamp dispenser. Holds Unforgettable, Topaze, Here's My Heart cream sachet. OSP $4.00 CMV $3.00 MB $1.00 BO

1972-73 BUTTERFLY COLOGNE
1½ oz. 3½" high, gold cap with 2 prongs. Holds cologne in Occur!, Topaze, Unforgettable, Somewhere & Here's My Heart. SSP $3.00, CMV $5.00 MB, $3.00 BO

1973-74 DOLPHIN MINIATURE
1.5 oz. clear glass, gold tail. Holds Charisma, Bird of Paradise or Field Flowers cologne. OSP $3.00 CMV $4.00 MB $3.00 BO

1973 BON BON COLOGNE
1 oz. black milk glass with black plastic cap. Holds Field Flowers, Bird of Paradise, Roses, Roses or Elusive. OSP $2.00 CMV $6.00 MB $4.00 BO

1972-73 BON BON COLOGNE
1 oz. white milk glass with white cap. Holds Unforgettable, Topaze, Occur!, Cotillion or Here's My Heart cologne. O.S.P. $2.00 CMV $4.00 MB $3.00 BO

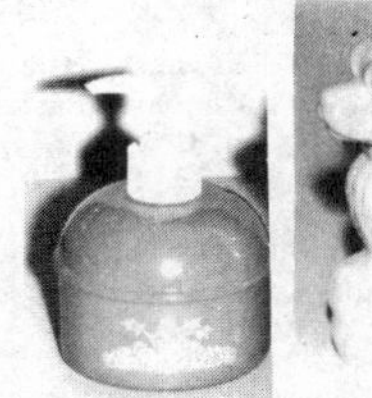

1974-79 COUNTRY KITCHEN MOISTURIZED HAND LOTION
10 oz. red glass with plastic top. Holds Moisturized Hand Lotion.
OSP $6.00 CMV $4.00 MB $3.00 BO
Reissued 1979

1974-76 LADY SPANIEL
1.5 oz. opal glass with plastic head. Holds Patchwork, Sonnet or Moonwind Cologne. OSP $3.00 CMV $4.00 MB $3.00 BO

1972-75 SECRETAIRE
7" high, pink paint over clear glass, gold cap. Holds 5 oz. of Foaming Bath Oil in Moonwind. O.S.P. $7.50 Charisma, Brocade, Lilac & Lemon Velvet. O.S.P. $6.00 CMV $6.00 MB $5.00 BO

1972-75 ARMOIRE DECANTER
7" high, 5 oz. white glass bottle with gold cap. Choice of Field Flowers, Bird of Paradise, Elusive or Charisma bath oil. S.S.P. $4.00 CMV $4.00 MB $3.00 BO
1975 Came in Field Flowers, Charisma & Bird of Paradise only. S.S.P. $4.00 CMV $4.00 MB $3.00 BO

1973-74 VICTORIAN WASH STAND
4 oz. buff painted with gray plastic simulated marble top with blue pitcher & bowl for cap. Came in Field Flowers, Bird of Paradise or Charisma Foaming Bath Oil. SSP $5.00 CMV $6.00 MB $5.00 BO

1972-74 REMEMBER WHEN SCHOOL DESK DECANTER
4 oz. black glass with light brown plastic seat front & desk top, red apple for cap. Came in Rapture, Here's My Heart, Cotillion, Somewhere Cologne. S.S.P. $5.00 CMV $7.00 MB $5.00 BO

1972-76 COUNTRY STORE COFFEE MILL
5 oz. ivory milk glass, white plastic cap & plastic handles on side with gold rim. Came in Sonnet, Moonwind, Bird of Paradise, Charisma Cologne. S.S.P. $6.00 C.M.V. $6.00 MB $4.00 BO Came in 2 different size boxes

1972-73 LITTLE DUTCH KETTLE
5 oz. orange painted clear glass with gold cap. Came in Cotillion, Honeysuckle Foaming Bath Oil or Lemon Velvet Bath Foam. SSP $5.00 CMV $5.00 MB $4.00 BO

LEFT 1977-79 DR. HOOT DECANTER
4 oz. white milk glass owl with blue plastic cap and white tassel. Came in Sweet Honesty or Wild Country. OSP $7.50 CMV $5.00 MB $4.00 BO

LEFT 1975-76 DR. HOOT DECANTER
4 oz. opal white glass, black cap, gold tassel. Holds Wild Country After Shave or Sweet Honesty Cologne. O.S.P. $5.00 CMV $5.00 MB $4.00 BO

CENTER 1972-74 PRECIOUS OWL CREAM SACHET
1½ oz. white bottle with gold eyes. Came in Moonwind, Field Flowers, Charisma, Roses, Roses. OSP $3.00 CMV $3.00 MB $2.00 BO

RIGHT 1976-77 SNOW OWL DECANTER
1.25 oz. frosted glass base and frosted plastic head with blue eyes. Came in Moonwind or Sonnet. S.S.P. $4.99 CMV $5.00 MB $4.00 BO

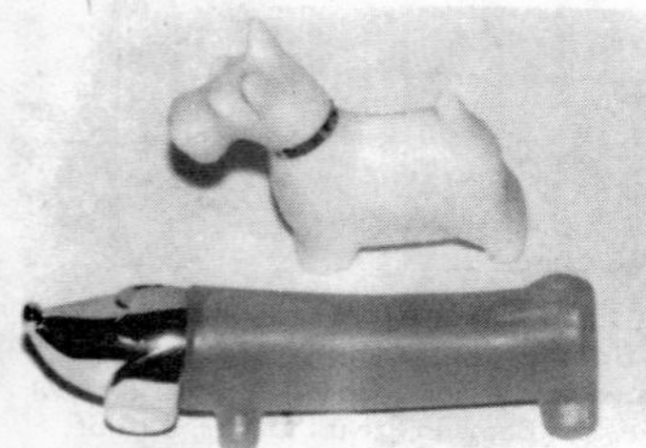

1973-76 QUEEN OF SCOTS
1 oz. white milk glass, white plastic head. Came in Sweet Honesty, Unforgettable, Somewhere, Cotillion, Here's My Heart. SSP $3.00 CMV $4.00 MB $3.00 BO

1973-74 DACHSHUND COLOGNE DECANTER
1.5 oz. frosted glass, gold cap. Came in Unforgettable, Somewhere, Topaze, Cotillion. SSP $3.00 CMV $4.00 MB $3.00 BO

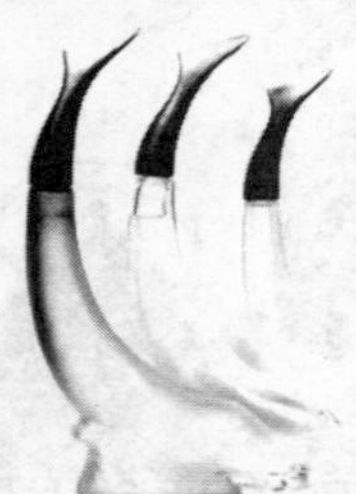

Right - EUROPEAN DOLPHIN
Bath oil, 165cc size, frosted glass, gold tail cap. Foreign Dolphin smaller than U.S. size. C.M.V. $25.00.

Left - 1968-69 DOLPHIN SKIN-SO-SOFT
8 oz. frosted glass with gold tail cap. Sold in U.S.A. SSP $4.00 CMV $6.00 MB $3.00 BO

Center - DOLPHIN FROM MEXICO
About same size as American Dolphin only bottle is clear glass, with gold tail. C.M.V. $20.00.

1975-76 KITTEN LITTLE COLOGNE DECANTER
1.5 oz. black glass with black head. Holds Sweet Honesty, Bird of Paradise or Roses, Roses, OSP $4.00 CMV $5.00 MB $4.00 BO

1975-76 TABATHA COLOGNE SPRAY
3 oz. black glass and plastic. Holds Imperial Garden, Bird of Paradise or Cotillion cologne. OSP $6.00 CMV $6.00 MB $5.00 BO

1974-76 KITTEN'S HIDEAWAY
1 oz. amber basket, white plastic kitten cap. Came in Field Flowers, Bird of Paradise or Charisma Cream Sachet. O.S.P. $4.00 C.M.V. $3.00 MB $2.00 BO

1975-76 BLUE EYES
1.5 oz. opal glass with blue rhinestone eyes. Available in Topaze, or Sweet Honesty cologne. OSP $4.00 CMV $5.00 MB $4.00 BO

1976-77 HEARTSCENT CREAM SACHET
.66 oz. white glass bottom with white plastic top. Gold dove design. Came in Charisma, Occur! or Roses, Roses. O.S.P. $3.00 CMV $3.00 MB $2.00 BO

1975-76 FOSTORIA COMPOTE
12 Skin-So-Soft capsules. Clear glass with glass top. OSP $8.00 CMV $8.00 MB $6.00 BO

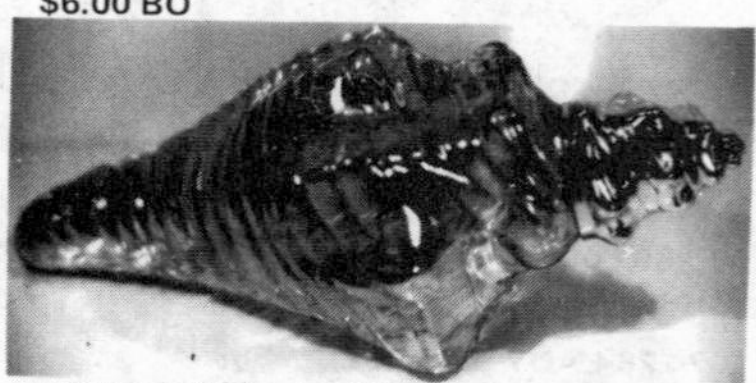

1971-72 SEA TREASURE FOAMING BATH OIL
5 oz. clear glass coated iridescent sea shell shaped bottle, gold cap. Came in Field Flowers, Charisma, Honeysuckle, Lilac. 7" long. SSP $5.00 CMV $8.00 MB $6.00 BO

1973-75 FLORAL BUD VASE
5 oz. white milk glass. Holds Roses, Roses or Lemon Velvet Bath Foam or Field Flowers or Honeysuckle Foaming Bath Oil. SSP $5.00 CMV $5.00 MB $4.00 BO

1973-76 SUZETTE DECANTER
5 oz. cream colored milk glass with cream colored plastic head & a pink-lavender bow around neck. Holds Field Flowers, Bird of Paradise or Cotillion Foaming Bath Oil. SSP $5.00 CMV $5.00 MB $4.00 BO

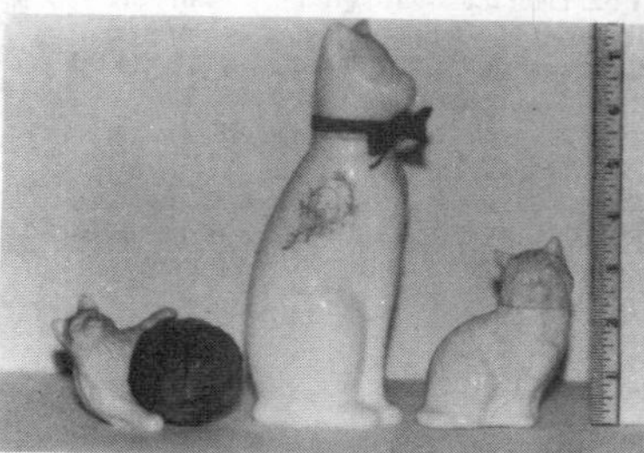

1973-74 KITTEN PETITE COLOGNE
1.5 oz. amber glass ball with white plastic cat for cap. Came in Sonnet or Moonwind. S.S.P. $3.00 C.M.V. $3.00 - $4.00 M.B.

1971 MING CAT COLOGNE
6 oz. white glass & head, blue trim & neck ribbon. Came in Moonwind, Bird of Paradise, Elusive, Charisma. S.S.P. $6.00 C.M.V. $9.00 MB

1972-76 KITTEN LITTLE COLOGNE
3½" high, white glass bottle holds 1½ oz. cologne in Occur!, Topaze, Unforgettable, Somewhere, Cotillion. S.S.P. $2.00 C.M.V. $3.00

1971 FRENCH TELEPHONE
6 oz. white milk glass base with gold cap & trim. Holds Foaming Bath Oil. Center of receiver holds ¼oz. of perfume in frosted glass. Came in Moonwind. O.S.P. $22.00 Bird of Paradise, Elusive or Charisma, O.S.P. $20.00 CMV $27.50 MB $20.00 BO

1970-72 SEA HORSE
Clear glass 6 oz. container holds Skin-So-Soft, gold cap. SSP $5.00 CMV $6.00 MB $4.00 BO

1973-76 SEA HORSE MINATURE COLOGNE
1.5 oz. clear glass, gold cap. Came in Unforgettable, Here's My Heart, Cotillion, SSP $3.00 CMV $4.00 MB $3.00 BO

1975-76 WINTER GARDEN
6 oz. clear glass with gold cap. Holds Here's My Heart, Topaze or Occur! cologne. OSP $5.00 CMV $4.00 MB $3.00 BO

1974-75 REGENCY DECANTER
6 oz. clear glass filled with Skin-So-Soft bath oil. OSP $5.00 CMV $4.00 MB $3.00 BO

1973-76 SEA SPIRIT FOAMING BATH OIL DECANTER
5 oz. light green glass with green plastic tail over cap. Holds Elusive, Topaze or Cotillion. OSP $5.00 CMV $5.00 MB $4.00 BO

1974-75 SONG OF THE SEA EMOLLIENT BATH PEARLS
80 bath pearls, aqua colored glass with plastic head. Holds Moonwind, Sonnet or Imperial Garden. O.S.P. $7.00 C.M.V. $7.00 MB $5.00 BO

1974-76 HONEY BEAR BABY CREAM DECANTER
4 oz. yellow painted glass with blue plastic bear on lid. SSP $4.00 CMV $4.00 MB $3.00 BO

1974-76 VICTORIAN SEWING BASKET
5 oz. white milk glass basket with lavender plastic top, gold cord holds pink flower. Came in Roses, Roses, Bird of Paradise or Charisma Perfumed Skin-So-Soft. O.S.P. $4.00 CMV $4.00 MB $2.00 BO

1975-76 VANITY JAR
5 oz. clear glass with silver lid. Choice of Rich Moisture Cream or SSS Skin conditioner. OSP $4.00 CMV $4.00 MB $2.00 BO

LEFT 1977-79 TREE MOUSE CREAM SACHET DECANTER
.66 oz. clear glass & clear plastic top. Gold mouse. Came in Sweet Honesty or Charisma. OSP $6.00 CMV $4.00 MB $3.00 BO

CENTER 1977 SILVER PEAR CREAM SACHET
.66 oz. silver plated over clear glass. Silver top. Came in Sweet Honesty or Charisma. SSP $3.99 CMV $3.00 MB $2.00 BO

LEFT 1976-78 ENCHANTED APPLE CREAM SACHET DECANTER
.66 oz. gold plated over clear glass. Gold top. Came in Charisma or Sonnet. OSP $5.50 CMV $4.00 MB $3.00 BO

1975-76 HIGH-BUTTONED SHOE
2 oz. clear glass with gold cap. Holds Occur! or Unforgettable cologne. O.S.P. $3.00 CMV $3.00 MB $2.00 BO

1976 GRACEFUL GIRAFFE
1.5 oz. clear glass with plastic top. Holds Topaze or To A Wild Rose cologne. OSP $4.00 CMV $4.00 MB $3.00 BO

1975-76 ULTRA COLOGNE
1 oz. clear glass with gold cap. Holds Timeless or Unspoken. O.S.P. $2.50 C.M.V. $1.00 M.B.

1974-75 PETIT POINT PERFUMED SKIN SOFTENER
5 oz. translucent purple glass with cloth petit point design on top. Holds Charisma Bird of Paradise or Field Flowers. O.S.P. $4.00 CMV $2.00 MB $1.00 BO

1974-76 PETIT POINT CREAM SACHET
1 oz. purple glass with cloth top on lid. Came in Field Flowers, Bird of Paradise or Charisma. OSP $4.00 CMV $2.00 MB $1.00 BO

1974-76 PETIT POINT PERFUME
.25 oz. purple glass jar with cloth top on lid. Holds Field Flowers, Bird of Paradise or Charisma. OSP $6.00 CMV $4.00 MB $3.00 BO

1974-76 PETIT POINT LIPSTICK
Not shown. CMV $1.00 MB

1974-76 CASTLEFORD COLLECTION EMOLLIENT BATH PEARLS
Holds 60 bath pearls. Clear glass. Came in Imperial Garden, Sonnet or Moonwind. OSP $8.00 CMV $9.00 MB $5.00 BO

1975-76 CASTLEFORD COLLECTION COLOGNE GELEE
4 oz. glass holds Raining Violets, Roses, Roses or Apple Blossom cologne gelee. OSP $8.00 CMV $8.00 MB $6.00 BO

1975 GOLDEN FLAMINGO DECANTER
6 oz. clear glass with gold flamingo on front. Holds Bird of Paradise, Charisma or Field Flowers. Foaming bath oil. O.S.P. $6.00 CMV $3.00 MB $2.00 BO
1975-76 ATHENA BATH URN
6 oz. clear glass. Holds Field Flowers, Bird of Paradise foaming bath oil or Roses, Roses creamy bath foam. OSP $6.00 CMV $3.00 MB $2.00 BO

1975-76 PEAR LUMIERE
2 oz. clear glass and plastic with gold leaf. Holds Roses, Roses, Charisma or Bird of Paradise cologne. O.S.P. $5.00 C.M.V. $5.00 MB $4.00 BO
1975-76 SONG OF LOVE COLOGNE MIST
2 oz. clear glass clear plastic top with white bird. Holds Bird of Paradise, Charisma or Sweet Honesty. O.S.P. $4.00 C.M.V. $4.00 MB $3.00 BO 1976 issued with blue base. Clear top in Moonwind & Here's My Hear. Same CMV.

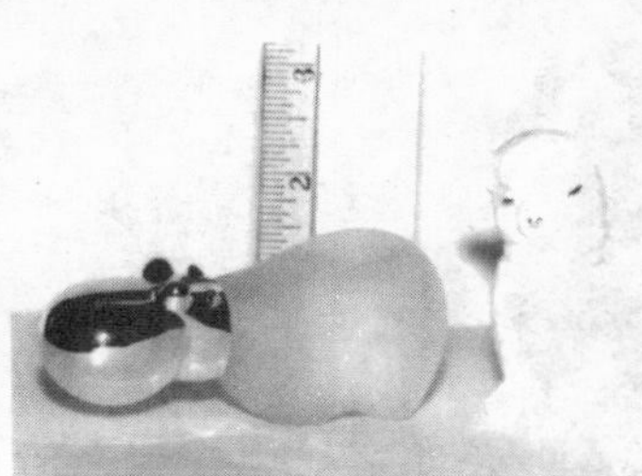

LEFT 1977-80 BABY HIPPO
1 oz. frosted glass with silver head. Came in Sweet Honesty or Topaze cologne. OSP $5.00 CMV $3.00 MB $2.00 BO
RIGHT 1977-78 LITTLE LAMB
.75 oz. white milk glass, white head. Came in Sweet Honesty or Topaze cologne. OSP $5.00 CMV $3.00 MB $2.00 BO

1975-76 CAMEO DECANTER CREAM SACHET
.66 oz. painted blue glass with blue and white plastic top. Came in Here's My Heart, Charisma, Topaze or To A Wild Rose. O.S.P. $4.00 CMV $4.00 MB $2.00 BO
1975-76 GATHER A GARDEN CREAM SACHET
.66 painted blue glass jar with floral design on plastic and metal lid. Came in Hawaiian White Ginger, Roses, Roses, Lemon Velvet, Lily of the Valley. O.S.P. $4.00 C.M.V. $4.00 MB $2.00 BO
1975-76 EMERALDESQUE CREAM SACHET
1 oz. green glass with green plastic top. Holds Here's My Heart, Occur! or Sweet Honesty. OSP $3.00 CMV $3.00 MB $1.00 BO

1973-76 ENCHANTED FROG CREAM SACHET
1.25 oz. cream colored milk glass with cream colored plastic lid. Came in Sonnet, Moonwind or Occur!. O.S.P. $3.00 C.M.V. $3.00 MB $2.00 BO
1975-76 HANDY FROG MOISTURIZED HAND LOTION
8 oz. white milk glass with red cap. OSP $6.00 CMV $5.00 MB $4.00 BO

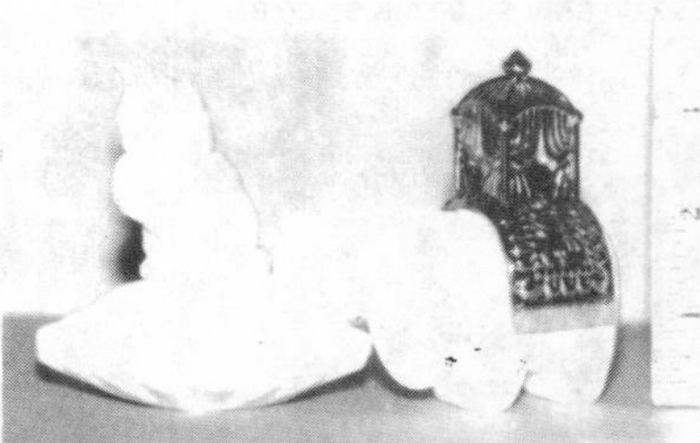

LEFT 1976-77 SITTING PRETTY COLOGNE DECANTER
1.5 oz. white milk glass base, white plastic top. Came in Charisma or Topaze. Pink ribbons painted on each corner. OSP $6.00 CMV $6.00 MB $5.00 BO
RIGHT 1977-79 ROYAL ELEPHANT
1/2 oz. white milk glass with gold snap on top. Came in Charisma or Topaze. OSP $6.00 CMV $3.00 MB $2.00 BO

1975-76 SNOW BUNNY
3 oz. clear glass with gold cap. Holds Moonwind, Charisma, Bird of Paradise or Sweet Honesty cologne. O.S.P. $4.00 CMV $4.00 MB $3.00 BO
1974-76 LA BELLE TELEPHONE
1 oz. clear glass with gold top. Holds Moonwind, Sonnet or Charisma Perfume Concentre'. OSP $7.00 CMV $8.00 MB $6.00 BO

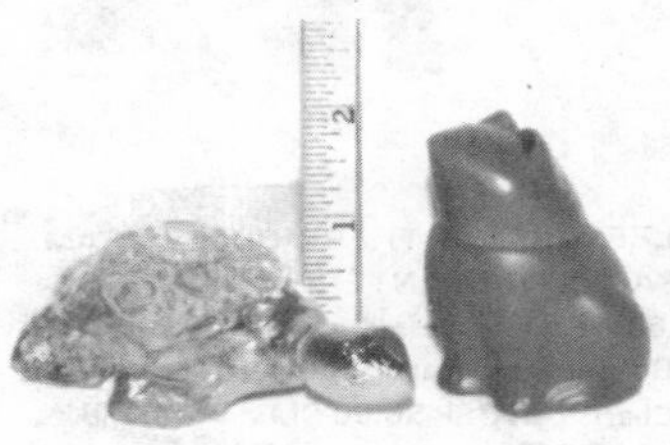

LEFT 1977 TREASURE TURTLE COLOGNE DECANTER
1 oz. clear glass turtle with gold cap. Came in Sweet Honesty or Charisma cologne. Avon on bottom & 'R' for reissue on tail. OSP $4.50 CMV $3.00 MB $2.00 BO
RIGHT 1977-79 EMERALD PRINCE FROG
1 oz. green frosted paint over clear glass. Came in Sweet Honesty or Moonwind cologne. OSP $5.00 CMV $3.00 MB $2.00 BO

1970-72 LOOKING GLASS COLOGNE
6½" high, clear glass mirror. Frame holds 1½oz. Cologne in Bird of Paradise, Elusive, Charisma, Brocade, Regence, Unforgettable, Rapture, Occur, Somewhere, Topaze, Cotillion, Here's My Heart, To A Wild Rose. With gold handle-cap. O.S.P. $3.50 C.M.V. $4.00, $6.00 MB

LEFT 1977-79 SILVER SWIRLS SALT SHAKER COLOGNE DECANTER
3 oz. silver plated over clear glass. Silver top. Came in Sweet Honesty or Topaze cologne. SSP $4.99 CMV $3.00 MB $2.00 BO
RIGHT 1977-78 ISLAND PARAKEET COLOGNE DECANTER
1.5 oz. blue glass base & blue & yellow plastic top. Approx. 4½" high. Came in Moonwind or Charisma cologne. OSP $6.00 CMV $4.00 MB $3.00 BO

LEFT - 1976-78 PRINCESS OF YORKSHIRE COLOGNE DECANTER
1 oz. off white over milk glass. Came in Sweet Honesty or Topaze cologne. OSP $6.00 CMV $4.00 MB $3.00 BO
CENTER 1974-75 ROYAL PEKINGESE
1.5 oz. white glass & white plastic head. Came in Unforgettable, Somewhere, Topaze. OSP $5.00 CMV $5.00 MB $3.00 BO
RIGHT 1977-79 FUZZY BEAR COLOGNE DECANTER
Tan flock over clear glass base & head. Came in Sweet Honesty or Occur! OSP $6.50 CMV $4.50 MB $3.00 BO

1976-77 HEARTHSIDE CREAM SACHET
.66 oz. bronze plated over clear glass. Came in Sweet Honesty or Occur. SSP $3.49 CMV $3.00 MB $2.00 BO
1976-77 GOLDEN ANGEL
1 oz. gold plated over clear glass. White angel head cap. Came in Sweet Honesty or Occur! SSP $2.99 CMV $2.00 BO $3.00 MB

LEFT 1975-76 COUNTRY STYLE COFFEE POT
10 oz. yellow speckled paint over clear glass. Came with yellow & white pump top. Came with moisturized hand lotion. OSP $6.00 CMV $6.00 MB $5.00 BO
RIGHT 1977-80 GOLDEN HARVEST
10 oz. ear of corn shaped clear & green glass bottle. Gold & plastic pump top. Came with Avon almond scented hand lotion. OSP $8.50 CMV $5.00 MB $4.00 BO

1976-78 TEDDY BEAR COLOGNE DECANTER
.75 oz. frosted glass, gold cap. Came in Sweet Honesty or Topaze. SSP $2.99 CMV $2.50 MB $2.00 BO
1976-78 PRECIOUS DOE COLOGNE DECANTER
1/2 ox. frosted glass bottle. Came in Field Flowers or Sweet Honesty. SSP $2.99 CMV $2.50 MB $2.00 BO

1975 FOAMING BATH OIL DECANTER
6 oz. clear glass with gold cap. Came in Cotillion, Field Flowers, Bird of Paradise, Charisma, Sonnet, Imperial Garden, Moonwind & Timeless. S.S.P. $2.88 This sold C26 - 1975 only. Very short issue. C.M.V. $8.00 M.B. This is the same bottle as the 1972-74 Emollient Freshener for After Bath. Only label & box is changed.

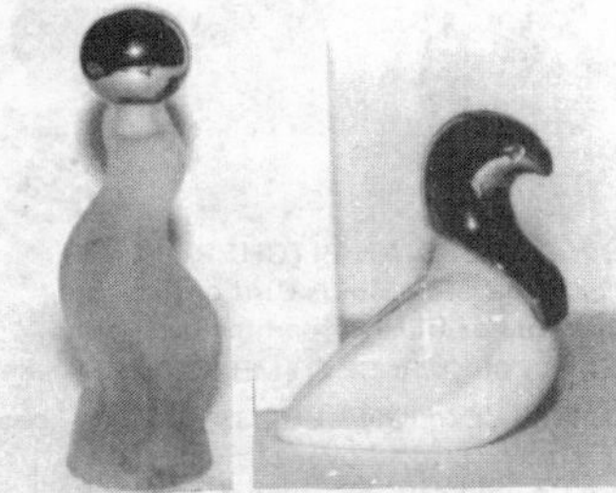

1976-77 LOVABLE SEAL
1 oz. frosted glass, gold cap. Came in Cotillion or Here's My Heart. O.S.P.$4.00 CMV $3.00 MB $2.00 BO
1978 LOVE BIRD DECANTER
1½ oz. milk glass bottle with gold cap. Came in Charisma or Moonwind cologne. SSP $3.99 CMV $3.00 MB $2.00 BO

1977-80 FLAVOR FRESH APOTHECARY DECANTER
6 oz. clear glass bottle & stopper. Holds mouth wash. O.S.P. $4.50 CMV $2.50 MB $1.00 BO

1973-75 LOVE SONG DECANTER
6 oz. frosted glass with gold cap. Holds Skin-So-Soft bath oil. O.S.P. $6.00 C.M.V. $5.00 MB $3.00 BO
1973-76 BATH TREASURE SNAIL DECANTER
6 oz. clear glass with gold head. Holds Skin-So-Soft. OSP $6.00 CMV $6.00 MB $4.00 BO

1976-78 COUNTRY JUG DECANTER
10 oz. gray painted over clear glass. Blue & gray plastic pump. Came with almond scented hand lotion. O.S.P.$8.00 CMV $5.00 MB $4.00 BO

1978-79 SEA FANTASY BUD VASE
6 oz. bottle. Gold & white fish & seaweed design on both sides. Holds Skin-So-Soft bath oil. S.S.P. $6.99 CMV $4.00 MB $3.00 BO

1974-75 DEW KISS DECANTER
4 oz. clear glass with pink lid. O.S.P. $3.00 CMV $3.00 MB $1.00 BO

1975-76 SEA LEGEND DECANTER
6 oz. clear glass with white cap. Holds Moonwind or Sonnet foaming bath oil or Roses, Roses creamy bath foam. O.S.P. $5.00 CMV $5.00, $3.00 BO

1971-73 KEEPSAKE CREAM SACHET
6½" high, gold lid on marbleized glass jar with flower in colors. Came in Moonwind. O.S.P. $5.00 Bird of Paradise, Field Flowers, Elusive, Charisma, S.S.P. $3.00 C.M.V. $4.00 $5.00 M.B.

1970-73 KEEPSAKE CREAM SACHET
5½" high gold metal tree lid on .66 oz. frosted glass jar. Came in Bird of Paradise, Elusive, Charisma, Brocade & Regence. S.S.P. $3.50 C.M.V. $4.00 $5.00 M.B.

1973-74 COUNTRY CHARM BUTTER CHURN DECANTER
1.5 oz. clear glass, gold bands & cap. Came in Field Flowers, Elusive, Occur!, Somewhere cologne. S.S.P. $3.00 C.M.V. $5.00 MB $4.00 BO

1972-74 GOLDEN THIMBLE
2 oz. clear glass with gold cap. Came in Bird of Paradise, Brocade, Charisma or Elusive cologne. SSP $2.00 CMV $3.00 MB $2.00 BO

1975-76 FLOWER FAIR SSS SKIN SOFTENER
5 oz. marbleized glass jar with plastic cap. Holds Skin-So-Soft Skin Softener. OSP $5.00 CMV $3.00 MB $2.00 BO

1975-76 FLOWER FAIR COLOGNE
3 oz. marbleized glass with plastic top. Holds Roses, Roses, Moonwind or Sonnet. O.S.P. $6.00 CMV $4.00 MB $3.00 BO

1974-76 BY THE JUG STRAWBERRY BATH FOAM
10 oz. beige plastic with pink top, brown cap looks like cork. S.S.P. $3.00 C.M.V. $3.00 Also came with left handed jug with label reversed. CMV $7.00

1974-75 BY THE JUG ASTRINGENT
10 oz. beige plastic with blue top, brown cap looks like cork. S.S.P. $3.00 C.M.V. $3.00.

1974-75 BY THE JUG BALSAM SHAMPOO
10 oz. beige plastic with orange top. Cap is brown looks like cork. S.S.P. $3.00 C.M.V. $3.00.

1974 BAROQUE CREAM SACHET
2 oz. white milk glass with gold top & bottom. Came in Imperial Garden, Sonnet or Moonwind. SSP $5.00 CMV $5.00 MB $4.00 BO

1973-75 COUNTRY STORE MINERAL SPRING BATH CRYSTALS
12 oz. clear glass with gold cap, holds green Mineral Springs Bath Crystals. S.S.P. $5.50 CMV $4.00 MB $2.00 BO

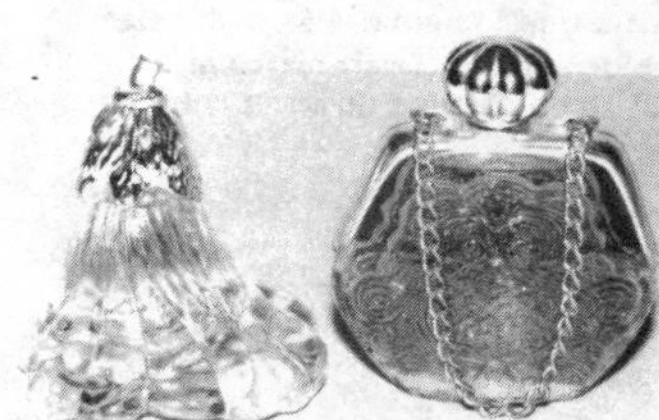

1969-70 PETTI FLEUR COLOGNE
1 oz. gold cap. Shaped like flower. Came in Elusive, Brocade, Charisma or Regence. OSP $2.50 CMV $5.00 MB $3.00 BO

1971 PURSE PETITE COLOGNE
1½ oz. embossed bottle with gold trim & cap & chain. Elusive, Charisma, Bird of Paradise, Field Flowers, Hana Gasa. O.S.P. $4.00 CMV $7.00 MB $5.00 BO

1974-76 PERSIAN PITCHER
6 oz. blue glass. Holds Bird of Paradise, Charisma or Elusive foaming bath oil. OSP $5.00 CMV $3.00 MB $2.00 BO

1971-72 COLOGNE ELEGANTE
4 oz. gold sprayed over clear glass & red rose on gold cap. 12" high. Came in Bird of Paradise, Hana Gasa, Elusive, Charisma. O.S.P. $8.50 Moonwind O.S.P. $10.00 CMV $10.00 MB $7.00 BO

1971 EMERALD BUD VASE COLOGNE
3 oz. green glass & glass top, 9" high. Came in Topaze, Occur, Unforgettable, Here's My Heart, To A Wild Rose. O.S.P. $5.00 CMV $3.00 MB $2.00 BO

1973-74 SAPPHIRE SWIRL
5 oz. blue glass with gold cap, holds Charisma or Bird of Paradise Perfumed Skin Softener. SSP $4.00 CMV $4.00 MB $3.00 BO

1972-73 PERIOD PIECE DECANTER
5 oz. frosted glass, came in Moonwind, Bird of Paradise, Charisma or Elusive. SSP $6.00 CMV $5.00 MB $4.00 BO
1976 Came with Charisma & Bird of Paradise. SSP $6.00 CMV $5.00 MB $4.00 BO

1973-76 APOTHECARY DECANTER
1973-74 8 oz. Spicy After Shave in light brown glass with gold cap.
1973-76 8 oz. Lemon Velvet Moisturized Friction Lotion light yellow glass with gold cap. Also came in light green or blue green glass.
1973 8 oz. Breath Fresh, dark green with gold cap. SSP $3.00 each, CMV $3.00 MB each $2.00 BO each.

1971 LOVELY TOUCH DECANTER
12 oz. clear glass, gold cap with dispenser cap, holds Vita Moist or Rich Moisture Body Lotion. S.S.P. $4.00 C.M.V. $4.00 M. MB $3.00 BO

1972-73 LOVELY TOUCH DECANTER
12 oz. clear glass with dispenser cap, holds Vita Moist or Rich Moisture Body Lotion SSP $4.00 CMV $4.00 MB $3.00 BO

1972-76 CLASSIC BEAUTY
10 oz. clear glass, holds Bird of Paradise or Field Flowers Hand & Body Cream. S.S.P. $5.00 CMV $4.00 MB $3.00 BO

1973-74 PINEAPPLE DECANTER
10 oz. clear glass with green plastic leaves, dispenser top. Holds Moisturized Hand Lotion. SSP $5.00 CMV $6.00 MB $4.00 BO

1973-75 BELL JAR COLOGNE DECANTER
5 oz. clear glass with bouquet of pink & white flowers, had gold cap & base with pink ribbon. Holds Field Flowers, Bird of Paradise, Charisma or Brocade cologne. SSP $7.00 CMV $7.00 BO $9.00MB
1976 sold only in Field Flowers, Bird of Paradise & Charisma. Same CMV

1973-74 CRUET COLOGNE SET
8 oz. clear glass with glass stopper & flat dish. Holds Imperial Garden, Patchwork, Sonnet or Moonwind Cologne. SSP$13.00 CMV $10.00 MB $7.00 BO & dish

1974-76 DOVECOTE COLOGNE DECANTER
4 oz. clear glass with gold roof & 2 white doves. Holds Field Flowers, Bird of Paradise, Charisma or Roses, Roses Cologne. SSP $3.00 CMV $3.00 MB $2.00 BO

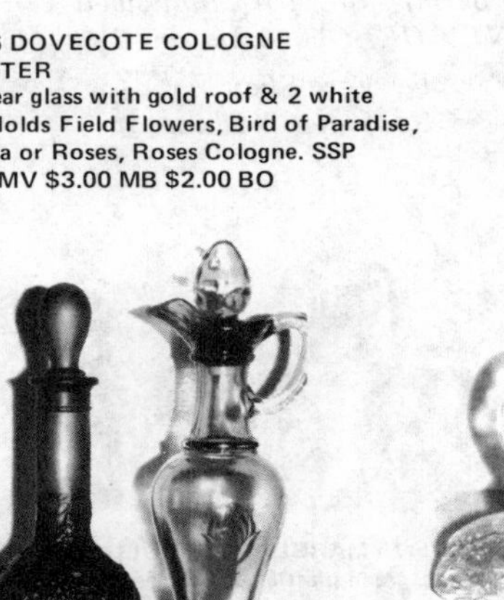

1973 GRAPE BUD VASE
6 oz. grape frosted glass holds Skin-So-Soft. SSP $5.00 CMV $5.00 MB $3.00 BO

1972-74 NILE BLUE BATH URN SKIN-SO-SOFT DECANTER
6 oz. deep blue glass with gold trim. SSP $6.00 CMV $8.00 MB $5.00 BO

1975 NILE GREEN BATH URN
same as above only green glass. CMV $8.00 MB $5.00 BO

1972-73 ROYAL APPLE COLOGNE
3 oz. frosted red glass with gold cap. SSP $4.00 CMV $4.00 MB $3.00 BO

1973-76 GARNET BUD VASE
3 oz. garnet colored translucent glass bottle & stopper. Came in Occur!, Somewhere, Topaze, To A Wild Rose cologne. SSP $5.00 CMV $4.00 MB $3.00 BO

1970 ROYAL VASE DECANTER
3 oz. Blue cologne bottle in Elusive, Charisma, Brocade or Regence. O.S.P. $5.00 CMV $5.00 MB $3.00 BO

1970-71 RUBY BUD VASE COLOGNE
3 oz. Red box holds ruby glass vase filled with Unforgettable, Rapture, Occur, Somewhere, Topaze or Cotillion. O.S.P. $5.00 CMV $5.00 MB $3.00 BO

1975 COLOGNE CRYSTALIQUE
4 oz. clear glass with glass stopper. Holds Moonwind, Sonnet or Imperial Garden. OSP $5.00 CMV $4.00 MB $3.00 BO

1975 COUNTRY PUMP
10 oz. clear glass with plastic top. Holds Rich Moisture or Vita Moist Body Lotion. OSP $5.00 CMV $4.00 MB $3.00 BO

1974 BREATH FRESH APOTHECARY DECANTER
8 oz. clear glass with gold cap. Holds Breath Fresh Mouth Wash. S.S.P. $3.00. CMV $3.00 MB $2.00 BO

THE AVON COLLECTOR

We Avon Collectors are DEFINITELY in a class all by our selves;
Spending small fortunes on bottles, just to line up neatly on shelves.

Each one collecting in his own special way;
Adding new treasures, one by one, day by day.

Off to a garage sale, a flea market, or still better yet
find the cache of a long time, hoarding type Avon Rep.

Finding a gift set, an old toy, or a mint box of soap;
Keep us ever searching with new rays of hope.

It's that suspense, the anticipation that keeps driving us on;
Many to the point where our savings are about gone.

Some people think we are silly, personally, I find it a thrill;
and I'm gonna keep right on collecting till I go over the hill.

Will my Avons be for sale when from this earth I depart;
My beautiful collection that is so dear to my heart?

You have got to be kidding, or just plain out of your tree;
I've already made arrangements to take all of them with me.

I first called on St. Peter, but he said, "I'm so sorry my dear;
We just don't allow wordly possessions up here."

"You might check with Satan, for so I've been told,
He might be willing to accept you into his fold."

I took that advice. I've been granted permission. Isn't that swell;
Can't you just imagine how HEAVENLY HELL'S gonna smell!!

By Vera Shaw
Spokane, Washington

LEFT 1975 CALIFORNIA PERFUME CO. ANNIVERSARY KEEPSAKE COLOGNE
Issued in honor of 89th Anniversary. 1.7 oz. bottle, pink ribbon & gold cap. Came in Charisma or Sweet Honesty cologne. Sold in 2 campaigns only. CMV $4.00, $6.00 MB. 1st issue
Avon Presidents Club Reps received this bottle with 4A design under bottom label. Regular issue had Avon on bottom. CMV for 4A $10.00 MB
Also came with 4A design & "M" for Managers. Given to Managers only. CMV $15.00 MB.
RIGHT 1976 CPC ANNIVERSARY KEEPSAKE COLOGNE
1.7 oz. clear glass bottle, gold cap. Bottle is embossed on back side (Avon 90th Anniversary Keepsake) Came in Moonwind or Cotillion cologne. Sold 2 campaigns only. OSP $6.00 CMV $6.00 MB $4,00 BO

1975-76 MARBLESQUE COLOGNE MIST
3 oz. green plastic coated glass bottle with gold plastic top. Holds Imperial Garden, Sonnet or Moonwind. O.S.P. $7.00 CMV $6.00 MB $5.00 BO
1975-76 TOPALENE SPRAY COLOGNE
(Non-aerosol)
2.5 oz. glass bottle with tortoise shell colored plastic top and gold band. Holds Moonwind, Patchwork or Roses, Roses. OSP $5.00 CMV $4.00 MB $2.00 BO
1976-77 CRYSTALPOINT SALT SHAKER
1.5 oz. blue glass. Holds Sonnet or Cotillion cologne. OSP $3.00 CMV $3.00 MB $2.00 BO

1971-73 ALADDIN'S LAMP
7½" long, 6 oz. green glass bottle with gold cap. Holds foaming bath oil in Charisma, Bird of Paradise, Elusive, Occur! or Unforgettable. SSP $7.00 CMV $7.00 MB $5.00 BO
1974-76 VENETIAN BLUE EMOLLIENT BATH PEARLS DECANTER
Frosted turquoise glass with turquoise plastic lid & gold tip. Holds 75 bath pearls. Came in Moonwind, Sonnet or Imperial Garden. SSP $6.00 CMV $6.00 MB $4.00 BO

1969 BATH SEASONS
3 oz. Bath oil, came in Charisma & Brocade, Black milk glass with silver cap & base. OSP $4.50 CMV $6.00 MB $4.00 BO
1972-74 EMOLLIENT FRESHENER FOR AFTER BATH
6 oz. clear glass with gold cap, holds Sonnet, Charisma or Moonwind pearlescent liquid. SSP $4.00 CMV $3.00 MB $1.00 BO
1973-75 AMBER CRUET
6 oz. light amber ribbed glass, holds Field Flowers, Bird of Paradise or Charisma foaming bath oil. S.S.P. $5.00 C.M.V. $4.00 MB $3.00 BO
1975 Came only in Field Flowers & Bird of Paradise.

1977-79 COUNTRY TALC SHAKER
3 oz. gray and blue speckled metal can shaker top. Came in Sweet Honesty or Charisma perfumed talc. OSP $7.50 CMV $4.00 MB $3.00 BO
1977-78 CALIFORNIA PERFUME CO. 1977 ANNIVERSARY KEEPSAKE
3.75 oz. blue can sold to public with Avon 1977 on the bottom. S.S.P.$2.99 CMV $2.50 MB $1.00 BO Was also given to Avon reps. during 91st Anniversary with "Anniversary Celebration Avon 1977" on the bottom. CMV $4.00 MB Came in Roses, Roses or Trailing Arbutus Talc.

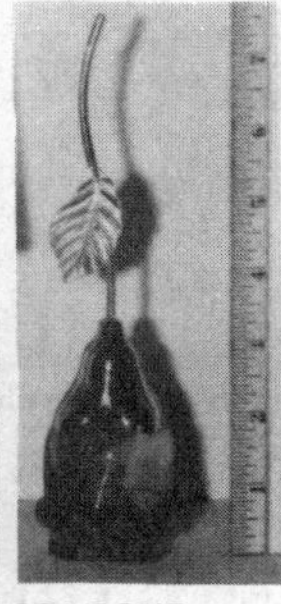

1974 COURTING ROSE COLOGNE
1.5 oz. Red glass rose with gold cap & stem. Came in Moonwind, Sonnet or Imperial Garden. S.S.P. $5.00 C.M.V. $9.00 M.B. Later issue painted red over clear glass. C.M.V. $5.00 M.B.

1974-76 SWEET TREAT COLOGNE DECANTER
White & brown painted glass with red cap. Came in pink & pretty cologne. S.S.P. $2.50 C.M.V. $2.50.

RIGHT 1977 COURTING ROSE 1.5 oz. amber coated over clear glass rose bottle with gold top. Came in Roses Roses or Moonwind cologne. OSP $6.00 CMV $5.00 MB, $4.00 BO

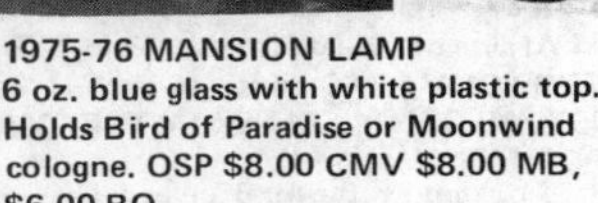

1975-76 MANSION LAMP
6 oz. blue glass with white plastic top. Holds Bird of Paradise or Moonwind cologne. OSP $8.00 CMV $8.00 MB, $6.00 BO

1975 EMPIRE GREEN BUD VASE
3 oz. green glass with silver base. Holds Moonwind, Sonnet or Imperial Garden cologne. OSP $6.00 CMV $5.00 MB $3.00 BO

1975-76 BUTTERFLY GARDEN BUD VASE
6 oz. black glazed glass with gold stopper. Holds Roses, Roses, Bird of Paradise or Topaze cologne. OSP $6.00 CMV, $6.00 MB, $4.00 BO

1972-73 SEAGREEN BUD VASE
5 oz. 9" high green glass bottle holds foaming bath oil in Field Flowers, Honeysuckle or Bird of Paradise. SSP $4.00 CMV, $4.00 MB, $2.00 BO

THE 1876 CAPE COD COLLECTION

CAPE COD 1876 COLLECTION
all are ruby red glass.

1979-80 1876 HOSTESS BELL
6½" high "Christmas 1979" on bottom. SSP $9.99, CMV $9.99 MB

1980-CAPE COD DESSERT PLATES
Box of 2 red glass plates marked Avon. SSP $10.99, CMV $10.99 MB

1975-80 CAPE COD CRUET
5 oz. red glass. Holds Skin So Soft. SSP $8.00, CMV $8.00 MB

1975-80 CAPE COD CANDLESTICK COLOGNE
5 oz. red glass. Came in Charisma, Patchwork or Bird of Paradise. SSP $8.00, CMV $8.00 MB

1977-80 CAPE COD WINE GOBLET
Red glass candle. SSP $4.99, CMV $4.99

1978-80 DESSERT BOWL & GUEST SOAPS
SSP $8.99, CMV $8.99 MB

1978-80 SALT SHAKER
May 1978 on bottom. SSP $4.00, CMV $4.00 MB. Latter issue not dated on bottom. CMV $3.00 MB

1976-80 CAPE COD WATER GOBLET
red glass candle. SSP $8.99, CMV $8.99 Also issued to reps with Presidents Celebration 1976 embossed on bottom. CMV $10.00 MB

1977-80 CAPE COD WINE DECANTER
16 oz. red glass holds bubble bath. SSP $13.99, CMV $13.99 MB

1976-1876 CAPE COD WINE GOBLET TEST
factory test in emereld green glass. Regular issue in red glass. EXPL embossed on bottom. Was never sold by Avon in green. CMV $50.00 green glass.

1970-71 PICTURE FRAME COLOGNE
4 oz. gold paint on clear glass. Gold cap & gold plastic frame to hold bottle. Came in Elusive, Charisma, Brocade, Regence, SSP $8.00 CMV $10.00 Mint $12.00 MB

1969 PYRAMID OF FRAGRANCE
Top is 1/8 oz. Perfume, gold cap. Center is 2 oz. Cologne. Bottom is 2-3 oz. cream sachet in black glass. 6" high, came in Charisma, Brocade or Regence. O.S.P. $12.50 CMV, $15.00 MB, $10.00 BO

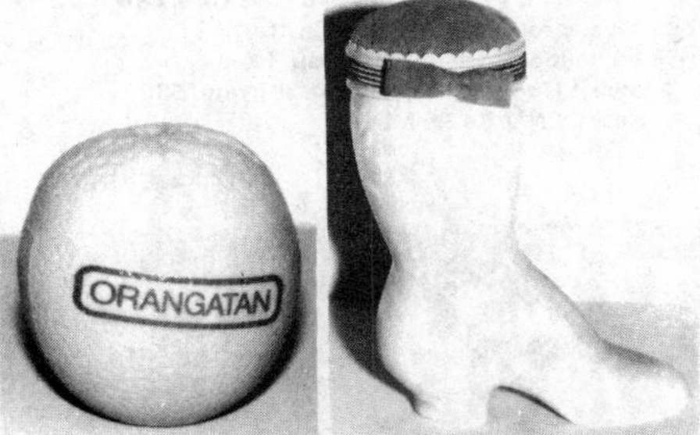

1976 ORANGATAN
6 oz. orange shaped and colored plastic bottle. Holds suntan lotion. OSP $4.00 CMV $3.00

1972-76 FASHION BOOT PIN CUSHION
5½" tall, blue milk glass with lavender bow & velvet cushion that fits over cap. Holds 4 oz. cologne, Roses, Roses or Charisma. Regular price $6.00 Sonnet or Moonwind SSP, $6.00 CMV, $6.00 MB, $4.00 BO

1973-74 COLOGNE ELEGANTE ATOMIZER DECANTER
3 oz. clear glass, gold cap with atomizer, also white plastic cap. Holds Imperial Garden, Patchwork, Sonnet or Moonwind. SSP, $6.00 CMV, $4.00 MB, $3.00 BO

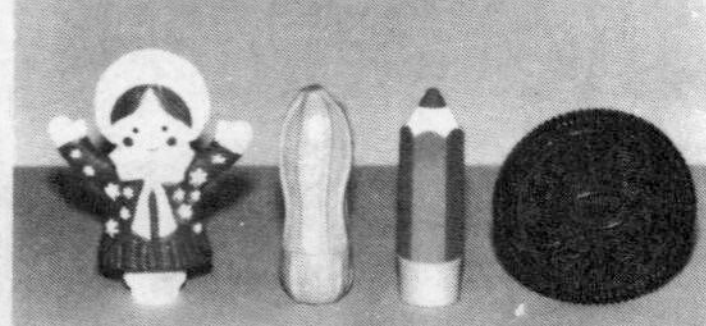

1975-77 SUNBONNET SUE DEMI STICK
.19 oz. red and white plastic. Pink & Pretty fragrance. OSP $2.50 CMV, $3.00 MB, $2.00 BO

1974-75 NUTSHELL COLOR MAGIC LIPSTICK
Peanut shaped case came in Pink Sorcery (blue lipstick) or Peach Sorcery (green lipstick). OSP $2.00 CMV, $3.00 MB, $2.00 BO

1975-76 SCHOOL DAYS PENCIL LIP POMADE
.13 oz. red, white & yellow plastic. Choice of strawberry, cherry or tutti-fruiti. OSP, $2.50 CMV, $3.00 MB, $2.00 BO

1975-76 SWEET LIPS LIP GLOSS COOKIE
brown plastic with 2 shades of lip gloss. OSP, $3.00 CMV, $3.00 MB, $2.00 BO

1974-76 ICE CREAM LIP POMADE
.13 oz. white plastic bottom with light pink, dark pink or red top for Cherry, Strawberry or Tutti-Frutti flavors. O.S.P. $2.00 CMV, $2.00 BO, $3.00 MB

1974-76 ICE CREAM CONE LIP POMADE
Yellow cone with different color tops for Cherry, Strawberry, Tutti-frutti, mint, chocolate. OSP, $2.00 CMV, $2.00 BO $3.00 MB

1973-74 LIP POP COLA'S
.13 oz. plastic tube with plastic top. Came in Cherry (light red case) Cola (brown case) Strawberry (pink case) lip pomade. Strawberry & Cherry also came solid red plastic (rare CMV, $7.00) others OSP, $1.50 CMV, $2.00 BO, $4.00 MB

1979-80 ROCKING HORSE TREE ORNAMENT DECANTER
.75 oz. clear glass rocker shaped bottle with gold plastic rocking horse top. Bottom of horse says 1979. Holds Sweet Honesty or Moonwind cologne. SSP $4.99 CMV $4.99 MB

LEFT TO RIGHT:

1979-80 SNOW OWL POWDER SACHET
1.25 oz. frosted glass. Holds Moonwind or Timeless powder sachet. Blue Rhine stone eyes. SSP $6.99 CMV $6.99 MB

1979-80 CUTE COOKIE DECANTER
1 oz. dark amber glass. Pink cap & point. Holds Hello Sunshine cologne. SSP $2.75 CMV $2.75 MB

1979-80 CHARMING CHIPMUNK DECANTER
.5 oz. clear glass painted frosted peach color. Holds Field Flowers or Sweet Honesty. SSP $3.99 CMV $3.99 MB

1980 PRECIOUS HEARTS DECANTER
heart embossed clear glass. 5 oz. Gold tone cap. Comes in Here's My Heart, Unforgettable, Moonwind, Topaze or Sweet Honesty. SSP $1.29 CMV $1.00 MB

1980 FLUFFY CHICK DECANTER
1 oz. clear glass yellow flock coated. Holds Hello Sunshine cologne. SSP $5.99 CMV $5.99 MB

1980 FLUTTERING FANCY DECANTER
1 oz. clear glass with pink butterfly on yellow frosted plastic cap. Holds Sweet Honesty or Charisma cologne. SSP $4.99 CMV $4.99 MB

1980 HUGGABLE HIPPO DECANTER
1.75 oz. white glass. Red hat. Holds Zany Cologne or Light Musk After Shave. Comes with card of stick-on decals. SSP $3.99 CMV $3.99 MB

1980 GREEN-BLUE-BROWN EYED SUSAN COMPACT
3 different color centers with yellow flower rim. SSP $4.99 CMV $2.50 EA. MB

1978 JOYOUS BELL
light blue frosted over clear glass. Silver cap. Came in Charisma or Topaze cologne. In blue & white box. SSP $2.99 CMV $2.99 MB

1978-79 SUNNY SHINE UP LIP GLOSS COMPACT
white plastic base with yellow screw on egg lid. SSP $2.99 CMV $2.00 MB

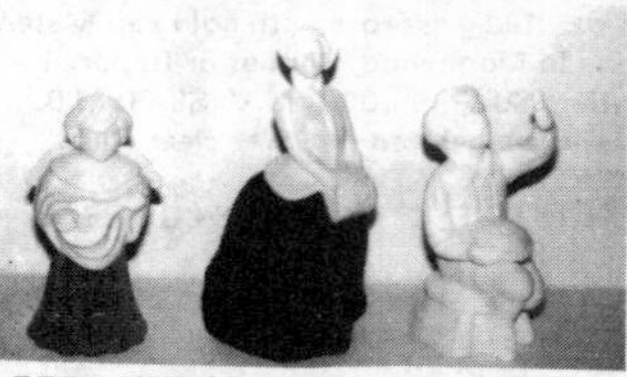

LEFT - 1979-80 ANGEL SONG WITH MANDOLIN DECANTER
1 oz. frosted over clear glass. White plastic top. Holds Moonwind or Unforgettable cologne. SSP $3.99 CMV $3.99 MB

1979-80 SKATER'S WALTZ DECANTER
4 oz. blue flock base over clear glass. Light blue plastic top. Holds Charisma or Cotillion cologne. SSP $7.99 CMV $7.99 MB

RIGHT

1979-80 LITTLE JACK HORNER DECANTER
1.5 oz. white glass painted white frosted. Came in Topaze or Roses Roses cologne. SSP $5.99 CMV $5.99 MB

1979-80 LADY SKATER TALC
3.75 oz. gold top can. Red cap. Choice of Ariane or Sweet Honesty Talc. SSP $3.99 CMV $3.00 mint. No Box.

1979-80 GENTLEMAN SKATER TALC FOR MEN
3.75 oz. gold top can. Blue cap. Choice of Clint or Trazarra Talc. SSP $3.99 CMV $3.00 Mint. No Box.

1979 CHRISTMAS TREE HOSTESS SET
9" high ceramic green tree. Comes with Mountain Pine fragrance wax chips & Rag Doll & Teddy Bear ceramic salt & pepper shakers. This was a very short issue at Xmas 1979. SSP $24.99 CMV $25.00 MB

LEFT TO RIGHT:
1979-80 MERRY MOUSE DECANTER
.75 oz. white milk glass bottle & head. Stick-on holly leaf. Choice of Zany or Cotillion cologne. SSP $4.99 CMV $4.99 MB

1979-80 PRECIOUS CHICKADEE DECANTER
1 oz. white glass. Red & white cap. Came in Here's My Heart or Sun Blossoms cologne. SSP $3.99 CMV $3.99 MB

1979-80 SNUG CUB DECANTER
1 oz. milk glass. Green cap. Pink & green paint. Comes in Occur! or Sweet Honesty cologne. SSP $2.99 CMV $2.99 MB

1979-80 CHRISTMAS BELLS DECANTER
1 oz. red glass. Silver cap. Holds Topaz or Sweet Honesty cologne. SSP $2.99 CMV $2.99 MB

1979-80 RED CARDINAL DECANTER
2 oz. clear glass painted red. Red cap. Holds Bird of Paradise or Charisma cologne. SSP $4.99 CMV $4.99 MB

1979-80 FESTIVE FACETS COLOGNE DECANTER
1 oz. with gold caps. Comes in Charisma "red glass", Sweet Honesty "green glass", and Here's My Heart in "blue glass". SSP $1.49 ea. CMV $1.49 MB ea.

1976 FAIRYTALE FROG
1 oz. clear glass with gold frog cap. Choice of Sweet Honesty or Sonnet Cologne. OSP $3.00 CMV $3.00 MB $2.00 BO

1976-80 LUCKY PENNY LIP GLOSS COMPACT
2" diameter copper colored. Contains 2 colors lip gloss. OSP $3.00 CMV $2.00 MB $1.00 no box

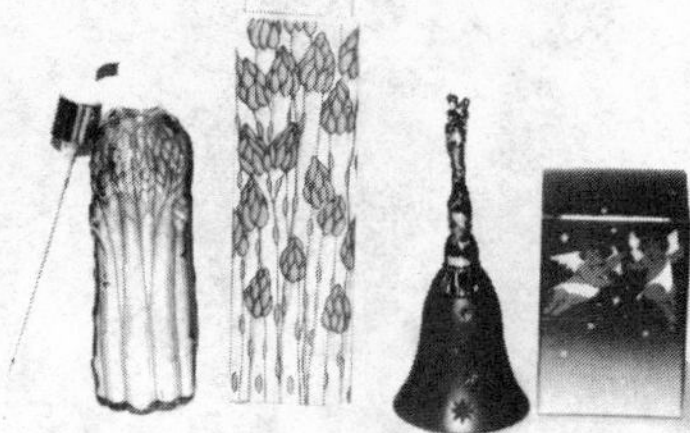

1979-80 GARDEN FRESH HAND LOTION DECANTER
10 oz. clear glass. Yellow & gold pump & cap. Green box. SSP $6.99 CMV $6.99 MB

1979-80 HEAVENLY CHERUB HOSTESS BELL
3.75 oz. clear glass painted frosted tan. Gold plastic handle. 1979 embossed on bottom. Comes in Topaze or Bird of Paradise cologne. SSP $6.99 CMV $6.99 MB

1973-75 CREAMY DECANTER
8 oz. yellow painted over clear glass with brown basket of blue & orange flowers. Holds Roses, Roses, Field Flowers, Bird of Paradise, hand & body cream lotion. OSP $5.00 CMV $5.00 MB $4.00 BO

1975-76 LIQUID MILK BATH
6oz. frosted glass bottle with gold cap. Holds Imperial Garden, Sonnet or Moonwind. OSP $5.00 CMV $4.00 MB $2.00 BO

(Left)
1978-80 AUTUMN ASTER DECANTER
.75 oz. clear glass, gold cap. Holds Topaze or Sun Blossoms cologne. S.S.P. $2.00, C.M.V. $2.00 M.B.

(Right)
1978-80 DOGWOOD DEMI DECANTER
.75 oz. flower shaped bottle, gold flower lid. Came in Apple Blossom or Moonwind , Topaze cologne. S.S.P. $2.99, C.M.V. $2.00 M.B.

1978-79 HUDSON MANOR COLLECTION

1978-79 SALTCELLAR CANDLE & SPOON
Silver plated. Comes with glass lined candle. Bottom says HMC Avon Silver plate on both pieces. Silver and white box. S.S.P. $18.99, C.M.V. $18.99 M.B.

1978-79 SILVER PLATED DISH AND SATIN SACHET
6 " silver plated dish with red satin sachet pillow. Bottom of dish says Avon Silver Plate HMC, Italy. S.S.P. $18.99, C.M.V. $18.99 M.B.

1978-79 SILVER PLATED HOSTESS BELL
5½" high silver plated bell. Avon silver plate HMC on bottom. S.S.P. $18.99, C.M.V. $18.99 M.B.

1978-79 SILVER PLATED BUD VASE AND SCENTED ROSE
8" high silver plated bud vase. Came with long stemmed fabric red rose and 2 Roses Roses fragrance pellets. S.S.P. $18.99, C.M.V. $18.99 M.B.

1978-79 DINGO BOOT
6 oz. camel tan plastic bottle and cap. Choice of Sweet Honesty Body Splash or Wild Country After Shave. S.S.P. $4.49, C.M.V. $3.00 M.B.

1978-79 VINTAGE YEAR "CHAMPAGNE BOTTLE"
2 oz. green glass, gold cap. 1979 embossed in bottom. Came in Sweet Honesty or Wild Country cologne. Green and gold box. S.S.P. $4.99, C.M.V. 4.99.

1978-79 ANNIVERSARY KEEPSAKE C.P.C.
1.5 oz. clear glass. Old style C.P.C. label and design. Pink neck ribbon. Came in Trailing Arbutus cologne. S.S.P. $4.99, C.M.V. $4.99 M.B.

1979-80 COUNTRY STYLE COFFEE POT
Came in special color up box. 10 oz. clear glass painted red or green, blue or yellow. Holds moisturized hand lotion. Comes with matching hand pump. S.S.P. $7.99, C.M.V. $7.99.

1979-80 FLOWER FANCY DECANTER
1.25 oz. clear glass, gold flower cap. Holds Field Flowers or Roses Roses. S.S.P. $3.99, C.M.V. $3.99 M.B.

1979-80 SPRING SONG DECANTER
1.5 oz. clear glass. Comes with plastic frosted flower stopper. Came in Lily of The Valley or Sweet Honesty cologne. S.S.P. $5.99, C.M.V. $5.99 M.B.

1978-80 SNIFFY "SKUNK" DECANTER"
1.25 oz. black glass, white trim. Holds Sweet Honesty or Topaze cologne. S.S.P. $4.99, C.M.V. $4.99 M.B.

1978-80 "CALCULATOR" IT ALL ADDS UP DECANTER
4 oz. black glass. Holds Deepwoods, after shave or Sweet Honesty body spash. S.S.P. $5.99, C.M.V. $5.99 M.B.

(Left to Right)

1979-80 WEDDING FLOWER MAIDEN DECANTER
1.75 oz. white painted over clear glass. Holds Unforgettable or Sweet Honesty cologne. S.S.P. $5.99, C.M.V. $5.99 M.B.

1978-79 GARDEN GIRL DECANTER
4 oz. pink painted over clear glass. Holds Charisma or Sweet Honesty cologne. S.S.P. $4.99, C.M.V. $4.99 M.B.

1978-79 ANGEL SONG DECANTER
1 oz. frosted glass base with off white plastic top. Holds Here's My Heart or Charisma cologne. S.S.P. $2.99, C.M.V. $2.99 M.B.

1978-79 ON THE AVENUE DECANTER
2 oz. blue painted over clear glass. Pink plastic top with lavendar hat. White detachable umbrella. Holds Topaze or Unforgettable cologne. S.S.P. $7.99, C.M.V. $7.99 M.B.

1978-80 PROUD GROOM DECANTER
2 oz. white painted over clear glass. Holds Sweet Honesty or Unforgettable cologne. S.S.P. $6.99, C.M.V. $6.99 M.B.

1979-80 TUG A BRELLA
2.5 oz. clear glass painted yellow, yellow plastic top. Black plastic umbrella on wire. Holds Moonwind or Cotillion cologne. S.S.P. $9.99, C.M.V. $9.99 M.B.

1978-80 GOOD FAIRY
3 oz. clear glass painted blue. Blue plastic top. Plastic wand. Blue and pink fabric purse and wings. Holds Delicate Daisies cologne. S.S.P. $5.99, C.M.V. $5.99 M.B.

1978-80 FRENCH RIBBON SACHET PILLOWS
Box holds 6 blue satin pillows with blue ribbon. S.S.P. $5.99, C.M.V. $5.00 M.B.

1979-80 GOLDEN NOTES "PARAKEET"
1.75 oz. clear glass coated light yellow. Yellow head. Came in Charisma or Moonwind cologne. S.S.P. $3.00, C.M.V. $3.00 M.B.

1979-80 CHURCH MOUSE GROOM
.75 oz. white glass, white plastic top. Holds Delicate Daisies cologne. S.S.P. $5.99, C.M.V. $5.99 M.B.

1979-80 FUZZY BUNNY
1 oz. clear glass coated with white flock. Pink ears, orange carrot. Holds Sweet Honesty or Honeysuckle cologne. S.S.P. $5.99, C.M.V. $5.99 M.B.

1978-79 KANGAROO TWO
8" red calico stuffed Kangaroo with Avon tag. Green neck ribbon. Came with .75 oz. frosted glass Kangaroo bottle with gold head. Holds Topaze or Sweet Honesty cologne. S.S.P. $9.99, C.M.V. $9.99 both M.B. Bottle only, $4.00. Stuffed toy, $5.00.

1979-80 SENTIMENTAL DOLL ADORABLE ABIGAIL
4.5 oz. clear glass painted beige. Beige plastic top. Comes in Regence or Sweet Honesty cologne. S.S.P. $9.99, C.M.V. $9.99 M.B.

1979-80 MRS. QUACKLES DECANTER
2 oz. clear glass painted off white. Off white plastic top with white lace and green bonnet. Comes in Delicate Daisies cologne. S.S.P. $5.99, C.M.V. $5.99 M.B.

1979-80 SWEET TOOTH TERRIER DECANTER
1 oz. white glass and white plastic top. Comes in Topaze or Cotillion cologne. S.S.P. $3.99, C.M.V. $3.99 M.B.

Left to Right)

1978-80 HEAVENLY MUSIC DECANTER

1 oz. clear glass, gold cap. Holds Charisma or Topaze cologne. S.S.P. $2.99, C.M.V. $2.99 M.B.

1978-79 LITTLE BURRO DECANTER

1 oz. light gray glass. Straw hat with red flower. Holds Sweet Honesty or Charisma cologne. S.S.P. $2.99, C.M.V. $2.99 M.B.

1978-80 HONEY BEE DECANTER

1.25 oz. amber coated over clear glass. Gold bee on lid. Holds Honeysuckle or Moonwind cologne. S.S.P. $3.99, C.M.V. $3.99 M.B.

1979-80 CURIOUS KITTY DECANTER

2.5 oz. clear glass, yellow cat cap. Came in Sweet Honesty or Here's My Heart cologne. S.S.P. $5.99, C.M.V. $5.99 M.B.

1978-79 PEEK A MOUSE CHRISTMAS STOCKING DECANTER

1.25 oz. green glass with gold mouse cap. Holds Sweet Honesty or Unforgettable cologne. Came with red velvet stocking with gold trim. S.S.P. $4.99, C.M.V. $4.99 M.B.

1979 AVONSHIRE COLLECTION COLOGNE DECANTER

6 oz. clear glass painted blue and white. Holds Charisma or Somewhere cologne. R on bottom for Reissue and dated May, 1979. S.S.P. $9.99, C.M.V. $9.99 M.B.

BATH OIL DECANTER

6 oz. clear glass painted blue and white. Holds Skin So Soft. R on bottom for reissue and dated May, 1979. S.S.P. $9.99, C.M.V. $9.99 M.B.

HOSTESS SOAPS

Blue box holds 3 white bars. S.S.P. $3.99, C.M.V. $3.99 M.B.

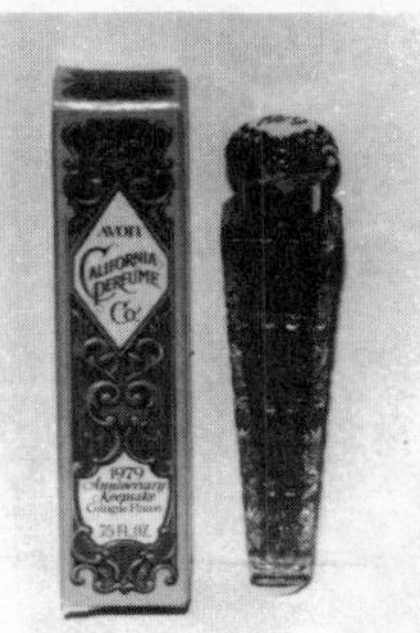

1979 ANNIVERSARY KEEPSAKE C.P.C. FLACON

.75 oz. clear glass. Silver cap has 1979 on top. Came with Sweet Honesty or Trailing Arbutus cologne. S.S.P. $4.99, C.M.V. $4.99 M.B.

1979 ANNIVERSARY KEEPSAKE EAU DE TOILETTE

Large 8 oz. clear glass bottle, CPC embossed on back side. Avon — 1979 on bottom. Gold Cap. Pink and green box. Came in Trailing Arbutus cologne, pink neck ribbon. S.S.P. $9.99, C.M.V. $9.99 M.B.

1978-79 ROYAL SIAMESE CAT

Light gray paint over clear glass. 4.5 oz. Gray plastic head has blue glass jewel eyes. Came in Cotillion or Moonwind cologne. S.S.P. $6.99, C.M.V. $6.99 M.B.

1978-79 EMERALD BELL

3.75 oz. light green glass. Gold and green plastic cap. Bottom has "Avon 1978" embossed. Came in Sweet Honesty or Roses Roses cologne. S.S.P. $5.99, C.M.V. $5.99 M.B.

1978-79 COLOGNE RONDELLE

.5 oz. clear glass, gold cap. Came in Sweet Honesty, Charisma, Cotillion, Topaze, Unforgettable, Moonwind, Heres My Heart, Sonnet, Occur, Bird of Paradise. Came in different color Christmas boxes. S.S.P. 99c, C.M.V. 99c M.B.

1978-79 BERMUDA FRESH MOUTHWASH DECANTER

6 oz. purple plastic, green top. S.S.P. $2.99, C.M.V. $1.50.

1978-79 COUNTRY CREAMERY "MILK CAN" DECANTER

10 oz. white painted over clear glass. Holds moisturized hand lotion. S.S.P. $5.99, C.M.V. $5.99 M.B.

1979-80 PRETTY PIGLET DECANTER

.75 oz. clear glass. Holds Roses Roses, pink cap; Honey Suckle, yellow cap; Hawaiian White Ginger, blue green cap. Fabric flower around neck. S.S.P. $3.00, C.M.V. $3.00 M.B.

1979-80 MONKEY SHINES DECANTER

1 oz. clear glass painted light gray, brown eyes and ears. Red cap and neck strap. Holds Sonnet or Moonwind cologne. SSP $5.99, CMV $9.79 MB

1979-80 BON BON DECANTER

.75 oz. dark amber glass. Pink and green top came with Sweet Honesty cologne or Cotillion with yellow and green top. S.S.P. $3.99, C.M.V. $3.99 M.B.

1979-80 GENTLE FOAL DECANTER

1.5 oz. dark amber glass and plastic head. Comes in Charisma or Sun Blossoms Cologne. S.S.P. $4.99, C.M.V. $4.99 M.B.

1978-79 DAPPER SNOWMAN

1 oz. white milk glass with black painted spots and black hat cap. Holds Moonwind or Sweet Honesty cologne. Brown, blue and red neck scarf. S.S.P. $2.99, C.M.V. $2.99 M.B.

1978-79 JOLLY SANTA

1 oz. clear glass, white painted beard. Red cap. Came in Here's My Heart or Topaze cologne. S.S.P. $1.49, C.M.V. $1.49.

1978-80 CUPID'S MESSAGE SACHET PILLOW AND STICK PIN
Red and white box holds 4" red satin heart with white lace trim. Avon on back side of arrow stick pin. Pillow has Timeless Fragrance. S.S.P. $7.99, C.M.V. $7.99 M.B.

1978-79 SCENT WITH LOVE "HEART COMPACT"
Pink box holds red plastic heart compact with Love in gold letters. Holds Sweet Honesty or Here's My Heart solid perfume. S.S.P. $2.99, C.M.V. $2.00 M.B.
1978-79 GOLDEN TURTLE COMPACT
.07 oz. gold plastic turtle holds Candid or Sweet Honesty solid perfume. S.S.P. $5.99, C.M.V. $4.00 M.B.

1965-66 SKIN-SO-SOFT DECANTER
10 oz. bottle with gold painted glass stopper. 1st issue came with solid painted gold band around center & later issue not solid band as pictured. OSP $5.00 CMV solid band $11.00 MB $7.00 BO Mint - not solid band $9.00 MB $5.00 BO Mint

1966 SKIN-SO-SOFT DECANTER (Left)
10 oz. bottle with glass & cork stopper. 10" high OSP $5.00 CMV $6.00 BO $8.00 MB
1967 SKIN-SO-SOFT DECANTER (Right) 8 oz. bottle with glass & cork stopper. 11" high. OSP $5.00 CMV $5.00 BO $7.00 MB

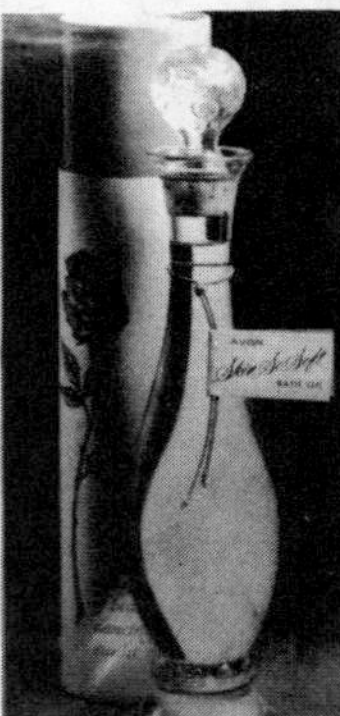

LEFT
1964 SKIN-SO-SOFT DECANTER
6 oz. gold crown top, came with gold neck tag. OSP $3.50 CMV $12.00 MB $7.00 bottle only with tag, Mint.

RIGHT 1962-63 SKIN-SO-SOFT DECANTER
5¾ oz. gold neck string with white label, pink & white box. OSP $3.50 CMV $12.00 MB Bottle only $7.00 mint with tag.

PERFUME GLACE

1967 PILL BOX PERFUME GLACE
Black & gold with red rose on top. Came in Occur! Rapture, Unforgettable, Somewhere, Topaze, Cotillion, Here's My Heart, To A Wild Rose, OSP $4.50 CMV $15.00 MB. Pill box only $10.00 mint

1969 DAISY PIN PERFUME GLACE
White & gold pin. Charisma, Brocade, Regence, O.S.P. $6.50. Rapture, Occur! Unforgettable O.S.P. $6.00. Somewhere, Topaze, Cotillion, OSP $5.75 CMV $6.00 $9.00 MB

1968-70 GOLDEN CHARMER LOCKET
Gold locket holds perfume glace in Somewhere, Topaze, Cotillion, Here's My Heart, To A Wild Rose, Unforgettable, Rapture, Occur! Brocade, & Regence. OSP $9.50 CMV $14.00 MB $9.00 locket only.

1965-66 PERFUME JEWEL GLACE
Gold & white box contains gold locket. Can be worn as pin or on a chain with solid perfume in Unforgettable, Rapture, Occur! Somewhere, Topaze, Cotillion, Here's My Heart, To A Wild Rose, & Wishing. O.S.P. $5.50 C.M.V. $17.00 ea. in box. $12.00 locket only.

1966-67 PERFUME GLACE NECKLACE
Special issue gold round box. Came with either silver with black stone or gold necklace with brown stone. CMV $20.00 MB as shown.

1969-70 GOLDEN LEAF PIN
Blue box contains gold leaf pin with pearl at stem. Perfume glace comes in Elusive, Charisma, Brocade, Regence, O.S.P. $7.00. Unforgettable, Rapture, Occur! Topaze, Somewhere, & Cotillion, Same pin also issued without glace. O.S.P. $6.50 CMV $9.00 MB $6.00 pin only.

1966-67 PERFUME GLACE NECKLACE
Silver with black stone & gold with brown stone. Came in Unforgettable, Rapture, Occur! O.S.P. $8.50 Somewhere, Cotillion, Topaze, O.S.P. $8.25 To A Wild Rose, Here's My Heart, Wishing. O.S.P. $8.00. C.M.V. $17.00 each M.B. $12.00 locket only.

1971-72 MANDOLIN PERFUME GLACE
2½" long gold mandolin. Choice of Moonwind, Elusive, Charisma, Brocade, Regence, or Bird of Paradise perfume glace. O.S.P. $9.00 CMV $14.00 in box. $8.00 no box. mandolin only.

1971-75 TORTOISE PERFUME GLACE
2½" long gold turtle with turquoise back came in same fragrances as Mandolin. OSP $9.00 CMV $10.00 MB $6.00 turtle only.

1971-75 MEMORY BOOK PERFUME GLACE - 1½" long gold book, choice of Moonwind, Elusive, Brocade, Regence, or Bird of Paradise perfume glace. OSP $7.00 CMV $9.00 MB $6.00. No box. $5.00 Book only.

1971-72 BABY GRAND PIANO PERFUME GLACE - 2" wide gold piano. Came in same fragrances as Memory Book, O.S.P. $10.00 CMV $14.00 MB $8.00 piano only.

1968-69 OWL PIN PERFUME GLACE
Gold metal pin with green eyes. Green & gold box. Came in Brocade, Regence, O.S.P. $6.50 Unforgettable, Rapture, Occur! O.S.P. $6.00. Cotillion, Here's My Heart, To A Wild Rose, O.S.P. $5.75 C.M.V. Owl only $7.00- $11.00 MB

1970-71 FLOWER BASKET PERFUME GLACE -
1½ x 1¼" gold tone pin. Choice of Bird of Paradise, Elusive, Charisma, Brocade, or Regence. OSP $7.00 CMV $10.00 MB $6.00 pin only.

1969-70 RING OF PEARLS GLACE
Perfume glace ring is gold with white pearls. Comes in Charisma, Regence, & Brocade. O.S.P. $7.50 C.M.V. $10.00 M.B. $7.00 ring only.

1970 CAMEO RING & PIN
Both are Perfume Glace, comes in Elusive, Charisma, Brocade, & Regence & Bird of Paradise. OSP $10.00 each. CMV $9.00 ea. $15.00 each MB

POMANDERS

Pomanders must be in the box to be Mint

1972-73 COCKATOO POMANDER
8½" tall blue scented wax pomander. Came in Floral Medley fragrance. SSP $5.00 CMV $7.00 MB

1975 CORAL EMPRESS POMANDER
6½" high coral colored wax figurine. Fragrant Seasons scent. O.S.P. $5.00 CMV $7.00 MB

1974-75 CHRISTMAS CAROLLERS POMANDER
7" high red wax pomander. Bayberry scented. OSP $6.00 CMV $7.00 MB

1977-78 FLORENTINE LADY POMANDER
Pink wax., approx. 9½" high. Came in Fragrant Seasons scent. O.S.P. $8.00 C.M.V. $5.00 M.B.

1972 ORIENTAL FIGURINE POMANDER
10" high. Scented pink wax figurine. O.S.P. $6.00 CMV $8.00 MB

1973 ORIENTAL FIGURINE POMANDER
Same as above except green. S.S.P. $6.00 CMV $8.00 MB

1973-74 HEARTSCENT CLOSET POMANDER
Wedgewood blue and white plastic heart with white tassel holds Potpourri scented chips. S.S.P. $3.00 C.M.V. $3.00 M.B.

1978-79 THE NESTLINGS
Yellow wax bird pomander. 6½" high. S.S.P. $5.99 C.M.V. $6.00 M.B.

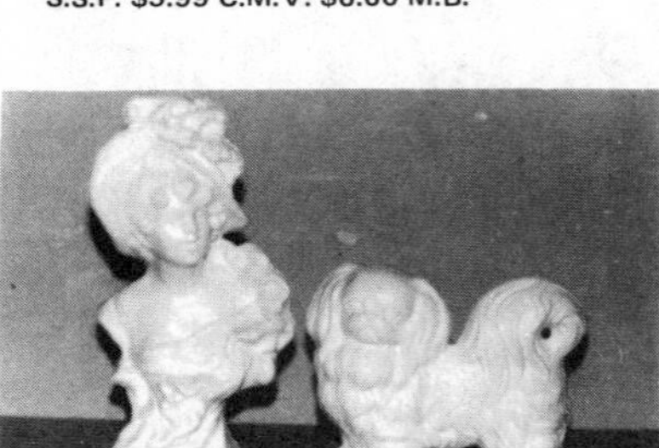

1976-77 PARISIAN MODE POMANDER
Pink wax. OSP $7.50 CMV $6.00 MB

1977-79 ROYAL PEKINGESE POMANDER
White wax. OSP $7.50 CMV $6.00 MB

1974-75 WISE EYES CLOSET POMANDER
Brown plastic with yellow cord & tassel. Came with Fernerie fragranced wax chips. O.S.P. $4.00 C.M.V. $3.50 M.B.

1974-76 PAMPERED PERSIANS DECANTER POMANDER
Wax sculptured cats with Floral Medley fragrance. SSP $5.00 CMV $5.00 MB
Yellow cat $7.00 MB

1974 SIGN OF SPRING POMANDER
6" high yellow fern-scented wax. O.S.P. $4.00 CMV $5.00 MB

1975-76 MEADOW BIRD POMANDER
6" high white and blue wax pomander, Fernerie scented. O.S.P. $6.00 C.M.V. $6.00 M.B.

1975-76 FLORENTINE CHERUB POMANDER
7½" high sculptured wax figurine. O.S.P. $6.00 C.M.V. $6.00 M.B.

1974-76 DELICATE DOVE POMANDER
4" high light green wax pomander scent Summer Breeze. O.S.P. $5.00 C.M.V. $5.00 M.B.

1974-75 DUCK DECOY DECORATIVE POMANDER
Wax statuette (not a bottle) scented with Deep Woods or Wild Country. O.S.P. $6.00 CMV $7.00 MB

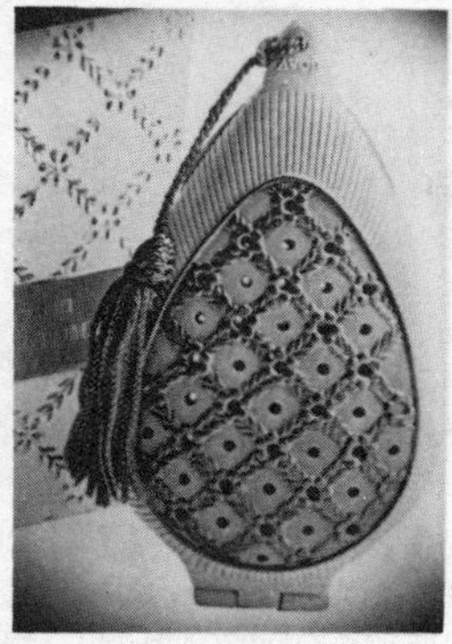

1967-69 LAVENDER POMANDER
Gold tassel on white, pink & gold plastic container. 4" high. Filled with Lavender Fragrance tablet. OSP $5.00 CMV $5.00 MB

1970 POTPOURRI POMANDER
Holder is yellow plastic & 4" high in same shape & design as Lavender Pomander. O.S.P. $5.00 C.M.V. $5.00 M.B.

1971 POTPOURRI POMANDER REFILL
Orange and white box holds refill in plastic bag. O.S.P. $2.50 C.M.V. $2.00 M.B.

1975-76 PICTURE HAT CLOSET POMANDER - Yellow & pink plastic hat with yellow cord & tassel. Came in Potpourri fragrance. O.S.P. $4.00 C.M.V. $3.00 M.B.

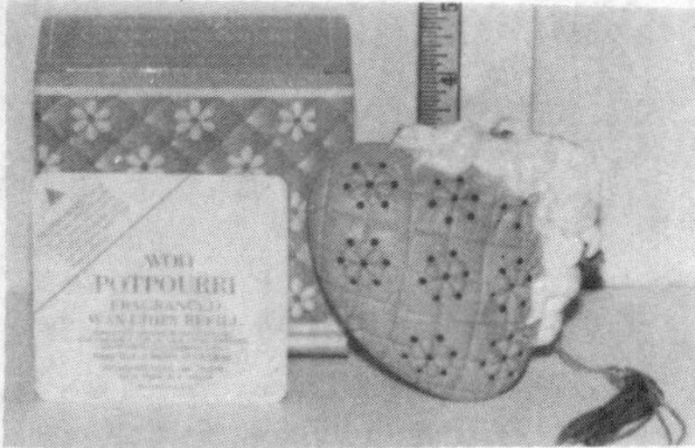

1977-78 SWEET CHERUBS CLOSET POMANDER
Blue & white plastic with blue tassel. Came in Potpourri fragrance wax chips. O.S.P. $5.00 C.M.V. $3.50 M.B.

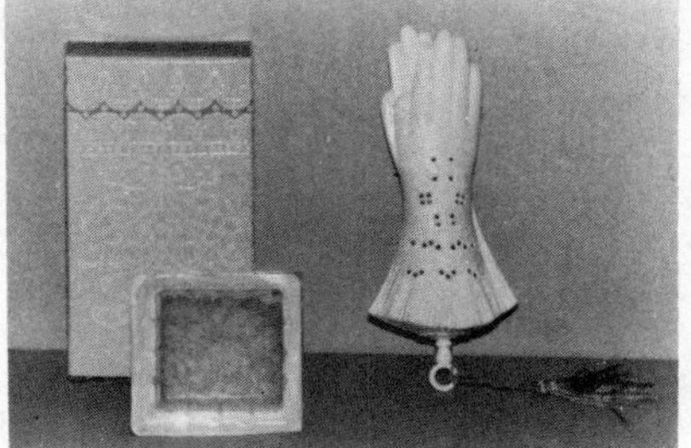

1979-80 LACY GLOVES CLOSET POMANDER
Lavender box holds Lavender plastic glove. It does not say Avon on it. Comes with packet of Gorlandia wax chips. SSP $3.00 CMV $3.00 MB

1979-80 TWO TURTLEDOVES POMANDER
Blue box holds white wax doves. SSP $8.99 CMV $8.99 MB

1979-80 UNDER THE MISTLETOE POMANDER
Light blue wax with wire hanging mistletoe. SSP $7.99 CMV $7.99 MB

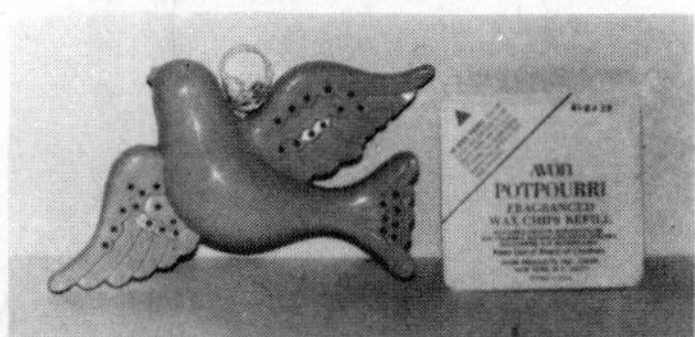

1979-80 FRESH FLIGHT CLOSET POMANDER
Blue plastic bird holds Potpourri wax chips. Came in colorful box. S.S.P. $3.99, C.M.V. $2.50 M.B.

1978-79 PAMPERED PIGLET CERAMIC POMANDER
Avon's 1st ceramic pomander is made in Brazil. White with pink and green flowers Came with Meadow Morn wax chip refill. Pink box. S.S.P. $7.99, C.M.V. $7.99 M.B.

1978-80 MEADOW MORN FRAGRANCE WAX CHIPS REFIL
Refill for Pomanders. S.S.P. $1.49, C.M.V. $1.00.

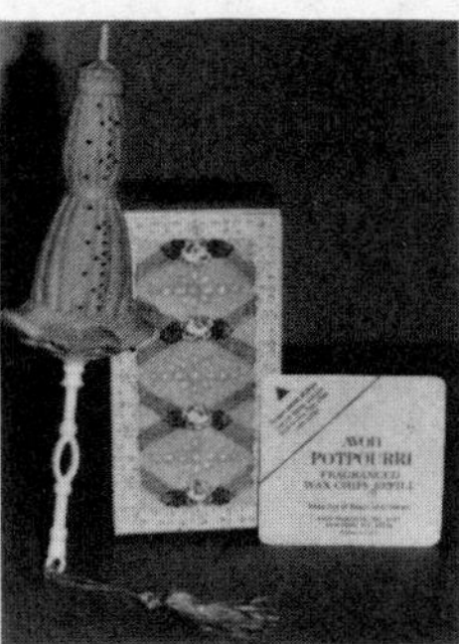

1975-77 PARASOL CLOSET POMANDER
Lavender with lavender cord & tassel. Came with Potpourri Fragrance wax chips. O.S.P. $3.00 C.M.V. $2.00 M.B.

1979-80 AUTUMN HARVEST POMANDER
10" long yellow and green wax. Hangs on wall. S.S.P. $7.99, C.M.V. $6.00 M.B.

1978-79 BOUNTIFUL HARVEST POMANDER
Red spiced apple with tan wax basket. S.S.P. $7.99, C.M.V. $7.99 M.B.

1978-79 VIENNESE WALTZ POMANDER
6½" high blue wax figurine, bottom label. S.S.P. $6.99, C.M.V. $6.99 M.B.

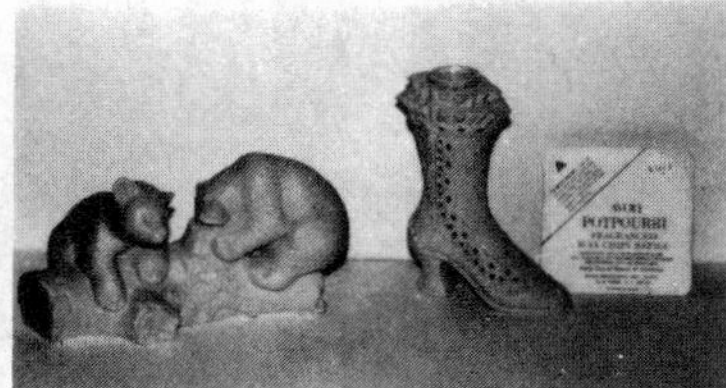

1979-80 HONEY BEARS POMANDER
Light yellow wax figure. S.S.P. $6.99, C.M.V. $6.99 M.B.

1978-79 FRILLY BOOT POMANDER
Pink plastic boot came with wax chip refill. S.S.P. $2.89, C.M.V. $2.50 M.B.

CANDLES

1974-75 OVALIQUE PERFUME CANDLE HOLDER - 4" high, clear glass, choice of Sonnet, Moonwind, Patchwork, Roses, Roses, Charisma, Bird of Paradise, Bayberry, Frankincense & Myrrh or Wassail. O.S.P. $8.00 C.M.V. $6.00 MB

1975-76 FACETS OF LIGHT FRAGRANCE CANDLETTE - 4" high, clear glass. Came with Bayberry Candle but any refill candlette will fit. O.S.P. $5.00 C.M.V. $5.00 M.B.

1974-75 GOLDEN PINE CONE FRAGRANCE CANDLETTE - Gold toned glass. Choice of Bayberry only. O.S.P. $5.00 C.M.V. $5.00 M.B.

LEFT 1977-78 DOVE IN FLIGHT CANDLETTE
Clear glass dove candle holder. Came in Meadow morn fragrance candlette. Refillable. S.S.P. $5.99 C.M.V. $5.00M.B.

RIGHT 1977-79 BUNNY CERAMIC PLANTER CANDLE HOLDER
3 different rabbits - one made in Brazil and recessed on bottom - one flat bottom made in U.S. and lighter in weight. 1978 issue same flat bottom only different type letters on bottom. Came with Floral Medley or Roses, Roses perfumed candle. S.S.P. $10.99 C.M.V. $10.00 M.B. each. Rabbit only $6.00 ea.

LEFT 1978 HEART AND DIAMOND FOSTORIA LOVING CUP PERFUMED CANDLE HOLDER
Approx. 7" high, clear fostoria glass. Came with Floral Medley perfumed candle. Embossed with "Avon 1978" on its base. Refillable. O.S.P. $15.00 C.M.V. $12.00 M.B. Glass only - $6.00.

RIGHT 1977-79 MOUNT VERNON SAUCE PITCHER
Approx. 5½" high. Blue fostoria glass. Came with Floral Medley perfumed candle. Refillable. Avon on bottom. O.S.P. $15.50 C.M.V. $12.00 M.B. Pitcher only - $6.00

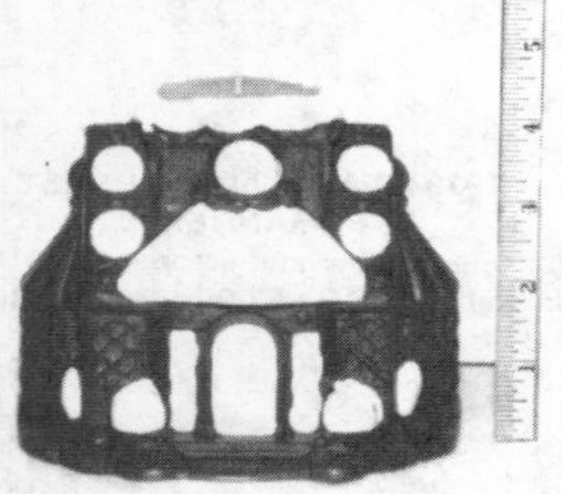

1977-79 GINGERBREAD HOUSE FRAGRANCE CANDLE
Brown & white candle. Came in Frankincense and Myrrh fragrance. O.S.P. $8.50 CMV $6.00 MB $3.00 No box.

1975-76 CATNIP FRAGRANCE CANDLE
4" high yellow plastic. Floral Medley fragrance. O.S.P. $3.00 C.M.V. $3.00 M.B.

1975-76 DYNAMITE FRAGRANCE CANDELETTE - Red & white. O.S.P. $4.00 C.M.V. $5.00 MB

1973-74 HEARTS & FLOWERS FRAGRANCE CANDLE - White milk glass with red, green & pink design. came in Floral Medley fragrance. SSP $4.00 CMV $4.00 MB $2.00 CO

1972-73 POTPOURRI FRAGRANCE CANDLE - White milk glass, came with Potpourri candle. SSP $4.00 CMV $3.00 CO $4.00 MB

1972 TURTLE CANDLE
White glass turtle candle with green glass shell top. O.S.P. $5.00 C.M.V. $5.00 $7.00 M.B.

1972 MUSHROOM CANDLE
White glass candle with pink glass mushroom top. O.S.P. $5.00 C.M.V. $5.00 - $7.00 M.B.

1970 DANISH MODERN CANDLE
Stainless steel candle holder with red candle. O.S.P. $8.00 C.M.V. $8.00 with candle. M.B.

1973 FLAMING TULIP FRAGRANCE CANDLE - Red candle in Floral Medley Fragrance. Gold holder. O.S.P. $7.00 CMV $6.00 CO $9.00 MB

1971-72 FLORAL MEDLEY PERFUMED CANDLES - Box holds yellow & purple frosted glass candle holders. O.S.P. $5.50 C.M.V. $6.00 M.B.

1974-75 LOTUS BLOSSOM PERFUMED CANDLE HOLDER - Black glass with green & white design. Available with candle fragrance: Bayberry, Frankincense & Myrrh, Wassail, Sonnet, Moonwind, Roses, Roses, Bird of Paradise or Charisma. O.S.P. $8.00 CMV $8.00 $12.00 MB

1971-72 DYNASTY PERFUMED CANDLE
6" high, white glass jar & lid. O.S.P. $7.50 CMV $7.00 - $10.00 MB

1972-73 CRYSTAL GLOW PERFUMED CANDLE HOLDER - Clear glass. Came with Moonwind, Bird of Paradise, Elusive, Charisma, Brocade, Regence, Wassail, Bayberry, Frankincense & Myrrh, Roses, Roses. S.S.P. $8.00 CMV $8.00 - $11.00 MB
1973 FOSTORIA PERFUMED CANDLE HOLDER - Clear glass. Came with Patchwork, Sonnet, Moonwind, Roses, Roses, Charisma, Bird of Paradise, Bayberry, Wassail, Frankincense & Myrrh candles. S.S.P. $6.00 C.M.V. $6.00 - $8.00 M.B.

1964-66 WHITE MILK GLASS CANDLE OSP $3.50 CMV $5.00 - $10.00 MB
1965-66 AMBER GLASS CANDLE Amber paint over clear glass. O.S.P. $4.00 C.M.V. $15.00 in box. $12.00 candle only.
1965-66 RED GLASS CANDLE Red paint over clear glass. O.S.P. $4.00 C.M.V. $11.00 - $15.00 in box. Dark red 1968 glass candle, not painted is from Europe. See foreign Avons for picture. C.M.V. $50.00

1972-73 CHINA TEA POT PERFUMED CANDLE - White china with blue flower design or without decal. Thousands came from factory, not sold by Avon, with or without decals, some had other color decals, some decals were on front, some on back. The factory rejects CMV $9.00 each. Came from Avon with Roses, Roses, Moonwind, Bird of Paradise, Elusive, Charisma, Brocade, Regence, Wassail, Bayberry, Frankincense & Myrrh candles. SSP $10.00 CMV $12.00 MB $8.00 BO

1971-75 FLORAL FRAGRANCE CANDLE - Metal gold leaf stand & pink or yellow flower candle. O.S.P. $8.50 CMV $6.00 - $9.00 MB
1972-73 WATER LILY FRAGRANCE CANDLE - Green lily pad base with white plastic petals with yellow center candle. OSP $5.00 CMV $3.00 CO $5.00 MB

1974-75 KITCHEN CROCK FRAGRANCE CANDLETTE - Yellow crock with red, yellow & blue flowers with crock cap. Came in Meadow Morn fragrance. S.S.P. $4.00 CMV $2.00 CO $3.00 MB
1969-70 WASSAIL BOWL CANDLE Silver paint over red glass with silver spoon. O.S.P. $8.00 C.M.V. $7.00 candle only - $10.00 M.B.

1970's CANDLE PERFUMED REFILLS Candle refills for the many candle holders Avon has made over the years. Comes in many fragrances. S.S.P. $2.50, C.M.V. $2.50 M.B.

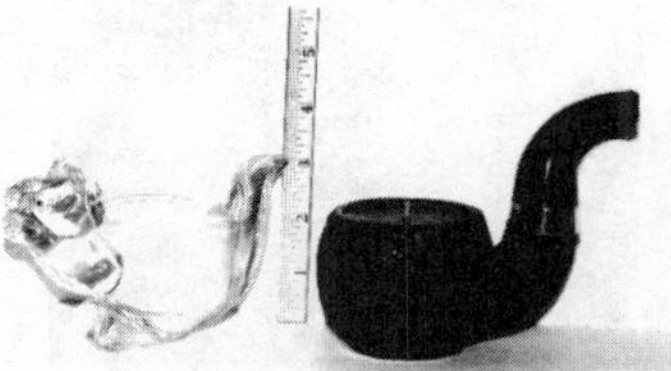

1978-79 BRIGHT CHIPMUNK CANDLETTE
Clear glass candle holder. Refillable. S.S.P. $5.99, C.M.V. $5.99 M.B.
1978-79 FRESH AROMA SMOKERS CANDLE
Non refillable brown wax like pipe with black plastic and chrome top. Bottom cardboard label. S.S.P. $6.99, C.M.V. $6.99 M.B.

1980 CRYSTAGLOW CLEARFIRE CANDLE
Clear glass. Avon in bottom under candle. SSP $9.99 CMV $9.99 MB
1980 - BUNNY BRIGHT CERAMIC CANDLE
White ceramic with Pink & green trim. 1980 Avon on bottom. SSP $11.99 CMV $11.99 MB.

1978-79 PLUM PUDDING CANDLE
4" high brown, green and white candle. Bottom label. S.S.P. $5.99, C.M.V. $5.99 M.B.
1978-79 WINTER LIGHTS CANDLETTE
Clear glass square candle holder. Holds glass candlette. Avon on bottom of both. S.S.P. $7.99, C.M.V. $7.99 M.B.

1979-80 REVOLUTIONARY SOLDIER SMOKERS CANDLE
Clear glass. Red & gold box. SSP $4.00 CMV $4.00 MB
1979-80 FOSTORIA CRYSTAL POOL FLOATING CANDLE
6" clear crystal dish - green & white flower candle. SSP $12.99 CMV $12.99

1979-80 MRS. SNOWLIGHT CANDLE
White, red & green wax candle. SSP $6.99 CMV $6.99 MB
1979-80 WINTER WONDERLAND CENTERPIECE CANDLE
White wax base, green wax trees, red & white wax house. Center holds glass candlette. SSP $14.99 CMV $14.99 MB

1967 FIRST CHRISTMAS CANDLE
Left - all gold, red inside 1967 had label on bottom and no Avon. OSP $5.00 CMV $6.00 CO $10.00 MB
1972 Reissued = Avon on bottom, no label CMV $7.00 MB $4.00 CO
FIRST CHRISTMAS CANDLE — FOREIGN
Right - All silver with red inside. C.M.V. $20.00

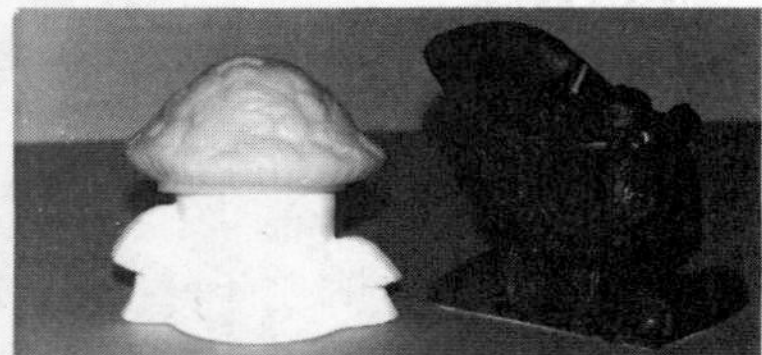

1975 ENCHANTED MUSHROOM FRAGRANCE CANDLE - White wax shell & yellow cover. Meadow Morn fragrance. OSP $4.00 CMV $4.00 MB $3.00 CO
1975-76 SLEIGH LIGHT FRAGRANCE CANDLE - 4" high, red & green. Bayberry scented. OSP $5.00 CMV $4.00 MB $3.00 CO

1976-77 TERRA COTTA BIRD CANDLETTE
Reddish brown clay bird candle holder. Avon in bottom. O.S.P. $8.00 C.M.V. $6.00 MB $3.00 bird only.
Also showm is fragrance candlette refill. C.M.V. $1.50

1975-77 WASHINGTON GOBLET FOSTORIA CANDLE HOLDER
Blue glass by Fostoria. Came with Frankincense & Myrrh or Floral Medley candle. OSP $9.99 CMV $11.00 MB $8.00 CO
1976-77 MARTHA WASHINGTON GOBLET
Blue glass Fostoria candle holder. OSP $12.50 CMV $11.00 MB $8.00 CO

LEFT 1967 REGENCE CANDLE
Gold paint over clear glass with green paper band. Lid makes base for bottom. OSP $6.00 CMV $20.00 in box, $15.00 candle only mint.
RIGHT:
1968-69 REGENCE CANDLE
Green glass candle holder with gold handle & base. OSP $10.00 CMV $12.00 candle only. $17.50 in box.

1975 FOSTORIA CANDLELIGHT BASKET - PERFUMED CANDLE HOLDER - Clear glass, gold handle. Choice of Sonnet, Moonwind, Patchwork, Charisma, Roses, Roses, Bird of Paradise, Wassail, Frankincense & Myrrh or Bayberry candle refill. OSP $9.00 CMV $9.00 MB $6.00 CO
1969-70 FOSTORIA SALT CELLAR CANDLE - Clear glass with small silver spoon. OSP $6.00 CMV $10.00 in box. $6.00 candle only. With spoon.

1970 NESTING DOVE CANDLE
White base glass & lid with dove on top. OSP $7.50 CMV $6.00 - $9.00 in box

1973 HOBNAIL PATIO CANDLE
White milk base clear glass top. came with Sonnet, Moonwind, Roses, Roses, Bird of Paradise, Charisma, Wassail, Bayberry & Frankincense & Myrrh candles. SSP $8.00 CMV $9.00 MB $6.00 CO

1975-76 BLACK-EYED SUSAN FRAGRANCE CANDLE - Yellow with brown center. Wild Flowers fragrance. O.S.P. $5.00 C.M.V. $5.00 MB $3.00 CO
1974-76 GREATFRUIT FRAGRANCE CANDLE - Yellow with red center. Has grapefruit fragrance. O.S.P. $3.00 C.M.V. $3.00 MB $2.00 CO

1969-70 CRYSTAL CANDLEIER
7" high, clear glass with blue crystals inside, gold handle on glass lid. O.S.P. $7.00 CMV $9.00 in box $6.00 candle only.
1969-70 GOLD & WHITE CANDLE
Painted gold & white over clear glass, lid makes stand for base. O.S.P. $8.00 C.M.V $9.00 in box. $6.00 candle only.

1968-69 GOLDEN APPLE CANDLE
Shiny gold over clear glass. O.S.P. $6.00 CMV $12.00 mint. $17.50 MB
1968 SILVER APPLE CANDLE
Factory test sample same as gold apple only in shiny silver over clear glass. Was not filled. C.M.V. $90.00 on silver top & bottom. Silver bottom with gold top C.M.V. $55.00

1967 FROSTED GLASS CANDLE
Gold band around edge, lid makes stand for base. OSP $5.00 CMV $10.00 MB $6.00 candle only.
1966-67 WHITE & GOLD CANDLE
White glass top & bottom with gold band. Top makes stand for base. O.S.P. $5.00 CMV $6.00 - $10.00 MB

1978-79 HEART AND DIAMOND CANDLESTICK
7" high heart embossed Fostoria clear glass candle, Avon 1979 on bottom. Comes with long red candle for one end or turn it over and insert the small glass candle holder on other end. Comes in red box. S.S.P. $12.99, C.M.V. $12.99 M.B.

1979-80 BUNNY CERAMIC PLANTER CANDLE
Made of ceramic in Brazil for Avon. Green, pink and yellow flowers. Brown eyes, pink inner ears. Comes with Floral Medley or Spiced Garden candle. S.S.P. $14.99, C.M.V. $12.00 M.B.
1979-80 TENDER BLOSSOM CANDLE
Light pink wax base with dark pink inner candle. S.S.P. $6.99, C.M.V. $6.00 M.B.

1979-80 GARDEN BOUNTY CANDLE
Beige and pink cart, red candle. S.S.P. $7.99, C.M.V. $7.99 M.B.
1979-80 COUNTRY SPICE CANDLE
Light blue green glass jar and lid. Wire bale. Comes with candle inside. S.S.P. $7.99, C.M.V. $7.99 M.B.
1979-80 FLOWER FROST COLLECTION WATER GOBLET CANDLETTE
Frosted glass goblet holds glass candle insert. S.S.P. $9.99, C.M.V. $9.99 M.B.

1979-80 SHIMMERING PEACOCK CANDLE
Box holds clear glass peacock. SSP $9.99 CMV $9.99 MB
1979-80 CLEARFIRE TRANSPARENT CANDLETTE REFILL
Did not come boxed. SSP $2.99 CMV $2.99 mint full

SOAP DISHES & SOAPS

See Page 5 for Grading Examples on Mint Condition

1970 HEAVENLY SOAP SET
White glass dish and 2 pink soaps. OSP $5.00 CMV $10.00 MB
1970 HEAVENLY FACTORY TEST DISH
Test dish was made in silver overlay. Never sold by Avon Reps. Rare. Not shown. C.M.V. $100.00 mint.

1977 FOSTORIA EGG SOAP DISH & SOAP
Blue soap came in Spring Lilacs fragrance. Egg dish about 4½" long clear glass. Avon on bottom. O.S.P. $15.00 C.M.V. $10.00 M.B. Egg dish only $5.00
1st issue had "Mothers Day 1977" on bottom CMV $12.00 MB

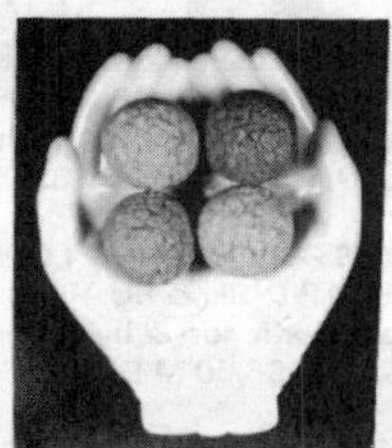

1969-70 TOUCH OF BEAUTY
White milk glass holds 4 small bars of pink soap. O.S.P. $5.00 C.M.V. $9.00 M.B.

1977-79 COUNTRY PEACHES SOAP JAR & SOAPS
Replica of a 19th century mason jar. Holds 6 yellow peach seed soaps. Blue glass jar with wire bail. Avon on bottom. OSP $8.50 CMV $7.00 MB Jar only - $3.00

1978 LOVE NEST SOAPS
Light green glass dish holds 3 yellow bird soaps in Special Occasion fragrance. S.S.P. $4.99 C.M.V. $5.00 M.B.

1977 "HEART AND DIAMOND" SOAP DISH & SOAP
Fostoria clear glass soap dish. Came with red heart shaped Special Occasion fragranced soap. Avon on dish. O.S.P. $9.00 C.M.V. $8.00 M.B.

1976-78 NATURE BOUNTIFUL CERAMIC PLATE & SOAPS
Wedgewood ceramic plate made in England, edged in 22K gold. Two soaps decorated with pears decals. Avon stamped on plate. O.S.P. $25.00 C.M.V. $16.00M.B. Plate only $7.00

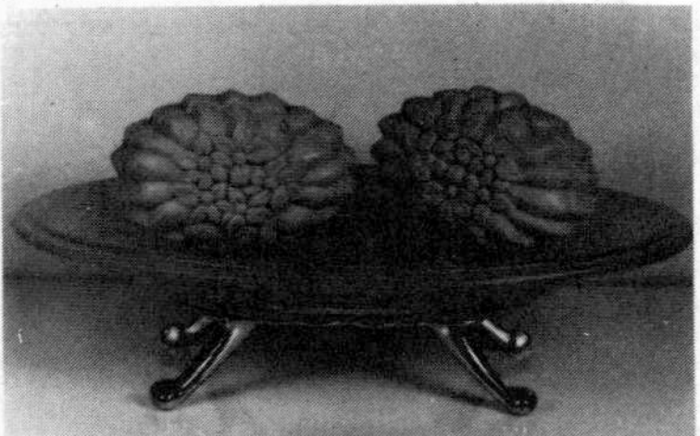

1971-73 DECORATOR SOAP DISH & SOAPS - 7" long frosted glass dish on gold stand. Came with 2 pink soaps. O.S.P. $7.00 CMV $8.00 MB

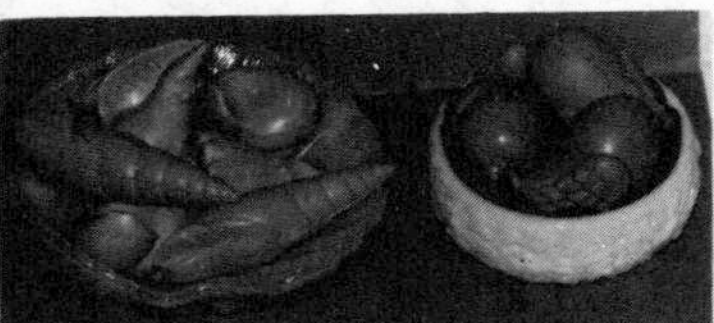

1972-73 GIFT OF THE SEA SOAP DISH & SOAPS - Iridescent white glass dish looks like a shell. 6 cakes, 1 oz. each, pink soap. 2 each of 3 different shells. S.S.P. $5.00 CMV $8.00 MB

1973-75 LOVE NEST SOAP DISH & SOAPS - White dish with green plastic lining, holds 2 aqua & 1 blue bird soap. OSP $4.00 CMV $6.00 MB

1970-71 DOLPHIN SOAP DISH AND HOSTESS SOAPS
Silver & Aqua plastic soap dish holds 4 blue soaps. OSP $8.00 CMV $11.00 MB

1971-73 OWL SOAP DISH
5½" long white glass soap dish with 2 owl eyes in bottom of dish. Holds 2 yellow bars of owl soap. O.S.P. $4.50 C.M.V. $8.00 M.B.

1972-74 FLOWER BASKET SOAP DISH & SOAPS - Clear glass dish with gold handle came with 5 cakes of soap (2 yellow, 3 pink) 1 oz. each. Hostess Fragrance. S.S.P. $5.00 CMV $8.00 MB

1974-76 BEAUTY BUDS SOAP DISH & SOAP - 6" long white milk glass with 4 yellow soaps. OSP $5.00 CMV $6.00 MB

1975-76 HOSTESS BLOSSOMS FLOWER ARRANGER SOAP DISH & SOAP - 4½" high white milk glass, plastic top & light green soap. O.S.P. $6.00 C.M.V. $6.00 M.B.

1975-76 BICENTENNIAL PLATE & SOAP - Clear glass plate with blue soaps embossed with the face of George & Martha Washington on each. Some have Avon on bottom and some don't. O.S.P. $7.00 C.M.V. $7.00 M.B.

1973-74 BUTTER DISH & HOSTESS SOAPS - Clear glass with 2 yellow 3 oz. butter pats. S.S.P. $7.00 C.M.V. $12.00 M.B.

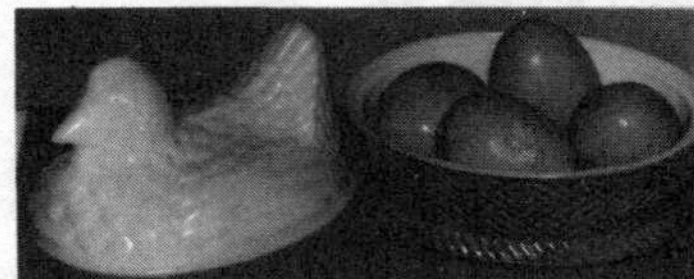

1973 NESTING HEN SOAP DISH & SOAP
White milk glass hen with beige painted nest. Holds 4 yellow egg soap, 2 oz. each. S.S.P. $7.00 CMV $10.00 MB

1974 LOVEBIRDS SOAP DISH & SOAPS
White milk glass dish with 2 - 4 oz. pink soaps. S.S.P. $6.00 C.M.V. $7.00 M.B.

1975-76 WINGS OF BEAUTY SOAP DISH & SOAP - White milk glass dish with 2 pink soaps. OSP $5.00 CMV $6.00 MB

1974-76 NUTTY SOAP DISH & SOAPS
Plastic dish with 2 peanut scented soaps. OSP $4.00 CMV $5.00 MB

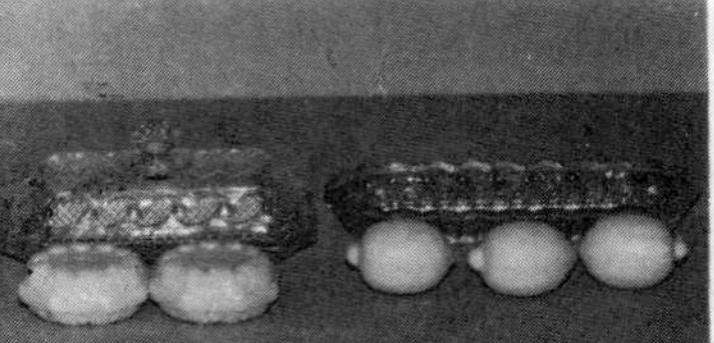

1975-76 CRYSTALUCENT COVERED BUTTER DISH & SOAP - 7" long clear glass with 2 yellow soaps. O.S.P. $10.00 C.M.V. $12.00 M.B.

1975-76 SUNNY LEMON SOAP DISH & SOAP
8½" long clear glass with 3 lemon scented yellow soaps. OSP $4.00 CMV $6.00 MB

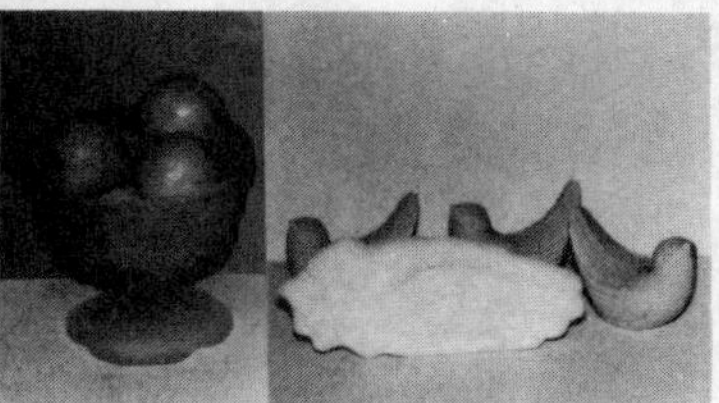

1979-80 FLOWER FROST SHERBET GLASS AND SOAPS
Frosted glass holds 6 yellow Avon balls of soap. S.S.P. $9.99, C.M.V. $9.00 M.B.

1978-80 BIRD IN HAND SOAP DISH AND SOAPS
5½" long white glass hand soap dish with 3 small blue bird soaps. S.S.P. $5.99, C.M.V. $5.00 M.B.

1979-80 BUTTERFLY FANTASY DISHES & SOAPS
2-4" porcelain with butterfly design. 1 Pink butterfly soap. SSP $9.99 CMV $9.99 MB

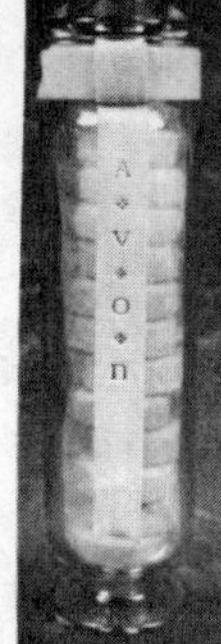

1965-66 AVON SOAP JAR
Pink ribbon on clear glass jar & lid. Came with 12 cakes of soap. O.S.P. $4.50 C.M.V. $20.00 in box, jar only with ribbon & no soap $6.00. Jar & soap with ribbons mint $16.00.

1975-76 HOSTESS FANCY SOAP DISH & SOAP - 8" wide clear glass with 5 pink soaps. O.S.P. $6.00 C.M.V. $6.00 M.B.

1979-80 FLOWER FROST COLLECTION CRESCENT PLATE & GUEST SOAPS
Frosted glass soap dish holds 3 yellow flower soap bars. SSP $12.99 CMV $12.00 MB

1979-80 MOUNT VERNON PLATE & SOAPS
9" long blue glass plate. Has Mount Vernon George and Martha Washington on front. Came with 2 white George and Martha bars of soap. S.S.P. $10.99, C.M.V. $10.99 M.B.

PLATES

1973-77 BETSY ROSS PLATE
White with colored scene, gold trim and lettering. 9" plate. SSP $13.00 CMV $18.00 MB

1974-77 FREEDOM PLATE
9" ceramic plate, blue trim with gold edge. Blue printing on back. Made by Wedgewood, England for Avon. S.S.P. $12.99 CMV $20.00 MB

1974-75 TENDERNESS PLATE
9¼" ironstone plate. Blue & white with gold edge. Made in Spain for Avon by Pontesa. The plate sold to public with word "Pontesa" on the back side in blue letters. This was also awarded to Avon Reps. with blue letters on the back and the work "Pontesa" in red letters. Plate was also sold with no inscription on back. CMV $20.00 MB regular issue $25.00 Rep Plate MB

1974-76 CARDINAL NORTH AMERICAN SONG BIRD PLATE
10" ceramic plate. Green letters on back. SSP $12.99 CMV $18.50 MB

1975-77 GENTLE MOMENTS PLATE
8¾" ceramic plate. Green letters on back. Made by Wedgewood, England. SSP $14.99 CMV $18.50 MB

1973-75 1973 "CHRISTMAS ON THE FARM" CHRISTMAS PLATE
White with colored scene, turquoise border, gold edge and lettering. 9" plate. SSP $13.00 CMV $55.00 MB
Rare 73 Xmas plate with Betsy Ross plate inscription on back CMV $100.00

1974-75 1974 COUNTRY CHURCH CHRISTMAS PLATE
9" ceramic plate. 2nd in a series of Christmas plates by Avon. Made by Wedgewood, England. Blue writing on back. Blue & white front, gold edge.
SSP $12.99 CMV $30.00 MB Rare issue came without Christmas 1974 on front of plate. CMV $50.00 MB

1978-79 STRAWBERRY PORCELAIN PLATE & GUEST SOAPS
7½" plate made in Brazil for Avon. Comes with 6 red strawberry soaps. S.S.P. $12.99 C.M.V. $12.00 M.B., $8.00 plate only.

1977-80 1977 "CAROLLERS IN THE SNOW" CHRISTMAS PLATE
8 3/4" ceramic blue & white plate, gold edge. Blue letters on back. Made by Wedgewood, England for Avon. S.S.P.$16.99 C.M.V. $15.00 M.B.

1976-80 1976 "BRINGING HOME THE TREE" CHRISTMAS PLATE
9" blue ceramic plate, gold edge. Blue printing on back. Made by Wedgewood, England for Avon. S.S.P. $15.99 C.M.V. $15.00 M.B.

1976-80 1975 "SKATERS ON THE POND" CHRISTMAS PLATE
8¾" ceramic green & white plate. Green letters on the back. Made by Wedgewood, England for Avon. This plate was not sold till 1976 Christmas selling season. S.S.P. $16.99 C.M.V. $15.00 M.B.

1978-79 1978 CHRISTMAS PLATE "TRIMMING THE TREE" (6th edition)
8 - 5/8" ceramic plate. Turquoise rim with gold edge trim. Made for Avon by Enoch Wedgewood in England. S.S.P. $19.99, C.M.V. $19.99 M.B

1979-80 1979 CHRISTMAS PLATE "DASHING THROUGH THE SNOW"
8¾" blue & white ceramic plate with gold trim. Christmas 1979 on front. Back of plate says made for Avon products by Enoch Wedgwood - in England. SSP $19.99 CMV $15.00 MB

1974-76 PINK ROSES CUP & SAUCER(left)
White China with pink flowers and green leaves with gold rim. Made by Stoke-on-Trent, England. OSP $9.99 CMV $12.00 MB
Also came with double printed letters on bottom. CMV $20.00 MB

1974-75 BLUE BLOSSOMS CUP & SAUCER
White China with blue & pink flowers and 22K gold trim. Made in England
OSP $9.99 CMV $12.00 MB

1976 CHRISTMAS PLATE TEST
8¾" test plate. Does not say Avon. Christmas 1976 on front 6 times in gold. Was never sold by Avon. Came from factory. Has blue border. CMV $75.00

1978 CHRISTMAS PLATE - 15 YEAR
Same plate as 15 year anniversary plate inscribed on back. We have no info on this or where it came from. Write Bud Hastin if you know what this plate is for. No Price established.

1973 CHRISTMAS "BETSY ROSS" PLATE
Factory mistake 1973 Christmas plate has inscription on back for Betsy Ross plate. Very Rare. CMV $80.00

MEN'S AFTER SHAVE & COLOGNES

ALL CONTAINERS PRICED EMPTY

See Page 5 for Grading Examples on Mint Condition

1972 EAGLE ORGANIZER BOTTLE
3 oz. clear glass, eagle embossed, gold cap. Came in set only in Deep Woods & Tai Winds. C.M.V. $3.00 ea.

1976 GIFT COLOGNE FOR MEN
2 oz. came in Deep Woods, Tai Winds, Wild Country, Everest, or Oland. SSP $1.99 CMV $1.00 MB .50 cent BO

1969-70 GENTLEMAN'S CHOICE
Red & silver box holds 2 oz. embossed bottles with silver, gold & black caps. Came in Excalibur, Wild Country, Tribute, Leather & Windjammer Cologne. O.S.P. $1.75 ea. CMV $2.00 ea. with black caps $4.00 ea.

1957 TRIUMPH
Special issue box holds 6 oz cologne for men. Silver label, red cap. O.S.P. $1.19 C.M.V. $22.50 M.B.

1977-78 COLOGNE MINIATURE FOR MEN
5 oz. smoked glass, black cap. Came in Clint, Everest or Wild Country. S.S.P. 88¢ C.M.V. 50¢

1975-78 ELECTRIC PRE-SHAVE LOTION
4 oz. plastic, blue cap. Spicy aroma. O.S.P. $1.00 C.M.V. 50¢

1976 BRACING LOTION FOR MEN
4 oz. plastic with green cap. O.S.P. $1.00 C.M.V. 50¢

1974-75 GIFT COLOGNE FOR MEN (CENTER)
2 oz. clear glass with gold cap. Came in Wild Country, Deep Woods, Oland or Tai Winds. O.S.P. $2.00 C.M.V. 75¢

1975-79 AFTER SHAVE (LEFT)
5 oz. clear glass, brown cap. Came in Deep Woods, Everest, Oland, Tai Winds, Wild Country & Clint. Different labels, same bottle. O.S.P. $3.00 C.M.V. $1.00 ea.

1975-76 GIFT COLOGNE FOR MEN (RIGHT)
2 oz. clear glass, gold cap. Choice of Wild Country, Tai Winds, Deep Woods or Oland, O.S.P. $2.00 C.M.V. $1.00

1951-52 SERVICE KIT AFTER SHAVE BOTTLE
4 oz. clear plastic with red cap. C.M.V. $12:00.

1970 GENTLEMEN'S SELECTION
2 oz. each with gold caps. Came in cologne in Oland, Tribute, Excalibur, Leather, Wild Country & Windjammer. O.S.P. $1.75 ea. C.M.V. $2.50 ea.

1964-66 4A AFTER SHAVE LOTION SAMPLE
Box holds 10 packet samples. CMV $5.00 box. mint.

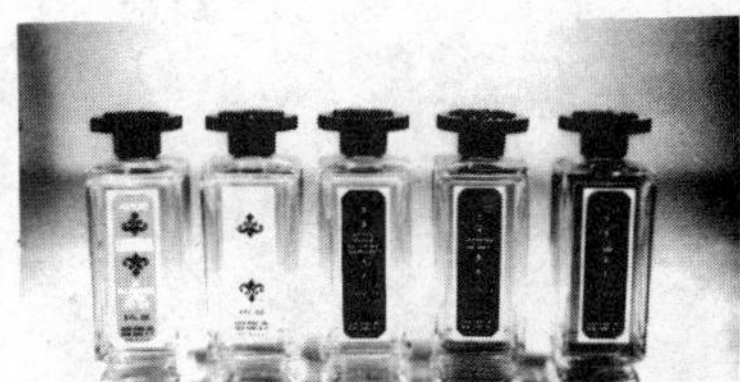

1965-66 AFTER SHAVE'S MISC.
2 oz. with 4A on black caps. Came in Island Lime, Blue Blazer, Leather, Tribute, Spicy, Bay Rum, Original, 4A After Shaves & Leather All Purpose Cologne & After Shower Cologne. Came in Bureau Organizer, Fragrance Wardrobe & After Shave Selection Sets only. C.M.V. each $8.00 MB 10 different $5.00 BO Add $3.00 for Blue Blazer.

1959-60 AFTER SHOWER FOR MEN
8 oz. gold cap with gold foil on neck & gold neck cord with Stage Coach on bottom. O.S.P. $2.50 C.M.V. with foil top & tag $45.00 mint, $60.00 MB

1970-72 COLOGNE SPRAY FOR MEN
4 oz. silver can with red cap in Leather. Brown cap in Wild Country. Tan cap in Oland. This can leaked & most boxes were ruined. OSP $5.00 CMV $10.00 each MB $4.00 can only

FOREIGN 4A AFTER SHAVE
4 oz. Foreign 4A on left with Invigorate. CMV $18.00 MB $25.00
1964-66 4A AFTER SHAVE
6 oz. 4A painted on clear glass, black cap with gold mirror on top. O.S.P. $2.00 CMV $17.00 BO MB $25.00

LEFT 1948-49 DEODORANT FOR MEN
2 oz. maroon cap & label. O.S.P. 59¢ C.M.V. $20.00.
RIGHT 1948 Only - COLOGNE FOR MEN
2 oz. size, maroon cap. Came in 1948 Pleasure Case Set only. C.M.V. $25.00

LEFT 1936-40 AFTER SHAVING LOTION SAMPLE
Maroon cap. CPC on back label. CMV $35.00 mint.
CENTER - 1940-49 AFTER SHAVE LOTION SAMPLE
½ oz. maroon cap. C.M.V. $35.00
RIGHT Only - HAIR TONIC SAMPLE
¼ oz. Maroon cap. C.M.V. $40.00 $45.00 M.B.

1979-80 COLOGNE ACCENT FOR MEN
.5 oz. clear glass. Blue cap. Blue & Silver box. SSP $1.25 CMV $1.00 MB

1961-63 DELUXE AFTER SHAVE "WOOD TOP"
6 oz. Some have gold letters on bottle, some have gold paper labels. Came in Deluxe Electric Pre-Shave Lotion, Deluxe After Shave Lotion, After Shave Lotion Spicy, Electric Pre-Shave Lotion Spicy. OSP $1.79 CMV ea. $25.00 MB $20.00 BO. mint 4 different fragrances.

1959-60 VIGORATE AFTER SHAVE
8 oz. clear glass with white cap. Bottle indented on botton with carriage. Box is black with red ribbon, gold bottom, plastic white insert on top with gold carriage. OSP $2.50 CMV $40.00 BO mint. $80.00 MB

1932-36 AFTER SHAVING LOTION
4 oz. black caps, 2 different yellow paper labels. OSP 37c CMV $40.00 BO mint ea. $50.00 MB

LEFT:
1978-79 GIFT COLOGNE FOR MEN
2 oz. clear glass, black cap. Holds Everest, Clint, Wild Country, or Deep Woods cologne. SSP $1.99 CMV $1.99 MB
RIGHT:
1978-79 COLOGNE MINIATURE FOR MEN
5 oz. clear glass, brown cap. Holds Wild Country, Clint, Everest, or Trazarra. SSP .99c CMV .99c MB

1979-80 AFTER SHAVE'S
3 oz. plastic bottle came in different color caps. No box. Came in Cool Sage, Light Musk, Brisk Spice. SSP $1.99 CMV .50c ea.
1979-80 COLOGNE'S FOR MEN
3 oz. clear glass bottle. Gold caps. Choice of Brisk Spice, Cool Sage or Light Musk. Came in box. SSP $2.99 CMV $1.00 ea. MB

1946-49 COLOGNE FOR MEN
6 oz. maroon cap. Shield on paper label. O.S.P. $1.50 C.M.V. $75.00 bottle only. In 2 different maroon boxs $85.00

MEN'S ITEMS, MISC.

ALL ITEMS' PRICES EMPTY - MINT

1948-49 CREAM HAIR LOTION
4 oz. maroon cap. O.S.P. 59¢ C.M.V. $20.00 $25.00 M.B.

1953-54 COLOGNE FOR MEN
4 oz. green label, red cap. Came in Before & After set only. C.M.V. $15.00.

LEFT:
1938-39 HAIR TONIC
6 oz. clear glass, maroon cap and label. OSP 52c CMV $30.00 BO mint $40.00 MB
RIGHT:
1940-49 HAIR LOTION
6 oz. maroon cap & box. OSP 69c CMV $40.00 in box. Bottle only $30.00 mint. Some labels say "formerly Hair Tonic"

1966-69 CREAM HAIR LOTION
4 oz. white plastic bottle with red cap and red label. Regular issue O.S.P. 98¢ C.M.V. $2.00. Very short issue sold 1966 only with red cap and red label with black border. CMV $4.00

1953-54 HAIR LOTION 1 OZ.
1 oz. bottle with red cap & green label. Came in Parade Dress set only. CMV $20.00 BO $25.00 MB
1953-54 CREAM HAIR LOTION 1 OZ'
1 oz. bottle with red cap. Came in Parade Dress set only. Green label. CMV $18.00 BO $25.00 MB in trial size box
1953-54 LIQUID SHAMPOO
1 oz. bottle with red cap & green label. Came in Parade Dress set only. CMV $22.00 BO $27.00 MB

1958-62 CREAM HAIR LOTION
4 oz. white plastic bottle, red cap. O.S.P. 89c CMV $7.00 MB $12.00.
1958-62 HAIR LOTION
4 oz. clear glass, red cap, black & white label. OSP. 79c CMV $14.00 MB $10.00 BO glass bottle on right also came in deer head box on left.

1936-38 HAIR TONIC EAU DE QUININE
For normal, dry or oily hair. 6 oz. turquoise cap. OSP 78c CMV $15.00. Also came in 16 oz. size. $25.00. Add $5.00 if MB

1949-58 HAIR LOTION
4 oz. silver label & red cap. OSP 59c
CMV $7.00 BO $12.00 MB
1949-58 CREAM HAIR LOTION
4 oz. bottle, silver label, red cap. OSP 59c CMV $7.00 BO $12.00 MB
1953-54 AFTER SHAVE LOTION
4 oz. silver label, red cap, as above.
CMV $15.00

1953-56 FIRST CLASS MALE
6 oz. cologne for men, box red & white.
OSP $1.50 CMV $25.00 MB as shown

1957 Only ROYAL ORDER
Red & green box holds 6 oz. Cologne for Men. Silver label. O.S.P. $1.50, C.M.V. $25.00 MB.

1949-58 COLOGNE FOR MEN
All three sizes have red caps & silver labels, 6oz. size 1949-57 O.S.P. $1.50, C.M.V. $15.00 MB 4 oz. size 1952-57, came in sets only. Also with green label. C.M.V. $9.00. 2 oz. size 1949-58, O.S.P. 69¢ C.M.V. $6.00.

1957 KING FOR A DAY
Box holds 4 oz. bottle of Electric Pre-Shave Lotion or choice of cologne for men, or 4 oz. deodorant for men. All had red caps. OSP 89c CMV $22.50 M.B.
1957-58 ELECTRIC PRE-SHAVE LOTION
4 oz. red cap, silver label. O.S.P. 89¢
C.M.V. $9.00 $10.00 M.B.

1954-57 DEODORANT FOR MEN
4 oz. red cap & green label. Came in sets only. CMV $9.00 MB $7.00 BO
1949-58 DEODORANT FOR MEN
2 oz. red cap & green label. OSP 63c
CMV $6.00 $8.00 MB

1949-58 DEODORANT FOR MEN SAMPLE
1/2 oz. bottle with red cap, green label.
C.M.V. $25.00 Mint

1949-58 AFTER SHAVING LOTION
4oz. bottle with silver label & red cap.
OSP 69c CMV $6.00 BO $9.00 MB
2 OZ. AFTER SHAVE 1957
Silver label. Came in Good Cheer set only.
C.M.V. $8.00.

1953-56 SHAVING BOWL
Wood Shaving Bowl, green label. No center handle. O.S.P. $1.25 C.M.V. $30.00 M.B. $40.00
1949-53 SHAVING BOWL
Wood Shaving Bowl, green label with red center handle. O.S.P. $1.10 C.M.V. $35.00 M.B. $45.00

1952-57 COLOGNE FOR MEN
4 oz. Clear glass bottle with red cap. Label is green & red. C.M.V. $9.00.

1949-58 COLOGNE FOR MEN SAMPLE
½ oz. red cap, silver label. CMV $25.00
1949-58 AFTER SHAVING LOTION SAMPLE
½ oz. red cap, green label. CMV $5.00

1966-68 ORIGINAL SOAP ON A ROPE
White bar with embossed carriage. O.S.P. $1.75 CMV $22.50 MB $15.00 soap only mint
1965-69 ORIGINAL AFTER SHAVE
4 oz. green label, red cap & red & green box. OSP $1.25 CMV $4.00 MB $5.00

1959-62 BRUSHLESS SHAVING CREAM
5 oz. black & white tube, red cap. O.S.P. 79¢ C.M.V. $8.00 MB.

1959-62 LATHER SHAVING CREAM
5 oz. black & white tube, red cap. O.S.P. 79¢ C.M.V. $8.00 MB.

1958-62 KWICK FOAMING SHAVE CREAM
6 oz. black & white can, red cap. O.S.P. 79¢ C.M.V. $8.00.

1959 Only TALC FOR MEN
Black & white can, red cap. O.S.P. 69¢, C.M.V. $12.00 MB, $10.00 can only mint.

1959-62 AFTER SHOWER POWDER FOR MEN
3 oz. black & white can, red cap. O.S.P. 89¢ C.M.V. $6.00 $7.00 M.B.

1955-57 KWICK FOAMING SHAVE CREAM
10 oz. green & white can, pointed red cap. OSP 98c CMV $8.00 $11.00 MB
1957-58 Same can with flat top, red cap. CMV $8.00 $11.00 MB

1949-57 SHAVING STICK
Green & red box holds Shaving Soap Stick with red plastic base. OSP 59c CMV $12.50 MB $4.00 stick only

1949-57 STYPTIC CREAM
1/3 oz. green tube with red cap. O.S.P. 39¢ C.M.V. $5.00. In box $8.00

1949-58 SHAVING CREAM SAMPLE
¼ oz. green tubes of lather & brushless shaving cream, red caps. C.M.V. $5.00 ea. mint. Also came in ½ oz. size sample tubes C.M.V. $6.00 ea. mint.

1949-59 LATHER & BRUSHLESS SHAVING CREAM
Green tubes, flat red caps, used in 1949-56. Tall red caps used 1957-59. O.S.P. 49¢ ea. C.M.V. $8.00 ea. in box, $6.00 tube only mint.

1949-57 CREAM HAIR DRESS
2¼ oz. green tube & box. Came with flat or tall red cap. O.S.P. 49¢ C.M.V. $12.00 M.B.

1962 AFTER SHOWER COLOGNE SPRAY
5.5 oz. white can & cap. OSP $1.75 CMV $7.00

1962-65 FOAM SHAVE CREAM SPICY
6 oz. white can, red cap. Came in regular or mentholated. OSP 89c CMV $6.00 MB $4.00 CO
Came with tall or flat red caps as shown.

1965-66 ORIGINAL AFTER SHAVE SPRAY
5½ oz. green can with red cap. O.S.P. $1.50 C.M.V. $6.00 can only mint, $9.00 M.B.

1949-58 TALC FOR MEN
2 5/8 oz. green can, red cap. O.S.P. 69¢ C.M.V. $5.00. M.B. $7.00. Also came in 2.6 oz. size.

1962-65 TALC FOR MEN SPICY
3 oz. white can, red cap. O.S.P. 89¢ C.M.V. $7.00. Also came in 3.1 oz. size.

1960-63 ROLL ON DEODORANT FOR MEN
1¾ oz. white plastic with red cap. OSP 89c CMV $5.00 MB $4.00 BO

1962-65 CREAM HAIR LOTION
4 oz. white plastic bottle, red cap. OSP 89c CMV $10.00 MB $7.00 BO

1962-65 LIQUID HAIR LOTION
4 oz. clear glass bottle, red cap. OSP 89c CMV $12.00 MB $8.00 BO

1962-65 HAIR TRAINER
4 oz. white plastic bottle, red cap. OSP 89c CMV $10.00 MB $7.00 BO

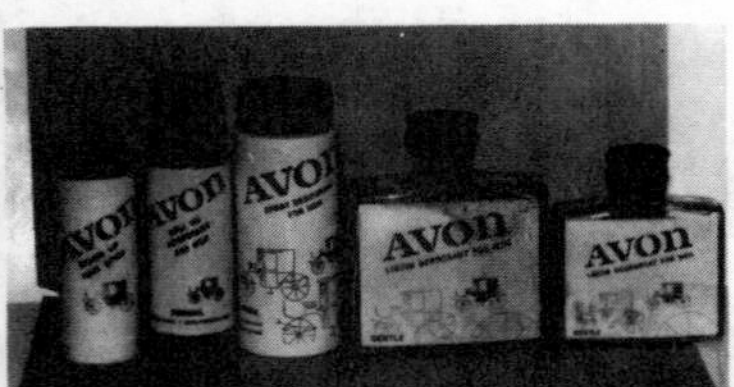

1962-65 STAND UP HAIR STICK
1½ oz. white plastic, red cap. OSP 89c CMV $4.00 MB $3.00 BO

1963-66 ROLL ON DEODORANT FOR MEN
1¾ oz. glass bottle, red cap. OSP 89c CMV $4.00 MB $3.00 BO

1962-66 SPRAY DEODORANT FOR MEN
2¾ oz. white plastic bottle, red cap. Came in gentle, normal or plain. OSP 89c CMV $3.00 MB $2.00 BO

1962-65 LIQUID DEODORANT FOR MEN GENTLE OR PLAIN
4 oz. & 2 oz. Clear glass bottle, red cap. OSP 79c CMV 2 oz. $6.00 4 oz. $7.00

1962-65 AFTER SHAVE LOTION SPICY
1962-65 ELECTRIC PRE-SHAVE LOTION SPICY
1962-65 AFTER SHOWER COLOGNE FOR MEN
1962-65 ORIGINAL AFTER SHAVE LOTION
1962-65 VIGORATE AFTER SHAVE LOTION
Each bottle is 4 oz. size with red caps. OSP ea. 89c on Spicy & Electric Pre-Shave & $1.00 ea. on Vigorate & After Shower Cologne. CMV ea. $7.00 BO $10.00 MB

1963-64 MEN'S SQUEEZE BOTTLE
2 oz. white plastic bottles with red caps & letters. Came in Vigorate, Spicy & Original After Shave Lotions, Electric Pre-Shave Lotion, Spicy Liquid Hair Lotion, Hair Trainer, Cream Hair Lotion, After Shower Cologne for Men, Liquid Deodorant for Men-gentle or plain. Came only in 1964 Xmas Trio Set & 1965 Jolly Holly Day Set. CMV $3.00 each.

1963-65 VIGORATE AFTER SHAVE, AFTER SHOWER SPRAY
1963-65 ORIGINAL AFTER SHAVE, AFTER SHOWER SPRAY SPICY
1963-65 AFTER SHAVE, AFTER SHOWER SPRAY SPICY
1963-65 AFTER SHOWER COLOGNE SPRAY
5½ oz. each. White can with red caps. O.S.P. Spicy & Original $1.50 ea. O.S.P. Cologne & Vigorate $1.75 ea. CMV $3.00 ea.

1962-65 AFTER SHAVE FOR DRY OR SENSITIVE SKIN SPICY 2 oz.
1962-65 LATHER SHAVE CREAM SPICY 4 oz.
1962-65 BRUSHLESS SHAVE CREAM SPICY 4 oz.
All three white tubes with red caps. OSP each 89c CMV $3.00 MB $6.00 ea.

1962-63 LATHER SHAVE CREAM
4 oz. tube, red cap. O.S.P. 89¢ C.M.V. $4.00 mint, $6.00 M.B.

1958 COLOGNE FOR MEN
2 oz. red cap, black & white label. Came in Happy Hours Set only. CMV $7.00 BO

1958-62 DEODORANT FOR MEN
2 oz. red cap. OSP 69c CMV $8.00 MB $6.00 BO

1958-59 COLOGNE FOR MEN
4 oz. black glass, red cap. OSP $1.25 CMV $15.00 MB $12.00 BO

1959-62 AFTER SHOWER SAMPLE
½ oz. black glass, red cap. CMV $6.00

1959-62 AFTER SHOWER FOR MEN
4 oz. black glass, red or gold cap. O.S.P. $1.25 C.M.V. $12.00

1959-60 AFTER SHOWER FOR MEN
2 oz. black plastic bottle with red cap. OSP $1.25 CMV $8.00

1959-60 AFTER SHAVE
2 oz. red plastic bottle & cap. Came in 1959 Lamplighter Set. CMV $8.00

LEFT TO RIGHT
1958-62 AFTER SHAVE LOTION SAMPLE
½ oz. red cap, black & white label. CMV $8.00
1958 AFTER SHAVE LOTION
2 oz. red cap. Came in sets only. C.M.V. $6.00
1958-62 AFTER SHAVE LOTION
4 oz. red cap, black & white label. O.S.P. 89¢ C.M.V. $4.00

1962-63 DELUXE STICK DEODORANT NORMAL
2½ oz. brown & gold plastic bottle. OSP $1.35 CMV $8.00 - $10.00 BO
1961-62 STICK DEODORANT FOR MEN A SPICY FRAGRANCE
2¾ oz. brown & gold plastic holder. OSP $1.35 CMV $9.00 - $11.00 MB

1960-61 STAGE COACH EMBOSSED BOTTLES
2 oz. size. Red or white caps. Came in First Prize Set only in After Shower for Men, Vigorate, Deodorant for Men, After Shave Lotion, Electric Pre-Shave Lotion, Liquid Hair Lotion. CMV ea. $18.00 MB $10 BO
1961 Only - 4 oz. size with white cap came in Spice After Shave Lotion. OSP $1.25 CMV $10.00 BO $14.00 MB
1960-61 8 oz. size with gold metal cap, came in Spice After Shave Lotion. OSP $1.98
After Shave Lotion OSP $1.79, Vigorate $2.50 & After Shower for Men OSP $2.50 CMV ea. $17.00 with indented gold cap $25.00 MB

1960-62 VIGORATE AFTER SHAVE
4 oz. frosted glass bottle, gold caps, painted labels. 2 different painted labels. O.S.P. $1.25 CMV $10.00 MB $15.00

1960-61 AFTER SHAVE FOR DRY & SENSITIVE SKIN
2 oz. white plastic bottle with red cap. O.S.P. 89¢ C.M.V. $7.00 B.O. $10.00 M.B. Also came in 2¾ oz.
1960-61 CREAM HAIR LOTION
2 oz. white plastic bottle with red cap. Came in 1st Prize Set only. C.M.V. $7.00 B.O. Also came in 2¾ oz. size. $10.00 M.B.

1959-62 ELECTRIC PRE-SHAVE LOTION
4 oz. red cap, black & white label. OSP 89c CMV $12.00 MB $8.00 BO
1960-62 AFTER SHAVING LOTION PLASTIC
3½ oz. white plastic bottle with red cap. Came in Overnighter Set only. C.M.V. $8.00
2 oz. After Shave, red plastic & cap as above came in 1959 Lamplighter Set. C.M.V. $8.00
1959-62 SPRAY DEODORANT FOR MEN
2¾ oz. white plastic bottle with red cap. OSP 89c CMV $6.00 MB $4.00 BO
1½ oz. size in white plastic, red cap, came only in 1959 Lamplighters Set. C.M.V. $7.00

1962-63 DELUXE AFTER SHAVE AFTER SHOWER SPRAY
5½ oz. brown can, gold cap. OSP $1.98 CMV $8.00 $10.00 MB
1961 Only - AFTER SHOWER POWDER SPICY
4 oz. brown can. OSP $1.35 CMV $12.00 - $14.00 MB

1962-63 DELUXE TALC FOR MEN
4 oz. brown can. OSP $1.35 CMV $8.00 - $10.00 MB
1962-63 DELUXE FOAM SHAVE CREAM
6 oz. brown can & cap. Regular or mentholated. OSP $1.35 CMV $8.00 - $10.00 MB

1961-62 AFTER SHAVE AFTER SHOWER SPRAY LOTION A SPICY FRAGRANCE
5½ oz. brown can, gold cap. OSP $1.79 CMV $12.00 mint. $14.00 MB

1959-61 STICK DEODORANT FOR MEN
2¾ oz. black & red plastic container. Came with two different caps, 1 flat, 1 indented. OSP $1.00 CMV $12.00 ea. $14.00 MB

1943-46 TALC FOR MEN
Maroon & ivory colored cardboard. One on left also came with black octaginal cap as shown and also with maroon or black round cap. One on right was smooth top. You punched holes in it. OSP 37c CMV $30.00 ea. mint.

1929 Only - TALC FOR MEN
Green can. O.S.P. 25¢ C.M.V. $50.00 mint
1930-36 TALC FOR MEN
Green can. O.S.P. 35¢ C.M.V. $40.00 mint

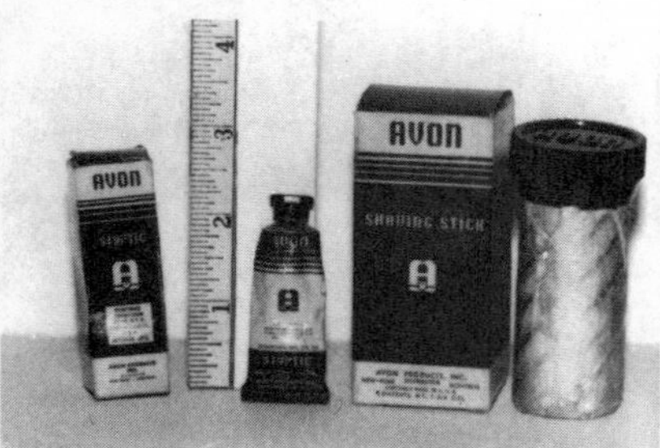

1936-49 STYPTIC CREAM
Maroon & ivory tube. OSP 17c. CMV $8.00 $15.00 MB
1936-49 SHAVING STICK
Avon on maroon base on Soap Stick. Maroon box. OSP 39c, CMV $6.00. $15.00 in box.

1929-33 SHAVING STICK
Green metal can. CPC on lid. OSP 35c CMV $45.00 Can only mint. $55.00 MB

1934-36 SHAVING STICK
Nickel metal container. OSP 36c CMV $45.00 MB $35.00 mint only.

1958-74 HAIR TRAINER LIQUID
4 oz. red plastic bottle, white cap. O.S.P. 89¢ C.M.V. $1.00
1959-62 ATTENTION CREAM HAIR DRESS
4 oz. red & white tube, red cap. O.S.P. 89¢ C.M.V. $8.00. M.B. $10.00
1958-65 STAND UP HAIR STICK
Red & white container with white cap. OSP 69c CMV $3.00 $7.00 MB

HAIR TRAINER BOXES 1958-61 LEFT TO RIGHT:
4 oz. red plastic bottle with 1958 box on left, 1962 box center, 1960-61 right. 1959 box came with basket ball player on front of box. CMV Ad $5.00 for each box mint.

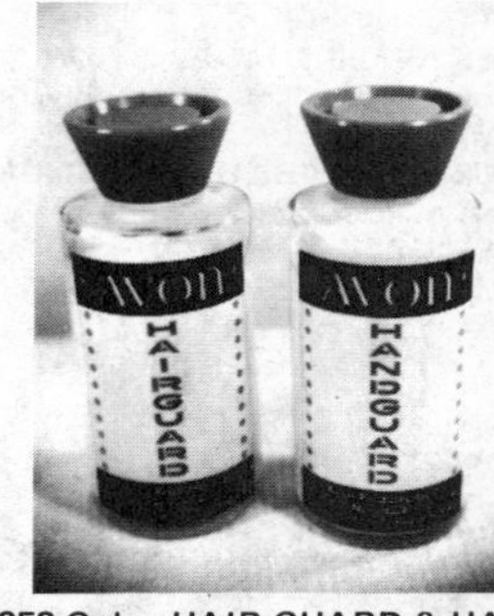

1958 Only - HAIR GUARD & HAND GUARD
Both 2 oz. bottles with red caps. Came in Avon Guard Set only. CMV Hand guard $16.00, Hair Guard $20.00

1965-67 BATH OIL FOR MEN
4 oz. silver paint over clear glass, red cap & red Avon plastic tag on gold neck cord. Came in silver box. OSP $2.50 CMV $7.00 - $10.00 MB. Foreign Bath Oil same as U.S. only shiny silver & no neck tag. CMV $12.00
1965-67 AFTER SHOWER FOAM FOR MEN
4 oz. silver can, black & red cap. Came in silver box. OSP $2.50 CMV $7.00 BO $10.00 MB

1955 CREAM HAIR LOTION
2 oz. clear glass. Red cap. Came in Space Scout set only. Rare CMV $20.00

1954-57 HAND GUARD & HAIR GUARD
2 oz. red cap on Hair Guard. 2 oz. green cap on Hand Guard. Both came in Back Field Set & Touchdown Set. Hair Guard also came in Pigskin Parade Set. C.M.V. $18.00 each.

1957 FOAMY BATH FOR CLEANER HIDES
2 oz. red cap, cow hide on label. Came in Trading Post Set only. C.M.V. $18.00
1957 HAIR TRAINER FOR TRAINING WILD HAIR
2 oz. red cap, cow hide on label. Came in Trading Post Set only. C.M.V. $18.00.

1967-68 BODY POWDER FOR MEN
6 oz. maroon cardboard box. OSP $4.00 CMV $8.00 MB $12.50

1975-76 TODAYS MAN SHAVE CREAM
5 oz. white with red & black design, black cap. O.S.P. $2.00 C.M.V. 50¢
1975-76 TODAYS MAN HAND CONDITIONER
5 oz. white plastic tube with black & red design, black cap. O.S.P. $1.69 C.M.V. 50¢
1975-76 TODAYS MAN AFTER SHAVE FACE CONDITIONER
5 oz. white with red & black. Black cap. O.S.P. $2.50 C.M.V. 50¢

1971-74 ANTI PERSPIRANT DEODORANT FOR MEN
4 oz. red, white & black can. O.S.P. $1.50 C.M.V. 25¢
1966-70 LIQUID DEODORANT FOR MEN
2 oz. red cap. O.S.P. 79¢ C.M.V. $2.00
1968-70 STICK DEODORANT FOR MEN
2.25 oz. red, white & black plastic. O.S.P. $1.25 C.M.V. $1.00
DEODORANT SOAP DRY FOREIGN
C.M.V. $3.00

1968 -72 STAY HAIR GROOM FOR MEN
7 oz. brown & black can. Black cap. O.S.P. $1.50 C.M.V. 50¢
1969-73 SKIN CONDITIONER FOR MEN
5 oz. black glass, red lid & red & black label. O.S.P. $2.50 C.M.V. $2.50 M.B.
1966-68 SKIN CONDITIONER ALL PURPOSE FOR MEN
5 oz. black glass, tan lid, gold label. O.S.P. $2.50 C.M.V. $5.00 M.B.

1969-72 BATH OIL
4 oz. black glass bottle, red cap. O.S.P. $2.50 C.M.V. $2.00
1969-72 AFTER SHAVE SOOTHER
4 oz. frosted glass bottle with red cap. O.S.P. $2.50 C.M.V. $2.00
1969-72 PROTECTIVE HAND CREAM FOR MEN
3 oz. black plastic tube with red cap. O.S.P. $1.50 C.M.V. $1.00

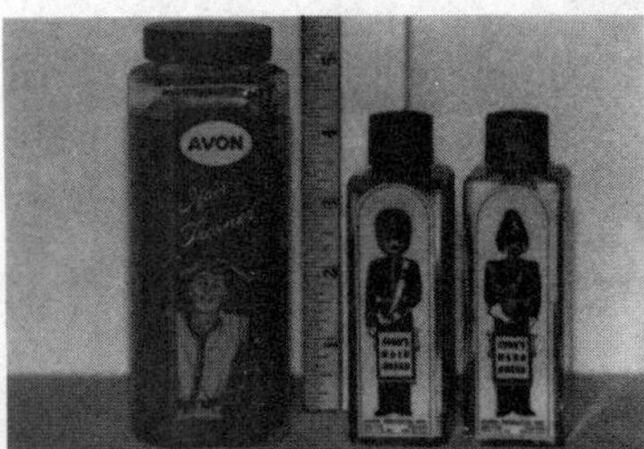

1957-58 HAIR TRAINER
6 oz. clear glass bottle with white or blue cap. Came in 1957 Hair Trainer Set. O.S.P. 79¢ C.M.V. $15.00
1951-52 HAND GUARD & HAIR GUARD
2 oz. clear glass with blue cap, Hair guard has red cap. Label is red, white & black. Came in Changing of the Guard Set only. C.M.V. $20.00 ea.

1972-76 PROTEIN HAIR CARE FOR MEN
Blue & white. Shampoo Concentrate 3 oz. O.S.P. $1.79 C.M.V. 50¢
DANDRUFF SHAMPOO 3 oz. O.S.P. $1.79 C.M.V. 50¢
CLEAR HAIR DRESS 4 oz. O.S.P $1.79 C.M.V. 50¢
HAIR & SCALP CONDITIONER 6 oz. O.S.P. $1.79 C.M.V. 50¢
1972-74 HAIR LOTION 6 oz. O.S.P. $1.75 C.M.V. 50¢
1974 (late) - 1976 HAIR/SCALP CONDITIONER (not shown) same as lotion. O.S.P. $2.50 C.M.V. 50¢
1972 Only HAIR SPRAY 7 oz. O.S.P. $1.75 C.M.V. 50¢
1973-76 HAIR MANAGING CONTROL (not shown) same as Hair Spray. O.S.P. $1.75 C.M.V. 50¢
1972-76 CREAM HAIR DRESS
4 oz blue tube, white cap. O.S.P. $1.79 C.M.V. 50¢

1977 TRAVEL-LITE
2 oz. light tan plastic bottle of shampoo 1.7 oz. spray deodorant, 2 oz. Wild Country after shave. All have brown caps. CMV $1.00 ea.

1970-77 FOAM SHAVE CREAM
11 oz. cans in Mentholated. Blue cap & regular, orange cap. O.S.P. $1.79 C.M.V. 50¢

1970-77 FOAM SHAVE CREAM
11 oz. can. Regular or Mentholated. Label is painted upside down. O.S.P.$1.79 Upside down label C.M.V. $8.00 Regular issue label 50¢

1966-72 ELECTRIC PRE-SHAVE LOTION
4 oz. white cap. O.S.P. $1.50 C.M.V. $1.00
1966-70 FOAM SHAVE CREAM
6 oz. red & white can in regular & green & white can in mentholated. O.S.P. 98¢ each. C.M.V. $1.00 each

1966-70 LIQUID HAIR LOTION
4 oz. clear glass bottle with white cap. O.S.P. 98¢ C.M.V. $2.00. 1970-71 bottle is plastic. C.M.V. $1.00.
1966-71 HAIR DRESS
4 oz. tube in Cream Clear & Clear for Extra Control. OSP 98c, CMV $2.00. Also came in 3 oz. tube. CMV $2.00 each.

BAY RUM

Also see CPC Bay Rum section, Bay Rum Keg in Men's Decanters

1964-65 BAY RUM AFTER SHAVE
4 oz. clear glass, black cap. OSP $1.25 CMV $8.50 bottle only. $12.50 MB
1962-65 BAY RUM JUG
8 oz. white painted bottom, green top over clear glass, black cap. Bay Rum After Shave. OSP $2.50 CMV $6.00 BO $10.00 MB
1964-65 BAY RUM TALC
4 oz. green paper container. OSP $1.25, CMV $10.00

1936-49 BAY RUM
4 oz. maroon cap. Both bottles have indented shoulders. Also came in 8 & 16 oz. size. OSP 52c CMV bottle only $22.00 BO, $30.00 MB
1936-49 AFTER SHAVING LOTION
4 oz. maroon cap, maroon & cream colored box. OSP 37c CMV $30.00 MB $22.00 BO

1964-65 BAY RUM SOAP
Green box holds 2 Bay Rum shaped soaps. OSP $1.25 CMV $27.50 MB

1964 BAY RUM GIFT SET
Green box holds 4 oz. Bay Rum After Shave with black cap & green 4 oz. paper Bay Rum Talc for men. OSP $2.50 CMV $35.00 MB

BLEND 7

1973-74 BLEND 7 EMOLLIENT AFTER SHAVE
5 oz. clear glass with black cap. SSP $4.00 CMV $3.00 MB $1.00 BO
1973-76 COLOGNE
5 oz. smoky glass with silver cap. SSP $4.00 CMV $3.00 MB $1.00 BO
1973-76 SOAP ON A ROPE
5 oz. yellow with black cord. SSP $2.00 CMV $4.00 MB

1974-76 BLEND 7 SPRAY TALC
7 oz. silver & black can with black cap. S.S.P. $3.00 C.M.V. 50¢
1974-76 BLEND 7 FRAGRANCE SAMPLES
10 foil samples in box. C.M.V. 50¢ box.

BLUE BLAZER

1964-68 BLUE BLAZER AFTER SHAVE
6 oz. blue glass with red square cap over small red cap. Horses on labels, came in gold or silver & with or without lines across horses. Some labels have 6 oz. at bottom of horse label. O.S.P. $2.50 C.M.V. $22.00 in box. $20.00 bottle only.

1964-68 BLUE BLAZER SOAP ON A ROPE
Blue soap on white rope. OSP $1.75 CMV $22.50 in box. $15.00 soap only mint.

1964-65 BLUE BLAZER II
Blue & red box holds Blue Blazer Talc & Spray Deodorant. O.S.P. $2.50 C.M.V. $25.00.

1964-65 BLUE BLAZER FOAM SHAVE CREAM
6 oz. blue can, red cap. OSP $1.25 CMV $10.00 MB $7.00 CO

1964-65 AFTER SHAVE SPRAY
Blue 6 oz. can, red cap. OSP $1.95 CMV $10.00 MB $7.00 CO

1964-65 TALC
3½ oz. blue paper box. OSP $1.25 CMV $12.00 MB $9.00 CO

1964-67 HAIR DRESS
4 oz. blue tube, red cap. OSP $1.25 CMV $8.00 MB $6,00 TO

1964-65 BLUE BLAZER I
Blue & red box holds 6 oz. Blue Blazer After Shave Lotion & Blue Blazer Soap on Rope. O.S.P. $3.45 C.M.V. $50.00 M.B.

1964-67 BLUE BLAZER SPRAY DEODORANT
2.75 oz. blue plastic bottles, red caps. 1 bottle has lines on horse design & 1 plain. The plain one is hardest to find. C.M.V. $8.00 O.S.P. $1.25 each. Different label on right. C.M.V. $7.00 with 2.75 oz. on front side.

1964 BLUE BLAZER TIE TAC
Silver Blue Blazer emblem Tie Tac. Came in Blue Blazer Deluxe Set only. In blue & red box. CMV $22.00 in box $10.00 pin only.

1965 BLUE BLAZER DELUXE
Blue & red box holds 6 oz. Blue Blazer After Shave, Blue Blazer Spray Deodorant & silver Blue Blazer Emblem Tie Tac. O.S.P. $5.50 C.M.V. $65.00.

1966-67 BLUE BLAZER SOAP & SPONGE SET
Red & blue box holds bar of blue soap & red & blue sponge. OSP $2.50 CMV set in box $22.50

BRAVO

1970 SANTA'S HELPER
Green box holds 4 oz. Bravo After Shave. Box came with foam stick on decorations. O.S.P. $1.98 C.M.V. $8.00 M.B. only.

1969 BRAVO AFTER SHAVE
4 oz. bottle with black cap, pink label. OSP $2.00 CMV $4.00 MB $2.00 BO

RIGHT 1970-72 BRAVO AFTER SHAVE
4 oz. black cap, pink label with black border around label. OSP $2.00 CMV $2.00 MB $1.00 BO

1969-72 BRAVO AFTER SHAVE SAMPLE
Box of 10 samples. CMV $1.00 MB

1969-72 BRAVO TALC
3.5 oz. pink & black paper container.
O.S.P. $1.25 C.M.V. $1.50

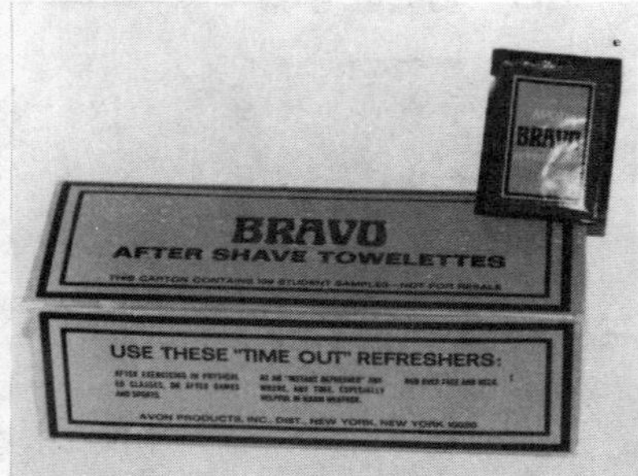

1969-72 BRAVO AFTER SHAVE TOWELETTES
Pink & black box holds 100 sample packets. CMV $10.00 MB or 10c per sample

CLINT

LEFT 1977-78 CLINT GIFT SET
Gray & green box with outer sleeve. Came with Clint soap on a rope & 5 oz Clint cologne. O.S.P.$12.50 C.M.V.$10.00 M.B.
RIGHT 1977 CLINT TRAVEL SET
Cardboard 1.5 oz. talc and 3 oz. Clint in plastic bottle with maroon cap. O.S.P. $3.49 C.M.V. $3.50 M.B.

1979-80 CLINT ROLL ON DEODORANT
2 oz. gray & maroon plastic. SSP $1.00 CMV .25c

1977 CLINT TRAVEL KIT
Comes empty, grey maroon & green bag. O.S.P. $14.00 C.M.V. $6.00 M.B.
1977-78 CLINT TALC
3.5 oz. cardboard talc container. O.S.P. $2.50 C.M.V. 50¢
1977=78 CLINT SOAP
3 oz. soap. O.S.P. $1.25 C.M.V.75¢
1977 CLINT SPRAY TALC
702 grey maroon & green can. O.S.P. $4.00 C.M.V. $1.00

LEFT 1977-79 CLINT AFTER SHAVE
5 oz. glass bottle, brown cap. OSP $5.00 CMV 75c
1977-78 CENTER CLINT SHOWER SOAP
Soap on green rope. OSP $5.00 CMV $3.50 MB
RIGHT 1976-79 CLINT COLOGNE
5 oz. bottle with Clint painted on front. OSP $7.50 CMV 75c

1977-79 CLINT STEIN COLOGNE
8 oz. Red plastic bottle came in Tall Ships Stein only. CMV $3.00

DEEP WOODS

1977-78 DEEP WOODS SOAP BAR
Brown wrapped soap, 3 oz. bar. OSP $1.25 CMV $1.00 mint
1977-78 DEEP WOODS TALC
3.5 oz. brown & green container. S.S.P. $1.49 C.M.V. 50¢

1972-79 DEEP WOODS PRODUCTS
1976-79 AFTER SHAVE
5 oz. brown cap. OSP $3.00 CMV 75c
1972-75 SHOWER SOAP ON A ROPE (CENTER) OSP $2.00 CMV $6.00 MB
1976-79 SHOWER SOAP ON A ROPE (RIGHT) OSP $3.00 CMV $3.00 MB
1972-79 DEEP WOODS FRAGRANCE SAMPLE CMV 25c box.

1972-78 DEEP WOODS
Light green with brown cap. Looks like a log.
1972-78 COLOGNE 5 oz. O.S.P. $6.50 C.M.V. $1.00
1973-75 COLOGNE SPRAY 3 oz. O.S.P. $5.00 C.M.V. $1.00
1973-77 SPRAY TALC 7 oz. O.S.P. $4.00 C.M.V. 50¢ Came in brown or green can.
1973-74 EMOLLIENT AFTER SHAVE S.S.P. $5.00 C.M.V. $2.00
1973-77 DEEP WOODS SPRAY TALC
7 oz. metal can with upside down painted label, brown plastic lid. This is a factory mistake. OSP $4.00 CMV $15.00

EXCALIBUR

1969-71 EXCALIBUR SOAP ON A ROPE
Blue soap on a rope. OSP $2.50 CMV $10.00 MB
1970-72 EXCALIBUR SPRAY TALC
7 oz. black can & cap. O.S.P. $3.00 C.M.V. $2.00

1969-73 EXCALIBUR COLOGNE FOREIGN & AMERICAN
Smaller foreign Excalibur on left. CMV $12.00. American on right. 6 oz. gold cap. Bottom of bottle appears to have rocks in glass. OSP $5.00 CMV $5.00 MB $2.00 BO
American rare issue came with sword pointing to right side low end of rocks CMV $15.00 mint

EVEREST

1977-79 EVEREST SOAP BAR
Blue wrapped 3 oz. bar.
SSP $1.25 CMV $1.00 mint.
1977-79 EVEREST TALC
3.5 oz. blue container OSP $2.50 CMV 50c

1975-79 EVEREST SOAP ON A ROPE
Blue soap, white rope. OSP $3.00 CMV $3.00 MB
1976-78 EVEREST AFTER SHAVE
5 oz. glass bottle with bronze cap. O.S.P. $4.00 C.M.V. 75¢
1975-79 EVEREST COLOGNE
5 oz. blue glass, blue cap. OSP $4.00 CMV 75c
1975-77 EVEREST SPRAY TALC
7 oz. blue & white with blue lid. O.S.P. $3.00 C.M.V. 50¢ mint.

1976-79 EVEREST STEIN COLOGNE
8 oz. blue plastic bottle came in 1976 to 1979 Collectors steins. CMV $3.00

1966-68 ISLAND LIME SOAP
Green soap on a rope. OSP $2.00 CMV $22.00 MB. Two different weave designs on soap.

ISLAND LIME

1974-76 ISLAND LIME SPRAY TALC
7 oz. green & yellow with dark green cap. O.S.P. $2.00 C.M.V. 50¢.
1966-69 ISLAND LIME AFTER SHAVE
1st issue 6 oz. dark yellow basket weave. CMV $12.00 MB $9.00 BO
1967 issue has light yellow weave on clear CMV $10.00. 1968 issue has light green weave. CMV $10.00. All 66 to 68 are clear glass bottles. 1969 issue is green glass bottle & low issue. CMV $20.00 MB $14.00 BO OSP ea. $3.00. All have green & yellow caps. Add $3.00 ea. MB Came with small or large flowers on caps.

1966-67 ISLAND LIME AEROSOL DEODORANT
4 oz. green & yellow checked can & green cap. OSP $1.50 CMV $3.00 CO $5.00 MB
1969-73 ISLAND LIME AFTER SHAVE
6 oz. green frosted glass & green cap with yellow letters. OSP $4.00 CMV $1.50
1973-74 Issue has gold cap, green letters. OSP $4.00 CMV $4.00 MB $2.00 BO

LEATHER

1966 ALL PURPOSE COLOGNE LEATHER (LEFT)
4 oz. black cap, red label. Came in Fox Hunt Set only. CMV $10.00
1968 AFTER SHAVE LOTION LEATHER (RIGHT)
3 oz. red cap, clear glass. Came in Boots & Saddle Set only. CMV $5.00

1966 LEATHER SOAP
One bar in brown & red box. OSP $1.75 CMV $17.00 MB

1966-67 LEATHER AEROSOL DEODORANT
4 oz. tan & red can with black cap. OSP $1.50 CMV $5.00 MB $3.00 Can only
1969-72 LEATHER SPRAY TALC
7 oz. tan & red can, black cap. O.S.P. $3.00 C.M.V. $2.00

OLAND

1970-77 OLAND COLOGNE
6 oz. embossed bottle with brown cap. O.S.P. $6.50 C.M.V. $2.00
1970-77 OLAND SPRAY TALC
7 oz. brown spray can with brown cap. O.S.P. $3.00 C.M.V. 50¢
1970-77 OLAND SOAP ON A ROPE
Tan bar of soap on green rope with plastic "O", OSP $4.00 CMV $7.00 MB, with plain rope - No "O" CMV $5.00 MB

1970 OLAND GIFT SET
Brown & silver box holds bar of Oland Soap, 3½ oz. Oland Talc & 6 oz. Oland Cologne. O.S.P. $8.00 C.M.V. $15.00

1970-72 OLAND SPRAY TALC
7 oz. can with O on brown cap. Painted label on can is upside down. Can was filled & sold by Avon by mistake. O.S.P. $3.00 C.M.V. on upside down label only $15.00
1970 OLAND AFTER SHAVE & COLOGNE
3½ oz. clear glass with gold cap. Came in Master Organizer only. C.M.V. $5.00 each.

SPICY

1967-75 AFTER SHAVE FOR DRY OR SENSITIVE SKIN - SPICY
2 oz. black, brown & white tube, brown or white cap. OSP 98c.
One has all white letters. CMV $1.00
One has black over print on white letters. Hard to find. CMV $3.00

1967-74 SPICY AFTER SHAVE
4 oz. clear glass, black cap. C.M.V. 50¢
4 oz. Amber glass with black cap. O.S.P. ea. $1.50. C.M.V. $2.00 M.B.

1966 FORE N AFTER SPICY
Spicy box holds 4 oz. Electric Pre-Shave Lotion Spicy & 4 oz. After Shave Lotion Spicy. White caps on both & wood grained paper labels. O.S.P. $1.96 C.M.V. $22.00 M.B.
1966 ELECTRIC PRE-SHAVE & AFTER SHAVE LOTIONS - SPICY
4 oz. white caps & wood grained paper labels. Came in Fore 'N' After Set only. C.M.V. $9.00 each.

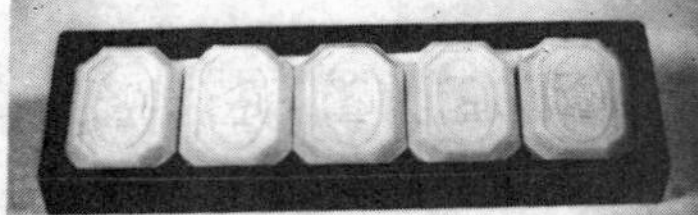

1965-66 SPICY SOAP SET
Five brown bars. OSP $2.00 CMV $22.50 MB

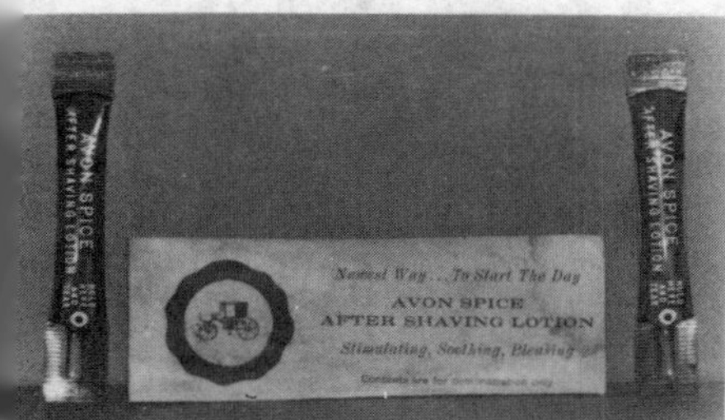

1961 SPICE AFTER SHAVE LOTION SAMPLES
Small white envelope holds 2 plastic samples. CMV $3.00

1965-67 AFTER SHAVE FOR DRY OR SENSITIVE SKIN - SPICY
2 oz. tan & white tube, tan cap. O.S.P. 89¢ C.M.V. $4.00 mint.
Upside down label on right - rare. C.M.V. $12.00 mint.

1965-67 TALC FOR MEN - SPICY
3½ oz. Bamboo style box. OSP 89c CMV $5.00 MB $3.00 CO

1965-67 AFTER SHAVE SPRAY-SPICY
5½ oz. Bamboo style can, tan cap. OSP $1.50 CMV $5.00 MB $3.00 CO

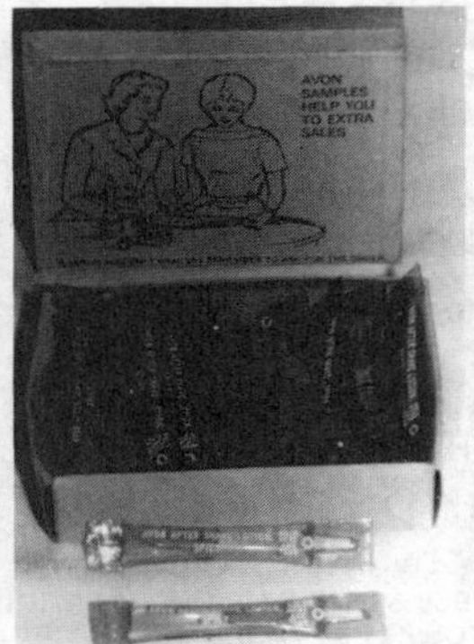

1961 SPICY AFTER SHAVE SAMPLES
Plastic sample tubes of Spicy After Shave Lotion. Full box of 30. Same samples also came in Cream Hair Dress, Rich Moisture Cream & Dew Kiss. CMV 25c each sample or $5.00 for full box of 30 mint.
Comes in 2 different boxes.

Left to Right: **1967-76 OATMEAL SOAP SPICY**
Large bath size & 3 oz. size in brown & white wrapper. OSP 60c CMV $2.00

1965-67 OATMEAL SOAP SPICY
Brown & white wrapping. O.S.P. 49¢ C.M.V. $7.00

1965 SPICY THREE
Brown box holds 2 bars of Spicy Oatmeal Soap & Spicy Talc for Men. OSP $1.85 CMV $22.50 MB

1967-74 TALC FOR MEN - SPICY
3½ oz. brown & white container. OSP 98c CMV $1.00 Upside down label CMV $8.00

1965-67 AFTER SHAVE SPRAY - SPICY
5½ oz. Bamboo style can, gold cap. O.S.P. $1.50 C.M.V. $6.00

1967 TWICE SPICE
Brown Striped box holds 4 oz. Spicy After Shave Lotion & Spicy Talc for Men. OSP $2.23 CMV $14.00 MB

1965-67 COLOGNE PLUS SPICY
2 oz. gold ribbed cap. O.S.P. $2.50 C.M.V. $20.00 in box. Bottle only $17.50

1965-67 AFTER SHAVE LOTION SPICY
4 oz. tan cap, O.S.P. 98¢ C.M.V. $7.00

1966 Only - SPICE 'O' LIFE SET
Box holds Spicy Talc for Men & 4 oz. After Shave Lotion. Came out at Fathers Day. OSP $1.96 CMV $22.50 MB

1968 SPICY TREASURES
Brown chest type box holds 4 oz. Spicy After Shave Lotion & 3½ oz. Talc for Men. O.S.P. $2.23 C.M.V. $14.00 M.B.

1965 HOLIDAY SPICE
Brown & white box holds Spicy Talc for Men & 4 oz. Spicy After Shave Lotion.
OSP $1.85 CMV $22.50 MB

1965-66 OVERNIGHTER
Brown vinyl zippered bag holds Spicy Talc, 4 oz. Spicy After Shave Lotion & bar of Spicy Oatmeal soap for Men.
OSP $7.50 CMV $22.50 MB

1965 CHRISTMAS WREATH
Gold box holds two 4 oz. bottles of Spicy After Shave Lotion with tan caps.
O.S.P. $1.95 C.M.V. $20.00 M.B.

1965 FIRST EDITION SPICY
Book type box holds 4 oz. Spicy After Shave Lotion & Spicy Talc for Men.
OSP $1.69 CMV $22.50 MB

SPORTS RALLY

1966-68 SPORTS RALLY BRACING LOTION
4 oz. glass bottle with blue cap. OSP $1.50 CMV $10.00 MB $6.00 BO

1966-68 BRACING TOWELETTE
Blue & white box holds 12 packets.
O.S.P. $1.25 C.M.V. $5.00 M.B.

1966-68 SPORTS RALLY SOAP ON A ROPE
4 oz. soap on white rope. OSP $1.50 CMV $12.00 $17.50 MB

1966-68 AEROSOL DEODORANT
4 oz. red, white & blue can, white cap.
OSP $1.25 CMV $3.00 MB $2.00 CO

1966-68 SPORTS RALLY HAIR DRESS
4 oz. red & white tube, red cap. OSP $1.00 CMV $3.00 $5.00 MB

1966-68 SPORTS RALLY ALL PURPOSE TALC
3½ oz. blue & white cardboard container.
OSP $1.00 CMV $3.00 $5.00 MB

1966-68 SPORTS RALLY CLEAR SKIN SOAP
2 bars with blue band around them. O.S.P. $1.00 C.M.V. $4.00 ea. bar. $10.00 set.

1966-68 SPORTS RALLY CLEAR SKIN LOTION
4 oz. white plastic bottle, red cap. OSP $1.25 CMV $4.00 MB $3.00 BO

1966-68 SPORTS RALLY BRACING TOWELLETTE
Contains 50 Towellettes in foil packet.
C.M.V. $10.00 M.B.

TAI WINDS

1971-72 TAI WINDS GIFT SET
5 oz. green glass bottle with green caps. Yellow bands 5 oz. embossed soap.
S.S.P. $6.99 C.M.V. $12.00 M.B.

1971-79 TAI WINDS COLOGNE
5 oz. green glass, blue-green cap & yellow ribbon. OSP $6.50 CMV 50c

1971-76 TAI WINDS SPRAY TALC
7 oz. blue-green & yellow can. O.S.P. $4.00 C.M.V. $1.00

1971-75 TAI WINDS AFTER SHAVE
5 oz. clear glass, blue-green cap, yellow ribbon. O.S.P. $5.00 C.M.V. $1.50 M.B.

1972-79 TAI WINDS SOAP ON A ROPE
Yellow soap on rope. OSP $4.00 CMV $3.00 MB

TRAZARRA

1978-80 TRAZARRA PRODUCTS
COLOGNE
4 oz. clear glass, gold cap. CMV 50c.
AFTER SHAVE
4 oz. clear glass, gold cap. CMV 50c.
TALC
3.5 oz. brown cardboard, plastic top & bottom. CMV 50c.
FRAGRANCE SAMPLE INCH
1 inch glass vile in paper holder. CMV 25c.
SOAP ON A ROPE
Tan soap on brown rope. CMV $2.00 MB.
ROLL ON DEODORANT
2 oz. brown plastic. CMV 50c. Pictured larger than actual size to other products.

TRIBUTE

1964-65 TRIBUTE SHAVE SET
Blue box holds 6 oz. After Shave Lotion & can of Foam Shave Cream. OSP $4.25 CMV $27.50 MB

1963-64 TRIBUTE GIFT SET NO. 1
Blue & silver box holds Tribute Talc, Foam Shave Cream & After Shave After Shower Spray. OSP $6.00 CMV $35.00 MB

1963-64 TRIBUTE GIFT SET NO. 2
Blue & silver box holds 6 oz. Tribute After Shave Lotion, Talc & Aerosol Deodorant OSP $6.50 CMV $35.00 MB

1963-68 TRIBUTE AFTER SHAVE SAMPLES
Box holds 30 foil samples. CMV $7.00 MB

1966-67 TRIBUTE SOAP
Blue & silver box holds 2 white bars with blue & silver centers. O.S.P. $1.75 C.M.V. MB $18.00
1963-66 TRIBUTE SOAP
Single bar in blue box. O.S.P. $1.75 CMV $22.50 MB

1963-66 TRIBUTE TALC
4 oz. blue & silver can, blue cap. O.S.P. $1.75 C.M.V. $6.00 mint.
1963-66 TRIBUTE AFTER SHAVE AFTER SHOWER SPRAY
5½ oz. blue & silver can & cap. O.S.P. $2.50 C.M.V. $6.00 mint.

1963-68 TRIBUTE AFTER SHAVE LOTION – LEFT
6 oz. silver & blue cap. O.S.P. $2.50 C.M.V. $6.00 mint
1968-72 TRIBUTE AFTER SHAVE RIGHT
4 oz. blue label, blue & silver cap. Same bottle also reads After Shave Lotion on label. O.S.P. $2.25 C.M.V. $2.50 mint.

1969-72 TRIBUTE SPRAY TALC
7 oz. blue can. O.S.P. $3.00 C.M.V. $1.00
Upside down label - rare. C.M.V. $15.00
1964-66 TRIBUTE SHAMPOO
Blue & silver tube. O.S.P. $1.75 C.M.V. $4.00
1963-66 TRIBUTE ELECTRIC PRE-SHAVE LOTION
4 oz. blue & silver cap. O.S.P. $1.75 C.M.V. $8.00 MB $5.00 BO

1963-67 TRIBUTE AEROSOL DEODORANT
3 oz. blue & silver can & cap. O.S.P. $1.75 CMV $6.00 MB $4.00 CO
4 oz. size same can, 1967 only. O.S.P. $1.50 CMV $6.00 MB $4.00 CO
1963-66 TRIBUTE CREAM HAIR DRESS
4 oz. blue & silver tube & cap. O.S.P. $1.75 C.M.V. $4.00 M.B.
1963-66 TRIBUTE FOAM SHAVE CREAM
6 oz. blue & silver can & cap. Came in regular & mentholated. O.S.P. $1.75 C.M.V. $6.00 M.B.

1964-66 TRIBUTE COLOGNE FOR MEN
4 oz. blue & silver top, cap & neck tag. O.S.P. $2.50 C.M.V. with tag $10.00 $12.00 mint.
1967-68 TRIBUTE ALL PURPOSE COLOGNE
4 oz. blue & silver top, cap & neck tag. O.S.P. $3.00 C.M.V. with tag $9.00 $12.00 mint.

1967-68 WILD COUNTRY BODY POWDER
6 oz. brown & white cardboard box. O.S.P. $4.00 CMV $8.00 mint.
1969-70 WILD COUNTRY COLOGNE SPRAY
2½ oz. white coated plastic bottle with silver cap. O.S.P. $4.00 C.M.V. $4.00 MB $2.50 BO

WEEK END

1979-80 WEEK END PRODUCTS
AFTER SHAVE
4 oz. emerald green glass wood cap. SSP $3.99 CMV .50c
COLOGNE
Same bottle as after shave. SSP $4.99 CMV .50c
WEEKEND SOAP FOR MEN
Green wrapped bar. SSP $1.00 CMV .50c
WEEKEND SAMPLES
Box of 10 green samples. CMV .25c
WEEKEND GET A WAY BAG
Green nylon bag. Does not say Avon. But has weekend tag. SSP $4.99 CMV $4.00 mint.

1979-80 WEEKEND PRODUCTS
Green packaging
SPRAY TALC
CMV .50c
ROLL-ON DEODORANT
CMV .50c
SHOWER SOAP ON A ROPE
Tan soap on green rope. CMV $3.00 MB

WILD COUNTRY

1976-80 WILD COUNTRY AFTER SHAVE
5 oz. bottle after shave, brown cap. OSP $5.00 CMV 50c
1977-79 WILD COUNTRY TALC
3.5 oz. cardboard container. OSP $2.50 CMV 50c
1976 WILD COUNTRY BELT BUCKLE
Sold by family fashions by Avon with purchase of other Wild Country products. OSP $1.99 CMV $3.00
1977-80 WILD COUNTRY SOAP
3 oz. soap. OSP $1.25 CMV $1.00

1977 WILD COUNTRY GIFT SET
Box holds 1.5 oz. talc & 3 oz. after shave in plastic bottle with brown cap. O.S.P. $3.49 C.M.V. $3.50 M.B.
1977-78 WILD COUNTRY GIFT SOAP
Metal container holds 5 oz. bar of white Wild Country soap. SSP $2.99 CMV $3.00 MB. Also came with label printed upside down on bottom of can. CMV $8.00

1973-74 WILD COUNTRY HAND CREAM
3 oz. brown & white plastic tube with brown cap. S.S.P. $1.75 C.M.V. $1.75
1975-77 WILD COUNTRY DEODORANT
4 oz. brown & white, white cap. O.S.P. $1.00 CMV 75c

1970-71 WILD COUNTRY SADDLE KIT
Brown & white cowhide kit holds Wild Country 6 oz. cologne, Foam Shave Cream & Spray Talc. OSP $16.00 CMV $17.00 MB

1975-77 WILD COUNTRY SPRAY DEODORANT - UPSIDE DOWN LABEL
4 oz. brown & white can, white cap. Was filled by mistake upside down at factory. OSP $1.00. CMV upside down label only $8.00

1970 WILD COUNTRY COLOGNE SAMPLES
Box of 10 sample packets. CMV .50c box

1978 WILD COUNTRY PENDANT
Silver & Ivory bull head. Neck chain for men. Avon on back. S.S.P. $8.99 C.M.V. $4.00 M.B.

1978 WILD COUNTRY ROLL ON DEODORANT
2 oz. white & brown plastic bottle. S.S.P. 99¢ C.M.V. 50¢

1967-76 WILD COUNTRY SOAP ON A ROPE
Ivory colored bar with bulls head in center. Round. O.S.P. $4.00 C.M.V. $4.00

1970-73 WILD COUNTRY FOAM SHAVE CREAM
11 oz. brown can. O.S.P. $1.75 C.M.V. $1.00

1969-77 WILD COUNTRY SPRAY TALC
7 oz. brown can. O.S.P. $4.00 C.M.V. 50¢ with special upside down label. C.M.V. $10.00

1971-76 WILD COUNTRY AFTER SHAVE
4 oz. silver label & black cap. O.S.P. $4.50 C.M.V. $1.00

1971-74-78 WILD COUNTRY TALC
3½ oz. brown shaker top container. O.S.P. $1.50 C.M.V. 50¢ Reissued in 1978

COLOGNE
6 oz. bottle with silver cap & label. O.S.P. $4.00 C.M.V. $2.50

1968-80 WILD COUNTRY ALL PURPOSE COLOGNE
6 oz. silver cap & label. OSP $6.50 CMV $1.00

1976-78 WILD COUNTRY SOAP ON A ROPE
Not shown- squared side, not round. OSP $4.00 CMV $4.00 MB

WINDJAMMER

1973 CANADIAN WINDJAMMER SOAP-ON-A-ROPE
C.M.V. $10.00 M.B.

1968 WINDJAMMER SPRAY TALC
7 oz. blue can. O.S.P. $2.50 C.M.V. $3.00

1969-72 WINDJAMMER RUB DOWN COOLER
10 oz. plastic bottle, blue & gold cap, lettering gold. Also came with blue lettering. OSP $3.00 CMV $1.00 $2.50 MB

1968-69 WINDJAMMER COLOGNE
5 oz. blue glass bottle & cap with ring. Painted label. OSP $4.00 CMV $8.00 MB $5.00 BO

Right: **1969-72 WINDJAMMER COLOGNE**
5 oz. blue glass & cap with blue paper label. OSP $4.00 CMV $2.00 BO $3.50 MB

MEN'S SETS OF 1930'S

WARNING!! Grading condition is paramount on sets. CMV can vary 50% on grade. Refer to page 5 on Grading.

1938-39 VALET SET
Speckled box holds 4 oz. After Shave, maroon can of Talc for Men, Smokers Tooth Powder & tube of Shaving Cream. O.S.P. $1.65 C.M.V. $100.00 set mint.

1936-38 MEN'S TRAVEL KIT
Leather case 7¼" x 6½" x 2" holds 4 oz. After Shave Lotion, Talc for Men, Shaving Cream & tube of Styptic. OSP $2.01 CMV $80.00 mint.

1938-42 MEN'S TRAVEL KIT
Brown leather zipper case holds maroon can of Talc for Men, tube of Shaving Cream & Styptic & 4 oz. After Shave Lotion. OSP $2.16 also came with inside case striped instead of checked as shown. CMV Both $65.00 MB

1934-35 MEN'S SHAVING SET
Wood grained box holds 4 oz. After Shave Lotion, can of Talc for Men & Smokers Tooth Powder & tube of Bayberry Shaving Cream. O.S.P. $1.65 C.M.V. $165.00 set.

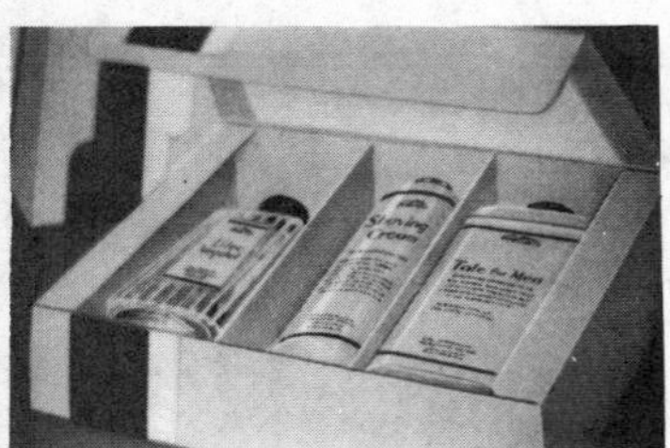

1931-36 ASSORTMENT FOR MEN
Green box holds tube of Shaving Cream & green can Talc for Men & choice of 4 oz. Bay Rum or 2 oz. Lilac Vegetal. O.S.P. $1.20 C.M.V. $110.00 M.B.

1938-39 HEADLINER FOR BOYS
Maroon & gray striped box holds tubes of Hair Dress & Tooth Paste with Tooth Brush. O.S.P. $1.10 C.M.V. $50.00 M.B.

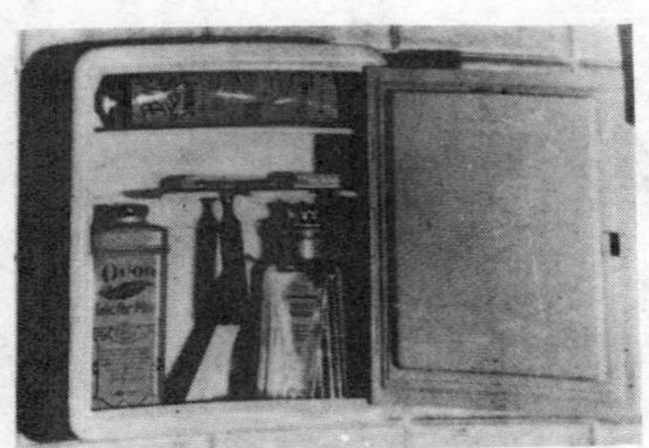

1931-34 SHAVING CABINET
White enamel cabinet with mirror on door. Cabinet is 8" high, 6½" wide & 2 3/8" deep. Label on door reads "Gem Micromatic Shaving Cabinet. Avon Products." O.S.P. $2.50 C.M.V. $75.00 empty.

1937-39 BRUSHLESS SHAVE SET
Speckled box holds 4 oz. After Shave Lotion, maroon can of Talc for Men & tube of Brushless Shaving Cream. O.S.P. $1.10 C.M.V. $75.00.

1930-32 HUMIDOR SHAVING SET
Gold & black metal box holds 4 oz. Bay Rum, 2 oz. Lilac Vegetal, Styptic Pencil, Tube of Menthol Witch Hazel Cream, Bayberry Shave Cream & green can of Talc for men. O.S.P. $2.50 C.M.V. $215.00 M.B.

1936-37 MEN'S PACKAGE
Maroon box holds can of Talc for Men, 4 oz. After Shave Lotion, turquoise can of Smokers Tooth Powder & tube of Shaving Cream. OSP $1.65 CMV $90.00 MB

1931-34 ASSORTMENT NO. 7 FOR MEN
Avon box holds can of Talc for Men, 4 oz. bottle of Bay Rum & tube of Bayberry Shaving Cream, 2 yellow Cannon wash cloths & 1 yellow Cannon towel. O.S.P. $2.00 C.M.V. $110.00 set mint

1933-36 MEN'S TRAVEL KIT
Black leather case 7¼" x 6½" x 2". Holds green tube of Bayberry Shaving Cream, 4 oz After Shave Lotion, Styptic Pencil & green can of Talc for Men. O.S.P. $1.95 C.M.V. $100.00 mint.

1938-39 SMOKERS TRIO
Green box holds 6 oz. Antiseptic, Tooth Brush & green can of Smokers Tooth Powder. O.S.P. $1.39 C.M.V. $70.00 M.B.

1936-37 ASSORTMENT FOR MEN
Wood grained paper box holds tube of Shaving Cream & can of Talc for Men & choice of 4 oz. Bay Rum or After Shave Lotion. O.S.P. $1.15 C.M.V. $80.00 M.B.

1938-39 ESQUIRE SET OR COUNTRY CLUB SET
Same set as above & same price, only name changed. C.M.V. $80.00 ea. set.

MEN'S SETS OF 1940'S

WARNING!!
Grading condition is paramount on sets.
CMV can vary 50% on grade.
Refer to page 5 on Grading.

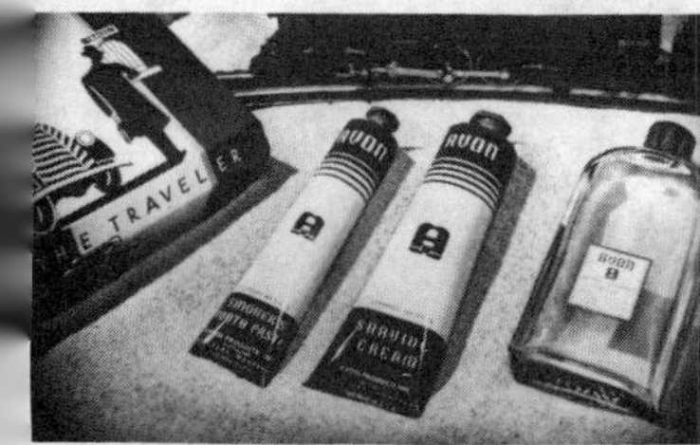

1941-45 TRAVELER SET
Maroon & ivory box holds 4 oz. After Shaving Lotion, maroon tubes of Smokers Tooth Paste & Shaving Cream. O.S.P. $1.00 C.M.V. $60.00 M.B.

1946-49 MEN'S TRAVEL KIT
Brown flip open leather case holds can of Talc for Men, 4 oz. After Shaving Lotion, Styptic Cream & choice of tube of Shaving Cream or Brushless Shaving Cream. OSP $4.17 CMV $75.00 MB

1946-49 TRAVELER SET
Maroon & white box holds 4 oz. After Shave Lotion, maroon tubes of Smokers Tooth Paste & Shaving Cream. OSP $1.25 CMV $65.00 MB

1940-41 ESQUIRE SET
Maroon box holds 4 oz. bottle of Bay Rum, tube of shaving cream, can of talc for men. O.S.P. $1.15 C.M.V. $75.00M.B.

1948 PLEASURE CAST SET
Blue box holds 2 oz. bottles with maroon caps in Deodorant for Men & Cologne for Men & tube of Brushless or Regular Shaving Cream. O.S.P. $1.69 C.M.V. $65.00 MB

1946-49 MODERN KNIGHT
Maroon & white box holds 2 oz. Deodorant for Men, can of Talc for Men & 4 oz. After Shaving Lotion. OSP $1.75 CMV $85.00 MB

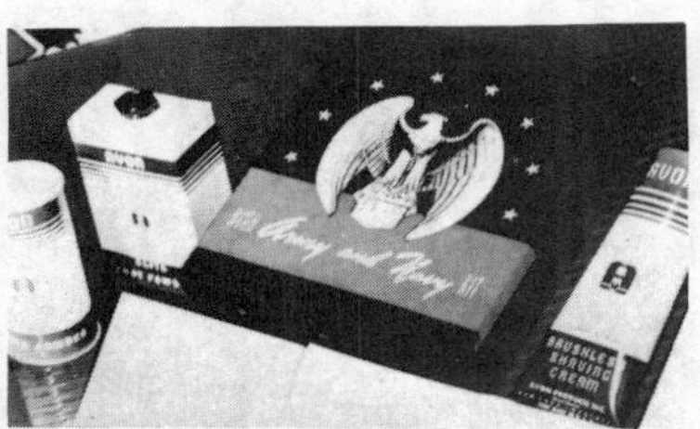

1943-46 ARMY & NAVY KIT
Blue & red box holds tube of Brushless Shaving Cream & maroon paper box of Elite Foot Powder & paper carton of Tooth Powder. O.S.P. $1.46 C.M.V. $80.00 M.B.

1941-42 ARMY & NAVY KIT
Blue & red box with Eagle on lid holds 4 oz. After Shave Lotion, maroon tube of Brushless Shaving Cream & maroon can of Elite Powder. Each in maroon & ivory boxes. O.S.P. $1.35 C.M.V. $75.00 M.B.

1940-42 BRUSHLESS SHAVE SET
Maroon & ivory box with man fishing, holds 4 oz. After Shave Lotion, maroon can of Talc for Men & tube of Brushless Shave Cream. O.S.P. $1.10 C.M.V. $65.00 M.B.

1943-46 BRUSHLESS SHAVE SET
Maroon & white box holds tube of Brushless Shave Cream, 4 oz. After Shave Lotion & maroon paper box of Talc for Men. O.S.P. $1.35 C.M.V. $75.00 M.B.

1946-49 BRUSHLESS SHAVE SET
Maroon & white box holds can of Talc for Men, tube of Brushless Shaving Cream, & 4 oz. After Shaving Lotion. O.S.P. $1.40 CMV $67.50 MB

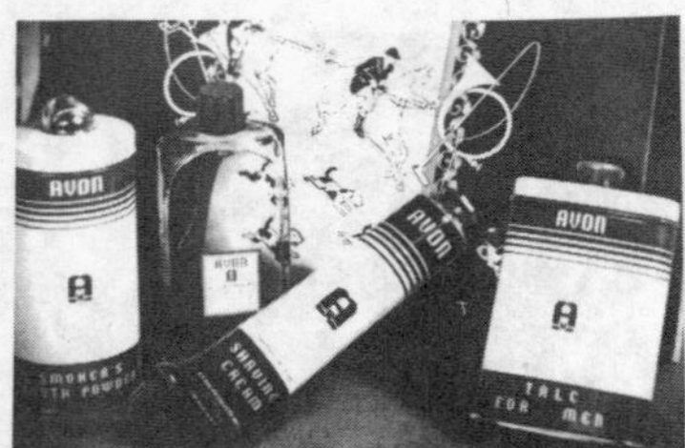

1940-42 VALET SET
Maroon & white box holds 4 oz. After Shaving Lotion, maroon cans of Talc for Men & Smokers Tooth Powder & tube of Shaving Cream. O.S.P. $1.69 C.M.V. $80.00 M.B.

1940-46 OLYMPIC SET
Maroon & ivory box holds 6 oz. bottle of Hair Lotion, tube of Shaving Cream & 4 oz. After Shaving Lotion. O.S.P. $1.29 C.M.V. $85.00

1939-41 COUNTRY CLUB SET
Box holds 4 oz. bottle of After Shave tube of shaving cream, can of talc for men. OSP $1.00 CMV $62.50 MB

1945-46 VALET SET
Maroon & ivory box holds 4 oz. After Shaving Lotion, tube of Shaving Cream, Talc for Men & Smokers Tooth Powder, both came in maroon paper containers with flat top lids & also pouring lids with caps. O.S.P. $1.85 C.M.V. $100.00 M.B.

1946-49 OLYMPIC SET
Maroon & white box holds tube of Shaving Cream, 6 oz. bottle of Hair Lotion & 4 oz. After Shaving Lotion. O.S.P. $1.65 C.M.V. $85.00 M.B.

1940-42 COUNTRY CLUB SET
Maroon & ivory box holds 4 oz. After Shaving Lotion, maroon can of Talc for men & tube of Shaving Cream. OSP $1.00 CMV $72.50 MB

1943-45 VALET SET
Maroon & ivory box holds 4 oz. After Shaving Lotion, 3 oz. tube in box of shaving cream. 2 5/8 oz. paper talc & 3.5 oz. paper side, tin flat top & bottom Smokers Tooth Powder. OSP $1.79 CMV $100.00 MB

1940-42 COMMODORE SET
Maroon & ivory box holds 4 oz. After Shaving Lotion, maroon can of Talc for Men & 2 white hankerchiefs. OSP $1.35 CMV $67.50 MB

1943-46 COUNTRY CLUB SET
Maroon & white box holds 4 oz. After Shave Lotion. 2 5/8 oz. paper box of Talc for men & 3 oz. tube of Shaving Cream. Talc came with flat paper top lid or cap lid as shown. OSP $1.15 CMV $75.00 MB

1946-49 VALET SET
Maroon box holds maroon can of Smokers Tooth Powder, Talc for Men, 4 oz. After Shaving Lotion & tube of Shaving Cream. O.S.P. $2.00 C.M.V. $75.00 M.B.

1943-46 COMMODORE
Maroon & white box holds 4 oz. After Shave Lotion, 2 white handkerchiefs & maroon paper box of Talc for Men. OSP $1.50 CMV $72.50

1943-46 COUNTRY CLUB SET
Maroon & white box holds 4 oz. After Shave Lotion, maroon flat top paper box of Talc for Men & tube of Shaving Cream. OSP $1.15 CMV $75.00 MB

MEN'S SETS OF 1950'S

WARNING!! Grading condition is paramount on sets.
CMV can vary 50% on grade.
Refer to page 5 on Grading.

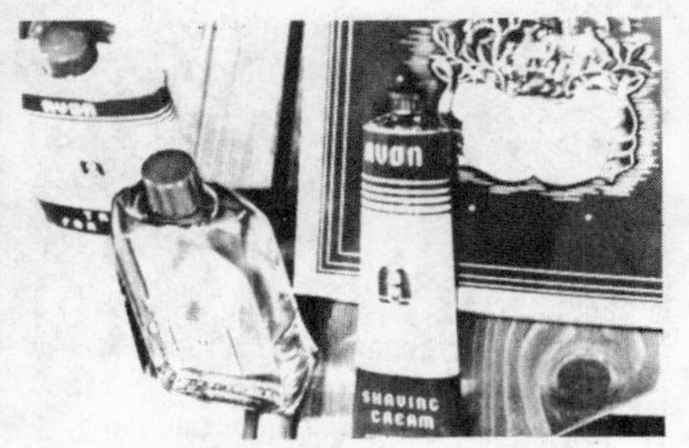

1946-49 COUNTRY CLUB
Maroon & white box holds tube of Shaving Cream, 4 oz. After Shaving Lotion & can of Talc for Men. OSP $1.35 CMV $67.50 MB

1953-54 BEFORE & AFTER
Silver, white & green box opens up to 4 oz. Cologne for Men & choice of cream or liquid Hair Lotion. O.S.P. $1.69 C.M.V. $40.00 M.B.

1957 MAN'S WORLD
Box has choice of 2 cream or liquid hair lotionsin 4 oz. size.. OSP $1.49 CMV $26.00 MB

1955 PIGSKIN PARADE
Red & green box holds tube of Creme Shappoo, youths tooth brush, Chap Check & 2 oz. bottle of Hair Guard & a plastic football OSP $1.95 CMV $52.50 MB

1956-57 TOUCHDOWN
Green, red & gold box holds 2 oz. bottles of Hair Guard with red cap & Hand Guard with green cap & small Football Soap. OSP $1.29 CMV $55.00 MB

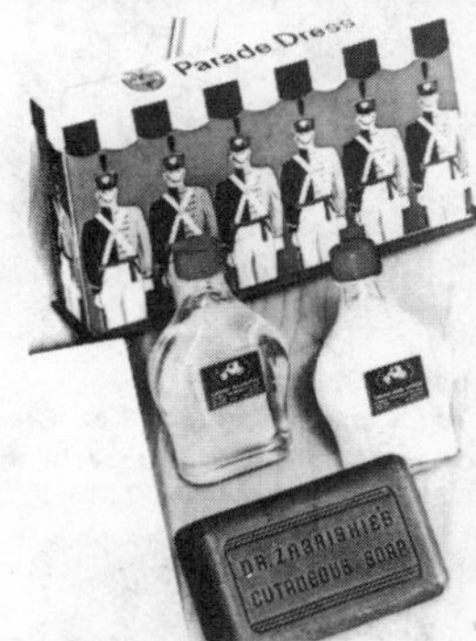

1953-54 PARADE DRESS
Red, white & blue soldier box holds 1 oz. bottle ofliquid shampoo & 1 oz. cream or liquid Hair Lotion, & 1 bar of Dr. Zabriskie's Soap. OSP $1.19 CMV $70.00 MB Set also came with 2 shampoo's & 1 hair lotion with no soap. Same CMV

1954 CLASSIC SET
Red & white box with horse head on box holds green can of talc for men, 2 oz. deodorant green label, 4 oz. cologne, silver label, all have red caps. Rare. O.S.P. $2.25 C.M.V. $75.00

1957 HAIR TRAINER & COMB SET
6 oz. bottle, white cap, red & white label. Came in box with comb. O.S.P. 79¢ CMV $15.00 BO $27.50 MB

1953-54 AVON SERVICE KIT
Green & red box holds tan plastic apron with 4 oz. plastic bottle of after shaving lotion with red cap, tube of brushless shaving cream, chlorophyll tooth paste, Dr. Sabriskie's Soap, comb & tooth brush. O.S.P. $3.95 C.M.V. $55.00 M.B.

1954 BACKFIELD
Red & green box holds 2 oz. bottle of Hair Guard with red cap & 2 oz. Hand Guard with green cap. Tube of Chap Check & small brown Football Soap. O.S.P. $1.95 C.M.V. $60.00 M.B.

1952 CHANGING THE GUARD
Red, white & blue guard house box holds 2 oz. Hair Guard with red cap & 2 oz. Hand Guard with blue cap. Came with outer box. OSP $1.00 CMV $60.00 MB

1953 ROUGH 'N' READY
White, red & green box holds 4 oz. Cream Hair Lotion, Chap Check & Dr. Zabriskie's Soap. OSP $1.25 CMV $47.50 MB

1957 ON THE GO
Brown leatherette bag holds green can of Talc for Men, 2 oz. Deodorant for Men, 4 oz. After Shave Lotion & can of Shaving Cream in choice of Kwick Foaming Lather, Brushless or Electric Pre-Shave Lotion. O.S.P. $8.95 C.M.V. $45.00 M.B.

1951-52 AVON SERVICE KIT
Red & green box holds canvas apron with 4 oz. plastic bottle of After Shaving Lotion with red cap. Dr. Zabriskie's Soap, tube or brushless shaving cream, tooth paste, tooth brush & comb. O.S.P. $3.90 C.M.V. $55.00 M.B.

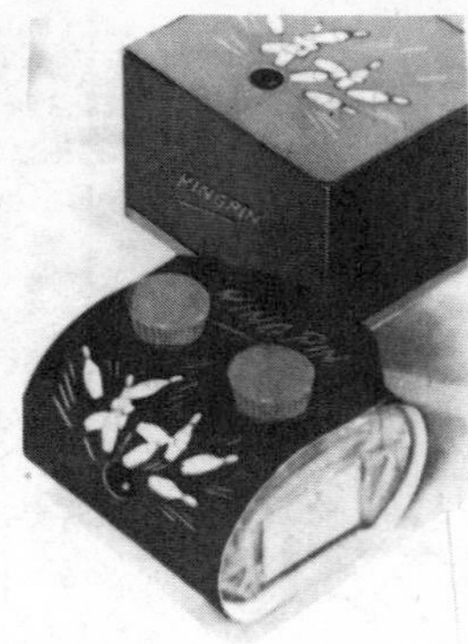

1953 KING PIN
Red & green box holds two 4 oz. bottles of After Shave Lotion wrapped in green King Pin wrappings. OSP $1.18 CMV $40.00 MB

1952-54 PLEASURE SHAVE
Green box with red & white barber pole holds 2 tubes of shaving cream in choice of brushless or lather. O.S.P. 98¢ C.M.V. $22.00 M.B.

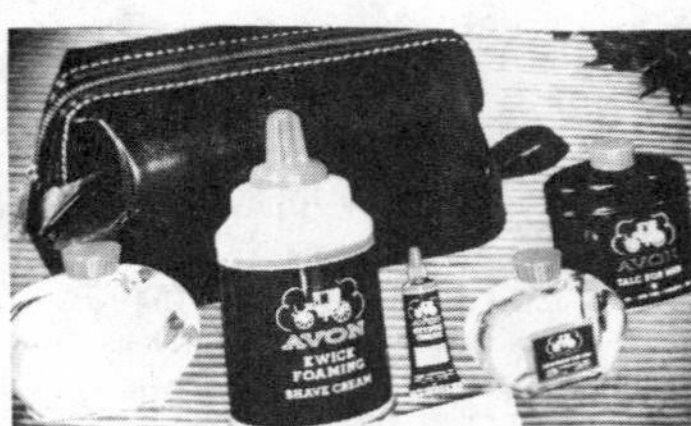

1956 THE TRAVELER
Brown leatherette bag holds choice of Shaving Cream in Kwick, Lather or Brushless, 4 oz. After Shaving Lotion, green can Talc for Men, 2 oz. Deodorant for Men & Styptic Cream. O.S.P. $7.95 C.M.V. $50.00 M.B.

1958 NEAT TRAVELER
Tan soft leather case holds 2 oz. Deodorant for Men, 4 oz. After Shaving Lotion choice of Kwick Foaming, Lather or Brushless Shaving Cream or Electric Pre-Shave Lotion & choice of Cream or Liquid Hair Lotion. O.S.P. $8.95 C.M.V. $45.00 M.B.

1950 Only YOUNG MAN SET
Red, white & green box holds tubes of Cream Hair Dress & Creme Shampoo, Comb & Nail file in brown leather case. O.S.P. $1.50 CMV $55.00 MB

1950-51 HI PODNER
White box holds 2 red leatherette cowboy Cuffs with tubes of cream hair dress & ammoniated tooth paste or dental cream and toothbrush. OSP $2.39 CMV $60.00 MB
1952 Hi Podner set is same except tube of cream hair dress was replaced with green tube of creme shampoo. CMV $60.00 MB

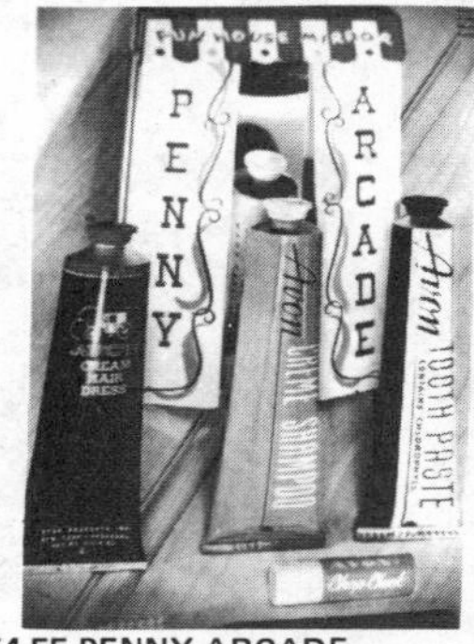

1954-55 PENNY ARCADE
Red & white with center foil mirror, holds tubes of Cream Hair Dress, Creme Shampoo & Chlorophyll Tooth Paste, Tooth Brush & Chap Check. O.S.P. $2.25 C.M.V. $55.00 M.B.

1953-55 MEN'S TRAVELING KIT
Choice of brown leatherette or plaid case. Holds 4 oz. After Shave Lotion, 2 oz. Deodorant for Men, Styptic Cream & green can of Talc for Men. OSP $7.50 CMV $52.00 MB

1957 ATTENTION
Red & green box holds two 4 oz. bottles in After Shave Lotion & choice of liquid or cream Hair Lotion. OSP $1.49 CMV $32.50 MB

1955-56 GOOD MORNING
Red box with Geese holds choice of two 4 oz. bottles of Cream or Liquid Hair Lotion. OSP $1.18 CMV $26.00 MB

1958 OVERNIGHTER
Tan case holds 2 oz. Deodorant for Men & 2 oz. After Shaving Lotion & choice of 4 oz. liquid or cream Hair Lotion. O.S.P. $2.98 CMV $32.50 MB

1954 SMOOTH SHAVING
Green tubes with red caps had choice of brushless or lather shaving cream. O.S.P. 98¢ C.M.V. $22.50 M.B.

1953 SPACE SHIP
Blue box holds plastic space ship with tubes of Chlorophyll Tooth Paste & Creme Shampoo & Tooth Brush. OSP $2.10 CMV $55.00 MB

1959-60 LAMPLIGHTER
Lamp post on covered box. 2 oz. red plastic bottle of After Shave Lotion, 1½ oz. white plastic bottle of Spray Deodorant for Men, 2 oz. black plastic bottle of After Shower for Men. All have red caps. O.S.P. $2.98 C.M.V. $42.50 M.B.

1958 AVON GUARD
Red & blue box holds 2 bottles of Hair Guard & Hand Guard with red caps, white Avon Rocket Soap sits on top of bottles. O.S.P. $1.39 C.M.V. $65.00 M.B.

1958 HAPPY HOURS
Cu-Cu Clock on black & brown box. 2 oz. cologne, deodorant & after shave lotion. All have red caps. OSP $1.98 CMV $40.00 MB

1959 GROOMING GUARDS
Black flip open box with red inner box holds can of After Shower Powder for Men, 2 oz. Spray Deodorant for Men in white plastic & tube of Attention Cream Hair Dress & choice of 4 oz. After Shower for Men or After Shaving Lotion. OSP $4.95 CMV $60.00 MB

1958 COAT OF ARMS
Red, white, blue & gold box holds 6 oz. Kwick Foaming Shave Cream, 2 oz. Deodorant for Men & 2 oz. After Shave Lotion OSP $1.98 CMV $37.50 MB

1958 HAPPY HOURS SUBSTITUTE SET
Outer sleeve marked Happy Hours Sub holds tan vinyl case with 2oz. cologne, After Shave Lotion & deodorant. This is a rare set. Factory ran out of regular issue box & used overnighter case for short period. OSP $1.98 CMV $45.00 Set MB. Must have outer sleeve.

1956 TOP OF THE MORNING
Red, white, green & silver box holds can of Kwick Foaming Shave Cream & 2 oz. After Shave Lotion. OSP $1.59 CMV $37.50 MB

1959 OUT IN FRONT
Box with soldier on horse holds 4 oz. cream or liquid Hair Lotion & 2¾ oz. Spray Deodorant for Men in white plastic bottles. OSP $1.98 CMV $27.50 MB

1959 CAPTAIN OF THE GUARD
White tube, red cap of Cream Hair Dress and white plastic bottle, red cap of Spray Deodorant for men. O.S.P. $1.98 C.M.V. $35.00.

1954 SPORT WISE
Red, white & green box holds two 4 oz. bottles of after shave lotions. O.S.P. $1.18 CMV $27.50 MB

1957 GOOD CHEER
Men playing bass fiddle on green & red box. 2 oz. bottles of cologne, deodorant & after shave lotions. All have red caps. O.S.P. $1.98 CMV $40.00 MB

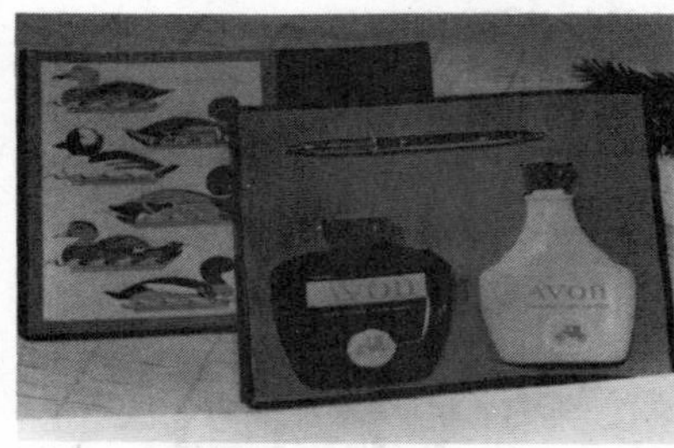

1958 MODERN DECOY
Blue & brown box with ducks on lid holds silver Paper Mate Capri Pen, 4 oz. Cream Hair Lotion & choice of 4 oz. After Shave Lotion, Cologne, Deodorant or Electric Pre-Shave Lotion. OSP $4.50 CMV $37.50 MB M.B.

1956 FATHER'S DAY SPECIAL SET NO. 1
Box with sail boat holds 2 - 4 oz. bottles of after shave with silver labels. Also came with choice of 4 oz. after shave and green can of talc for men or 4 oz. deodorant & 4 oz. after shave lotion. O.S.P. $1.39 C.M.V. $35.00 M.B.

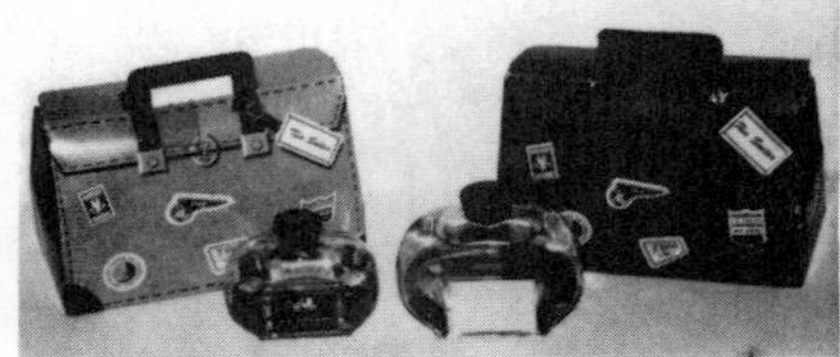

1953-54 TWO SUITER SET
2 different Olive tan box with airlines painted on sides, holds choice of 2 2 oz. deodorants for men or 1 2 oz. deodorant and 4 oz. after shave or 2 oz. deodorant and 2 oz. cologne for men. Sold at Father's Day. OSP $1.26 CMV $50.00 MB Light color box. $55.00 MB Dark color box.

1957 SAILING, SAILING
4 oz. clear glass, red cap, silver label. Choice of any 2 bottles of After Shaving Lotion, Electric Pre-Shave Lotion or Deodorant for Men. O.S.P. $2.07 C.M.V. $30.00 M.B.

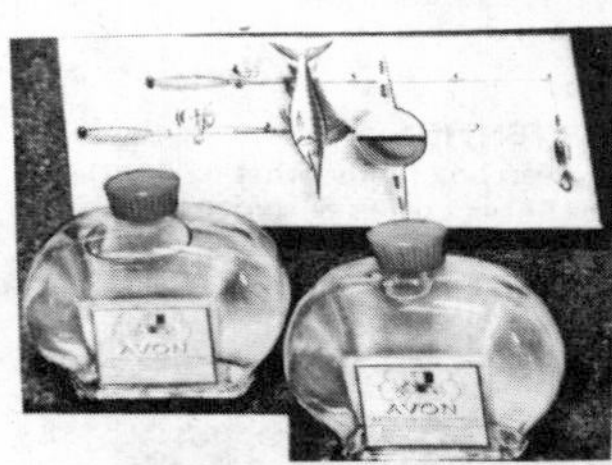

1955 PLEASURE CAST
Green & white box holds two 4 oz. bottles of After Shaving Lotion. O.S.P. $1.25 CMV $27.50 MB

1957 REFRESHING HOURS
Red & green hourglass box holds 4 oz. After Shaving Lotion & 4 oz. Deodorant for Men. OSP $1.69 CMV $27.50 MB

1959 TRIUMPH
Triumph box holds choice of 5 combinations of two 4oz. after shave lotions or electric pre-shave lotion & after shave lotion or after shave lotion & after shower powder for men. OSP ea. set $1.78 CMV ea. set $30.00 MB M.B.
Electric Pre-Shave Lotion & After Shower for Men in black glass, or After Shower Powder for Men & After Shower for Men in black glass. O.S.P. ea. set $2.14 C.M.V. $30.00 MB

1951 VALET
Green flip open box holds 2 oz. Deodorant for Men & tube of brushless or lather Shaving Cream & 4 oz. cream or liquid Hair Lotion. O.S.P. $2.00 C.M.V. $45.00 M.B.

1955-56 SHAVE BOWL SET
Bronze box holds wood shave bowl & bronze 4 oz. Deodorant for Men. O.S.P. $2.39 C.M.V. $55.00 M.B.

1955 SPACE SCOUT
Blue box holds wall charts of planets & tooth brush, white tooth paste, bottle of hair guard, tube of antiseptic cream & chap check. OSP $2.25 CMV $47.50 MB

1955 SATURDAY NIGHT
Plaid box holds 4 oz. Deodorant for Men, plaid bow tie & choice of 4 oz. cream or liquid hair lotion. O.S.P. $2.69 C.M.V. $42.50 MB

1956 VARSITY
Same set as Saturday Night only name changed. OSP $2.19 CMV $42.50 MB

1959-60 CAROLLERS
Xmas box with red & gold base holds red & black Stick Deodorant for Men & black & white can of After Shower Powder for Men & choice of 4 oz. After Shower for Men in black glass or Electric Pre-Shave Lotion or After Shave Lotion. O.S.P. $3.75 CMV $50.00 MB

1955 FLYING HIGH NO. 1 & NO. 2
Red & green box has 4 oz. After Shave Lotion & 4 oz. Deodorant for Men. No. 2 box has 4 oz. Deodorant for Men & green can Talc for Men. O.S.P. $1.49 C.M.V. $30.00 ea. set MB

1956 MORE LOVE THAN MONEY
Red, black & gold box holds 4 oz. Cologne for Men, 4 oz. After Shave Lotion & 2 oz. Deodorant for Men. Brown leather wallet with a new 1956 penny in it. O.S.P. $5.95 CMV $47.50 MB

1957 TRADING POST
Red & brown box holds 2 oz. bottle of Foamy Bath & Hair Trainer. Both have red caps. OSP 98c CMV $52.50 MB

1949-51 COUNTRY CLUB
Green flip open box with red inner box, holds green can of Talc for Men, 4 oz. After Shaving Lotion & choice of Lather or Brushless Shaving Cream. O.S.P. $1.85 CMV $47.50 MB

1957 SEND OFF
Red, white & black box holds two 4 oz. After Shave Lotions. O.S.P. $1.49 C.M.V. $27.50 M.B.

1958 STAGE COACH
Yellow stage coach box holds 2 oz. bottles of Hair Trainer & Foamy Bath. Both have red caps. OSP 98c CMV $50.00 MB

1954 PLEASURE CAST NO. 2
Green & white boxholds 4 oz. After Shave Lotion & green can of Talc. O.S.P. $1.25 C.M.V. $32.50 M.B.

1954 PLEASURE CAST NO. 1
Red & white box holds 2 oz. Deodorant for Men & 4 oz. After Shave Lotion O.S.P. $1.25 C.M.V. $32.50 M.B.

1957 MERRILY
Red, white & green box holds can of Kwick Foaming Shaving Cream & 2 oz. Deodorant for Men & 2 oz. After Shave Lotion. O.S.P. $1.98 C.M.V. $30.00 M.B.

1956-57 OVERNIGHTER
Brown aligator type bag holds 2 oz. After Shaving Lotion & 2 oz. Deodorant for Men, & choice of 4 oz. cream or liquid Hair Lotion. O.S.P. $2.75 C.M.V. $40.00 M.B.

1952-53 AVON CLASSIC
Silver & green box holds 2 oz. Deodorant for Men, green can Talc for Men & 4 oz. Cologne for Men. O.S.P. $2.25 C.M.V. $47.50 MB

1951 CLASSIC SET
Green box holds 4 oz. Cream Hair Lotion, tan bar of soap & 2 oz. deodorant. O.S.P. $1.75 set $55.00 M.B.

1957 MONEY ISN'T EVERYTHING
Red box with money written all over lid, holds 4 oz. Cologne for Men, 4 oz. After Shave Lotion & 2 oz. Deodorant for Men, plus brown leather Billfold. O.S.P. $5.95 C.M.V. $55.00 M.B.

1953 MANS SAMPLE CASE
Very rare brown leather case has three partitions inside to hold a Gilette brass razor, ½ oz. green sample tube brushless shaving cream, 3/4 oz. blue, white & green sample tooth paste tubes, 1 oz. bottle liquid shampoo, green label, 1 oz. bottle cream hair lotion, green label, 1/2 oz. bottle shaving lotion, green label 1/2 oz. bottle deodorant for men, green label, 1/2 oz. bottle cologne for men, silver label. All bottles have red caps. C.M.V. $125.00 complete set mint.

1949-51 PLEASURE SHAVE
Green box holds green can of Talc for Men, wood shaving bowl. 4 oz. after shave lotion with silver label. O.S.P. $2.35 C.M.V. $65.00 M.B.

1956 BEFORE AND AFTER
Red & silver box holds 4 oz. Electric Pre-Shave Lotion & 4 oz. After Shave Lotion. OSP $1.59 CMV $27.50 MB

1955 ROUND THE CORNER
Red & white striped box holds 2 oz. Deodorant for Men & can of Kwick Foaming Shave Cream. O.S.P. $1.59 C.M.V. $35.00 M.B.

1949-51 DELUXE TRIO
Stage coach on green flip open box with green & red inner box. Holds choice of 4 oz. cream or liquid hair lotion and 2 oz. deodorant for men and 2 oz. cologne for men. O.S.P. $2.00 C.M.V. $50.00 M.B.

1952 DELUXE TRIO
Same as 1949 set only has green removable lid. O.S.P. $2.00 C.M.V. $50.00 M.B.

1954-56 PERSONAL NOTE SET
Green & red box holds 4 oz. Cologne & Deodorant for Men with green label & gold ball point pen. OSP $2.95 CMV $50.00 MB

1949-50 VALET SET
Green box with choice of green can Talc for Men or Shaving Soap & 4 oz. Cologne for Men. O.S.P. $1.65 C.M.V. $40.00 M.B.

1952-53 U.S. MALE
Green & white mail box choice of two 4 oz. After Shave Lotions or 4 oz. After Shave Lotion & 2 oz. Deodorant for Men. O.S.P. $1.22 CMV $35.00 MB

1954-56 BLACK SHEEP
Red, white, green & black box holds black sheep soap with gold bell on neck & 4 oz. Cologne for Men & 4 oz. Deodorant for Men. OSP $2.50 CMV $90.00 MB

1957 HOLIDAY HOLLY
Green & White box holds 4 oz. After Shave Lotion & green can of Talc for Men. O.S.P. $1.39 C.M.V. $25.00

1954-55 COUNTRY CLUB
Red box holds green can of Talc for Men, 4 oz. After Shaving Lotion & tube of Brushless or Lather Shaving Cream. O.S.P. $1.85 CMV $47.50 MB
1956 Country Club Set came in green box with Golf Ball & Red Flag on lid & red lined box. Same contents as 1954 set. OSP $2.19 CMV $47.50 MB

1957 NEW DAY
Red top box holds 4 oz. Electric Pre-Shave Lotion & 4 oz. After Shaving Lotion. OSP $1.59 CMV $27.50 MB

1949-53 COMMODORE
Stage coach on green flip open box holds 2 oz. cologne & 2 oz. deodorant for men & green tube of brushless or lather shaving cream. O.S.P. $1.90 C.M.V. $45.00 M.B.

1953-54 QUARTET
Green & red box holds 2 tubes of Shave Cream brushless or lather, 2 oz. Deodorant for Men, green label & 4 oz. After Shave Lotion with silver label. O.S.P. $2.20 CMV $55.00 MB

1952-53 COUNTRY CLUB
Stage coach on green box lid with inner box in red. Holds green Talc for Men 4 oz. After Shave Lotion & tube of brushless or lather Shave Cream. OSP $1.85 CMV $47.50 MB

1953-56 DELUXE TRIO
Tan leatherette bag holds 2 oz. Cologne for Men & 2 oz. Deodorant for Men & choice of 4 oz. cream or liquid Hair Lotion. Avon on bag. Fold open top, no zipper. O.S.P. $2.25 C.M.V. $45.00

1957 CUFFLINKS
Black velour covered box holds 2 gold Cufflinks and 4 oz. Cologne & Deodorant for Men. O.S.P. $3.50 C.M.V. $45.00 M.B.

MEN'S SETS OF 1960'S

WARNING!! Grading condition is paramount on sets.
CMV can vary 50% on grade.
Refer to page 5 on Grading.

1965 ORIGINAL SET
Horse box holds two 4 oz. bottles of Original After Shave with red caps. O.S.P. $1.96 C.M.V. $20.00 M.B.

1965 CHRISTMAS CALL
Red box holds two 4 oz. bottles of Original After Shave Lotion. Red caps. OSP $1.95 CMV $20.00 MB

1961 GOLD MEDALLION GIFT SET
Gold box holds three individual men's grooming products in 2 oz. glass or plastic bottles. Glass bottles are: Spicy After Shave Lotion, Vigorate After Shaving Lotion, After Shaving Lotion,, After Shower Lotion, Electric Pre-Shave Lotion, Liquid Hair Lotion & Deodorant for Men. Plastic bottles are: After for Dry Sensitive Skin & Cream Hair Lotion. Set of 3 bottles. OSP $2.50 CMV $50.00 MB with outer sleeve

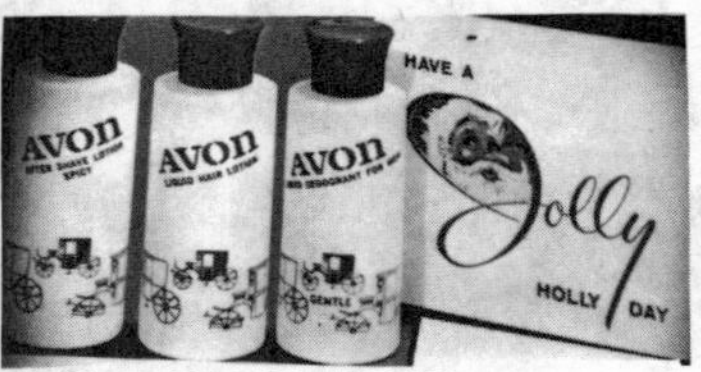

1963 JOLLY HOLLY DAY
Green & white box holds three 2 oz. white plastic bottles with red caps in choice of Vigorate, Spicy & Original After Shave Lotions, Electric Pre-Shave Lotion, liquid or cream Hair Lotion, Hair Trainer, After Shower Cologne for Men, & Liquid Deodorant for Men-gentle. O.S.P. $1.98 C.M.V. $20.00 M.B.

1962-63 DELUXE SET FOR MEN
Brown & gold box holds can of Deluxe Foam Shave Cream, Deluxe After Shave, After Shower Spray, & Deluxe Stick Deodorant normal. O.S.P. $4.98 C.M.V. $40.00 MB

1965 KING FOR A DAY
Box holds 3 white plastic bottles with red caps in choice of any 3 After Shave Lotions. Spicy, Original & Vigorate After Shave, After Shower Cologne for Men, Cream or Liquid Hair Lotion, Liquid Deodorant for Men, Electric Pre-Shave Lotion. O.S.P. $1.98 C.M.V. $20.00 M.B.

1962-63 HOLLY TIME
Red, white & green box holds choice of 2 plastic bottles in Cream Hair Lotion or Liquid Hair Lotion in glass bottle. O.S.P. $1.78 CMV $22.50 MB

1962-63 CHRISTMAS CLASSIC
Blue box holds choice of two 4 oz. bottles of 'Vigorate' After Shave Lotion, After Shower Cologne for Men, Original After Shave Lotion O.S.P. $1.79 C.M.V. $22.50 MB.

1960 FIRST PRIZE
Black, gold & red box holds three 2 oz. embossed Stage Coach bottles in choice of After Shower for Men, 'Vigorate' After Shaving Lotion, Cream Hair Lotion, Deodorant for Men, Liquid Hair Lotion, Electric Pre-Shave Lotion, After Shave for dry or sensitive skin. OSP $2.50 CMV $50.00 Set of 3 MB with outer sleeve

1962-63 UNDER THE MISTLETOE
Green box holds 4 oz. Electric Pre-Shave Lotion Spicy & After Shave Lotion Spicy. Red caps. OSP $1.78 CMV $22.50 MB

1964 CHRISTMAS TRIO FOR MEN
Winter scene box holds three 2 oz. red & white plastic bottles of any three of: Spicy After Shave Lotion, Original After Shave Lotion, 'Vigorate' After Shave Lotion, After Shower Cologne, Spicy Electric Pre-Shave Lotion, Liquid Deodorant for Men, Liquid Hair Lotion, Cream Hair Lotion or Hair Trainer. OSP $1.98 CMV $22.50 MB

1962 TRAVEL DELUX SET
Tan plastic bag with front & top zipper. Holds only 2 items. After Shave lotion & roll on deodorant as pictured. Outer sleeve list only 2 contents. O.S.P.$6.95 C.M.V. $35.00 M.B.

1960-62 OVERNIGHTER
Tan plastic travel case holds After Shaving Lotion, Roll on Deodorant for Men & Cream Hair Lotion, Cream Hair Lotion or Hair Trainer. OSP $1.98, CMV $22.50 MB.

1967 SMART MOVE
Orange & black box holds three 2 oz. plastic bottles of After Shave. Original or Spicy in red, Tribute or Spicy in black. White bottle came in both Original & Spicy. O.S.P. $4.00 C.M.V. $40.00 M.B.

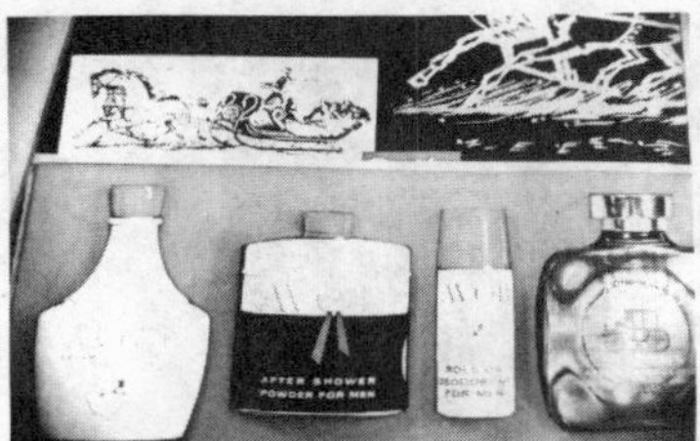

1960-61 DASHING SLEIGHS
Black, gold & red box holds 4 oz. plastic bottle of Cream Hair Lotion, can of After Shower Powder for Men, Roll on Deodorant for Men & choice of Vigorate or After Shower for Men in 8 oz. embossed stage coach bottle. OSP $5.17 CMV $62.50 MB

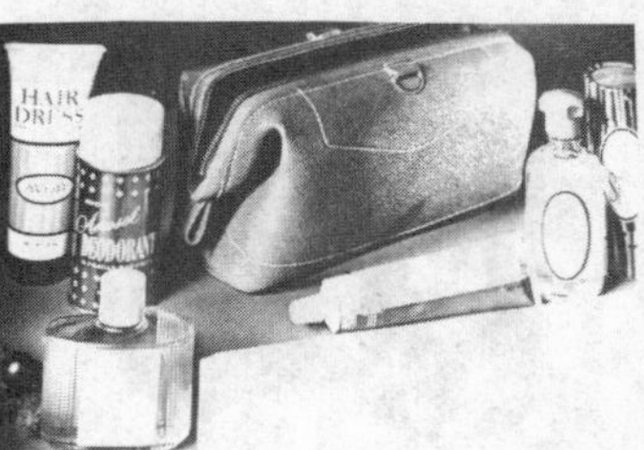

1966 MEN'S TRAVEL KIT
Brown travel bag holds Smoker's tooth paste, Clear Hair Dress, Spicy After Shave Lotion, Spicy Talc for Men, Aerosol Deodorant & choice of Electric Pre-Shave Lotion or Foam Shave Cream in regular or mentholated. O.S.P. $12.95 C.MV. $30.00 M.B.

1963-64 MEN'S TRAVEL KIT
Black leather bag holds can of After Shave After Shower Spray, Spicy, tube of Cream Hair Dress, tooth brush, Smokers tooth paste, Spray Deodorant for Men & choice of Foam Shave Cream, Spicy or Electric Pre-Shave Lotion. O.S.P. $11.95 C.M.V. $32.50 MB

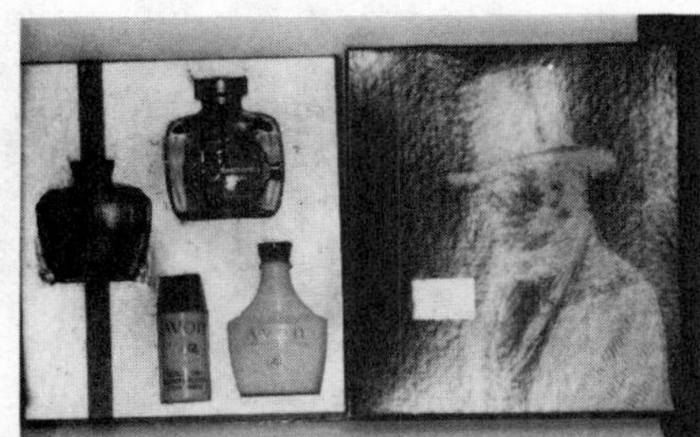

1961 FOR GENTLEMEN
Black, gold & red box holds 4 oz. plastic Cream Hair Lotion, Roll on Deodorant for Men, choice of Vigorate or After Shower for Men in 8 oz. embossed Stage Coach bottle & choice of 6 oz. Kwick Foaming Shave Cream or 4 oz. Electric Pre-Shave Lotion. OSP $5.17 CMV $62.50 ea. set MB, 2 different sets are shown.

1968 BOOTS & SADDLE
Cowhide type box holds 3 oz. bottles of Leather After Shave Lotion with red cap & Wild Country After Shave with black cap. O.S.P. $3.00 C.M.V. $18.00 M.B.

1966-67 BUREAU ORGANIZER
Wood grained plastic tray is 12¾" x 5½" Came with 2 oz. bottles with black 4A embossed caps in Tribute After Shave Lotion, Blue Blazer After Shave, Spicy After Shave & Leather All Purpose Cologne. O.S.P. $11.95 CMV $45.00 MB. Tray $15.00

1967 TAG-ALONGS
Box holds 3½ oz. red plastic bottle of After Shave Lotion Spicy & tan 3 oz. plastic bottle of Squeeze Spray Deodorant. Both have black caps. O.S.P. $2.50 C.M.V. $12.00 MB Bottles only $3.00 ea.

1959-60 TRAVEL DELUXE
Brown soft leather case holds After Shave Lotion, choice of Spray Deodorant or Roll on Deodorant for Men, 4 oz. Hair Lotion in Cream or Liquid or Attention & choice of Shave Cream in Kwick Foaming, Lather or Brushless or Electric Pre-Shave Lotion. O.S.P. $9.95 C.M.V. $35.00 M.B.

1969 THE TRAVELER
Box holds 2 plastic bottles in Bravo or Spicy After Shave & Spray Deodorant. OSP $2.50 CMV $8.00 MB

1968 OVERNIGHTER
Black box holds 3 oz. white plastic bottle of Squeeze Spray Deodorant & 3½ oz. black plastic bottle of Spicy After Shave Lotion. OSP $2.50 CMV $9.00 MB

1969 STRUCTURED FOR MEN
Silver box holds black plastic stair step base with 3 oz. bottles of Glass, Wood & Steel Cologne. O.S.P. $8.50 C.M.V. $15.00 in box, bottles & base only $10.00

1966-67 FRAGRANCE CHEST
Brown chest type box holds four 1 oz. bottles with silver caps, of after shave lotion in Tribute, blue glass, Leather in amber glass, Spicy in clear glass, Island Lime in green glass. OSP $4.00 CMV $40.00 MB. with outer sleeve $37.00 as pictured.

1966 AFTER SHAVE SELECTION
Fathers day box holds three 2 oz. bottles in choice of Leather All Purpose Lotion for Men, Blue Blazer, Island Lime, Tribute, After Shave Lotion Spicy, Bay Rum, Original & 4A After Shave Lotions. O.S.P. $2.98 C.M.V. $33.00 boxed with sleeve.

1969-70 COLOGNE TRILOGY
Brown & gold plastic box holds three 1½ oz. bottle with gold caps & labels, in Wild Country, Windjammer & Excalibur Cologne. Box is 6" high. O.S.P. $8.00 C.M.V. $17.50 M.B.

1968 GENTLEMAN'S COLLECTION
Brown plastic box holds three 2 oz. bottles with gold, silver & bronze caps. Came in Leather, Windjammer & Wild Country Cologne. O.S.P. $8.00 C.M.V. $20.00 M.B.

1965 MEN'S FRAGRANCE WARDROBE
Red box holds three 2 oz. bottles of After Shave Lotion in choice of Set A: Leather, Blue Blazer, After Shower Cologne. Set B: Leather, Tribute, Spicy. Set C: "4-A", Tribute, Original. Or Set D: Spicy, Bay Rum. Original. O.S.P. $3.50 ea. set. C.M.V. $33.00 ea. set boxed with sleeve.

1964 HOLLY STAR
Red, white & green box holds 4 oz. After Shave Lotion, Spicy & 3 oz. Talc for Men, Spicy. O.S.P. $1.59 C.M.V. $22.00 M.B.

1964 Only, SANTA'S TEAM
Blue box holds 4 oz. each of After Shave Lotion Spicy & Liquid Deodorant for Men. O.S.P. $1.59 C.M.V. $22.00 M.B.

1968 AFTER SHAVE CADDY
6 oz. rectangular bottle with silver cap & top fits in brown plastic box. Came in Leather & Island Lime After Shave. O.S.P. $7.00 CMV $14.00 MB

1964 HOLIDAY GREETINGS
Gold box holds 4 oz. bottle of Electric Pre-Shave Lotion Spicy & After Shave Lotion Spicy. O.S.P. $1.78 C.M.V. $22.00 M.B.

1962-63 GOOD CHEER
Red & gold box holds Spicy Talc for Men & choice of Spicy or Original After Shave Lotion. O.S.P. $1.78 C.M.V. $22.00 M.B.

1966 FOX HUNT
Fox hunt box holds two 4 oz. bottles with black caps in Leather All Purpose Cologne. O.S.P. $4.00 C.M.V. $30.00 M.B.

962-63 CHRISTMAS DAY
artridge box holds 4 oz. Liquid Deodorant or men-gentle & choice of Spicy or Original After Shave Lotion. O.S.P. $1.78 C.M.V. 22.00 M.B.

1964 CHRISTMAS MORNING
Red & gold box holds two 4 oz. bottles of After Shave Lotion Spicy. O.S.P. $1.78 C.M.V. $22.00 M.B.

1967-68 MEN'S AFTER SHAVE CHOICE
Black box holds 2 oz. After Shave Lotion in Wild Country with silver cap, Leather with gold cap & Tribute with blue cap. Late issue set came with all silver or gold caps. O.S.P. $5.00 C.M.V. $18.00 with color caps. $15.00 with silver or gold caps.

MEN'S SETS OF 1970'S

WARNING!! Grading condition is paramount on sets.
CMV can vary 50% on grade.
Refer to page 5 on Grading.

1978 WILD MALLARD
Brown & green ceramic organizer and white Clint Soap-On-A-Roap. Bottom says "Made in Brazil for Avon, May 1978". SSP $19.99 CMV $16.00 MB

1970 MASTER ORGANIZER
Wood grained plastic flip open box, holds choice of 3½ oz. Cologne or After Shave in Oland with tan bar of soap or Excalibur with blue bar of soap. O.S.P. $25.00 CMV $30.00 MB

1979 FRAGRANCE GIFT SET FOR MEN
Box holds choice of After Shave in plastic bottles in Cool Sage, Brisk Spice, or Light Musk or the same fragrances in cologne in glass bottles & matching talc. SSP $3.99 cologne set glass. CMV $3.99 MB, SSP $2.99 plastic, CMV $2.99 MB

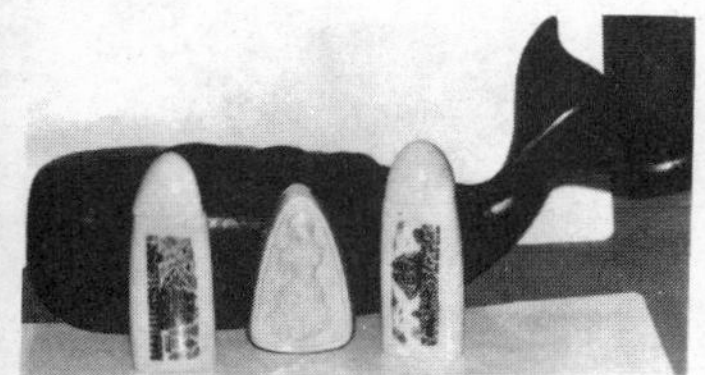

1973 WHALE ORGANIZER
Brown plastic whale holds 2-3 oz. ivory milk glass bottles and 5 oz. bar of soap. Came in Blend 7 or Deep Woods After Shave and Cologne. SSP $27.00, CMV $25.00 MB.

1974-75 TRAVEL SET FOR MEN
Brown box holds 3 oz. white plastic bottle with white cap. Choice of Deep Woods, Wild Country, Oland or Spicy After Shave and 1.5 oz. brown plastic bottle, white cap of Talc in choice of same fragrances. Short issue O.S.P. $4.00 C.M.V. $5.00 M.B.

1971 Only COLLECTORS ORGANIZER
Plastic brown duck holds two 3 oz. bottles of Cologne & After Shave. Tai Winds & Wild Country. Painted duck design on bottles & gold caps. 1 yellow bar of duck soap. O.S.P. $25.00 C.M.V. $27.50 M.B.

1972 AMERICAN EAGLE BUREAU ORGANIZER
Plastic case, wood carved like finish. Case holds 2 clear glass bottles with embossed eagles & a 5 oz. bar of soap. The bottles hold 3 oz. one has cologne & one after shave. Came in Deep Woods or Tai Winds. S.S.P. $20.00 C.M.V. $25.00 M.B.

APPLE BLOSSOM

1974-78 APPLE BLOSSOM PERFUMED POWDER MIST UP SIDE DOWN LABEL
Regular issue can went thru the assembly line and was filled upside down. O.S.P. $3.00 C.M.V. $10.00 upside down label only, mint.

1941-42 APPLE BLOSSOM PERFUME
1/8 oz. gold cap. OSP 75c CMV in box $45.00, $27.50 BO. This bottle has two different gold labels and round or flat top caps.

1941-42 APPLE BLOSSOM TOILET WATER
2 oz. pink cap, blue label. OSP $1.04 CMV $30.00 BO $40.00 in box shown

1925 APPLE BLOSSOM COMPLEXION SOAP
Yellow & pink wrapping on 3 bars of soap. O.S.P. 69¢ C.M.V. $80.00 M.B.

1974-77 APPLE BLOSSOM AFTER BATH FRESHENER
8 oz. pink plastic pink cap. O.S.P. $3.00 C.M.V. 50¢

1974-76 APPLE BLOSSOM PERFUMED POWDER MIST
7 oz. white and pink can with pink lid. O.S.P. $3.00 C.M.V. 50¢

1974-76 APPLE BLOSSOM COLOGNE MIST
2 oz. clear bottle with clear cap has inner pink & white cap. O.S.P. $3.00 C.M.V. 50¢

1974-76 APPLE BLOSSOM COLOGNE GELLE
3 oz. clear glass pink & white cap. O.S.P. $3.00 C.M.V. 50¢

1974-78 APPLE BLOSSOM CREAM SACHET
.66 oz. clear glass, pink & white cap. O.S.P. $1.25 C.M.V. 25¢

1974-78 APPLE BLOSSOM PERFUME DEMI STICK
.19 oz. pink and white. O.S.P. $1.25 C.M.V. 25¢

1974-78 APPLE BLOSSOM FRAGRANCE SAMPLES
10 foil packetts per box. C.M.V. 25¢

1941-43 APPLE BLOSSOM PERFUME
Box holds 1/8 oz. bottle with gold cap and label. OSP 75c, CMV $27.50 BO mint, $40.00 MB as shown.

1941-42 APPLE BLOSSOM TOILET WATER
2 oz. pink, white & blue. OSP $1.04 CMV $30.00 BO $45.00 MB as shown

1941-48 APPLE BLOSSOM BEAUTY DUST
6 oz. blue and white paper box. O.S.P. $1.10 C.M.V. $20.00 M.B. $15.00 for Beauty Dust only mint.

1941-44 APPLE BLOSSOM BODY POWDER
Blue feather design, flat sifter top container in special issue box as shown. O.S.P. 65¢ C.M.V. $25.00 M.B. as shown. Can only $22.00 mint.

1941-43 APPLE BLOSSOM COLOGNE
6 oz. bubble sided bottle with pink cap. OSP $1.00 CMV $45.00 BO $60.00 MB

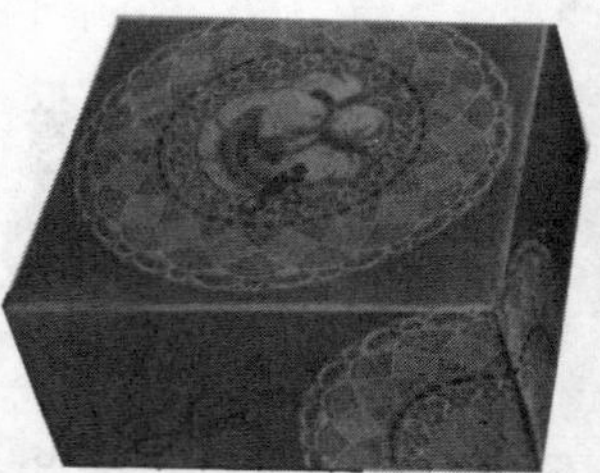

1942-43 APPLE BLOSSOM MOTHERS DAY BEAUTY DUST
Special issue blue, pink and white lace design box. Holds feather dèsign Apple Blossom beauty dust. Sold at Mothers Day only in this special box. O.S.P. $1.10 C.M.V. $30.00 M.B. as shown.

1941-48 APPLE BLOSSOM BEAUTY DUST
6 oz. size blue and white feather design paper container. O.S.P. $1.10 C.M.V. $18.00 mint. The Feather Plume outer box shown was issued Christmas 1942 only. Add $7.00 for this box.

1946 APPLE BLOSSOM BEAUTY DUST
Special short issue box holds regular issue beauty dust. O.S.P. $1.10 C.M.V. M.B. as shown $20.00

1943-45 APPLE BLOSSOM BEAUTY DUST
Blue & white feather design paper box. O.S.P. $1.10 C.M.V. $35.00 mint. $40.00 M.B. Outer box pictured in 1943 Christmas issue only. This is rare. C.M.V. $45.00 M.B. as shown.

1943 FLOWERTIME SET
Green satin lined box with flower carts on lid. Holds 6 oz. Apple Blossom cologne and Apple Blossom Body Powder. O.S.P. $1.65 C.M.V. $90.00

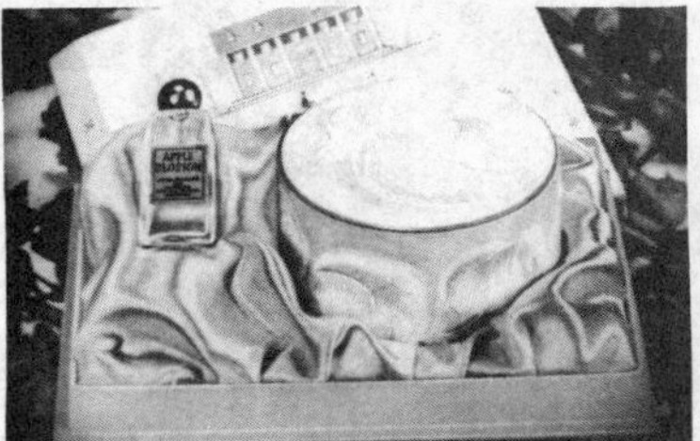

1941-42 COLONIAL SET
Satin lined box holds Apple Blossom Perfume with gold cap & blue feather box of Face Powder. O.S.P. $1.35 C.M.V. $80.00 M.B. Also came with perfume on right side of box.

1941 BLUE BIRD SET
Blue satin lined box holds Apple Blossom Perfume & Apple Blossom Body Powder & blue feather box of Face Powder. O.S.P. $1.65 C.M.V. $90.00 M.B.

1941 BLUE BIRD SET
Satin lined box holds Apple Blossom Body Powder, blue feather box of Face Powder & turquoise & gold lipstick. O.S.P. $2.25 C.M.V. $70.00 M.B.

1943-44 PETAL OF BEAUTY
Blue flowered box, pink satin lining, holds 6 oz. Apple Blossom cologne, pink cap and blue feathered Apple Blossom Beauty Dust. O.S.P. $2.20 C.M.V. $100.00 M.B.

ARIANE

1977-80 ARIANE PRODUCTS
SATIN BEAUTY DUST
Red plastic with silver rim. OSP $8.50 CMV $2.00

1977-80 PERFUME
.25 oz. glass stopper sealed in plastic. Came in red velvet bag in red box. OSP $15.00 CMV $10.00 MB in bag.

1977-80 ULTRA COLOGNE SPRAY
1.8 oz. clear glass bottle, red and silver cap. Red box. First Edition bottle was sold 2 campaigns only. Never pictured in Avon catalog. Regular issue does not say 1st edition. OSP $7.50 CMV 50c regular issue - 1st Edition bottle CMV $5.00 MB. Rare issue came with 1st Edition marked on backside. CMV not established.

1977-80 ARIANE ULTRA COLOGNE SAMPLE
Small sample packet came 10 to a box for 35¢ O.S.P. C.M.V. 10¢ each packet.

1977 ARIANE NECKLACE
Silver container holds small vial of Ariane cologne. 3 different ones came in red velvet bag. Used by Reps to demonstrate fragrance. 1 for Avon Reps C.M.V. $10.00 in bag. 1 for Presidents Club members only with P.C. on back of necklace C.M.V. $15.00 in bag and 1 for Managers, back side says (August Conference 77) C.M.V. $30.00 in bag. All came in red velvet bags, black tie string on Rep bag, silver string on on Presidents Club and red string on Managers.

1977-80 ARIANE SOLID PERFUME COMPACT
Red and silver box holds red and silver plastic compact. OSP $3.75 CMV 50c

1977 ARIANE FRAGRANCE SAMPLE
Red and silver packet holds small vial of cologne. Came with introduction sheet. Used by Reps only. Marked Not for Re-sale. C.M.V. 50¢

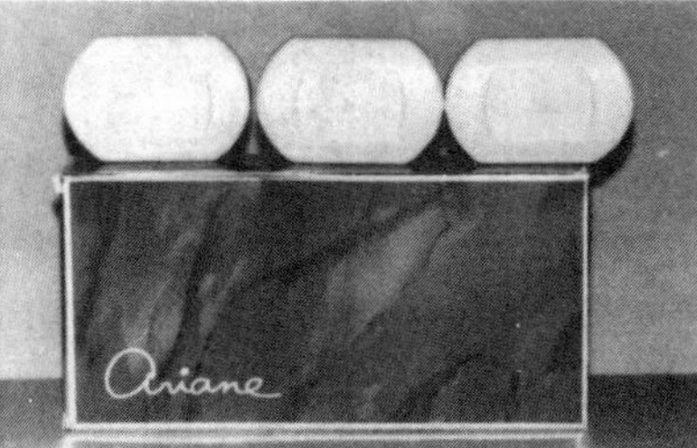

1978 ARIANE PERFUMED SOAPS
Red box holds 3 white soaps.
S.S.P. $4.95 C.M.V. $4.95 M.B.

1977 ARIANE ADDRESS BOOK
Red velvet booklet with note pad and address book. Chrome pen has no markings. Given to team leaders. C.M.V.$4.00

1978 ARIANE ULTRA CREME PERFUME
.66 oz. glass jar, silver cap. O.S.P. $4.50 C.M.V. 50¢

1978 ARIANE SATIN PERFUMED TALC
3 oz. red and silver container. O.S.P. $3.00 C.M.V. 50¢

1942 ATTENTION SACHET CHRISTMAS BOX
1¼ oz. bottle with turquoise cap sold 1942-48. Regular issue box in Misc. Powder Sachet section. The box pictured here is special issue for Christmas. O.S.P. 25¢ C.M.V. $18.00 M.B. as shown. $12.00 BO mint.

1942 ATTENTION SACHET
Special 1st issue blue box as shown. 1¼ oz. bottle, turquoise cap. O.S.P. $1.04. C.M.V. $20.00 M.B. as shown in this box. See Misc. Powder Sachet section for further details, on regular issue bottles and box.

See Page 5 for Grading Examples on Mint Condition

ATTENTION

Check index misc. section for Attention Powder Sachets & Bath Salts

1943 ATTENTION SACHET 57th ANNIVERSARY BOX
Special issue purple and pink box with flowers. Holds regular issue Attention powder sachet. Sold for 25¢ to celebrate Avons 57th Anniversary. C.M.V. $20.00 as shown. M.B.

1943-47 ATTENTION COLOGNE
6 oz. bubble sided bottle with pink tall or short cap. OSP $1.50 CMV $45.00 BO $60.00 MB

1941-43 ATTENTION BODY POWDER
Pink box, flat sifter top on paper container. O.S.P. 65¢ C.M.V. $25.00 M.B., can only $20.00 mint.

1943-44 then 46-48 ATTENTION BATH SALTS
Tulip "A" box holds 9 oz. or 8½ oz. glass jar with turquoise lid. O.S.P. 63¢ C.M.V. $25.00 M.B. $15.00 BO mint

1943-47 ATTENTION BODY POWDER
Blue & white cardboard with feather design. O.S.P. 65¢ C.M.V. $25.00 M.B. container only $20.00 mint

1942 Only - ATTENTION TOILET WATER
Special issue Christmas box holds 2 oz. Attention Toilet Water with purple cap and label. OSP 25c CMV $45.00 MB as shown $30.00 BO

1943-45 FLOWERTIME SET
Box holds 6 oz. Attention cologne & Attention Body Powder. O.S.P. $1.65
1943 set is green satin lined box with flower carts on lid. C.M.V. $90.00 M.B.
1944 set in plain box with flower design on lid. C.M.V. $90.00 M.B.
1945 set in white box with boy & girl in 1700 style dress under a tree. C.M.V. $90.00

1944 FLOWERTIME SET
Box with flowers on lid holds 6 oz. Attention cologne & Attention body powder. O.S.P. $1.65 C.M.V. $85.00M.B.

1943-45 PINK RIBBON SET
Blue & pink box holds blue & pink can of Attention Body Powder & paper box of Attention Bath Salts. O.S.P. $1.61 C.M.V. $60.00 for set in box.
1943-45 ATTENTION BODY POWDER
Blue & pink cardboard container. Came in Pink Ribbon set only. C.M.V. $25.00.
1943-45 ATTENTION BATH SALTS
9 oz. blue & pink cardboard container. Came in Pink Ribbon set only. C.M.V. $25.00.

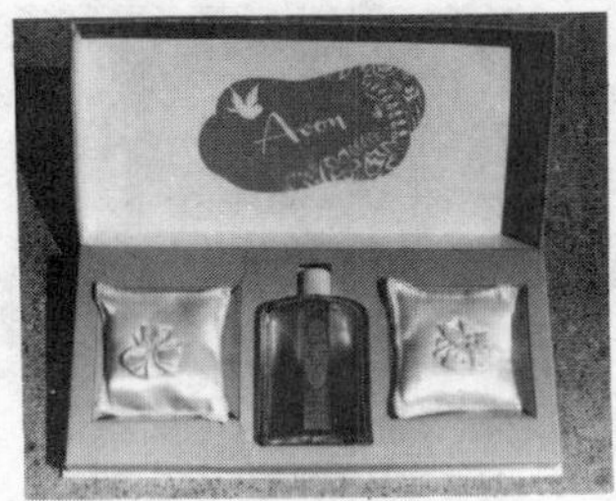

1943 Only SCENTIMENTS
2 oz. clear bottle toilet water, gold foil label, white cap or gold cap. White & pink satin sachet pillows. O.S.P. $1.85 C.M.V. $65.00 M.B.

LEFT 1942 Only ATTENTION TOILET WATER
2 oz. purple cap. O.S.P. 25¢ C.M.V. $40.00 B.O. $45.00 M.B.
1943-46 ATTENTION TOILET WATER
2 oz. bottle, came with gold ribbed cap or plastic cap. OSP $1.04 CMV $25.00 BO mint $35.00 MB

BABY PRODUCTS

1915 C.P.C. BABY BOOK
CMV $30.00 mint.

1946-50 LANOLIN BABY SOAP
Pink box holds 2 wrapped bars. O.S.P. 86¢ C.M.V. $35.00 M.B.

1955-61 BABY SOAP
Blue & white box holds Castile & Lanolin white cake baby soap. O.S.P. 29¢ C.M.V. $12.00 MB also came with "Castile with Lanolin" on box and printed on soap horizontal. Same CMV.

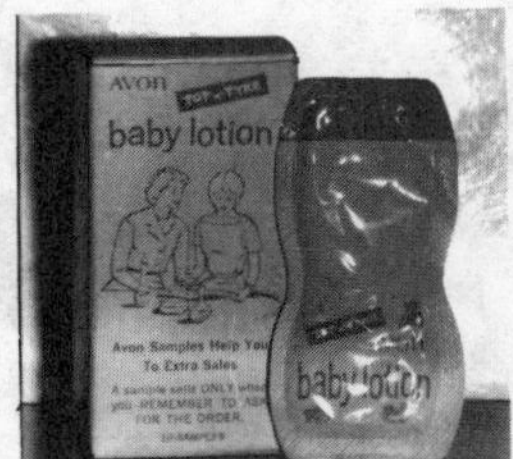

1964-68 BABY LOTION SAMPLES
White foil with pink & blue design. Came 10 to a box. CMV $4.00 box or 50c per sample.

1962-64 SWEETEST ONE BABY SET
Pink and white box holds 1 bar Baby Soap, Baby Powder & Lotion or Oil. Bar of soap came with blue ends, white center and white ends with blue center. OSP $2.07 CMV $40.00 MB.

1966 TREE TOTS SET
Box holds white plastic hair brush, 3 oz. plastic tube Non-Tear Gel Shampoo, 3 oz. Baby Soap with Lanolin & 6 oz. Nursery Fresh Room Spray. O.S.P. $3.00 C.M.V. $20.00 MB.

1973-76 BABY BRUSH & COMB SET
Yellow box holds small yellow plastic brush and comb. Avon on both. O.S.P. $3.50 C.M.V. $3.00 M.B.

1957-58 BABY & ME SET
Clear glass bottle baby lotion, white cap & Cotillion Toilet Water gold cap, pink paper around neck. Box white, blue & pink. OSP $1.98 CMV $45.00 MB

1951-55 BABY TALC
Blue & white box & can. O.S.P. 52¢ C.M.V. $18.00 in box. $13.00 can only.
1951-55 LANOLINBABY SOAP
Blue & white box & wrapping, holds 2 bars. O.S.P. 69¢ C.M.V. $25.00 in box.
1951-55 BABY LOTION
4 oz. white plastic bottle, blue cap. O.S.P. $1.00 C.M.V. $12.00 in box, bottle only $8.00.

1961-64 BABY CREAM
2 oz. blue & white tube. O.S.P. 89¢ C.M.V. $4.00
1961-64 BABY SOAP
Blue & white wrapper. O.S.P. 39¢ C.M.V. $8.00
1959-64 TOT 'N TYKE BABY SHAMPOO - 6 oz. white plastic bottle, blue cap. OSP 98c CMV $6.00 BO $7.00 MB
1958-64 BABY LOTION
6 oz. white plastic bottle, blue cap. OSP 98c CMV $5.00
1960-64 BABY OIL
6 oz. white plastic bottle, blue cap. OSP 98c CMV $6.00
1955-64 BABY POWDER
9 oz. blue & white can. OSP 79c CMV $10.00

1896 CALIFORNIA BABY SOAP
4 oz. white embossedbar in wrapping. O.S.P. 15¢ C.M.V. $60.00 M.B.

1954-56 BABY POWDER
2 oz. pink can & cap with paper label around can. Came in Little Lamb Set. Rare. C.M.V. $25.00
1954-56 BABY POWDER
2 oz. blue, white & pink can, pink cap. Came in Little Lamb Set. C.M.V. $20.00

1962-64 BABY SOAP
Came in Sweetest One baby set. White ends and blue center line. C.M.V. $6.00 mint.

1955-60 BABY OIL
8 oz. bottle with indented sides, white cap. O.S.P. 79¢ C.M.V. $15.00

1956-57 BABY LOTION
8 oz. bottle with indented sides, white cap. O.S.P. 89¢ C.M.V. $12.50 B.O. $15.00 M.B.

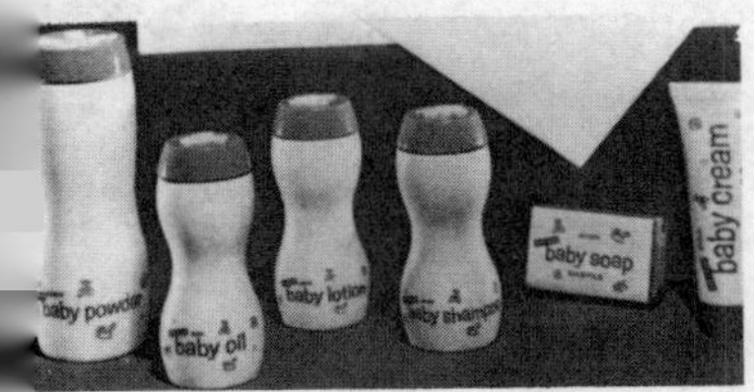

1964-68 BABY SHAMPOO
6 oz. white plastic bottle with blue cap. O.S.P. 98¢ C.M.V. $5.00
1964-68 BABY LOTION
6 oz. white plastic bottle with blue cap. O.S.P. 98¢ C.M.V. $5.00
1964-68 BABY CREAM
2 oz. blue & white tube with blue cap. O.S.P. 98¢ C.M.V. $3.00
1964-68 BABY POWDER
9 oz. white plastic bottle, blue cap. O.S.P. 98¢ C.M.V. $5.00
1964-66 BABY OIL
6 oz. white plastic bottle with blue cap. O.S.P. 98¢ C.M.V. $6.00
1964-68 TOT 'N TYKE BABY SOAP
Blue & white wrapper, white cake of baby soap. O.S.P. 39¢ C.M.V. $7.00

1968-75 BABY PRODUCTS
1969-74 SHAMPOO - blue, white & pink, 6 oz. plastic bottle. O.S.P. 98¢ C.M.V. 50¢
1968-79 NURSERY FRESH ROOM SPRAY - 6 oz. blue, white & pink can. OSP $1.50 CMV 50c also came with upside-down label CMV $8.00
1969-72 BABY POWDER
9 oz. blue, white & pink plastic bottle. OSP 98c CMV $2.00
1969-75 BABY CREAM
2 oz. tube, blue, pink & white. OSP 98c CMV 50c
1969-75 BABY SOAP
3 oz. bar wrapped in blue, pink & white paper. OSP 59c CMV 75c
1969-75 BABY LOTION
6 oz. blue, white & pink plastic bottle. OSP 98c CMV 50c

AVON COLOGNE

1941 AVON COLOGNE
6 oz. flat sided bottle. Soon after Avon Cologne was introduced the name was changed to Orchard Blossoms Cologne. O.S.P. 60¢ C.M.V. $50.00 B.O. $65.00 M.B.

1943 AVON COLOGNE, REPRESENTATIVE GIFT
6 oz. clear bottle, maroon & gold label, blue cap. Bottom label reads "This is a gift to our representatives & must not be offered for sale". Came in blue & pink box, pink ribbon on box & bottle. 57th Anniversary Campaign Card. C.M.V. bottle only $100.00 mint. M.B. $150.00. As shown.

AVONSHIRE BLUE

1975-76 AVONSHIRE BLUE BRUSH & COMB
Blue and white plastic. S.S.P. $4.00 C.M.V. $4.00 M.B.
1975-76 AVONSHIRE BLUE VANITY MIRROR
9½" long blue and white plastic. Avon on handle. S.S.P. $3.00 C.M.V. $3.00 M.B.

1971-74 AVONSHIRE BLUE
Wedgewood blue and white over clear glass.
COLOGNE DECANTER
6 oz. comes in Field Flowers, Brocade, Elusive, Charisma SSP $5.00 CMV $6.00 MB $3.00 BO
PERFUME CANDLE
holds Patchwork, Sonnet, Moonwind, Bird of Paradise, Charisma, Wassail, Roses, Roses, Bayberry, Frankincense & Myrrh. SSP $8.00 CMV $8.00 MB $6.00 CO
BATH OIL DECANTER
6 oz. holds Skin-So-Soft or Field Flowers, Bird of Paradise. SSP $6.00 CMV $6.00 MB $4.00 BO
SOAP
3 bars 2 oz. blue soap. SSP $2.00 CMV $6.00 MB

1972 AVONSHIRE BLUE SOAP DISH & SOAP - 6" long blue dish trimmed in white with white bar of soap. Came with oval soap & round soap. O.S.P. $4.50 CMV $8.00 oval, $23.00 round soap MB

BALLAD

1939-45 BALLAD PERFUME
3 dram glass stoppered bottle with gold neck cord & gold label at base of bottle. Front of box lays down. O.S.P. $3.50 C.M.V. $125.00 in box. Bottle only $90.00
See misc. perfume for 1 dram Ballad Perfume.

1945-53 BALLAD PERFUME
Gold & white box holds 3 dram glass stoppered bottle with gold neck cord & gold label at base of bottle. O.S.P. $3.50 C.M.V. $125.00 in box. $90.00 bottle only.

1945 BALLAD AWARD PERFUME
Avon label on bottom, Ballad label across top, glass stopper. C.M.V. $375.00 mint box.

1945 Only BALLAD PERFUME
3 dram, clear glass with gold neck cord & label, box gray, white & gold. O.S.P. $3.50 C.MV. $135.00 in this box. $90.00 bottle only.

BIRD OF PARADISE

1971-73 BIRD OF PARADISE PERFUMED SKIN SOFTENER
5 oz. blue glass jar with blue & gold lid. O.S.P. $4.00 C.M.V. $1.00
1973-76 BIRD OF PARADISE PERFUME SKIN SOFTENER
Jar plastic, lid same. (not shown) S.S.P. $2.00 C.M.V. 50¢.
1969-72 BIRD OF PARADISE COLOGNE FLUFF
3 oz. blue plastic coated bottle with gold top. Blue & gold neck tag. O.S.P. $5.00 C.M.V. $2.00.
1971-77 BIRD OF PARADISE PERFUMED POWDER MIST
7 oz. blue and gold can, gold cap. O.S.P. $4.00 C.M.V. 50¢

1971-78 BIRD OF PARADISE PERFUMED TALC
2 different labels. Left and center same labels but top is turquoise on one and dark blue on other. One on right is dark blue label and top. Each is 3½ oz. size. OSP $1.35 CMV 50c
Also came with upside down label CMV $8.00

1970-78 BIRD OF PARADISE SAMPLES
Bottle has white cap, blue foil envelopes. C.M.V. 25¢ ea.
1970-78 BIRD OF PARADISE DEMI-STICK
.19 oz. solid perfume, white cap. O.S.P. $2.00 C.M.V. 50¢
1971-76 BIRD OF PARADISE EMOLLIENT MIST
4 oz. blue & turquoise can with turquoise cap. O.S.P. $4.00 C.M.V. 50¢
1972-76 BIRD OF PARADISE HAND & BODY LOTION
8 oz. & 16 oz. turquoise plastic bottle & cap. O.S.P. $3.50 & $6.00 C.M.V. 50¢ ea.

1970-72 BIRD OF PARADISE PERFUME GLACE RING
Gold ring with turquoise top. Perfume glace inside. O.S.P. $10.00 C.M.V. $7.00.
1970-72 BIRD OF PARADISE ½ OZ. COLOGNE
½ oz. bottle with gold cap. O.S.P. $2.00 C.M.V. $2.00 M.B.

1977-78 BIRD OF PARADISE FOAMING BATH OIL
6 oz. blue plastic bottle and cap. O.S.P. $7.50 C.M.V. 50¢
1976-78 BIRD OF PARADISE CREAM SACHET
.66 oz. clear glass bottom, blue and gold cap. O.S.P. $3.00 C.M.V. 50¢

1970 BIRD OF PARADISE AVON AWARDS
Gold pin, bracelet & earrings with turquoise stones. C.M.V. pin $12.00, bracelet & earrings $20.00 M.B.

1970-76 BIRD OF PARADISE PERFUME ROLLETTE
1/3 oz. bottle with gold cap, turquoise & green box. O.S.P. $3.00 C.M.V. $1.00 M.B.

1970-72 BIRD OF PARADISE COLOGNE DECANTER
8" high 5 oz. clear glass with gold head. OSP $6.00 CMV $4.00 BO $6.00 MB

1970 BIRD OF PARADISE ROBE
Blue terry cloth robe given to Reps for selling 24 Bird of Paradise 3 oz. cologne mists in C-19-1970. Came S-M-L size. Bird of Paradise on pocket. C.M.V. $35.00

BIRD OF PARADISE ORDER BOOK COVERS
Left - Canadian. Presidents Club earned for eligibility into Presidents Club.
Honor Award earned for sales goal. Each came with pen in matching design. C.M.V. $5.00 ea. with pen.

1970 BIRD OF PARADISE ORDER BOOK COVER
Blue & turquoise, awarded for qualifying for Presidents Club, has matching pen. C.M.V. $7.50

1970 BIRD OF PARADISE SCARF
Awarded for selling cologne mists. Blue & turquoise silk. C.M.V. $10.00.

1973-76 BIRD OF PARADISE PERFUMED SKIN SOFTENER
5 oz. blue plastic jar gold and blue lid. O.S.P. $3.00 C.M.V. .25¢

1974-75 BIRD OF PARADISE SOAP
3 oz. blue bar with blue wrapper and floral center. O.S.P. $1.00 C.M.V. $1.00 mint.

1976-78 BIRD OF PARADISE SOAP
3 oz. blue bar with blue wrapper. O.S.P. $1.00 C.M.V. $1.00 mint

1970-71 BIRD OF PARADISE BATH BRUSH & SOAP
Blue box holds blue plastic bath brush & blue soap. O.S.P. $6.00 C.M.V. $8.00 M.B.

1969-75 BIRD OF PARADISE BATH OIL EMOLLIENT
6 oz. gold cap & neck tag. O.S.P. $7.50 C.M.V. $1.00

1969-72 BIRD OF PARADISE 4 OZ. COLOGNE COLOGNE
4 oz. gold cap & neck tag. O.S.P. $5.00 C.MV. $2.00.

1969-74 BIRD OF PARADISE BEAUTY DUST
6 oz. turquoise & gold paper box. O.S.P. $5.00 C.M.V. $3.00.

1970-76 BIRD OF PARADISE COLOGNE MIST
3 oz. blue plastic coated bottle with gold cap & neck tag. O.S.P. $7.00 C.M.V. $1.00.

1969-75 BIRD OF PARADISE CREAM SACHET
.66 oz. blue glass with gold lid. O.S.P. $3.00 C.M.V. 50¢.

1970-76 BIRD OF PARADISE SOAP
3 oz. bars blue soap in blue & turquoise box. 1st issue no flower on soap. 1972 soap had flower. SSP. $3.00 CMV $4.00 MB No flowers $6.00 MP

1971-72 BIRD OF PARADISE SCENTED HAIR SPRAY
7 oz. blue can & lid. OSP $1.50 CMV $3.00

1971-74 FOAMING BATH OIL
6 oz. blue plastic bottle with gold cap & blue & gold neck tag. O.S.P. $4.00 C.M.V. $2.00.

BLUE LOTUS

1967-72 BLUE LOTUS AFTER BATH FRESHENER
6 oz. glass bottle with blue cap. O.S.P. $3.00 C.M.V. $2.00

1968-72 BLUE LOTUS CREAM SACHET
.66 oz. blue frosted glass with blue cap. O.S.P. $2.50 C.M.V. $1.00.

1970-73 BLUE LOTUS FOAMING BATH OIL
6 oz. plastic bottle with blue cap. O.S.P. $3.50 C.M.V. $1.50.

1969-72 BLUE LOTUS CREAM LOTION
5 oz. plastic bottle with blue cap. O.S.P. $2.00 C.M.V. $1.50

1969-73 BLUE LOTUS DEMI STICK
.19 oz. white plastic with blue and green center. O.S.P. $1.00 C.M.V. $1.00.

1967-71 BLUE LOTUS PERFUME SOAP
3 oz. blue, white & purple wrapper. O.S.P. 75¢ C.M.V. $2.00.
1967-71 BLUE LOTUS PERFUMED TALC
3½ oz. cardboard container with plastic shaker top. O.S.P. $1.10 C.M.V. $2.00.
1967-71 BLUE LOTUS AFTER BATH FRESHENER SAMPLES
Box holds 10 samples. C.M.V. $1.50 per box

BRISTOL BLUE

1975 BRISTOL BLUE COLOGNE
5 oz. translucent blue glass filled with Moonwind, Sonnet or Imperial, Garden Cologne. OSP $6.00 CMV $4.00 BO $5.00 MB
1975-76 BRISTOL BLUE BATH OIL
5 oz. blue opaline glass decanter with plastic inner bottle that holds Skin-So-Soft bath oil. OSP $6.00 CMV $4.00 BO $5.00 MB
1975-76 BRISTOL BLUE SOAP DISH & SOAP
Translucent blue opaline glass dish with Moonwind, Sonnet or Imperial Garden soap. OSP $5.00 CMV $6.00 MB

BRIGHT NIGHT

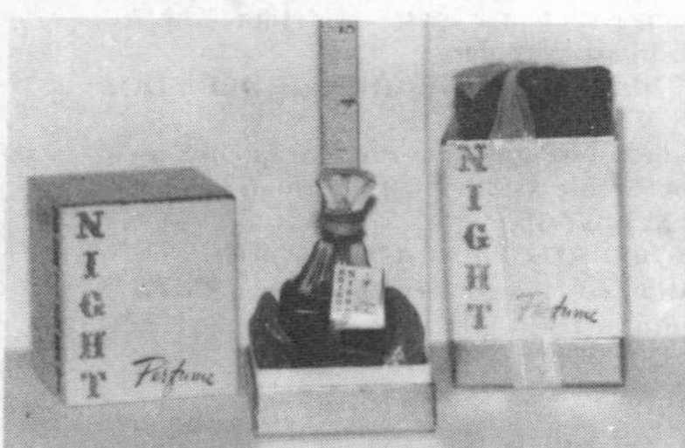

1954-59 BRIGHT NIGHT PERFUME
Gold & white box holds ½ oz. glass stoppered bottle with white label on gold neck cord. OSP $7.50 CMV $120.00 MB. Bottle only $75.00 mint. Also came with 1 dram perfume in felt wrapper on top of lid. Add $15.00 for 1 dram perfume with ribbon around box.

1956 MAGIC HOURS
Gold & white box holds Bright Night 2 oz. Toilet Water & white Cologne stick. O.S.P. $3.50 C.M.V. $45.00.

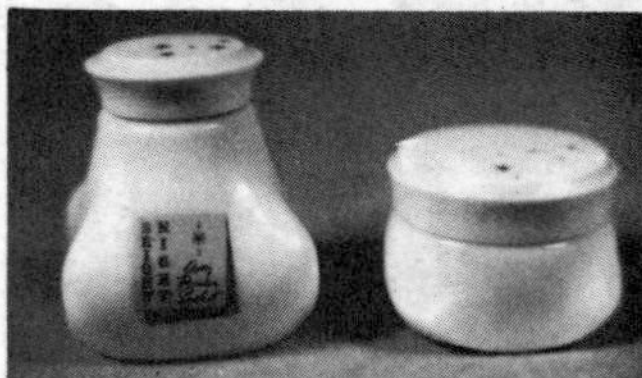

1955-61 BRIGHT NIGHT POWDER SACHET
.9 oz. 1¼, 1½ oz. white glass jar with stars on white lid. Front paper label. O.S.P. $1.50 C.M.V. $8.00 M.B. $10.00 1½ oz. rare, C.M.V. $20.00 M.B.
1954-61 BRIGHT NIGHT CREAM SACHET
White glass jar with stars on white lid. O.S.P. $1.50 C.M.V. $6.00 M.B. $8.00.

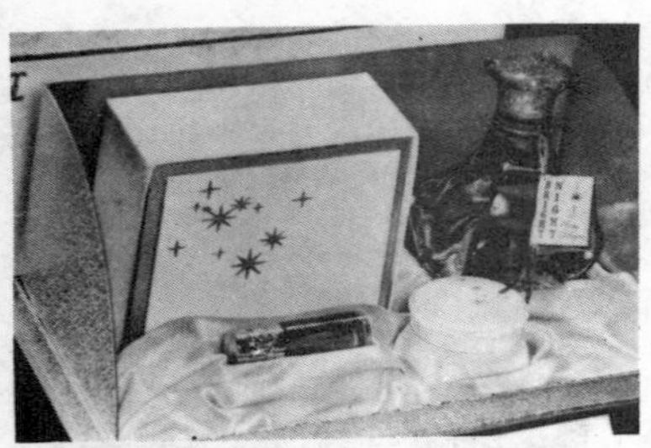

1955-56 MELODY
Gold & white box holds Bright Night 1 dram perfume, Cream Sachet, 4 oz. Cologne & Beauty Dust. O.S.P. $8.75 C.M.V. $85.00.

1958-61 BRIGHT NIGHT COLOGNE MIST
3 oz. white plastic coated over clear glass. Gold speckled cap, gold neck cord with white paper label. Came with 2 different caps. O.S.P. $2.75 C.M.V. $20.00 in box. $14.00 bottle only mint.

1958 GOLDEN GLAMOR
Gold & white box holds Bright Night Cologne Mist, 1 dram perfume, cream sachet & beauty dust. O.S.P. $8.95 CMV $95.00 MB.

1954-61 BRIGHT NIGHT COLOGNE
4 oz. gold speckled cap with gold neck cord & white paper label. OSP $2.50 CMV $20.00 MB $14.00 BO mint.

1955-61 BRIGHT NIGHT TOILET WATER
2 oz. gold speckled cap with white paper label on gold neck cord. OSP $2.00 CMV $20.00 MB $14.00 BO

1959-61 BRIGHT NIGHT BEAUTY DUST
White plastic box with gold stars on lid. OSP $2.95 CMV $8.00 CO $12.00 MB

1957 GOLDEN BEAUTY
Gold base box lined with gold acetate with gold plastic lid, holds Bright Night Beauty Dust, 4 oz. cologne, cream sachet & 1 dram perfume. O.S.P. $8.95 C.M.V. $85.00.

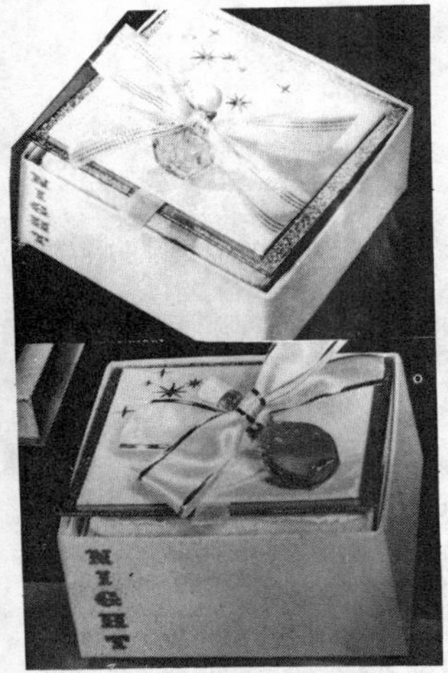

Top, 1957-58 BRIGHT NIGHT BEAUTY DUST
White cardboard box trimmed in gold. Came at Xmas with 5/8 dram Snowflake Perfume bottle with white ribbon & cap. O.S.P. $2.50 C.M.V. $30.00 M.B.
Bottom, 1956 BRIGHT NIGHT BEAUTY DUST
Same as above. Came at Xmas 1956 with long neck perfume bottle with white cap & ribbon. O.S.P. $2.50 C.M.V. $30.00 M.B.
1954-59 BRIGHT NIGHT BEAUTY DUST
Same powder box without perfume. O.S.P. 75¢ C.M.V. $18.00 Mint.

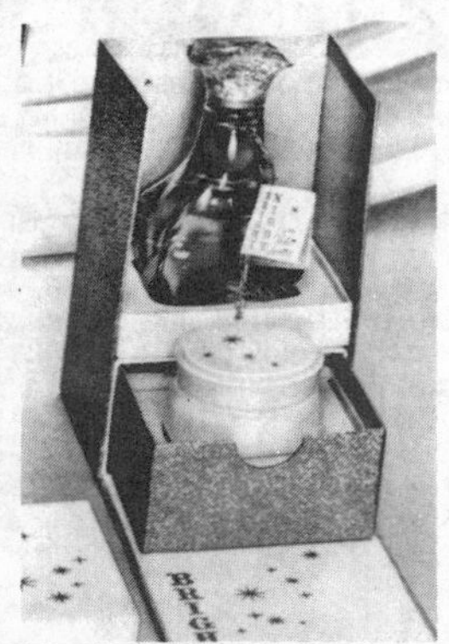

1957 BRIGHT NIGHT GEMS
Gold & white flip open box holds Bright Night 2 oz. Toilet Water in top & Cream Sachet in pull-out drawer in bottom. O.S.P. $3.50 C.M.V. $45.00 Mint.

BROCADE

1968-75 BROCADE CREAM SACHET
.66 oz. brown ribbed glass, designed cap. O.S.P. $3.00 C.M.V. 50¢.
1967-68 BROCADE CREAM SACHET
.66 oz. brown ribbed glass, label on top. OSP $3.00 CMV $2.00 BO $3.00 MB
1968 BROCADE TALC
2¾ oz. metal talc, brown, white and gold. Sold only in Perfume Pair set. C.M.V. $2.00

1967-71 BROCADE BEAUTY DUST
Brown ribbed plastic, patterened lid. OSP $6.00 CMV $6.00 MB $9.00
1971-75 BROCADE BEAUTY DUST
Pattern printed cardboard, non-refillable. OSP $5.00 CMV $3.00 CO $4.00 MB. Also came with upside down lettering CMV $6.00

1967-72 BROCADE 4 OZ. COLOGNE
Frosted ribbed glass with brown & white cap. OSP $6.00 CMV $2.00 MB $3.00
1967-72 BROCADE COLOGNE MIST
3 oz. ribbed frosted glass with brown & white cap. Some lids have design only & some say Brocade on top. OSP $6.00 CMV $2.00 BO $3.00 MB
1967-72 BROCADE COLOGNE MIST REFILL
3 oz. brown plastic coated bottle, white cap. OSP $4.00 CMV $3.00 BO $4.00 MB

1967-72 BROCADE PERFUME GLACE
Gold case. O.S.P. $5.50 C.M.V. $6.00 M.B. $9.00.

1967 BROCADE DELUXE GIFT SET
Brown & white box with white lining holds Brocade Beauty Dust, Perfume Rollette & Cream Sachet. O.S.P. $12.95 C.M.V. $35.00 M.B.

1967-74 BROCADE PERFUME POWDER MIST
Left: 7 oz. brown & white painted can with gold cap. O.S.P. $4.00 C.M.V. 50¢.
Right: 7 oz. brown & white paper label with gold cap, O.S.P. $4.00 C.M.V. $3.00.
Some came with 7 oz. weight in center label and some at bottom of can in front.

1969 MANAGERS BROCADE DEMO KIT
Brocade box holds round Brocade Talc & cologne mist. CMV $27.50 MB

Left-1969-72 BROCADE PERFUMED SKIN SOFTENER
5 oz. ribbed sides, brown glass, designed top. OSP $4.00 CMV $2.00 BO $3.00 MB
Center-1968-69 BROCADE PERFUMED SKIN SOFTENER
5 oz. ribbed sides, brown glass, label printed on top OSP $4.00 CMV $5.00 MB $3.00 BO
1968 only, BROCADE PERFUMED SKIN SOFTENER - Right
Manufactured during glass strike, 5 oz. round smooth brown glass, label painted on top. O.S.P. $4.00 C.M.V. $15.00 mint

BROCADE

1967-72 BROCADE PERFUME ROLLETTE
Left to Right: Brown frosted glass gold cap with 4A design. Ribs horizontal. OSP $3.00 CMV $3.00
Same as above only no 4A design OSP $3.00 CMV $3.00
Brown carnival glass, gold cap. Verticle ribs. O.S.P. $3.00 C.M.V. $8.00.
Brown frosted glass, brown & white paper label on cap. Ribs horizontal. O.S.P. $3.00 C.M.V. $4.00.

1968 BROCADE SOAP
Brown & white wrapper. Came in perfume pair only. C.M.V. $4.00 Mint.

1969-72 SCENTED HAIR SPRAY
7 oz. brown & white can OSP $1.50 CMV $3.00
1969-72 BROCADE PERFUMED TALC
3½ oz. brown & white cardboard O.S.P. $1.25 C.M.V. $1.50.

1967-69 BROCADE PERFUME OIL
½ oz. frosted brown glass with gold cap. O.S.P. $6.00 C.M.V. $5.00 M.B. $7.00.
1970-71 BROCADE ½ OZ. COLOGNE
Ribbed clear glass with gold cap. OSP $2.00 CMV $2.00 MB $1.00 BO

BUTTONS 'N BOWS

1949 BUTTONS & BOWS SONG SHEET
Green song sheet with words to help sell Quaintance products. 4¼" wide x 6½" high. C.M.V. $5.00

1961-63 CUTE AS A BUTTON
Pink & white box holds Buttons N Bows Nail Polish with white cap & pink & white lipstick. OSP $1.58 CMV $17.00 MB

1968-70 BROCADE COLOGNE SILK
3 oz. frosted bottle with gold cap. OSP $4.50 CMV $2.00 MB $4.50
1968-72 BROCADE FOAMING BATH OIL
6 oz. plastic bottle with gold cap. O.S.P. $4.00 C.M.V. $2.00.

1960-63 BUTTONS N BOWS BEAUTY DUST
Pink & white cardboard box with clear plastic lid. O.S.P. $2.25 C.M.V. $16.00.
1960-63 BUTTONS N BOWS CREAM SACHET
Pink glass jar with white & pink lid. OSP $1.35 CMV $8.00 BO $12.00 MB

1961-63 BUTTONS N BOWS NAIL POLISH
Pink & white box holds nail polish with white cap. OSP 69c CMV $8.00 in box $6.00 bottle only
1961-63 BUTTONS N BOWS LIPSTICK
Pink & white box holds pink & white striped lipstick. OSP 89c CMV $7.00 in box, $4.00 tube only.

1960-63 BUTTONS N BOWS COLOGNE
2 oz. clear glass, white cap, lettering pink, came with pink ribbon bow around neck. OSP $1.35 CMV $12.00 MB $9.00 BO
1960-63 BUTTONS N BOWS COLOGNE MIST
2½ oz. pink plastic with white cap. Bottom is 2 shades of pink. OSP $2.25 CMV $7.00 $12.00 MB
1962-63 BUTTONS N BOWS ROLL-ON DEODORANT
1¾ oz. white & pink painted label on clear glass, pink cap. OSP 89c CMV $6.00 BO $10.00 MB

1962-63 PRETTY CHOICE
2 oz. frosted plastic bottle Cream Lotion. White cap. Cologne, clear glass, white cap, light pink ribbon on neck. Had choice of Cream Lotion or Bubble Bath. O.S.P. $2.70 C.M.V. $30.00 M.B.

1962-63 BUTTONS N BOWS CREAM LOTION
4 oz. pink plastic bottle with white cap. O.S.P. $1.35 C.M.V. $6.00 M.B. $10.00
1962-63 BUTTONS N BOWS BUBBLE BATH
4 oz. pink plastic, white cap, pink lettering. O.S.P. $1.35 C.M.V. $6.00 $10.00 M.B.
BUTTONS & BOWS
Cream lotion & bubble bath both came in solid pink plastic & clear frosted plastic bottle. Pink has pink letters. Frosted has white letters.

1961-63 BUTTONS N BOWS SOAP
Pink box & soap. OSP $1.35. Some buttons have thread through holes. CMV $25.00 MB No threads $27.50 with threads.

1961-62 BUTTON BUTTON
Pink & white box holds Buttons N Bows 2 oz. Cologne & Beauty Dust. O.S.P. $3.60 C.M.V. $40.00 M.B.

CAMEO

1966 CAMEO SOAP
Blue & white box holds 4 white Cameo Soaps. OSP $2.00 CMV $20.00 MB
1965 CAMEO SET
White, gold & green box holds Cameo Compact, Lipstick & Cameo Brooch. O.S.P. $6.50 C.M.V. $30.00.
1965-66 CAMEO LIPSTICK
White lipstick with gold base & ladies face on top. OSP 98c CMV $2.00 $3.00 MB
1965-66 CAMEO COMPACT
White plastic with gold edge & pink ladies face on top. OSP $2.50 CMV $6.00 CO $8.00 MB

1973-74 CAMEO SET
Redish brown plastic with white Cameo Beauty Dust 6 oz. came in Sonnet, Moonwind, Hana Gasa, Charisma, Unforgettalbe, Rapture, Somewhere, Cotillion, Here's My Heart, Topaze, Occur!, To A Wild Rose. S.S.P. $4.00 C.M.V. $4.00 Brush & Comb set. S.S.P. $6.00 C.M.V. $6.00 Mirror S.S.P. $4.00 C.M.V. $4.00.

1969 CAMEO SOAP ON A ROPE
Blue box holds blue soap on white or blue & white rope. OSP $1.75 CMV $5.00 $12.00 MB
1961-63 CAMEO SACHET
Gold metal base holds pink painted over milk glass jar with white lid with ladies face. Came in Topaze, Cotillion, Somewhere OSP $3.25 To A Wild Rose OSP $2.75 Persian Wood & Here's My Heart OSP $3.00 CMV $7.00 BO $11.00 MB
1965 CAMEO BROOCH
Gold brooch with pink & white ladies face. Came in Cameo set only. CMV $15.00 MB. $7.00 brooch only.

CANDID

1976 CANDID BAG FOR MANAGERS
Maroon and white canvas bag. Back side says Avon, New York, London, Paris. C.M.V. $10.00

1977 CANDID TOTE BAG
Light colored canvas bag given to Reps for going to C-10 sales meeting. C.M.V. $3.00. They could also win a Candid matching purse organizer. C.M.V. $3.00

1977-78 CANDID PERFUMED TALC
3.5 oz. O.S.P. $3.00 C.M.V. 50¢
1977-78 CANDID ULTRA COLOGNE SPRAY
1.8 oz. gold cap. O.S.P. $7.50 C.M.V. 50¢
1977-78 CANDID ULTRA COLOGNE
2 oz., gold cap. O.S.P. $6.50 C.M.V. 50¢
1977-78 CANDID ULTRA PURSE COLOGNE
.5 oz. O.S.P. $3.00 C.M.V. 50¢
1978 ULTRA PURSE SPRAY COLOGNE
Refillable .33 fl. oz. S.S.P. $3.95 C.M.V. 50¢

1977 CANDID SALES LEADER TROPHY
Wood base with brass plaque with bottle of Candid cologne mist glued in base. Given to 1 Rep. in each district who sold the most Candid cologne mist on its introduction. C.M.V. $12.50

1977 CANDID MAKEUP DEMO KIT
For Reps only. Box lid Candid is in different position then regular set sold. Came with outer sleeve and says (Not for Resale) on back side. Box holds 5 items. Makeup, lip color, eye color, cheek color, mascara with lash builders. C.M.V. $10.00 MB with outer sleeve only. Sold to public for $10.95. Same CMV.

CANDID PRODUCTS
1976-78 CANDID FRAGRANCE SAMPLE
Small plastic vial. Came in matchbook like cover.
1976-78 CANDID COLOR FOR EYES
.25 oz. C.M.V. 25¢
1977-78 CANDID SOLID PERFUME COMPACT
Plastic container. O.S.P. $3.75 C.M.V. 25¢
1976-78 CANDID COLOR FOR CHEEKS
Plastic, .15 oz. O.S.P. $3.50 C.M.V. 25¢
1976-78 CANDID MASCARA
.25 oz. O.S.P. $3.00 C.M.V. 25¢
1977-78 CANDID FRESH & FOAMING BODY CLEANSER
6 oz. plastic tube O.S.P. $4.50 C.M.V.25¢

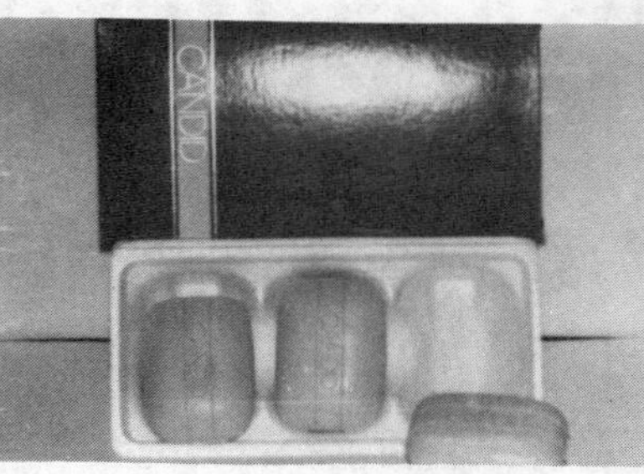

1977-78 CANDID PERFUMED SOAPS
Open end box, 3 cakes each 3 oz., white bars. O.S.P. $7.00 C.M.V. $5.00 M.B.

1977-78 CANDID PERFUMED SKIN SOFTENER
5 oz. plastic jar. S.S. P. $2.49 C.M.V. 50¢
1977-78 CANDID MAKEUP
1.5 oz. glass bottles, gold cap. Came in 3 shades. O.S.P. $3.50 C.M.V. 50¢

1977-78 UNDER MAKEUP MOISTURIZER
2 oz. clear glass bottle, gold cap. O.S.P. $3.50 C.M.V. 50¢

CERTAIN LOOK

1972 BLUSH PETITE COMPACT
.19 oz. white with pink & blue picture. Came with brush. S.S.P. $3.00 C.M.V. $1.00.
1972 CERTAIN LOOK EYE SHINE
.25 oz. white with pink & lavender. S.S.P. $1.00 C.M.V. 25¢.
1972-74 CERTAIN LOOK DEW GLOW
2.25 oz. pink frosted glass with white cap & pink & blue picture. S.S.P. $3.00 C.M.V. $1.00.
1972 CERTAIN LOOK LIPSTICK
White with pink & blue picture. SSP $1.00 CMV $1.00
1974-76 CERTAIN LOOK LONG LASH MASCARA
CMV $1.00

1979-80 CANDID SHEER SUNSHINE FACE COLOR
1.5 oz. tube, gold cap. SSP $1.50 CMV .25c
1979-80 CANDID ULTRA CREME PERFUME
.66 oz. clear glass, gold cap. SSP $1.00 CMV .25c

COME SUMMER 1978-80

1976-78 COME SUMMER PERFUMED TALC
3.5 oz. green and white container. O.S.P. $2.00 C.M.V. 50¢

1976-78 COME SUMMER BUBBLE BATH GELEE
4 oz. tube, white flower design and cap. O.S.P. $3.50 C.M.V. 50¢

1977-78 COME SUMMER - A TOUCH OF COLOGNE
.33 oz. ribbed glass bottle, white cap. O.S.P. $1.75 C.M.V. 50¢

1975-78 COME SUMMER BODY SPLASH
12 oz. white plastic with painted label & white cap. O.S.P. $3.00 C.M.V. 25¢.

1975-78 COME SUMMER PERFUMED POWDER MIST
7 oz. green & white with white cap. O.S.P. $3.00 C.M.V. 50¢.

1975-78 COME SUMMER COLOGNE ICE
2.25 Solid Cologne. White & green with white cap. O.S.P. $4.00 C.M.V. 50¢.

1975-76 COLOGNE MIST
2 oz. clear glass with green band on bottle & white cap with green band. O.S.P. $3.00 C.M.V. 50¢.

1975-78 COME SUMMER FRAGRANCE SAMPLES
Box of 10 samples. C.M.V. 50¢ box.

1975 CHARISMA SOAP
3 pink Charisma Soap in special Christmas 1975 Design Box. O.S.P. $3.00 C.M.V. $7.00 MB

1970-76 CHARISMA SOAP
Red box holds 3 bars. OSP $3.50 CMV $5.00 MB

CHARISMA

1970-71 CHARISMA FOAMING BATH OIL
Left - 6 oz. red plastic bottle with red band on gold cap. Red paper label with gold lettering on bottom. O.S.P. $3.50 C.M.V. $2.00

1971-73 CHARISMA FOAMING BATH OIL
Middle - Same as above only cap has no red band. Bottom label is white with red lettering. OSP $4.00 CMV $2.00 MB

1973-74 CHARISMA FOAMING BATH OIL
Right - Same as above only front lettering says Foaming Bath Oil. Bottom label has number in red. OSP $4.00 CMV $2.00 MB

1968 CHARISMA JEWELRY SET AWARD
Red & gold Necklace, Bracelet & Earrings. Given for meeting or exceeding a prize goal. CMV +35.00 set. $12.00 each MB

1968-70 CHARISMA TRAY
Left - Dark red plastic with gold rim. 11" diameter. This one used as introduction. CMV $8.00 MB
Right - Lighter red plastic with gold rim. 10" diameter. OSP $3.00 CMV $3.00 to $4.00 MB

1968-78 CHARISMA DEMI STICK
Red & gold with white cap. O.S.P. $2.50 C.M.V. $1.00

1968-78 CHARISMA SAMPLES
Clear glass with white cap. C.M.V. 25¢
Red foil envelope, 10 in box. C.M.V. 25¢

1968 CHARISMA ORDER BOOK COVER
Introducing Charisma. Came with red pen. C.M.V. $5.00. With pen $6.00.

1969 CHARISMA COLOGNE SILK
3 oz. frosted glass, red cap. O.S.P. $4.50 C.M.V. $4.00.

1970-71 CHARISMA COLOGNE SILK
3 oz. clear glass, red cap. O.S.P. $4.50 C.M.V. $2.00.

1969-72 CHARISMA SKIN SOFTENER
5 oz. red glass jar with red & gold cap. 1974 Skin Softener changed to plastic. O.S.P. $4.00 CMV 50c $1.00 MB

1968-76 CHARISMA CREAM SACHET
.66 oz. red glass jar with red & gold lid. O.S.P. $4.50 C.M.V. 50¢.

1969-72 CHARISMA COLOGNE
½ oz. red glass, gold cap. O.S.P. $1.75 C.M.V. $2.00.

1968-76 CHARISMA BEAUTY DUST
6 oz. red plastic powder box trimmed in gold. OSP $10.00 CMV $6.00 MB $3.00 CO

1970-72 CHARISMA SCENTED HAIR SPRAY
7 oz. red can. OSP $1.50 CMV $3.00

1970-76 CHARISMA PERFUMED TALC
3½ oz. red cardboard. O.S.P. $1.35 C.M.V. 50¢.

1971-76 CHARISMA PERFUME POWDER MIST
7 oz. red & gold can, gold top, painted label. No longer boxed. O.S.P. $5.00 C.M.V. 50¢.

1969-70 CHARISMA PERFUMED POWDER MIST
7 oz. red & gold can, gold top, has paper label. Also came boxed. O.S.P. $3.50 C.M.V. $3.00.

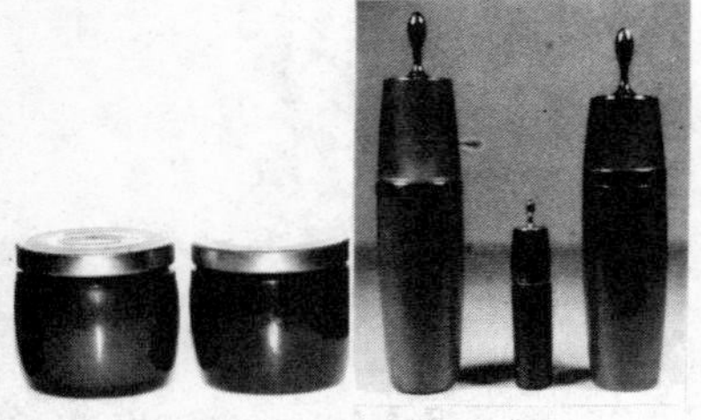

1969-71 CHARISMA SKIN SOFTENER
5 oz. dark red glass jar has red & gold metal caps, or red & silver metal caps. Bottom labels are red with gold lettering. OSP $4.00 CMV $1.00 BO $2.00 MB

1972 CHARISMA SKIN SOFTENER
5 oz. light red glass, caps are red & gold metal. Paper labels on bottoms are white with red lettering. OSP $4.00 CMV $2.00 MB $1.00 BO

1973-78 CHARISMA SKIN SOFTENER
(Not Shown) 5 oz. red plastic with gold & red cap. O.S.P. $5.50 C.M.V. 25¢.

1969-72 CHARISMA COLOGNE
4 oz. red glass, some are silver tip (rare) with red plastic cap trimmed in gold. O.S.P. $6.00 C.M.V. $3.00.

1968-76 CHARISMA COLOGNE MIST
3 oz. red plastic coated, trimmed in gold. O.S.P. $8.00 C.M.V. $1.00.

1968-76 CHARISMA PERFUME ROLLETTE
.33 oz. red glass trimmed in gold. O.S.P. $4.50 C.M.V. $1.00.

COTILLION

See Page 5 for Grading Examples on Mint Condition

1961-68 COTILLION CREAM LOTION
4 oz. pink plastic, white cap. O.S.P. $1.50 C.M.V. $3.50.

1961-64 COTILLION BODY POWDER
4 oz. pink plastic, white cap. O.S.P. $2.25 C.M.V. $6.00. M.B. $8.00.

1962-63 COTILLION BEAUTY DUST
Gold and white paper box with clear plastic lid with 4A design on lid. Came in 1962-63 Fragrance Magic sets only. CMV $17.00 mint.

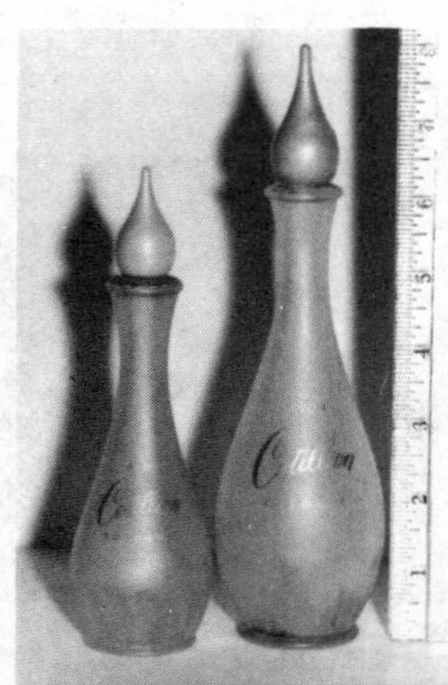

1961-71 COTILLION COLOGNE
2 oz. frosted glass with white cap. O.S.P. $2.00 C.M.V. $1.00.

1961-63 COTILLION COLOGNE
4 oz. frosted glass with white cap. O.S.P. $3.00 C.M.V. $10.00.

1961-70 COTILLION BEAUTY DUST
White frosted plastic bottom with clear plastic lid. OSP $4.00 CMV $3.00 $5.00 MB
Some with yellow plastic bottom. CMV $6.00 $8.00 MB

1961-74 COTILLION PERFUMED TALC
2.75 oz. bright pink can with white cap. O.S.P. $1.00 C.M.V. $1.00.

1964-73 COTILLION PERFUMED SKIN SOFTENER
5 oz. pink glass jar with gold & white lid. Some came with silver lid. O.S.P. $3.50 C.M.V. gold 50¢, silver $1.00.
Regular issue came pink painted over clear glass. C.M.V. 50¢ Some came pink painted over white milk glass. C.M.V. $5.00

1973-75 COTILLION PERFUME SKIN SOFTENER
5 oz. pink plastic with white & gold cap. O.S.P. $3.50 C.M.V. 50¢.

1966-70 COTILLION SCENTED HAIR SPRAY
7 oz. pink can. OSP $1.50 CMV $3.00

1966-72 COTILLION PERFUME POWDER MIST
Left - 7 oz. (1966-70) pink can has paper label & pink cap & came in white box lined in pink. O.S.P. $3.50 C.M.V. $2.00.
Right - 7 oz. (1970-71) pink can, pink cap. Label was painted. Not boxed. O.S.P. $3.50 C.M.V. $1.00.

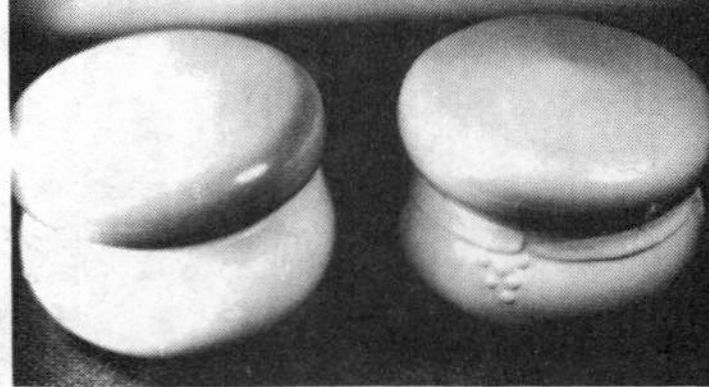

1953-57 COTILLION CREAM SACHET
Pink lid, white glass bottom. O.S.P. $1.25 C.M.V. $8.00. M.B. $10.00.

1957-61 COTILLION CREAM SACHET
Pink lid, pink glass bottom. O.S.P. $1.50 C.M.V. $7.00. M.B. $9.00.

961-66 COTILLION PERFUMED BATH
IL
oz. pink plastic bottle, white cap. O.S.P.
2.50 C.M.V. $6.00.
966-74 COTILLION FOAMING BATH
IL
oz. pink plastic bottle, white cap.
SP $3.00 CMV $1.00 BO $2.00 MB

1969-72 COTILLION COLOGNE
½ oz. white cap, clear glass. O.S.P. $1.50
C.M.V. $1.00
1964-69 COTILLION PERFUMED OIL
½ oz. frosted glass with white cap. OSP
$4.00 CMV $5.00 BO $7.00 MB
1963-64 COTILLION PERFUME OIL
FOR THE BATH
½ oz. frosted glass with white cap. OSP
$4.00 CMV $7.00 BO $9.00 MB

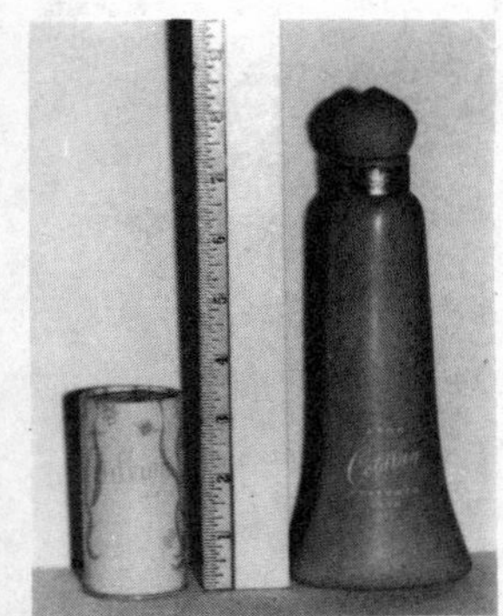

1950 Only - COTILLION TALC
2 oz. white cardboard, pink top & bottom.
Came in Always Sweet Set only. C.M.V.
$15.00.
1959-61 COTILLION PERFUMED BATH
OIL
8 oz. pink plastic, pink cap. O.S.P. $2.50
C.M.V. $10.00.

1974-77 COTILLION PERFUME TALC
3.5 oz. pink & gold, cardboard. O.S.P.
$1.00 C.M.V. 50¢
1975-78 COTILLION CREAM SACHET
.66 oz. clear glass with gold & pink cap.
O.S.P. $2.00 C.M.V. 25¢
1975-78 COTILLION PERFUME
DEMISTICK
.19 oz. white with pink & gold. O.S.P.
$1.00 C.M.V. 25¢.

1961-74 COTILLION COLOGNE
MIST
3 oz. white plastic coated bottle with
white cap. OSP $4.00 CMV $1.00
Same bottle with yellow plastic coated
bottom. CMV $10.00 MB $7.00 BO
1975-76 Issue has white cap, pink top &
pink painted label. O.S.P. $5.00
C.M.V. $1.00.

1946-50 COTILLION COLOGNE
6 oz. pink cap. OSP $1.50 CMV $45.00
BO $60.00 MB
1946-50 COTILLION BODY POWDER
4.5 oz. light pink cardboard. Blue
metal sifter top. OSP .75c CMV $15.00
MB $20.00
Came in sets in 5 oz. size with pink &
white plastic sifter top. Same CMV

1959-61 COTILLION BEAUTY DUST
Pink plastic bottom, white plastic top
with gold center. OSP $2.95 CMV $6.00
CO $12.00 MB

Left - 1959-61 COTILLION COLOGNE
MIST
3 oz. pink plastic coated bottle with
white cap & paper label. OSP $2.95 CMV
$12.00 BO $17.00 MB
Center - 1958-59 COTILLION COLOGNE
MIST
3 oz. pink plastic coated bottle. OSP
$2.50 CMV $16.00 $20.00 MB
Right - 1958 Only - COTILLION
COLOGNE MIST
Rare 3 oz. pink plastic bottle. OSP
$2.50 CMV $42.50 BO $52.50 MB

1953-54 COTILLION TALC
4 oz. clear glass bottle with pink cap & pink
or white (rare) painted label. 1955 was
called Talcum in painted label, pink &
white box. O.S.P. $1.00, C.M.V. $15.00
ea. in box. Bottle only $10.00.

1953-61 COTILLION TOILET WATER
2 oz. gold cap, pink band around neck,
pink painted label. OSP $1.50 CMV
$15.00 MB $10.00 BO mint. Some
have white painted label.
1953-61 COTILLION 4 OZ. COLOGNE
Gold cap, pink band around neck, pink
painted label. OSP $2.00 CMV $15.00
MB $10.00 BO mint. Some have white
painted label.

1957 Only - COTILLION COLOGNE
3 dram, white cap. Came in Fragrance Rainbow Set only. CMV $8.00 BO $10.00 with neck bow.

1961 Only - COTILLION COLOGNE
2 oz. gold cap, pink band around neck, painted label. O.S.P. $1.50 C.M.V. $20.00. $22.00 M.B.

1954-59 COTILLION BATH OIL
4½ oz. pink cap, pink painted label, pink & white box. OSP $1.35 CMV $15.00 in box. $9.00 bottle only mint

1954-61 COTILLION CREAM LOTION
4½ oz. pink cap & pink painted label. Pink & white box OSP .95c CMV $12.00 in box. $6.00 bottle only mint.

1960 Only - COTILLION COLOGNE
4 oz. clear glass, gold cap, pink paper band around neck with pink painted label. Pink & god box. OSP $2.50 CMV $22.00 in this box.

1953-59 COTILLION BEAUTY DUST
Pink paper sides with pink & white tin top. OSP $1.95 CMV $12.00 MB $16.00

1956-58 COTILLION TALC
3 oz. frosted glass with pink lid & paper label, pink & white box. OSP $1.00 CMV $14.00. in box $9.00 bottle only mint.

1958-59 BODY POWDER
3 oz. frosted glass with pink cap & paper label. Pink & white box. OSP $1.00 CMV $15.00 in box. $11.00 bottle only mint

Left - 1947 Only - COTILLION TALCUM
Pink paper box, white shaker top. OSP .39c. CMV $25.00 MB $30.00

Center - 1942-46 COTILLION TALCUM
2.75 oz. turquoise & white all paper box. War time. Paper top fits over top of box, shaker top. CMV without top $20.00 in mint. OSP .39c CMV $25.00 mint

Right - 1944-46 COTILLION TALCUM
Turquoise & white paper box, plastic octagonal cap. OSP .39c CMV $25.00 mint.

1940-43 then 1946-50 COTILLION TALCUM
14.5 oz. metal can, turquoise & white. O.S.P. $1.04 C.M.V. $20.00. Add $5.00 for CPC label.

1943-46 COTILLION TALCUM
14.5 oz. paper box used during war. Rare. O.S.P. $1.19 C.M.V. $35.00

1939-42 COTILLION FACE POWDER
Gold & turquoise powder box. OSP .78c CMV $8.00 MB $10.00. Add $3.00 for CPC label.

1957-61 COTILLION POWDER SACHET NO LABEL
Pink paint over clear glass. Pink cap. Rare issue came with no painted label. Plain pink all over. CMV Add $5.00 to price of regular issue.

1951-53 COTILLION CREAM SACHET
White glass jar with pink & white lid. O.S.P. $1.25 C.M.V. $15.00.

1950-53 COTILLION TOILET WATER
2 oz. pink cap, pink & white label & white box. Box came solid & with open window so label shows through. O.S.P. $1.25 C.M.V. $22.00 in box, $18.00 bottle only.

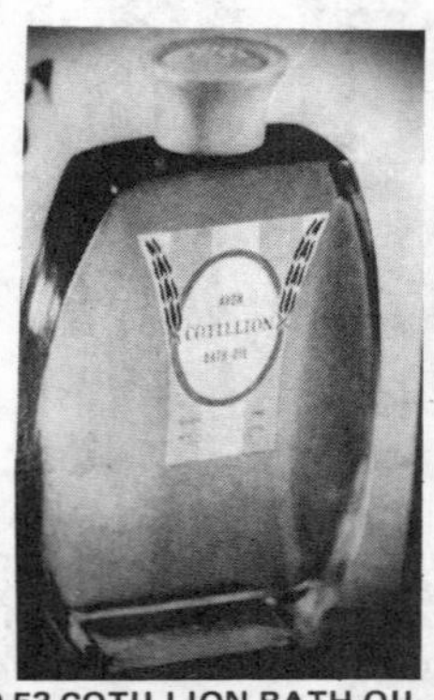

1950-53 COTILLION BATH OIL
6 oz. pink & white label & pink cap. Pink & white box. O.S.P. 95¢ C.M.V. $22.00 in box. $18.00 bottle only.

48 COTILLION TALC
hite, pink & blue paper container came in
ir Ribbon Set only. C.M.V. $12.00.
51 COTILLION TALC
oz. blue, white & pink paper container.
me in 1951 Always Sweet Set. C.M.V.
2.00.

950-53 COTILLION TALC
ink & white can with pink cap. O.S.P.
3¢ C.M.V. $12.00. M.B. $15.00.
950-53 COTILLION BODY POWDER
oz. pink & white paper box, sifter on top
with metal lid & bottom. O.S.P. 75¢ C.M.V.
17.00. M.B. $20.00.

1950-53 COTILLION BEAUTY DUST
Pink & white container. O.S.P. $1.75
CMV $20.00 mint. $25.00 MB

1950-53 COTILLION CREAM LOTION
6 oz. pink & white label, pink cap & pink & white box. O.S.P. 89¢, C.M.V. $22.00 in box. $18.00 bottle only.
1950-53 COTILLION COLOGNE
4 oz. bottle with pink cap & label. O.S.P. $1.75 C.M.V. $22.00 in box. $18.00 bottle only.

1937-38 COTILLION SACHET
1¼ oz. ribbed glass bottle with turquoise cap. O.S.P. $1.04 C.M.V. $24.00 M.B. $18.00 BO mint.

1939 Only - COTILLION TOILET WATER
Flowered box & label. 2 oz. bottle, white plastic cap. Sold for .20c with purchase of other Avons. May 2-22, 1939. CPC on box and back side of label. CMV $50.00 MB $35.00 BO mint

1946-49 COTILLION TOILET WATER
2 oz. pink, gold or white cap. OSP $1.19 CMV $35.00 in box. $25.00 BO mint

1939 Only - COTILLION PERFUME
2 dram. Ribbed cap with "A" on cap. Sold for one campaign only for 20¢ with purchase of other Avons. C.M.V. in box $75.00. Bottle only $55.00.

1951-52 COTILLION PERFUME
3 dram glass stoppered swirl glass bottle. White, pink & blue flower design around neck with neck tag. Pink & white box. O.S.P. $3.50 C.M.V. $125.00 in box. Bottle only with tag & flower design $100.00

1948-50 COTILLION SWIRL PERFUME
3 dram glass stoppered bottle is swirl glass design, gold neck tag. Purple & white flowered box. O.S.P. $3.00 C.M.V. $75.00 Mint. $100.00 M.B.

1935 Only - COTILLION PERFUME
¼ oz. gold cap, green & yellow label & box. For 77th birthday of D.H. McConnell. O.S.P. 20¢ C.M.V. $80.00 in box. Bottle only $60.00.

1937 COTILLION PERFUME
2 dram, gold cap. O.S.P. 20¢ C.M.V. in box $70.00. Bottle only $50.00.

1953-58 COTILLION PERFUME
3 dram bottle with gold cap, pink band around neck with painted label. In pink & white box. O.S.P. $4.50 C.M.V. $100.00 in box. $65.00 bottle only. Came with perfume 1 dram smooth glass with gold scroll cap in gold wrapper with pink snap & white & gold ribbon. O.S.P. $6.00 C.M.V. $12.00. Complete set C.M.V. $115.00 with white & gold ribbon.

1950 COTILLION PERFUME
1/8 oz. pink cap. Very rare. O.S.P. $1.00 C.M.V. $70.00. M.B. $85.00.

1936 Only - COTILLION PERFUME
2 dram, gold ribbed cap. Sold for 20¢ July 7-27, 1936 only, with purchase of other Avons. In honor of Mr. McConnell's 78th birthday. C.M.V. $80.00 M.B. Bottle only $60.00.

1934 COTILLION PERFUME
¼ oz. metal cap. First Cotillion bottle issued in honor of Mr. McConnell's birthday. O.S.P. 20¢ C.M.V. $55.00 B.O. $75.00 M.B.

1943 COTILLION TALCUM CHRISTMAS BOX
Pale blue and pink outer box issued only at Christmas 1943 with cardboard large size talc. O.S.P. 98¢ C.M.V. $35.00 M.B. as shown.

1952 COTILLION SACHET VALENTINE BOX
1¼ oz. Pink cap. Came in gold, pink and white Valentine box. Rare in this box. C.M.V. $25.00 M.B. as shown.

1941 ONLY - COTILLION SACHET BOX
Special issue box to Avon ladies only, for 20¢. Holds regular issue Cotillion sachet, 1939 - 1944. C.M.V. $20.00 M.B. as shown.

1939 COTILLION SACHET SPECIAL ISSUE BOX
Special issue box is blue with lace design. Holds regular issue powder sachet. O.S.P. 20¢ C.M.V. $18.00 M.B. as shown.

1940 Only - COTILLION PERFUME
2 dram, ribbed gold cap with "A" on top. Also came plain gold cap. Sold for 20¢ with purchase of other Avons. C.M.V. in box $75.00. Bottle only $55.00

1941 ONLY - COTILLION TALCUM BOX
Blue box with fan. 2.75 oz. can. Sold to Reps for .10c to use as demonstrator. CMV $30.00 MB as shown

1940-41 COTILLION TALCUM CHRISTMAS BOX
Special issue blue and white Christmas box holds regular issue metal can of Cotillion Talcum in large size. O.S.P. 89¢ RARE. C.M.V. $30.00 M.B. as shown.

1957 COTILLION SACHET CHRISTMAS BOX
.9 oz. pink painted glass, pink cap. Bottle sold 1957-61. Pink, green and blue triangle box sold 1957 only. O.S.P. $1.50 C.M.V. $15.00 M.B. as shown.

LEFT 1950-53 COTILLION POWDER SACHET
1¼ oz. pink cap & pink & white label. OSP $1.19 CMV $15.00 MB $20.00
CENTER 1957-61 COTILLION POWDER SACHET
1¼ oz. or .9 oz. pink cap & pink bottom with painted label. Came light or dark pink bottom & also white or pink painted lettering. OSP $1.50 CMV $9.00 MB $13.00
RIGHT 1953-56 COTILLION POWDER SACHET
1¼ oz. clear glass, pink cap & pink painted label. Also white lettering (rare) OSP $1.25 CMV $8.00 MB $12.00 White lettering $18.00

LEFT 1937 COTILLION SACHET
On left - red and green box sold Christmas only for 25¢, CPC on box and bottle. CMV $25.00 MB $18.00 BO mint
RIGHT 1937 Blue and white box special issue. CMV $25.00 MB Bottle only - ribbed glass, turquoise cap, sold 1937-38. OSP $1.04 CMV $18.00 BO mint

1957 Only - 1 oz. COTILLION COLOGNE
Pink cap. Came in Beautiful Journey Set. C.M.V. $15.00.
1956 Only - COTILLION COLOGNE
2 oz. white caps. Came in Bath Bouquet only. C.M.V. $20.00 mint.
1956 Only - COTILLION BATH OIL
2 oz. white caps. Came in Bath Bouquet only. C.M.V. $20.00 mint.

1938-50 COTILLION TALCUM
2.75 oz. Turquoise can. Box marked 2¾ oz. size. Can sold 1938-43 then 1946-50. OSP .37c CMV $10.00 can only. $15.00 MB mint.

1956-61 COTILLION PERFUMED TALC
White can with pink cap & design. Also came just Talc. O.S.P. 69¢ C.M.V. $8.00 in box. Can only $5.00

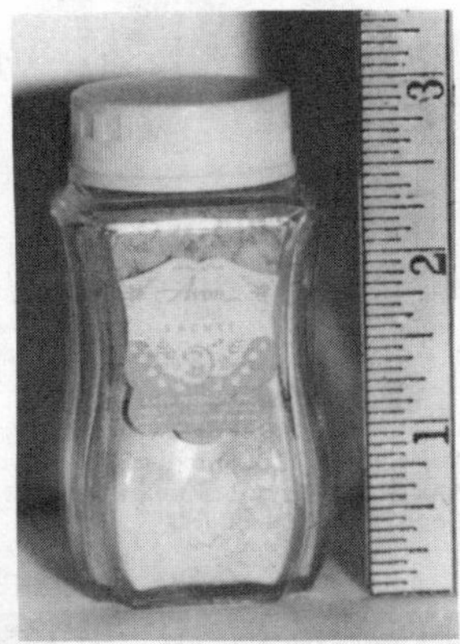

1952 COTILLION VALENTINE SACHET
1¼ oz., whtie cap. O.S.P. 98¢ C.M.V. $25.00 M.B. See Misc Powder Sachet section for box. C.M.V. B.O. mint $18.00

1939 Only - 53rd ANNIVERSARY COTILLION TALCUM
Special 53rd Anniversary Box to first introduce Cotillion Talcum. May 23 to June 12, 1939. 2.75 oz. turquoise & white can. This can sold 1939-43 then 1946-50. O.S.P. 37¢ C.M.V. can only $10.00. In special 53rd box $25.00.

1961-75 COTILLION CREAM SACHET
.66 frosted glass with pink & white lid, gold or silver lettering. O.S.P. $2.00 C.M.V. 25¢.
1961-67 COTILLION POWDER SACHET
9/10 oz. frosted glass with pink & white cap. OSP $2.00 CMV $8.00 MB $6.00 BO
1944-45 COTILLION SACHET
1¼ oz. paper box, pink plastic flowers on lid. O.S.P. $1.15 C.M.V. $20.00 M.B. $18.00 B.O. Mint

1955-56 COTILLION BATH OIL
2 oz. clear glass bottle with pink cap, label pink & white. Came in That's For Me Set only. C.M.V. $15.00.
1949 HAND LOTION
2 oz. clear glass bottle with pink & blue label, blue cap. Came in Your Charms & Hair-Ribbons Set. C.M.V. $15.00.

1946-47 COTILLION SACHET
1¼ oz. pink glass & cap with painted label. (Rare) Sold only in Cotillion Garland Set. Same set in 1947 was called Cotillion Duet. C.M.V. $20.00. M.B. $22.00.
1946-49 COTILLION SACHET
1¼ oz. clear glass, pink cap, paper label. O.S.P. $1.15 C.M.V. $16.00. M.B. $18.00.
1939-44 COTILLION SACHET
1¼ oz. turquoise cap, clear glass, paper label OSP $1.04 CMV $12.00 BO $16.00 MB

1964-68 COTILLION PERFUME MIST
2 dram, pink & white metal with gold band. OSP $3.25 CMV $6.00 $7.00 MB
1961-63 COTILLION SPRAY PERFUME
2 dram, pink & white metal with gold band. OSP $3.50 CMV $10.00 MB
1960-61 COTILLION SPRAY PERFUME
Rose, white & gold box holds rose & gold metal spray container. OSP $2.95 CMV $14.00

1953-61 COTILLION SOAP
Pink & white box holds 3 pink or white bars. O.S.P. 89¢ Box came as sleeve top with round edge white soaps. 1953-56 C.M.V. $35.00 M.B. 1956-61 came sleeve top box with 3 flat edge pink soaps. CMV $32.50 MB

1958 COTILLION BOUQUET
Pink & white box holds Cotillion Cologne Mist & pink glass Cream Sachet. O.S.P. $3.95 C.M.V. $65.00 M.B.

1964 COTILLION DUO
White, pink & gold box holds Cotillion Powder Sachet & 1 dram perfume. O.S.P. $4.50 CMV $22.50 MB

1957 THE COTILLION
Pink & white box holds Cotillion Beauty Dust, Cream Sachet with white glass bottom & 4 oz. Cologne. O.S.P. $4.95 C.M.V. $45.00.

1962 COTILLION BATH OIL
6 oz. pink & white plastic bottle. Came n in Bath Bouquet Set only. CMV $6.00
1949-50 COTILLION COLOGNE
2 oz. pink cap. O.S.P. $1.25 C.M.V. $22.50 $25.00 M.B.

1961-67 COTILLION SOAP
Gold & white box holds 3 bars with gold centers. OSP $2.00 CMV $22.50 MB

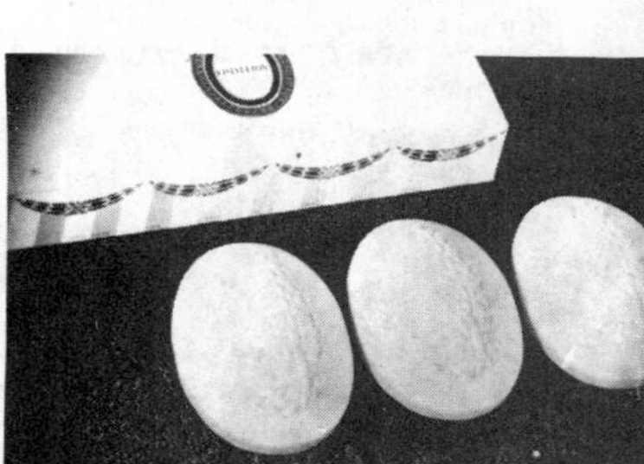

1950-53 COTILLION SOAP
Pink & white box holds pink bars. OSP .69¢ CMV $37.50 MB

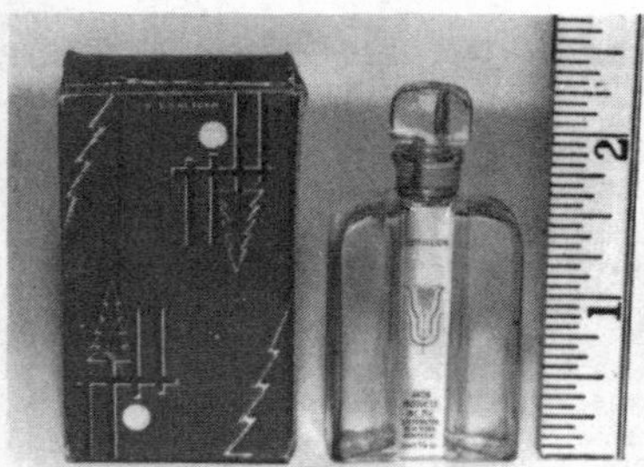

1935 COTILLION TULIP PERFUME CHRISTMAS BOX
Red and green Christmas box holds 1/4 oz. glass stoppered perfume with gold label. This bottle sold 1934-39. With this box 1935 Christmas only. O.S.P. $1.04 C.M.V. $90.00 M.B. as shown. See Misc Perfumes for other fragrances in same bottle.

1961-62 COTILLION DEBUT
White & gold box holds Cotillion Beauty Dust & Cream Sachet & Cologne Mist, in satin lined flip open compartment. O.S.P. $10.00 C.M.V. $35.00.

1963 DEBUTANTE
Pink, white & gold box holds Cotillion Cologne Mist & Beauty Dust. Comes in 2 different inner boxes. OSP $8.50 CMV $20.00 MB

1953-56 ENCHANTMENT SET
Pink & white box holds Cotillion Powder Sachet & 1 dram Perfume. O.S.P. $3.00 CMV $37.00 MB

1956 COTILLION PRINCESS SET
Pink, white & gold box holds Cotillion Beauty Dust & 4 oz. Cologne. O.S.P. $3.95 C.M.V. $40.00.

1961-62 SOMEONE LIKE YOU
Pink & white box holds Cotillion 2 oz. Cologne & Cream Sachet. O.S.P. $4.00 C.M.V. $20.00.

1957 COTILLION TREASURES
Gold, white & pink box holds 3 oz. bottles of Cotillion Bath Oil & Cologne with gold caps, 1 pink bar of Cotillion Soap. O.S.P. $2.75 C.M.V. $75.00 M.B.

1954-55 COTILLION GARLAND SET
Pink & white box holds 4½ oz. Cotillion Bath Oil & Cream Lotion. O.S.P. $2.15 CMV $37.50 MB

1945-47 COTILLION PERFUME
3 dram glass stopper bottle with gold neck tag. Came in blue, pink and white box as shown. O.S.P. $3.00 C.M.V. $100.00 B.O. mint $125.00 M.B.

1956 COTILLION CAROL
Pink & white box holds Cotillion Cream Sachet with white glass bottom & Cotillion Talc. O.S.P. $2.25 C.M.V. $35.00.

1953-55 COTILLION DUET
Pink & white flowered box with pink satin lining holds Cotillion 4 oz. Cologne & Cotillion Talc. O.S.P. $3.00 C.M.V. $42.00 MB

1950 COTILLION GARLAND
Pink, white & green box holds Cotillion Talc & 2 oz. Toilet Water. O.S.P. $1.85 CMV $52.50

1950-52 COTILLION BATH ENSEMBLE
Pink & white box holds 2 drawers with Cotillion Talc, Powder Sachet & 2 bars of pink soap in top drawer. Bottom drawer holds Cotillion Cream Lotion, Toilet Water, Bath Oil & 1 dram Perfume. O.S.P. $8.25 C.M.V. $175.00 M.B.

1953-55 COTILLION DELUXE SET
Pink & white box flips open in center. Holds Cotillion 1 dram Perfume, 4 oz. Cologne, Powder Sachet & Talcum. Same set also came with lift off lid. OSP $6.00 CMV $60.00 MB

1956 Only – COTILLION BATH BOUQUET
Pink & white box holds 2 oz. Cotillion Cologne, 2 oz. Cotillion Bath Oil & 1 bar of Cotillion Soap. O.S.P. $2.25 C.M.V. $55.00.

1952 COTILLION FANTASY
Pink & white Cotillion Body Powder with Crean Sachet on top under clear plastic lid. O.S.P. $1.95 C.M.V. $40.00 M.B.

1950-52 THE COTILLION
Pink & white box with green lining holds Cotillion Cream Lotion & Cologne. OSP $2.60 CMV $52.50

1951-52 JOLLY SURPRISE SET
Pink & white box holds Cotillion Powder Sachet & 1 dram Perfume in pink net lining. OSP $1.99 CMV $42.00 set.

1951 COTILLION ENCHANTMENT
Pink, white & green box holds Cotillion Toilet Water & Cream Sachet. O.S.P. $2.50 CMV $52.50 MB

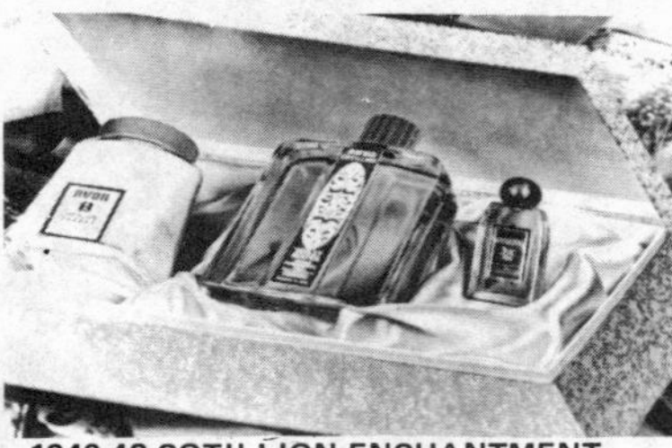

1940-43 COTILLION ENCHANTMENT SET
Silk lined gold & green box holds Cotillion Powder Sachet, 2 oz. Toilet Water & 1 dram Perfume with gold cap. O.S.P. $2.85 C.M.V. $95.00 M.B.

1938-39 COTILLION ENCHANTMENT
White box with satin lining holds Cotillion 2 dram glass stoppered perfume, 2 oz. Cotillion toilet water & powder sachet. O.S.P. $2.95 C.M.V. $150.00 M.B.

1940-41 COTILLION CLASSIC
Satin lined box with people dancing on lid holds 2 oz. Cotillion Toilet Water & gold box of Cotillion Talc. O.S.P. $1.50 C.M.V. $65.00 M.B.

1947-48 COTILLION DUET
Pink box holds 2 oz. Cotillion Toilet Water with gold cap & Powder Sachet. O.S.P. $2.39 C.M.V. $70.00 M.B.

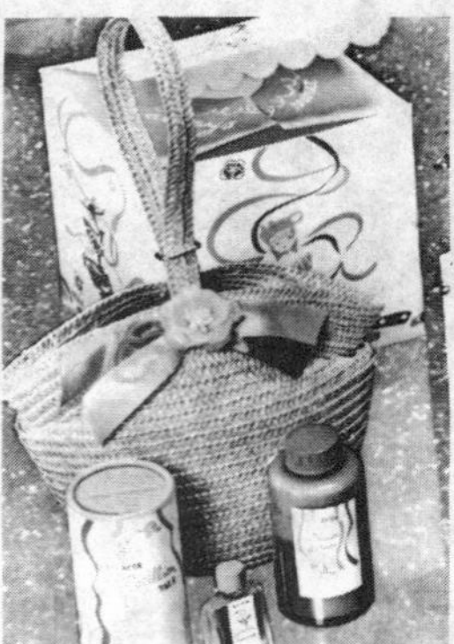

1950 ALWAYS SWEET SET
Pink & white box holds straw handbag with green & yellow ribbon & pink flower. Holds bottle of cream lotion with blue cap, Cotillion Talc & 5/8 dram Cotillion Perfume. O.S.P. $2.39 C.M.V. $90.00 M.B.

1949 YOUR CHARMS SET
White, blue & pink box with or without ribbon band around lid came with gold heart & arrow charm on lid. Box contains pink & blue paper box of Cotillion Talc, 2 oz. Avon Hand Lotion, pink & blue label with blue cap. 5/8 dram Cotillion Perfume with blue cap. Set came with & without perfume. O.S.P. $1.59 C.M.V. $60.00 with perfume. $47.00 without perfume.

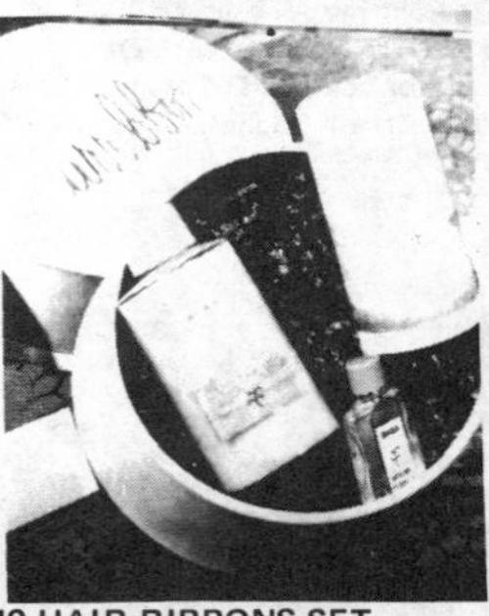

1948-49 HAIR RIBBONS SET
Pink & white box has bottle of Avon Hand Lotion, Cotillion Talc, 5/8 dram bottle of Cotillion Perfume. Also came, this box, with hand lotion & Cotillion Talc from 1949 Your Charm Set. Set came with or without perfume. O.S.P. $1.59 C.M.V. $60.00 with perfume, C.M.V. $47.00 without perfume.

1946-47 COTILLION CLASSIC
Pink flowered box holds Cotillion 6 oz. Cologne & Body Powder. O.S.P. $2.48 C.M.V. $90.00.

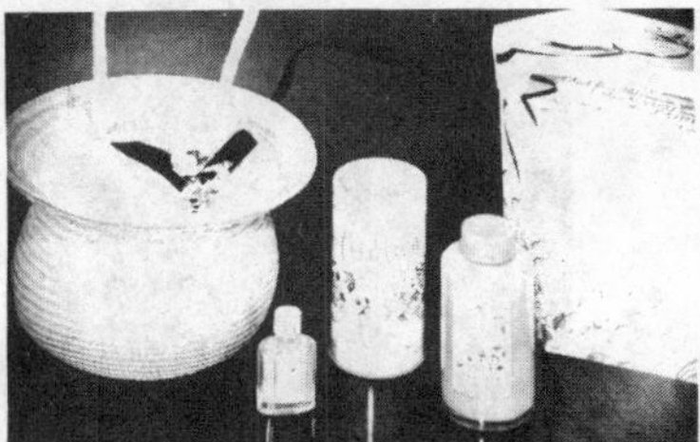

1951 ALWAYS SWEET SET
White, blue & pink box with girls hat on lid, holds straw handbag containing Cotillion Talc, 5/8 dram perfume & cream lotion with blue cap. O.S.P. $3.00 C.M.V. $90.00 M.B.

1946 COTILLION GARLAND/COTILLION DUET
Pink round box holds Cotillion Toilet Water & pink painted powder sachet. This set was introduced as Cotillion Duet then changed to Cotillion Garland for Xmas 1946. O.S.P. $2.84 C.M.V. $75.00.

COUNTRY GARDEN

1971-73 COUNTRY GARDEN FOAMING BATH OIL
4" high, 6 oz. white glass bottle, white cap, green ribbon on neck. Came in Bird of Paradise, Elusive or Charisma. O.S.P. $5.50 CMV $5.00 MB $3.00 BO
1971-72 SOAP DISH & SOAP
4" long white soap dish with bar of Country Garden Soap. OSP $4.50 CMV $6.00 MB
1971-72 BEAUTY DUST
4½" high, 5 oz. white glass jar with white lid & green ribbon. Came in Bird of Paradise, Elusive or Charisma. OSP $6.00 CMV $6.00 MB $4.00 BO
1971-73 POWDER SACHET
3" high, 1¼ oz. white glass jar with white lid & green ribbon. Came in Bird of Paradise, Elusive or Charisma. OSP $4.50 CMV $4.00 MB $2.00 BO

COURTSHIP

1937 Only - COURTSHIP PERFUME
2 dram, gold cap. Sold for .20c with other purchase during Founders Campaign July 6-26, 1937. CMV $55.00 MB $40.00 BO mint

See Misc. perfumes & Toilet Water for other Courtship bottles.

1938 Only - COURTSHIP PERFUME
2 dram bottle, gold cap. OSP .20c CMV $55.00 MB $40.00 BO mint.

CRIMSON CARNATION

1946-47 CRIMSON CARNATION PERFUME
Blue & white box holds 3 dram bottle with white cap. O.S.P. $3.75 C.M.V. $100.00 M.B. Bottle only $60.00.
See misc. perfumes for other Crimson Carnation Perfumes.

1946-48 CRIMSON CARNATION TOILET WATER
2 oz. gold or plastic caps. OSP $1.19 CMV $35.00 BO $45.00 MB

1940-44 COURTSHIP PERFUME
Box holds 1/8 oz. bottle, gold cap and label. OSP .75c CMV $25.00 mint. $35.00 MB as shown

CRYSTAL

1976-80 BEAUTY DUST CRYSTALIQUE
Clear glass, holds all Beauty Dust refills. (Sold empty) O.S.P. $5.00 C.M.V. $5.00 M.B.

1966 CRYSTAL BEAUTY DUST
All glass powder dish. OSP $5.00 CMV $18.00 $21.00 MB
1966-70 CRYSTAL COLOGNE
4 oz. 5½'' high. Glass bottle with matching plastic cap, gold trim. Came in Unforgettable, Rapture, Occur, O.S.P. $5.00. Somewhere, Topaze, Cotillion, O.S.P. $4.00. Here's My Heart, To A Wild Rose, O.S.P. $3.50 CMV $2.00 BO $3.00 MB

Left - 1972 CRYSTALIQUE BEAUTY DUST
Clear crystal plastic powder box & lid with gold base. OSP $8.00 CMV $6.00 MB $5.00 CO
Right - 1972 CRYSTALIQUE BEAUTY DUST
Clear glass came with choice of powder. Moonwind, Charisma, Regence, Elusive, Rapture, Occur! Somewhere, Topaze, Cotillion, Unforgettable or Here's My Heart, with matching puffs. SSP $7.00 CMV $12.00 MB $10.00 CO

DAISIES WON'T TELL

1959 DAISY TREASURES
Pink box with yellow slide open cover with lt. blue ribbon on Daisy flower. Holds 3 bottles of Nail Polish with white caps & Nail File. O.S.P. $2.75 C.M.V. $55.00 M.B.

1960 DAISY PINK SET
Daisies box holds Daisy Pink nail polish, white cap and pink metal pomade in box. O.S.P. $1.25 C.M.V. $20.00 M.B.

1962-64 DAISY POMADE LIPSTICK
Pink box holds pink with gold base lip stick. O.S.P. 59¢ C.M.V. $4.00 M.B.

1960 FIRST WALTZ SET
Blue & white Daisies Won't Tell box holds First Waltz Nail Polish & pink Pomade. OSP $1.25 CMV $20.00 MB

1960 FIRST WALTZ LIPSTICK
Blue flowered box holds pink lipstick. Came in Daisy Won't Tell. OSP 50c CMV $6.00 MB.

1962-64 DAISIES WON'T TELL COLOGNE MIST
2 oz. white plastic coated bottle with wh cap & blue painted label. O.S.P. $2.25 C.M.V. $7.00 B.O. $9.00 M.B.
1962-64 DAISIES WON'T TELL CREAM LOTION
4 oz. white plastic bottle & cap. Blue painted label. O.S.P. $1.19 C.M.V. $6.00 B.O. $8.00 M.B.

1957 Only - ONE I LOVE
Floral box contains 2 oz. Cologne, Cream Lotion & Bubble Bath in Daisies Won't Tell. White flower caps with yellow centers. Any sets you find with pink caps are taken off Cotillion bottles. OSP $2.49 CMV $50.00 MB

1963-64 DAISIES WON'T TELL CREAM SACHET
Pink glass jar with white plastic lid. O.S.P. $1.10 CMV in box $11.00. Jar only $9.00

1959-61 DAISIES WON'T TELL CREAM SACHET
Pink glass jar with floral metal lid. O.S.P. $1.19 C.M.V. $11.00. M.B. $13.00.

1959-61 DAISY SHAMPOO
4 oz. white plastic bottle & cap.
OSP $1.19 CMV $10.00 BO $12.00 MB

1963-64 DAISY SOAP ON A ROPE
Pink, white & yellow box holds white soap with yellow center on a white rope. O.S.P. $1.19 CMV $20.00 MB

1959-62 DAISY SOAP ON A ROPE
Blue white & pink flowed box holds white Daisy Soap with yellow center, on a blue rope. OSP $1.19 CMV $20.00 MB

1958 HEARTS 'N' DAISIES
Blue & white box holds 2 oz. Daisy Won't Tell Cologne & Pink Pomade Lipstick. O.S.P. $1.59 C.M.V. $22.00 M.B.

1959 LOVE ME - LOVE ME NOT
Blue, white & green box holds Daisies Won't Tell Spray Cologne & Cream Sachet in pink glass. O.S.P. $2.50 C.M.V. $30.00.

1958-61 DAISY DUST
2 oz. white plastic bottle & cap. OSP . $1.19 $1.19 CMV $10.00 BO $12.00 MB

1958-61 DAISY CREAM LOTION
4 oz. white plastic bottle & cap. Two different labels. Newer has large letters & painted address at bottom. Older one is smaller letters & embossed address at bottom. OSP $1.19 CMV $10.00 BO $12.00 MB

1958-61 DAISY BUBBLE BATH
4 oz. white plastic bottle & cap OSP $1.19 CMV $10.00 BO $12.00 MB

1958 FAIRY TOUCH
Blue & white box holds 2 blue & white tubes with yellow caps of Daisies Won't Tell Hand Cream. OSP .79c CMV $16.00 MB

1956 WEE TWO
Blue, white & yellow box has two tubes with yellow caps of Dasies Won't Tell Hand Cream & Cream Shampoo. O.S.P. .89c CMV $18.00

1957 DAINTY HANDS
Pink, white & yellow box holds 2 tubes with pink hearts & yellow caps of Daisies Won't Tell Hand Cream. O.S.P. 79¢ CMV $18.00 M.B.

1956 LITTLE CHARMER
Black & white plastic basket with flowers on top holds Daisies Won't Tell 2 oz. Cologne. Gold Pomade & tube of Daisy Hand Cream. OSP $3.50 CMV $60.00 MB

CENTER-1957 Only - DAISIES WON'T TELL SPRAY COLOGNE
1½ oz. blue plastic coated bottle with white cap & painted label. O.S.P. $1.59 C.M.V. $13.00 . M.B. $15.00

LEFT 1958-60 DAISIES WON'T TELL SPRAY COLOGNE
Pink plastic coated bottle with white cap OSP $1.59 CMV $10.00 BO $12.00 MB

RIGHT 1962-64 DAISIES WON'T TELL COLOGNE
2 oz. glass bottle, white cap & painted label. OSP $1.19 CMV $6.00 BO $9.00 MB

1958-59 DAISY POMADE
Blue & white flowered holder holds pink Daisy Pomade. Also came in lime green color. OSP .59c CMV $12.50 in holder, $2.00 Pomade only.

1960 DAISY PINK NAIL POLISH
Blue and white box holds Daisy Won't Tell nail polish, white cap. O.S.P. 69¢ C.M.V. $8.00 M.B., $6.00 B.O. mint.
1960 FIRST WALTZ NAIL POLISH
Blue and white box holds Daisy Won't Tell nail polish, white cap. O.S.P. 69¢ C.M.V. $8.00 M.B., $6.00 B.O. mint.
1960-61 DAISY POMADE LIPSTICK
Blue & white box holds pink & gold Pomade in shades of 1st Waltz or Daisy Pomade. OSP .69c CMV $6.00 MB

1958-62 DAISIES WON'T TELL COLOGNE
2 oz. white cap & painted label. OSP $1.19 CMV $7.00 MB $10.00. Same bottle came in Bubble Bath & Cream Lotion in sets only. Same CMV.
1956-57 DAISIES WON'T TELL BUBBLE BATH
4 oz. bottle with rib around center. Painted label, white flower cap. OSP $1.10 CMV $8.00 MB $10.00
2 oz. Bubble Bath is same type bottle. Came in One I Love set and Daisies Wont Tell set. CMV $12.00

1956-57 DAISIES WON'T TELL CREAM LOTION
Yellow & white box holds 2 oz. bottle with rib around center & white flower cap, painted label. O.S.P. 69¢ C.M.V. $12.00 M.B. $10.00 bottle only.
1962-64 DAISIES WON'T TELL HAND CREAM
Pink tube with white flower cap. In pink & blue box. O.S.P. 59¢ C.M.V. $7.00 in box, $5.00 tube only.

Left - 1957 DAISIES WON'T TELLLL BEAUTY DUST
Blue, white & yellow paper powder box with girl on lid. OSP $1.29 CMV $20.00 $25.00 MB
1959-60 DAISY FLUFF ON
Blue paper powder box with Daisy Puff & clear plastic lid. O.S.P. $1.98 C.M.V. $12.00 MB $16.00

1956 DAISIES WON'T TELL BEAUTY DUST
Yellow, white & blue paper box. Short issue. OSP $1.29 CMV $20.00 mint $25.00 MB. Also came with Blue sided container

1960 GAY DAISIES
Blue, white & pink box holds Daisy Soap On A Blue Rope & choice of Daisy Bubble Bath, Daisy Dust, Cream Lotion or Daisy Shampoo. OSP $2.35 CMV $35.00 MB

1956 DAISIES WON'T TELL COLOGNE WITH ATOMIZER
Yellow, white & pink box holds 2 oz. bottle with rib around middle, white & gold spray atomizer. Short issue. O.S.P. $1.25 C.M.V. $15.00. M.B. $20.00
1957-58 DAISIES WON'T TELL COLOGNE
2 oz. bottle with rib around center & painted label. Came in Daisy Sets only. C.M.V. $9.00 B.O. $12.00 M.B.

1962-64 DAISIES WON'T TELL BUBBLE BATH
4 oz. white plastic bottle & cap with blue painted label. O.S.P. $1.19 C.M.V. $6.00 B.O. $8.00 M.B.
1962-64 DAISY DUST
2 oz. white plastic bottle & cap with blue painted label. O.S.P. $1.19 C.M.V. $6.00 B.O. $8.00 M.B.
1958-61 DAISIES WON'T TELL HAND CREAM
Blue & white box holds blue & white tube with both flat or tall yellow cap. O.S.P. 49¢ C.M.V. $6.00 in box, $4.00 tube only.
2 oz. Bubble Bath is same type bottle. Came in One I Love Set & Daisy Won't Tell set.

963-64 DAISY CHAIN GIFT SET
nk & white box holds 2 oz. Daisy Won't ll Cologne & pink tube of Daisy Hand eam. O.S.P. $1.78 C.M.V. $22.00 M.B.

962-64 FIRST RECITAL
nk & blue fold-over box holds Daisy Soap n Rope & choice of Daisy Cream Lotion, ubble Bath, Daisy Dust. O.S.P. $2.38 M.V. $35.00 M.B.

1963-64 PICK A DAISY
Pink & blue box holds Daisy Soap On A Rope & Daisies Won't Tell Cream Sachet. OSP $2.38 CMV $32.50 MB

1959-60 DAISY BOUQUET
Blue & white flowed box holds 4 oz. Daisy Cream Lotion. Daisv Bubble Bath & 2 oz. Daisy Dust OSP $3.50 CMV $37.50 MB M.B.

1958 DAISIES WON'T TELL BEAUTY DUST
Blue & white box holds blue & white paper powder box with white daisy on top. OSP $1.49 CMV $23.00 MB. Beauty Dust only $18.00 mint.

1957 DAISY BOUQUET
Blue, white & yellow box holds Daisies Won't Tell 2 oz. Cologne, Beauty Dust & Lime Yellow Pomade. OSP $2.95 CMV $45.00 MB. Yellow Pomade $5.00

1956 BLOSSOMS
Daisy box holds 2 oz. Daisies Won't Tell Cologne with blue ribbon & gold Pomade. OSP $1.59, CMV $27.50 MB gold pomade CMV $5.00

1956 MISS DAISY SET
Daisy box holds Daisies Won't Tell 2 oz. Cologne & Beauty Dust. Top of bottle sticks through top of box. O.S.P. $2.35 CMV $37.50

1957 DAISY PETALS
Yellow & white box with pink hearts holds 2 oz. Daisies Won't Tell Cologne & lime yellow pomade lipstick in corner of box. OSP $1.59 CMV $25.00 MB

1956 DAISIES WON'T TELL SET
Daisy box holds 2 oz. Daisies Won't Tell Cologne & Bubble Bath with center rib on each & can of 3¼ oz. Daisy Talc. O.S.P. $2.25 C.M.V. Talc can only $20.00 C.M.V. $60.00 MB with outer sleeve

1958 FIELD OF DAISIES
Blue & white flowered box holds 2 oz. bottles of Daisies Won't Tell Cologne, Cream Lotion with red ribbon, & Bubble Bath. O.S.P. $2.19 C.M.V. $50.00 M.B.

1961 PRETTY BEGINNER
Blue, white & yellow box holds Daisies Won't Tell 2 oz. Cologne & choice of Daisy Soap, Daisy Dust, Cream Lotion, Shampoo or Bubble Bath. O.S.P. $2.38 C.M.V. $25.00. C.M.V. with soap $35.00 M.B.

1957 DAISIES WON'T TELL SET
Box holds 2 oz. each in Bubble Bath Cream Lotion & Cologne. White & yellow daisy caps. OSP $2.49. Came with outer sleeve. CMV $60.00 MB

1958 DAISY DARLING
Blue box with Daisies & red ribbon holds Daisies Won't Tell Spray Cologne & Beauty Dust. O.S.P. $2.98 C.M.V. $40.00 M.B.

1956 PLAYMATE
Daisies Carrying Case holds Daisies Won't Tell 2 oz. cologne, cream lotion & gold or black Pomade with plastic doll with movable arms & legs, with satin & net dress. Eyes open & shut. OSP $3.95 CMV $85.00 MB

1957 MY DOLLY
White, yellow & green box holds Daisies Won't Tell 2 oz. Cream Lotion, Cologne, Pink or Yellow Pomade & plastic doll with movable arms, black hair, blue hat, yellow dress trimmed in pink satin. O.S.P. $3.95 CMV $85.00 MB

DELFT BLUE

1972-74 DELFT BLUE
White milk glass with blue flowers.
SKIN-SO-SOFT SOFTENER 5 oz. S.S.P. $4.00 CMV $5.00 MB $4.00 BO
FOAMING BATH OIL 5 oz. holds Patchwork, Moonwind or Sonnet. S.S.P. $6.00 C.M.V. $7.00 MB $6.00 BO
PITCHER & BOWL 5 oz. S.S.P. $8.00 C.M.V. $10.00 MB $7.00 BO & bowl
SOAP DISH & SKIN-SO-SOFT SOAP 3 oz. SSP $4.00 CMV $6.00 MB

DELICATE DAISIES

1977-78 DELICATE DAISIES COLOGNE
2 oz. bottle with white painted daisies on front. White cap. O.S.P. $3.50 C.M.V. $1.00 M.B.

1977-78 DELICATE DAISIES BRUSH
Blue plastic with Avon on handle. O.S.P. $5.50 C.M.V. $1.00 M.B.

1977-78 DELICATE DAISIES PERFUMED TALC
2 oz. blue talc, white plastic top and bottom. OSP $2.00 CMV .50c. Also came with upside down label. CMV $8.00

1977-78 DELICATE DAISIES HAND CREAM
1.5 oz. tube. O.S.P. $2.00 C.M.V. 25¢

1978 DELICATE DAISIES EAR RINGS
Green and gold flower design, for pierced ears. S.S.P. $4.99 C.M.V. $2.00

1978 BUSY BEE BRACELET
Gold daisy on bracelet. S.S.P. $4.99 C.M.V. $2.00 M.B.

ELEGANTE

1957 SPARKLING BURGUNDY
Round neck & silver box with red sati lining. Holds Elegante 4 oz. Cologne, Cream Sachet. 1 dram Perfume & Beauty Dust. O.S.P. $8.95 C.M.V. $115.00 MB

1956-59 ELEGANTE PERFUME
Red & silver box holds ½oz. bottle with silver cap & neck tag with red neck ribbo O.S.P. $7.50 C.M.V. $125.00 in box. $75.00 bottle only with neck tag & ribb

956-59 ELEGANTE BEAUTY DUST
ed paper sides with tin top & bottom. lver letters on lid. OSP $2.25 CMV 15.00 MB $20.00.

956-59 ELEGANTE COLOGNE
Red & silver box holds 4 oz. bottle with lver cap & neck tag & red ribbon. OSP 2.50 CMV $40.00 in box, $20.00 bottle nly with neck tag & ribbon.

957-59 ELEGANTE TOILET WATER
Red & silver box holds 2 oz. bottle with ilver cap & neck tag & red ribbon. OSP 2.00 CMV $40.00 in box. Bottle only ith tag & ribbon $20.00.

957-59 ELEGANTE POWDER SACHET
/10 oz. bottle with silver cap. OSP $1.50 MV $12.00 BO $17.00 MB

956-59 ELEGANTE CREAM SACHET
66 oz. jar with silver cap. OSP $1.50 MV $8.00 BO $13.00 MB

1957 SNOW DREAMS SET
White box with red ribbon holds Elegante 2 oz. Toilet Water, Cream Sachet & 1 dram Perfume, in red wrapper. O.S.P. $5.50 C.M.V. $75.00 M.B.

1969-74 ELUSIVE BEAUTY DUST
Pink plastic with gold or silver trim. O.S.P. $6.00 CMV $3.00 $5.00 MB

1969-74 ELUSIVE SAMPLES
10 samples to a box. C.M.V. 50¢

1969-75 ELUSIVE ROLLETTE
.33 oz. frosted glass. O.S.P. $3.00 C.M.V. 75¢

1970-73 ELUSIVE PERFUMED DEMI STICK
Paper center, white cap. O.S.P. $1.75 C.M.V. $1.00

1969-75 ELUSIVE ½ oz. COLOGNE
½ oz. pink frosted glass. O.S.P. $2.00 C.M.V. $1.00

1969-75 ELUSIVE CREAM SACHET
Pink frosted glass. O.S.P. $3.00 C.M.V. 50¢

1970-72 ELUSIVE PERFUMED SKIN SOFTENER
Pink frosted glass. Lid came with gold or silver trim. O.S.P. $4.00 C.M.V. $1.00

1970-71 ELUSIVE TRAY
Pink plastic, gold trim. O.S.P. $4.00 CMV $6.00 MB $4.00 Tray only

ELUSIVE

1970-72 ELUSIVE SCENTED HAIR SPRAY
7 oz. pink can & cap with gold letters. O.S.P. $1.50 CMV $3.00

1971-74 ELUSIVE PERFUMED POWDER MIST
7 oz. pink painted label. O.S.P. $4.00 C.M.V. 50¢

1970-71 ELUSIVE PERFUMED POWDER MIST
7 oz. pink paper label. O.S.P. $4.00 C.M.V. $2.00

1971-74 ELUSIVE PERFUMED TALC
3½ oz. pink paper container. O.S.P. $1.35 C.M.V. 50¢

1969-74 ELUSIVE COLOGNE MIST
3 oz. pink plastic coated bottle. O.S.P. $6.00 C.M.V. 50¢

1970-72 ELUSIVE FOAMING BATH OIL
6 oz. pink plastic with pink cap. O.S.P. $3.50 CMV $2.00

1970-74 ELUSIVE PERFUMED SOAP
3 pink bars in pink box. O.S.P. $3.50 CMV $5.00 MB

1969 ELUSIVE BLOUSE & CUFFLINKS
Blouse lt. lavendar silk with label with S.M. Kent signature & Avon. Cufflinks are gold with pink sets. Awarded for selling Elusive Cologne Mists. C.M.V. $10.00 blouse, $5.00 cufflinks.

1969-74 ELUSIVE COLOGNE MIST
Left - Pink painted bottle with pink & gold cap. Paint doesn't go to bottom. Right - Later issue pink plastic coated bottle, pink & gold cap. O.S.P. $6.00 C.M.V. painted $1.00. Plastic coated 50¢.

1969 ELUSIVE CLUTCH PURSE
Pink leather with gold trim. Awarded for selling Cologne Mists. C.M.V. $10.00

1969 ORDER BOOK COVER
Pink plastic with gold "Avon Honor Award" on cover, came with pink & gold pen. C.M.V. $7.50

1969 ELUSIVE BALLAD
Small black record marked Avon in pink sleeve. C.M.V. $6.00

1969 ELUSIVE PINK& GOLD SCARF
Given to Avon sales ladies on first Elusive Sales Campaign. White box has 4A design & signed by S.M Kent, designer. C.M.V. $7.50 M.B.

1977 EMPRISE NECKLACE GIFT
Gold double E necklace given to Avon Team Leaders to introduce the new fragrance. T.L. on back side and it came in an Avon Box. C.M.V. $10.00. District Managers also got one marked D.M. on back and in D.M. Avon box. C.M.V. $15.00 M.B. Was also given to Division Managers C.M.V. $15.00 M.B. Emprise Money Clip for male Reps. C.M.V. $15.00 M.B.

1977-78 EMPRISE ULTRA GIFT SET
Box came with 1.8 oz. Ultra cologne spray and .33 oz. Ultra purse concentre. O.S.P. $11.50 C.M.V. $9.00 M.B.

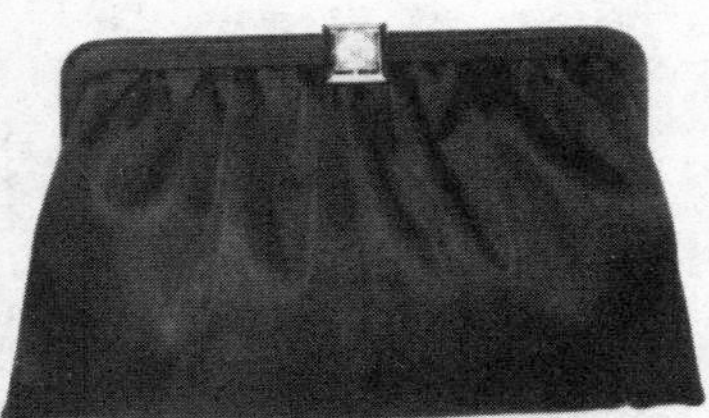

1977 EMPRISE PURSE AWARD
Black satin purse with jewel snap. Has gold carrying chain inside. Purse does not say Avon on it. Given to Reps for top sales of Emprise products. Came in clear plastic bag marked Avon. Designed by S.M. Kent. C.M.V. $10.00

1977-80 EMPRISE PERFUME
Box holds 1/4 oz bottle with glass stopper with plastic base seal. O.S.P. $15.00 C.M.V. $10.00 M.B.

EMPRISE

1977-78 EMPRISE PERFUMED SOAPS
Open end box holds 3 beige color bars. O.S.P. $7.00 C.M.V. $5.00 M.B

1977-78 EMPRISE PERFUMED SKIN SOFTENER
5 oz. plastic jar, gold and black cap. O.S.P. $6.00 C.M.V. 25¢

1977-78 EMPRISE ULTRA CREME PERFUME
.66 oz. frosted glass jar, gold cap. O.S.P. $4.50 C.M.V. 25¢

1977-80 EMPRISE FOAMING BATH OIL
6 fl. oz. bath oil. O.S.P. $5.50 C.M.V. 50¢

1977 EMPRISE PERFUMED POWDER MIST
7 oz. spray can. O.S.P. $5.00 C.M.V. 50¢

1976-80 EMPRISE ULTRA PURSE CONCENTRE
.33 oz. fluid. O.S.P. $5.00 C.M.V. 50¢

1977-80 EMPRISE PERFUMED TALC
3.5 oz. O.S.P. $3.00 C.M.V. 50¢

1976-80 EMPRISE ULTRA COLOGNE SPRAY
1.8 oz. non aerosol spray. O.S.P. $7.50 C.M.V. 50¢

1977-80 EMPRISE ULTRA COLOGNE
2 oz. O.S.P. $6.50 C.M.V. 50¢

ENGLISH PROVINCIAL

1972-74 ENGLISH PROVINCIAL
White milk glass with blue & pink flowers & aqua blue lid with flowers. Came in Charisma, or Bird of Paradise

FOAMING BATH OIL 8 oz. S.S.P. $5.00 C.M $5.00 MB $3.00 BO

COLOGNE 5 oz. SSP $5.00 CMV $5.00 MB $3.00 BO

POWDER SACHET
1.25 oz. SSP $4.00 CMV $4.00 MB $3.00 BO

SOAP DISH & SOAP
1.25 oz. SSP $4.00 CMV $4.00 $6.00 MB

1976-78 FIELD FLOWERS PERFUMED SOAP - 3 oz. white with flowered band around center. O.S.P. $1.00 C.M.V. $1.00

1972-76 FIELD FLOWERS AFTER BATH FRESHENER - 8 oz. green plastic bottle with aqua cap. O.S.P. $4.00 C.M.V. 50¢

1974-75 FIELD FLOWERS PERFUMED SOAP - 3 oz. yellow green wrapper with flowers in center. O.S.P. $1.00 C.M.V. $1.00

1974-75 FIELD FLOWERS HAND & BODY LOTION - 8 oz. yellowgreen plastic with yellow green plastic cap. O.S.P. $2.00 C.M.V. 50¢

1975-78 FIELD FLOWERS CREAM SACHET - .66 oz. clear glass with gold & green cap. O.S.P. $2.00 C.M.V. 25¢

1973-76 FIELD FLOWERS PERFUMED SKIN SOFTENER - 5 oz. yellow green plastic jar, gold lid. O.S.P. $3.00 C.M.V. 50¢

FIELD FLOWERS

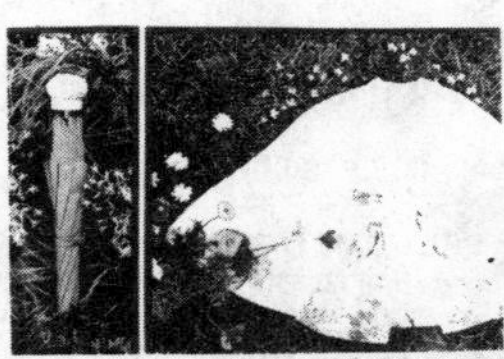

1971 FIELD FLOWERS UMBRELLA
18" Spring-green nylon umbrella has cream colored floral-relief handle. Given for making sales goal. C.M.V. $10.00

1971 FIELD FLOWERS RAIN CAPE
Given to Pres. Club Representatives only for making sales quota. Beige with floral sash. C.M.V. $20.00

1971 FIELD FLOWERS TOTE BAG
Cream-colored wet-looking vinyl Tote Bag. Field Flowers pattern inside. Given for achieving sales goal. C.M.V. $12.00

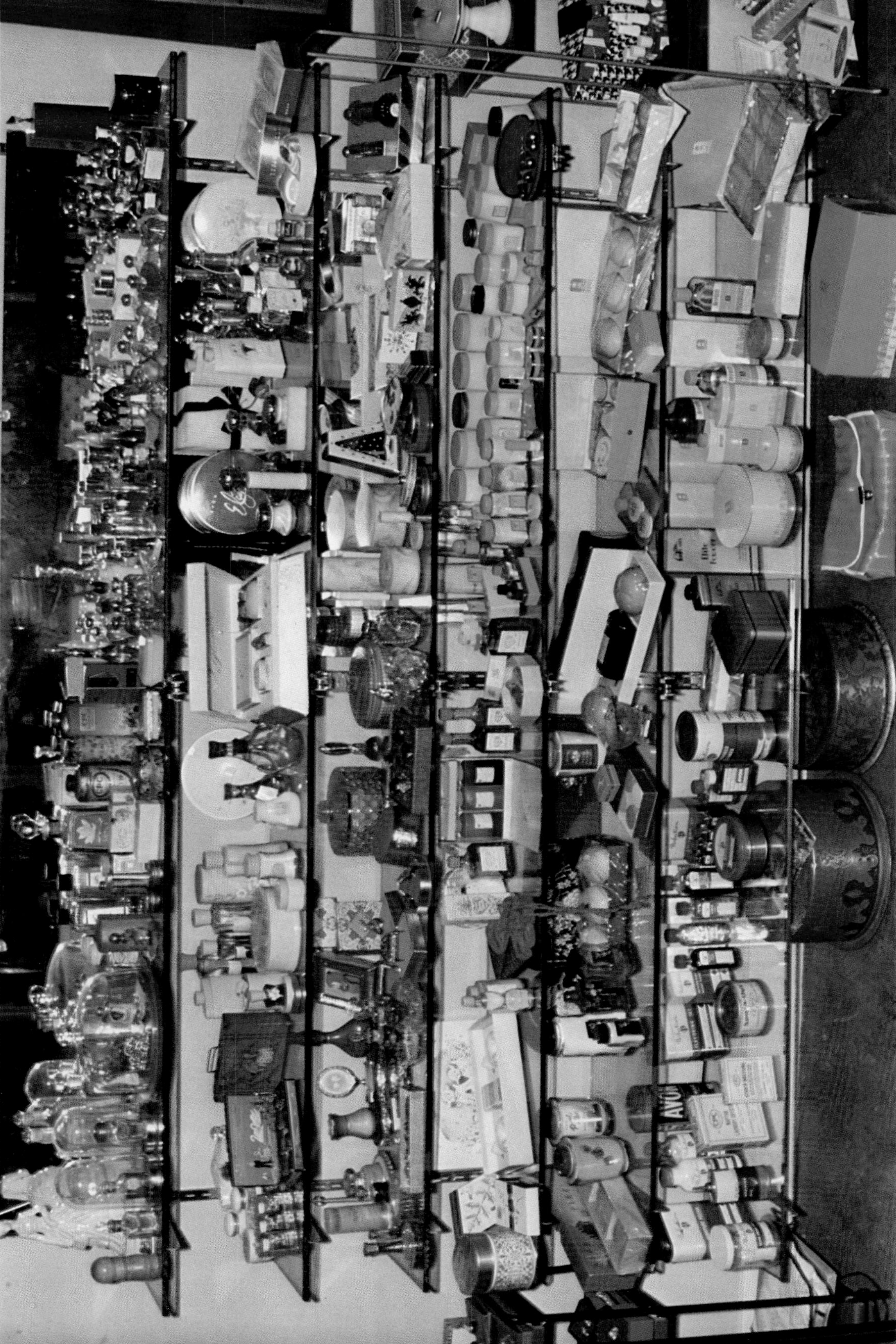

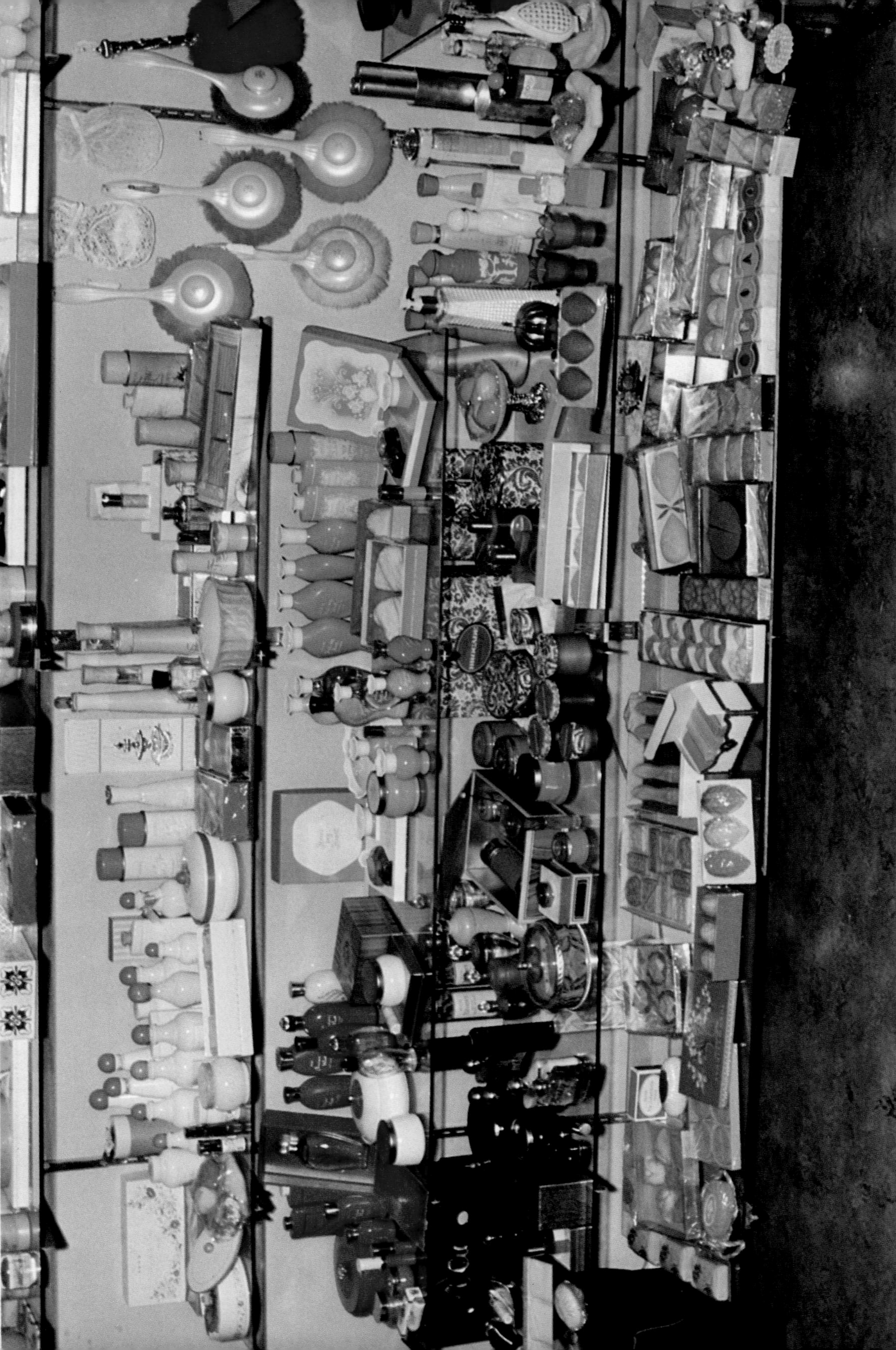

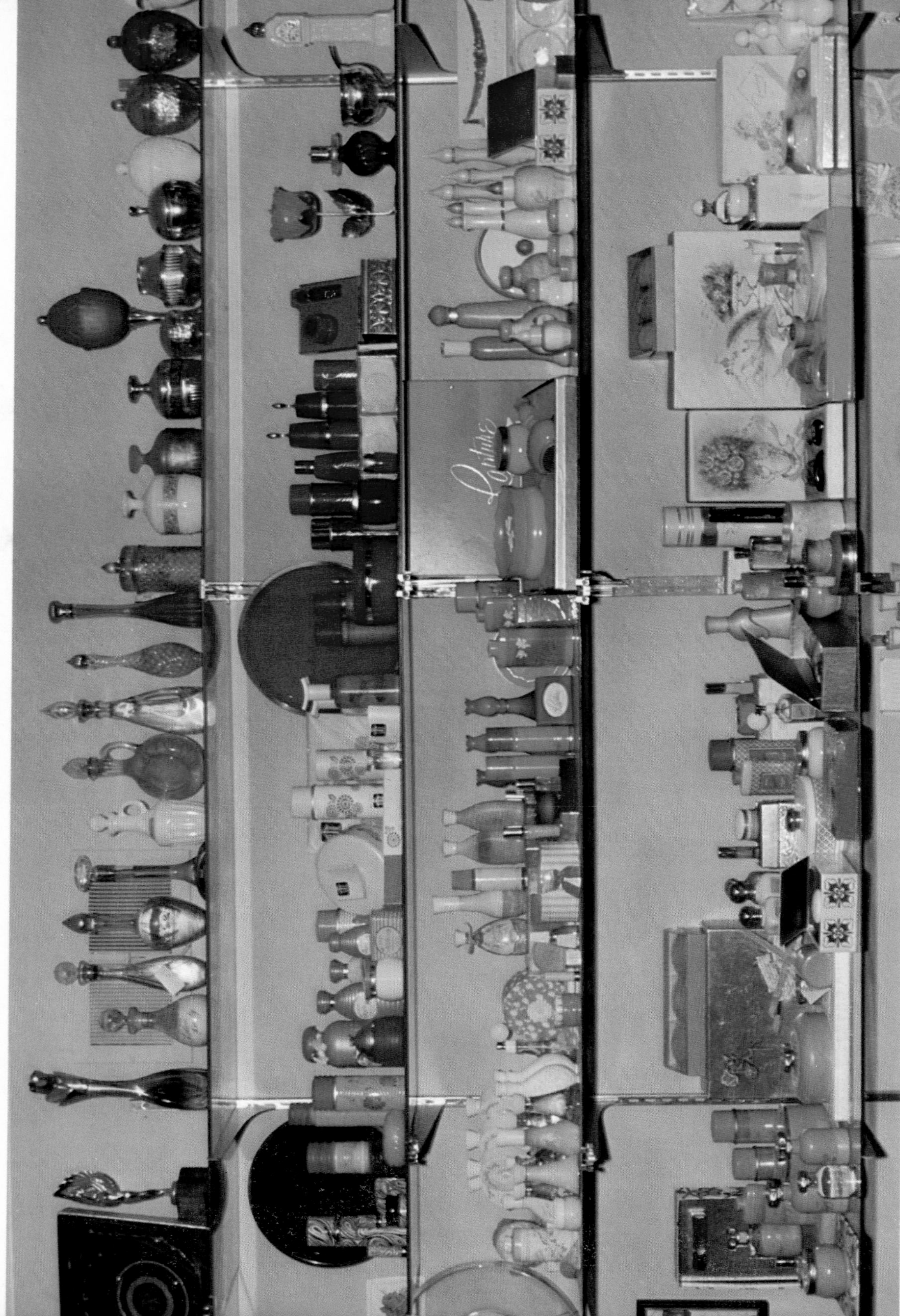

971-76 FIELD FLOWERS COLOGNE IST - 3 oz. green plastic coated over glass, ellow cap. O.S.P. $7.00 C.M.V. $1.00
971-72 FIELD FLOWERS COLOGNE ELEE - 3 oz. green ribbed glass & range cap. O.S.P. $4.00 C.M.V. $1.50
971-73 FIELD FLOWERS PERFUMED KIN SOFTENER 5 oz. green glass, bright r pale blue cap. O.S.P. $4.00 C.M.V. $1.00
971-75 FIELD FLOWERS CREAM ACHET - .66 oz. green ribbed glass with purple cap. O.S.P. $3.00 C.M.V. 50¢
1971-76 FIELD FLOWERS PERFUMED POWDER MIST 7 oz. green, white & pink can. OSP $4.50 CMV 50c. Also came with upside down label. CMV $8.00
1971-76 FIELD FLOWERS SOAP Flowered box holds yellow, pink & green flower bars. OSP $5.00 CMV $6.00 MB
1971-72 FIELD FLOWERS FOAMING BATH OIL - 6 oz. green plastic bottle with pink flowered cap. O.S.P. $4.00 C.M.V. $1.00
1971-72 FIELD FLOWERS SCENTED HAIR SPRAY - 7 oz. pink & green can with green cap. OSP $1.50 CMV $3.00

1971 FIELD FLOWERS ORDER BOOK COVER & PEN - Presidents Club. One was given for being eligible for membership. Honor Award was earned for sales goal. Cover on left - Canadian Presidents Club Honor Award Each came with Avon Pen. C.M.V. $5.00 ea. with pen.

1971-72 FIELD FLOWERS BATH BRUSH & SOAP - Pink brush approx. 16" long & 5 oz. flower embossed pink Soap. O.S.P. $6.00 C.M.V. $8.00 M.B.

1970-73 FIELD FLOWERS PERFUMED TALC - 3½ oz. green paper label. O.S.P. $2.00 C.M.V. $1.00. 1973-77 Perfume Talc had pink label. C.M.V. 50¢
1970-78 FIELD FLOWER DEMI STICK - Green paper band, white cap. O.S.P. $2.00 C.M.V. 50¢
1970-77 FIELD FLOWERS FRAGRANCE SAMPLES - 10 samples in a box. C.M.V. 50¢
1970-78 FIELD FLOWERS COLOGNE SAMPLE - Clear glass, white cap. C.M.V. 25¢

FLOWER TALK

1972-73 FLOWER TALK
White with orange, blue, yellow, green & purple designs.
PERFUMED TALC - 3.5 oz. S.S.P. $1.00 C.M.V. $1.00
COLOGNE MIST - 3 oz. S.S.P. $4.00 CMV $2.00 MB $1.00 BO
ROLLETTE - .33 oz. S.S.P. $1.00 C.M.V. $1.00
DEMI STICK - .19 oz. S.S.P. $1.00 C.M.V. 50¢
SAMPLE FLOWER TALK - C.M.V. 25¢
CREAM SACHET - .66 oz. S.S.P. $2.00 CMV $1.00 BO $2.00 MB

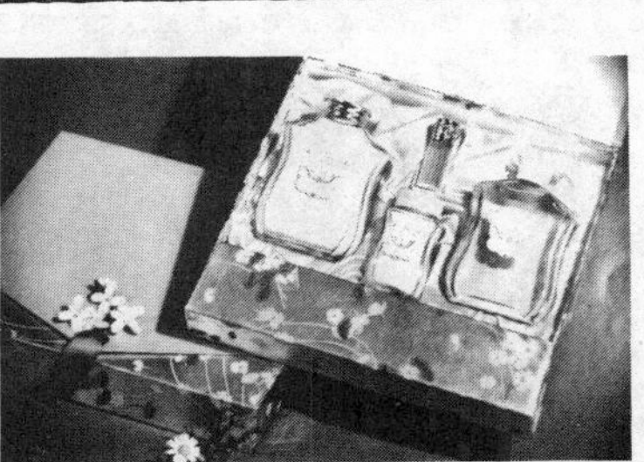

1950-52 FLOWERS IN THE WIND
Blue & silver flip-open box with pink satin lining holds Flowertime Cologne, Talc, Powder Sachet & 1 dram Perfume. O.S.P. $5.50 C.M.V. $90.00 M.B.

FLOWERTIME

1949 FLOWER CLUSTER
Blue & gold box contains box of Face Powder, Gold Lipstick, & 1 dram Flowertime Perfume. O.S.P. $3.00 C.M.V. $50.00 M.B.

1950-53 FLOWERTIME POWDER SACHET
1½ oz. with indented pink cap. O.S.P. $1.19 CMV $15.00 in box, $10.00 bottle only
1949-53 FLOWERTIME TALC
5 oz. bottle with brass shaker top. O.S.P. 89¢ CMV $23.00 in box, $18.00 BO mint.

1952 VALENTINE GIFT SACHET
In special red & white gift box. Came in Flowertime, Golden Promise, Quaintance, Cotillion. OSP 98c CMV $17.00 MB as shown. $10.00 BO mint

1949 DOUBLY YOURS SET
White & blue swing open box holds 2 oz. bottles of Cologne with pink caps in Cotillion & Flowertime. OSP $2.10 CMV $65.00 MB

1949-53 FLOWERTIME COLOGNE
4 oz. pink cap. OSP $1.75 CMV $20.00 in box. $16.00 bottle only. Same bottle came in 2 oz. size in sets only. CMV $20.00
1949-53 FLOWERTIME TOILET WATER
2 oz. pink cap. OSP $1.25 CMV $23.00 in box. $18.00 bottle only.
1949-50 FLOWERTIME POWDER SACHET
1¼ oz. bottle has flat or indented pink cap. OSP $1.19 CMV $15.00 in box $13.00 bottle only.

1949-52 FLOWERTIME SET
Turquoise & gold box with satin lining holds 4 oz. Flowertime Cologne & Talc. O.S.P. $2.75 C.M.V. $60.00 M.B.

FOREVER SPRING

ALL ITEMS' PRICES EMPTY - MINT

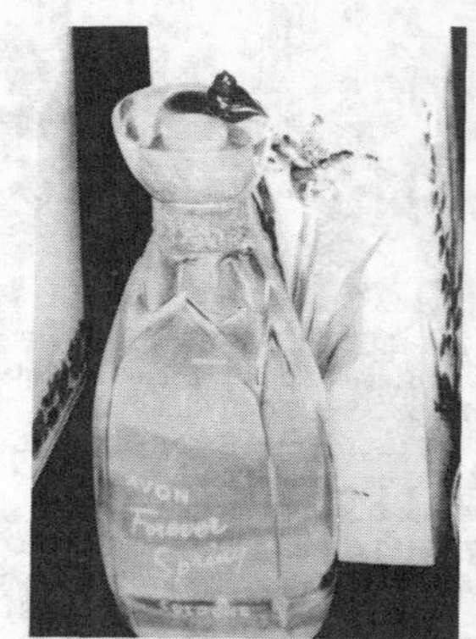

1956-59 FOREVER SPRING COLOGNE
4 oz. bottle with blue bird on yellow cap, painted label, yellow & white flowered bo
O.S.P. $2.00 C.M.V. in box $20.00. Bottle only with bird $15.00

1956-59 FOREVER SPRING CREAM SACHET - Yellow glass bottom & cap with flowers on all 3 lids shown. O.S.P. $1.25, CMV $8.00, $11.00 MB.
1956-59 FOREVER SPRING POWDER SACHET - 9/10 oz. Yellow glass & cap. OSP $1.25, CMV $9.00, $12.00 MB
1956-59 FOREVER SPRING BODY POWDER - Frosted glass jar with flowere cap, painted label. O.S.P. $1.00 C.M.V. $12.00 BO $17.00 MB

1956-59 FOREVER SPRING CREAM LOTION
4 oz. green painted glass bottle with yellow cap. OSP 95c, CMV $20.00 in box, $17.00 bottle only, mint.

1956 SPRINGTIME
Yellow & white box holds Forever Spring Beauty Dust & 4 oz. Cologne. O.S.P. $3.95 C.M.V. $50.00

1953 FOREVER SPRING SET
Green & white box with green net lining holds Forever Spring Body Powder, Cream Sachet & 1 dram Perfume in green felt sleeve. O.S.P. $3.95 C.M.V. $55.00 M.B.
1952 FOREVER SPRING SET is same as above only did not have 1 dram Perfume. O.S.P. $2.75 C.M.V. $37.50 M.B.

1951 FOREVER SPRING REPRESENTATIVE GIFT SET - CMV $80.00 MB.

1951-52 SPRING CORSAGE
Green box with clear plastic lid & bouquet of flowers holds Forever Spring 4 oz Cologne & 1 dram Perfume. O.S.P. $4.50 C.M.V. $50.00

1953 SPRING SONG
Blue & green box holds Forever Spring 4 oz. Cologne & 1 dram Perfume. O.S.P. $3.50 C.M.V. $40.00 M.B.

1952-53 SPRING MELODY
Forever Spring Body Powder & Cream Sachet setting on top under clear plastic lid. O.S.P. $1.95 C.M.V. $35.00 M.B.

1956 MERRY MERRY SPRING
Yellow, white & blue box holds Forever Spring 2 oz. Toilet Water & Cream Sachet. O.S.P. $2.75 C.M.V. $37.50 M.B.

1956 FOREVER SPRING POWDER BOX COLOGNE
1/16 oz. size bottle came in special beauty dust box set only. Came tied to silk ribbon. CMV $12.00 BO mint $15.00 mint with ribbon.

1956-59 FOREVER SPRING CREAM LOTION - 4 oz. clear glass with yellow cap, painted label. No bird on cap. Came in yellow & white box. O.S.P. 95¢ C.M.V. in box $14.00 Bottle only $12.00 mint.

1956-59 FOREVER SPRING TOILET WATER - 2 oz. yellow cap with tiny blue bird, painted label. Came in yellow & white flowered box. O.S.P. $1.50 C.M.V. in box $20.00. Bottle only with bird $15.00 mint.

1951-56 FOREVER SPRING CREAM SACHET - Green box holds white glass jar with green lid. O.S.P. $1.25 C.M.V. $12.00 in box. $9.00 jar only - mint.

1956-59 FOREVER SPRING PERFUME
Yellow & white box with purple base holds ½ oz. bottle with blue bird on yellow cap & painted label. O.S.P. $5.00 C.M.V. in box $100.00, bottle only with bird $85.00.

1953 SPRING CREATION
Green box with net lining holds Forever Spring Cream Sachet & 1 dram Perfume. O.S.P. $2.75 C.M.V. $40.00 M.B.

1951-56 FOREVER SPRING TOILET WATER - 2 oz. yellow tulip cap & green painted label. Came in green box. O.S.P. $1.50 C.M.V. $20.00 in box. $17.50 B.O. mint

1951-56 FOREVER SPRING BODY POWDER - Green & white paper container. O.S.P. 95¢ C.M.V. $18.00

1957-59 FOREVER SPRING PERFUMED TALC - 2.75 oz. Yellow & white can, yellow cap. O.S.P. 69¢ C.M.V. $10.00, M.B. $12.00

1951-52 FOREVER SPRING 1 DRAM PERFUME - 1 dram, ribbed glass, gold cap. Came in green felt folder. O.S.P. $1.75 C.M.V. $17.00 in sleeve. $12.00 B.O.

1951-56 FOREVER SPRING BEAUTY DUST - Green & white can. O.S.P. $1.75 CMV $20.00 $25.00 MB

1956-59 FOREVER SPRING BEAUTY DUST - Yellow & white paper box with tin top & bottom. O.S.P. $1.95 C.M.V. $16.00 $20.00 MB

1957 SPRING GODDESS
Yellow & white box holds Forever Spring Beauty Dust, Cream Sachet & 4 oz. Cologne. O.S.P. $4.95 C.M.V. $50.00 M.B.

1951-56 FOREVER SPRING PERFUME
Yellow & green box with blue & green ribbon holds 3 dram glass stoppered bottle with blue ribbon on neck & neck tag. O.S.P. $5.00 C.M.V. $100.00 in box, $85.00 bottle only with tag & ribbon.

1956 SPRING MOOD
Yellow & white box holds Forever Spring Body Powder & 4 oz. Cream Lotion in green glass. O.S.P. $1.95 C.M.V. $40.00 M.B.

1956-57 APRIL AIRS
Yellow & white box with blue ribbon top holds Forever Spring Body Powder & Cream Sachet. O.S.P. $2.25 C.M.V. $40.00 MB.

1951-56 FOREVER SPRING COLOGNE
4 oz. with yellow tulip cap & green painted label. Came in green box. O.S.P. $2.25 CMV $20.00 in box, $16.00 mint bottle only.

1953-56 FOREVER SPRING POWDER SACHET - 1¼ oz. bottle with yellow cap & green painted label. Came in green box. O.S.P. $1.25 C.M.V. $15.00 in box. $11.00 Bottle only mint

GARDEN OF LOVE

See Misc. perfumes for Garden of Love Perfumes

LEFT 1946-48 GARDEN OF LOVE POWDER SACHET
1¼ oz. turquoise ribbed plastic cap & flowered label. O.S.P. $1.19 C.M.V. $20.00 in box $17.00 bottle only.
CENTER 1944-45 GARDEN OF LOVE SACHET
1¼ oz. pink paper sachet. Came with pink plastic flower on lid. O.S.P. $1.15 C.M.V. $18.00 mint, $20.00 M.B.
RIGHT 1940-46 GARDEN OF LOVE POWDER SACHET
1¼ oz. bottle with black or turquoise metal cap. OSP $1.04, CMV $20.00, $15.00 bottle only.

1948 Only - GARDEN OF LOVE SWIRL PERFUME
3 dram glass stoppered bottle is swirl glass design with gold neck tag. Purple & white flowered box. O.S.P. $3.00 C.M.V. $90.00 B.O. mint, $120.00 M.B.

1940-44 GARDEN OF LOVE PERFUME
Orange lid, gold base box holds 3 dram glass stoppered bottle with gold neck tag. O.S.P. $2.50 C.M.V. $100.00 mint, B.O. $125.00 M.B.

GOLDEN PROMISE

ALL CONTAINERS PRICED EMPTY

See Page 5 for Grading Examples on Mint Condition

1947-56 GOLDEN PROMISE COLOGNE
4 oz. painted label, gold cap. O.S.P. $2.25 C.M.V. $18.00 M.B. $22.00

1953-56 GOLDEN PROMISE TOILET WATER - 2 oz. gold cap & painted label. O.S.P. $1.50 C.M.V. $20.00 M.B. $24.00

1948 GOLDEN PROMISE SACHET
Special gold box 62nd anniversary issue. 1¼ oz. ribbed gold plastic cap or threaded brass cap. OSP $1.25 CMV $17.50 MB as shown.

1953-56 GOLDEN PROMISE CREAM SACHET
White glass, square base with yellow flowered cap. OSP $1.00 CMV $8.00 BO $11.00 MB

1947-56 GOLDEN PROMISE BODY POWDER
Gold & white shaker Top can. OSP $1.50 CMV $16.00 CO mint $20.00 MB

Left - 1947-56 GOLDEN PROMISE BEAUTY DUST
Standard issue Gold & white can. OSP $1.50 CMV $18.00 CO mint $22.00 MB

Right - 1947-51 GOLDEN PROMISE BEAUTY DUST
Smaller then regular issue came in sets only. CMV $20.00 mint

1947-49 GOLDEN PROMISE 3 PIECE SET - Gold & white box holds Golden Promise 1 dram Perfume, 4 oz. Cologne & Beauty Dust. O.S.P. $4.95 C.M.V. $82.50 MB

1947 GOLDEN PROMISE PERFUME GIFT - Clear bottle, gold cap. Label is gold with red lettering, says "Golden Promise Perfume with Best Wishes of Avon Products, Inc., Pasadena, Cal." Came in gold box with same statement. C.M.V. $75.00 M.B. $50.00 B.O.

1953-54 GOLDEN JEWEL
White & gold box with gold jewel on front. Holds Golden Promise 2 oz. Toilet Water & 1 dram Perfume. Toilet Water cap fits through top of box. O.S.P. $2.75 C.M.V. $40.00 M.B.

1949 Only - GOLDEN PROMISE PERFUME
¼ oz. glass bottle fits in gold metal case. Came in Golden Duet & Evening Charm Sets. C.M.V. $25.00

1947-49 GOLDEN PROMISE 2 PIECE SET - Gold & white box holds Golden Promise 4 oz. Cologne & Body Powder. OSP $2.95 CMV $60.00 MB

1947-50 GOLDEN PROMISE PERFUME
Gold & white flip open box holds ½ oz. bottle with gold cap & painted label. O.S.P. $3.95 C.M.V. $175.00 in box. Bottle only $100.00 mint

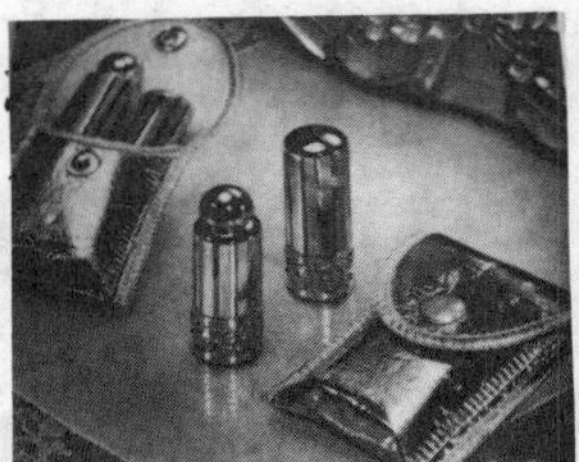

1949 GOLDEN DUET
Small gold purse holds Lipstick & gold metal case with ½ dram bottle of Golden Promise Perfume inside. O.S.P. $2.50 C.M.V. $35.00 mint. $40.00 M.B.

1947 GOLDEN PROMISE BODY POWDER CHRISTMAS DEMO
Regular issue talc in gold box given to Avon ladies in special outer Merry Christmas demo box. OSP $1.50 CMV $30.00 MB with outer box shown

1950-51 GOLDEN PROMISE SET
Gold box with clear plastic cover & gold tie down ribbon holds Golden Promise 4 oz. Cologne & Beauty Dust. O.S.P. $3.95 CMV $60.00 MB

1952-54 GOLDEN PROMISE DELUXE
Gold box with clear plastic lid & gold satin lining holds Golden Promise 4 oz. Cologne, Powder Sachet, 1 dram Perfume & Body Powder. Gold ribbon around box. O.S.P. $6.25 C.M.V. $100.00 M.B.

Left to Right:
1952-56 GOLDEN PROMISE POWDER SACHET
1¼ oz. yellow plastic cap. OSP $1.25 CMV $12.00 MB $9.00 BO
1951-52 GOLDEN PROMISE POWDER SACHET
1¼ oz. gold cap. OSP $1.25 CMV $12.00 MB $9.00 BO
1948-50 GOLDEN PROMISE POWDER SACHET
1¼ oz. Smooth gold cap. OSP $1.19 CMV $12.00 MB $9.00 BO

1950-54 GOLDEN PROMISE PERFUME
Gold & white box holds 3 dram glass stoppered bottle with gold base label & neck cord. O.S.P. $4.00 C.M.V. $125.00 in box. Bottle with label & cord $100.00

1954-56 GOLDEN PROMISE PERFUME
Gold & white box holds ½ oz. bottle with flat glass stopper & gold & white label. O.S.P. $3.95 C.M.V. $125.00 in box. $90.00 bottle only mint.

HANA GASA

1970-74 HANA GASA FRAGRANCE SAMPLES - 10 in a box. C.M.V. 50¢ box.
1970-74 HANA GASA COLOGNE SAMPLE - Sample bottle, white cap. C.M.V. 25¢
1970-75 HANA GASA COLOGNE
½ oz. clear glass, yellow cap. O.S.P. $2.00 C.M.V. $1.00
1970-74 HANA GASA PERFUME ROLLETTE - Yellow painted glass, yellow cap. O.S.P. $3.00 C.M.V. $1.00
1970-75 HANA GASA CREAM SACHET
.66 oz. yellow painted over milk glass with yellow lid. OSP $3.00 CMV .50c
1970-76 HANA GASA BEAUTY DUST
6 oz. yellow plastic. O.S.P. $8.50 C.M.V. $3.00 CO $5.00 MB

1971 HANA GASA HAIR SPRAY
7 oz. yellow can OSP $1.50 CMV $3.00
1971-74 HANA GASA PERFUME POWDER MIST - 7 oz. yellow can. O.S.P. $4.00 C.M.V. $1.00
1971-74 HANA GASA PERFUME TALC
3½ oz. yellow cardboard. O.S.P. $1.35 C.M.V. $1.00
1971-77 HANA GASA FOAMING BATH OIL
6 oz. clear plastic bottle, also yellow plastic bottle, yellow cap. OSP $4.50 CMV $1.00
1970-76 HANA GASA COLOGNE MIST
3 oz. yellow plastic coated glass, yellow cap. O.S.P. $6.00 C.M.V. $1.00
1971-75 HANA GASA SOAP
3 yellow bars in pink & yellow box. O.S.P. $5.00 C.M.V. $5.00 M.B.

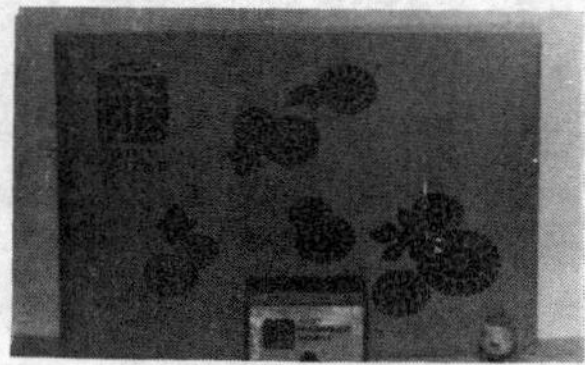

1970-71 HANA GASA GIFT NOTES
Yellow with pink flowers, has 15 notes & envelopes. 18 seals. O.S.P. $2.00 C.M.V. $2.00

1970 HANA GASA UMBRELLA
Bamboo painted in Hana Gasa colors. Used at sales meetings at introduction of Hana Gasa. Came in Avon Box. Very rare. C.M.V. $100.00 in box.

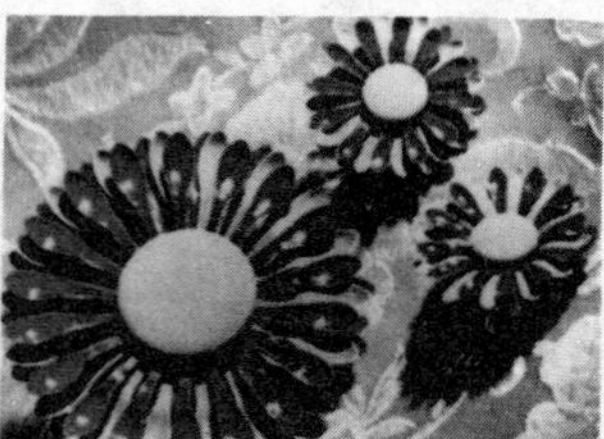

1970 HANA GASA JEWELRY
Enameled pin & clip-on earrings are deep red & purple. Given when someone a representative recommended was appointed as a representative. C.M.V. $15.00 set

70 HANA GASA HAPPI-COAT
ellow with orange & green flowers. Given hen someone a representative recommended as appointed as a representative. One size ts all. C.M.V. $10.00 mint.

HAPPY HOURS

1948-49 HAPPY HOURS SET
Pink & blue box holds Happy Hours Talc, Cologne & Perfume. O.S.P. $2.00 C.M.V. $115.00 MB

1948-49 HAPPY HOURS TALC
2¾ oz. metal shaker cap. Sold in sets only. CMV $20.00 mint
1948-49 HAPPY HOURS COLOGNE
1 oz. plastic cap. Came in sets only. CMV $20.00 mint
1948-49 HAPPY HOURS PERFUME
3 drams, pink cap. Rare. Came in sets only. CMV $50.00 mint

1948-49 MEMENTO
Blue & pink box holds Happy Hours Cologne & perfume. OSP $1.50 CMV $90.00 MB

1948-49 STAR BOUQUET
Green & pink box holds Happy Hours Talc & Cologne. OSP $1.25 CMV $65.00 MB

HAWAIIAN WHITE GINGER

1968-72 HAWAIIAN WHITE GINGER CREAM SACHET - Both .66 oz. green frosted jars & flowered caps. Short jar 1967 same as Lily of The Valley jar. C.M.V. $2.00.
Tall green jar in 1969 O.S.P. C.M.V. $1.00

1976-78 HAWAIIAN WHITE GINGER COLOGNE SPRAY
1.8 oz. flower embossed bottle, gold cap. O.S.P. $5.00 C.M.V. 50¢
1976-78 HAWAIIAN WHITE GINGER BODY SPLASH
8 oz plastic bottle, white cap. O.S.P.$5.00 C.M.V. 50¢

LEFT 1967-72 BATH FRESHENER
6 oz. glass bottle with white cap. O.S.P. $2.50 C.M.V. $2.00
CENTER 1968-76 HAWAIIAN WHITE GINGER FOAMING BATH OIL
8 oz. plastic bottle. O.S.P. $3.00 C.M.V. 50¢
RIGHT 1969-72 HAWAIIAN WHITE GINGER CREAM LOTION
5 oz. plastic bottle. O.S.P. $2.00 C.M.V. 75¢

1972-76 HAWAIIAN WHITE GINGER AFTER BATH FRESHENER - 8 oz. white plastic bottle with white cap. O.S.P. $5.00 C.M.V. 50¢
1971-72 HAWAIIAN WHITE GINGER COLOGNE MIST - 2 oz. lt, green glass bottle with white cap. O.S.P. $4.25 CMV $1.00 $2.00 MB
1965-67 HAWAIIAN WHITE GINGER AFTER BATH FRESHENER - 5 oz. bottle with white painted label & cap. Also came with & without gold 4A design O.S.P. $2.00 C.M.V. $6.00 in box, $5.00 bottle only.

1972-76 HAWAIIAN WHITE GINGER COLOGNE MIST - 2 oz. clear glass bottle with clear plastic cap with inner cap of green, red & white. O.S.P. $5.00 C.M.V. 75¢

1972-74 HAWAIIAN WHITE GINGER ROLLETTE - .33 oz. clear bottle, white cap with colored band. O.S.P. $2.50 C.M.V. 50¢

1970-78 HAWAIIAN WHITE GINGER DEMI STICK - .19 oz. green, red & white, white cap. O.S.P. $1.75 C.M.V. 50¢

1973-78 HAWAIIAN WHITE GINGER CREAM SACHET
.66 oz. glass jar, white, green & red cap. This has 3 different lid labels. Early ones — no zip code. .66 oz. Next — zip but no numbers. Doesn't have weight on lid. Later ones have zip & numbers but no weight on lid. O.S.P. $2.50 C.M.V. 50¢.

1972-73 FLORAL DUET HAWAIIAN WHITE GINGER - Came with Rollette & bar of soap. O.S.P. $3.25 CMV $5.00 MB

1970-78 HAWAIIAN WHITE GINGER SOAP - 3 oz. single bar soap (same as shown in set) OSP $1.00 CMV $1.00

1969-75 WHITE GINGER FRAGRANCE KWICKETTES (Not Shown) - Box holds 14 packets. OSP $1.50 CMV $1.00 box.

LEFT 1968 Only - HAWAIIAN WHITE GINGER TALC
2.75 oz. green & white Talc sold in perfume pair only. C.M.V. $2.00

CENTER 1968-73 HAWAIIAN WHITE GINGER TALC
3.5 oz. multi-colored cardboard, gold letter label. O.S.P. $2.00 C.M.V. $1.00
1974-77 Talc came with pink letter label. C.M.V.

RIGHT 1972 HAWAIIAN WHITE GINGER BEAUTY DUST
Multi-colored cardboard. O.S.P. $3.00 CMV $4.00 mint, $5.00 MB

GARDENIA

1940-42 GARDENIA PERFUME
Gold speckled box holds 3/8 oz. bottle with gold octagonal cap. OSP $1.50 CMV $50.00 BO mint $80.00 MB

1948-52 GARDENIA PERFUME
3/8 oz. or 3 dram bottle with flowered cap. Came in satin lined box with clear plastic lid. OSP $2.50 ea. CMV $80.00 MB $50.00 bottle only mint

1933-36 GARDENIA PERFUME "RIBBED"
½ oz. ribbed glass with black octagonal cap. Came in Gold box set. CMV $45.00 mint

1933-36 GARDENIA PERFUME "OCTAGONAL"
6 sided bottle & black octagonal cap. Came in Little Folks set & Handkerchief set. CMV $45.00 mint

HELLO SUNSHINE

1979-80 HELLO SUNSHINE PRODUCTS
LIP BALM
Pink-white & yellow CMV .50c
HAND CREAM
White, yellow & pink 1.5 oz. tube. Green cap. CMV .50c
FUN SHINE NAIL TINT
.5 oz. clear glass, pink cap. CMV .75c MB
COLOGNE
2.5 oz. clear glass. yellow cap. Yellow & pink decal on glass. CMV $1.00

HER PRETTINESS

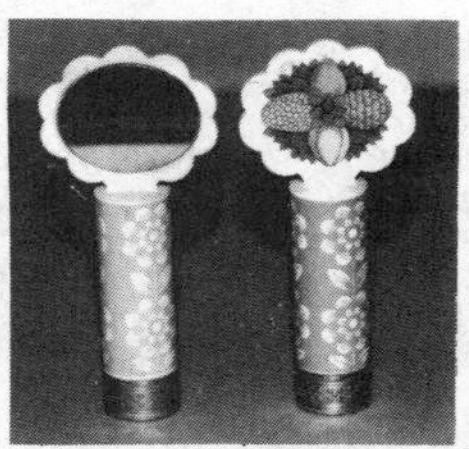

1970-71 HER PRETTINESS LIP KISSES
Lip Pomade, tubes blue & white, pink & white, orange & white in cherry, chocolate or peppermint. Mirror on back side of cap. OSP $1.95 CMV $2.00 ea. $3.00 MB

1970 ROYAL FOUNTAIN CREME SACHET — Blue base with silver & gold fountain top. Contains Her Prettiness Creme Sachet. O.S.P. $3.00 C.M.V. $5.00 M.B.

1970-71 HER PRETTINESS TALC
3½ oz. flowered paper box. O.S.P. $1.00 C.M.V. $2.00

969-71 PRETTY ME DOLL
oz. plastic bottle with gold hair, cap
pink neck ribbon. Holds Powdered
ubble Bath. 6½" high. O.S.P. $6.00
MV $8.00, $6.00 BO
969-72 FLOWER BELLE COLOGNE
IIST - Blue top with yellow base has 2 oz.
ler Prettiness Cologne Mist. O.S.P. $3.50
.M.V. $4.00
969-72 BRUSH & COMB SET
ink box with yellow comb & brush.
).S.P. $3.50 C.M.V. $5.00
969-72 BUNNY PUFF
½ oz. white plastic rabbit with pink
luff tail. Holds Her Prettiness Talc.
).S.P. $3.75 C.M.V. $5.00
976 BUNNY FLUFF PUFF
leissued - Same except holds
ink & Pretty. O.S.P. $4.00, C.M.V. $4.00
Also has R on bottom for reissue.
1979 reissued in yellow rabbit.
It is shown in childrens toy sections.

1969-72 HER PRETTINESS ENCHANTED COLOGNE MIST - Brown tree base holds 3 oz. Cologne Mist in green bubble top & green bird spray button. O.S.P. $5.00 C.M.V. $6.00 M.B. $7.00
1969-72 MAGIC MUSHROOM CREAM SACHET - Green, pink & blue plastic. O.S.P. $3.00 C.M.V. $4.00
1969-72 LADY BUG FRAGRANCE GLACE - Red, black & green plastic bug. O.S.P. $3.00 C.M.V. $3.00 M.B. $4.00
1969-71 LOVE LOCKET FRAGRANCE GLACE - Gold locket & chain, in yellow, gold & pink box. O.S.P. $4.50 C.M.V. $10.00 M.B.
1969-72 SECRET TOWER ROLLETTE Red cap on bottle. O.S.P. $1.75 CMV $3.00 MB

1969-70 HER PRETTINESS ART REPRODUCTION PRINT - 14"x18" Pink, green & white, was free with purchase of any Her Prettiness products. Came in cardboard tube with Her Prettiness sticker & a poem "Her Prettiness Serves Ten In The Garden" C.M.V. $8.00 three pieces. $4.00 print alone.

1969-72 HER PRETTINESS COLOGNE SAMPLE
1/8 oz. clear glass white cap. Painted label. Came in envelope. CMV $1.00 mint in envelope.

HERE'S MY HEART

1946-48 HERE'S MY HEART PERFUME
½ oz. glass stoppered bottle with painted label & pink neck ribbons. Bottle is tied to pink satin heart shaped base & box. O.S.P. $7.50 C.M.V. in box $140.00. Bottle only with ribbon $100.00.

1960-66 HERE'S MY HEART PERFUMED BATH OIL
6 oz. blue plastic, white beaded cap. OSP $2.25 CMV $5.00 BO $6.00 MB
1966-68 FOAMING BATH OIL
6 oz. blue plastic, white beaded cap. OSP $2.75 CMV $6.00 MB $4.00 BO

1959 POWDER SACHET CHRISTMAS BOX
Blue box with gold butterflies sold Christmas only 1959 with choice of Powder sachet in Here's My Heart, Persian Wood, Nearness, Cotillion (pink painted), Bright Night and To a Wild Rose. O.S.P. $1.50-$1.75 C.M.V. $15.00 each M.B. as shown.

1948-49 HERE'S MY HEART PERFUME
½ oz. glass stoppered heart shaped bottle. Painted label, pink satin ribbon & heart shaped box & base. Very rare. O.S.P. $7.50 C.M.V. bottle only $125.00 Bottle in box $175.00.

1961 HERE'S MY HEART COLOGNE SPECIAL ISSUE
Blue and white box (short issue) holds 4 oz. cologne. O.S.P. $3.00 C.M.V. $16.00 MB as shown.

1957-58 HERE'S MY HEART COLOGNE MIST
3 oz. blue plastic coated bottle with indented heart, 2 hearts on gold cap. Also plain lid. OSP $3.00 CMV $18.00 BO mint. $23.00 MB

1963 HERE'S MY HEART PERFUME OIL FOR THE BATH - ½ oz. painted label & white beaded cap. Came in blue & white box. O.S.P. $3.50 C.M.V. $15.00 M.B. Bottle only $12.00.
1970-71 HERE'S MY HEART ½ OZ. COLOGNE - ½ oz. painted label, white beaded cap, blue & white box. O.S.P. $1.50 CMV $1.00 BO $1.50 MB

1959-62 HERE'S MY HEART TOIL WATER - 2 oz. painted label & whit beaded cap. Came in blue & white b O.S.P. $2.50 C.M.V. $12.00 in box, $10.00 bottle only.
1960-63 HERE'S MY HEART 4 OZ. COLOGNE - 4 oz. bottle with white beaded cap & painted label. Came in blue & white box. O.S.P. $3.00 C.M. $12.00 in box, bottle only $10.00.

1964-68 HERE'S MY HEART PERFUME OIL - ½ oz. painted label & white beaded cap. Came in blue & white box. O.S.P. $3.50 C.M.V. $8.00 in box. $6.00 bottle only.
1958-61 HERE'S MY HEART LOTION SACHET - 1 oz. blue plastic coated bottle with white beaded cap & painted label. Blue & white box. O.S.P. $2.00 C.M.V. $8.00 in box. $5.00 bottle only.
1961-68 HERE'S MY HEART 2 OZ. COLOGNE - 2 oz. white beaded cap & painted label, blue & white box. First introduced in red & white rose box. O.S.P. $1.75 C.M.V. in rose box $8.00 In blue box $3.00. Bottle only $2.00
1958-76 HERE'S MY HEART COLOGNE MIST - 3 oz. blue plastic coated bottle with white beaded cap & painted label. Blue & white box. O.S.P. $7.00 C.M.V. $1.00.

1967-68 HERE'S MY HEART PERFUME ROLLETTE - .33 oz. ribbed glass, smooth gold cap. O.S.P. $3.00 C.M.V. $3.00
1963-65 PERFUMED CREAM ROLLETTE .33 oz. 4A embossed bottle with gold cap. O.S.P. $1.75 C.M.V. $3.00 mint.
1960-66 HERE'S MY HEART POWDER SACHET - 9/10 oz. blue glass, white beaded plastic cap. O.S.P. $2.00 C.M.V. $8.00. M.B. $10.00.
1958-60 HERE'S MY HEART POWDER SACHET - Blue & white plastic squeeze bottle with white beaded cap. O.S.P. $1.75 C.M.V. $10.00. M.B. $12.00.
1975-78 HERE'S MY HEART DEMI STICK - .19 oz. blue & white, white cap. O.S.P. $1.00 C.M.V. 25¢
1976-77 HERE'S MY HEART CREAM SACHET - .66 oz. clear glass, gold, blue & white lid. O.S.P. $2.00 C.M.V. 25¢

1958-62 HERE'S MY HEART PERFUMED TALC
2.75 oz. blue & white can, white beaded cap. OSP. .79c CMV $3.00 CO $4.00 MB
1966-70 HERE'S MY HEART SCENTEL HAIR SPRAY — 7 oz. blue & white can 4A on cap. OSP $1.50 CMV $3.00
1962-72 HERE'S MY HEART PERFUM TALC - 2.75 oz. blue & white can with white cap. O.S.P. 79¢ C.M.V. $1.00.

1950 HERE'S MY HEART PERFUME SAMPLE - With gold lid. C.M.V. $30.00
1957-58 HERE'S MY HEART LOTION SACHET - 1 oz. blue plastic coated bottle with hearts on gold cap, painted label. O.S.P. $2.00 C.M.V. $15.00. M.B. $18.00.

1958 LOTION SACHET
½ oz. clear glass fan shaped bottle with blue cap. Came in Here's My Heart & Persian Wood. Came in Wishing Set only. CMV $8.00 ea. MB $4.00 BO
1961-63 HERE'S MY HEART BODY POWDER - 4 oz. blue plastic bottle with white beaded cap, painted label. O.S.P. $1.95 CMV $8.00 MB $5.00 BO

1958-68 HERE'S MY HEART CREAM LOTION - 4 oz. bottle with painted label & white beaded cap. O.S.P. $1.00 C.M.V. $2.00 BO $3.00 MB
1958-63 HERE'S MY HEART SPRAY PERFUME - Blue, white & gold box hold blue tin container with gold cap with hea on top. O.S.P. $3.50 C.M.V. $12.00 in b $8.00 container only.

1959-75 HERE'S MY HEART CREAM SACHET
.66 oz. white beaded cap. Came blue painted over clear glass. CMV .50c or blue paint over white milk glass. CMV $3.00 OSP $3.00
1964-73 HERE'S MY HEART PERFUMED SKIN SOFTENER
5 oz. blue painted over milk glass or clear glass jar with gold & white lid. OSP $3.00 CMV $1.00
1958-70 HERE'S MY HEART BEAUTY DUST
White plastic powder box with beaded edge. Some with yellow lid & white handle CMV $10.00 OSP $3.00 white issue CMV $3.00 CO $4.00 MB

1959-64 HERE'S MY HEART SOAP
Blue & white box, holds 2 white heart shaped bars. OSP $1.29 CMV $22.50 MB M.B.

1964 HEARTS IN BLOOM
Blue & white box holds Here's My Heart Cologne Mist, Cream Sachet & Cream Lotion. O.S.P. $6.50 C.M.V. $35.00 M.B.

1961 SENTIMENTAL HEART
Blue box with blue satin lining holds Here's My Heart Cologne Mist & Beauty Dust. O.S.P. $6.50 C.M.V. $30.00 M.B.

1966-67 HERE'S MY HEART SOAP
Blue & white box holds 3 heart shaped bars. OSP $1.75 $22.50 MB

1965-66 HERE'S MY HEART PERFUMED SOAP - 3 oz. white soap in blue & white wrapper. O.S.P. 39¢ C.M.V. $3.00
1964-68 HERE'S MY HEART PERFUME MIST - 2 dram blue & white metal with gold band OSP $3.00 CMV $5.00 $6.00 MB
1970-73 HERE'S MY HEART FRAGRANCE SAMPLE - 10 foil samples in a box. C.M.V. 75¢ box
1960-66 HERE'S MY HEART POWDER SACHET SAMPLE - C.M.V. $1.00

1964 HEART FELT SET
Blue & white box holds Here's My Heart 2 oz. Cologne & Cream Sachet. O.S.P. $3.50 C.M.V. $22.50 MB.

1960 ROMANTIC MOOD
Blue & white box with blue satin lining with Here's My Heart Cologne Mist, Cream Sachet & Beauty Dust. O.S.P. $8.25 C.M.V. $40.00 M.B.

1962-65 HERE'S MY HEART SOAP
Blue & white box holds 2 white heart shaped soaps. OSP $1.29 CMV $22.50 MB

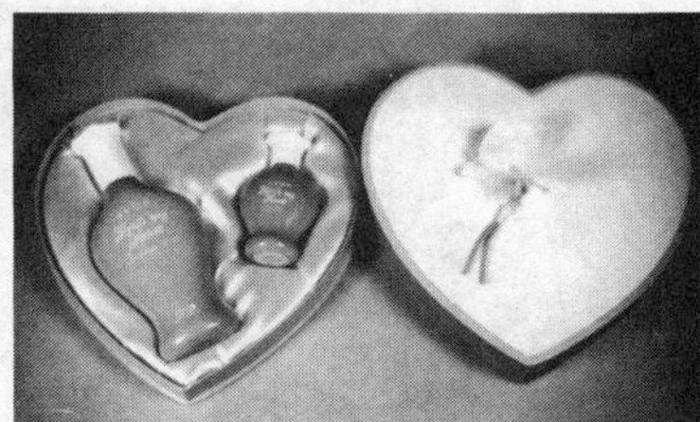

1958 SWEETHEARTS
Blue & white heart shaped box with white satin lining & white rose on lid. Holds Here's My Heart Cologne Mist & plastic Powder Sachet or Lotion Sachet. O.S.P. $5.00 C.M.V. $45.00 M.B.

1959 HEART O'MINE
Blue & white box with blue heart on lid with white rose & blue satin lining holds Here's My Heart Cologne Mist, Cream Sachet, Beauty Dust & Spray Perfume. O.S.P. $11.95 C.M.V. $45.00 M.B.

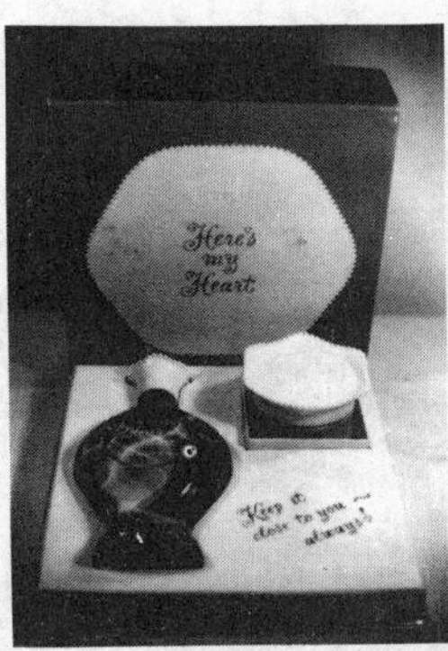

1961 TWO HEARTS GIFT SET
Blue & white box holds 2 oz. Here's My Heart Cologne & Cream Sachet. O.S.P. $3.50 C.M.V. $25.00 M.B.

1963 NEW REMEMBRANCE
Blue & white box holds Here's My Heart Cologne Mist & Beauty Dust. O.S.P. $6.95 C.M.V. $30.00 M.B.

IMPERIAL GARDEN

1973 IMPERIAL GARDEN CERAMIC VASE TEST
Test vase from factory never sold by Avon. Has gold ban around top of cap & bottom is glazed over Avon. Blue & green flowers on front different from regular issue. CMV $25.00

1973 IMPERIAL GARDENS AWARDS
Earned for selling certain number Cologne Mist for each level.
Level 1 - BUD VASE - white china with orange & gold trim. C.M.V. $8.00 M.B.
Level 2 - TRAY - white plastic with orange & gold trim. C.M.V. $10.00 $15.00 M.B.
Level 3 - GINGER JAR - white china with orange & gold trim. C.M.V. $25.00 M.B.
Level 4 - ROBE - beige with orangish pink trim & floral sash. C.M.V. $25.00 M.B.

HONEYSUCKLE

1967-72 HONEYSUCKLE AFTER BATH FRESHENER - 8 oz. bottle with orange cap & center band label. O.S.P. $3.00 C.M.V. $1.00
1972-76 HONEYSUCKLE AFTER BATH FRESHENER - 8 oz. yellow plastic bottle with yellow cap. O.S.P. $5.00 C.M.V. 50¢
1967-76 HONEYSUCKLE FOAMING BATH OIL - 8 oz. plastic bottle with orange cap. OSP $4.50 CMV $1.00
1969-72 HONEYSUCKLE CREAM LOTION 5 oz. yellow plastic bottle. O.S.P. $2.00 C.M.V. 50¢
1967-77 HONEYSUCKLE PERFUMED TALC - 3½ oz. yellow & white paper container. O.S.P. $2.00 C.M.V. 50¢
1968-69 HONEYSUCKLE SOAP 6 sided box holds 3 yellow bars. OSP $3.00 CMV $9.00 MB
1970-74 HONEYSUCKLE PERFUMED DEMI STICK - .19 oz. yellow, green & white. Yellow cap. O.S.P. $1.75 C.M.V. $1.00
1971-72 HONEYSUCKLE COLOGNE MIST - 2 oz. yellow glass bottle, yellow cap. O.S.P. $4.25 C.M.V. $1.00
HONEYSUCKLE CREAM SACHET SAMPLE - Sample in foil. C.M.V. 25¢
1971-73 HONEYSUCKLE KWICKETTES Box holds 14 Kwickettes. O.S.P. $1.75 C.M.V. $1.00
1967-78 HONEYSUCKLE PERFUMED SOAP - 3 oz, bar in yellow & orange wrapper. O.S.P. $1.25 C.M.V. $1.25
1967-75 HONEYSUCKLE CREAM SACHET .66 oz. yellow frosted glass with orange lid. O.S.P. $2.50 C.M.V. 50¢

1972-73 HONEYSUCKLE FLORAL DUET - Box came with Rollette & bar of soap. O.S.P. $3.25 C.M.V. $5.00 M.B.

LEFT TO RIGHT
1973-77 HONEYSUCKLE CREAM SACHE .66 oz. clear glass jar. Green, orange & whit lid. O.S.P. $2.50 C.M.V. 50¢
1975-78 DEMI STICK .19 oz. Yellow, green & white with white cap. O.S.P. $1.75 C.M.V. 50¢
1972-74 HONEYSUCKLE ROLLETTE .33 oz. clear bltt
.33 oz. clear bottle, white cap with colored band. O.S.P. $2.50 C.M.V. $1.00
1972-75 HONEYSUCKLE COLOGNE MIST
2 oz. clear glass bottle with clear plastic cap with inner cap of yellow & green. O.S.P. $5.00 C.M.V. 75¢

1974-76 IMPERIAL GARDEN PERFUMED SOAP - Three 3 oz. cakes white soap. Came in white & orange box. S.S.P. $6.00 C.M.V. $7.00 MB
1974-77 IMPERIAL GARDEN PERFUMED POWDER MIST - 7 oz. orange painted can, white lid. O.S.P. $5.00 C.M.V. 50¢
1974-76 IMPERIAL GARDEN PERFUMED SKIN SOFTENER - 5 oz. orange plastic, white & gold cap. O.S.P. $5.50 C.M.V. 50¢
1973 IMPERIAL GARDEN COASTERS 4 white plastic, orange design. C.M.V. $25.00 M.B. set.

1974-76 IMPERIAL GARDEN PERFUME TALC - 3.5 oz. White, gold & orange, cardboard. O.S.P. $1.00 C.M.V. 25¢
1974 Only - IMPERIAL GARDEN BEAUTY DUST - 6 oz. white plastic with orange & gold. O.S.P. $5.00 CMV $5.00 $6.00 MB
1974-76 IMPERIAL GARDEN EMOLLIENT MIST - 4 oz. white with gold & orange. Has orange cap. O.S.P. $3.00 C.M.V. 50¢

1973 IMPERIAL GARDEN TEA SET
White Bone China with Imperial Garden design. Given to one representative in each district when her recommendation name was drawn at the Christmas Party. C.M.V. $175.00 M.B.

1973-75 IMPERIAL GARDEN CERAMIC VASE
Some came with short neck & tall cap & some with long neck & short caps. White with orange flowers & gold stems. 18 oz. Ceramic Vase. Bath Crystals 7" high. SSP $16.00 CMV $16.00 MB

1973-77 COLOGNE MIST - 3 oz. S.S.P. $8.00 C.M.V. $1.00

1973-77 CREAM SACHET - .66 oz. S.S.P. $4.50 C.M.V. 50¢

1973-77 ROLLETTE - .33 oz. S.S.P. $4.50 C.M.V. 25¢

1973-77 SAMPLE BOTTLE COLOGNE C.M.V. 25¢

1973-77 SAMPLE - C.M.V. 25¢ box. Box of 10 samples.

1973-77 IMPERIAL GARDEN COLOGNE MIST
3 oz. white with orange flowers & gold stems. 2 different designs as pictured. OSP $8.00 CMV $1.00 each.

1977 IMPERIAL GARDEN SOAP ON A ROPE - CANADA
Orange rope, white bar C.M.V. $4.00

JARDIN D' AMOUR

See Misc. Perfume & Powder Section for additional Jardin D.Amour bottles.

1930'S JARDIN D' AMOUR PERFUME
1 oz. clear glass bottle with frosted glass stopper. Silver & blue CPC label. If you have any information on when or what this bottle was sold or given for please contact Bud Hastin. Very rare. CMV $150.00 mint.

1954 Only - JARDIN D'AMOUR PERFUME SET
Blue & gold bucket with gold tie down cord. Holds 1½ oz. bottle with gold label, clear plastic cap with blue stone in gold set. Bottom of bucket holds 1 dram perfume. Came in blue, white & gold lay down box. OSP $15.00 CMV in box complete $200.00 1½ oz. bottle in bucket mint $175.00. 1 dram perfume $15.00 1½ oz. bottle only. $100.00 mint

1929-36 JARDIN D'AMOUR TALC
Frosted glass with brass shaker top. Front paper label. O.S.P. $1.04 CMV $60.00 BO mint $70.00 MB

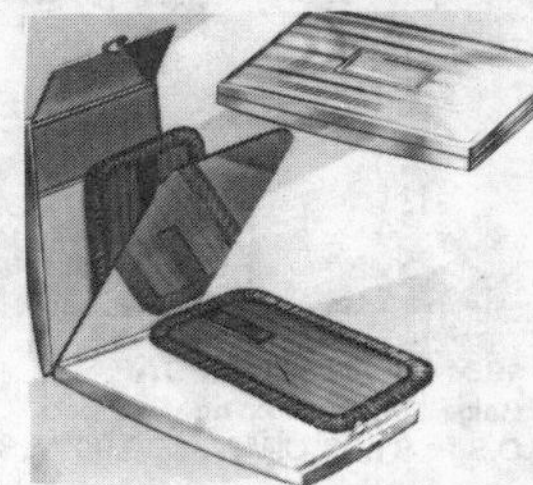

1929-32 JARDIN D'AMOUR VANITY COMPACT - Silver Compact. O.S.P. $2.25 C.M.V. $40.00 in box. Compact only $35.00 mint.

1934-36 JARDIN d. AMOUR SACHET
1¼ oz, ribbed glass jar, black cap. OSP $1.04 CMV $25.00 mint BO $30.00 MB

1929-33 JARDIN D'AMOUR PERFUME
Orange box with gold base for 1 & 2 oz. glass stoppered bottle. Black label at neck. O.S.P. $3.50 & $6.50 C.M.V. bottle only $100.00. In box $135.00.

JASMINE

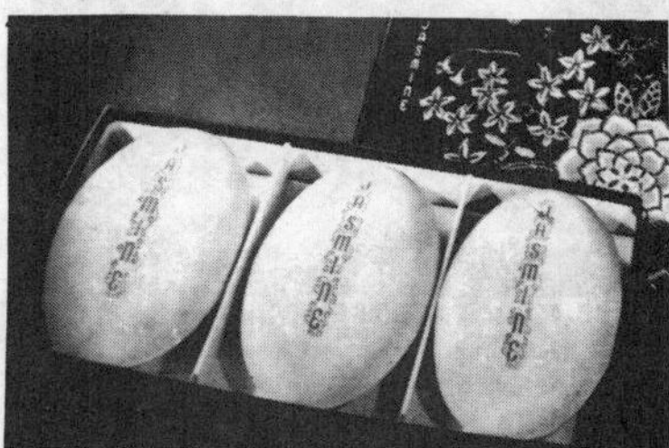

1948-49 JASMINE SOAP
Xmas only. Black flowered box holds 3 white bars. O.S.P. $1.28 C.M.V. $40.00 M.B.

1934-36 JASMINE SOAP
Beige & gold box holds 3 bars.
O.S.P. $1.02 C.M.V. $50.00 M.B.

1946-47 FANTASY IN JASMINE
Black box with pink flowers holds 2 bars of Jasmine Soap & 9 oz. bottle of Jasmine Bath Salts. O.S.P. $1.95 C.M.V. $75.00 MB. Set also came with 2 bottles in boxes of 1¼ oz. Jasmine Sachet in place of soaps. CMV with boxed sachets $100.00 MB

1966-67 JASMINE GIFT SOAP
Floral box contains 3 yellow Jasmine Soaps. O.S.P. $2.00 C.M.V. $20.00 M.B.

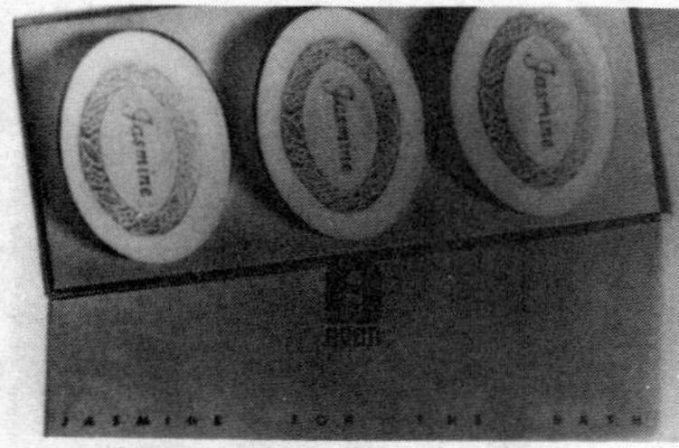

1936-45 JASMINE SOAP
Turquoise & gold box holds 3 embossed bars. O.S.P. $1.02 C.M.V. $45.00 M.B.

1945 Only - FANTASY IN JASMINE
Black box with pink flowers holds Jasmine Bath Salts & 2 Jasmine Soaps.
O.S.P. $1.60 C.M.V. $75.00 M.B.

1942-44 FANTASY IN JASMINE SET
Green box holds 2 bars. Jasmine Soap & 9 oz. Jasmine Bath Salts with turquoise lid. O.S.P. $1.35 C.M.V. $60.00 M.B.
Same set sold Christmas 1942 in blue flowered box. Same CMV.

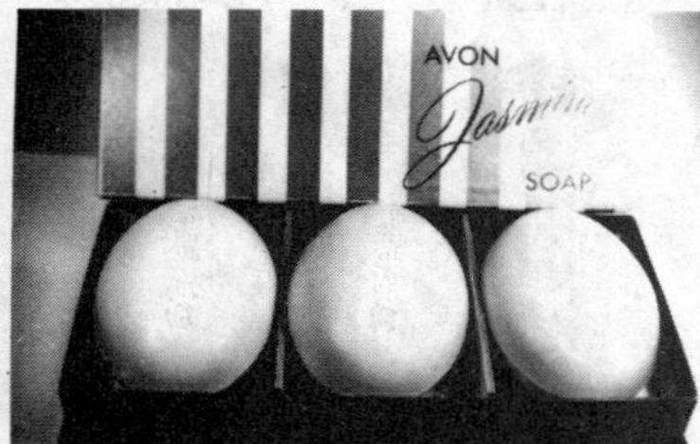

1939 Only - JASMINE SOAP
Gold striped box holds 3 bars. Avon on back of soap. O.S.P. $1.25 C.M.V. $60.00 M.B.

1956-57 FANTASY IN JASMINE
White box with yellow flowers holds 2 bars Royal Jasmine Soap & 2 oz. Royal Jasmine Bath Oil with white cap & black label. O.S.P. $1.95 C.M.V. $45.00 M.B. C.M.V. 2 oz. Bath Oil $25.00 B.O.

1948 FANTASY IN JASMINE
Black box with pink flowers holds 2 bars Jasmine Soap & 2 oz. Jasmine Toilet Water.
O.S.P. $2.39 C.M.V. $75.00 M.B.

1940-43 BATH ENSEMBLE
Blue flowered flip open box holds Jasmine Bath Salts, Jasmine 2 oz. Toilet Water. 2 bars of Jasmine Soap & can of Dusting Powder. O.S.P. $3.50 C.M.V. $150.00 M.B. set.

1946-53 JASMINE SOAP
Black flowered box holds 3 bars.
OSP $1.25 CMV $37.50 MB

1954-57 ROYAL JASMINE SET
Yellow & white flowered box holds 8 oz. Royal Jasmine Bath Salts & bar of Royal Jasmine Soap. O.S.P. $1.39 C.M.V. $37.50

1946-50 JASMINE POWDER SACHET
1¼ oz. bottle with black cap & label. Came in black box. O.S.P. $1.19 C.M.V. $20.00 in box. $15.00 bottle only.

1947-50 JASMINE DUSTING POWDER
13 oz. black & gold tin can with pink flowers on lid. O.S.P. $1.50 C.M.V. $25.00. M.B. $30.00.

1945-52 JASMINE BATH SALTS
9 oz. clear glass with black cap & label. Label came with either a large or small pink flower on front. Came in black box. OSP 75c CMV $40.00 in box. $30.00 bottle only mint.

1949 JASMINE POWDER SACHET
1¼ oz. clear glass bottle, black cap & label. O.S.P. $1.25 C.M.V. $20.00 $25.00 M.B.

1949 JASMINE TOILET WATER
2 oz. black cap & label. O.S.P. $1.25 C.M.V. $35.00. M.B. $40.00

1957-59 ROYAL JASMINE BATH OIL
Yellow, white & green box holds 8 oz. bottle with yellow cap & flowered label. O.S.P. $1.95 C.M.V. $25.00 M.B. Bottle only $20.00.

1946-48 JASMINE TOILET WATER
2 oz. gold cap, also came in black flowered box. Turquoise box shown. O.S.P. $1.19 C.M.V. in box $40.00 Bottle only $30.00 mint.

1964-68 JASMINE AFTER BATH FRESHENER - 8 oz. glass bottle with yellow cap & painted label. Yellow flowered box. O.S.P. $2.50 C.M.V. $2.00 BO $3.00 MB

1966-70 JASMINE FOAMING BATH OIL
8 oz. frosted plastic bottle with yellow cap, green or white painted label, yellow box. O.S.P. $2.50 C.M.V. $1.50

1964-66 JASMINE PERFUMED BATH OIL
8 oz. plastic bottle, green cap. Green or white painted label. O.S.P. $2.50 C.M.V. $2.50

1964-68 JASMINE PERFUMED TALC - 3½ oz. yellow flowered paper container with plastic shaker top. O.S.P. 89c CMV $2.00

1964-67 JASMINE PERFUMED SOAP - 3 oz. bar in yellow flowered wrapping. O.S.P. 39¢ C.M.V. $2.00

1967-72 JASMINE CREAM SACHET
.66 oz. yellow frosted glass with gold & white lid. OSP $2.50 CMV 50c

1967-72 JASMINE FRAGRANCE KWICKETTES - 14 foil Towellettes in box. O.S.P. $1.25 C.M.V. $1.00 box.

1954-57 ROYAL JASMINE BATH SALTS - Yellow & white flowered box holds 8 oz. bottle with yellow cap. O.S.P. 89¢ C.M.V. $25.00 M.B. $20.00 B.O.

1954-59 ROYAL JASMINE SOAP
Box holds 3 bars, with round edges. Box lid lifts off. O.S.P. $1.69 C.M.V. $25.00 M.B.

1959-66 ROYAL JASMINE SOAP
Same box only lid flips back and not off. The soap has flat edges. CMV $22.00 MB

1936-44 JASMINE BATH SALTS
9 oz. glass jar, turquoise lid. O.S.P. 63¢ CMV $20.00 BO mint, $25.00 MB

LAVENDER

1977-78 LAVENDER BOUQUET SACHET PILLOWS
Pink box holds 6 satin lavender filled sachet pillows. Came with pink ribbon around them. S.S.P. $4.99 C.M.V. $4.00

1946-48 LAVENDER ENSEMBLE
Blue and pink flowered flip open box holds 4 oz. bottle, pink cap of Lavender Toilet Water, 2 pink bars of Lavender Soap and 2 paper wrapped cakes of sachet. O.S.P. $2.75 C.M.V. $90.00 M.B.

1945 LAVENDER SOAP
Pink box holds 3 Lavender embossed bars. OSP 85c, CMV $60.00 MB.

1946-48 LAVENDER SACHET CAKES
Box holds 2 flower design wrapped cakes of sachet. OSP 79c, CMV $25.00 MB.

1945-46 LAVENDER SACHETS
Beige box holds 2 foil wrapped cakes of Sachet. O.S.P. 79¢ C.M.V. $25.00 M.B.

1946 Only - LAVENDER SOAP SET
Box holds 3 lavender bars of soap. O.S.P. 85¢ C.M.V. $50.00 M.B.

1934-38 LAVENDER ENSEMBLE
Lavender box holds 4 oz. Lavender Toilet Water, 2 bars lavender soap & package of Lavender Blossoms. O.S.P. $1.50 C.M.V. $125.00 M.B. set. Lavender Blossoms only $50.00 M.B.

1938 Only - LAVENDER ENSEMBLE
Lavender flip open box holds 4 oz. Lavender Toilet Water with same label as 1934 Lavender Toilet Water, 2 bars of lavender soap, 2 lavender sachet cakes. O.S.P. $1.50 C.M.V. $100.00 M.B. Bottle only $45.00.

1935 Only - LAVENDER SOAP
Box holds 3 lavender bars of soap. O.S.P. 67¢ C.M.V. $75.00 M.B.

1938-40 LAVENDER ENSEMBLE
Lavender flip open box with cardboard liner holds 4 oz. Lavender Toilet Water, 2 bars of Lavender Soap wrapped in lavender paper & 2 Sachet Cakes with lavender band around them. O.S.P. $1.50 C.M.V. $80.00 M.B.

1940-43 LAVENDER ENSEMBLE
Lavender flowered box with satin lining holds 4 oz. Lavender Toilet Water, 2 bars Lavender Soap & 2 Lavender Sachet Cakes. O.S.P. $1.75 C.M.V. $90.00 M.B.

1941 Only - LAVENDER ENSEMBLE
Box holds 2 Lavender Sachet Cakes, bottle of Lavender Toilet Water & 2 lavender bars of soap. O.S.P. $1.50 C.M.V. $85.00 M.B. set.

1970-72 LAVENDER & LACE
Lavender & white box holds 1.7 oz. white glass bottle of Lavender Cologne with lavender ribbon. A lavender & white lace handkerchief came with it. O.S.P. $4.50 C.M.V. $5.00 set. Bottle only $2.00 M.B.

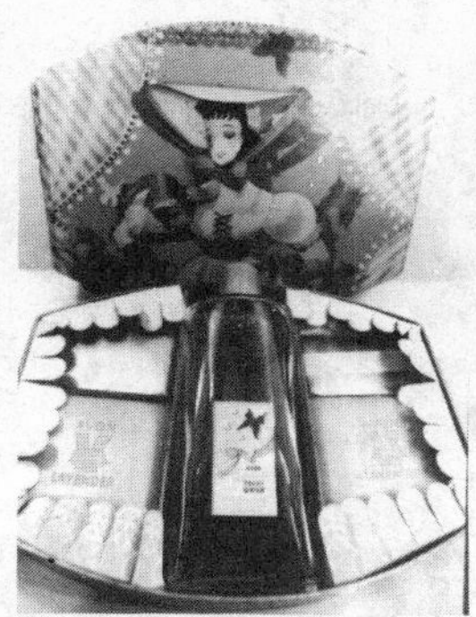

1945-46 LAVENDER ENSEMBLE
Blue, pink & white box with silver bottom holds 4 oz. Lavender Toilet Water, 2 bars Lavender Soap & 2 Sachet Cakes. O.S.P. $1.95 C.M.V. $90.00 M.B.

1961-68 LAVENDER POWDER SACHET
.9 oz. pink & white label & neck band, glass & plastic stopper. One with 4A design in place of size. $4.00 BO $6.00 MB on 9 oz. CMV $10.00 in box, $8.00 BO

1946 LAVENDER ENSEMBLE
Blue, pink and green flowered box with satin lining holds 2 bars of Lavender soap, 4 oz. bottle of Lavender toilet water, and 2 flower wrapped cakes of sachet. O.S.P. $2.75 C.M.V. $95.00 M.B.

LEFT 1946-48 LAVENDER TOILET WATER
4 oz. pink cap. OSP $1.19 CMV $35.00 BO $40.00 MB
RIGHT 1934-37 LAVENDER TOILET WATER
4 oz. ribbed bottle with blue or gold cap. Lavender label. OSP 75c CMV $45.00 mint BO $55.00 MB

1935-38 LAVENDER BLOSSOMS
Lavender & pink box holds package of Lavender Blossoms. O.S.P. 50¢ C.M.V. $40.00 M.B.

1944-45 AVON LAVENDER SACHET
Beige box holds 2 lavender wrapped cakes of Sachet. One set has lavender flowers on band around lavender colored celephane. Other set has lavender foil wrapper with lavender colored paper bands. Came both ways. O.S.P. 79¢ C.M.V. $25.00 M.B. ea. set. Also came as pictured on top. Lavender paper cover with flowers on band. O.S.P. 79c CMV $25.00 MB. Some boxes have label printed on box & some boxes plain.

Left - 1938-43 LAVENDER TOILET WATER - 4 oz. lavender cap. O.S.P. 78¢ C.M.V. $35.00 B.O. $40.00 M.B. C.P.C. on box, 1938-39 add $5.00.
Right - 1945-46 LAVENDER TOILET WATER - 4 oz. lavender cap. O.S.P. 89¢ C.M.V. $40.00 B.O. $45.00 M.B.

LEMON VELVET

1973 LEMON VELVET MOISTURIZED FRICTION LOTION
8 oz. lt. yellow glass with gold cap. OSP $4.00 CMV $2.00 BO $3.00 MB
1973-75 LEMON VELVET PERFUMED POWDER MIST
7 oz. yellow, green & white, green lid. OSP $4.00 CMV 50c
1972-76 LEMON VELVET COLOGNE MIST
2 oz. clear glass bottle with clear plastic cap with inner cap of yellow & green. OSP $4.25 CMV 75c
1972-74 LEMON VELVET ROLLETTE
.33 oz. clear bottle with green & yellow cap. OSP $2.50 CMV 50c
1973-76 LEMON VELVET PERFUMED SKIN SOFTENER
5 oz. yellow plastic jar with gold, yellow & green lid. OSP $2.00 CMV 50c
1975-77 LEMON VELVET CREAM SACHET
Not shown. .66 oz. white, yellow, green cap. OSP $3.00 CMV 50c

1969-77 LEMON VELVET PERFUMED SOAP - Yellow flowered box holds 3 yellow bars. OSP $3.00, CMV $4.00

1969-73 PERFUMED SKIN SOFTENER 5 oz. yellow frosted glass jar with green flowered lid. O.S.P. $3.50 C.M.V. 50¢

1969-76 BATH FOAM 8 oz. yellow plastic bottle with green cap. O.S.P. $3.50 C.M.V. 50¢

1969-76 MOISTURIZED FRICTION LOTION - 10 oz. yellow plastic bottle with green cap. First issue green smooth cap, second issue green cap with flower on top. O.S.P. $3.00 C.M.V. 50¢

1969-74 FRAGRANCE KWICKETTES Yellow box holds 14 packets. O.S.P. $1.50 C.M.V. 50¢ box.

1969-74 BEAUTY DUST 6 oz. yellow paper box with clear plastic lid. OSP $3.50 CMV $2.00 $4.00 MB

1971-75 CREAM SACHET .66 oz. yellow glass & cap. OSP $3.00 CMV 50c

1971-75 PERFUMED DEMI STICK Yellow & green plastic tube with white cap. OSP $1.75 CMV 50c

1971-72 BATH MIT Yellow Bath Mit Sponge. OSP $1.50 CMV $1.00

1971-74 CLEANSING GEL 6 oz. yellow tube. OSP $3.00 CMV 50c

1968-77 LILAC SOAP Box holds lavender bars. O.S.P. $5.00 C.M.V. $5.00

1940 LILAC TOLIET WATER 2 oz., gold ribbed cap with 'A' on top, gold label. Blue box. Has Avon Products Inc. label. OSP 78c CMV $35.00 BO mint $40.00 MB. Same bottle sold 1934 to 1939 only bottom of label only says Toilet water & does not say Avon Products. CPC on backside of label. Same CMV as above.

LILAC

1964-68 LILAC AFTER BATH FRESHENER - 8 oz. class bottle with pink. cap & pink or white painted label. Pink box. O.S.P. $2.50 C.M.V. $2.00

1964-66 LILAC PERFUME BATH OIL - 8 oz. frosted plastic bottle with pink cap & painted label, pink box. Later issue says "Foaming Bath Oil" C.M.V. 25¢ O.S.P. $2.50 C.M.V. $2.50

1964-76 LILAC PERFUMED TALC 3½ oz. pink paper container with plastic shaker top. OSP $2.00 CMV $1.00

1971-73 LILAC FRAGRANCE KWICKETTES - Box holds 14 towelettS. O.S.P. $1.75 C.M.V. $1.00

1970-76 LILAC PERFUMED DEMI STICK - .19 oz. Lavender label with white cap & bottom. O.S.P. $1.75 C.M.V. 50¢

1968-70 LILAC PERFUMED DEMI STICK - .19 oz. Lavender label & cap & bottom. O.S.P. $1.75 C.M.V. $1.00

1964-67 PERFUMED SOAP 1 bar in pink flowered wrapping. OSP 39c CMV $2.50 mint

1967-75 LILAC CREAM SACHET .66 oz. purple frosted glass with gold & white lid. O.S.P. $2.50 C.M.V. 50¢

1975-76 LILAC CREAM SACHET .66 oz. clear glass, white cap with lilacs on top. O.S.P. $3.00 C.M.V. 25¢

1966-75 LILAC FOAMING BATH OIL 8 oz. plastic bottle. Pink cap. O.S.P. $2.50 C.M.V. 50¢

1966 LILAC SOAP Lavender box holds 3 piece lavender soap in cellophane wrapper. O.S.P. $2.50 C.M.V. $15.00 M.B.

1966-68 LILY OF THE VALLEY SOAP Green box holds 2 green cakes. O.S.P. $2.00 CMV $18.50 MB

LILY OF THE VALLEY

ALL CONTAINERS PRICED EMPTY - MINT

See Page 5 for Grading Examples on Mint Condition

1934-40 LILY OF THE VALLEY 2 oz., gold ribbed cap, 'A' on top. Gold front label. OSP 78c CMV $35.00 BO mint. $40.00 MB

1979-80 LILY OF THE VALLEY PRODUCTS

COLOGNE ICE STICK Yellow & green plastic. SSP $2.49 CMV 50c

PERFUMED TALC 3.5 oz. cardboard sides, plastic top & bottom. SSP $1.29 CMV 25c

CHATEAU OF FLOWERS BOOK Green hardback book on story of Lily of the Valley. Book does not say Avon on it. Must be in Avon box cover as shown. SSP $2.00 CMV $2.00 MB

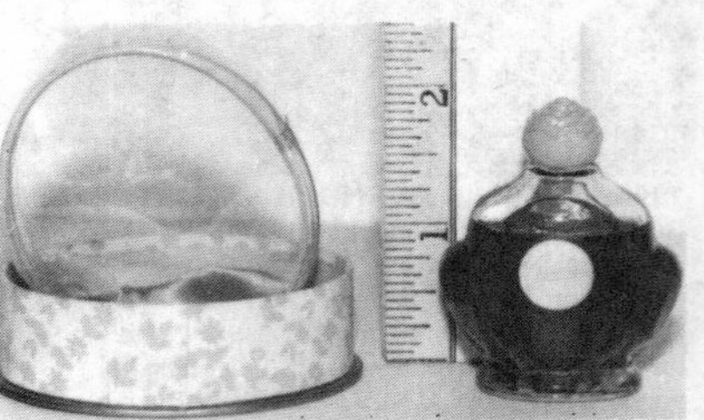

1948-52 LILY OF THE VALLEY PERFUME 3 dram bottle with flower cap. Came in satin lined box with clear plastic lid. OSP $2.50 CMV $80.00 MB $50.00 BO mint.

1979 LILY OF THE VALLEY SCENTED PILLOW
10" x 10" lace green & white scented pillow. SSP $11.99 CMV $8.00 MB.

1949-52 LILY OF THE VALLEY TOILET WATER - 2 oz. white cap. O.S.P. $1.25 C.M.V. $45.00 M.B. $35.00 bottle only

1946-49 LILY OF THE VALLEY TOILET WATER - Green box holds 2 oz. bottle with gold cap & label. O.S.P. $1.19 CMV $40.00 MB $30.00 BO mint.

1974 Only - LILY OF THE VALLEY CREAM SACHET - .66 oz. clear embossed glass with white cap with flowers. First issued with this jar. O.S.P. $1.25 C.M.V. $1.00 BO $2.00 MB

1975-76 LILY OF THE VALLEY CREAM SACHET - .66 oz. clear ribbed glass with white cap with flowers. O.S.P. $1.25 C.M.V. 50¢

1974-76 LILY OF THE VALLEY PERFUME DEMI-STICK - .19 oz. white with flowers. O.S.P. $1.00 C.M.V. 50¢

1964-68 LILY OF THE VALLEY AFTER BATH FRESHENER - 8 oz. glass bottle with green cap, painted label in green or white letters, green box. O.S.P. $2.50 CMV $2.00 MB $1.00 BO

1964-66 PERFUMED BATH OIL
8 oz frosted plastic bottle with green cap, painted label in green or white letters, green box. O.S.P. $2.50 C.M.V. $3.00

1964-70 PERFUMED TALC
3½ oz. green paper container with plastic shaker top. O.S.P. 89¢ C.M.V. $1.50

1964-67 PERFUMED SOAP
3 oz. bar with green & white flowered wrapping. O.S.P. 39¢ C.M.V. $3.00 Mint.

1966-70 LILY OF THE VALLEY FOAMING BATH OIL - 8 oz. white plastic, green label & cap. O.S.P. $2.50 C.M.V. $2.00

1967-75 CREAM SACHET
.66 oz. green frosted glass jar with gold & white lid. O.S.P. $2.50 C.M.V. 50¢

1964-68 LILY OF THE VALLEY KWICKETTES
Box of 14 fragrance samples. O.S.P. $1.25 C.M.V. $2.00 M.B.

LUCY HAYS

See Misc. Perfumes for other Lucy Hays Perfumes.

1936 Only - LUCY HAYS PERFUME
2 dram, gold cap. Sold for 20¢ with other purchase to celebrate Mr. & Mrs. McConnell 51st wedding anniversary. Lucy Hays was Mrs. McConnell's maiden name. Sold March 3 to 23, 1936 only. C.M.V. in box $85.00 bottle only $65.00 mint.

LULLABYE

1955-56 LULLABYE SET
Blue & pink box holds Baby Oil & Baby Powder. O.S.P. $1.39 C.M.V. $36.00 MB

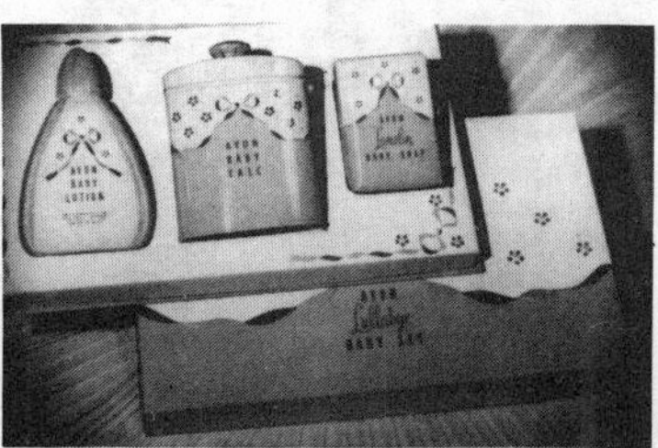

1951-55 LULLABYE BABY SET
Blue, pink & white box holds Baby Lotion, Baby Talc, Lamolin Baby Soap. O.S.P. $2.35 C.M.V. $65.00 M.B.

1964-66 LULLABYE BABY SET
Pink & blue box holds 2 bars Baby Soap & choice of Tot N Tyke Baby Oil, Baby Lotion or Baby Shampoo. OSP $1.96 CMV $26.00 MB

1946-50 LULLABYE BABY SET
Pink box holds Lullabye Baby Oil, Lullabye Baby Soap, Lullabye Baby Cream & Lullabye Baby Talc. O.S.P. $3.55 C.M.V. $135.00 M.B.

1946-50 LULLABYE BABY TALC
5 oz. pink paper container with pink & white plastic top & bottom. O.S.P. 65¢ C.M.V. $25.00 M.B. $20.00 Talc only mint.
1946-50 LULLABYE BABY OIL
6 oz. clear glass bottle, back side flat. Pink cap & painted label. O.S.P. $1.00 CMV $50.00 MB $40.00 BO
1940-50 LULLABYE BABY CREAM
White milk glass jar with pink lid & label. O.S.P. 89¢ C.M.V. $25.00 M.B. $20.00 jar only.
1946-50 LULLABYE BABY SOAP
Plastic wrapper with pink painted bow & flowers on wrapper. O.S.P. 39¢ C.M.V. $15.00 mint

LUSCIOUS

Left - 1950-55 LUSCIOUS PERFUME
1 dram, painted label with smooth gold cap. Came in felt wrapper. O.S.P. $1.75 C.M.V. in wrapper $15.00. Bottle only $10.00 mint.
Right - 1955-56 LUSCIOUS PERFUME
1 dram, painted label, embossed gold cap. Came in felt wrapper. O.S.P. $1.75 C.M.V. in wrapper $15.00, bottle only $8.00

1950 LUSCIOUS PERFUME
3 dram glass stoppered bottle, came with painted label or with gold neck tag label. O.S.P. $2.25 C.M.V. $125.00 in box. $100.00 bottle only.

1950 LUSCIOUS PERFUME AWARD
Gold & purple box holds 3 dram, ribbe glass stopper. Stopper different from regular issue. Given when Luscious was first issued. C.M.V. $150.00 in box. $100.00 bottle only.
1950 LUSCIOUS PERFUME
1 dram clear bottle with gold cap, & label. Came in brown felt wrapper. O.S.P. $1.75 C.M.V. $12.00 bottle only. $18.00 in wrapper.

MARIONETTE

1939-40 MARIONETTE TOILET WATER - 2 oz. plastic cap, long fro label. O.S.P. 20¢ C.M.V. $45.00 in b $35.00 bottle only.

LEFT 1940 ONLY MARIONETTE SACHET SPECIAL ISSUE BOX
Short issue blue & pink box holds regular issue Marionette Powder Sachet on left in 1¼ oz. size. Sold for 20c with regular order. CMV $25.00 MB in this box only.
RIGHT 1938 ONLY MARIONETTE SACHET
1¼ oz. ribbed glass bottle with turquoise plain metal cap or ribbed plastic turquoise cap. OSP $1.04 CMV $24.00 BO $28.00 MB.

1940-46 MARIONETTE TOILET WATER
2 oz., gold ribbed cap & gold label. Also came with plastic caps. OSP $1.04 CMV $30.00 BO mint $35.00 MB.

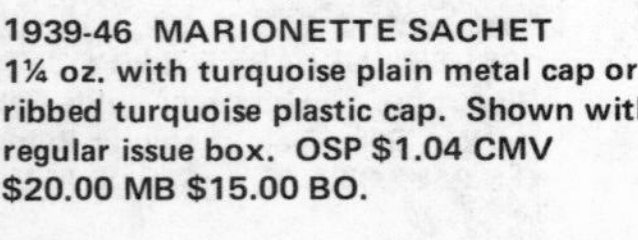

1939-46 MARIONETTE SACHET
1¼ oz. with turquoise plain metal cap or ribbed turquoise plastic cap. Shown with regular issue box. OSP $1.04 CMV $20.00 MB $15.00 BO.

1938 MARIONETTE PERFUME
¼ oz. size. Gold ribbed cap with CPC on label. Sold in honor of M McConnell's birthday. O.S.P. 20¢ CMV $50.00 MB $40.00 BO

MINERAL SPRINGS

973-75 MINERAL SPRINGS BATH OAM - 8 oz. marbleized plastic bottle ith marbleized cap. O.S.P. $3.00 C.M.V. 0¢

972-76 MINERAL SPRINGS SPARKLING RESHENER - 8 oz. amber plastic bottle arbleized cap. O.S.P. $3.00 C.M.V. 50¢

972-74 MINERAL SPRINGS CLEANSING EL - 6 oz. amber plastic tube with marbleized d. O.S.P. $2.00 C.M.V. 75¢

972-74 MINERAL SPRINGS MOISTURIZING ODY RUB - 8 oz. amber bottle with marbleized ap. O.S.P. $3.00 C.M.V. 75¢

1972-73 MINERAL SPRINGS SOAP
2 bars in gold & yellow box. O.S.P. $2.00 C.M.V. $4.00 M.B.

1972-74 MINERAL SPRINGS PERFUMED POWDER MIST - 7 oz. yellow, gold, brown, & beige with beige cap. O.S.P. $2.00 C.M.V. $1.00

1973 BATH MITT
9" long sponge with white cord. Sold for use with all bath gelee. O.S.P. $1,00 C.M.V. $1.00 mint.

1972-77 MINERAL SPRINGS BATH CRYSTALS - 12 oz. amber plastic bottle with marbelized cap. O.S.P. $4.00 C.M.V. 50¢

1972-77 MINERAL SPRINGS BATH CRYSTALS SAMPLE - Yellow, gold & beige foil packets in box. C.M.V. 50¢ each box.

MERRIMENT

1955 JOLLY SURPRISE
Pink & blue flip open box holds choice of 4 oz. bottle of Merriment Cologne. O.S.P. $1.75 or Bubble Bath O.S.P. $1.50 with pink caps. C.M.V. in box $55.00 ea. Bottle only $40.00 ea.

1976-78 MINERAL SPRINGS BATH CRYSTALS
12 oz. green container. O.S. P. $6.00 C.M.V. 50¢

MISS LOLLYPOP

1967 MISS LOLLY POP LIP POP
1st issue pink and white dots, mirror top with face on back. O.S.P. $1.50 CMV $4.00 MB, $2.00 lip pop

1968 MISS LOLLY POP LIP POP
Same box came with 2 pink and white dot lip pops, no mirror top. O.S.P. $1.75 C.M.V. $3.00 M.B.

1968 MISS LOLLYPOP HAND CREAM
Left - 2 oz. white plastic tube, white boots & purse, yellow cap. O.S.P. 75¢ C.M.V. $3.00

1968 MISS LOLLYPOP HAND CREAM
Right - 2 oz. white plastic tube, black boots & purse, yellow cap. O.S.P. 75¢ C.M.V. $3.00

1968-70 MISS LOLLYPOP ICE CREAM PUFF
3½ oz. yellow plastic bottom with pink fluff. Holds Talc. OSP $3.00 CMV $4.00 BO $6.00 MB

1968-70 MISS LOLLYPOP DOUBLE DIP BUBBLE BATH
5 oz. orange & white plastic bottle, red cap. OSP $2.00 CMV $4.00 BO $5.00 MB

1967-69 MISS LOLLYPOP LIP POPS
Girls face on handle. Pink lemonade, cherry, rasberry, peppermint & cola. OSP $1.75 ea. CMV $2.00, $3.00 MB

1968-69 MISS LOLLYPOP ROLLETTE
Pink, yellow & white cap. 1/3 oz. size. OSP $1.50 CMV $3.00 MB $2.00 BO

1968-70 MISS LOLLYPOP PERFUMED TALC
3½ oz. paper container with plastic shaker top. OSP $1.00 CMV $5.00 MB $4.00 CO

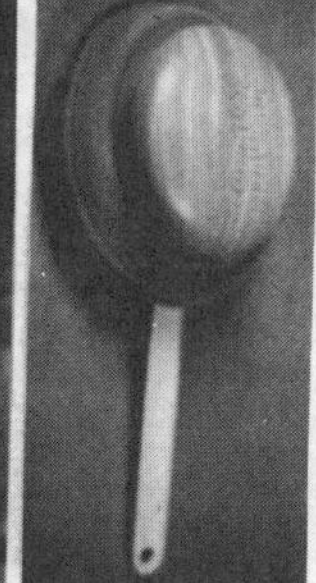

1968-70 MISS LOLLYPOP POWDER MITT - Yellow, orange & white plastic mitt filled with powder. Pink & white box. O.S.P. $2.50 C.M.V. $5.00 M.B.

1967-70 MISS LOLLYPOP SOAP & SPONGE - Pink soap & 9" long sponge. Pink & white box. O.S.P. $2.50 C.M.V. $12.00 M.B.

1967-69 MISS LOLLYPOP COLOGNE BOOT - 2 oz. glass boot with gold cap & red tassel. Red & white box. O.S.P. $2.00 C.M.V. $8.00 M.B. Bottle only with tassel $5.00

1967-70 MISS LOLLYPOP CREAM SACHET -.66 oz. dark or light yellow glass jar with white kitten on red, white & pink cap. Kittens eyes are blue or black, head als turns on some. O.S.P. $2.00 C.M.V. $5.00 M.B. $4.00 B.O. Also came with white base. C.M.V. $7.00 M.B. $6.00 B.O.

1967-70 MISS LOLLYPOP COLOGNE MIST - 3 oz. pink plastic coated bottom with red band, white hat with red & yellow ribbon. O.S.P. $3.00 C.M.V. $6.00 MB, $5.00 BO

1968 PRETTY ME
Box with white plastic tray holds Miss Lollypop Perfume Rollette & Lip Pop in choice of peppermint, pink lemonade, cherry, raspberry or cola. OSP $3.25, CMV $10.00

1967-68 MISS LOLLYPOP POWDERETTE
3½ oz. container of perfumed talc, red plume on top is long handled puff. O.S.P. $2.50 C.M.V. $10.00 M.B.

1969 PRETTY TOUCH
Yellow, pink, green & orange plastic light switch plate. O.S.P. 29¢ with purchase of Miss Lollypop items. Hard to find. Sold only 1 campaign. C.M.V. $9.00 M.B.

MOONWIND

1973-78 MOONWIND PERFUMED TALC
3.5 oz. blue cardboard trimmed in silver. O.S.P. $2.50 C.M.V. 25¢

1972-73 MOONWIND BATH PEARLS
Blue plastic jar with silver trim. Contained 75 capsules of Emollient Oil. O.S.P. $5.00 CMV $3.00, $5.00 MB

1971-78 MOONWIND FRAGRANCE SAMPLES - 10 foil samples in box. C.M.V. 25¢

1971-78 MOONWIND COLOGNE SAMPLES - Clear glass bottle with white cap. C.M.V. 25¢

1973 MOONWIND COLOGNE AND BATH OIL
4 oz. clear glass bottles, gold caps. Came in Treasure Chest set only. C.M.V. $3.00

972-73 MOONWIND PIN/SCARF IOLDER
ilver with blue enamel & blue set. SSP 6.00 CMV $6.00 MB

1971-80 MOONWIND FRAGRANCE
All are blue trimmed in silver.
Left to Right -
1971-75 COLOGNE MIST
3 oz. blue with silver painted top. OSP $7.50 CMV $1.00
1975-80 COLOGNE MIST
Blue with flat top, 2.7 oz. size. OSP $8.00 CMV 50c
1972 FOAMING BATH OIL
6 oz. OSP $5.00 CMV $1.50
1971-76 PERFUME ROLLETTE
1/3 oz. OSP $4.50 CMV 50c
1971-76 BEAUTY DUST
6 oz. OSP $10.00 CMV $3.00, $6.00 MB
1972-77 PERFUMED POWDER MIST
7 oz. OSP $5.00 CMV 50c Some with upside down painted label. CMV $8.00
1972-73 PERFUMED SOAPS
3 bars, blue, in blue box. OSP $6.00 CMV $7.00 MB
1972-73 PERFUMED SKIN SOFTENER
5 oz. blue glass. OSP $5.00 CMV 50c
1971-75 CREAM SACHET
.66 oz. OSP $4.00 CMV 50c
1976-78 CREAM SACHET
Blue with silver cap. OSP $4.50 CMV 25c

1975-78 MOONWIND PERFUMED SOAP
3 cakes blue soap. Blue & silver lid slides over gold box. O.S.P. $4.00 C.M.V. $4.00 M.B.

1971 MOONWIND ORDER BOOK COVERS - Dark blue with silver trim. Presidents Club cover earned for entry into President's Club. Honor Award earned for sales goal. Each came with pen. C.M.V. $4.00 Honor Cover with pen. $6.00 Presidents Cover with pen.

1975-76 MOONWIND EMOLLIENT MIST - 4 oz. blue & silver, blue cap. O.S.P. $3.00 C.M.V. 50¢
1973-78 MOONWIND PERFUMED SKIN SOFTENER - 5 oz. blue plastic jar with blue & silver lid. Came with 2 different lids, one has silver edge and one is blue edged. O.S.P. $3.00 C.M.V. 25¢
1974 MOONWIND DEMI STICK
.19 oz. White with blue & silver.
O.S.P. $1.00 C.M.V. 25¢
1975-78 MOONWIND POWDER SACHET
1.25 oz. blue & silver, cardboard.
O.S.P. $2.00 C.M.V. 25¢
1976-78 MOONWIND PERFUMED SOAP
3 oz. blue bar with blue and silver wrapper. O.S.P. $1.00 C.M.V. $1.00
1974-75 MOONWIND PERFUMED SOAP
(on right) 3 oz. blue bar with blue wrapper & multi-colored center. O.S.P. $1.00 C.M.V. $1.00

1971 MOONWIND TRAY
Blue glass tray trimmed in silver emblem of Diana in center. Given for selling 10 Moonwind Cologne Mist during C18-19. C.M.V. $22.00. M.B. $25.00
1971 MOONWIND JEWELRY BOX
Blue & silver. Emblem of Diana on top in silver. Given for selling 20 Moonwind Cologne Mist in C-18-19. C.M.V. $25.00 $30.00 M.B.
1971 MOONWIND ROBE
Blue, zipper front with silvery trim. Zipper pull is emblem of Diana. Given to Presidents Club representatives for selling 35 Moonwind Cologne Mists. C.M.V. $30.00. M.B. $35.00.

NEARNESS

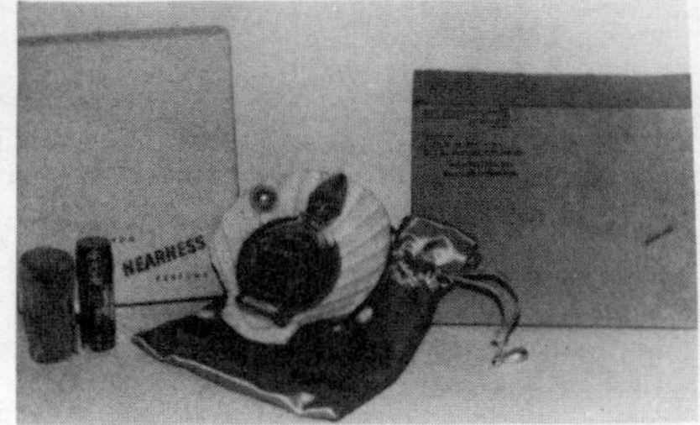

1956 NEARNESS GIFT PERFUME COMBO SET
½ oz. Nearness perfume on the clam shell in blue satin bag. Came with 1 dram Nearness perfume in blue felt wrapper in white box & outer sleeve. OSP $7.95 CMV $130.00 MB.

LEFT 1957-59 NEARNESS COLOGNE MIST
3 oz. blue plastic coated bottle with blue cap, blue & gold box. O.S.P. $2.75 C.M.V. $25.00 in box. $20.00 bottle only.
RIGHT 1959-61 NEARNESS COLOGNE MIST
3 oz. blue plastic coated bottle with pearl on pearl colored cap. Cap will turn gray in sun light & not considered mint. Blue & gold box. O.S.P. $2.95 CMV $24.00 MB $18.00 BO mint.

1955-59 NEARNESS 1 DRAM PERFUME
1 dram, clear smooth glass, gold scroll cap. Came in blue felt wrapper. O.S.P. $2.25 CMV $8.00 BO $15.00 in wrapper.
1956-57 TWO PEARLS SET
Blue & gold box with 2 pearls on lid holds Nearness Body Powder & Cream Sachet. O.S.P. $2.50 C.M.V. $40.00 M.B.

1956-61 NEARNESS TOILET WATER
2 oz. bottle with blue cap & see through label on back side. Came in blue & gold box. O.S.P. $2.00 C.M.V. $20.00 in box. $15.00 bottle only.

1955-61 NEARNESS COLOGNE
4 oz. bottle with blue cap & see through label on back side. Came in blue & gold box. O.S.P. $2.50 C.M.V. $20.00 in box. $15.00 bottle only.

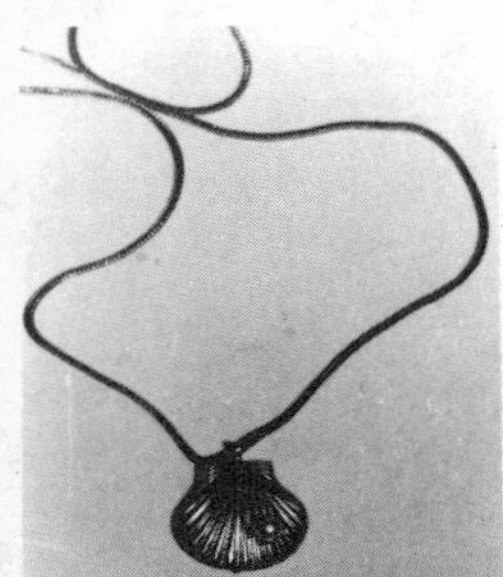

1956 Only - NEARNESS SEA SHELL NECKLACE - Gold finished pendant with pearl on fine chain. Came only in Always Near Set. C.M.V. $25.00

1957 ONLY - NEARNESS COLOGNE
½ oz. clear glass. Sold in **Gems & Crystals** Set only. Came with 2 different caps. Available in 4 fragrances. C.M.V. $12.50

1955-61 NEARNESS CREAM SACHET
Blue glass bottom, blue metal cap. O.S.P. $1.50 C.M.V. $8.00 B.O. $10.00 M.B.

1955-59 NEARNESS PERFUME
Blue satin draw bag holds clam shell with pearl & ½ oz. bottle with blue cap & see through label on back side. O.S.P. $7.50 C.M.V. in bag $100.00. Bottle only $75.00

1957 Only - NEARNESS CHARM
Blue box holds Nearness Toilet Water & can of Talc. O.S.P. $2.50 C.M.V. $40.00 M.B.

1956-58 NEARNESS BODY POWDER
Frosted glass bottle with blue cap & label. Blue & gold box. O.S.P. $1.00 C.M.V. $16.00 in box. Bottle only $12.00

1957-61 NEARNESS PERFUMED TALC
Blue can & cap. O.S.P. 69¢ C.M.V. $10.00 in box. Can only $7.00

1956-61 NEARNESS POWDER SACHET
1¼ oz. blue glass bottle with blue cap & label. O.S.P. $1.50 C.M.V. $12.00 in box. $8.00 bottle only.

1958 SEA MIST SET
Blue & gold box with net lining holds Nearness Cologne Mist & Cream Sachet. O.S.P. $3.95 C.M.V. $60.00 M.B.

1957 CIRCLE OF PEARLS
Blue plastic box with blue plastic cover holds Nearness 2 oz. Toilet Water, Cream Sachet & Pearl Necklace. O.S.P. $5.95 CMV $65.00 MB

1956-59 NEARNESS BEAUTY DUST
Blue cardboard container with tin bottom OSP $2.25 CMV $20.00 MB $15.00 container only, mint. CMV $22.00 for special 1956 Christmas issue box as shown MB.

FOREIGN NEARNESS PERFUMED TALC - Blue can from Canada. C.M.V. $15.00

RIGHT 1959-61 NEARNESS BEAUTY DUST
Plastic powder box has pearl colored lid, gray band & blue bottom. O.S.P. $2.95 C.M.V. $15.00 in box. $10.00 container only mint.

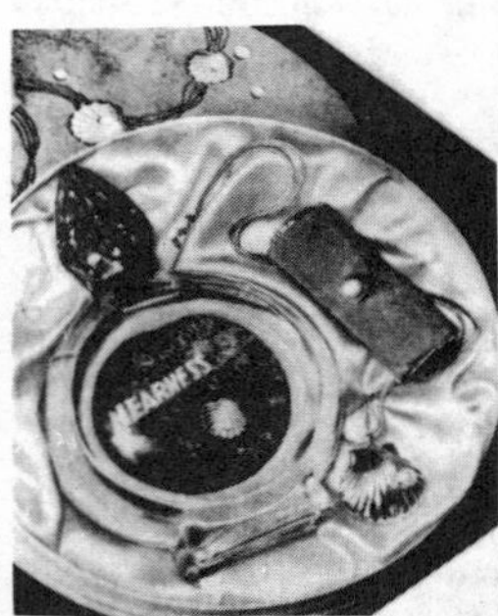

1956 ALWAYS NEAR SET
Blue sea shell box with pink satin lining holds Nearness 2 oz. Toilet Water, 1 dram Perfume & gold sea shell necklace with pearl. O.S.P. $5.95 C.M.V. $75.00 M.B.

OCCUR!

1965 OCCUR! DELUXE SET
Black & gold box holds Occur! Beauty Dust, Perfumed Skin Softener & Cologne Mist. O.S.P. $13.95 C.M.V. $35.00

1964-65 OCCUR! FRAGRANCE FORTUNE SET - Black & gold box holds Occur! 2 oz. Cologne & ½ oz. Perfume Oil. Both have gold caps. O.S.P. $6.95 C.M.V. $30.00 M.B.

1963-67 OCCUR! POWDER SACHET
9/10 oz. black glass & cap, painted label. OSP $2.50 CMV $9.00 MB $7.00 BO
1963-75 OCCUR! CREAM SACHET
.66 oz. black glass & cap. 2 caps - 1 says Occur! 1 says Occur! Cream Sachet. O.S.P. $3.00 C.M.V. 50¢
1976-78 OCCUR! CREAM SACHET
.66 oz. clear glass with black & gold lid. O.S.P. $3.00 C.M.V. 25¢

1963 OCCUR! PERFUME OIL FOR THE BATH - Black & gold box holds ½ oz. bottle with gold cap & painted label. O.S.P. $5.00 CMV $12.00 in box, $8.00 BO
1963-66 OCCUR! COLOGNE MIST
2 oz. frosted glass with black cap & gold painted label. Came in black & gold box. OSP $3.00 CMV $4.00 MB $2.00 BO
Also came with 4A embossed bottle with black neck label & gold plastic cap. OSP $2.50 CMV $4.00 MB $2.00 BO

1965-67 OCCUR! SOAP
Black & gold box holds 3 yellow bars. OSP $2.25 CMV $16.00 MB

1963-64 OCCUR! SOPHISTICATE SET
3 oz. Occur! Cologne Mist, Perfume Cream Rollette & Beauty Dust. Black & gold box. O.S.P. $12.95 C.M.V. $35.00 M.B.

1964 OCCUR! ELEGENCE SET
Black & gold box holds Occur! 4 oz. Cream Lotion, Perfumed Talc & 2 oz. Cologne. O.S.P. $5.75 C.M.V. $35.00 M.B.

1971-75 OCCUR! BEAUTY DUST
6 oz. black cardboard, non-refillable. OSP $8.50 CMV $3.00, $4.00 MB
1963-70 OCCUR! BEAUTY DUST
Black plastic box with gold handle on black lid. OSP $5.00 CMV $3.00, $5.00 MB
1964-72 OCCUR! PERFUMED SKIN SOFTENER
5 oz. black painted over white milk glass or clear glass jar with black & gold lid. OSP $1.75 CMV, $1.00. Also came white milk glass painted black. CMV $7.00
1965-68 OCCUR! PERFUMED SOAP
Black wrapped soap. OSP 49c CMV $2.00

1964-74 OCCUR! PERFUMED TALC
2.75 oz. black can & cap, gold painted label. O.S.P. $1.00 C.M.V. 50¢
1966-74 OCCUR! FOAMING BATH OIL - 6 oz. black plastic bottle with gold cap & painted label. Came in black & gold box. OSP $3.50 CMV $3.00 MB $2.00 BO
1963-76 OCCUR! COLOGNE MIST
3 oz. black plastic coated bottle with gold cap & painted label. Came in black & gold box. Older issue was gold bottom under plastic coating CMV $3.00. Came with and without 3 oz. on front of bottle. CMV $2.00 OSP $7.00 CMV $11.00

1964-65 OCCUR! PERFUMED BATH OIL - 6 oz. black plastic bottle with gold cap & painted label. Black & gold box. O.S.P. $2.75 C.M.V. $5.00 B.O. $6.00 M.B.

1964-68 OCCUR! CREAM LOTION
4 oz. gold cap & painted label. Came in black & gold box. OSP $1.75 CMV $4.00 MB $2.00 BO
1970-71 OCCUR! ½ OZ. COLOGNE
½ oz. size with gold cap & painted letters. Came in black & gold box. OSP $1.50 CMV $1.00 BO $1.50 MB
1964-69 OCCUR! PERFUME OIL
½ oz. gold cap & painted label. Came in black & gold box. OSP $5.00 CMV $6.00 MB $4.00 BO
1964-71 OCCUR! 2 OZ. COLOGNE
2 oz. bottle with gold cap & painted label. Came in black & gold box. OSP $2.50 CMV $1.00 in box. Bottle only 75c.

1966-70 OCCUR! SCENTED HAIR SPRAY
7 oz. black can with black cap. OSP $1.50 CMV $3.00
1965-69 PERFUME ROLLETTE
.33 oz. gray ribbed carnival glass, gold cap. OSP $2.50 CMV $6.00 BO $7.00 MB
1963-65 PERFUMED CREAM ROLLETTE
.33 oz. 4A embossed bottle with gold cap. OSP $2.50 CMV $2.00 MB $3.00
1963-68 OCCUR! PERFUME MIST
Gold box holds 2 dram black & gold metal case with white cap. OSP $3.75 CMV $6.00 MB $5.00 BO

ORCHARD BLOSSOMS

1943-44 PETAL OF BEAUTY
Blue box with pink satin lining holds 6 oz. Orchard Blossoms Cologne & blue feather design Beauty Dust or Apple Blossom Beauty Dust. OSP $2.20 CMV $100.00 MB.

1945-46 PETAL OF BEAUTY
Blue & white box holds 6 oz. Orchard Blossoms Cologne & blue & white box Beauty Dust. O.S.P. $2.20 C.M.V. $100.00 M.B.

PATCHWORK

1972 PATCHWORK COOKER AWARD
Patchwork design. Level 4, earned for selling Cologne Mists. C.M.V. $30.00 M.B. $35.00

1972 PATCHWORK COOKIE JAR AWARD - Level 2 - Earned for selling Cologne Mists. White glass with orange, green, red & yellow. C.M.V. $12.00 M.B. $15.00

LEFT 1941-45 ORCHARD BLOSSOMS COLOGNE
6 oz. bubble sided bottle, short front label has tree with flowers on it. OSP $1.50 pink cap. CMV $50.00 BO $60.00 MB
RIGHT 1945-46 ORCHARD BLOSSOMS COLOGNE
Same as above with long blue & white front label, pink cap. OSP $1.50 CMV $65.00 MB $55.00 BO

1973-76 PATCHWORK PRODUCTS
White with orange, red & green designs.
1973-76 SOAP - 3 cakes, yellow, orange & green. SSP $5.00 CMV $6.00 MB
1973-76 COLOGNE MIST - 3 oz. S.S.P. $4.00 C.M.V. $1.00
1973-76 PERFUME POWDER MIST
7 oz. S.S.P. $2.00 C.M.V. 50¢
1973-76 PERFUME ROLLETTE - .33 oz S.S.P. $3.00 C.M.V. 50¢
1973-77 CREAM SACHET - .66 oz. S.S.P. $3.00 C.M.V. 25¢
1973-76 COLOGNE SAMPLE BOTTLE - C.M.V. 25¢

1972 PATCHWORK CANISTER AWARD - Level 3 - Earned for selling Cologne Mists. White glass 3 pc. caniste set with patchwork decals. C.M.V. $25.00 set M.B.

1973-77 PATCHWORK PRODUCTS
1973-74 HAND & BODY LOTION
8 oz. S.S.P. $2.00 C.M.V. 50¢
1973-75 FOAMING BATH OIL
6 oz. S.S.P. $3.00 C.M.V. $1.00
1973-74 PERFUME CANDLE
S.S.P. $6.00 C.M.V. $6.00
1973-76 COLOGNE GELEE -
3 oz. S.S.P. $4.00 C.M.V. $1.00
1973-74 EYESHADOW - S.S.P. $4.00 C.M.V. $1.00
1973-76 SAMPLES in foil pouch. C.M.V. 25¢ box.
1973-76 PATCHWORK CREAM SACHET - 5 oz. white plastic jar with red, yellow & orange lid. O.S.P. $3.00 C.M.V. 50¢
1973-76 PERFUMED SKIN SOFTENE
5 oz. Plastic jar. O.S.P. $4.50 C.M.V. 25

972 PATCHWORK REFRIGERATOR AWARDS - Level 1 - Earned by selling Cologne Mists. White plastic with orange, reen, red & yellow, patchwork decals. C.M.V. $10.00 set. $12.00 M.B.

1973 PATCHWORK BINGO CARD
9½" paper bingo card used by Reps at meetings. C.M.V. $2.00

PERSIAN WOOD

RIGHT 1958-62 PERSIAN WOOD PERFUMED TALC
Red & gold box holds red can with brass cap & trim. OSP 79c CMV $5.00 MB $3.00 can only, mint.
LEFT 1962-68 PERSIAN WOOD PERFUMED TALC
Same as above only with a white plastic cap. OSP 79c CMV $3.00 MB $2.00 can only.

PENNSYLVANIA DUTCH

973-76 PENNSYLVANIA DUTCH DECANTERS
ellow painted over clear glass with ange fruit and yellow caps. All items MV $3.00 BO $5.00 MB
973-76 HAND & BODY LOTION
0 oz. Came in Patchwork or Sonnet nly. SSP $5.00
973-74 COLOGNE DECANTER
Salt or peper shaker) Holds Moonwind, atchwork, or Sonnet. 4 oz. SSP $5.00
973-76 FOAMING BATH OIL
oz. SSP $5.00
973-75 POWDER SACHET SHAKER
.25 oz. SSP $5.00
973-76 PERFUMED SKIN SOFTENER
oz. OSP $5.00

PATTERNS

1969 PATTERNS
1969-70 TRAY- 10" black plastic tray with gold edge when held to light shows purple, red, gray, these are transparent. There is an opaque black one - rare. CMV red, gray & purple $4.00 MB $2.00 TO Reissued in 1975. Black (no light comes through) $7.50
1969-70 POWDER SHADOW COMPACT
Black & white plastic. O.S.P. $5.00 C.M.V. $2.00
1969-70 LIPSTICK - Black & white metal tube. O.S.P. $1.50 C.M.V. $1.00
1969-74 CREAM SACHET - .66 oz. Black & white glass jar, plastic lid. O.S.P. $3.00 C.M.V. 50¢
1969-72 COLOGNE MIST
3 oz. black & white spray can & cap. O.S.P. $6.00 C.M.V. $1.00
1969-74 PERFUME ROLLETTE
.33 oz. black & white bottle & cap. O.S.P. $3.00 C.M.V. $1.50
1969-70 PATTERNS PERFUME GLACE RING - Black, white & red box holds gold ring with black set. O.S.P. $6.00 . C.M.V. in box $6.00. Ring only $3.00

1964-66 PERSIAN WOOD PERFUME OIL
Red & gold box holds ½ oz. bottle, white lettering & gold cap. OSP $3.50 CMV $10.00 in box $8.00 BO
1961-66 PERSIAN WOOD COLOGNE
2 oz. clear glass, gold lettering, gold cap. In red & gold box. OSP $1.75 CMV $6.00 in box. $4.00 BO
1960-63 PERSIAN WOOD COLOGNE
Red & gold box holds 4 oz. bottle with gold lettering & gold cap. OSP $2.75 CMV $10.00 in box $8.00 bottle only.

LEFT TO RIGHT
1959-76 PERSIAN WOOD CREAM SACHET
.66 oz. red bottoms with smooth gold lid. CMV $6.00 BO $7.00 MB. Gold embossed cap with curved sides. CMV $4.00 BO $5.00 MB. Same cap with straight sides. CMV 50c. Came red paint over clear or milk glass.

1960-64 PERSIAN WOOD PERFUMED SKIN SOFTENER
5 oz. off-white glass bottom with straight sides. Red & gold cap with either curved or straight sides. OSP $3.00 CMV $5.00 MB $3.50 BO
1964-66 PERSIAN WOOD PERFUMED SKIN SOFTENER
5 oz. white glass, round bottom, red & gold cap. OSP $3.00 CMV $3.00 BO $4.00 MB

1963-67 PERSIAN WOOD PERFUME MIST
2 drams, red base, white cap, in gold box. OSP $3.25 CMV $6.00, $7.00 MB
1957-63 PERSIAN WOOD SPRAY PERFUME
2 dram, red metal with gold cap, red & gold box. OSP $3.50 CMV $10.00 in box. $8.00 container only.

1957-66 PERSIAN WOOD POWDER SACHET - 1¼ oz. red plastic squeeze bottle, gold cap, red & gold box. O.S.P. $2.00 C.M.V. $10.00 M.B. $7.00 bottle only

1957-61 PERSIAN WOOD LOTION SACHET
Red plastic coated, gold cap. Came in red & gold box. O.S.P. $2.00 C.M.V. $10.00 M.B. $7.00 bottle only.

1960-62 PERSIAN WOOD 4 OZ COLOGNE - Red & gold flip open box holds 4 oz. Persian Wood Cologne. OSP $3.00 CMV $20.00 MB

1957-60 PERSIAN WOOD BEAUTY DUST
Red glass bottom with red & gold tin lid. Lid also came in cardboard just like tin lid shown. Same CMV. OSP $3.00 CMV $10.00 mint $15.00 MB

1960-66 PERSIAN WOOD BEAUTY DUST
White plastic with red design around gold handle. OSP $3.25 CMV $8.00 mint $12.00 MB

1959-61 PERSIAN WOOD TOILET WATER
2 oz. gold cap, painted label. Came in red & gold box. OSP $2.50 CMV $10.00 MB $8.00 BO

1957-59 PERSIAN WOOD MIST
3 oz. red plastic coated glass, smooth gold cap. Came in red & gold box. OSP $3.00 CMV $10.00 BO $12.00 MB

1956-59 PERSIAN WOOD MIST
3 oz. red plastic coated glass, raised gold cap with 4A on top. Came in red & gold box. OSP $3.00 CMV $10.00 BO $12.00 MB

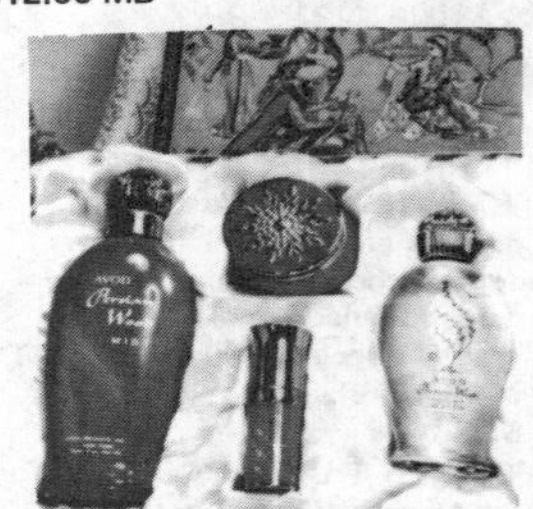

1959-60 PERSIAN TREASURE
Fancy gold box with white satin lining holds Persian Wood Mist, 2 oz. Toilet Water, Perfume Spray & Cream Sachet. OSP $10.75 CMV $60.00 MB

1961-62 PERSIAN MAGIC
Red & gold box holds Persian Wood 2 oz. Cologne & Cream Sachet. O.S.P. $3.50 CMV $22.00 MB

1963-64 PERSIAN INTRIGUE
Red & gold box holds Persian Wood Mist, Cream Lotion & Perfumed Cream Rollette. OSP $6.50 CMV $32.50

1959-64 PERSIAN WOOD MIST
3 oz. red plastic coated glass, gold crown cap. Came in red & gold box. O.S.P. $3.00 C.M.V. $6.00 in box. $5.00 bottle only.

1964-76 PERSIAN WOOD COLOGNE MIST - 3 oz. red plastic coated glass, gold crown cap. Came in red & gold box. OSP $7.00 CMV $1.00, $2.00 MB

1963 PERSIAN WOOD PERFUME OIL FOR THE BATH - ½ oz. bottle with gold cap, painted label. Came in red & go box. O.S.P. $3.50 C.M.V. $12.00 bottle only. $15.00 in box.

1961-66 PERSIAN WOOD CREAM LOTION
4 oz. clear glass, gold lettering, gold cap Came in red & gold box. OSP $1.25 CMV $5.00 MB $3.00 BO

1960-66 PERSIAN WOOD PERFUME BATH OIL
6 oz. red plastic bottle with gold cap. Came in red & gold box. OSP $2.25 CMV $8.00 MB $6.00 BO

1961-63 PERSIAN WOOD BODY POWDER
4 oz. red plastic bottle with gold cap, i red & gold box. OSP $1.95 CMV $12. in box $8.00 bottle only.

1957-58 PERSIAN FANCY
Red & gold box with red lining ho Persian Wood Mist & Lotion Sache or Powder Sachet. O.S.P. $5.00 C. $40.00 M.B.

961-62 PERSIAN LEGEND
ed & gold box with red satin lining holds ersian Wood Mist & Beauty Dust. O.S.P. 6.50 C.M.V. $40.00 M.B.

1960s PERSIAN WOOD BEAUTY DUST REFILL
Box holds plain paper refill pack with red powder puff. O.S.P. $2.98 C.M.V. $6.00 M.B.

1964 PERSIAN MOOD
Red & gold box with white lining holds Persian Wood Cream Sachet & 1 dram Perfume. OSP $4.00, CMV $22.00 MB M.B.

1962-63 PERSIAN WOOD COLOGNE
2½ oz. clear glass, gold cap. Red label on front of flat sided bottle. Came in Refreshing Hours Set only. C.M.V. $10.00.

1975-76 PERSIAN WOOD CREAM SACHET - .66 oz. clear glass, red & gold cap. O.S.P. $1.50 C.M.V. 50¢

PINE & ROYAL PINE

See Page 5 for Grading Examples on Mint Condition

1942-51 PINE BATH OIL
6 oz. flat sided bottle with turquoise cap. O.S.P. 95¢ C.M.V. $22.00. M.B. $28.00

1955-57 PINE BATH OIL
4 oz. bottle with green cap. Came in Pinehurst Set only. C.M.V. $30.00

1963-68 ROYAL PINE BATH OIL
8 oz. green plastic bottle & cap. O.S.P. $2.00 C.M.V. $6.00 M.B. $4.00 B.O. See Misc. Bottle section under Mis. Bath Oils for different labels.

1954-57 ROYAL PINE BATH SALTS
8 oz. clear glass with green lid. Green & brown label. O.S.P. 75¢ C.M.V. $20.00 $25.00 M.B.

Left - 1944-45 PINE BATH OIL
6 oz. flat sided bottle with green cap & brown label. O.S.P. $1.00 C.M.V. $25.00 $30.00 M.B.

Right - 1955-57 ROYAL PINE BATH OIL - 6 oz. flat sided bottle, green cap. O.S.P. $1.25 C.M.V. $25.00 B.O. $30.00 M.B.

1955-56 PINE BATH OIL
2 oz., pink cap. Pink and white curtain label. Came in "That's for Me Set" only. C.M.V. $15.00

1957-59 ROYAL PINE BATH OIL
8 oz. bottle with green cap & pine cones on label in yellow, white & green box. O.S.P. $1.95 C.M.V. $25.00 in box. $22.00 bottle only.

1959 PINE SOAP
Plain green box with gold printing on lid. 3 green flat edge bars. CMV $30.00 MB

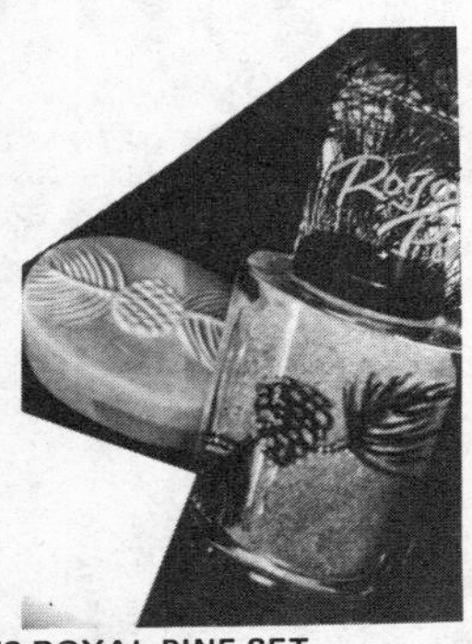

1953 ROYAL PINE SET
Pine box holds 1 bar of Pine Soap & 8 oz. jar with green lid & pine cone & branch painted on bottle. O.S.P. $1.25 C.M.V. $45.00

1955-57 PINEHURST
Pine box holds 2 green bars of Pine Soap & 4 oz. bottle of Pine Bath Oil with green cap. OSP $1.75 CMV $52.50 MB

1954-57 ROYAL PINE SET
Pine covered box holds 8 oz. jar with green lid of Royal Pine Bath Salts & green bar of Pine Soap. O.S.P. $1.39 C.M.V. $35.00 set. Bottle only $20.00

1943 ROYAL PINE SET
Beige box with pine cones & crest on lid, holds 6 oz. Royal Pine Bath Oil & 2 bars Pine Soap. Came in 2 different size boxes as shown. OSP $1.60 CMV $60.00 MB each set.

1940 Only - PINE SOAP
Special box holds 3 green bars of Pine Soap. O.S.P. 69¢ C.M.V. $45.00 M.B.

1940-42 BREATH OF PINE
Green & white box holds 2 green bars of Pine Soap & 9 oz. bottle of Pine Bath Salts. O.S.P. $1.25 C.M.V. $55.00 M.B.

1940-43 ROYAL PINE
Pine cones on lid of box, holds 2 green bars of Pine Soap & 6 oz. bottle of Pine Bath Oil. O.S.P. $1.35 C.M.V. $55.00 M.B.

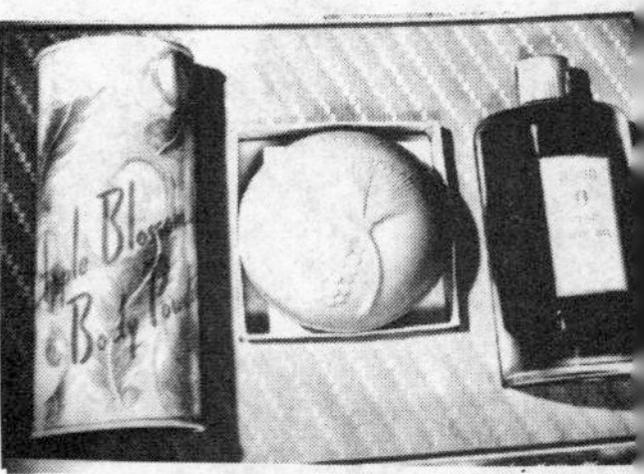

1941-42 TOWERING PINE
Pine cones on lid of box, holds Appl
Blossoms Body Powder, green bar of
Pine Bath Soap & 6 oz. bottle of Pin
Bath Oil. O.S.P. $1.65 C.M.V. $65.0
M.B.

1940 Only - BREATH OF PINE
Box holds 9 oz. bottle of Pine Bath S
& 2 green bars of Pine Soap. O.S.P. $
C.M.V. $60.00 M.B.

1940-59 PINE SOAP
Green box with pine cone on lid h
3 green round bars of Pine Soap. (
69¢ C.M.V. $30.00 M.B.

1959-65 ROYAL PINE SOAP
Same design box & same design on
only edge of soap is flat instead of
OSP $1.25 CMV $25.00 MB

1953 PINE BATH SALTS
8 oz. clear glass jar, green lids, painted
branch. Came 2 different ways. Both c
in 1953 Royal Pine Set only. C.M.V.
$30.00 ea. mint.

1940 PINE SOAP SUBSTITUTE
3 green bars of pine soap came in brown and green box that was the Royal Pine set box. A letter from Avon stating the regular soap boxes were not available & Royal Pine set box was substituted. RARE. with letter. O.S.P.
C.M.V. $45.00 M.B. with letter as shown.

1964-65 JUST PEACHY
Pink & white box holds Peach Soap On A Rope & Peach Pomade. O.S.P. $2.35 C.M.V. $40.00 M.B.

1964 PEACH SURPRISE SET
Pink & white box holds Pretty Peach 2 oz. Cologne with choice of 4 oz. Bubble Bath or Cream Lotion. O.S.P. $2.85 C.M.V. $20.00 M.B.

1965 PEACH DELIGHT
Box holds Pretty Peach Necklace, Beauty Dust & Cologne. O.S.P. $5.95 C.M.V. $55.00 M.B. set.

PRETTY PEACH

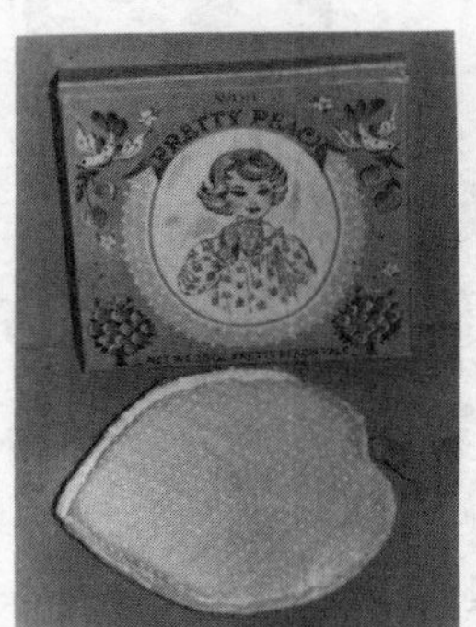

1965-66 PRETTY PEACH TALC PUFF
Pink box holds pink & white puff filled with powder. O.S.P. $1.50 C.M.V. $6.00 MB Puff only $2.00 mint.

1964-67 PRETTY PEACH CREAM SACHET - Yellow glass jar with peaches on lid. O.S.P. $1.00 C.M.V. $7.00 in box. $5.00 jar only.
1964-67 PEACH POMADE
Foam peach with green leaf holds Pomade Lipstick. O.S.P. $1.00 C.M.V. $16.00. M.B. $18.00

1964-67 PRETTY PEACH CREAM LOTION & BUBBLE BATH - 4 oz. pink plastic bottle with peach on cap, painted label, pink box. O.S.P. $1.35 C.M.V. Cream Lotion $8.00 M.B. $10.00. C.M.V. Bubble Bath $6.00. M.B. $8.00

1966-67 PRETTY PEACH SOAP & SPONGE - Pink box holds pink & white sponge & soap. O.S.P. $2.25 C.M.V. in box $12.00. Soap & Sponge only $8.00.

FOREIGN PRETTY PEACH EAU DE COLOGNE - Peach cap & painted label. C.M.V. $10.00
FOREIGN PRETTY PEACH HAND CREAM - C.M.V. $6.00

1964-67 PRETTY PEACH COLOGNE
2 oz. bottle with peach cap with green leaf & painted label. Pink box. O.S.P. $1.50 CMV $7.00 in box $4.00 bottle only.

1964-66 PRETTY PEACH SOAP
Pink box holds 2 peach halves & brown seed center soap. O.S.P. $1.50 C.M.V. $24.00 in box $12.50 soap only.

1964-67 PRETTY PEACH "SODA" COLOGNE MIST - 2 oz. pink plastic coated bottle with pink top with white flowers & blue straws. Came in 2 different silver stands. OSP $2.50 CMV $8.00 each $12.00 MB

1964-67 PRETTY PEACH PERFUMED TALC - 2½ oz. pink & white paper container. O.S.P. 79¢ C.M.V. $6.00. M.B. $8.00

1964-67 PRETTY PEACH BEAUTY DUST - Pink & white cardboard box. O.S.P. $2.50 C.M.V. $10.00. M.B. $14.00

1964-65 PRETTY PEACH SOAP ON A ROPE - 5 oz. peach shaped soap on white rope. OSP $1.35 CMV $17.00 MB $11.00 soap only.

1965 PRETTY PEACH NECKLACE
Small peach on gold chain. Came in Peach Delight Set only. C.M.V. $20.00 $25.00 on card.

1964-67 PRETTY PEACH SACHET SAMPLES - Box holds 10 peach shaped samples of Cream Sachet packets. C.M.V. $2.50 box of 10.

1965 PEACH SMOOTH
Peach box holds 2 tubes of Pretty Peach Hand Cream. O.S.P. $1.35 C.M.V. $12.00 MB $4.00 tube only mint.

1965-66 PRETTY PEACH PRINCESS
Box holds Pretty Peach Talc & Cream Sachet. OSP $2.25 CMV $20.00 MB

1964-65 MISS AVON SET
Blue & black plastic case holds Pretty Peach Cologne, Bubble Bath, Perfumed Talc & 10 Lip Dew Samples in a bag. Al Talc samples. O.S.P. $7.50 C.M.V. $50. set in blue case. $55.00 set M.B.

QUAINTANCE

1948-56 QUAINTANCE POWDER SACHET - 9/10 oz. or 1¼ oz. clear glass with red cap, painted label. O.S.P. $1.19 C.M.V. $11.00 in box. $10.00 jar only.

Right - 1948 Only - QUAINTANCE POWDER SACHET - 9/10 oz. clear glass with red cap & larger painted label. O.S.P. $1.19 CMV $20.00 MB $16.00 BO. Also came in 1¼ oz. size with large size label. CMV $20.00 MB $16.00 BO

1955-56 QUAINTANCE COLOGNE
2 oz. bottle with blue cap, came in Dantiness Set & Bath Bouquet Sets. C.M.V. $15.00 Quaintance Cream Lotion in same sets. C.M.V. $12.00

1953-56 QUAINTANCE CREAM SACHET
White square glass jar with red rose on white cap. O.S.P. $1.25 C.M.V. $12.00 in box. $10.00 jar only

1949-56 QUAINTANCE BATH OIL
4 oz. clear glass, white painted label. Rose cap. O.S.P. $1.25 C.M.V. $20.00 in box. Bottle only $16.00 mint.

1949-56 QUAINTANCE CREAM LOTION - 4 oz. clear glass, white paint label. Rose cap. O.S.P. 89¢ C.M.V. $14 in box. $12.00 bottle only mint.

1948-56 QUAINTANCE 4 OZ. COLOGN
4 oz. clear glass, green painted label, ribb corners, rose cap with green leaf. O.S.P. $ C.M.V. $15.00 in box. Bottle only $13.0

1948-50 QUAINTANCE 2 OZ. COLOGN
2 oz. bottle with rose cap, painted label & ribbed corners. Came in Quaintance Set & Quaintance Bow Knot Set only. C.M.V $20.00

1953-56 QUAINTANCE TOILET WATE
2 oz. clear glass, green painted label, ribb corners, rose cap with green leaf. O.S.P. $ C.M.V. $20.00 in box. $15.00 bottle onl

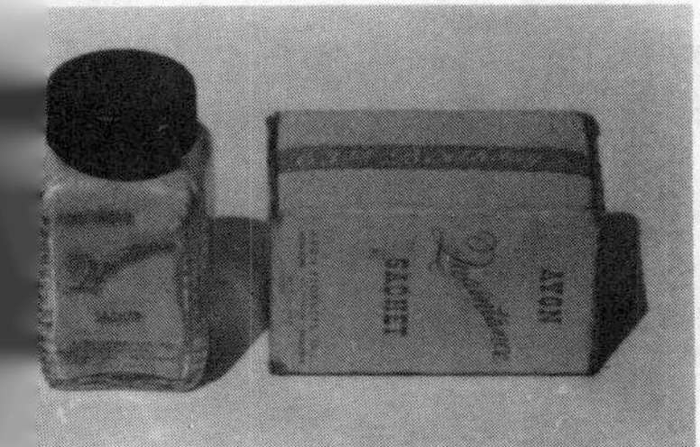

1949 QUAINTANCE SACHET 63RD BIRTHDAY BOX
Regular issue powder sachet came in special issue Avon's 63rd Birthday box. $15.00 MB as shown.

1948-56 QUAINTANCE POWDER SACHET - 9 oz. clear glass, white cap & painted label. Cap same as Bright Night without stars, but came this way. C.M.V. $15.00 M.B.

1948 Only - 62nd. ANNIVERSARY QUAINTANCE COLOGNE - 1st issued in white lace design box. 4 oz. size. Given to Reps. for selling 62 Avon items on 62nd anniversary celebration. C.M.V. $55.00 M.B.

1955-56 QUAINTANCE BATH OIL
2 oz. pink cap, pink and white label. Came in That's For Me set only. C.M.V. $15.00 mint.

1955 BATH BOUQUET
White & blue box with red rose on lid holds 2 oz. bottles of Quaintance Cream Lotion & Cologne with blue caps. Blue bar of Quaintance Soap. O.S.P. $1.95 CMV $52.00 MB.

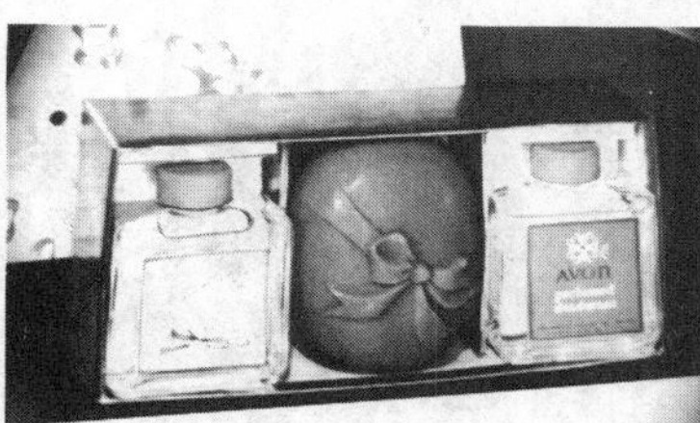

1955 DAINTINESS SET
White box with pink & blue ribbons holds 2 oz. bottles of Perfumed Deodorant & Quaintance Cologne with blue caps & blue bar of Quaintance Soap. O.S.P. $1.95 CMV $52.00 MB.

1949-56 QUAINTANCE PERFUME
3 dram glass bottle, painted label, rose flowered cap & green leaf. Box green felt. Diary has white cover with red rose & turquoise design. O.S.P. $4.00 C.M.V. $150.00 in box.

1952 QUAINTANCE SACHET VALENTINE BOX
Short issue box at Valentine time. Holds regular issue powder sachet. OSP $1.19 CMV in this box $19.00 mint.

1948-56 QUAINTANCE BODY POWDER
5 oz. red & white paper box, shaker top. O.S.P. 75¢ C.M.V. $16.00 in box. $12.00 container only.

1948-50 QUAINTANCE PERFUME
1 dram size with red rose cap, painted label. Blue & white box. O.S.P. $1.50 C.M.V. $80.00 in box. $70.00 bottle only.

1948-57 QUAINTANCE BEAUTY DUST
Red rose on tin lid, white paper sides & tin bottom, white box. O.S.P. $1.50 CMV $18.00 in box $12.00 Beauty Dust only mint.

1950 QUAINTANCE PERFUME
White box with white lace trim holds 3 dram perfume with plain red cap & green leaf. O.S.P. $4.00 C.M.V. $125.00 in box.

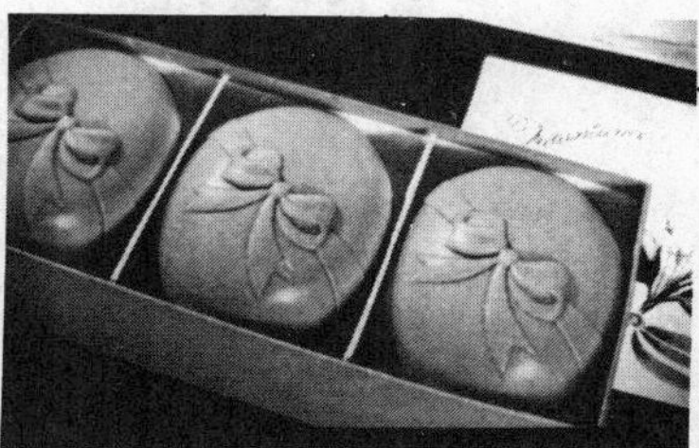

1955-56 QUAINTANCE SOAP
3 blue bars with embossed bows. O.S.P. $1.59 C.M.V. $40.00 M.B.

1956 DAINTINESS SET
White box with pink & blue ribbon holds 2 oz. bottles of Quaintance Cream Lotion & Cologne with blue caps & blue bar of Quaintance Soap. O.S.P. $1.95 C.M.V. $52.00 MB

1950 QUAINTANCE BOW KNOT
Box holds Quaintance 2 oz. Cologne & Powder Sachet. O.S.P. $2.25 C.M.V. $50.00

1948 QUAINTANCE SET
Blue & white box contains 2 oz. Quaintance Cologne & Powder Sachet, both have red caps. O.S.P. $2.35 C.M.V. $45.00 M.B.

1954-56 ROSE GAY SET
Blue & white box holds Quaintance 4 oz. Cream Lotion & Body Powder. O.S.P. $1.95 CMV $52.00 MB

1954-55 QUAINTANCE HARMONY
Blue & white flip open box holds Quaintance Cologne & Cream Lotion. OSP $2.15 CMV $52.00 MB

1954-55 LEISURE HOURS SET
Blue & yellow fold up box holds 4 oz. Quaintance Bath Oil & Cream Lotion. OSP $2.75 CMV $52.00

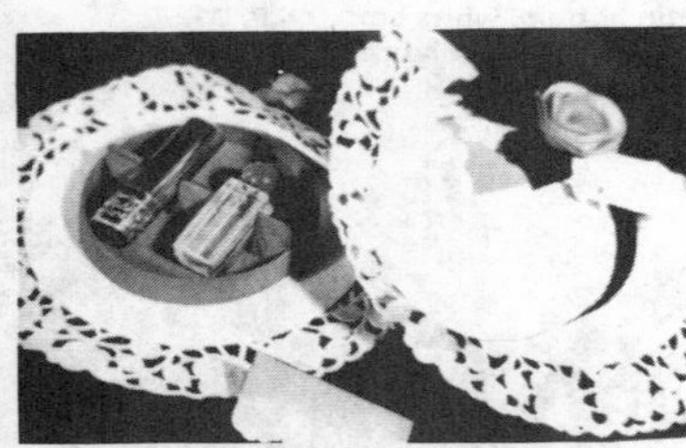
1948 GAY BONNET SET
White hat shaped box with black ribbon & red rose around hat lid contains gold lipstick & 1 dram bottle of Quaintance Perfume with rose cap. O.S.P. $2.35 CMV $105.00 MB

1952-53 QUAINTANCE HARMONY
Box with blue ribbon on clear plastic lid holds 4 oz. Quaintance Cream Lotion & Cologne. O.S.P. $2.75 C.M.V. $45.00 set M.B. C.M.V. 4 oz. Cologne with rose cap $20.00

1952-53 MISS QUAINTANCE SET
Blue & white octagonal box holds Quaintance Body Powder & 4 oz. Cream Lotion. O.S.P. $1.95 C.M.V. $47.50 MB

1950-51 QUAINTANCE ROSE GAY SET
Blue & white box with red roses holds Quaintance Body Powder & 4 oz. Cream Lotion. OSP $1.85 CMV $47.00 MB

1950-51 QUAINTANCE HARMONY
White box with blue ribbon over clear plastic lid holds Quaintance 4 oz. Cologne & Body Powder. O.S.P. $2.95 C.M.V. $50.00 M.B.

1949 QUAINTANCE PERFUME AWARD
Given to representatives in 63rd anniversary campaign for selling 63 pieces of Avon. Green felt cover trimmed in gold, holds 3 dram bottle with rose flowered cap & painted label, green leaf around neck. Not shown in picture. Must have leaf to be mint. 63rd anniversary inscribed inside cover. C.M.V. $100.00 M.B.

LEFT 1949 BEAUTY MUFF SET
Red, white & blue box with blue ribbon on lid contains white lambswool muff with 1 dram Quaintance Perfume with rose cap & gold lipstick. OSP $2.35 CMV $100.00
RIGHT 1950 BEAUTY MUFF SET
Same set & box only came with 1 dram gold scroll top perfume. CMV $65.00 MB

QUEEN'S GOLD

1975-76 QUEEN'S GOLD FRAGRANCE SAMPLES - 10 foil packets in box. C.M.V. 25¢ box.
1975-76 QUEEN'S GOLD FOAMING BATH OIL - 10 oz. yellow plastic bottle with gold cap. O.S.P. $5.00 C.M.V. 50¢
1975-76 QUEEN'S GOLD COLOGNE MIST - 3 oz. yellow plastic coated bottle, gold cap. O.S.P. $5.00 C.M.V. 50¢
1975-76 QUEEN'S GOLD CREAM SACHET - .66 oz. clear glass with gold & yellow cap. O.S.P. $3.00 C.M.V. 25¢
1974-76 QUEEN'S GOLD DEMI STICK .19 oz. white with brown, pink & blue. O.S.P. $1.00 C.M.V. 25¢
1974-75 QUEEN'S GOLD PERFUME POWDER MIST - 7 oz. gold, brown, pink & blue. O.S.P. $2.00 C.M.V. 50¢

1975 "WE WANT TO PAMPER YOU" SAMPLE - Sent to all President Club Members campaign 3, 1975 introducing new fragrance Queen's Gold. Clear glass bottle with white cap. White envelope with yellow printing. C.M.V. $2.00

RAINING VIOLETS

1974-76 RAINING VIOLETS COLOGNE MIST - 2 oz. clear plastic with clear plastic lid with purple & blue inner cap. O.S.P. $5.00 C.M.V. 50¢
1974-76 RAINING VIOLETS MOISTURIZING BATH OIL - 6 oz. white plastic, pink cap. O.S.P. $2.00 C.M.V. 50¢
1974-76 RAINING VIOLETS PERFUME DEMI STICK - .19 oz. white with violets. O.S.P. $1.00 C.M.V. 50¢
1974-76 RAINING VIOLETS CREAM SACHET - .66 oz. clear glass with metal lid with violets. O.S.P. $3.00 C.M.V. 50¢

1973-75 RAINING VIOLETS
White with violet & lavender caps.
CLEANSING GEL - 6 oz. S.S.P. $2.00 C.M.V. 50¢
MOISTURIZED FRICTION LOTION 10 oz. S.S.P. $3.00 C.M.V. 50¢
EMOLLIENT MIST - 4 oz. S.S.P. $2.00 C.M.V. 50¢
PERFUMED POWDER MIST 7 oz. S.S.P. $2.00 C.M.V. 50¢
COLOGNE GELEE - 3 oz. S.S.P. $3.00 C.M.V. $1.00

RAPTURE

1965 RAPTURE DELUXE
Turquoise box contains Beauty Dust, Perfumed Skin Softener & Cologne Mist in Rapture. OSP $13.95 CMV $32.50

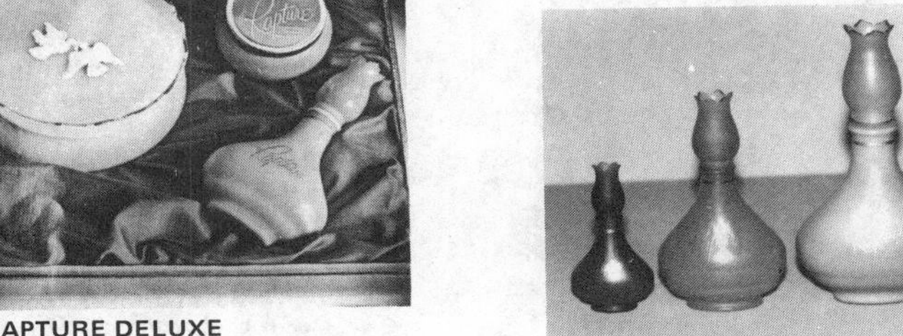

1966-72 RAPTURE FOAMING BATH OIL
6 oz. blue plastic bottle & cap. OSP $2.75 CMV $2.00
1965-66 RAPTURE PERFUMED BATH OIL
6 oz. blue plastic bottle & cap. OSP $2.75 CMV $3.00 BO $4.50 MB
1965-68 RAPTURE CREAM LOTION
4 oz. blue plastic bottle & cap. OSP $1.75 CMV $2.00 BO $3.00 MB

1964-69 RAPTURE PERFUME OIL
½ oz. green glass & cap. OSP $5.00 CMV $4.00, $6.00 MB
1964-71 RAPTURE COLOGNE
2 oz. blue glass & cap. OSP $2.50 CMV $1.00 BO $2.00 MB
1964-74 RAPTURE COLOGNE MIST
3 oz. turquoise plastic coated cap, all have gold letters. OSP $5.00 CMV $1.00 BO $1.50 MB Pictured above with regular issue box on right & special issue 1970 box on left. Add $1.00 for 1970 box.

1964-66 RAPTURE POWDER SACHET
9/10 oz. blue frosted glass with blue lid with 2 white doves. O.S.P. $2.50 C.M.V. $6.00 in box, $4.00 BO

1964-75 RAPTURE CREAM SACHET
.66 oz. dark purple glass jar with 2 white doves on purple plastic lid. O.S.P. $3.00 C.M.V. 50¢

1965-68 RAPTURE SOAP
Blue box holds 3 blue bars with 2 doves embossed. OSP $2.00 CMV $16.00 MB.

1964-73 RAPTURE PERFUMED SKIN SOFTENER - 5 oz. with blue & gold lid. Came blue painted over clear glass. C.M.V. $1.00. Also came blue painted over white milk glass. C.M.V. $3.00. O.S.P. $3.50

1964-70 RAPTURE BEAUTY DUST
Light blue plastic, white doves on lid. OSP $5.00 CMV $3.00 CO $5.00 MB

1969-72 RAPTURE ½ OZ. COLOGNE
½ oz. green cap. O.S.P. $1.50 C.M.V. $1.00

1964-65 RAPTURE PERFUMED CREAM ROLLETTE - Gold cap, embossed 4A design on 1/3 oz. bottle. O.S.P. $2.50 C.M.V. $3.00

1965-69 RAPTURE PERFUMED ROLLETTE
1/3 oz. blue ribbed glass, gold cap. O.S.P. $2.50 C.M.V. $6.00. M.B. $7.00

1964-68 RAPTURE PERFUME MIST
2 dram, dark turquoise & white metal with gold band. O.S.P. $3.25 C.M.V. $5.00. M.B. $6.00

1966-67 RAPTURE PERFUMED SOAP
3 oz. soap in turquoise wrapper. O.S.P. 49¢ C.M.V. $4.00

1964 RAPTURE PERFUMED SKIN SOFTENER SAMPLE - Turquoise foil packet holds Skin Softener. C.M.V. $2.50 box of 10

1964 RAPTURE COLOGNE SAMPLE
10 foil samples per box. CMV $1.50 box.

1964 RAPTURE POWDER SACHET SAMPLE - Paper folder with sample inside. C.M.V. $1.00 each.

1966-70 RAPTURE SCENTED HAIR SPRAY - 7 oz. blue can. O.S.P. $1.50 CMV $3.00

1965-72 RAPTURE PERFUMED TALC
2.75 oz. blue can. O.S.P. $1.00 C.M.V. $1.00
Foreign Rapture Perfume Talc is 2.75 oz. blue can, but shorter than U.S. can. C.M.V. $2.00

1971-74 RAPTURE BEAUTY DUST
6 oz. blue & gold cardboard. O.S.P. $4.50 CMV $3.00 CO $5.00 MB

1966 only RAPTURE COLOGNE MIST
2 oz. medium blue glass, gold trim. OSP $3.00

1966 only RAPTURE COLOGNE MIST
2 oz. dark blue glass. OSP $3.00

1965-66 RAPTURE COLOGNE MIST
2 oz. light blue glass, no gold trim. OSP $3.00

1965-66 RAPTURE COLOGNE MIST
2 oz. very light appears almost frosted glass. CMV each $4.00 BO $5.00 MB

1965 RAPTURE AWARD BOWL
Fostoria glass bowl with Rapture Doves etched in bottom. Given to each representative in the winning district during the 79th Anniversary Campaign. C.M.V. $35.00. M.B. $40.00.

1964 RAPTURE PIN
Silver gray in color. C.M.V. $15.00 pin only $18.00 on Avon card pictured.

1965 RAPTURE BLOUSE AWARD
Cotton blouse with 2 doves on upper left side of shirt. Came in blue and white. Won by Avon Reps. Modeled by Sally Omann. Avon neck label made by Lady Manhatten. Won by selling 50 Rapture and/or Occur products. C.M.V. $20.00

1964-65 RAPTURE RHAPSODY TRAY
Rapture Powder Sachet, 1 dram Perfume & 2 oz. Cologne sit on blue velvet, trimmed in gold. Rapture mirror in center with 2 doves on mirror. O.S.P. $10.95 C.M.V. $30.00 tray, set mint. $40.00 set MB

REGENCE

1966 REGENCE HAND MIRROR
Green & gold metal 4½" long. Came in Regence gift set. CMV $10.00 in box. $7.00 mirror only.

1967-71 REGENCE FRAGRANCE SAMPLE
Foil packet. CMV $1.00 box of 10.

1970-71 REGENCE ½ OZ. COLOGNE
½ oz. clear glass bottle with gold cap. OSP $1.75 CMV $2.00 MB $1.00 BO
1968-69 REGENCE PERFUME OIL
½ oz. gold cap. Came with either clear bottom label or gold neck tag label. OSP $6.00 CMV $4.00 BO $6.00 MB
1967-69 REGENCE COLOGNE
2 oz. gold cap. OSP $3.00 CMV $2.00 MB $1.00 BO
1968-70 REGENCE COLOGNE SILK
3 oz. gold cap, frosted glass bottle. OSP $4.50 CMV $2.00 MB $1.00 BO
SO SOFT
6 oz. gold cap. OSP $5.00 CMV $2.00 MB $1.00 BO

1969-71 REGENCE 4 OZ. COLOGNE
4 oz. gold cap. OSP $6.00 CMV $2.00
1969-72 REGENCE FOAMING BATH OIL
6 oz. light green plastic bottle with gold cap. OSP $4.00 CMV $1.00 BO $2.00 MB
1966-71 COLOGNE MIST REFILL
3 oz. green plastic coated. OSP $4.00 CMV $3.00 BO $4.00 MB

1966-71 REGENCE COLOGNE MIST
3 oz. green & gold plastic. Base is gold on older ones and green on newer ones. OSP $6.00 CMV gold base $3.00 green base $2.00 MB $1.00 BO
1968-71 HAIR SPRAY
7 oz. green & gold with green cap. OSP $1.50 CMV $3.00
1966-73 REGENCE BEAUTY DUST
Green & gold plastic bottom, clear plastic lid with gold crown. OSP $6.00 Paper side older CMV $8.00 MB Plastic side newer CMV $5.00 MB $2.00 less each for no box.

1966-69 REGENCE PERFUME
½ oz. frosted glass with gold plastic cap. Bottle trimmed in gold, green & white box. Gold neck tag. O.S.P. $15.00 C.M.V. $15.00 B.O. $25.00 M.B.

1966-69 REGENCE PERFUME
1 oz. frosted glass bottle & stopper, trimmed in gold, green & white box. Gold neck tag. OSP $30.00 CMV $25.00 BO $37.50 MB

1968-71 REGENCE PERFUME SKIN SOFTENER - 5 oz. green ribbed glass, small silver edged cap. Gold center & multi-color cap. O.S.P. $4.00 C.M.V. $2.00
1971-74 REGENCE PERFUMED SKIN SOFTENER - 5 oz. green ribbed glass, large silver edged, gold center & multi-color green cap. O.S.P. $4.00 C.M.V. $1.00
1967-68 REGENCE PERFUMED SKIN SOFTENER - 5 oz. green ribbed glass, small silver edge cap with gold center & plain green cap. O.S.P. $4.00 C.M.V. $3.00 $4.00 M.B.

1966-67 REGENCE CREAM SACHET
Green painted glass with green paper band. Green & gold cap, gold base. OSP $3.00 CMV $2.00, $3.00 MB
1968-75 REGENCE CREAM SACHET
Solid green glass, green plastic cap. OSP $3.00 CMV 50c. Both also came green painted over clear or milk glass. Same CMV.

1966 REGENCE COLOGNE MIST STOCKHOLDERS GIFT - White, green & gold box. Given to Stockholders on introduction of Regence, says "Your introduction to a Fragrance masterpiece by Avon" C.M.V. $35.00 M.B.

1967-68 REGENCE PERFUME ROLLETTE
.33 oz. ribbed glass, smooth gold cap. OSP $3.00 CMV $2.00 MB $1.50 BO
1969-73 REGENCE PERFUME ROLLETTE
.33 oz. ribbed glass & green cap. OSP $3.00 CMV $1.00 BO $1.50 MB
1967-70 REGENCE PERFUMED GLACE
Green & gold box holds green & gold Glace Compact. OSP $5.50 CMV $8.00 in box. $5.00 compact only.

1968-72 REGENCE TALC
3½ oz. green paper box. O.S.P. $1.25 C.M.V. $1.00
1967-72 REGENCE PERFUMED POWDER MIST - 7 oz. green can with gold cap. O.S.P. $4.00 C.M.V. $1.00

1968 REGENCE CREAM SACHET
.66 oz. clear glass painted green. Green & gold tone cap & base. Sides are smooth no design. CMV $4.00 MB $3.00 jar only.

FOREIGN ROSE GERANIUM CREAM SACHET - Frosted rose colored glass, gold cap. C.M.V. $2.00

1966 REGENCE GIFT SET
Green box holds Cream Sachet, Cologne Mist, green & gold hand mirror. O.S.P. $12.50 C.M.V. $37.50

1966 REGENCE EARRINGS
Gold with turquoise settings, Customer service award campaign 14-18, 1966. Has green velvet box. C.M.V. $60.00 in box.
1966 REGENCE NECKLACE
Crown performance award. Gold with turquoise settings & gold crown set in center, can also be worn as a pin. Has green velvet box. C.M.V. $50.00 in box.

ROSE GERANIUM

1964-68 ROSE GERANIUM AFTER BATH FRESHENER
8 oz. glass bottle with rose colored cap, red flowered box. OSP $2.50 CMV $4.00 MB $3.00 BO
1964-67 PERFUMED BATH OIL
8 oz. frosted plastic bottle with rose color cap. Red flowered box. OSP $2.50 CMV $3.00 MB $2.00 BO
1964-66 PERFUMED TALC
3½ oz. rose covered paper container with plastic shaker top. OSP 89c CMV $4.00 MB $3.00 CO Also came with upside down label. CMV $8.00
1964-66 PERFUMED SOAP
3 oz. bar with rose design wrapping. OSP 39c CMV $4.00

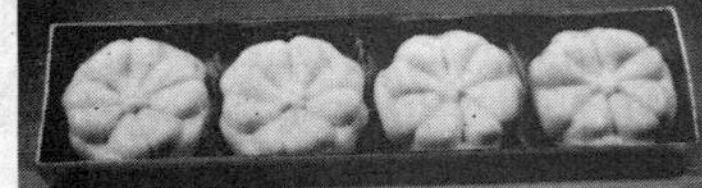

1966-67 ROSE GERANIUM SOAP
Flowered box holds 4 flower shaped soaps. O.S.P. $2.25 C.M.V. $18.00 M.B.

LEFT 1942 only ROSE GERANIUM LIQUID SOAP FRAGRANCE
6 oz. flat sided bottle came in Rainbow Wings & Bath Bouquet Set only. CMV $45.00 MB
RIGHT 1943-48 ROSE GERANIUM BATH OIL
6 oz. flat sided bottle, pink cap. OSP 95c CMV $25.00 BO $35.00 MB

1957-58 ROSE GERANIUM BATH OIL
8 oz. bottle with red cap. OSP $1.95 CMV $20.00 MB $15.00 BO

1943-50 ROSE GERANIUM BATH OIL
6 oz. flat sided bottle has Tulip A label, pink cap. OSP 95c CMV $25.00 MB $30.00

1974-77 ROSES PERFUME TALC
3.5 oz. pink & gray cardboard. O.S.P. $1.00 C.M.V. 25¢
1976-78 TOUCH OF ROSES SOAP
3 oz. pink soap, pink & gray wrapper. O.S.P. $1.00 C.M.V. $1.00
1974-75 ROSES, ROSES SOAP
3 oz. pink soap, pink wrapper with floral band. O.S.P. $1.00 C.M.V. $1.00
1973-76 ROSES, ROSES PERFUMED SKIN SOFTENER - 5 oz. pink plastic with pink & gold metal lid. O.S.P. $3.00 C.M.V. 25¢
1975-78 SACHET OR ROSES CREAM SACHET
.33 oz. clear glass with pink metal lid. O.S.P. $3.00 C.M.V. 25¢

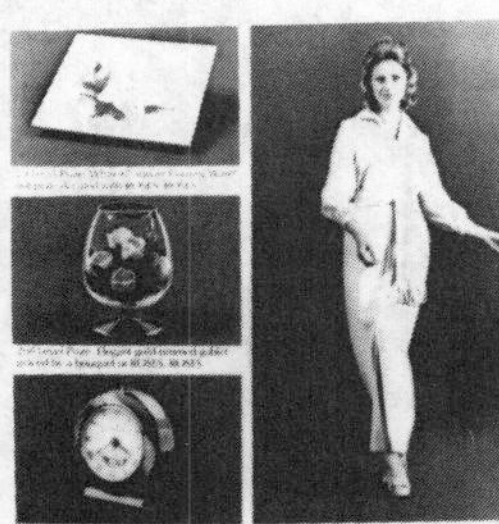

1972 ROSES, ROSES HOT PLATE
6" square, white Corning Ware with pink & green rose. Given for selling Mist of Roses Cologne. C.M.V. $12.00 M.B.
1972 ROSES, ROSES GOBLET
Gold trimmed goblet with bouquet of pink artificial roses. Came with card of congratulations. Given for selling Mist of Roses Cologne. C.M.V. $18.00 M.B.
1972 ROSES, ROSES CLOCK
3" clock by Hamilton, 4 small roses on front. Given for selling Mist of Roses Cologne. C.M.V. $15.00 M.B.
1972 ROSES, ROSES GOWN
Pink floor length gown with sash. Given for selling Mist of Roses Cologne. C.M.V. $20.00 mint. $25.00 M.B.

ROSES, ROSES

1972-75 ROSES, ROSES FRAGRANCE KWICKETTS - 14 per box, pink foil packets. O.S.P. $1.00 C.M.V. 50¢
1972-77 ROSES, ROSES AFTER BATH FRESHENER - 8 oz. pink plastic bottle, pink cap. O.S.P. $5.00 C.M.V. 50¢
1972-78 ROSES, ROSES FRAGRANCE SAMPLES - 10 samples per box, C.M.V. 25¢ box.
1972-78 ROSES, ROSES COLOGNE SAMPLE - Clear glass with white lid. C.M.V. 25¢
1973-77 ROSES, ROSES HAND & BODY LOTION - 8 or 16 oz. pink plastic bottle with pink lid. O.S.P. $3.50 8 oz. $6.00 16 oz. C.M.V. 50¢ each.
1972-76 ROSES, ROSES PERFUME POWDER MIST - 7 oz. pink & gray can, pink lid. O.S.P. $4.50 C.M.V. 50¢
1973-77 ROSES, ROSES BATH GELEE
4 oz. clear plastic tube with pink cap. O.S.P. $3.50 C.M.V. 25¢

1972 ROSES, ROSES ORDER BOOK & PEN - Redesigned size is larger than older Order Books, pink with darker pink rose & green leaves. Given to all President Club members. C.M.V. $5.00 mint.

1972-73 GLOW OF ROSES PERFUMED CANDLE - 4½" high, pink frosted glass. SSP $6.00 CMV $4.00 BO $5.00 MB
1972-73 SCENT OF ROSES DECANTER
6 oz. red glass jar with gold lid, filled with Cologne Gelee. S.S.P. $5.00 C.M.V. $3.00
1972-73 DEW OF ROSES PERFUMED SKIN SOFTENER - 5 oz. frosted pink glass jar with gold lid. S.S.P. $2.00 C.M.V. $2.00
1972-76 SCENT OF ROSES COLOGNE GELEE - 3 oz. clear pink glass jar, gold lid. S.S.P. $2.00 C.M.V. 75¢

1976 ROSES ROSES PERFUMED SOAP BAR
3 oz. bar wrapped in red paper. O.S.P. $1.25 C.M.V. 75¢
1977-78 ROSES ROSES COLOGNE SPRAY
1.8 oz. flower embossed bottle, gold cap. O.S.P. $5.00 C.M.V. 50¢

1972-77 MIST OF ROSES COLOGNE MIST
3 oz. pink plastic coated bottle, gold cap. O.S.P. $7.00 C.M.V. $1.00
1972-76 FOAM OF ROSES CREAMY BATH FOAM - 5 oz. pink plastic bottle with gold cap. O.S.P. $5.00 C.M.V. 50¢
1972-77 TOUCH OF ROSES PERFUMED SOAP - pink box holds 3 pink flowered soaps. O.S.P. $5.00 C.M.V. $5.00 M.B.
1972-75 ROSES CREAM SACHET
.66 oz. pink glass jar with pink rose on gold lid. O.S.P. $3.00 C.M.V. 50¢

SEA GARDEN

1970-73 SEA GARDEN PERFUMED BATH SOAP - 6 oz. blue bar with blue box. OSP $2.00 CMV $4.00 MB
1970-73 SEA GARDEN EMOLLIENT MIST - 4 oz. dark or light blue spray can with green cap. O.S.P. $3.00 C.M.V. $1.00 each color.
1970-74 SEA GARDEN PERFUMED POWDER MIST - 7 oz. blue can with green lid. O.S.P. $3.75 C.M.V. 50¢
1970-75 SEA GARDEN EMOLLIENT BATH FOAM - 5 oz. green & white frosted bottle with green cap. O.S.P. $5.00 C.M.V. 75¢

SILK 'N HONEY

1969-74 SILK & HONEY BATH FOAM
6 oz. gold plastic bottle & cap. O.S.P. $3.00 C.M.V. 50¢
1969-74 CREAMY LOTION
6 oz. gold plastic bottle & cap. O.S.P. $2.50 C.M.V. 50¢
1969-74 CREAMY MASQUE
3 oz. gold ribbed plastic jar & cap. O.S.P. $2.50 C.M.V. 50¢
1969-71 SOFTALC
3 oz. gold plastic bottle & cap. O.S.P. $1.50 C.M.V. $1.50
1970-76 PERFUMED POWDER MIST
7 oz. gold & yellow can. O.S.P. $4.50 C.M.V. 50¢
1969-70 BATH GELEE
4½ oz. gold frosted glass jar with gold behive lid & gold spoon. O.S.P. $6.00 CMV $7.00 MB $5.00 BO with spoon.

1970-71 SILK & HONEY PERFUME POWDER MIST - 7 oz. yellow & gold paper label, yellow cap. O.S.P. $3.75 C.M.V. $2.00
7 oz. Yellow & gold painted can, yellow cap. "Shake vigorously before use" on front of can, newer issue. O.S.P. $3.75 C.M.V. $1.00

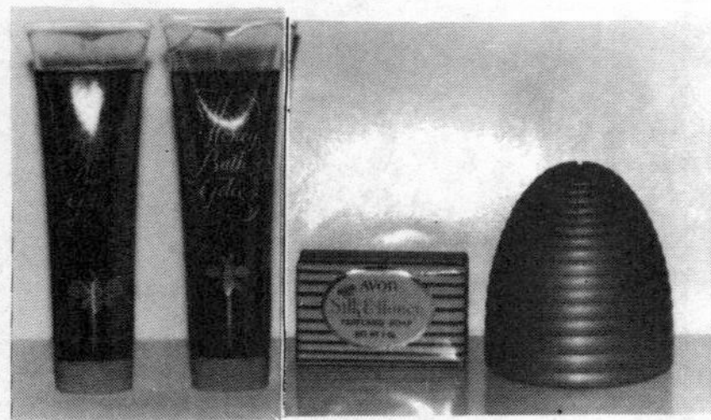

1975-76 SILK & HONEY BUBBLE BATH GELEE - 4 oz. plastic tube. O.S.P. $3.50 C.M.V. 25¢
1973-74 SILK & HONEY BATH GELEE
4 oz. clear plastic tube with yellow cap. O.S.P. $2.00 C.M.V. 50¢
1970-76 SILK & HONEY PERFUME SOAP - 3 oz. gold & yellow wrapper. O.S.P. $1.25 C.M.V. $1.25
1969 SILK & HONEY BANK
Yellow plastic Beehive Bank. C.M.V. $10.00

1970-71 SILK & HONEY MILK BATH
6 oz. gold plastic milk can bottle with flowers around neck. O.S.P. $5.00 C.M.V. $4.00

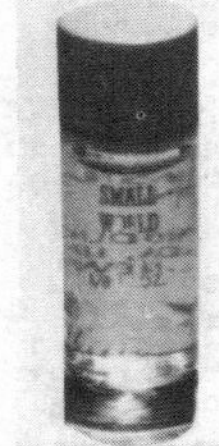

1974 SMALL WORLD COLOGNE SAMPLE - CANADA
1/8 oz. clear glass, white cap. Used by Avon Reps. as sample in Canada. CMV $3.00.

1970-73 SMALL WORLD PRODUCTS
Back row left to right -
1971-72 CREAM LOTION (WENDY)
5 oz. 5" high cowgirl plastic bottle. OSP $5.00 CMV $6.00, $8.00 MB
1971-72 BUBBLE BATH (BRITISH MISS)
4½" high, 3 oz. pink plastic bottle. OSP $5.00 CMV $6.00, $8.00 MB
1971-72 COLOGNE MIST (GIGI)
5" high, 5 oz. blue plastic coated bottle with white collar & blue & red hat. OSP $3.50 CMV $6.00, $8.00 MB
1971-72 NON-TEAR SHAMPOO (SENORITA)
5" high, 5 oz. orange plastic bottle with pink flower in hair on cap. OSP $3.50 CMV $6.00 BO $8.00 MB
Front row left to right -
1971-72 CREAM SACHET
.66 oz. white jar with pink & white lid. OSP $2.50 CMV $3.00 MB $2.00 BO
1970-73 LIPKINS
3" high with pink, yellow & orange caps in Dutch Chocolate, Tropical Fruit or French Mint. OSP $1.75 CMV $3.00 ea. MB $2.00 BO
1970-73 LOVE DOVE CREAM SACHET
White jar & dove lid. OSP $3.00 CMV $4.00, $5.00 MB

SMALL WORLD

1970-73 SMALL WORLD PRODUCTS
Back row left to right -
1970-72 COLOGNE (SPLASHU)
2 oz. 4½" high. O.S.P. $3.50 C.M.V. $6.00
1970-71 BUBBLE BATH (BUBBLY-O-BATH) - 5" high, 5 oz. green plastic bottle. O.S.P. $3.50 C.M.V. $6.00
1971-73 PERFUMED TALC
3½ oz. blue paper container. O.S.P. $1.25 C.M.V. $4.00
Front row left to right -
1970-73 LOVE CAKES SOAP
3 pink heart shaped bars in blue box. OSP $2.00 CMV $9.00 MB
1971-72 ROLLETTE
3" high, .33 oz. Indian design. O.S.P. $1.75 C.M.V. $3.00
1970-73 DEMI STICK
3" high with pink cap. O.S.P. $1.50 C.M.V. $2.00
1970-71 PIN PAL PERFUME GLACE
Black hair, white & red body. O.S.P. $2.50 C.M.V. $4.00
1970-71 NON-TEAR SHAMPOO (POOLU) 5½" high, Red bottle, black hair. O.S.P. $3.50 C.M.V. $6.00
1970-71 COLOGNE MIST (HEIDI) - 3 oz. 5"-high, purple bottle, yellow hair. O.S.P. $5.00 C.M.V. $6.00

Add $2.00 each item MB.

1970 SMALL WORLD SUCKER
Sent to representatives at introduction of Small World. Red & yellow wrapper says "Avon Watch for the Small World" CMV $17.00 mint.
1971-72 SMALL WORLD PERFUME GLACE
Blue with white polka-dots. OSP $2.50 CMV $4.00, $5.00 MB
1971 SMALL WORLD GLACE WATCH
Orange with striped band. OSP $3.00 CMV $6.00 MB $8.00

SOMEWHERE

ALL CONTAINERS PRICED EMPTY

See Page 5 for Grading Examples on Mint Condition

1966-76 SOMEWHERE PRODUCTS
Left ro right -
1966-75 CREAM SACHET
White glass trimmed in green & gold. .66 oz. O.S.P. $3.00 C.M.V. 50¢
1966-72 SKIN SOFTENER
Green & gold lid, 5 oz. glass jar came in green paint over clear glass. C.M.V. $1.00, or green paint over white milk glass., C.M.V. $3.00. O.S.P. $3.50
1966-69 PERFUME OIL
½ oz. green label, gold cap. O.S.P. $4.00 CMV $4.00, $6.00 MB
1966-71 COLOGNE
2 oz. gold cap. O.S.P. $2.50 C.M.V. $1.50
1966-76 COLOGNE MIST
3 oz. green plastic coated, gold cap, green label. O.S.P. $7.00 C.M.V. $1.00

SOMEWHERE
Green & white design.
1976 - CREAM SACHET - Gold & green lid. O.S.P. $1.00 C.M.V. 50¢
1975-76 DEMI STICK O.S.P. $1.00 C.M.V. 50¢
1970-71 COLOGNE - ½ oz. gold cap. OSP $1.00 CMV $2.00 MB $1.00 BO
1967-68 CREAM LOTION
4 oz. gold cap. OSP $1.50 CMV $3.00 BO $4.00 MB
1973-76 SOMEWHERE TALC
3.5 oz. green cardboard round container. OSP $2.00 CMV $1.00

1966-71 SOMEWHERE SCENTED HAIR SPRAY - 7 oz. green can. O.S.P. $1.50 CMV $3.00
1966-67 SOMEWHERE SOAP - Single bar in green wrapper. O.S.P. 49¢ C.M.V. $4.00
1966-72 SOMEWHERE TALC - 2¾ oz. Green & white can, green cap. O.S.P. $1.00 C.M.V. $1.00

1966-72 SOMEWHERE FOAMING BATH OIL
6 oz. green plastic bottle with gold cap. OSP $3.50 CMV $2.00 BO $3.00 MB
1966-68 SOMEWHERE PERFUME MIST
2 dram, white cap, green bottom. OSP $3.25 CMV $6.00 MB $5.00 BO

1962-63 UNFORGETTABLE SET
Pink, yellow & blue box holds Somewhere Cologne Mist, Cream Sachet & Beauty Dust. OSP $10.95 CMV $45.00 MB

1964 DREAM CASTLE
Pink & green box holds 2 oz. bottle of Somewhere Cologne & Cream Sachet. O.S.P. $4.00 C.M.V. $30.00 M.B.

1967-70 SOMEWHERE BEAUTY DUST
White plastic with green around bottom. Gold handle. OSP $4.00 CMV $10.00 MB $6.00 CO
1968- PERFUME TALC
3½ oz. green cardboard with gold trim. Came with Fluff Puff set. CMV $2.00

1967-Only - SOMEWHERE POWDER SACHET (on left) 9/10 oz. white glass bottom, white & gold cap with green ribbon. Issued during bottle strike in 1967. Bottom is same as Wishing Powder Sachet. O.S.P. $2.00 C.M.V. $23.00 $25.00 M.B.
1966-68 SOMEWHERE POWDER SACHET
9/10 oz. white glass, green label, white lid with gold band. Hard to find. O.S.P. $2.00 CMV $18.00 MB $15.00 BO

1962-66 SOMEWHERE POWDER SACHET
1¼ oz. pink glass bottom, pink jeweled lid. OSP $2.00 CMV $6.00 MB $4.00 BO
1962-66 SOMEWHERE CREAM SACHET
Pink glass & pink jeweled lid. O.S.P. $2.00 CMV $1.00 - $3.00 MB. Some came pink paint on milk glass. Same CMV.

1961-66 SOMEWHERE DUSTING POWDER - Pink plastic bottom, clear plastic top with pink jeweled crown. OSP $4.00 CMV $10.00 MB $6.00

1963 SOMEWHERE PERFUMED OIL FOR THE BATH
½ oz. clear glass, white lettering, pink cap. OSP $4.00 CMV $7.00 BO $10.00 MB
1964-66 SOMEWHERE PERFUMED OIL
½ oz. clear glass, white lettering, pink cap. OSP $4.00 CMV $5.00 BO $7.00 MB

1961-63 SOMEWHERE PERFUME
1 oz. pink jewel cap, jewels in glass around bottom of bottle. Has 4 Butterflies on lid. O.S.P. $20.00 C.M.V. $80.00 in box. $50.00 BO mint.

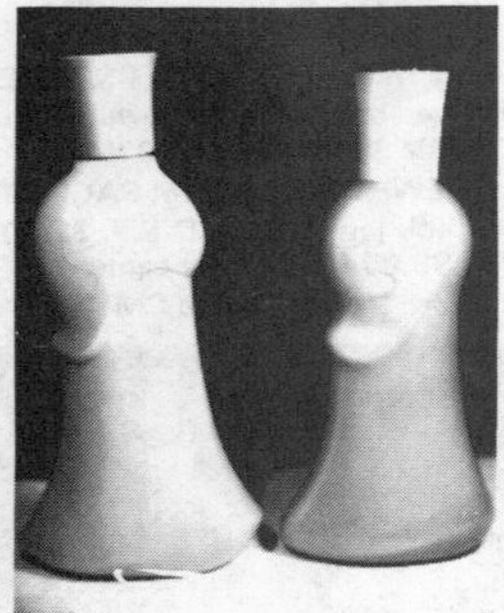

1962-66 SOMEWHERE BATH OIL
6 oz. pink plastic bottle & cap. OSP $2.50 CMV $3.00 BO $5.00 MB
1961-66 SOMEWHERE COLOGNE MIST - 3 oz. pink plastic coated glass, pink jeweled lid. OSP $4.00 CMV $3.00 BO $5.00 MB

1963-66 SOMEWHERE CREAM LOTION
4 oz. pink lid without jewels. OSP $1.50 CMV $3.00 - $5.00 MB
1961-66 SOMEWHERE COLOGNE
2 oz. pink jeweled lid. OSP $2.00 CMV $3.00 - $5.00 MB

1964-66 SOMEWHERE PERFUMED SKIN SOFTENER
5 oz. pink glass jar with pink & gold
1965 SOMEWHERE PERFUMED SOAP
3 oz. pink soap with pink & white wrapper. O.S.P. 39¢ C.M.V. $4.00 mint.

1962-66 SOMEWHERE TALC
2¾ oz. pink can & lid. O.S.P. 89¢ C.M.V. $3.00 - $5.00 MB
1964-66 SOMEWHERE 2 DRAM PERFUME MIST - White lid, pink bottom, gold band. O.S.P. $3.25 C.M.V. $9.00 in box. $7.00 Mist only.

1961 PERFUME MIST AWARD
Given to each representative sending in an order during the 75th Anniversary Campaign. This was also the introduction to a new fragrance - Somewhere. C.M.V. $15.00 M.B.

1968-69 SOMEWHERE SOAP
3 white bars in green box. O.S.P. $3.0
CMV $13.00 MB

1966-68 SOMEWHERE SOAP
Green & white box holds 3 bars. O.S.P. $2.00 C.M.V. $16.00 M.B.

1962-66 SOMEWHERE SOAP
Pink box holds 3 bars with embossed O.S.P. $1.75 C.M.V. $20.00 M.B.

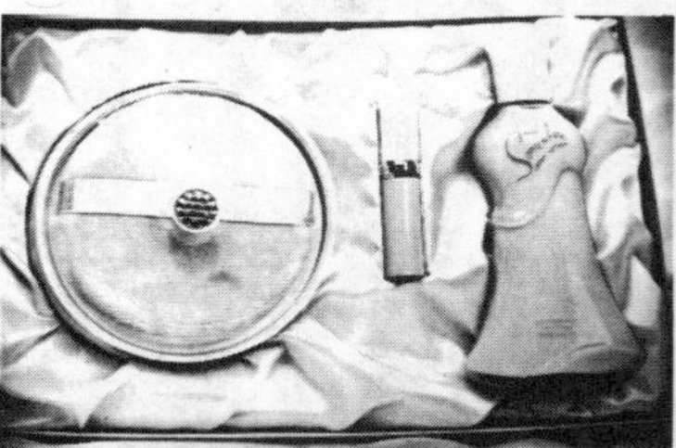

1964 DREAMS OF SOMEWHERE
Box holds 2 dram bottle of Somewhere Perfume Mist, 6 oz. Beauty Dust & 4 oz. bottle of Cream Lotion. O.S.P. $9.25 C.M.V. $40.00 M.B.

SONNET

1943-44 BLUE BIRD
Blue and white box, blue satin lining holds feather design face powder, cardboard or plastic lipstick and Sonnet or Apple Blossom Body Powder. O.S.P. $2.25 C.M.V. $75.00

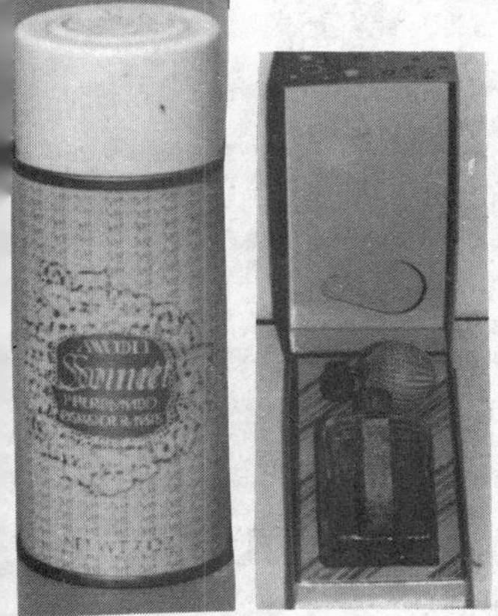

1973-77 SONNET PERFUME POWDER MIST (double stamped label)
Regular issue can came out with double stamp label on entire can. Rare. C.M.V. $8.00

1940-42 FRAGRANCE MIST SONNET
Blue & gold box holds 2 oz. Sonnet Toilet Water, gold cap and label and spray atomizer. Also came in other fragrances. See Fragrance Mist Sets of 1940's. O.S.P. $1.35 C.M.V. $50.00 M.B. $35.00 B.O. mint.

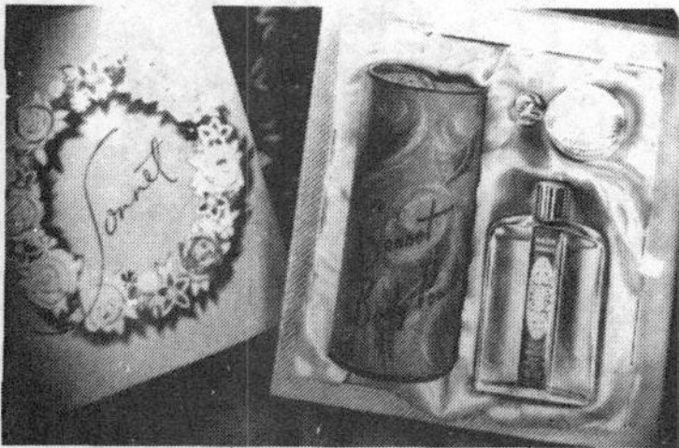

1941-42 SONNET SET
Satin lined lavender box holds 2 oz. Sonnet Toilet Water with gold top atomizer & Sonnet Body Powder. O.S.P. $2.00 C.M.V. $70.00 M.B.

1973-78 SONNET PRODUCTS
White & gold design.
1973-77 PERFUMED POWDER MIST
7 oz. metal can, white cap. S.S.P. $2.00 C.M.V. 50¢
1973-77 PERFUME POWDER MIST (double stamped label)
Can came out of factory with a double stamped label all over can. Rare. C.M.V. $8.00
1973-78 PERFUMED TALC
3.5 oz. cardboard with plastic top & bottom. O.S.P. $2.50 C.M.V. 25¢
1973-76 CREAM SACHET
.66 oz. jar. O.S.P. $4.50 C.M.V. 50¢
1973-76 BEAUTY DUST
6 oz. plastic, pink puff. O.S.P. $10.00 CMV $2.00, $5.00 MB
1973-78 PERFUME SKIN SOFTENER
5 oz. plastic jar. O.S.P. $5.50 C.M.V. 50¢
1973-75 PERFUMED ROLLETTE
.33 oz. bottle. S.S.P. $2.00 C.M.V. 25¢
1973-78 COLOGNE MIST
3 oz. spray bottle. O.S.P. $8.00. 1st issue 1973. Issued with no gold ring around neck. C.M.V. $2.00 1973-78 issued with gold ring around neck. C.M.V. 50¢
1973-74 FOAMING BATH OIL
6 oz. white plastic bottle, gold cap. SSP $2.00 CMV $1.00 BO $2.00 MB

1973-74 SONNET HAND & BODY LOTION - 8 oz. white plastic. O.S.P. $2.00 C.M.V. 75¢
1975-76 SONNET EMOLLIENT MIST
4 oz. white & gold with white cap. O.S.P. $3.00 C.M.V. 50¢
1975-78 SONNET POWDER SACHET
1.25 oz. white & gold cardboard. O.S.P. $2.00 C.M.V. 50¢
1976-78 SONNET PERFUMED SOAP
3 oz. white bar with gold & white wrapper. O.S.P. $1.00 C.M.V. $1.00
1974-75 SONNET PERFUMED SOAP
3 oz. white with multi-colored center. O.S.P. $1.00 C.M.V. $1.00
1974-78 SONNET PERFUMED DEMI STICK - .19 oz. white & gold. O.S.P. $1.00 C.M.V. 25¢

1972 SONNET AWARDS
All earned for selling Cologne Mist.
VANITY TRAY - 10" white plastic, gold trim. C.M.V. $10.00
VANITY BOX - white plastic, gold trim. C.M.V. $18.00 M.B.
THREE PANEL MIRROR - white & gold. C.M.V. $24.00 M.B.
HOSTESS ROBE - white satin, gold trim. (Won by Presidents Club members only) C.M.V. $30.00 M.B.

1973 SONNET COLOGNE & SONNET SKIN SO SOFT BATH OIL
4 oz. clear glass bottles, cap is gold. Came in Treasure Chest set only. C.M.V. $3.00 each.

1941 Only SONNET TOILET WATER
2 oz. purple cap & label. 2 different labels. One has yellow dress on box & label and the other has green dress on box and label. OSP 20c CMV $30.00 BO $40.00 MB each.

1941-46 SONNET TOILET WATER
2 oz. gold ribbed cap and gold front label. OSP $1.04 CMV $30.00 BO mint. $35.00 MB.
1941-43 SONNET BODY POWDER
Angel on box, blue & white paper container with plastic shaker top. OSP 65c CMV $22.00 MB $18.00 CO

1974-77 SONNET PERFUMED SOAP
3 oz. Three pink oblong shaped bar soap, in gold & white box. O.S.P. $4.00 C.M.V. $4.00 M.B.
1972-74 SONNET PERFUMED SOAP
3 oz. Three pink round shaped bars soap, in gold & white box. O.S.P. $3.00 C.M.V. $6.00 MB

1941-43 SONNET BODY POWDER
Flat sifter top, scroll box. OSP CMV $22.00 MB can only $18.00 mint.

SPORTIF

1980 SPORTIF PRODUCTS
Green in color
COLOGNE SPRAY
1.8 oz. CMV 50c.
COLOGNE SAMPLES
Box of 10 CMV 25c
COLOGNE INCH SAMPLE
Small glass vial in folder. CMV 25c.

STRAWBERRY

1975-78 STRAWBERRY BUBBLE BATH GELEE - 4 oz. plastic tube. O.S.P. $3.50 C.M.V. 25¢
1973-74 STRAWBERRY BATH GELEE
4 oz. clear tube, red cap. S.S.P. $2.00 C.M.V. 50¢
1973-74 BIG BERRY
10 oz. red plastic with green cap top. Holds Bath Foam. S.S.P. $4.00 CMV $2.00 - $3.00 MB.

LEFT TO RIGHT
1979-80 STRAWBERRY BODY LOTION
6 oz. white plastic. SSP $2.99 CMV 25c.
1979-80 STRAWBERRY FAIR BUBBLE BATH
8 oz. white plastic. SSP $2.99 CMV 25c.
1979-80 STRAWBERRY FAIR PERFUMED TALC
3.5 oz. white, green & red paper sides, plastic top & bottom. SSP $1.49 CMV 25c.
1979-80 BERRY NICE STRAWBERRY COMPACT
Small red & green plastic holds lip gloss. SSP $3.49 CMV $2.50 MB.
1979-80 STRAWBERRY FAIR SHOWER SOAP
Red strawberry soap on a green rope. SSP $3.49 CMV $3.49 MB.
1979-80 SUNNY MORN STRAWBERRY SHAMPOO
8 oz. pink plastic. SSP $1.69 CMV 25c.

1979 STRAWBERRY PORCELAIN SUGAR SHAKER & TALC
Box holds white porcelain shaker & 3.5 oz. box of strawberry perfumed talc. Made in Brazil. Avon 1978 on bottom of shaker. SSP $11.99 CMV $12.00 MB set. Early orders & demos had 1978 on bottom of sugar shaker & regular issue had only "Avon" & no date on bottom. Talc only CMV $2.00, shaker only CMV $8.00 no date, CMV $12.00 1978 date. Talc also came with upside down label from factory by mistake. CMV $8.00 upside down label on talc.

1971-72 STRAWBERRY BATH GELEE
4 oz. red strawberry base & gold cap & spoon. OSP $7.00 CMV $4.00 - $6.00 MB
1971-72 STRAWBERRY GUEST SOAP
Red box holds 3 strawberry soaps. OSP $3.00 CMV $7.00 MB.
1971-72 STRAWBERRY BATH FOAM
4 oz. red glass & top. 6" high. OSP $4.00 CMV $4.00 - $5.00 MB.

1978-79 STRAWBERRY PORCELAIN NAPKIN RINGS & SOAP SET
Box holds 2 porcelain napkin rings and 1 red strawberry shaped soap. Porcelain made in Brazil. S.S.P. $9.99, C.M.V. $9.99 M.B. set.

1970 STRAWBERRIES & CREAM BATH FOAM - 4 oz. white milk glass, red cap & design or orange cap & design. O.S.P. $3.50 C.M.V. red cap $6.00, Orange cap $4.00

1969-70 STRAWBERRY FAIR SOAP Red soap in yellow plastic basket with green grass, wrapped in cellophane & bow. OSP $3.00 CMV $7.00, $10.00 MB.

1979-80 STRAWBERRY PORCELAIN DEMI CUP CANDLETTE
Box holds 4" saucer & 2¼" high cup. Strawberry design. Made in Brazil for Avon 1978 on bottom of each. SSP $7.00 CMV $7.99 MB

SUN BLOSSOM

1978 BURST OF SPRING SCARF
Yellow, green and white acetate scarf designed by S.M. Kent. 28" square. O.S.P. $2.50 C.M.V. $2.50

1978 SUN BLOSSOMS PERFUMED TALC
Yellow flower design 3.5 oz. container. S.S.P. $1.00 C.M.V. 25¢

1978 BURST OF SPRING BEAUTY DUST CONTAINER
Yellow, pink and green metal can to put beauty dust in. Sold empty. S.S.P. $4.99 C.M.V. $4.00 M.B.

1978 SUN BLOSSOM COLOGNE SPRAY
1.8 oz. flower embossed bottle, gold cap. S.S.P. $2.50 C.M.V. 25¢

1978 SUN BLOSSOM COLOGNE
1/2 oz. bottle, yellow cap. S.S.P. $1.00 C.M.V. 50¢

SWAN LAKE

1947-50 SWAN LAKE 3 PIECE SET
Blue & white box holds 9 oz. blue boxes of Swan Lake Bath Salts & Body Powder & 4 oz. Cologne with white cap. O.S.P. $3.00 C.M.V. $110.00 M.B.

1947-49 SWAN LAKE 2 PIECE SET
Blue & white box holds 6 oz. Swan Lake Bath Oil & 9 oz. blue box of Swan Lake Body Powder. O.S.P. $2.00 C.M.V. $100.00 MB.

1947-49 SWAN LAKE BATH OIL
6 oz. flat sided bottle, pink cap, painted label. O.S.P. $1.25 C.M.V. $55.00 $65.00 M.B.

1947-50 SWAN LAKE COLOGNE
4 oz. pink cap, painted label. O.S.P. $1.35 C.M.V. $45.00 B.O. mint - $55.00 M.B.

1947-49 SWAN LAKE BODY POWDER
9 oz. blue, pink & white paper box. O.S.P. 85¢ C.M.V. $30.00 M.B. $35.00. Also came 4½ oz. size in sets. C.M.V. $30.00 mint.

1947-49 SWAN LAKE BATH SALTS
9 oz. blue, pink and white paper box. O.S.P. 85¢ C.M.V. $30.00 M.B. $35.00

SWEET HONESTY

1977 SWEET HONESTY RECORD
Small 33 1/3 size cut out plastic record in green folder. Sent to Avon managers on introduction of Sweet Honesty. CMV $4.00 mint.

1977 SWEET HONESTY SCARF
Red, white, blue and green scarf sold for $1.00 with order of Sweet Honesty products. C.M.V. $1.50 in Avon plastic bag.

1973-76 SWEET HONESTY PRODUCTS
COLOGNE MIST - 2 oz. S.S.P. $3.00 C.M.V. $1.00
GENTLE MOISTURE GEL - 1.8 oz. S.S.P. $1.00 C.M.V. 25¢
JUST ENOUGH COLOR LIQUID FOUNDATION - 1.5 oz. S.S.P. $1.00 C.M.V. 25¢
CREAM SACHET - .66 oz. S.S.P. $1.50 C.M.V. 25¢
LIP GLOSS POT - .12 oz. S.S.P. $1.00 C.M.V. 25¢
VERY REAL BLUSH - .25 oz. S.S.P. $1.00 C.M.V. 25¢
COMPACT - 5 oz. S.S.P. $2.50 C.M.V. $1.00

1977-78 SWEET HONESTY GIFT SET
Came with 2 oz. cologne and 2 perfumed soaps. O.S.P. $9.00 C.M.V. $7.00 M.B.

1973-78 SWEET HONESTY PRODUCTS
1973-76 AFTER BATH FRESHENER
10 oz. O.S.P. $3.00 C.M.V. 50¢
1973-77 PERFUME POWDER MIST
7 oz. O.S.P. $2.00 C.M.V. 50¢
1973-78 PERFUME TALC
3.5 oz. O.S.P. $1.00 C.M.V. 25¢
1973-77 COLOGNE GELEE
1.5 oz. O.S.P. $1.00 C.M.V. 25¢
FACE BEAMER
1.5 oz. O.S.P. $1.00 C.M.V. 25¢
BRIGHT & SHINING SHADOW
.25 oz. O.S.P. $1.00 C.M.V. 25¢
LIP COLOR AND/OR SUNNY LIP GLEAMER
.13 oz. O.S.P. $1.00 C.M.V. 25¢
WIDE EYES MASCARA
.15 oz. O.S.P. $1.00 C.M.V. 25¢
1973-78 DEMI STICK
.19 oz. O.S.P. $1.00 C.M.V. 25¢
1973-77 ROLLETTE
.33 oz. O.S.P. $2.00 C.M.V. 25¢
1973-78 FRAGRANCE SAMPLES
10 foil samples per box. C.M.V. 25¢

1978 SWEET HONESTY PERFUMED SOAPS
Boxed 3 cakes, 3 oz. each. O.S.P. $6.50 C.M.V. $5.50 M.B.
1976-77 SWEET HONESTY BY THE JUG BUBBLE BATH
10 oz. plastic jug. O.S.P. $5.00 C.M.V. $1.50

1976-78 SWEET HONESTY BUBBLE BATH
10 oz. plastic bottle, pink cap. O.S.P. $4.50 C.M.V. 50¢
1977-78 SWEET HONESTY COLOGNE
2 oz. bottle, gold and pink cap. O.S.P. $5.00 C.M.V. 50¢

TEMPO

1979-80 TEMPO PRODUCTS
Colors are beige, silver & red.
ULTRA SOFT BODY SATIN
6 oz. plastic.
PERFUMED TALC
3.5 oz. Paper, plastic top & bottom.
PERFUMED SKIN SOFTENER
5 oz. plastic
ULTRA CREAM PERFUME
.66 oz. glass
CMV 25c each all products.

TENDER BLOSSOM

1978 TENDER BLOSSOMS TALC
3½ oz. Came in Field Flowers, Roses, Roses, Hawaiian White Ginger and Honeysuckle. O.S.P. $2.00 C.M.V. 50¢
1977-79 TENDER BLOSSOMS FRAGRANCE CANDLE
Came in Floral Medley fragrance. OSP $6.50 CMV $4.50 MB
1977 TENDER BLOSSOMS BEAUTY DUST CONTAINER
Flower shaped metal container with Tender Blossoms design O.S.P. $6.50 C.M.V. $4.50 M.B.
1977-79 COLOGNE
1/2 oz. bottle. Came in Field Flowers, Honeysuckle, Raining Violets, Roses, Roses, Hawaiian White Ginger, Apple Blossom. Each cologne had different colored caps. Box shown in Tender Blossoms design issued Christmas 1977 only. O.S.P. $2.00 C.M.V. $1.50 M.B. as shown.

TASHA

1979-80 TASHA PRODUCTS
DREAM DIARY
Given to Reps. CMV $1.00
ULTRA COLOGNE SPRAY
1.8 oz. CMV 50c.
ULTRA COLOGNE
.33 oz. gold cap. CMV 50c.
LIGHT PERFUME
.5 oz. gold cap. CMV 50c.
PERFUMED SOAP
Single bar. CMV 75c.
PERFUMED POWDER MIST
4 oz. can. CMV 50c.
LUXURY BATH FOAM
6 oz. plastic. CMV 50c.
ULTRA COLOGNE
2 oz. glass, gold cap. CMV 50c.
TASHA ULTRA COLOGNE
2 oz. not shown. CMV 50c.
1979-80 SSP $4.50 50c.

1980 TASHA ULTRA CREME PERFUME
.66 oz. clear glass, gold tone lid. CMV 50c.
1980 TASHA PERFUMED TALC
3.5 oz. purple color. SSP $1.75 CMV 50c.
1980 TASHA LUXURY BATH FOAM
Not shown. 6 oz. plastic. CMV 50c.

TIMELESS

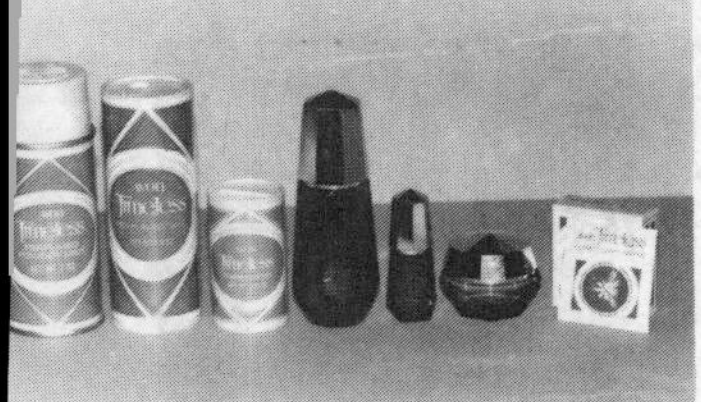

1975-78 TIMELESS
Yellow & light amber
1975-77 PERFUMED BOWDER MIST
7 oz. O.S.P. $3.00 C.M.V. 50¢
1975-78 PERFUMED TALC
3.5 oz. cardboard. O.S.P. $1.50 C.M.V. 25¢. Also came with upside down label C.M.V. $6.00
1975-78 POWDER SACHET
1.25 oz. cardboard. O.S.P. $3.50 C.M.V. 75¢
1975-77 ULTRA PERFUME ROLLETTE
.33 oz. gold cap. O.S.P. $3.00 C.M.V. 50¢
1975-78 ULTRA CREAM SACHET
.66 oz. gold cap. O.S.P. $3.00 C.M.V. 25¢
1975-78 ULTRA COLOGNE SAMPLE
10 foil packets per box. C.M.C. 25¢
1978-80 ULTRA PERFUME CONCETRE
.33 oz. gold cap CMV 25c

1974 TIMELESS ULTRA COLOGNE MIST FOR PRESIDENTS CLUB ONLY
2 oz. size, gold cap
RIGHT - 2 oz. size, gold cap. 1st issue to Avon Presidents Club members only, had 4A design on bottom under label. Regular issue had Avon on bottom. Box also came with special card saying it was collectors edition, fall 1974. C.M.V. $6.00 M.B. as shown.
1974-78 LEFT
Regular issue is 1.8 oz. size, gold cap. Avon on bottom. O.S.P. $7.50 C.M.V. 50¢

1975 TIMELESS MANAGERS GIFT SET - Gold box holds Perfume Rollette, Cologne Mist & Creme Perfume. Given to Avon Managers only at introduction of Timeless. C.M.V. $35.00 M.B.

1977-78 TIMELESS BEAUTY DUST CONTAINER
Amber plastic base and lid. O.S.P. $9.50 C.M.V.$4.00 M.B.
1976-78 TIMELESS PERFUMED SOAP
3 oz. bar. O.S.P. $1.25 C.M.V. 75¢
1976-78 TIMELESS ULTRA COLOGNE
2 oz. amber glass bottle, gold cap. O.S.P. $7.50 C.M.V. 50¢

1975-78 TIMELESS SOAP
3 cakes amber soap in amber gold & yellow box. O.S.P. $4.00 C.M.V. $4.00 M.B.
1975-78 TIMELESS PERFUMED SKIN SOFTENER - 5 oz. lt. amber plastic jar with gold lid. O.S.P. $2.00 C.M.V. 50¢

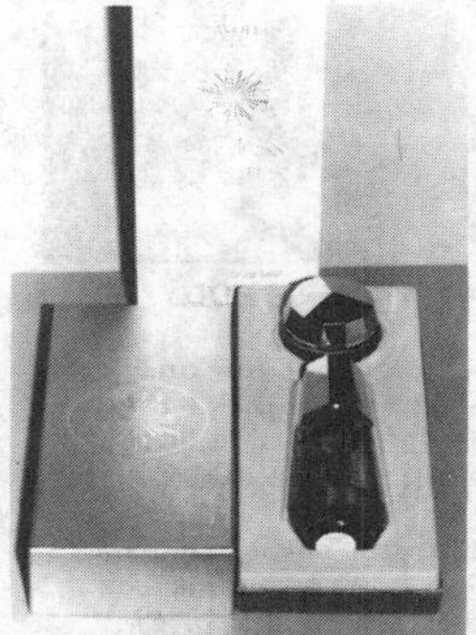

1976 TIMELESS GIFT SET
Amber bottles with gold caps. Box yellow & gold. Contains Ultra Cream Sachet & Cologne Mist. O.S.P. $10.00 C.M.V. $10.00 M.B.

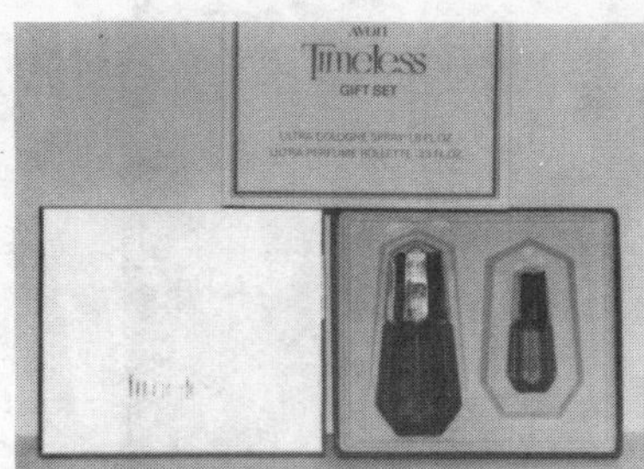

1977-78 TIMELESS ULTRA GIFT SET
Box came with 1.8 oz. Ultra cologne spray and .33 oz. Ultra perfume rollette.
O.S.P. $11.50 C.M.V. $9.00 M.B.

TO A WILD ROSE

1960-61 TO A WILD ROSE 4 OZ. COLOGNE - Pink, green & white Xmas box holds 4 oz. white glass bottle with pink cap & neck ribbon. No flower band around base, as shown, but also came with a paper flower band around base. O.S.P. $2.50 C.M.V. $25.00 in box pictured.

1960-61 TO A WILD ROSE 4 OZ, COLOGNE - Pink & white box holds 4 oz. white glass bottle, pink cap, painted label, pink silk ribbon on neck. O.S.P. $2.50 CMV $15.00 BO with ribbon mint. $17.00 MB. Came with and without painted flowers around base.

1955-63 TO A WILD ROSE COLOGNE
4 oz. white glass bottle, pink cap, has flowered paper border around base. O.S.P. $2.50 C.M.V. $15.00 - $17.00 M.B.

1950-55 TO A WILD ROSE BODY POWDER - 5 oz. blue paper container 2 different bottoms. One is refillable from the bottom. O.S.P. 85¢ C.M.V. $15.00, $20.00 MB. Some issued as shown with To A Wild Rose Body Powder on side & some only say Avon Body Powder.

1956-62 TO A WILD ROSE TOILET WATER
2 oz. white glass, pink cap, has paper flower band around base. OSP $1.50 CMV $10.00 BO $12.00 MB

1963 TO A WILD ROSE PERFUME OIL FOR THE BATH
½ oz. white glass, pink cap, pink & white box. OSP $1.50 CMV $10.00 MB $8.00 BO

1956 TO A WILD ROSE TOILET WATER
½ oz. size. Same size & design as Perfumed Oil shown above. White glass with pink cap & lettering. Came in Special Date Set, rare. CMV $27.00 mint.

1955-67 TO A WILD ROSE POWDER SACHET - White glass, white lid with painted rose. Paper band around bottom with roses. Came in 9 oz. & 1.25 oz. O.S.P. $1.25 C.M.V. $7.00 in box $6.00 bottle only.

1964-68 TO A WILD ROSE PERFUME OIL - ½ oz. white glass, pink letters & cap. OSP $3.50 CMV $6.00 BO $8.00 MB

1959-75 TO A WILD ROSE COLOGNE MIST - 3 oz. white plastic coated with pink flower on cap. O.S.P. $5.00 CMV $1.00, $2.00 MB

1976 TO A WILD ROSE COLOGNE MIST - 3 oz. white bottle, pink letters, pink cap - no flower. O.S.P. $7.00 C.M.V. 50¢

1964-68 TO A WILD ROSE PERFUMED MIST - 2 dram, pink & white, gold band. OSP $3.00 CMV $7.00 in box, $6.00 Mist only.

1958-59 TO A WILD ROSE COLOGNE MIST - 3 oz. white plastic coated over clear glass, pink cap. Came with or without embossed rose on lid. OSP $2.50 CMV $17.00 BO $22.00 MB

1966-67 TO A WILD ROSE SOAP
3 oz. white embossed soap in pink & green wrapper. O.S.P. 49¢ C.M.V. $2.00

1955-59 TO A WILD ROSE BODY POWDER
4 oz. white glass & cap with rose on lid, paper label around bottom, pink letters. OSP $1.00 CMV $10.00 BO $13.00 MB

1961-63 TO A WILD ROSE BODY POWDER
4 oz. white hard plastic bottle, white lid with roses. OSP $1.79. Also came 3 oz. size and with short issue pink cap. CMV $12.00 pink cap. CMV $8.00 BO $10.00 MB

1955-59 TO A WILD ROSE BODY POWDER
4 oz. white glass & cap with rose on lid, paper label. OSP $1.00 CMV $10.00 BO $13.00 MB

1959-61 TO A WILD ROSE PERFUMED BATH OIL
8 oz. white plastic bottle with pink cap. OSP $2.25 CMV $5.00 BO $7.00 MB

1961-66 TO A WILD ROSE PERFUMED BATH OIL
Same only 6 oz. size. CMV $6.00 MB $4.00 BO

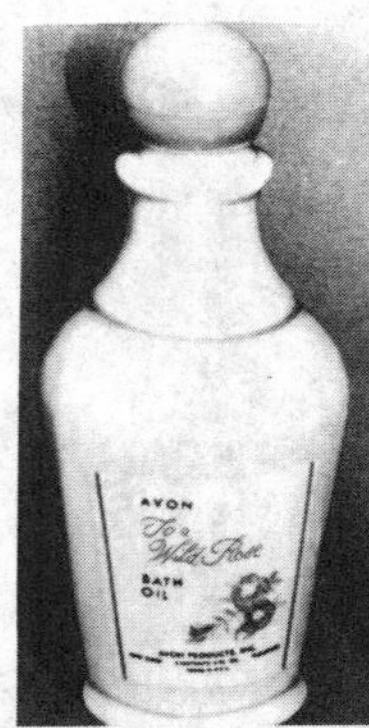

1956-59 TO A WILD ROSE BATH OIL
4 oz. white glass bottle with pink cap. OSP $1.35 CMV $12.00 in box, $10.00 bottle only. 2 oz. white glass bottle with pink cap, same label came in Trilogy Set only. C.M.V. $15.00

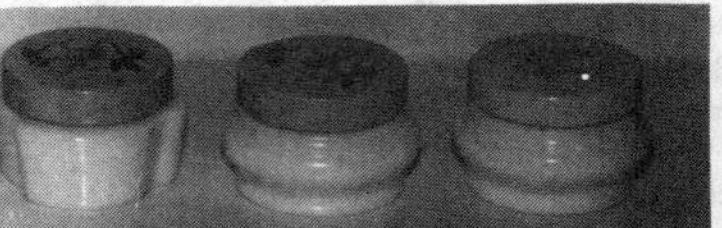

LEFT - 1950-55 TO A WILD ROSE CREAM SACHET
Blue cap with pink flowers, white glass, 3 cornered shape. OSP $1.25 CMV $10.00 MB $8.00 BO

RIGHT - 1955-72 TO A WILD ROSE CREAM SACHET
White glass, white lid with painted rose. OSP $1.25 CMV 50c, $1.00 MB

CENTER - TO A WILD ROSE CREAM SACHET
Same shaped jar as one on right only has blue lid as on the left jar. Lid will not interchange with jar on right. Also came with white lid label with no zip code, is older. Rare. CMV $9.00 BO $11.00 MB

957 TO A WILD ROSE LOTION
oz. white glass with paper label & pink ap. Came in Trilogy Set only. CMV 16.00 mint.
957 TO A WILD ROSE COLOGNE
oz. white glass with paper label, pink ap. Came in Trilogy Set only. CMV 16.00 mint.

1965-68 TO A WILD ROSE CREAM LOTION
4 oz. painted label, white glass, pink cap. OSP $1.25 CMV $4.00 BO $5.00 MB
1956-65 TO A WILD ROSE CREAM LOTION
4 oz. white glass, pink cap, paper label. OSP $1.25 CMV $5.00 BO $7.00 MB

1961-68 TO A WILD ROSE 2 OZ. COLOGNE - 2 oz. white glass, pink letters & cap. Came with & without painted flowers around base. O.S.P. $1.50 C.M.V. $3.00
1960-63 TO A WILD ROSE SPRAY PERFUME REFILL
Box holds small metal refill. CMV $4.00 MB $2.00 refill only.

1964-70 TO A WILD ROSE BEAUTY DUST - White plastic trimmed in pink. OSP $3.25 CMV $4.00 - $6.00 MB
1959-70 TO A WILD ROSE PERFUMED SKIN SOFTENER - 5 oz. white glass, pink & white lid. O.S.P. $3.50 C.M.V. $2.00

1970-71 TO A WILD ROSE COLOGNE
½ oz. white glass with pink cap & letters. OSP $1.75 CMV $2.00 MB $1.00 BO
1962-72 TO A WILD ROSE PERFUMED TALC
2¾ oz. white & pink can with pink cap. OSP $1.00 CMV $1.00
1954-55 TO A WILD ROSE TALC
Blue can & cap with pink flowers. OSP 49c CMV $8.00 CO $10.00 MB

1956-72 TO A WILD ROSE TALC
White can with pink flowers & cap. OSP 69c CMV $5.00 - $7.00 MB. Add $3.00 for 1959 Christmas box shown.
1966-68 TO A WILD ROSE FOAMING BATH OIL
6 oz. white plastic bottle with pink cap. OSP $2.50 CMV $3.50, $5.00 MB

1962-63 TO A WILD ROSE BEAUTY DUST - Pink & green flowers, clear plastic top, cardboard. Came in Fragrance Magic Sets only. C.M.V. $16.00 mint.
1955-59 TO A WILD ROSE BEAUTY DUST - Pink ball on top, trimmed in pink, tin lid & bottom. Sides cardboard. OSP $1.75 CMV $12.00 - $16.00 MB.

1950-55 TO A WILD ROSE BEAUTY DUST - Blue can with flowers on lid. OSP $1.75, CMV $15.00 CO, $20.00 MB

1954 TO A WILD ROSE COLOGNE OR CREAM LOTION
2 oz. clear glass with blue caps. Came in Bath Bouquet Set. CMV $17.50 each mint.

1954 TO A WILD ROSE COLOGNE BATH OIL - CREAM LOTION
2 oz. clear glass with white cap, blue label. Came in Miss Coed Set only. CMV $20.00 each.

1955 TO A WILD ROSE COLOGNE OR CREAM LOTION - 2 oz. clear glass with white caps. Came in Bath Bouquet Set. CMV (each) $17.50 mint.

1950-56 TO A WILD ROSE PERFUME
Pink flowers on pink & blue box. 3 dram bottle with blue cap & flower around neck. O.S.P. $4.50 C.M.V. in box $110.00. Bottle only with tag $75.00
1960-63 TO A WILD ROSE SPRAY PERFUME - Red, white & gold box holds pink & white metal spray perfume with pink flowers. OSP $2.95 CMV in box $11.00 Spray only $7.00

ALL ITEMS' PRICES EMPTY - MINT

See Page 5 for Grading Examples on Mint Condition

1956 TO A WILD ROSE BATH OIL & COLOGNE - Both 2 oz. bottles with white caps. Came in 1956 Bath Bouquet Set only. CMV (each) $17.50 mint

1955-59 TO A WILD ROSE PERFUME
Pink & white box holds ½ oz. white glass bottle with pink cap & painted label. O.S.P. $5.00 C.M.V. $100.00 in box. Bottle only $70.00

1954 MISS COED
Blue box holds three 2 oz. bottles of To A Wild Rose Cologne, Cream Lotion & Bath Oil. All have white caps. OSP $2.35 CMV $75.00 set, $15.00 each bottle.

1953-55 TO A WILD ROSE SACHET
1¼ oz. blue cap with embossed flower on top. Blue box. CMV $15.00 MB $12.00 BO mint.

1956 SWEETHEARTS SET
White & pink box holds To A Wild Rose Beauty Dust & 4 oz. Cologne. O.S.P. $3.95 C.M.V. $45.00 M.B.

1950-55 TO A WILD ROSE TOILET WATER
2 oz. blue cap, with or without embossed roses. Three cornered bottle. OSP $1.50 CMV $20.00 MB, $17.00 BO
1953-55 TO A WILD ROSE CREAM LOTION
4 oz. blue cap & label, with or without embossed roses. OSP 89c, CMV $15.00 bottle only, $17.00 in box.

1950-55 TO A WILD ROSE COLOGNE
4 oz. clear glass, blue caps, blue label. OSP $2.00 CMV $20.00 MB $16.00 BO.
1953-55 TO A WILD ROSE POWDER SACHET
1¼ oz. blue smooth top cap, blue label, clear glass. OSP $1.25 CMV $12.00 $15.00 MB
1975-76 TO A WILD ROSE CREAM SACHET
.66 oz. clear glass jar, red & gold lid. OSP $3.00 CMV 25c.

1956 TO A WILD ROSE SPECIAL DATE SET - Pink & gold box holds black lipstick, Powder Pak & ½ oz. of To A Wild Rose Toilet Water. O.S.P. $2.50 C.M.V. $45.00 MB.

1956 ADORABLE SET
Pink & white box with pink ribbon on lid holds To A Wild Rose Body Powder & Cream Sachet. O.S.P. $2.25 C.M.V. $32.50 M.B.

1958 A SPRAY OF ROSES
Pink & white box holds To A Wild Rose Cologne Mist & Cream Sachet. O.S.P. $3.95 CMV $37.00 MB

1955 SWEETHEARTS
Pink & white box holds To A Wild Rose Beauty Dust with pink ribbon & 4 oz. Cologne. O.S.P. $3.95 C.M.V. $50.00 M.B.

1957 TO A WILD ROSE TRILOGY SET - Box holds 3 To A Wild Rose 2 oz bottles of Bath Oil, Cream Lotion & Cologne. OSP $2.95 CMV $57.50 MB M.B.

3-55 TO A WILD ROSE BATH OIL
z. bottle with blue cap, with or without
bossed roses. Blue label. O.S.P. $1.25
.V. $20.00 in box. Bottle only $17.00

1953-54 ROSE PETALS
2 clear glass bottles, blue caps, holds Bath Oil & Cream Lotion. O.S.P. $2.15 CMV $47.50 MB.

1954-55 PETAL OF BEAUTY
Blue & pink box with blue ribbon around outside holds 4 oz. Cologne & Beauty Dust. OSP $3.75 CMV $52.00 MB.

1957 ROSES ADRIFT
Pink & white box holds To A Wild Rose Beauty Dust, Cream Sachet & Cologne. O.S.P. $4.95 C.M.V. $50.00 M.B.

1961 LOVELY AS A ROSE
Pink & white box holds 2 oz. To A Wild Rose Cologne & Cream Sachet. O.S.P. $3.50 C.M.V. $20.00 M.B.

1955 PINK BELLS
Pink box holds 2 blue cans of To A Wild Rose Talc. OSP $1.00 CMV $22.50 MB.

1955-56 ADORABLE SET
ink & white box with pink flowers on top holds To A Wild Rose Body Powder & Cream Sachet. O.S.P. $2.25 C.M.V. $32.50 M.B.

1963-64 HOLIDAY ROSES
Box holds To A Wild Rose Beauty Dust, Splash Cologne, Cream Lotion, with paper label. Same set in 1964 with painted label. OSP $6.50 CMV $37.00 each set MB.

1953 WILD ROSES
To A Wild Rose Body Powder with Cream Sachet on top. Pink ribbon around set. O.S.P. $1.95 C.M.V. $35.00 M.B.

1961 SPRAY OF ROSES
White & pink box with pink satin lining holds To A Wild Rose Beauty Dust & Cologne Mist. O.S.P. $5.90 C.M.V. $30.00 M.B.

1964 WILD ROSES
Multi-pink flowered box holds 2 oz. bottle of To A Wild Rose Cologne & Cream Sachet. OSP $3.50 CMV $25.00 MB.

1950-52 TO A WILD ROSE SET
Blue & pink box holds To A Wild Rose Body Powder & 4 oz. Cologne. O.S.P. $2.85 CMV $52.50 MB.

1956 BATH BOUQUET SET
White & pink box holds To A Wild Rose Cologne & Bath Oil with white caps & 1 bar of soap. O.S.P. $2.25 C.M.V. $52.00 MB. Also came with 2 bath oils as substitutes.

1955 BATH BOUQUET SET
White & pink box holds To A Wild Rose 2 oz. Cologne & Cream Lotion with white caps & 1 bar of soap. O.S.P. $1.95 C.M.V. $52.00 MB

1954 BATH BOUQUET SET
Pink and blue box. To A Wild Rose 2 oz. Cologne & Cream Lotion with blue caps, and white soap. O.S.P. $1.95 C.M.V. $52.00 MB. One box had sleeve top and one with a lift off lid. Came with and without flowers on bottom of box.

1969-73 TO A WILD ROSE SOAP
(Bottom) Floral box holds 3 white bars. OSP $3.00 CMV $7.00 MB.

1957-68 TO A WILD ROSE SOAP
(Top) Pink & white box holds 3 bars in 2 different size boxes. OSP $1.59 CMV $15.00 each box MB.

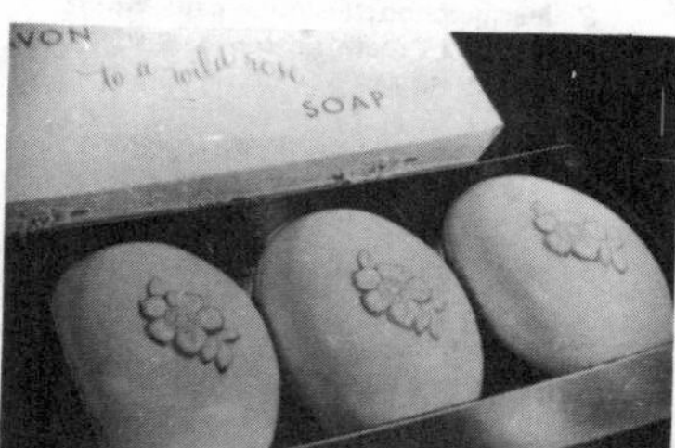

1952-56 TO A WILD ROSE SOAP
Box holds 3 white bars. O.S.P. $1.50 CMV $26.50.

1953 PETAL OF BEAUTY SET
Pink box holds blue and pink satin bag or all blue bag with To A Wild Rose 4 oz. Cologne & Beauty Dust, with 5/8 dram Perfume (small square bottle) with ribbon tied around it inside beauty dust. OSP $5.25 CMV in box $75.00, bag and contents only $55.00 1950-52 set sold without 5/8 dram perfume. CMV $55.00 MB $35.00 no box.

1956 ANNIVERSARY SPECIAL
Pink & white box holds 2 cans of To A Wild Rose Talc. OSP $1.10 CMV $20.00 MB

1966-69 TO A WILD ROSE SCENTED HAIR SPRAY
7 oz. pink & white can, pink cap. O.S.P. $1.50 C.M.V. $3.00
1968-73 TO A WILD ROSE PERFUMED POWDER MIST
7 oz. pink & white can, 2 different labels 1 paper C.M.V. $4.00, 1 painted label $2.00 O.S.P. $3.50 each.

1969 TO A WILD ROSE TALC
2.75 oz. pink and white can, pink cap. Came in 1969 Perfumed Pair set only. C.M.V. $2.00
1955-56 TO A WILD ROSE BATH OIL
2 oz. pink cap and label. Came in "That's Me Set" only. C.M.V. $15.00 mint.

TOPAZE

1959-63 TOPAZE PERFUME
1 oz. amber glass & amber jeweled glass stopper. Bottle cut like a gem. In yellow & white box. O.S.P. $20.00 C.M.V. in box $135.00. Bottle only $100.00

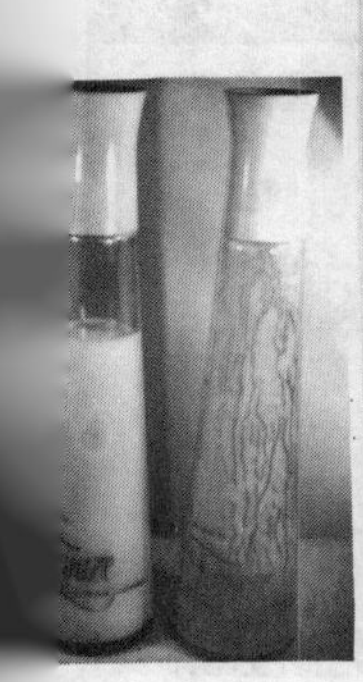

9-68 TOPAZE COLOGNE MIST
z. yellow plastic coated, yellow jewel
lid, in round yellow box. OSP $7.00
V $3.00 in round box.
59-76 issue came in square box. Same
tle. CMV $1.00.

59-67 CREAM LOTION
oz. yellow cap. OSP $1.50 CMV $2.00
so came with yellow cap with jewel
re). CMV $8.00.
OPAZE BODY LOTION – FOREIGN
MV $6.00

59-63 TOPAZE 4 OZ. COLOGNE
ld cap. O.S.P. $3.00 C.M.V. $10.00
plain yellow box $14.00
60-71 TOPAZE 2 OZ. COLOGNE
ld cap, painted label. O.S.P. $2.00
M.V. $1.00. M.B. $2.00

935 Only - TOPAZE PERFUME
oz. gold cap, gold & white label & box.
ntroducing Topaze for the 50th Wedding
nniversary of Mr. & Mrs. D.H. McConnell.
.S.P. 20¢ C.M.V. bottle only $50.00
70.00 M.B.

1959-67 TOPAZE POWDER SACHET
Both 9/10 oz. yellow glass, yellow caps.
O.S.P. $2.00 common issue with large cap.
CMV $6.00 MB, $5.00 BO. CMV small
cap $6.00 BO, $7.00 MB

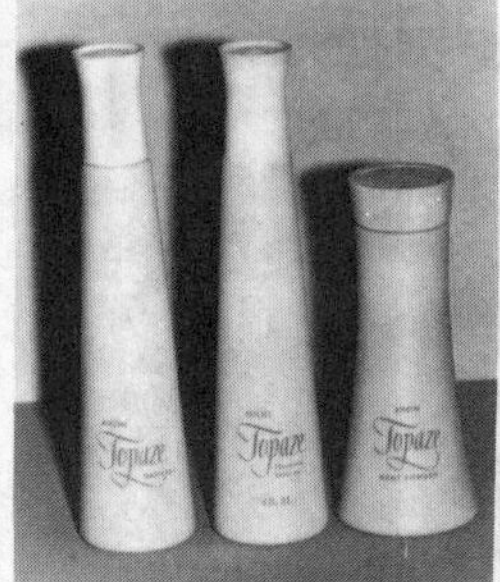

1961-66 TOPAZE BATH OIL
6 oz. yellow plastic bottle & cap. O.S.P.
$2.50 C.M.V. $4.00
1966-73 TOPAZE FOAMING BATH OIL
6 oz. yellow plastic bottle & cap. O.S.P.
$2.75 C.M.V. $1.50
1961-63 TOPAZE BODY POWDER
4 oz. yellow plastic bottle & cap. O.S.P.
$2.25 CMV $7.00 - $9.00 MB.

1974-76 TOPAZE PERFUME TALC
3.5 oz. yellow with gold, cardboard. OSP
$1.00 CMV 50c.
1975-78 TOPAZE PERFUME DEMI
STICK
.19 oz. white with yellow & gold. OSP
$1.00 CMV 50c.
1975-76 TOPAZE CREAM SACHET
.66 oz. clear glass, gold & yellow cap.
OSP $2.00 CMV 50c.

1965-69 TOPAZE PERFUME ROLLETTE
.33 oz. ribbed carnival glass, gold cap. OSP
$2.00 CMV $6.00 BO $7.00 MB
1966-70 TOPAZE SCENTED HAIR SPRAY
7 oz. yellow can. OSP $1.50 CMV $3.00

1960-70 TOPAZE DUSTING POWDER
Yellow plastic bottom, white lid with
yellow jewel. OSP $4.00 CMV $3.00 -
$5.00 MB
1964-72 TOPAZE PERFUMED SKIN
SOFTENER
5 oz. yellow painted over white milk
glass or clear glass, gold & white lid.
OSP $3.50 CMV $2.00 MB $1.00 BO.

1964-68 TOPAZE PERFUME MIST
2 dram yellow bottle, white top with gold
band, box gold. OSP $3.25 CMV $5.00 -
$6.00 MB
1959-63 TOPAZE SPRAY PERFUME
Yellow box holds 2 dram metal spray
perfume, gold top & yellow bottom.
OSP $3.75 CMV $12.00.

1960-61 TOPAZE TEMPLE OF LOVE
Yellow & gold. Holds yellow & white plastic
holder. Came with .75 oz. Topaze Cream
Sachet. OSP 75c CMV in box $18.00
$10.00 holder only, $5.00 for .75 oz.
Cream Sachet only.
1960-75 TOPAZE CREAM SACHET
.66 oz. yellow paint on clear or milk
glass, yellow cap. OSP $3.00 CMV 25c

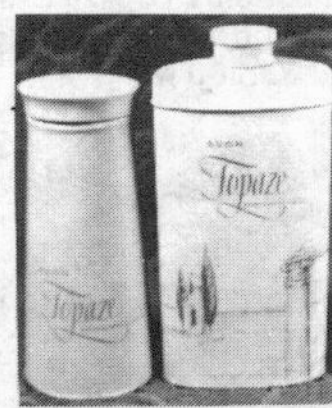

1961-62 TOPAZE PERFUMED TALC
2¼ oz. yellow round can & cap. OSP
$1.00 CMV $5.00 - $7.00 MB.
1962-74 TOPAZE PERFUMED TALC
2¾ oz. yellow & white can, yellow cap.
OSP $1.00 CMV $1.00.
1975-76 TOPAZE PERFUMED TALC
3.5 oz. yellow paper cylinder. OSP
$2.00 CMV 50c.

1960-61 GOLDEN TOPAZE
Gold box with plastic cover holds Topaze Cream Sachet, Cologne Mist & Beauty Dust. O.S.P. $9.95 C.M.V. $40.00 M.B.

1961 GOLDEN GEM
Gold box holds 2 oz. Topaze Cologne & Cream Sachet in .75 oz. size. O.S.P. $4.00 C.M.V. $25.00 M.B.

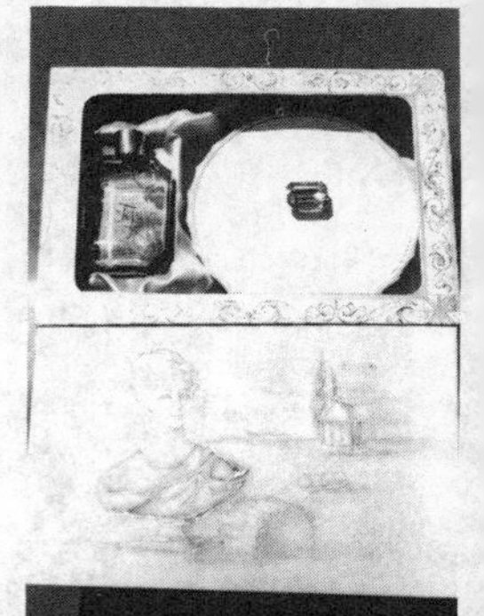

1960 TOPAZE TREASURE
Yellow & gold satin lined box holds Topaze Beauty Dust & 2 oz. Cologr
O.S.P. $5.95 C.M.V. 37.50 M.B.

1961 TOPAZE JEWEL
Gold box holds Topaze Cologne Mist & Cream Lotion. O.S.P. $4.95 C.M.V. $30.00 M.B.

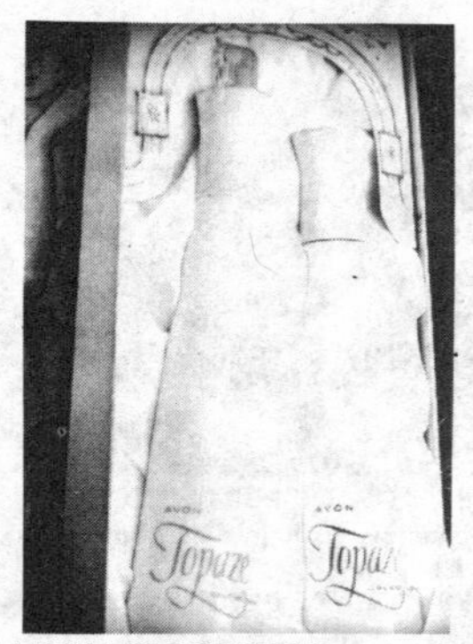

1964 TOPAZE PRINCESS
Gold box holds Topaze 3 oz. Cologne Mist & 4 oz. Cream Lotion. O.S.P. $5.95 C.M.V. $25.00 M.B.

1959-61 TOPAZE 4 OZ. GIFT COLOGNE
Gold cap, clear glass in yellow & gold satin lined box. O.S.P. $3.75 C.M.V. in box $17.00. Bottle only $8.00

1963 TOPAZE ELEGANCE
Gold & white box holds Topaze Beauty Dust, 4 oz. Creme Lotion & 2 oz. Cologne. OSP $7.95 CMV $35.00 MB

1970-71 TOPAZE ½ OZ. COLOGNE
Gold cap & painted label. OSP $1.50 CMV $2.00 MB $1.50 BO
1963 TOPAZE PERFUME OIL FOR THE BATH
½ oz., gold cap, painted label. OSP $4.00 CMV $40.00 BO $45.00 MB
1964-69 TOPAZE PERFUME OIL
½ oz., gold cap & painted label. OSP $4.00 CMV $4.00 MB $6.00.

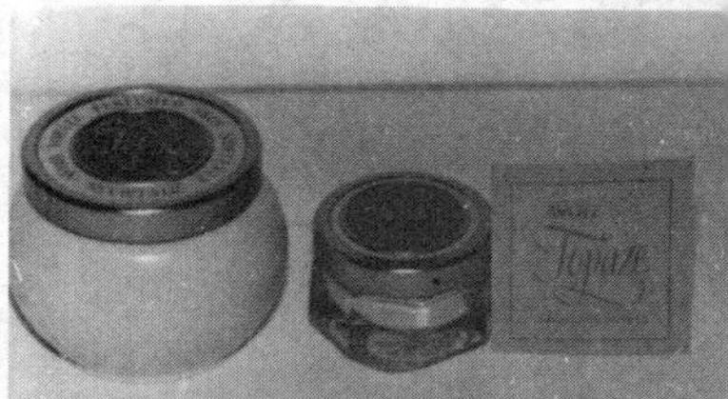

1977-78 TOPAZE PERFUME SKIN SOFTENER
5 oz. plastic jar, yellow and gold lid. O.S.P. $6.00 C.M.V. 50¢
1976-78 TOPAZE CREAM SACHET
.66 gem like cut glass base. Gold and brown cap. S.S.P. $1.50 C.M.V. 50¢
1970s TOPAZE FRAGRANCE SAMPLE
Yellow packet came 10 to a box. C.M.V. 50¢ box of 10

1964 TOPAZE SETTING
Yellow box holds 2 oz. bottle of Topaze Cologne & Powder Sachet. O.S.P. $4.00 C.M.V. $25.00 M.B.

1965-66 TOPAZE SOAP COLUMN
Holds 3 yellow bars. O.S.P. $1.75 CMV $22.00 - $26.00 MB

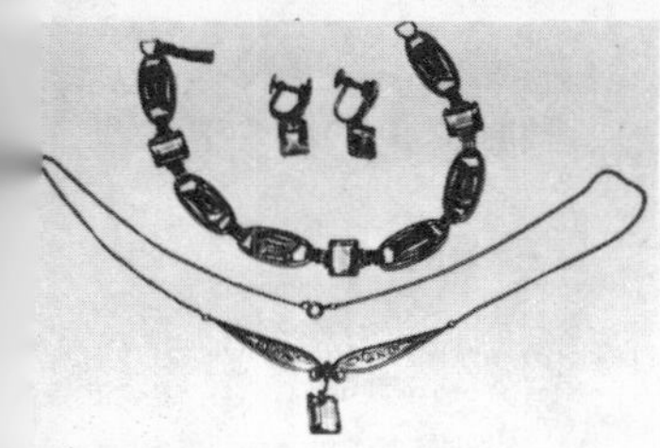

960 TOPAZE JEWELRY - AWARDED FOR SALES OF TOPAZE PRODUCTS
12 carat gold filled with imported Topaze stones. CMV Necklace $30.00 - $40.00 MB, Bracelet $30.00 - $40.00 MB, Earrings $20.00 - $30.00 MB.

1976-78 TOPAZE COLOGNE SPRAY
2 oz. clear glass gold cap. S.S.P. $3.99 C.M.V. 50¢
1977 TOPAZE PERFUMED POWDER MIST
7 oz. yellow and brown can, plastic cap. O.S.P. $5.00 C.M.V. 50¢
1976-78 TOPAZE FOAMING BATH OIL
6 oz. yellow plastic bottle and cap. S.S.P. $5.55 C.M.V. 50¢

1961-64 TOPAZE SOAP
Yellow box holds 2 bars of Topaze Soap. OSP $1.50 CMV $22.00 MB

1965-69 UNFORGETTABLE PERFUME OIL
LEFT — Clear glass, gold cap, no neck trim. OSP $5.00 CMV $7.00 MB $6.00 BO
CENTER LEFT — Clear glass, gold cap, cut out gold neck trim. OSP $5.00 CMV $7.00 MB $6.00 BO
CENTER RIGHT — Clear glass, gold cap, solid gold neck trim, scolloped edge. OSP $5.00 CMV $7.00 MB $6.00 BO
RIGHT — Solid gold neck trim with . smooth edge. CMV $7.00 MB $6.00 BO.

UNFORGETTABLE

LEFT TO RIGHT
1966-68 UNFORGETTABLE POWDER SACHET
9 oz. pink glass, gold pattern printing & gold cap. No neck trim. OSP $2.50 CMV $6.00 MB $8.00
1965 ONLY - UNFORGETTABLE POWDER SACHET
9 oz. pink glass, gold lettering, cap & trim. Neck trim has cut out pattern. OSP $2.50 CMV $8.00 MB $6.00 BO.
UNFORGETTABLE POWDER SACHET
9 oz. pink glass, no trim. OSP $2.50 CMV $6.00 - $8.00 MB
1965 ONLY - UNFORGETTABLE POWDER SACHET
9 oz. pink glass, gold lettering, cap & trim. No holes in trim. OSP $2.50 CMV $6.00 MB $8.00

1966-68 UNFORGETTABLE CREAM LOTION
4 oz. orange plastic bottle with gold cap. OSP $1.75 CMV $2.00 - $3.00 MB.
1966-72 UNFORGETTABLE FOAMING BATH OIL
6 oz. orange plastic bottle with gold cap. OSP $3.00 CMV $2.00 BO $3.00 MB.

1965-76 UNFORGETTABLE COLOGNE MIST - 3 oz, pink plastic coated, gold cap. 2 different gold trims aroundneck. O.S.P. $5.00 C.M.V. 50¢ with holes in gold trim. $4.00 on solid gold neck trim.
1965-75 UNFORGETTABLE CREAM SACHET
Pink painted over clear or milk glass bottom with gold plastic cap & gold trim. OSP $2.50 CMV 50c.

1965-70 UNFORGETTABLE BEAUTY DUST
Pink plastic trimmed in gold. OSP $5.00 CMV $3.00 - $6.00 MB
1965-73 UNFORGETTABLE SKIN SOFTENER
5 oz. pink painted over clear or milk glass, pink & gold lid. OSP $3.50 CMV $1.00

1966-71 UNFORGETTABLE SCENTED HAIR SPRAY
7 oz. orange & gold can. OSP $1.50 CMV $3.00
1971-73 UNFORGETTABLE BEAUTY DUST
Orange & gold 6 oz. cardboard box. OSP $4.50 CMV $3.00 mint, $5.00 MB.
1968-72 UNFORGETTABLE PERFUMED POWDER MIST
7 oz. orange and gold can, 2 different labels. OSP $3.75 CMV $1.00

1965 UNFORGETTABLE PERFUMED SOAP
3 oz., pink & gold wrapper. OSP 49c CMV $4.00
1965-74 UNFORGETTABLE CREAM SACHET SAMPLE
Pink, gold plastic. CMV box of 10 $1.50.
1965-76 UNFORGETTABLE FRAGRANCE SAMPLE
Box holds 10 samples in pink foil. CMV 50c box.
1966-68 UNFORGETTABLE POWDER SACHET SAMPLE

1965-68 UNFORGETTABLE SOAP
Orange box holds 3 orange soaps with gold centers. O.S.P. $2.25 C.M.V. $19.00 MB.

1970-71 UNFORGETTABLE COLOGNE
½ oz. with gold cap. OSP $1.75 CMV $2.00 MB $1.50 BO

1966-74 UNFORGETTABLE PERFUMED TALC
2¾ oz. pink can & cap. OSP $1.00 CMV $1.00

1965-66 UNFORGETTABLE HEIRLOOM
Gold & white tray holds 1½ oz. pink & gold cardboard Perfumed Talc. C.M.V. $15.00. 9/10 oz. Powder Sachet, gold cap & ½ oz. Perfume Oil with gold cap. O.S.P. $10.95.
For set CMV $30.00, $40.00 MB.

1966-71 UNFORGETTABLE COLOGNE
2 oz. gold cap, painted label. O.S.P. $2.50 C.M.V. $2.00

1964-68 UNFORGETTABLE PERFUME MIST - 2 dram, rose colored bottom, white cap, gold trim, all metal. O.S.P. $3.25 CMV $5.00 - $6.00 MB.

1965 UNFORGETTABLE DELUXE
Gold & white box holds Beauty Dust, Cream Sachet & Cologne Mist. O.S.P. $12.95 C.M.V. $32.50 M.B.

1965 UNFORGETTABLE INTRODUCTION BROCHURE
Gold cover has red and gold 3D glasses inside cover and 8 pages of introducing new Unforgettable products for Reps only. C.M.V. $30.00

VIOLET BOUQUET

1946-49 VIOLET BOUQUET COLOGNE
6 oz. bottle. Came in different color caps. OSP $1.00 CMV $80.00 MB $70.00 BO

1945 VIOLET BOUQUET REPRESENTATIVE GIFT - Avon's 59th Anniversary Gift to each representative. Violet colored net ribbon around white cap. 16 oz. crackle glass bottle. C.MV. $150.00 mint $175.00 M.B.

UNSPOKEN

1976-77 UNSPOKEN ULTRA GIFT SET
Box came with 1.8 oz. Ultra cologne spray and .33 oz. Ultra perfume rollette. OSP $10.50, CMV $7.00 MB.

1976-78 UNSPOKEN FOAMING BATH OIL
6 oz. bath oil, also came in 12 oz. size. O.S.P. $5.50 C.M.V. 25¢. 12 oz. size - O.S.P. $8.50 C.M.V. 25¢

1977 UNSPOKEN PERFUMED POWDER MIST
7 oz. size. O.S.P. $5.00 C.M.V. 50¢

1976-78 ULTRA COLOGNE SPRAY
1.8 oz. size. O.S.P. $7.50 C.M.V. 25¢

1977-78 ULTRA COLOGNE
2 oz. size. O.S.P. $6.50 C.M.V. 25¢

1977-78 ULTRA PURSE SPRAY COLOGNE
Refillable .33 fl. oz. S.S.P. $3.95 C.M.V. 50¢

1975 UNSPOKEN PRESIDENTS CLUB VELVET BAG
1.8 oz. bottle, silver top & cap, in blue velvet bag with Presidents Club tag. Came in plastic bag. CMV $10.00 bag. The bottle did not come with the bag.

75-76 UNSPOKEN PRODUCTS
75-78 FOAMING BATH OIL
oz. light blue and dark blue. O.S.P. .00 C.M.V. 25¢ Also came in 12 oz. ze C.M.V. 25¢
75-78 ULTRA CREAM PERFUME
lear glass with silver lid. O.S.P. $3.00 .M.V. 25¢
975-77 ULTRA PERFUME ROLLETTE
33 oz. clear glass, silver cap. O.S.P. 3.00 C.M.V. 25¢
975-78 UNSPOKEN FRAGRANCE SAMPLE
0 foil packets to box. C.M.V. 25¢
975-78 ULTRA COLOGNE SPRAY
non aerosol) 1.8 oz. clear glass with silver cap. O.S.P. $5.00 C.M.V. 25¢
975-78 PERFUME SOAPS
3 oz. light blue soap in two-toned blue box. O.S.P. $4.00 C.M.V. $4.00 M.B.

1976-78 UNSPOKEN PERFUMED TALC
3.5 oz. blue paper carton. O.S.P. $2.50 C.M.V. 25¢
1976-78 UNSPOKEN PERFUMED SKIN SOFTENER - 5 oz. blue plastic jar, silver & blue lid. O.S.P. $5.50 C.M.V. 25¢

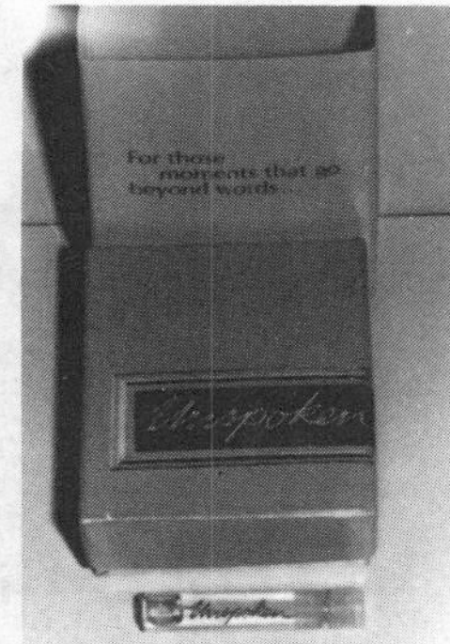

1975 UNSPOKEN PERFUME VIAL
Blue box holds small 1 5/8" vial Unspoken Perfume. Given to managers only. Outside sleeve on box. CMV $10.00 box.

WHITE MOIRE

1946 WHITE MOIRE SACHET 60TH ANNIVERSARY BOX
1¼ oz. regular issue bottle, white cap. Came in special issue blue and white box with white ribbon and blue & silver tag saying "Avon Diamond Anniversary 60th Year". O.S.P. $1.15 C.M.V. $30.00 M.B. as shown.

1946 WHITE MOIRE SACHET
White cap & small plain paper label. C.M.V. $30.00 B.O. $35.00 M.B.

1948-49 WHITE MOIRE POWDER SACHET
1¼ oz. clear glass, blue & white label, blue cap. OSP $1.15 CMV $20.00, $25.00 MB
1946-47 WHITE MOIRE POWDER SACHET - Right
1¼ oz. clear glass, white or blue plastic cap. OSP $1.15 CMV $18.00 - $23.00 MB. Both bottles pictured have same label.

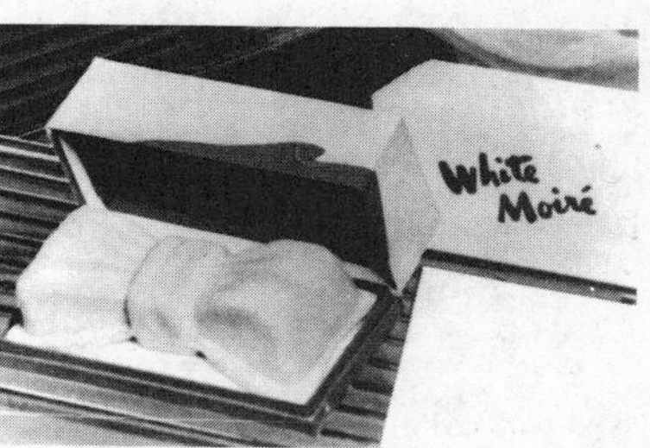

1946-49 WHITE MOIRE SOAP
Blue & white box, white bow tie soap. OSP $1.22 CMV $47.50 MB

1945-49 WHITE MOIRE BODY POWDER
5 oz. or 4½ oz. size, blue & white paper container with plastic sifter top, came in blue & white box. OSP 65c CMV $30.00 MB, $25.00 container only, mint.
1945-49 WHITE MOIRE COLOGNE
6 oz. white or blue cap. Blue & white label. OSP $1.75 CMV $65.00 BO, $75.00 MB

1945-49 WHITE MOIRE SET
Blue & white box with white silk bow on lid contains 6 oz. White Moire Cologne with white cap. Blue & white label. Also 5 oz. White Moire Body Powder, blue & white cardboard. O.S.P. $2.50 C.M.V. $110.00 M.B.

WISHING

1963 Only - WISHING SET
White & gold box holds Wishing 2 oz. Cologne & Cream Sachet. O.S.P. $3.10 C.M.V. $25.00 M.B.

1964 WISHING PERFUMED PAIR
White box holds Wishing Perfumed Talc & bar of soap in white wrapper. O.S.P. $3.50 CMV $19.00 MB

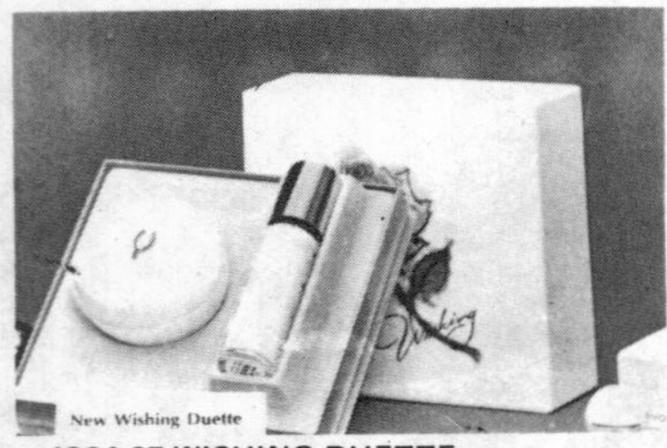
New Wishing Duette

1964-65 WISHING DUETTE
White, gold & pink box holds Wishing Cream Rollette & Cream Sachet. O.S.P. $3.50, CMV $19.00 MB

1964-66 WISHING BATH OIL
6 oz. white plastic bottle, gold lettering, white box. O.S.P. $2.25 C.M.V. $12.00 in box, $10.00 bottle only.

1964-67 WISHING PERFUME OIL
½ oz. clear glass, white cap, gold lettering with small gold wishbone on gold string. White box. OSP $3.50 CMV $8.00 BO $10.00 MB
1963-67 WISHING COLOGNE
2 oz. clear glass, white cap, gold lettering with gold wishbone on neck, white box. OSP $1.75 CMV $7.00 MB $4.00 BO.

1964-68 WISHING POWDER SACHET
9/10 oz. white glass bottom. Bottle on right has white plastic cap, bottle on left has yellow plastic cap, not faded. Both have wishbone in center of cap. White box. O.S.P. $1.75 C.M.V. yellow cap $10.00, white cap $6.00, add $2.00 MB ea.
1963-70 WISHING CREAM SACHET
White glass bottom with white plastic cap, gold wishbone in center of cap. Also came with Wishing written on lid. C.M.V. $2.00 with wishbone. $10.00 with Wishing lettering. O.S.P. $1.75

1963-70 WISHING COLOGNE MIST
2½ oz. white plastic coated, gold trim. Gold wishbone on neck, white box. O.S.P. $2.95 C.M.V. $3.00
1963-66 WISHING BUBBLE BATH
4 oz. white plastic bottle & cap, white box. O.S.P. $1.35 C.M.V. $7.00 in box. $5.00 bottle only.
1963-67 WISHING CREAM LOTION
4 oz. white plastic bottle & cap. White box. O.S.P. $1.35 C.M.V. $6.00 in box. $5.00 bottle only.

1963-66 WISHING SOAP
White box holds 3 white wishbone emboss soaps. OSP $1.35 CMV $25.00 MB

FOREIGN WISHING EAU DE COLOGNE MIST - 3 oz. white plastic coated, gold 4 leaf clover on gold string in place of wishing bone. C.M.V. $10.00
FOREIGN WISHING CREAM SACHET
White glass with gold 4 leaf clover on lid. C.M.V. $6.00

1963-67 WISHING BEAUTY DUST
4 oz. white plastic trimmed in gold. O.S.P. $2.95 C.M.V. $8.00. - $10.00 M.B.
1964-69 WISHING PERFUMED SKIN SOFTENER - 5 oz. white glass jar with gold & white lid. O.S.P. $3.00 C.M.V. $4.00 in box, $2.50 jar only.

1965-67 WISHING PERFUME MIST
2 dram, white metal, gold trim, white box. O.S.P. $3.00 C.M.V. $6.00
1963-66 WISHING PERFUMED TALC
2.75 oz. white can, gold lettering. O.S.P. 79¢ C.M.V. $4.00

6-67 WISHING SCENTED HAIR
AY - 7 oz. white can with gold lettering,
te cap. OSP $1.50 CMV $4.00
5-66 WISHING PERFUMED SOAP
z. white soap with white & gold
pper. O.S.P. 39¢ C.M.V. $4.00 mint.

52 WISHING TOILET WATER (left)
oz. white cap. Same as Flowertime
ttle. OSP $1.25 CMV $25.00 BO
0.00 MB.
947-49 WISHING TOILET WATER
ight) 2 oz. white cap. OSP $1.25 CMV
35.00 MB $30.00 BO. Also came in
ld 61st Anniversary box. CMV $40.00
B.

1947 WISHING COLOGNE
4 oz. bottle with gold cap, painted label.
Same bottle as Golden Promise Cologne.
Came in fancy open front & top box.
Given to Avon Representatives for calling
on 61 customers during 61st Anniversary
Campaign in campaign 9-1947. C.M.V.
$85.00 bottle only. $110.00 M.B.

YOUNG HEARTS

1964-65 WISHING NECKLACE
22K Gold wishbone necklace, came in Charm of Wishing Set only. C.M.V. $25.00 in small pink & white box. $17.00 necklace only.

1963-65 SECRET WISH SET
White box holds Wishing Perfumed Talc & 4 oz. Cream Lotion. O.S.P. $2.10 C.M.V. $20.00 M.B.

1963-64 WISH COME TRUE SET
White & gold box holds Wishing Bubble Bath & 2 oz. Cologne with wishbone on neck. OSP $3.10 CMV $26.00 MB.

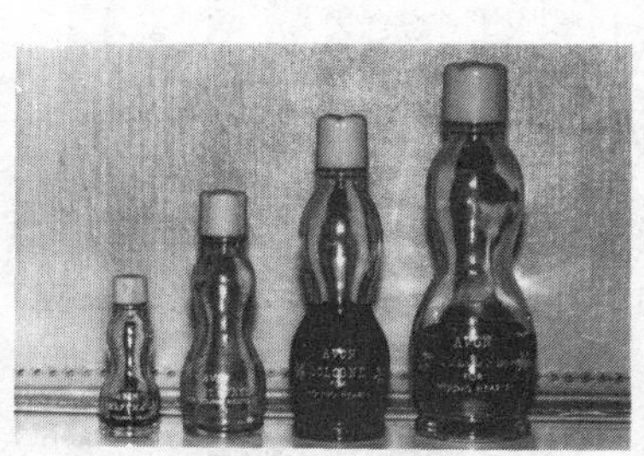

1952-54 YOUNG HEARTS
1 dram perfume, pink cap & painted label. Came in sets only. CMV $60.00 ½ oz. Toilet Water with pink cap & painted label. Came in sets only. CMV $30.00 1 oz. Cologne with pink cap. Came in sets only. CMV $30.00

1965 WISHING DATE SET
White & gold box holds Wishing Perfume Skin Softener, Perfume Rollette & white vinyl covered Wishing Date Book. OSP $6.00 CMV $32.50 MB.

1964-65 CHARM OF WISHING
Gold & white box holds Wishing Beauty Dust, Cologne Mist & 22K gold plated Wishbone Necklace on 9" chain. O.S.P. $8.50 CMV $62.50 MB.

1952-54 YOUNG HEARTS KIDDIE BUBBLE BATH
2 oz. bottle with pink cap & white Foam Cat Head on cap. Blue & white box, painted label. OSP $1.10 CMV $50.00 in box with foam head, $30.00 bottle only. Add $10.00 for foam head.

1952-53 YOUNG HEARTS KIDDIE COLOGNE
2 oz. bottle with white foam cat head over pink cap, painted label. Blue & white box. OSP $1.25 CMV $50.00 in box with cat head. $30.00 bottle only. Add $10.00 for foam head.

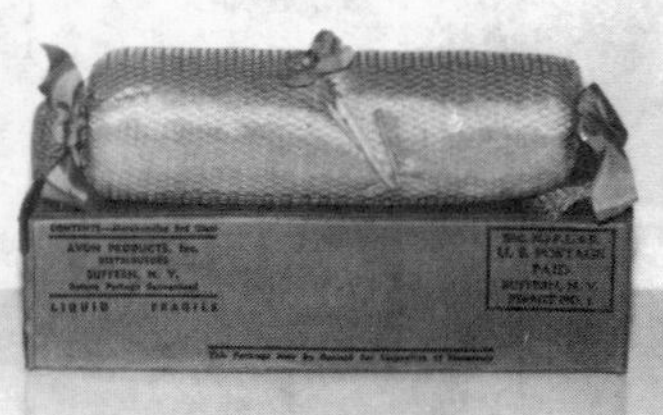

1945-46 YOUNG HEARTS SACHET
One pink lace net with pink ribbons on each end. Came in For Young Hearts set only. CMV $25.00 MB.

1952-53 YOUNG HEARTS CREAM LOTION
2 oz. pink cap. Came in set only C.M.V. $20.00 mint.
1952-53 YOUNG HEARTS POLISH REMOVER
2 oz. pink cap. Came in 'N Everything Nice set only. C.M.V. $20.00 mint.

1953 HONEY BUN SET
Blue & pink round box holds 2½ oz. Young Hearts Toilet Water with pink & gold Pomade Lipstick. O.S.P. $1.19 CMV $50.00 MB.

1945-46 YOUNG HEARTS SACHET
Box holds two pink lace net sachets with pink ribbons on each end and flower in the middle. Refills for the Young Hearts Set. CMV $40.00 MB.

1952-53 YOUNG HEARTS TALC
1 2/3 oz. cardboard Talc, came in sets only. C.M.V. $20.00
1952-54 YOUNG HEARTS COLOGNE
2 oz. cologne with pink cap and painted label. O.S.P. $1.25 C.M.V. $30.00 B.O. mint.
1952-54 YOUNG HEARTS BUBBLE BATH
2 oz, pink cap and painted label. O.S.P. $1.25 C.M.V. $30.00 B.O. mint.

1952 HONEY BUN SET
Pink & white 8 sided box holds Young Hearts Toilet Water & gold Pomade Lipstick. OSP $1.19 CMV $50.00 MB

1954-55 KIDDIE COLOGNE
2 oz. bottle of Young Hearts Cologne has pink cap with white foam dog head on cap, in yellow, white & blue box. OSP $1.25 CMV $50.00 MB $25.00 BO. Add $15.00 for foam head on bottle only mint.
1954-55 YOUNG HEARTS BUBBLE BATH
White foam dog head on pink cap, in yellow, white & blue box. OSP $1.10 CMV $25.00 BO. Add $15.00 for foam head on bottle only mint. $50.00 MB.

1954 HONEY BUN SET
Blue, white and yellow box holds Young Hearts Toilet Water, and gold Pomade Lipstick. OSP $1.19 CMV $50.00 MB.

1954 YOUNG HEARTS CREAM LOTIO
Bottle has pink cap, in pink & white hear shaped box. O.S.P. 50¢ C.M.V. $25.00 in box. $20.00 bottle only.

1954-55 YOUNG HEARTS TALC
Pink and white metal can.
COLOGNE - pink cap.
BUBBLE BATH - pink cap.
All 3 came in sets only. CMV $25.00 each, mint.

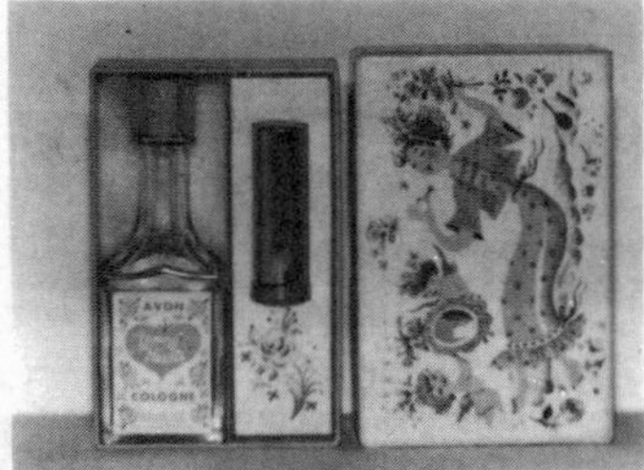

1954-55 HONEY BUN SET
Young Hearts Cologne & gold Lipstick in white, blue & yellow box. O.S.P. $1.19 C.M.V. $45.00 M.B.

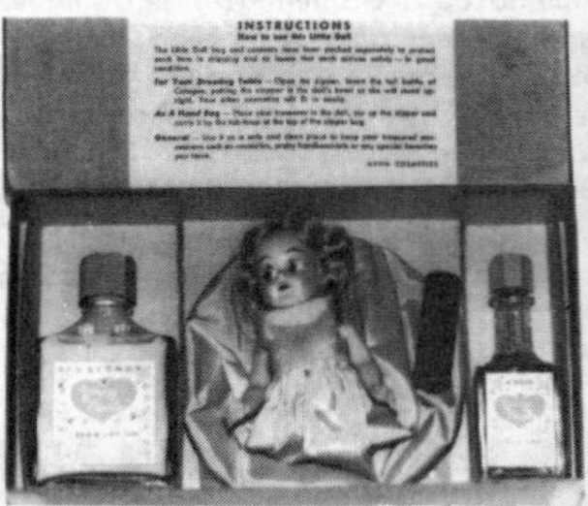

1954-55 LITTLE DOLL SET
Plastic doll with blond hair. Blue dress is a zipper handbag containing Young Hearts Cream Lotion, Cologne & Gold Pomade. OSP $2.95 CMV $115.00 set MB.

953 YOUNG HEARTS SET
lue & white box holds Young Hearts Cologne, Bubble Bath & Talc. O.S.P. 1.75 CMV $95.00 MB.

945-46 FOR YOUNG HEARTS SET BOTTLES
Each are 2 oz. frosted glass with pink caps. In Cotillion Toilet Water, Cream Lotion and Bubble Bath. CMV $22.50 each.

1945-46 FOR YOUNG HEARTS SET
Pink box holds three 2 oz. frosted glass bottles of Cotillion Toilet Water, Cream Lotion & Bubble Bath. All have pink caps. Pink net sachet in top of box. O.S.P. $3.75 CMV $110.00 set MB, or $22.50 each bottle. $20.00 for Net sachet.

1954-55 MISS FLUFFY PUFF SET
Young Hearts Beauty Dust & Cologne in blue & pink. Pink çap in pink & white box. O.S.P. $2.35 C.M.V. $60.00 M.B.

1954-55 NEAT & SWEET SET
Young Hearts Cologne & Cream Lotion with pink heart shaped soap. Pink caps in yellow, white & blue box. 1955 set came with green & gold spray atomizer. OSP $2.50 CMV $75.00 MB. Add $10.00 for atomizer set.

1954-55 YOUNG HEARTS BEAUTY DUST - Blue, white & yellow paper box. O.S.P. $1.19 C.M.V. $20.00 - M.B. $25.00.

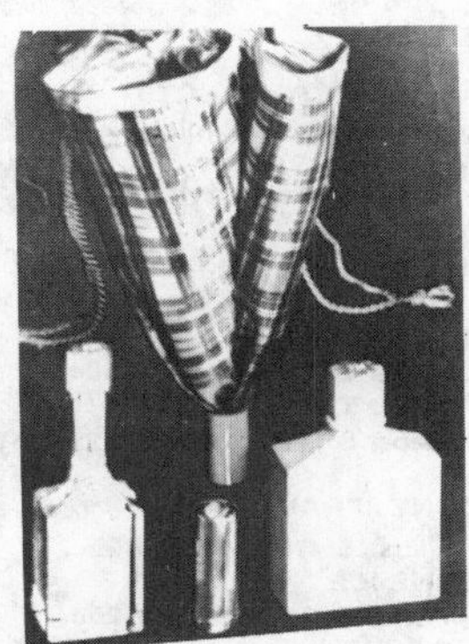

1954-55 RAIN DROPS SET
Red umbrella hand bag holds Young Hearts Cologne, Pomade & Cream Lotion. O.S.P. $3.25 C.M.V. $90.00 set M.B.

1952 RAIN DROPS
Red umbrella bag holds 1 oz. Young Hearts Cologne, Perfume & Cream Lotion. All have pink caps. OSP $2.95 CMV $125.00 MB.

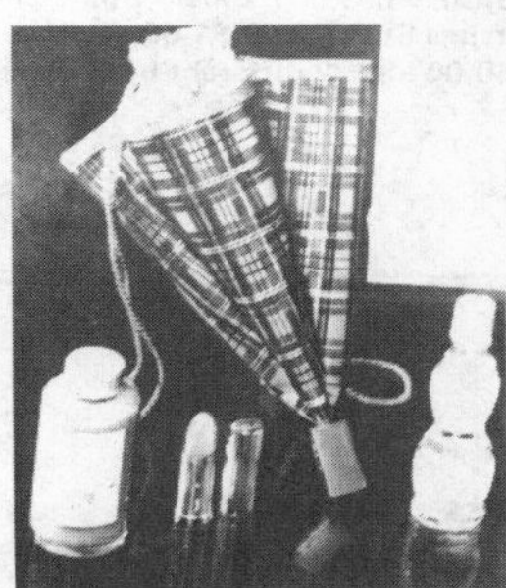

1953 RAIN DROPS
Red umbrella hand bag holds Young Hearts Cologne, Pomade & Cream Lotion. Pink caps. O.S.P. $2.95 C.M.V. $90.00 set M.B.

1954-55 YOUNG HEARTS SET
Cologne, Talc & Bubble Bath with pink caps & pink hearts on labels, in pink & white box. O.S.P. $1.95 C.M.V. $85.00 M.B.

1953 'N EVERYTHING NICE
Box holds Young Hearts Cream Lotion, Polish Remover with pink caps & Nail Polish, white cap, Emery Board and Orange Stick. OSP $1.65, CMV $60.00 MB. 2 different box lids.

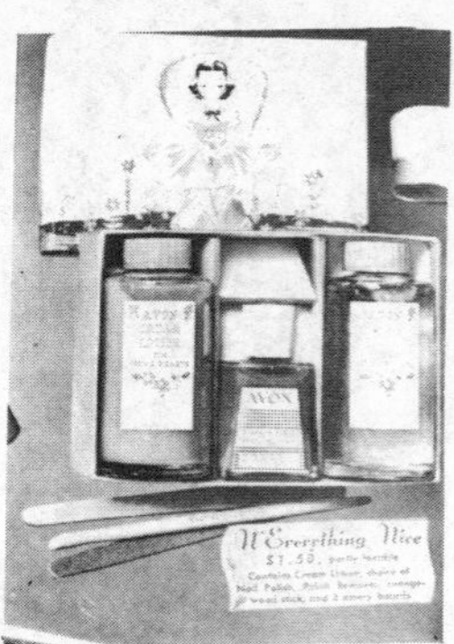

1952 'N EVERYTHING NICE
Box holds Young Hearts Cream Lotion, pink cap. Polish Remover, pink cap. Nail Polish, white cap, Emery Board and Orange Stick. O.S.P. $1.50 C.M.V. $60.00 M.B.

1952 YOUNG HEARTS SET
Blue, white & pink box holds Young Hearts Cologne, Talc & Bubble Bath. OSP $1.50 CMV $85.00 MB.

ZANY

1979 ZANY RADIO
Orange & pink Zany bottle shaped AM radio made in Hong Kong for Avon Products. Given to Avon customers in a drawing. Came in pink bag & certificate. CMV $25.00 MB, $20.00 mint in bag complete, radio only $15.00.

1979 ZANY BAG AWARD
Given to reps for ordering 10 Zany products. Orange canvas bag. CMV $4.00 mint.

1979-80 ZANY PRODUCTS
The colors are orange & pink.
ZANY BUBBLE BATH
10 oz. plastic SSP $3.49 CMV 25c.
BODY SPLASH
Not shown. 10 oz. plastic. SSP $3.49 CMV 25c.
PURSE CONCENTRE
.33 oz. glass. SSP $1.99 CMV 50c.
PERFUMED TALC
3.5 oz. paper & plastic. SSP $1.25 CMV 25c.
COLOGNE SPRAY
1.8 oz. glass. SSP $3.99 CMV 25c.
COLOGNE ICE
1 oz. plastic. SSP $2.75 CMV 25c.
CREME PERFUME
.66 oz. glass. SSP $1.99 CMV 25c.
ZANY INCH
Small demo vial of Zany on demo card used by reps. CMV 25c.

1979-80 ZANY PRODUCTS
BUBBLE BATH
10 oz. pink plastic jug. Pink cap. SSP $4.99 CMV 50c.
SHAMPOO
10 oz. orange plastic jug. Pink cap. SSP $4.99 CMV 50c.
Neither came in box.

WOMEN'S SETS OF 1930'S

WARNING!! Grading condition is paramount on sets.
CMV can vary 50% on grade.
Refer to page 5 on Grading.

1932-33 VANITY SET
Gray velvet lined blue box contains blue & gold double Compact & Lipstick. OSP $2.50 CMV $52.00 MB

1931-32 VANITY BOOK
Silver & blue box contains blue & silver Compact & Lipstick. O.S.P. $1.82 C.M.V. $60.00 M.B.

1939 SPECTATOR
Turquoise & white box holds 2 dram bottle with gold cap of Trailing Arbutus Perfume, Lipstick & Rouge Compact. O.S.P. $1.56 C.M.V. $80.00

1939 COLONIAL SET
Blue & gold box holds 2 dram Gardenia Perfume & Face Powder in choice of Ariel or Cotillion. O.S.P. $1.30 C.M.V. $65.00 M.B.

1933 VANITY BOOK
Silver & blue box contains blue & silver double compact & Lipstick. O.S.P. $1.75 C.M.V. $60.00 M.B.

1938-40 WINGS TO BEAUTY
Hinged lid box holds 4 oz. bottle of Lotus Cream & choice of Ariel or Cotillion Face Powder & choice of astringent or skin freshener. O.S.P. $1.60 C.M.V. $60.00 M.B.

1935 GIFT SET "K"
Box contains blue Compact, 2 dram perfume in Gardenia & blue & silver lipstick. OSP $2.54 CMV $115.00 MB

1934-35 VANITY BOOK
Blue & silver box holds blue & silver compact & Lipstick. O.S.P. $2.27 CMV $52.00 MB

1937 LYRIC SET
White & gold box holds Trailing Arbutus Toilet Water, turquoise & white can, Daphne Talcum , turquoise & white can, turquoise cap, white jar, turquoise lid Cold Cream. O.S.P. $1.65 C.M.V. $70.00 M.B.

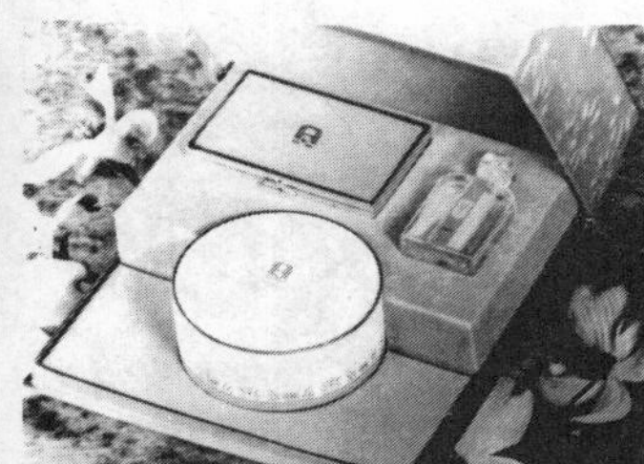

1939 MAYFAIR SET
Blue lid box holds 2 dram glass stoppered bottle of Bolero Perfume, box of Face Powder & turquoise double Compact. O.S.P. $3.57 C.M.V. $110.00 M.B.

1936-37 VANITY BOOK
Satin lined box holds green & gold Compact & Lipstick. OSP $2.27 CMV $47.50 MB
1938-40 SPORT WISE
Same set as 1936-37 Vanity Book only name changed. OSP $2.27 CMV $47.50 MB.

1935 GIFT SET "D"
Blue & yellow box contains choice of Ariel or Vernafleur face powder in silver & blue box & 2 dram Ariel perfume with gold cap & Ariel Sachet with silver label. O.S.P. $2.34 C.M.V. $100.00 M.B.

1936 GIFT SET "D"
Blue & yellow box contains Ariel or Vernafleur Face Powder in green & gold & 2 dram Ariel perfume with gold cap & Ariel Powder Sachet with black cap. O.S.P. $2.34 C.M.V. $90.00 MB.

1935 GIFT SET "A"
Satin lined box contains face powder in Ariel or Vernafleur & 2 dram bottle of Gardenia perfume with gold ribbed cap. OSP $1.30, CMV $80.00 MB

1936-37 GIFT SET "A"
Box has box of face powder, 3 dram size of Ariel, Vernafleur or Gardenia perfume with gold caps. OSP $1.30 CMV $65.00 MB.

1938-39 BEAUTY KIT FOR FINGERS
Green box holds bar of Lemonal Soap, turquoise tube of Hand Cream, bottle of Polish Remover & Cream or Nail Polish. O.S.P. $1.35 C.M.V. $60.00 M.B. Same set also came in gold design box as substitute.

1933-36 PERFUME HANDKERCHIEF SET - Two small bottles of Ariel & 391 Perfume or Bolero, with black caps, 4 handkerchiefs under green & red flower cutout. O.S.P. $1.00 C.M.V. $85.00 M.B.

1931-33 ATOMIZER SET NO. 6
Blue & silver box contains red 1 oz. glass bottle with silver atomizer with Ariel or Vernafleur perfume, in 1 oz. bottle with cork stopper. Set comes in 2 different boxes. OSP $2.86 CMV $150.00 MB.

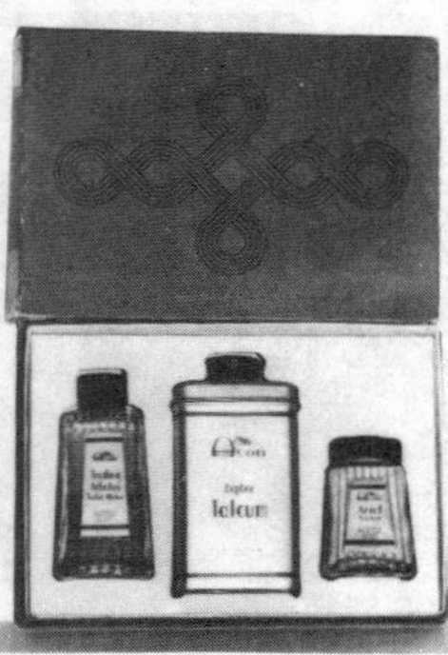

1934-35 TRIO SET
Red & blue box contains Trailing Arbutus Toilet Water, Daphne Talcum & Ariel Sachet. O.S.P. $1.60 C.M.V. $110.00 M.B.

1936 Only - HANDKERCHIEF SET
Avon box holds 2 perfume bottles of Bolero & Ariel. O.S.P. $1.00 C.M.V. $90.00 MB

1933-35 GIFT SET NO. 21
Contains box of face powder & table rouge. Silver & blue. Blue Lipstick in green, white & red box. O.S.P. $1.56 C.M.V. $55.00 M.B.

1939 Only - HANDKERCHIEF SET
Gardenia & Cotillion Perfumes with 4 handkerchiefs. O.S.P. $1.00 C.M.V. $70.00 MB.

1937-38 PERFUME HANDKERCHIEF SET - Two 1/8 oz. bottles of Gardenia & Cotillion Perfume on four colored handkerchiefs. O.S.P. $1.00 C.M.V. $70.00 MB.

1936-37 GIFT SET NO. 21
Striped box holds turquoise & white box Face Powder, turquoise & white cake rouge, turquoise & gold lipstick. O.S.P. $1.56 C.M.V. $50.00 M.B.

1934 GIFT SET NO. 36
Red & green box contains bottle of Rosewater Glycerine, Lily of the Valley Toilet Water, can of Daphne Talcum & Vernafleur Bath Salts. O.S.P. $1.95 C.M.V. $160.00 M.B.

1936-37 GIFT SET "B"
Green & silver box holds green & gold lipstick & rouge with 3 dram Trailing Arbutus Perfume with gold cap. OSP $1.56 CMV $80.00 MB.

1935 BATH ENSEMBLE
Box contains Jasmine Bath Salts, 2 bars Jasmine Bath Soap, Avon Dusting Powder in silver can & bottle of Trailing Arbutus Toilet Water. O.S.P. $3.50 C.M.V. $175.00 M.B.

1934 GIFT SET NO. 24
Holly decorated box contained box of face powder, rouge & jar of vanishing cream. O.S.P. $1.56 C.M.V. $75.00 M.B.

1936-37 GIFT SET "W"
Satin lined box holds two ribbed bottles of Nail Polish & Polish Remover, green & gold lipstick and rouge. O.S.P. $1.67 C.M.V. $75.00 M.B.

1936-39 BATH ENSEMBLE
Plaid box holds 9 oz. Jasmine Bath Salts, 2 oz. Trailing Arbutus Toilet Water, 2 bars of Jasmine Soap & can of Beauty Dust. O.S.P. $3.50 C.M.V. $140.00 M.B.

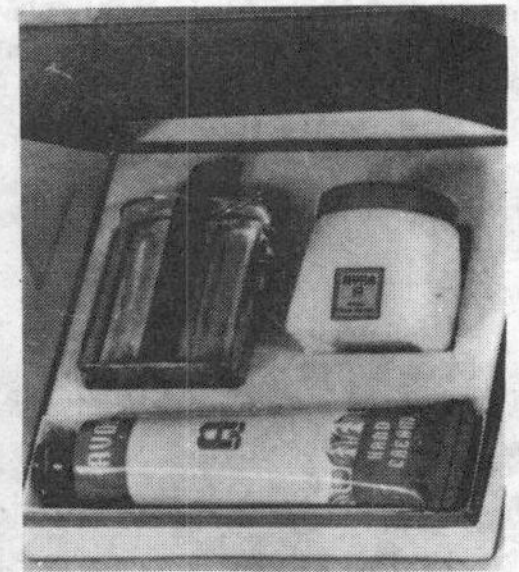

1937 HARMONY SET
Blue & white box contains Lily of the Valley Toilet Water, gold cap & label. White milk glass jar with turquoise cap of Rose Cold Cream & turquoise & white tube Hand Cream. O.S.P. $1.80 C.M.V. $65.00 M.B.

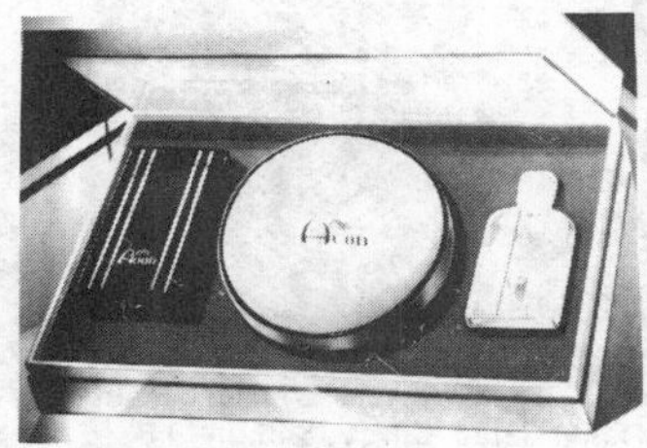

1934-35 THREESOME SET
Silver & blue box contains compact, face powder & 2 dram bottle of Bolero Perfume. O.S.P. $3.57 C.M.V. $110.00 M.B.

1931-32 ASSORTMENT SET FOR WOMEN
Contains 2 bars Verna Fleur Toilet soap, blue & silver can Avon Dusting Powder, bottle of Verna Fleur Bath Salts, 1 bath towel & 2 wash cloths. All in orange & blue box. O.S.P. $3.50 C.M.V. $110.00

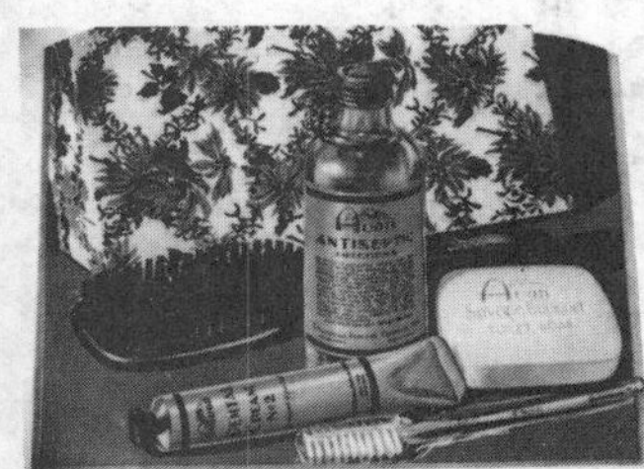

1934 GIFT SET NO. 19
Red & green box contains Deluxe Hair Brush, Toothpaste, 1 bar of Savona Soap, bottle of antiseptic & tube of Dental Cream No. 2. O.S.P. $1.85 C.M.V. $100.00 M.B.

1936-37 THREESOME SET
Box has green & gold compact, box of face powder & glass stoppered 3 dram of Bolero Perfume. OSP $3.57 CMV $110.00 MB.

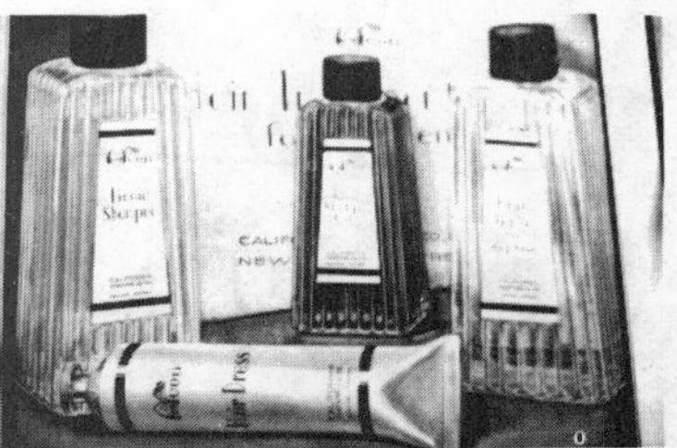

1931-35 HAIR TREATMENT SET FOR MEN
6 oz. Liquid Shampoo, 2 oz. Pre-Shampoo, 6 oz. Hair Tonic. All have blue caps. Silver tube Hair Dress. White box. O.S.P. $1.98 C.M.V. $135.00 M.B.

1931-35 AVON HAIR TREATMENT SET FOR WOMEN
Contains Liquid Shampoo, Pre-Shampoo Oil, Wave Set & Hair Tonic. All have blue plastic caps, blue & white box. O.S.P. $2.00 C.M.V. $150.00 M.B.

1935 GIFT SET "B"
Box contains blue & silver lipstick & rouge compact & 2 dram bottle of Trailing Arbutus perfume. O.S.P. $1.56. C.M.V. $85.00 M.B.

1937-39 BATH DUET
Box holds turquoise & white can of Daphne Talc with choice of bath salts in Jasmine, Pine, Ariel or Verna Fleur. O.S.P. $1.00 C.M.V. $55.00 M.B.

1935 AVON GIFT SET "F"
Red & gold box contains blue compact, face powder in Ariel or Verna Fleur & lipstick. O.S.P. $2.80 C.M.V. $65.00 M.B.

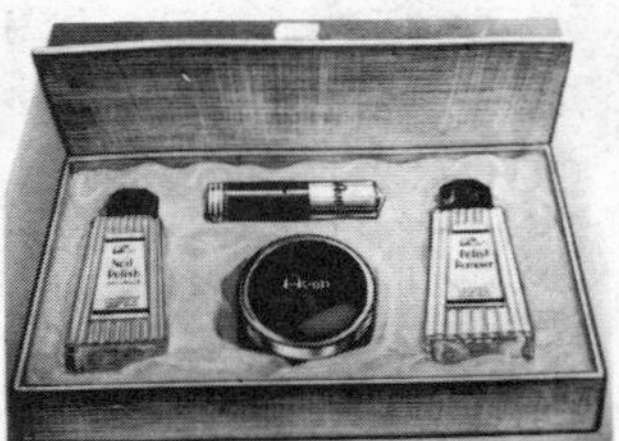

1935 GIFT SET "W"
Box contains nail polish, lipstick, rouge compact & polish remover. O.S.P. $1.67 CMV $90.00 MB.

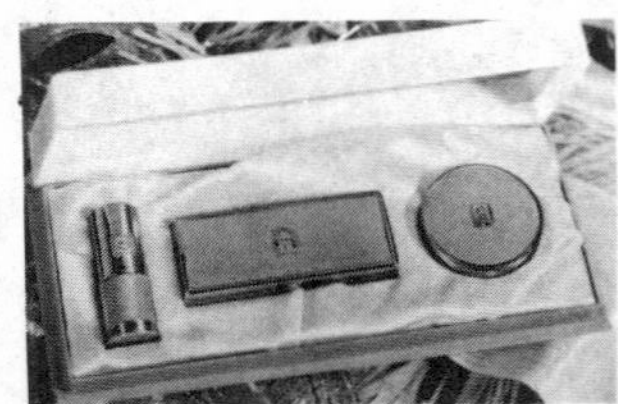

1938-41 CHARMER SET
Satin lined box contains lipstick, mascara & rouge. All green & gold. O.S.P. $2.15 C.M.V. $55.00 MB

1936-37 POWDER COMPACT SET
Box holds box of face powder & green & gold compact. O.S.P. $2.50 C.M.V. $45.00 M.B.
1938 ARISTOCRAT
Same set as Powder Compact Set only name changed in 1938. O.S.P. $2.50 C.M.V. $45.00 MB.

1936-37 AVON GIFT SET "F"
Box holds green & gold compact, lipstick & box of face powder in Ariel or Vernafleur. OSP $3.05 CMV $55.00 MB
1938 MASTERCRAFT
Same set as Gift Set "F" only name changed in 1938. OSP $3.05 CMV $55.00 MB.

1936 TRIO GIFT SET
Box holds 2 oz. trailing Arbutus toilet water with tulip label & gold ribbed cap. Silver can of Daphne Talcum & ribbed glass Ariel powder sachet. O.S.P. $1.29 C.M.V. $100.00 M.B.

1939-42 FAIR LADY
Green, yellow & white flowered box with gold base holds 4 perfumes in Narcissus, Gardenia, Cotillion, Trailing Arbutus, or Sweet Pea. Each came in different colored caps. OSP 94c CMV $100.00 MB.

1936-37 GIFT SET "K"
Blue & gold box has green & gold lipstick & compact & 2 dram perfume with gold cap. O.S.P. $2.79 C.M.V. $80.00.
1938 EMPRESS
Same set as Gift set "K" only name is changed. C.M.V. $80.00.

WOMEN'S SETS OF 1940'S

WARNING!! Grading condition is paramount on sets.
CMV can vary 50% on grade.
Refer to page 5 on Grading.

40-41 MILADY SET
tin lined box contains two small bottles perfume in Gardenia, Cotillion or Ballad d white lace edged hankey. O.S.P. $2.25 M.V. $85.00 M.B.

1946 DOUBLE DARE SET
Red & gold box holds bottle of Double Dare nail polish & gold Bamboo lipstick. O.S.P. $1.25 CMV $50.00 MB.

1940 MAYFAIR SET
Blue box contains 1 dram perfume with gold cap. Green & gold compacts & box of face powder in Ariel or Cotillion. O.S.P. $3.35 C.M.V. $75.00 M.B.

1943 COLONIAL DAYS
6 oz. clear glass bottle, pink cap Cream Lotion & cardboard Body Powder, shaker cap. O.S.P. $1.60 C.M.V. $65.00 M.B.

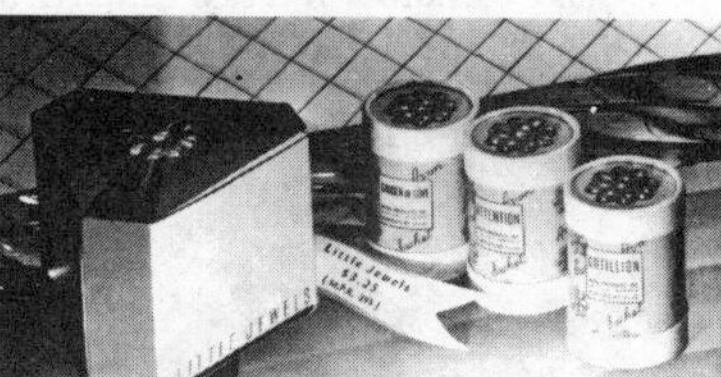

1944-45 LITTLE JEWELS
Pink box holds 3 paper powder sachets in 1¼ oz. Cotillion, Attention, Garden of Love. OSP $3.25 CMV $62.50 MB, mint.

1940-41 COLONIAL SET
Feather Face Powder & Garden of Love Perfume in blue box. O.S.P. $1.25 C.M.V. $55.00 M.B.

1940 COLONIAL SET
Blue box holds 1 dram Garden of Love perfume, gold cap and label and box of face powder. O.S.P. $1.25 C.M.V. $55.00 M.B.

1946 Only - LEADING LADY
Red, blue & gold box holds Bamboo lipstick & nail polish. OSP $1.00 CMV $42.50 MB

1943 PEEK-A-BOO SET
Pink & blue box with yellow satin lining holds blue & white feather design card board compact, cardboard lipstick & rouge. OSP $2.50 CMV $60.00 MB.

1940 SPECTATOR SET
Box contains green and gold rouge, 1 dram Garden of Love perfume, gold cap, green and gold lipstick. O.S.P. $1.56 C.M.V. $65.00 M.B.

1941-42 ELYSIAN SET
Satin lined box contains lipstick, rouge & 1 dram perfume with gold cap. O.S.P. $1.75 C.M.V. $75.00 M.B.

1940-43 MR. & MRS. SET
Blue & pink box contains Smokers Tooth-powder, After Shaving Lotion for Men, Cotillion Toilet Water & Cotillion Talcum for women. OSP $2.50 CMV $120.00 MB

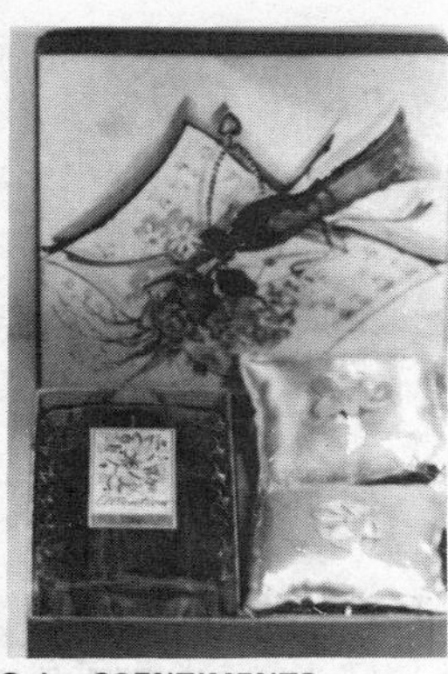

1945 Only - SCENTIMENTS
Box holds 6 oz. Attention Cologne & 2 satin sachet pillows. O.S.P. $2.50 C.M.V. $90.00 M.B.

1943-44 BATH BOUQUET
Blue box holds 6 oz. of Rose Geranium Bath Oil & Apple Blossom Beauty Dust. O.S.P. $2.35 C.M.V. $65.00 M.B.

1940-42 HANDKERCHIEF SET
Box holds, white, pink, blue & yellow handkerchiefs, 1/8 oz. Cotillion Perfume with red cap, Gardenia Perfume with blue cap. O.S.P. $1.00 CMV $57.50 MB.

1940-43 BATH DUET
Blue, pink & white box holds can of Daphne or Cotillion Talc & choice of Jasmine, Pine, Ariel or Vernafleur Bath Salts. OSP $1.00 CMV $55.00 MB.

1943-44 RAINBOW WINGS
Box holds 6 oz. bottles of Cream Lotion & Rose Geranium Bath Oil with pink caps. Both **bottles** are flat on one side. Butterflies on box. O.S.P. $2.00 C.M.V. $60.00 M.B.

1942 MINUET
Box with music notes on lid, satin lined holds lipstick, powder compact, rouge, and face powder. All are blue & white feather design. O.S.P. $2.95 C.M.V. $60.00 M.B.

1940-42 MERRIMENT SET
Rouge, lipstick & eyebrow pencil. All green & gold. O.S.P. $1.50 C.M.V. $45.00 M.B.

1945-46 RAINBOW WINGS
Pink box holds two 6 oz. flat sided bottles of Cream Lotion & Rose Geranium Bath Oil. Pink net ribbon on top of box. O.S.P. $2.00 C.M.V. $70.00 M.B. with net.

1943-44 MINUET
Pink & blue box with yellow satin lining holds blue plastic rouge compact, cardboard feather design lipstick, Cotillion perfume with gold cap & neck tag & blue satin sachet pillowette. O.S.P. $3.9 C.M.V. $90.00 M.B.

1947-49 THAT'S FOR ME SET
Multi-colored box contains choice of Cream Cake or Cake Make-up, gold lipstick & ½ oz. nail polish. O.S.P. $2.00 CMV $37.00 MB.

1940 ORCHID SET
Red & white box, green & gold lipstick & rouge. Cream polish with green cap. O.S.P. $ C.M.V. $50.00.

1941 WINGS TO BEAUTY
Red designed box contains choice of 2 2 oz. skin conditioner, astringent, finishing lotion or Lotus Cream, and box of face powder. O.S.P. $1.00 C.M.V. $55.0 M.B.

1944 Only - PEEK-A-BOO
Blue, white & pink box with yellow satin lining holds cardboard compact covered with pink satin & white net. Cake rouge in blue plastic compact & cardboard feather design lipstick. O.S.P. $2.50 CMV $55.00 MB.

1948-49 FAIR LADY SET
Pink & blue box contains four 1/8 oz. perfumes in Lily of the Valley, Garden of Love, Quaintance, Gardenia & Cotillion. All have blue caps. O.S.P. $1.50 C.M.V. $100.00 M.B.

1945-47 FAIR LADY SET
Blue & white box holds 4 small bottles with colored caps of perfume in Cotillion, Lily of the Valley, Gardenia & Garden of Love, Trailing Arbutus & Sweet Pea. O.S.P. $1.50 C.M.V. $90.00 M.B. Also came with all blue caps.

1941 TANDEM SET
Box holds gold Bamboo compact & turquoise & gold lipstick. OSP $1.75 CMV $47.00 MB.

1942 TANDEM SET
Same set only with matching bamboo lipstick. CMV $47.00 MB.

1941-42 RECEPTION SET
Satin lined box holds gold compact, blue box of face powder & 1/8 oz. perfume. O.S.P. $2.75 C.M.V. $70.00 M.B.

1947 BEAUTY BASKET
Straw basket with pink ribbon holds two 6 oz. bottles of Avon Cream Lotion & Rose Gardenia Bath Oil. Both bottles are flat on the back side & have pink caps. OSP $2.00 CMV $65.00 basket mint with bottles. $85.00 mint in box.

1949-50 COLOR MAGIC TWO PIECE SET
Multi-colored box contains gold lipstick & ½ oz. nail polish with green cap. O.S.P. $1.35, CMV $38.00 MB

1947-54 PERFUMED DEODORANT SET
Turquoise box holds two 2 oz. bottles of Perfumed Deodorant. O.S.P. 98¢ C.M.V. set $15.00 MB

1949-50 COLOR MAGIC THREE PIECE SET
Multi-colored box holds gold lipstick, gold rouge & ½ oz. nail polish with green cap. O.S.P. $2.19 C.M.V. $45.00 M.B.

1948 BEAUTY MARK
Red & gold box contains gold lipstick & ½ oz. nail polish with green cap. O.S.P. $1.35, CMV $37.00 MB

1948 COLOR CLUSTER
Red & gold box contains gold lipstick, gold rouge & ½ oz. nail polish with green cap. O.S.P. $2.00 C.M.V. $40.00 M.B.

1946-47 COLOR CLUSTER SET
Red & gold box holds gold Bamboo Lipstick & Rouge with ½ oz. Nail Polish with black cap. O.S.P. $2.15 C.M.V. $45.00 MB

1950 FRAGRANT MIST
Turquoise & gold box holds 2 oz. Toilet Water with green & gold atomizer in choice of Flowertime, Cotillion, Lily of the Valley & Wishing. O.S.P. $2.35 C.M.V. $45.00 MB.

1940-42 FRAGRANT MIST
Blue & gold box holds 2 oz. toilet water with gold or plastic cap & label & spray atomizer. Came in Cotillion, Marionette, Sonnet, Jasmine or Apple Blossom. OSP $1.35 CMV $50.00 MB.

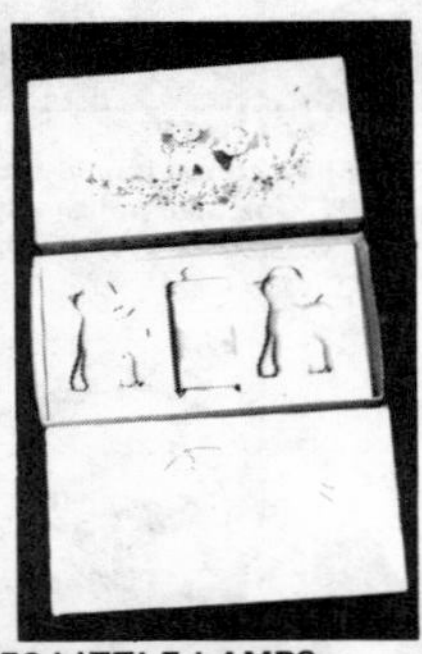

1954-56 LITTLE LAMBS
Box holds 2 lamb soaps & can of Baby Powder. Two different boxes. One has 2 lambs & the other has 2 lambs holding a umbrella. OSP $1.30 CMV $65.00 each set.

WOMEN'S SETS OF 1950'S

WARNING!! Grading condition is paramount on sets. CMV can vary 50% on grade. Refer to page 5 on Grading.

1951-52 FRAGRANCE MIST
Turquoise box with pink & gold inside holds 2 oz. Toilet Water & 1 dram perfume in choice of Cotillion, Flowertime & Lily of the Valley. O.S.P. $2.35 C.M.V. $50.00 MB.

1954 HOUSE OF CHARM
Pink box holds four 5/8 dram bottles of perfume with turquoise caps or white caps Choice of To A Wild Rose, Cotillion, Golden Promise & Quaintance. O.S.P. $1.95 C.M.V. $110.00 M.B.

1952-53 HOUSE OF CHARM
With windows open. You find four 1/8 oz. or 5/8 dram bottles of perfume: Lily of the Valley, Cotillion, Golden Promise or Quaintance. In pink box, all blue caps. OSP $1.95 CMV $100.00 MB

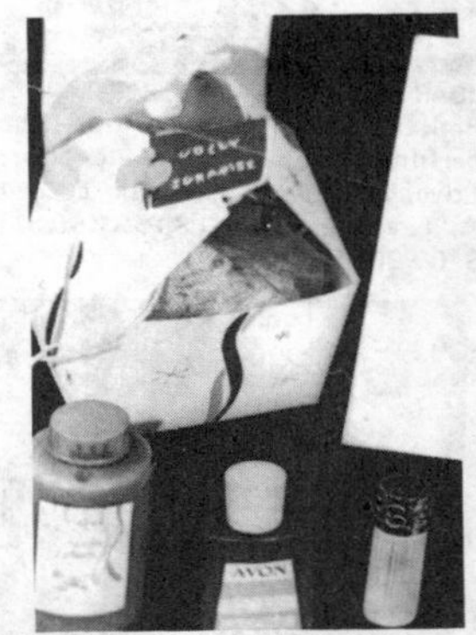

1950 Only - JOLLY SURPRISE
Pink, white & green Santa box holds 2 oz. Cream Lotion, Nail Polish & 1 dram perfume in ribbed glass. O.S.P. $1.95 C.M.V. $55.00 M.B.

HOUSE OF CHARM PERFUMES
Shown only to identify size & labels. Left square bottle is 1954 set only. Center bottle has same label as short one on left issued in 53-54. Right one issued 1952-53 sets only.

1954 FRAGRANCE RAINBOW
Flowers on top of box. Choice of Cotillion, To A Wild Rose, Forever Spring, Quaintance, cologne in ½ oz. bottles, white caps & painted labels. O.S.P. $2.50 CMV $65.00 MB

1957 GEMS IN CRYSTAL
½ oz. bottles of Nearness, Bright Night, Cotillion & To A Wild Rose. Pointed plastic caps. O.S.P. $2.95 C.M.V. With flat top caps. $65.00 $75.00 with pointed caps. M.B.

1953-55 CHRISTMAS ANGELS
Blue and white box holds gold lipstick & Cream Sachet in To A Wild Rose, Quaintance, Cotillion, Forever Spring & Golden Promise. To A Wild Rose pictured sold 1955 only and 1953-54 came with older 3 corner white jar with blue cap. Both are same C.M.V. O.S.P. $2.00 C.M.V. $27.50

1957 RAINBOW SET
Blue box holds 4 Cream Sachet jars in Cotillion, To A Wild Rose, Bright Night & Nearness. Jars are white glass with green, yellow & have two pink lids. O.S.P. $3.25 CMV $50.00 set MB, $55.00 MB with outer box as shown, $8.00 each jar.

956 Only - FRAGRANCE RAINBOW SET
ox holds four 3 dram bottles with white ainted caps. Came in To A Wild Rose, earness, Bright Night, Cotillion, uaintance & Forever Spring. O.S.P. 2.75 CMV $75.00 MB

1958 WISHING COIN TRIO
Blue & gold box holds choice of Cream Sachet, Lotion Sachet & ½ oz. Cologne in To A Wild Rose, Cotillion, Nearness, Forever Spring, Bright Night, Elegante, Here's My Heart & Persian Wood fragrances. Blue caps on all 3. O.S.P. $2.50 C.M.V. $40.00 M.B.

1950 AVON BLOSSOMS SET
Four 1/8 oz. or 5/8 dram perfume bottles set in white foam with wire fence behind it. Flowers around bottles. Plastic cap. Quaintance, Cotillion, Luscious, & Golden Promise. OSP $2.00 CMV $85.00 set only $100.00 MB.

1953 FRAGRANCE TIE INS
White box with bows holds four ½ oz. bottles with white caps. Came in Cotillion, Forever Spring, Quaintance & To A Wild Rose Cologne. O.S.P. $2.50 C.M.V. $65.00 MB

1955 CUPID'S BOW
White & pink box holds four ½ oz. bottles of Cologne with white caps. Bright Night, To A Wild Rose, Quaintance & Cotillion. OSP $2.50 CMV $60.00 MB.

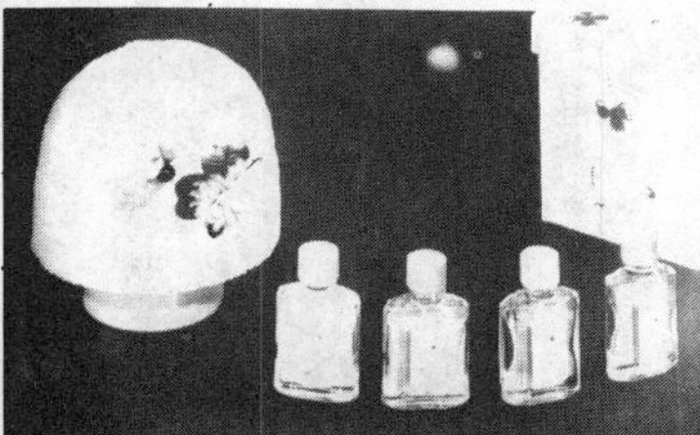

1951 SWEET AS HONEY "BEE HIVE"
Foam beehive holds four 5/8 dram bottles of perfume in Cotillion, Quaintance, Golden Promise, Luscious, Forever Spring & To A Wild Rose. All have different colored caps. OSP $2.50 CMV in box $115.00 Beehive and bottles only $90.00 mint.

1956 CREAM SACHET PETITES
Gold box holds 4 plastic Cream Sachets in blue boxes. Came in Cotillion, Bright Night, Nearness & To A Wild Rose. O.S.P. $3.25 C.M.V. $55.00 set. $10.00 each jar in box.

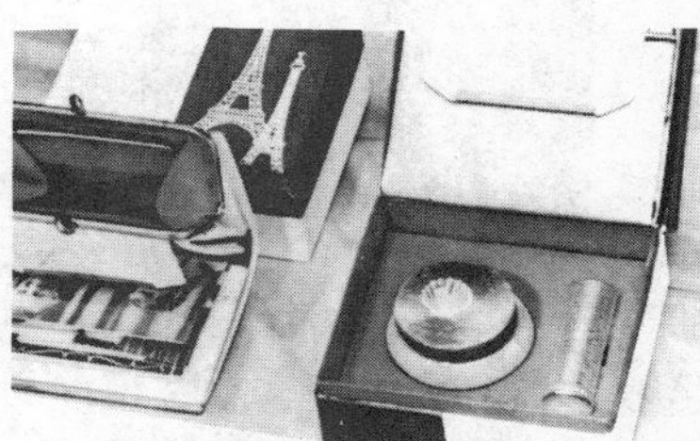

1957 TRI COLOR SET
Blue & white box holds Nearness or Choice Cream Sachet, gold satin sheen lipstick & white leather purse trimmed in gold. OSP $7.75 CMV $45.00 MB.

1958 DRAMATIC MOMENTS SET
Essence de Fleurs Cologne Mist & paper box of powder in blue box. Came in To A Wild Rose, Cotillion, Forever Spring. O.S.P. $5.00 Nearness, Elegante & Bright Night. O.S.P. $5.25 C.M.V. $40.00 M.B.

1955 BATH DELIGHTS
Box holds bottle of Avon Bubble Bath & choice of Body Powder in Golden Promise, Quaintance or Forever Spring. O.S.P. $2.10 C.M.V. $50.00 M.B.

1955-56 THAT'S FOR ME
Pink box holds four 2 oz. bottles with pink caps of Bath Oil. Quaintance, To Wild Rose, Cotillion & Pine. O.S.P. $2
C.M.V. $85.00 M.B.

1958 SAFE JOURNEY
Gold & white zippered travel kit holds 6 plastic containers of Perfumed Talc, Hand Lotion, Lotion Sachet, Cleansing Cream, Rich Moisture Cream & Deodorant. O.S.P. $6.95 C.M.V. $35.00 mint.

1955 SHOWERS OF STARS
Silver box with fluff on top holds Cream Sachet & Body Powder in choice of Golden Promise, Quaintance & Forever Spring. O.S.P. $2.10 C.M.V. $40.00 M.B.

1956 FOR YOUR BEAUTY SET
Blue & gold box holds Cleansing Cream in plastic bottle, 2 oz. bottle of Skin Freshener & Rich Moisture Cream in jar. O.S.P. $2.95 CMV $22.00 MB

1950-51 ADORABLE SET
White box holds blue satin with white lace pillow with powder pak & lipstick inside. OSP $2.95 CMV $35.00 MB

1954 SILVER WINGS SET
Box holds Cream Sachet & Body Powder in choice of To A Wild Rose, Quaintance, Golden Promise or Forever Spring. O.S.P. $2.10 C.M.V. $40.00 each. set M.B.

1958 BEAUTIFUL YOU
Pink & white box with ladies face holds 3½ oz. Rich Moisture Cream, 2 oz. of Skin Freshener & Rich Moisture Suds or Deep Clean. O.S.P. $3.50 C.M.V. $22.50 M.B.

1950 ADORABLE
Foam holder has powder pak & gold lipstick. Trimmed in blue feathers & pink ribbon & flowers. Came in green box. OSP $2.00 CMV $35.00 mint as shown $40.00 MB.

954-55 LADY BELLE
'hite bell shaped box trimmed in blue &
ld has two 1 dram perfumes. Ribbed glass
ith gold cap. Choice of Cotillion, To A
'ild Rose, Golden Promise, Quaintance,
right Night, or Forever Spring. OSP
3.00 CMV $80.00 MB.

1955 JEWELLED LIPSTICK
Blue & gold box with gold lipstick with pearl & rhinestones on top. O.S.P. $1.75 CMV $18.00 MB

1955 CHARMER SET
White, gold & red brocade case holds jewelled lipstick & 1 dram perfume. O.S.P. $3.00 C.M.V. $25.00 mint.

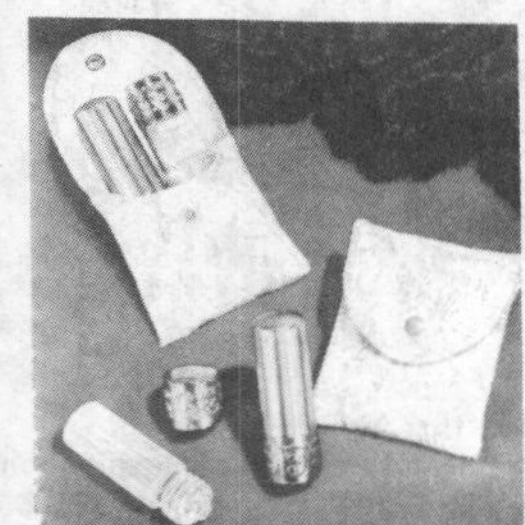

1950-51 AVONETTE
Blue & white brocade bag holds 1 dram perfume & deluxe gold lipstick. OSP $2.65 CMV $22.00, $25.00 MB

1954 CONCERTINA
Two gold fashion lipsticks in red, white & green box. OSP $1.10 CMV $35.00 MB

1958 FASHION FIRSTS
White & gold box holds 2 light tan fashion lipsticks. OSP $1.69 CMV $15.00 MB.

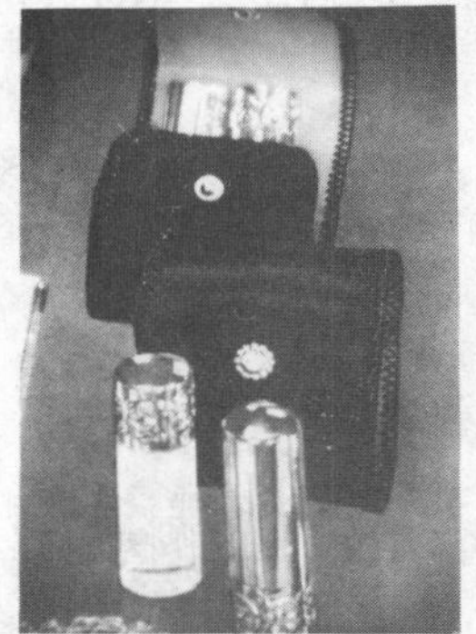

1953-54 AVONETTE
Black case holds 1 dram perfume & gold deluxe lipstick. O.S.P. $2.50 C.M.V. $22.00 $25.00 M.B.

1957 BEAUTIFUL JOURNEY SET
Pink zippered bag holds 1 oz. bottles of Cotillion Cologne, Deep Clean Cleansing Cream, Deodorant, Hand Lotion, Skin Freshener & ½ oz. jar of Rich Moisture Cream with peach colored cap. $10 each bottle; $15 Cotillion Cologne; $7 Rich Moisture Cream. O.S.P. $5.95 C.M.V. set $70.00 M.B.

1957 TWO LOVES
Red Christmas tree hang on box came with Black fashion lipstick and liquid rouge. OSP $1.10 CMV $33.00 MB

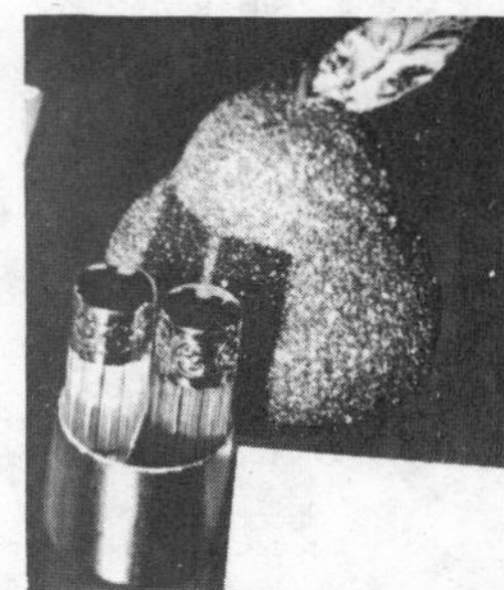

1953 PRECIOUS PEAR
Gold bell box holds 1 dram perfumes in Golden Promise, Quaintance, Cotillion, To A Wild Rose & Forever Spring. O.S.P. $2.75 C.M.V. $75.00 M.B.

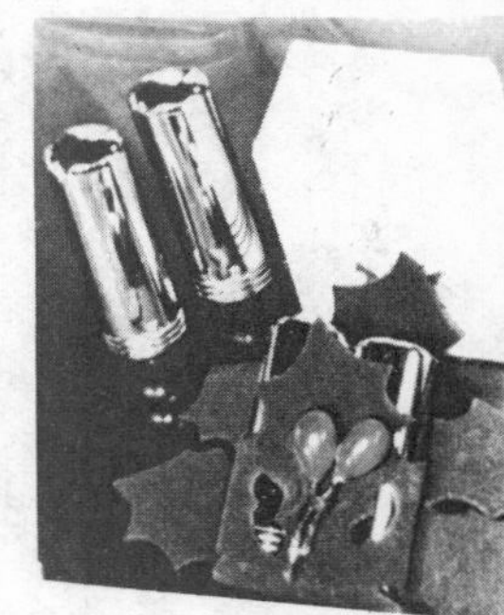

1953 HOLIDAY FASHION
White box holds 2 gold fashion lipsticks in green holly leaves. OSP $1.10 CMV $25.00 MB

1959 2 LIPS
2 white enamel lipsticks, white box with pink & gold design. O.S.P. $1.69 C.M.V. $14.00 M.B.

1957 BEAUTY PAIR
White, blue & yellow box with 2 black & pink fashion lipsticks. OSP $1.49 CMV $27.00 MB

1952 TIME FOR BEAUTY
Blue, white & pink box with pink ribbon holds gold lipstick & nail polish. O.S.P. $1.65 CMV $30.00 MB

1952-53 SUNNY HOURS
White umbrella holds 1 dram perfume & deluxe gold lipstick. O.S.P. $2.50 C.M.V. in box $50.00 Umbrella & contents only $30.00.

1958 TOUCH OF PARIS
Box holds white lipstick & compact. O.S.P. $2.10 C.M.V. $16.00 M.B.

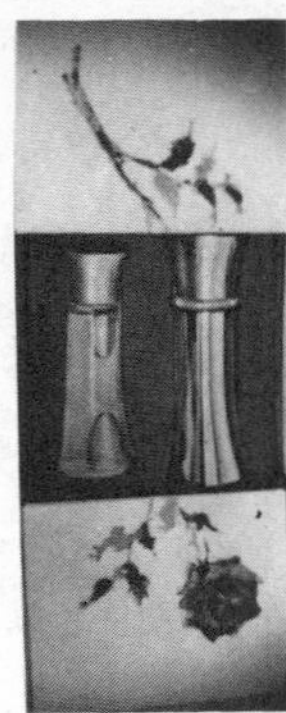

1959 TOPS STYLE BEAUTY
Red & white box holds lipstick & 1 dram Top Style Perfume. O.S.P. $2.95 C.M.V. $20.00 MB

1956 TWO LOVES SET
Box holds 2 black lipsticks. O.S.P. $1.40 C.M.V. $33.00 M.B.

1955 TWO LOVES
Red, white, blue & gold Christmas tree ornament box holds 2 gold fashion lipsticks. OSP $1.10 CMV $33.00 MB.

1959 CLEAR-IT-SKIN CARE KIT
White box holds shampoo & lotion in white plastic bottles & bar of Clear Skin Soap. OSP $2.50 CMV $20.00 MB

1954-55 GADABOUTS
Gold & white box holds turquoise & whi compact & gold lipstick. O.S.P. $2.10 C.M.V. $18.00 M.B.

1955-56 BEAUTY BOUND
Turquoise & white plastic compact, jeweled lipstick. Box pink & turquoise O.S.P. $2.75 C.M.V. $17.00 M.B.

1959 PEARL FAVORITES
Blue, green & white box holds white compact & white enamel lipstick. O.S.P. $2.19 C.M.V. $16.00 M.B.

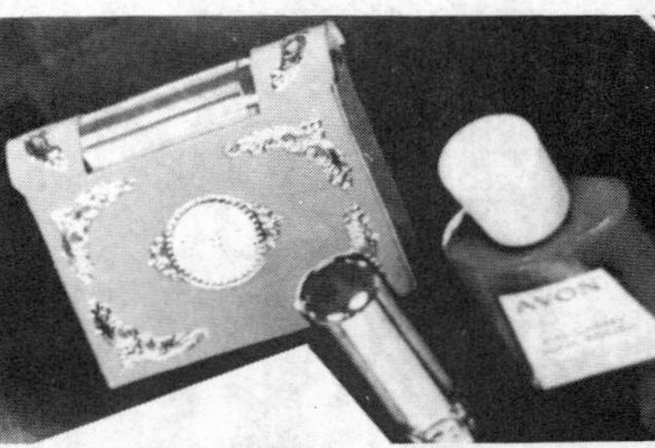

1954 BEAUTY PAIR
Red & gold box holds gold Deluxe Lipstick & nail polish. O.S.P. $1.50 C.M.V. $25.00 MB

50-51 LADY FAIR
ed, white & silver box holds gold Deluxe
pstick & bottle of nail polish. O.S.P.
.65 C.M.V. $30.00 M.B.

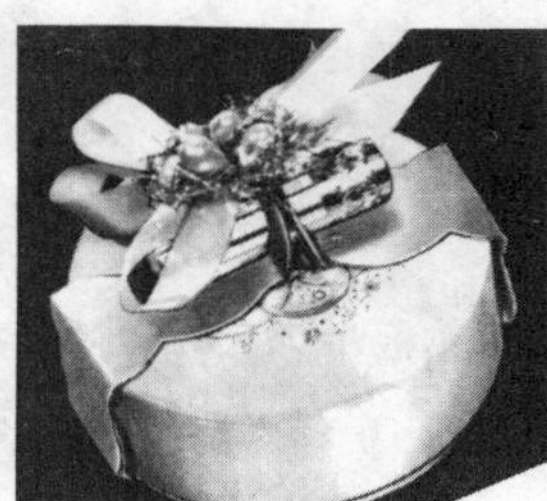

1954-55 COLOR CORSAGE
Turquoise box of face powder with gold lipstick on top. O.S.P. $1.90 C.M.V. $25.00 M.B.

1958 MAKEUP MATES
Green box holds lipstick & face powder. OSP $1.98 CMV $17.00 MB.

1957 MODERN MOOD
Pink & gold box holds 2 cans of Talc in choice of Cotillion or To A Wild Rose. Same box in blue & gold holds 2 cans of Talc in choice of Nearness or Forever Spring. O.S.P. $1.29 C.M.V. $22.50 ea. set. M.B.

1957 AVON JEWELS
Box contains liquid rouge, nail polish & longlife gold lipstick. OSP $2.50 CMV $25.00 MB.

1956 SINGING BELLS
White bell box holds 2 cans of Talc in Cotillion or To A Wild Rose. O.S.P. $1.10 CMV $20.00 MB

1952-53 GADABOUTS
Gold & white box holds compact & Cologne stick. Both are turquoise in color. O.S.P. $2.25 C.M.V. $25.00 M.B.

1955-56 TOP STYLE
Box holds gold lipstick, ½ oz. nail polish & liquid rouge. O.S.P. $1.95 C.M.V. $22.00 M.B.

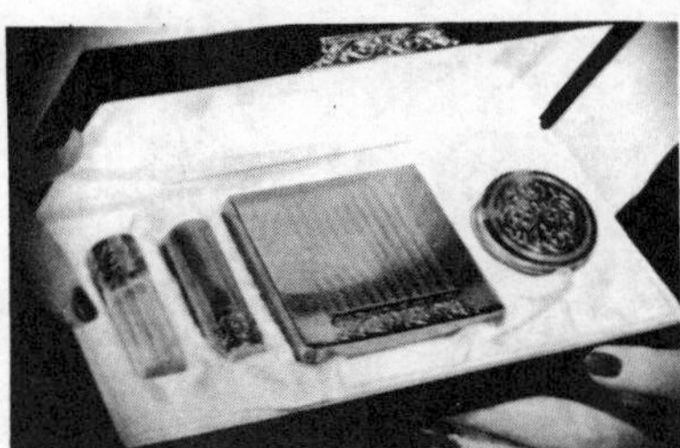

1950-54 HIGH FASHION
Black case with white satin lining holds 1 dram perfume, gold lipstick, gold compact & gold rouge compact. OSP $10.00 CMV $40.00 MB.

1958 CLASSIC STYLE
Black & gold box holds Top Style lipstick & gold Top Style compact. O.S.P. $5.00 CMV $20.00 MB.

1955 SPECIAL DATE
Blue & white box holds gold lipstick, powder pak & ½ oz. Cotillion Toilet Water. OSP $1.95 CMV $37.00 MB.

1954-55 FASHION JEWELS
Black velvet case holds 1 dram perfume, jeweled lipstick & gold compact. O.S.P. $10.50 C.M.V. $35.00 M.B.

1951 SPECIAL SET
Blue & pink Xmas box holds 2 bottles of hand lotion. OSP $1.00 CMV $30.00 MB

1955-57 SPECIAL NAIL CARE
Red and white box contained Silvery Base and Top Coat. O.S.P. $1.10 C.M.V. $10.00 M.B.

1956 Only - SHOWER OF FRESHNESS
Turquoise & white box holds 2 bottles of Perfumed Deodorant. O.S.P. $1.38 CMV $12.00 MB

1957 BOUQUET OF FRESHNESS
Pink & lavender box holds 2 two oz. bottles of Perfumed Deodorant. O.S.P. $1.38 CMV $12.00 MB

1952-53 TWIN PAK
Silver box holds 2 bottles of Hand Lotion. White caps, red ribbon on box. O.S.P. $1.10 CMV $30.00 MB

1954-55 FOR YOUR LOVELINESS
Green & silver box holds 3½ oz. jar of Moisture Cream & choice of 4 oz. bottle of Hand Lotion or Skin Freshener. O.S.P. $2.75 CMV $18.00 MB

1955 FOAM 'N SPRAY SET
Green box holds can of Avon Hair Spray & 6 oz. bottle of Cream Lotion Shampoo. OSP $2.19 CMV $20.00 MB

1954 HAND BEAUTY
Red box holds two bottles of hand lotion. OSP $1.10 CMV $18.00 MB.

1955 HAND BEAUTY
Pink box holds two 4 oz. bottles of hand lotion with turquoise caps. O.S.P. $1.18 CMV $18.00 MB.

1956 DOUBLY YOURS SET
Blue & gold box holds two bottles of hand lotion. OSP $1.29 CMV $18.00 MB.

1957 A THING OF BEAUTY
White, pink & black box holds 6 oz. Avon Cleansing Cream, 2 oz. Skin Freshener & 3½ oz. Rich Moisture Cream. O.S.P. $3.50 C.M.V. $22.50 M.B.

1956 BEAUTY DUST WITH COLOGNE
At Xmas only a 5/8 dram bottle with white flat cap & neck ribbon came in Beauty Dust. Elegante with red ribbon, Nearness, lavender ribbon, Cotillion, & To A Wild Rose, pink ribbons, Forever Spring, purple ribbon, Quaintance, blue ribbon, each ribbon has gold edge. Add $12.00 to each Beauty Dust if bottle has ribbon.

1954 HAPPY TRAVELER SET
Black & white bag holds Perfumed Deodorant Hand Cream, Rich Moisture Cream, Skin Freshener, Cleansing Cream & a plastic jar. OSP $5.95 CMV $35.00 MB.

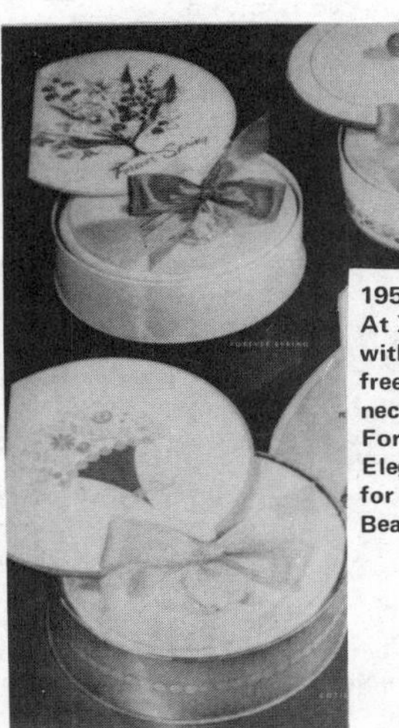

1957-58 BEAUTY DUST WITH COLOGNE
At Xmas only a 5/8 dram snow flake bottle with white round cap of cologne was given free with purchase of Beauty Dust. Matching neck ribbons on each bottle. Cotillion, Forever Spring, To A Wild Rose, Nearness, Elegante, Bright Night, CMV add $8.00 for each bottle with ribbon to price of Beauty Dust.

1953-55 BEAUTY DUST WITH COLOGNE
At Xmas only a 5/8 dram bottle of cologne with silk ribbon came in Beauty Dust in Quaintance, To A Wild Rose, both pink & white also blue container, Golden Promise, Forever Spring & Cotillion. O.S.P. $1.75 ea. CMV add $9.00 to price of Beauty Dust if bottle has ribbon & $5.00 without ribbon.

1955-56 HAPPY TRAVELER SET
Black bag with pink & blue stripes holds Cleansing Cream, Skin Freshener, Rich Moisture Cream, Hand Cream, Flowing Cream Deodorant, 1 empty plastic jar packette of tissues. OSP $5.95 CMV $35.00 MB.

1951 HOME PERMANENT REFILL KIT
Kit contains 4 oz. permanent wave lotion. C.M.V. $25.00 Neutralizer, end tissues. O.S.P. $1.00 C.M.V. $45.00 M.B. set.

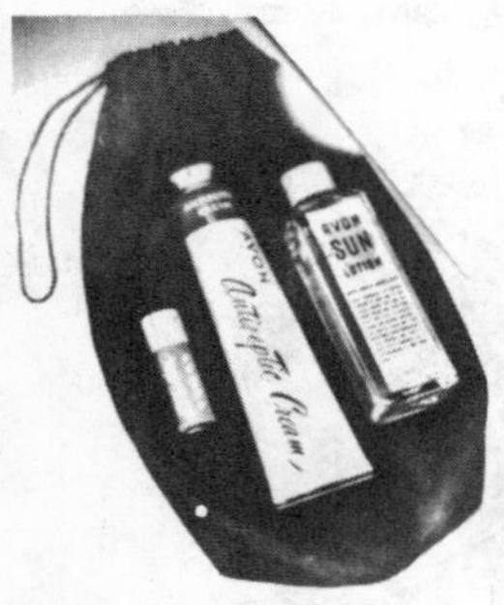

1954 CAMPING KIT
Navy blue cotton twill draw string bag. Came with 2 oz. Sun Lotion, Chap Check, Antiseptic Cream & choice of either Creme Shampoo or Cream Hair Dress. O.S.P. $1.95 Value complete set $50.00 MB

1955 FALL BAZAAR GIFT BOX
Special issue Christmas box holds 2 turquoise tubes of hand cream. O.S.P. 89¢ C.M.V. $17.00 M.B.

1955½ HAPPY TRAVELER SET
Black zipper bag with pink and blue stripes came with pack of Kleenex tissues, 2 turquoise and white plastic jars, tube of hand cream and cleansing cream and rare 2 oz. bottle of skin freshener with turquoise cap. O.S.P. $5.95 C.M.V. $35.00 mint $40.00 MB

WOMEN'S SETS OF 1960'S

WARNING!! Grading condition is paramount on sets.
CMV can vary 50% on grade.
Refer to page 5 on Grading.

1966-67 COLOGNE GEMS
Gold & white box contains two 1 oz. Gem Colognes, clear glass with plastic caps. Came in Unforgettable, Rapture, Occur! Somewhere, Topaze, Cotillion, Here's My Heart, To A Wild Rose. O.S.P. $3.50 CMV $10.00 MB

1968 FRAGRANCE FLING TRIO
½ oz. cologne, gold cap. Set of 3. Came in Charisma, Brocade, Regence, Occur, Unforgettable, Rapture, Somewhere, Topaze Cotillion, Here's My Heart, Wishing, To A Wild Rose, Persian Wood. O.S.P. $4.00 CMV $10.00 MB

1967-68 GIFT MAGIC
3½ oz. clear glass rocker bottle with gold label & lid. Box red & purple with gold & white sleeve. Came in choice of Brocade, Regence, Unforgettable, Rapture, Occur!, Somewhere, Topaze, Cotillion, Here's My Heart, To A Wild Rose, Wishing & Persian Wood Cologne. O.S.P. $2.98 C.M.V. $15.00 M.B.

1965 FRAGRANCE ORNAMENTS
3 bottles 5/8 dram Perfume Oil. Same as the Bullet bottle. White paper trimmed in gold. Gold & white box. Set A: Wishing, Somewhere, Occur. Set B: Rapture, Topaze, To A Wild Rose. Set C: Unforgettable, Here's My Heart & Cotillion. OSP $4.50 CMV $40.00 MB

1964 FRAGRANCE GOLD SET
Box holds 3 heart shaped ½ oz. colognes in Occur, Somewhere, Wishing, Topaze, Cotillion, Here's My Heart, Persian Wood, To A Wild Rose. OSP $3.50 CMV $20.00 MB

1965 FRAGRANCE FAVORITES
Box holds 3 heart shaped ½ oz. colognes in Unforgettable, Rapture, Occur, Cotillion, Somewhere, Topaze, Here's My Heart, Persian Wood, To A Wild Rose, Wishing. OSP $3.50 CMV $20.00 MB.

1966-67 RENAISSANCE TRIO
3ox holds 3 boxes with ½ oz. Colognes in Jnforgettable, Rapture, Occur, Somewhere, Topaze, Cotillion, Here's My Heart, To A Wild Rose & Wishing. O.S.P. $3.50 CMV $16.00 MB

1963-64 WOMAN'S TRAVEL KIT
White floral bag holds moisturized Hand Cream, Perfumed Talc, 4 oz. Skin-So-Soft, 2 oz. Perfumed Deodorant & choice of Night Cream. O.S.P. $11.95 C.M.V. $25.00 M.B.

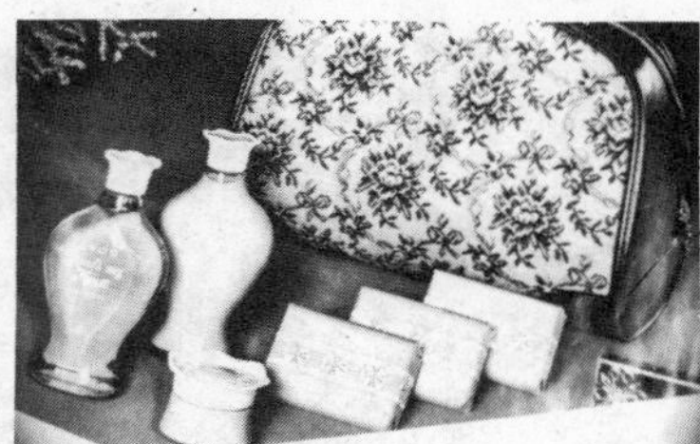

1962 TOTE ALONG SET
Tapestry bag holds 4 oz. Cologne & Cream Lotion, Cream Sachet, 3 cakes of wrapped soap in Somewhere, Topaze, Cotillion, Here's My Heart, Persian Wood & To A Wild Rose. O.S.P. $12.95 C.M.V. $32.00 M.B.

65 FRAGRANCE GOLD DUET
vo heart shaped ½ oz. Colognes in gold & ite box. Came in Rapture, Occur!, tillion, Somewhere, Topaze, Here's My art, Persian Wood, To A Wild Rose, shing & Unforgettable. O.S.P. $2.50 MV $16.00 MB

1962-63 FRAGRANCE MAGIC
Matching boxes holds Cologne Mist & Beauty Dust with clear plastic top. Came in To A Wild Rose, Persian Wood, Here's My Heart, Somewhere, Cotillion & Topaze. OSP $6.00 to $8.00 CMV $35.00 MB each.

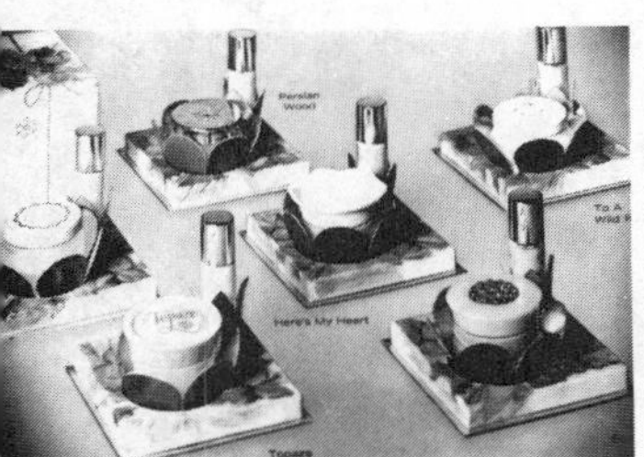

1963-64 FLOWER FANTASY
Cream Sachet & Cream Rollette in Here's My Heart, Persian Wood, To A Wild Rose, Cotillion, Somewhere, Topaze, Occur!. OSP $5.00 CMV $17.00 MB.

965 FLOWER FANTASY
loral box holds Cream Sachet & Perfume ollette in Here's My Heart, To A Wild ose, Wishing, Somewhere, Cotillion, Topaze Occur!. O.S.P. $5.00 C.M.V. $15.00 ea. B $18.00 with carnival glass rollette.

1963-64 BEAUTY SCENTS
Box holds 5 oz. Perfumed Skin Softener & matching Perfume Creme Rollette in Somewhere, Topaze, Cotillion, To A Wild Rose, Here's My Heart & Persian Wood. OSP $5.25 CMV $16.00 MB.

1965 Beauty Scents issued same box but with Perfume Rollette and dropped Persion Wood and added Rapture and Occur! O.S.P. $5.25 C.M.V. $15.00 ea. MB $17.00 with carnival glass rollette.

1959-60 TWO LOVES SETS
Matching boxes hold Cologne Mist & Cream Sachet in To A Wild Rose, Here's My Heart. CMV $20.00 each, Nearness CMV $38.00, Cotillion CMV $23.00, 1959 only for Persian Wood CMV $27.00 & Bright Night CMV $30.00 OSP $4.25 to $4.75.

1959-60 ON THE WING SET
Blue plastic bag holds choice of Perfumed Talc, in Here's My Heart, Persian Wood, To A Wild Rose, Nearness, Cotillion & Floral. Skin Freshener, Deep Clean & 2 oz. plastic bottle of choice of 1½ oz. jar of Vita Moist or Rich Moisture Cream. O.S.P. $6.25 C.M.V. $30.00 M.B.

1964 FRAGRANCE FORTUNE
Matching boxes hold 2 oz. Cologne & ½ oz. Perfume Oil in Somewhere, Here's My Heart, Cotillion, To A Wild Rose, Persian Wood & Topaze. O.S.P. ea. $4.98 C.M.V. $25.00 MB.

1967 FLUFF PUFF SET
Issued during bottle strike. Green box holds 2 boxes 3.5 oz. of powder. White plastic bottle, gold base & pink puff. Does not say Avon. Came in Unforgettable, To A Wild Rose, Cotillion, Regence. O.S.P. $5.50 C.M.V. $18.00 M.B. Regence came in dark pink & light pink & green. Green is rare. C.M.V. green only $25.00 M.B.

1965-66 WOMEN'S TRAVEL KIT
Yellow floral "hat box" contains cream deodorant, Skin-So-Soft, hand cream, wh Velex Cleansing cream, Hormone Cream, Rich moisture, Vita Moist & Cream Supreme. O.S.P. $12.95 C.M.V. complete set $30.00 M.B. Hat box only $12.00.

1960 LADIES CHOICE
Matching boses hold 4 oz. Cologne & Beauty Dust in Cotillion, Persian Wood, To a Wild Rose, Here's My Heart. OSP $5.45 to $6.25 CMV $40.00 each set MB.

67 FLUFF PUFF
ɔral box contains one puff & Beauty Dust. ite plastic. Comes in Unforgettable, To A ld Rose, Cotillion & Regence. O.S.P. .50 CMV $12.00 MB Also came in ite puff in Regence. CMV $20.00.

65 BATH BOUQUET
reen box contains 1½ oz. green card-ard talc, 2 oz. bath oil & ½ oz. cologne in ere's My Heart, To A Wild Rose, ishing, O.S.P. $4.00 Somewhere, Topaze, otillion O.S.P. $4.25 Rapture & Occur! S.P. $4.50 C.M.V. $35.00 M.B.

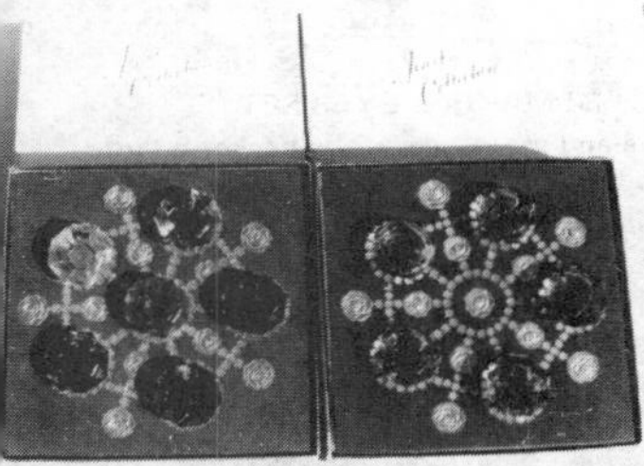

964 JEWEL COLLECTION
Vith 6 gem shaped bottles of perfume oil & old caps. Blue & gold box. Somewhere, Topaze, Cotillion, Persian Wood, Here's My Heart & To A Wild Rose. OSP $5.95 CMV $50.00 MB

964 JEWEL COLLECTION - CANADA
Box is same as American set only center ottle hole is not punched out. Came in Somewhere, Topaze, Cotillion, Here's My Heart, To A Wild Rose in perfume oils, /8 dram each. Very rare set. OSP $6.95 CMV $200.00 MB.

1959-60 PARIS MOOD
Gift set came with spray Essence, Beauty Dust & Cream Sachet in Persian Wood, Here's My Heart, Cotillion, To A Wild Rose, Bright Night & Nearness fragrances. OSP $7.95 CMV $47.00 MB. See stock holders gifts for additional information. information.

1967-70 ROLL-A-FLUFF
Fluff holds 3½ oz. Beauty Dust. Red puff is Charisma. Green puff is Regence, White puff is Brocade. Gold top & handle. O.S.P. $13.50 CMV $15.00 MB.

1968 FLUFF PUFF'S
3½ oz. Talc & matching puff comes in Somewhere with green puff, Honeysuckle with yellow puff, Here's My Heart with blue puff & To A Wild Rose with pink puff. OSP $6.00 CMV $10.00 MB.

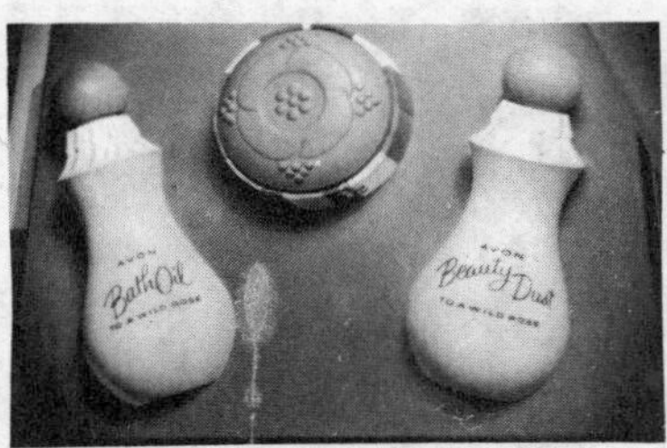

1960-61 MODERN SIMPLICITY
Lavender blue & white box contains soap, 4 oz. bath oil, 3 oz. Beauty Dust in choice of Cotillion, To A Wild Rose, & Here's My Heart. O.S.P. $3.98 C.M.V. $42.50 M.B.

1965 JUST TWO
3 oz. each, Tribute After Shave, black glass. Clear Rapture Cologne with gold tags. OSP $5.50 CMV $70.00 MB Bottles only with tags, black, $25.00 clear $20.00.

1960 CLASSIC HARMONY
Red, pink & gold box holds top style lipstick, compact & perfume. Came in choice of shades & fragrances. O.S.P. $6.95 C.M.V. $25.00 M.B.

1968 SPLASH & SPRAY SET
Purse size cologne spray & 2½ oz. splash cologne bottle with refill funnel. Both trimmed in gold. Gold box. Came in Brocade & Regence, O.S.P. $7.00 Unforget-table, Somewhere & Topaze, O.S.P. $6.50 CMV $20.00 MB.

1965-66 GOLDEN VANITY
Gold metal stand with removable mirror in center. Came with perfume rollette & gold refillable lipstick. O.S.P. $10.00 C.M.V. complete set. $30.00 M.B. Stand with mirror only $15.00

1966 FRAGRANCE VANITY TRAY
Three hearts on tray. ½ oz. Cologne, Heart shaped bottles on 1966 glass tray with Avon insignia on tray. O.S.P. Tray $1.25 CMV $3.00 tray - MB $4.00 colognes, OSP $3.75 CMV $2.00 each bottle, $4.00 MB CMV set $18.00 MB.

1967 MANICURE TRAY
Dark brown plastic tray with 4A design. Came with tubes of Nail Beauty & Cuticle remover, ½ oz. bottle of Double Coat & Nail Enamel with white caps & box of 10 Enamel Remover pads, 1 orange stick & emery board. OSP $5.00 CMV complete set $16.00 MB, tray only $5.00. Also came in amber color tray CMV $10.00 tray.

1960 GOLDEN RINGS SET
Red & gold box holds 2 pink & white lipsticks. OSP $1.79 CMV $15.00 MB

1966 PERFUME OIL PETITES (PIN CUSHION)
Gold box with red velvet pin cushion top & inner box holds three 5/8 dram heart shaped bottle with gold cap & label. Came in choice of Set A: Wishing, Somewhere, Occur!, Set B: Rapture, Topaze, To A Wild Rose. Set C: Here's My Heart, Unforgettable, Cotillion. O.S.P. $4.50 CMV $42.50 MB.

1965-66 MANICURE TRAY
White plastic tray & tissue holder. Came with pink box of Kleenex Tissue with 4A design on box. 8½ in. x 6 x 3 in. O.S.P. $5.00 CMV tray only $5.00, MB $7.00 Avon Kleenex box mint $7.00. Complete set MB $14.00

1968 GOLDEN HEIRLOOM CHEST
6" long gold metal, glass lid, red velvet in bottom of chest. Avon on bottom. Came in perfume rollette in Brocade or Regence & deluxe refillable gold lipstick. Came in pink box. O.S.P. $15.00 C.M.V. complete set in box $35.00 chest only $25.00.

1964-65 VANITY SHOW CASE
Silver & gold plastic holder. Avon on bottom. Came with 1 dram ribbed perfum & deluxe silver lipstick with 4A on top. O.S.P. $5.00 C.M.V. complete set $20.00 in box. Holder only $6.00.

1962-64 MANICURE TRAY
Clear plastic, Avon on bottom, 4A design Came with 3 oz. bottle on Oily Polish Remover, ½ oz. bottle of Nail Polish & Base Coat or Double Coat & 2 tubes of Cuticle Remover & Nail Beauty. O.S.P. $3.98. CMV complete set $20.00 tray only $7.00

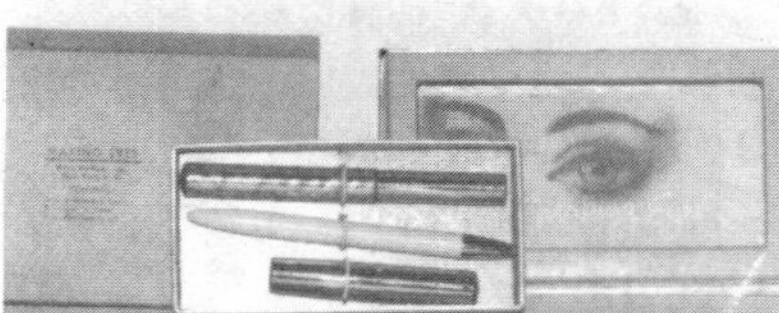

1961-62 MAKING EYES SET
Blue and green box with checker board top holds Eye Shadow Stick, Curl N Color and Eyebrow Pencil. Box came with outside sleeve. OSP $3.95 CMV $25.00 MB

1969 FLUFF PUFF
Cardboard Talc, blue & gold design on white; Puff white with marbleized handle, white knob with 4A. Came 3 different colors, Rapture, turquoise. Occur!, yellow & Unforgettable, coral, O.S.P. $4.99 CMV $10.00 MB

1. Elusive

2. Bird of Paradise

3. Charisma

1970 TWO LOVES
Cream Sachet & Perfume Rollette in Elusive in pink & gold box, Bird of Paradise in turquoise & gold box & Charisma in red and gold box with white gold or red liner. O.S.P. $6.00 each. CMV $12.00 each MB.

1967 MERRY LIPTINTS
Red flocked sleeve holds 2 white and gold Encore lipsticks with boxes to match sleeve but not flocked. O.S.P. $1.99 C.M.V. $9.00 MB.

1968 VANITY TRAY
Brown plastic tray. Came with brown plastic fashion lipstick shown on right & perfume rollette in choice of Unforgettable, Rapture, Occur, Somewhere, Topaze, Cotillion, Here's My Heart or To A Wild Rose. O.S.P. $6.00 C.M.V. complete set $11.00 in box. Tray only $6.00 MB.

1969 SCENTIMENTS
Box holds ½ oz. clear glass jar with gold cap with Cream Sachet in Unforgettable, Rapture, Occur, Somewhere, Topaze, or Cotillion with 4A embossed soap. O.S.P. $3.50 C.M.V. $9.00 M.B. Each fragrance came with different color soap.

1963 FASHION STAR
Blue, pink & white box holds two Fashion lipsticks. OSP $1.69 CMV $12.00 MB.

1962 COLOR TRICK
Blue & gold foil box has 2 black fashion lipstick tubes, gold bottom. OSP $1.96 CMV $15.00 MB.

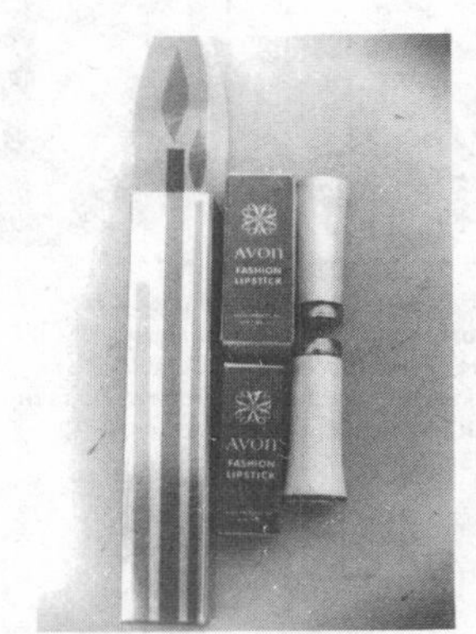

1965 FASHION TWINS
Multi-colored box holds 2 Cameo lipsticks. OSP $1.95 CMV $14.00 MB

1964 GOLDEN ARCH
Gold arch box holds 2 floral Fashion lipsticks. O.S.P. $1.96 C.M.V. $16.00 M.B.

1967 MERRY FINGERTIPS
Pink velvet box holds 2 bottles of nail polish. OSP $1.70 CMV $12.00 MB.

1965 PRETTY NOTIONS
Pink vinyl case contains pink compact & Cameo lipstick. O.S.P. $4.50 C.M.V. $10.00 set only. $12.00 M.B.

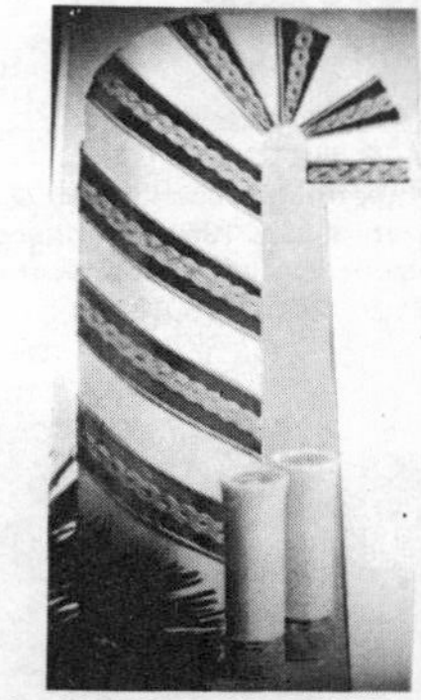

1966 CANDY CANE TWINS
Candy cane box holds 2 Cameo lipsticks. OSP $1.96 CMV $20.00 MB.

1962 FASHION TWIN SET
Blue & white silk cosmetic case holds gold & black compact & lipstick. O.S.P. $3.29 C.M.V. $15.00 $17.00 M.B.

1968-69 SCENTIMENTS
Gold, white & silver box holds Cream Sachet & Perfumed Rollette in Brocade, Regence, Unforgettable, Rapture, Occur, Somewhere, Topaze or Cotillion. O.S.P. $4.00 C.M.V. $10.00.

1962 CLEVER MATCH SET
Pink & red box holds black lipstick & nail polish with white cap. 1961 set same only has white plastic lipstick with pink flowered top. OSP $1.83 CMV $15.00 MB.

1969 TWO LOVES
Red & gold box with red felt inside holds perfume rollette & cream sachet in Charisma, Brocade or Regence. O.S.P. $6.00 C.M.V. $12.00 M.B.
Brocade is gray inside box.

1963 COLOR NOTE
Gold & white box holds bottle of nail polish & pink fashion lipstick. O.S.P. $1.67 CMV $14.00 MB.

1967 TWO LOVES
Gold & green box has Cream Sachet & Perfume Rollette in Unforgettable, Rapture, Occur! Somewhere, Topaze, Cotillion, Here's My Heart & To A Wild Rose. O.S.P. $5.00 C.M.V. $12.00 M.B.

1963-64 TOUCH-UP TWINS
Multi-colored box holds lipstick & perfume cream rollette in Here's My Heart, Persian Wood, To A Wild Rose, O.S.P. $3.10 each. Somewhere, Topaze, Cotillion, O.S.P. $3.35; Occur! O.S.P. $3.85 CMV $17.00 MB.

1965 Only - TOUCH-UP TWINS
Angel box holds deluxe lipstick & perfume rollette in Here's My Heart, Wishing, To A Wild Rose, O.S.P. $2.70; Somewhere, Topaze, Cotillion, O.S.P. $2.95; Rapture, Occur! O.S.P. $3.45 CMV $12.00 MB. Add $2.00 for carnival glass rollette.

1964 PAIR TREE
Gold, white & blue holds nail polish & floral fashion lipstick. O.S.P. $1.83 CMV $14.00 MB.

1966 SLEIGH MATES
Red & gold box holds Fashion Cameo lipstick & bottle of nail enamel. O.S.P. $1.83 C.M.V. $17.00 M.B.

1962-63 HAWAIIAN DELIGHTS
Box holds 4 bottles of nail polish. White caps. O.S.P. $2.98 C.M.V. $18.00 M.B.

1964 COLOR GARDEN
Red & white floral box holds 4 nail polish bottles with white caps. Came with pearl or cream polish only. OSP $2.76 CMV $20.00 MB.

5 STAR ATTRACTIONS
conatins ½ oz. cologne & metal lip-
k in Rapture, Occur! Somewhere, Topaze,
illion, Here's My Heart, Persian Wood, To
Vild Rose & Wishing. O.S.P. $2.50 C.M.V.
.00 MB.

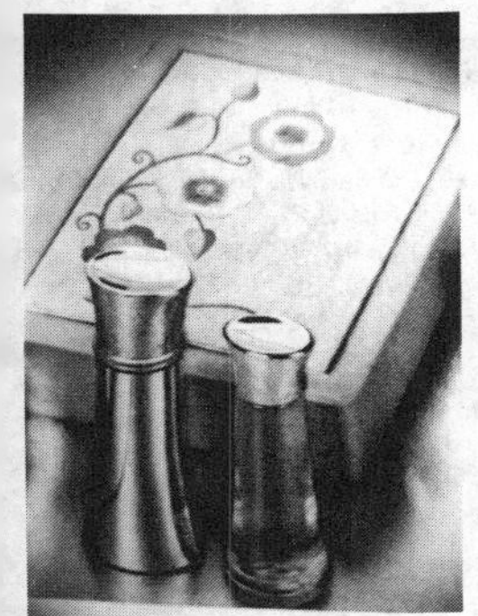

960 PARTY FUN
lue & gold box holds gold lipstick & 1
ram perfume in Topaze, Here's My
eart, Persian Wood, Cotillion, To A
Vild Rose, Bright Night, Nearness.
.S.P. $3.50 C.M.V. $22.00 M.B.

1965 PERFUMED PILLOWETTES
Box contains two sachet pillows & gold top powder sachet in Occur! Rapture, O.S.P. $3.75; Lavender, Somewhere, Cotillion, Topaze, O.S.P. $3.25; Here's My Heart, To A Wild Rose & Wishing, O.S.P. $3.00 C.M.V. $20.00 M.B.

1962-63 BATH CLASSIC
1½ oz. with gold design, gold cap in gold box with large red powder puff. Box has clear plastic top. Cologne came in Somewhere, Cotillion, Topaze, O.S.P. $5.00; Here's My Heart, Persian Wood, O.S.P. $4.75; To A Wild Rose, O.S.P. $4.50 C.M.V. $35.00 M.B.

1963-64 FLORAL ENCHANTMENT
Floral box holds Cologne Mist & Cream Sachet in Occur! Persian Wood, Here's My Heart, To A Wild Rose, Topaze, Somewhere & Cotillion. Came with 2 different bottles. CMV $17.00 MB.

1965 BATH SPARKLERS
Silver box holds 3 colored tubes of bubble bath powder in Lilac, Jasmine & Lily of the Valley. O.S.P. $2.50 C.M.V. $25.00 M.B.

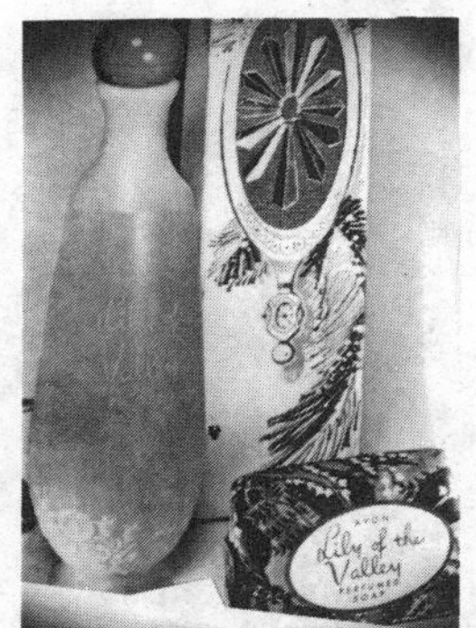

1963 BATH BOUQUET
Gift box holds 8 oz. plastic bottle of bath oil & soap in Lily of the Valley, Lilac. OSP $2.39 CMV $13.00 each MB.

1962-63 REFRESHING HOURS
Red & white box holds 2¾oz. can of Perfumed Talc & 2½ oz. bottle of Cologne in Somewhere, Topaze, Cotillion, Here's My Heart, Persian Wood & To A Wild Rose. O.S.P. $2.50 C.M.V. $25.00 ea. set.

1965 FLORAL TALC TRIO
Floral box holds three 3½ oz. talcs in Lily of the Valley, Lilac & Jasmine. OSP $2.65 CMV $10.00 MB

1964 BATH BOUQUET
Pink box holds white plastic 6 oz. bottle of perfumed bath oil & perfumed soap in Topaze, Somewhere, To A Wild Rose, Persian Wood, Here's My Heart & Cotillion fragrances. O.S.P. $2.89 CMV $13.00 each MB.

1963 BATH BOUQUET
8 oz. plastic bottle of bath oil & soap in Royal Jasmine, Royal Pine, Rose Geranium. OSP $2.39 CMV $13.00 each MB.

1960 BEGUILING SET
Multi-colored box holds spray essence & cream sachet in Bright Night, Nearness, To A Wild Rose, Cotillion, O.S.P. $4.50; Here's My Heart & Persian Wood, O.S.P. $5.00 C.M.V. $25.00 M.B.

1966 FRAGRANCE CHIMES
Red & gold box holds perfumed talc & cream sachet in Rapture, Occur! Unforgettable, Somewhere, Topaze, Cotillion, Here's My Heart & To A Wild Rose & Wishing. O.S.P. $2.89 C.M.V. $12.00 M.B.

1967 FLORAL MEDLEY
Floral box contains perfumed talc & cream sachet in Honeysuckle, O.S.P. $3.48, Jasmine, Lily of the Valley, Lilac. OSP $2.89 CMV $12.00 each set.

1966 FRAGRANCE DUETTE
Blue & gold box holds 2 oz. splash on cologne & perfumed rollette in Occur! Rapture & Unforgettable. O.S.P. $5.00 C.M.V. $15.00 M.B.

1964 FLOWER BATH SET
Talc and 2 bars of soap in choice of Lily of the Valley, Lilac, Jasmine & Rose Geranium. OSP $1.67 CMV $13.00 MB.

1964 DECORATION GIFT SET
Purple, gold & white box holds cream sachet & spray essence in Here's My Heart, Persian Wood, To A Wild Rose, Somewhere, Cotillion & Topaze. OSP $5.50 CMV $20.00 MB.

1962-63 FRAGRANCE GEMS
Box holds creme sachet & cream lotion in Topaze, Cotillion, Somewhere, Persian Wood, Here's My Heart & To A Wild Rose. OSP $2.75 CMV $16.00 MB

1962 BATH BOUQUET
White & gold box holds 6 oz. pink & white plastic bottle of bath oil & wrapped soap in Somewhere, Cotillion, Here's My Heart, Topaze, Persian Wood, Royal Jasmine Rose Geranium, Royal Pine, Floral & To A Wild Rose. O.S.P. $2.79 C.M.V. $15.00 M.B.

1967-68 KEEPSAKES
Gold, floral & white box holds 3 oz. cologne mist, perfume rollette in Occur! Rapture, & Unforgettable. O.S.P. $8.50 C.M.V. $14.00 M.B.

1965 DOUBLE PAK SET
Box in green, pink & red foil design. Came with choice of 2 tubes of moisturized hand cream or Avon hand cream or silicone glove or bottle of hand lotion as shown. O.S.P. $1.29 C.M.V. $10.00 M.B.

WOMEN'S SETS OF 1970'S

WARNING!! Grading condition is paramount on sets.
CMV can vary 50% on grade.
Refer to page 5 on Grading.

1971-73 PRECIOUS PAIR
ulti-colored box holds matching 1½ oz. erfumed Talc & ½ oz. Cologne in Occur! apture, Unforgettable, Somewhere, opaze & Cotillion. O.S.P. $4.00 C.M.V. 5.00 M.B.

1973 MINUETTE DUET
5 oz. cologne in clear bottle with gold cap. 1.5 oz. talc in paper cylinder with Christmas scene. Came in set of Unforgettable, To A Wild Rose, Occur! Somewhere, Topaze or Cotillion. S.S.P. $3.00 C.M.V. $5.00 M.B.

1973-75 FRAGRANCE TREASURES
.66 oz. clear glass cream sachet with pink & gold lid. Pink & gold soap wrapper & box. Choice of Sonnet, Charisma or Moonwind. O.S.P. $3.00 C.M.V. $4.00 M.B.

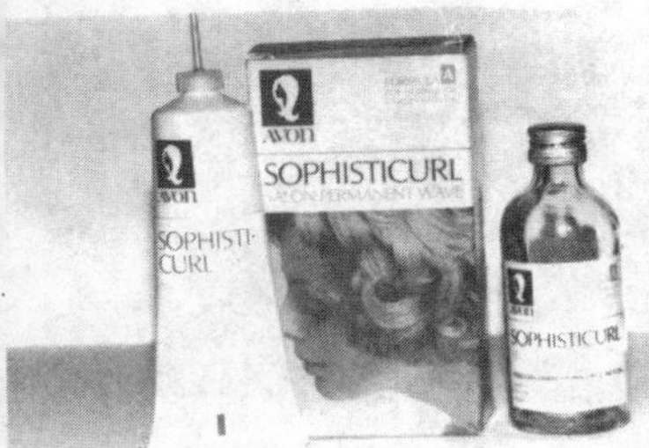

1971 SOPHISTICURL
A salon permanent wave used only in Avon Beauty Salons. Box holds 4 oz. bottle of waving lotions and 3.75 oz. white tube of neutralizer. C.M.V. $10.00 set M.B.

1978-79 FRAGRANT NOTIONS
Floral design box with gold & blue felt inner box holds .33 oz. bottle, gold cap & porcelain thimble with Avon stamped in bottom. Box came with outside sleeve. Choice of Ariane or Timeless Cologne. SSP $6.99 CMV $6.99 MB.

1972-75 FRAGRANCE FANCY
Pink, blue & white. Has .33 oz. rollette & 1.5 oz. perfume talc. Choice of Unforgettable, Somewhere, Cotillion, Occur! Topaze, Here's My Heart or Rapture. O.S.P. $3.00 C.M.V. $4.00 M.B.

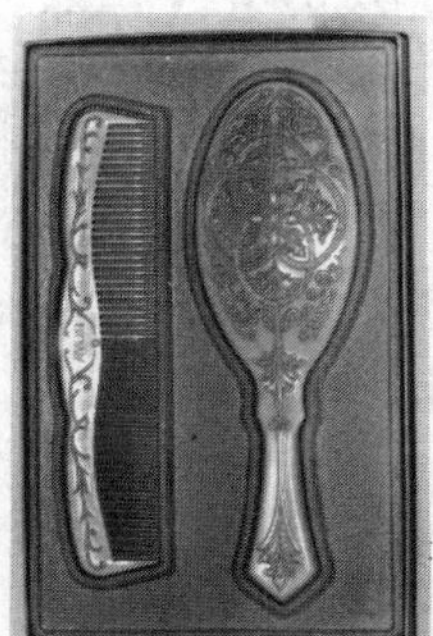

1972-73 PAST & PRESENT BRUSH & COMB SET - Antique ivory colored, nylon bristled, plastic brush & comb. S.S.P. $4.00 C.M.V. $5.00 M.B.

1970 ULTRA-FLUFF SET
Box holds 3½ oz. Beauty Dust, 1/8 oz. Perfume, Lamb's Wool Puff & white pedestal dish in Brocade, Charisma & Regence. O.S.P. $10.00 C.M.V. $12.00 M.B.

1971-74 HAIR PERFECT SET
Blue & white box holds 2 oz. brown glass bottle of Color Perfect & 2 oz. white plastic bottle of cream developer. O.S.P. $2.50 C.M.V. $4.00 M.B.

1973 TREASURE CHEST SET
White plastic chest with deep purple velour inside & on top. Bottles are clear glass with white on front & gold rose & gold cap. One bottle holds 4 oz. Skin-So-Soft, other holds 4 oz. cologne in Moonwind or Sonnet. Soap 5 oz. in Moonwind (blue) or Sonnet (pink) S.S.P. $20.00 C.M.V. $25.00 M.B.

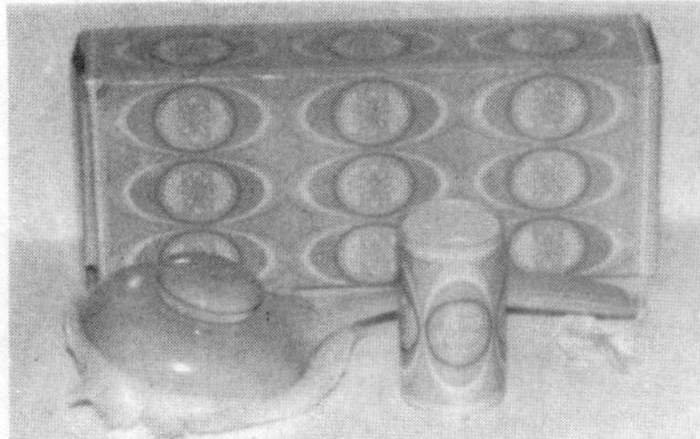

1977-78 FLUFF PUFF SET
Perfumed talc dispenser. Pink plastic holder approx. 11½" long. Came with 2 oz. cardboard talc in Roses, Roses, or Sonnet. S.S.P. $5.99 C.M.V. $4.50 M.B.

1971 CURL SUPREME SALON PERMANENT WAVE
Purple box holds 3.75 oz. white tube of neutralizer and 4 oz. bottle of waving lotion. Used only in Avon beauty salons. Not sold. C.M.V. $10.00 M.B.

1969 HAIR COLOR SET
2 oz. brown glass bottle of hair color & 2 oz. white plastic bottle of cream developer in blue box. Short issue. O.S.P. $2.50 C.M.V. $15.00 M.B.

1971 BUILT-IN BODY SALON PERMANENT WAVE
White box holds 4 oz. bottle of waving lotion and 4 oz. bottle of neutralizer. Used only in Avon beauty salons and nc sold. C.M.V. $10.00 M.B.

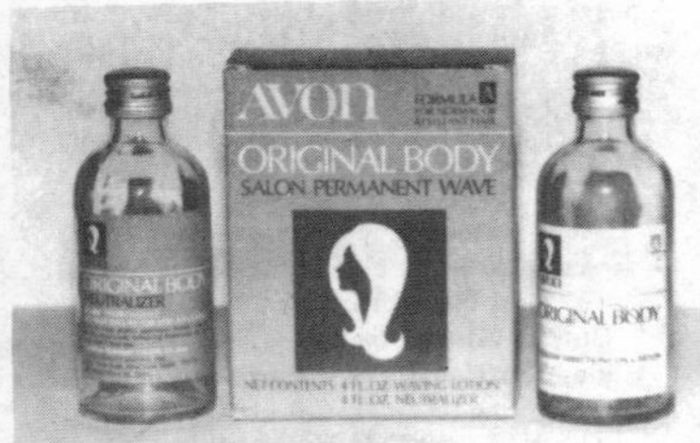

1971 ORIGINAL BODY SALON PERMANENT WAVE
Pink box holds 4 oz. bottle of neutralizer and waving lotion. Used only in Avon beauty salons. Not sold. C.M.V. $10.00 M.B.

1977-78 FRAGRANCE NOTES
Fragranced writing paper & sealing wax. Came with 18 notes scented with Earth Flowers fragrance, sealing wax stick, and goldtone seal. O.S.P. $9.00 C.M.V. $7.00 M.B.

1936-37 FACIAL SET
Turquoise flip up box holds Ariel face powder, 2 oz. jar cleansing cream, tissue cream, & 2 oz. bottle of astringent. All products are marked CPC. Also came with packet of tissues. OSP $1.60 CMV $50.00 MB.

1969-72 LIGHTS & SHADOWS COLOGNE
Lights is clear glass & gold cap. Shadows is smoked glass & cap. 2 oz. each. OSP $4.00 CMV $4.00 MB
1969 LIGHTS & SHADOWS SAMPLES
Each sample has both fragrances. Box of 10 sample packets. CMV 50c each

AVON FACIAL SETS

WARNING!! Grading condition is paramount on sets.
CMV can vary 50% on grade.
Refer to page 5 on Grading.

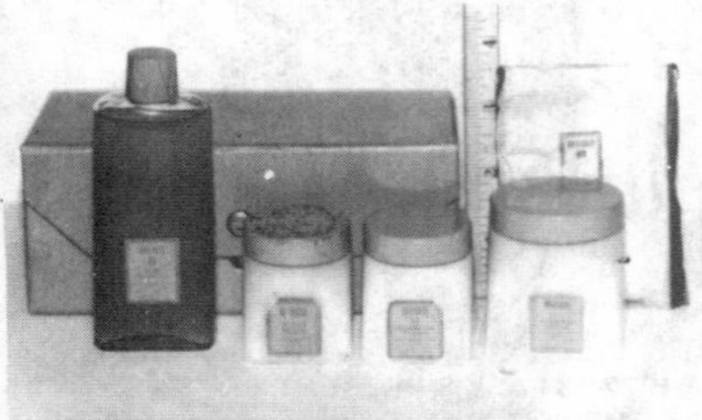

1937-38 FACIAL SET
Green box contains choice of 2 oz. bottle of Skin Freshener or Astringent, green caps, 2 oz. jar of Cleansing Cream, 1 oz. jar of Tissue Cream and Ariel or Vernafleur Face Powder. C.M.V. $65.00 M.B. O.S.P. $1.68

1941-48 FACIAL SET
Green box contains jar of Cleansing Cream, Foundation Cream, Night Cream with green lids. Skin Freshener, 2 oz. green cap & box of Face Powder, blue & white feather design, 2 packs of Avon Facial Tissues. O.S.P. $1.89 C.M.V. $50.00 M.B.

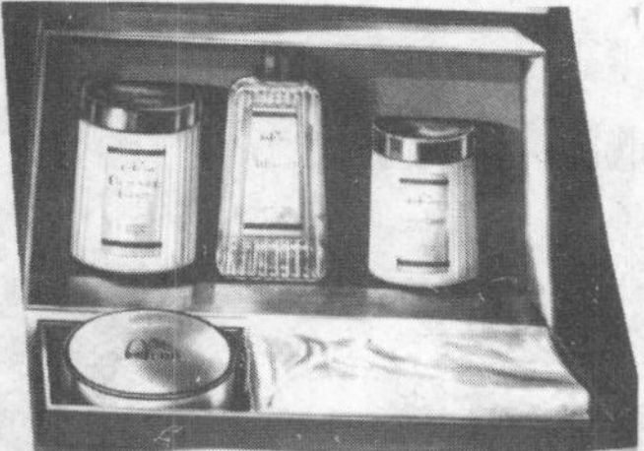

1934-36 FACIAL SET
Silver & blue box contains 2 oz. jar of cleansing cream & 1 oz. jar of tissue cream, 2 bottles of astringent, silver box of Ariel face powder, package of tissues. O.S.P. $1.68 C.M.V. $110.00 M.B.

1938-40 FACIAL SET
Green box holds 4 oz. bottles of Astringent & Lotus Cream, jars of Tissue Cream & Cleansing Cream & box of Face Powder in Ariel or Cotillion. O.S.P. $1.89 C.M.V. $65.00 M.B.

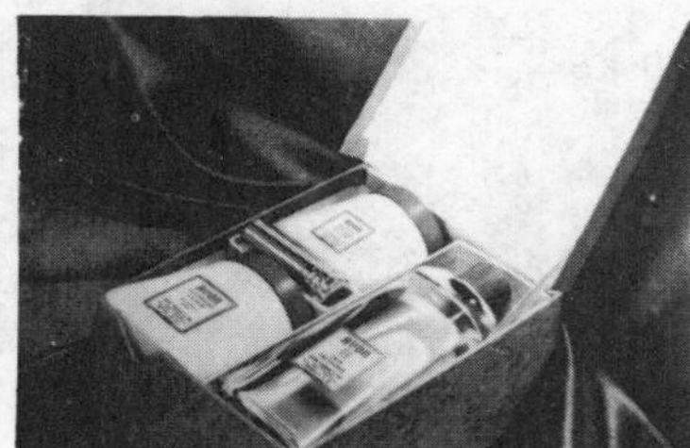

1949-54 FACIAL SET FOR DRY SKIN - Green box contains Fluffy Cleansing Cream, Skin Freshener, Special Dry Skin Cream & Lipstick.
SAME SET FOR OILY SKIN - Contained liquefying Cleansing Cream, Astringent, Night Cream & Lipstick. O.S.P. $3.39 ea. set. C.M.V. $50.00 M.B. ea. set.

GOLD BOX SETS

1947-48 GOLD BOX SET
Three 1/8 oz. perfume bottles, gold caps. pink labels. Ballad, Garden of Love, Cotillion. O.S.P. $2.50 C.M.V. $80.00 M.B.

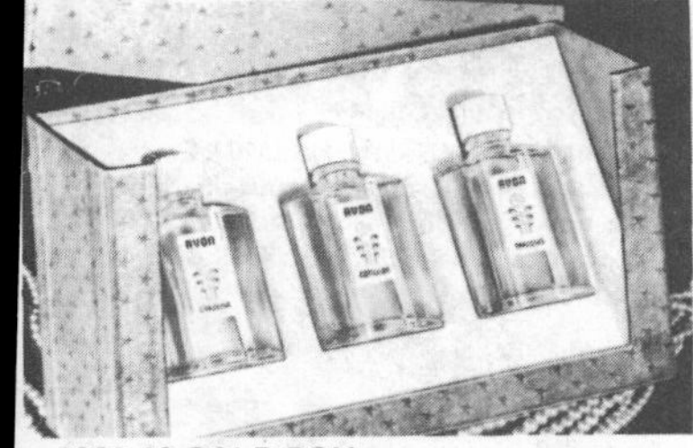

1939-40 GOLD BOX
Gold open front box holds 3 bottles of perfume in Gardenia, Cotillion, Narcissus, or Trailing Arbutus, white plastic caps on all. O.S.P. $1.25 C.M.V. $85.00 M.B.

1944 GOLD BOX
Ribbons & flower design box holds three 1/8 oz. perfumes in Trailing Arbutus, Cotillion & Gardenia. O.S.P. $1.50 C.M.V. $85.00 M.B.

1945-46 GOLD BOX
Pink & white box holds three 1/8 oz. bottles in Crimson Carnation, Gardenia, & Cotillion perfume. O.S.P. $1.50 C.M.V. $80.00 M.B.

1933-36 GOLD BOX SET
Gold box contained three ½ oz. bottles of Verna Fleur, Ariel, 391, Bolero or Gardenia. Black caps. O.S.P. $1.46 C.M.V. $125.00 M.B.

1937-38 GOLD BOX SET
Gold box holds three 1/8 oz. bottles of Cotillion, Narcissus & Gardenia perfumes. O.S.P. $1.25 C.M.V. $80.00 M.B.

1949 GOLD BOX SET
Turquoise plastic bottom with gold insert, clear plastic lid contains three 1 dram bottles of Cotillion, Flowertime & Golden Promise perfumes. All have gold caps and labels. O.S.P. $2.25 C.M.V. $80.00 M.B.

1941-44 GOLD BOX SET
Pink & gold box contains 1/8 oz. perfumes in Gardenia, Cotillion, & Trailing Arbutus, white caps, pink & gold box. O.S.P. $1.35 C.M.V. $85.00 M.B.

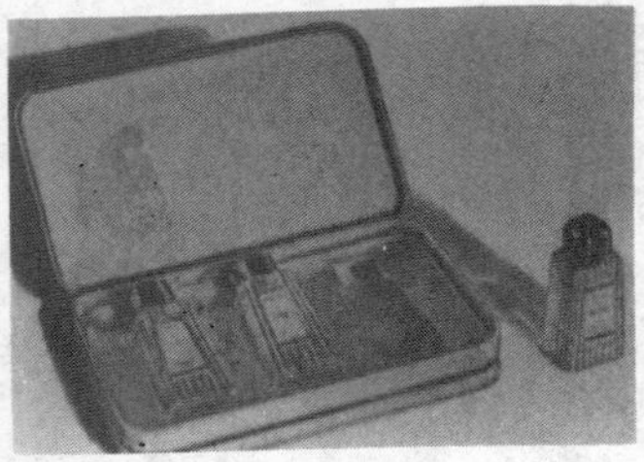

1932 GOLD BOX SET
Metal gold with black strips . Can holds 3½ oz. ribbed glass bottles of 391, Ariel, and Vernafleur perfume. All have black octagonal caps. This is the same metal can as the 1925-30 manicure set. O.S.P. $1.40 C.M.V. $135.00

MAKE-UP ENSEMBLE SETS

1952-53 MAKE-UP ENSEMBLE
Turquoise & gold box holds gold compact, lipstick & face powder or powder pak. OSP $2.75 CMV $30.00 MB.

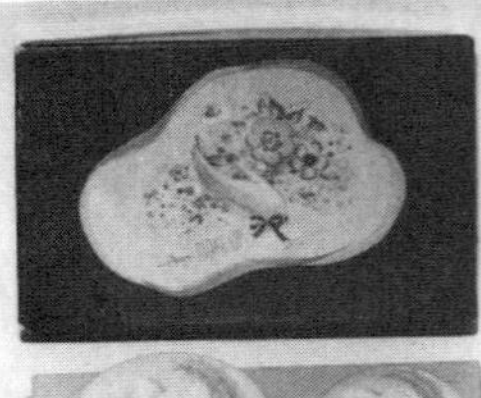

1943-44 MAKE-UP ENSEMBLE
Blue & pink box holds feathered box of face powder, rouge & plastic or card-board lipstick. OSP $1.75 CMV $40.00 MB.

1939-40 MAKE-UP EMSEMBLE
Box holds can of face powder in choice of Cotillion, Ariel, or Vernafleur, and table rouge in green and gold boxes. Lipstick in green and gold. OSP $1.40 CMV $37.00 MB.

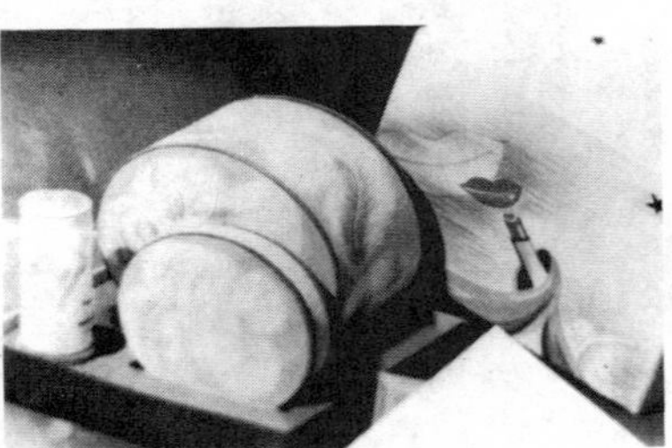

1945 MAKE-UP ENSEMBLE
Lipstick designed box holds feather design face powder, lipstick & rouge. Also came with metal bamboo lipstick. OSP $1.75 CMV $37.00 MB.

1949-51 MAKE-UP ENSEMBLE
Blue, pink & white box contains face powder, gold lipstick & rouge. Eiffel Tower on box. O.S.P. $2.35 C.M.V. $30.00 M.B.

1941-42 MAKE-UP ENSEMBLE
Contains face powder, rouge in feather design boxes, turquoise & gold lipstick. OSP $1.52 CMV $37.00 MB

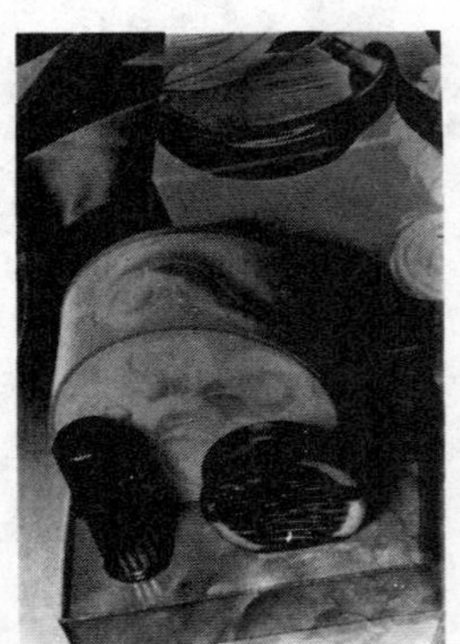

1946 Only - MAKE-UP ENSEMBLE
Pink & blue feather design box holds gold bamboo lipstick, rouge & box of face powder. O.S.P. $2.25 C.M.V. $40.00 M.B.

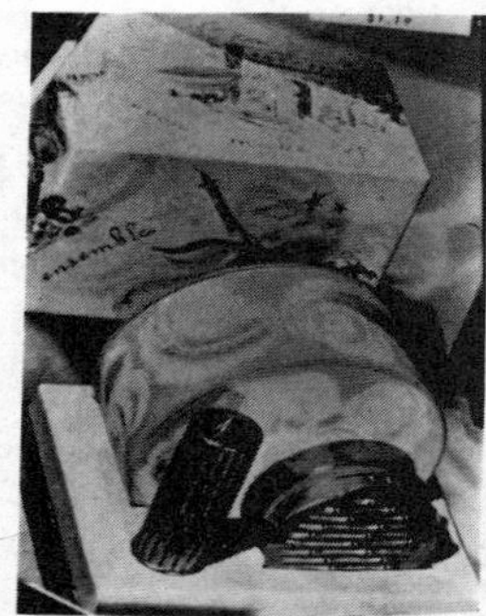

1947 Only - MAKE-UP ENSEMBLE
White, pink box with Eiffel Tower on box holds pink & blue feather design powder with bamboo lipstick & rouge. O.S.P. $2.35 C.M.V. $40.00 M.B.
1948 MAKE-UP ENSEMBLE - Same except lipstick gold with swirl design around bottom. O.S.P. $2.35 C.M.V. $40.00 M.B.

MANICURE SETS

WARNING!! Grading condition is paramount on sets.
CMV can vary 50% on grade.
Refer to page 5 on Grading.

957 COLOR CHANGE
ink, turquoise & gold design on white lastic case, holds 2 oz. bottle, white cap, ily nail polish remover & top coat & nail olish. O.S.P. $1.95 C.M.V. $18.00 M.B.

1950-52 DELUXE MANICURE SET
Black & red box holds bottles of cuticle softener, nail polish, oily polish remover & Cling Tite. O.S.P. $2.50 C.M.V. $25.00 M.B.

1958 COLOR BAR SET
White plastic tray holds 4 bottles of nail polish or silvery base coat, top coat, and cuticle softener. Mix or match. O.S.P. $3.00 C.M.V. $15.00 complete. $18.00 M.B.

1955 LITTLE FAVORITE SET
Plastic turquoise case holds bottles of nail polish, oily polish remover & cuticle softener, all have white caps. O.S.P. $1.50 C.M.V. $18.00 M.B.

1956-57 POLKA DOT
Red & white plastic case holds ½ oz. bottles of nail polish, top coat & 2 oz. oily polish remover. O.S.P. $1.69 C.M.V. $18.00 M.B.

1950-51 DELUXE MANICURE SET
Black & red box holds three ½ oz. bottles nail polish, ½ oz. bottle of clear nail polish, ½ oz. bottle cuticle softener, 1 orange stick, 1 white nail white pencil & booklet. O.S.P. $2.75 C.M.V. $25.00 M.B.

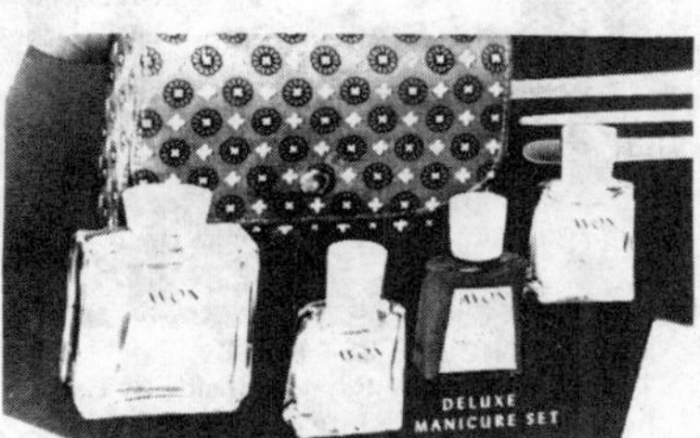

1953-54 MANICURE SET DELUXE
Gray case holds ½ oz. bottles of cuticle softener, nail polish, double coat, 2 oz. oily polish remover, white caps on all. O.S.P. $2.65 C.M.V. $22.00 M.B.

1956-57 MANICURE SET DELUXE
Pink plastic container holds ½ oz. bottles of polish remover, cuticle softener, silvery base, top coat & polish. All have white caps. O.S.P. $3.25 C.M.V. $25.00 M.B.

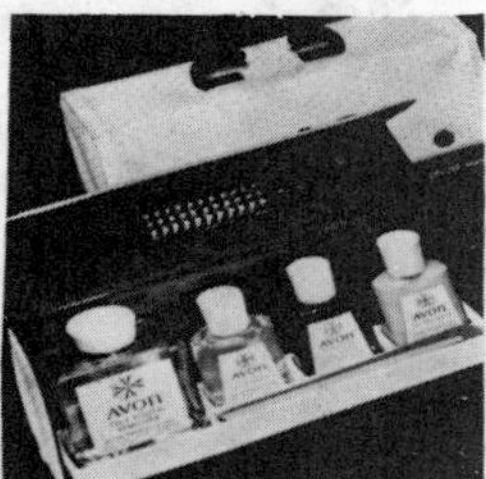

1955 DELUXE MANICURE SET
White plastic with gold dots, red lining holds Oily Nail Polish Remover, Cuticle Softener, Silvery Base, choice of Nail Enamel, all white caps & Emery Board. O.S.P. $2.95 C.M.V. $25.00 M.B.

1950-52 AVON THREESOME
Red & white box holds 3 nail polish bottles with white caps. OSP $1.29 CMV $28.00 MB.

1944-49 MANICURE SET DELUXE
Black & red bag holds 5 bottles of nail polish, top coat, nail polsh base, cuticle softener, oily polish remover. All have black or turquoise caps. White nail white pencil, orange stick & 2 nail files. O.S.P. $3.00 C.M.V. $45.00 M.B.

1949 MANICURE SET DELUXE
Same black & red bag only holds 4 bottles with turquoise caps in Cling Tite nail polish, nail polish remover & cuticle softener. O.S.P. $2.50 C.M.V. $40.00 M.B.

1960-61 MANICURE PETITE
Black vinyl case holds top coat, oily polish remover & cream or pearl nail polish. White caps. O.S.P. $2.98 C.M.V. $12.00 M.B.

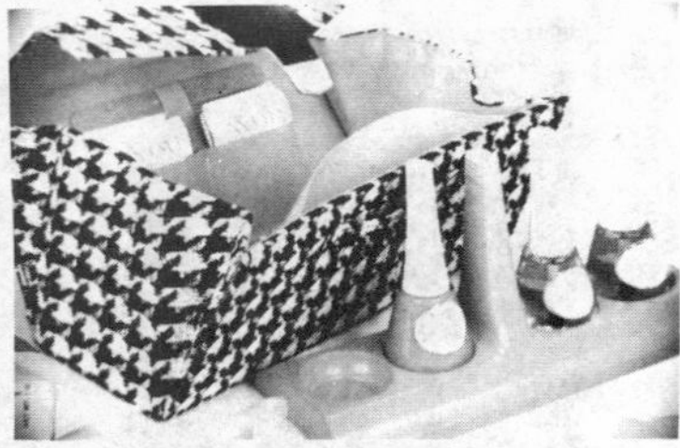

1968-69 MANICURE BEAUTI-KIT
Black & white vinyl case holds ½ oz. bottles of nail enamels, 1 oz. plastic tube cuticle conditioner, 1 oz. plastic tube cuticle remover, 10 enamel remover pads, ½ oz. bottle of enamel set, long-last top coat & emery boards. Red plastic tray. O.S.P. $12.00 CMV $12.00 MB.

1942-43 AVON THREESOME
Pink & white box has 3 small bottles with turquoise caps of cream polish, nail polish base & oily polish remover. Comes with story booklet on hands. OSP 85c CMV $40.00 MB.

1940 MANICURE SET NO. 2
Brown case holds fingernail file, orange stick, white Avon nail white pencil, ½ oz. bottles of clear or cream nail polish, polis remover, cuticle softener & cuticle oil. Turquoise or black caps. O.S.P. $2.25 C.M.V. $55.00 M.B.

1941-43 MANICURE SET DELUXE
Same set as above only name changed. O.S.P. $2.25 C.M.V. $55.00 M.B.

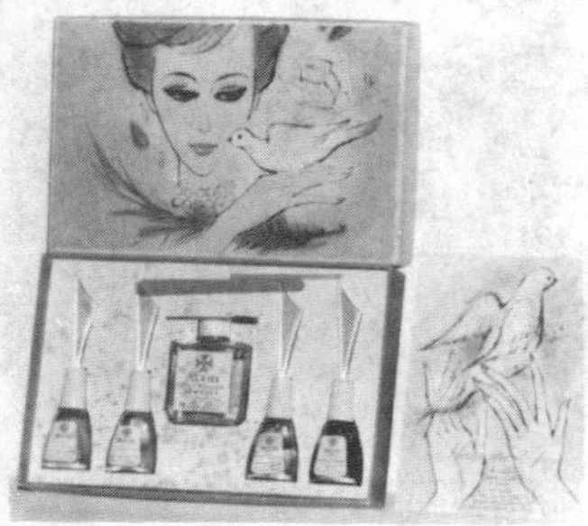

1959 MANICURE DELUXE
Box holds cuticle softener, silvery base, oily polish remover, top coat & cream polish. O.S.P. $3.95 C.M.V. $20.00 M.B.

1936-37 MANICURE SET NO. 1
Green & white box has bottles of nail polish & polish remover with 2 rolls of cotton and booklet "What Story do your Hands Tell?" O.S.P. 52¢ C.M.V. $45.00 M.B.

1938-49 NAIL POLISH THREESOME
Turquoise & white box holds ½ oz. double coat, ½ oz. nail polish, ½ oz. oily polish remover, 2 rolls cotton & booklet. O.S.P. 85¢ C.M.V. $42.50

1960-61 DELUXE MANICURE
Black vinyl case holds silvery base, oily polish remover, cuticle softener, top coat & cream nail polish. All have white caps. O.S.P. $4.98 C.M.V. $15.00 M.B.

1937 MANICURE SET NO. 2
Turquoise & white lid, gold inside box holds cans of nail white & nail cream, bottles of polish remover, cuticle softener & nail polish, orange stich, nail file, 3 cotton rolls in glass tube and booklet "What Story do your Hands Tell?" O.S.P. $1.67 C.M.V. $80.00 M.B.

1945-50 NAIL POLISH TWOSOME
Turquoise box holds 1/2 bottles of cream polish and cuticle softener and small 30 page booklet. O.S.P. 85¢ C.M.V. $30.00 M.B.

1948-49 AVON THREESOME
Red, white & green tray with green box holds three ½ oz. bottles with white caps for oily polish remover, clingtite & nail polish. OSP $1.19 CMV $28.00 MB

1938-39 MANICURE SET NO. 2
Brown case holds orange stick, nail file, can of nail white, nail cream, bottles of cuticle softener, cream polish & polish remover. O.S.P. $1.89 C.M.V. $55.00 M.B.

1966 MANICURE KIT
Gold & white plastic case holds 1 bottle of nail enamel, long last base coat, enamel set, cuticle remover cream, nail beauty, 10 enamel remover pads, emery board & orange stick. OSP $8.50 CMV $15.00 complete set. MB.

938-49 MANICURE SET NO. 1
'urquoise box holds ½ oz. nail polish and ream polish, 2 cotton rolls and booklet 'What Story Do Your Hands Tell?". CPC n box. 2 different boxes. Some say nanicure set No. 1 at top of box and some t bottom of box. Add $5.00 for CPC box)SP 52c CMV $30.00 MB.

1938-49 AVON TWOSOME
Turquoise and white box holds ½ oz. of nail polish & ½ oz. of cuticle softener, 2 cotton rolls and booklet "What Story do your Hands Tell?" C.P.C. on box in 1938-39. Add $5.00 for C.P.C. box. O.S.P. 52¢ C.M.V. $30.00

1930 MANICURE SET NO. 1
Silver box holds 2 small bottles of nail polish & polish remover. Black caps. O.S.P. 52¢ C.M.V. $60.00 M.B.

1941-44 ROYAL WINDSOR SET
Blue box holds choice 1/2 oz. nail polish base and 1/2 oz. cream polish or 1/2 oz. to top coat. O.S.P. 52¢ C.M.V. $15.00 M.B. as shown.

1931-36 MANICURE SET NO. 2
Silver box holds 3 small ribbed glass bottles of polish remover, nail polish, cuticle softener. All have black caps. Two small silver cans of nail white & nail cream, 1 fingernail file & booklet "What Story Do Your Hands Tell?" OSP $1.67 CMV $110.00 MB. Same set also came with no stripe on box as shown & 2 different linings inside box as shown.

1974 NAIL BUFFER SET
Box holds .25 oz. tube of nail buffing cream & nail buffer. OSP $3.00 CMV $1.50 MB

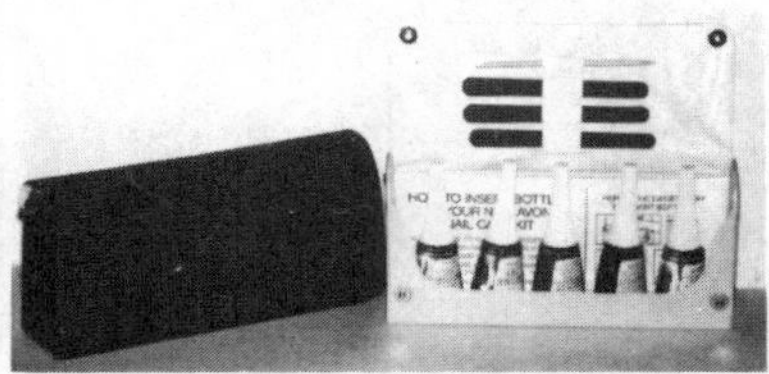

LEFT 1979-80 NAIL CARE KIT
Blue plastic kit holds 5 bottles of Avon nail care products. 3 emery boards & wood cuticle stick. SSP $6.50 CMV $5.00 MB.
RIGHT 1978-79 NAIL CARE KIT
Same as above only beige color aligator grain case. CMV $5.00 MB

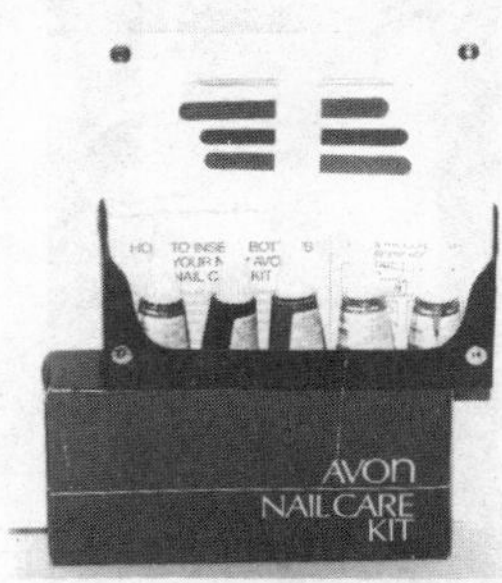

1979-80 NAIL CARE KIT
Blue plastic kit holds 5 bottles of nail care products & 3 emery boards & 1 cuticle stick. SSP $6.99 CMV $5.00 MB complete.

PERFUME PAIR SETS

1962 PERFUMED PAIR
Box holds 2¾ oz. can of Perfumed Talc & Perfumed Soap in Somewhere, Topaze, Cotillion, Persian Wood, Here's My Heart & To A Wild Rose. O.S.P. $1.18 C.M.V. $15.00 M.B.

1963 PERFUMED PAIR
Gold & white box with perfumed talc & bar of soap in To A Wild Rose, Here's My Heart, Persian Wood, Topaze, Somewhere & Cotillion. O.S.P. $1.18 C.M.V. $14.00 M.B. each set.

1964 PERFUMED PAIR
Box holds perfumed talc & soap in Here's My Heart, Persian Wood, To A Wild Rose, O.S.P. $1.18. Somewhere, Topaze, Cotillion, O.S.P. $1.28 C.M.V. $14.00 M.B.

1966 PERFUMED PAIR
Brown, gold & white box holds 2¾ oz. perfumed talc & wrapped soap in Unforgettable, Rapture, Occur! Cotillion, Somewhere, Topaze, Here's My Heart, To A Wild Rose & Wishing. O.S.P. $1.39 C.M.V. $11.00 M.B.

1970 PERFUMED PAIR
Each box contains perfumed talc & matching soap in Hawaiian White Ginger, Honeysuckle, Elusive, Blue Lotus, Bird of Paradise & Charisma. O.S.P. $2.25 C.M.V. $6.00 M.B.

1969 PERFUMED PAIR
Box holds perfumed talc & bar of soap in Charisma, Brocade, Blue Lotus, White Ginger, Honeysuckle & To A Wild Rose. OSP $2.00 CMV $7.00 MB.

1968 PERFUMED PAIR
Box holds 2¾ oz. can of talc & matching soap in Brocade, Regence, Unforgettable, Hawaiian White Ginger, Honeysuckle & To A Wild Rose. O.S.P. $1.79 C.M.V. $8.00 M.B.

1967 PERFUMED PAIR
Box contains perfumed talc & matching soap. Comes in Unforgettable, Here's My Heart, To A Wild Rose, Somewhere, Topaze, Cotillion, Rapture & Occur! O.S.P. $1.49 C.M.V. $10.00 M.B.

1974-75 PERFUMED PAIR
1.5 oz. perfumed talc & .5 oz. cologne. Choice of Roses, Roses, Unforgettable Cotillion, Sonnet and Moonwind. Cam in 2 different boxes. O.S.P. $3.00 C.M. $4.00 M.B.

PURSE SETS-WOMEI

1949 EVENING CHARM SET
Black purse holds gold compact, lipstic & 1 dram bottle in gold metal case wit Golden Promise perfume. Also came w beige purse. OSP $10.00 CMV $40.00 M.B.

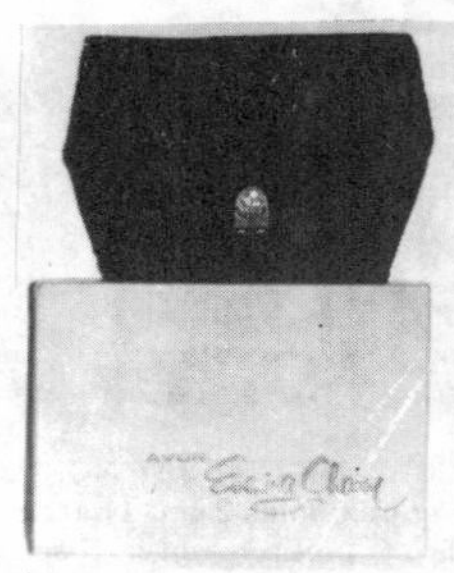

1953 EVENING CHARM PURSE
Avon box holds black velvet purse. Av on tag inside. C.M.V. $15.00 M.B. pur only $6.00

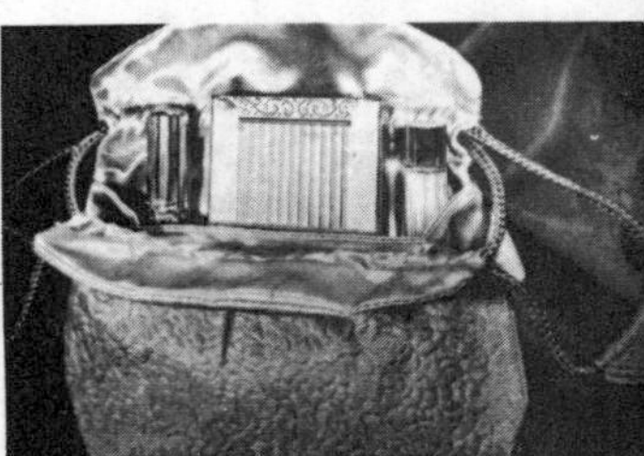

1952 EVENING CHARM SET
Gold purse holds 1 dram perfume, lipstic & gold deluxe compact. O.S.P. $10.95 CMV $30.00 MB.

1953 EVENING CHARM SET
Choice of black velvet bag or brocade bag. Came with 1 dram embossed top perfume, gold deluxe compact & gold jeweled lipstick. O.S.P. $10.95 CMV $30.00 MB

1955-56 DRESS UP SET
Black & gold reversible purse holds 1 dram perfume, gold compact & gold jeweled lipstick. OSP $10.95 CMV $30.00 complete MB.

1964 PURSE COMPANIONS SET
Brocade beige purse with pockets to hold floral fashion lipstick & cameo compact. O.S.P. $6.50 C.M.V. $17.00 M.B.
Same set in 1965 only with cameo lipstick. OSP $6.50 CMV $15.00 MB.

1961 CHAMPAGNE MOOD SET
Gold & white sequin bag holds deluxe lipstick & compact. O.S.P. $6.50 CMV $20.00 MB.

1964 BEAUTY BOUND SET
Black leather handbag holds deluxe compact & lipstick & choice of creme rollette. O.S.P. $14.95 C.M.V. $18.00 M.B.

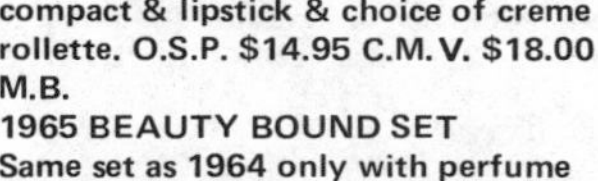

1965 BEAUTY BOUND SET
Same set as 1964 only with perfume rollette instead of creme rollette. O.S.P. $14.95 C.M.V. $18.00 M.B.

1957 MAKE-UP TUCK IN SET
Black striped purse contains pink powder-pak, liquid rouge & lipstick. O.S.P. $3.50 CMV $25.00 MB.

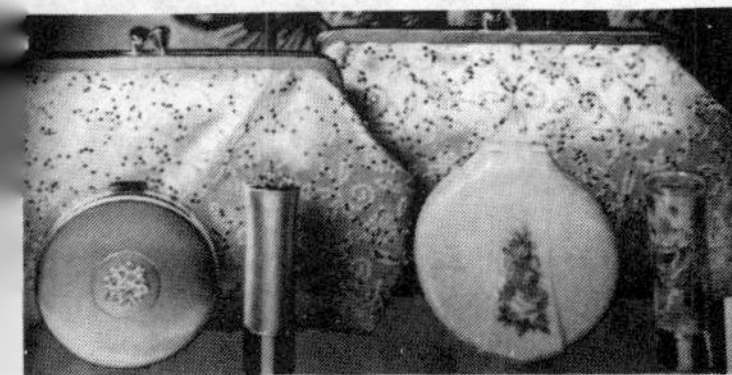

1963 MODERN MOOD SET
Gold & white purse holds deluxe compact & lipstick. On left - O.S.P. $7.00 C.M.V. $17.50 MB Or pearl pink compact & floral fashion lipstick, O.S.P. $4.75 C.M.V. $15.00 M.B.

1954 EVENING CHARM SET
Choice of black velvet or white brocade purse with 1 dram perfume, gold deluxe compact & gold jeweled lipstick. Both have zipper tops. OSP $12.50 CMV $30.00 MB.

1960 GOING STEADY SET
Gray bag holds white compact & lipstick. Purse does not say Avon on it. O.S.P. $3.50 C.M.V. $15.00 M.B.

1955 DRESS UP SET
Black & gold purse with gold satin lining holds 1 dram perfume, jeweled lipstick & deluxe gold compact. O.S.P. $10.95 CMV $32.50 MB.

1965 Only - EVENING LIGHTS PURSE SET - White box with gold purse came with Deluxe compact, lipstick & perfume rollette. OSP $14.95 CMV $20.00 MB.

1958 ON THE AVENUE SET
Black purse holds top style lipstick & top style compact with Here's My Heart or Persian Wood spray perfume. O.S.P. $12.95 C.M.V. $30.00 M.B.

1956 AROUND TOWN SET
Black leather bag holds gold lipstick, powder compact, 1 dram perfume & cologne stick. O.S.P. $12.50 C.M.V. $35.00 M.B.

1951 EVENING CHARM SET
Brocade hand bag, or black satin bag with gold trim. CAme with same contents as 1953 Evening Charm Set listed. OSP $10.95 CMV purse only $6.00 complete set MB $30.00.

1978-79 POLISHED GOLD EVENING BAG
Gold plastic purse. Does not say Avon on it. Comes in white Avon box. SSP $6.50 CMV $4.00 MB.

1959 PAK-PURSE SET
White leather purse holds lipstick, 1 dram perfume & compact. O.S.P. $8.95 C.M.V. $20.00 M.B.

1960 HIGH STYLE SET
Blue satin lined bag holds gold deluxe compact & lipstick. O.S.P. $5.95 C.M.V. $15.00 M.B.

1962 DELUXE TWIN SET
Blue clutch bag holds deluxe compact & lipstick. OSP $7.50 CMV $16.00 MB.

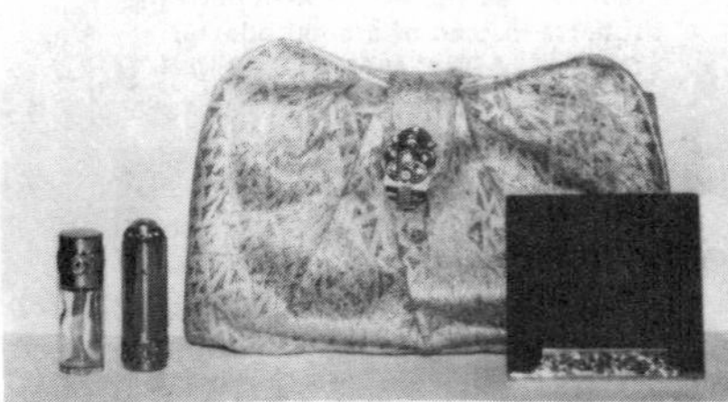
1955 EVENING CHARM SET
Gold brocade purse. Has Avon tag inside. Also came in matching black satin bag. Holds 2 dram embossed top perfume, gold deluxe compact, and gold jeweled lipstick. OSP $12.50 CMV $30.00 MB.

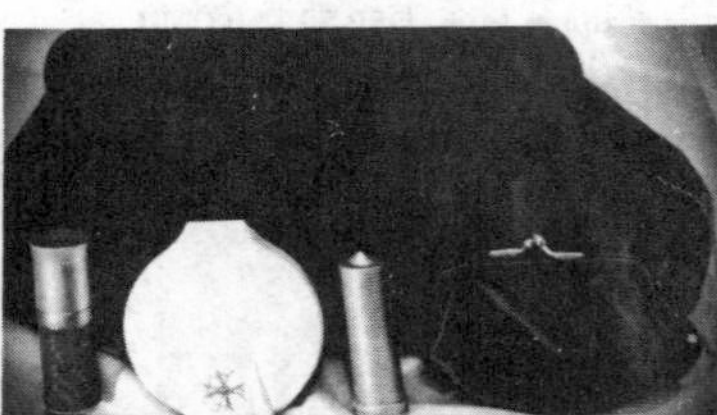
1957 IN STYLE SET
Black satin purse holds Persian Wood Spray perfume, white compact, gold lipstick & black coin purse. O.S.P. $12.95 C.M.V. $32.00 M.B.

1956 LADY FAIR SET
Gold box holds 1 dram perfume, gold lipstick & red leather billfold. OSP $5.95 CMV $35.00 MB.

C.P.C. SOAPS

All Soaps Must Be Mint For CMV

1906 JAPAN TOILET SOAP
Box of 3 cakes. O.S.P. 25¢ C.M.V. $85.00 M.B.

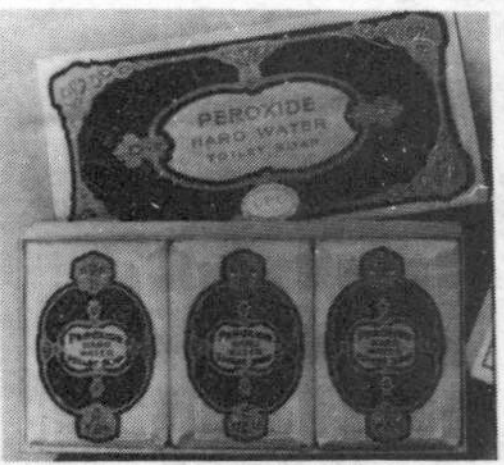

1915 PEROXIDE TOILET SOAP
Box of 3 cakes. O.S.P. 50¢ C.M.V. $75.00 M.B.

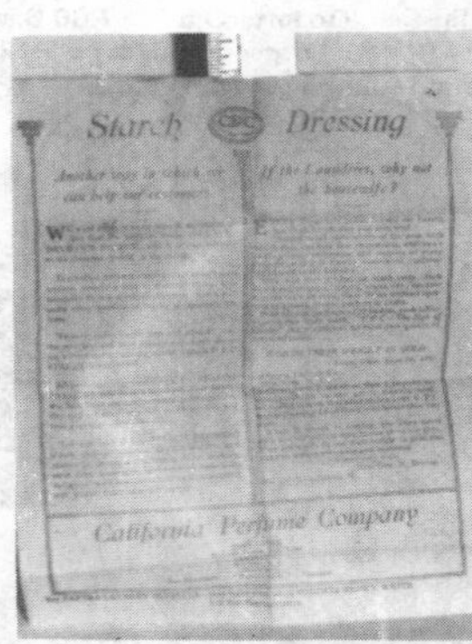

1911 STARCH DRESSING DIRECTI SHEET
Came in box of Starch Dressing. Print on both sides. C.M.V. $5.00 mint

1906 ALMOND, BUTTERMILK & CUCUMBER SOAP
3 bars in yellow box with pink flowers on box. O.S.P. 40¢ C.M.V. $85.00 M.B.

1920 ABC TOILET SOAP
Yellow, pink & green box & wrapping holds 3 bars soap. O.S.P. 40¢ C.M.V. $75.00 M.B.

1925 ALMOND BOUQUET TOILET SOAP
Yellow, green & pink wrapping around 3 bars of soap. Soap is embossed. O.S.P. 30¢ C.M.V. $75.00 M.B.

1906 ALMOND MEAL TOILET SOAP
Box of 3 cakes. O.S.P. 25¢ C.M.V. $85.00 M.B.

1931-36 CASTILE IMPORTED SOAP
Box holds 2 silver wrapped bars. O.S.P. 60¢ C.M.V. $40.00 M.B.

1908 CPC IMPORTED CASTILE SOAP
5 oz. cake. First came out about 1893. O.S.P. 25¢ C.M.V. $50.00 M.B.

1925 CASTILE SOAP
One bar of soap. O.S.P. 33¢ C.M.V. $40.00 M.B.

1931-36 CASTILE IMPORTED SOAP
Box holds 2 silver wrapped bars. O.S.P. 60¢ C.M.V. $45.00 M.B. Same box also came with 1 large bar. O.S.P. 33¢ C.M.V. $35.00 M.B.

1936-43 CASTILE SOAP
2 white bars wrapped in silver paper & turquoise box. O.S.P. 62¢. C.M.V. $20.00 M.B.

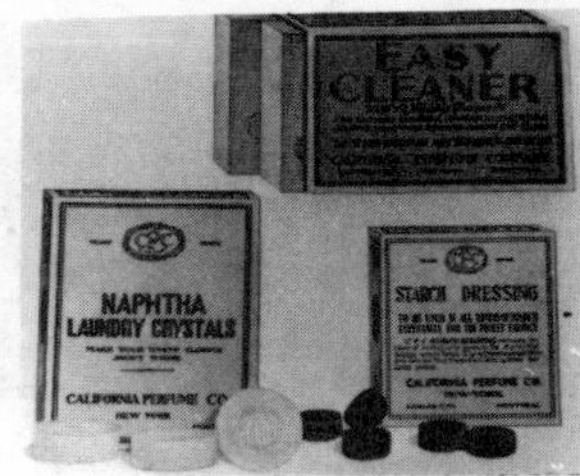

1925 EASY CLEANER
Box of 2½ lb. cakes. OSP 33c CMV $40.00 MB.

1925 NAPTHA LAUNDRY CRYSTALS
2 different box labels. 1 box has blue letters & 1 box has green letters. 13 white crystals in box, with instruction sheet. CMV $35.00 MB OSP 33c.

1925 STARCH DRESSING
25 tablets in box. Each tablet is marked CPC & has instruction sheet in box. OSP 33c CMV $35.00 MB.

1915 CPC STARCH DRESSING
Paper box holds 25 blue tablets. O.S.P. 25¢ C.M.V. $40.00 M.B.

1915 CPC NAPTHA LAUNDRY CRYSTALS
13 white tablets, paper box. O.S.P. 25¢ C.M.V. $40.00 M.B.

1896 SAVONA BOUQUET SOAP
Maroon colored box & wrapping. 2 bars. O.S.P. 50¢ C.M.V. $90.00 M.B.

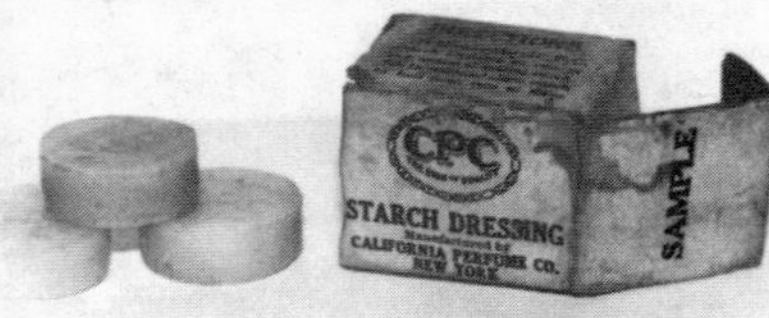

1915 STARCH DRESSING SAMPLE
1" size box holds 3 samples. CMV $40.00 MB.

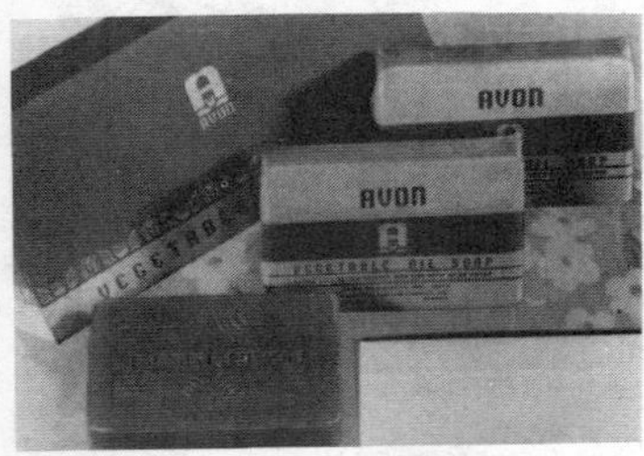

1936-38 VEGETABLE OIL SOAP
3 light orange colored bars wrapped in turquoise & white paper & box. O.S.P. 46¢ C.M.V. $45.00 M.B.

1936-43 SAVONA BOUQUET TOILET SOAP - Turquoise & white box holds 6 square bars. O.S.P. 72¢ C.M.V. $55.00 M.B.

1932-36 SAVONA BOUQUET TOILET SOAP - Box of 6 bars. O.S.P. 50¢ C.M.V. $60.00 M.B.

Left - 1936 SAVONA BOUQUET SOAP SAMPLES - C.M.V. $15.00 each.
Right - 1929 SAVONA BOUQUET TOILET SOAP SAMPLES - C.M.V. $15.00 each.

1931-36 VEGETABLE OIL SOAP
Box of 3 bars. O.S.P. 45¢ C.M.V. $50.00 M.B.

1956-62 DR. ZABRISKIES SOAP
Turquoise box holds 1 green bar. OSP 43c CMV $20.00 MB.

DR. ZABRISKIES SOAP

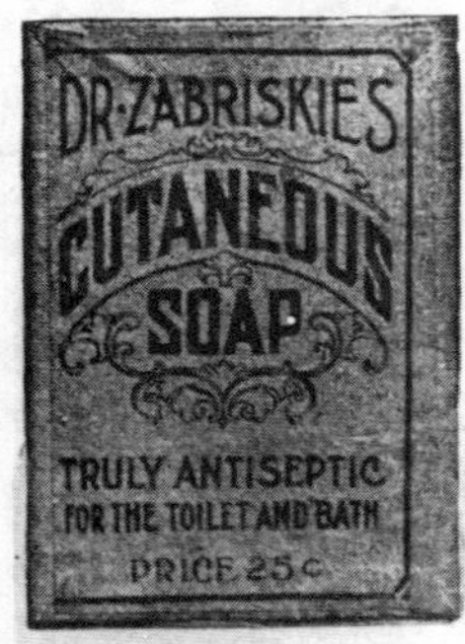

1893 DR. ZABRISKIES CUTANEOUS SOAP - 1 bar in box. O.S.P. 24¢ C.M.V. $60.00 M.B.

1920 DR. ZABRISKIES CUTANEOUS SOAP - Green cake & box. O.S.P. 24¢ C.M.V. $40.00 M.B.

1915 DR. ZABRISKIES SOAP
Green bar embossed, came in blue box. O.S.P. 25¢ C.M.V. $45.00 M.B.

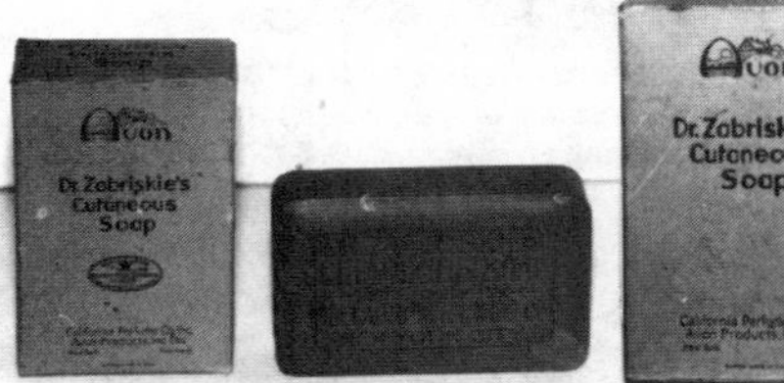

1931-33 DR. ZABRISKIES CUTANEOUS SOAP
Gray box on right holds 1 bar. OSP 31c CMV $30.00 MB.
1933-36 DR. ZABRISKIES SOAP
Gray box holds 1 bar. CPC & Avon on box & soap. 2 different labels on boxes. OSP 33c CMV $30.00 MB.

1936-56 DR. ZABRISKIES CUTANEOUS SOAP - Green bar in turquoise box. O.S.P. 33¢ C.M.V. $20.00 M.B.

1940-47 DR. ZABRISKIES CUTANEOUS SOAP
3 oz. green bar and box. O.S.P. 33¢ C.M.V. $20.00 M.B.

MEN'S SOAP

1963-64 MOST VALUABLE SOAP SET
Yellow box holds 3 yellow bars. O.S.P. $1.35, CMV $25.00 MB

1949-57 SHAVING SOAP
Two bars in green & red box. O.S.P. 59¢ C.M.V. $30.00 M.B.

1978-79 BARBER SHOP DUET MUSTACHE COMB AND SOAP SET
Box holds white bar mans face soap and small brown plastic mustache comb. S.S.P. $3.99, C.M.V. $3.99 M.B. set.

1978-79 ROYAL HEARTS SOAPS
King and queen box holds 2 white bars with King and Queen of Hearts soaps. S.S.P. $4.99 C.M.V. $4.49 M.B.

1978-79 SUITABLY GIFTED SOAP
Blue box holds blue bar that is shaped like a shirt and tie. S.S.P. $4.99, C.M.V. $4.49 M.B.

1977-78 ON DUTY 24 SOAP
Deodorant soap. O.S.P. 3 for 99¢ C.M.V. 35¢ each.

1908 CPC SHAVING SOAP
White bar embossed. Came in yellow box. O.S.P. 20¢ C.M.V. $60.00 M.B.

1930-36 SHAVING SOAP
White bar. O.S.P. 25¢ C.M.V. $30.00 M.B.
1930 STYPTIC PENCIL
O.S.P. 10¢ C.M.V. $5.00 M.B.

1936-49 SHAVING SOAP
Two bars in maroon box, white soap. O.S.P. 31¢ C.M.V. $40.00 in box.

1960-62 CARRIAGE SHOWER SOAP
Red, white & black box contains 6 oz. cake embossed Stage Coach soap on red or white rope. O.S.P. $1.35 C.M.V. $30.00

1961-63 OATMEAL SOAP
Two brown bars. O.S.P. $1.35 C.M.V. $22.00 M.B.

1963-64 OATMEAL SOAP FOR MEN SPICY - Embossed stage coach on brown bar of soap. O.S.P. 39¢ C.M.V. $10.00 in wrapping.

1972-73 SHAMPOO SHOWER SOAP FOR MEN
5 oz. bar on red & black rope. Also came with white rope. Red & black box. OSP $2.50, CMV $6.00 MB.

1966-67 BATH SOAP FOR MEN
2 white soaps with red buttons, silver & white box. OSP $2.50 CMV $22.50 MB.

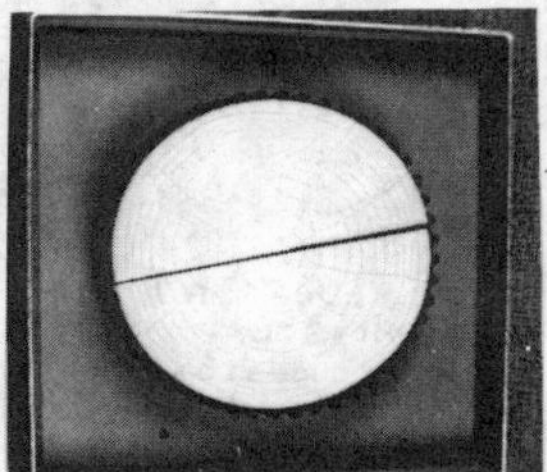

1966-67 LONESOME PINE SOAP
Green & gold box holds woodgrained soap cut in half. OSP $2.00 CMV $20.00 MB.

1975 GOLF BALL SOAPS
3 white soaps in yellow & green box. Spicy scented. O.S.P. $2.00 C.M.V. $4.00 MB.

1975 1928 MODEL 'A' SOAP SET
Two 3 oz. white bars of soap with dark & light blue wrapper & box. O.S.P. $3.00 C.M.V. $4.00 M.B.

WOMEN'S SOAP

ALL SOAPS MUST BE MINT FOR CMV

1978 A TOKEN OF LOVE HOSTESS SOAPS
All three pieces are special occasion fragranced soaps. Light pink outside, dark pink inside soap. O.S.P. $6.00 C.M.V. $6.00 M.B.

1963 SOAP TREASURE
Gold & white box holds 5 bars of perfumed soap in choice of Lilac, Lily of the Valley, Floral, Lemonol, Cotillion, Here's My Heart, Rose Geranium, To A Wild Rose, Royal Jasmine, Persian Wood, Somewhere, Royal Pine & Topaze set. Came with 2 different kinds of soap as shown. O.S.P. $1.95 CMV $22.00 MB set each.

1945-55 FACIAL SOAP
Box holds 2 bars. O.S.P. 89¢ C.M.V. $25.00 M.B.

1978 ANGEL FISH HOSTESS SOAPS
Box holds 3 blue fish soaps. S.S.P. $3.66 C.M.V. $3.50 M.B.

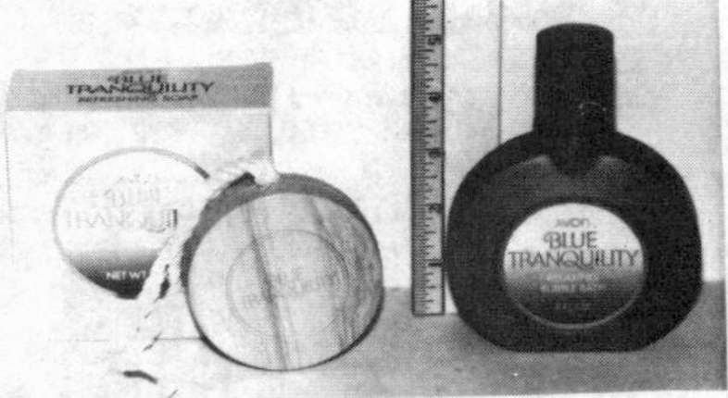

1976 LITTLE CHOIR BOYS HOSTESS SOAPS
Box holds 3 pink soaps. Came in light or dark pink. S.S.P. $2.88 C.M.V. $4.00

1979-80 PERFUMED SOAP CHRISTMAS WRAP
Single fragrance bar in red - Tempo or Ariane, Bronze - Candid, Blue - Emprise or Unspoken. SSP 99c CMV 75c mint.

1978-80 BLUE TRANQUILITY REFRESHING SOAP
5 oz. blue embossed bar on white rope. Blue box. SSP $2.99 CMV $2.50 MB.

1978-80 BLUE TRANQUILITY RELAXING BUBBLE BATH
8 oz. blue plastic bottle. Came without a box. SSP $2.99 CMV 25c.

1955-61 FACIAL SOAP
Turquoise box holds 2 bars. O.S.P. 89¢ C.M.V. $18.00 M.B.

1977-78 WINTER FROLICS HOSTESS SOAPS
Came with 2 Festive Fragrance scented soaps with long lasting decals. 3 oz. each O.S.P. $5.50 C.M.V. $5.00 M.B.

1977 MERRY ELFKINS GUEST SOAPS
Box holds 3 green soaps. O.S.P. $5.50 C.M.V. $5.50 M.B.

1978-80 COUNTRY GARDEN SOAPS
Box holds 2 Avon bar flower soaps with 2 different flower decals. S.S.P. $3.99, C.M.V. $3.99 M.B.

1978-79 CHRISTMAS CAROLLERS SOAPS
Box holds 2 turquoise color carollers soaps. S.S.P. $2.99, C.M.V. $2.99 M.B.

1978-79 TREASURE BASKET GUEST SOAPS
Silver basket holds 2 yellow & 2 pink tulip soaps. S.S.P. $8.98 C.M.V.$8.00M.B.

1976-1876 WINTERSCAPES HOSTESS SOAPS
Two Currier & Ives scenes soaps. Came in Special Occasion fragrance. O.S.P. $5.50 C.M.V. $5.50 M.B.

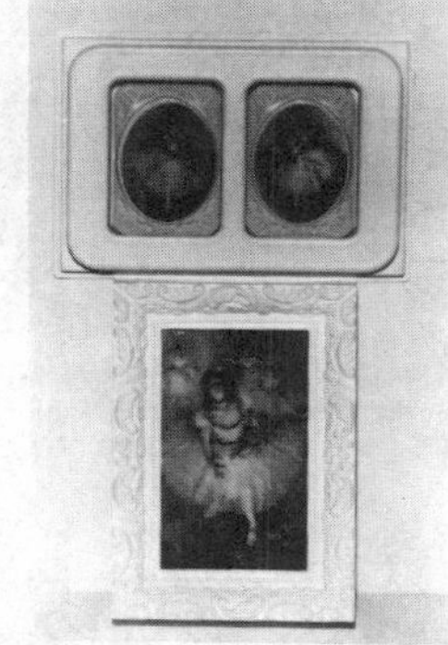

1978-80 BALLET PICTURE SOAPS
White plastic box and lid holds 2 blue picture decal bars of soap. S.S.P. $6.99, C.M.V. $6.99 M.B.

1977-78 TENDER BLOSSOMS GUEST TOWELS & SOAPS
Came with 12 paper hand towels & three special occasion fragranced soaps. O.S.P. $6.50 C.M.V. $6.00 M.B.

1977 PERFUMED SOAP HOLIDAY WRAPPING
Came in Charisma & Touch of Roses in Red poinsetta wrap. Sonnet & Field Flowers in green, and Moonwind and Bird of Paradise in blue. S.S.P. $1.25 C.M.V. $1.00 ea.

1977-78 SUMMER BUTTERFLIES HOSTESS SOAPS
Two scented soaps with long lasting decals. 3 oz. each. O.S.P. $5.50 C.M.V. $3.50 M.B.

1975-76 PICK-A-BERRY STRAWBERRY SOAPS & CONTAINER - 4½" high red plastic with 6 strawberry scented soaps. O.S.P. $6.00 C.M.V. $6.00 M.B.

1973 MELLON BALL GUEST SOAP
1 oz. honey-dew & cantelope colored balls inside cantelope shaped plastic container S.S.P. $4.00 C.M.V. $6.00 M.B.

1974-75 RECIPE TREASURES
5 orange scented soaps in yellow & orange decorative metal file box. O.S.P. $5.00 C.M.V. $6.00 M.B.
1974-75 COUNTRY KITCHEN SOAP DISH & SOAP - Red plastic scooped dish contains 5 green apple fragranced soaps. OSP $6.00 CMV $7.00 MB.

1972-75 HIDDEN TREASURE SOAP
Two 3 oz. turquoise soaps with pearl colored & shaped 1/8 oz. bottle of perfume. Came in Bird of Paradise only. S.S.P. $5.00 CMV $8.00 MB

1975-76 PETIT FOURS GUEST SOAPS
Eight 1 oz. soaps, 3 pink hearts, 2 yellow squares, 3 rounds. O.S.P. $4.00 C.M.V. $4.00 M.B.
1975 BAYBERRY WREATHS GIFT SOAPS - 3 Bayberry scented soaps in Christmas box. O.S.P. $3.00 C.M.V. $4.00 M.B.

1975-76 ANGEL LACE SOAPS
3 blue soaps in blue & white box. O.S.P. $3.00 C.M.V. $4.00 M.B.
1975 TOUCH OF LOVE SOAPS
3 white soaps in lavender box. Spring lavender fragrance. O.S.P. $4.00 C.M.V. $4.00 M.B.

1972-73 LACERY HOSTESS BATH SOAP
Cream colored with foil center design. Box gold & pink. SSP $3.00 CMV $6.00 MB.

1974-76 GOLDEN BEAUTIES HOSTESS SOAP - 2 oz. each, 3 cakes yellow soap. SSP $2.00 CMV $4.50 MB

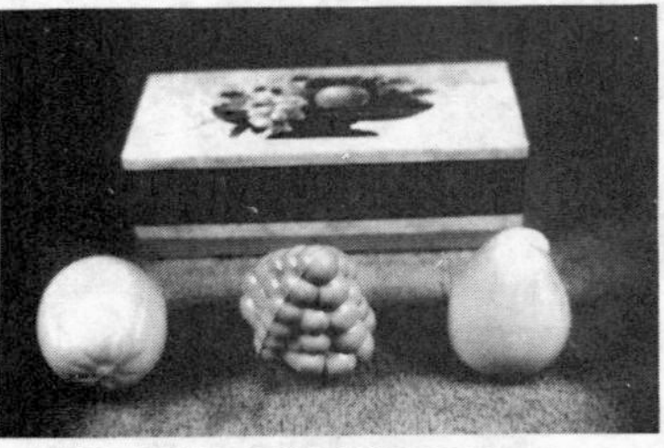

1969 FRUIT BOUQUET SOAP
Orange, lavender, and green soap. O.S.P. $3.00 C.M.V. $9.00 M.B.

1973 SOAP FOR ALL SEASONS
1.5 oz. each, 4 soaps, yellow, green, blue & orange. SSP $3.00 CMV $7.00 MB.

1972-73 CUP CAKE SOAP
Green, pink & orange soap, 2 oz. each. SSP $2.50 CMV $7.00 MB

1972-75 FRAGRANCE & FRILLS SOA
4 lavender soaps in lavender plastic box. In center a 1/8 oz. bottle of Dazzling perfume in Field Flowers or Bird of Paradise. SSP $6.00 CMV $8.00 MB.

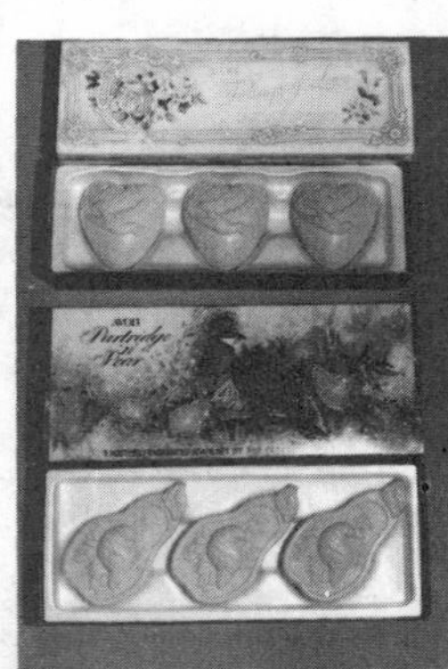

1976 TIDINGS OF LOVE SOAPS
3 pink soaps in pink & white box. O.S.P. $3.00 C.M.V. $4.00 M.B.
1974-75 PARTRIDGE 'N PEAR HOSTE SOAP - 3 yellow soaps in festive Christm box. O.S.P. $3.00 C.M.V. $4.00 M.B.

2-73 HOSTESS BOUQUET GUEST
.P - 3 pink bars shaped like flower
quet tied with green ribbon. Came in
& blue bouquet box. O.S.P. $3.50
.V. $6.00 M.B.

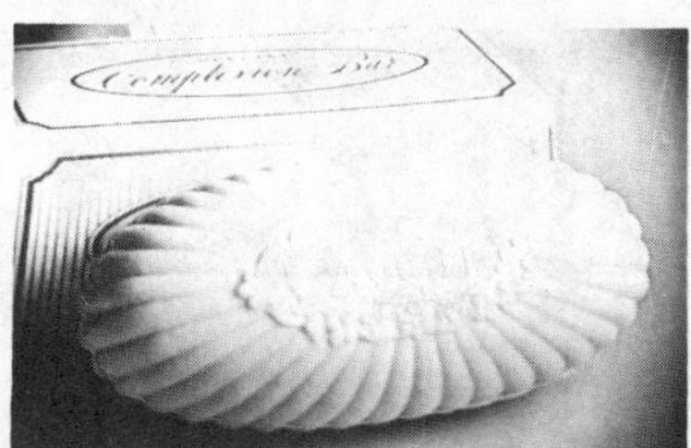

1966-70 COMPLEXION BAR
4 oz. bar. O.S.P. $1.25 C.M.V. $2.50 M.B.

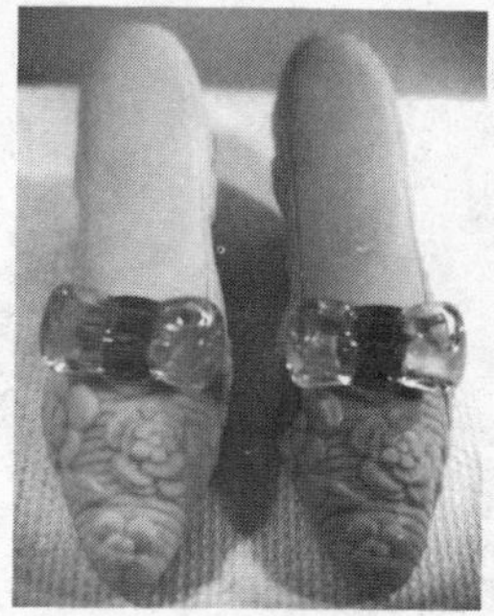

1970-71 SLIPPER SOAP & PERFUME
1/8 oz. bow tie perfume sits in light pink slipper soap in Cotillion, & dark pink soap in Charisma. OSP $5.00 each CMV $8.00 MB $6.00 soap & perfume only, mint.

971-72 GRADE AVON HOSTESS SOAPS
lastic carton holds 2 blue & 2 pink egg shaped oaps. O.S.P. $4.50 C.M.V. $7.00 M.B.

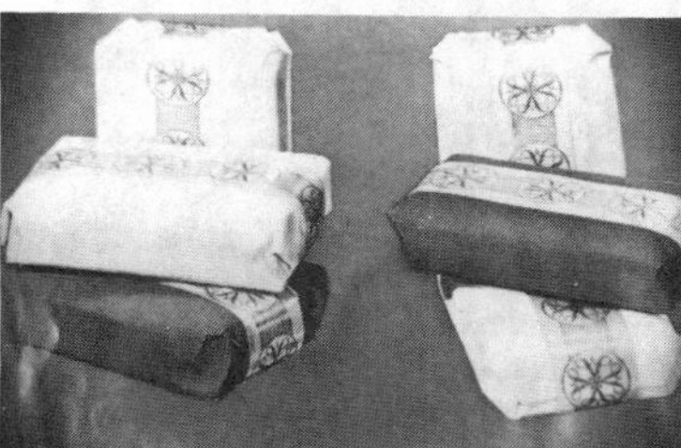

1961-64 PERFUMED SOAPS & PERFUMED DEODORANT SOAPS
1 bar each in Lemonol, Persion Wood, Somewhere, Facial, Floral, Royal Pink, Royal Jasmine, Here's My Heart, Cotillion, To A Wild Rose, Topaze, & Rose Geranium. O.S.P. 39¢ C.M.V. $3.00 ea. mint.

1968 WHIPPED CREAM SOAP
Green, blue, pink & yellow soap. O.S.P. $3.00 C.M.V. $9.00 M.B.

1973 SOAP SAVERS
9 oz. total of 6 green soaps in spearmint fragrance. SSP $3.00 CMV $6.00 MB.

1967 BAY BERRY SOAP
Blue & gold box holds 3 wrapped bars in plastic holder. OSP $3.00 CMV $22.00 MB M.B.

1970-73 PINE CONE GIFT SOAPS
Box contains blue, yellow & green pine scented soaps. O.S.P. $3.00 C.M.V. $8.00 M.B.

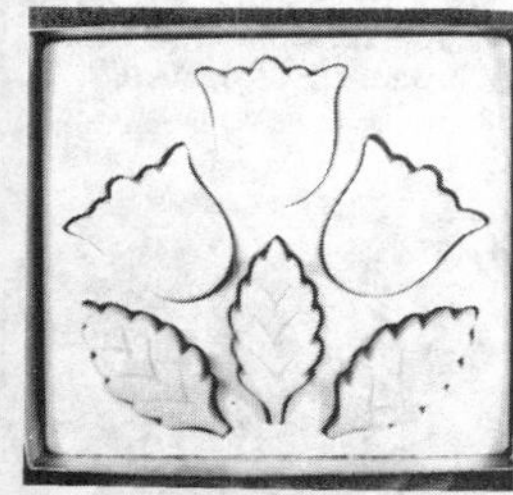

1970-73 SPRING TULIPS SOAP
Blue & pink box holds 6 green, white & pink soaps. O.S.P. $3.50 C.M.V. $8.00 M.B.

1968-70 PARTRIDGE & PEAR SOAPS
Two green pears & white partridge. O.S.P. $3.00 C.M.V. $8.00 M.B.

1976-77 BOUQUET OF PANSIES SOAP
Blue box holds 2 flower decorated special occasion white soaps. O.S.P. $5.50 CMV $5.00 MB.

1966-67 CHERUB SOAP SET
Blue box holds 2 pink angel soaps.
OSP $2.00 CMV $21.00 MB.

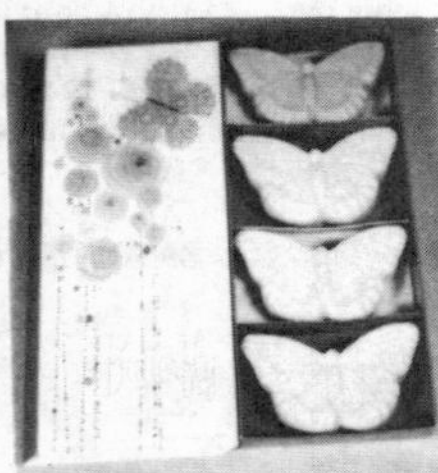

1966-67 BUTTERFLY SOAP
4 bars in box. O.S.P. $2.00
CMV $21.00 MB.

1969 DECORATOR SOAPS
Pink box holds 3 egg shaped soaps in green, pink & blue. O.S.P. $3.00 C.M.V. $9.00 M.B.

1959-61 HOSTESS BOUQUET SOAP
Pink & yellow box holds 4 bars. O.S.P. $1.39 CMV $21.00 MB.

1964-65 HOSTESS SOAP SAMPLER
Floral box holds 12 cakes of soap.
O.S.P. $2.50 C.M.V. $20.00 M.B.

1962-64 GIFT BOWS SOAP
Box holds 6 bow tie soaps.
OSP $2.25 CMV $23.00 MB.

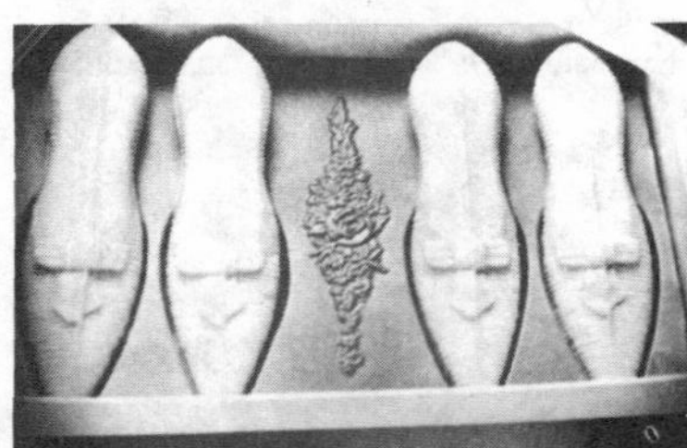

1965-66 LADY SLIPPERS SOAP
4 shoe soaps in box. O.S.P. $2.25
CMV $23.00 MB.

1963-67 PERFUMED DEODORANT SOAP
O.S.P. 39¢ C.M.V. $3.00 mint.

1971-73 SCENTED SOAPS
3 oz. bars in matching soap & wrapping. Mint, Pine Tar, Almond, Camomile, Papaya, Avocado, O.S.P. 75¢ C.MV. $3.00 each MB.

1966-67 LEMONOL SOAP
Blue and yellow box holds six 2½" yello
bars. O.S.P. $2.25 C.M.V. $22.50 M.B.

1941-58 LEMONOL SOAP
Yellow & green lemon box holds 3 yellow bars with round edges & flat on bottom. OSP $1.00 CMV $30.00 MB.

1958-66 LEMONOL SOAP
Yellow & green lemon box holds 3 yellow bars with flat edges. Box comes lift off - older - & flip up as shown. OS
$1.19 CMV $22.50 MB.

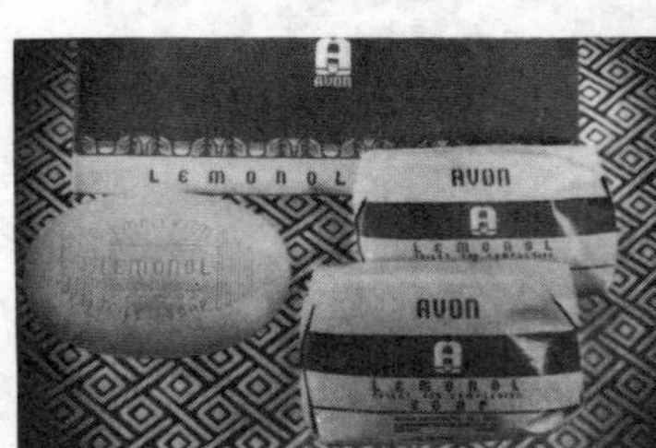

1936-41 LEMONOL TOILET SOAP - Three yellow bars in turquoise & white box & wrapping. O.S.P. 51¢ C.M.V. $40.00 M.B. Box of 12 bars O.S.P. $1.79 C.M.V. $60.00 M.B.
Add $3.00 per bar for CPC label, mint.

1923-31 LEMONOL TOILET SOAP
Box of 3 bars. O.S.P. 45¢ C.M.V. $60.00 M.B.

1923-31 LEMONOL SOAP
Box of 12 cakes. O.S.P. $1.65
C.M.V. $80.00 M.B.

1931-36 LEMONOL TOILET SOAP
Yellow soap wrapped in blue & silver paper. Came in box of 3. O.S.P. 50¢ C.M.V. $45.00 M.B. Box of 12 bars $1.75 C.M.V. $65.00 M.B.

SOAPS WITH SPONGES

(Left to Right)
1979-80 BATH BLOSSOM SPONGE AND SOAP
Box holds yellow, green and blue sponge and yellow soap. S.S.P. $5.99, C.M.V. $4.00 M.B.
1979-80 SWEET PICKLES WORRIED WALRUS SOAP AND SPONGE
Purple, green and brown sponge. Comes with wrapped bar of Sweet Pickles childrens bath soap. S.S.P. $4.99, C.M.V. $3.50 M.B.
1979-80 FEARLESS FISH SPONGE AND SOAP
Green fish sponge and Sweet Pickles wrapped soap with fish on a scooter. S.S.P. $3.99, C.M.V. $3.00 M.B.

1965-66 BATH FLOWERS SOAP & SPONGE - Pink & white floral box contains 1 bar To A Wild Rose soap, pink, green & white sponge. O.S.P. $2.50 C.M.V. $12.00 M.B.

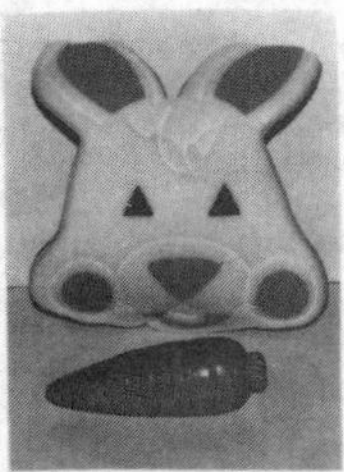

1974 GOOD HABIT RABBIT BATH MITT & SOAP - White & pink foam mitt with yellow carrot soap. S.S.P. $2.50 CMV $4.50 MB.

1977-80 PINK PANTHER SPONGE MITT & SOAP
Pink mitt, yellow eyes. Blue green & pink wrapped soap. OSP $6.00 CMV $3.50 MB.

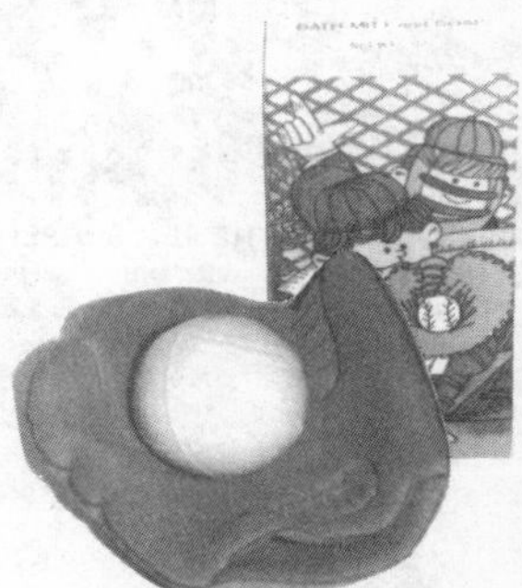

1972 LITTLE LEAGUER SOAP AND SPONGE
Tan sponge mit & white baseball soap. Sponge is different from Little Pro soap & sponge in 1966. C.M.V.$8.00 MB $4.00 soap & sponge only, mint.

1969-71 CHARLIE BROWN BATH MITT & SOAP - Red & white sponge with white bar of Snoopy embossed soap. O.S.P. $3.00 CMV $6.00 MB.

1966 LITTLE PRO SOAP
White baseball soap & brown sponge. O.S.P. $2.25 C.M.V. $10.00 M.B. $6.00 soap & sponge only.

1965-66 MINNIE THE MOO SOAP & SPONGE - White foam cow with yellow ears & black eyes. Soap is in green wrapper. O.S.P. $1.75 C.M.V. $6.00 soap & sponge only mint. $11.00 MB.

1969-70 POLLY PARROT PUPPET SPONGE & SOAP - Green & orange sponge with bar of soap. OSP $3.00 CMV $7.00 MB soap & sponge only $4.00.

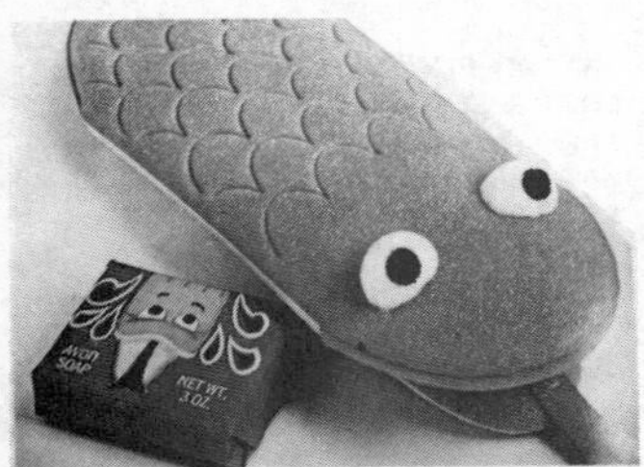

1968-69 CLARENCE THE SEA SERPENT
Orange & yellow sponge with bar of serpent soap in blue & yellow wrapper. O.S.P. $2.25 CMV $7.00 MB.

1970-71 HUBIE THE HIPPO SOAP & SPONGE - Turquoise & red sponge with Hippo wrapped soap. O.S.P. $4.00 CMV $6.00 MB.

1967-68 NEST EGG SOAP & SPONGE
Box holds yellow nest sponge & pink soap. OSP $2.25 CMV $12.00 MB.

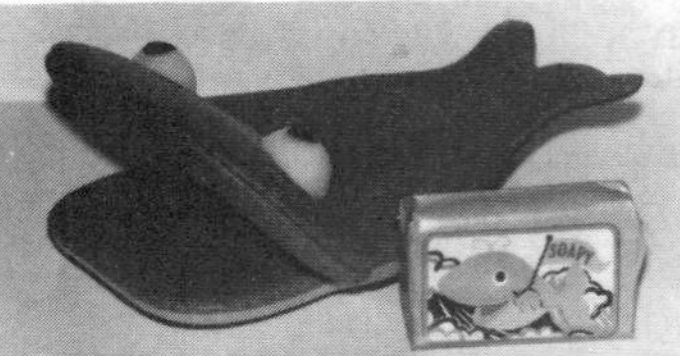

1973-74 SOAPY THE WHALE BATH MITT & SOAP - 8½" long blue & red sponge mitt with blue soap. S.S.P. $3.00 C.M.V. $5.00 MB.

1973 CEDRIC SEA SERPENT SPONGE & SOAP
9½" long, green & pink sponge, white soap. OSP $2.50 CMV $6.00 MB.
1974-75 CEDRIC SEA SERPENT SPONGE & SOAP (Right)
9½" long, purple & pink sponge. OSP $3.00 CMV $5.00 MB.

1966-67 SPONGAROO SOAP & SPONGE
Brown kangaroo sponge is 15" x 5¾". White kangaroo soap. OSP $2.25 CMV $12.00 MB soap only $7.00 mint.

1969 BATH BLOSSOMS
Pink & yellow sponge with pink soap. O.S.P. $3.50 C.M.V. $8.00 M.B. $4.00 soap & sponge only.

1980 SPIDERMAN SPONGE & SOAP
Blue & red sponge. Red wrapped soap. SSP $4.00 CMV $3.00 MB.

1978-79 YAKETY-YAK TAXI SOAP & SPONGE
Box holds yellow taxi sponge & bar of wrapped sweet pickles soap. SSP $3.99 CMV $3.00 MB.

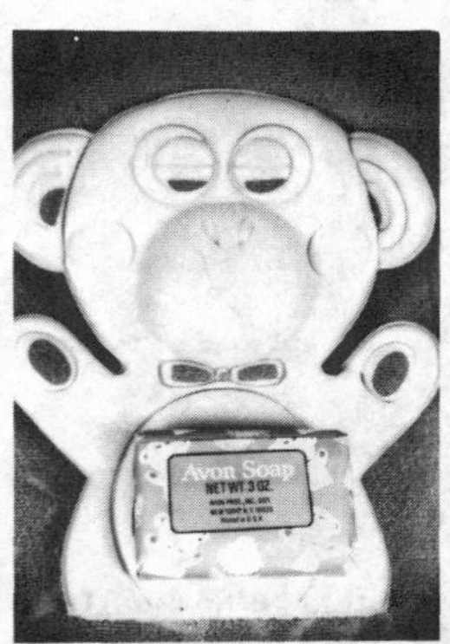

1969 MONKEY SHINES
Brown & pink sponge & bar of soap. OSP $3.00 CMV $7.00 MB. Soap & sponge only $3.00.

CHILDREN'S SOAPS

EFT 1956 SANTA'S HELPER SOAP
ox holds 3 green, yellow & red soaps.
SP $1.19 CMV $60.00 MB.
IGHT 1955 SANTA'S HELPER SOAP
ox holds green, red & yellow soap. Red
anta soap much larger than 1956 set.
SP $1.49 CMV $60.00 MB.

1956-57 CASEY JONES JR.
Red, white & blue box holds red engine soap, yellow passenger car & red caboose. OSP $1.19 CMV $55.00 MB.

1955 KIDDIE KENNEL SOAP
Blue & yellow box holds blue, yellow & pink dog soaps. O.S.P. $1.49 C.M.V. $60.00 MB.

LEFT 1977-79 M.C.P. SOAP
Tan color Male Chauvinist Pig soap. Came in Deep Woods scent. OSP $5.00 CMV $3.00 MB.
RIGHT 1977-79 BUTTON BUTTON GUEST SOAPS
Cardboard spool containers holds 5 blue button shaped soaps. OSP $6.00 CMV $3.00 MB.

1956 BEST FRIEND SOAP
Blue & white box holds blue dog soap. OSP 59c CMV $35.00 MB.

1955 AWAY IN THE MANGER SOAP SET
Box holds 4 bars of pink, blue & white & yellow soap. 2 different scenes as shown. Remove panel on bottom picture to show inner panel as shown on top picture. OSP $1.49 CMV $60.00 each set, MB.

1957 FIRE ENGINE SOAP
Red box contains red fire truck soap. OSP 59c CMV $40.00 MB.

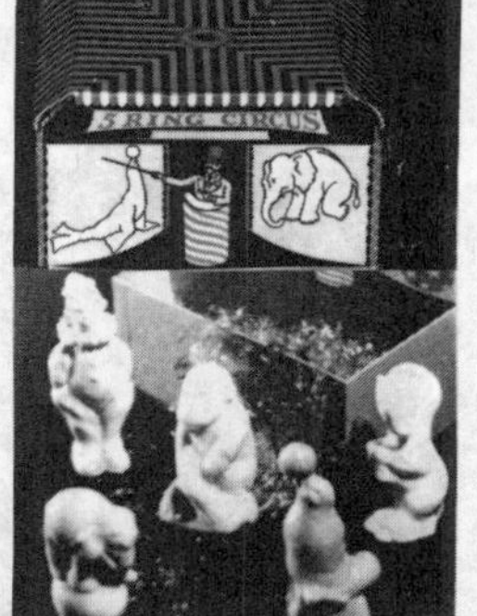

1939-41 CIRCUS SOAP SET
5 ring circus on box holds 5 figural soaps. This set is Avons first figurals. Soaps are clown, Elephant, Monkey, Seal, Horse, OSP $1.19 CMV $250.00 MB. Very rare.

1954 THREE LITTLE BEARS SOAP SET
3 brown bear soaps. O.S.P. $1.19 C.M.V. $60.00 MB.

1953-54 BO PEEP SOAP
Blue & green box holds 3 white sheep soaps. OSP $1.00 CMV $62.50 MB.

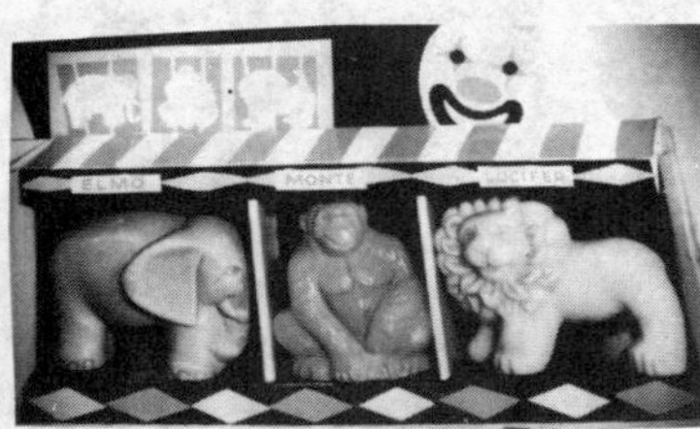

1957-58 CIRCUS WAGON SOAP SET
Pink, yellow, black & white circus wagon box contains 1 blue elephant, 1 pink monkey, 1 yellow lion soaps. O.S.P. $1.25 CMV $65.00 MB.

1958 "OLD 99" SOAP
Yellow train engine soap.
OSP 69c CMV $40.00 MB.

1959 POOL PADDLERS SOAP
Pond display box holds green frog, yellow fish & blue turtle soap.
OSP $1.39 CMV $35.00 MB.

1958 FORWARD PASS
7½ oz. brown football soap on a white rope on side of soap. O.S.P. $1.00 CMV $30.00 MB.

1959 HIGH SCORE
Green net box holds brown basketball soap on a rope. O.S.P. $1.19 C.M.V. $15.00 soap only, mint. $27.50 MB.

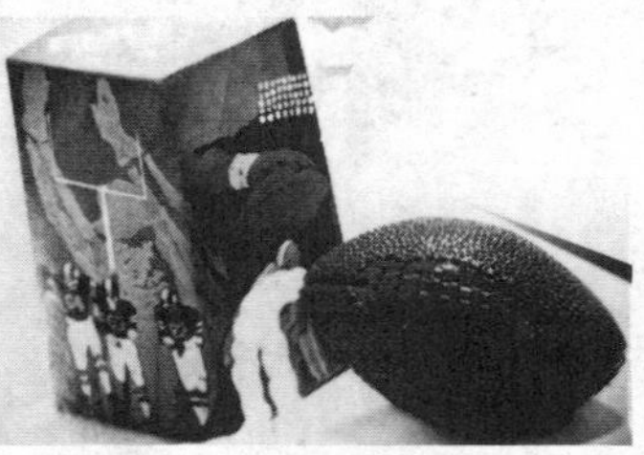

1970-71 FIRST DOWN SOAP
Box holds brown 5 oz. football soap on a rope. This soap is different from older one. Rope is on end of football. OSP $2.00 CMV $7.00 MB.

1960 FRILLY DUCK SOAP
Box contains yellow & blue soap 5¾ oz.
OSP 89c CMV $20.00 MB.

1960-61 AVONLITE SOAP ON A ROP
Green bowling ball shaped soap in greer box. Brochure says "Bowl 'em Over" Soap says "Avon Lite" O.S.P. $1.19 CMV $35.00 MB. Soap only $20.00 mi mint.

1961-62 LI'L FOLKS TIME SOAP ON A ROPE - Red box holds yellow clock soap on a rope. O.S.P. $1.19 C.M.V. $26.00 MB.

1961-62 A HIT! SOAP ON A ROPE
Box holds white base ball soap on a rope.
OSP $1.19 CMV $25.00 MB.

1962-63 SHERIFF'S BADGE SOAP
Box holds yellow soap on a rope with embossed sheriff's badge. O.S.P. $1.19 CMV $28.00 MB.

1966-67 LITTLE SHAVER SOAP
Yellow shaver soap on a rope. O.S.P. $1.35 C.M.V. $20.00 M.B.

1958 TEXAS SHERIFF SOAP
Box holds 2 blue pistol soaps & silver sheriff's badge. Box comes with band around outside of box as shown at top. OSP $1.19 CMV $55.00 MB.

1962-63 LIL TOM TURTLE SOAP
Box holds green turtle soap with white hat. OSP 98c CMV $20.00 MB.

1962-64 "WATCH THE BIRDIE" SOAP - White molded camera soap on a rope. OSP $1.19 CMV $22.00 MB.

1965 HANSEL & GRETEL SOAP
Blue & pink soap in box. O.S.P. $1.35 CMV $25.00 MB.

1963-64 LIFE PRESERVER SOAP
White life preserver soap on a rope. OSP $1.19 CMV $22.00 MB.

1964-65 PACKY THE ELEPHANT SOAP - Green box holds pink elephant with white hat. OSP 98c CMV $20.00 MB.

1966 SPEEDY THE SNAIL
Green snail soap on a rope. OSP $1.35, CMV $20.00

1966-67 GOLDILOCKS SOAP
5 oz. yellow soap. O.S.P. $1.00 C.M.V. $10.00 M.B.

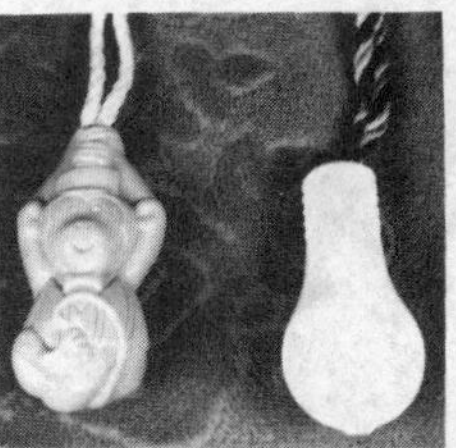

1965 MR. MONKEY SOAP ON A ROPE
Brown monkey soap. OSP $1.35 CMV $15.00 MB.

1967 LIGHT BULB SOAP ON A ROPE
Yellow soap on black, orange & yellow rope. OSP $1.50 CMV $15.00 MB.

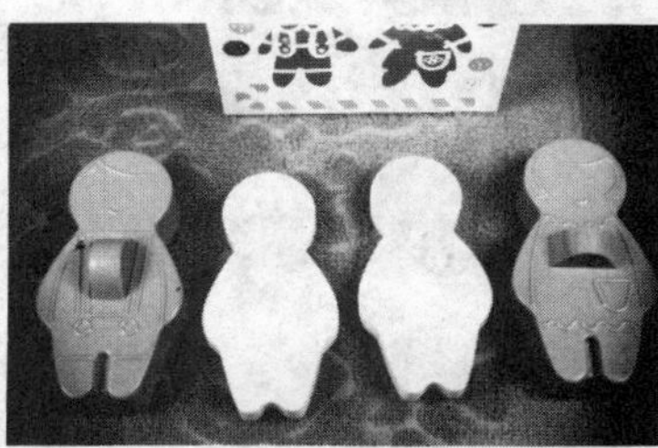

1965 GINGER BREAD SOAP TWINS
Pink, white & brown box holds 2 blue plastic gingerbread cookie cutters with 2 yellow bars of gingerbread soap. OSP $1.50, CMV $25.00

1966 SUNNY THE SUNFISH SOAP
Yellow fish soap on a rope. O.S.P. $1.19 CMV $16.00 MB.

1964-66 SEA BISCUIT - THE SEA HORSE SOAP ON A ROPE - Box holds green soap on a rope. Sea Horse. O.S.P. $1.25 C.M.V. $18.00 MB.

1966-67 CHICK-A-DEE SOAP
Yellow soap on a rope.
O.S.P. $1.35 C.M.V. $15.00 M.B.

1966-67 YO YO SOAP SET
Pink & red wood Yo Yo & pink soap.
OSP $1.50 CMV $20.00 MB. Yo Yo only $6.00

1967 BUNNY'S DREAM SOAP ON A ROPE - Box holds orange carrot soap on a green rope. O.S.P. $1.25 C.M.V. $15.00 M.B.

1968 EASTER QUACKER SOAP ON A ROPE - Yellow soap. O.S.P. $1.35 CMV $11.00 MB.

1968-69 RUFF, TUFF, & MUFF SOAP SET - Blue, pink & yellow dog soaps.
O.S.P. $1.25 C.M.V. $7.00 M.B.

1969 TUB RACERS SOAP
Green box holds red, yellow & green racer soap. O.S.P. $1.75 C.M.V. $7.00 M.B.

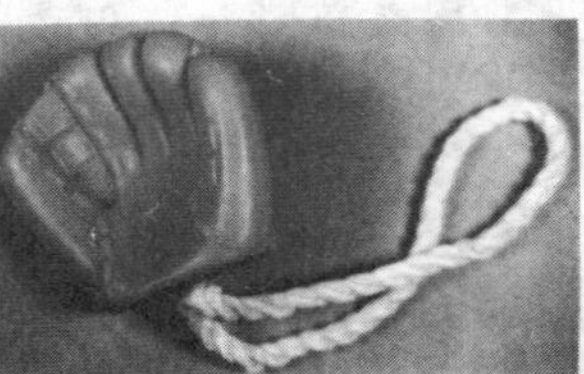

1969-72 MIGHTY MIT SOAP ON A ROPE - Brown soap. O.S.P. $2.00 CMV $7.00 MB.

1969-70 YANKEE DOODLE SHOWER SOAP - White drum shaped soap on a rope. OSP $2.00 CMV $8.00 MB.

1971 TWEETSTERS SOAPS
Yellow box holds 3 pink bird soaps.
OSP $2.00 CMV $7.00 MB.

1969-70 MODELING SOAP
Pink 6 oz. soap in blue & pink box
OSP $2.00 CMV $6.00 MB.

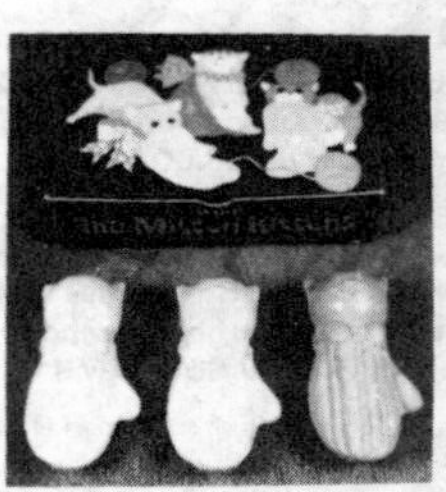

1969-70 MITTENS KITTENS SOAP
Pink, green & yellow soap. Blue box. OSP $1.50 CMV $7.00 MB.

1970 PEEP A BOO SOAP ON A ROPE
Yellow chick soap on pink or white rope.
OSP $1.35 CMV $8.00 MB.
1970 EASTER BONNET SOAP ON A ROPE
Yellow soap. OSP $1.35 CMV $8.00 MB.

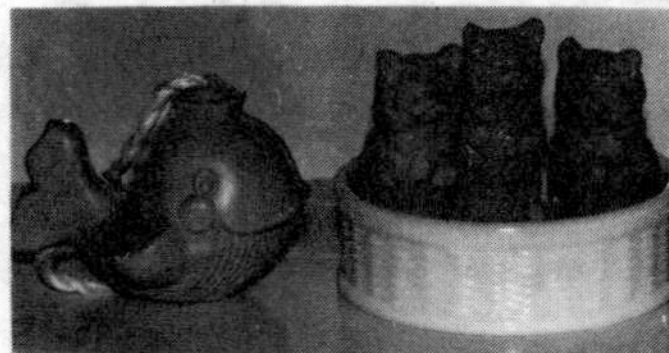

1974-75 WILBUR THE WHALE SOAP ON A ROPE
5 oz. blue soap with white rope. SSP $2.00 CMV $5.00 MB.
1973-75 SITTIN' KITTENS SOAP DISH AND SOAPS
White milk glass dish with 3 kitten soaps in gold colored, yellow and orange. SSP $4.00 CMV $6.50 MB.

1974-75 TUBBY TIGERS SOAP SET
3 orange soaps in orange and green box. OSP $2.00 CMV $4.00 MB.

1974-75 FOOTBALL HELMET SOAP-ON-A-ROPE - yellow soap, white cord. OSP $2.00 CMV $4.00 MB.

1972-73 PERCY PELICAN SOAP ON A ROPE
5 oz. yellow soap on white rope. SSP $1.50 CMV $5.00 MB.
1973-74 PETUNIA PIGLET SOAP ON A ROPE
5 oz. pink soap on white rope. SSP $2.00 CMV $5.00 MB.

1971 SCRUB TUG
4" long plastic boat scrub brush holds 2 oz. yellow boat soap. OSP $2.50 CMV brush & soap $5.00 MB, brush only $1.00
1973-75-79 PIG IN A TUB
3" long yellow scrub brush holds 2 oz. pink pig soap. SSP $2.20 CMV $3.00 MB. Reissued 1979.

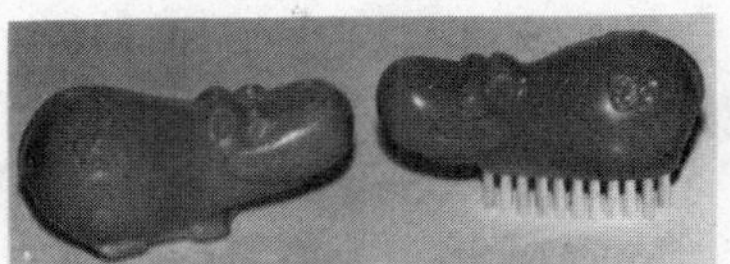

1973-74 HAPPY HIPPOS NAIL BRUSH & SOAP
3" long pink nail brush with yellow soap SSP $2.00 CMV $5.00 MB.

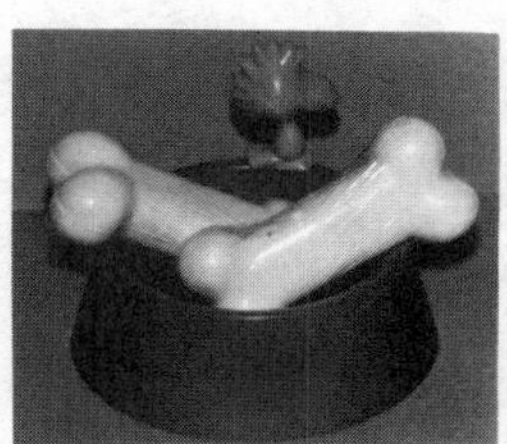

1973-74 SNOOPY'S PAL SOAP DISH & SOAPS
4½" diameter red plastic dish says Snoopy on front with yellow bird. Comes with two 2 oz. white bone shaped soaps. S.S.P. $3.00. C.M.V. $6.00 MB.

1973-75 HOOTY AND TOOTY TUGBOAT SOAPS
2 oz. yellow & orange tugboat shaped soaps. SSP $2.00 CMV $4.00 MB.

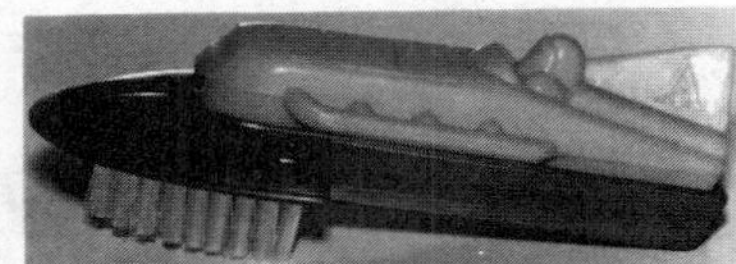

1972-73 HYDROJET SCRUB BRUSH & SOAP - Red plastic jet with yellow soap. SSP $2.00 CMV $4.50 MB.

1973-75 SURE WINNER SOAPS
3 snowmobile soaps in blue, red & yellow. SSP $2.00 CMV $4.00 MB.
1972-73 SURE WINNER SHOWER SOAP
White with blue cord. SSP $2.00 CMV $6.00 MB.

1972 BLUE MOO SOAP ON A ROPE
5 oz. blue cow soap on a rope. OSP $1.75 CMV $5.00 MB.
1971-72 HONEY LAMB SOAP ON A ROPE
5" high yellow soap on blue rope. OSP $1.19 CMV $5.00 MB.
1971-72 AL E. GATOR SOAP ON ROPE
5" high green soap on white rope. OSP $2.00 CMV $5.00 MB.

1971-72 THREE MICE SOAPS
Box holds green, white & pink mice soaps. OSP $2.00 CMV $6.00 MB.

1974 HOOPER THE HOUND SOAP HOLDER AND SOAP
White and black plastic head with pink, green and yellow hoops, has yellow soap. S.S.P. $4.00 C.M.V. $5.00 M.B.

1978-79 FURRY, PURRY, AND SCURRY SOAPS
Red box with white dots holds 3 kitten shaped soaps in yellow, bue and green. S.S.P. $2.99, C.M.V. $3.00 M.B.

1978-80 TUBBO THE HIPPO SOAP DISH AND SOAP
Blue box holds light green plastic hippo soap dish and 3 oz. pink embossed wrapped bar of hippo soap. S.S.P. $4.99 C.M.V. $4.99 M.B. Soap dish only $1.00 Soap only wrapped $1.50

1978-79 ALKA SELTZER SOAPS
Blue and white and red box holds 2 white embossed bars. S.S.P. $4.00, C.M.V. $4.00 M.B.

1978-79 SAFE COMBINATION BANK
Black and gold tin bank comes with two yellow bars of soap embossed "Avon, 99.9 mint" Bottom of bank says "Made in England, exclusively for Avon". S.S.P. $7.99, C.M.V. $7.99 M.B.

1970-72 TREE TOTS SOAP
Red & green box holds 3 squirrel soaps. O.S.P. $1.75 C.M.V. $6.00 M.B.

1971 ARISTOCAT KITTENS SOAP
Box holds white, brown & blue kitten soaps. O. S.P. $2.00, C.M.V. $6.00 MB.

1970-72 TUB RACERS
Three Speed Boat soaps in red, blue & yellow. O.S.P. $2.00, C.M.V. $5.00 MB.

1970-72 PEANUTS GANG SOAP
Red Lucy, yellow Charlie, white Snoopy soaps. O.S.P. $2.00, C.M.V. $6.00 MB.

1977-78 PINK PEARL SCRUB AWAY NAIL BRUSH AND SOAP
3 oz. soap, pink plastic brush shaped like pink pearl eraser. OSP $4.00 CMV $3.00 MB.

CHILDREN'S TOYS

All items are priced mint condition. See pages 5 & 14 for grading examples.

LEFT 1977-78 TERRIBLE TUBBLES FLOATING SOAP DISH & SOAP
Blue plastic dish with 3 oz. soap. OSP $5.50 CMV $3.00 MB.

RIGHT 1976-77 RANDY PANDY SOAP DISH & SOAP
Black, light blue and red rubber soap dish & 3 oz. blue & white soap. S.S.P.$3.99 C.M.V. (Panda only) $1.00. Set $3.00 M.B.

1971-72 CHOO-CHOO TRAIN
Soap coach is 4" long plastic soap dish with yellow bar of soap. OSP $1.50 CMV $4.00 MB, with soap. $1.00 soap coach only. Caboose is pink plastic bottle 3" long with Non Tear Shampoo. OSP $2.00 CMV $4.00 MB. Puffer Chugger is 4" long green plastic bottle with yellow cap & nose. Holds bubble bath. OSP $2.00 CMV $4.00 MB.

1973-75 ROTO-BOAT FLOATING SOAP DISH & SOAP
9"long blue & white boat with red rudder holds 3 oz. blue soap. SSP $3.00 CMV $4.00

1973-74 SNOOPY COME HOME SOAP DISH & SOAP
6" long, brown raft with whitesail, has 3 oz. brown soap. S.S.P. $3.00 CMV $5.00 MB.

1975-76 GREAT CATCH, CHARLIE BROWN SOAP HOLDER & SOAP
Red, white, black and brown plastic. OSP $4.00 CMV $5.00 MB.

1974-75 QUACK AND DOODLE FLOATING SOAP DISH & SOAP
Yellow rubber with yellow soap. OSP $3.50 CMV $4.00 MB.

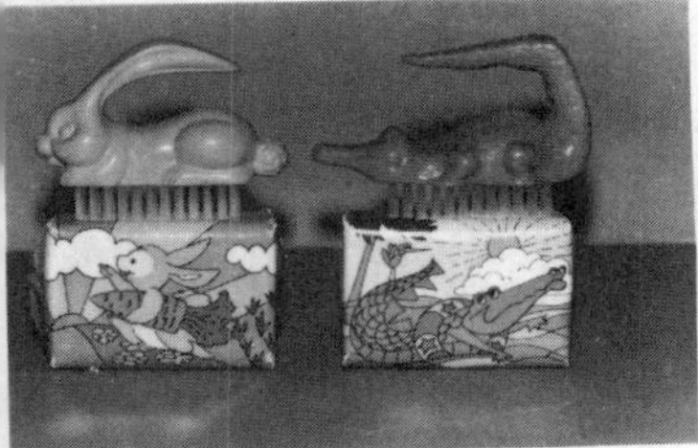

1975 GOOD HABIT RABBIT SCRUB BRUSH & SOAP
Pink plastic with white bristles. OSP $2.50 CMV $3.00 MB.

1974-75 GAYLORD GATOR SCRUB BRUSH & SOAP
Green plastic with white bristles. OSP $2.50 CMV $3.00 MB.

1970-72 CLEAN SHOT
Orange net holds orange basketball sponge & 1 bar of clean shot soap. OSP $4.50 CMV $6.00 MB set.

1969-70 FREDDIE THE FROG
Green rubber frog soap dish & green vest soap. Pink lips & pink band around hat. O.S.P. $1.75. C.M.V. Frog only $2.00, with soap $6.00 MB.

1965-66 FREDDIE THE FROG
Green Rubber frog with yellow hat & eyes, pink lips, green soap. O.S.P. $3.00 C.M.V. Frog only $5.00, with soap $10.00 M.B.

1973 REGGIE RACOON HAIR BRUSH & COMB
6½" long, tan & black with tan comb. S.S.P. $3.00, C.M.V. $3.00 M.B.

1970-71 REGINALD G' RACCOON III
Black, brown & white rubber soap dish & 3 oz. pink vest soap. O.S.P. $3.50, C.M.V. Raccoon only $2.00 $6.00 set MB.

1972-74 RANDY PANDY SOAP DISH
Black, white & pink rubber soap dish & 3 oz. white soap O.S.P. $3.50. CMV Panda only $2.00, set $5.00 MB.

1973-74 CLANCEY THE CLOWN SOAP HOLDER & SOAP
Orange, pink & white clown holds green & white, pink & orange 3 oz. soap. SSP $3.50 CMV $5.00 MB.

1967-69 GAYLORD GATER
10" long green & yellow rubber soap dish with yellow soap. O.S.P. $2.25, CMV gater only $2.00, $6.00 set MB.

1973-74-79 TOPSY TURTLE FLOATING SOAP DISH & SOAP
7" long green rubber soap dish with 3 oz. pink soap. SSP $2.00 CMV $3.00 MB. Reissued 1979. Some came light green body & dark green head. Also came matching body & head.

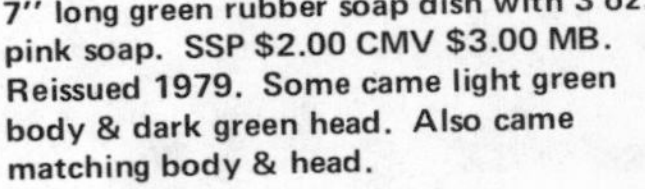

1973-74 SOAP BOAT' FLOATING SOAP DISH & SOAP
7½" long blue and red boat with white sail and white soap. S.S.P. $2.00 CMV $5.00 MB.

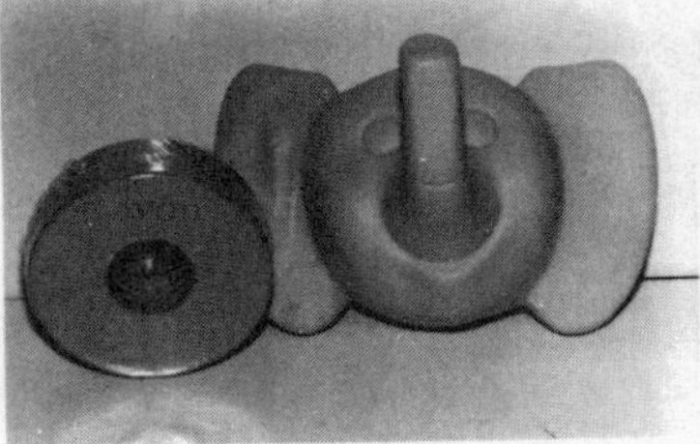

1966-67 RING AROUND ROSIE
Pink rubber elephant sticks on wall with blue bar of Avon soap. O.S.P. $2.25 CMV $15.00 MB, soap only $6.00 elephant only $4.00.

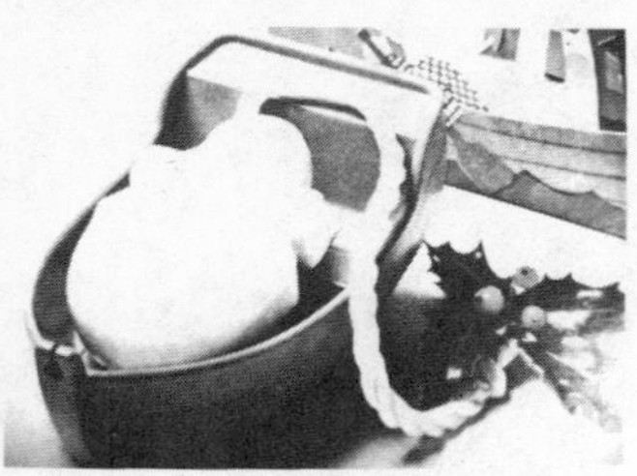

1966-67 WASH AWEIGH SOAP & DISH - Green plastic boat dish & yellow anchor soap on a rope. O.S.P. $1.98, C.M.V. Boat $6.00, Anchor soap $9.00, set $18.00 MB.

1971-72 BARNEY BEAVER SOAP DISH & SOAP - 10½" long, brown soap dish & brown vest soap. O.S.P. $3.50 CMV $5.00 MB. beaver only $2.00. only $2.00.

1974-75 SNOOPY'S SKI TEAM
7 oz. white plastic bottle, red skis, yellc "Woodstock". Holds bubble Bath. OS $5.00 CMV $3.00 MB.

1975-78 WOODSTOCK BRUSH & COMB
Yellow plastic brush, green comb. OSP $4.00 CMV $1.00 BO $2.00 MB.

1965-67 FIRST DOWN
Large box holds real junior size football & 6 oz. brown football soap on a rope. Rope comes out side of soap. O.S.P. $3.95 Avon soap & ball. C.M.V. soap $9.00 M.B. C.M.V. ball $15.00 CMV set in box $27.50 MB. M.B.

1970 FREDDY THE FROG MUG
5 oz. white glass with red top & white cap. Holds bubble bath. OSP $3.50 CMV $5.00, $7.00 MB.

1970-72 GAYLORD GATOR MUG
5 oz. white glass mug with yellow top & white cap. Holds Non Tear Shampoo. OSP $3.50 CMV $5.00, $7.00 MB.

1968-72 CHARLIE BROWN
4 oz. red, white & black plastic bottle of Non Tear Shampoo. OSP $2.50 CMV $5.00 MB $3.00 BO

1970-72 LUCY
4 oz. red, white & black plastic bottle holds Bubble Bath. OSP $2.50 CMV $5.00 MB $3.00 BO

1969-72 SNOOPY MUG
5 oz. white glass, 5 inches high. Came 2 ways, red or blue top. Blue top is more rare. Also came with tall decal or round decal. OSP $3.50 CMV $7.00 red top MB, $9.00 blue top MB, $2.00 less no box.

1978-79 1913 BUFFALO NICKEL SOAP DISH AND SOAP
5" nickel plated Buffalo nickel metal soap dish and light gray or off white color soap. S.S.P. $7.99, C.M.V. $7.99 M.B.

1971-75 SNOOPY COMB &BRUSH SET
5½" long black & white brush & white comb. OSP $3.50 CMV $3.00 MB. M.B.

1975-76 GRIDIRON SCRUB BRUSH & SOAP - Brown Plastic with yellow soap. OSP $4.00 CMV $3.00 MB M.B.

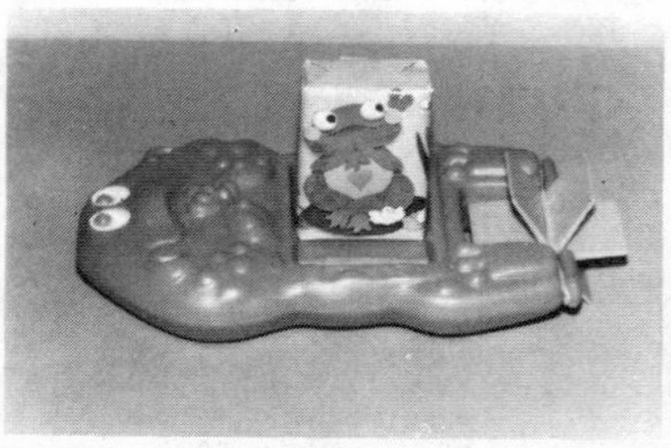

1975-76 PADDLEWOG FROG FLOATING SOAP DISH & SOAP
Green plastic with pink propeller and yellow soap. O.S.P. $4.00 C.M.V. $3.00 M.B.

1966-67 PERRY THE PENGUIN
Black & white penguin soap dish and white vest soap. OSP $1.98 CMV penguin $4.00, vest soap $5.00, set $12.00 MB.

1968-76 SNOOPY SOAP DISH
White bar of Avon soap sets in black & white plastic soap dish. OSP $6.00 CMV $5.00 MB, Snoopy only $1.00.

1979-80 SPACE PATROLLER DECANTER
8 oz. gray plastic, black cap & stick on decals SSP $4.99 CMV $3.00

1979-80 SPIDER MAN TOOTHBRUSH & HOLDER
Red & blue plastic. Yellow & green Avon toothbrushes. SSP $4.99 CMV $2.50 MB.

1969-70 LUCY MUG
5 oz. white glass, yellow top & label. White cap, Non Tear Shampoo. O.S.P. $3.50, C.M.V. $8.00.

1969-70 CHARLIE BROWN MUG
5 oz. white glass, blue top & label. White cap. Bubble bath. O.S.P. $3.50 C.M.V. $8.00.

1973-74 BO BO THE ELEPHANT
6 oz., pink plastic with squeeze head. Filled with baby shampoo. SSP $3.00 CMV $2.00 BO $4.00 MB.

1973 SNOOPY'S SNOW FLYER
10 oz. red, white & black. Holds bubble bath. SSP $4.00 CMV $4.00 MB $2.00 BO.

1972 CHARLIE BROWN COMB & BRUSH
4½" long, red, black & white with white comb. S.S.P. $3.00, C.M.V. $4.00 MB.

1973-74 GRID KID BRUSH & COMB
4½" long, red, black & white with white comb. S.S.P. $3.00, C.M.V. $3.00 M.B.

1969-72 SNOOPY & DOG HOUSE
8 oz. white plastic dog & red plastic 3" high dog house, holds Non Tear Shampoo. OSP $3.00 CMV $3.00, $5.00 MB

1968-74 LINUS
Red, white & green plastic 4 oz. tube of Gel Bubble Bath with red, white & black plastic Linus, plastic holder. OSP $3.50 CMV $4.00 MB. $2.00 Linus & tube only.

1971-72 SNOOPY'S BUBBLE TUB
5" long, 12 oz. blue & white plastic tub, bottle holds Bubble Bath. OSP $4.00 CMV $2.00 BO $4.00 MB.

1971-72 PEANUTS PALS SHAMPOO
6 oz. plastic, white, red & black bottle with yellow cap. 6" high. OSP $3.50 CMV $4.00 MB $2.00 BO

1970-72 SCHROEDER
6 oz. red, white, black & yellow plastic bottle holds bubble bath. OSP $3.50 CMV $2.00 - $4.50 MB.

1970-72 LINUS
4 oz. red, white & black plastic bottle holds Non Tear Shampoo. OSP $3.00 CMV $4.50 MB, $2.00 BO.

1969 TUB TALK TELEPHONE (Blue)
6 oz. blue plastic telephone with yellow cap & holder. Holds No Tear Shampoo. OSP $2.25 CMV $5.00, $7.00 MB.

1964-65 VERY OWN TELEPHONE
(Red) 6 oz. red plastic telephone & base, holds Baby Shampoo. OSP $1.98 CMV $9.00 BO $13.00 MB.

1967-68 TUB TALK TELEPHONE
(Yellow) 6 oz. yellow telephone with red cap & holder. Holds Tot 'N Tyke Shampoo. OSP $1.75 CMV $7.00 BO $10.00 MB.

1969 SNOOPY THE FLYING ACE
4 oz., 6" high white plastic with blue hat, yellow glasses, holds Bubble Bath. OSP $3.00 CMV $2.00, $5.00 MB.

1969-73 JUMPIN' JIMMINY
8 oz., 6" high, green, red & yellow pull toy with yellow cap, holds bubble bath. OSP $3.50 CMV $3.50 MB $2.00 BO.

1978 POP A DUCK GAME
6 oz. blue plastic with red orange cap. Came with 3 green balls. Pink, orange & yellow ducks & red orange ball holder. Bottle holds Bubble Bath for children S.S.P. $3.99 C.M.V. $3.00 M.B.

The #1 spot in the nation is through an ad in the AVON TIMES. A monthly publication of the Bud Hastin's National Avon Club. This is the world's largest Avon Collectors Club. Thousands of "Hard Core Avon Collectors" read the large want ad section of AVON TIMES each month. Avons advertised in AVON TIMES bring top prices.

Join the 1,000's of other Avon Collectors who know by experience it's a must to receive the Avon Times if you buy, sell or trade Avons.

Tell your friends about the AVON TIMES. It costs 15c per word to run a (quick results) ad in the AVON TIMES. Or you may join the Bud Hastin National Avon Club for $11.00 per year ($11.00 in Canada, U.S. money orders only), and receive 3 free ad coupons worth $22.50 in free advertising. Plus you get 12 monthly issues of AVON TIMES bringing you the latest on Avon collecting. It tells you where Avon Bottle Shows are held around the nation. It features monthly articles on different trends in Avon collecting, bringing you the news first when a "rare" or "odd" Avon is discovered so you will know what to look for. Plus the largest Avon advertising section in the United States. You get first hand information on buying Avon Club Bottles that double in value the first year. Club bottles issued in 1972 are now selling for $600.00 and only cost $11.95 seven years ago.

Don't miss the NEW LOOK of the AVON TIMES
NOW professionally typeset and printed.

YOU CAN'T AFFORD NOT TO BELONG TO BUD HASTIN'S NATIONAL AVON CLUB AND GET THE AVON TIMES WITH $22.50 WORTH OF FREE ADS, DISCOUNT'S ON THE AVON ENCYCLOPEDIA. DON'T DELAY - TELL YOUR FRIENDS - JOIN TODAY!

It Doesn't Cost You—It Pays You To Belong

JOIN BUD'S BUNCH

Send 15c per word for ads or send $11.00 for 1 year (Canada - $11.00 for 1 year, U.S. money orders only) membership with $22.50 worth of free ad coupons.

Send Order To:

BUD HASTIN
P. O. Box 8400, Ft. Lauderdale, FL 33310

MEMBERSHIP AND AD RATES
SUBJECT TO CHANGE WITHOUT NOTICE

▪-61 CLEAN AS A WHISTLE
Red & white plastic bottle, Real
…tle cap. Came in bubble bath.
…P. $1.79 C.M.V. $15.00, M.B.
…00 BO.

1966-67 THREE BEARS
4¾'' high each. 3 oz. each. White plastic bottles with blue caps. OSP $1.25 each. Papa Bear holds baby oil, CMV $10.00 BO, $14.00 MB. Mama Bear holds baby lotion, Baby Bear holds shampoo, CMV $8.00 BO $12.00 MB each.

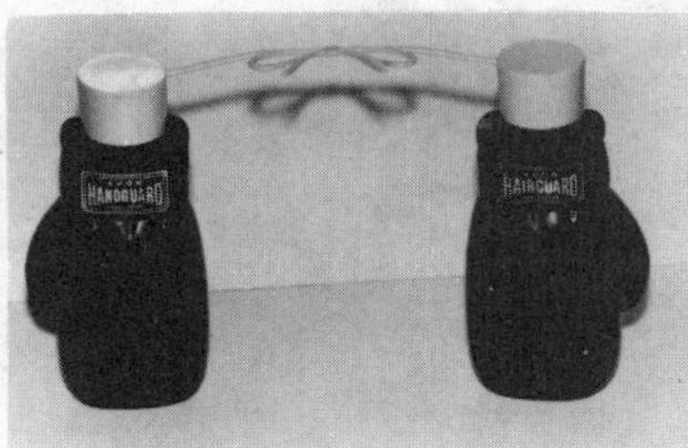

1960-62 A WINNER
4 oz. maroon plastic Boxing Gloves with white Caps. Tied together with white plastic cord. Hand Guard & Hair Guard. O.S.P. $1.98 C.M.V. $20.00 M.B. $7.00 ea. bottle.

…64-65 BUBBLE BUNNY
…ng & white rabbit puppet with
…oz tube of bubble bath gel. O.S.P.
…1.98, C.M.V. $5.00 puppet only,
…11.00 MB.

1967 GOOD HABIT RABBIT
3 oz. 4½'' high. White plastic Rabbit, green hat & orange carrot. Came in Tot N'Tyke Shampoo. O.S.P. $1.50, CMV $8.00, $11.00 MB.

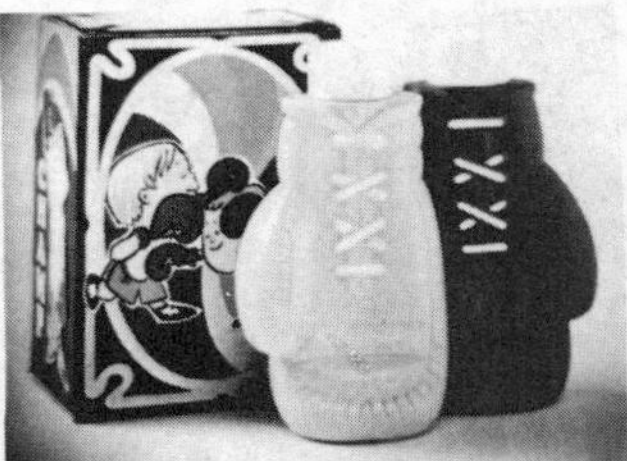

1967-68 LITTLE CHAMP
½ oz. each with white caps. Blue boxing glove holds Non Tear Shampoo, yellow glove holds Hair Trainer. O.S.P. $2.50, CMV $17.00 set in box. Each glove $5.00

1965 BUGLE
6 oz. blue plastic bugle with yellow cap. Holds Tot 'N Tyke Shampoo. OSP $1.79 CMV $10.00 BO $15.00 MB.
1965 FIFE
6 oz. yellow plastic bottle with red cap. Came in Hand Lotion or Hair Trainer. OSP $1.49 CMV $10.00 BO $15.00 MB.

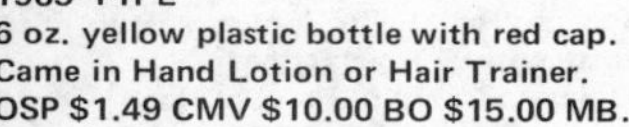

1967-68 THREE LITTLE PIGS
3 oz. each. 4½ inches high. Blue pigs yellow hat holds bubble bath, yellow pig, green hat holds baby shampoo & pink pig with pink hat holds baby lotion. OSP $1.35 each, CMV $5.00 each, $8.00 MB.

1965-66 MR. MANY MOODS
6 oz. white plastic bottle with blu… & yellow hat, red nose & mouth, black eyes. Holds shampoo. O.S.P. $1.98, C.M.V. $8.00, $10.00 M.B.
1968 MR' PRESTO CHANGO
6 oz. yellow plastic bottle with red hat, black eyes & pink lips. Holds No Tear Shampoo. O.S.P. $2.25, C.M.V. $5.00, $6.00 M.B.

1970-72 RING 'EM UP CLEAN
8 oz. orange plastic bottle with red or white cap holds Non Tear Shampoo OSP $2.50 CMV $2.50, $4.00 MB.

1965 SAFE SAM
8 oz. red & black plastic safe holds bubble bath. OSP $1.98 CMV $8.00, $11.00 MB.

1966-67 WHISTLE TOTS
6¾" high. 4 oz. white plastic bottle with whistle cap. Red cap fireman holds Tot 'N Tyke Shampoo. Blue cap policeman holds Hair Trainer & green clown holds bubble bath. O.S.P. $1.50 ea. C.M.V. $7.00 BO mint $10.00 MB.

1970-72 MOON FLIGHT GAME
4 oz. white Space Capsule holds Non Tear Shampoo. Comes with black game sheet. O.S.P. $4.00, C.M.V $4.00 M.B. $1.50 B.O.

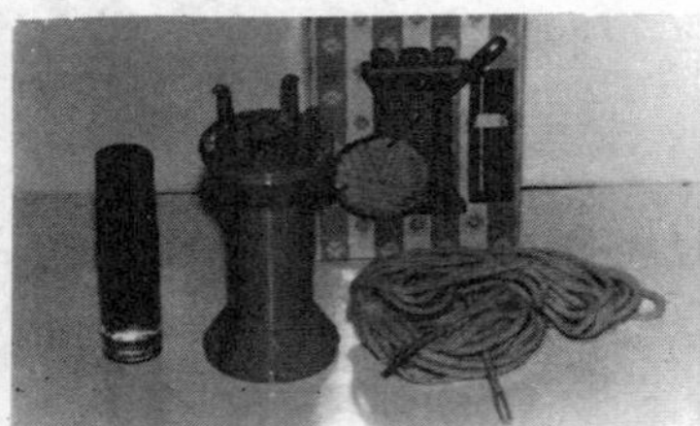

1972-73 SPOOL-A-DOO ROLLETTE
.33 oz. Rollette with red cap. Came with yellow plastic spool, eight yards of pink yarn & blue & pink plastic needles. S.S.P. $2.00 C.M.V. $4.00 M.B.

1966-67 GLOBE BANK
10 oz. blue plastic globe holds bubble bath. Black base. Bank has 5 different colored sets of stick on countries., North America came in orange, blue, tan, pink or yellow. OSP $2.50 CMV $16.00 MB $10.00 BO

1970 MAD HATTER
6 oz. bronze plastic with pink hat & clock. Came in bubble bath. OSP $3.00 CMV $4.00 MB, $2.00 BO

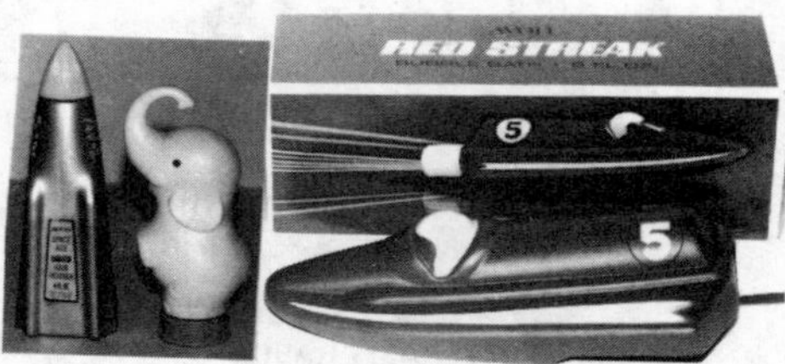

1968-69 SPACE ACE
4 oz. silver & yellow plastic rocket holds liquid hair trainer. OSP $1.50 CMV $3.00, $5.00 MB.

1970 BO BO THE ELEPHANT
5 oz. light or dark pink plastic bottle of Non Tear Shampoo. OSP $2.50 CMV $2.50, $4.00 MB.

1972-73 RED STREAK BOAT
5 oz. red plastic boat, white cap. Holds bubble bath. OSP $2.00 CMV $5.00 MB $3.00 BO.

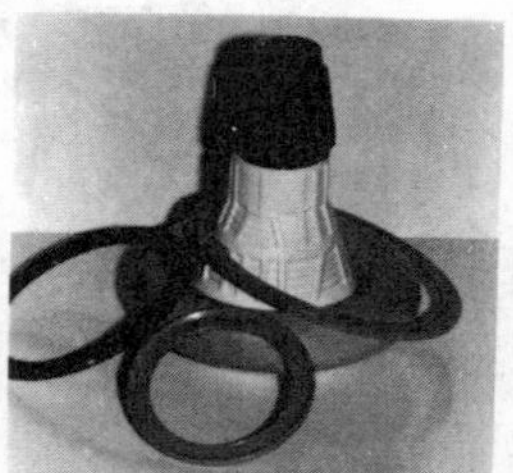

1970-71 SPLASH DOWN BUBBLE BATH
8 oz. white plastic bottle with red cap & yellow base ring. Came with 3 plastic toss rings. OSP $4.00 CMV $3.00 MB, bottle only $1.00.

1966-67 SCHOOL DAYS
8 oz. red & white plastic ruler holds Non Tear Shampoo. Yellow cap. OSP $1.98 CMV $7.00, $10.00 MB.

1968-69 MILK BATH
6 oz. pink plastic milk can holds powdered bubble bath. OSP $4.00 CMV $2.00 BO $3.00 MB.

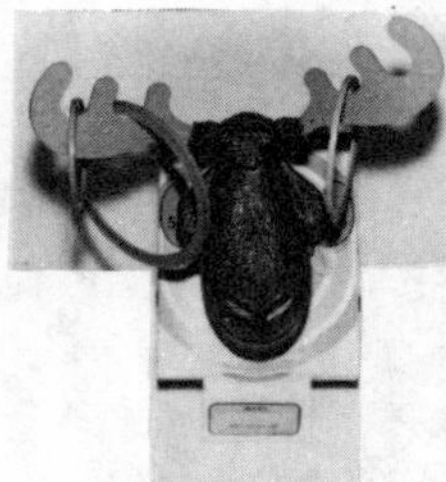

1972-75 LOOP-A-MOOSE GAME & SOAP - 7" high brown plastic moose, yellow antlers, has green, pink & yellow rings to toss. Comes with 3 oz. yellow soap. S.S.P. $3.00, C.M.V. $3.00 M.B.

1964 TOY SOLDIERS
4 oz. ea. Red, white & blue plastic bottles, black caps. Came in Hair Trainer, Shampoo, Hand Lotion, Bubble Bath. O.S.P. $1.25 ea. C.M.V. $10.00 ea. B.O. $12.00 M.B.

1970-72 CONCERTINA
8 oz. blue / yellow plastic squeeze bottle holds bubble bath. Musical cap with pink strap. OSP $2.50 CMV $5.00 MB $3.00 BO.

1962-65 CONCERTINA
8 oz. red & yellow plastic squeeze bottle with musical cap. Holds bubble bath. OSP $1.98 CMV $12.00, $15.00 MB.

1967 MR. LION
4 oz. white plastic bottle with red bubble pipe over white cap. Holds bubble bath. OSP $1.50 CMV $5.00 BO $7.00 MB.

1967 TIN MAN
4 oz. white plastic bottle with blue bubble pipe over white cap. Holds Non Tear Shampoo. OSP $1.50 CMV $5.00 BO $7.00 MB.

1967 STRAW MAN
4 oz. white plastic bottle with yellow bubble pipe over white cap. Holds hand lotion. OSP $1.50 CMV $5.00 BO $7.00 MB.

1971-72 MR' ROBOTTLE
8" high plastic bottle with blue body & red legs & arms. silver & yellow cap. Holds bubble bath. Came with white plastic wrench to put together. O.S.P. $3.50, C.M.V. $3.50 B.O. $5.00 MB.

1969 BIRD HOUSE
7" high orange plastic bottom with tan roof. Holds 8 oz. of Powdered Bubble Bath. O.S.P. $3.75, C.M.V. $5.00 BO $7.00 MB.

1971-72 KANGA WINKS
7" high yellow & orange plastic bottle with pink hat holds 8 oz. of bubble bath. Box also holds black & white plastic target & package of 16 plastic chips for tiddlywinks. O. S.P. $4.00, C.M.V. $4.00 complete set $1.00 Kangaroo only.

1961-62 AVONVILLE SLUGGER
6 oz. tan plastic bat holds shampoo. OSP $1.49 CMV $12.00 BO $17.00 MB.

1973 SURE WINNER SLUGGER DECANTER
6 oz. yellow plastic bat. Holds Sure Winner Bracing Lotion or Liquid Hair Trainer or Avon Spicy After Shave. SSP $2.00 CMV $3.00 mint.

1965 (Only) TOPSY TURVEY CLOWN
10 oz. red, white & yellow plastic clown. Blue hat, black feet. Holds bubble bath. O.S.P. $2,50, C.M.V. $16.00 MB $11.00 BO mint.

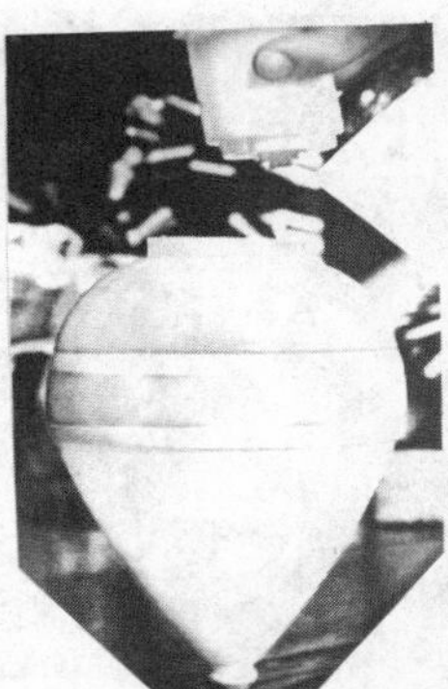

1966-67 SPINNING TOP
4 oz. red & white top holds bubble bath, yellow top spinner. O.S.P. $1.75 CMV $10.00 MB $6.00 BO

1963-64 FIRST MATE SHAMPOO
8 oz. blue & white plastic sailor with white hat. O.S.P. $1.98. C.M.V. $14.00 in box, $10.00 BO .

1963-64 CAPTAIN'S BUBBLE BATH
8 oz. white, yellow & black plastic bottle with blue hat. OSP $1.98 CMV $14.00 MB $10.00 BO

1968-69 ONE TWO LACE MY SHOE
8 oz. bubble bath. Pink plastic shoe with orange tie on & yellow cap. Green or yellow roof. OSP $2.98 CMV $5.00 BO $8.00 MB.
1968-69 TIC TOC TURTLE
8 oz. 5½" high. Green turtle, yellow clock face with pink hands. Bubble bath. OSP $2.50 CMV $5.00 BO $8.00 MB.

1961-62 LAND HO
8 oz. blue & white plastic telescope holds Hair Trainer, OSP $1.49 CMV $17.00 MB $12.00 BO mint.
1961-62 NAUGHTY-LESS
8 oz. red & white submarine with white & blue cap. Holds bubble bath. OSP $1.79 CMV $15.00 BO mint $20.00 MB.

1961-64 LIL FOLKS TIME
8 oz. yellow & white plastic clock with yellow cap & red time hands, holds bubble bath. OSP $1.79 CMV $10.00 MB $6.00 BO
1967-69 TIC TOC TIGER
8 oz. orange & white plastic clock with yellow cap & hands, holds bubble bath. OSP $1.75 CMV $4.00 BO $6.00 MB.

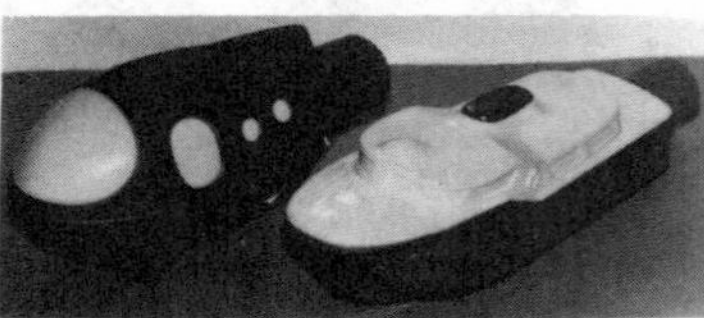

1964-65 AQUA CAR
8 oz. red & white plastic bottle of bubble bath. OSP $1.98 CMV $10.00 - $15.00 MB
1970-71 S.S. SUDS
8 oz. blue & white plastic boat holds No Tear Shampoo. OSP $3.00 CMV $3.00 $5.00 MB.

1967-68 BIRD FEEDER
11" high, black & white plastic center with red base & yellow top. Holds 7½ oz. powdered bubble bath. O.S.P. $3.50 C.M.V. $7.00 bottle only. $9.00 M.B.

1964-65 SANTA'S CHIMNEY
Red & white box holds 5 oz. of powdered bubble bath. Top of box makes a puzzle game. OSP $1.98 CMV $20.00 MB.

1966-67 LITTLE MISSY ROLLING PIN
12" long, 8 oz. pink plastic center with orange ends. Holds Non Tear Shampoo. O.S.P. $2.25 C.M.V. $9.00 B.O. mint $13.00 MB.

1967-68 SANTA'S HELPER
Red & white sponge with 6 oz. tube of Gel Bubble Bath. O.S.P. $2.50 C.M.V. $7.00 M.B.

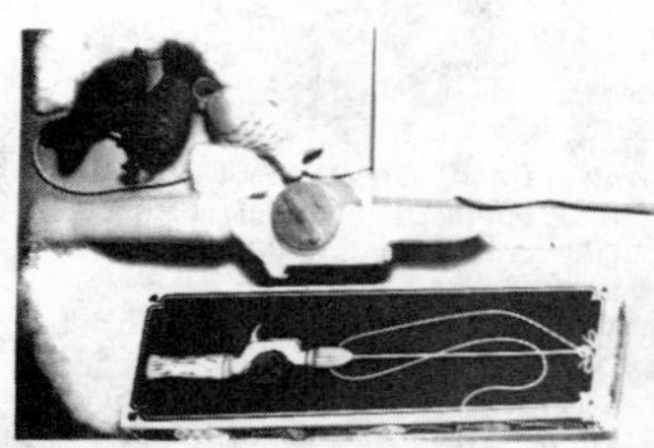

1968-69 TUB CATCH
2 ft. long yellow rod & reel holds 6 oz. of bubble bath. Pink, green & blue plastic fish. OSP $3.50 CMV $9.00 MB.

1971-72 HICKORY DICKORY CLOCK
5½" high, 8 oz. yellow plastic cheese clock with orange face & pink hands, purple mouse cap. Contains Non Tear Shampoo. OSP $4.50 CMV $5.00 MB $3.00 BO

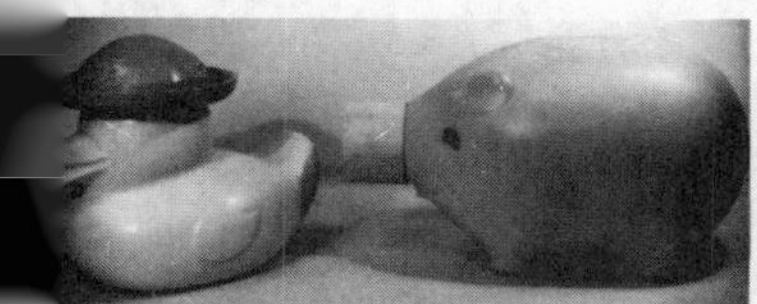

1960-62 FRILLY DUCK
3 oz. yellow plastic duck with blue cap. Came in baby oil, baby lotion & Tot N' Tyke shampoo. OSP 98c CMV $9.00 $13.00 MB
1960-62 PIG IN A POKE
8 oz. pink plastic pig holds bubble bath Came in pink bag. OSP $1.79 CMV $13.00 MB $9.00 BO.

1971-72 MAZE GAME
6 oz. green plastic bottle, white cap, holds Non Tear Shampoo. OSP $2.50 CMV $5.00 MB $3.00 BO
1971-72 HUGGY BEAR
8 oz. brown plastic bottle with lace-up vest, holds bubble bath. OSP $3.50 CMV $5.00 MB $3.00 BO

1964-65 PACKY THE ELEPHANT
3 oz. each. O.S.P. $1.10 each. Each has white hat. Blue holds baby oil, yellow holds baby shampoo, baby lotion in red. CMV red & blue $10.00 BO each $15.00 MB, yellow $15.00 BO $20.00 MB.

1973 LITTLE WIGGLEY GAME & BUBBLE BATH - 8 oz. green with pink legs, red & yellow hoops. Holds bubble bath. SSP $3.50 CMV $3.00 MB.

1962-64 LITTLE HELPER IRON
8 oz. blue plastic iron with white handle, holds bubble bath. OSP $1.98 CMV $13.00 mint $17.00 MB.
1962-64 WATERING CAN
8 oz. yellow plastic bottle holds bubble bath. Blue cap. OSP $1.98 CMV $13.00 mint $17.00 MB.

1965 (Only) JET PLANE
3 oz. red, white & blue plastic tube with white plastic wings came in Gel bubble bath, children's Gel shampoo or Hair Trainer. OSP $1.50 CMV $10.00 mint $15.00 MB.

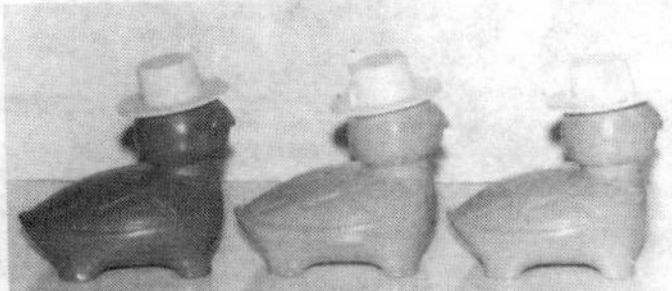

1961-63 LIL TOM TURTLES
3 oz. plastic turtles. O.S.P. $1.10 each. Each has white hat. Yellow holds baby shampoo, blue has baby oil & baby lotion in red. CMV $10.00 each, $15.00 MB.

LEFT 1978 EASTER DEC-A-DOO FOR CHILDREN
8 oz. plastic yellow base, pink top. Came with stick on decals. This is different from 68-69 issue. Old one does not say for children on label. Holds bubble bath. SSP $3.99 CMV $3.00 MB $2.00 BO
RIGHT 1978-79 DUSTER D. DUCKLING FLUFF PUFF
3.5 oz. yellow plastic & fluff top. Holds Delicate Daisies perfumed talc. SSP $4.44 CMV $3.00 MB $2.00 BO

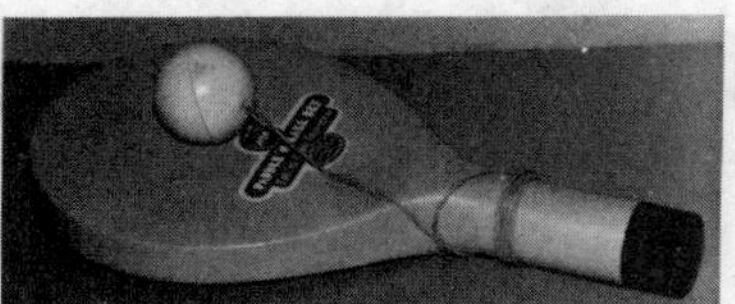

1966-67 PADDLE N' BALL SET
6 oz. tan plastic paddle with red cap, holds shampoo. Rubber ball hooked to paddle. 8" long by 4½" wide. O.S.P. $1.75 C.M.V. $12.00 - $15.00 M.B.

1969-71 MICKEY MOUSE
4½ oz. red pants, black & white plastic Mickey with yellow feet. Holds bubble bath. OSP $3.50 CMV $4.00 BO $6.00 MB
1970-71 PLUTO
4 oz. yellow & black plastic dog with red collar, holds Non Tear Shampoo. OSP $3.50 CMV $4.00 BO $6.00 MB.

1971-72 ARISTOCAT
4 oz. gray cat with pink collar holds Non Tear Shampoo. OSP $3.00 CMV $4.00 MB $3.00 BO
1971 CLUCK A DOO
8 oz. yellow bottle, pink hat, came with stick on decals. Holds bubble bath. OSP $3.00 CMV $5.00 MB $3.00 BO.

1976-78 CUSTOM CAR
7 oz. blue plastic bottle with red tire cap. Filled with bubble bath for children. OSP $5.00 CMV $2.00 MB $1.00 BO
1977-78 TRICERATOPS
8½ oz. green plastic bottle. Came with bubble bath for children. OSP $5.50 CMV $2.00 MB $1.00 BO

1969-70 CHIEF SCRUBBEM
4 oz. red & yellow plastic Indian holds liquid soap. OSP $2.50 CMV $4.00 MB $3.00 BO

1968-69 SCRUB MUG
6 oz. blue plastic mug with blue brush lid. Holds liquid soap. OSP $2.50 CMV $5.00 MB $3.00 BO

1971-72 POP A DUCK
6 oz. blue plastic bottle holds bubble bath. 3 plastic ducks & ball. C.M.V. $5.00 complete set M.B. O.S.P. $3.50

1968-69 EASTER DEC A DOO (Left)
8 oz. pink & yellow plastic egg holds bubble bath. Came with stick on decorations. OSP $2.50 CMV $5.00 MB $3.00 BO

1963-65 HUMPTY DUMPTY (Right)
8 oz. plastic bottle of bubble bath. Blue bottom, white top, black belt. OSP $1.98 CMV $8.00 MB $5.00 BO

1967-68 SMILEY THE WHALE
9" blue plastic whale holds 9 oz. bubble bath. OSP $1.98 CMV $5.00 BO $8.00 MB

1959-62 WHITEY THE WHALE
8 oz. white plastic whale holds bubble bath. OSP $1.79, CMV $15.00 MB $10.00 BO

1968-69 MARY NON TEAR SHAMPOO
3 oz. pink plastic bottle. OSP $1.35 CMV $5.00 BO $7.00 MB.

1968-69 LITTLE LAMB BABY LOTION
3 oz. white plastic lamb with blue cap. OSP $1.35 CMV $5.00 BO $7.00 MB.

1968-69 LITTLE RED SCHOOLHOUSE
3 oz. red plastic school with yellow cap. Contains bubble bath. OSP $1.35 CMV $5.00 BO $7.00 MB.

1976-78 TYRANNOSAURUS REX
4 oz. green plastic bottle, green rubber head. Holds bubble bath for children. SSP $2.99 CMV $1.00 BO $2.00 MB.

1978-79 TUB SUB
6 oz. yellow plastic, 10" long. Holds bubble bath for children. SSP $3.99 CMV $3.00 MB $1.00 BO.

1975-76 ROCKABYE PONY DECANTER
6 oz. yellow plastic, holds clearly gentle baby lotion. OSP $4.00 CMV $2.00 BO $3.00 MB

1975-76 JACK-IN-THE-BOX
4 oz. yellow & pink plastic, holds baby cream. OSP $4.00 CMV $2.00 BO $3.00 MB

1963-64 TOOFIE TWOSOME
This is the 1st issue of the Toofie series 3½ oz. green & blue tube & green cap. Choice of red, yellow, blue or green tooth brush. O.S.P. $1.25, CMV $8.00 MB. Tube only $3.00

1967-68 TOOFIE TOOTH PASTE
3½ oz. white tube with racoon & pink cap & tooth brush, pink & white box. O.S.P. $1.25 C.M.V. $6.00 MB $2.00 tube only.

1966-67 TOOFIE THE TIGER
3½ oz. Green & orange tube, green cap, tooth brush. O.S.P. $1.35, C.M.V. $6.00 M.B. in box, $3.00 tube only mint.

1968-69 TOOFIE ON GUARD
3½ oz. red, white & blue tube, blue cap. Avon tooth brush. O.S.P. $1.25, C.M.V. Tube only $2.00. mint $5.00 MB.

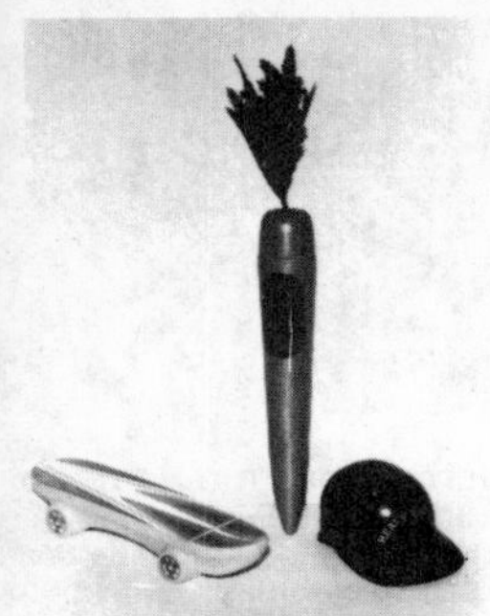

1978-79 HANG TEN SKATEBOARD DECANTER
.5 oz. yellow plastic with top stick n decal. Holds bubble bath for children. S.S.P. $4.99, C.M.V. $2.50 M.B.

1978-79 14 KARROT TAN DECANTER
4 oz. orange plastic with green leaf top. Holds Bronze Glory tanning lotion. S.S.P. $4.99, C.M.V. $2.50 M.B.

1978-79 HEAVY HITTER DECANTER
4 oz. dark blue plastic. White letters. Holds non tear shampoo. S.S.P. $4.99, C.M.V. $2.50 M.B.

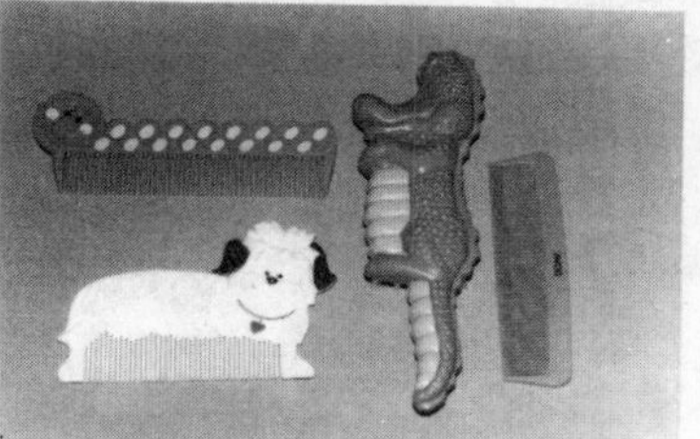

1974-75 CURLY CATERPILLAR COMB
6" long green and pink plastic. OSP $1.50 CMV $1.00 MB

1975-76 SHAGGY DOG COMB
5" long white plastic. OSP $1.25 CMV $1.00 MB.

1974 AL E. GATOR COMB & BRUSH
5" long green plastic with green comb. OSP $3.00 CMV $3.00 MB.

1969-70 TOOFIE TOOTHPASTE
3½ oz. blue & green tube with pink cap & tooth brush in blue & green box. OSP $1.35 CMV $5.00 MB $2.00 tube only.

KIDS' PLASTIC TOYS

1978-79 SWEET PICKLES FUN BOOK AND RECORD
Book and record issued by Avon Products. Came in an envelope. There are 4 different ones. S.S.P. $1.99, C.M.V. $1.99 complete mint.

1978-79 ACCUSING ALLIGATOR
6 oz. green, yellow, and tan plastic. Holds bubble bath. S.S.P. $4.99, C.M.V. $3.50 M.B.

1978-79 SUPERMAN BUBBLE BATH
8 oz. blue, red and gray plastic. Holds bubble bath. Box came with 2 red and yellow plastic cut out capes. S.S.P. $5.99, C.M.V. $4.00 M.B.

1978-79 ON THE RUN "JOGGING SHOE"
6 oz. blue plastic with white stripes. Holds Wild Country after shave or Sweet Honesty Body Splash. S.S.P. $3.99, C.M.V. $3.00 M.B.

1978-79 CONAIR "HAIR DRYER"
6 oz off white plastic. Blue letters and cap. Holds Naturally Gentle Shampoo. S.S.P. $4.99, C.M.V. $3.50 M.B.

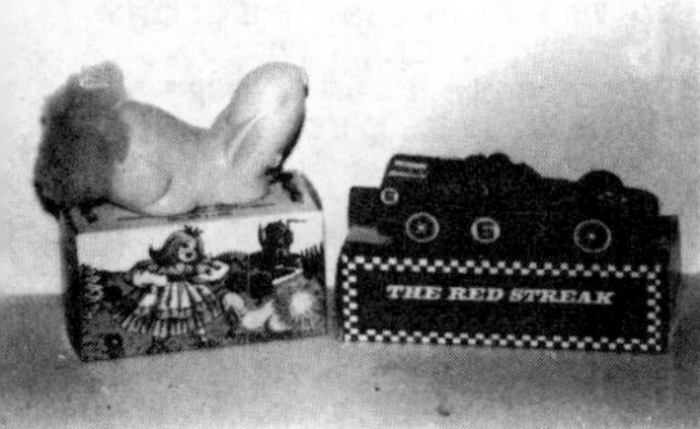

1979-80 BUNNY FLUFFPUFF
3.5 oz. yellow plastic with yellow fluff tail and pink eyes and ears. Holds childrens talc. S.S.P. $5.99, C.M.V. $3.50 M.B.

1979-80 RED STREAK CAR
7 oz. red plastic with blue and silver stick on decals. Holds bubbble bath for children. S.S.P. $3.99, C.M.V. $2.00 M.B.

1978-79 BATMOBILE
6 oz. blue and silver plastic with stick on decals. Came in bubble bath for children. S.S.P. $4.99, C.M.V. $3.00 M.B.

1978-79 LIP POP POMADE "PEPSI"
Dark amber plastic. Gray cap. Looks like Pepsi Cola bottle. S.S.P. $2.99, C.M.V. $1.50 M.B.

1979 TOOTH BRUSH DUO (CHILDRENS)
Red and pink box holds 1 red and 1 white tooth brush for kids. S.S.P. 89c, C.M.V. 50c M.B.

1979 PINK PANTHER TOOTH BRUSH HOLDER
Pink plastic holder. Yellow and red tooth brush. Blue and pink box. S.S.P. $4.99, C.M.V. $3.00 M.B.

1979-80 COMBSICLE
Popsicle box holds brown and beige Avon comb. S.S.P. $1.99, C.M.V. $1.00 M.B.
1979-80 CHOCOLATE CHIPLICK COMPACT
Tan and brown plastic, holds lip gloss. S.S.P. $3.49, C.M.V. $2.00 M.B.
1979-80 POWER DRILL
5 oz. yellow plastic with silver plastic drill cap. Holds Wild Country or Electric Pre Shave. S.S.P. $5.99, C.M.V. $4.00 M.B.

1978-79 BED OF NAILS COMB
5½" comb, tan white and red. S.S.P. $2.49, C.M.V. $2.00 M.B.
1978-79 WONDER WOMAN MIRROR
7½" long plastic mirror. S.S.P. $5.99, C.M.V. $4.00 M.B.
1978-79 SWEET PICKLES ZANY ZEBRA HAIR BRUSH
White, black, pink and green plastic. S.S.P. $4.99, C.M.V. $2.50 M.B.
1978-79 TASTI MINT LIP GLOSS COMPACT
Green and silver plastic. S.S.P. $2.99, C.M.V. $2.00 M.B.

1973 BARNEY BEAVER TOOTH-BRUSHES AND HOLDER
4" high, brown plastic with white & blue. Has pink & blue tooth brushes. Comes with a sticker to put on wall. S.S.P. $2.50 C.M.V. $4.00 MB.
1973 'I LOVE TOOFIE' TOOTH-BRUSHES AND HOLDER
5" high, white & pink, holds red & blue toothbrushes. Comes with sticker to put on wall. S.S.P. $2.00, CMV $4.00 MB.

1973-74 BABY SHOE PIN CUSHION
7 oz. white plastic with pink pin cushion & blue bow, filled with baby lotion. SSP $4.00 CMV $4.00 BO $5.00 MB.
1973-76 SUNNY BUNNY BABY POMANDER
Wax figurine with nursery fresh fragrance. SSP $5.0J CMV $5.00 BO $6.00 MB.
1973-74 SAFETY PIN DECANTER
8 oz. yellow plastic filled with baby lotion, SSP $3.00 CMV $3.00 BO $4.00 MB.

1970-72 TOPSY TURVEY
4 oz. green plastic bottle with white cap holds bubble bath. OSP $2.00 CMV $3.00 MB $1.00 BO
1972-73 BALL & CUP
4 oz. blue bottom with green cup & ball. Holds shampoo. OSP $2.00 CMV $4.00 MB $2.00 BO

1965-66 CUCKOO CLOCK
10 oz. red, white & blue plastic clock holds bubble bath. O.S.P. $2.50 C.M.V. $8.00 - $9.00 M.B.
1969-70 WRIST WASH BUBBLE BATH
2 oz. orange plastic clock with blue cap. OSP $3.00 CMV $6.00 MB $3.00 BO.

1968 LITTLE RED RIDING HOOD
4 oz. yellow plastic bottle, red cap. Holds bubble bath. OSP $1.50 CMV $2.00 BO, $6.00 with glasses MB.
1968 WOLF
4 oz. yellow & blue plastic bottle, green cap, holds Non Tear Shampoo. OSP $1.50 CMV $2.00 BO $6.00 MB with white fang teeth.

1962-63 SIX SHOOTER
6 oz. gray plastic & white gun with N Tears Shampoo. O.S.P. $1.98 C.M.V. $18.00 BO mint, $24.00 MB.

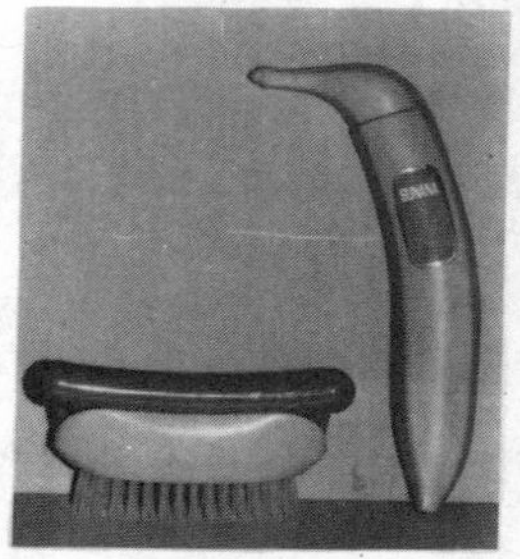

1975-76 HOT DOG! BRUSH & COMB
Yellow & red plastic comb. OSP $3.00 CMV $1.00, $2.00 MB
1974-76 SUNANA BRONZE GLORY TANNING LOTION
6 oz. yellow plastic banana. OSP $2.75 CMV $2.00 MB $1.00 BO.

1974-75 GRID KID LIQUID HAIR TRAINER
8 oz. red, black & white plastic. OSP $2.00 CMV $1.00 BO $2.00 MB.
1975-76 ARCH E. BEAR BRUSH & COMB
Red, white & blue brush with white comb. OSP $3.00 CMV $1.00, $2.00 MB.

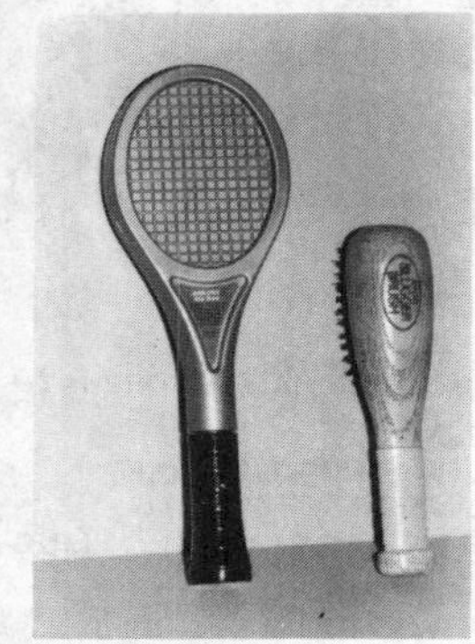

1975-76 TENNIS ANYONE?
5 oz. gray & black plastic, holds Sweet Honesty After Bath Freshener or Avon Spicy After Shave. O.S.P. $3.00 C.M.V. $1.50
1974-75 SLUGGER BRUSH
7" long brown & black plastic. O.S.P. $3.50 C.M.V. $1.00

1978-79 LOVING LION DECANTER
8 oz. plastic, purple, yellow, pink & orange. Holds Non Tear Shampoo. SSP $4.99 CMV $3.50 MB.
1978-79 THREE RING CIRCUS CHILDREN'S TALC
5 oz., 2 sections of center turn around. SSP $2.49 CMV $2.00 MB.
1978-79 OCTUPUS TOOTHBRUSH HOLDER
Purple & orange plastic toothbrush holder. Comes with orange & white Avon toothbrush. SSP $3.99 CMV $2.50 MB.

LEFT 1979-80 MOST VALUABLE GORILLA
4 oz. orange & blue plastic stick on front & back decals in any letter. Holds bubble bath for children. SSP $5.99 CMV $3.50 MB.
CENTER 1979-80 WILLIE WEATHER-MAN
6 oz. tan plastic, pink cap. Blue umbrella changes color with the weather. Holds Non Tear Shampoo. SSP $4.99 CMV $3.00 MB
RIGHT 1980 IMP THE CHIMP BATH BRUSH
Brown plastic, yellow, black & pink trim. 10" long. SSP $6.99 CMV $4.00 MB.

1974-75 TOOFIE TRAIN
Red plastic train, yellow plastic cup. Red & blue toofie toothbrushs & yellow with red cap Toofie toothpaste. O.S.P. $5.00 CMV $5.00 MB.

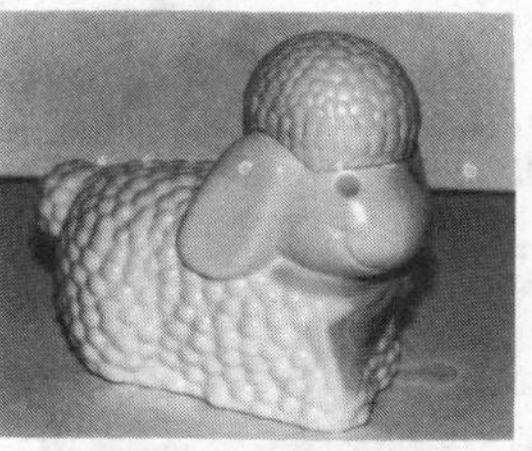

1975-76 PRECIOUS LAMB BABY LOTION
6 oz. white plastic lamb with blue bow. Holds baby lotion. SSP $2.99 CMV $3.00 MB.

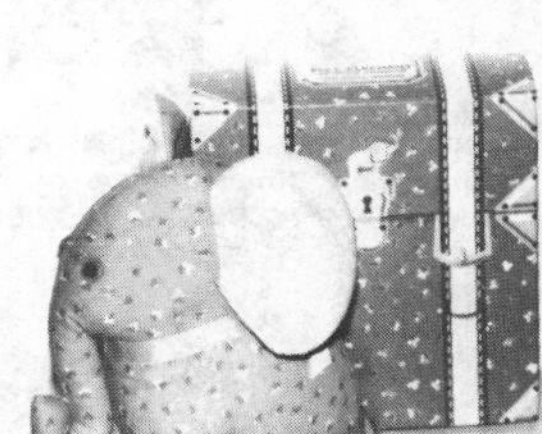

1979-80 ELLA ELEPHANT SCENTED STUFFED ANIMAL
Pink box holds pink scented elephant with turquoise ears & pink ribbon. Has Avon tag. Made in Taiwan. SSP $7.99 CMV $6.00 MB.

1974-75 SURE WINNER CATCHER'S MITT
6 oz. brown plastic with brown cap. Holds Avon liquid hair trainer. OSP $2.00 CMV $2.00
1975-76 WINKIE BLINK CLOCK BUBBLE BATH
8 oz. yellow with blue clock hands & blue cap. OSP $4.00 CMV $2.00 MB, $1.00 BO

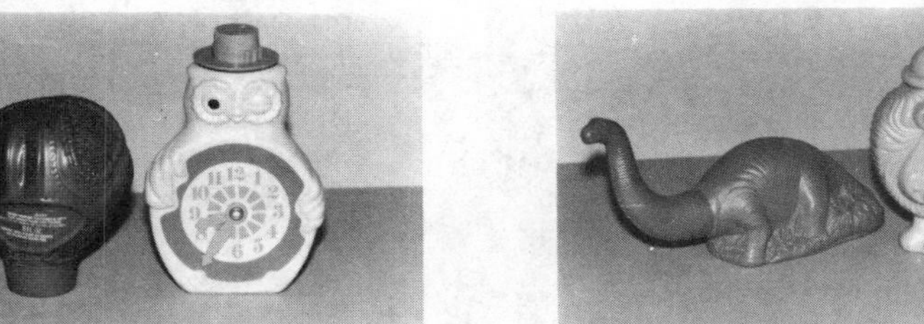

1975-76 BRONTOSAURUS BUBBLE BATH
10 oz. blue gray plastic. OSP $3.50 CMV $1.00 BO $2.00 MB.
1974-76 LOVABLE LEO
10 oz. yellow plastic, pink cap. Children's shampoo. OSP $3.00 CMV $1.00 BO $2.00 MB.

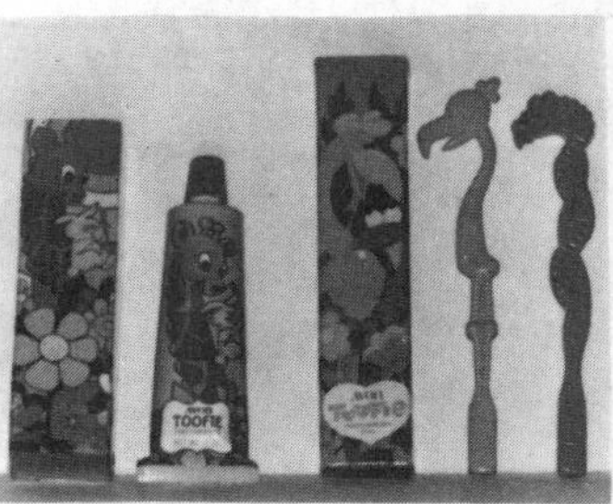

1971-73 TOOFIE TOOTHPASTE
3½ oz. yellow & orange tube & box. OSP 89c CMV $1.00, $2.00 MB
1973-74 TOOFIE TOOTHBRUSH DUO
Pak of 2, green worm & yellow bird. SSP $2.00 CMV $2.00 MB.

1976 TOOFIE TIGER TOOTHBRUSHES & HOLDER
Yellow, black, white & pink. Has one pink & one white toothbrush. OSP $2.50 CMV $2.00 MB.
1971-73 TOOFIE TOOTHBRUSH DUO
1 yellow giraffe, 1 pink rabbit brush. OSP $1.00 CMV $2.00 MB.
1975-76 TORTOISE 'N HARE TOOTHBRUSH DUO
Green tortoise and yellow hare. OSP $1.80 CMV $1.00 MB.

1978 TOOFIE THE CLOWN
Orange, yellow and white plastic tooth brush holder. Blue and pink tooth brushes. S.S.P. $2.99 C.M.V. $2.00 M.B.

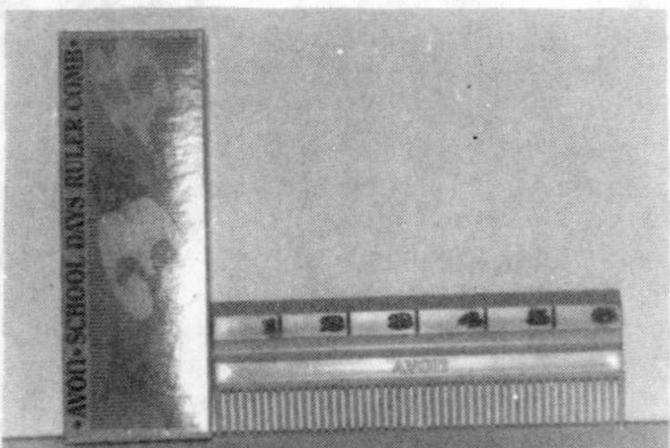

1976-79 SCHOOL DAYS RULER COMB
Box holds yellow plastic 6" ruler comb. O.S.P. $3.00 C.M.V. $1.00 M.B.

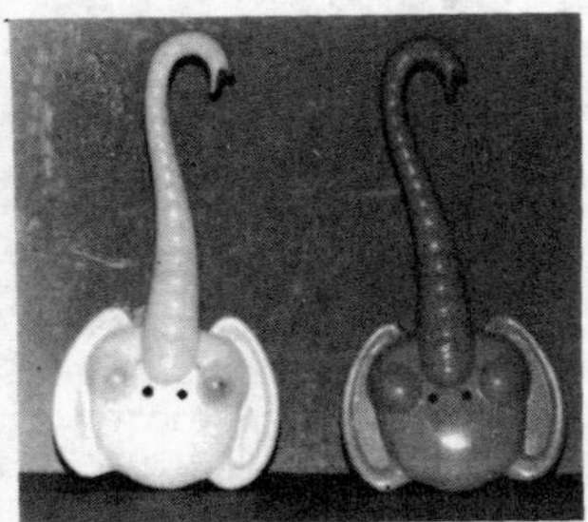

1975 SCRUBBO THE ELEPHANT BATH BRUSH
White plastic - pink ears and cheeks. S.S.P. $2.99 C.M.V. $2.00 M.B.
1976 issue was all pink plastic. Each is 8" long. S.S.P. $2.99 C.M.V. $2.00 M.B.

1974-75 TED E. BEAR TOOTH BRUSH HOLDER
Box holds tan, pink and white plastic holder and pink and white Avon tooth brushes. O.S.P. $2.75 C.M.V. $2.00 M.B.

1976-77 SPOTTY TO THE RESCUE TOOTHBRUSH HOLDER
Red, white and black plastic toothbrush holder holds 2 Avon tooth brushes. S.S.P. $2.49 C.M.V. $2.00 M.B.

1977-78 WALLY WALRUS TOOTH BRUSH HOLDER & TOOTH BRUSH
Adhesive back holder sticks to wall. Came with 2 child sized Avon toothbrushes in red and white. Plastic holder is Blue and red with white hat and trim. S.S.P. $2.00 C.M.V. $1.50 M.B.

1977-79 KISS 'N MAKEUP LIP GLOSS COMPACT
Came with Frostlight Peach and Frostlight Pink lip gloss. Red plastic container. O.S.P. $4.00 C.M.V. $1.00

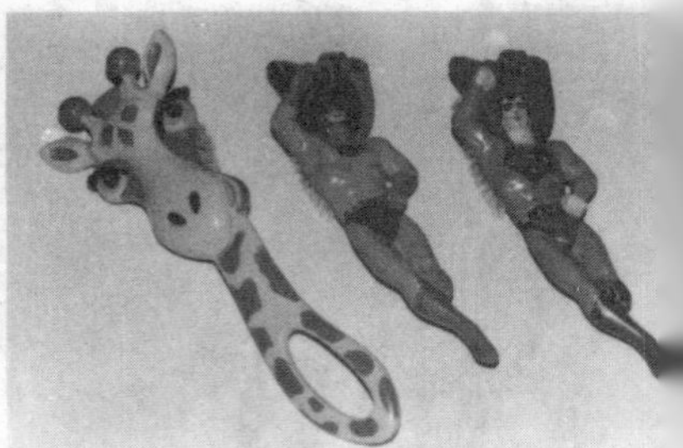

LEFT 1977-79 GIRAFFABATH BATH BRUSH
Orange and beige plastic. Blue eyes. O.S.P. $6.00 C.M.V. $2.50 M.B.
CENTER 1977-78 BATMAN STYLING BRUSH
Blue, grey, and black plastic brush. O.S.P. $6.00 C.M.V. $2.50 M.B.
RIGHT 1977 SUPERMAN STYLING BRUSH
Red and blue plastic brush. O.S.P. $6.00 C.M.V. $2.50 M.B.

LEFT 1975-76 JACK KNIFE COMB & BRUSH
Blue & silver plastic comb. Cub Scout gold label on top. O.S.P. $5.00 C.M.V. $2.00 M.B.
CENTER 1977-78 ICE CREAM COMB
Orange plastic comb with pink & brown ice cream & red cherry on top. O.S.P. $3.00 C.M.V. $1.00 M.B.
RIGHT 1977 REGGIE RACCOON HAIR BRUSH & COMB
6¼" long. Brown, white, pink and black brush and white comb. S.S.P. $3.99 C.M.V. $2.00 M.B.

1972-74 TURN A WORD BUBBLE BATH - 8 oz. pink plastic bottle with white cap & green lettered sides. O.S.P. $3.50, C.M.V. $2.00.
1972 LOVE LOCKET GLACE
CMV $6.00 MB $4.00 CO.

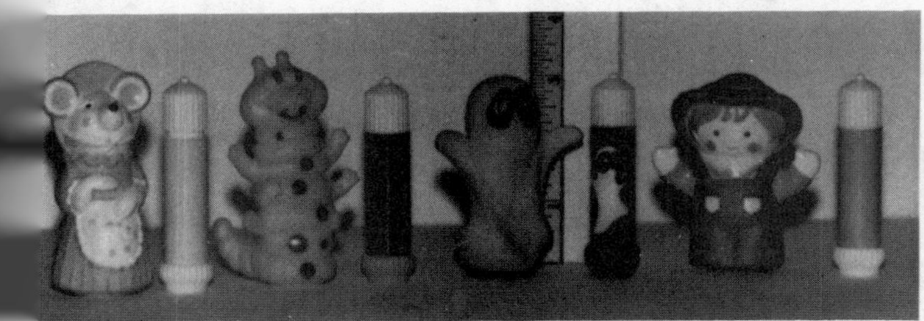

LEFT TO RIGHT
1977-78 MILLICENT MOUSE DEMI STICK
Came with Pink & Pretty fragrance demi stick. Colors are pink and white. O.S.P. $3.75 C.M.V. $2.00 M.B.
1977-79 GLOW WORM
Came with Care Deeply lip balm. White rubber top with purple spots. Demi stick is blue and green. O.S.P. $3.50 C.M.V. $2.00 M.B.

1977-78 GILROY THE GHOST
Came with Care Deeply lip blam. White and black rubber top with black, green and white demi stick. O.S.P. $3.50 C.M.V. $2.00 M.B.
1977-78 HUCK L. BERRY
Came with Care Deeply lip balm. Blue, yellow and white rubber top with yellow and white demi stick. O.S.P. $3.75 C.M.V. $2.00 M.B.

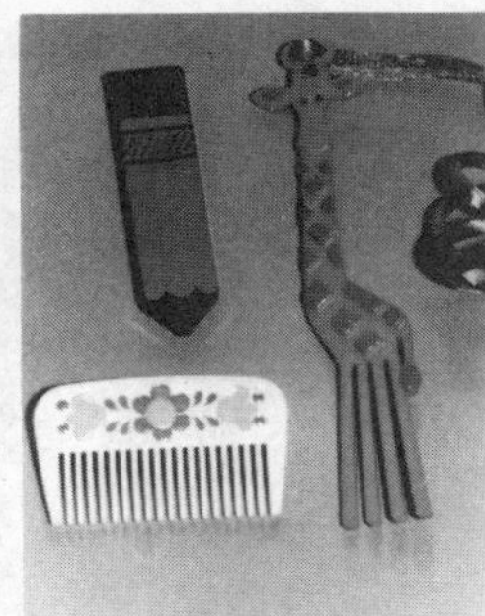

1973-75 SCHOOL DAYS BARRETTE
Brown & yellow S.S.P. $1.50 C.M.V. $1.50 M.B.
1973 COMB BARRETTE
2'' long, white plastic with red, pink & green design S.S.P. $1.50, C.M.V. $2.00 M.B.
1973 JENNY GIRAFFE
Yellow & brown with coral cord. S.S.P. $1.50, C.M.V. $2.50 M.B.

1974-76 ICE CREAM CONE LIPS POMADE
Plastic yellow base with red, pink, lavender colored tops. Came in Strawberry, Cherry, Mint, Chocolate, or Tutti-Frutti flavored lip gloss. SSP $2.00 CMV $2.00 $3.00 MB.
1974-75 RAPID RABBIT PIN PAL
White plastic with pink and green. Feet swing, filled with perfumed glace. SSP $2.00 CMV $2.00, $3.00 MB.
1974 MYRTLE TURTLE PIN PAL
Green plastic with pink and green. Filled with perfumed glace. SSP $2.00 CMV $2.00, $3.00 MB.

1976 JACK IN A BOX GLACE
White plastic with pink & green trim. SSP $1.99 CMV $2.50 MB.
1977 CHICK A PEEK GLACE
Yellow plastic back & chick with purple plastic egg. SSP $1.99 CMV $2.50 MB.

LEFT 1971 LOONEY LATHER BUBBLE BATH
6 oz. spray can, pink cap. OSP $2.00 CMV $4.00
RIGHT 1971 LOONEY LATHER SHAMPOO
6 oz. size, green cap. OSP $2.00 CMV $4.00

CHILDREN'S FUN JEWELRY
Top row left to right.
1973 LUV-A-DUCKY
Yellow & orange. SSP $2.00 CMV $2.50, $4.00 MB
1973 FLY-A-KITE
Red, white & blue. SSP $2.00 CMV $2.50, $4.00 MB
1973-74 FUZZY BUG
Blue with green fur. SSP $2.00 CMV $2.50, $4.00 MB.

Second row left to right.
1973 PANDY BEAR PIN
Black & white. SSP $1.50 CMV $2.50 $4.00 MB.
1973 PERKY PARROT
Red & green. SSP $1.50 CMV $2.50 $4.00 MB.

1975-76 BOBBIN' ROBIN PIN
White cage, red bird (bird movable)
O.S.P. $1.99 C.M.V. $2.00 M.B.
1975-76 PEDAL PUSHER PIN
Blue elephant with green jacket and pink bike. O.S.P. $1.89 C.M.V. $2.00 M.B.
1975-76 MAGIC RABBIT PIN
White and pink rabbit with grey hat
O.S.P. $1.99 C.M.V. $2.00 M.B.

1974-75 MINUTE MOUSE PIN
White with blue clock, orange hands & numbers O. S.P. $1.99 C.M.V. $2.00 M.B.
1974-76 LICKETY STICK MOUSE PIN
White plastic with green hat and pink stripped stick. O.S.P. $1.99 C.M.V. $2.00 M.B.
1976-78 COTTON TAIL GLACE
Yellow and pink with white tail.
O.S.P. $1.99 C.M.V. $2.00 M.B.

1975 PUPPY LOVE PIN PAL GLACE
Beige dog with black ears and pink pillow. OSP $1.99 CMV $3.00 MB.
1974-75 WEE WILLY WINTER PIN PAL GLACE
White snowman with pink hat, scarf & mittens. OSP $1.88 CMV $3.00 MB.
1974-75 SUNNY FRESH ORANGE GLACE NECKLACE
Orange and yellow with green cord.
OSP $2.99 CMV $3.00 MB
1975-76 PETER PATCHES PIN PAL GLACE
Yellow with red and blue trim. OSP $1.99 CMV $3.00 MB.

1975 CHICKEN LITTLE PIN PAL GLACE
Yellow chicken with pink flower & green leaf. OSP $2.49 CMV $3.00
1974-75 WILLIE THE WORM PIN PAL GLACE
Red apple, green worm. OSP $1.99 CMV $3.00 MB
1975-77 ROCK-A-ROO PIN PAL GLACE
Pink with dark pink rocking pouch.
OSP $1.99 CMV $2.00 MB.

1973-74 BUMBLEY BEE PINS
Yellow with black stripes. One with big stripes & 1 with narrow stripes. OSP $2.00 CMV $3.00, $5.00 MB.

CHILDREN'S PERFUME GLACE PIN PALS Top row left o right. Add $1.00 each MB.
1973-74 FUNNY BUNNY
Pink & white. SSP $2.00 CMV $3.00
1973 CALICO CAT
Red with white dots. Also came red & no dots. SSP $2.00 CMV $3.00.
1974-75 CALICO CAT
Blue with white dots. Also came blue with no dots on bottom half. OSP $2.00 CMV $2.00 each.
1972 BLOUSE MOUSE
Green and pink. Also came green with white trim. SSP $2.00 CMV $3.00

Second row left to right.
1974 BLUE MOO
Blue & pink. SSP $2.00 CMV $2.00
1972-75 SNIFFY PIN PAL
Black, pink & white. SSP $2.00 CMV $2.00
1973 ELPHIE THE ELEPHANT
Yellow & pink. SSP $2.00 CMV $3.00

Bottom row.
1973 GINGER BREAD PIN PAL
Brown and pink. Also came brown and white. SSP $2.00 CMV $4.00 pink, $5.00 white.

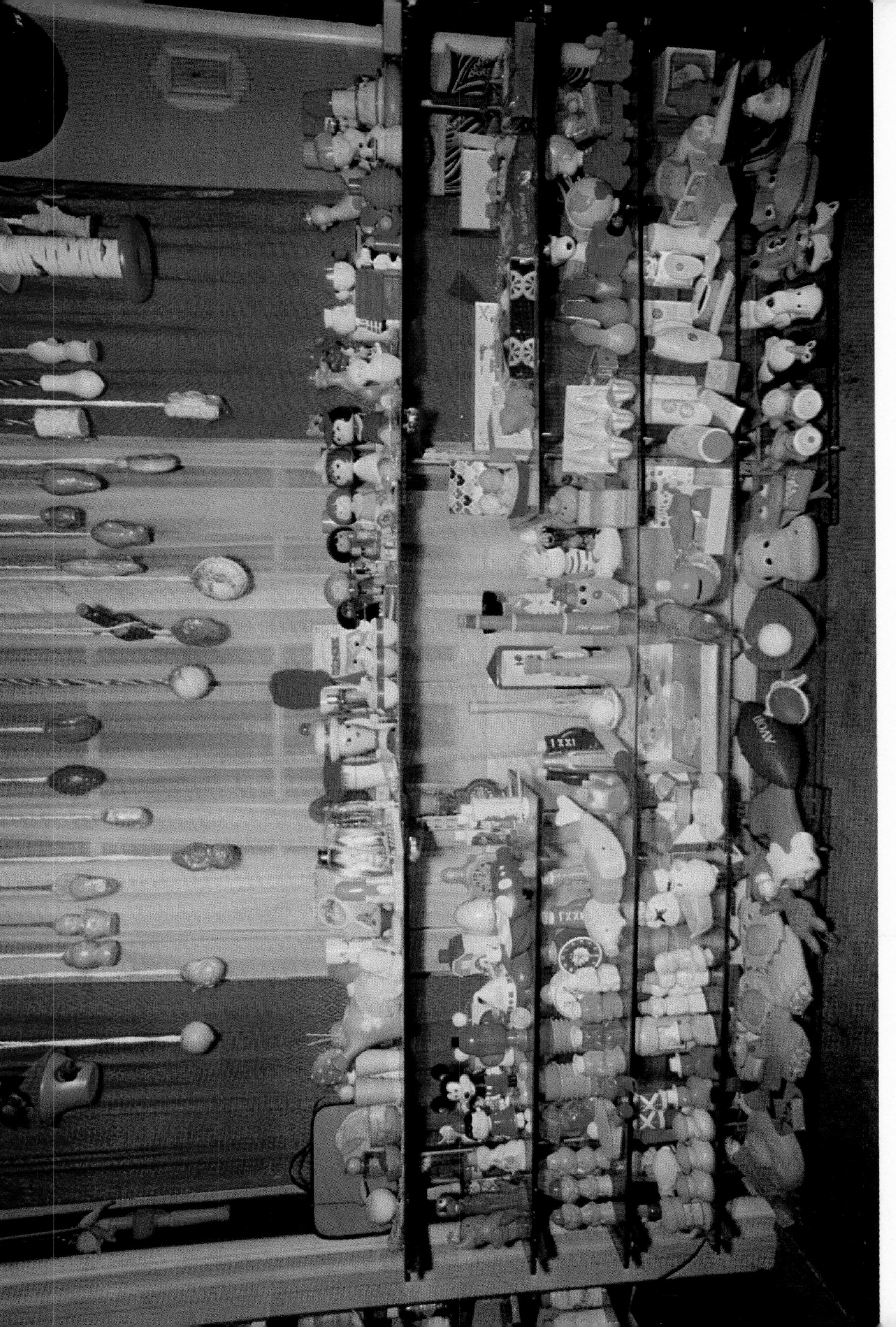

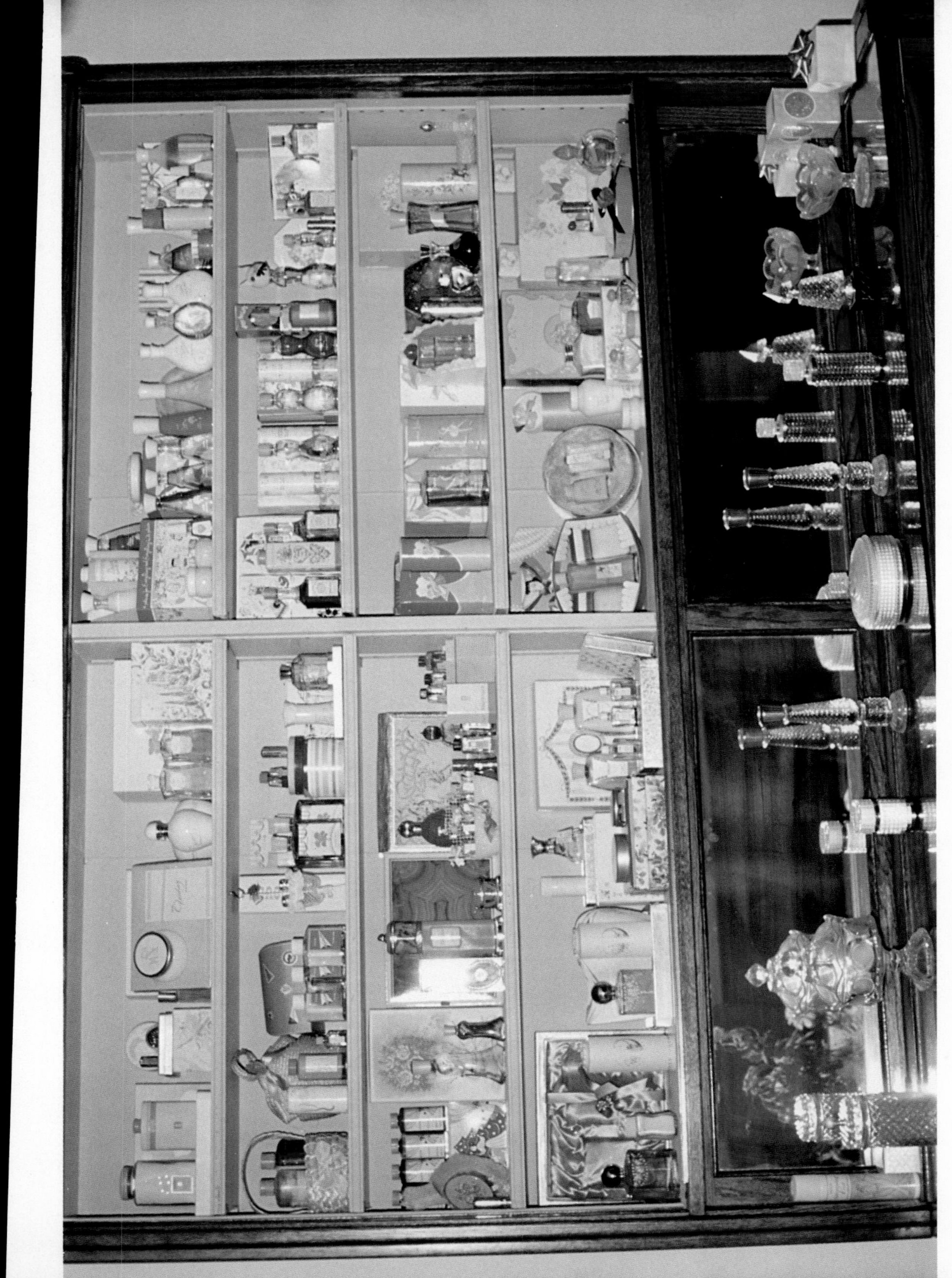

Display by Chris Martikan

MISC. AVONS - BOTTLES - ETC.

ALL CONTAINERS PRICED EMPTY

See Page 5 for Grading Examples on Mint Condition

1936-54 BRILLIANTINE
2 oz. green cap & label, 3 different labels. OSP 59c CMV $20.00 MB $15.00 BO. Add $5.00 for CPC label.

1930-36 ASTRINGENT
Came in 2 & 4 oz. size as pictured on right for size comparison. Both are ribbed glass bottles with dark blue caps & silver & blue labels. OSP 75c - 4 oz., 40c - 2 oz., CMV $40.00 MB, $35.00 BO. Mint each size.

1930-36 SKIN FRESHENER
4 or 2 oz. ribbed glass, blue or black cap. OSP 75c, 2 oz. size came in sets only. CMV $40.00 BO, $45.00 MB each.

1936-54 ASTRINGENT
2 oz. and 4 oz. size with turquoise caps. O.S.P. 78¢ C.M.V. in box $15.00. Bottle only $12.50each mint. Add $5.00 for C.P.C. label.

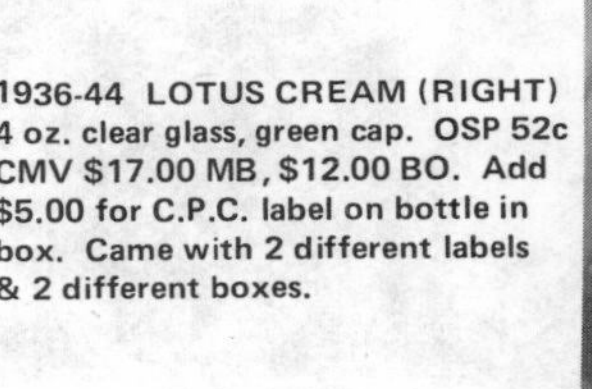

1936-44 LOTUS CREAM (RIGHT)
4 oz. clear glass, green cap. OSP 52c CMV $17.00 MB, $12.00 BO. Add $5.00 for C.P.C. label on bottle in box. Came with 2 different labels & 2 different boxes.

1930-36 LIQUID POWDER
4 oz. ribbed glass bottle with dark blue cap, silver & blue label. O.S.P. $1.00 C.M.V. $40.00 in box. $35.00 bottle only.

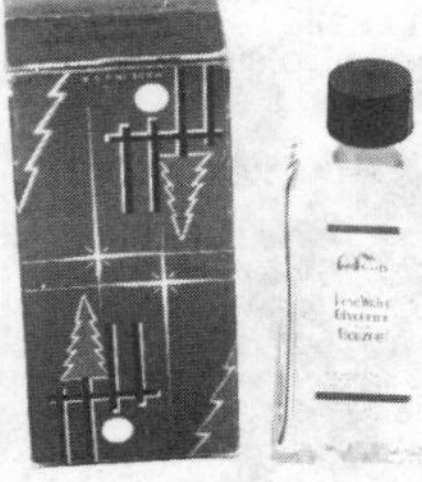

1930-36 ROSE WATER, GLYCERINE & BENZOIN
4 oz. ribbed glass bottle, blue cap. OSP 75c CMV $40.00 BO, $45.00 MB. Add $5.00 for 1935 special issue Christmas box shown.

1938-50 FINISHING LOTION
2 oz. clear glass bottle with turquoise cap. OSP 52c CMV in box $17.00, bottle only $12.50. Add $5.00 for CPC label on bottle in box.

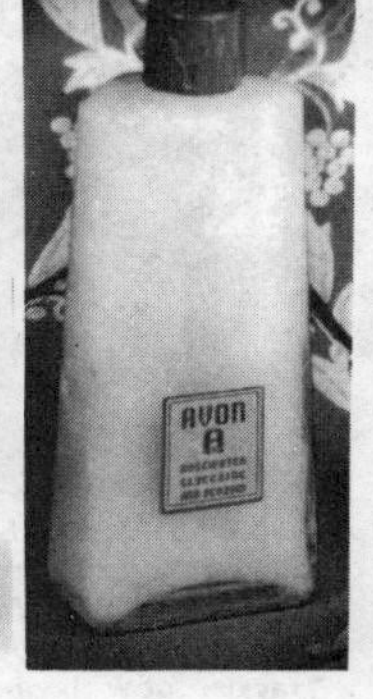

1936-44 ROSE WATER, GLYCERINE & BENZOIN
4 oz. bottle with turquoise cap. OSP 52c CMV $17.00 MB, $12.00 BO. Add $5.00 for C.P.C. label on bottle in box.

1936-41 LIQUID POWDER RACHEL OR PEACH
4 oz. green cap, clear glass. OSP $1.04 CMV $20.00 MB, $15.00 BO. Add $5.00 for C.P.C. label on box.

1954-65 SKIN FRESHENER
4 oz. bottle with green cap & label. OSP 89c CMV $1.00 each. 1965 bottle has For Dry Skin & For Normal Skin added to label. CMV $2.00 BO, $3.00 MB.
1954-65 ASTRINGENT
4 oz. bottle with green cap & label. OSP 89c CMV $3.00 MB, $2.00 BO.
1965 ASTRINGENT FRESHENER FOR OILY SKIN
Same 4 oz. bottle as 1954-65 Astringent only name is changed. OSP $1.25 CMV $3.00 BO, $4.00 MB.

1943-45 LIQUID SHAMPOO
6 oz. round shoulder bottle, black cap. This bottle is rare with round shoulders. OSP 59c, CMV $30.00 mint, $35.00 M

1931-36 BRILLIANTINE
2 oz. ribbed glass bottle with dark blue cap & silver & blue label. O.S.P. 52¢ C.M.V. $45.00 in box. $40.00 bottle only.

1955 SKIN FRESHENER
Rare 2 oz. glass bottle with embossed flowers around neck. Turquoise cap. Came in 1955 Happy Traveler Set only. C.M.V. $12.00 mint.
1930-36 LOTUS CREAM (LEFT)
4 oz. ribbed glass bottle, blue cap. O.S.P. 75¢ C.M.V. $40.00 M.B. $35.00 B.O.

1950-51 FOUNDATION LOTION
2 oz. bottle with turquoise cap. O.S.P. 59¢ Formally called Finishing Lotion. C.M.V. $20.00 MB, $15.00 BO.
1943-49 LEG MAKE-UP
4 oz. clear glass with black cap, or turquoise cap on left. 2 different bottles as shown. O.S.P. 69¢ C.M.V. $20.00 M.B. $15.00 B.O. each.

1954-58 SKIN FRESHENER
2 oz. bottle with turquoise cap & label. Came in Beautiful You set, A Thing of Beauty set. For your Beauty set & Happy Traveler set with white cap. CMV $3.00

LEFT TO RIGHT
1936-54 SKIN FRESHENER
2 and 4 oz. size bottles. Both 4 oz. bottles in center have 2 different labels. Turquoise caps. O.S.P. 78¢ C.M.V. in box $15.00. Bottle only $12.50 each. Add $5.00 for C.P.C. label on bottle or box.

1943-48 SUN CREAM
4 oz. clear glass, turquoise cap. O.S.P. 85c CMV $20.00 MB, $15.00 BO.

1951-55 COCOANUT OIL SHAMPOO
1 pint bottle with black pouring, or flat black cap. O.S.P. $1.19 C.M.V. $22.50 B.O. $27.50 M.B.

1956-57 LIQUID COCOANUT OIL SHAMPOO
1 pint with green label and double pouring cap. OSP $1.59 CMV $18.00 BO, $22.00 MB.

1930-36 LIQUID SHAMPOO
1 pint size. Metal cap. O.S.P. $1.02 C.M.V. $35.00 B.O. $40.00 M.B.

1931-36 LIQUID SHAMPOO
6 oz. ribbed glass bottle with dark blue cap & silver & blue label. O.S.P. 75¢ C.M.V. $40.00 in box. $35.00 bottle only.

1953-55 CREME HAIR RINSE (LEFT)
6 oz. clear glass bottle with green cap and label. OSP 89c, CMV $10.00 in box, $6.00 BO.

1954-56 CREME LOTION SHAMPOO (RIGHT)
6 oz. bottle with turquoise cap, painted label. 1956 label has 4A design, OSP $1.00 CMV $9.00 MB, $5.00 BO.

1937-50 LIQUID SHAMPOO
1 pint size with raised pouring or flat cap. O.S.P. $1.19 C.M.V. $20.00 B.O. $25.00 M.B. 1937-39 has C.P.C. label. $30.00

1937-50 LIQUID SHAMPOO
6 oz. turquoise cap. Indented top of bottle. OSP 59c, CMV $20.00 MB, $15.00 BO. Add $5.00 for C.P.C. label on bottle in box.

1956 Only CREME LOTION SHAMPOO
6 oz. clear glass, green cap. OSP $1.00 CMV $9.00 MB, $5.00 BO mint.

1956-57 LIQUID COCOANUT OIL SHAMPOO
6 oz. clear bottle with green cap, painted label. OSP 79c, CMV $9.00 MB, $5.00 BO

1956 CREME HAIR RINSE
6 oz. bottle with white cap & painted label with 4A design. OSP 89c, CMV $9.00 MB, $5.00 BO.

1951-55 COCOANUT OIL SHAMPOO
6 oz. bottle with turquoise cap & label. OSP 59c, CMV $17.00 MB, $12.00 BO.

1936-38 PRE-SHAMPOO OIL
2 oz. bottle with turquoise cap & label. OSP 52c CMV $22.00 MB, $18.00 BO. Add $5.00 for C.P.C. label on bottle in box.

1946-49 SOAPLESS SHAMPOO
6 oz. turquoise cap. O.S.P. 59¢ C.M.V. $20.00 B.O. $25.00 M.B. Also came in 16 oz. round size with same label. 1946-49 O.S.P. $1.19 C.M.V. $20.00 B.O. $25.00 M.B.

1931-36 PRE-SHAMPOO OIL
2 oz. ribbed glass bottle with dark blue cap, silver & blue label. O.S.P. 52¢ C.M.V. $40.00 in box. $35.00 bottle only.

1931-36 WAVE SET
4 oz. ribbed glass bottle with dark blue cap & silver & blue label. O.S.P. 52¢ C.M.V. $40.00 in box. $35.00 bottle only.

1930-36 WITCH HAZEL
4 oz. ribbed glass bottle with dark blue plastic cap, green label. O.S.P. 50¢ C.M.V. $45.00 in box. $40.00 bottle only. Also came in 8 & 16 oz. size.

1936-48 WITCH HAZEL
4 oz. green cap & label. Also came with black cap. OSP 37c, CMV $15.00 BO, $20.00 MB. Add $5.00 for C.P.C. label on bottle in box. (also came in 8 & 16 oz. size).

1936-44 WAVE SET
4 oz. bottle with turquoise cap & label. OSP 52c, CMV $20.00 MB, $15.00 BO. Add $5.00 for C.P.C. label on bottle in box.

1931-36 HAIR TONIC EAU DE QUININE FOR OILY HAIR - 1 pint size. Silver metal cap. (For dry hair, same price & date) O.S.P. $1.75 C.M.V. $45.00 M.B. $40.00 B.O.

1931-36 HAIR TONIC EAU DE QUININE
6 oz. ribbed glass bottle with dark blue cap with silver & blue label. Came in Tonic for Dry Hair & for Oily Hair. O.S.P. 90¢ C.M.V. $40.00 in box. $35.00 bottle only.

1942-49 CREAM LOTION
6 oz. pink cap, back side of bottle is flat, Flowered box shown sold 1942 only. O.S.P. 79¢ C.M.V. $30.00 M.B. $25.00 B.O.

1954 SUN LOTION
2 oz. bottle, white cap. Came in camping kit set only. C.M.V. $22.00

1955-57 SUN FOAM
Peach colored can & cap. O.S.P. $1.35 CMV $6.00 MB, $4.00 can only.

1942-43 CREAM LOTION BOX
Box shown sold 1942-43 only. 6 oz. fl sided bottle with pink cap sold 1942-4 O.S.P. 49¢ as pictured. C.M.V. $30.00 M.B. as shown. $25.00 B.O.mint.

1951-54 HAND LOTION
4 oz. pink or white plastic cap, blue & pin label. O.S.P. 59¢ C.M.V. $15.00 in box. $13.00 bottle only.

1948 HAND LOTION
2 oz. glass bottle with blue cap. Came in 1948 Hair Ribbons Set. C.M.V. $15.00

1943-50 HAND LOTION
4 oz. clear glass, turquoise cap. O.S.P. 59¢ C.M.V. $17.00 in box. $12.50 bottle only.

1950 HAND LOTION
4 oz. pink cap. Same bottle as Cotillion of that period. This was a substitute bottle. Rare. OSP 59c, CMV $15.00 BO, $20.00 MB.

1942 Only HAND LOTION ROSE WATER, GLYCERINE & BENZOIN LOTION
6 oz. flat sided bottle. Came in sets only. CMV $40.00 mint.

1966-70 HAND LOTION
Pink plastic bottle with pink cap, gold lettering. 1966-70 - 10 oz. size. O.S.P. $1.50 C.M.V. $1.00. 1966-67 - 4 oz. size. O.S.P. 79¢ C.M.V. $1.00

1950 Only HAND LOTION
4 oz. clear glass, turquoise cap & label. OSP 59c, CMV $14.00 mint.

1968-74 BRONZE GLORY TANNING OIL - 4 oz. brown plastic with yellow cap. O.S.P. $1.00 C.M.V. 50¢
1972-74 BRONZE GLORY TANNING LOTION - 4 oz. yellow plastic with brown cap. O.S.P. $1.00 C.M.V. 50¢
1967-74 KWICK TAN
4 oz. white, orange & red. O.S.P. $1.00 C.M.V. 25¢
1973-74 BRONZE GLORY TANNING BUTTER - 7 oz. brown can with yellow cap. O.S.P. $1.00 C.M.V. 50¢

1958-65 TAN MOISTURIZED SUNTAN LOTION
4 oz. white plastic bottle with brown cap. OSP 98c, CMV $2.00 BO, $3.00 MB.
1954-58 HAND LOTION
4 oz. green cap & label. OSP 59c, CMV $1.00 BO, $3.00 MB.

1956-57 GIFT HAND LOTION
8 oz. bottle with pump dispenser, indented front & back. 1956 box has Xmas tree on it. 1957 box shown. O.S.P. $1.39 C.M.V. $15.00 in box. $10.00 bottle only.

1949-58 SUN LOTION
4 oz. bottle with white cap. Montreal label to 1954. C.M.V. $11.00. Pasadena label 1954-58 O.S.P. $1.00 C.M.V. $10.00 B.O. $12.00 M.B.

1959 MERRY CHRISTMAS HAND LOTION
Christmas box holds 6 oz. white pearl plastic bottle with blue cap of White Pearl hand lotion. Sold Christmas only. O.S.P. 98¢ $6.00 B.O. C.M.V. $10.00 M.B.

1973-76 MOISTURIZED HAND LOTION
10 oz. plastic bottle. O.S.P. $1.00 C.M.V. 25¢
1965-66 HAND LOTION - 4 oz. white & turquoise plastic. O.S.P. 79¢ C.M.V. $2.00

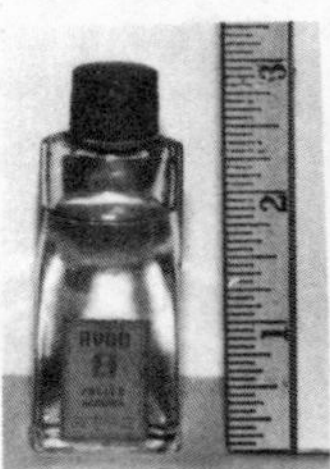

1936-39 POLISH REMOVER
½ oz. bottle, turquoise cap. C.P.C. on label. OSP 31c, CMV $15.00 BO, $20.00 MB.

1936-37 NAIL POLISH
Clear glass with turquoise cap, C.P.C. label. OSP 37c, CMV $15.00 BO, $20.00 MB.

1963-64 HAND LOTION
8 oz. gold stripes on bottle, gold & white pump. Also came without gold neck band. OSP $2.50 CMV $8.00 MB, $3.00 BO.
1964-65 LOTION LOVELY
8 oz. gold painted label. Came in Wishing, Here's My Heart, Persian Wood, To A Wild Rose - OSP $3.00; Somewhere, Topaze, Cotillion - OSP $3.50; Occur! Rapture - OSP $4.00, CMV $7.00 MB, $3.00 BO.

1936-39 CUTICLE SOFTENER
½ oz. bottle with turquoise cap. C.P.C. on label. CMV $15.00 BO, $20.00 MB.
1955-62 OILY POLISH REMOVER
2 oz. white cap & label. O.S.P. 49¢ C.M.V. $4.00

1931-36 NAIL POLISH
Ribbed glass bottle with black octaginal cap. Gray and blue box. O.S.P. 50¢ C.M.V. $30.00 M.B. mint.
1931-36 POLISH REMOVER
1931-36 CUTICLE SOFTENER
Both ½ oz. ribbed glass, black 8 sided caps. Silver labels. O.S.P. 50¢ C.M.V. $25.00 ea. B.O. $30.00 M.B.

1965-66 VITA MOIST BODY LOTION
1965-66 RICH MOISTURE BODY LOTION
Both 8 oz. white pump on gold top. OSP $3.50 CMV each $2.00 BO, $5.00 MB.

1946-50 OILY POLISH REMOVER
2 oz. bottle with turquoise cap. OSP 43c, CMV $15.00 MB, $10.00 BO.
1950-53 OILY POLISH REMOVER
2 oz. white cap. OSP 49c, CMV $6.00 BO, $10.00 MB.

1962-68 OILY ENAMEL REMOVER (Left)
3 oz. white cap. O.S.P. 75¢ C.M.V. $2.00
1968-77 OILY ENAMEL REMOVER (Right) 3 oz. bottle with white lid. O.S.P. 90¢ C.M.V. 25¢
1970-74 CUTICLE SOAK
3 oz. plastic bottle with white cap. O.S.P. $1.00 C.M.V. 25¢

1954-58 NAIL POLISH
With 4A design on label, came in long last nail polish, cuticle softener, silvery base, top coat, oily polish remover. O.S.P. 39¢ to 59¢ C.M.V. $2.00 for nail polish bottles & $3.00 for all others.

1938-50 NAIL POLISH
½ oz. & ¼ oz. bottle came in polish remover, cream polish, cuticle softener, cuticle oil, oily polish remover, nail polish base & top coat. 1946-50 Same bottles & labels with black caps. Also came in double coat, nail polish & cling tite. O.S.P. 29¢ to 43¢ C.M.V. in box $7.00. Bottle only $6.00. Nail polish bottles only $5.00

1946-47 DOUBLE DARE NAIL POLISH
½ oz. black cap, red paper label. O.S.P. 43¢ C.M.V. $8.00 B.O. $10.00 M.B.

1967 FLOWER PRINT NAIL ENAMEL
1/2 oz. bottle, white cap. Flower on label and box. O.S.P. $1.25 C.M.V. $2.00 M.B.

1950-54 NAIL POLISH
½ oz. bottle with white cap & gold line through label. Came in nail polish, cuticle softener, cling-tite, oily polish remover, clear nail polish & double coat. O.S.P. 39¢ to 49¢ C.M.V. $3.00 on nail polish bottle, $3.50 on all others.

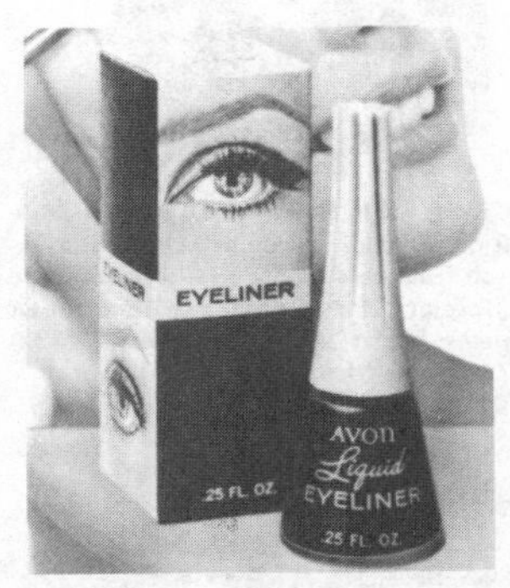

1969-72 LIQUID EYELINER
.25 oz. bottle. O.S.P. $2.00 C.M.V. $1.00 M.B.

1966 ICE CREAM NAIL ENAMEL
½ oz. nail enamel in tangerine, toffee, raspberry, blueberry, pistachio, whipped cream & sugar frost, white caps. O.S.P. $1.25 ea. C.M.V. $3.00 in box, 50¢ bottle only.

1967 FIRE WORKS NAIL POLISH
½ oz. each, with white caps. Came in blue, orange, violet, green, pink & base coat. O.S.P. $1.25 C.M.V. $2.00 ea. B.O. $3.00 M.B.

1951 CREAM LOTION
2 oz. bottle with blue cap. Came in 1951 Always Sweet Set. C.M.V. $18.00

1950-51 CREAM LOTION
2 oz. clear glass with turquoise cap, label has red, yellow, & blue streamers. Came in 1951 Always Sweet Set & 1950 Jolly Surprise. C.M.V. $12.00

1944-45 LIQUID TWIN-TONE
2 oz. bottles. OSP 89c, CMV $15.00 BO, $20.00 MB.

1959-63 BATH OILS - MISC.
Royal Pine Bath Oil, green plastic. Rose Geranium, pink; Floral, lavender; & Jasmine, yellow. All are 8 oz. plastic bottles with matching caps. O.S.P. $2.00 C.M.V. $3.00 each.
1959-63 BUBBLE BATH
8 oz. pink plastic bottle & cap. O.S.P. $1.69 C.M.V. $2.00

1962 BATH OIL
6 oz. plastic bottles, white caps. Came in 1962 Bath Bouquet set only, in Somewhere, Cotillion, Here's My Heart, Topaze, Persian Wood, Royal Jasmine, Rose Geranium, Royal Pine, Floral and To a Wild Rose. C.M.V. $6.00
1978 SMOOTH AS SILK BATH OIL TRIAL SIZE
1 oz. plastic bottle, pink cap. C.M.V. 29¢ C.M.V. 30¢

1960-61 BATH OILS - MISC.
4 oz. white plastic bottle with blue lid. Came in Modern Simplicity Set only in To A Wild Rose, Here's My Heart & Cotillion. C.M.V. $15.00 each.

1945 TOILET WATER, CREAM LOTION & BUBBLE BATH - All are 2 oz. size, frosted glass & pink caps. Came in 1945 Young Hearts Set. C.M.V. $20.00 ea. Toilet Water is in Cotillion fragrance.

1974-76 FOAMING BATH OIL
6 & 12 oz. plastic bottle with cap, colored to match fragrance, came in Charisma, Moonwind, Sonnet, Bird of Paradise, Field Flowers or Timeless. O.S.P. $4.50 for 6 oz. & $7.50 for 12 oz. 1977 Imperial Gardens was sold. C.M.V. 50¢ each.

1954-72 PERFUMED DEODORANT
On left - 2 oz. turquoise cap & label with 4A design. O.S.P. 79¢ C.M.V. 50¢
1942-54 PERFUMED DEODORANT
On right - 2 oz, green cap, old Avon label. OSP 59c, CMV $9.00 MB, $6.00 BO.

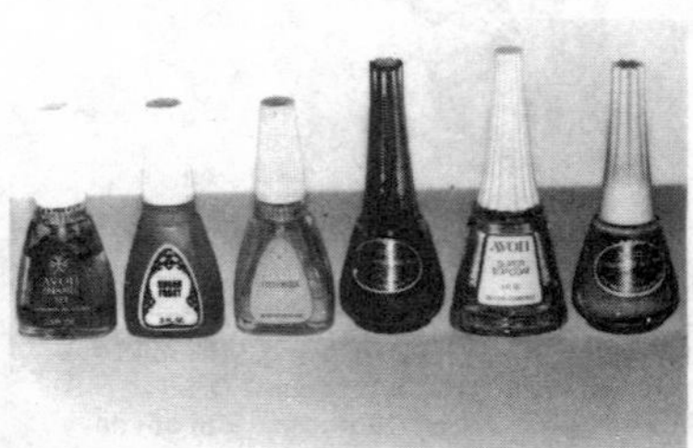

1970's MISCELLANEOUS NAIL ENAMELS - C.M.V. 50¢ each.

LEFT TO RIGHT
1979-80 ON DUTY ROLL-ON DEODORANT
2 oz. black & blue plastic, blue cap. Anti-stain, quick drying. SSP $1.00 CMV 25c.
1979-80 ON DUTY AEROSOL DEODORANT
4 oz. black can. Ozone safe formula. SSP $1.59 CMV 25c.
1979-80 DRI 'N DELICATE AEROSO DEODORANT
4 oz. pink & white can, white cap. Ozo safe formula. SSP $1.59 CMV 25c.

1965 BATH OILS - MISC.
Came in Bath Bouquet Set only. 2 oz. gold cap & label. Came in Rapture, Occur! Somewhere, Topaze, Cotillion, Here's My Heart, To A Wild Rose & Wishing. C.M.V. $9.00 each.
1967-68 PERFUMED DEODORANT
4 oz. size. Turquoise cap & label. O.S.P. $1.25 CMV $1.50 BO, $2.50 MB.

1966-70 TOUCH ON DEODORANT
1¾ oz. white cap, clear glass, white design & green & white label. O.S.P. $1.25 C.M.V. $1.00
1960-66 FLOW ON DEODORANT
1¾ oz. green cap & painted label, green & white label on clear glass. O.S.P. 89¢ C.M.V. $3.00
1966-67 ROLL ON DEODORANT
1¾ oz. green cap & green & white 4A design & label on clear glass. O.S.P. 89¢ C.M.V. $2.00

61-62 STICK DEODORANT
oz. white cap, green glass jar with
inted label. OSP 89c, CMV $5.00
.00 M.B.
56-61 STICK DEODORANT
een cap & label on clear glass jar, 2
fferent caps. Older has 4A design on
p and newer one has (New) spelled on
. O.S.P. 79¢ C.M.V. $6.00 $7.00 M.B.
ch.

1931-36 DEODORANT
2 oz. ribbed glass bottle with silver label
& dark blue cap. O.S.P. 50¢ C.MV. in box
$40.00. Bottle only $35.00

1936-48 DEODORANT (LEFT)
2 oz. turquoise cap & label. OSP 52c, CMV $20.00 in box, $14.00 bottle only. Add $5.00 for C.P.C. label on bottle in box. 1946-48 Came with black applicator with sponge end. CMV $25.00 MB, $20.00 BO.

1944-45 LIQUID DEODORANT (RIGHT)
2 oz. turquoise cap with applicator. OSP 59c, CMV $20.00 BO, $25.00 MB.

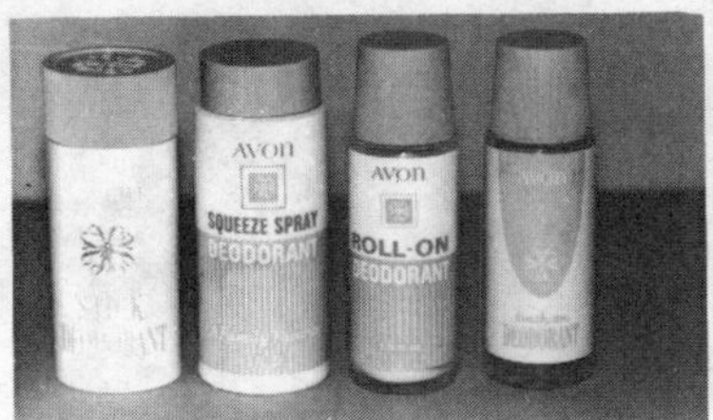

Left to Right - 1965-68 STICK DEODORANT
2.75 oz. white plastic with aqua cap. O.S.P. $1.00 C.M.V. $1.50
1968-70 SQUEEZE SPRAY DEODORANT
3 oz. white, blue, green plastic with blue cap. O.S.P. 98¢ C.M.V. $1.50
1968-69 ROLL-ON DEODORANT
1¼ oz. clear glass with painted blue, white & green label with blue cap. O.S.P. 98¢ C.M.V. $1.50
1965-66 TOUCH ON DEODORANT
1.75 oz. clear glass, painted label, white & aqua with aqua cap. O.S.P. $1.00 C.M.V. $2.00

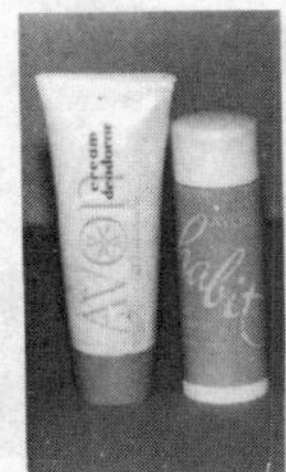

1960-66 CREAM DEODORANT
1.75 oz. white tube with aqua cap. Also sold with word "Normal" on tube. O.S.P. 79¢ C.M.V. $1.00
1970 Only - HABIT DEODORANT
1.25 oz. aqua with white cap. O.S.P. $1.00 C.M.V. $1.50

1966-67 SPRAY DEODORANT
3 oz. turquoise plastic bottle with white cap. O.S.P. 98¢ C.M.V. $2.00

1968-70 AEROSOL DEODORANT
7 oz. blue & white can. O.S.P. $1.75 C.M.V. $1.00

1973-77 DRY 'N DELICATE DEODORANT
4 oz. pink & white can with pink cap. O.S.P. $1.00 C.M.V. 25¢
1976 ULTRA DRY DEODORANT
7 oz. blue, white & gold with white cap for powder. Same design only red, white & gold with white cap for scented. O.S.P. $1.98 C.M.V. 50¢
1968-76 AEROSOL PERFUMED DEODORANT - 4 oz. white, gold & aqua can with aqua cap. O.S.P. $1.00 C.M.V. 25¢

early 1970's PROFESSIONAL HAIR CARE CARE PRODUCTS
Used in Avon beauty salons only, not sold.
HAIR SPRAY - 13 oz. pink, blue & white can C.M.V. $5.00
INSTANT LOTION CONDITIONER
16 oz. frosted plastic bottle, orange letters. C.M.V. $4.00
SHAMPOO FOR DRY HAIR
16 oz. plastic bottle. C.M.V. $4.00
HAIR NET - 8 oz. plastic bottle. Oily hair, green letters; Normal hair, purple letters. C.M.V. $3.00 each.
BEAUTY SALONS RAIN HAT
Pink and white case holds clear plastic rain bonnet. Used in Avon beauty salons only, not sold. C.M.V. $3.00

1978-79 PEARL NAIL ENAMEL
.5 oz., white cap, gray & white box. SSP 99c, CMV 25c MB.

1978-79 COLORWORKS SAMPLES
LASTING COLOR EYE SHADOW
Box of 10 samples
SUPERSHINE LIP GLOSS
Box of 10 samples
CMV 50c each box.

1978-80 NEW VITALITY PRODUCTS
CONDITIONING SETTING LOTION
8 oz. plastic, pump top. CMV 50c.
EXTRA BODY CONDITIONER
8 oz. plastic, yellow cap. CMV 50c.
BLOW DRY CONDITIONER
8 oz. plastic, pump top. CMV 50c.
CONDITIONING SHAMPOO
8 oz. plastic, yellow cap. CMV 50c.
HOT CONDITIONING TREATMENT
Box holds 3 plastic tubes. CMV $1.00 MB.

1978-79 DEW KISS PRODUCTS
Frosted or pink plastic containers.
Left to Right.
DEW KISS SAMPLE - CMV 25c.
LIP DEW - CMV 25c.
UNDER MAKEUP MOISTURIZING CREAM - 3 oz. CMV 25c.
UNDER MAKEUP MOISTURIZING LOTION
Gold cap. Came in 5 oz., 3.5 oz. or 1.5 oz. size. CMV 25c each.

1979-80 ALL OVER FACE COLOR
1 oz. plastic, gold cap. CMV 25c.
1979 CREME NAIL ENAMEL
White cap in special color up box. CMV 25c.
1970'S CREME HAIR RINSE
6 oz. pink plastic, pink 4A cap. CMV 50

1979-80 MOISTURE GARDEN PRODUCTS
BODY LOTION
10 oz. plastic, CMV 25c.
PUMP DISPENSER
for body lotion. CMV 50c MB.
FACIAL LOTION
4 oz. plastic bottle, not shown. CMV 25c.
HAND CREAM
4 oz. plastic jar, not shown. CMV 25c.
1979 MOISTURE GARDEN FLOWER GARDEN
Avon box holds planter & packet of seeds
Box came with white outside sleeve. CMV $1.00 MB.

1978-80 FEELING FRESH PRODUCTS
1978 FEELING FRESH COOLER BAG
White & blue zipper bag given to Avon reps only. CMV $4.00
BODY SPLASH WITH MOISTURIZERS
8 oz. plastic. CMV 50c.
DEODORANT BODY POWDER WITH BAKING SODA
8 oz. plastic. CMV 50c.
FOOT COMFORT SPRAY
3 oz. metal can. CMV 50c.
ROLL-ON DEODORANT
2 oz. plastic. CMV 50c.
1979-80 FEELIN' FRESH AEROSOL DEODORANT
4 oz. white can & cap. Blue & green letters. Ozone safe formula. SSP $1.59 CMV 25c.

LEFT 1970'S SKYLIGHTERS NAIL ENAMEL
.5 oz., white cap. In New York City designed box. CMV $2.00 MB.
CENTER 1970 STROKE OF BRILLIANTS NAIL POLISH
.5 oz., white cap. CMV $2.00 MB
1971 SHINE DOWN STICK
.6 oz. brown & gold plastic tube. CMV $1.00 MB.

1978-80 FRIVOLIE PRODUCTS
All are green & yellow.
SPARKLING BODY SPLASH
8 oz. plastic. CMV 50c.
BUBBLING BUBBLE BATH
8 oz. plastic. CMV 50c.
TANTALIZING TALC
3.5 oz. cardboard & plastic. CMV 50c.
COLOGNE ICE
1 oz. plastic. CMV 50c.

1979-80 CRYSTAL LIGHTS
Nail Enamel - CMV 50c MB.
Creamy Powder Eye Shadow - CMV 50c MB
Lip Stick - CMV 50c MB.

1978-80 FEELIN' FRESH SOAP
Regular issue bar on left, CMV 50c.
Introductory trial size bar on right, short issue. CMV $2.00.

1965-66 ENAMEL REMOVER PADS
Red & white box holds 10 samples. CMV $2.00 MB.
1969 NAIL ENAMEL
½ oz., white tall cap. CMV $1.50 MB.

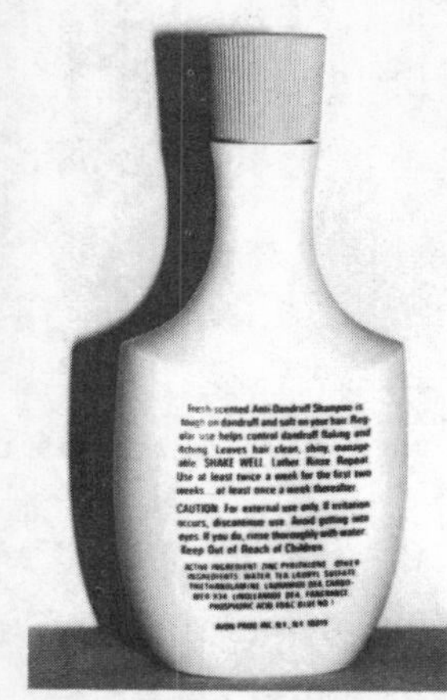

1978 KEEP CLEAR ANTI-DANDRUFF SHAMPOO
8 oz. white plastic bottle, blue cap. OSP 89c, CMV 25c. Also came with back label on both sides with front label missing, factory mistake. CMV $8.00

1978-79 GOOD & GLOSSY ROLL-ON LIP GLOSS
.33 oz. clear glass, white caps. One with blue band around cap & blue letters. One with pink band & white letters. One with green band & white letters. SSP 82c each CMV 50c each.

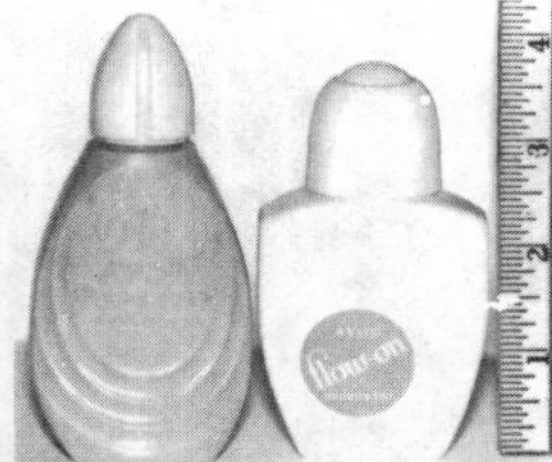

1955-59 FLOWING CREAM DEODORANT
2 oz. turquoise plastic bottle with white cap. OSP 79c, CMV $2.00 BO, $4.00 MB.
1958-60 FLOW ON DEODORANT
2 oz. white plastic bottle. O.S.P. 89¢ C.M.V. $2.00 B.O. $3.00 M.B.

1978-80 CUCUMBER COOLER PRODUCTS
FACIAL FRESHENER
8 oz. plastic, white cap. CMV 50c.
PEEL OFF FACIAL MASK
3 oz. tube, white cap. CMV 50c.
SPLASH OFF CLEANSER
6 oz. plastic, white cap. CMV 50c.

1971 Only - HABIT ANTI PERSPIRANT DEODORANT - 1.25 oz. size. Pink & white plastic bottle. O.S.P. $1.25 C.M.V. $1.50
1972-75 HABIT ANTI PERSPIRANT DEODORANT- 1.5 oz. pink & white bottle. O.S.P. $1.50 C.M.V. 25¢
1971-76 ROLL-ON ANTI PERSPIRANT DEODORANT - 2 oz. clear glass with white & pink label. Pink cap. O.S.P. 98¢ C.M.V. 25¢
1960-70 HABIT CREAM DEODORANT
1¼ oz. turquoise plastic container & cap. O.S.P. $1.25 C.M.V. $1.00 mint
Also came for normal skin.

1948-51 BUBBLE BATH
4 oz. bottle with blue cap. Round blue & pink box with top of bottle sticking through lid. O.S.P. $1.29 C.M.V. $25.00 in box. Bottle only $15.00
1951-58 BUBBLE BATH
Same bottle as above in a square box of same design. O.S.P. $1.29 C.M.V. $20.00 in box. Bottle only $15.00.

Left to right
1970 Only - ULTRA DRY ANTI PERSPIRANT - 7 oz. orange & yellow can. O.S.P. $1.89 C.M.V. $2.00
1971-76 ULTRA DRY ANTI PERSPIRANT
7 oz. orange & yellow can. O.S.P. $1.89 C.M.V. 25¢ Upside down label C.M.V. $8.
1970 Only AEROSOL DEODORANT
7 oz. blue & white can. O.S.P. $1.75 C.M.V. $2.00
1971-76 AEROSOL DEODORANT
7 oz. blue & white can. O.S.P. $1.75 C.M.V. 25¢

1965-67 BUBBLE BATH
8 oz. white plastic bottle and white cap. O.S.P. $1.98 C.M.V. $1.00
1972-78 BUBBLE BATH
16 oz. pink plastic bottle with white cap. O.S.P. $4.00 C.M.V. 25¢
1973-78 BUBBLE BATH
8 oz. pink plastic bottle with white cap. O.S.P. $2.00 C.M.V. 25¢
1975-76 BUBBLE BLOSSOM BUBBLE BATH DECANTER
14 oz. pink plastic bottle with white cap. O.S.P. $5.00 C.M.V. 50¢

1944-48 BUBBLE BATH
Blue & white box with pink ribbon holds 8 oz. bottle with blue cap & label. O.S.P. $2.25, C.M.V. in box $45.00 Bottle only $35.00.

1966-69 DEW KISS
Came in 1½ oz. & 3½ oz. size. White cap with label band around cap from 1966-69. C.M.V. $1.00 1969-76 label is on front of bottle. O.S.P. $1.50 & $3.00 C.M.V. $1.00 each.

LEFT TO RIGHT
1973 DEW KISS DECANTER
4 oz. clear glass with gold cap. SSP $3.00 CMV $3.00 MB
1974 DEW KISS DECANTER
4 oz. clear glass with gold cap. SSP $2.50 CMV $2.00 MB, $1.00 BO
1960-66 DEW KISS
1½ oz. pink lid, gold string with pink & gold tag, with 4A design. OSP $1.25 CMV $5.00 MB $3.00 bottle with tag.

1968-70 MOUTHWASH & GARGLE
10 oz. bottle with white cap. Came in glass changed to plastic, glass bottle bigger. O.S.P. $1.25 C.M.V. $1.00 in glass. 50¢ in plastic.
1968-74 BREATH FRESH
10 oz. bottle with white cap. Came in glass changed to plastic, glass bottle bigger. O.S.P. $1.25 C.M.V. $1.00 in glass 50¢ in plastic.

1970-72 BREATH FRESH CONCENTRATED MOUTHWASH
1 oz. glass bottle with white cap. O.S.P. $1.75 CMV 50c BO, $1.50 MB.

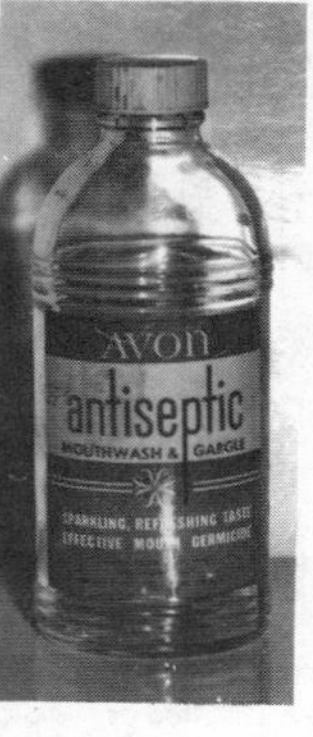

1955-59 ANTISEPTIC MOUTHWASH
(Left) 7 oz. white cap. Label says antiseptic only. OSP 59c, CMV $7.00 BO BO, $10.00 MB.
1959-68 ANTISEPTIC MOUTHWASH
(Right) 7 oz. white cap. OSP 59c, CMV $6.00 MB, $5.00 BO.

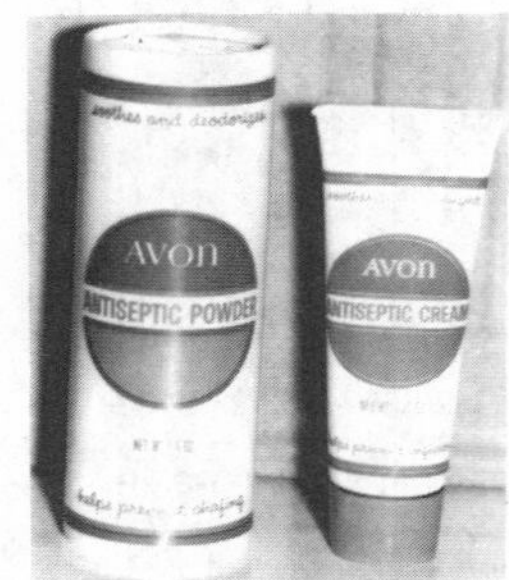

1969-71 ANTISEPTIC POWDER
3½ oz. cardboard container, plastic shaker top. O.S.P. 89¢ C.M.V. $1.00
1969-71 ANTISEPTIC CREAM
1.75 oz. plastic tube, blue cap. O.S.P. 89¢ C.M.V. $1.00.

1933-36 ANTISEPTIC (LEFT)
Metal cap, green label. 6 oz. size OSP 36c, CMV $35.00 MB, $30.00 BO
Also came in 12 oz. size with same label OSP 62c, CMV $40.00 in box, $35.00 bottle only.
1936-40 ANTISEPTIC (RIGHT)
6 oz. metal cap. Turquoise box & label. OSP 36c, CMV $35.00 MB, $30.00 mint BO.

1946 Only ANTISEPTIC
6 oz. round bottle, black cap. Rare.
O.S.P. 39¢ C.M.V. $45.00 M.B. $40.00 B.O

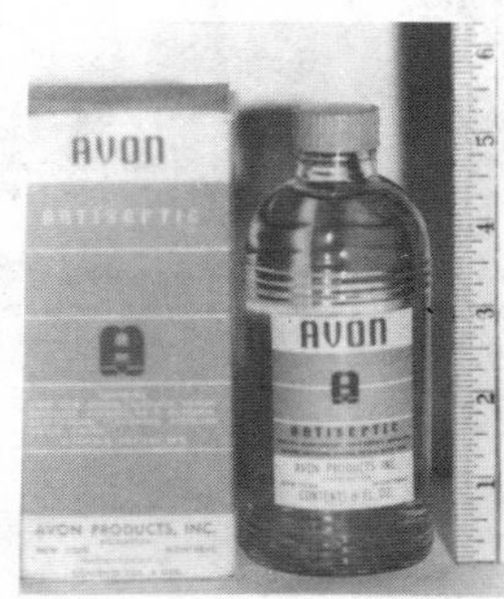

1940-50 ANTISEPTIC
6 oz. clear glass bottle with turquoise cap. Early issue had metal cap. Also came in 12 oz. size. OSP 62c, OSP 36c, CMV - 6 oz. size, $12.00 BO $16.00 MB - 12 oz. size, $16.00 BO $20.00 MB. Add $5.00 for C.P.C. label.

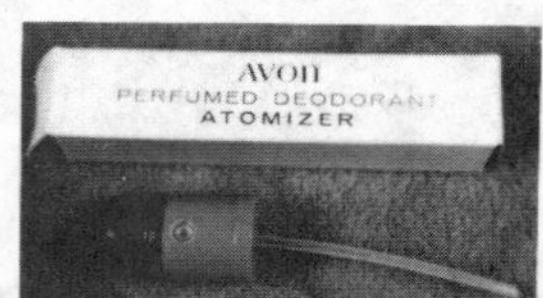

1950's & 60's AVON ATOMIZER
Red & black also turquoise & white. O.S.P. 69¢ C.M.V. $3.00 in box.

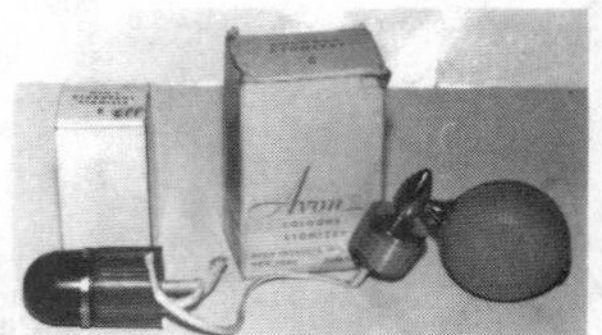

1960's ATOMIZER - MENS DEODORANT
(Left)
Black & red also came in turquoise. O.S.P. 69¢ C.M.V. $4.00 in box.
1940's-50's ATOMIZER FOR COLOGNES
(right)
Turquoise bulb, 24K gold plated. C.M.V. $5.00 in box.

1977-78 DELICATE BEAUTY
2 oz. glass bottle liquid makeup. Gold cap. O.S.P. $5.00 C.M.V. 25¢

1965-66 AVON DIRT
Gold cap frosted glass bottle is same as Crown Top powder sachet bottle. Front label reads "4A design at top, Avon Dirt - Contains handfull of 100% dehydrated mud to be used by clean people". Back label reads "Directions: For people unacustomed to having dirty hands. Moisten hands lightly and rub on Avon Dirt to a gooey mess. Now you can use Avon Soap to remove Avon Dirt". This is a rare bottle. Only one found to date. If you know what or where it was used, please notify Bud Hastin. No value established.

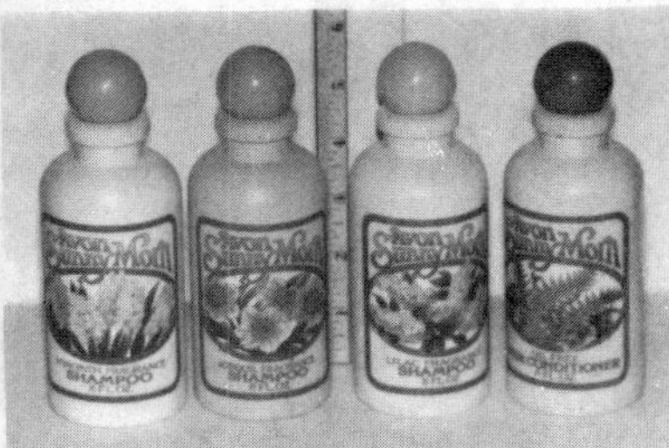

1977-80 SUNNY MORN SHAMPOO
8 oz. plastic bottle in different colors. Came in Hyacinth, Jonquil, Lilac, Strawberry & Clover fragrances. OSP $2.29 CMV 25c.
1977-80 SUNNY MORN HAIR CONDITIONER
8 oz. plastic oil free conditioner. OSP $2.29 CMV 25c.

1977 SUNNY MORN SHAMPOO — DOUBLE STAMP LABEL
8 oz. plastic bottle. Label has been stamped 4 times at factory by mistake. CMV $8.00.

1971 HAIR BEAUTY PACK
1.25 oz. tube used in Avon beauty salons. C.M.V. $3.00
1971 AVON COFFEE CUP HOLDER
Used in Avon beauty salons. White plastic. C.M.V. $3.00

1971 HAIR DRESSING & CONDITIONER
11 oz. pink spray can and cap. C.M.V.$5.00
1971 SHAMPOO FOR COLOR TREATED HAIR
12 oz. pink plastic bottle, white cap. C.M.V. $4.00
1971 SETTING LOTION
16 oz. plastic bottle. C.M.V. $4.00
1971 HAIR THICKENER
16 oz. plastic bottle. C.M.V. $4.00
All of these items used only in Avon beauty salons. Not sold.

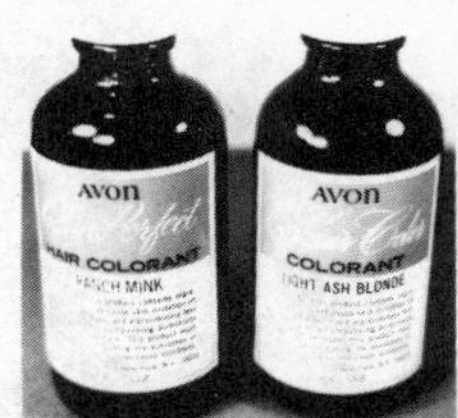

1971-72 COLOR PERFECT HAIR COLOR
2 oz. brown glass with white cap & Avon on bottom. C.M.V. $1.50
1969 HAIR COLOR COLORANT
2 oz. brown glass with white cap. Has 4A on cap. No Avon on bottom. C.M.V. $5.00

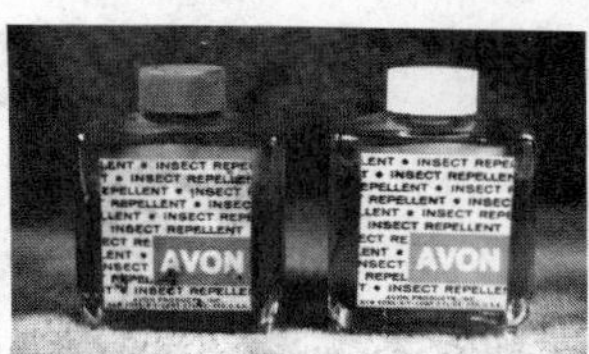

1959-65 INSECT REPELLENT
2 oz. bottle with red & white caps. OSP 59c, CMV $5.00 MB, $3.00 BO

1976-78 BODY SPLASH
8 oz. plastic bottle. Came in Field Flowers, Honeysuckle, Hawaiian White Ginger, Apple Blossom, Roses, Roses, and new in 1978, Sun Blossoms. Each came in a different color container and cap. S.S.P. $2.50 C.M.V. 50¢ each.

1957 BEAUTIFUL JOURNEY BOTTLES
1 oz. clear glass bottles came in Beautiful Journey Set only. Pink caps. Came in Hand Lotion, Skin Freshener, Deep Clean, Deodorant and Cotillion Cologne. C.M.V. $10.00 each.

1962-63 CLEAR-IT SUDS
6 oz. white plastic with clear plastic lid with red on inside white cap. O.S.P. $1.25 C.M.V. $3.00
1960-63 CLEAR-IT SHAMPOO
3 oz. white plastic with clear plastic lid with red on inside white cap. Also came in 6 oz. O.S.P. 79¢ C.M.V. $2.50

1972-75 EAU DE COOL
6 oz. light blue glass, silver cap. OSP $5.00 CMV $2.00 MB, $1.00 BO.

1966-67 ULTRA SHEER LIQUID FOUNDATION - 1 oz. gold top, embossed bottle. O.S.P. $2.25 C.M.V. $2.00
1968-74 ULTRA SHEER NATURAL VEIL - 1 oz. embossed bottle, same as Liquid Foundation only name changed. O.S.P. $2.25 C.M.V. 50¢
1965-72 EYE & THROAT OIL
1 oz. gold cap, painted label. O.S.P. $2.50 C.M.V. $1.00

LEFT TO RIGHT
1954-58 FASHION FILM
1 oz. white cap. OSP 95c, CMV $4.00 BO
1951-54 FASHION FILM
1 oz. white cap. OSP 75c, CMV $5.00 BO
1958-61 FASHION FILM
1 oz. pink cap. OSP $1.10 CMV $4.00 BO
Add $1.00 each for each box.

1967 EYE & THROAT OIL
1 oz. gold cap. Issued during glass strike in 1967 only. Short issue. O.S.P. $2.50 CMV $4.00 BO $5.00 MB.

1954-59 LIQUID ROUGE (RIGHT)
1/8 oz. gold embossed cap. OSP 69c, CMV $7.00 MB, $5.00 BO
1959-66 LIQUID ROUGE (LEFT)
¼ oz. smooth brass cap, 2 different labels. OSP 89c, CMV $4.00 MB, $3.00 BO.

1966-69 SKIN FRESHENER
4 oz. glass bottles, 3 different color labels & caps. Normal skin in blue, Astringent Freshener for Oily Skin in peach & Dry Skin in pink. O.S.P. $1.25 C.M.V. $1.00 each.

1975-78 COUNTRY CUPBOARD BUBBLING BATH FOAM
6 oz. plastic bottle. Came in Green Apple, Peach or Strawberry. O.S.P. $4.50 C.M.V. 25¢
1975-78 COUNTRY CUPBOARD PERFUMED TALC
5 oz. cardboard container. Came in Green Apple, Peach or Strawberry. O.S.P. $2.50 C.M.V. 25¢

1978-80 CLEAR SKIN MEDICATED LIQUID CLEANSER
10 fl. oz. plastic white bottle, blue cap. OSP $2.49 CMV 25c.
1978-80 CLEAR SKIN MEDICATED ASTRINGENT
12 fl. oz. white plastic bottle, blue cap. OSP $2.99 CMV 25c
1978-80 CLEAR SKIN MEDICATED LOTION
4 fl. oz. white plastic bottle, blue cap. OSP $1.89 CMV 25c.
1978-80 CLEAR SKIN MEDICATED CLEANSER PLUS
3 oz. white tube, blue cap. OSP $1.29 CMV 25c.
1978-80 CLEAR SKIN MEDICATED SOAP
3 oz. bar. OSP 99c, CMV 60c.

1973-78 CARE DEEPLY HAND CREAM
4 oz. white and black tube. OSP $1.00 CMV 25c.
1975-78 CARE DEEPLY LIP BALM
White and black, black cap. OSP $1.00 CMV 25c. Also with sunscreen.
1974-78 CARE DEEPLY LOTION
16 oz. white plastic with white cap. SSP $2.50 CMV 50c.
1974-78 CARE DEEPLY HAND CREAM
6 oz. black and white. OSP $1.50 CMV 25c.

EFT TO RIGHT
977-80 FIRM & NATURAL HAIR PRAY
oz. non-aerosol plastic pump spray. OSP $2.29 CMV 25c.
977-80 KEEP CLEAR ANTI-DANDRUFF HAMPOO
oz. plastic bottle. OSP $2.29 CMV 25c.
977-80 KEEP CLEAR ANTI-DANDRUFF HAMPOO SAMPLE
oz. plastic bottle. OSP 25c, CMV 25c.
977-80 ON DUTY DEODORANT
4 oz. non-aerosol pump spray in plastic bottle. OSP $2.49 CMV 25c.

1970-80 CLEAR SKIN PRODUCTS
1970-76 Labels are silver & blue, silver caps.
1977-80 Labels changed to dark and light blue with dark blue caps.
4 oz. Shampoo Concentrate, blue cap.
4½ oz. Cleansing Grains
3 oz. Bar of Soap
2 oz. Liquid Make-Up, silver cap.
Cover Stick, 4 oz. Lotion; 6 oz. Astringent, silver cap old, blue cap new issue. CMV 50c each.
1971-72 — 3 oz. Facial Mask, silver cap old, blue cap new issue; 5 oz. Cream Cleanser, silver cap; 12 oz. Astringent, silver cap old, blue cap new issue; 6 oz. Cleansing Gel, blue cap; Oil Free Blotting Cream .65 oz. tube. CMV 50c each.

1960-63 CLEAR SKIN SOAP
Brown bar in gray & white box. O.S.P. 49¢ C.M.V. $3.00
1964-69 CLEAR SKIN SOAP
Brown bar in gray & white wrapper. O.S.P. 59¢ C.M.V. $2.00

1957-59 CLEAR SKIN LOTION
6 oz. bottle with white cap. O.S.P. $1.00 CMV $5.00 MB, $4.00 BO
1963-69 CLEAR SKIN LOTION
3 oz. white plastic bottle with red cap. O.S.P. 59¢ C.M.V. $1.00
1959-63 CLEAR SKIN LOTION
3 oz. white plastic with clear plastic lid with red on inside white cap. O.S.P. 79¢ C.M.V. $2.50
1970-73 CLEAR SKIN BLOTTING CREAM - .65 oz. white tube with blue cap. O.S.P. $1.50 C.M.V. 25¢

1971-75 AMERICAN SPORTSTER
SUPERSTICK - white tube, blue & red design. O.S.P. $2.50 C.M.V. 50¢
1971-73 SHOWERING SOAP SHAMPOO
White plastic bottle, blue & red design, blue cap. O.S.P. $2.50 C.M.V. $1.50
OUTDOOR SHIELD
White plastic compact with blue & red design. O.S.P. $2.50 C.M.V. $1.00
SKIN COMFORT GEL
White plastic tube, red & blue design. O.S.P. $2.50 C.M.V. 75¢

1973-76 ESSENCE OF BALSAM
7 oz. Hair Spray - light green with green cap. O.S.P. $2.00 C.M.V. 25¢
7 oz. Hair Spray for Heated Rollers Green with white cap. O.S.P. $2.00 C.M.V. 25¢
8 oz. Lotion Shampoo - green with white lid. O.S.P. $2.00 C.M.V. 25¢
8 oz. Lotion Conditioner - yellow with white lid. O.S.P. $2.00 C.M.V. 25¢
1973-77 Lotion Conditioner
8 oz., yellow with white lid. O.S.P. $2.00 C.M.V. 25¢

1970-76 CLEAR SKIN CLEANSING GRAINS - 4.5 oz. white, silver & blue cardboard. O.S.P. $1.75 C.M.V. 50¢
Other Picture - Same with label upside down. C.M.V. $5.00

1974-78 PERFECT BALANCE
PEACH COLORED OR WHITE
4 oz. TissueOff Cream. O.S.P. $2.00 C.M.V. 25¢; 6 oz. Toning Freshener. O.S.P. $2.00 C.M.V. 25¢; 4.5 oz. Cleansing Grains. O.S.P. $1.00 C.M.V. 25¢; 6 oz. Toning Astringent, O.S.P. $2.00 C.M.V. 25¢; 4 oz. Wash-Off Lotion, O.S.P. $2.00 C.M.V. 25¢; 3 oz. Night Time Moisturizer O.S.P. $2.00 C.M.V. 25¢; 2.5 oz. Night Cream, O.S.P. $2.00 C.M.V. 25¢
.75 oz. Eye Cream, O.S.P. $2.00 C.M.V. 25¢

1973 SUMMER DEW MOISTURIZING BODY CREME
5 oz. white with pink & blue design. SSP $4.00 CMV $2.00 MB, $1.00 BO
1973 SUMMER DEW MOISTURIZING BODY FLUFF
4 oz. white with pink & blue design. SSP $4.00 CMV $2.00 MB, $1.00 BO

1976-78 EVEN TONE MAKE-UP
Off white, plastic. Choice of Dewy Make-Up or Matt in light, medium or heavy coverage. O.S.P. light & medium $1.50 each. O.S.P. Heavy cover $2.00 each. C.M.V. 25¢ ea.

ULTRA SHEER - White & Gold
1972-74 UNDER MAKEUP MOISTURIZER SAMPLES - Box of 10. C.M.V. 50¢
UNDER MAKEUP MOISTURIZER
2 oz. came in mauve, apricot, aqua, untinted. S.S.P. $3.00 C.M.V. $1.00
ULTRA SHEER PRESSED POWDER
5 oz. mirrored compact with lamb's wool applicator. S.S.P. $3.00 C.M.V. $1.00
ULTRA SHEER LIP GLOSS POT
.10 oz. white plastic with gold Avon on lid. Choice of 3 colors. S.S.P. $1.00 C.M.V. 50¢ M.B.

ROUND COMPACT - .5 oz. S.S.P. $3.00 C.M.V. $1.00
1971 SHEER COMPANIONS - White plastic case held white & gold lipstick & compact. S.S.P. $5.00 C.M.V, $4.00 M.B.

1976-78 DELICATE BEAUTY SKIN CARE
Sample - **GENTLE WHIPPED NIGHT CREAM** - C.M.V. 25¢ each.
GENTLE FRESHENER - 5 oz. turquoise & white. O.S.P. $2.00 C.M.V. 50¢
GENTLE LOTION CLEANSER - 4 oz. turquoise & white. O.S.P. $2.00 C.M.V. 50¢
GENTLE WHIPPED NIGHTCREME
3 oz. turquoise & white. O.S.P. $3.00 C.M.V. 50¢
Sample - **GENTLE LOTION CLEANSER** C.M.V. 25¢ each.

1975-78 CLEARLY GENTLE WHITE & BLUE - 7 oz. Nursery Spray O.S.P. $1.00 C.M.V. 25¢; 4 oz. Ointment O.S.P. $1.00 C.M.V. 25¢; 10 oz. Lotion O.S.P. $1.00 C.M.V. 25¢; 3 oz. Soap O.S.P. 50¢ C.M.V. 50¢; 10 oz. Liquid Cleanser O.S.P. $1.00 C.M.V. 25¢

1972-76 RESILIENT HAIR CARE
Yellow & black with yellow caps.
4 oz. Hair Texturizer O.S.P. $2.00 C.M.V. 25¢; 8 oz. Creme Rinse O.S.P. $2.00 C.M.V. 25¢; 8 oz. Lotion Shampoo O.S.P. $3.00 C.M.V. 25¢; 7 oz. Hair Spray O.S.P. $1.50 C.M.V. 25¢
1973-76 HONEY GIRL - 4.7 oz. yellow with yellow plunger. O.S.P. $1.00 C.M.V. 25¢
1973 RESILIENT CREME RINSE SAMPLE - 1 oz. yellow tube. C.M.V. $1.00

1966 Only - GOLD SATIN
Eye Highlight - gold case, came in box with girls picture on front. O.S.P. $1.75 C.M.V. $2.00; Complexion Highlight - cardboard with girls picture on top & box. O.S.P. $1.75 C.M.V. $3.00 M.B.; Fingertip Highlight - clear glass with white cap. Came in box with girls picture. O.S.P. $1.75 C.M.V. $2.00 M.B.
Powder Eye Shadow Brush - O.S.P. $1.50 C.M.V. $1.00

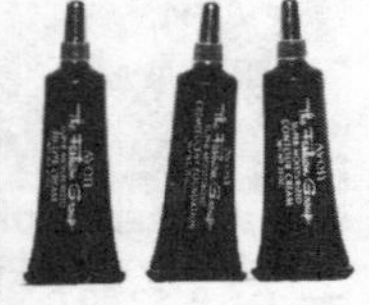

1972 FASHION GROUP CUSTOM FOUNDATION KIT - Gold & black cardboard with black plastic tubes. .25 oz. Cremelucent Foundation, .25 oz. Hi-Lite Cream, .25 oz. Contour Cream. O.S.P. $4.50 C.M.V. $4.00 M.B.

1978 MOISTURE SECRET PRODUCTS TRIAL SIZE
All are pink plastic and introductive size in 1.7 oz. tube. Enriched Cremegel Cleanser, 1 oz. tube Enriched Freshener, and 1/2 oz. tube of Enriched Daytime Moisturizer. All with PMB and .47 oz. jar of Enriched Night Concentrate. C.M.V. 50¢ each.

1975-78 NATURAL SHEEN HAIR DRESS & CONDITIONER - 3 oz. brown & white tube. O.S.P. $2.00 C.M.V. 25¢
1975-76 NATURAL SHEEN AEROSOL HAIR GLOSSER - 7 oz. brown & white can. O.S.P. $3.00 C.M.V. 50¢
1975-76 PERFECT CARE BODY LOTION DRY ASHY SKIN - 6 oz. brown & white plastic bottle. O.S.P. $3.00 C.M.V. 50¢
1975-76 SHADES OF BEAUTY LIQUID FOUNDATION - 1.5 oz. brown & white plastic bottle. O.S.P. $2.00 C.M.V. 50¢
1975-76 SHADES OF BEAUTY CREAMY BLUSH - .25 oz. Brown & white tube. O.S.P. $2.00 C.M.V. 25¢

1970-78 PROTEM PRODUCTS
Back Row - 7 ox. Hair Spray O.S.P. $2.00 C.M.V. 25¢; 12 oz. Conditioner O.S.P. $4.00 C.M.V. 25¢; 6 oz. Cream Rinse O.S.P. $2.00 C.M.V. 25¢; 6 oz. Hair Set O.S.P. $2.00 C.M.V. 25¢; 6 oz. Conditioner (New style cap) O.S.P. $2.00 C.MV. 25¢; 6 oz. Conditioner (Old style cap) O.S.P. $2.00 C.M.V. 25¢
Front Row - 1970-73 Hair Gloss - O.S.P. $1.00 C.M.V. 75¢; 6 oz. Creme Shampoo (Old style lid) O.S.P. $2.00 C.M.V. 25¢; 3 oz. Dandruff Shampoo O.S.P. $1.00 C.M.V. 25¢; 3 oz. Super Rich Conditioner O.S.P. $1.00 C.M.V. 25¢

1966-75 ULTRA SHEER LOOSE POWDER
1966-74 1¾ oz. white cardboard trimmed in gold. O.S.P. $2.50 C.M.V. 50¢
1973-74 Fluff Foundation
2 oz. white can with gold. O.S.P. $3.50 C.M.V. 50¢
1968-74 FINISHING GLO
.75 oz. white can trimmed in gold. O.S.P. $2.50 C.M.V. 50¢
1967-74 LIPSTICK
White & gold plastic. O.S.P. $1.75 C.M.V. 50¢

1975-80 HI LIGHT SHAMPOO FOR NORMAL HAIR
6.5 oz. plastic with white cap. O.S.P. $1.00 C.M.V. 25¢
1972-76 SHAMPOO FOR COLOR TREATED HAIR
8 oz. clear plastic with white cap..
1971 had outline of girls head on front. O.S.P. $1.00 C.M.V. 25¢
1970-75 SUPER HI LIGHT SHAMPOO
12 oz. clear plastic white cap. O.S.P. $1.00 C.M.V. 25¢
1967 Only - NON TEAR SHAMPOO
12 oz. white & pink with pink cap. O.S.P. $1.50 C.M.V. $2.00

1975-79 CREAM HAIR RINSE
12 oz. white plastic bottle with white cap. OSP $1.00 CMV 25c.
1975-79 BUBBLE BATH FOR CHILDREN
12 oz. white plastic bottle with white cap. OSP $2.00 CMV 25c.
1975-79 NON TEAR SHAMPOO
12 oz. white plastic bottle, white cap. OSP $2.00 CMV 25c.

1973-75 FASHION GROUP BODY MAKE UP
2 oz. gold can, black lid. Black applicator with sponge. O.S.P. $3.00 C.M.V. $3.00 M.B.

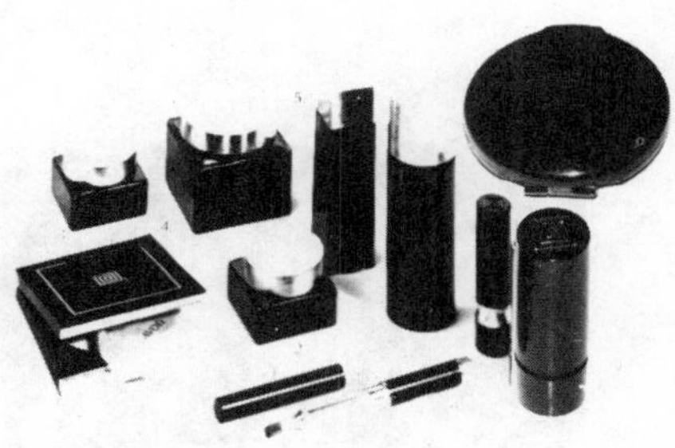

1971-78 FASHION GROUP
All items are black with gold caps & trim Compact, Contour Cream, Cremelucent Foundation, Hi Lite Cream 1976 issue round jar, Blushing Stick, Under Make Up Moisture Veil, Blushstick & Lipstick, Creamy Rouge compact.
1975-76 LIQUID LUCENT FOUNDATION
C.M.V. 50¢ ea.

1971 Only - PRIMA NATURA PRODUCTS
All items are white with gold letters.
NIGHT VEIL CONCENTRATE
2½ oz. OSP $6.00
THERMAL FACIAL
3 oz. OSP $6.50 Came with cloth mask.
CLEANSING FORMULA
4 oz. OSP $5.50
MOISTURIZING FRESHENER
4 oz. OSP $3.50
TONING FRESHENER
4 oz. OSP $3.50
EYE CREAM CONCENTRATE
.75 oz. OSP $4.00
CMV All items above $1.00 BO, $1.50 MB
CREME OF SOAP
5 oz. with white spatula. OSP $4.50 CMV $2.50 MB, $1.50 BO.

1978 HI LIGHT SHAMPOO 1/3 EXTRA
8.7 oz. plastic bottles with 1/3 extra free on top. Came in normal, oily, and dry hair shampoo. S.S.P. 99¢ C.M.V. 25¢ each.

1975-78 FLAVOR FRESH MOUTH-WASH (Backward label)
14 oz. plastic with embossed star on back side of bottle. Should be on front side. Factory mistake. O.S.P. $1.00 C.M.V. $8.00

1957-60 RICH MOISTURE SUDS
6 oz. turquoise plastic bottle, white cap. OSP $1.50, CMV $3.00 MB, $2.00 BO
1962 WASH OFF FACIAL CLEANSER
6 oz. pink plastic bottle, pink cap. 1963 came out for dry or oily skin. OSP $1.25 CMV $3.00 MB, $2.00 BO
1958-65 MOISTURE BATH
6 oz. white plastic bottle, turquoise cap. OSP $1.25 CMV $3.00 MB, $2.00 BO.

AVON

1975-78 MOISTURIZED HAND LOTION
16 oz. plastic bottle with white cap.
O.S.P. $2.00 C.M.V. 25¢
1975-78 FLAVOR FRESH MOUTHWASH
14 oz. plastic bottle with white cap.
O.S.P. $1.00 C.M.V. 25¢
1960-62 HI LIGHT SHAMPOO FOR OILY HAIR
6 oz. white plastic clear plastic cap. Also came for Normal or Dry Hair. O.S.P. $1.19 CMV $3.00 MB, $2.00 BO
1957-60 DEEP CLEAN CLEANSING CREAM
6 oz. white with gold lettering, aqua cap.
O.S.P. $1.39 C.M.V. $3.00 Mint
1964-76 AVON CURL SET
8 oz. plastic with aqua lid. O.S.P. $1.50 C.M.V. 25¢

1968-74 BUBBLE BATH
8 oz. white plastic with white cap. 1972 Christmas box. O.S.P. $2.00 C.M.V. 25¢
C.M.V. $3.00 mint with box shown.

1961-76 VITA MOIST BODY LOTION
Yellow plastic, white cap.
1961-64 4 oz. S.S.P. $1.00 C.M.V. $2.0
1966-74 8 oz. S.S.P. $1.50 C.M.V. 50¢
1974-78 16 oz. S.S.P. $2.75 C.M.V. 25¢

1957-61 MOISTURIZED HORMONE LOTION
6 oz. green plastic bottle with 4A embossed turquoise cap. O.S.P. $2.00 C.M.V. $2.00.

1957-65 HAIR COSMETIC
3 oz. pink plastic with white cap. O.S.P. $1.00 C.M.V. $2.00 Mint.

1966-69 DEEP CLEAN CLEANSING LOTION FOR DRY SKIN
6 oz. light pink with dark pink cap. O.S.P. $1.25 C.M.V. $1.00
1966-69 DEEP CLEAN WASH-OFF CLEANSER FOR NORMAL SKIN
6 oz. light green with dark green cap.
O.S.P. $1.25 C.M.V. $1.00
1966-69 DEEP CLEAN WASH-OFF CLEANSER FOR DRY SKIN
6 oz. light peach with dark peach cap. Also came for oily skin. O.S.P. $1.25 C.M.V. $1.00

1958 LOTION SACHET
Came in Safe Journey only. White plastic with turquoise cap. C.M.V. $5.00 Mint.

1974-78 ONE STEP CREME HAIR RINSE
8 & 16 oz. white plastic with white cap.
O.S.P. $2.00 & $3.00 C.M.V. 50¢ ea.

1969-75 UNDER MAKE UP MOISTURIZER
2 oz. white milk glass jar, white & gold lid. O.S.P. $3.00 C.M.V. 25¢

1969-74 ASTRINGENT
4 oz. clear plastic, white cap, green label.
O.S.P. $1.00 C.M.V. 50¢
1969-74 SKIN FRESHNER
4 oz. clear plastic, white cap, pink label.
O.S.P. $1.00 C.M.V. 50¢

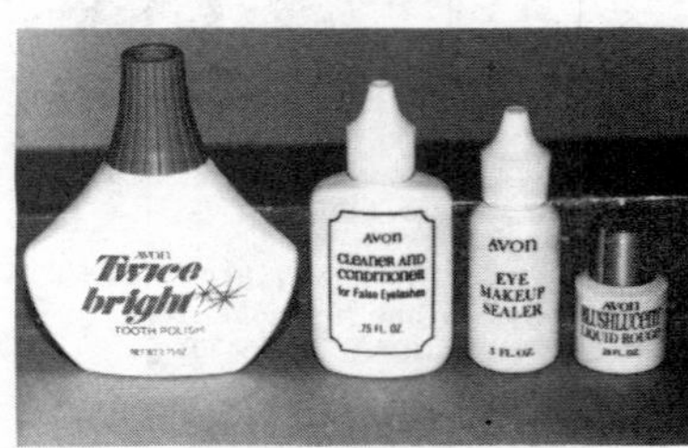

1974-76 TWICE BRIGHT TOOTH POLISH
2.75 oz. white plastic, blue lid. O.S.P. $1.00 C.M.V. 25¢
1970-74 CLEANER & CONDITIONER FOR FALSE EYELASHES
.75 oz. white plastic. O.S.P. $1.00 C.M.V. 50¢
1971-73 EYE MAKE UP SEALER
.5 oz. white plastic. O.S.P. $1.00 C.M.V. 50¢
1973-76 BLUSHLUCENT LIQUID ROUGE
.25 oz. white plastic with gold cap.
O.S.P. $1.00 C.M.V. 25¢

1974-78 NATURALLY GENTLE CREME RINSE
8 oz. plastic with yellow cap and plunger.
O.S.P. $2.00 C.M.V. 25¢
1974-78 NATURALLY GENTLE SHAMPOO
16 oz. plastic with yellow cap. O.S.P. $3.00 C.M.V. 25¢
1965-74 PROTECTIVE HAND LOTION
7.75 oz. light green with white cap.
O.S.P. $1.00 C.M.V. 50¢
1973 SPECIAL COMPLEXION GRAINS
4.5 oz. pink, white and gold. O.S.P. $1.00 C.M.V. $1.00

1969 GENTLE LOTION SHAMPOO
8 oz. yellow plastic bottle with white cap. O.S.P. $1.00 C.M.V. $1.00
1975-77 NATURALLY GENTLE CONCENTRATE
6 oz. clear plastic, yellow cap. O.S.P. $2.00 C.M.V. 25¢
1975-78 HI-LIGHT SHAMPOO FOR OILY HAIR
6.5 oz. clear plastic with white cap. O.S.P. $1.00 C.M.V. 25¢
1967-1973 AEROSOL HAIR CONDITIONER
2 oz. pink, white & gold. 1973 only changed top and added white lid over spray. O.S.P. $3.00 C.M.V. $1.00

1970-76 STEPPING OUT FOOT COMFORT SPRAY
5 oz. blue & white can. Short one rare. O.S.P. $2.00 C.M.V. Tall 50¢ C.M.V. Short $6.00

1970-76 EVENTONE
1.5 oz. plastic white cap. O.S.P. $1.00 C.M.V. 25¢
1960-66 EVEN TONE
1½ oz. plastic bottle, gold lid (1961-62) 1962-66 same bottle with white plastic lid in same shape. O.S.P. $1.35 C.M.V. $1.00 white cap, $2.00 gold cap. Also came 1.75 oz. size.

1973-74 ULTRA SHEER FLUFF FOUNDATION
2 oz. white & gold can, white cap. O.S.P. $2.00 C.M.V. 25¢
1967-73 FINISHING GLO
.75 white and gold. O.S.P. $2.75 C.M.V. 50¢
1971-74 TRANSPARENT FACE TINT
1.5 oz. white tube white cap. O.S.P. $2.00 C.M.V. 50¢
1971-75 FROSTY OR TRANSPARENT GEL BLUSH
.5 oz. white & gold tube with white cap. (Frosty sold only 1975) O.S.P. $1.00 C.M.V. 25¢

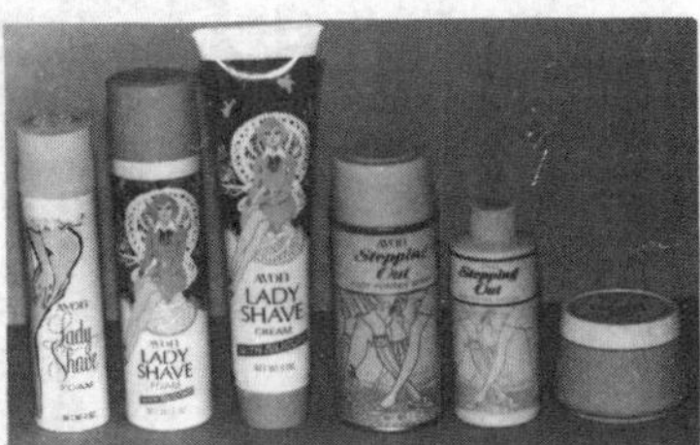

1971-75 LADY SHAVE FOAM
4 oz. white & pink can, pink cap. O.S.P. $1.00 C.M.V. 25¢
1976 LADY SHAVE FOAM
6 oz. white yellow & green, yellow cap. O.S.P. $1.00 C.M.V. 25¢
1976 LADY SHAVE CREAM
6 oz. white tube, yellow cap. O.S.P. $1.00 C.M.V. 25¢
1973-76 STEPPING OUT FOOT POWDER SPRAY
7 oz. blue & white with blue cap. O.S.P. $1.00 C.M.V. 25¢
1971-74 STEPPING OUT SOOTHING LOTION
4 oz. white & blue plastic, blue cap. O.S.P. $1.00 C.M.V. 25¢
1969-76 STEPPING OUT FOOT CARE CREAM
4 oz. blue jar, white cap. O.S.P. $1.00 C.M.V. 25¢

SKIN-SO-SOFT

1966 FRAGRANCE TRIO
Box holds 3 bottles of Skin-So-Soft, 1 oz. each, gold cap in choice of Unforgettable, Rapture, Occur! Somewhere, Topaze, Cotillion, Here's My Heart, To A Wild Rose & Wishing. O.S.P. $4.50 C.M.V. $10.00 MB.

1965 SHOWER MATES
Green & white box holds 4 oz. can of After Shower Foam & 2 bars of SSS Soap. OSP $3.20 CMV $10.00 MB.

1967 SKIN-SO-SOFT COMPLEMENTS
Box holds 3 oz. box of Satin Talc & 2 bars of SSS Soap. O.S.P. $2.50 C.M.V. $8.00 MB.

1968 SKIN-SO-SOFT SMOOTHIES
Box holds 4 oz. bottle of Skin-So-Soft & 3 oz. Satin Talc. O.S.P. $3.50 C.M.V. $6.50 MB.

1970 SKIN-SO-SOFT
Clear glass container holds 2 oz. Skin-So-Soft, gold cap. Comes in Bird of Paradise, Elusive, Charisma, Brocade, Unforgettable, Field Flowers, Occur!, Rapture & To A Wild Rose. OSP $2.50 CMV $1.00
1971-72 SKIN-SO-SOFT "2 OZ."
2 oz. 7 layer glass bottle with gold cap. 4½" high. Came in Bird of Paradise, Elusive, Charisma, Brocade, To A Wild Rose. OSP $2.50 CMV $1.00

1966-67 SKIN-SO-SOFT (Left)
1 oz. gold cap with painted leaf. Came in set of three only. Unforgettable, Rapture, Occur!, Somewhere, Topaze, Cotillion, Here's My Heart, To A Wild Rose, Wishing. CMV $3.00 MB, $2.00 BO
1969 SKIN-SO-SOFT (Right)
1 oz. gold cap & paper label. Came in Unforgettable, Rapture, Occur!, Somewhere, Topaze, Cotillion, To A Wild Rose & Here's My Heart. OSP $1.50 each, CMV $3.00 MB, $2.00 BO.

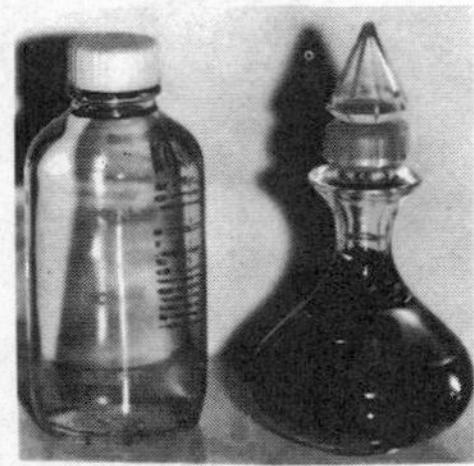

1967 SKIN-SO-SOFT
4 oz. white cap. This bottle has no S embossed on side. Issued during glass strike. OSP $2.25 CMV $10.00
1969-70 SKIN-SO-SOFT SCENTED BATH OIL
2 oz. clear glass bottom, clear plastic top. This top is the same as the clear Just II. Came in Charisma, Brocade, Rapture, Unforgettable, Occur!, Here's My Heart, Cotillion, To A Wild Rose & Regence. OSP $2.50 CMV $3.00 MB, $2.00 BO.

1964-65 BATH MATES
Box holds 4 oz. bottle of Skin-So-Soft Bath Oil & 2 cakes of soap. OSP $3.23 CMV $10.00 MB.

1969-78 SKIN-SO-SOFT
4 oz. in clear plastic bottle with turquoise cap. O.S.P. $3.00 C.M.V. 25¢
1969-78 SKIN-SO-SOFT
8 oz. clear plastic bottle with turquoise cap. O.S.P. $5.00 C.M.V. 25¢
1972-78 SKIN-SO-SOFT
16 oz. clear plastic bottle with turquoise cap. O.S.P. $8.50 C.M.V. 25¢

1965 SKIN-SO-SOFT DISH & SOAP
Blue & white plastic soap dish with white bar of SSS soap. O.S.P. $1.50 C.M.V. $10.00 M.B. Soap & dish $8.00, Dish only $3.00

1966-67 BATH LUXURY
Box holds 4 oz. bottle of Skin-So-Soft & pink bath sponge. Came with 2 different sponges. Course as shown & fine grain. OSP $4.50 CMV $10.00 MB.

Right to Left) 1961-69 SKIN-SO-SOFT
4 oz. glass bottle with three S's on side. Turquoise cap. O.S.P. $2.25 C.M.V. $1.00
1964-69 SKIN-SO-SOFT
8 oz. glass bottle with three S's on side. Turquoise cap. O.S.P. $4.00 C.M.V. $1.00
1965-74 SKIN-SO-SOFT SOAP
3 oz. bar. O.S.P. 49¢ C.M.V. $1.00 mint.
1965-67 SKIN-SO-SOFT AFTER SHOWER FOAM - 4 oz. white spray can with turquoise cap. O.S.P. $2.25 C.M.V. $1.00

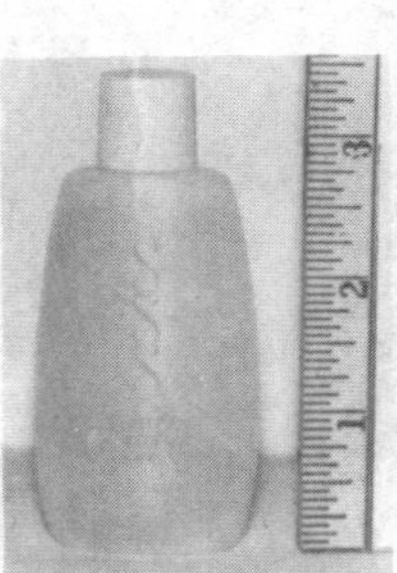

1977-78 SKIN SO SOFT TRIAL SIZE
1 oz. plastic bottle, white lid.
O.S.P. 25¢ C.M.V. 25¢
1968-78 SATIN TALC
3 oz. size. 2 different labels as shown.
O.S.P. $2.00 C.M.V. 50¢ each.

SKIN-SO-SOFT PRODUCTS
White & gold with aqua lids.
1973-78 SKIN SOFTENER - 5 oz. plastic jar. O.S.P. $4.50 C.M.V. 25¢
1960's BATH OIL SAMPLE
C.M.V. 50¢
1973-77 SATIN POWDER SPRAY
7 oz. can. O.S.P. $4.50 C.M.V. 50¢
1970's BATH OIL SAMPLE
C.M.V. 25¢
1974-78 EMOLLIENT SHOWER GEL
6 oz. O.S.P. $4.00 C.M.V. 25¢
1970's EMOLLIENT SHOWER GEL SAMPLE - C.M.V. 25¢

1980 SMOOTH AS SILK SKIN SOFTENER
5 oz. pink plastic. CMV 25c
1980 SKIN SO SOFT SKIN SOFTENER
5 oz. blue plastic. CMV 25c.

1979-80 SKIN SO SOFT TRIAL SIZE
1 oz. plastic bottle, blue cap. CMV 25c.
1979-80 SKIN SO SOFT LIGHT BOUQUET
16 oz. plastic bottle, blue cap. SSP $5.99
CMV 25c. All plastic bottle Skin So Soft products, CMV 25c each.

1970'S SKIN-SO-SOFT SAMPLES
Box of 10 packets, marked not for resale. CMV $1.00 MB.

BATH SALTS - MISC.

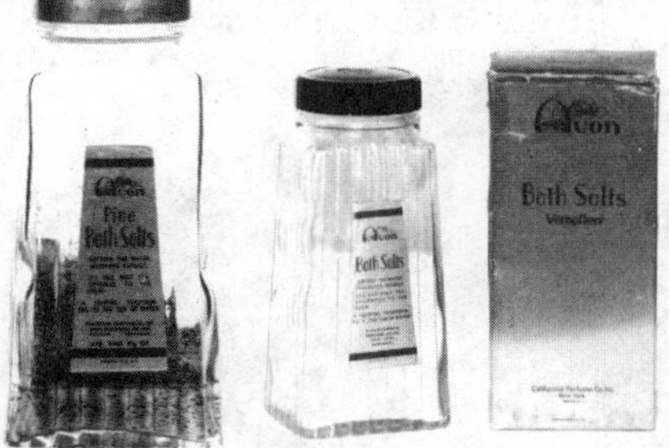

1931-33 BATH SALTS
10 oz. ribbed glass bottle with blue lid, silver label, 2 different labels. OSP 75c.
CMV $60.00 MB.
1933-37 BATH SALTS
8½ oz. ribbed glass jar with dark blue cap, Came in Ariel & Vernafleur from 1933-37 Pine & Jasmine from 1935-37. OSP 63c. each. CMV $60.00 each in box.

1933-37 BATH SALTS SAMPLE
Ribbed glass bottle with blue cap. Came in Ariel, Vernafleur, C.M.V. $60.00. Pine & Jasmine C.M.V. $55.00 ea.

1954-57 BATH SALTS
8 oz. bottle with turquoise cap & label. Came in Jasmine & Pine. O.S.P. 89¢ each. CMV $20.00 MB, $15.00 BO.

BEAUTY DUST POWDERS, TALC-MISC.

1936 BATH SALTS
8½ or 9 oz. glass jars with turquoise lids from 1936-44, small paper label. 9 oz. jars from 1943-53 came in Ariel 1936-44 C.M.V. $30.00 Pine 1936-44 then 46 to 53 C.M.V. $25.00 Vernafleur 1936-44 C.M.V. $35.00 & Jasmine 1936-44 C.M.V. $25.00 Attention 1943-44 then 46-48 O.S.P. each 63¢ C.M.V. $25.00. Add $5.00 for box. See Attention Fragrance for regular issue box.

1943-45 BATH SALTS
5 oz. red and white paper containers. Came in Attention, Jasmine, Pine, Vernafleur. O.S.P. 69¢ each. C.M.V. $25.00 each mint. $30.00 M.B.

1929-30 BATH SALTS
10 oz. bottle with metal lid, silver & blue label. Ribbed glass sides. O.S.P. 75¢ C.M.V. $60.00 B.O. $65.00 M.B.

1936-49 DUSTING POWDER REFILL
13 oz. turquoise & white cardboard box. O.S.P. 78¢ C.M.V. $15.00 M.B. Add $5.00 for C.P.C. label.

1943-44 DUSTING POWDER
Turquoise & white paper box. O.S.P. $1.39 C.M.V. $35.00 - $40.00 M.B.

1935-36 DUSTING POWDER
13 oz. metal gold colored can. Came in Bath Ensemble Set only. C.M.V. $35.00 mint.
1935-36 DUSTING POWDER
Same as gold can only general issue was silver & blue can. O.S.P. $1.20 C.M.V. $30.00 can only mint. $40.00 MB.

1940-41 DUSTING POWDER CHRISTMAS BOX
Special issue blue and white Christmas box holds regular issue metal can of dusting powder. O.S.P. $1.00 C.M.V. $35.00 M.B. as shown.

1945-48 DUSTING POWDER
6 oz. blue & white cardboard with ladies face on lid. Also contained Apple Blossom Beauty Dust. O.S.P. $1.35 C.M.V. $25.00
1936-49 DUSTING POWDER
13 oz. turquoise & beige can with "A" on top. 1st (1936-39) issue had CPC on bottom CMV $30.00. 1940-49 Avon Products label only. OSP $1.39 CMV $20.00. Add $5.00 each for MB.

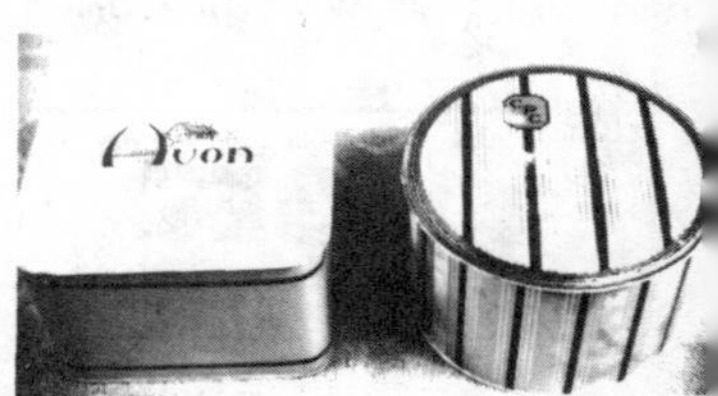

1930-34 DUSTING POWDER
8 oz. blue & silver square can. OSP $1.35 CMV $40.00 MB, $30.00 can only mint.
1925-29 DUSTING POWDER
Gold metal can with black stripes. Came in Daphne, Vernafleur, Trailing Arbutus, California Rose, Baby Powder & Super Rite Talcum. OSP $1.00, CMV $50.00 MB, $40.00 can only.

1943-46 DUSTING POWDER
13 oz. paper box, turquoise & ivory. O.S.P. $1.39 C.M.V. $35.00 M.B. $30.00 box only mint.

1936-49 DUSTING POWDER REFILL
Round cardboard container. Came in Jasmine or Avon dusting powder. O.S.P. 89¢ C.M.V. $15.00 M.B.

1966-68 MIX & MATCH - BEAUTY DUST DEMO
White box, came in choice of beauty dust refill & different fragrance empty container. CMV $10.00 MB.

1936-48 ELITE POWDER
Large family size on left, turquoise & white can. OSP $1.19, CMV $25.00 - $30.00 MB.
1936-54 – 2.9 oz. or 3 oz. size on right, turquoise & white can, 2 different boxes. OSP 43c, CMV $10.00 CO, $12.00 MB. Add $3.00 for C.P.C. label.

1931-36 ELITE POWDER
Silver & blue can with blue cap is general issue in regular size on right. OSP .37c CMV $25.00. Family size 1 lb. can on left OSP $1.04 CMV $30.00. Add $5.00 MB

1934-35 ELITE POWDER
Same design & shape cans, came in sets only in gold & blue cans. CMV small size $35.00. Large family size $35.00, add $5.00 ea. MB

1941 DUSTING POWDER MOTHERS DAY BOX
Special issue lavender box with white lace holds regular issue dusting powder. Sold during Mothers Day. O.S.P. $1.00 C.M.V. $30.00 M.B. as shown.

1943 DUSTING POWDER CHRISTMAS BOX
Outer box special issue for Christmas. Holds square cardboard beauty dust. C.M.V. $40.00 M.B. as shown.

1944 BEAUTY DUST CHRISTMAS BOX
Special issue Christmas box. Holds feather design paper container of beauty dust. OSP $1.10 CMV $27.00 MB as shown, beauty dust only mint, $22.00.

1966-68 BEAUTY DUST DEMO
Avon embossed boxes had mix or match Beauty Dust and refill. Used by Reps only. CMV $10.00 MB.

1943-46 ELITE FOOT POWDER
Maroon and cream colored paper box. 2.75 oz. Black screw off octaginal cap. O.S.P. 43¢ C.M.V. $25.00 mint.

1943-46 ELITE FOOT POWDER
2.75 oz. maroon & white victory paper box. Flat punch out top with paper lift off lid. OSP 43c, CMV $25.00 mint.

Left to Right

1942-48 BEAUTY DUST
6 oz. blue feather design cardboard. Came in Avon Beauty Dust & Apple Blossom. O.S.P. $1.19 C.M.V. $22.00 - $25.00 M.B.

1942-48 FACE POWDER
1¾ oz. blue feather design cardboard. O.S.P. 89¢ C.M.V. $8.00 mint - $12.00 M.B.

1946-48 HEAVENLITE FACE POWDER
2½ oz. same feather design paper box. O.S.P. 89¢ C.M.V. $8.00 - $12.00 M.B.

1942-49 ROUGE
Blue Feather design, paper container on right. O.S.P. 55¢ C.M.V. $5.00 - $7.00 M.B.

1942-46 FEATHER DESIGN LIPSTICK
Blue plastic top and bottom with cardboard sides. Also came with red plastic top and bottom. O.S.P. 59¢ C.M.V. $5.00 $8.00 M.B.

1965 BEAUTY DUST REFILL
White outer box holds colorful inner box with plain beauty dust refill. Came in choice of Persian Wood, Cotillion, To a Wild Rose, Somewhere, Topaze, Occur, Here's My Heart, and Rapture. O.S.P. $2.98 C.M.V. $7.00 as shown M.B.

1943-46 ELITE POWDER
Turquoise & white paper boxes in family size. O.S.P. $1.19 C.M.V. $30.00. Regular size O.S.P. 43¢ C.M.V. $20.00

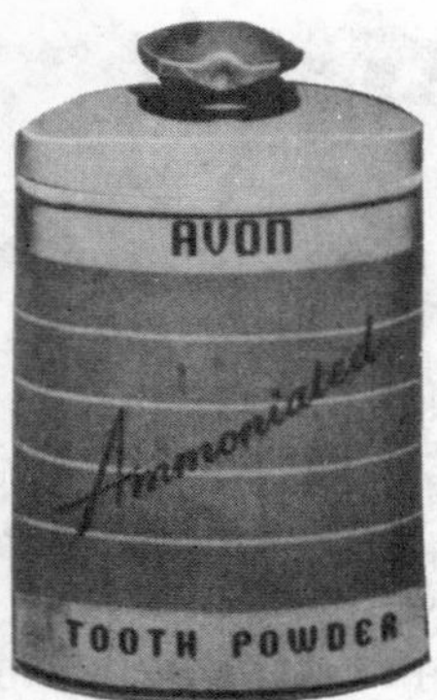

1949 ONLY - AMMONIATED TOOTH POWDER
3 oz. turquoise can and tilt cap. This can with this style cap was a very short issue. O.S.P. 49¢ C.M.V. $15.00 M.B., $13.00 can only mint.

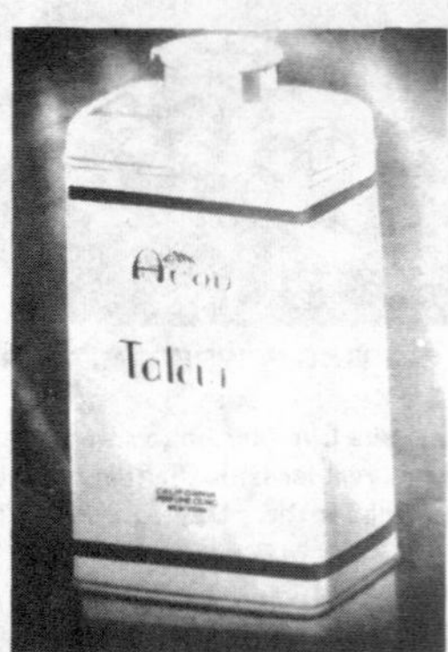

1930-32 TALCUM POWDER
Silver & blue can came in regular & family size. O.S.P. 50¢ C.M.V. $35.00 $40.00 M.B. 1 lb. family size O.S.P. $1.00 C.M.V. $35.00 - $40.00 M.B.

LEFT 1943-46 SMOKERS TOOTH POWDER "PAPER"
Maroon & cream paper sides, tin top & bottom. OSP 36c, CMV $20.00 mint.
RIGHT 1943-46 TALC FOR MEN "PAPER"
Maroon & cream paper container. Metal screw on cap in black or maroon. OSP 37c, CMV $20.00 mint.

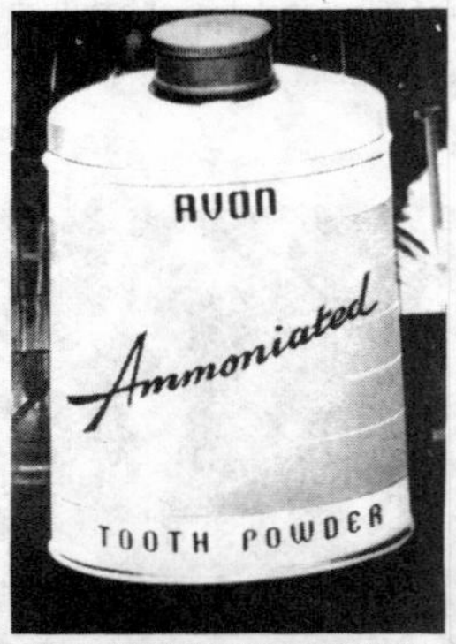

1949-55 AMMONIATED TOOTH POWDER - 3 oz. turquoise & white can with turquoise lid. O.S.P. 49¢ C.M.V. $9.00 - $12.00 M.B.

1943-46 ELITE POWDER
2.75 oz. or 3 oz. paper box. OSP 43c. CMV $18.00 mint.
1943-46 TOOTH POWDER
3 oz. paper box. OSP 39c, CMV $20.00 mint.
1943-46 SMOKER'S TOOTH POWDER
3½ oz. paper box with metal top & bottom. OSP 59c, CMV $20.00 mint.
All are turquoise and white.

LEFT TO RIGHT
1936-49 SMOKER'S TOOTH POWDER
Metal cap 3½ oz. turquoise & white can. O.S.P. 36¢ C.M.V. $16.00 - $18.00 M.B.
1950-54 SMOKER'S TOOTH POWDER
3½ oz. turquoise & white can, turquoise tilt cap. O.S.P. 57¢ C.M.V. $14.00 $16.00 M.B.
1946-50 SMOKER'S TOOTH POWDER
3½ oz. turquoise & white can, turquoise plastic cap. O.S.P. 57¢ C.M.V. $14.00 $16.00 M.B.

1932-36 SMOKER'S TOOTH POWDER
Green can. O.S.P. 51¢ C.M.V. $35.00 M.B. $25.00 can only.

LEFT 1930-36 TOOTH POWDER
Green metal can. O.S.P. 35¢ C.M.V. $30.00 M.B. $25.00 can only mint.

RIGHT 1936-50 TOOTH POWDER
Turquoise and white metal can, silver cap. O.S.P. 36¢ C.M.V. $14.00 in box. $10.00 can only.

1944-46 SMOKERS TOOTH POWDER
Turquoise and white paper container. Plastic cap. OSP 57c, CMV $22.00 mint. mint.

1936-49 TALC FOR MEN
Maroon & cream colored can with maroon cap. O.S.P. 37¢ C.M.V. $15.00 in box. $12.00 can only.

1938-49 SMOKER'S TOOTH POWDER
Maroon & cream colored can. Came in Men's Sets only. C.M.V. $16.00 mint.

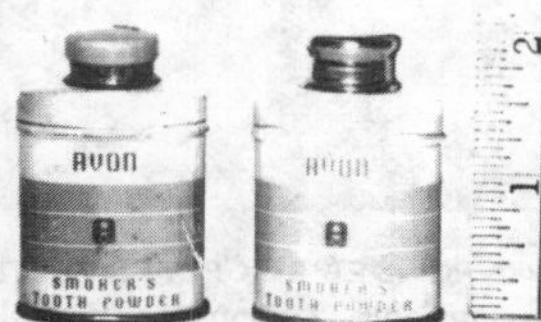

SMOKERS TOOTH POWDER SAMPLES
Left – 1936-40 Small ¼ oz. turquoise & white can. C.P.C. label, turquoise sifter cap. CMV $35.00 mint.
Right – 1940-49 Same can only has chrome lift off cap. CMV $30.00 mint.

1930-36 FACE POWDER
Silver & blue paper box came in Ariel & Vernafleur. O.S.P. 78¢ C.M.V. $16.00 in box. $12.00 container only mint.

1943-46 TOOTH POWDER
Flat metal top, paper side container. 3 oz. size. Turquoise and white. O.S.P. 39¢, CMV $25.00 MB, $20.00 can only mint. mint.

1944 HEAVENLIGHT FACE POWDER
General issue feather design paper box. Shown in 1944 pink design box. 2½ oz. contents. Powder only sold in 1944-48. C.M.V. $12.00 M.B. as shown. Powder box only $8.00.

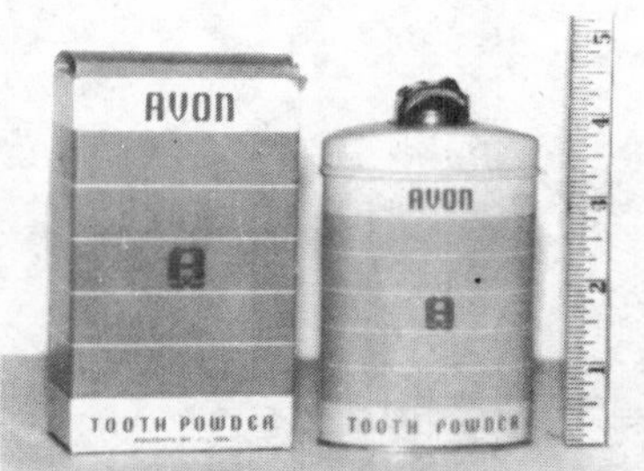

1936-49 TOOTH POWDER
Box holds 2¼ oz. turquoise and white can. Silver slide open cap. O.S.P. 49¢ C.M.V. $14.00 M.B. as shown.

1958-66 AQUA DENT
7 oz. green color can with white cap. OSP 79c, CMV $3.00 - $4.00 MB.

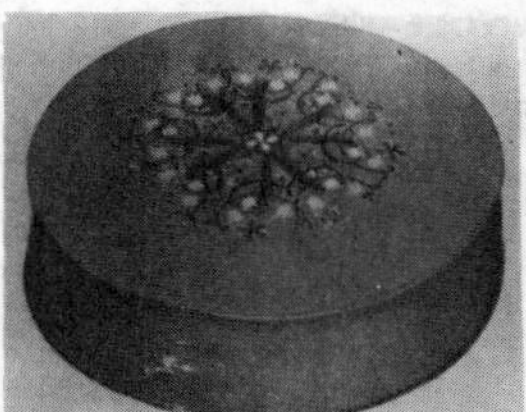

1955-57 SHEER MIST FACE POWDER
Turquoise cardboard with white & pink flowers & gold 4A design on lid. O.S.P. $1.10 C.M.V. $4.00 - $5.00 M.B.

1936-39 FACE POWDER
3" diameter, turquoise and cream container, cardboard. Came in Cotillion, Ariel or Vernafleur fragrance. Choice of natural, rose, peach, Rachel No. 1, Rachel No. 2 orchre, orchre-rose and suntan shades. O.S.P. 78¢ C.M.V. $10.00 $12.00 M.B.

1958-59 SHEER MIST FACE POWDER
2½ oz. white cardboard box with pink rose on lid & pink rim around edge. OSP $1.10 CMV $1.00 box only, $3.00 MB.

1960-63 FACE POWDER
Same design as Sheer Mist only has plastic lid, no pink rim. OSP $1.25 CMV $1.00, $1.50 MB.

1963-67 FASHION FINISH FACE POWDER - 1½ oz. white plastic box. O.S.P. $2.25 C.M.V. 50¢

1976 FINISHING FACE POWDER EVEN TONE - 1½ oz. pink plastic box same as 1969-75 white box. O.S.P. $3.00 C.M.V. 50¢

1973-76 HEAVY DUTY POWDERED HAND CLEANSER - 10 oz. blue, white, pink & black cardboard with plastic top & bottom. O.S.P. $2.25 C.M.V. 25¢

1965 BATH BOUQUET TALC
1½ oz. green paper box. Came in Bath Bouquet Set only in all fragrances of that set. C.M.V. $8.00 mint.

1960-61 BEAUTY DUST
3 oz. white plastic bottle, has paper label or painted label, turquoise cap. This came in Modern Simplicity Set only. Came in Cotillion, To A Wild Rose & Here's My Heart. C.M.V. $15.00

1940-50'S DUSTING POWDER PUFF
Envelope holds Avon puff. Rare. CMV $10.00

LEFT 1956-62 ANTISEPTIC POWDER
3 oz. gray & white can, red cap. OSP 59c, CMV $2.00
RIGHT 1962-64 ANTISEPTIC POWDER
3 oz. gray & white can, red cap. OSP 69c CMV $1.50
RIGHT 1965-68 ANTISEPTIC POWDER
Same as 1962-64 can only 2¾ oz. size. OSP 69c, CMV $1.00

1970-71 POWDER PUFFERY BEAUTY DUST - 5 oz. white plastic base with pink puff in Charisma, Brocade, Cotillion & To A Wild Rose. O.S.P. $5.00 C.M.V. $3.00 $5.00 M.B.

1963 SACHET PILLOWS
Green and white holder contains powder sachet pillow. Came 6 to a pack. O.S.P. 50¢ C.M.V. for set of 6 $7.00 mint.

1940's TRIM TONE COSMETIC STOCKING - Beige with gold band, box turquoise. O.S.P. $1.50 C.M.V. $25.00 M.B.

1966-68 PAT 'N POWDER MITT
Lace Mitt contains Beauty Dust in Occur! Rapture, & Unforgettable. O.S.P. $2.50 C.M.V. $3.00 M.B.

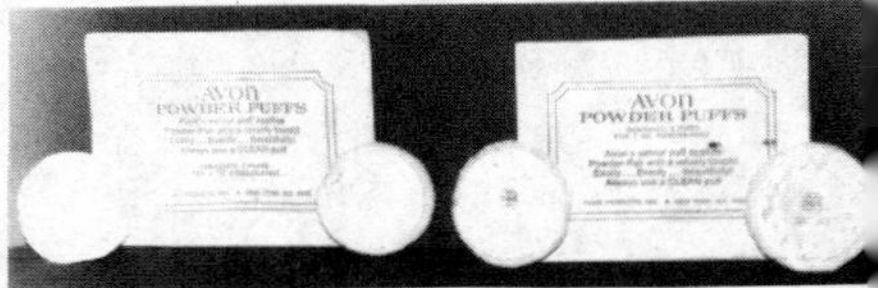

1960-70'S POWDER PUFF COMPACT REFILLS
2 different puffs & package for compacts. CMV $3.00 each mint.

1940s POWDER PAK PUFFS REFILL
Envelope holds 2 compact puff refills. C.M.V. $5.00 mint
1960s POWDER PUFF REFILLS
Envelope holds 2 puff refills. C.M.V. $3.00

OLOGNES - MISC.

52-56 COLOGNE STICK
rquoise plastic cologne stick came in olden Promise, Cotillion, Quaintance, orever Spring & To A Wild Rose. 1956 ly Nearness & Bright Night came in hite plastic of same design. OSP $1.50 MV each $10.00

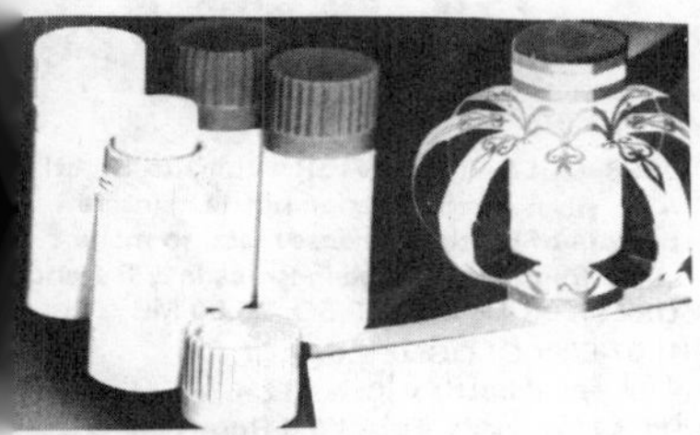

1956-58 COLOGNE STICK
White plastic with colored cap. Gold, white & red paper ornament package. Xmas only in 1957-58. Came in Nearness, Elegante, Bright Night O.S.P. $1.50 To A Wild Rose, Forever Spring, Cotillion O.S.P. $1.25 C.M.V. stick only $6.00. In package $18.00

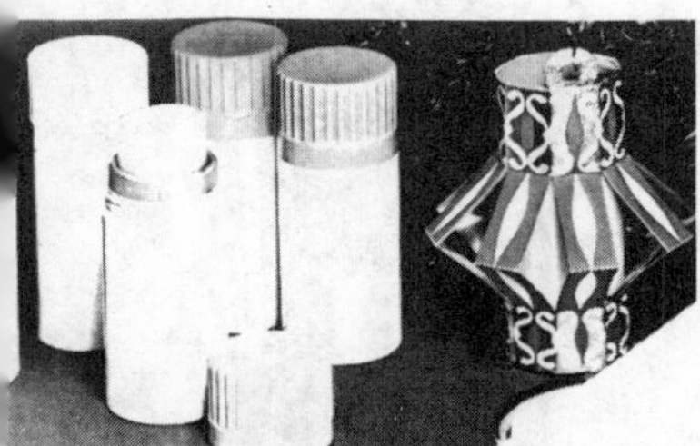

1956-58 COLOGNE STICK
White plastic with colored caps. came in Nearness, Bright Night O.S.P. $1.50; Cotillion, Quaintance, To A Wild Rose, Forever Spring, O.S.P. $1.25. Came in blue, white & gold paper ornament at Christmas only. CMV in ornament $18.00, stick only $6.00.

1953-54 COLOGNE STICKS CHRISTMAS PACKAGING
Green & red on white cardboard, pink ribbon in top. CMV $18.00 MB.
1952 Only - COLOGNE STICK CHRISTMAS PACKAGING (Right)
Red & white candy striped cardboard, red ribbon top. CMV $18.00 MB.

1931-36 HEADACHE COLOGNE
4 oz. ribbed glass bottle with dark blue cap & silver label. O.S.P. 75¢ C.M.V. $50.00 bottle only. $60.00 M.B.

1957-58 SNOW FLAKE COLOGNE
1/8 oz. round white caps. Came in Beauty Dust only in Cotillion, Forever Spring, To A Wild Rose, Nearness, Elegante & Bright Night. No labels on bottles. C.M.V. $9.00 ea. Flat top bottle came in all Beauty Dust at Christmas 1963. CMV $8.00 each.

1936-40 INHALANT COLOGNE
4 oz. bottle with turquoise cap & label. Turquoise & white box. O.S.P. 52¢ CMV $35.00 MB, $30.00 BO.

1956 POWDER BOX COLOGNE
1/16 oz. Came in Beauty Dust only with ribbons attached, in Cotillion, Forever Spring, Golden Promise, To A Wild Rose & Quaintance. CMV $10.00 BO, $12.00 mint with ribbon.

1940-41 REFRESHING COLOGNE
4 oz. bottle with turquoise cap & label. Turquoise box. OSP 52c, CMV $35.00 MB, $30.00 bottle only.

1979-80 PURSE CONCENTRE
.33 oz. clear glass, gold tone cap. Comes in Here's My Heart, Unforgettable, Sonnet, Bird of Paradise, Occur!, Cotillion. SSP $1.50 CMV $1.00 MB.

1978-79 ULTRA COLOGNE .33 OZ.
.33 oz. clear glass. Came in gold & silver caps in Timeless, Ariane, Tempo, Candid, Emprise, Unspoken, Each comes with different color bands on caps & different boxes. SSP $1.50 CMV $1.00 MB.

COLOGNE & COLOGNE MIST SPECIAL ISSUE BOXES
Left To Right
1968 COLOGNE - CMV $2.00 box
1969 COLOGNE - CMV $2.00 box
1974 COLOGNE MIST - CMV $1.00 box
1974 COLOGNE MIST - CMV $1.00 box
Each was sold with choice of fragrance on a short selling period.

COLOGNE MIST SPECIAL ISSUE BOXES
Each came in choice of fragrance & was sold for a short period.
Left To Right
1975 COLOGNE MIST
1975 COLOGNE MIST
1976 COLOGNE MIST
1978 ULTRA COLOGNE SPRAY
Add $1.00 to CMV of each bottle for each box shown.

LEFT 1979 ANNIVERSARY COLOGNE PETITE
.5 oz. clear glass, gold cap, special box. Comes in Regence, Persian Wood, Rapture, or Brocade. SSP $1.25 CMV $1.00 MB
CENTER 1979-80 COLOGNE CLASSIQUE
.5 oz. clear glass, gold cap. Comes in 11 fragrances. SSP $1.25 CMV $1.00 MB.
RIGHT 1979-80 PURSE CONCENTRE
.33 oz. octaginal shaped bottle. Different color stripe on cap for 9 different fragrances. SSP $1.50 CMV $1.00 MB.

1966-69 COLOGNE GEMS
1 oz. clear glass with flat plastic top. Came in Cotillion, Rapture, Unforgettable, Somewhere, Occur! Topaze, Here's My Heart & To A Wild Rose. O.S.P. $1.75 C.M.V. $2.00 BO. $4.00 MB.

1969-75 DAZZLING PERFUME
1/8 oz. gold cap. Came in Unforgettable, Rapture, Occur! O.S.P. $3.25; Somewhere, Topaze, Cotillion, Here's My Heart, To A Wild Rose, O.S.P. $2.75; Charisma, Brocade, Regence, Bird of Paradise, Elusive & Moonwind. OSP $3.75 CMV $1.00
1969-70 MINUETTE COLOGNE
½ oz. gold cap. Elusive, Charisma, Brocade, Regence, Unforgettable, Rapture, Somewhere, Topaze, Occur!, Cotillion. OSP $1.50 CMV $1.00
1968-69 FRAGRANCES FLING COLOGNE
½ oz. gold cap. Came in Charisma, Brocade, Regence, Occur!, Unforgettable, Rapture, Somewhere, Topaze, Cotillion, Here's My Heart, To A Wild Rose, Wishing, Persian Wood. OSP $4.00 CMV $2.00
Unforgettable, Rapture, Occur! O.S.P. $2.50 Somewhere, Topaze, Cotillion, Here's My Heart, To A Wild Rose, O.S.P. $2.00.
.33 oz. with gold 4A design on cap.
C.M.V. 50¢

1958 COIN FAN BOTTLES
½ oz. clear glass with turquoise caps. Bo pink & gold. Came either cologne or lotion sachet, choices of To A Wild Rose Cotillion, Nearness, Forever Spring, Brig Night, Elegante, Here's My Heart & Persi Wood. Came in Wishing Coin Set only. CMV $3.00 BO each, $8.00 MB.

1968 COLOGNE RIVIERA (Left to Right)
4 oz. silver cap & silver on bottle. Unscrew bottom of bottle & reverse metal to make stand for bottle. Came in Brocade & Regence OSP $6.00 CMV $4.00 BO, $6.00 MB
1967-68 COLOGNE CLASSIC
4 oz. spiral bottle with gold cap, came in Here's My Heart, To A Wild Rose, OSP $3.50; Somewhere, Topaze, Cotillion, OSP $4.00; Unforgettable, Rapture, Occur!, OSP $5.00. CMV $2.00 BO, $3.00 MB.
1969 GIFT COLOGNE
4 oz. gold cap. Came in Topaze, To A Wild Rose, Somewhere, Here's My Heart, Cotillion & Rapture. OSP $4.00 CMV $2.00 BO, $3.00 MB.

1962-63 BATH CLASSIC
1½ oz. clear glass with gold design & gold cap. Came in Bath Classic Set only. Came in Somewhere, Cotillion, Topaze, Here's My Heart, Persian Wood & To A Wild Rose. CMV $10.00 BO mint.

956 FRAGRANCE COLOGNES
dram bottle with white painted label & cap. Came in Fragrance Rainbow Set only in Nearness, Cotillion, Bright Night & To A Wild Rose. CMV $15.00 mint.

1953-55 BEAUTY DUST COLOGNE
(Right) 5/8 dram bottle with no label & flat white or round white cap. Came in Beauty Dust at Christmas only. Each had a silk neck ribbon with gold edge. Quaintance, blue ribbon; To A Wild Rose, pink ribbon; Forever Spring, purple ribbon; Cotillion, pink ribbon; Nearness, pink ribbon; Elegante, red ribbon. CMV with ribbon $12.00 bottle only $8.00

1957 Only - ½ OZ. GEMS IN CRYSTAL COLOGNES - ½ oz. bottle in 2 different shapes. Both came with pointed & flat top plastic caps. Each came in To A Wild Rose, Cotillion, Bright Night, Nearness, each has matching tops & labels. All came in Gems in Crystal Set only. C.M.V. $15.00 flat cap. $18.00 pointed cap.

1967-68 GOLD CAP ROCKER COLOGNE
½ oz. gold round cap. Came in Brocade, Regence, Unforgettable, Rapture, Occur!, Somewhere, Topaze, Cotillion, Here's My Heart, To A Wild Rose, Persian Wood & Wishing. OSP $1.25, CMV $2.00 each BO, $3.00 MB.

1959-62 FLAT TOP ROCKER COLOGNE
½ oz. flat plastic cap. Came in Persian Wood, Here's My Heart, Cotillion, To A Wild Rose, Topaze, Somewhere, Regence, Bright Night & Nearness. OSP $1.00 each. CMV $3.00 BO, $5.00 MB. Add $1.00 for Nearness & Bright Night.

1953-55 ½ OZ. COLOGNE
½ oz. size with white cap & painted label. Came in Cupids Bow, Fragrance Tie Ins, Fragrance Rainbow & Special Date Set only. Came in Forever Spring, Cotillion, Quaintance & To A Wild Rose. C.M.V. $10.00 ea. Bright Night, C.M.V. $14.00 ea. mint.

1964-66 ½ OZ. HEART SHAPED COLOGNE
Left is gold band on plastic cap. Came in Unforgettable, Rapture, Occur! Cotillion, Somewhere, Topaze, Here's My Heart, Persian Wood, To A Wild Rose & Wishing. O.S.P. $1.25 CMV $4.00 MB, $2.00 BO

FOREIGN HEART SHAPED EAU DE COLOGNE (Right) - No gold band around plastic cap. C.M.V. $8.00

1966 COLOGNE ½ OZ.
Has embossed leaves in glass, gold cap. Came in Unforgettable, Rapture, Occur! Somewhere, Topaze, Cotillion, Here's My Heart, To A Wild Rose or Wishing. Came in red & gold box in Renaissance Trio only. CMV $4.00 MB $3.00 BO.

1962-63 REFRESHING HOURS COLOGNE
2½ oz. gold cap, front side of bottle is flat, trimmed in gold. Came in Somewhere, Topaze, Cotillion, Here's My Heart, Persian Wood, To A Wild Rose Cologne. Came in Refreshing Hours Set only. CMV $8.00 mint.

1970-71 MINUETTE COLOGNE
5 oz. clear glass cologne bottle with gold cap. Came in Bird of Paradise, Elusive, Charisma, Brocade, Regence, Unforgettable, Rapture, Occur! Somewhere, Topaze, To A Wild Rose, Cotillion & Here's My Heart. OSP $1.50 CMV $2.00 MB, $1.00 BO

1973-75 DEMI COLOGNE
½ oz. clear glass, gold cap. came in Imperial Garden, Patchwork, Sonnet, Moonwind, Roses, Roses, Field Flowers, Bird of Paradise, Charisma, Unforgettable, Topaze, Occur! Here's My Heart. S.S.P. $1.00 C.M.V. $1.00 M.B.

1962-63 FAN ROCKER
½ oz. cologne, gold cap with neck cord. Came in To A Wild Rose, Here's My Heart, Persian Wood, Cotillion, Somewhere, Topaze, OSP $1.00 CMV $3.00 BO - $5.00 MB.

1975-77 COLOGNE
2 oz. clear glass with gold cap. Name of cologne on side in gold. Came in Moonwind, Charisma, Topaze, Sonnet, O.S.P. $4.00 C.M.V. 50¢

1975-76 DEMI-COLOGNE (Pepper Mill Shape) - ½ oz. clear glass with gold cap. Holds Sonnet, Moonwind, Charisma, Patchwork, Somewhere, Topaze, Occur! Cotillion. O.S.P. $2.00 C.M.V. 50¢

LEFT 1976-79 COLOGNE PETITE
½ oz. Came in Charisma, Moonwind, Topaze, Here's My Heart, Unforgettable, Sweet Honesty, Cotillion, Occur!, Persian Wood, Regence, Rapture & Brocade. Gold cap. SSP 99c, CMV 50c.

CENTER & RIGHT 1977-78 ULTRA COLOGNE
.33 oz. Came in Unspoken, Emprise, Ariane, Timeless, Candid. Came with silver or gold caps. SSP $1.50 CMV 50c MB.

1966-70 COLOGNE SILK
3 oz. frosted glass bottle, gold cap, colored neck labels. Came in Here's My Heart, To A Wild Rose, OSP $3.50; Somewhere, Topaze, Cotillion, OSP $3.75; Unforgettable, Rapture, Occur! OSP $4.00. CMV $1.00, $2.00 MB.

1968-69 BUD VASE COLOGNE
4 oz. gold neck trim, colored paper labe in Here's My Heart, To A Wild Rose, Somewhere, Topaze, Cotillion, OSP $4. Unforgettable, Rapture, Occur! OSP $5.00. CMV $2.00 BO, $3.00 MB.

LEFT 1977-78 COLOGNE MINIATURE FOR MEN
1/2 oz. Came in Clint, Everest or Wild Country. Smoked glass, gray cap. S.S.P. 88¢ C.M.V. 50¢ M.B.

CENTER 1977 CHRISTMAS CANDLE COLOGNE DECANTER
1 oz. green glass. Came in Charisma, Sweet Honesty, Topaze or Moonwind. S.S.P. $1.29 C.M.V. $1.00 M.B.

RIGHT 1977 FRAGRANCE FACETTES
1/2 oz. colognes. Came in Moonwind, Charisma, Topaze, Occur!, Unforgettable, Here's My Heart, Cotillion, Sweet Honesty, Sonnet or Bird of Paradise, with gold cap. S.S.P. $1.00 C.M.V. 50¢ M.B.

1977-78 COLOGNE 1/2 OZ.
.5 oz. Came in Field Flowers, Honeysuckle, Hawaiian White Ginger, Apple Blossom, Raining Violets, Roses, Roses. Different fragrances came with different colored caps. O.S.P. $2.00 C.M.V. 50¢ each.

COLOGNE MIST - MISC.

1959-66 SPRAY ESSENCE
1 oz. black plastic coated, gold & blue lid. Came in Cotillion, To A Wild Rose, Bright Night, Nearness, OSP $3.00; Persian Wood, Here's My Heart, OSP $3.25; Somewhere 1962-66, OSP $3.50; Rapture, Occur! 1965-66, OSP $4.00. CMV $2.00 BO, $5.00 MB.

1957-59 ESSENCE DE FLEURS
1 oz. black plastic coated, gold & blue lid. Came in Nearness, Elegante, To A Wild Rose, Cotillion, Bright Night, & Forever Spring. OSP $3.00 CMV $4.00 BO, $7.00 MB.

1966-68 COLOGNE MIST
2 oz. gold cap with 4A design on cap. Came in Here's My Heart, To A Wild Rose, OSP $2.25; Somewhere, Topaze, Cotillion, OSP $2.50; Unforgettable, Rapture, Occur!, OSP $3.00. CMV $1.00 BO, $2.00 MB each.

1966-67 SPRAY ESSENCE
1¼ oz. plastic coated glass with gold cap. Came in Here's My Heart, To A Wild Rose, Wishing, OSP $3.50; Somewhere, Topaze, Cotillion, OSP $3.75; Unforgettable, Rapture, Occur!, OSP $4.00. CMV $2.00 BO, $3.00 MB.

1967-70 SPRAY ESSENCE
1¼ oz. All had gold caps. Eight different fragrances with 8 different colored bands around neck. Unforgettable, Rapture, Occur! O.S.P. $4.00, Somewhere, Topaze, Cotillion, O.S.P. $3.75, Here's My Heart, To A Wild Rose O.S.P. $3.50 C.M.V. $1.50 B.O. $2.00 M.B.

1962-64 CRYSTAL GLORY
Does not say Spray Essence on cap. Plastic gold top & base. 1 oz. refillable bottle. Came in Topaze, Somewhere, Cotillion, Here's My Heart, Persian Wood, To A Wild Rose, OSP $4.50 - $5.00, CMV $10.00 BO, $12.00 MB.
1962-64 CRYSTAL GLORY SPRAY ESSENCE
Gold top & base. Same fragrances as above. OSP $4.50 - $5.00. CMV $8.00 BO $10.00 MB.
1962 SILVER TOP CRYSTAL GLORY SPRAY ESSENCE
Metal on top & base is silver instead of gold. Rare. Same fragrances as above. OSP $4.50 - $5.00 CMV $30.00
1962-64 CRYSTAL GLORY REFILL
(Right) 1 oz. spray bottle fits inside Crystal Glory bottle. Came in all fragrances above. OSP $2.00, CMV $6.00 MB.

1979-80 COLOGNE SPRAY 1.8 OZ.
1.8 oz. clear glass, gold & silver caps with matching neck bands, boxes & label. Comes with Moonwind, Charisma, Sonnet, Topaze, Here's My Heart, Bird of Paradise, Cotillion, Occur!, & Unforgettable. SSP $3.99 CMV 25c each.

1969-70 COLOGNE MIST
2 oz. gold cap, frosted glass. Came in Charisma, Brocade, & Regence. O.S.P. $4.25 C.M.V. $2.00
1969-71 SPRAY ESSENCE
1¼ oz. gold cap, ribbed glass. Came in Charisma. Brocade, Regence. O.S.P. $4.50 C.M.V. $2.00

1975-76 CARNATION COLOGNE MIST (Left to Right) - 2 oz, clear glass, gold cap. O.S.P. $3.00 C.M.V. 50¢
1975-76 COLOGNE MIST
1 oz. clear glass, gold cap, white neck label. Came in Sonnet, Bird of Paradise, Moonwind, Charisma, Field Flowers or Roses, Roses. O.S.P. $2.00 C.M.V. 50¢
1974-75 COLOGNE MIST
2 oz. clear glass, gold cap. Came in Imperial Garden, Sonnet, Charisma or Moonwind. O.S.P. $4.00 C.M.V. 50¢
1975-76 COLOGNE MIST
2 oz. clear glass, gold cap. Came in Occur! Topaze, Unforgettable, Here's My Heart, Cotillion, To A Wild Rose, Field Flowers, Regence, Brocade, Bird of Paradise. O.S.P. $4.00 C.M.V. $1.00

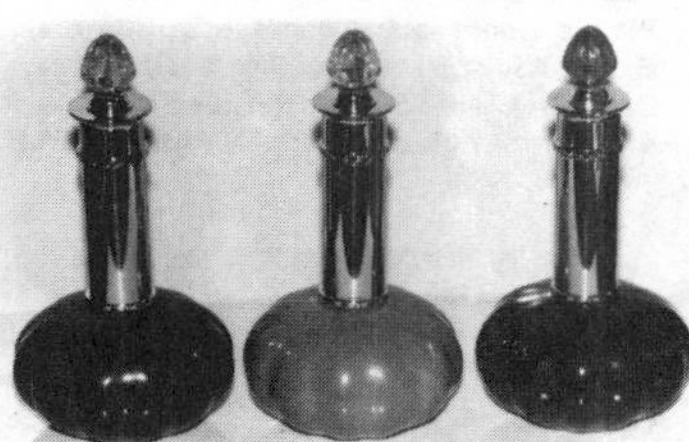

1972 DECORATOR COLOGNE MIST
4 oz. plastic coated bottle in color to match fragrance. Long gold cap with top matching fragrance color. Came in Moonwind (deep blue) Charisma (crimson red) Bird of Paradise (pale blue) Field Flowers (spring green) SSP $5.00 CMV $5.00 MB, $3.00 BO

1970-76 PURSE SPRAY ESSENCE
¼ oz. glass bottle with gold cap in Elusive, Charisma, Brocade, Regence, Unforgettable, Rapture, Occur! Somewhere, Topaze & Cotillion, Bird of Paradise & Hana Gasa. O.S.P. $3.50 C.M.V. $1.00 M.B.
1971-75 COLOGNE MIST
2 oz. silver top. Came in Bird of Paradise, Hana Gasa, Elusive, Charisma, Brocade & Regence. O.S.P. $4.25 C.M.V. $1.00

1968-72 COLOGNE MIST
2 oz. gold cap, gold & white band. Came in Here's My Heart, Topaze, To A Wild Rose, Somewhere, Cotillion, O.S.P. $2.50 C.M.V. $1.00
1963-66 COLOGNE MIST
Embossed bottles with gold plastic caps, came with black & gold paper label & green & gold cloth type label and green and white paper label. Held 2 oz. of Occur!, Somewhere, Topaze, Cotillion, Persian Wood, Here's My Heart & To A Wild Rose. O.S.P. $2.50 C.M.V. $5.00 each MB, $3.00 BO.

SACHETS CREAM - MISC.

1973-75 CREAM SACHET JARS
Clear ribbed glass jar with colored border on lid & colored flower to match fragrance. .66 oz. came in Gardenia, Violet & Carnation. S.S.P. $1.25 C.M.V. 50¢ ea.

CREAM SACHET BOXES
Special short issue boxes came with cream sachets in several fragrances.
Left To Right — 1956, 1964, 1958, 1954
CMV - See bottle in each fragrance line & add $5.00 each for these boxes.

1958 CREAM SACHET CHRISTMAS BOX
Special issue blue and gold box came with choice of cream sachet in To a Wild Rose, Cotillion, Forever Spring, Nearness, Bright Night, Elegant. O.S.P. $1.50 each. See jar in each fragrance line and add $5.00 for this box.

1957 CREAM SACHET CHRISTMAS BOX
Special issue box at Christmas. Pink,and white, came in choice of Cotillion, Nearness, Forever Spring, Bright NIght, To a Wild Rose, Elegante cream sachet. O.S.P. $1.50 See bottle in each fragrance line and add $6.00 for this box.

LEFT 1963 POWDER SACHET CHRISTMAS BOX
Short issue box came in 6 fragrances at Christmas. Add $4.00 to CMV of bottle for this box.
RIGHT 1965 POWDER SACHET CHRISTMAS BOX
High top boot design box was short issue. Came in 8 fragrances. Add $4.00 to CMV of bottle for this box.

1974-76 MAGNOLIA CREAM SACHET
.66 oz. clear embossed glass with white lid & pink & yellow on flower. O.S.P. $1.25 C.M.V. 25¢
1974-77 MAGNOLIA DEMI STICK
.19 oz. white with floral colored center. O.S.P. $1.25 C.M.V. 25¢
1974-76 HYACINTH CREAM SACHET
.66 oz. clear embossed glass with pink flowers on lid. O.S.P. $1.25 C.M.V. 25¢
1974-77 HYACINTH DEMI STICK
.19 oz. white with pink flowers. O.S.P. $1.25 C.M.V. 25¢

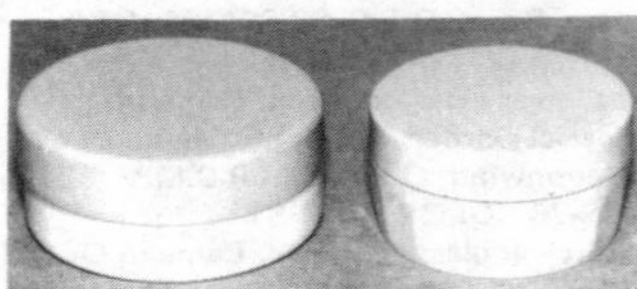

1957 CREAM SACHET - white jar with green, yellow or pink lid. Came in Cotillion, To A Wild Rose, Bright Night, & Nearness. Came in Rainbow Set. C.M.V. $8.00 ea.
1956 CREAM SACHET PETITES
Plastic cream sachet came in Cotillion, Bright Night, Nearness, To A Wild Rose. Came in Cream Sachet Petites Sets only. 4 different colors. C.M.V. $10.00 ea. M.B.

1960 CREAM SACHET DECOR
Ribbed clear plastic with removable bottom, sold for 50¢ at Xmas with purchase of Cream Sachet in Bright Night, Nearness, Cotillion, To A Wild Rose, Persian Wood, & Here's My Heart. C.M.V. $8.00 holder only, $12.00 MB

1969 SCENTIMENTS CREAM SACHET
1/2 oz. clear glass jar, gold lid, 4A design on lid. Came in Scentiments Set only in Unforgettable, Rapture, Occur, Somewhere, Topaze or Cotillion.
C.M.V. $4.00 mint.

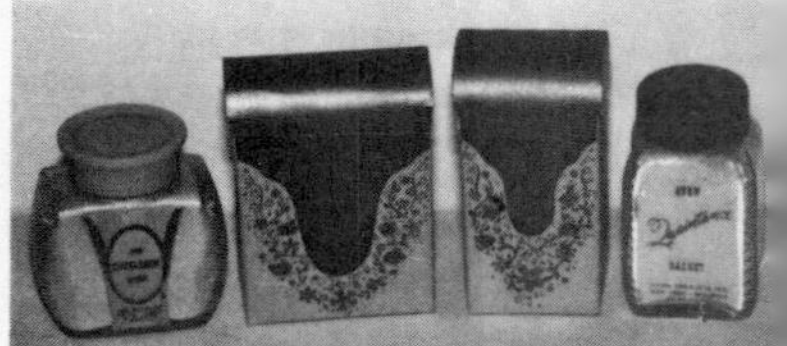

1952 VALENTINE GIFT SACHET
Short issue box in red & white. Came in Flowertime, Golden Promise, Cotillion, & Quaintance. Cotillion came in same design, different shaped box. Add $7.00 CMV to price of each bottle for this box.

1956 POWDER SACHET CHRISTMAS BOX
Special issue Christmas box came with choice of 6 fragrances. Add $5.00 to CMV of bottle for this box.

1958 CREAM SACHET
.3 oz. white glass jar. turquoise flower lid. Came in 1958 Wishing Trio set. Pink and gold box. CMV $5.00 jar only, $10.00 MB

SACHETS POWDER - MISC.

1936-38 POWDER SACHET
1¼ or 2 oz. ribbed glass bottle with turquoise cap & label. Came in Ariel 1936-38 C.M.V. $24.00, Cotillion 1937-38 C.M.V. $20.00, Marionette 1938 only C.M.V. $24.00, Jardin D'Amour 1936-38 or Jardin Sachet C.M.V. $22.00. O.S.P. each $1.04. All prices are mint only. Add $4.00 M.B.

EFT 1930-34 POWDER SACHET
lear glass bottle with brass cap & silver
blue label. Came in Ariel. O.S.P. 78¢
Jardin D'Amour O.S.P. $1.04 C.M.V.
60.00 each mint.
IGHT 1934-36 POWDER SACHET
¼ oz. ribbed glass bottle with dark blue
ap & silver & blue label. Came in Jardin
'Amour O.S.P. $1.04 & Ariel O.S.P. 78¢
.M.V. $28.00 ea. mint. $33.00 M.B.

1965-66 CROWN TOP POWDER SACHET
.9 oz. frosted bottle with gold cap. Came in perfume pillowette set in Rapture, Wishing, Occur! Lavender, Somewhere, Topaze, Cotillion, Here's My Heart, To A Wild Rose. CMV $8.00 BO, $10.00 MB

1969-70 POWDER SACHET
1½ oz. painted red over clear glass, red neck bow with silver lid. Comes in Cotillion, Charisma, Unforgettable, and To A Wild Rose. O.S.P. $4.50 C.M.V. $6.00 in box. $5.00 bottle only.
1970-71 POWDER SACHET
Crystal-like glass bottle holds 1¼ oz. of powder sachet in Elusive, Charisma, Unforgettable, and Topaze. O.S.P. $4.00 CMV $3.00 BO, $4.00 MB

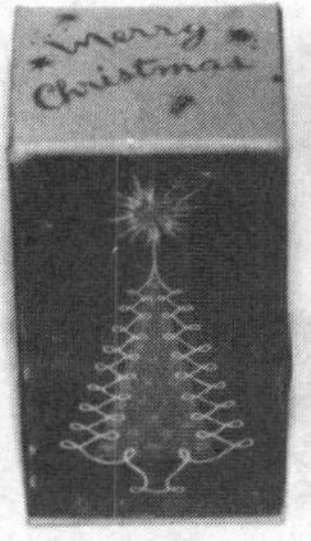

1952 ONLY - POWDER SACHET CHRISTMAS BOX
Special issue red and green box for all powder sachet at Christmas, Came in Cotillion, Golden Promise, Quaintance, and Flowertime. See bottle in each fragrance line and add $5.00 for this box.

1958 POWDER SACHET CHRISTMAS BOX
Special issue pink and white box came with powder sachet in choice of To a Wild Rose, Cotillion, Forever Spring, Nearness, Bright Night, Elegante. O.S.P. $1.50 ea. See jars in each fragrance line for C.M.V. and add $5.00 for this box.

1957 POWDER SACHET X-MAS BOX
Pyramid shaped box in pink, green, blue, and white. Came in To a Wild Rose, Forever Spring, Cotillion, Nearness, Bright Night and Elegante powder sachet. Short issue RARE, O.S.P. $1.50 ea. See bottle in each fragrance line and add $6.00 for this box mint.

1939-48 POWDER SACHET
1¼ oz. glass bottle with turquoise cap & label. Came in Jardin D'Amour (1939-40) C.M.V. $20.00. Ariel (1939-42) C.M.V. $20.00, Cotillion (1939-46) C.M.V. $12.00 Garden of Love, Turquoise or black cap (1940-46) C.M.V. $18.00. Attention (1942-48) C.M.V. $15.00 Marionette, (1939-46) C.M.V. $17.00 - O.S.P. $1.04 each. Add $3.00 M.B.

1944-45 POWDER SACHET
1¼ oz. pink paper sachet boxes. Came in Attention, Garden of Love, Cotillion, Marionette, pink plastic flower on lid. O.S.P. $1.15 ea. C.M.V. $18.00 ea. $20.00 M.B.

1973-75 TURN-OF-CENTURY POWDER SACHET SHAKER
1.25 oz. clear glass with gold cap. Came in Roses Roses, Charisma, Unforgettable. OSP $4.50 CMV $3.50 MB, $2.00 BO
1972-73 POWDER SACHET SHAKER
(Right) 3½" high, 1.25 oz. white glass jar with gold cap. Came in Moonwind, OSP $5.00; Bird of Paradise, Unforgettable, Field Flowers, SSP $3.00. CMV $3.00 BO, $5.00 MB.

PERFUMED TALCS - MISC.

1959-60 FLORAL PERFUMED TALC
Lavender & white can. Matching box.
OSP 69c, CMV $5.00 can only, $7.00 MB

1959 PERFUMED TALC CHRISTMAS BOX
Short issue box in choice of 6 fragrances of talcs. Add $4.00 CMV for this box to price of talc.

PERFUMED TALC SPECIAL ISSU CHRISTMAS BOXES
Left To Right
1966 Christmas, 1967 Christmas, 1969 Christmas, 1970 Christmas.
Each came in choice of talc. Add $2.00 each box to CMV of the talc it holds.

1958 PERFUMED TALC CHRISTMAS BOX
Special issue X-mas box for perfumed talc in choice of To A Wild Rose, Cotillion, Nearness & Forever Spring. O.S.P. 69¢ each. Check fragrance line for C.M.V. on talc and add $5.00 for this box.

TOILET WATERS - MISC.

Left to Right - 1940 Only TOILET WATER
2 oz. plastic caps, blue & gold label with tulip. Came in Cotillion, Vernafleur, Lily of the Valley, White Rose, Lilac, Trailing Arbutus, Marionette, Lilac Vegetal. O.S.P. 78¢ C.M.V. $35.00 B.O. mint. $40.00 M.B.

1940-46 TOILET WATER
2 oz. gold ribbed cap & gold label. Also came with plastic caps. Came in Cotillion, Jasmine, Marionette, Lilac, Lily of the Valley, Trailing Arbutus, Apple Blossom, Sonnet & Attention. O.S.P. $1.04 C.M.V. $30.00 B.O. mint. $35.00 M.B.

1934-40 TOILET WATER
2 oz. gold cap with A on top of cap. Blue & gold tulip label. CPC on back of label. Came in same as 1st toilet water on left. O.S.P. 78¢ C.M.V. $35.00 B.O. mint $40.00 M.B.

1933-34 TOILET WATER
2 oz. ribbed bottle came in Trailing Arbutus, Vernafleur, Lily of the Valley, White Rose, Lilac Vegetal. Black or blue cap. OSP 75c, CMV $50.00 bottle only mint, $60.00 MB.

PERFUMES - MISC.

ALL ITEMS' PRICES
EMPTY--MINT

1931-34 GIFT ATOMIZER PERFUME
1 oz. red glass bottle with screw on metal top & white squeeze bulb. came in atomizer set No. 6 only. Does not say Avon or C.P.C. Also comes in green glass. CMV $85.00

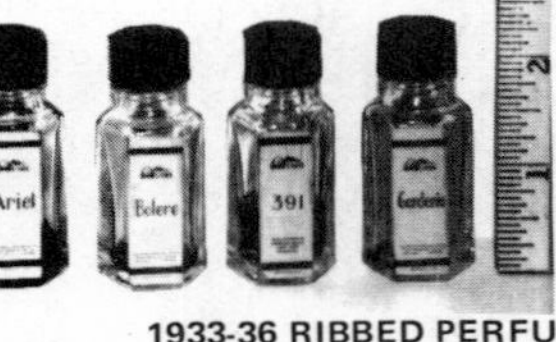

1933-36 RIBBED PERFUME (Left)
½ oz. ribbed glass bottle with black octogonal cap & gold label. Came in Gold Box set in Bolero, 391, Gardenia, Ariel, Vernafleur, C.M.V. $45.00 mint.

1933-36 PERFUMES (Right)
Small six sided bottle with silver label & black caps. Came in Ariel, Bolero, Gardenia, Trailing Arbutus, 391, Vernafleur, came in Little Folks set & Handkerchief Set. CMV $45.00 mint.

1931-33 391 PERFUME (Left)
Silver & blue box holds 1 oz. glass stopper. Blue ribbon on neck. OSP $2.60 CMV bottle only $125.00, in box $150.00.
1931-33 391 PERFUME FLACONETTE
(Center) Small embossed bottle with glass stopper with long dabber. Brass cap with 391 on it. OSP $1.30 CMV $85.00 BO $95.00 MB.
1933-36 391 PERFUME (Right)
½ oz. ribbed glass bottle with black octagonal cap. Came in gold box set. CMV $45.00 mint.

1946-50 1/8 OZ. PERFUME OR 1 DRAM
Gold box, gold label. Some have metal gold caps. Came in Crimson Carnation, Lily of the Valley, Gardenia, Cotillion, Golden Promise, Garden of Love, Ballad, Quaintance, Flowertime. OSP $1.00, CMV $20.00 Crimson Carnation $30.00. Add $5.00 each MB. Also came in gold box set of 1947-49.

1934-39 7 DRAM TULIP PERFUME
Glass stoppered bottle, gold label with tulip. Came in Jardin D'Amour, Bolero, Cotillion, Ariel, Narcissus, Rose, Lily of the Valley, Trailing Arbutus, Gardenia, Sweet Pea, Marionette, Topaze, Courtship, Lucy Hays. O.S.P. $2.00 C.M.V. $125.00 M.B. $100.00 B.O.

1951-53 PERFUMES 5/8 DRAM
Bottle with pink, yellow, green or blue caps came in Cotillion, Quaintance, Golden Promise, Luscious, Lily of the Valley. Came in 1952-53 House Of Charm, 1951 Always Sweet Set & Sweet As Honey Beehive Set. CMV $12.00 each, mint.

1950 PERFUMES
5/8 dram each. Quaintance, Cotillion, Golden Promise, Luscious, green, blue pink & yellow caps. Came in Avon Blossoms Set. CMV $12.00 each mint.

1937-46 PERFUME
1/8 oz. bottle on right has flower on label with 3 branches on each side. came in sets only in Gardenia, Cotillion, C.M.V. $14.00. Narcissus, Trailing Arbutus, Sweet Pea, C.M.V. $17.00 each. White, blue, red, green or yellow plastic caps. 2 dram size or ¼ oz. on left came in 1939-40 Gold Box Sets & Little Folks Sets in same fragrances and caps. CMV $25.00 each.

(Left) 1940-42 MISC. 1/8 OZ. PERFUME
1 dram or 1/8 oz. gold cap & label. Came in Cotillion, Ballad, Gardenia, Garden of Love, Apple Blossom, Marionette, Trailing Arbutus, Lily of the Valley, Sweet Pea. CMV $25.00 BO, mint, $35.00 MB.
(Right) 1940-44 MISC. 1/8 OZ. PERFUME
Gold metal or plastic caps & gold label. Came in Garden of Love, Gardenia, Marionette, Sweet Pea, Lily of the Valley, Trailing Arbutus, Ballad, Courtship, Apple Blossom, Cotillion. OSP 75c, CMV $25.00 BO mint, $30.00 MB.

LEFT 1946-50 PERFUME
1/8 oz. clear glass, gold cap, painted label. Available in Crimson Carnation, Lily of the Valley, Gardenia, Cotillion, Golden Promise, Garden of Love, Ballad, Quaintance, Flowertime. O.S.P. $1.00 C.M.V. $20.00 B.O. $25.00 M.B.
RIGHT 1954 Only 5/8 DRAM PERFUME
Came in 1954 House of Charms Set only. Blue caps, pink, blue & white label. Came in Cotillion, Quaintance, To A Wild Rose, Golden Promise, Lily of the Valley - rare. C.M.V. $22.00 each.

PERFUMES FOR SIZE COMPARISON ONLY
Left to Right — 2 dram or ¼ oz., 1/8 oz. or 1 dram, 5/8 dram, 5/8 dram.

1944 Only - FLORAL PERFUMES
3 dram gold cap & label. Came in yellow feather design box in Trailing Arbutus, Gardenia, Sweet Pea, Lily of the Valley, Bottle also came in Cotillion, in sets only. not in this box. O.S.P. $2.50 C.M.V. in box $85.00. Bottle only $60.00 mint.

1945 Only - FLORAL PERFUMES
3 dram gold cap & labels, came in yellow feather design box in Trailing Arbutus, Cotillion, Gardenia, Sweet Pea, Lily of the Valley, Marionette. O.S.P. $1.65 C.M.V. $60.00 bottle only, mint with tag. $85.00 M.B.

1966-67 PERFUME FLACON
1 dram, gold ribbed cap, ribbed glass. Came in Here's My Heart, Wishing, To A Wild Rose, Somewhere, Topaze, Cotillion, Unforgettable, Regence, Rapture, Occur!. OSP $2.50, CMV $1.00 BO, $3.00 MB.

1946 Only - 1/8 OZ. PERFUME
1/8 oz. plastic cap. Came in Gardenia, Cotillion, Garden of Love, Lily of the Valley, Trailing Arbutus, Sweet Pea. OSP 75c, CMV $25.00 BO, $30.00 MB each mint.
(Right) 1941-46 1/8 OZ. PERFUME
1/8 oz. size, white paper label, gold metal caps & plastic caps. Came in Gardenia, Sweet Pea, Courtship, Apple Blossom, Cotillion, Trailing Arbutus, Lily of the Valley, Garden of Love, Marionette. OSP 75c, CMV $25.00 BO, $30.00 MB.

(Left) 1946-53 1/8 OZ. PERFUME
Flower on label, plastic cap. Came in Trailing Arbutus, Cotillion, Crimson Carnation, Quaintance, Lily of the Valley, Gardenia, Garden of Love, Sweet Pea. Came in Fair Lady, Your Charms, & Hair Ribbons Sets. CMV each $15.00, CMV Crimson Carnation & Sweet Pea $25.00 mint. Same label came on 5/8 dram size "smaller bottle" but has no size on label. Same CMV.
(Right) 1941-45 1/8 OZ. PERFUMES
1/8 oz. , 2 different flat gold caps and also plastic caps. White paper label. Came in Courtship, Sweet Pea, Lily of the Valley, Trailing Arbutus, Marionette, American Ideal, Apple Blossom, Cotillion, Ballad, Gardenia, Garden of Love. OSP $1.00 CMV bottle only $30.00 mint. $40.00 MB.

1964-65 ONE DRAM PERFUME GOLD BOX
4A embossed gold box. Ribbed bottle, gold cap. Came in Somewhere, Topaze, Cotillion, Here's My Heart, Persian Wood, To A Wild Rose, Wishing, Occur!, Rapture, and Unforgettable. Same bottle sold in regular issue box 1962-66. O.S.P. $2.25 to $2.50 CMV $8.00 MB in gold box. 1965 Christmas special issue box on right. CMV $8.00 MB.

1934-39 2 DRAM TULIP PERFUME
¼ oz. or 2 drams, gold cap & label with tulip. CPC on back of label & Avon on bottom of bottle. Came with 2 different labels as shown, came in Jardin D'Amour, Bolero, Cotillion, Ariel, Narcissus, Rose, Lily of the Valley, Trailing Arbutus, Gardenia, Sweet Pea, Marionette, Courtship, Lucy Hays, Topaze, O.S.P. 78¢ C.M.V. $65.00 M.B. $55.00 B.O. mint.

1934-39 ¼ oz. TULIP PERFUME
Glass stopper, gold label with tulip. Came in Lucy Hays, Topaze, Jardin D'Amour, Bolero, Cotillion, Ariel, Narcissus, Rose, Lily of the Valley, Trailing Arbutus, Gardenia, Sweet Pea, Marionette, Courtship. O.S.P. $1.04 CMV $75.00 BO, $90.00 MB.

1934-39 7 DRAM TULIP PERFUME
Glass stopper, gold label with tulip. Came i Lucy Hays, Topaze, Jardin D'Amour, Boler Cotillion, Ariel, Narcissus, Rose, Lily of the Valley, Trailing Arbutus, Gardenia, Sweet Pea, Marionette, Courtship, O.S.P. $2.60 C.M.V. $125.00 in box. Bottle only $100.0 mint.

1946-47 MISC. FLORAL PERFUMES
Blue & white box holds 3 dram bottle with plastic cap. Came in Crimson Carnation, Gardenia, Lily of the Valley, O.S.P. $3.75 C.M.V. $75.00 in box. Bottle only $50.00 Crimson Carnation. CMV $100.00 MB, $60.00 BO.

1940-42 FLORAL PERFUME
3/8 oz. gold cap & label in gold speckled box. Came in Sweet Pea, Gardenia, Trailing Arbutus, Lily of the Valley, O.S.P. $1.50 CMV $50.00 BO mint, $80.00 MB. 00 M.B.

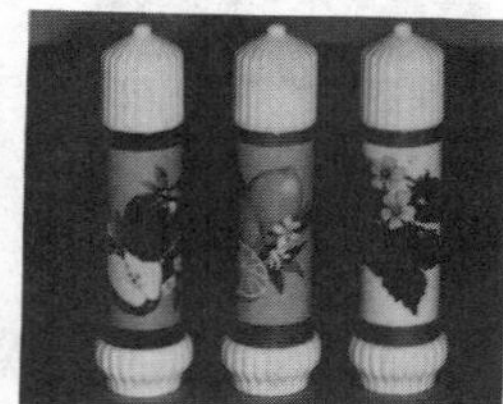

1975 FRUIT STIX PERFUMED
DEMI STICK - .19 oz. Available in apple, (pink & red) lemon (yellow & gold) or strawberry (pink & red) O.S.P. $1.00 C.M.V. $1.00 M.B.

940-44 BOUQUET PERFUMES
dram, glass stopper, box is gold base & range lid. Came in Garden of Love, Apple Blossom, Marionette, Courtship, Cotillion, Gold neck tag. O.S.P. $2.50 ea. C.M.V. $100.00 B.O. mint. $125.00 M.B.

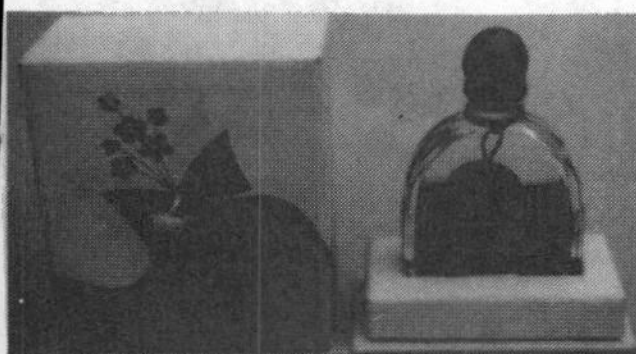

1945-47 BOUQUET PERFUMES
Blue, pink & white box holds 3 dram glass stoppered bottle with gold neck tag. Came in Courtship, Cotillion, Garden of Love, O.S.P. $3.00 C.M.V. $125.00 M.B. $100.00 B.O.

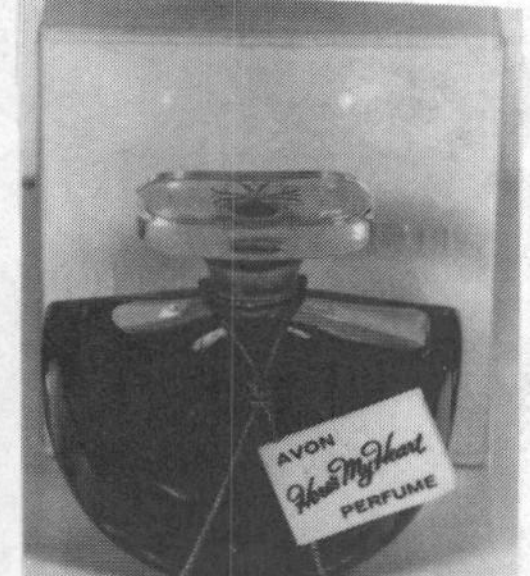

1959-63 ROCKER PERFUME
White box holds 1 oz. bottle with flat glass stopper with 4A on top. Gold cord criscrossed bottle with white tag label. Came in Here's My Heart, Persian Wood, O.S.P. $17.50; To A Wild Rose, Bright Night, Nearness, O.S.P. $15.00; Cotillion, O.S.P. $20.00; C.M.V. in box $65.00. Bottle only with tag $50.00. C.M.V. Nearness & Bright Night $80.00 in box. $65.00 bottle with tag.

1959-62 TOP STYLE PERFUME
Shown with general issue box. 1 dram size, gold cap. Came in Topaze, Persian Wood, Here's My Heart, To A Wild Rose, Cotillion, Bright Night, & Nearness. OSP $2.50 CMV $5.00 BO, $7.00 MB.

1963-71 1 OZ. HEART PERFUME
Gold box, 4A insignia on glass stopper. Gold neck tag. Came in Unforgettable & Occur!, OSP $25.00; Somewhere, Topaze, Cotillion, OSP $20.00; Here's My Heart, Persian Wood, Rapture, To A Wild Rose, OSP $17.50. CMV $35.00 BO, $60.00 MB.

1962-66 ONE DRAM PERFUME
Ribbed bottles with gold caps held Somewhere, Topaze, Cotillion, Here's My Heart, Persian Wood, To A Wild Rose, Wishing, Unforgettable, Rapture, Occur! OSP $2.50 CMV $5.00 MB, $4.00 BO.

1969-72 ½ OZ. PERFUME
Pink box holds jewel like clear glass bottle 4" high. Comes in Elusive, Charisma, Brocade, Regence, O.S.P. $15.00. Unforgettable, Rapture, Occur!, Somewhere, Topaze, Cotillion, OSP $12.50 CMV $10.00 MB, $5.00 bottle only.

1966-69 PERFUME
½ oz., gold cap, meatl leaves around base. White & gold box. Came in Unforgettable, Rapture, Occur! O.S.P. $12.50. Somewhere, Topaze, Cotillion, O.S.P. $11.00. Here' My Heart, To A Wild Rose, Wishing, O.S.P. $10.00 C.M.V. $14.00 M.B. Bottle only $7.00 Mint.

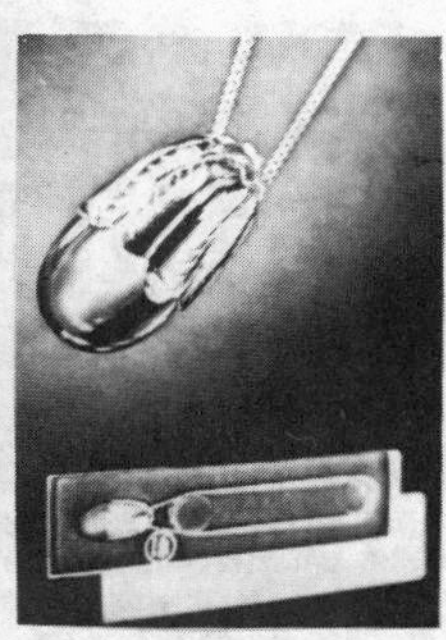

1971-72 GOLDEN MOMENTS PENDANT PERFUME - Antiqued brass pendant on 32" gold chain. Holds 1/8 oz. perfume in Moonwind, O.S.P. $15.00 Bird of Paradise, Elusive, Charisma O.S.P. $14.00 C.M.V. Pendant on chain only $10.00 mint, $16.00 MB.

1970 PERFUME PENDANT
Gold pendant with ruby teardrop, holds 1 dram liquid perfume. Comes in Charisma, Elusive, Brocade, & Regence. O.S.P. $14.00 C.M.V. $15.00 in box. $10.00 pendant only mint.

1959-60 TOP STYLE CHRISTMAS PERFUME
Sold only at Christmas time in box shown. Came in all regular fragrances of Top Style perfume. OSP $2.50 CMV $15.00 MB in this box only.

1944 Only - BOUQUET PERFUMES
Blue & pink box holds 3 dram perfume, glass stopper. Came in Marionette, Cotillion, Garden of Love, Gold neck tags. O.S.P. $3.00 C.M.V. in box $140.00. Bottle only $100.00.

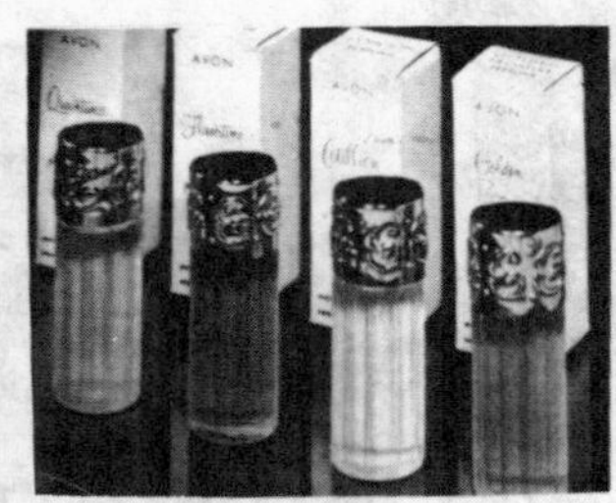

1950-55 PERFUMES "1 DRAM"
Ribbed bottles with gold caps came in Cotillion, Quaintance, Ballad, Golden Promise, Gardenia, Lily of the Valley, Forever Spring, & To A Wild Rose. OSP $1.50 CMV $12.00 MB, $8.00 BO.

1955-59 PERFUMES "1 DRAM"
Clear smooth glass, gold scroll cap with felt like wrapper, Nearness, blue; Bright Night, black; Elegante, violet; To A Wild Rose, pink; Forever Spring, green; Cotillion, gold; simulated grain leather, Luscious 1st issue 1950. tan; O.S.P. $2.25 C.M.V. $14.00 each in wrapper mint, $8.00 BO.

1958 ONE DRAM GIFT PERFUME
1 oz. smooth clear glass bottle, cap either smooth or embossed. Box blue, white & gold. Choice of Elegante, Nearness, Bright Night, Forever Spring, To A Wild Rose or Cotillion. O.S.P. $2.00 C.M.V. $20.00 M.B. as shown, $8.00 B.O. Nearness & Bright Night $10.00 B.O.

1941 VALENTINE'S DAY PERFUME
1/8 oz. clear glass bottle with gold cap with Ballad Perfume. Box red & white. Came in several fragrances. C.M.V. $75.00 M.B.

1961 GOLDEN GIFT PERFUME
Blue, gold & green box holds 1 dram top style perfume. Came in Cotillion, To A Wild Rose, Nearness, Bright Night, Somewhere, Here's My Heart, Persian Wood, Topaze. OSP $2.25 CMV $12.00 MB.

1965-69 PERFUME ROLLETTES
.33 oz. glass bottles available in Somewhere, Topaze, Cotillion, Here's My Heart, To A Wild Rose, Wishing, Regence, Occur!, Rapture, Unforgettable, Brocade & Persian Wood. Issued in carnival glass or clear ribbed glass. OSP $1.75 to $3.00. CMV clear $2.00 MB, $1.00 BO; CMV carnival $7.00 BO, $9.00 MB. Box pictured is 1966 Christmas box. Add $1.00 extra for this box.

Left - 1951-52 WITH LOVE PERFUMES
Pink heart box opens to 1 dram ribbed bottle & cap in Lily of the Valley, To A Wild Rose, Luscious, Quaintance, Golden Promise, Cotillion, Ballad, Flowertime, Gardenia, O.S.P. $1.75 C.M.V. $25.00 M.B. as shown.
Right - 1951 CHRISTMAS BELL PERFUME
Gold bell box holds 1 dram, ribbed bottle & cap in Forever Spring, To A Wild Rose, Luscious, Cotillion, Flowertime, Quaintance, Golden Promise, Ballad, Gardenia & Lily of the Valley. O.S.P. $1.60 C.M.V. $25.00 M.B. as shown.

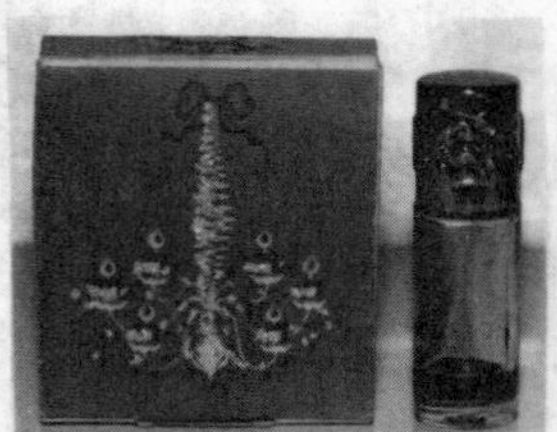

1955 XMAS PERFUME
1 dram, gold cap in red, white, blue & gold Xmas box. Came in To A Wild Rose, Cotillion, Forever Spring, Golden Promise, Luscious, & Quaintance. O.S.P. $1.75 C.M.V. $25.00 M.B.

1953 VALENTINE PERFUMES
1 dram ribbed perfume came in To A Wild Rose, Forever Spring, O.S.P. $1.75 Cotillion, Golden Promise, Quaintance O.S.P. $1.50 C.M.V. $25.00 M.B. as shown.

1953-54 PERFUME
Green & pink fold out box holds 1 dram ribbed glass bottle with gold scroll cap. Came in To A Wild Rose, Cotillion, Forever Spring, Quaintance, Golden Promise, Luscious. OSP $1.75 CMV $25.00 MB as shown.

1972-75 PERFUME PENDANT
Gold with 2 simulated half pearls, 32" chain. Came in Sonnet or Moonwind perfume. OSP $10.00 CMV $10.00 MB. Pendant only $5.00

FT 1973-74 SCENTIMENT PERFUME
LLETTE
oz. white base with blue bird & pink
wers, gold trim & cap. Holds Moonwind,
tchwork, Sonnet. SSP $2.50 CMV $3.00
), $4.00 MB
GHT 1974 SCENTIMENT PURSE
RAY ESSENCE
5 oz. blue plastic coated bottom, white
pink bird design on paper label with
ld cap. Came in Field Flowers, Bird
Paradise or Charisma. SSP $3.00 CMV
3.00 BO, $4.00 MB.

1963-65 PERFUME CREME ROLLETTE
4A embossed bottles with gold caps. Came in Here's My Heart, Persian Wood, To A Wild Rose, O.S.P. $2.00 Cotillion, Somewhere, Topaze, & Wishing $1.75. Occur! & Rapture, OSP $2.50 CMV $5.00 MB, Rollette only $3.00 mint.

PERFUME OILS

1966 PERFUME OIL PETITES (PIN CUSHION) 5/8 dram, clear bottle, gold cap & label. Came in Pin Cushion Set only. Came in Somewhere, Wishing, Occur! Rapture, Topaze, To A Wild Rose, Here's My Heart, Unforgettable, Cotillion, C.M.V. $10.00 each mint.

1971 PERFUME HALF OUNCE
1/2 oz. bottle with clear plastic top in a pink & gold box. Came in Somewhere Topaze, Cotillion, Unforgettable, Rapture, Occur! O.S.P. $12.50. Regence, Brocade, Charisma, Elusive O.S.P. $15.00
CMV $15.00 MB as shown, $5.00 BO.

1969-73 PERFUME OIL (Left)
½ oz. gold caps. Came in Elusive, Hana Gasa, Charisma, Brocade, Moonwind, Regence and Bird of Paradise. O.S.P. $6.00 Unforgettable & Occur, O.S.P. $5.00 C.M.V. $2.00, $3.00 M.B.

1965 BULLET PERFUME OIL (Right)
5/8 dram, gold top. Came in Wishing, Somewhere, Occur! Rapture, To A Wild Rose, Topaze, Unforgettable, Here's My Heart, Cotillion, came in Fragrance Ornaments Set only. CMV $10.00 BO

Left - 1964-65 JEWEL PERFUME OIL
5/8 dram, gold cap. Perfume Oil came in Jewel Collection only. Came in Cotillion, Topaze, Persian Wood, Here's My Heart, To A Wild Rose. C.M.V. $6.00 ea. mint.
Right - FOREIGN JEWEL EAU DE COLOGNE - ½ oz. gold cap. C.M.V. $20.00

1951-53 PERFUME "1 DRAM"
Verticle ribbed bottle and ribbed gold cap with scroll on cap. Came in Cotillion, Golden Promise, Quaintance, To A Wild Rose, Forever Spring. O.S.P. $1.75.
C.M.V. $14.00 M.B., $12.00 B.O. mint.

COMPACTS & LIPSTICK - MISC.

ALL ITEMS' PRICES EMPTY - MINT

See Page 5 for Grading Examples on Mint Condition

1933-36 MASCARA COMPACT
Blue & silver metal compact. O.S.P. $1.04 C.M.V. $20.00 mint, $25.00 M.B.

1931-33 TRIPLE COMPACT
Blue & silver metal compact. Avon on lid. O.S.P. $1.30 C.M.V. $25.00 - $30.00 M.B.

1934-36 DOUBLE COMPACT
Blue & silver compact & puffs. O.S.P. $1.75 C.M.V. $22.00 mint, $27.00 M.B.

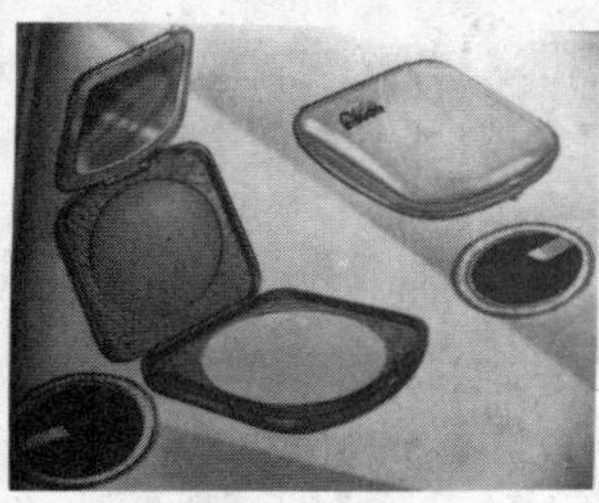

1930-32 COMPACT
Silver metal compact in single size. O.S.P. $1.35 Double size O.S.P. $1.85 C.M.V. $20.00 ea. $25.00 M.B.

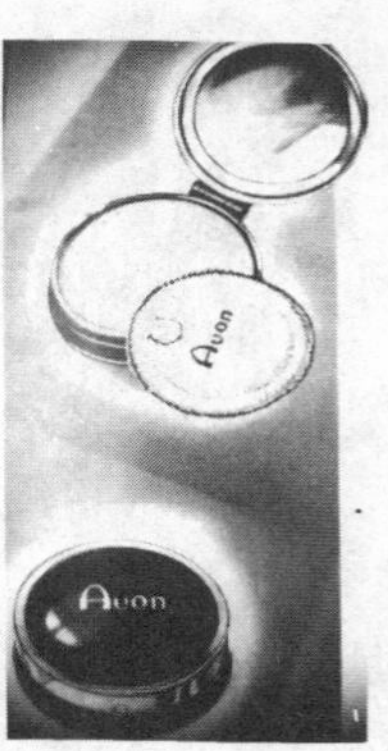

1930-36 SINGLE ROUGE COMPACT
Blue & silver metal compact, O.S.P. 52¢ C.M.V. $10.00 - $15.00 M.B.
1930-33 EYE LASH CREAM
Blue compact with mirror, same as above rouge compacts. OSP $1.00, CMV $12.00 - $17.00 MB

1936-42 POWDER ROUGE REFILL
Turquoise & white box. Refill fits double compact. O.S.P. 52¢ C.M.V. $6.00 M.B.
1936-42 CREAM ROUGE COMPACT
Turquoise & gold metal case. O.S.P. 78¢ C.M.V. $7.00 - $9.00 M.B.
1936-42 SINGLE ROUGE COMPACT
Turquoise & gold metal case. O.S.P. 52¢ C.M.V. $7.00 - $9.00 M.B.

1930-36 CREAM ROUGE COMPACT
Blue metal compact as above. O.S.P. 75¢ C.M.V. $10.00 - $15.00 M.B.

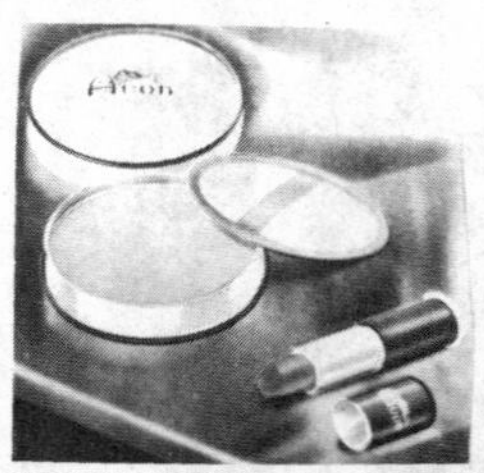

1930-36 DRESSING TABLE ROUGE
Silver & blue paper box. O.S.P. 47¢ C.M.V. $12.00 mint, $16.00 M.B.
1930-36 LIPSTICK
Blue & silver metal tube. O.S.P. 52¢ C.M.V. $8.00 - $12.00 M.B.

1937-39 NAIL WHITE
1937-39 NAIL CUTICLE CREAM
Both turquoise & white small metal cans. Came in Manicure Set only. C.M.V. $7.00 ea. mint.
1932-33 COMPACT
Octaginal shaped blue & gold. Avon lid shown closed & open. Came in 1932-33 Vanity Set only. C.M.V. $30.00 mint.

1931-33 FAN COMPACT
Silver & blue metal compact. O.S.P. $2.00 C.M.V. $25.00 mint, $30.00 M.B.

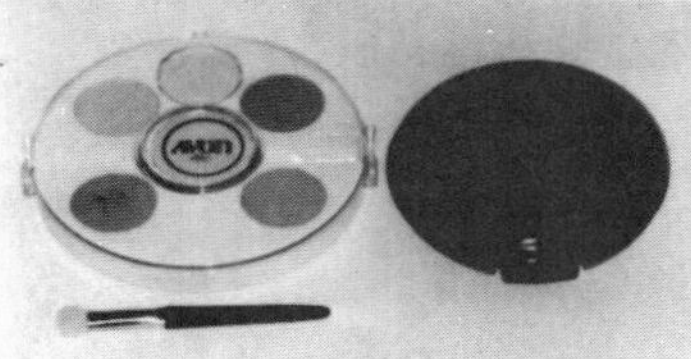

1973-74 DIAL A SHADOW
White and clear plastic holder holds 5 powder eye shadows and applicator. O.S.P. $6.00 C.M.V. $1.00 M.B.
1976-78 ABOUT TOWN COMPACT
Brown plastic with weave design on lid. O.S.P. $3.50 C.M.V. 50¢

1936-42 FACE POWDER SAMPLE
Cream colored metal can. Came in Verna Fleur Ariel in 5 shades. C.M.V. $5.00 C.P.C. label $8.00 Add $2.00 M.B.
1936-42 DRESSING TABLE ROUGE
Turquoise and gold cardboard with turquoise and white box. Came in 5 shades. O.S.P. 47¢ C.M.V. $5.00 - $8.00 M.B. Add $2.00 for C.P.C. label.

1936-41 MASCARA COMPACT
Turquoise and gold. O.S.P. $1.04 C.M.V. $12.00 - $15.00 M.B.
1936-41 LIPSTICK
Turquoise and gold. O.S.P. 52¢ C.M.V. $8.00 mint - $10.00 M.B.

1944-46 LIPSTICK - PLASTIC
Blue feather design plastic lipstick. OSP 52c CMV $6.00 MB, lipstick only $2.00

1949-52 MASCARA
Gold metal case. O.S.P. $1.00 C.M.V. $8.00 in box. $5.00 case only.

1942-48 MASCARA COMPACT
Gold metal, bamboo design. Sold 1942-43 then 1946-48 O.S.P. $1.19 C.M.V. $12.00 $15.00 in box.
1942-48 BAMBOO LIPSTICK
Gold metal bamboo design. O.S.P. 79¢ C.M.V. $6.00 - $8.00 M.B.
1942-48 BAMBOO SINGLE ROUGE COMPACT
Gold metal bamboo design. O.S.P. 79¢ C.M.V. $7.00 - $9.00 M.B.
1942-48 BAMBOO CREAM ROUGE COMPACT
Gold metal bamboo design. O.S.P. 69¢ C.M.V. $7.00 - $9.00 M.B.

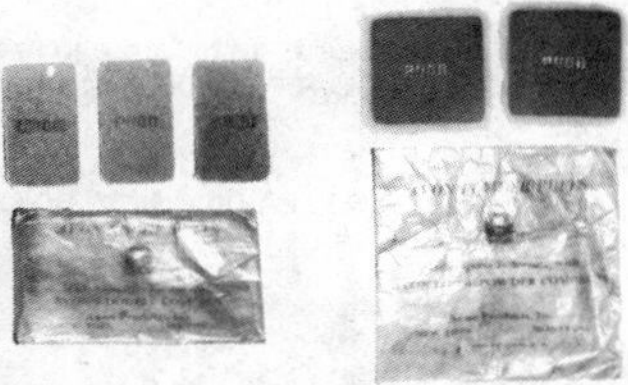

LEFT 1940'S ROUGE PUFFS REFILLS
Avon package holds 3 small turquoise rouge double compact puffs. CMV $3.00 package mint.
RIGHT 1940'S POWDER COMPACT PUFFS REFILLS
Avon package holds 2 turquoise puff refills. CMV $3.00 package mint.

1943-44 FACE POWDER COMPACT
Feather design cardboard compact with mirror inside. 3½" across. C.M.V. $20.00 $25.00 M.B.

1974-75 AVON COMPACT
Black plastic. C.M.V. 50¢
1975-76 BLUSH COMPACT
Brown plastic, gold trim. O.S.P. $3.00 C.M.V. 50¢
1976-78 MAKING EYES EYE SHADOW
Turquoise plastic case. O.S.P. $1.00 C.M.V. 25¢
1972-74 TANTALEYES COLLECTION COMPACT
Brown case with 2 eye shadows, plus mascara has brush and sponge tip applicator. O.S.P. $3.00 C.M.V. $1.00 M.B.

1934-36 COMPACT REFILLS
Avon on small and large size, blue and silver puff with refill cake. Came in gray box. C.M.V. $4.00 each.

1943-49 MASCARA
Blue and white feather design paper box. O.S.P. 69¢ C.M.V. $14.00 mint - $17.00 M.B.
1942-49 FACE POWDER SAMPLE
Blue & white feather design, metal case. Paper box. 1943-46 C.M.V. $4.00 mint.

1943-45 HEAVENLIGHT COMPACT
Blue plastic or metal with white feather, came in rouge or face powder. O.S.P. 59¢ C.M.V. $8.00 - $10.00 M.B.
1945-49 EYE SHADOW
Blue plastic compact with white feather. Same as 1943 Rouge Feather compact above. O.S.P. 79¢ C.M.V. $7.00 - $9.00 M.B.

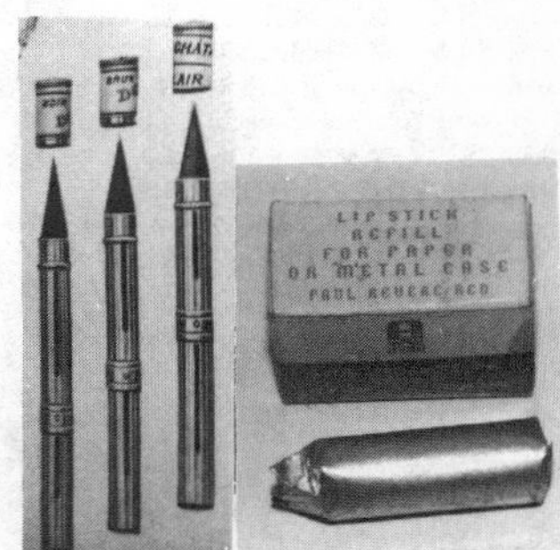

1916-20 CPC EYEBROW PENCILS
Metal tubes. O.S.P. 30¢ C.M.V. $15.00 ea. $25.00 M.B.
1944 LIPSTICK REFILL
Foil wrapped lipstick in plastic case, for metal or paper case. Came in green and white box. 2 different boxes. Some are white top, green bottom as shown or reversed. CMV $10.00 each MB.

1931-36 NAIL WHITE
1931-36 NAIL CREAM
Both small silver & blue or gold & blue cans. Came in manicure sets only. CMV $8.00 each mint.

1936-42 COMPACTS
Single compact. O.S.P. $1.25. Double compact O.S.P. $1.75 both Turquoise and gold.metal. C.M.V. $14.00 ea. - $17.00 ea. M.B.

1942-49 BAMBOO COMPACT
Gold metal, bamboo design. O.S.P. $2.35 for double size, $1.75 for single size in same design. Sold 1942-43 then 1946-49 C.M.V. $15.00 ea. mint - $18.00 ea. M.B.

1949-57 ROUGE COMPACT
Small gold embossed cream compact. O.S.P. 79¢ Larger cake rouge compact in same design. O.S.P. 89¢
C.M.V. ea. $9.00 in box $7.00 compact only.
1949-56 EYE SHADOW
Same gold case design as 1949 rouge compacts above. O.S.P. 79¢ C.MV. $7.00 $9.00 M.B.

1952-58 MASCARA COMPACT
Turquoise plastic O.S.P. $1.00 C.M.V. $5.00 Also came in white plastic C.M.V. $4.00
1954-58 CREAM MASCARA
Turquoise plastic container holds mascara tube and brush. O.S.P. 69¢ C.M.V. $5.00 Later issue came in pink tube & holder. C.M.V. $4.00

1968-74 EYEBROW BRUSH-A-LINE
Tortoise colored plastic with gold trim. S.S.P. $1.00 C.M.V. 25¢
1974 ABOUT TOWN COMPACT
Tortise colored plastic with gold design. S.S.P. $3.00 C.M.V. $1.00

1968-70 GLACE FASHION COMPACT
.12 oz. brown compact, gold top. O.S.P. $2.00 C.M.V. $1.00 $2.00 M.B.
1973-75 AVONSHIRE BLUE PERFUME GLACE COMPACT
.12 oz. blue and white plastic available in Moonwind, Charisma or Elusive. O.S.P. $2.50 C.M.V. $2.00 M.B.

1970's EYE BROW BRUSH-A-LINE
Miscellaneous cases. C.M.V. 50¢ each.

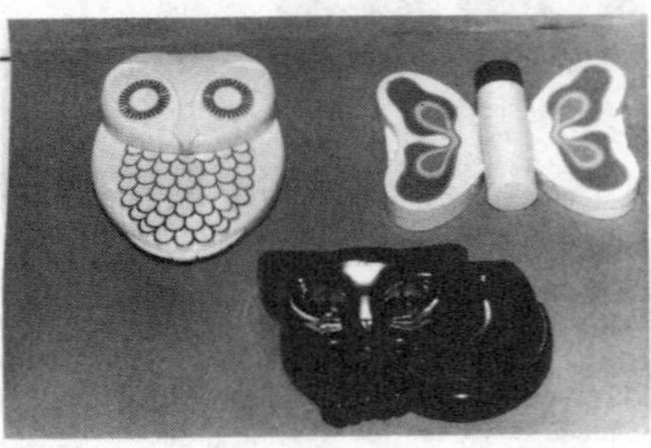

1972 OWL MAKE UP
White plastic gold trim. SSP $6.00 CMV $3.00 - $4.00 MB.
1970-71 BUTTERFLY COLLECTION
White plastic, turquoise, pink & gold, tube of 1 lipstick in center. SSP $6.00 CMV $4.00 MB, $3.00 CO
1973 HONEY CAT MAKE UP COLLECTION
Brown plastic with sponge tipped application. SSP $7.00 CMV $3.00 MB, $2.00 cat only.

1970-71 COLOR EYES QUARTETTE (LEFT)
Black and gold compact. O.S.P. $5.50 C.M.V. $2.00
1969-71 SPARKLING CREAM SHADOW COLLECTION
Brown compact with raised gold flower design. O.S.P. $3.50 C.M.V. $2.00.

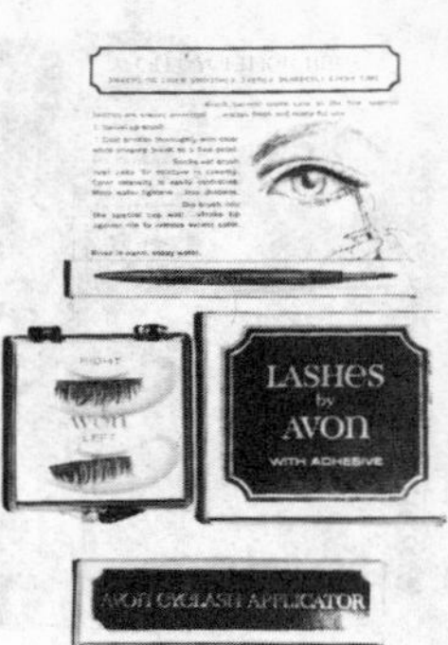

1969-74 EYE LINER BRUSH
Brown plastic. O.S.P. $1.00 C.M.V. 50¢
1969-75 FALSE LASHES
Choice of black or brown. Came in brown and white case. O.S.P. $4.00 C.M.V. $2.00 M.B.
1969-73 EYELASH APPLICATOR
Gold toned. O.S.P. $1.00 C.M.V. 50¢ M.B.

1967-68 APPLIQUE LIPSTICK
Gold case with pop-up mirror and lipstick inside. Two different designs. O.S.P. $3.50 C.M.V. $4.00 - $5.00 M.B.

1968-69 GADABOUTS COMPACT
Black and white plastic compact also had yellow and white compact each had matching lipsticks. O.S.P. compact $1.50 C.M.V. $2.00

1965-66 IMPERIAL JEWEL COMPACT
Gold compact with rhinestone clasp with 4A design. O.S.P. $6.00 C.M.V. $8.00 - $10.00 M.B.

951-55 POWDER PAK COMPACT
urquoise plastic with white scroll design.
lot 4A. O.S.P. $1.10 C.M.V. $3.00

964-66 PLATINUM ROSE COMPLEXION
IGHLIGHT - Tan & white box. O.S.P.
1.35 C.M.V. $1.00

1967-68 IMPERIAL COMPACT (TOP)
Gold compact O.S.P. $7.00 C.M.V. $6.00
$7.00 M.B.

1966-68 COMPETITE COMPACT (BOTTOM)
Basketweave style compact. O.S.P. $4.50
CMV $4.00 - $5.00 MB.

1970-72 COLOR EYES DUET
Black plastic. OSP $2.00 CMV 50c

1968-69 SPARKLING CREAM EYE SHADOW
Clear plastic OSP $1.75 CMV 50c.

1960'S CREAM ROUGE
Clear plastic. OSP $1.25 CMV 50c.

1973-76 ULTRA SHEER LIP GLOSS POT
White plastic. OSP $2.00 CMV 50c.

1970-76 POWDER SHADOW DUET
OSP $2.00 CMV 50c.

1962-65 GOLDEN HIGHLIGHT
Clear plastic. OSP $1.25 CMV $1.00

1971-75 EYE GLEAM
Brown plastic. OSP $1.00 CMV 50c.

1973-74 ULTRA SHEER LIP POT GLOSS
White plastic, Avon on top. OSP $2.25 CMV
CMV 50c.

BOTTOM RIGHT - 1967-74 CAKE EYELINER
Blue plastic with 4A design on lid. OSP
$1.50 CMV 50c.

1960-63 CURL 'N COLOR MASCARA
Gold metal tube, with Avon embossed on it.
O.S.P. $2.00 C.M.V. $2.50

1957-66 EYE SHADOW STICK
Same type gold tube as Curl 'N Color
Mascara. O.S.P. $1.00 C.M.V. $2.00

1966 FASHION AWARD COMPACT
Pink marbleized plastic case. O.S.P. $1.75
C.M.V. $2.00 - $3.00 M.B.

Left to right back row

1967-73 ULTRA SHEER PRESSED POWDER
White plastic and gold trim. O.S.P. $3.00
C.M.V. $1.00

1969-71 BLUSH COMPACT
Brown plastic with gold trim. Came with a
brush. O.S.P. $3.00 C.M.V. $1.00

Front row left to right

1972-74 FASHION GROUP COMPACT
Black plastic with gold trim. O.S.P. $4.50
C.M.V. $2.00

1970-73 SILVERY POWDER SHADOW COLLECTION
Jade like, mirrored, with gold trim. O.S.P.
$5.00 C.M.V. $2.00

1970-72 LIP TWINS
Jade like plastic, gold trim, holds 2 lipsticks,
mirror on back. S.S.P. $3.00 C.M.V. $2.00

Front Row

1965-67 DRESSING TABLE FACE POWDER
All pink plastic. OSP $1.25 CMV $2.00
$4.00 M.B.

Second Row left to right
White plastic compact with 4A design.
O.S.P. C.M.V. $1.50

1972-75 FASHION LACE COMPACT
White plastic with cut out design. O.S.P.
$3.50 C.M.V. $1.00

1972-74 FASHION LACE LIPSTICK
White plastic with cut out design. O.S.P.
$1.50 C.M.V. 50¢

1958-61 TOP STYLE COMPACT
All gold compact with 4A in center of gold
mesh lid. OSP $3.50 CMV $6.00, $7.00 MB

1961-63 FASHION COMPACT
Black bottom & gold lid. OSP $2.00 CMV
$3.00, $4.00 MB.

1972-74 CREMESTICK FOUNDATION
.85 oz. white plastic with gold trim.
O.S.P. $2.00 C.M.V. 50¢

1973-76 MOISTURE STICK
.7 oz. pink & gold. O.S.P. $1.00 C.M.V. 25¢

1969-75 GLO GETTER BLUSH STICK
1 oz. brown & gold. O.S.P. $1.00 C.M.V. 50¢

1971-74 GO TOGETHER
One side is foundation, other side blush.
O.S.P. $4.00 C.M.V. $1.00

1976 GREAT BLUSH FROST STICK
.85 oz. brown plastic. O.S.P. $3.00
C.M.V. 25¢

1963-65 POWDER-PAK COMPACT (Left)
Left to Right - Top - Pink plastic. OSP
$1.50 CMV $2.00, $3.00 MB

1970-71 BLUSHMAKER COMPACT (Right)
Green with gold, also has green handle
brush. OSP $5.00 CMV $1.00.

1973 Only - DESIGNERS ACCENT COMPACT
On bottom, pink with pink & dark pink
design. Called Accent in Mauve. Sold
for 3 campaigns only. OSP $1.50 CMV
$1.50, $2.00 MB.

1949-52 GAY LOOK
Gold deluxe compact & lipstick in black taffeta snap shut case. O.S.P. $5.00 C.M.V. $15.00 mint.
1953-56 GAY LOOK
Black covered metal case holds same as above. O.S.P. $5.75 C.M.V. $15.00 mint.
1949-56 DELUXE COMPACT
Gold compact. OSP $3.95 CMV $10.00 MB, $8.00 compact only, mint.

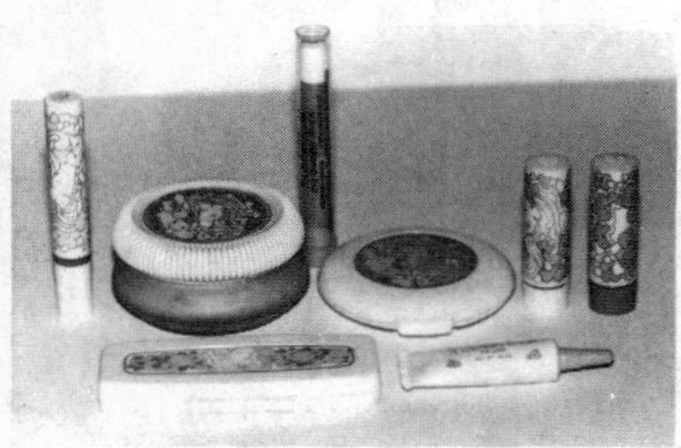

1970-76 CERTAIN LOOK PRODUCTS
Back Row - MASCARA, O.S.P. $2.00 C.M.V. 25¢
DEW GLOW - O.S.P. $2.50 C.M.V. 50¢
EYE SHADOW STACK - O.S.P. $1.00 C.M.V. 50¢
COMPACT - O.S.P. $2.00 C.M.V. 50¢
LIPSTICK - (has white base) O.S.P. $1.00 C.M.V. 50¢
LIP BEAMER (has purple base) O.S.P. $1.00 C.M.V. 50¢
Front Row - SHADOW & LINER TRIO O.S.P. $2.00 C.M.V. $1.00
EYE SHINE - O.S.P. $1.00 C.M.V. 25¢

Left to Right back row
1960-66 COMPACT DELUXE & LIPSTICK DELUXE - Silver & gold. O.S.P. Compact $3.50 C.M.V. $5.00 - $6.00 M.B.
O.S.P. Lipstick $1.35 C.M.V. $3.00 - $4.00 M.B.
1971-73 ENCORE COMPACT & LIPSTICK
Green ribbed plastic, gold 4A design on top. O.S.P. Compact $3.50 C.M.V. $2.00. O.S.P. Lipstick $1.35 C.M.V. $1.00
Front
1971-73 SIMPLICITY COMPACT
Pink plastic gold design. O.S.P. $2.75 CMV $1.00, $2.00 MB.

1966-67 BLUSHMATES
Maroon plastic case holds white compact & make up brush. O.S.P. Avon blush $5.50 Sparkling Blush $6.00. C.M.V. $10.00

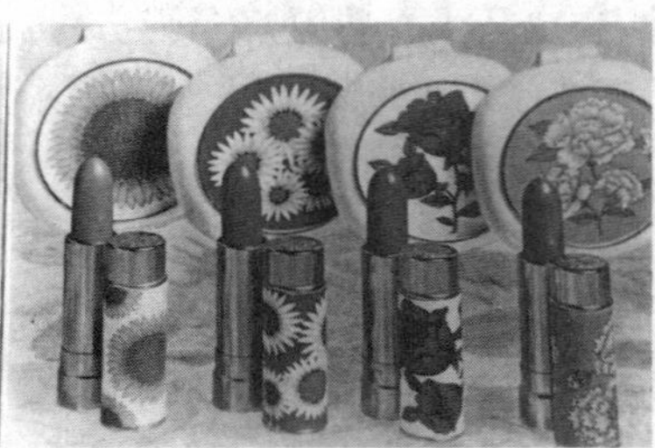

1967 FLOWER PRINT COMPACT & LIPSTICK - 4 compacts with matching lipsticks. Designs are Sunflower, Daisy, Poppy & Carnation. Compacts O.S.P. $2.50 C.M.V. $2.00 - $3.00 M.B.
Lipsticks O.S.P. $1.50 C.M.V. $2.00 M.B.
Also came in flower print lipstick. See Misc. Bottles.

1968-69 JEWELED LIPSTICK
Gold lipstick with simulated diamond. O.S.P. $6.00 C.M.V. $5.00 - $6.00 M.B.
1968-69 JEWELED COMPACT
Gold powder compact with simulated diamonds. O.S.P. $10.00 C.M.V. $12.00 M.B. Compact only $8.50

1969 CAPTIVATORS COMPACT & LIPSTICK - Leopard, Zebra & Tiger design plastic compacts. O.S.P. $3.50 C.M.V. $3.00 each. Matching lipsticks O.S.P. $1.75 C.M.V. $1.50. Add $1.00 each - M.B.

1969 RING FLING
Plastic tube of lipstick with beaded ring to match. White top lipstick, white & black beads. Lime green top, lime green & green beads. Blue top, dark blue & light blue beads. Pink top, dark pink & light pink beads. Yellow top, red & yellow beads. Orange top, yellow & orange beads. O.S.P. $2.00 CMV $4.00 with rings, MB.
1969 SWING FLING COMPACT
.5 oz. dark pink with colored design. OSP $2.00 CMV $2.00 - $2.50 MB.
1969 ENAMEL FLING
.5 oz. clear glass, white cap. OSP $1.00 CMV $1.00, $1.50 MB.

1970-71 EMPRESS LIPSTICK
Green, blue & gold lipstick. OSP $3.00 CMV $1.00, $2.00 MB
1970-71 EMPRESS COMPCAT
Green, blue & gold compact. OSP $7.50 CMV $4.00 MB, $3.00 CO

Left to Right
Top - 1968 FESTIVE FANCY LIPSTICK & COMPACT - Green plastic with white flowers. O.S.P. compact $3.00 C.M.V. $2.00 Lipstick O.S.P. $1.75 C.M.V. $1.00
1971-72 LIPSTICK-A-LA-MODE
White plastic - top holds glace, bottom lipstick. O.S.P. $4.50 C.M.V. $1.00
1967-73 FASHION LIPSTICK & COMPACT - Brown plastic with gold trim O.S.P. lipstick $1.35 C.M.V. 50¢
O.S.P. compact $2.25 C.M.V. 75¢
1968-71 ENCORE COMPACT & LIPSTICK
Gray with gold trim. OSP lipstick $1.25 C.M.V. 75¢ O.S.P. Compact $2.00 C.M.V. $1.50

958-64 POWDER PAK
ink plastic box, 7 oz. size. OSP $1.10
MV $2.00, $3.00 MB
957-64 POWDER PAK COMPACT
earl color plastic compact. OSP $1.25
MV $2.00, $3.00 MB.

1963-65 PETTI PAT COMPACT
White plastic compact with pink design. O.S.P. $1.10 C.M.V. $2.00
1963-65 CAKE ROUGE - Small white plastic compact O.S.P. $1.50 C.M.V. $2.00 M.B.

1967-69 COMPACT & LIPSTICK DELUXE
Gold compacts O.S.P. $5.50 ea. C.M.V. $4.00
Gold lipstick O.S.P. $2.00 C.M.V. $2.00
Add $1.00 for boxes.

1968-70 BLUSHING CREAM
.25 oz. clear plastic. gold 4A design. O.S.P. $2.00 C.M.V. 50¢
1971-75 BLUSHING CREAM
.25 oz. white plastic base, pink top, gold 4A design. O.S.P. $2.00 C.M.V. 25¢

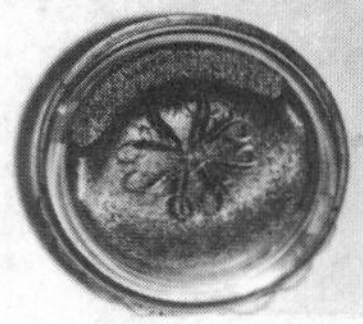

1962-65 GOLDEN HIGHLIGHT CREME FOR EYES
Clear plastic. OSP $1.25 CMV $2.00 MB

Left to Right
1955-57 POWDER PAK PLAQUE
Turquoise powder refill. O.S.P. 69¢ C.M.V. $3.00
1958-60 Same only pink. O.S.P. 69¢ C.M.V. $2.00
1949-55 POWDER PAK
Gold & turquoise cardboard powder box. OSP 95c, CMV $3.00, $4.00 MB
1955-57 POWDER PAK (Not shown)
Gold & turquoise cardboard powder box. Face powder same design only bigger box. 4A emblem on lid. OSP 95c, CMV $3.00
1955-57 POWDER PAK COMPACT
Turquoise & white compact with 4A design. OSP $1.10, CMV $2.00 - $3.00 MB.

Left to Right - Top to Right
1966-72 ULTRA SHEER POWDER
White plastic. 1¾ oz. O.S.P. $2.50 C.M.V. $1.00
1967-69 FINISHING FACE POWDER
Pink & brown box 2½ oz. O.S.P. $1.50 C.M.V. $2.00 mint.
1950-55 DRESSING TABLE ROUGE
Turquoise & gold cardboard 1/3 oz. size. O.S.P. 69¢ C.M.V. $3.00 - $4.00 M.B.
1949-55 FACE POWDER
Turquoise cardboard 2½ oz. size. OSP 89c, CMV $5.00 - $7.00 MB.

1930-41 BLACKHEAD REMOVER
Made of metal. Came in CPC Avon envelope. OSP 15c, CMV $7.00 mint in envelope only.

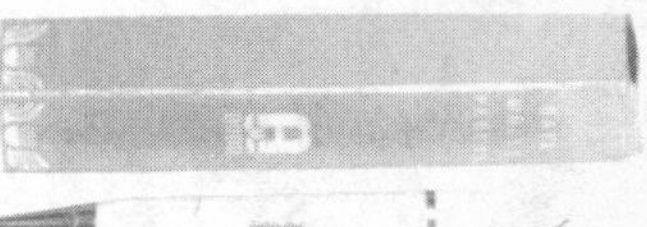

1941-48 NAIL WHITE PENCIL
White plastic pencil in turquoise box. OSP 29c, Avon on pencil, CMV $2.00 pencil only, $5.00 MB.

1961-68 CREAM ROUGE
Clear plastic with 4A design on lid. OSP $1.00 CMV 50c, $1.00 MB.
1962-64 EYE SHADOW
Same container as above. Came in Eye Shadow. OSP $1.00 CMV 50c, $1.00 MB

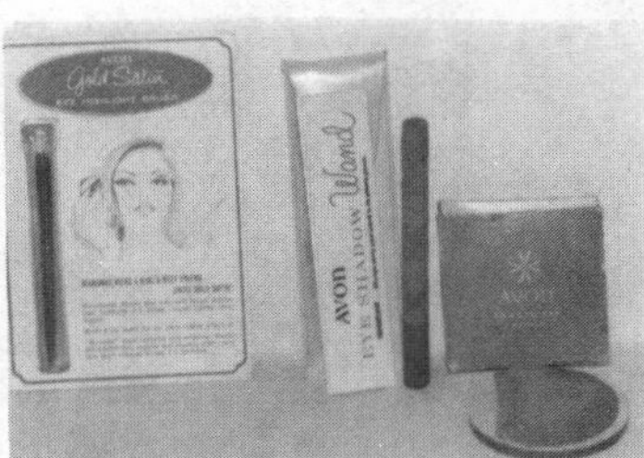

LEFT 1970'S GOLD SATIN EYE BRUSH BRUSH
Small eye brush. C.M.V. 50¢ on card.
CENTER 1960s EYE SHADOW WAND
Eight tier eye shadow in packet. C.M.V. 50¢
RIGHT 1971 POWDER PACK REFILL
Pink box holds metal powder refill. C.M.V. $1.00 M.B.

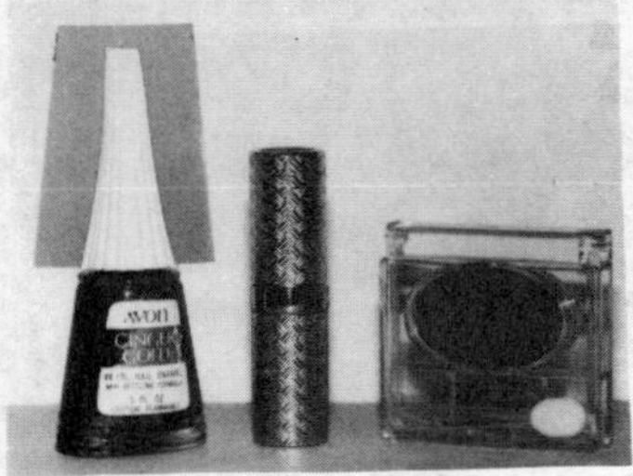

1978-79 POLISH GOLD COLLECTION
Each comes in gold & white box. All 3 pieces sold for $6.50 for the set. Nail Enamel, Gold Lipstick, Creamy Powder Eye Shadow. CMV 25c each.

1979-80 FLAVOR SAVERS LIP GLOSS
All in different colors. Strawberry, lime, chocolate, cherry, orange & grape. SSP $1.00 each, CMV 25c each.

1973-74 SUNNY LIP GLEAMER
Clear pink top, white plastic tube. O.S.P. $1.00 C.M.V. 50¢
1973-74 COLOR MAGIC
White case with colorful butterfly. O.S.P. $1.00 C.M.V. 50¢
1973-75 LOOKING PRETTY MIRRORED LIPSTICK - Green plastic. O.S.P. $2.00 CMV $1.00
1972-73 POP TOP LIPSTICK
Turquoise plastic, gold design. O.S.P. $1.50 C.M.V. 50¢
1973-75 POP TOP LIPSTICK
Brown plastic, gold design. O.S.P. $1.50 C.M.V. 50¢

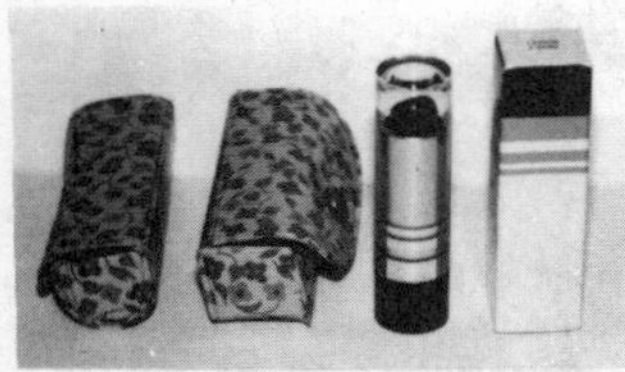

1978 LIPSTICK CASE
2 different green plastic cases with mirror inside lid. Holds lipstick. Sold 1 campaign only. 1 case is square bottom & 1 is round bottom. SSP $1.00 CMV $1.00

1965-68 NATURAL BLUSH
White plastic O.S.P. $1.50 C.M.V. $1.00
1966-68 BLUSH
White plastic, brown label. O.S.P. $2.00 C.M.V. $1.00
1966-68 SPARKLING BLUSH
White plastic. O.S.P. $2.00 C.M.V. $1.00
1970-72 BLUSHING CREAM
Pink lid, white bottom. O.S.P. $2.00 C.M.V. 75¢

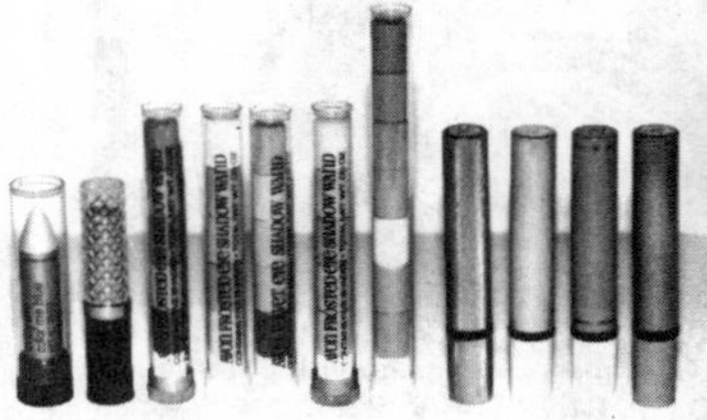

Left to Right
1975-76 EYE SHADOW CRAYON
Black base, clear top. O.S.P. $1.00 C.MV. 50¢
1970-74 CRYSTAL SHADOWS
Black base, clear top. O.S.P. $1.00 C.M.V. 50¢
1971-78 EYE SHADOWS WANDS
Came frosted or velvet. Different years different colors available. O.S.P. $1.00 C.M.V. 50¢
1962 EYE SHADOW WAND
6 stack up shades. O.S.P. $1.35 C.M.V. $1.00
1962-78 MASCARA
Lash Supreme - gold case; Making Eyes, pink case; Sweet Honesty, blue & white
1976 Making Eyes, turquoise case. O.S.P. $1.00 C.M.V. 25¢ each.

1970 PETIT PINK LIPSTICK
Black, pink & green floral lipstick & box. CMV $3.00 MB
1979 ABOUT TOWN TRIAL OFFER LIPSTICK
Box came with Candid lipstick. Made in Spain on label. OSP 79c, CMV $1.00 MB.

LEFT TO RIGHT
1979-80 SMOOTH DAYS AHEAD LIP BALM
White, blue & red calender on side. CMV 50c.
1968 FESTIVE FANCY DEMI STICK
Green & gold. CMV 50c, $1.00 MB.
1960'S LIPSTICK
Black & white. CMV $1.00 - $2.00 MB
1958-61 TOP STYLE LIPSTICK
Brass. CMV $3.00, $4.00 MB.

1954 JEWELED LIPSTICK
Gold Christmas box holds gold lipstick with jewel on top. OSP $1.75 CMV $15.00 in box shown.
1954-56 JEWELED LIPSTICK
Gold lipstick with white jewel on top. OSP $1.75 CMV lipstick only $4.00, $6.00 MB.

1970's MISCELLANEOUS EYEBROW PENCILS & MASCARA, EYE LINER REFILLS & LIP BRUSH. C.M.V. 25¢ each.

1963-65 FASHION LIPSTICK
Pink flowered plastic case with gold base. O.S.P. 98¢ C.M.V. $1.50 in demonstrator case as shown $5.00, lipstick only $1.00 - $2.00 MB.

1969-78 LIP DEW
Gold & white case. O.S.P. $1.00 C.M.V. 50¢
1970-71 LIP MAKER
Pink & red. O.S.P. $1.00 C.M.V. 50¢
1971-75 LIP FOUNDATION
Red, purple & white case. O.S.P. $1.00 C.M.V. 50¢
1968-73 QUICK COVER
Tan & brown case. O.S.P. $1.00 C.M.V. 50¢
1970-74 HIDE 'N LITE
White with green & gray stripes. O.S.P. $1.00 C.M.V. 25¢
1973 Only SUN SAFE STICK
Gold, tan & white. O.S.P. 89¢ C.M.V. 25¢

LEFT TO RIGHT
1948-58 DELUXE LIPSTICK
Gold metal case. OSP 95c, CMV $3.00 $5.00 MB
1962-63 FASHION LIPSTICK
Black metal case. OSP 98c, CMV $2.00 - $3.00 MB
1967-68 ENCORE LIPSTICK
Gold & white plastic. OSP $1.00 CMV $1.00, $1.50 MB.
1968-69 GADABOUTS
Black & white or yellow & white plastic. OSP 99c, CMV $1.50 each MB.
1957-60 FASHION CASE LIPSTICK
White metal. OSP 89c, CMV $2.00 - $3.00 MB
1968 ULTRA SHEER LIPSTICK
White plastic, gold base. OSP 99c, CMV $1.00.

1956-57 FASHION CASE LIPSTICK
Clear plastic base with black cap. O.S.P. 79c, CMV $4.00 mint, $6.00 MB.
1936 LIPSTICK SAMPLES
Turquoise and brass metal sample. C.M.V. 50¢ mint each.

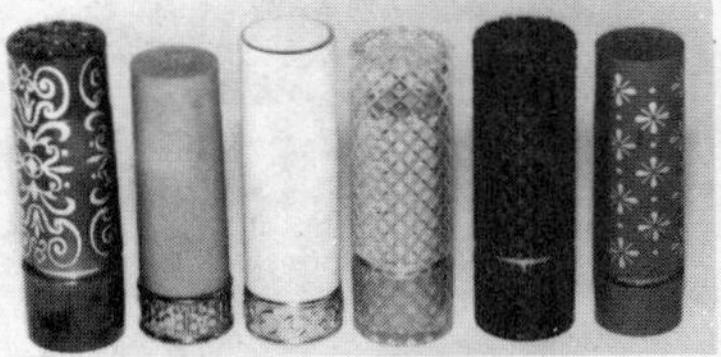

1974-78 ABOUT TOWN LIPSTICK
Brown & gold. O.S.P. $3.00 C.M.V. 25¢
1969 RING FLING LIPSTICK
Plastic top, white, black, lime green, blue, pink or yellow. OSP $2.00 CMV $1.00, $2.00 MB
1966-74 ULTRA SHEER LIPSTICK
White plastic. OSP $1.00 CMV 50c.
1972-73 ENCORE LIPSTICK
Clear plastic. OSP $1.00 CMV 75c.
1973-78 WINDSOR LIPSTICK
Dark blue plastic. OSP $2.00 CMV 25c.
1968-71 ENCORE LIPSTICK
Gray & gold plastic. OSP $1.00 CMV $1.00.

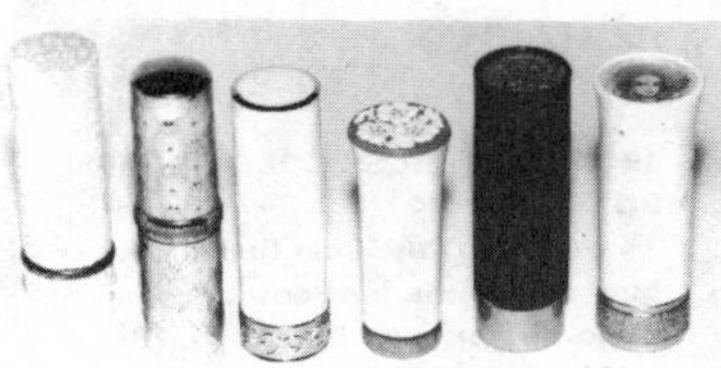

1970-71 DELUXE LIPSTICK
Carved ivory design. O.S.P. $2.00 C.M.V. $1.00
1965-67 LIPSTICK REFILLABLE
Gold metal case. Held Encore Lipstick. O.S.P. $2.00 C.M.V. $2.00
1966-74 ULTRA SHEER
White plastic. O.S.P. $1.00 C.M.V. 50¢
1960-61 FASHION LIPSTICK
White & pink plastic. O.S.P. 98¢ C.M.V. $2.00
1967-72 FASHION LIPSTICK
Tortoiseshell case. O.S.P. $1.00 C.M.V. 50¢
1964-66 FASHION CASE CAMEO LIPSTICK
White plastic with cameo on lid. O.S.P. 98¢ C.M.V. $2.00

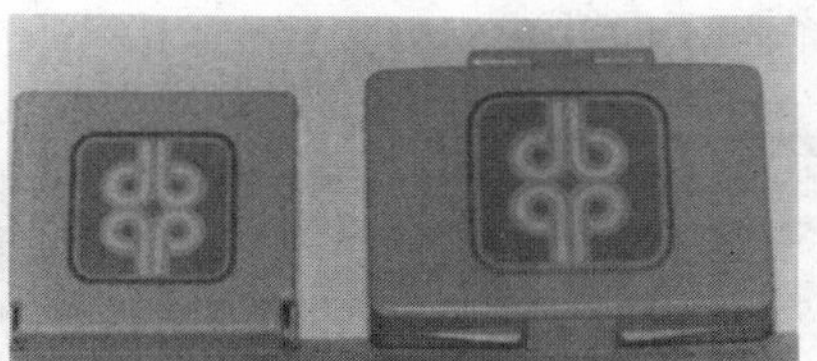

LEFT 1976-78 DELICATE BEAUTY POWDER EYE SHADOW
Gray plastic. O.S.P. $3.50 C.M.V. 50¢
RIGHT 1976-78 DELICATE BEAUTY TENDER PEACH 100% FRAGRANCE FREE POWDER BLUSH
Gray plastic. O.S.P. $5.00 C.M.V. 50¢

1972-73 MIRROR MIRROR
Silver box, holds white plastic reversable mirror. O.S.P. $3.50 CMV $2.00 - $3.00 MB

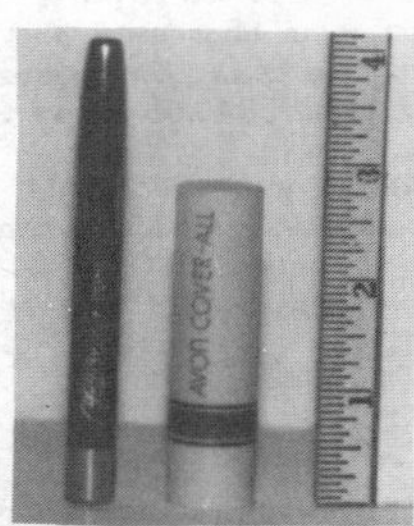

1977-78 COLORSTICKS FOR EYES AND LIPS
Make up colors in pencil form.
O.S.P. $3.50 C.M.V. 25¢
1977-78 COVER ALL
Concealing stick. O.S.P. $3.25 C.M.V. 25¢

1974-78 DELICATE BEAUTY
Beige & White Design
Back Row - Left to Right -
AUTOMATIC EYELINER - O.S.P. $3.00 C.M.V. 25¢
CREAM FOUNDATION - O.S.P. $3.00 C.M.V. 25¢
AUTOMATIC MASCARA - O.S.P. $2.00 C.M.V. 25¢
UNDER MAKEUP MOISTURIZER
O.S.P. $3.00 C.M.V. 25¢
BLUSH STICK - O.S.P. $4.00 C.M.V. 25¢
LIPSTICK - O.S.P. $1.50 C.M.V. 25¢
Front Row -
PRESSED POWDER COMPACT
O.S.P. $3.00 C.M.V. 50¢
POWDER SHADOW DUET - O.S.P. $2.00 C.M.V. 25¢
BLUSHING CREAM - O.S.P. $2.00 C.M.V. 25¢

CREAM JARS-MISC.

1930-34 VIOLET NUTRI CREAM
White jar, metal lid, silver & blue label. 2 & 4 oz. size. O.S.P. 78¢ on 4 oz. & 52¢ for 2 oz. C.M.V. $40.00 in box. $35.00 jar only.

1930-34 CLEANSING CREAM
4 oz. white glass ribbed jar with aluminum lid. Silver & blue label. O.S.P. $1.00 C.M.V. $35.00 jar only. $40.00 in box.

1933-36 CREAM JARS - MISC.
Ribbed white glass jar with blue metal caps. Following came in 2 & 4 oz. size. Rose Cold Cream, Violet Nutri Cream, 4 oz. size only in Cleansing Cream, 2 oz. size only in Bleach Cream, Vanishing Cream, Tissue Cream. O.S.P. 78¢ C.M.V. on 4 oz. & 52¢ on 2 oz. size. C.M.V. $30.00 ea. $35.00 M.B.

1936-55 CREAM JARS - MISC.
This style bottle was sold from 1936-55. Came in Tissue Cream, Rose Cold Cream, Special Formula Cream, Foundation Cream, Violet Protective Cream, All-Purpose Cream, Bleach Cream, Cleansing Cream, Night Cream, Violet Nutri Cream, Complexion Cream, Vanishing Cream, Super Rich Cream, 1947 Special Dry Skin Cream 1948 Facial Mask Cream, white glass jars came in small, medium & large size with turquoise metal caps. Paper caps were used 1943-46. O.S.P. 52¢ to 89¢. C.M.V. $4.00 ea. Add $3.00 ea. for turquoise paper caps. C.M.V. with CPC labels on jar or box 1936-39 $8.00 jar only. $12.00 CPC label on box mint.

1954-55 ANTISEPTIC CREAM
3½ oz. large size jar only. O.S.P. 89¢ C.M.V. $4.00 $5.00 M.B.

1946 Only - COLOR PICK-UP CREAM
7/8 oz. white glass jar, turquoise lid. O.S.P. 89¢ C.M.V. $15.00 mint, $18.00 M.B.

1940 ONLY - ROSE COLD CREAM BOX
1¾ oz. jar of Rose Cold Cream came in special issue box for Reps. to use as demonstrator only. Cost Reps. 10¢. C.M.V. $15.00 M.B. as shown.

1942 ROSE COLD CREAM SPECIAL ISSUE BOX
Special issue blue and pink rosebud box holds regular issue large size jar of Rose Cold Cream. OSP 49c, CMV $14.00 MB as shown.

1930-34 TISSUE CREAM
Ribbed white glass, metal lid, silver & blue label. 2 oz. size. 75c

1931 VANISHING CREAM
2 oz. white glass jar with aluminum lid. Silver & blue label. O.S.P. 52¢ C.M.V. $40.00 in box. $35.00 jar only.

1930-34 ROSE COLD CREAM
2 & 4 oz. white glass ribbed jars with aluminum lids. Silver & blue labels. O.S.P. 2 oz. 52¢ 4 oz. size 78¢ C.M.V. $40.00 ea. in box. $30.00 jar only.

1932-33 BLEACH CREAM
3 oz. frosted glass jar, metal lid, silver & blue label. OSP 78c, CMV $50.00 - $55.00 MB.

1941 ROSE COLD CREAM SPECIAL ISSUE BOX
Special issue rose color box with girls face on side. Came with regular issue middle size jar of Rose Cold Cream for 10¢ with regular order. CMV $14.00 MB as shown.

1953 CREME SHAMPOO
4 oz. jar very short issue. RARE. OSP $1.00, CMV $13.00 MB, $10.00 jar only mint.

1939 ONLY - CREAM DEODORANT
White glass jar. Turquois lid. O.S.P. 37¢ This jar is Rare. CMV $16.00 MB, $12.00 jar only, mint.

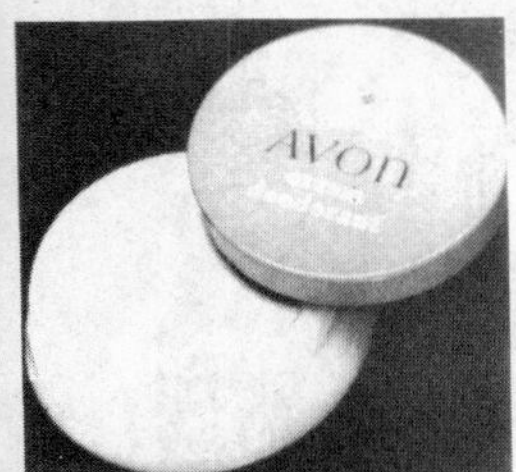

1954-59 CREAM DEODORANT
White glass jar, turquoise lid. O.S.P. 49¢ C.M.V. $4.00 in box. $2.50 jar only.

1936-54 CREAM DEODORANT
1 oz. white glass jar, turquoise lid. O.S.P. 39¢ C.M.V. $7.00 jar only. $10.00 M.B. Add $4.00 CPC label.

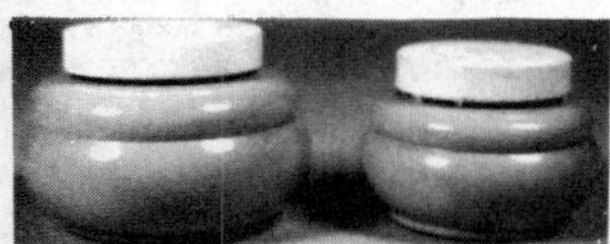

1957-60 RICH MOISTURE CREAM
In 3½ & 2 oz. turquoise jars with 4A on white lids. O.S.P. 2 oz. $1.50, 3 oz. $2.50 CMV $3.00 MB, $2.00 jar only, mint.

1961-72 RICH MOISTURE CREAM
2 oz. & 3½ oz. turquoise glass jar with 4A on white lid. O.S.P. 3½ oz. $2.50 2 oz. $1.50 C.M.C. 25¢ ea. on 1972 jar the 4A design was dropped.
1961-65 HORMONE CREAM
2 oz. turquoise glass jar with 4A on white lid. Same as Rich Moisture Cream jar. O.S.P. $2.00, CMV $1.00 MB, 50c jar only.

1954-57 RICH MOISTURE CREAM
Turquoise jar & cap in 2 oz. & 3½ oz. size. O.S.P. $1.50 for 2 oz. $2.50 for 3½ oz. 2 oz. jar came with 2 different size neck & caps. CMV $4.00 each size MB, $3.00 jar only.

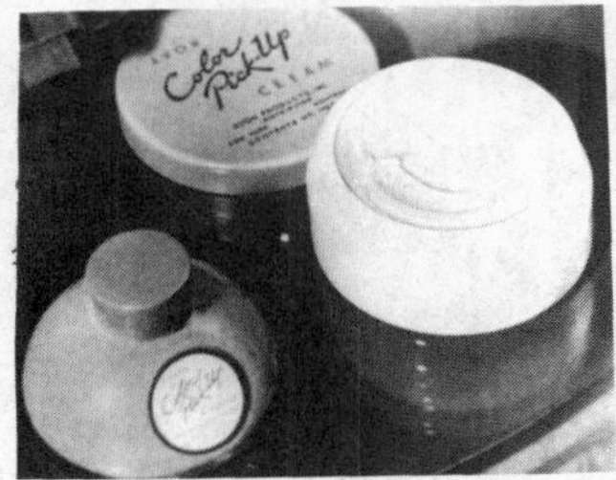

1946-50 COLOR PICK-UP LIQUID
1 oz. clear glass bottle with turquoise cap. OSP 89c, CMV $8.00 - $11.00 MB
1946-54 COLOR PICK-UP CREAM
1 7/8 oz. white glass jar with turquoise lid. OSP 89c, CMV $6.00 - $10.00 MB
Also came 1 oz. jar. Same lid & jar.

1946-47 COLOR PICK UP CREAM
Painted over twin tone lid. 1 7/8 oz. white glass jar with green lid. O.S.P. 89¢ C.M.V. $10.00 - $12.00 M.B.

1943-46 TWIN TONE MAKE UP CREAM
1 7/8 oz. white jar, turquoise paper lid & metal lid. O.S.P. 89¢ C.M.V. metal lid $9.00, Paper lid $12.00
1943-46 TWIN TONE MAKE UP CREAM
7/8 oz. white glass jar, turquoise paper lid. OSP 89c, CMV $10.00 - $14.00 MB.

1945 Only - HAND CREAM
3½ oz. clear glass jar, turquoise lid. Rare. C.M.V. $25.00 - $30.00 M.B.

1939 ONLY - ROSE COLD CREAM BOX
2 oz. white glass jar, turquoise lid in special short issue design box. C.P.C. on box. O.S.P. 10¢ C.M.V. $15.00 M.B. as shown.

1954-61 AVON CREAMS
White glass jar with green lid & label. Came in: HORMONE CREAM; SUPER RICH CREAM; CLEANSING CREAM & ANTISEPTIC CREAM in large and small jars. O.S.P. 89¢ C.M.V. $2.00 each.
1967-69 STAY FAIR NIGHT CREAM
2¼ oz. light blue base, blue and white lid. O.S.P. $2.00 C.M.V. $1.00

1959-61 VITA MOIST CREAM
2 oz. yellow glass jar with white smooth cap. O.S.P. $3.00 C.M.V. $1.50
1961-68 VITA MOIST CREAM
1 oz. yellow glass jar with white smooth cap. O.S.P. $1.75 C.M.V. 75¢
1965-69 SUPER RICH CREAM
2¼ oz. pink glass bottom, white & pink cap. O.S.P. $3.00 C.M.V. 75¢
1969-74 SUPER RICH CREAM
2¼ oz. blue glass jar with white & blue cap. O.S.P. $3.00 C.M.V. 25¢

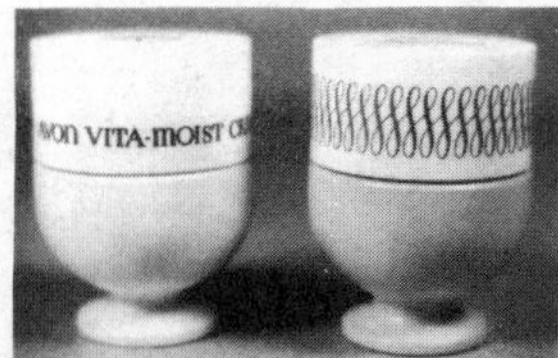

1961-69 VITA MOIST CREAM
2¼ oz. yellow glass jar with white smooth cap. O.S.P. $3.00 C.M.V. 50¢
1969-72 VITA MOIST CREAM
2.25 oz. yellow glass jar with ribbed white cap. O.S.P. $3.00 C.M.V. 50¢
1961-69 CREAM SUPREME
2¼ oz. Pink glass jar with white cap with gold design around edge. O.S.P. $3.00 C.M.V. 75¢
1969-72 CREAM SUPREME
2¼ oz. pink glass jar with pink 4A on white ribbed cap. O.S.P. $3.00 C.M.V. 50¢

1940-50 NAIL & CUTICLE CREAM
1 oz. white glass jar, turquoise lid. O.S.P. 43¢ C.M.V. $5.00 - $7.00 M.B.

1951-54 NAIL BEAUTY
1 oz. white glass jar, white lid. O.S.P. 49¢ C.M.V. $4.00 - $5.00 M.B.

1954-57 NAIL BEAUTY
1 oz. white jar with white lid. O.S.P. 59¢ C.M.V. $3.00

1970 MAKE UP SETTING PADS
Pink frosted jar, white cap. Has 45 pads per box. O.S.P. $2.75 C.M.V. $5.00

1957-63 FRENCH FROSTING
1 oz. clear glass jar with pink plastic lid with gold center. O.S.P. $1.25 C.M.V. $2.00 jar only. $5.00 in box.

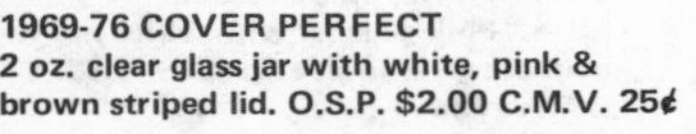

1969-76 COVER PERFECT
2 oz. clear glass jar with white, pink & brown striped lid. O.S.P. $2.00 C.M.V. 25¢

1967-71 HAIR CONDITIONER
6 oz. white jar, pink metal cap. O.S.P. $2.50 C.M.V. $1.00

1956 STRAWBERRY COOLER
Frosted glass jar with strawberry on white lid. OSP $1.50 CMV $3.00 - $5.00 MB.

1974-78 RICH MOISTURE CREAM
7 oz. blue plastic with white lid. O.S.P. $4.00 C.M.V. 25¢. Also came 2 oz. size C.M.V. 25¢

1972-75 RICH MOISTURE CREAM
3.5 oz. blue plastic with white lid. (No lettering on front) O.S.P. $2.00 C.M.V. 25¢

1976-78 AVON COLD CREAM
3.1 oz. white plastic, blue lid. O.S.P. $1.00 C.M.V. 25¢

1975-77 VITA MOIST
3.5 oz. yellow plastic, white lid. C.M.V. 25¢

1977-78 TANNING BUTTER
1.75 oz. bronze plastic container O.S.P. $1.49 C.M.V. 25¢

1969-70 STEPPING OUT
4 oz. blue jar, white lid. O.S.P. $2.00 CMV $1.00 MB, 50c jar only.

1971-76 STEPPING OUT - Is same only 5 oz. size. Blue jar. O.S.P. $2.00 C.M.V. 25¢

1973-74 SKIN-SO-SOFT SOFTENER VANITY JAR
5 oz. clear glass with antiqued gold lid. SSP $4.00 CMV $2.50 MB, $2.00 jar only.

1973-75 CREAM SACHET VANITY JAR
1 oz. clear glass with antiqued silver lid. Holds Field Flowers, Charisma or Topaze. SSP $3.00, CMV $2.50 MB, $2.00 jar only.

1973 RICH MOISTURE CREAM VANITY JAR
5 oz. clear glass with antiqued silver lid. SSP $2.50 CMV $2.50, $2.00 jar only.

1974-76 VITA MOIST CREAM
3.5 oz. yellow plastic with white & yellow lid. O.S.P. $2.00 C.M.V. 25¢

1975-78 VITA MOIST CREAM
7 oz. yellow plastic with white & yellow lid. O.S.P. $3.00 C.M.V. 25¢

1976-77 HORMONE CREAM
3.25 oz. white plastic with white & gold lid. O.S.P. $2.00 C.M.V. 25¢

1970-73 DEEP CLEAN CLEANSING CREAM - 4 oz. white plastic, blue lid. O.S.P. $1.00 C.M.V. 50¢

1965-76 HORMONE CREAM
2.25 oz. white glass jar with gold tip on white lid. O.S.P. $1.50 C.M.V. 25¢

1960-74 EYE CREAM
White glass jar with eye on metal lid. O.S.P. $1.50 C.M.V. 25¢

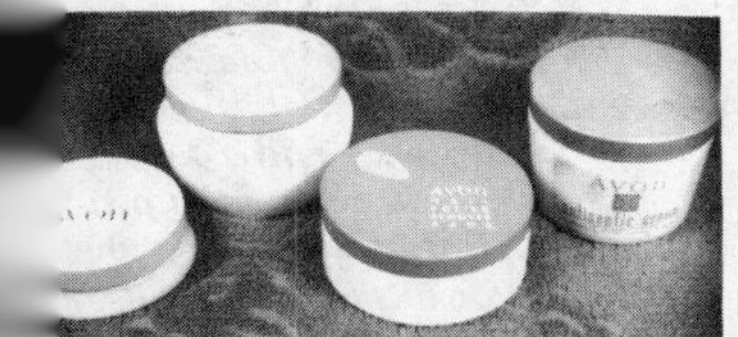

55-57 COLOR PICKUP CREAM
ıite glass jar with pink lid. O.S.P. 95¢
MV $6.00 each MB, $4.00 jar only.
961-65 WHITE VELVET CREAM
oz. white glass jar with 4A on turquoise
. O.S.P. $1.25 C.M.V. $1.00 - $2.00 M.B.
963-66 POLISH REMOVER PADS
hite glass jar with red lid, holds 20
ds. O.S.P. 98¢ C.M.V. $2.00 - $3.00
.B.
954-58 ANTISEPTIC CREAM
½ oz. white glass jar with gray lid.
.S.P. $1.00 C.M.V. $2.00 - $3.00
.B.

1954 RICH MOISTURE CREAM
1½ & 3½ oz. turquoise glass jars with turquoise plastic lids. O.S.P. $1.50 CMV $3.00 - $4.00 MB.
1963-66 CREAM FOUNDATION
1 oz. white glass jar with white plastic lid with gold center. O.S.P. $1.35 C.M.V. $1.50

1961-65 COLOR CAKE
2 oz. white cap & pink base. OSP $1.95 CMV $1.00, $2.00 MB
1947-54 CAKE MAKE-UP
1¾ oz. pink base, white cap. OSP $1.00 CMV $3.00, $4.00 MB.

LEFT 1955-57 CREAM CAKE
Avon in center of pink lid, white glass bottom. OSP 95c, CMV $3.00, $4.00 MB.
RIGHT 1948-55 CREAM CAKE
Dove on top of pink lid, white glass bottom. O.S.P. 95¢ C.M.V. $4.00 $5.00 M.B.

BRUSHES & COMBS - MISC.

1969-73 COMPLEXION BEAUTY BRUSH
Pink & white box holds white plastic brush. CMV $1.00 MB.

1978 COMB & BRUSH VALET
Brown plastic. Deer on top, brown box. S.S.P. $6.99 C.M.V. $3.00 M.B.

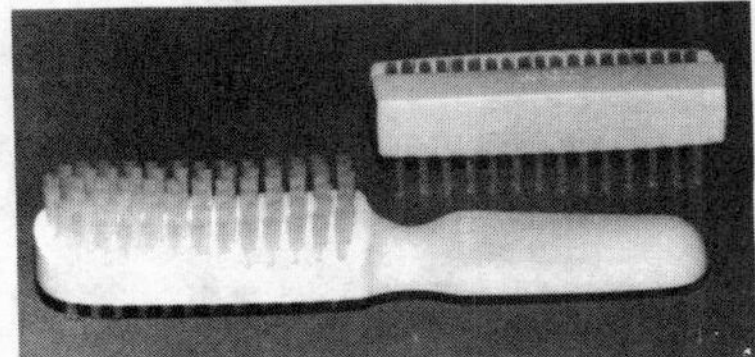

1970-73 NAIL BRUSH
White plastic nylon bristles. O.S.P. $1.00 C.M.V. 50¢ M.B.
1973-76 AVON HAND & NAIL BRUSH
White plastic, nylon bristles. (with long handle). O.S.P. $1.88 C.M.V. 50¢ M.B.

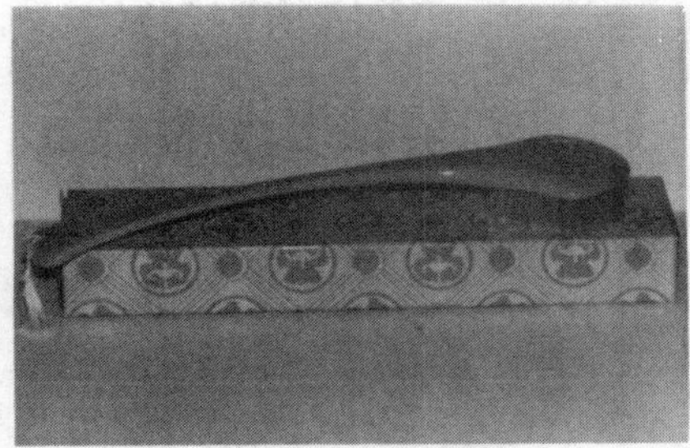

1977-78 BATH BRUSH
Approx. 15½" long, plastic brush. Came in blue, ivory or yellow. SSP $6.99, CMV $2.00 each MB.

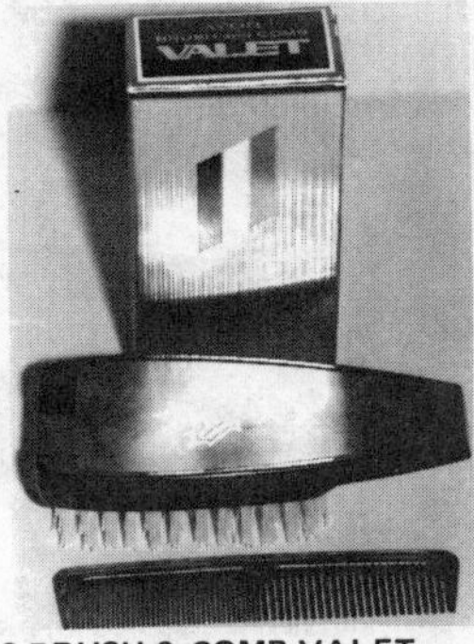

1970 BRUSH & COMB VALET
Black brush & comb with copper colored insert. O.S.P. $3.00 C.M.V. $3.00

1975-78 PLAQUE CONTROL
2 brushes, 1 blue, 1 yellow. O.S.P. $1.00 C.M.V. $1.00 M.B.
1973-78 TOOTHBRUSH DUO
2 brushes, 1 brown, 1 white. O.S.P. $1.25 C.M.V. $1.25 M.B.
1972-73 SAF-T-DENT TOOTHBRUSH
1 brush, pink or blue. O.S.P. $1.00 C.M.V. $1.00 M.B.
1973-76 STIMU-TEX TOOTHBRUSHES
2 brushes, 1 white, 1 blue. O.S.P. $1.00 C.M.V. $1.00 M.B.
1970-73 DECORATOR TOOTHBRUSH TRIO PAK - 3 brushes, either 1 of each, yellow, green or pink or all three same color. O.S.P. $1.00 C.M.V. $1.00 M.B.
1965-70 DECORATOR TOOTHBRUSH TRIO PAK - 3 brushes, choice of red, yellow or blues, box matching color of brushes. O.S.P. $1.00 C.M.V. $1.00 M.B.

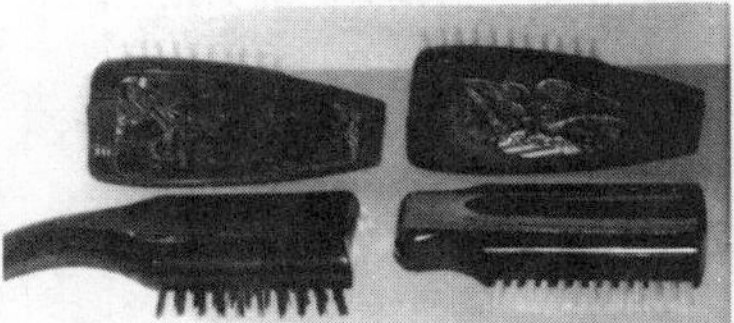

Back row left to right -
1974-75 OUTDOORSMAN BRUSH & COMB SET - 5" long, brown plastic with decorative panel. Comb is brown. O.S.P. $4.00 C.M.V. $2.00 M.B.
1975 AMERICAN EAGLE BRUSH & COMB VALET - 5½" long, black plastic with eagle on top, red & blue shield. O.S.P. $5.00 C.M.V. $2.00 M.B.
1970-73 CLUB BRUSH - Black with black bristles. O.S.P. $2.00 C.M.V. $1.00 M.B.
1972 VALET TRIO
Brown plastic with brown comb & silver shoe horn. O.S.P. $3.00 C.M.V. $2.00 M.B.

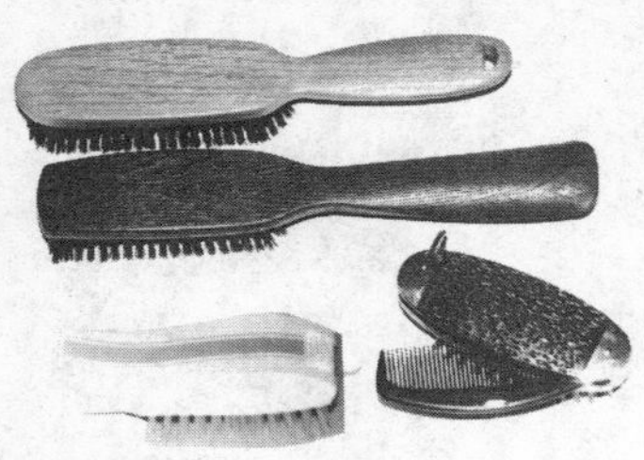

1974 FAMILY CLOTHES BRUSH
9" long, simulated wood grain, black bristles. O.S.P. $4.00 C.M.V. $2.00 M.B.
1974-76 CLOTHES BRUSH VALET WITH SHOE HORN - 10" long, brown plastic. O.S.P. $2.50 C.M.V. $1.50 M.B.
1972-73 SURE WINNER COMB & BRUSH
White with blue stripe. O.S.P. $3.00 C.M.V. $1.50 M.B.
1974-76 JACK KNIFE COMB & BRUSH
Black & silver with black comb. O.S.P. $4.00 C.M.V. $2.50 M.B.

1973-75 CHARM BRACELET & CHARMS GOLD FINISH - Bracelet - S.S.P. $4.00 No. 1 Owl Charm S.S.P. $3.00; No 2 Victorian Pitcher S.S.P. $3.00; No. 3 French Telephone S.S.P. $3.00; No. 4 Country Store Coffee Mill S.S.P. $3.00; No. 5 Fashion Boot S.S.P. $3.00; No. 6 Sweet Shoppe S.S.P. $3.00. 1973 Fashion Boot & Victorian Pitcher still available.

JEWELRY

PLEASE NOTE: Avon Jewelry is not considered a collectable item by most avid collectors & bottle dealers. Most collectors agree that most people buying Avon Jewelry are buying it to wear, not to put it in a collection.

Avon Products, Inc. is now the world's largest retailer of costume jewelry and are making vast amounts of jewelry in large volume. Because of these reasons, Avon Jewelry should not be considered collectable at this time as a collectors item. We show you some of the older jewelry pieces to identify with. I do not encourage you to buy Avon Jewelry as a collectors investment, as you are sure to never recover your original investment. Buy it only for your personal use as Avon is making some very beautiful pieces of jewelry.

No C.M.V. is given on jewelry shown. Only O.S.P. from Avon.

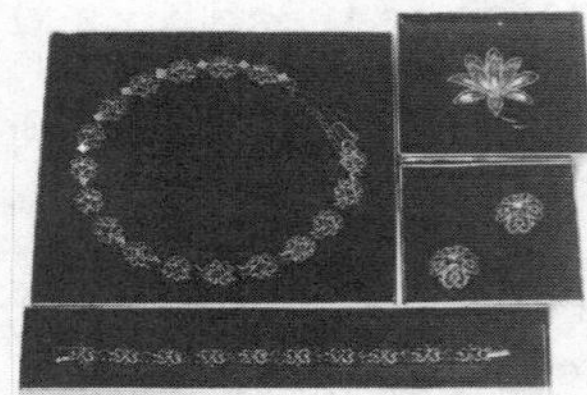

1971 PRECIOUS PRETENDERS GOLD FINISH - Necklace S.S.P. $9.00; Bracelet 1971-73 S.S.P. $6.00; 1971-73 Pin S.S.P. $5.00; Earrings S.S.P. $4.00

1978-79 DECORATOR'S JEWELRY CHEST
Wood box sold empty. Lift up lid. Bottom drawer only opens. Bottom gold label says "Avon Decorator's Jewelry Chest 1978 Made in Taiwan." Very short issue. Same box sold in other stores. Must have Avon label on bottom. SSP $6.00 with a $10.00 purchase of other Avon products. CMV $30.00 with Avon label only in box.

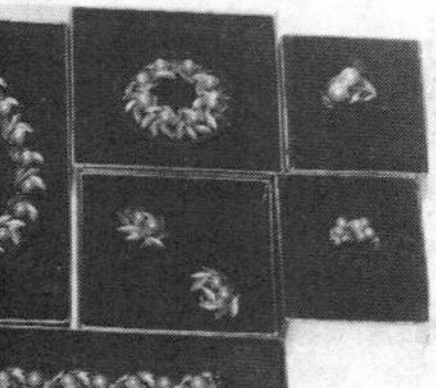

1971 EVENING CREATION
Gold wash with pearls. Necklace S.S.P. $11.00; 1971-73 Bracelet S.S.P. $8.00 1971-73 Pin S.S.P. $7.00; Earrings (clipped) S.S.P. $5.00; Earrings (pierced) S.S.P. $7.00; Cluster Ring S.S.P. $8.00; Duet Ring S.S.P. $6.00

1972-73 BAMBOO MAGIC
Gold finish. Ring S.S.P. $6.00; Pin S.S.P. $6.00; Pierced earrings S.S.P. $9.00; Clip earrings S.S.P. $6.00

1972 BLUE TEARDROP
Silver color with aqua sets. Necklace S.S.P. $8.00; Earrings S.S.P. $6.00

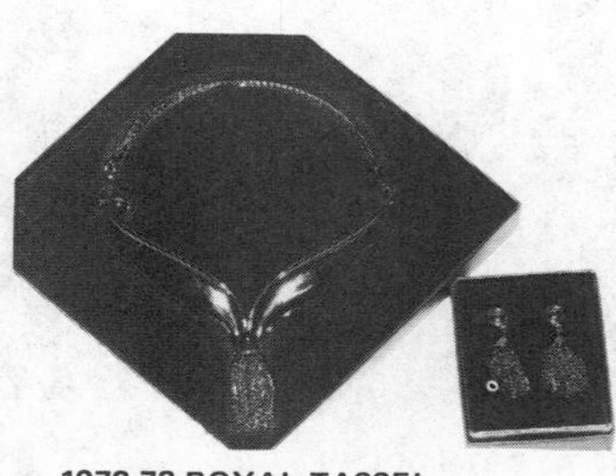

1972-73 ROYAL TASSEL
Gold finish. Necklace S.S.P. $9.00 Pierced earrings S.S.P. $8.00

1975-78 JEWELRY DEMO DISPLAY CASE - Case for representatives to demonstrate jewelry. Blue case. C.M.V. $4.00

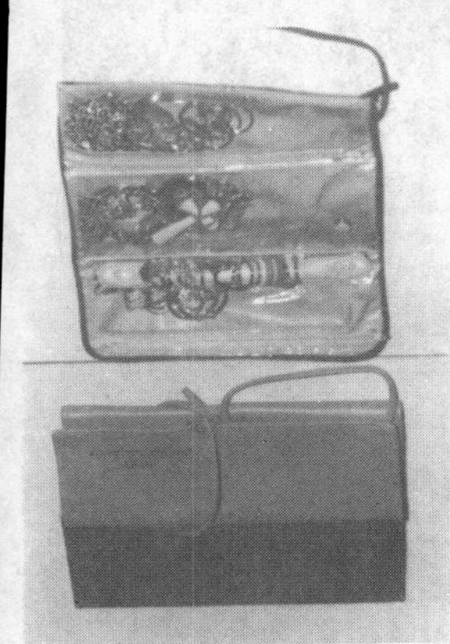

1977 14K GOLD FILLED JEWELRY DEMO CASE
Gray leatherette demo case used by Avon Reps to show 14K gold jewelry. Avon on outside. Cost Avon Reps. $2.50 C.M.V. $3.50
1977 JEWELRY WRAP CASE
Blue velvet wrap case, clear plastic inside, Avon tag on inside. Sold for $3.50 with purchase of 2 jewelry items. C.M.V. $2.50

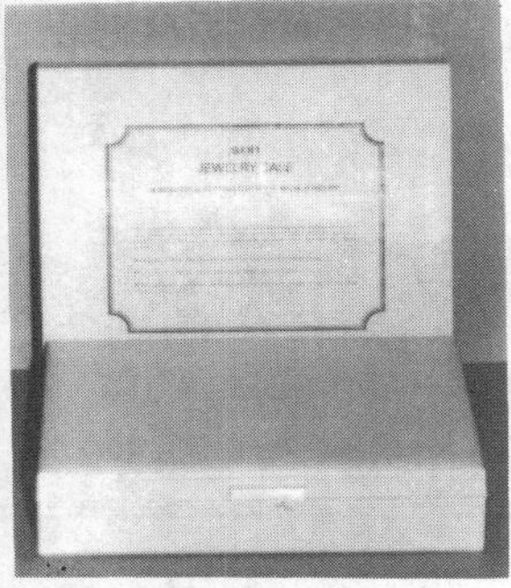

1977-78 JEWELRY CASE
White jewelry case 10½"x 8½"x 2". Dark blue velvet inside. S.S.P. $5.00 C.M.V. $4.00 Avon on bottom and outer sleeve.

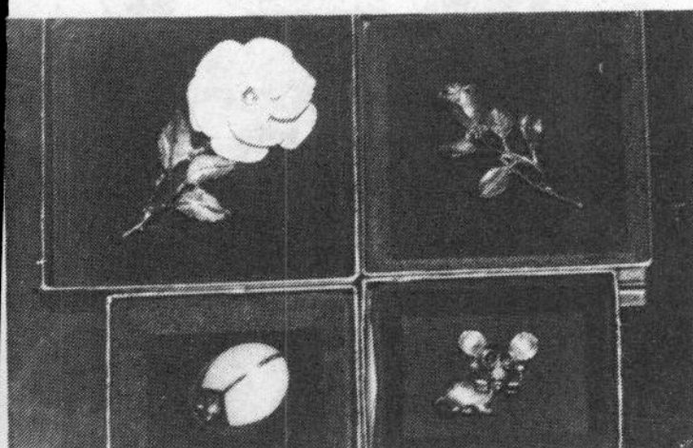

1972-73 SNOW FLOWER PIN
Gold with white enamel petals. S.S.P. $7.00
1972-73 GILDED ROSE PIN
Gold with pink sapphire S.S.P. $4.00
1972-73 LADY BUG PIN
Silver with white body & rhinestones. S.S.P. $6.00
1973 SPECTACULAR MOUSE PIN
Gold with moveable glasses. S.S.P. $4.00

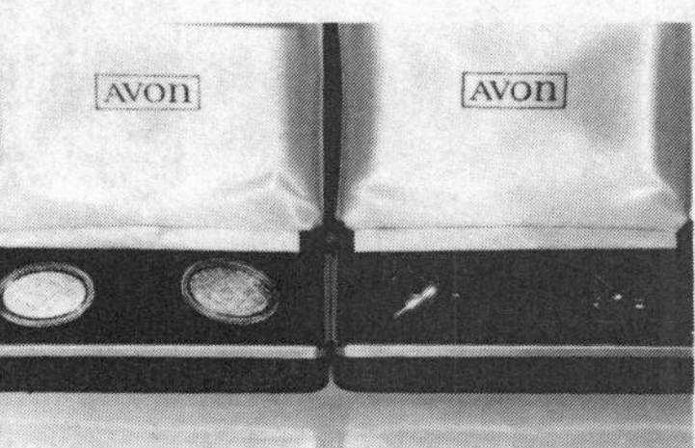

1971 BRUSHED OVAL CUFF LINKS
Gold florentine-brushed finish. S.S.P. $6.00
1971 GEOMETRIC CUFF LINKS
Gold finish S.S.P. $7.00

1971 STARBURST CUFF LINKS & TIE BAR - Gold with simulated sapphire sets. S.S.P. $9.00
1971 CLASSIC ACCENT
Gold & simulated black onyx stone. Tie Tac S.S.P. $3.oo S.S.P. Cuff Links $7.00

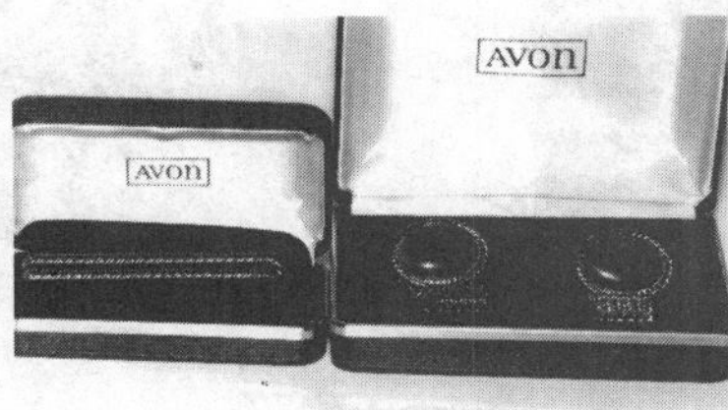

1971 ROPE TWIST BAR
Gold finish S.S.P. $4.00
1971 CONVERTIBLE CUFF LINKS
Gold with simulated tiger eye. Removable wrap around links. S.S.P. $11.00

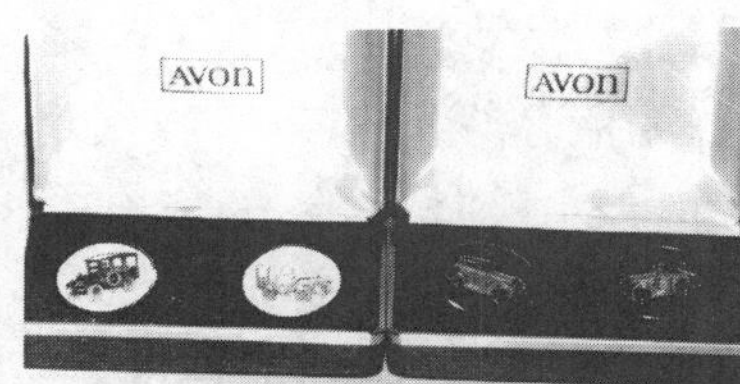

1972 STATION WAGON CUFF LINKS
Gold with white background, brown, green & red car. S.S.P. $8.00
1972-73 ROLLS ROYCE CUFF LINKS
Silver with black background & orange & brown car. S.S.P. $8.00

1972-73 STAR FLOWER
Gold florentine finish. Bracelet S.S.P. $9.00; Pin S.S.P. $5.00; Earrings S.S.P. $5.00

1972 BUTTON COVERS
Gold finish S.S.P. $4.00; Blue enamel S.S.P. $4.50

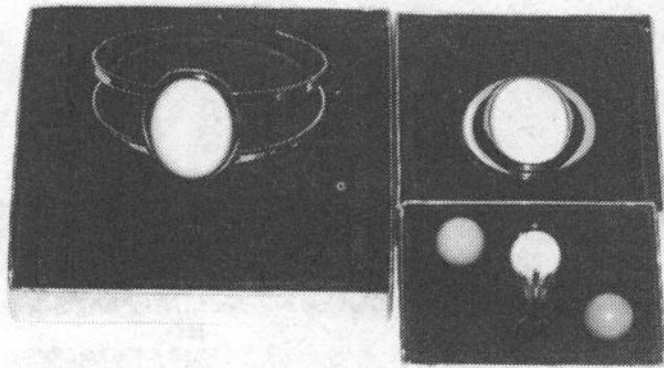

1972 ACCENT-IN-WHITE
Gold with white set. Bracelet S.S.P. $8.00 Pin S.S.P. $6.00
1972-73 COLOR RING FLING
Gold with coral, aqua, white pop in beads. S.S.P. $8.00

1973 SWEET VIOLETS LOCKET
Gold with white front & bouquet of violets. Holds 2 pictures. S.S.P. $8.00
1973-75 GODDESS DIANA PENDANT NECKLACE - Silver with etched frosted glass. S.S.P. $9.00
1973-75 AUTUMN GLORY CONVERTIBLE NECKLACE/PIN - Gold with pearls. S.S.P. $9.00

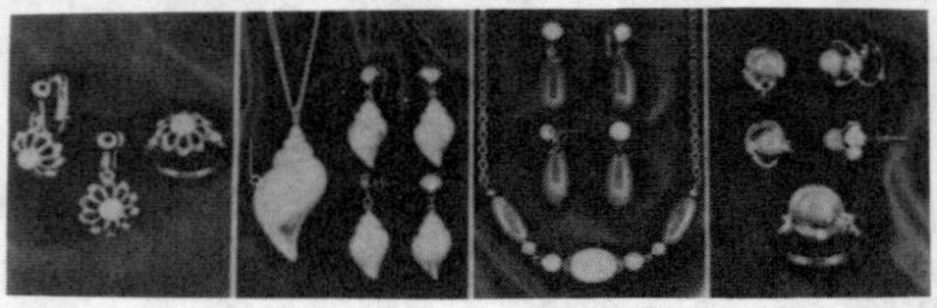

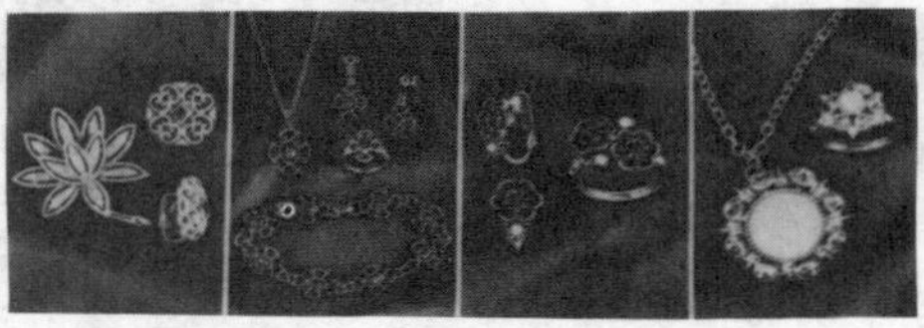

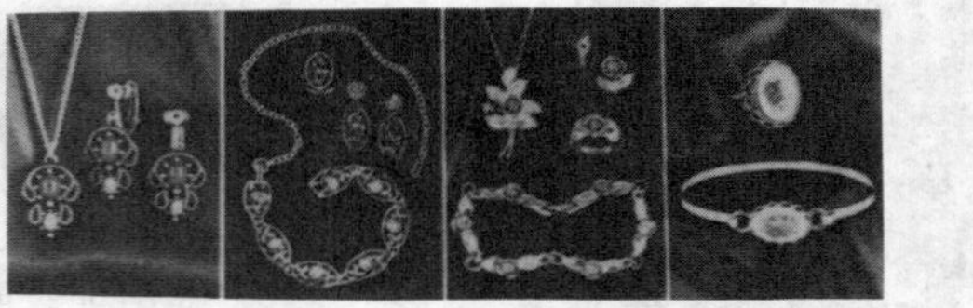

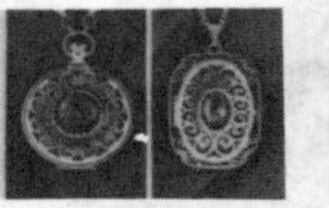

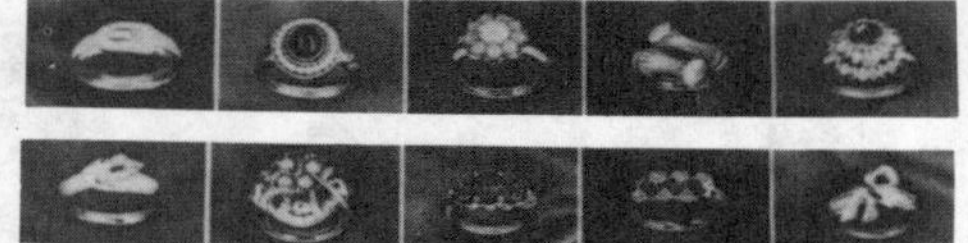

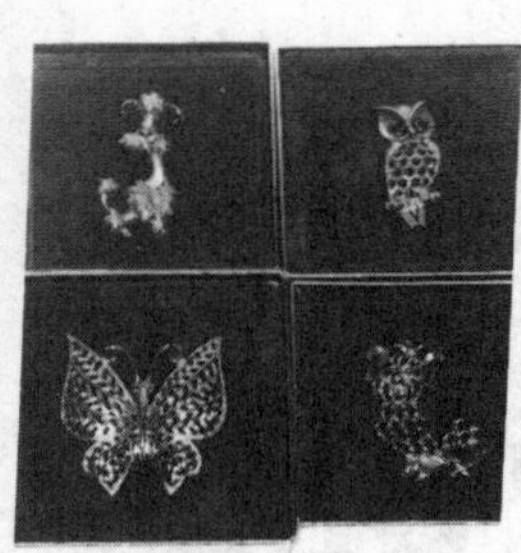

1972-73 POODLE PIN - Gold finish S.S.P. $4.00
1972 BUTTERFLY PIN - Silver finish with blue sets. S.S.P. $6.00
1972-73 OWLETTE PIN - gold finish with red eye sets. S.S.P. $4.00
1972-73 PEKINESE PIN - gold finish with green eye sets. S.S.P. $4.00

1974-75 PALE FIRE COLLECTION
Silver toned with simulated coral, surrounded by rhinestones. Necklace with 24" chain. S.S.P. $8.00. Ring S.S.P. $7. Earrings S.S.P. $8.00

1972 ROPE TWIST NECKLACE
Gold with turquoise. S.S.P. $10.00

1973 SONNET CONVERTIBLE NECKLACE/BRACELET - White with gold. S.S.P. $9.00

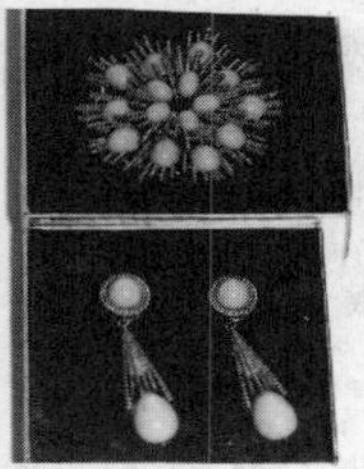

72 AZURENE PIN
ld with turquoise sets. S.S.P. $8.00
72 AZURENE CLIP EARRINGS
ld with turquoise sets. S.S.P. $6.00

72 LOVE BLOSSOMS
ld with blue flowers & rhinestone nters. Convertible necklace/pin. S.S.P. .00, pierced earrings with removable tals, S.S.P. $6.00, clip earrings S.S.P. .00

1973-75 ROYAL OCCASION
Gold with simulated topaze. Necklace S.S.P. $5.00. Pierced earrings S.S.P. $7.00 Ring S.S.P. $7.00

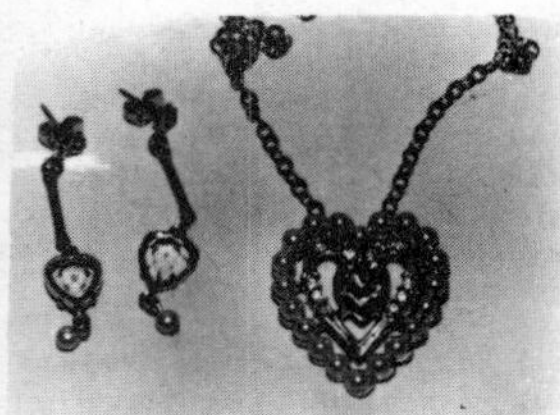

1974-75 DEAR HEART COLLECTION
Silver tone with simulated pink sapphire with pearls and rhinestones.
Pierced earrings S.S.P. $8.00. Necklace with 18" chain S.S.P. $7.00.

1972-73 MULTI-STRAND CONVERTIBLE
Necklace/Bracelet. Silver finish. S.S.P. $10.00

1972-73 CONVERTIBLE CREATION
Necklace/Bracelet/Belt. Gold finish. 36" long. S.S.P. $12.00

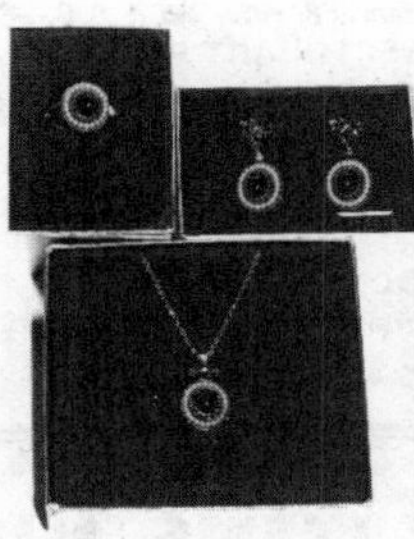

1973 BLACK CABOCHON
Black Cabachon circled with pearls.
1973-76 Ring S.S.P. $7.00, Necklace S.S.P. $6.00, Convertible earrings S.S.p. $7.00.

1973-76 BARONESS JEWELRY
Gold with jade like stones. Ring S.S.P. $6.00, Earrings S.S.P. $6.00, Necklace S.S.P. $7.00, Bracelet S.S.P. $8.00

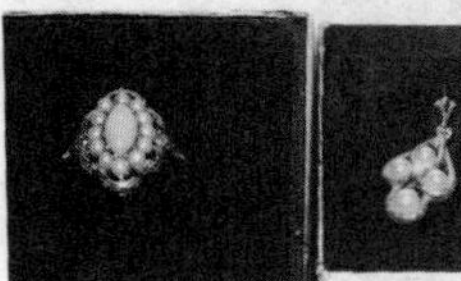

1972-73 SERENA RING
Gold with pearls & large pink stone. S.S.P. $8.00
1972-73 TOUCH OF BEAUTY PIERCED EARRINGS
Gold with pearls & one pink set, S.S.P. $7.00

1973-75 SIERRA JEWELRY
Silver & simulated turquoise. Necklace S.S.P. $8.00, Ring S.S.P. $5.00, Bracelet S.S.P. $9.00

1974-75 QUEENSBURY JEWELRY
Antiqued gold with simulated amethyst and pearls. Ring S.S.P. $7.00, Pierced Earrings S.S.P. S.S.P. $8.00, Necklace with 24" chain S.S.P. $7.00

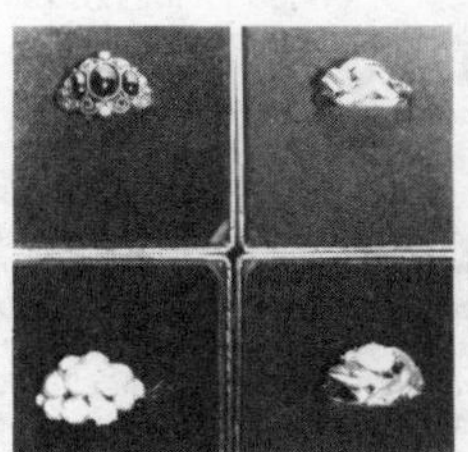

1972-76 MIDNIGHT SPLENDOR RING
Silver with black stones. S.S.P. $8.00
1973 FRENCH KNOT RING
Silver finish. S.S.P. $6.00
1972-73 ARABESQUE CLUSTER RING
Gold with pink sets & 2 rhinestones. S.S.P. $8.00
1972-73 FIRE FLOWER RING
Gold with simulated fire opal. S.S.P. $7.00

1972-73 CREATION-IN-BLUE
Silver with blue stone surrounded by rhinestones. Necklace/Pin S.S.P. $10.00, convertible pierced earrings S.S.P. $8.00, Ring S.S.P. $9.00

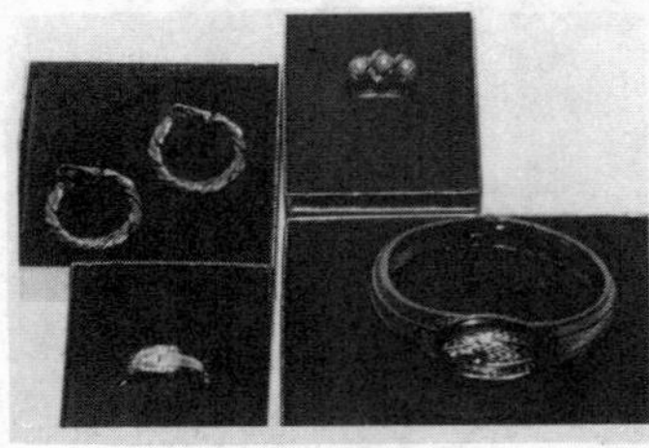

1972-75 TWISTED HOOP CLIP EARRINGS
Gold finish. S.S.P. $5.00
1973-75 BUCKLE RING
Gold finish with rhinestones. S.S.P. $8.00
1973-76 TRIPLE TWIST RING
Gold with pearls. S.S.P. $6.00
1972-73 BUCKLE BRACELET
Gold finish. S.S.P. $9.00

1973 OVALESQUE PENDANT NECKLACE
Gold tone. S.S'P. $8.00
1973 GRANADA PENDANT NECKLACE
Gold with ruby stone. S.S.P. $8.00
1972-75 PURPLE PENDANT NECKLACE
Gold with amethyst surrounded with seed pearls. S.S.P. $9.00

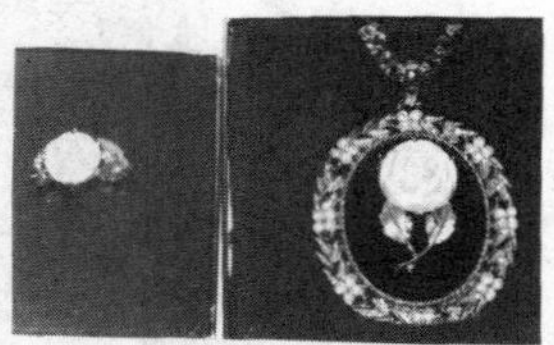

1973 SERENA ROSE
Gold with coral rose. Ring S.S.P. $7.00
Necklace mirrored back S.S.P. $9.00

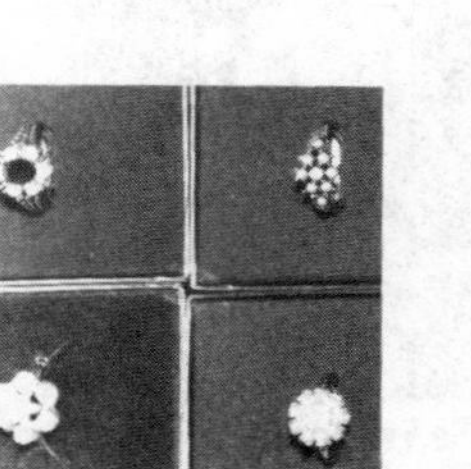

1973-76 ROSE GLOW RING
Gold with pearls & ruby set. S.S.P. $8.00
1973-75 SWEETHEART RING
Gold with pearls & turquoise beads. S.S.P. $6.00
1972-73 LUSTRE RING
Gold with pearls & turquoise sets. S.S.P. $8.00
1973-76 MOONLUSTER RING
Gold with pink beads / baroque pearl. S.S.P. $7.00

1973-76 EVENING SPLENDOR
Silver with pearls. Ring has rhinestone and pearls. Pierced earrings S.S.P. $7.00
Ring S.S.P. $7.00

PAPER ITEMS MISC.

CATALOGS - AVON 1930-57
Top Row - Left to Right -
1930-36 10" x 7" dark blue, silver Avon on cover. C.M.V. $20.00 to $50.00 depending on condition. 1936-48 7¼" x 10½" size, green cover, gold tulip A. C.M.V. $15.00 to $40.00. 1948-54 7¼" x 10½", green cover, Avon in gold letters. C.M.V. $10.00 to $30.00.
Bottom Row - Left to Right -
1954 a special gold cover catalog for Honor Presidents Award Reps. C.M.V. $20.00 ea. 1954-57 general issue was green cover 7½" x 10½", gold Avon & 4A design. C.M.V. $10.00 - $20.00. 1956 Honor Award, red cover catalog, gold Avon & 4A design. C,M.V. $25.00
Each of these catalogs was made to install or remove pages. The dates given reflect the years that each cover was used. Each catalog was changed each year on the inner pages. WANTED: If you have any Avon Sales Catalogs for 1941-43-44-45 -47 & wish to sell them, please contact Bud Hastin, Box 9868, Kansas City, Mo. 64134.

1920's-30's SALES BROCHURES
Fold out sales brochures given to customers by CPC & Avon representatives. Each one shows all items sold in regular sales catalog. These are rare and in color. Left to right - 1926 C.M.V. $50.00; C.M.V. 1929 $35.00; 1931 to 33 same cover C.M.V. $35.00; 1935 C.M.V. $35.00; 1939 C.M.V. $25.00; A 1933 brochure is laid out on bottom to see all the products offered

1916-29 CPC SALES CATALOG
On bottom is black hard bound CPC Sales Catalog with 32 to 40 color pages. Book is 10½" x 16" in size. The hard bound book was first issued in 1916 in the big size & last used in 1921. Gold lettering on front. 1922 to 1929 the black catalog is soft cover & 34 pages in color. 10" x 14½" in size. These catalogs are usually not dated & very hard to find. CMV range from $25.00 to very bad condition to $200.00 for a mint new condition catalog. Each year a new book was issued.

TALOGS CPC
6 CPC Catalog shown on top left - right 1898, bottom right 1908 & tom left is 1915. Each one shows the n sold during that period by CPC & s prices. 1915 was the last small catalog ted, 1916 they went to the large black d bound color books. For comparison size, the 1896 is 4½ in. wide & 6 5/8 in. h. No value can be set on this type of k because of their rarity. If you have owledge of any old CPC Catalogs or tlooks for sale, please contact Bud stin, Box 9868, Kansas City, . 64134, as he is always in the market buy them for information to pass on to u, the collector.

ORDER BOOKS Left to Right
1920's CPC on cover (white cover)
C.M.V. $20.00
1930's Tulip A design (white cover)
C.M.V. $15.00
1940's Script A design (blue cover)
C.M.V. $10.00
1950's 4A design (green cover)
C.M.V. $5.00
1960's 4A design (white cover)
C.M.V. $2.00
All must be in new condition for C.M.V. given.

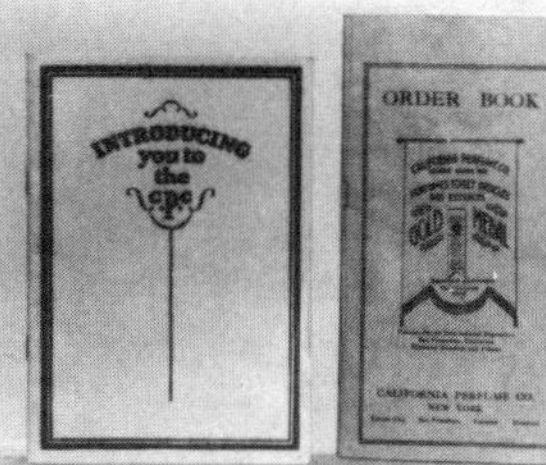

LEFT 1928 CPC INTRO BOOKLET
30 page booklet used by reps to start selling Avon. CMV $25.00 mint.
RIGHT 1922 CPC ORDER BOOKLET
Used by reps to keep records of their orders. CMV $12.00 mint.

1916-18 CPC MAIL ORDER CATALOG
(Left) 4½" x 6" gray cover 40 page booklet sent to customers in areas where CPC reps did not call. Rare. No price established.
1898 CPC CATALOG
(Right) 5" x 7" size blue cover & 64 pages in blue paper. Used by CPC reps to sell products. Eureka Trade Mark on back cover. Very Rare. No price established.

FROM THE ONSTOT COLLECTION
LEFT TO RIGHT
1912 INSTRUCTION MANUAL
Used by CPC Sales Managers. CMV not established
1912 CATALOG - CPC
64 page sales catalog used by reps. CMV not established
1909 WOMAN BEAUTIFUL BOOKLET
Small booklet on massage cream. CMV not established.

937 POCKET CATALOG
A small fold out leaflet brochure left with he customer to buy Avon products .M.V. $25.00 mint.

ORDER BOOKS — Left to Right
1933, 1937, 1942. Far right 1939 green order book cover. CMV $15.00 each mint.

FROM THE ONSTOT COLLECTION
LEFT TO RIGHT
1920 BABY BOOK
CMV not estabilshed
1898 CATALOG CPC
62 page sales catalog. Only has illustrations, not pictures, of products. Book is dated 1898. CMV not established.
1897 CATALOG - CPC
62 page sales catalog. Book is dated 1897. CMV not established.

1967 CALENDAR
Avon Calling calendar. CMV $8.00 mint.

LEFT 1896 CPC CALLING CARD
Has list of products on backside & CPC Co. 126 Chambers St., New York on front. CMV $25.00.
RIGHT 1893 CPC SALES CATALOG
Small 30 page booklet on products. Contains no pictures. Rare. No price established.

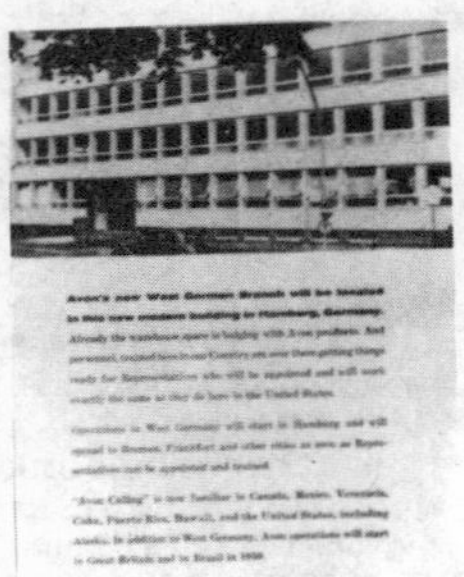

1959 WEST GERMAN BRANCH OPENING CARD
Card introducing the starting of Avon operations in Hamburg, Germany. CMV $10.00 mint.

1959 CHRISTMAS CARD - CANADA
Avon Christmas card given to customers by reps in Canada. CMV $3.00

GREETING CARDS FROM AVON
Left to Right
1977 FATHERS DAY CARD
Red & white card. CMV $1.00
1977 SEYMOUR KENT CARD
Red card, came with white lace handkerchief made by Desco. CMV $1.50
1969 FATHERS DAY CARD
Straight 8 on front. CMV $1.50

1980 ORDER BOOK COVER
You never looked so good on cover. CMV 50c.
1980 COLORCREME EYE SHADOW SAMPLE
Blue & white card. CMV 25c.

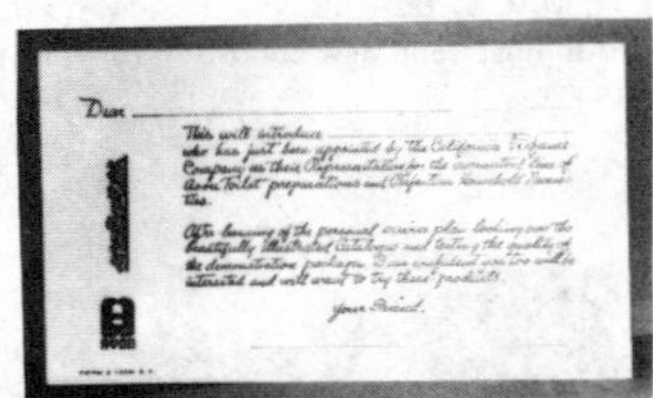

1930'S CPC LADY INTRODUCTION CARD
3½" x 5¼" card used by reps to introduce themselves to customers. CMV $2.00

1970'S GREETING CARDS - AVON
Many different cards used by Avon managers & reps for different occassions. CMV about 50c each

1978 AVON NOTE CARDS
Box of blank Avon note cards. CMV $4.00 MB

LEFT 1978 NAPKIN 'SWEET DREAMS'
White napkin with moon & sunrise scene. CMV $1.00
RIGHT 1979 NAPKIN 'GETTING BETTER EVERY DAY'
For Presidents Club members. White napkin, red letters. CMV $1.00
BOTTOM 1978 NAPKIN 'GROUND BREAKING CEREMONY'
Red napkin from Pasadena branch ground breaking ceremony, April 13, 1978. CMV $1.50

1976 WASHINGTON'S ACCEPTANCE SPEECH
Reprinted for Avon reps in C2-76. Outer cover holds copy of Washington hand written letter. Avon printed on back. CMV $7.00 mint.

1972 DEEP WOODS - ST. REGIS CARD
Special thank you card for Avon reps. from St. Regis Paper Co. CMV $1.00
1970'S DAVE'S WAITING PICTURE
Picture of David Mitchell, Chairman of Avon Products. No price established.
1960'S SALES CHART
Green & white paper. CMV $2.00

1976 MOTHERS DAY CARD
Given to customers in Mothers Day orders 1976 by Avon reps. CMV $1.00

1980 CALENDAR - AVON
Large Avon calendar given to customers by Avon reps. Came in big envelope. CMV $1.00 each mint in envelope.

1960 ORDER BOOK
CMV $2.00
1958 CALL TAG PADS
Pad of tear off sheets left by Avon lady. CMV $3.00 pad.

LEFT CPC BOOKLET
Cover says 'Introducing You To The CPC' CMV $25.00
RIGHT 1945 GREAT OAK BOOKLET
20 page, blue cover. Given to reps in 1945. Written by D. H. McConnel, founder of CPC in 1903. Came with letter from Russel Rooks who bacame President of Avon. Rare. CMV $50.00 with letter.

1979 TEAM LEADER ORGANIZER
10½" x 12" size light brown binder organizer. Came in white box. Team Leader Organizer on front of binder. CMV $7.00 MB.

70'S AUTO HANDBOOK
ed plastic 2 ring instruction manual employees of Avon with company ised cars. CMV $5.00

LEFT 1935 BUSINESS INTRO BOOK
20 page booklet on how to be a Avon lady. Used by Reps. CMV $5.00
RIGHT 1931 BUSINESS INTRO BOOK
17 page booklet on how to be a Avon lady. Used by reps. CMV $5.00

978 IVORY COAST AFRICA
ST ISSUE AVON CATALOG
7 page catalog given to each Avon manager in U.S. with letter from Avon Products announcing expansion into Africa. CMV $4.00

1948 HOW TO CONDUCT GOOD SALES MEETINGS - BOOKLET
Black leatherette spiral bound. Booklet used by Avon managers. CMV $10.00

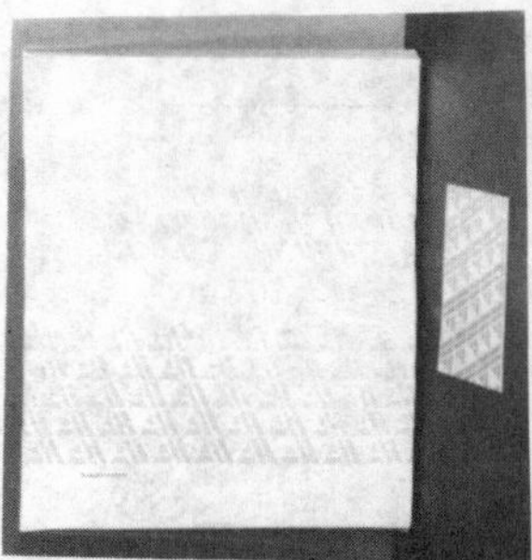

1978 NOTE SET PEOPLE TO PEOPLE
Box with matching outer sleeve with A's on it used by managers. About 100 notes in box & envelopes. CMV $8.00 MB.

1978 AVON CATALOG - HONG KONG
Sales Catalog from Hong Kong. CMV $2.00

1953 PROMISE TO MYSELF BOOKLET
23 page booklet published by Irene Nunemaker & Avon Products Inc. CMV $5.00

1960'S NOTEBOOK COVERS - MANAGERS
3 different blue plastic binders used by Avon managers. One is Avon Beauty Notes, Group Meetings & Avon on 3rd one. Small one is red. CMV $3.00 each.

1973 CIRCLE OF EXCELLENCE ITEMS
Given to managers on C of E trip to Bermuda. White plastic airline ticket holder, CMV $10.00 Menu, Program of Events, Airline Menu, CMV $5.00 each item. Honor Roll Booklet, blue & gold booklet listing all C of E managers for 1973. CMV $10.00

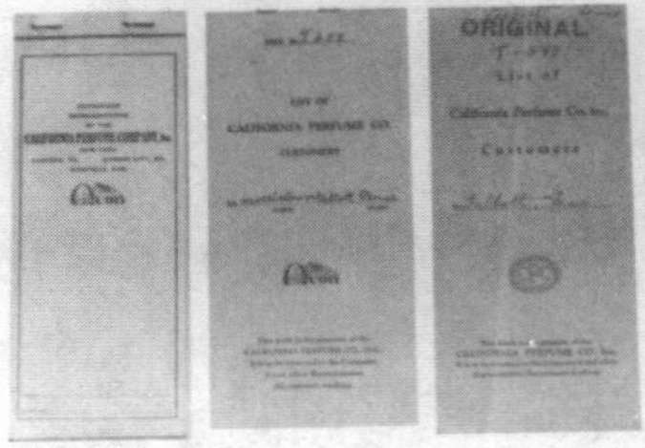

LEFT 1930 ORDER BOOK CPC AVON
C.M.V. $15.00 mint.
CENTER 1930 AVON CUSTOMER LIST BOOKLET
8 pages C.M.V. $5.00 mint.
RIGHT 1928 CPC CUSTOMER LIST BOOKLET
12 pages C.M.V. $8.00 mint

1950's CHRISTMAS CARD
C.M.V. $1.00 each.
1970 AVON COASTER
Different varieties. C.M.V. $1.00 each.

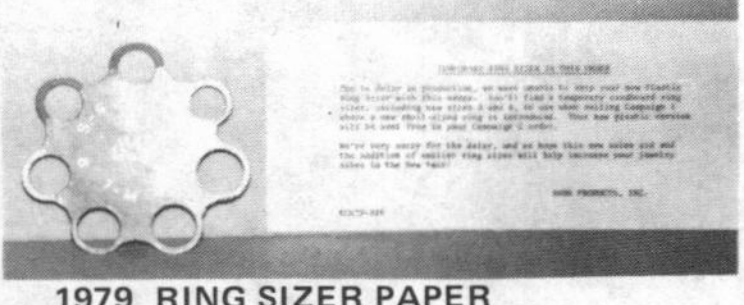

1979 RING SIZER PAPER
Blue & white paper Avon ring sizer issued before plastic sizers were delivered. Very short issue to Avon reps, issued C25-79. Size 3 to 9. CMV $1.00 mint.

1930's-40's GREEN ADDRESS BOOK
Green leather, gold A design. C.M.V. $10.00
1956 HONOR AWARD BOOK COVER
Red plastic, gold design. C.M.V. $7.50
1900 JOE JEFFERSON CPC PAD
50 sheets, scratch pad. C.M.V. $35.00 mint.

1927 CALOPAD SANITARY NAPK
Cardboard box holds 12 napkins. O.S
50¢ C.M.V. $35.00 M.B.

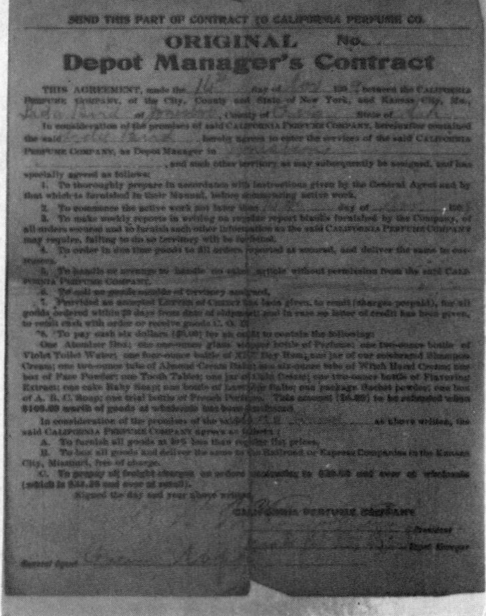

SEND THIS PART OF CONTRACT TO CALIFORNIA PERFUME CO.
ORIGINAL No.
Depot Manager's Contract
THIS AGREEMENT, made the 14th day of 190 , between the CALIFORNIA PERFUME COMPANY, of the City, County and State of New York, and Kansas City, Mo.,

1909 DEPOT MANAGERS CONTRACT CPC
Paper agreement between CPC & sales lady.
C.M.V. $40.00 mint

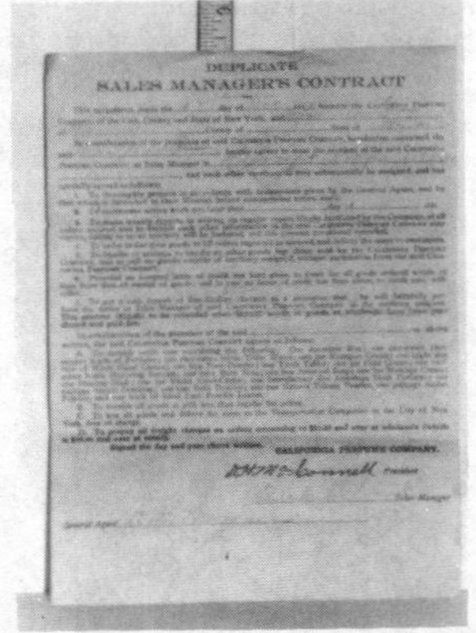

1913 SALES MANAGERS CONTRACT
Paper agreement for Avon ladies in early 1900s. Signed by D.H.McConnell, founder of Avon. C.M.V. $25.00

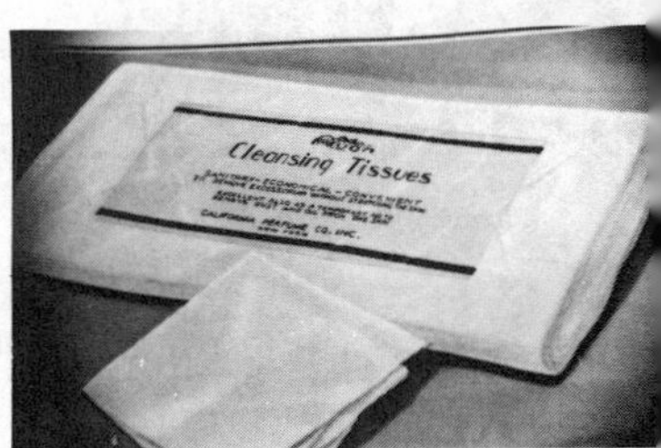

1930-32 CLEANSING TISSUE
Wrapped in cellophane. Package of 135 sheets. O.S.P. 50¢ C.M.V. $15.00 mint.

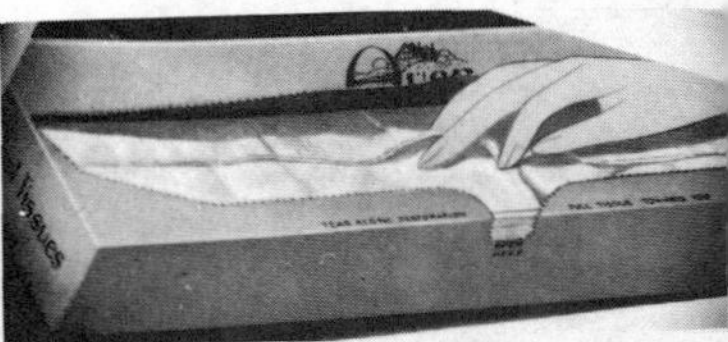

1932-36 FACIAL TISSUES
Box of 160 tissues. O.S.P. 50¢
C.M.V. $20.00 mint.

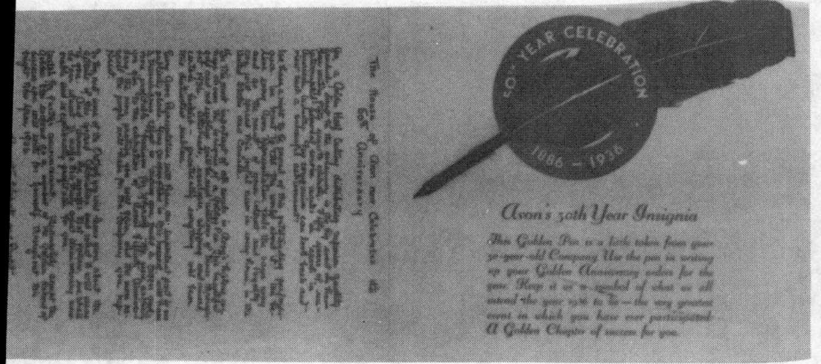

36 50TH ANNIVERSARY GOLD UILL PEN & LETTER
nt to representatives to announce the th year celebration. The circle stands the "Avon Family Circle", the feather d quill indicated the opportunities to Feather your nests. Comes complete with attached 50th anniversary letter. It folds in center. Did not come separate. C.M.V. complete as pictured, $45.00 mint.

CHRISTMAS AVON CATALOGS
Starting in the early 1930's thru 1956, Avon printed a special Xmas Sales Catalog showing many gifts never sold at any other time. These catalogs are rare & hard to find. C.M.V. 1930's $40.00 each. 1940's $35.00 each. 1950's $25.00 each.

1967 CHRISTMAS CATALOG
In upper right part of picture is special hard bound edition. C.M.V. $15.00 mint.

1905 - 74 OUTLOOK
Outlooks were first printed in 1905 & given only to sales reps. of CPC & Avon. They were to show new items coming out & also show awards they could win. The Outlook was discontinued in 1974 & the name was changed to (Avon Calling). If you have any old Outlooks 1939 or older & want to sell them, please contact Bud Hastin

Outlooks were given for each sales campaign during the year. C.M.V. 1905 to 1930, $5.00 to $15.00; 1930 to 1939 $2.00 to $5.00; 1940-49 $1.00 to $5.00; 1950 to 1959 $1.00 to $4.00; 1960 to 1965 $1.00 to $3.00; 1966 to 1969 50¢ to $1.00; 1970 to 1976 10¢ to 25¢ each Outlook,

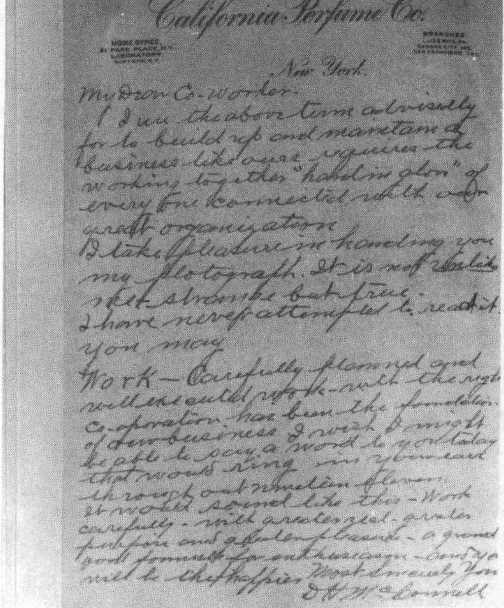

California Perfume Co.

New York.

My Dear Co-worker.
I use the above term advisedly for to build up and maintain a business like ours requires the working together "hand in glove" of every one connected with our great organization.
I take pleasure in handing you my photograph. It is not [illegible] but true. I have never attempted to reach it you may.
Work — Carefully planned and well executed work — with the right co-operation has been the foundation of our business. I wish I might be able to say a word to you today that would ring in your ears throughout nineteen eleven. It would sound like this — Work carefully — with greater zeal — greater purpose and abundant pleasure — a grand good formula for enthusiasm — and you will be the happier. Most sincerely Yours
D.H. McConnell

1900's CPC D.H. McCONNELL LETTER
On CPC Letterhead. Hand written by D.H. McConnell, founder of Avon to his factory workers. C.M.V. for any hand written D.H. McConnell letter dated 1890's to 1930's would be $25.00 to $50.00 depending on buyer.

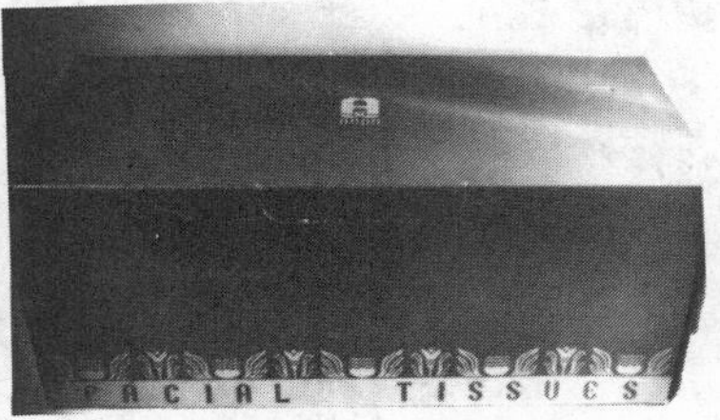

1937-44 AVON FACIAL TISSUE
Turquoise & white paper box - Rare O.S.P. 50¢ C.M.V. $20.00 mint.

1971 DESIGNERS COLLECTION CHRISTMAS CARDS - Box of 25 Avon Xmas cards, all the same design. Came in 36 different designs, No. 1 shown. O.S.P. $4.00 to $10.00 per box. Back of each card marked Avon Products, Inc. & gives the card number. C.M.V. ea. card 50¢ to $1.00.

1909 CPC CALENDAR
C.M.V. $75.00

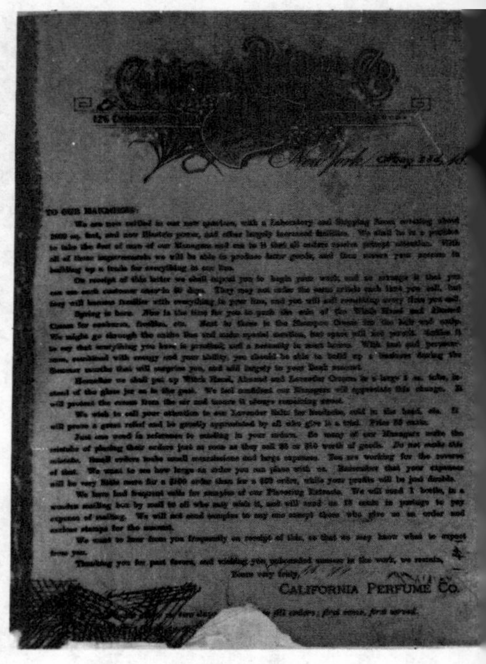

TO OUR MANAGERS:

CALIFORNIA PERFUME CO.

1896 LETTER FROM CPC
On CPC Letterhead. Letter to CPC managers. C.M.V. $45.00

1975 AVON HERITAGE ALMANAC
1975 calendar given to District Managers only. Duplicate of 1929 calendar, each page shows different outlook, Limited edition, 2,678 given. C.M.V. $25.00

1910 CPC CALENDAR
9" wide - 12 5/16" high. Printed in 6 colors. C.M.V. $75.00

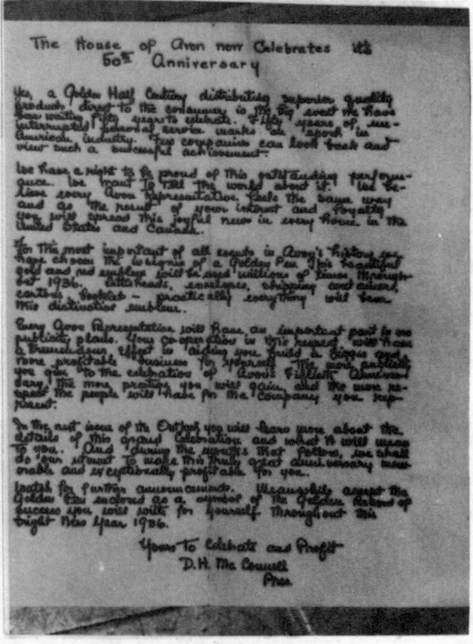

The House of Avon now Celebrates its 50th Anniversary

Yours to Celebrate and Profit
D.H. Mc Connell
Pres.

1936 LETTER FROM AVON
Misc. letters from Avon may vary in price depending on the year. Any letters personally signed by D.H. McConnell, founder of Avon in his own hand writing should be worth at least $25.00. Letter shown is a copy. C.M.V. $15.00 mint.

The 500 Club Certificate

1930's CPC FIVE HUNDRED CLUB CERTIFICATE - Sent to a representative when she completes $500.00 worth of net business. C.M.V. $20.00 mint.

EARLY 1900's CPC CHRISTMAS GREETING CARD - 1¢ Post card sent out at Xmas time. 126 Chambers Street, New York is the return address. C.M.V. $25.00

1960's-70's ORDER BOOK
Misc. Avon Order Books used by Reps. C.M.V. 50¢ each.

EARLY 1930's CPC AVON FIVE HUNDRED CLUB - Certificate given to representatives for selling $500.00 worth of Avon products. C.M.V. $15.00 each. Mint.

1960's-70's CHILDREN'S COLOR BOOKS
Small World, Mickey Mouse, Peanuts, I Wish I Could. C.M.V. $2.00 each.

1968 BUSINESS CARD - AVON
C.M.V. $3.00 box.

1961 ROSE STAMPS
Page of 75 Rose Stamps for Avon Rep. use in C-2-1961. Stamps say "Avons 75th Year". C.M.V. $20.00

1966 CALENDAR
Quarterly calendar for Sept., Oct., Nov., Dec. showing Avon for the 1966 Christmas selling season.
C.M.V. $5.00

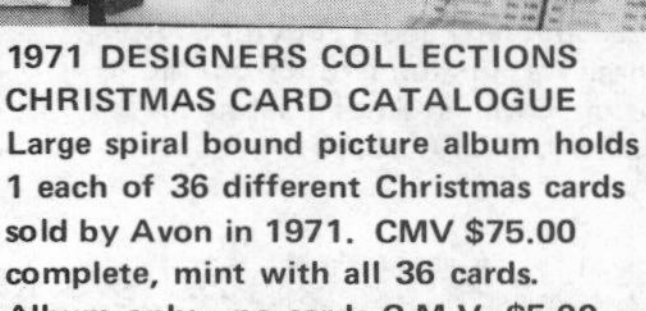

1971 DESIGNERS COLLECTIONS CHRISTMAS CARD CATALOGUE
Large spiral bound picture album holds 1 each of 36 different Christmas cards sold by Avon in 1971. CMV $75.00 complete, mint with all 36 cards.
Album only - no cards C.M.V. $5.00

1971 PLACE MATS
Four Seasons - Robert Woods signed plastic place mats for Avon. Had choice of one of the four when you bought certain products.
C.M.V. $3.00 each.

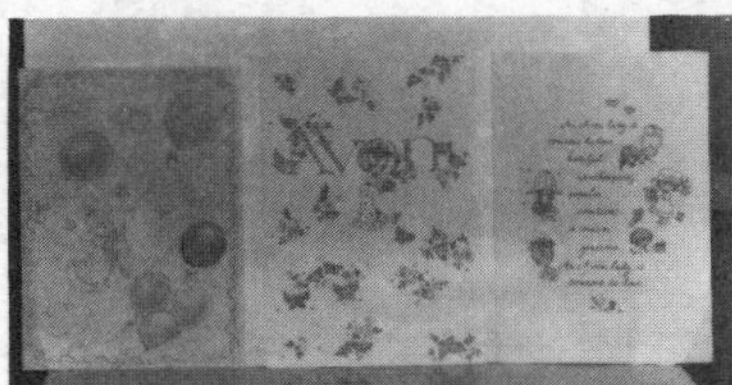

1970's AVON CARDS
Sent to representatives. C.M.V. $2.00 each. Many different ones.

1950's AD DISPLAYS
Magazine advertising on hard backs.
C.M.V. $15.00 each.

1973 PLAN BOOKS FOR MANAGERS
C.M.V. $5.00

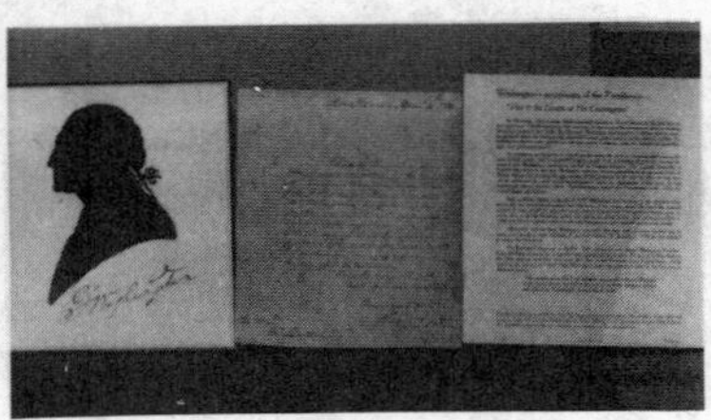

1976 GEORGE WASHINGTON REPRESENTATIVE GIFT LETTER
Folder (on left) and a copy of a letter George Washington wrote from Mt. Vernon. Given at Sales Meeting in February. C.M.V. $5.00

1962 MANAGERS SALES MEETING NOTE BOOK - Campaign 15, 16, 17, 18. Sales meeting plans. Red with white Xmas Tree. C.M.V. $25.00

1935 AVON BEAUTY SERVICE BOOK
30 page booklet showing how to apply Avon cosmetics. Used by Reps. Came in Avon CPC envelope. C.M.V. $10.00 mint with envelope.

1975 BIRTHDAY CARD — AVON
Birthday cards made only for Avon & sent to Reps on their birthday. Avon on back and inside. This type of card has been used for years. C.M.V. $1.00 each.

1920 CPC INSTRUCTIONAL MANUAL
14 page booklet used to train early day Avon Reps. Tells them how and what to do to be a sales lady for CPC. No pictures. C.M.V. $20.00

1937 PAVING THE WAY
Booklet used by Reps in 1930s to help train them for better sales. Tulip A on cover. C.M.V. $8.00

1964 BEAUTY BOOK
128 page book used by Reps on beauty counciling. C.M.V. $4.00
1967 BEAUTY BOOK
140 page book used by Reps on beauty counciling. C.M.V. $4.00

1972-74 CREATIVE NEEDLECRAFT FROM AVON - Embroidery kits included picture, yarn, needle & instructions. Came in many patterns. C.M.V. $8.50 mint set.

1972 MANAGERS INTRODUCTION BOOK
Turquoise binder holds 25 glossy pages. Managers use to get new Avon ladies to sell Avon. C.M.V. $7.00

1945 MANAGERS INFORMATION BOOKLET
8¼"x 9" 18 page booklet for managers to show new Avon Reps for general information on Avon products. The cover of this booklet is the same art work Avon products used to make the 1977 National Association of Avon Clubs plate advertised in C26-77 Avon Calling. C.M.V. $15.00

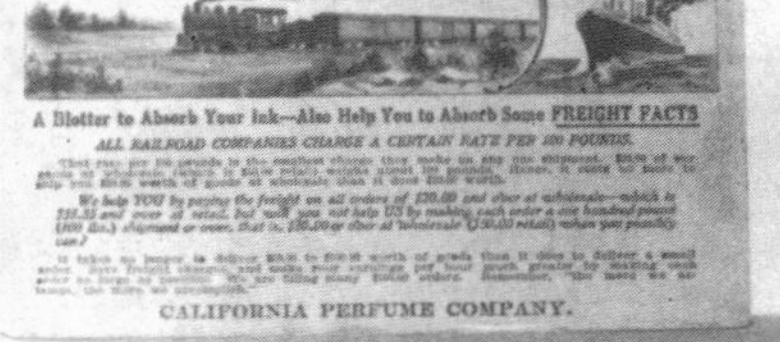

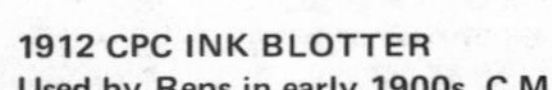

1912 CPC INK BLOTTER
Used by Reps in early 1900s. C.M.V. $25.00

Avon Advertising

Avon and magazine advertising began in March, 1906, but was rather short lived with only a few California Perfume ads appearing in Good Housekeeping magazine. For the next thirty years the company relied on their representatives and the worth of their products to spread their name and gain new customers.

By 1936 a dramatic change took place in the company's attitude and in April of that year a national advertising campaign was begun. Once again the ever popular Good Housekeeping was used as their advertising vehicle. The first advertisements were black and white and not very impressive in comparison to their competitor's full color, full page layouts. Public response was good enough, however, to continue the series and in 1938 Avon ads began to appear in the Christian Science Monitor as well as Good Housekeeping. The following year Woman's Home Companion was added and so on until by the end of the 1940's Avon ads were appearing in 15 of the nations leading publications.

Along the way, color ads and full page ads, as well as some two page ads were introduced. To date Avon ads have appeared in over 40 different magazines and in 1975 found their way into some metropolitan newspapers.

We do not know how many Avon collectors have already begun to collect the ads, but the number is certain to grow once everyone is aware of their existance. Not only do they reflect the company's public appearance, but they also picture many of Avon's now collectable products.

To date Avon has produced over 500 different magazine advertisements; a spectacular number by any standard. Of these, many were published in as many as 12 magazines at the same time while others were produced for a specific market and appeared in only one publication making them quite naturally difficult to obtain. Other factors involved in valuing ads are the content, number of products shown and their collectability and naturally, age. Other considerations are size, ½ or full page and if it is in color or black and white.

The prices shown here are mainly in relation to age and degree of difficulty to find. The other factors mentioned will cause this price to fluctuate and the value shown should be considered only as a broad guide and by no means a definite price. This "Avon Advertising" section was prepared by Dalene Thomas, 8612 W. Warren Lane, Lakewood, CO 80227. For more information on "Avon Advertising", write to Dalene Thomas, enclosing a self-addressed, stamped envelope, if you wish to reply.

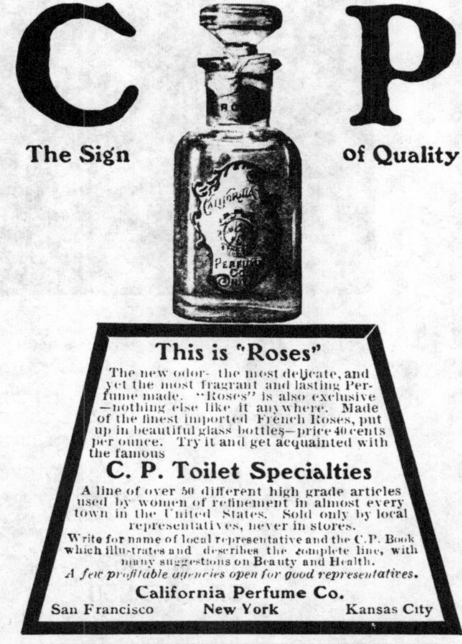

March 1906
Good Housekeeping Only
C.M.V. $5.00

March 1937
C.M.V. $1.50

April 1936
Good Housekeeping Only
C.M.V. $2.00

October 1939
C.M.V. $1.00

March 1945
C.M.V. $1.00

June 1946
C.M.V. $1.00

September 1947
C.M.V. $1.75

November 1949
C.M.V. $1.50

March 1952
C.M.V. $1.50

only Avon brings these
flattering fragrances to you!

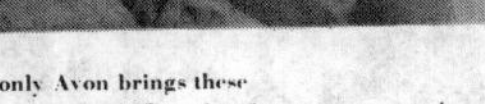

Your Avon Representative gives you friendly help in selecting your Avon Cosmetics and Toiletries

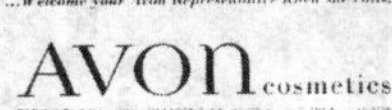

June - July 1954
C.M.V. 75¢

AVON'S NEW

FINDS A YOUNG MAN'S SPIRIT!

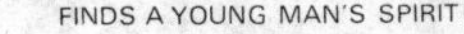

October 1962
C.M.V. 75¢

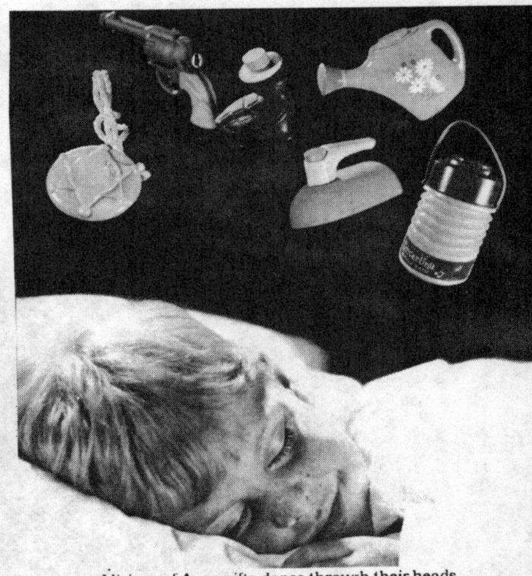

Visions of Avon gifts dance through their heads

AVON cosmetics

October 1964
C.M.V. $1.50

Women love these new Avon Cosmetics and

Imagine! You can select the newest, the finest, the most beau fully packaged cosmetics in the world *without stirring from yo home.* Glamorous make-up in all its intriguing new forms . scientifically formulated creams and lotions for the loving care your complexion . . . a wide and wonderful variety of fragranc for you to spray on, splash on, dust on, cream on — you choo these with the help of your Avon Representative.

AVON COSMETICS FOR ALL THE FAMILY ARE BROUGHT TO YOUR HOME BY YOUR AVON REPRESENTATI

January 1960
C.M.V. $1.50

September 1966
C.M.V. 75¢

November 1967
C.M.V. 75¢

November 1969
C.M.V. $2.00

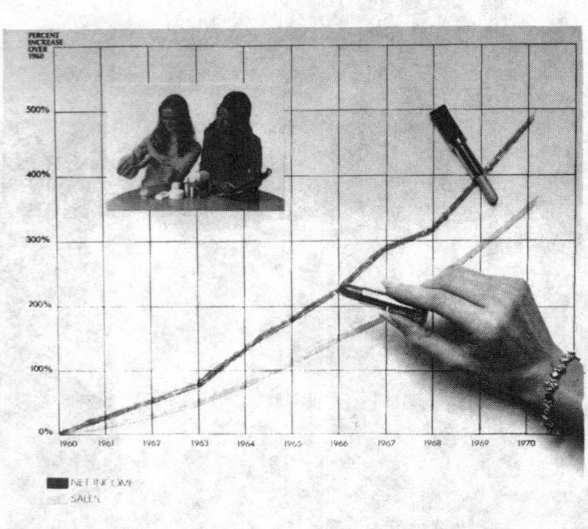

A graphic reminder from the world's leading manufacturer of cosmetics and toiletries.

May 1971
C.M.V. $2.00

PERFECTION ALL PRODUCTS

WARNING!! Grading condition is paramount on sets.
CMV can vary 50% on grade.
Refer to page 5 on Grading.

See Page 5 for Grading Examples on Mint Condition

940's PERFECTION RECIPE BOOK
ame in food coloring or flavoring sets. MV $12.00 mint.

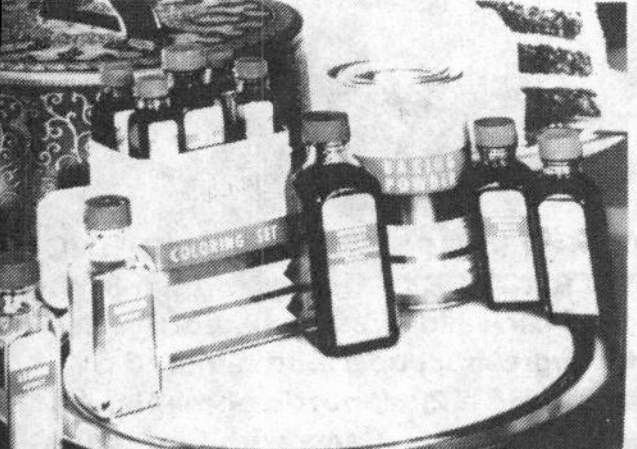

941-42 PERFECTION CAKE CHEST
rown & red designed cake chest has oloring set in can, 2 oz. bottles of lemon almond extract, 2 oz. bottles of maple black walnut falvoring, & 4 oz. bottle f vanilla. All bottle have red plastic caps. an of baking powder, recipe book, cake hest is same as 1938 to 1941. Avon erfection in bottom of cake pan. O.S.P. 3.95 C.M.V. set complete $110.00 M.B. hest only $35.00 mint.

1930s FOOD COLORING DIRECTIONS
Came in Perfection Food Coloring sets. CPC on back. CMV $10.00 mint.

1938-41 PERFECTION CAKE CHEST
Gold, red, brown, black cake chest. Contains can of baking powder, coloring set of 4 oz. vanilla extract. 2 oz. each of lemon & almond extract, 2 oz. each of black walnut & maple flavors. All have metal caps. recipe book. Avon Perfection in bottom of cake pan. O.S.P. $3.50 C.M.V. set complete $135.00 M.B. Chest only $35.00 mint.

1933-38 PERFECTION CAKE CHEST
Blue & gold cake pan 10½" in diameter contains Perfection coloring set, metal caps. Can of Perfection baking powder. Bottles contain lemon, maple, black walnut, almond & vanilla flavoring & recipe book. Avon Perfection in bottom of cake pan. O.S.P. $3.50 C.M.V. set complete $135.00. Chest only $35.00 mint.

1906 FOOD FLAVORING DEMONSTRATOR SET - Black leather covered wood case holds 24 - 1 oz. bottles of food flavoring. C.M.V. mint with all labels, $2,000.00 complete

1895-1920 HARMLESS COLORING SET
Set of 8 - ½ oz. bottles with cork stoppers came in wood box. Lemon, chocolate, lilac, coffee, orange, red, violet & green. O.S.P. 50¢ C.M.V. $400.00 set in box or $45.00 each bottle.

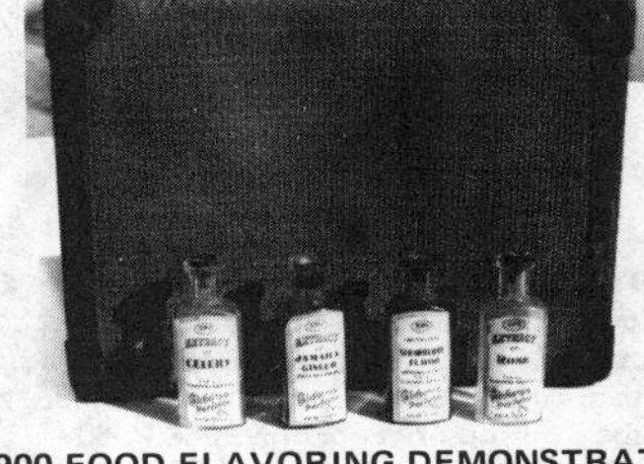

1900 FOOD FLAVORING DEMONSTRATOR SET - Straw covered wood case holds 20 bottles of food flavoring extracts. C.M.V. complete set mint $1,600.00

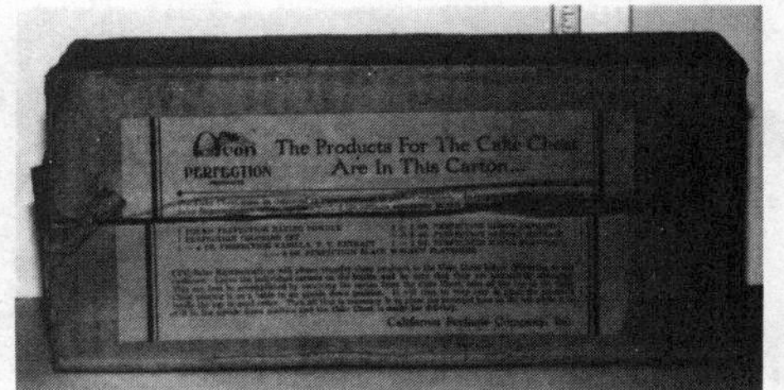

193 CAKE CHEST PRODUCT BOX
CPC box with list of all contents that came in perfection cake chest. CMV $10.00 box only.

1920 HARMLESS COLORS SET
Cardboard box holds 8 - ½ oz. bottles with cork stoppers, Red, chocolate, green, coffee, lemon, velvet, orange, lilac. O.S.P. 50¢ C.M.V. $300.00 M.B.

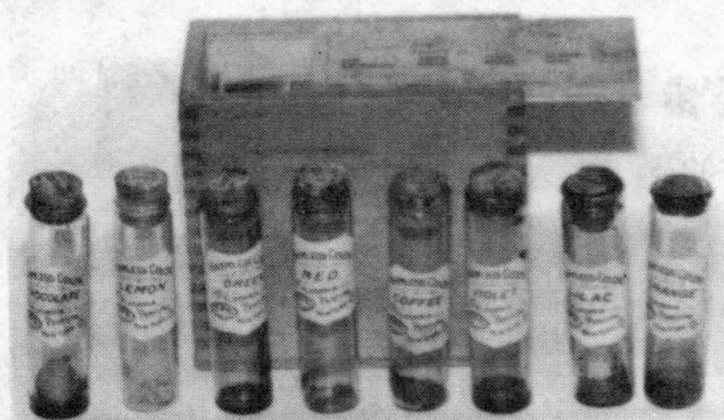

1915 HARMLESS COLORS SET
Wood box with slide open lid, paper label on top. Holds 8 - ½ oz. bottles with cork stoppers. Paper labels on top of cork & front of bottles also. Came in chocolate, lemon, green, red, coffee, violet, lilac & orange. OSP 50c, CMV $350.00 MB.

1934-41 PERFECTION COLORING SET
Orange, brown & white metal cans hold 4- ½ oz. bottles in blue, yellow, brown & green coloring & 2 oz. bottle of red. All have metal caps. Came with Perfection Cook Booklet. O.S.P. 85¢ C.M.V. $75.00 M.B. Can only $15.00 mint.

1930-34 PERFECTION FLAVORING EXTRACT SET - In orange, brown & white can, has 2 oz. vanilla & ½ oz. ea. of almond, lemon, peppermint, & winte green extract. All have cork stoppers. O.S.P. $1.00 C.M.V. $125.00. Can only $15.00 mint.

1910-15 HARMLESS COLORS SET
Wood box, slide open lid, holds 8 - ½ oz. bottles with cork stoppers. Red, chocolate, green, coffee, lemon, velvet, orange, lilac. Labels on top of corks only. O.S.P. 50¢ C.MV. $350.00 M.B.

1941-48 PERFECTION COLORING SET
Orange, brown & white can holds 2 oz. red coloring & ½ oz. ea. of yellow, brown, blue & green coloring, red plastic caps. O.S.P. 98¢ C.M.V. $65.00 M.B. Set came with Avon Recipe Booklet. Add $10.00 for Recipe Booklet. Can only $15.00 mint. This set also came in 1934-41 can. Only can is marked Avon and not C.P.C. Came with red caps and 1941-48 labels. C.M.V. $70.00 M.B.

1934-41 PERFECTION FLAVORING EXTRACT SET - Orange, brown & white metal can holds four ½ oz. bottles in wintergreen, peppermint, almond & lemon and a 2 oz. bottle of maple. All have metal caps. Came with Perfection Cook Booklet. C.M.V. booklet only $10.00. O.S.P. $1.00. C.M.V. $75.00 M.B. Can only $15.00 mint.

1920-30 PERFECTION COLORING SET
Bottles of green, yellow, blue, brown in ½ oz. size. Red in 2 oz. size. All have cork stoppers. O.S.P. 74¢ C.M.V. $250.00

1941-48 PERFECTION FLAVORING SET - Red, white & bronze can holds 2 oz. bottle of vanilla, ½ oz. bottle of maple, black walnut, almond & lemon. All have red plastic caps. O.S.P. $1.15 C.M.V. $60.00 complete set mint. Set came with Avon Recipe Booklet in can. Add $10.00 for Recipe Booklet. Can only $12.00 mint.

1930-34 PERFECTION COLORING SET
Brown & orange paper box. Red coloring in 2 oz. size, brown, blue, yellow, green coloring in ½ oz. size. All have cork stoppers. O.S.P. 85¢ C.M.V. $160.00 M.B. Box only $20.00 mint.

1893-1908 FLAVORING EXTRACT
8 & 16 oz. bottle, glass stopper. Came in all flavors listed under smaller bottles of 1893 Flavoring Extracts. O.S.P. $1.00 C.M.V. $110.00 B.O. $125.00 M.B.

1893-1912 FLAVORING EXTRACTS
2 oz. bottle shown is same shape as 4 oz. bottle. Paper label. Came in almond, banana, blood orange, celery, cinnamon, cloves, lemon, nutmeg, onion, orange, peach, pear, peppermint, pineapple, pistachio, quince, jamaica, ginger, raspberry, rose, strawberry, vanilla & wintergreen. O.S.P. 25¢ & 45¢ C.M.V. $100.00 in box, $85.00 bottle only mint. Also came in 16 oz., 1 qt., ½ gal., & 1 gal. C.M.V. $100.00

1914 FOOD FLAVORING SET
Box holds 2 oz. bottle of vanilla tonka, a 2 oz. bottle of lemon, & four 1 oz. bottles of any other flavor. O.S.P. $1.00 C.M.V. $450.00 for set.

920 FLAVORING EXTRACT SET
ox holds two 2 oz. bottles & four 1 oz. ottles of any flavor desired. 1, 2 & 4 oz. ottles shown. O.S.P. $1.90 C.M.V. 450.00 set mint in box.

920-21 NO ALCOHOL FLAVORING SET
et came with 5 small tubes & 1 large tube. hoice of Vanilla, lemon, pineapple, banana, aple, almond, orange, strawberry, jamaica, inger, peppermint, nutmeg, wintergreen, innamon, rose, celery, onion, pistachio & aspberry. O.S.P. $2.00 C.M.V. $200.00 M.B.

921 NO ALCOHOL FLAVOR IN TUBES
Metal tubes came small & large size, available n flavors as set. O.S.P. small tube 30¢, large ube 55¢ C.M.V. small tube $30.00 Large tube $30.00

1896 VANILLA TONKA & VANILLIN FLAVOR - Small sample bottle, clear glass, cork stopper. C.M.V. $100.00 mint.

1906 "EXTRACT CONCENTRATED" VANILLA EXTRACT - 2 & 4 oz. glass bottle with cork stopper. O.S.P. 50¢ & 90¢ C.M.V. $100.00 - $115.00 in box.

1908 FRUIT FLAVORING
4 oz. embossed Fruit California Perfume Co. Flavors. Had paper label on reverse side. CMV $25.00 BO $75.00 mint with paper label, $90.00 MB. Some came with reversed "A"s in California. Add $5.00 for reverse As.

1923-30 PERFECTION FLAVORING EXTRACT - 2 oz. clear glass bottle, cork stopper. Lemon, orange, grape, cherry, raspberry, logganberry. CMV $45.00 - $50.00 MB.

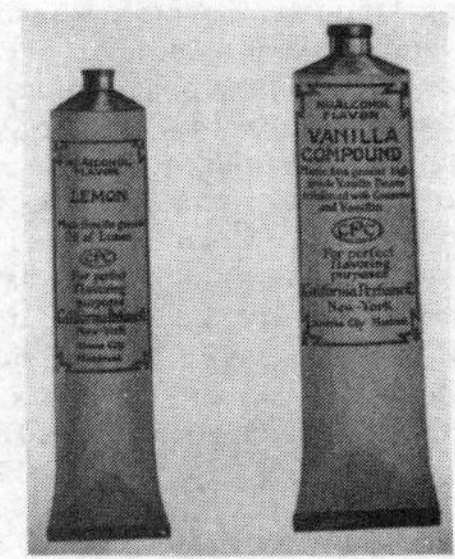

1923 NO ALCOHOL FLAVORS IN TUBES
Lemon & vanilla only in small & large size tubes. O.S.P. 24¢ & 45¢ C.M.V. $30.00 in box mint. Tube only $20.00 mint.

FROM THE ONSTOT COLLECTION

1898 EXTRACTS - FRUIT FLAVORING
2 oz. clear glass. Fruit Flavors California Perfume Co. embossed on backside. Pineapple & wintergreen shown. Cork stopper. OSP 25c, CMV $110.00 BO mint, $130.00 MB.

1915 ROOT BEER EXTRACT
2 oz. cork stopper, clear glass. Very rare. OSP 45c, CMV $100.00 mint. $125.00 MB.

1923-30 PERFECTION CONCENTRATED FLAVORING EXTRACT - 2, 4 & 8 oz. sizes, & 1 pt & 1 qt. Came in flavors of lemon, vanilla tonka, almond, orange, peppermint, wintergreen, pure vanilla, cork stoppers. Yellow labels. O.S.P. 39¢ to $4.45 C.M.V. in box $60.00 - $45.00 bottles only with mint labels.

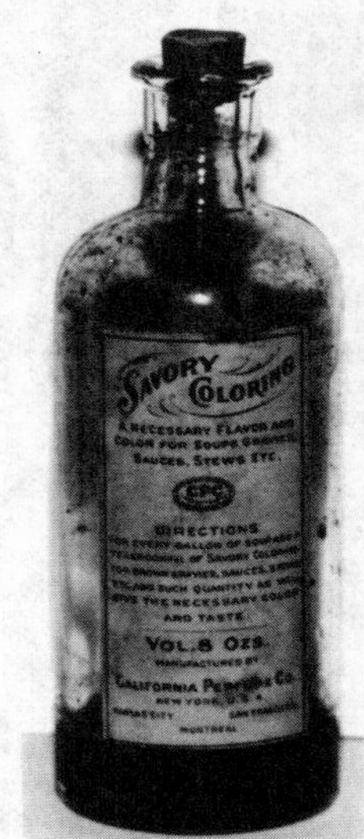

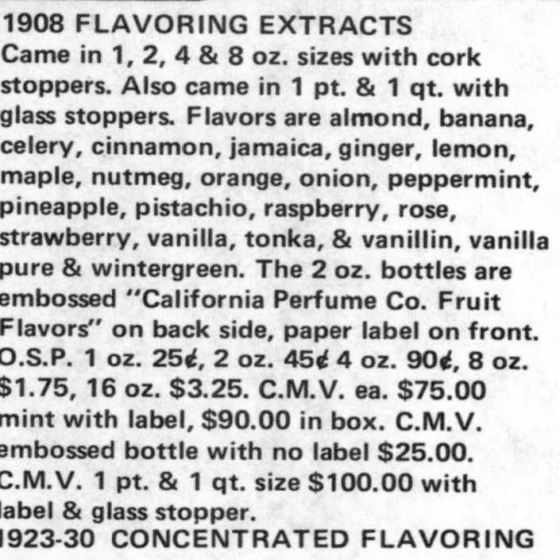

1908 FLAVORING EXTRACTS
Came in 1, 2, 4 & 8 oz. sizes with cork stoppers. Also came in 1 pt. & 1 qt. with glass stoppers. Flavors are almond, banana, celery, cinnamon, jamaica, ginger, lemon, maple, nutmeg, orange, onion, peppermint, pineapple, pistachio, raspberry, rose, strawberry, vanilla, tonka, & vanillin, vanilla pure & wintergreen. The 2 oz. bottles are embossed "California Perfume Co. Fruit Flavors" on back side, paper label on front. O.S.P. 1 oz. 25¢, 2 oz. 45¢ 4 oz. 90¢, 8 oz. $1.75, 16 oz. $3.25. C.M.V. ea. $75.00 mint with label, $90.00 in box. C.M.V. embossed bottle with no label $25.00. C.M.V. 1 pt. & 1 qt. size $100.00 with label & glass stopper.

1923-30 CONCENTRATED FLAVORING EXTRACT
8 oz. size with handle. Same label as 1923-30 extracts. This bottle is very rare with handle. Label in poor condition. CMV $75.00 mint.

1934-41 PERFECTION EXTRACT
Metal caps on ½ oz. 2, 4 & 8 oz. bottles. Flavors are vanilla tonka, lemon, almond, orange, peppermint, wintergreen, pure vanilla, black walnut, maple. O.S.P. 2 oz. size 50¢, 4 oz. size 75¢, & 8 oz. size, O.S.P. $1.45. C.M.V. ea. 2 oz. & 4 oz. $12.50 ea. 8 oz. size $20.00. C.M.V. ½ oz. $12.00 ea.

1915 SAVORY COLORING
8 oz. clear glass. Cork stopper. Rare in 8 oz. size. CMV $125.00 mint, $150.00 MB.

RIGHT 1934-39 VANILLA TONKA ¼ OZ. SAMPLE
¼ oz. size, 2 3/8" high, metal cap. On right shown next to ½ oz. size, on left, that came in food flavor sets. CMV $25.00 ¼ oz. size sample mint, CMV ½ oz. size $15.00 mint.

1923 FRUIT FLAVORS BROCHURE
Introducing new line of CPC Perfection fruit flavors. 1 page. CMV $10.00.

1923-30 CONCENTRATED FLAVORING EXTRACT
8 oz. size with handle. Same label as 1923-30 extracts. This bottle is very rare with handle. Label in poor condition. CMV $75.00 mint.

936-41 BAKING POWDER SAMPLE
range, brown & white 1 oz. can, 2¼" igh. 2 different size samples. Rare. MV $40 mint each.

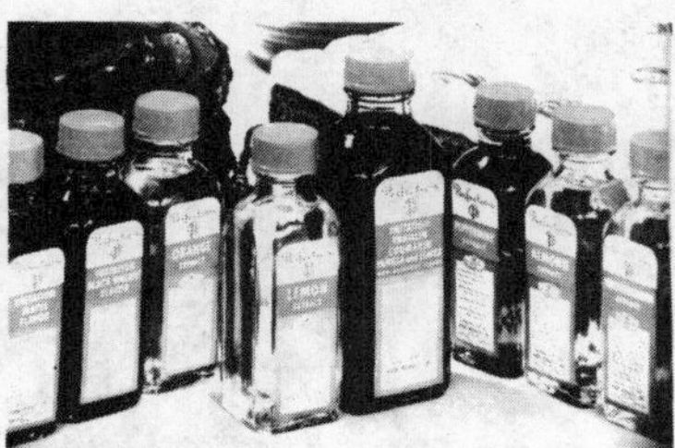

1941-48 PERFECTION FLAVORING EXTRACTS - Vanilla & lemon came in 2 & 4 oz. sizes. 2 oz. size only in maple, black walnut, orange, peppermint, almond, wintergreen, all have red plastic caps. O.S.P. 49¢ 2 oz. & 89¢ 4 oz. C.M.V. $9.00 ea. ½ oz. size came in Extract Set only. C.M.V. $12.00 - $15.00 M.B.

1941-48 FOOD COLORING
Red plastic caps. Savory coloring came in 4 oz. bottle. O.S.P. 39¢, red, yellow, blue, brown & green came in 2 oz. bottles. O.S.P. 29¢ all but red & savory coloring came in ½ oz. bottles in coloring set. C.M.V. $12.00 ea. size. $15.00 ea. M.B.

934-41 FLAVORING EXTRACT
oz. bottle plus cap. came in vanilla tonka, mon. almond, orange, peppermint, winter-een, pure vanilla, black walnut & maple. .S.P. $1.45 C.M.V. $25.00 M.B. Bottle nly $15.00

1908 FOOD COLORING
2 & 4 oz. bottles with cork stoppers & paper labels. Came in coffee, violet, lilac, orange, chocolate, red, green & lemon. O.S.P. 25¢ & 45¢ C.M.V. $75.00 bottle with label. $90.00 in box.

1920 PERFECTION CONCENTRATED COLORING - ½ oz. bottles with cork stopper. Came in blue, brown, green & yellow. Came in Coloring Set only. 2 oz. bottle of red, All yellow labels & same shape. C.M.V. $60.00 each mint.

1941-48 SAVOURY COLORING
4 oz. bottle with the word Savoury spelled different. Regular spelling is Savory. O.S.P. 39¢ C.M.V. $15.00 B.O. mint, $17.00 M.B.

1939-41 PERFECTION IMITATION VANILLIN COUMARIN VANILLA & TONKA SAMPLE
¼ oz. size bottle. Metal cap. CMV $25.00 mint.

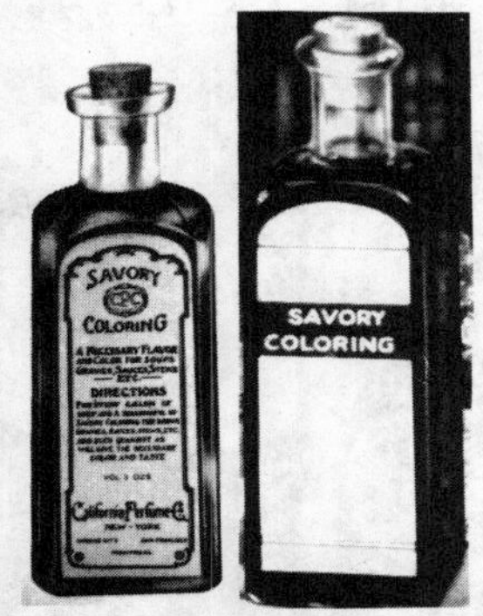

1923-30 SAVORY COLORING
2 & 4 oz. bottle with yellow labels & brown letters, cork stoppers, came in red, yellow, blue brown & green. Also came with brown label & yellow letters. OSP 33c, & 59c. CMV each with mint label $45.00 - $55.00 in box. ½ oz. bottle came in Coloring Set only. CMV same as above.

1931-34 PERFECTION SAVORY COLORING
4 oz. cork stopper, CPC label. OSP 35c, CMV $35.00 in box, $30.00 bottle only.

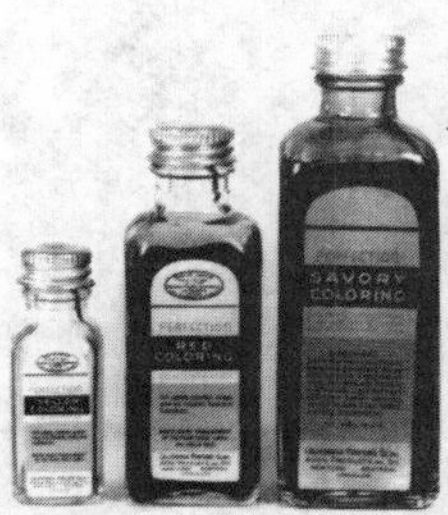

1934-41 PERFECTION COLORING
½ oz. size in green, yellow, blue & brown. Came in Coloring Set. C.M.V. $15.00 ea. 2 oz. size in same colors plus red. O.S.P. 25¢ C.M.V. $17.00. 4 oz. size in savory coloring O.S.P. 35¢. All have metal caps. C.M.V. $17.00. Add $3.00 ea. M.B.

1915 SAVORY COLORING
3 oz. clear glass bottle, cork stopper. 3 oz. size is rare. O.S.P. 25¢ C.M.V. $75.00 with mint label. $90.00 M.B.

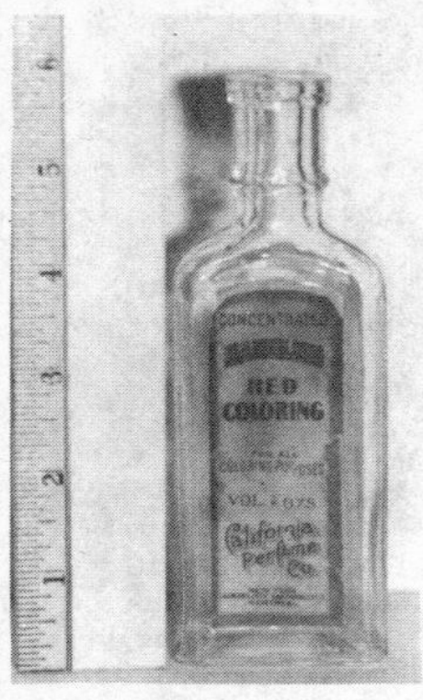

1915 HARMLESS RED COLORING
2 oz. clear glass, cork stopper. O.S.P. 25¢ C.M.V. $75.00 mint - with label $90.00 M.B.

PERFECTION CAKE PAN
Tin pan marked "Perfection" We believe this was sold by Perfection Stove Co. & not by Perfection of Avon Products. If you have information on this please write to Bud Hastin.

1920-30 PERFECTION CONCENTRAT COLORING
2 oz. No coloring listed on label. Cork stopper. O.S.P. 33¢ C.M.V. $45.00 B.O. mint, $55.00 M.B.

1906 BAKING POWDER
½ & 1 lb. can. O.S.P. 25¢ & 45¢ C.M.V. $75.00 mint.

1906-1915 BAKING POWDER
5 lb. container, paper label, metal can. O.S.P. 25¢ 1 lb. C.M.V. $50.00 mint. Pictured next to 1923-30 1 lb. can, for size conparison.

1940'S PERFECTION MEASURING CUP
Metal cup.

1940'S PERFECTION PIE PAN
9" pie pan with removable bottom. Center of pan says "Trade Mark Perfection Patented" We believe both items were sold by Perfection Stove Co. & not by Perfection of Avon Products. No value established.

1931-41 PERFECTION OLIVE OIL
1 pt. orange, brown & white can, 2 different labels. OSP $1.35 CMV $30.00 in box, $25.00 can only mint.

1943-46 BAKING POWDER
16 oz. paper container used during war. OSP 45c, CMV $25.00 mint.

1937 VANILLA TONKA AND VANILLIN SPECIAL ISSUE BOX
Regular issue 2 oz. bottle came in special issue box for 15¢ with regular order. C.M.V. $20.00 M.B. as shown.

1923-30 PERFECTION BAKING POWDER
(Left) 1 lb. can. Also came in ½ lb. & 5 lb. sizes. O.S.P. 45¢ C.M.V. $40.00 mint $45.00 M.B.

1931-41 PERFECTION BAKING POWDER
(Right) 1 lb. orange, brown & white can. O.S.P. 45¢ C.M.V. $25.00 - $30.00 M.B. Add $5.00 CPC label.

95 OLIVE OIL
oz. glass bottle with cork stopper. O.S.P. ¢ C.M.V. $75.00 bottle only - $85.00 box. Also came in 1 pt., 1 qt., ½ gal., 1 gal. size. C.M.V. $100.00

1905 OLIVE OIL
16 oz. bottle. O.S.P. $1.25 C.M.V. $75.00 mint.

1941-43-46-48 PERFECTION BAKING POWDER
16 oz. red & white can. OSP 45c, CMV $17.00 mint, $22.00 MB.

1915 OLIVE OIL
8 oz. glass bottle with cork stopper. O.S.P. 50¢ C.M.V. $85.00 in box - $75.00 bottle only mint. Also came in 16 oz., 1 qt., ½ gal., 1 gal. size. C.M.V. $100.00

1915 BAKING POWDER
16 oz. container. O.S.P. 25¢ C.M.V. $50.00 in box - $45.00 container only mint. Also came in 1 lb. & 5 lb. size. C.M.V. $50.00 mint.

1941 PERFECTION SAMPLES
Sample size each. Perfection flavor sample came 20 in a box for 50¢. Baking powder came 16 for 50¢. C.M.V. Flavoring bottle $20.00 each. Baking powder $40.00 each.

1923 SUPREME HUILE D'OILVE OIL
Green & yellow can in 1 pt. size. O.S.P. $1.35 C.M.V. $45.00 M.B. $35.00 can only mint. Also came in qt. size can. O.S.P. $2.50 C.M.V. $50.00 M.B. - $40.00 can only mint.

LEFT 1915 FURNITURE POLISH
8 oz. clear glass bottle, cork stopper. C.M.V. $85.00 B.O. mint. $100.00 M.B. Same label as on rare amber bottle.

RIGHT 1943-46 PERFECTION FURNITURE POLISH
12 oz. bottle, metal cap. OSP 69c, CMV $18.00, $22.00 MB.

1941 FURNITURE POLISH - All green, bronze & white metal can. 12 oz. can as pictured 1941-43 then 1946-48. O.S.P. 69¢ C.M.V. $12.00 - $15.00 M.B. 16 oz. can as pictured 1948-51 O.S.P. 79¢ C.M.V. $12.00. 1 qt. size can as pictured 1941-43 O.S.P. $1.29 C.M.V. $15.00. Add $3.00 M.B.

1906 CPC FURNITURE POLISH
(Left) 8 oz. bottle with cork stopper. OSP 50c, CMV $100.00, $115.00 in box.

1912 FURNITURE POLISH
(Right) 8 oz. bottle, cork stopper, label also reads for automobile bodies. OSP 50c, CMV $125.00 in box, $100.00 bottle only.

1916 FURNITURE POLISH
11 oz. metal can with green label. O.S.P. 50¢ C.M.V. $75.00 in box - $65.00 can only mint. Also came in qt. size. O.S.P. $1.20, ½ gal. size O.S.P. $2.25 C.M.V. $75.00 mint

1915 FURNITURE POLISH
8 oz. amber glass, cork stopper. Very rare. C.M.V. $150.00 bottle only mint. $175.00 M.B.

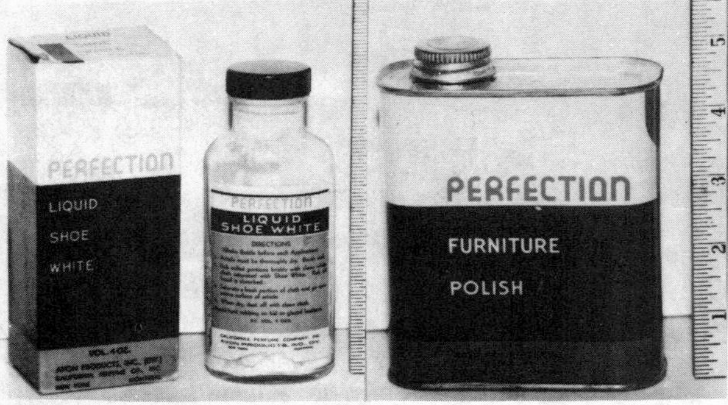

1935-41 PERFECTION LIQUID SHOE WHITE
Box holds 4 oz. bottle with brown cap. Brown, orange and white label. OSP 50c, CMV $25.00, $30.00 MB.

1936-41 PERFECTION FURNITURE POLISH
12 oz. brown, orange & white can. OSP 75c, CMV $15.00, $20.00 MB

1946-58 LIQUID SPOTS OUT
4 oz. bottle, green smooth or threaded cap. 2 different labels. 1 box brown & 1 box bronze. OSP 50c, CMV in box $20.00, bottle only $15.00

1931-36 PERFECTION FURNITURE POLISH
12 oz. brown, orange & white can. OSP 75c, CMV $15.00, $20.00 MB.

1944 Only - FURNITURE POLISH
12 oz. bottle, black cap. O.S.P. 79¢ C.M.V. $40.00 B.O. $45.00 M.B.

1941-57 PERFECTION LIQUID SHOE WHITE
4 oz. green smooth or threaded cap. 2 different labels. OSP 37c, CMV $10.00 bottle, only. $12.50 in box.

1918 FURNITURE POLISH
½ pt. bottle. cork stopper, clear glass. O.S.P. 50¢ C.M.V. $100.00 - $125.00 in box.

1925 FURNITURE POLISH
12 oz. metal can with blue label. O.S.P. 48¢ Same as above only in 32 oz. blue metal can. O.S.P. $1.20. Back side labels in French on both cans. C.M.V. $45.00 can only mint, $55.00 M.B. ea.

1920 SHOE WHITE
Green box holds 5 oz. sack of powder. O.S.P. 25¢ C.M.V. $45.00 M.B.

1931-35 PERFECTION LIQUID SHOE WHITE
Box holds 4 oz. bottle with brown cap. brown orange and white label. OSP 50c, CMV $25.00, $30.00 MB.

1925-30 LIQUID SHOE WHITE
4 oz. glass bottle with cork stopper. O.S.P. 35¢ C.M.V. $50.00 in box, $45.00 bottle only mint.

1918 SHOE WHITE
Box holds 5 oz, sack of Shoe White Powder. O.S.P. 25¢ C.M.V. $45.00 M.B.

1918 SPOTS OUT
Metal can. O.S.P. 33¢ C.M.V. $50.00 can only mint. $65.00 M.B.

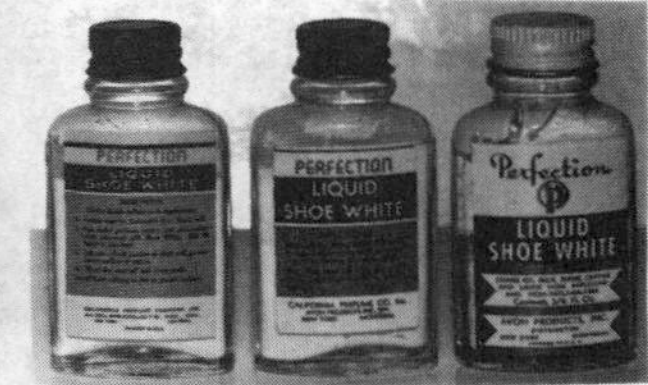

LEFT TO RIGHT
1935-41 LIQUID SHOE WHITE SAMPLE
½ oz., black cap. CPC on label. CMV $40.00
1935-41 LIQUID SHOE WHITE SAMPLE
Same as above, different label. CMV $40.00
1941-57 LIQUID SHOE WHITE
¾ oz. white cap, green & brown label. CMV $35.00.

1925-29 LIQUID SPOTS OUT
4 oz. clear glass bottle, black cork cap, blue label. O.S.P. 40¢ C.M.V. $40.00 M.B. $35.00 B.O. mint.

1931-41 SPOTS OUT
½ lb. orange, brown & white can. O.S.P. 40¢ C.M.V. $25.00 M.B. $20.00 can only mint.

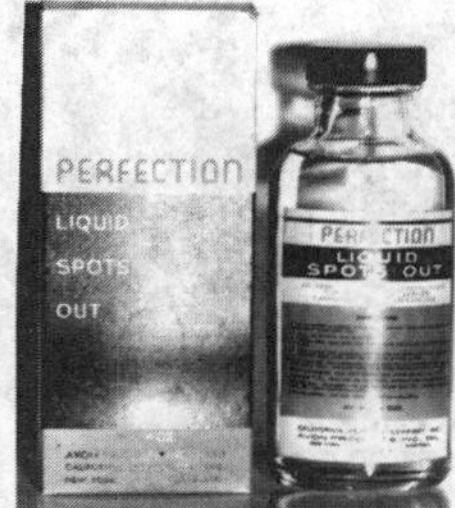

1934-41 LIQUID SPOTS OUT
4 oz. bottle, orange, brown & white label. Black cap. O.S.P. 40¢ C.M.V. in box $30.00 Bottle only $25.00

1941-43 SPOTS OUT
8 oz. green, brown & white can. Sold 1941-43 then 1946-48. O.S.P. 45¢ C.M.V. $15.00. - $18.00 M.B.

1938-41 LAUNDRY CRYSTALS PERFUMED
Brown, orange, & white paper sides, tin top & bottom. Top cut out to be used as bank. Held 13 crystals. Came with Avon & CPC labels. OSP 27c, CMV $22.50 Avon label, $27.00 CPC label.

1915 CARPET RENOVATOR SOAP
Paper box with one bar carpet soap. 2 different boxes shown. First issued about 1893. O.S.P. 35¢ C.M.V. $50.00. Each mint.

1925 MOTHICIDE
½ lb. metal can with blue label. O.S.P. 48¢ C.M.V. $40.00 in box. $30.00 can only mint.

LEFT 1929 PERFECTION SPOTS OUT LIQUID - 4 oz. bottle with CPC on black cork stopper & blue label. O.S.P. 50¢ C.M.V. $40.00 in box. $35.00 bottle only.

RIGHT 1931-34 PERFECTION LIQUID SPOTS OUT - 4 oz. size. CPC on cork stopper. O.S.P. 40¢ C.MV. $40.00 in box, $32.50 bottle only.

1923 SPOTS OUT
8 oz. metal can. O.S.P. 33¢ C.M.V. $40.00 mint. 16 oz. can not shown, O.S.P. 59¢ C.M.V. $45.00 mint. Add $10.00 ea. M.B.

1931-41 PERFECTION MOTHICIDE
½ lb. orange, brown & white can. O.S.P. 50¢ C.M.V. $25.00 in box. $17.50 can only mint. Add $5.00 CPC label.

1923 MOTHICIDE
1/2 lb. metal can 3¼" across. Paper label in English and French. O.S.P. 48¢ C.M.V. $35.00 mint.

1929-31 POWDERED CLEANER
12 oz. blue box. O.S.P. 25¢ C.M.V. $30.00 mint - $35.00 M.B.

1931-36 PERFECTION LAUNDRY CRYSTALS
Brown, orange & white paper box. OSP 25c, CMV $30.00 MB.

1934-36 LAUNDRY CRYSTALS PERFUMED
(Right) Brown, white & orange box holds 13 white crystals. OSP 25c, CMV $30.00 mint.

1941-48 PERFECTION LAUNDRY CRYSTALS PERFUMED
Green, brown and white can with green lid holds 13 crystals. Metal top and bottom and paper sides sold 1941-46. All metal sold 1946-48. O.S.P. 29¢. C.M.V. $20.00 mint each.

1943-46 PERFECTION LAUNDRY CRYASLS PERFUMED
All cardboard wartime packaging. C.M.V. $25.00 mint. Also came with white top and bottom.

1931-34 POWDERED CLEANER
Red, white & blue. 16 oz. can. O.S.P. 35¢ C.M.V. $25.00 mint. $30.00 M.B.

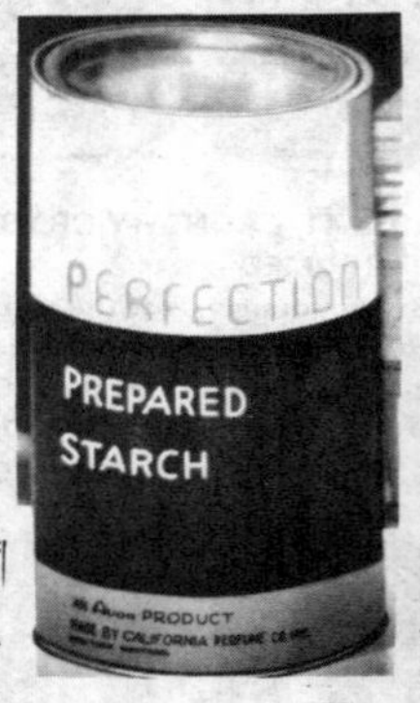

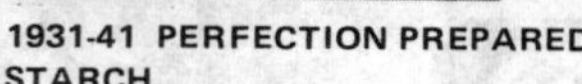

1931-41 PERFECTION PREPARED STARCH
(Left) 6 oz. brown, orange & white can. Sold 1931-36. CMV $25.00, $30.00 MB. Same can in 8 oz. size sold 1936-41 CMV $20.00, $25.00 MB.

1941-48 PERFECTION PREPARED STARCH
(Right) 8 oz. brown, green & white can. 2 different labels. Shiny top or painted top. OSP 39c, CMV $15.00 mint, $18.00 MB.

1934-41 PERFECTION POWDERED CLEANER
16 oz. orange, brown & white can. 2 different labels. Cardboard sides, metal top & bottom. OSP 35c, CMV $25.00 MB, $20.00 can only, mint.

1943-46 POWDERED CLEANER
16 oz. paper can, green, bronze & white. O.S.P. 39¢ C.M.V. $15.00 mint - $20.00 M.B.

1941-43 then 1946-57 POWDERED CLEANER - 16 oz. paper sides with metal top & bottom. Green, bronze & white. O.S.P. 39¢ C.M.V. $10.00 - $12.00 MB. 5 different labels.

1925 MOTHICIDE
1 lb. metal can on right. Paper label around can is in English and French. O.S.P. $1.00 C.M.V. $40.00 mint. C.M.V. as shown with spots $20.00. ½ lb. metal can on left O.S.P. 50¢, C.M.V. $40.00 mint.

954-57 PERFECTION MOTHICIDE
½ oz. bronze metal can, green top, 2 ifferent edges on lid. Sold 1954-57 CMV $10.00. Red metal can sold 1957 only. CMV $12.00, OSP each 55c, add $2.00 MB each.

1931-41 PERFECTION KWICK METAL POLISH - ½ lb. orange, brown & white can. O.S.P. 35¢ C.M.V. $25.00 M.B. $20.00 can only mint. 1954-57 Green & brown 13 oz. can on right. O.S.P. 55¢ C.M.V. $10.00 mint.

1941-52 PERFECTION SILVER CREAM POLISH - Green, brown & white. 8 oz. can. Sold 1941-43 then 1946-52. O.S.P. 49¢ C.M.V. $12.00 mint, $15.00 M.B.

1943-46 MOTHICIDE
Glass jar with white lid. O.S.P. 55¢ C.M.V. $20.00 - $25.00 M.B.
1941-43 then 1946-54 MOTHICIDE
8 oz. green, bronze & white metal can O.S.P. 55¢ C.M.V. $12.00 - $15.00 M.B.

1941-48 KWICK METAL POLISH
8 oz. green, brown & white can. Sold 1941-43 then 1946-48. O.S.P. 39¢ C.M.V. $15.00 - $17.00 M.B.

1896 SILVER PLATE POLISH
4 oz. glass bottle with metal cap. O.S.P. 25¢ C.M.V. $100.00 - $115.00 in box.

1918 CPC SILVER CREAM POLISH
6 oz. jar, metal lid. O.S.P. 30¢ C.M.V. $85.00 mint.

1923 KWICK CLEANING POLISH
8 oz. metal can, brown label. O.S.P. 24¢ C.M.V. $45.00 in box. $35.00 can only mint. Also came in 16 oz. can. O.S.P. 45¢ C.M.V. $50.00 in box. $40.00 can only mint.

1923 SILVER CREAM POLISH
8 oz. metal can. O.S.P. 30¢ C.M.V. $40.00 mint. 16 oz. can O.S.P. 54¢ C.M.V. $45.00 mint. Add $5.00 M.B.

1943-46 PERFECTION SPOTS OUT
9½ oz. glass jar, white metal lid. O.S.P. 45¢ C.M.V. $22.00 - $25.00 M.B.
1943-46 PERFECTION KWICK METAL POLISH - 11 oz. glass jar with white metal cap. O.S.P. 39¢ C.M.V. $22.00 - $25.00 M.B.
1943-46 PERFECTION SILVER CREAM POLISH - 10½ oz. glass jar with white metal lid. O.S.P. 49¢ C.M.V. $22.00 - $25.00 M.B.

1925 KWICK METAL POLISH
½ lb. metal can with brown label. O.S.P. 24¢ C.M.V. $40.00 in box. $30.00 can only mint.

1931-41 PERFECTION SILVER CREAM POLISH - ½ lb. brown, orange & white can. O.S.P. 35¢ C.M.V. $25.00 M.B. $20.00 can only mint.

1943 SILVER CREAM POLISH
Stick on white & green label over name of other product on can. Used during shortage of products during war. OSP 49c, CMV $20.00 mint with label shown.

LEFT 1930-33 AUTO LUSTRE
Blue 1 pt. can. OSP 75c, CMV can only $30.00 mint, $35.00 MB.
RIGHT 1930-33 AUTO LUSTRE SAMPLE
1 oz. blue metal can. Rare. CMV $75.00

1933-36 PERFECTION AUTO POLISH
1 pt. brown, orange & white can. Two different labels. OSP 75c, CMV $25.00 in box, $20.00 can only, mint.

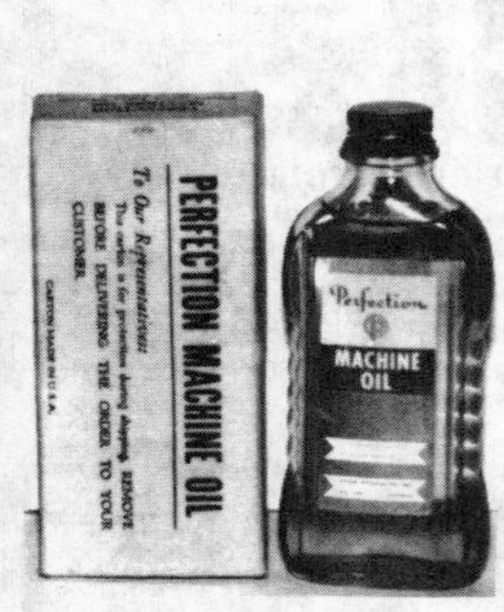

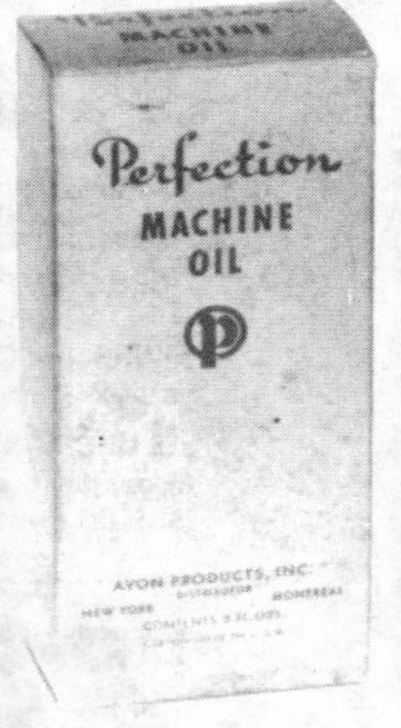

1943-46 PERFECTION MACHINE OIL
3 oz., smooth side glass, metal cap. OSP 29c, CMV $20.00 BO, $25.00 MB.
1945 MACHINE OIL "RIBBED SIDE"
Short issue 3 oz. ribbed sided bottle, metal cap. OSP 29c, Came in 2 different boxes as shown. CMV $25.00 BO, $30.00 MB.

1931-41 PERFECTION MACHINE OIL
3 oz. brown, orange & white can. Two different labels. OSP 26c, CMV $18.00 in box, $12.50 can only, mint.

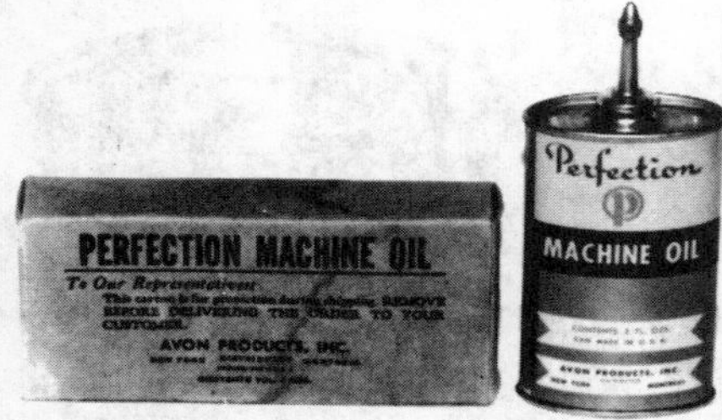

1941-48 PERFECTION MACHINE OIL
3 oz. brown, green & white can. Sold 1941-43 then 1946-48. O.S.P. 29¢ C.M.V. $15.00 in box. $10.00 can only.

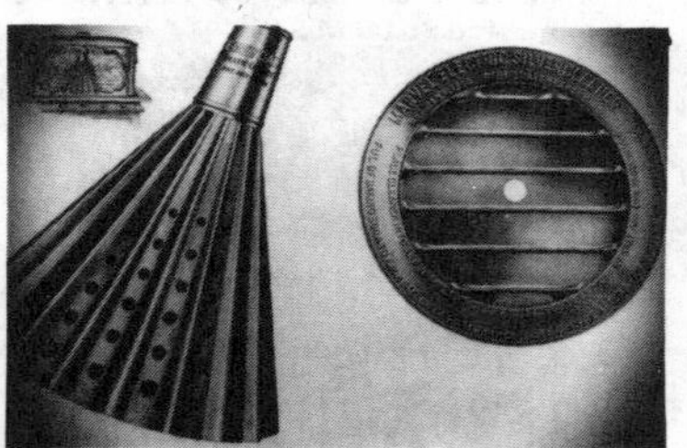

1918 CPC EASYDAY AUTOMATIC CLOTHES WASHER - made of pure zinc. Has Easyday name at top & Pat. July 4, 1916. O.S.P. $2.00 C.M.V. $100.00
1918 CPC MARVEL ELECTRIC SILVER CLEANER - Metal plate has Marvel name & Pat. Jan. 11, 1910. O.S.P. 75¢ C.M.V. $50.00

1932-41 PERFECTION MENDING CEMENT - Brown, orange & white tube. O.S.P. 25¢ C.M.V. $12.00 in box. Tube only $7.00 mint.
1941-48 PERFECTION MENDING CEMENT - White, green & brown tube. O.S.P. 29¢ C.M.V. $10.00 in box. $7.00 tube only mint.

SAMPLES & DEMONSTRATOR KITS

936 REPRESENTATIVE DEMO CASE
Black case with metal mirror in lid. Handle s on opposite side of lid opening. Inner shelf is dark blue and lifts out of case. Storage area under shelf. Case came complete with 1936 sales catalog, 1/4 oz. glass stopper perfume in Cotillion,metal cap 1/4 oz. perfume in Gardinia, blue and silver lipstick and rouge compact. Silver box of face powder, ribbed glass bottle of skin freshener (2 oz.), astringent (2 oz.) Lotus Cream (4 oz.), Rosewater Glycerin and Benzoin (4 oz.). All with black caps. 2 oz. jars of vanishing cream and tissue cream and 4 oz. jars of cleansing cream. C.M.V. $1000.00 M.B. complete set.

1951 CLEANSING CREAM DEMONSTRATOR KIT
Demo box holds 2 white glass jars with turquoise lids of Cleansing Cream and 1 jar of Night cream. Used by Reps to show products. CMV $20.00 MB. Comes in 2 different boxes.

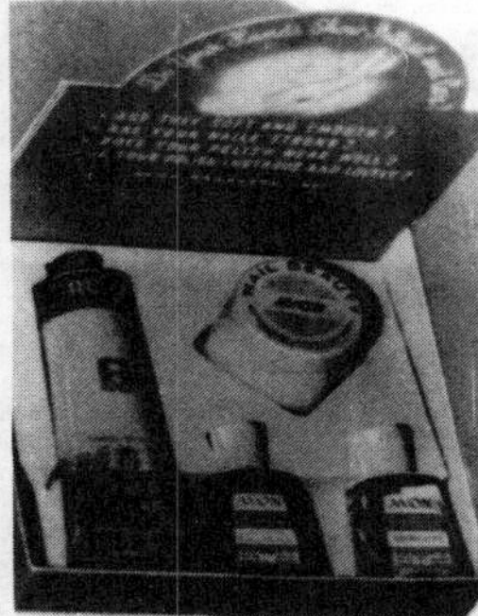

1953 HAND CARE DEMONSTRATOR KIT - Box holds 2 bottles of nail polish, 1 tube of hand cream, jar of nail beauty. C.M.V. $37.50 M.B.

1948 SKIN CARE DEMO KIT
Demo box holds blue 2¼ oz. tube of Fluffy Cleansing Cream, 4 oz. bottle of Skin Freshener, and tube of Special Dry Skin Cream. Not sold to public. Used by reps as demonstrator. CMV $55.00 MB

1940 REPRESENTATIVE DEMO KIT
Box holds jars of cleansing cream, night cream, foundation cream & bottle of skin freshener. O.S.P. $1.00 C.M.V. $45.00 M.B.

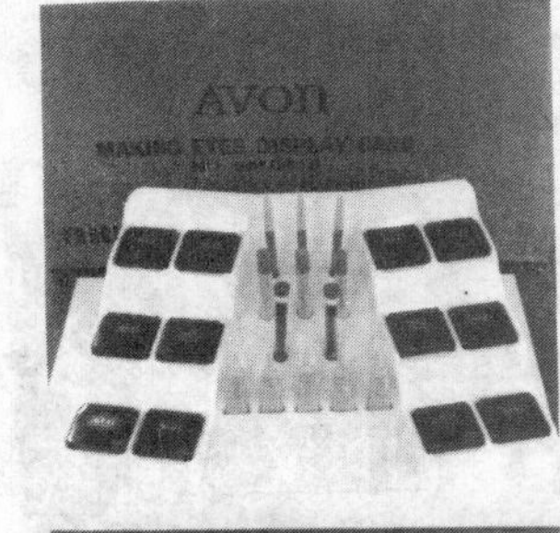

1976 C-17 MAKING EYES DISPLAY
Plastic base used by managers to display new turquoise color eye makeup products. Base holds 12 powder eye shadows, 5 cream eye shadows, 2 eye shadow wands, 3 mascaras, 3 brow and liner pencils. C.M.V. $45.00 M.B. as shown full. Products 25¢ each empty. C.M.V. base only $15.00

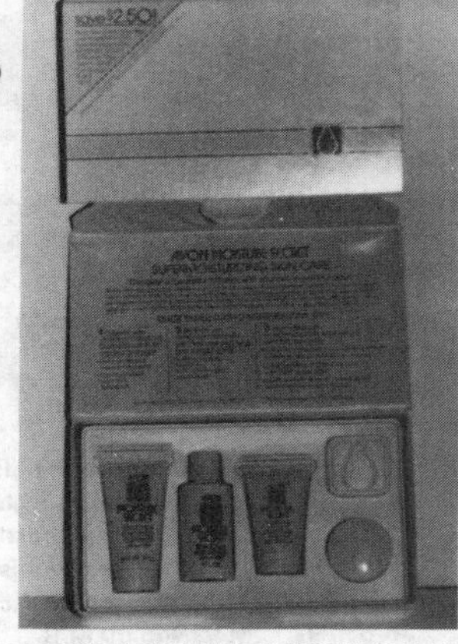

1978 MOISTURE SECRET SKIN CARE KIT
White and pink plastic kit holds pink plastic tubes of Moisture Secret Enriched Cremegel Cleanser, Enriched Freshener & Enriched Daytime Moisturizer. All with PMB, and pink plastic jar of Enriched Night Concentrate. All are trial size. Came with outer sleeve over kit. S.S.P. $2.50 C.M.V. $2.50 M.B.

1942GIFT DISPLAY ENSEMBLE DEMO
A special hand carrying box used by Reps at Christmas time. Came with several sets to show customers. To determine price of this kit look up each set and get price. Then add $25.00 for the demo box.

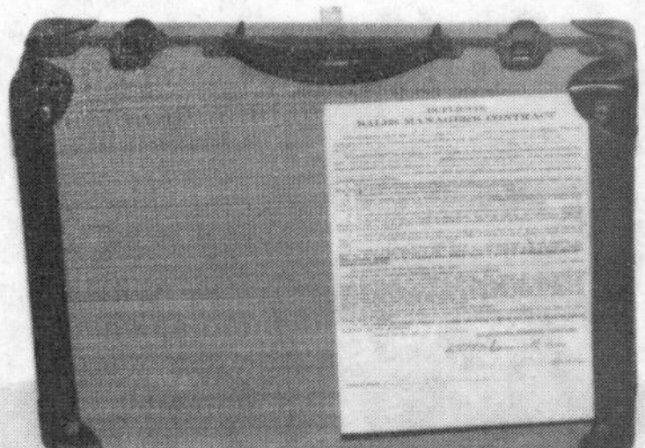

1913 CPC SALES MANAGERS DEMO BAG
Leather bound straw bag used by early day Avon ladies to show their products.

Measures 14" wide, 4" deep, 10" high. does not say CPC on case. C.M.V. $75.00 mint.

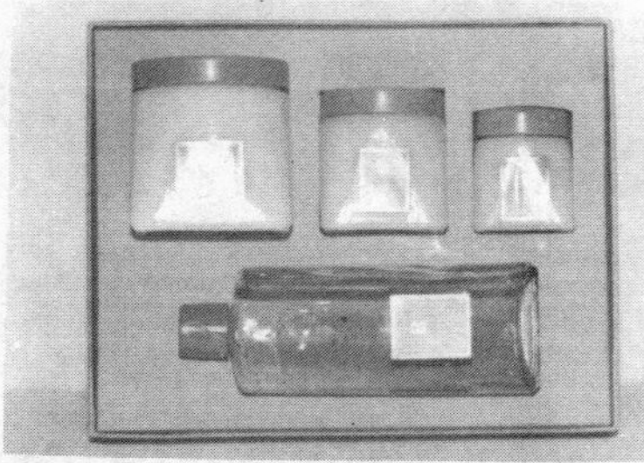

1940s FACIAL DEMO KIT
Green lid box with pink base holds white glass jars of cleansing cream, night cream, foundation cream and 4 oz. bottle of skin freshener. All have turquoise caps. Used by Reps to demonstrate facial products. C.M.V. $45.00 M.B.

1952 SKIN CARE DEMO KIT
Flip open display box holds 1 jar each of Cleansing Cream and Night Cream and a bottle of Skin Freshener. Used by Reps to show products. C.M.V. $30.00 M.B.

1942 Only - DEMONSTRATOR KIT
Box holds jar of cream deodorant & 1 bar of Lemonol Soap. C.M.V. $40.00 M.B.

1941 DEMO KIT XMAS
For representatives only. C.M.V. complete $350.00

1948 HAND LOTION & HAND CREAM DEMO KIT
Demo box holds tube of hand cream and 4 oz. bottle of hand lotion. Not sold. Used by Reps to sell products. C.M.V. $30.00 M.B.

1949 DEMONSTRATOR KIT
Demo box holds tubes of hand cream and creme shampoo and jar of perfumed deodorant. Used by Reps to show products. C.M.V. $25.00 M.B.

1943 GIFT DISPLAY ENSEMBLE DEMO
A special hand carrying box used by Reps at Christmas time to show Christmas sales items and sets. To determine price of this kit, look up each set and get their price, then add $25.00 for this demo box.

1936 MAKE UP TRIO DEMO KIT
Brown box holds 1¾ oz. box of Ariel Suntan Face Powder, turquoise & gold rouge Compact in crusader red & matching Lipstick in crusader red. Came with fold out display card. C.M.V. $55.00 M.B.

1947 SHAMPOO DEMO KIT
Box holds 2 bottles of soapless & liquid shampoo. For reps. only. C.M.V. $50.00 mint.

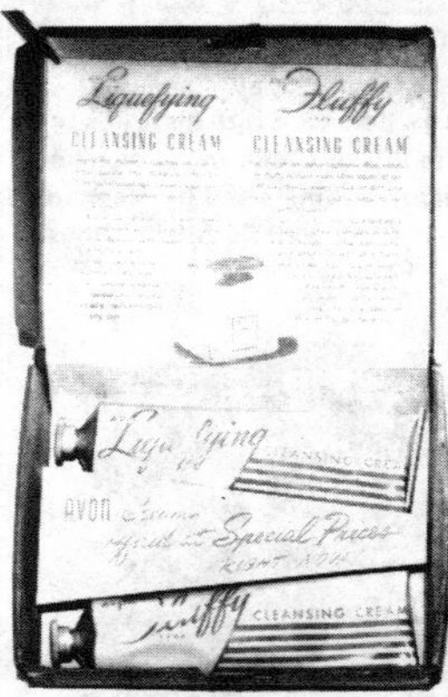

1947 CLEANSING CREAM DEMO KIT
Box with lady's face on lid holds tube of liquifying & fluffy cleansing cream. Pink tubes, 2¼ oz. each. Tubes were never sold to public. For reps only. CMV Rare $45.00 MB.

62 - 76th ANNIVERSARY CELEBRATION
EMO KIT - Pink cardboard box holds 2 oz. tillion Cologne, Cotillion Cream Sachet, oz. Perfumed Deodorant, 6 oz. Rosiest ray Sachet, Silver Notes Eye Shadow Hi Light Shampoo. C.M.V. $27.50.

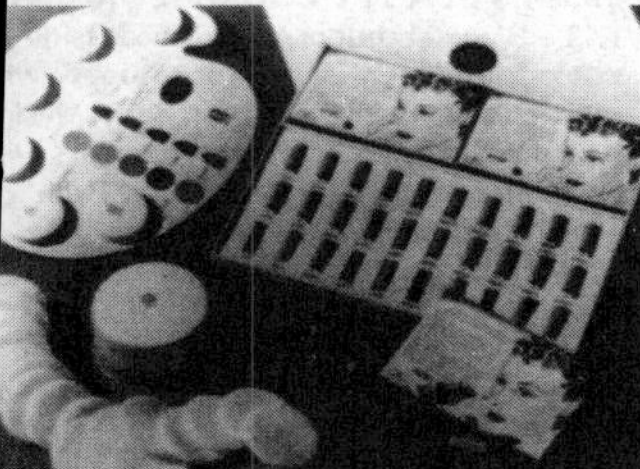

1940 DEMONSTRATOR KIT
Box with gold Avon seal on lid holds lipstick sample box, face powder pallette, box of face powder & 30 cotton puffs. C.M.V. complete set $75.00 M.B.

1938 HAND CREAM SAMPLES
Box of 24 - ¼ oz. turquoise & white tubes. C.M.V. $3.00 ea, tube. Mint complete $100.00.

1938 CLEANSING CREAM SAMPLES
Same box as hand cream samples. Box of 24 - ¼ oz. tubes. CMV $3.00 each tube mint, complete set, $100.00

1951 BIRTHDAY CAKE
Blue & white box holds foam cake with five 1 dram ribbed perfumes, To A Wild Rose, Golden Promise, Cotillion, Quaintance, & Flowertime. This was a demonstrator kit, for reps. CMV $90.00 cake & bottle only mint, $125.00 MB.

1953 PACK UP YOUR SKIN TROUBLES
DEMONSTRATOR KIT - Cardboard carrying case holds jars of cleansing cream & tissue cream & 4 oz. bottle of astringent. C.M.V. $45.00 M.B.

1942 FACIAL DEMONSTRATOR KIT
Box holds 3 tubes of night cream, jar of night cream, foundation cream & 4 oz. bottle of skin freshener. O.S.P. 69¢
C.M.V. $45.00 M.B.

1942 CLEANING CREAM DEMONSTRATOR KIT - Box holds jar & 3 sample tubes of cleansing cream. C.M.V. $35.00 M.B.

1949 DENTAL DEMO KIT
Box holds tube of Ammoniated tooth paste, and can of Ammoniated tooth powder. Not sold to public. Used by Reps to show products. CMV $37.50 MB.

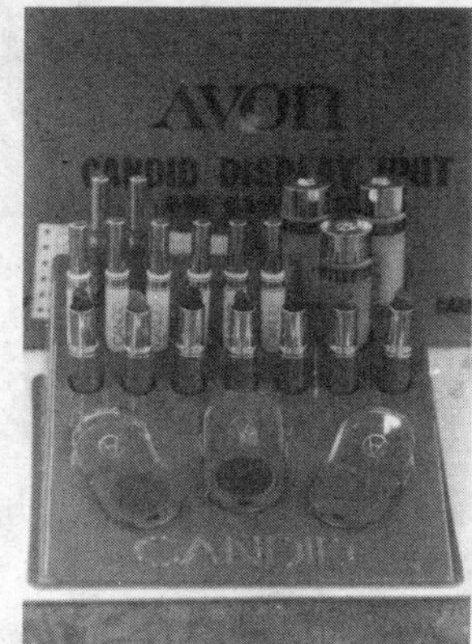

1976 CANDID MANAGERS DISPLAY
Orange plastic display for Avon managers to display new Candid products. Base holds 7 Candid lipsticks, 6 eye colors, 2 mascaras, 3 cheek colors, and 3 1½ oz. bottles of makeup. C.M.V. complete set full in box $45.00, empty items 25¢ ea., base only $15.00

1963 - 77th ANNIVERSARY DEMO SET
Demo kit for Avon reps. on 77th Anniversary Top of box has rose in left corner & says - Celebrating Avon's 77th Anniversary.
Box holds 2 oz. cologne mist with 4A's embossed on side, jar of cream foundation, 4 oz. skin-so-soft & petti pat compact.
C.M.V. $32.50 M.B.

1977 COLORWORKS DEMO KIT
Silver and white box with outer sleeve holds Oil Free Liquid Makeup, Oil Free Cheekblush, Supershine Lip Gloss, Lasting Color Eye Shadow and Lashes, Lashes Mascara. Used by Avon Reps to sell New Colorworks products.
Rep cost - $4.50 C.M.V. $5.00 M.B. complete

1977 FASHION MAKEUP GROUP COLLECTION
Demo kit used by Reps to sell Fashion Makeup products. Box is black and gold with white base. Outside sleeve. Cost Rep. - $5.47 C.M.V. $5.50 M.B. complete

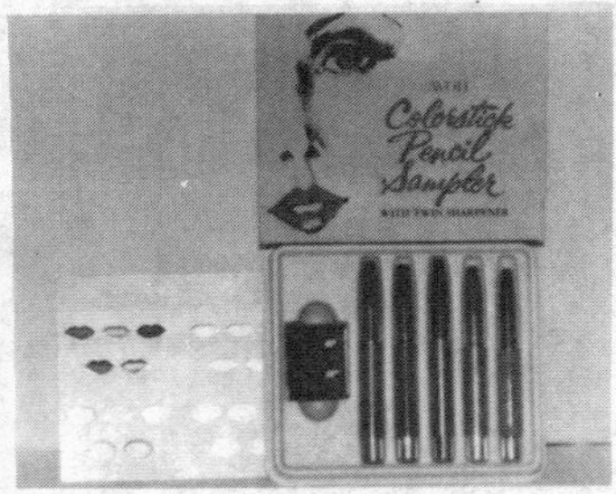

1977 COLORSTICK PENCIL SAMPLER
Plastic base with sleeve lid holds color chart and 5 Colorstick pencils and brown plastic 2 hole pencil sharpener, marked Avon. Used by Reps to sell Colorstick products. Rep cost - $3.99 C.M.V. $4.00 M.B., complete.

1965 MANAGERS DEMO KIT
White box holds eye & face make up CMV $55.00 MB.

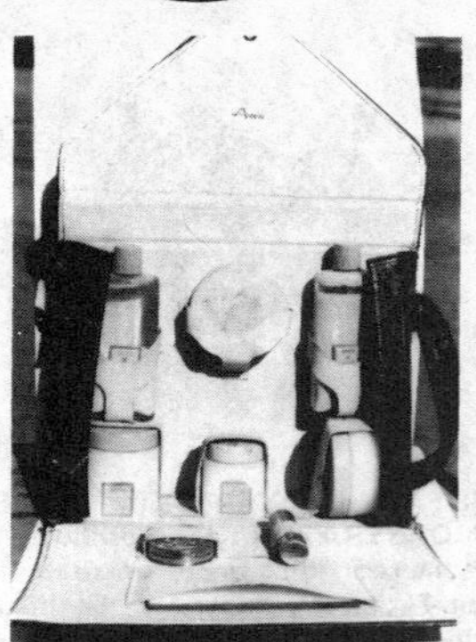

1948 REPRESENTATIVE DEMONSTRATOR KIT - Black leather kit. C.M.V. $90.00 mint.

1946 DEMONSTRATOR KIT
Box holds tube of tooth paste & hand cream & bottle of antiseptic. C.M.V. $40.00 M.B.

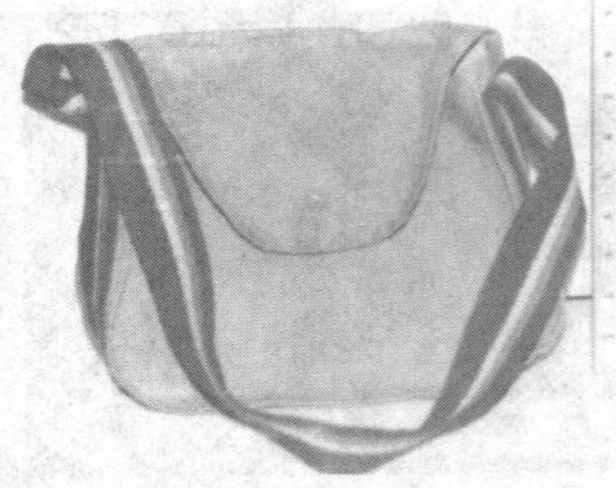

1977 COLORWORKS SHOULDER BAG
Given to customers who bought all 5 colorworks products. Sold to Reps for $2.50 as a Demo. Tan canvas bag with red, yellow and green strap. Measures 8½"c 10". C.M.V. $3.00

1970 REPS DEMO AND ORDER CASE
Blue plastic snap shut case. Has order pad, and fragrance samples and color brochures. C.M.V. $10.00 mint.

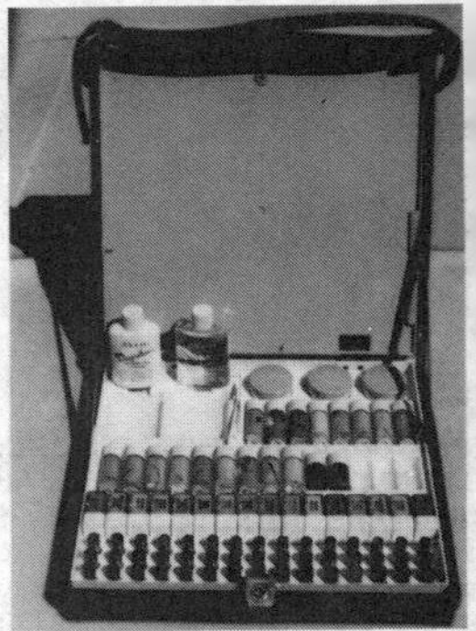

1959-60 BEAUTY COUNSELOR DEM KIT - Black shoulder bag with outside pocket holds removable turquoise & w plastic inner case with Avon & 4A desi on lid containing 3 white plastic jars w turquoise lids holding .46 oz. of Rich Moisture Cream, Vita Moist Cream & Strawberry Cooler, 1 oz. glass bottle sample of Skin Freshener, 1¼ oz. white plastic sample bottle Deep Clean Cleans Cream, 17 sample bottles of Liquid Pov 5 liquid Rouge samples in small bottles, gold metal lipstick samples & 16 plastic shaker powder samples. CMV $200.00 complete.

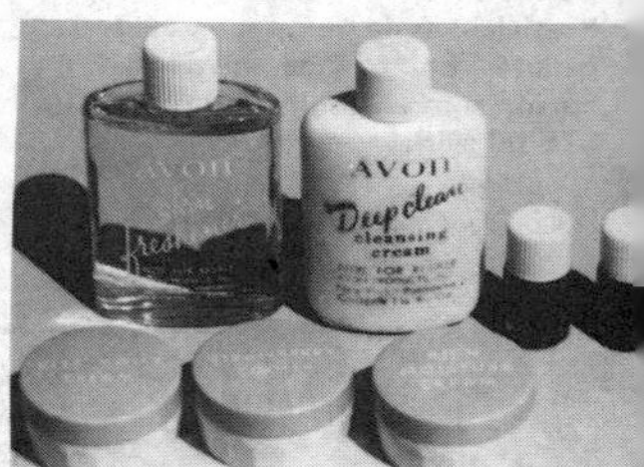

1956-60 BEAUTY COUNSELOR DEMO KIT SAMPLES - Front row left to right - White plastic jars with turquoise caps, ca in VITA MOIST CREAM, STRAWBERR COOLER, RICH MOISTURE CREAM, C.M.V. $6.00 ea. Back row left to right - SKIN FRESHENER, clear glass, white cap. $10.00; DEEP CLEAN CLEANSING CREAM, white plastic, gold lettering, white cap. C.M.V. $6.00. Rouge, clear glass, white cap. C.M.V. $6.00 ea.

1956 SKIN CARE DEMONSTRATOR
Plastic case holds plastic bottle of Deep Clean Cleansing Cream, 1 oz. glass bottle of Skin Freshener, 2 white jars of Rich Moisture & Hormone Cream & plastic spoon. C.M.V. $37.50 M.B.

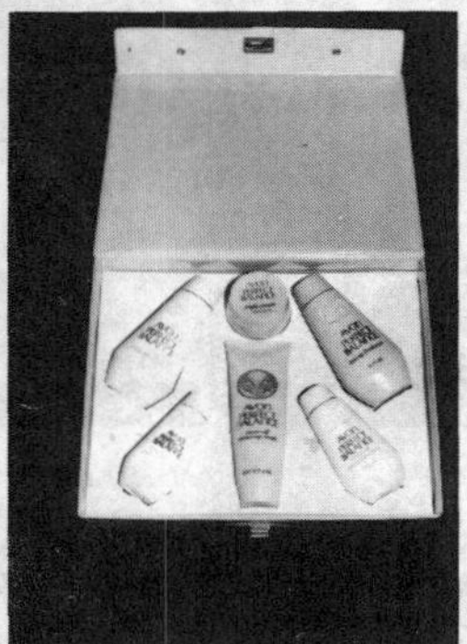

1974 PERFECT BALANCE MANAGERS DEMO KIT - Contained Tissue-Off cleansing cream, Toning Freshener, night cream, Wash-off cleansing lotion, Toning astringent, night time moisturizer. C.M.V. $35.00 M.B.

1964 PERFUME SAMPLE
Small 1/8 oz. bottle came in Occur! Somewhere, Cotillion, Topaze, Here's My Heart, Persian Wood, To A Wild Rose. C.M.V. $8.00 each.

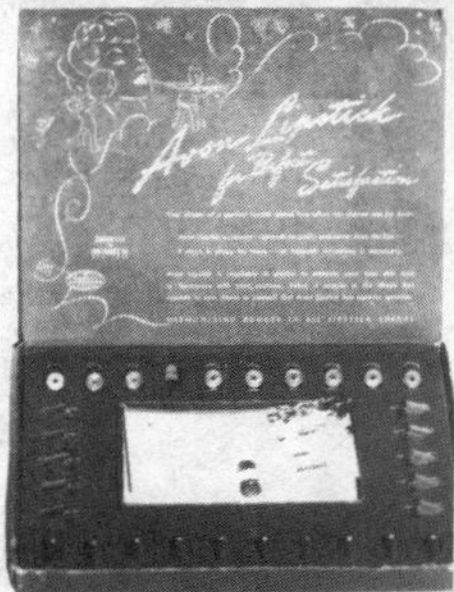

1942 LIPSTICK DEMONSTRATOR CASE
Box holds 30 turquoise plastic or metal samples or 30 brass bamboo samples. CMV $40.00 MB. Lady's face on top of box.

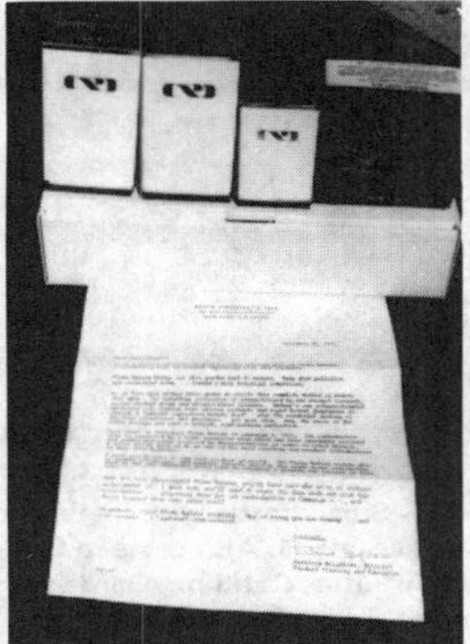

1970 PRIMA NATURA PRODUCTS INTRODUCTION DEMO KIT FOR MANAGERS ONLY - White Avon embossed box holds Creme of Soap, Night Veil Concentrate, Toning Freshener, Moisturizing Freshener. C.M.V. $25.00

1935 PERFUME SAMPLE
Very small glass vial with cork stopper in envelope. Came in Gardenia, Jardin D' Amour, Bolero, Cotillion, Ariel, Narcissus, Rose, Lily of the Valley, Sweet Pea, Trailing Arbutus. CPC on package. CMV $18.00 each in envelope mint.

1960 EYE SHADOW DEMONSTRATOR CARD - 6 gold metal eye shadow tubes. C.M.V. $12.00 mint.

1952 LIPSTICK DEMONSTRATOR
Box holds 4 full size gold embossed lipsticks & 1 refill. Used early to mid 50's. C.M.V. $30.00 M.B.

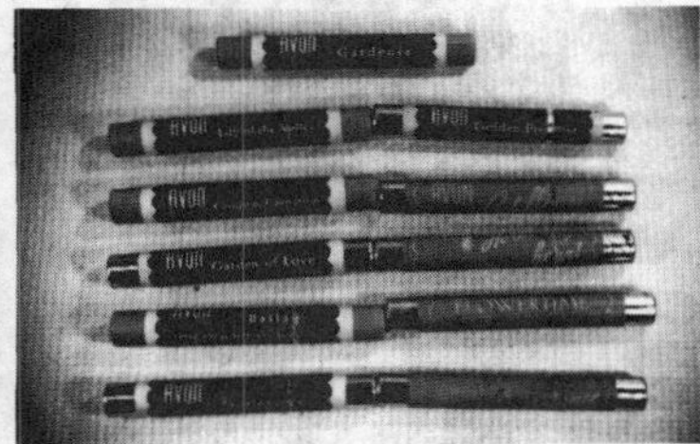

1947-50 PERFUME SAMPLES
Small sample tubes with glass vials of perfume inside. Gardenia, Lily of the Valley, Crimson Carnation, Luscious, Garden of Love, Ballad, Quaintance, & Golden Promise. CMV $20.00 each with vials. Here's My Heart, Flowertime, Quaintance & Cotillion came in pink or blue tubes. CMV $15.00 each mint.

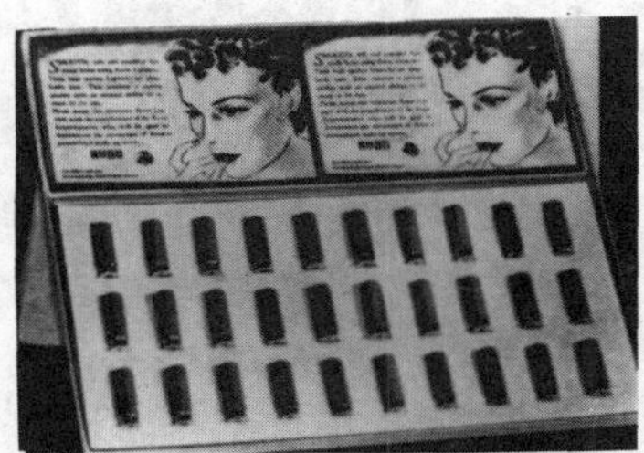

1940 LIPSTICK DEMONSTRATOR
Box holds 30 metal lipstick samples, with cards. CMV $35.00 MB with all 30 cards.

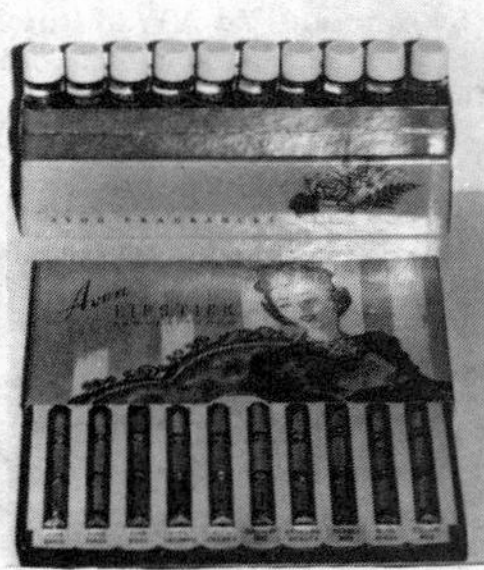

1960 FRAGRANCE SAMPLES — WOMEN'S
Pink & gold box holds 10 - 1 dram bottles, white caps. C.M.V. $12.00
1949 - early 1950's LIPSTICK JEWEL ETCHED SAMPLES - Box holds 30 metal lipstick samples. C.M.V. $30.00

LIPSTICK SAMPLES
(Left) 1947 red box holds 30 brass samples. Also came 2 boxes in a plain carton from Avon. CMV $30.00, CMV $60.00 box of 2 sets.
(Right) 1951 white plastic tray holds 30 brass lipstick samples. CMV $25.00.

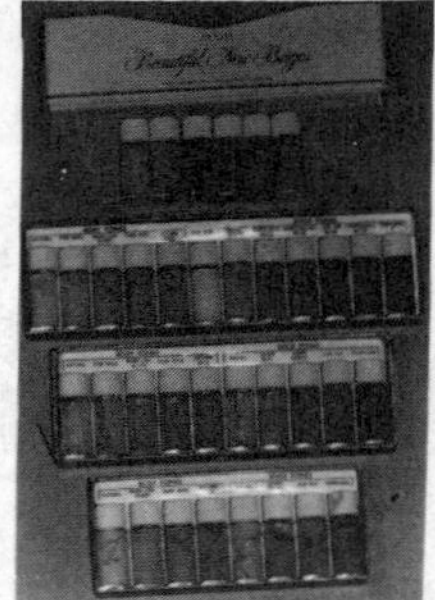

1960'S FOUNDATION DEMONSTRATORS
Clear glass bottles with white plastic lids. Top to Bottom — 12 bottle set, only 6 showing, 12 bottle set, 10 bottle set. Front row 8 bottle set. CMV all sets $5.00 MB.

MEN'S AFTER SHAVE SAMPLES
2 on left are 1960's. Box red, & silver bottles have red caps. CMV $10.00
2 on right are late 60's and early 70's. Box is red woven design & black. Bottles have red caps. Came with 2 different outer sleeves as shown. CMV $6.00 each MB.

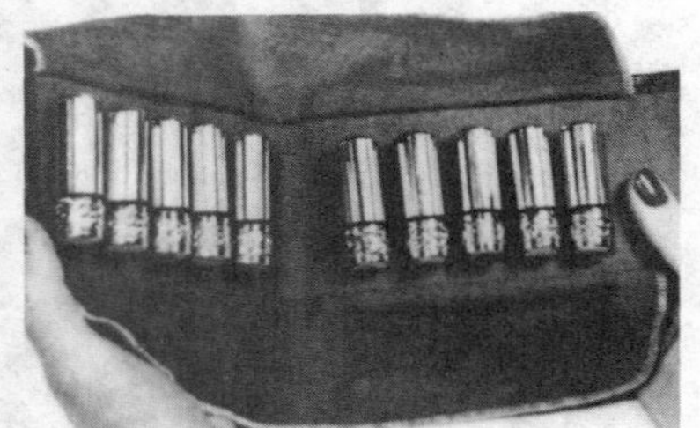

1949 LIPSTICK DEMONSTRATOR KIT - Black flannel roll-up kit holds 10 gold full size lipsticks. CMV $30.00 mint.

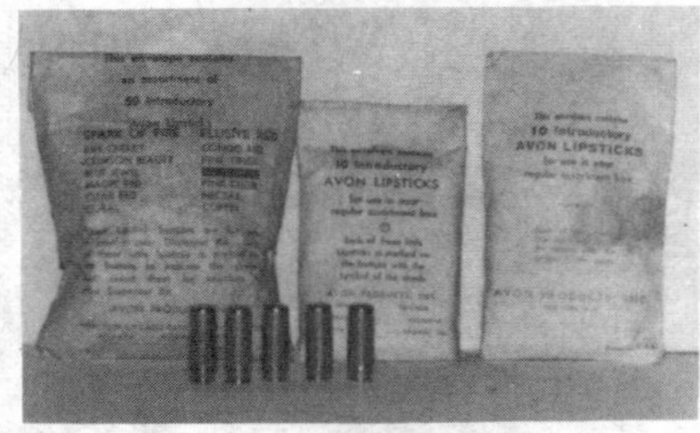

1950s LIPSTICK PACKS
2 different packs of 10 brass lipsticks. C.M.V. $6.00 complete pack or 50 sample pack, brass - C.M.V. $15.00 complete.

1941 GARDEN OF LOVE PERFUME SAMPLE - Small bottle with metal cap in sample envelope. Also came in Ballad, Trailing Arbutus, Cotillion, Gardenia, Merriment, Sweet Pea, Courtship, Lily of the Valley, Jardin D' Amour. CMV $18.00 each in envelope only. Add $2.00 for CPC on envelope.

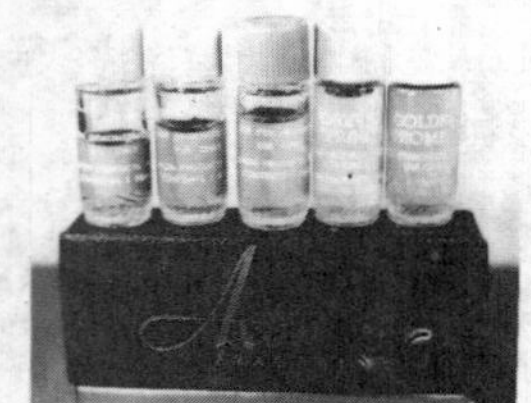

EARLY 1950's COLOGNE DEMONSTRATOR SET - 1 dram bottles of Cotillion, Quaintance, Forever Spring, Golden Promise, & To A Wild Rose. In green & gold box. Came in 5 & 6 bottle sets. C.M.V. $17.00 M.B.

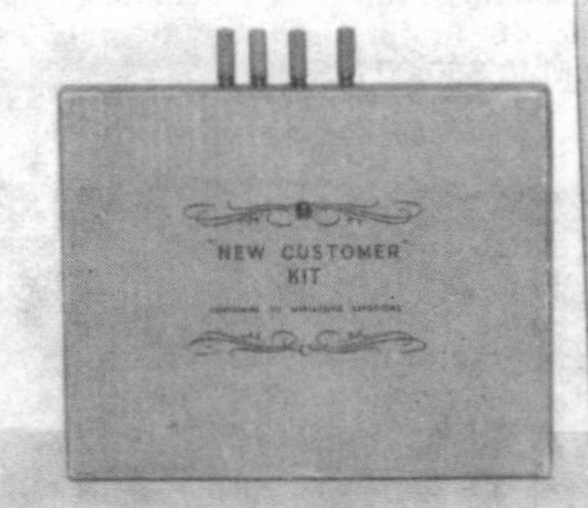

1936-40 NEW CUSTOMER KIT
Turquoise box holds 30 turquoise metal lipstick samples with 30 sample cards. CMV $45.00 set MB with all cards.

1940 LIPSTICK SAMPLE
Gold metal case on display card. Came in 2 different size and style cards as shown. CMV $1.00 on card. Lipstick only 25c.
1938 LIPSTICK SAMPLE
Same card as 1940 card only came with turquoise metal lipstick sample. CMV $1.00 on card, mint.

1956 HARMONY ROUGE SAMPLES
5 sample bottles. CMV $15.00
1950 COLOGNE SAMPLES
Green box holds 6 samples, colored lids. CMV $12.00 MB.
1968 COLOGNE SAMPLES
Green box with woven design holds 7 samples, all have yellow caps. CMV $5.00 MB.

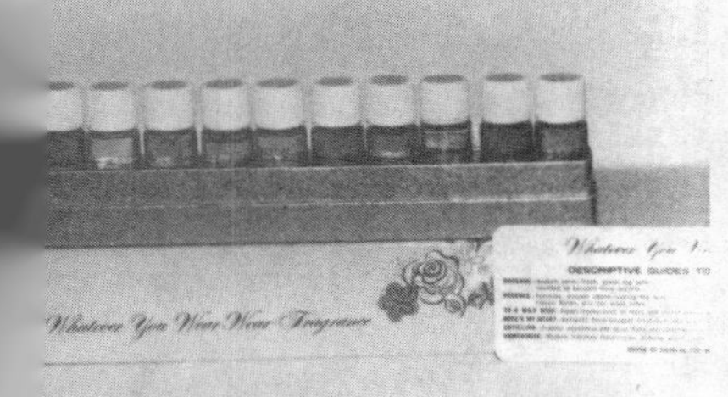

1965 FRAGRANCE COLOGNE SAMPLES
Pink and gold box holds 10 cologne samples with white caps. C.M.V. $7.00 M.B.

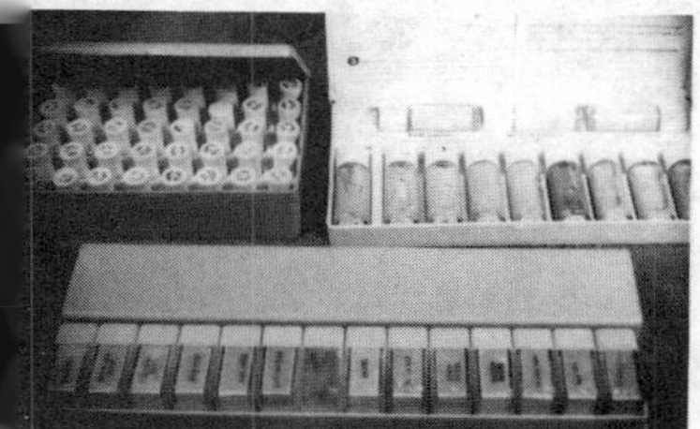

1958 POWDER SAMPLES - 14 samples, square container. C.M.V' $10.00 M.B.
1967 LIQUID POWDER SAMPLES (upper right) Box of 12 samples, clear plastic top. CMV $8.00 MB.

1956 COLOGNE DEMONSTRATOR SET - 1 dram bottles of To A Wild Rose, Forever Spring, Bright Night, Nearness, Elegante, & Cotillion, All different color caps, in pink & gold box. C.M.V. $15.00 M.B. Also came out in Canada in all white caps. C.M.V. $15.00 M.B.

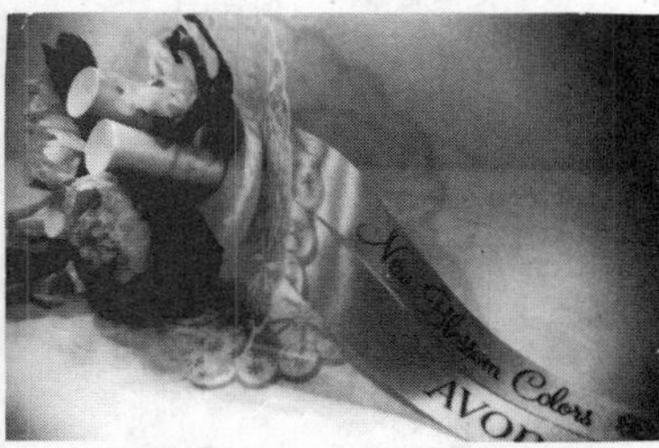

1960 NOSE GAY LIPSTICK DEMO KIT
White foam, pink ribbon & flowers. Holds 4 white lipsticks. Came only in plum, orange, peach, & cherry blossom. Made up like flower bouquet. CMV $65.00 mint.

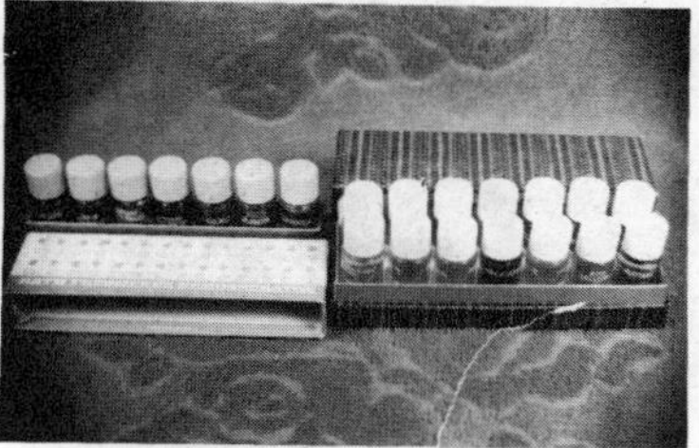

1968 BATH FRESHENER SAMPLES
Colored caps. 7 samples. C.M.V. $6.00 M.B.
1968 COLOGNE SAMPLES - 14 samples, white caps. C.M.V. $7.00 M.B.

1957 NAIL POLISH DEMONSTRATOR
Six ½ dram bottles with white caps. CMV $20.00 MB. B.

1940-41 PERFUME DEMO KIT
Green & gold box holds 3 - 1 dram bottles with colored caps. Perfume sample set used by representatives. Came in Marionette Garden of Love, Cotillion, & Gardenia, OSP 30c, CMV $67.50 MB.

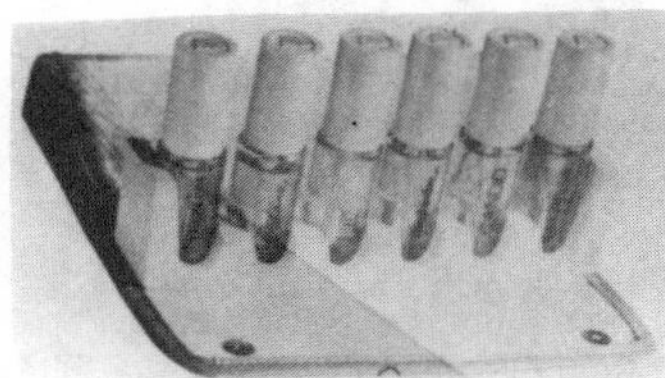

1978 FRAGRANCE DEMO KIT
Plastic demo kit holds 6 sample bottles of Avon fragrance. C.M.V. $2.00

1953 LIPSTICK DEMONSTRATOR
Green leatherette zippered case holds 5 gold lipsticks. CMV $27.50 mint.

1940's HEAVENLIGHT FACE POWDER SAMPLE - Blue metal case, white feather on lid. C.M.V. $2.00 mint.

1978 SAMPLE & DEMO PRODUCTS
1977-78 Lipstick samples – Pack of 10 white plastic lipstick samples. C.M.V. 25¢ a pack,
1976-78 Ring sizes – White plastic Avon marked ring sizes. Used by Reps to sell Avon rings. C.M.V. 25¢
1977-78 FRAGRANCE SAMPLE DEMO KIT
Blue plastic, white inside has plastic tray with room for 38 sample 1/8 oz. bottles of both womens and mens fragrances. C.M.V. $2.00 case.

1973 FOUNDATION MAKEUP DEMO
Box holds 7 bottles with white caps. Used by Reps only. C.M.V. $3.00 M.B.

1940s FACE POWDER SAMPLE BOX
Light green box holds 30 plain blue face powder samples. Avon on back. C.M.V. $25.00 box complete mint.

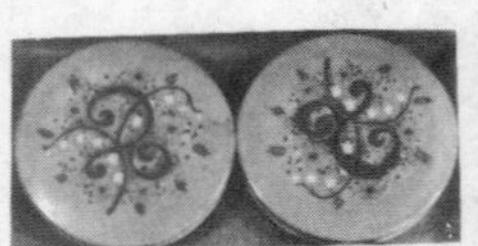

1949-55 FACE POWDER SAMPLES
Green metal samples. C.M.V. $1.50 each mint.
1930-36 FACE POWDER SAMPLE
Small silver can, came in Ariel or Vernafleur. C.M.V. $6.00 mint.

1944 FACE POWDER DEMONSTRATOR PALETTE - Board holds 8 paper box samples. C.M.V. $32.00 mint.

1942 FACE POWDER SAMPLES
Box holds 30 blue feather design samples. C.M.V. $42.00 M.B.

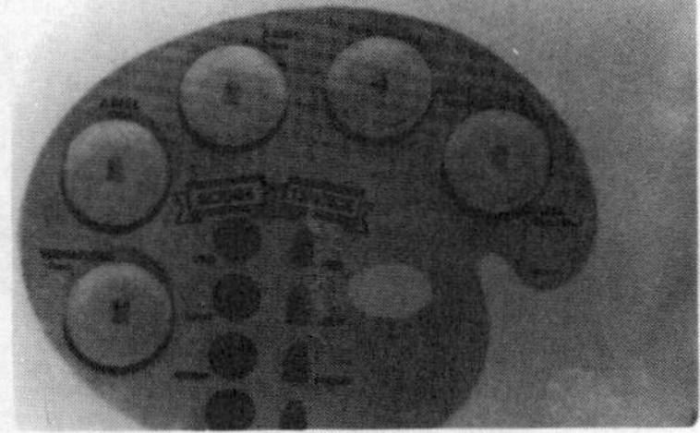

1938 FACE POWDER DEMONSTRATOR PALETTE - Board holds 5 samples in Ariel, & Vernafleur. C.M.V. $32.00 mint.

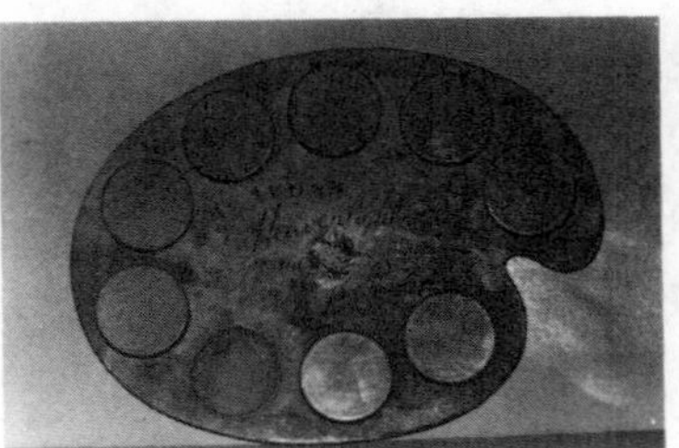

1946 HEAVENLIGHT FACE POWDER SAMPLE PALETTE - Each pink sample has Heavenlight written across each top. C.M.V. $30.00

1940 FACE POWDER DEMONSTRATOR PALETTE - Board holds 8 metal samples. C.M.V. $32.00 mint.

(Left to Right to Bottom)
FACE POWDER DEMONSTRATOR PALETTES
1946-49 HEAVENLIGHT - Blue board holds 9 feather design samples. C.M.V. $27.00
1949-54 FACE POWDER PALETTE
Turquoise board holds 8 to 10 samples. C.M.V. $22.00
1954-55 FACE POWDER PALETTE
Turquoise board holds 10 samples. C.M.V. $22.00

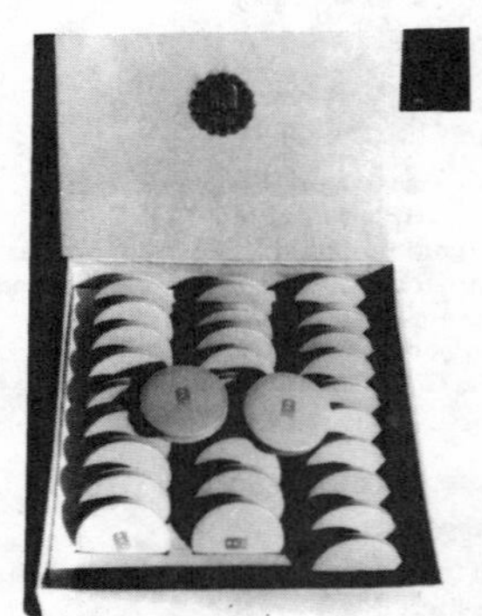

1942 FACE POWDER SAMPLE SET
Box holds 30 metal face powder samples. O.S.P. 50¢ C.M.V. $45.00 set M.B. $1.00 each sample.

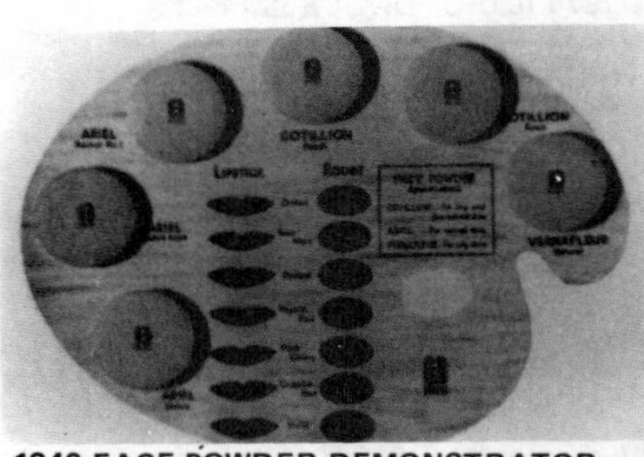

1940 FACE POWDER DEMONSTRATOR PALETTE - Board holds 6 metal samples in Ariel, Cotillion & Vernafleur. C.M.V. $30.00

1957 FACE POWDER DEMONSTRATOR PALETTE - Turquoise board holds 10 samples with clear plastic tops. C.M.V. $22.00 mint.

1946-49 HEAVENLIGHT FACE POWDER SAMPLES - Box holds 30 feather design samples. O.S.P. 50¢ C.M.V. $35.00 M.B. Samples came both in cardboard & tin.

1971-72 CUSTOM CONDITIONER
¾ oz. bottle with white cap. Used in Avon beauty shops for professional use only. C.M.V. $10.00
1971-72 NEW DIMENSION EXTRA & REGULAR
¾ oz. glass bottle. Used in Avon Beauty Shops for professional use only. Top of bottle must be broken to use contents. C.M.V. $10.00

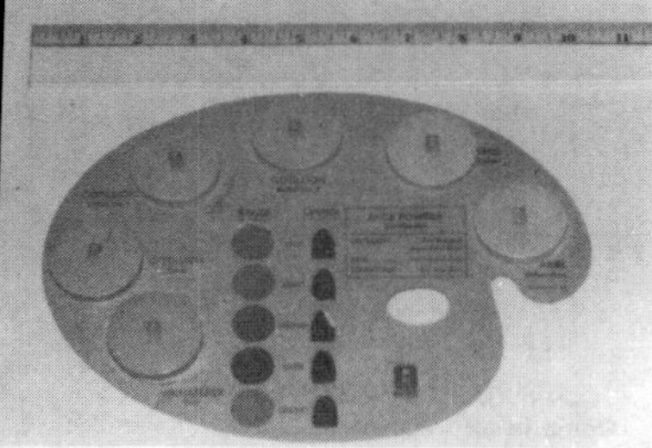

1939 FACE POWDER DEMONSTRATOR PALETTE
Board holds 6 different face powder samples with tulip A on lid in Cotillion, Ariel, or Vernafleur. C.M.V. $30.00 mint

1953 SALES BAG
Black bag used by Avon reps. in early 50's. C.M.V. $22.00 mint.

1941-43 DELIVERY BAG
Black imitation leather waterproof bag used by Reps to deliver Avon products. Base of bag measures 15½" long, 7" wide, 10" high and has a 21 inch zipper. Cost a Rep. $1.49. C.M.V. $15.00 mint.

1944 DELIVERY BAG PRIZE
Black waterproof bag, zipper top, metal buttons on bottom to set on. Given to Reps for placing order of $150.00 or more. Used to deliver Avon products. C.M.V. $15.00 mint.

1950s FACE POWDER PALETTE DEMONSTRATOR
Board holds 10 sample powders. Came in pink envelope. Used by Reps. Same palette came in different envelopes. C.M.V. $22.00 with envelope.

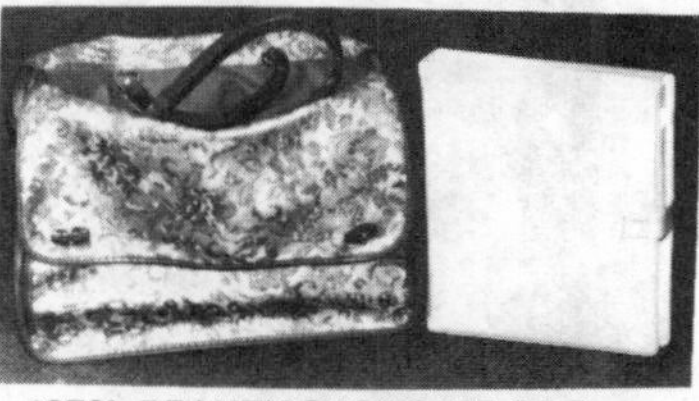

1970's BEAUTY SHOWCASE BAG
Blue & green vinyl came with blue plastic holder for samples. C.M.V. $10.00 for both or $5.00 each.

1970's DELIVERY BAG
White, blue & green design used by Avon ladies. C.M.V. $6.00

1970 REPRESENTATIVES DEMO BAG
White background with bright colored flowers. Silver 4A emblem under handle. CMV $6.00 mint.

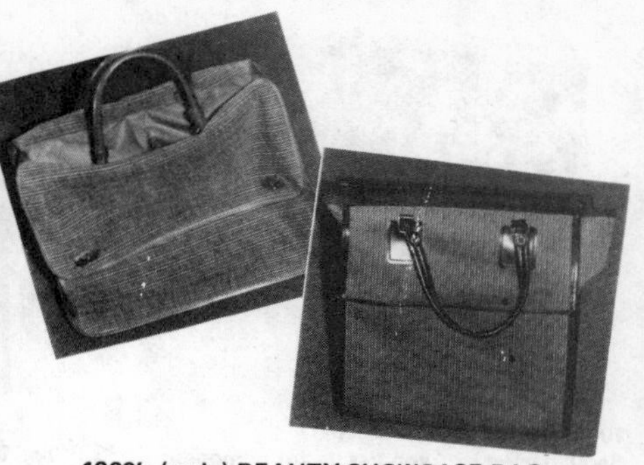

1960's (early) BEAUTY SHOWCASE BAG
Two toned blue with black trim. Used by reps. C.M.V. $6.00

1960's (late) BEAUTY SHOWCASE BAG
Two toned blue & blue trim. Used by reps. C.M.V. $5.00

1960's DELIVERY BAG
Two toned blue silver 4A emblem under handle. C.M.V. $6.00

DELIVERY BAGS
Left - 1929 Black leatherette C.M.V. $30.00. Middle - 1948 Black leatherette front opening lays flat. C.M.V. $20.00 Right - 1942 Black leatherette C.M.V. $20.00

1950's DELIVERY BAG
Black leatherette C.M.V. $17.00 mint.

1949 TISSUE DEMONSTRATOR
Small packet of Avon tissues for demonstrators. C.M.V. $12.00 mint.

1937-44 FACIAL TISSUES SAMPLES
Beige & green paper wrapper. C.M.V. $10.00 mint.

1950'S POWDER SACHET PACKETS
Came in all fragrances, 10 in an envelope. CMV $1.00 each or $7.00 for packet of 10 mint.

1963 TRIBUTE AFTER SHAVE SAMPLES
Left - Box of 10. C.M.V. $5.00
1965 OCCUR! CREAM SACHET SAMPLES - Box of 30. C.M.V. ea. $5.00
1961 CREAM HAIR DRESS SAMPLES
Box of 30 tubes. C.M.V. M.B. $5.00 each tube 25¢

1964 EYE SHADOW TRY-ONS
(Bottom) Demo paper container with 50 match samples, double sided. CMV $6.00 mint.
(Top) Eye Shadow Try-Ons holds 15 match samples. CMV $5.00 mint.

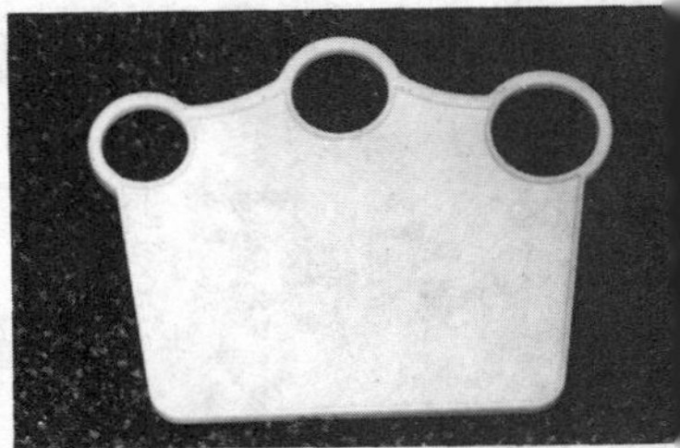

1972-77 RING SIZER
Pink plastic Avon ring sizer for reps. to sell Avon rings in correct size. C.M.V. $1.00

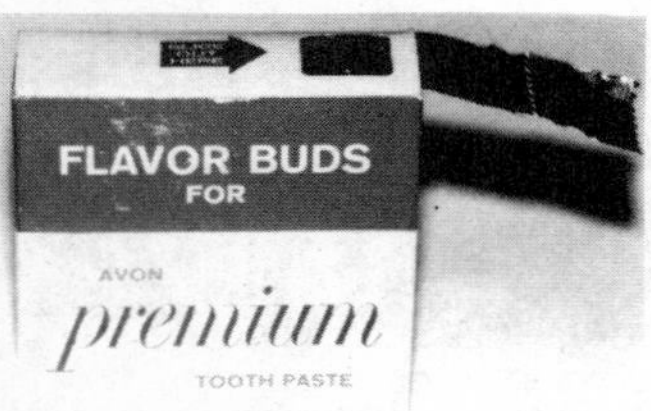

1950's FLAVOR BUDS TOOTHPASTE SAMPLE - Red & white box with foil tear off samples. CMV $7.00 MB.

1960's CLEAR 'N' COVER SAMPLE
C.M.V. $1.00
1960 LUMINOUS CREAM EYE SHADOW
C.M.V. $1.00

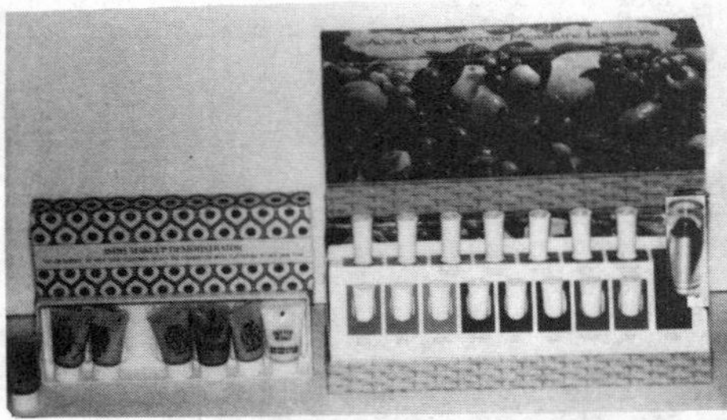

1977 FOUNDATION MAKE-UP DEMO
Box holds 7 Even-Tone foundation tubes with white caps. Marked not for resale on back. CMV $2.00 MB.
1978 COLORCREME MOISTURE LIPSTICKS DEMO SET
Fruit backet design box holds 15 small white plastic sample lipsticks & 1 full size lipstick in silver and blue tube. Box came with outer sleeve. CMV $2.00 MB.

1949-55 CREAM CAKE SAMPLES
Holds 6 shades of Cream Cake. C.M.V. $8.00 mint.

1976 FRAGRANCE SAMPLES
25 to a box. Came in all fragrances. C.M.V. 75¢ each box.

1970'S RICH MOISTURE CREAM SAMPLES
10 packets. CMV 25c box.
1970'S FASHION GROUP SAMPLES
Box of 10 packets. CMV 25c box.

1940-1950'S FACE POWDER SAMPLES
Avon envelope holds 10 sample packets of face powder. CMV $3.00 mint.

1979-80 SAMPLE TRIAL SIZE PRODUCTS
Bottles are all plastic.
Left to Right.
Smooth as Silk Bath Oil — 1 oz. CMV 25c.
Bubble Bath — 1 oz. CMV 25c.
New Vitality Extra Body Conditioner — 2 oz. CMV 25c.
Rich Moisture Hand Cream — ½ oz. CMV 25c.
Nurtura Replenishing Cream — Box of 10 samples. CMV 25c.
Care Deeply Lotion For Problem Dry Skin — 2 oz. CMV 25c.

1979-80 ENVIRA MAKE-UP DEMO KIT & PRODUCTS
Pink lid box with outer sleeve & white plastic inner base holds 1 each of Envira Products which are also sold separate.
CONDITIONING MAKE-UP CMV 25c
PURE COLOR BLUSH CMV 25c
GENTLE EYE COLOR CMV 25c
PURE COLOR LIPSTICK CMV 25c
SOFT EYE DEFINER CMV 25c
CONDITIONING MASCARA CMV 25c
CMV complete set in demo box, mint $7.50.
SAMPLES CONDITIONING MAKE-UP
Box of 10 CMV 25c
SAMPLES PURE COLOR BLUSH
Box of 10 CMV 25c.

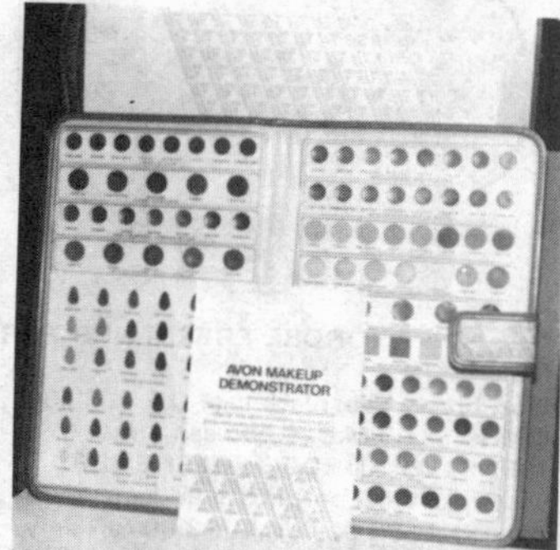

1979 MAKE-UP DEMO CASE
Large tan vinyl case. CMV $10.00 MB.

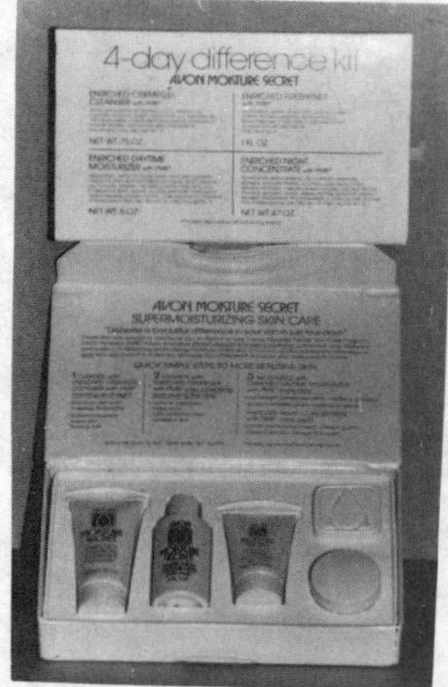

1980 MOISTURE SECRET KIT
Outer sleeve holds white & pink plastic case. 4 small pink plastic containers of creams. SSP $3.50 CMV $3.50 MB.

1940'S CLEANSING CREAM SAMPLE SET
Box holds 10 turquoise ¼ oz. sample tubes of cleansing cream. Also came with 2 stacks of your skin can be beautiful pamphlets. CMV $35.00 MB.

1979 FRESH LOOK MAKE-UP DEMO KIT
Used by reps only. Peach color box. CMV $5.00 MB.

1949-50 FACE POWDER DEMO SAMPLES
Pink & white feather box holds 50 demo packets of face powder. Used by reps. Packets are different. Was not sold to public. CMV $15.00 MB

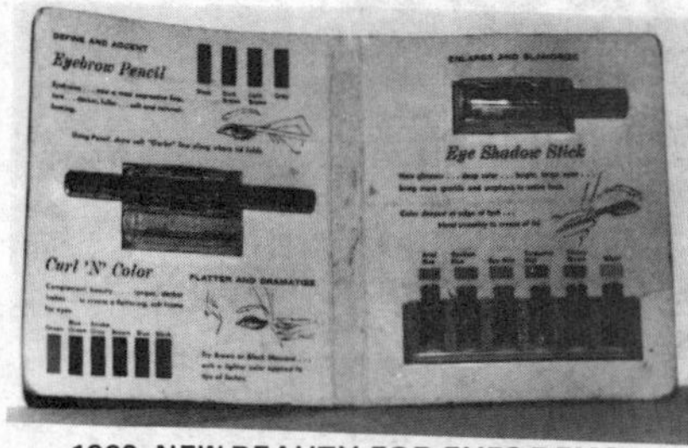

1960 NEW BEAUTY FOR EYES DEMO
Cardboard card opens up with 6 brass lipstick samples, brass eye shadow stick, eyebrow pencil & curl 'n' color. Used by reps. CMV $12.50 mint.

SPRAY CANS - MISC.

ALL ITEMS' PRICES EMPTY - MINT

1965-67 WARDROBE FRESHENER FOR MEN (Left)
6 oz, brown can, black cap. O.S.P. $2.00 C.M.V. $4.00 M.B. $3.00 can only.
1967-68 WARDROBE FRESHENER (Center) 6 oz. purple & gold can, white cap. O.S.P. $2.00 C.M.V. $3.00 can only. $4.00 M.B.
1968-78 WARDROBE FRESHENER (Right) 6 oz, red, black & gold with black cap. O.S.P. $1.00 C.M.V. 25¢

1954-57 AVON NET HAIR SPRAY
Green and white can, white caps. Came in 5 oz. size. O.S.P. $1.25 , & 11 oz. size, O.S.P. $2.00. C.M.V. $7.00 M.B. $6.00 each, can only.

1974-76 ORIENTAL IRIS
7 oz. White can lavender flowers and cap. S.S.P. $2.00 C.M.V. 25¢
1976-78 COUNTRY MEADOWS ROOM FRESHENER
7 oz. green can and cap. O.S.P. $1.49 C.M.V. 25¢ regular can. Pictured with rare upside down label. C.M.V. $8.00

1957-58 AVON NET HAIR SPRAY
White & pink spray can came in 5 & 11 oz. sizes. O.S.P. $1.25 & $2.00 C.M.V. $5.00 ea.
1958-60 AVON NET FOR FINE HAIR
5 oz. blue & white can & cap. O.S.P. $1.25 C.M.V. $5.00.
1959-64 AVON NET REGULAR
5 oz. pink & white can & cap. O.S.P. $1.25 C.M.V. $4.00.
1956 LATHER FOAM SHAMPOO
Green can and cap, short issue. O.S.P. $1.29 C.M.V. $6.00 mint

LEFT 1977-78 GENTLE RAIN ROOM FRESHENER
7 oz. blue spray can, blue top. O.S.P. $1.49 C.M.V. 50¢
1978 BURST OF SPRING ROOM FRESHENER
7 oz. yellow and green can, yellow top. O.S.P. $1.49 C.M.V. 50¢
RIGHT 1971-73 ENAMEL SET SPRAY
7 oz. white can, red cap. Red design. O.S.P. $1.00 C.M.V. 50¢

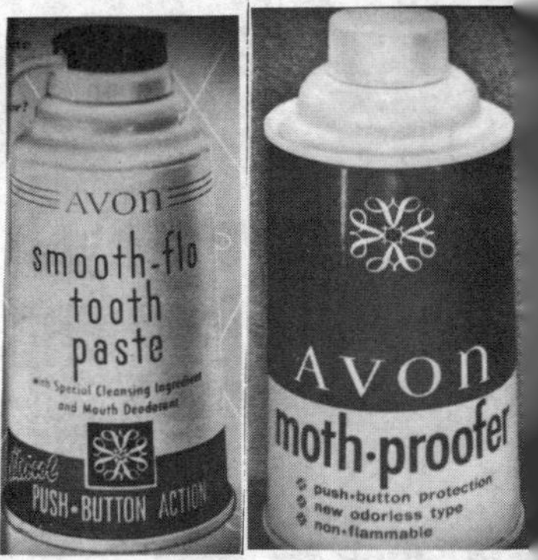

LEFT 1959-61 SMOOTH-FLOW TOOTHPA
5½ oz. white, red & gray metal can, red cap. O.S.P. 89¢, C.M.V. $4.00 can only $5.00 M.B.
RIGHT 1956-60 MOTH PROOFER
12 oz. red & white spray can, white cap. O.S.P. $1.89, C.M.V. $4.00.
1968-72 MOTH PROOFER
11 oz. red & white spray can with white cap. O.S.P. $1.89, C.M.V. 50¢

1973-78 ROOM FRESHENER'S
1973-78 SCOTTISH HEATHER - can with pink cap. C.M.V. 50¢
1973-78 SWISS SNOWDROPS - can with dark green cap. C.M.V. 50¢
1973-74 WASSIAL BOWL - can with red cap. C.M.V. 75¢
1973-78 EVERGREEN - can with green cap. C.M.V. 50¢
1973-76 DUTCH TULIP - can with pink cap. C.M.V. 50¢ - O.S.P. $2.00 all scents.

1971-73 INSTANT COOL
4 oz. white & blue can, white cap. OSP $2.00 CMV 75c.
1968-70 HAIR SPRAY (Unscented)
7 oz. white & gold with pink cap. OSP $1.00 CMV $1.00
1975-79 ON DUTY DEODORANT
7 oz. black & white with black cap. OSP $1.00 CMV 25c. Also came with upside down label. CMV $8.00
1979-80 came in 4 oz. can. Same CMV.

1979-80 HELLO SPRING ROOM FRESHENER
7 oz. white can, green cap. SSP $1.11 no box. CMV 25c. Also came with upside down label. CMV $8.00.
1979-80 HAIR SPRAY FULL CONTROL
6 oz. brown can & cap. SSP $1.79, CMV 25c.
1979-80 HAIR SPRAY FIRM & NATURAL
6 oz. green & white can & green cap. SSP $1.79, CMV 25c.

1958-68 KLEAN AIR
12 oz. Spray can 1958-63 came in Mint with blue cap. C.M.V. $2.00. Bouquet 1958-63 with pink cap, C.M.V. $2.00. 1961-67 Citrus, orange cap, C.M.V. $1.00. Meadow Fresh 1961-67 in pink cap, C.M.V. $1.00. Pine 1961-67 in green cap, C.M.V. $1.00. Spice 1962-67, brown cap, C.M.V. $1.00. Sudden Spring 1966-68 turquoise cap, C.M.V. 75¢. Indoor Garden 1964-67, yellow cap, C.M.V. $1.00 O.S.P. $1.89 ea.

1958-73 SPRAY SACHET
Box holds 6 oz. can of Spray Sachet in Lavender. 1958-72 with lavender cap. C.M.V 50¢. 1961-72 Rosiest, pink cap. C.M.V. 50¢. Sunny Morning, 1961-63, blue cap. C.M.V. $4.00. Bayberry 1963-72 green cap. C.M.V. 50¢ Carnation 1964-68, red cap. C.M.V. $2.00. Ribbons N Lace 1967-72, Pink cap. C.M.V. 50¢, 1969-72 Potpourri, red cap. C.M.V. 50¢ 1970-72 Sheer Fancy, green cap. C.M.V. 50¢. 1971-72 Lemon Verbena, light green cap. C.M.V. 50¢ O.S.P. $1.50 - $2.00 each.

EFT TO RIGHT
971-74 MATTER MINITS MASQUE
75 oz. yellow, brown & white with
ellow cap. O.S.P. $1.50 C.M.V. 50¢.
974-75 AEROSOL HAIR CONDITIONER
oz. Pink, white & gold with white
p. O.S.P. $2.00 C.M.V 25¢.
970-72 ASSURA SPRAY
oz. Blue & white can, white cap.
S.P. $1.00 C.M.V. $1.00
973-74 ASSURA SPRAY
oz. Blue & white can, white cap.
powder spray) or green & white
with green cap (dry mist). O.S.P. $1.00
.M.V. 50¢.

LEFT 1956-58 KLEAN AIR
12 oz. blue & white spray can with white cap. Mint scented. OSP $1.89. CMV $5.00 mint. Also came 3 oz. pink & white. Same shape can. CMV $7.00
RIGHT 1970-73 KLEAN AIR
12 oz. citrus blossoms can with yellow green cap. O.S.P. $1.98, C.M.V. $1.00.
12 oz. Mountain Mist can with turquoise cap. O.S.P. $1.98, C.M.V. $1.00.

1974-78 ROOM FRESHENERS
Yellow & white can, yellow cap. Pink, green & white can, light pink cap. Lavender & white can, lavender cap. Red & green can, red cap.
1974-77 BAYBERRY
O.S.P. $1.00 C.M.V. 25¢
12 oz. yellow & green, yellow cap. OSP $1.50 CMV 75c. Also came 3 oz. size. CMV $1.00
1971-74 JAMAICAN WATERFALL
12 oz. pink & white with pink cap. OSP $1.50 CMV 75c. Also came 3 oz. size. CMV $1.00.
1971-76 SURFACE DISENFECTANT
White 12 oz. can, white cap. OSP $1.50 CMV 25c.

1968 KLEAN AIR CONCENTRATE
3 oz. Citrus, green can; Sudden Spring, yellow can; Jamaican Waterfall, pink can. OSP $1.69, CMV $1.00 each.
1965-68 BEAUTIFACIAL
3.75 oz. metal can. OSP $2.50, CMV $2.00

1970-74 ROOM FRESHENERS
1970-72 Country Strawberry can with red cap. C.M.V. $1.00
1970-73 Green Apple can with green cap. C.M.V. $1.00
1972-74 Hawaiian Pineapple can with yellow cap. C.M.V. 50¢
1972-73 Fresh Mellon can with yellow-green cap. C.M.V. $1.00
1973-74 Really Raspberry can with red cap. C.M.V. 50¢
1970-72 Tangy Tangerine can with orange cap. C.M.V. $1.00. O.S.P. all scents $2.00

TEST BOTTLES & COMPS

The following definition of test bottles is "A very limited run by one to seven glass factories in 'flint' (clear) or colored glass samples. The size, shape or features may vary somewhat. Avon decides the final color to be used; the unused and discarded colors may be rejects, oddities, facimilies of issue - and coveted sample or TEST bottle." Avon Test Bottles are not sold by the Avon Representative. They are a very limited run of bottles made at the factory to check the color, size, glass thickness and shape of an Avon bottle before it goes into production. Usually no more than 1,000 test bottles are made of any 1 item and in most cases only a few dozen to a few hundred are made in test samples. In most cases the test bottle is run off in a different color than the regular production model is. Sometimes it will be run in more than 1 color as a test to see which looks the best. Test bottles are not supposed to be taken from the factory and are supposed to be destroyed when the test bottles are perfected as to Avon desires. They are hard to find and most test bottles come from New Jersey and Ohio where the test bottles are tested. Because of the very limited production of test bottles and the fact they are hard to find, the prices sometimes command a high price. WARNING! WHAT TODAY MAY BE A VALUABLE TEST BOTTLE, MAY BE TOMORROW REGULAR ISSUE. Avon more and more are using the same bottle over the years in a different color, which often will be the same as the original test bottle. When this happens, unless you can see the definite difference, the price of the test bottle will not be worth any more than the regular issue.

Many bottles are being painted over clear glass or white milk glass by Avon. Always unscrew the cap to see what color of glass your bottle actually is.

You also have to be aware that Avon is selling all over the world in the same bottle, only the color will changed in several different countries. Use the foreign bottle section to help you identify bottles in a different color.

COMPS *are the artist's model, made up and painted to see what the item will look like before the production mold is made. Comps are also used to photograph for Avon Catalogs. Some are made of solid lucite, plastic and other materials different from the production model. Comps are extremely rare and most are made 1 of a kind.*

Avon Products since 1977 has been giving the National Association of Avon Clubs 1 each of about 40 different comps each year at the big Annual N.A.A.C. Collectors Convention. Each comp given comes with a letter signed by an Avon Vice President stating that the comp is 1 of a kind & was never sold by Avon Products. These comps are either auctioned off or sold by raffle and bring prices from $150.00 up to $500.00. You will have to contact members of the more than 150 Avon Collectors Clubs around the U.S. to find comps. The CMV varies widely so be sure you get the letter from Avon with it as it will be of little value without the letter to prove it is an original comp.

Avon test bottles are a very exciting part of Avon collecting, but we suggest you use caution in buying them at big prices until you know what you are getting. WARNING! Many items are issued in other countries in the same color as a U.S. test bottle which destroys the value of the U.S. test bottle.

1977 VIKING SHIP COMP.
Blue green paint over clear glass, matching plastic cap. Red & white tin sail. Used only to photograph for Avon brochures. Given to NAAC with letter from Avon on 1 of a kind. RARE. C.M.V.$300.00 with letter from Avon.

1977 COLORWORKS DEMO KIT COMP BOX
Hand painged white & gray box, used to photograph for Avon Brochure. Given to NAAC from Avon with letter on 1 of a kind. RARE. C.M.V. $50.00 with Avon letter.

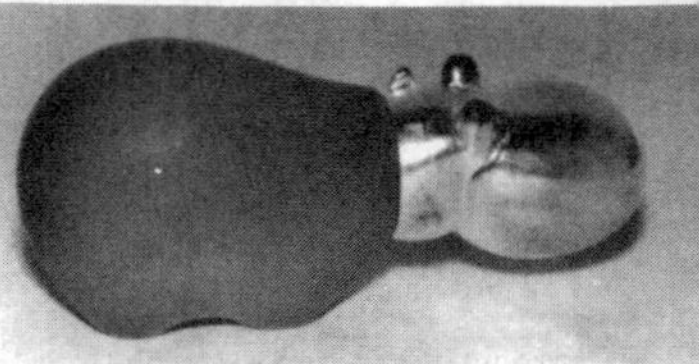

1977 BABY HIPPO PHOTO COMP.
Solid lucite body & silver head. Was used to take pictures for Avon catalogs before bottle was manufactured. RARE 1 of a kind. C.M.V. $350.00

1977 SUMMER BUTTERFLIES SOAP COMPS.
2 mock up plastic decorated soaps used only to photograph for Avon brochures. Avon donated this to NAAC with letter on 1 of a kind. RARE. C.M.V. $145.00 with letter from Avon.

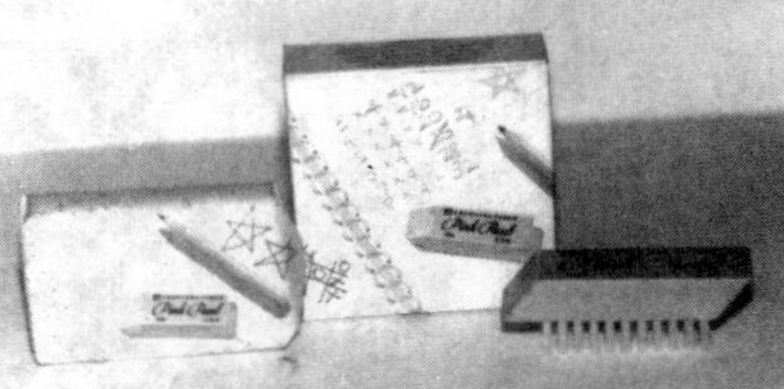

1977 SCRUB AWAY NAIL BRUSH & SOAP COMP.
Box, soap & brush are not real. Used only to photograph for Avon brochures. Given to NAAC 2 July, 77 with letter from Avon on 1 of a kind. RARE. C.M.V. $75.00 with Avon letter.

EFT 1977 TYRANNOSAURUS REX OMP.
lastic base - rubber head, blue green color. Used by Avon to photograph r Avon brochures. Given to NAAC ith letter from Avon on 1 of a kind. ARE. C.M.V. $300.00 with Avon letter.
IGHT 1977 SKATERS WALTZ ECANTER COMP.
lastic base flocked in red, pink plastic. op. Used to photograph for Avon rochures. Given to NAAC with letter rom Avon on 1 of a kind. RARE. .M.V. $350.00 with letter from Avon.

EFT 1977 TEDDY BEAR COLOGNE OMP.
an flock over clear glass used by Avon o photograph for Avon brochures. Given o NAAC with letter from Avon on of a kind. RARE C.M.V. $425.00 ith letter from Avon.
IGHT 1977 MALE CHAUVINIST PIG OMP.
ucite mock up used to photograph for von brochures. Given to NAAC with etter from Avon on 1 of a kind. RARE. .M.V. $265.00 with letter from Avon.

1972-74 DELFT BLUE PITCHER & BOWL REJECT
White milk glass. No decals painted on at factory. C.M.V. $15.00

LEFT 1977 HARD HAT COMP
Yellow paint over clear glass. Yellow cap used to photograph for Avon brochures. Given to NAAC and sold with letter from Avon on 1 of a kind. C.M.V. $200.00
RIGHT 1977 FAITHFUL LADDIE COMP
Amber glass & matching plastic top. Used only to photograph for Avon brochures. Given to NAAC. Came with letter from Avon on 1 of a kind. C.M.V. $160.00 with letter from Avon.

1976-77 PLASTIC TEST
Misc. factory test items in plastic & rubber. Used at factory in designing items for general delivery by Avon. These were never issued to public like shown. C.M.V. $5.00 each.

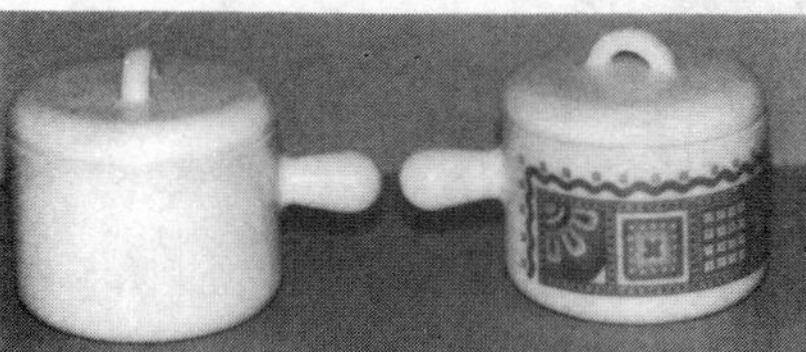

PATCHWORK CANDLE TEST JAR
Avon stamped in bottom. The outside design was not put on jar. C.M.V. $10.00

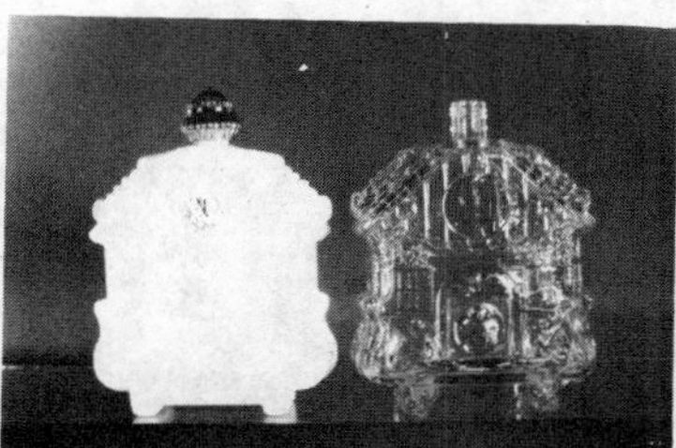

1972 ENCHANTED HOURS CUCKOO CLOCK TEST
Left - white milk glass, C.M.V. $45.00.
Right - clear glass, C.M.V. $75.00.
Issued in blue milk glass.

1970 INDIAN HEAD PENNY TEST BOTTLE
Bottle was issued bronze paint over clear glass. This bottle is shiny silver over clear glass. C.M.V. $25.00 mint

1977 TALC COMPS.
Candid & Deep Woods. Outside shell wrapped around regular container. Used only to photograph for Avon brochures. Candid is orange and Deep Woods is green. Given to NAAC with letter from Avon on 1 of a kind. RARE. C.M.V. $25.00 each with letter from Avon.

1969 STRAIGHT EIGHT TEST
Dark amber, issued dark green. C.M.V. $65.00.

1970 PACKARD ROADSTER TEST
Clear glass, issued light amber. C.M.V. $40.00.

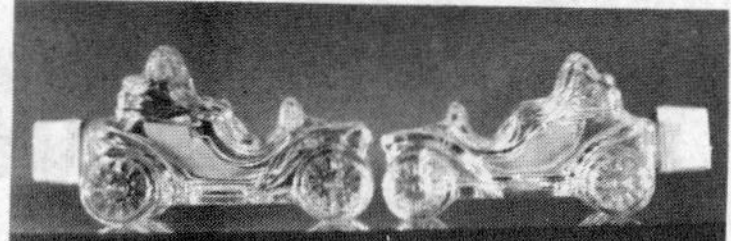

1970 ELECTRIC CHARGER TEST
Clear glass, test is 2 sizes, issued black glass, larger size. C.M.V. large $40.00. Small $45.00. Test also in Dark amber glass. C.M.V. $75.00.

1971 STANLEY STEAMER TEST
Clear glass, issued blue glass.
C.M.V. $35.00.

1971 VOLKSWAGEN TEST
Clear glass, test must have side vent windows. Issued black glass & clear glass painted red or blue. C.M.V. $20.00.

1972 MAXWELL '23 TEST
Clear glass, issued green glass, other tests in light green, kelly green, light blue & turquoise. C.M.V. $35.00 ea.

1973 JAGUAR TEST
Clear glass, issued green glass. C.M.V. $35.00.

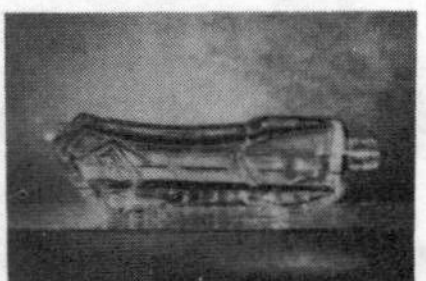

1973 SNOWMOBILE TEST
Clear glass, issued blue glass.
C.M.V. $35.00.

1973 HAYNES-APPERSON 1902 TEST
Clear glass, issued in green glass.
C.M.V. $35.00.

1973 ROAD RUNNER TEST
Clear glass, issued blue glass. C.M.V. $30.00
1973 COUNTRY VENDOR TEST
Clear glass, issued dark amber glass.
CMV $35.00

1968 STERLING SIX TEST BOTTLE
Clear glass factory test bottle. C.M.V. $45.00, issued amber or green glass.
1968 STERLING SIX GOLD TEST BOTTLE - This bottle is smooth all over & no spokes on wheels & has the appearance of being gold filled in amber glass. The numbers 1268 are embossed on front grill. C.M.V. $150.00

1971 STATION WAGON TEST
Above clear glass, below turquoise glass, issued green glass. C.M.V. $35.00 ea.

1973 MACK TRUCK
Clear glass, issued green glass.
C.M.V. $35.00.
1975 MALLARD IN FLIGHT
Clear glass, issued brown glass.
C.M.V. $50.00.

1971 DUNE BUGGY TEST
Clear glass, issued blue glass.
C.M.V. $35.00.

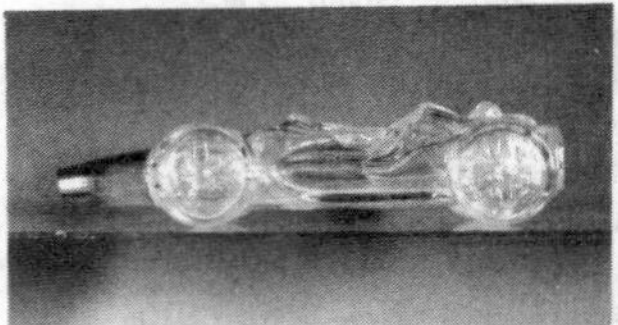

1972 SURE WINNER TEST
Clear glass, issued blue glass.
C.M.V. $45.00.

1969 TOURING "T" TEST
Left - dark amber glass, right clear glass. Issued black glass. C.M.V. amber $45.00, clear $40.00

1972 REO DEPOT WAGON TEST
Clear glass, issued brown glass.
C.M.V. $35.00.

1972 CAMPER TEST
Clear glass, issued green glass.
C.M.V. $35.00.

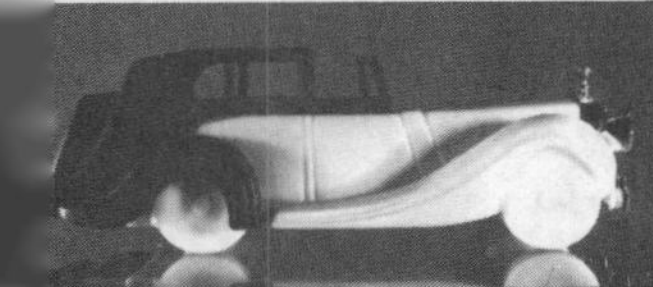

1972 ROLLS ROYCE TEST
Custard glass, issued clear glass painted gray. C.M.V. $75.00.

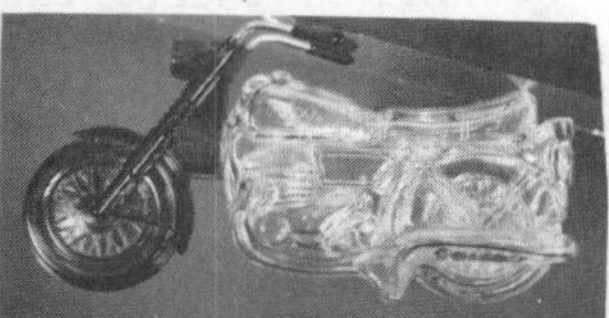

1972 SUPER CYCLE TEST
Clear glass (will not stand by itself) Tests also in light gray, dark amber & purple. Issued in gray glass. C.M.V. $35.00 ea.

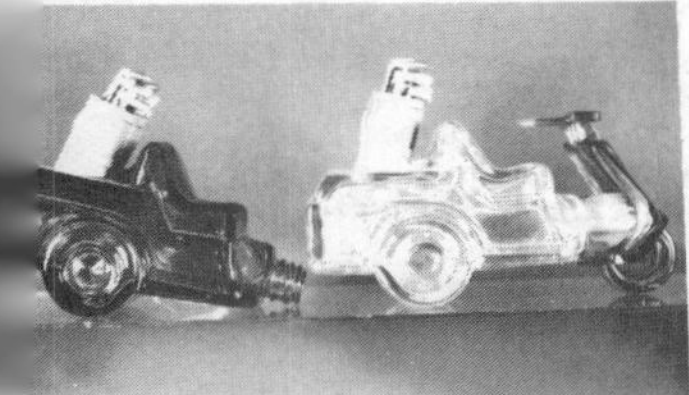

972 AVON OPEN TEST
.eft - Light green glass. C.M.V. ;20.00. Right - Clear glass, C.M.V. $25.00. Test also came in kelly green. C.M.V. $25.00. Issued in green glass.

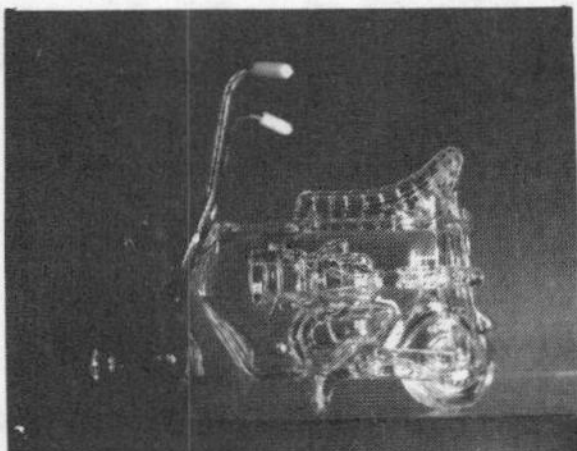

1972 MINI BIKE TEST
Clear glass bottle, issued light amber. C.M.V. $40.00.

1970 STAGECOACH TEST
Clear glass, issued dark amber. C.M.V. $45.00.

1966 CLEAR PONY POST TEST
The tall pony post was introduced in C 16, 1966. The Avon catalog has a picture of a man holding a amber Pony Post. This would be clear glass with after shave making it amber in color. Later catalogs changed to green glass. 8 oz. bottle on right is the same size in all details as the green glass Pony Post. Avon claims a few of this one were filled & sold. O.S.P. $4.00, C.M.V. $250.00. The 1973 Gold painted Pony Post from Mexico is clear glass. The only sure way to tell the U.S. Pony Post is the bottom of bottle does not have Avon or a mold number on bottom where Mexico bottles all have mold number but not all have Avon on bottom.

1966 CLEAR TEST BOTTLE
on left is about ¼" shorter than full size. The cap is smaller & fits on the short green Pony head After Shave. The mane on this horse head is much narrower than on the left. This bottle was made too small to hold 8 oz. so was rejected at factory. . Both have gold ring & caps. C.M.V. $350.00.

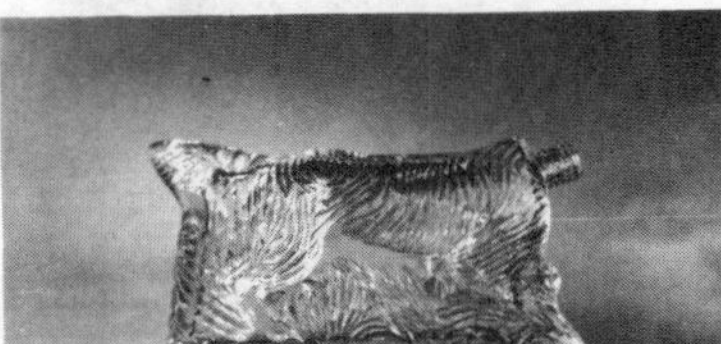

1973 AT POINT TEST
Clear glass, issued redish amber glass. C.M.V. $35.00.

1972 OLD FAITHFUL DOG TEST
Clear glass, issued dark amber. C.M.V. $35.00.

1970 COVERED WAGON TEST
Clear glass, issued dark amber. C.M.V. $40.00.

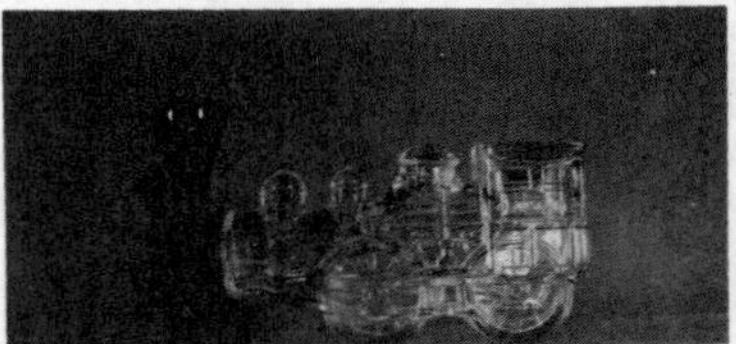

1971 GENERAL 4-4-0 TEST
Clear glass, issued blue glass. C.M.V. $40.00.

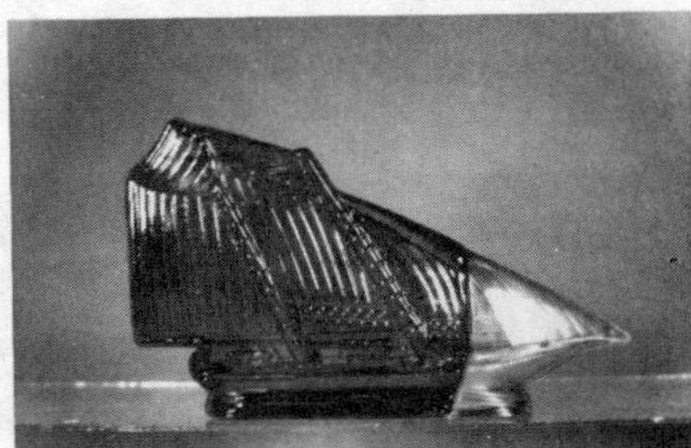

1972 SCHOONER TEST
Blue glass, issued clear glass sprayed blue. C.M.V. $20.00.

1971 SIDE WHEELER TEST BOTTLE
5 oz. clear glass factory test bottle. C.M.V. $50.00.

1971 PONY EXPRESS TEST
Clear glass, issued dark amber. C.M.V. $35.00.

1972 PHEASANT TEST
Clear glass. Issued dark amber.
C.M.V. $30.00

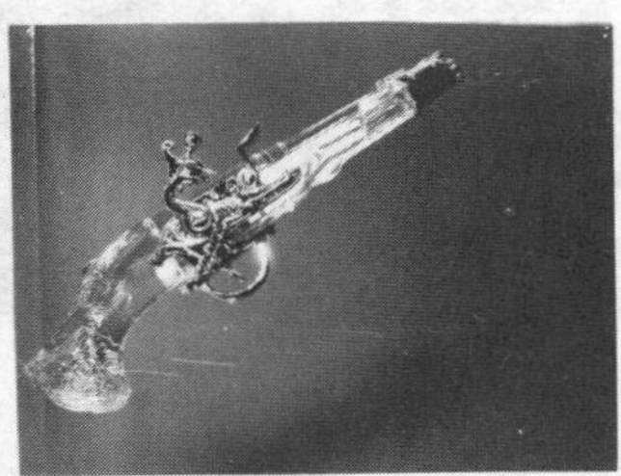

1973 DUELING PISTOL 1760 TEST
Clear glass, issued dark amber. C.M.V. $35.00.

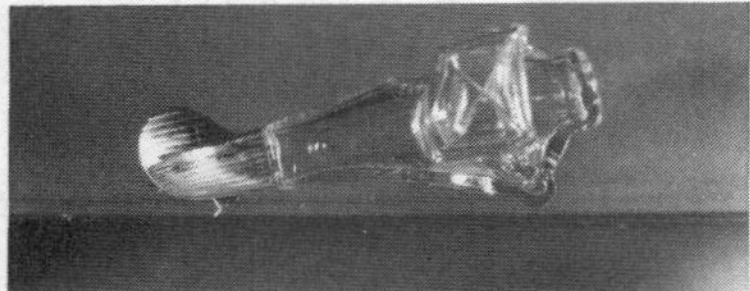

BI PLANE TEST
Clear glass. C.M.V. $50.00.
Never issued.

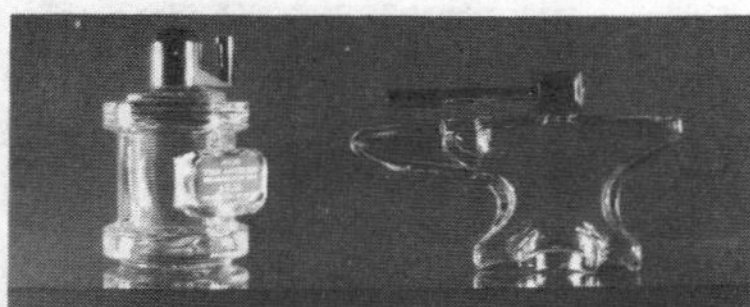

1970 ANGLER TEST
Clear glass, issued blue glass. C.M.V. $35.00.

1972 ANVIL TEST
Clear glass, issued black glass. C.M.V. $35.00.

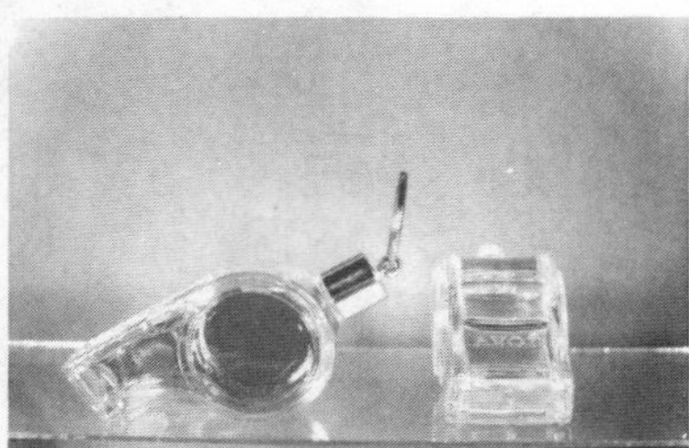

1972 BIG WHISTLE TEST
Clear glass, issued blue glass, photo shows front & side view. C.M.V. $35.00.

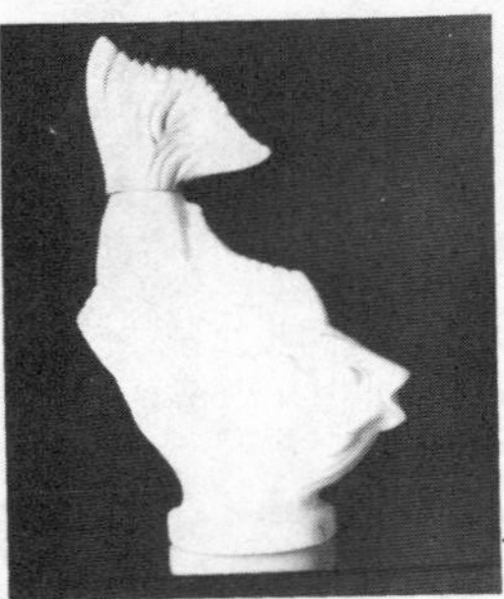

1973 SEA SPIRIT TEST
White milk glass, issued green milk glass. C.M.V. $35.00.

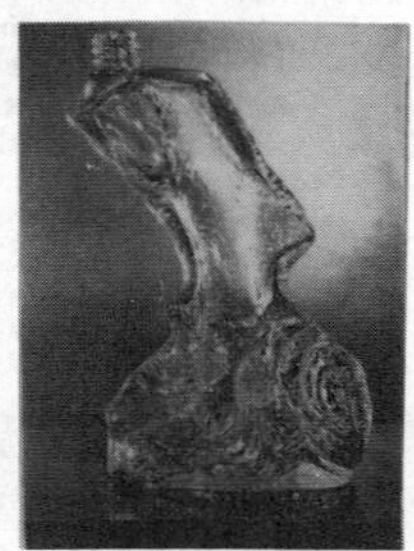

1973 RAINBOW TROUT TEST
Clear glass, issued green glass.
CMV $30.00

1972 SEA TROPHY TEST
Clear glass, issued light blue glass.
C.M.V. $35.00.

1967 MALLARD DUCK TEST
Dark amber, issued in green glass.
C.M.V. $45.00.

1971 WESTERN SADDLE TEST
Clear glass, issued dark amber.
C.M.V. $35.00.

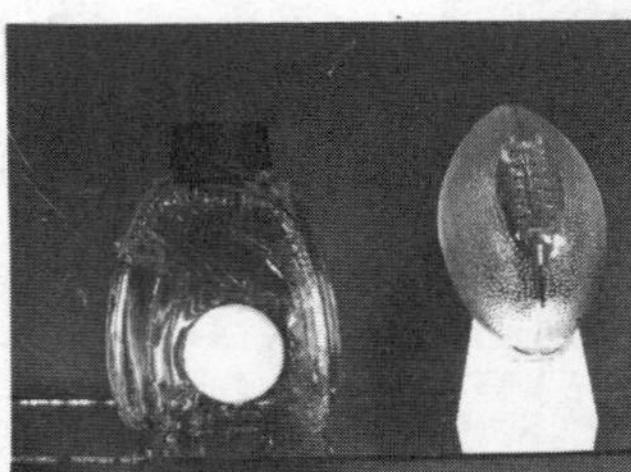

1972 FIELDER'S CHOICE TEST
Clear glass bottle, issued dark amber g
C.M.V. $50.00.

1970 FIRST DOWN TEST
Clear glass bottle issued dark amber glass. C.M.V. $45.00.

1973 LONG DRIVE TEST
Clear glass, issued dark amber. C.M.V
$35.00.

1973 MARINE BINOCULARS TEST
Clear glass, issued black glass.
CMV $35.00

1965 BOOT TEST
Clear glass, issued amber glass. C.M.V. $75.00.

1967 SPRAY BOOT COLOGNE TEST
Dark amber, issued clear glass with beige plastic coating C.M.V. $15.00.

1970 CAPITOL TEST
Left - clear glass, right - dark glass, issued in light amber. C.M.V. clear $30.00, dark amber $35.00.

1966 DEFENDER CANNON TEST
Clear glass, issued light amber. C.M.V. $100,00.

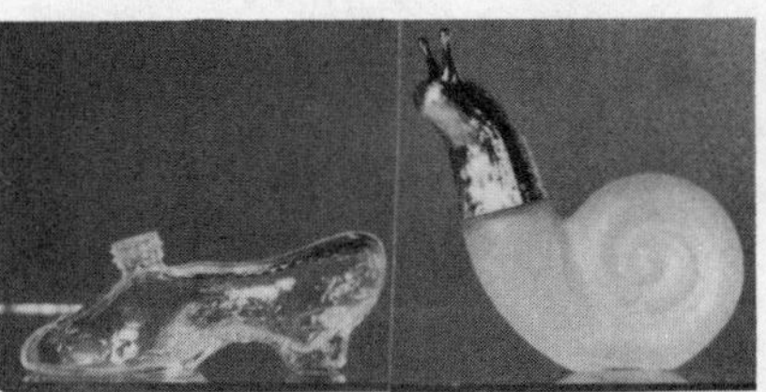

1973 SLIPPER TEST
Clear glass, issued frosted. C.M.V. $25.00.

1968 SNAIL TEST
Frosted glass, issued clear glass. C.M.V. $18.00. (NOTE - frosting can be done by acid or sandblasting by those familiar with either process.)

1971 LIBERTY BELL TEST
Clear glass, issued light amber glass & clear glass, baked on yellow paint. The above 2 bells have many distinct differences from issue, mainly the inscriptions. C.M.V. left- $100.00 Right- $35.00.

1968 TOWN PUMP TEST
Clear glass, left bottle is smooth, right has rough embossing. Test also in dark amber glass. Clear - C.M.V. $100 Dark Amber - C.M.V. $150.00

1966 CANDLE & 1967 FROSTED GLASS CANDLE TEST
Clear glass, issued in milk glass. C.M.V. $100.00.
Frosted glass, 4A design in lid is embossed, issued with sticker. CMV $50.00. Embossed 4A lid is only difference from regular issue candle.

1973 CLASSIC LION TEST
Clear glass, issued green glass. C.M.V. $35.00.

1973 HARVESTER DECANTER TEST
Clear glass, issued light amber. C.M.V. $35.00.

1969 WEATHER-OR-NOT TEST
Clear glass, issued dark amber glass, C.M.V. $75.00.

1974 ELECTRIC GUITAR TEST
Clear glass, issued dark amber glass. C.M.V. $35.00.

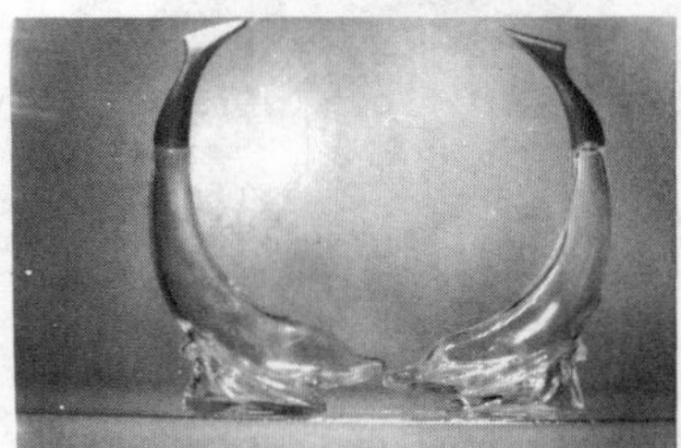

1968 DOLPHIN TEST
Left -Clear glass, issued frosted glass. Right - Mexican in clear, but different. C.M.V. $75.00 each.

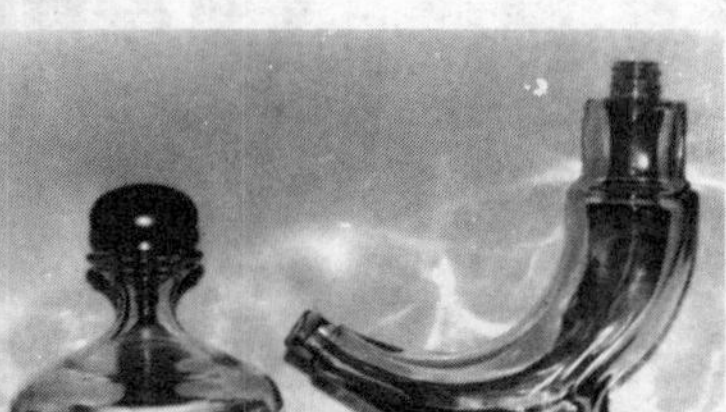

1964 CAPTAINS CHOICE TEST
Clear glass, issued green glass. C.M.V. $75.00.

1966 VIKING HORN TEST
Clear glass bottle, issued dark amber. C.M.V. $75.00.

1971 FLORAL MEDLEY TEST
Clear glass, issued yellow & purple frosted glass. C.M.V. $10.00.

1972 PERIOD PIECE DECANTER TEST - Clear glass, issued frosted glass. C.M.V. $40.00.

1972 VICTORIAN POWDER SACHET TEST - left - bottom is clear glass. C.M.V. $25.00. Top is white milk glass. C.M.V. $15.00. Issued marbled, light & dark green colored swirl glass.

1972 VICTORIAN SOAP DISH TEST
Right - Clear glass, issued marbled light & green colored swirl glass. C.M.V. $20.00.

1966 REGENCE COLOGNE TEST
Black glass, issued clear glass. C.M.V. $45.00.

1966 COLOGNE GEMS TEST
Dark amber glass bottle issued clear glass. C.M.V. $40.00.

1970 NESTING DOVE CANDLE TEST
Clear glass factory test sample candle holder. C.M.V. $50.00.

1972 VICTORIAN LADY TEST
Left - Custard glass. C.M.V. $25.00. Right - Custard glass also but sprayed white. C.MV. $30.00. Test also in clear glass (not pictured) C.M.V. $35.00. Issued white milk glass.

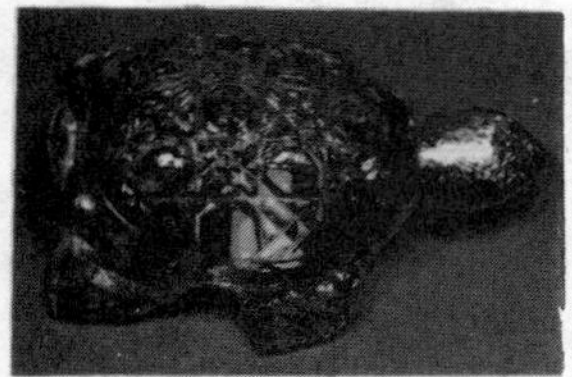

1971 TREASURE TURTLE TEST
Clear glass, issued dark amber. C.M.B. $20.00. 1977 Reissued in clear glass, but reissued has (R) embossed in bottom.

LEFT 1969 WISE CHOICE OWL TEST BOTTLE
4 oz. clear glass factory test bottle. CMV $30.00

RIGHT 1967 WARRIOR HEAD TEST BOTTLE
6 oz. dark amber glass. C.M.V. $60.00

LEFT 1972 RADIO TEST
Clear glass, issued dark amber. C.M.V. $35.00

CENTER 1973 HOMESTEAD DECANTER TEST
Clear glass, issued dark amber. C.M.V. $20.00

RIGHT 1973 COLLECTOR'S PIPE DECANTER TEST
Clear glass, issued dark amber. C.M.V. $40.00

LEFT 1973 WESTERN BOOT TEST
Clear glass, issued dark amber glass. C.M.V. $35.00

RIGHT 1970 PAID STAMP TEST
Clear glass, issued dark amber. C.M.V. $40.00

TOP 1972 SMALL WONDER CATER-PILLAR TEST
Clear glass, issued frosted glass. C.M.V. $30.00

BOTTOM 1971 SCENT WITH LOVE TEST
Clear glass, issued frosted glass. C.M.V. $35.00

LEFT 1970 TIFFANY LAMP TEST
Clear glass, issued dark amber glass. CMV $30.00

RIGHT 1969 SWINGER TEST
Clear glass or dark amber glass, issued in black glass. C.M.V. $50.00 clear, $60.00 amber.

LEFT 1971 EAGLE TEST
Clear glass, issued dark amber & black glass. C.M.V. $35.00

RIGHT 1973 CANADA GOOSE TEST
Clear glass, issued dark amber. C.M.V. $35.00

LEFT 1972 DREAM GARDEN TEST
Clear glass, issued pink frosted glass. C.M.V. $30.00

RIGHT 1973 VICTORIAN WASH STAND TEST'
Clear glass, issued baked on yellow paint. Top is clear plastic or issued gray marbelized plastic. C.M.V. $75.00

LEFT 1972 BULLDOG PIPE TEST
Clear glass, issued custard glass. C.M.V. $35.00.

CENTER 1972 PIANO TEST
Clear glass, issued dark amber. C.M.V. $35.00

RIGHT 1971 FIELDER'S CHOICE (Comp)
Issued dark amber. Comp is sold lucite. C.M.V. $200.00

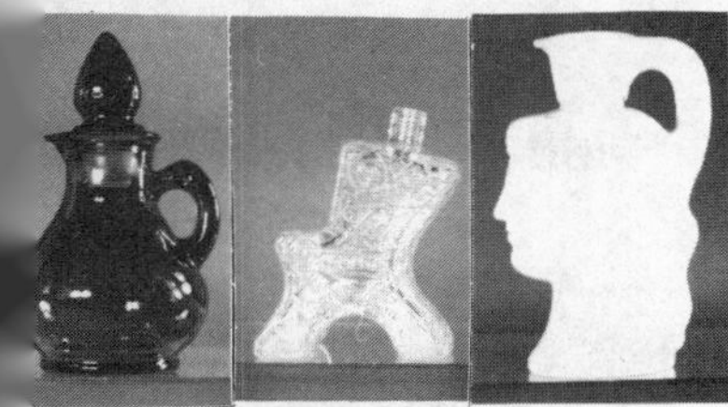

LEFT 1971 STRAWBERRY BATH FOAM TEST
Light red & uneven color, issued in ruby red glass. C.M.V. $20.00
CENTER 1972 SCHOOL DESK TEST
Clear glass, issued dark amber. C.M.V. $37.00
RIGHT 1972 GRECIAN PITCHER TEST
Custard glass, issued white milk glass. C.M.V. $25.00

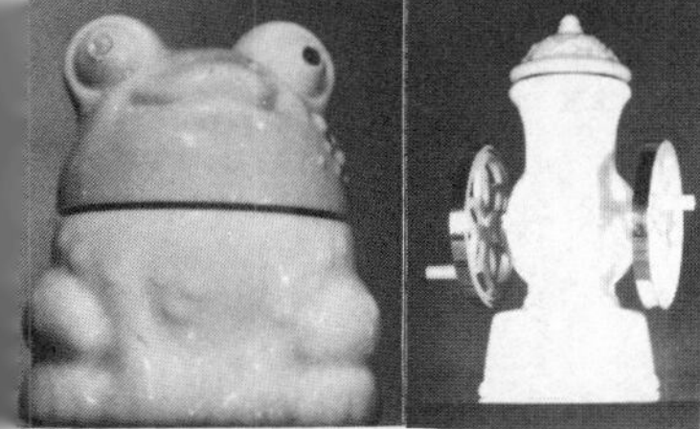

RIGHT 1972 ENCHANTED FROG TEST
White milk glass, issued custard glass. C.M.V. $35.00
LEFT 1972 COUNTRY STORE COFFEE MILL TEST
White milk glass, issued custard glass. C.M.V. $40.00

LEFT 1973 HEARTH LAMP TEST
Clear glass, issued black glass. C.M.V. $35.00
CENTER 1972 EAU DE COOL TEST
Several colors in test, issued smokey blue glass. C.M.V. $7.00
RIGHT 1969 POT BELLY STOVE TEST
Clear glass. C.M.V. $35.00. Test also in carnival glass. C.M.V. $100.00 Issued in black glass.

LEFT 1972 PRECIOUS OWL TEST
Clear plastic head, issued cream colored. C.M.V. $45.00
CENTER 1968 OPENING PLAY TEST BOTTLE
Clear glass factory test bottle. C.M.V. $75.00
RIGHT 1973 KITTEN PETITE TEST
Clear glass ball, issued light yellow, amber. C.M.V. $25.00

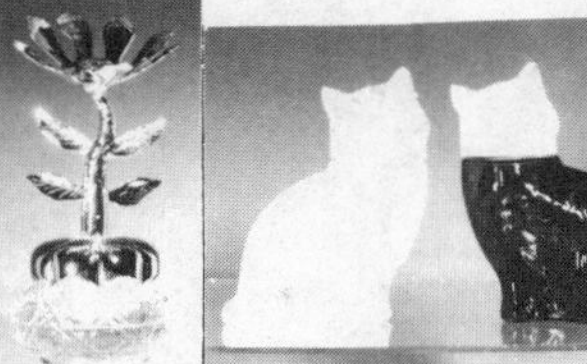

LEFT 1971 EMERALD BUD VASE TEST
Left is clear glass, right is blue glass, issued in green glass. C.M.V. $20.00 ea.
RIGHT 1972 CLASSIC BEAUTY TEST
Clear glass, no neck design, issued clear glass with embossed neck design. C.M.V. $35.00

LEFT 1970 KEEPSAKE CREAM SACHET TEST
Clear glass, issued frosted glass. C.M.V. $15.00
RIGHT 1972 KITTEN LITTLE TEST
Left - White milk glass, C.M.V. $25.00.
Right - Dark amber, C.M.V. $30.00.
Issued clear glass sprayed white.

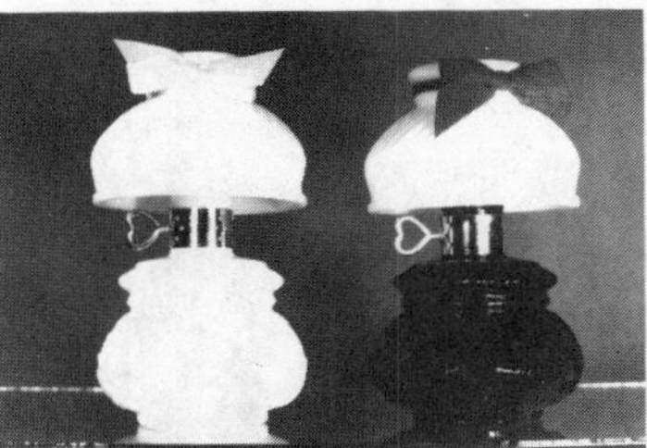

1970 COURTING LAMP TEST
Left - white milk glass. CMV $100.00
Right - ruby red glass. CMV $200.00
Test also in dark carnival glass (not pictured) CMV $100.00. Test also in light painted pink over clear glass CMV $150.00.

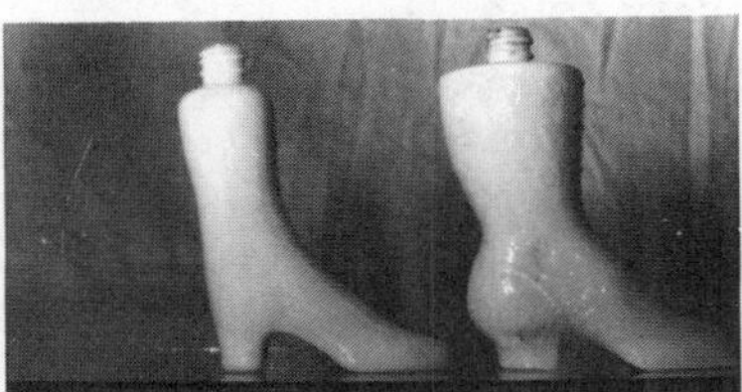

1972 FASHION BOOT PINCUSHION TEST (NOT A COMP)
Issued in blue milk glass. Left shows bottle first stage before being blown into boot at right.

LEFT 1971 PARLOR LAMP TEST
Clear glass bottom. C.M.V. $20.00
Top dark amber. C.M.V. $30.00
Issued yellow frosted bottom with iridescent top.
RIGHT 1971 PARLOR LAMP (Comp)
Issued in frosted yellow bottom with iridescent top. Comp is solid lucite. C.M.V. $250.00 mint.

1972 MOONWIND PERFUMED SKIN SOFTNER TEST
Clear glass, issued dark blue. C.M.V. $15.00.
1971 Moonwind cream sachet test
Clear glass or light blue.
Issued dark blue. C.M.V. $10.00 ea.

1971 ALADDIN'S LAMP TEST
Clear glass, issued in green, left has threaded middle spout. C.M.V. $45.00.

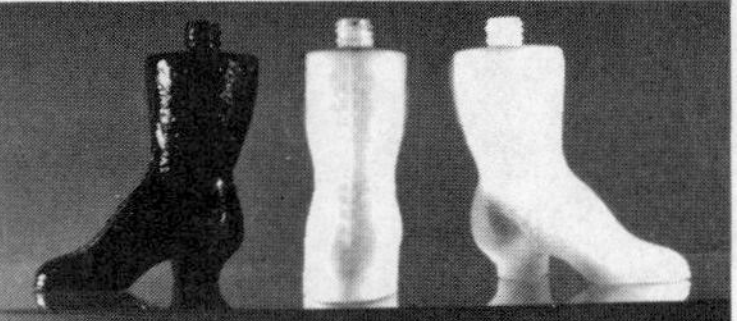

1972 FASHION BOOT PIN CUSHION TEST - Left to Right
Dark amber, C.M.V. $25.00.
Light blue milk glass, C.M.V. $30.00.
White milk glass, C.M.V. $30.00.
Issued in medium blue milk glass.

1972 NILE BLUE BATH URN TEST
Left - Clear glass, C.M.V. $25.00.
Right - Dark amber, C.M.V. $20.00.
Issued blue glass.

1972 BREATH FRESH DECANTER TEST - Pale green almost clear, issued in turquoise, yellow & amber.
C.M.V. $20.00.
1971 AVONSHIRE BLUE COLOGNE TEST - Clear glass, issued to resemble Wedgewood. C.M.V. $20.00.
1970 RUBY BUD VASE TEST
Left - clear glass,other half red, issued ruby red glass. C.M.V. $20.00.

1972 DELFT BLUE PITCHER & BOWL TEST
Bowl is clear glass, C.M.V. $40.00.
Pitcher is blue milk glass. C.M.V. $50.00. Both issued in white milk glass.

LEFT 1973 INDIAN TEST BOTTLE
Clear glass test bottle of Indian sitting. Never issued by Avon. Avon on bottom. CMV $40.00
1972 AVONSHIRE BLACK SOAP DISH
Black painted over white milk glass. Avon on bottom. Was sold very short time only by early trend setter reps only on East coast area. CMV $35.00

1971 VICTORIAN PITCHER TEST
Left - Pitcher & stopper are white milk glass. C.M.V. $80.00.
Right - Pitcher is clear, top dark amber glass. C.M.V. Pitcher $75.00. Stopper $8.00. Issued marbled light & dark green colored swirl glass.

1971 SCRUB TUG (COMP) TEST
Issued in red plastic boat with yellow soap. Comp both parts are plastic. C.M.V. $150.00.

1971 PUFFER TRAIN (COMP)
Issued in 3 plastic parts with soap. Comp is in solid plastic parts.
C.M.V. $300.00 complete mint.

LEFT 1971 VICTORIAN PITCHER & BOWL TEST
White milk glass, issued green marblized.
C.M.V. $80.00
RIGHT 1973 AMBER CRUET TEST
Dark amber, clear stopper, issued light amber. C.M.V. $35.00

1973 PEACOCK DECANTER TEST
Clear glass, issued turquoise glass.
C.M.V. $35.00.

LEFT 1972 BREATH FIRST DECANTER (Comp)
Issued in various colors, Comp is solid lucite. C.M.V. $200.00
RIGHT 1973 COFFEE KLATCH TEST BOTTLE
White milk glass, issued yellow glass.
C.M.V. $30.00

1970 CANDLESTICK COLOGNE TEST BOTTLE
Clear glass test. Regular issue was red glass. Never issued in clear. CMV $30.00
1974 BEN FRANKLIN TEST BOTTLE
Clear glass test. Regular issue was clear glass painted white. Paint cannot be removed. CMV $15.00 test.
1974 THUNDERBIRD TEST
Clear glass test. Regular issue was blue glass. Clear was never sold. CMV $20.00 clear.

1978 QUAKER STATE HAND CLEANER COMP SALES AID
Mock up container with cardboard false top with no holes used by Avon managers at sales meetings to introduce product. CMV $5.00

1974 CHRISTMAS BELL - REJECTS
Shiny red general issue on right. Silver coated on left is a base coat under the final red coating. The see thru red coating in center was red coated over clear glass that never got the silver base coat. The silver & clear red was never filled or sold by Avon. No price established.

1976 HOSPITALITY BELL TEST BOTTLES
Avon 1976 embossed on bottom. One is cobalt blue glass & one is light green glass. Regular issue came out light blue. Test also came in clear glass, flint & blue green. CMV $50.00 each.

1978 LITTLE BURRO - PHOTO COMP
Solid lucite comp used by Avon to photograph for the sales brochures before the actual bottle was made. Came with a letter from Avon Products stating it as a 1 of a kind. It was sold at public auction at the 1978 National Association of Avon Clubs Convention in Houston, Texas, & donated by Avon Products. Box is also a comp. Came with stick on label & burro. CMV $150.00 with letter from Avon in comp box.

MARY MARY COLOGNE DECANTER REJECT
Water bucket on left came from factory with no handle or pouring spout. This is a factory reject that got thru quality control. Add $10.00 value over regular issue on right.

The following is a list of some of the comps given by Avon Products at the Annual N.A.A.C. Collectors Convention. If no price is quoted, the price range is from $150.00 to $500.00, depending on the buyer. Be sure to get the letter from Avon with a comp. Please read introduction to this section to better understand what a comp is.

Bed of Nails Comb/Carton
Conair[R] 1200 Blow Dryer Decanter/Carton
Dingo[R] Boot Decanter/Carton
Avon Flowerfrost Collection Sherbert Glass & Hostess Soaps/Carton
Fuzzy Bunny Cologne Decanter/Carton
Gentlemen's Talc
"Heart and Diamond" Convertible Candlestick/Carton
It All Adds Up! Decanter
Moisture Garden Rosewater & Glycerin Body Lotion, Hand Cream and Facial Lotion
On The Mark After Shave Decanter
Peek-A-Mouse Christmas Stocking and Cologne Decanter/Carton
Quaker State Avon Heavy Duty Powdered Hand Cleanser Decanter
Sweet Pickles Outraged Octopus Toothbrush Holder, Brushes/Carton
Sweet Pickles Fearless Fish Sponge Mask, Soap/Carton - CMV $150.00 with letter
Sweet Pickles Yakety Yak Sponge, Soap/Carton - CMV $200.00 with letter
Sweet Pickles Zany Zebra Hair Brush/Carton
Sweet Pickles Puzzles
Sweet Tooth Terrier Cologne Decanter/Carton
Tubbo The Hippo Soap Dish and Soap/Carton
Weekend Decision Maker/Carton - CMV $150.00 with letter
Duster D. Duckling - CMV $200.00 with letter
1876 Centennial Express - CMV $300.00 with letter

1970 COURTING LAMP TEST
Clear glass base with pearl essence finish. White glass top. Not sold by Avon. Factory test bottle. CMV $100.00

1978 COUNTRY COFFEE POT - PHOTO COMP
A clear glass bottle that was hand painted yellow & white, & hand painted pump. Was sold at auction by Avon Products in Houston at the N.A.A.C. Collectors Convention. It came with a letter from Avon as 1 of a kind. CMV $150.00 with letter from Avon Products.

1976 CHRISTMAS SUPRISE BOOT TEST BOTTLE
1 oz. light blue tint glass test bottle from factory. Regular issue in green glass. CMV blue test bottle, $20.00

LEFT TO RIGHT
LANTERN - SOLID LUCITE COMP
Painted red. Letter 1 of a kind, from Avon. CMV $200.00 with letter.
EMERALD BELL- COMP
Solid lucite light green, silver top. CMV $200.00 with letter from Avon.
1978 CAPE COD CANDLE TEST
Emerald green glass, EXPL embossed on bottom. Never sold by Avon. General issue came in ruby red glass. CMV $35.00 green.
1976 HOSPITALITY BELL TEST
Light green glass, silver top. General issue came in blue. Green never sold in U.S. CMV $35.00 green.

FOREIGN AVONS

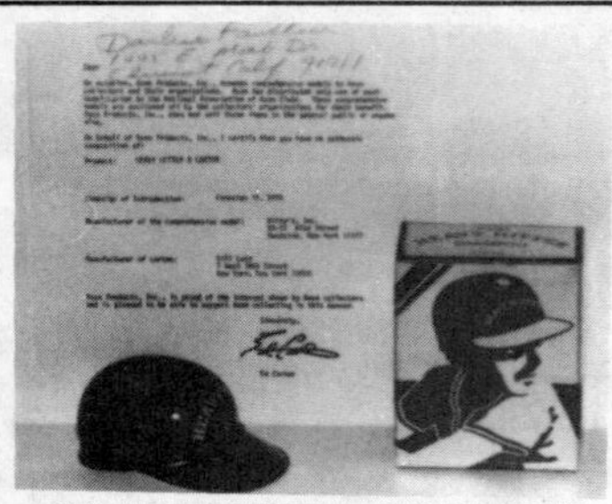

1978 HEAVY HITTER PHOTO COMP
1 of a kind comp made of blue painted plaster. Hat is in 2 pieces. Box also is hand made with stick on design. Came with letter from Avon as 1 of a kind. Sold at auction by Avon at N.A.A.C. Avon Collectors Convention in Houston, Texas, June, 1978. CMV $200.00 with letter from Avon, mint.

ANGLER DECANTER - CANADIAN
Darker blue glass than American. C.M.V. $8.00

1975 MG CAR DECANTER
England, Spain & Germany. Green glass. CMV $14.00 MB.

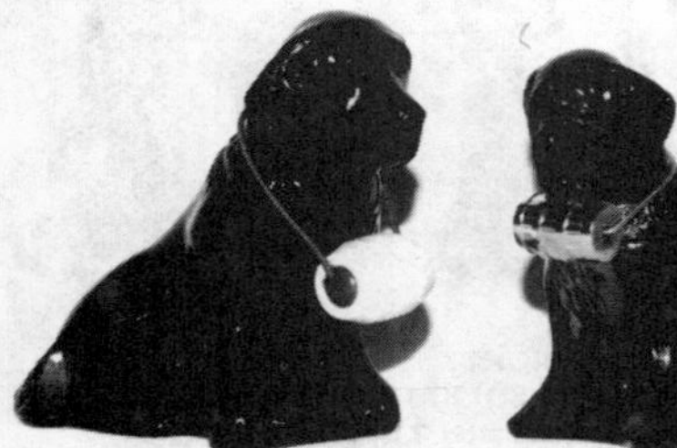

LEFT 1979 ST. BARNARD - SPAIN
150 ml, dark amber glass. Brown plastic neck strap with beige plastic keg around neck. Bottle is same size issued in U.S. Keg & strap are different. CMV $15.00 MB

RIGHT 1972 ST. BERNARD - GERMANY
100 ml, dark amber glass. Silver keg & neck strap. Smaller than U.S. & Spain bottle.

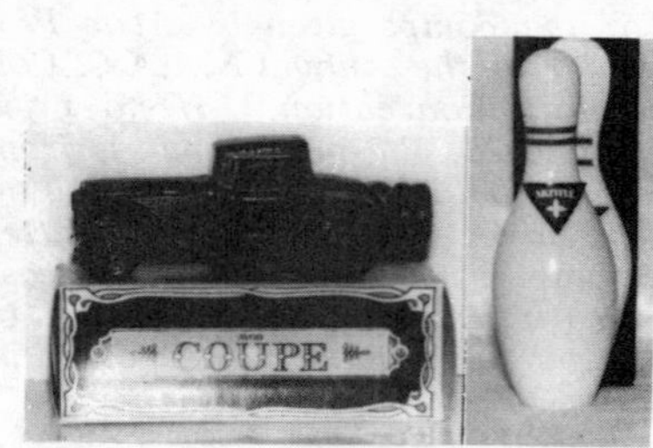

1975 COUPE AFTER SHAVE - MEXICO
Same as the Sterling 6 in U.S. CMV $12.00 MB

1970 SKITTLE BOWLING PIN - GERMAN
120 cc white glass bottle holds After Shave. Red neck stripes & label. C.M.V. $12.00 M.B.

SHORT PONY AFTER SHAVE - CANADA
Emerald green on left - C.M.V. $10.00
1973 Light amber - Canada, C.M.V. $6.00
Dark amber - Australian C.M.V. $100.00

UNICORN COLOGNE
Canada - C.M.V. $10.00 - Mexico is Her Prettiness - C.M.V. $20.00

1973 PONY POST - MEXICO
Shiny gold, painted over clear glass bottle. This bottle is same as American clear glass Pony Post only Mexican bottle has mold number on bottom. Mexico came both with & without Avon in bottom where U.S. clear Pony Post never had Avon in bottom. C.M.V. $25.00 M.B. $20.00 B.O. mint.

1974-75 MINI BIKE - SPAIN
120 cc green glass holds after shave. C.M.V. $12.00

1974-75 BOOK END COLOGNE FOREIGN
2 oz. dark amber glass, paper label. Sold in Europe, Australia. C.M.V. $10.00 Mexico issued in green glass, paper label. C.M.V. $12.50

1974-75 1ST EDITION BOOK – Foreign
60 ml. size, amber glass. Painted label. C.M.V. $10.00

1971-72 FOREIGN CHESS PIECE SHAVE LOTION
150 cc,gold cap, white painted bottle over clear glass. C.M.V. $10.00 M.B. $8.00 B.O.

1979 NOBLE PRINCE DECANTER, EUROPE
90 ml, dark amber glass shown with American issue on left for size comparison. CMV $10.00 MB.

1979-80 CHAMPAGNE DECANTER, MEXICO
58 ml, green glass with gold plastic top. CMV $6.00 MB

1978 CHAMPAGNE DECANTER, EUROPE
30 ml, green glass with plastic gold top. CMV $5.00 MB

1978 CHAMPAGNE DECANTER, AUSTRALIA
30 ml, green glass with gold plastic cap. CMV $5.00 MB.

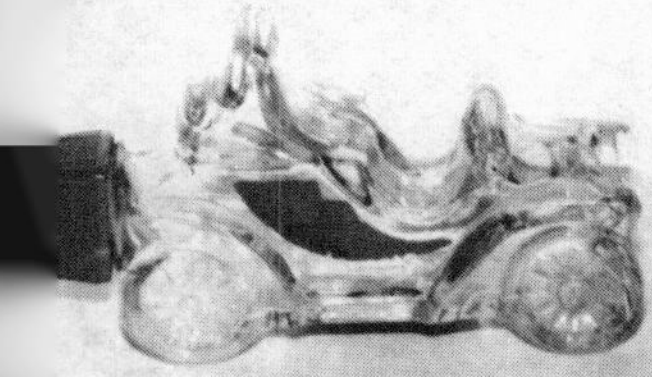

72 ELECTRIC CHARGER - MEXICO
ear glass, red cap & red bottom label.
me in After Shave. CMV $30.00

1960'S VIKING HORN, EUROPE
205 cc, dark amber glass. Foreign label on bottom. Goldtone top & horn tip. CMV $20.00

1979-80 BUGATTI, 1927, EUROPE
195 ML, black glass, cream colored plastic top. CMV $10.00 MB.
1979 BUGATTI, FATHERS DAY CARD
Grey, Avon marked card. CMV $4.00

1969 PIPE DREAM, EUROPE
177 cc size dark amber glass. Came in gold & maroon box without the plastic base stand. Avon cosmetics label on bottom. Same size as U.S. CMV $30.00 MB.

1980 SOCCER PLAYER DECANTER, MEXICO
90 ml, green glass with light green plastic top. CMV $12.50 MB.
1980 FORD PICKUP, 1973 MEXICO
148 ml, emerald green glass with green plastic pickup bed & decals. CMV $10.00 MB
1980 PONY POST MINIATURE, MEXICO
45 ml, dark amber glass. CMV $6.00 MB
1980 EL TORO BULL, MEXICO
130 ml, dark amber glass with white plastic horns. CMV $8.50 MB.

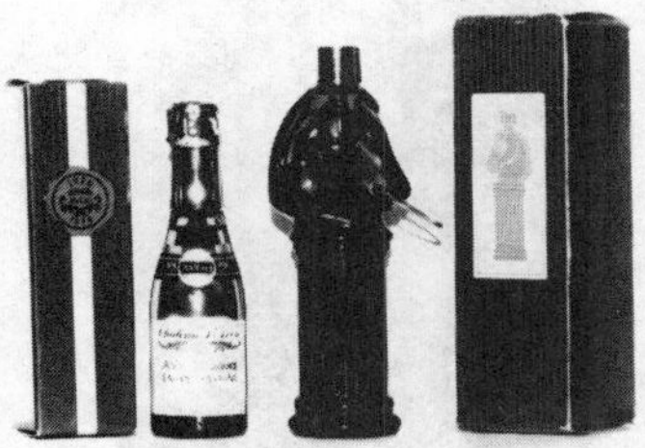

LEFT 1978 CHATEAU D' AVON, CHAMPAGNE - EUROPE
30 ml size green glass bottle. Came in green box. CMV $7.00
RIGHT 1979 ARIETE PONY POST - MEXICO
5¼" high dark amber glass, gold cap. Brass ring. Brown box. CMV $6.00

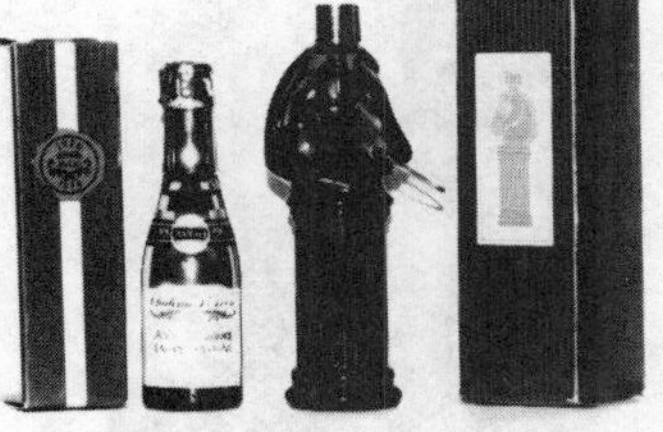

1966 HIGH SOCIETY ORB, EUROPE
237 cc, clear glass, red letters & gold crown cap. Red felt neck band. Bottle same as our Royal Orb, only painted letters on front say "Avon High Society 237 ccm" CMV $75.00 mint.

STRUCTURED COLOGNE - MEXICO
Clear glass, clear plastic top. C.M.V. $5.00.
EDICION DE LUJO BOOK - MEXICO
Same as 1st Edition Book. C.M.V. $10.00.

PONY DECANTER SHORT - GERMAN
120 cc After Shave, emerald green glass C.M.V. $15.00 in box. More common issue is greenish brown. C.M.V. $10.00 M.B.

1970 PERFUME AWARD - GERMAN
Falconette Perfume given to German Avon ladies in red Avon box. C.M.V. $20.00 M.B.
1970 FALCON AFTER SHAVE - GERMANY
150 cc amber glass bottle, gold falcon head cap. C.M.V. $30.00 M.B.

CAPTAINS CHOICE AFTER SHAVE
CANADA - Emerald green glass, C.M.V. $9.00
TOUCH-DOWN AFTER SHAVE - MEXICO
Dull silver on blue glass. This bottle is easy to duplicate with silver paint. Use caution. C.M.V. $15.00 mint.

AVON

1972 WINE SERVER
After Shave - Mexican green. CMV $25.00
After Shave - Mexican clear. CMV $30.00 (flat caps)
Cologne - Canadian green. CMV $20.00 (round cap)

1975 DUNE BUGGY – MEXICO
148 ml. size. Green glass. Black cap. Came in after shave. CMV $10.00

1976 STANLEY STEAMER – MEXICO
158 ml, light green glass. Black seats and caps. C.M.V. $12.50
1975 PACKARD ROADSTER – EUROPE
175 ml, mediam amber glass., darker than U.S.issue. C.M.V. $10.00

1977 RALLY CAR – EUROPE
60 ml. size cobalt blue color. Same as the U.S. Porche car only different color. C.M.V. $9.00

1976 CRUZEIRO – BRAZIL
115 ml. size clear glass bottle. Gold cap. Brazil on one side and 1949-1-Cruzeiro on the other side. Came in after shave. C.M.V. $15.00

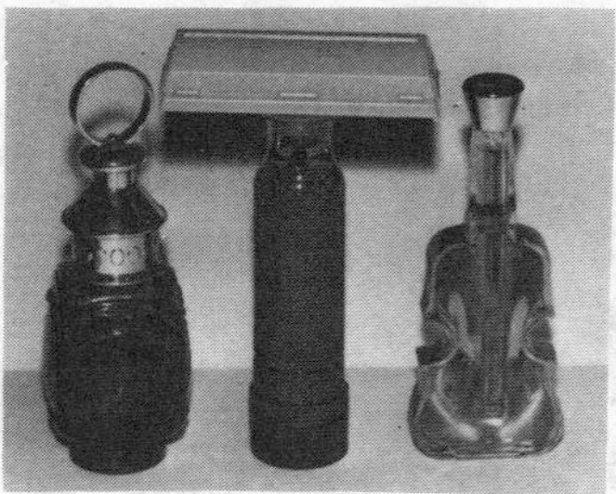

1975 OIL LANTERN – MEXICO, FOREIGN
Green glass, silver cap. After shave. C.M.V. $8.00
1976 SUPER SHAVER – FOREIGN
112 ml. size green glass - grey plastic top. After shave. C.M.V. $8.00
1976 VIOLIN - MEXICO, SPAIN
88 ml. size clear glass, gold cap. Cologne. CMV $15.00

LEFT 1972 PONY POST IMPERATOR FOREIGN
Green glass pony post 9" tall. 2 7/16" wide across the base. Came with gold cap and nose ring. C.M.V. $25.00
RIGHT 1974 UNICORN – FOREIGN
Emerald green glass, silver cap. Held cologne. RARE. Same size as Canada, clear. C.M.V. $150.00 green glass.

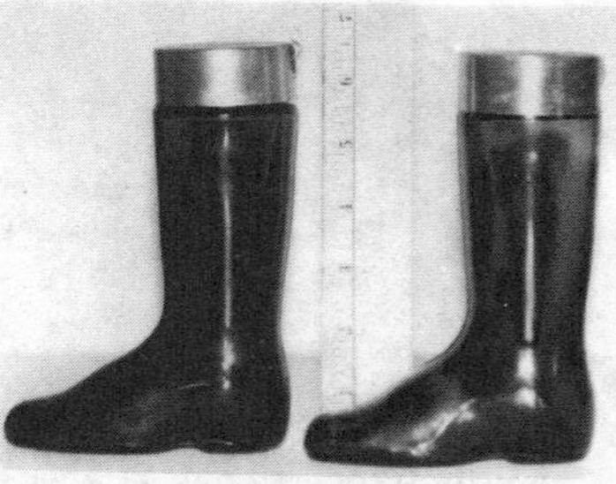

1973 BOOT – MEXICO
Dark brown amber boot on left pictured with American boot on right which is much lighter. Gold cap and bottom spanish label. C.M.V. $15.00

1977 CRYSTALSONG BELL – MEXICO & EUROPE
118 ml. light green glass, clear plastic handle. CMV $12.00
1977 SUPER CYCLE – MEXICO
118 ml light green glass and cap. C.M.V. $12.50

1976 SEIGE CANNON – EUROPE
60 ml. size amber glass. After shave. C.M.V. $10.00 M.B.
1976 ROCKET 022 – EUROPE
120 ml. size black glass. Gold cap. CMV $12.00 MB

1977 VOLKSWAGEN – MEXICO
120 ml, black painted over clear glass. Holds after shave. C.M.V. $8.00
1973 RADIO – CANADA
5 oz. amber glass, gold cap. Holds after shave. Gold front decal has 600 on station number. C.M.V. $5.00
1977 CAPE COD WINE GOBLET & CANDLE – EUROPE
light purple glass, Avon on bottom. CMV $8.00

1976-77 RACING MOTORBIKE EUROPE
100 ml. size black glass, black cap. Looks purple next to bright light. CMV $18.00 MB.

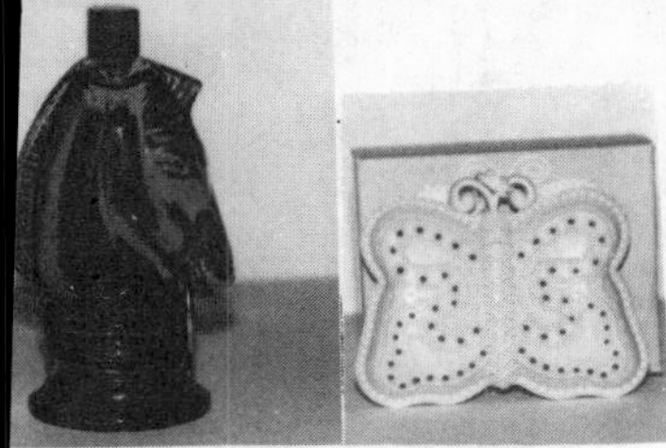

LEFT 1976-77 PONY DECANTER – JAPAN
118 ml. size light amber glass. Appears green when full of after shave. C.M.V. $12.00. Pony also came in dark green glass from Japan. C.M.V. $12.00. Light green glass from Mexico, C.M.V. $10.00. Light amber from Australia, C.M.V. $10.00 and light green from Australia, C.M.V. $10.00.
RIGHT 1976 BUTTERFLY POMANDER EUROPE
Pink plastic. C.M.V. $6.00 M.B.

LEFT 1976 BARBER POLE – CANADA
3 oz. white glass and red painted stripes. Came in after shave. White cap. C.M.V. $5.00
RIGHT 1976 BARBER POLE – MEXICO
88 ml. size clear glass painted gray or white with paper stripe label. White cap. C.M.V. $8.00 ea.
1977 CPC ANNIVERSARY KEEPSAKE EUROPE
15 ml. clear glass, black cap. CMV $5.00 Back of bottle is embossed "Avon Anniversary Keepsake" U.S. issue says 90th on back. C.M.V. $8.00 M.B. Rare issue with clear plastic cap, C.M.V. $10.00.
1976 COLOGNE – CANADA
(far right) .5 oz. clear glass, white cap. C.M.V. $3.00

1976 PRECIOUS BELLS – EUROPE
30 ml. clear glass, gold cap. Cologne. C.M.V. $6.00 M.B.
1976 ROYAL SWAN – EUROPE
30 ml. size clear glass, gold cap. Cologne. C.M.V. $12.50 M.B.

LEFT TO RIGHT
1977 ZODIAC HOROSCOPE – MEXICO
Cobalt blue glass, gold caps. Blue and gold labels. Came in all 12 zodiac signs in choice of Charisma or Wild Country. C.M.V. $8.00 each.
1977 CHRISTMAS SURPRISE BOOT – CANADA
1 oz. green glass, red cap. Different from U.S. issue. C.M.V. $3.00
1975 AFTER SHAVE – EUROPE
30 ml. clear glass with yucky green cap. C.M.V. $5.00
1975 ½ OZ. COLOGNE – CANADA
Clear glass, black cap. C.M.V. $3.00

1977 PLUMIERE (INK WELL) – MEXICO
175 ml. dark amber glass, tan plastic feather pen, black cap. C.M.V. $10.00
1978 INKWELL – EUROPE
180 ml. Dark amber glass, black cap, gold feather pen. CMV $10.00

LEFT TO RIGHT
1977 BLOOD HOUND PIPE – ENGLAND
150 ml. white milk glass, black cap, silver band, came in after shave. CMV $10.00
1978 PONY EXPRESS RIDER PIPE – MEXICO
88 ml. dark amber glass, white and gold handle. C.M.V. $8.50
1976 CORN COB PIPE – MEXICO
90 cc dark amber glass, black and gold cap. C.M.V. $8.50.
1975 PIPE FULL PIPE – MEXICO
60 ml. light green glass, black and silver cap. C.M.V. $8.50.

LEFT TO RIGHT
1978 - 1886 PERFUME ON ROLLETTE – GERMANY
Clear glass, red cap. C.M.V. $5.00
1977 - 1886 EAU DE COLOGNE – EUROPE
1886 embossed on clear bottle, red cap. C.M.V. $8.00
1978 - 1886 EAU DE COLOGNE SPRAY – GERMANY
50 g. clear glass, red cap. C.M.V. $11.00
1976 - 1886 EAU DE COLOGNE – EUROPE
100 ml. 1886 embossed on clear glass, red cap. C.M.V. $9.00.

1976 EXCALIBUR – MEXICO
Clear glass, gold cap. Blue painted label on front of bottle and black and gold neck label. C.M.V. $10.00
1975 LEATHER BOOT – MEXICO
Dark amber glass and cream color cap, plastic. Cologne for men. C.M.V. $10.00
1977 LEATHER BOOT – MEXICO
Dark amber glass and gold plastic cap. Cologne for men. C.M.V. $8.00

LEFT TO RIGHT
1978 ELEY GRAND PRIX – EUROPE
60 ml. red plastic, gold cap. C.M.V. $5.00. Holds after shave.
1978 SOCCER FOOTBALL – MEXICO
Yellowish tan plastic bottle. CMV $5.00 Issued in Europe 1979 rust color. CMV $5.00
1978 SPICY AFTER SHAVE LOTION -
15 ml. clear glass, black cap. C.M.V. $5.00.

AVON

1976 COURTING LAMP — MEXICO
Blue paint over clear glass base. Blue ribbon, white shade top. Lighter blue than one from England. C.M.V. $15.00

1976 PINK COURTING LAMP — BRAZIL
Pink painted glass bottom. Pink ribbon on white glass top. 140 mo. C.M.V. $50.00

1977 NOVIA (BRIDAL MOMENTS) MEXICO
147 ml. dull white paint over clear glass, white plastic top. Came all white. C.M.V. $8.00
Some are showing up with painted flowers on cap. It is very easy to paint this so don't pay a big price for one that someone has probably painted the flowers to get more money out of. C.M.V. $10.00 with painted flowers. Pictured in Mexican Avon catalog all white.

1971 KEEPSAKE CREAM SACHET ENGLAND - Lavender frosted glass bottom gold tree top. C.M.V. $10.00 M.B.

1971 FRAGRANCED LANTERN ENGLAND - 30 cc Lantern shaped cologne bottle, gold cap. C.M.V. $12.00 M.B. Also came in 30 cc Skin So Soft, gold cap. CMV $10.00 MB

COLOGNE BELLS - FOREIGN
15 cc each. One has gold & clear plastic handle. C.M.V. $30.00 - Right - gold cap & neck tassel. C.M.V. $35.00

1972 COURTING LAMP - YELLOW GERMAN - 150 m/l yellow glass bottom with white glass top. Holds cologne. Yellow box. C.M.V. $20.00 in box. Also came in blue as U.S. Also in green - Mexico. C.M.V. $25.00 in green glass.

1972 SKIN SO SOFT MINIATURE GERMAN
30 ml crown shaped bottle, gold cap. C.M.V. $5.00 M.B.

LEFT 1977 COMMEMORATION CROWN EUROPE
30 ml. size clear glass different from U.S. crown. Gold cap. Came in cologne. Sold from Queens Coronation Celebration. C.M.V. $7.00 M.B.

RIGHT 1976 SUN BURST COLOGNE MEXICO
14.5 ml. size clear glass, gold cap. Came in cologne. C.M.V. $7.00

1975 PETIT TELEPHONE — EUROPE
30 ml. clear glass. One plastic cap is ivory and one is peach ivory color. C.M.V. $8.00 ea. M.B.

1968 CANDLE - RED GLASS ENGLAND
Dark red glass candle on left not coated as in American red candle on right. Both same size. Avon in bottom of glass. C.M.V. for red glass only - $50.00

1975 CHIMNEY LAMP — CANADA
2 oz. clear glass, plain frosted top shade Holds cologne. C.M.V. $5.00 M.B.

1976 RECOLLECTIONS CRUET EUROPE
Amethyst color glass cruet and stopper. C.M.V. $10.00

1976 RECOLLECTION CANDLE STICK COLOGNE — EUROPE
150 ml. size amethyst color glass. C.M.V. $10.00

1976 FRAGRANCE HOURS CLOCK EUROPE
180 cc size olive color glass. Cologne CMV $12.00

1980 TREE MOUSE DECANTER - MEXICO
18 g. dark amber glass with gold mouse. CMV $5.00 MB.
1980 BOSTONIAN GLASS 1876 CANDLE MEXICO
Dark cobalt blue glass. CMV $10.00 MB.
1980 LITTLE BURRO - MEXICO
Dark amber glass with straw hat and pink flower. 28 ml. CMV $5.50 MB.

1968 KEYNOTE - EUROPE
7 cc. clear glass key, gold cap. Bottle is same as U.S. only has foreign label on bottle & box. Different from 1979 Fragrant Key. CMV $25.00 MB.

1980 CHURCH MOUSE DECANTER – EUROPE
White milk glass with pink and white plastic head & cloth veil. CMV $10.00 MB.
1980 CHURCH MOUSE DECANTER - MEXICO
Same as above only clear glass painted white. CMV $7.00 MB
1980 SEASON SONG BIRDBATH - EUROPE
30 ml. frosted glass with plastic top & blue bird. CMV $7.00 MB
1980 PETITE TELEPHONE - EUROPE
30 ml. clear glass painted gold with gold plastic top. CMV $10.00 MB.

1980 BLUE EYED CAT - MEXICO
45 ml. white milk glass. CMV $6.00 MB
1980 CHRISTMAS ANGEL - MEXICO
2.8 ml. clear glass with white plastic head. CMV $5.00 MB.
1980 LOVE BIRD - MEXICO
Frosted glass with gold cap. 43 ml. CMV $7.00 MB.

1976 PRECIOUS RABBIT - MEXICO
30 ml size. Smaller than U.S. gold plastic head. CMV $8.00 MB.

1973 FUNNY FLOWER POT - ENGLAND
120 ml yellow painted glass bottle with green plastic flower pot lid with green, pink, blue & yellow plastic flowers. Holds cologne. CMV $15.00 MB.

1977 LOOKING GLASS - FOREIGN, MEXICO
Gold handle, dark amber glass. Mirror in center. 43 ml size. CMV $8.50 MB
1976 KITTEN PETITE - MEXICO
Green glass ball, white cat cap. CMV $8.50 MB.

LEFT TO RIGHT
1977 SCREW DRIVER – MEXICO
Clear glass - silver top on left. U.S. issue on right. CMV $8.00
1974 STRAWBERRIES & CREAM BATH FOAM – EUROPE
120 cc. white milk glass, red top. Strawberries are smaller than the U.S. issue on right. C.M.V. $6.50
1977 GIFT COLOGNE FOR MEN – EUROPE
30 ml. clear glass, blue cap. Smaller than U.S. issue on right. C.M.V. $5.00

1974 COFFEE MILL COLOGNE – CANADA
Cream color milk glass, 5 oz. size. Same as U.S. issue only no gold trim. C.M.V. $6.00
1976 SECRETAIRE – SPAIN
Light pink milk glass, gold cap. Holds cologne. C.M.V. $10.00
1974 FLOWER MAIDEN – CANADA
4 oz. dull yellow frosted paint over clear glass. Plain white plastic dap. U.S. issue has painted flower on cap. C.M.V. $7.00

LEFT TO RIGHT
1978 MINUETTE – MEXICO
88 g size white glass, green painted neck band. C.M.V. $6.00
1977 RENAISSANCE CANDLE – AUSTRALIA
Blue glass with cameo lady on side. CMV $20.00
1978 JARRA PERSA – MEXICO
180 g clear glass cream lotion. Blue and pink and green front label. C.M.V. $8.00

1980 MOISTURE SECRET SET, EUROPE
White vinyl case contains skin care products in light tan packaging. Same set in U.S. was pink packaging. CMV $8.00 MB

1980 FISH BUBBLE BATH, EUROPE
400 ml, plastic fish container with white top. Holds pink bubble bath. CMV $6.00

1980 GOLF BALL, EUROPE
45 ml. green, yellow & white plastic. ½ size of U.S. issue. CMV $6.50 MB.

1980 ENCHANTED ISLES DECANTER - AUSTRALIA, MEXICO
60 ml. clear glass with gold top. CMV $7.00 MB

1980 SPANISH SENORITA - AUSTRALIA, MEXICO
115 ml. clear glass painted red & white with pink plastic top. CMV $10.00 MB

1980 LITTLE BURRO - AUSTRALIA
25 ml. light smoked glass with plastic cap, straw hat, & red flower. CMV $6.00 MB

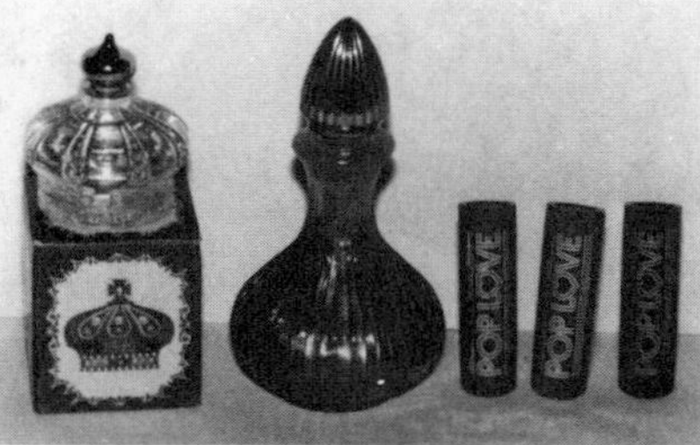

1980 ROYAL CROWN - MEXICO
28 ml. clear glass, gold cap. Glass design different from others issued. CMV $5.50 MB.

1976 COLOGNE BODY SILK - MEXICO
Clear glass with gold top. 77 g. CMV $6.00 MB

1980 POPLOVE LIPSTICKS - MEXICO
Plastic tube came in 3 shades. CMV $2.50 each MB.

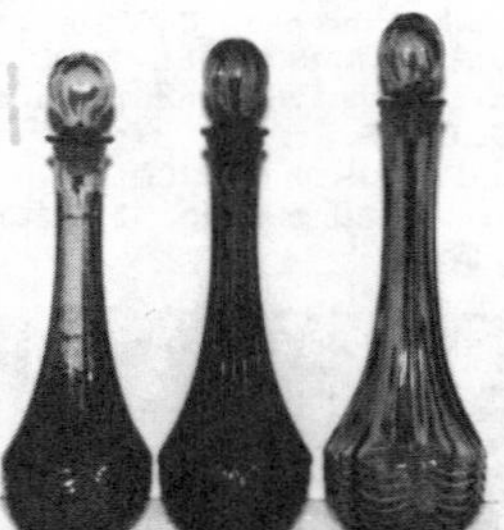

LEFT TO RIGHT

1976 NOVA BUD VASE — SPAIN
100 cc green glass and top. C.M.V. $12.00

1973 NOVA BUD VASE — ENGLAND
100 cc purple glass and cap. C.M.V. $12.00

U.S. issue on right was called Sea Green Bud Vase is shown to show size.

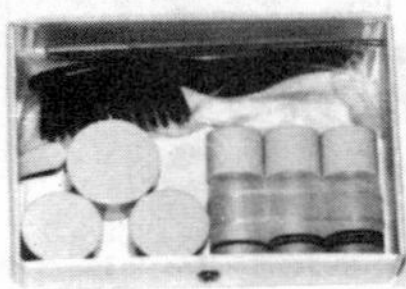

1979 TRAVEL KIT - JAPAN
White plastic case, Avon on clasp & 4A design on lid holds Avon comb, brush, 3 plastic jars & 3 plastic bottles. All are marked Avon. CMV $20.00

1980 PRECIOUS RABBIT - EUROPE
30 ml. size goldtone over clear glass. CMV $10.00 MB.

1979 GIVING DECANTER - EUROPE
60 ml., clear glass, flower gift card on front of box. CMV $6.50 MB.

1979 CARD, MOTHERS DAY - EUROPE
Pink flowered card in envelope. CMV $3.00

1976 BATH SEASONS — EUROPE
90 ml. white glass. Bubble bath. White cap. Blue painted band around neck. C.M.V. $7.00 M.B.

1976 SWIRL PITCHER — EUROPE
150 ml. clear glass swirl bottle and cap. C.M.V. $7.00 M.B.

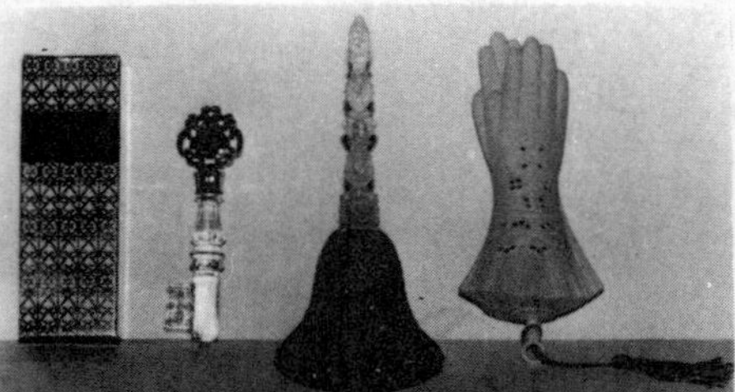

1979 FRAGRANT KEY - EUROPE
Same as U.S. issue of 1967 only does not have 4A design on cap. Different label on box. CMV $7.00 MB.

1979 ROSE POINT BELL - AUSTRALIA
115 ml. size clear glass coated light pink. No date on bottom. CMV $8.50 MB.

1980 LADY'S GLOVE POMANDER - EUROPE
Lavender plastic, smaller in size than U.S. issue. CMV $5.00 MB.

1979 HOSPITALITY BELLS - MEXICO, EUROPE
Mexico came in dark blue glass with silver handle. CMV $8.50 MB
European came in deep cobalt blue glass with silver handle. CMV $10.00 MB
1979 ANNIVERSARY KEEPSAKE - EUROPE
Came with pink atomizer. CMV $12.50 MB.

1978 VANITY JARS – JAPAN
Clear glass bottom, one has yellow cap, and one has white cap. One is 140 g and 130 g size. CMV $12.00 each.
1978 CALAMINE LOTION – JAPAN
120 ml. size frosted glass, white cap. C.M.V. $7.00

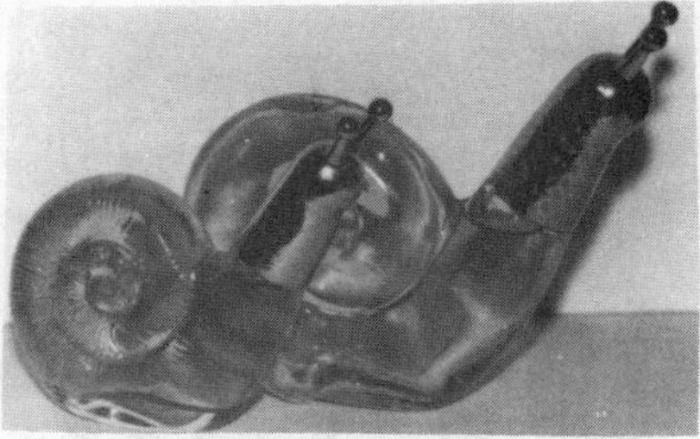

1976 BATH TREASURE SNAIL – EUROPE
90 ml. size. Clear glass, gold cap. Shown next to the larger U.S. snail. CMV $9.00

LEFT TO RIGHT
1974 SERENADE IN BLUE DEMI-CUP – MEXICO
White glass, blue decal and cap. C.M.V. $10.00
1978 PERFUMED SKIN SOFTENER – JAPAN
White glass and gold cap. C.M.V. $8.00
1978 COCKER SPANIEL – MEXICO
42 ml. white glass and cap. C.M.V. $6.50

LEFT TO RIGHT
1979 SANTA CLAUS - MEXICO
29 ml. all clear glass with red cap. U.S. had painted face. CMV $5.00 MB
1980 BIRD OF SPLENDOUR - EUROPE
75 ml. clear glass with gold plastic top. CMV $10.00 MB.
1980 BIRD OF PARADISE - MEXICO
43 ml. dark blue glass with darker blue plastic head. CMV $6.50 MB. Also issued in Spain with lighter blue plastic head. CMV $8.50 MB.

LEFT TO RIGHT
1977 FLIGHT TO BEAUTY – MEXICO
Pale blue painted over clear glass, white plastic dove top. C.M.V. $7.00
1978 GOOD LUCK ELEPHANT – MEXICO
43 ml. clear glass, silver cap. C.M.V. $8.50
1977 MINIATURE LOCION – MEXICO
57 g. clear glass, gold flower cap. C.M.V. $6.00
1978 KOFFEE KLATCH – MEXICO
148 g. blue painted over clear glass. Yellow plastic cap. C.M.V. $8.50.

LEFT TO RIGHT
1978 BOW BOTTLE – JAPAN, EUROPE, & AUSTRALIA
30 ml. clear glass, gold cap. Cologne. C.M.V. $6.50
1976 PRECIOUS SWAN – CANADA
4 ml. clear glass, gold cap. C.M.V. $8.00.
1977 PRECIOUS DOE – MEXICO
13 ml. frosted glass, frosted head cap. C.M.V. $6.50

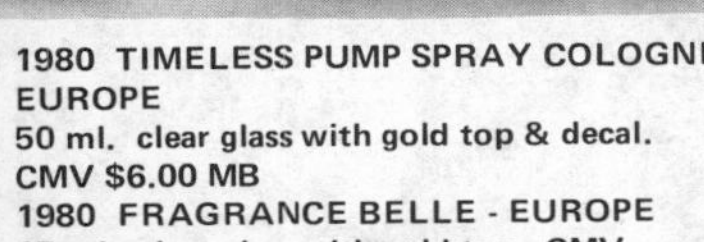

1980 TIMELESS PUMP SPRAY COLOGNE EUROPE
50 ml. clear glass with gold top & decal. CMV $6.00 MB
1980 FRAGRANCE BELLE - EUROPE
15 ml. clear glass with gold top. CMV $3.50 MB
1980 ROSE BOTTLE - MEXICO
Clear glass with gold top. CMV $5.00 MB
1980 V.S.O.P. DECANTER - EUROPE
30 ml. green glass with black top. CMV $6.00 MB.

LEFT TO RIGHT
1978 ROCKER COLOGNE – EUROPE
15 ml. gold cap, red label. C.M.V. $5.00
1978 PARFUME CONENTRE – EUROPE
15 ml. clear glass, gold cap. C.M.V. $8.00
1978 EAU DE PARFUME – EUROPE
15 ml. clear glass, gold cap. Embossed flowers around center. C.M.V. $6.00
1977 ROSETTE COLOGNE – CANADA
½ oz. white cap, clear glass. Different flowers than Europe bottle on left side. C.M.V. $4.00
1975 BUTTER CHURN COLOGNE – CANADA
1½ oz. clear glass, gold cap. C.M.V. $6.00

LEFT TO RIGHT
1977 TEDDY BEARS – EUROPE
22 ml. clear glass, gold cap. C.M.V. $6.00 U.S. issue frosted glass.
Mexico - 50 ml. frosted glass, frosted head. CMV $15.00
Mexico - 50 ml, dark brown frosted glass and matching head. C.M.V. $18.00
Spain - 50 ml lighter brown frosted glass and matching head. CMV $20.00

LEFT TO RIGHT
1974 GRAPE BUD VASE – EUROPE
180 ml. purple glass holds perfumed bath oil. C.M.V. $8.00
1977 EMERALD BUD VASE – AUSTRALIA
85 ml. emerald green glass holds cologne. C.M.V. $8.00
1978 CREAM LOTION – JAPAN
150 ml. clear glass, gold cap. C.M.V. $10.00
1976 EAU DE COLOGNE – EUROPE
50 ml. clear glass with white cap, came in many fragrances. C.M.V. $8.00

LEFT TO RIGHT
1977 FROSTED COLOGNE – JAPAN
59 ml. frosted glass, clear top. Same as ours just two bottles in 1965, C.M.V. $10.00.
1974 HOBNAIL BELL – MEXICO
58 ml. frosted glass, gold handle. Belt on bottom. C.M.V. $11.00
1977 ANGEL – EUROPE
30 ml. clear glass, gold cap. C.M.V. $6.50
1974 BELL COLOGNE – EUROPE
25 cc size. Same as our 1968 U.S. Bell on right only smaller in size. C.M.V. $8.00.

1972 FRAGRANCE ORNAMENT CANADA - 5/8 dram bullet perfume bottle, gold cap, in paper ornament. C.M.V. $10.00 M.B.
1973 CHRISTMAS ORNAMENT ENGLAND - Paper ornament holds small bottle of perfume, frosted cap. C.M.V. $12.00 M.B.

1977 FIGA FIST - BRAZIL
55 cm. dark amber glass and matching plastic fist cap. CMV $30.00 MB
1980 HEARTH LAMP COLOGNE DECANTER - BRAZIL
Light green glass with green & white plastic shade & cloth daisies. 235 cm CMV $25.00 MB.
1980 LITTLE DUTCH KETTLE - BRAZIL
150 cm. clear glass painted grey. Blue flowers & blue cap. CMV $20.00 MB
1980 PRECIOUS RABBIT - BRAZIL
Clear glass with white plastic head. CMV $20.00 MB.

LEFT 1975-77 FRAGRANCE HOURS FOREIGN
180cc light amber glass, gold cap. Holds cologne. CMV $12.50
RIGHT 1977 SPANISH FIGURINE
Pink plastic cap. Red and white frosted painted base over clear glass.
C.M.V. $11.00 each M.B. Spanish figurine pictured is from Spain. Also came from Mexico with dull red paint and Australia with shiny red paint. C.M.V. $9.00

CANDLE SET - CANADA
Red box holds wood candle holder with red scented candle. C.M.V. $9.00 M.B.
WEATHER OR NOT - CANADA
5 oz. dark amber glass, plain gold cap. C.M.V. $10.00 M.B.

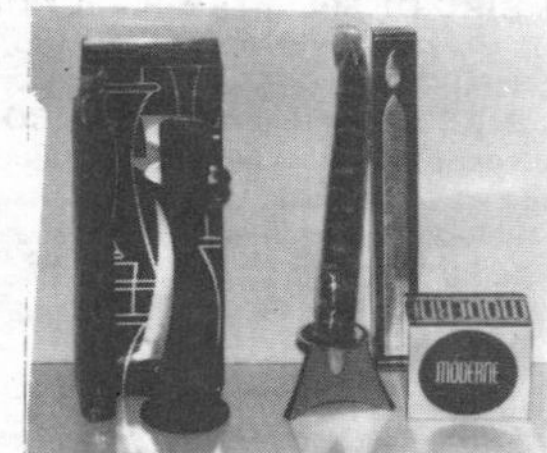

1972 FESTIVE CANDLE – ENGLAND, AUSTRALIA, GERMAN
Wooden candle holder does not say Avon. Perfumed candle not marked, must be in box. C.M.V. $9.00
1973 MODERNE CANDLE – ENGLAND
Silver based candle holder marked Avon. Red candle wrapped in Avon paper. C.M.V. $8.00 M.B.

1972 EVENING LIGHT PERFUME GERMAN - Box holds small perfume bottle in pink hang on carton. C.M.V. $12.00 M.B.
1970 FALCONETTE PERFUME GERMAN - 1 dram bottle in gold & white box. C.M.V. $7.00 M.B.

1974 COLOGNE - CANADA
2 oz. clear glass bottle with light gold cap. Came in Hawaiian White Ginger, Blue Lotus, Honeysuckle, Lilac. C.M.V. $4.00 M.B.

1972 ROCKER COLOGNE – EUROPE
½ oz. gold indented top, pink or white label. 2 different labels. C.M.V. $9.00 each, M.B.

969 FROSTED CANDLE — FOREIGN
rosted glass. C.M.V. $20.00

1969 LOTION LUXURY - FOREIGN
Clear glass bottle & stopper. C.M.V. $10.00, $12.00 M.B.

1974 LOTION LUXURY — AUSTRALIA
Came in all fragrances. C.M.V. $6.00
1971 BATH SEASONS - GERMAN
90 cc white glass bottles trimmed in green Honeysuckle, blue, Lily of the Valley, red Strawberry, lavender, Lilac, each holds bath foam. C.M.V. $10.00

1972 GENTLEMEN'S COLLECTION SET - ENGLAND - Box holds 50 cc bottle, brown cap, bar of soap. C.M.V. $12.00 M.B.

1975 SNOWMAN DECANTER — CANADA, AUSTRALIA - 1 oz. white glass, pink cap. Holds cologne C.M.V. $5.00 M.B.
1975 CIRCUS TALC - CANADA
Cardboard sides, white plastic top & bottom. C.M.V. $2.00
1975 SPRING PROMISE COLOGNE MIST - CANADA - 3 oz. lavender plastic coated over clear glass bottle, matching plastic top. C.M.V. $5.00

LEFT TO RIGHT
BATH SEASONS — ENGLAND
90 mm white glass with dark flowers. C.M.V. $10.00
1978 LANTERN COLOGNE — ENGLAND
15 mm clear glass, gold cap. C.M.V. $8.00. Also issued in Canada, C.M.V. $3.00
LAVENDER BATH OIL — ENGLAND
150 mm white plastic, lavender ribbon & label. C.M.V. $8.00
1974-75 BLUE NILE DECANTER — CANADA
6 oz. blue glass & cap, gold neck band. Holds Foaming Baith Oil. O.S.P. $4.75 CMV $8.00

1975 COLOGNE PETITE — CANADA
½ oz. clear glass, gold cap. Came in all fragrances. C.M.V. $4.00 M.B.
PINEAPPLE COLOGNE DECANTER CANADA - 3 oz. clear glass, comes in Field Flowers, Hana Gasa, Bird of Paradise, Elusive & Charisma cologne. C.M.V. $5.00 M.B. Also sold in Mexico under name of Colonia Magnifiscents, C.MV. $10.00 M.B.

1972 SEA TREASURE DECANTER
MEXICO - Clear glass bottle with gold cap. C.M.V. $10.00 M.B.

1975 WILD COUNTRY SADDLE KIT — CANADA - Box holds all brown plastic kit with box containing 6 oz. Wild Country After Shave & 7 oz. Spray Talc. C.M.V. $20.00

1973 INTERNATIONAL MEN'S SET
ENGLAND -Green & white box holds 50 ml size bottle with green cap. Holds After Shave Lotion & 1 white bar World embossed soap. CMV $12.00 MB.

1972 CARTE BLANCHE MEN'S GIFT SET - CANADA - Box holds Carte Blanche After Shave & Soap On A Rope. CMV $15.00 MB

1973-76 BATH SEASONS - ENGLAND - SPAIN - 90 ml white glass bottle with pink ribbon, red & green strawberry design. Holds strawberry cream bath foam. C.M.V. $5.00 M.B.

1973 - ENGLAND - FLORAL DEMI CUPS 90 ml white glass cup, white metal lid with pink cap. Red & green flower design. Holds bath oil. C.M.V. $9.00 M.B.

1979 PERFUMED PAIR SETS - EUROPE Box holds talc & soap. Container & product different color and design for each fragrance. Timeless, Ariane, Lily of the Valley, Honeysuckle, Unspoken, Moonwind. Moonwind and Unspoken have 2 different package designs. CMV $8.00 each MB.

LEFT 1979 GIFT SET FOR MEN - MEXICO
48 g. plastic talc, brown and white, and 45 ml. clear glass cologne with brown cap CMV $8.50 MB

RIGHT 1979 PERFUMED PAIR - MEXICO
Clear glass petite perfume with red top and 48 g. talc in flowered cardboard container CMV $7.00 MB.

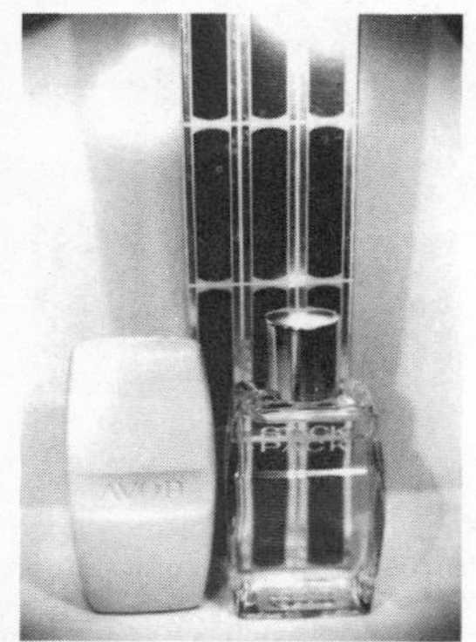

STACK PACK SET - FOREIGN
Bronze box holds bar of soap & 50 cc bottle of shave lotion. C.M.V. $15.00 M.B.

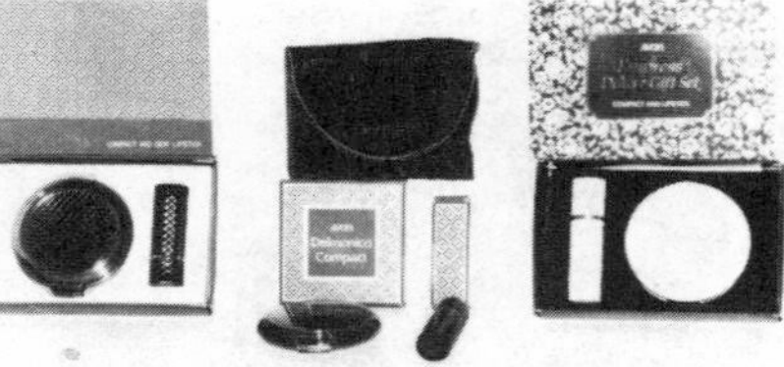

1979 DELMONICO DUET - JAPAN
Blue box holds blue compact & blue lipstick. CMV $15.00 MB

1979 DELMONICO COMPACT AND LIPSTICK - JAPAN
Blue plastic compact & lipstick holder. Came with blue velvet pouch. CMV $12.00 MB

1979 EMPRESS DELUXE GIFT SET - JAPAN, AUSTRALIA
Box holds bone style, flower embossed lipstick and compact, with brass trim. CMV $17.50 MB Japan, CMV $10.00 MB Australia.

1980 CHIC SELECTED SUMMER FRUITS SET - EUROPE
Box holds nail polish, lipstick & wand style eye shadow. CMV $12.00 MB

1980 FASHION MAKE-UP GROUP SET - EUROPE
Box holds eye shadow, 60 ml. cremelucent foundation, mascara & lipstick. CMV $16.00 MB.

1979 FRAGRANCE DUET SETS - EUROPE
Box holds soap & perfume rollette. Each fragrance has different color design and bottle. Elegance, green; Ariane, pink; Timeless, tan; Unspoken, blue; Moonwind, blue; Charisma, red. CMV $7.00 MB

1969 GENTLEMAN'S COLLECTION FOREIGN - Red & silver box holds bar of soap & 6 cc bottle of shave lotion with copper cap. C.M.V. $15.00 M.B.

1979 MOONWIND GIFT SET - JAPAN
Blue box holds 4 bars Moonwind soap & 70 ml. bottle Moonwind cologne. CMV $22.00 MB.

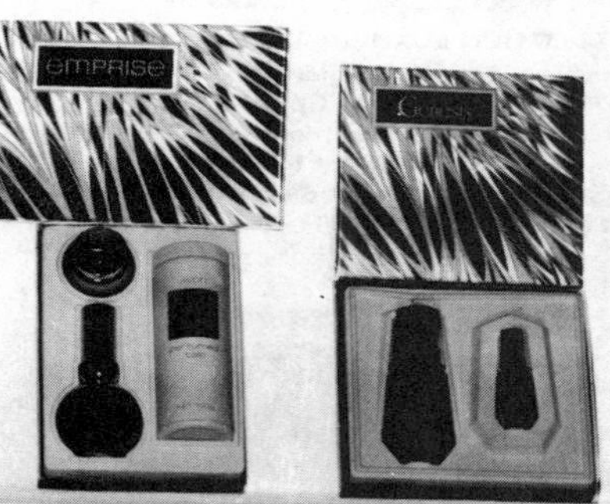

1980 EMPRISE GIFT SET - AUSTRALIA
Black, gold & white box holds 18 g. Ultra creme perfume, 100 g. perfumed talc, & 50 ml. Ultra cologne spray. CMV $20.00 MB

1980 GENESIS GIFT SET - AUSTRALIA
Brown & gold box holds 50 ml. Ultra cologne spray, same as U.S. Timeless, & 9 ml. Ultra perfume concentrate. CMV $20.00 MB.

1977 ESTUCHE VIA JERO SET – MEXICO
Blue box holds 90 ml size blue plastic bottle, gold caps in after shave and deodorant or brown box with brown bottles and gold caps. C.M.V. $8.00 each set.

LEFT TO RIGHT
1976 DAILY DOUBLE SET – AUSTRALIA
Brown and white box holds choice of mens fragrance with 100 g talc and 150 ml plastic after shave. Blend 7 pictured. C.M.V. $10.00 M.B.
1977 GENTLEMANS COLLECTION SET – AUSTRALIA
Box holds choice of mens fragrance in 100 g. talc and 150 ml plastic bottle of after shave. Windjammer pictured. C.M.V. $10.00

1975 MISS LOLLY POP TALCO PERFUMADO – MEXICO
Metal shaker top can. C.M.V. $5.00.
1978 BABY LOCION – MEXICO
White plastic bottle with blue cap. C.M.V. $3.00.
1975 FLUFF PUFF SET – MEXICO
Box holds pearl white puff and can of Talco Perfumado. C.m.V. $12.00.

1975 ELEGANCE GIFT SET – SOUTH AMERICA
Light green and white box with clear lid holds cologne spray and perfumed talc. C.M.V. $20.00 M.B.

1973 SIDE BY SIDE - ENGLAND
Light green box holds yellow soap & bottle of cologne, gold cap. C.M.V. $10.50 MB.

1975 FRAGRANCE FANCY SET CANADA - Box holds Perfumed Talc & Perfume Rollette. C.M.V. $5.00
1975 SIDE BY SIDE SET - CANADA
Box holds bar of soap & ½ oz. Cologne. C.M.V. $6.00

1969 FRAGRANCE FLING SET - FOREIGN
15 cc Cologne & green soap. C.M.V. $15.00 M.B.

1974 PERFUMED TALC SET - CANADA
Box holds 3 metal Talc cans. CMV $10.00 MB.

1972 BABY BRUSH & COMB SET
White brush & comb in box. C.M.V. $4.00
1972 HAIR CARE PORTABLES SET CANADA - Box holds Chic 'N' Sure hair spray can & Avon brush. C.M.V. $5.00

1972 SIDE BY SIDE SET - GERMAN
Blue box holds soap & 15 m/l Cologne bottle. C.M.V. $10.00 M.B.
1971 SIDE BY SIDE BAMBOO SET GERMAN - Blue & green box holds green bar of soap & frosted 15 cc cologne with silver cap. C.M.V. $13.00 M.B.

1973 SNOW DROPS SET - CANADA
Box holds cologne & soap. CMV $7.00 MB
1972 GIFTABLES SET - CANADA
Box holds cologne & soap. CMV $8.00 MB

1973 DOUBLETTE SET – EUROPE
Yellow box holds yellow flower shaped soap & 25 cc cologne. C.M.V. $12.00 M.B.

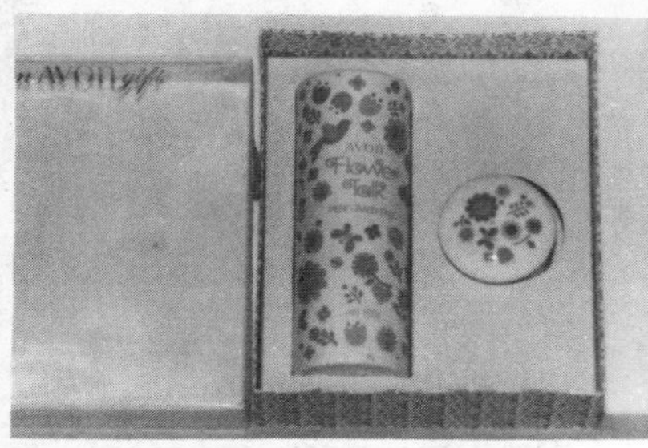

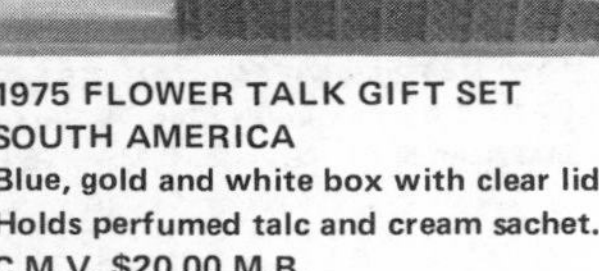

1975 FLOWER TALK GIFT SET SOUTH AMERICA
Blue, gold and white box with clear lid. Holds perfumed talc and cream sachet. C.M.V. $20.00 M.B.

1974 ELEGANTE SET – MEXICO
Yellow and gold box holds cologne and perfume rollette. CMV $17.00 MB.

LEFT 1977 SKIN SO SOFT SMOOTHIES – AUSTRALIA
Gold and blue box holds 85 g Satin Talc and 100 ml plastic bottle of Skin So Soft, bath oil. C.M.V. $7.00 M.B.
RIGHT 1976 SKIN SO SOFT SMOOTHIES – AUSTRALIA
Blue and gold box holds 85 g Satin Talc and 100 ml plastic bottle of Skin So Soft bath oil C.M.V. $9.00 M.B.

1975 FRAGRANCE FANCY – CANADA
Box holds perfumed talc and perfume rollette. C.M.V. $6.00 M.B.

1975 RICH MOISTURE DOUBLE PAK – CANADA
Pink and white box holds 2 pink and white tubes of rich moisture hand cream in French and English. C.M.V. $6.00
1977 PERFUMED PAIR – MEXICO
Pink and white box holds matching 48 g metal talc and 13 ml bottle of cologne. Came in Elegante pictured and Somewhere and Charisma. C.M.V. $7.00 M.B.

1976 SIDE BY SIDE SET FOREIGN
Box holds 15 ml. clear glass bottle cologne, gold cap, 1 bar soap. C.M.V. $6.00 M.B.

1976 MERRY TINTS SET – EUROPE
Box holds nail enamel and 1 blue lip stick. C.M.V. $8.00

1976 FRAGRANCE TWINS – EUROPE
Box holds cream sachet and bar of soap. C.M.V. $6.00

1975 FRAGRANCE FAVORITES CANADA
Box holds cream sachet and perfumed talc. C.M.V. $6.00 M.B.

1978 PRETTY PEACH PRINCESS GIFT SET – AUSTRALIA
Pink box holds 100 g white plastic Pretty Peach Talc and yellow glass cream sachet. C.M.V. $8.00 M.B.
1978 SWEET VIOLETS GIFT SET
Box holds Sweet Violets Talc and cream sachet. C.M.V. $8.00 M.B.

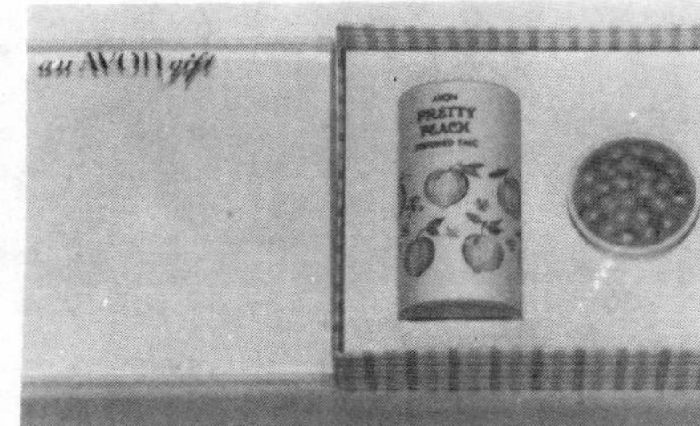

1975 PRETTY PEACH GIFT SET SOUTH AMERICA
Pink box with clear top holds Pretty Peach Talc and Cream Sachet. C.M.V. $20.00 M.B.

1972 PRETTY PEACH - EUROPE
Soap On A Rope - C.M.V. $8.00 in box. Talc - C.M.V. $7.00; Hand Cream - C.M.V. $2.50, Cream Sachet - C.M.V. $5.00 in box.

LEFT TO RIGHT
1974 DAISY TALCO PERFUMADO
White plastic bottle. C.M.V. $5.00
1974 PRETTY PEACH TALCO
Metal can, plastic top. C.M.V. $5.00
1978 PRETTY PEACH COLOGNE - MEXICO
57 ml clear glass, peach cap. No leaf. C.M.V. $4.00
1978 PRETTY PEACH CREAM LOTION – MEXICO
118 g peach plastic, peach cap, no leaf. C.M.V. $3.00
1974 CHIPPY TALCO
Metal can, plastic top. C.M.V. $5.00

1972 PRETTY PEACH - EUROPE
Bubble bath C.M.V. $8.00 in box.
Shampoo C.M.V. $8.00 in box.
Cologne C.M.V. $8.00 in box.

1976 COOL EAU D'AVON ROLL ON EUROPE - Octagonal shaped blue glass bottle with silver 4A design cap. C.M.V. $4.00 M.B.

1976 COOL EAU D'AVON - EUROPE - 60 cc Blue glass bottle with silver 4A design cap. C.M.V. $4.00 M.B.

1977 COOL EAU DE COLOGNE SPRAY EUROPE
57 g. light blue glass bottle, blue paper neck label. Clear and silver plastic cap. C.M.V. $5.00

1975 EAU DE COOL - CANADA
6 oz. C.M.V. $3.00 M.B.

LEFT TO RIGHT
1976 MENS COLOGNE – EUROPE
60 ml clear glass, indented sides., black cap. C.M.V. $4.00
1975 TORERO AFTER SHAVE – EUROPE
120 cc clear glass, black cap. Pink label. C.M.V. $6.00
1978 BLEND 7 HAIR TONIC – JAPAN
150 ml. clear glass, brown cap. C.M.V. $9.00
1978 BLEND 7 AFTERSHAVE – JAPAN
150 ml. clear glass, brown cap. C.M.V. $9.00
1976 BLEND GOLD – CANADA
Amber glass bottle with gold 7 painted on front. Brown cap. C.M.V. $4.00

LEFT TO RIGHT
1976 SQUEEZE SPRAY DEODORANT – EUROPE
81 ml Torero - red plastic with black cap. C.M.V. $.4.00
1978 SQUEEZE SPRAY DEODORANT – MEXICO
90 ml Tai Winds - light green plastic with dark green cap. C.M.V. $2.50
1976 SQUEEZE SPRAY DEODORANT – EUROPE
90 ml Wild Country - white plastic with brown cap. C.M.V. $3.00
1977 SQUEEZE SPRAY DEODORANT – MEXICO
90 ml Wild Country - white plastic with brown cap. C.M.V. $2.50
1978 ROLL ON DEODORANT – EUROPE
90 ml Wild Country - white plastic with brown cap. C.M.V. $3.00
1978 SQUEEZE SPRAY DEODORANT – MEXICO
80 ml Spicy - white and brown plastic with brown cap. C.M.V. $2.50
1973 SQUEEZE SPRAY DEODORANT – BRAZIL
105 ml brown bottle with dark brown cap. C.M.V. $10.00

LEFT TO RIGHT
1975 AEROSOL DEODORANT – EUROPE
71 g size metal cans in Windjammer, blue - and Tai Winds in green. C.M.V. $4.00 each.
1978 DEODORANT SQUEEZE BOTTLE – MEXICO
4 on right are plastic bottle in Blend 7 - Squeeze Spray Deodorant, Desodorante Perfumado, and Desodorante Pulveizador. C.M.V. $2.50 each.

TALC'S FROM MEXICO
1975 Windjammer CMV $8.00
1975 Carriage Talc - green, C.M.V. $6.00
1977 Blend 7, Spicy, Blue Blazer, Deep Woods, Cavalier, New World, Tai Winds, Oslo, Wild Country. C.M.V. $4.00 each.

LEFT TO RIGHT
1976 BLUE BLAZER TALC – EUROPE
100 g blue metal can, red cap. C.M.V. $5.00
1965 BAY RUM TALC – CANADA
2.6 oz. green matal can, black cap. C.M.V. $20.00
1976 TAI WINDS TALC – EUROPE
100 g green metal can, white cap. C.M.V. $6.50
1974 EXCALIBUR TALC – EUROPE
100 g black cardboard side, plastic top and bottom. C.M.V. $6.00

1978 TALC'S FOR MEN – AUSTRALIA, EUROPE
100 g size plastic with painted or paper labels. Older issue in cardboard sides. Came in Blend 7 - 2 different, Spicy, - 3 different, Tai Winds - 2 different, Endeavour, Everest, Wild Country - 3 different, Clint, Oland, Windjammer, Deep Woods, Blue Blazer. C.M.V. $3.00 each.

1978 AFTER SHAVE'S – AUSTRALIA
Each is 150 ml plastic bottle with Blend 7 brown cap, Windjammer blue cap. C.M.V. $4.00 each. Bay Rum tan cap, Leather red cap, Island Lime green cap. C.M.V. $5.00 each.

1971 LOCION PARA – MEXICO
Green and red box holds 4 oz. bottle, red cap, green and red label. Came in after shave or cologne. C.M.V. $5.00 each M.B.

1970 DESODORANTE – FOREIGN
2 oz. clear glass bottle, white caps. Red and black label. C.M.V. $4.00 M.B.

1978 LLAMA SPORT - MEXICO
TALCO 100 g. metal can. CMV $4.00
LOCION JUVENILE 120 ml size, clear glass orange cap. CMV $5.00
DESODORANTE 90 ml. white plastic, orange cap. CMV $4.00

1975 COLOGNES FOR MEN – FOREIGN
60 cc bottles, flat on face side, gold caps. Windjammer & Spicy fragrance. C.M.V. $3.00 ea.

1977 TAI WINDS MINIATURE EUROPE
15 ml. size green glass and cap. C.M.V. $5.00 M.B.
1976 ENDEAVOUR MINIATURE EUROPE
15 ml. size clear glass, blue cap. C.M.V. $5.00 M.B.
1976 WILD COUNTRY MINIATURE EUROPE
15 ml. size clear glass, brown cap. C.M.V. $5.00 M.B.
1976 WINDJAMMER MINIATURE EUROPE
15 ml. size blue glass and cap. C.M.V. $5.00 M.B.

LEFT TO RIGHT
1976 CAVALIER AFTER SHAVE – MEXICO
120 ml clear glass black cap and pink and black label. Also came in cologne. C.M.V. $6.00 each.
1976 CAVALIER SQUEEZE DEODORANT MEXICO
9 ml pink and black plastic bottle. C.M.V. $3.00
1978 OSLO – MEXICO, SPAIN
168 ml clear glass, brown marbleized cap. Came in after shave or cologne. C.M.V. $6.00 each
1978 OSLO – SQUEEZE DEODORANTE – MEXICO
90 ml cream color and brown plastic bottle. C.M.V. $3.00

LEFT TO RIGHT
1970 COLOGNE – MEXICO
Green and white plastic bottle, silver soccer ball cap. CMV $8.00
1970 DEODORANTE - MEXICO
Same as cologne above. CMV $8.00
1976 LEATHER AFTER SHAVE – MEXICO
Clear glass, red label, black cap. C.M.V. $6.00
1975 AFTER SHAVE AND COLOGNE – MEXICO
After shave in black cap and cologne in gold cap. C.M.V. $8.00 each.

1971 EMPERATOR SHAVE LOTION ENGLAND - 150 cc size, clear ribbed bottle blue & silver neck band & cap. C.M.V. $10.00 $14.00 MB.
RIGHT 1970s TALC DEODORANT EUROPE
85 g. white and blue paper container with plastic top and bottom. C.M.V. $2.00

1980 WINDJAMMER AFTER SHAVE - EUROPE
30 ml. clear glass with navy blue top. CMV $5.00 MB
1980 CLINT AFTER SHAVE - MEXICO
1.5 ml. clear glass bottle with blue top & red writing. CMV $5.00 MB
1980 EVEREST AFTER SHAVE - MEXICC
1.5 ml. clear glass with dark blue top. CMV $5.00 MB.

1979 THE TRAVELLER SET - AUSTRALIA
Brown box holds 1 100 ml light brown plastic Tai Winds after shave and 1 dark brown 75 ml squeeze spray deodorant. CMV $6.50 MB
1979-80 LEATHER AFTER SHAVE - MEXICO
118 ml clear glass with brown top and label. CMV $5.00 MB
1979-80 LEATHER TALC - MEXICO
100 g cardboard container. CMV $3.00 MB.

1980 CLINT PRODUCTS - JAPAN
Left To Right
COLOGNE
120 ml size. CMV $8.00 MB
HAIR TONIC
150 ml size. CMV $9.00 MB
HAIR LIQUID
150 ml size. CMV $9.00 MB
AFTER SHAVE
120 ml size. CMV $8.00 MB
1980 CLINT PRODUCTS - MEXICO
TALC
100 g size. CMV $3.00 MB
DEODORANT
90 ml. CMV $2.50 MB.

1980 AFTER SHAVES - EUROPE
All are 75 ml size plastic bottles. Hud, grey with silver cap; Tai Winds, green with gold cap; Wild Country, brown with silver cap; Windjammer, blue with gold cap. CMV $3.50 each.

1980 AFTER SHAVES - EUROPE
Left to Right, all 50 ml. size in Tai Winds, Wild Country, and Nexus. CMV $5.00 each MB. Windjammer and Spicy on far right 100 ml size are from Australia. CMV $5.00 each MB.

1973 HAIR TONIC - EUROPE
180 m/l bottle with oil, orange label, with out oil, green label. Both black caps. C.M.V. $6.00 ea. M.B.

COLONIA - MEXICO
4A design on black cap. C.M.V. $8.00
1974-76 COLONIA - MEXICO
C.M.V. $4.00

BLUE BLAZER - MEXICO
Dark blue glass, 2 different paper labels. Cologne & After Shave, red caps. C.M.V $18.00 ea.

BLUE BLAZER - EUROPE
Soap On A Rope - C.M.V. $5.00
Talc Can - C.M.V. $5.00 - Talc Cardboard C.M.V. $5.00, Spray Deodorant - C.M.V. $5.00, After Shave Lotion - 170 cc clear glass bottle, large red round cap. C.M.V. $15.00

1975 BLUE BLAZER AFTER SHAVE — FOREIGN
Clear glass. Left - English, right - Spain (cut out label). C.M.V. $10.00 each
1978 BLUE BLAZER COLOGNE — SPAIN
Same as center bottle, Clear glass. C.M.V.$10.00

1972 BOOT - SPAIN
236 cc amber bottle, gold cap. Leather Cologne. C.M.V. $10.00
1972-76 ELECTRIC PRE-SHAVE - SPAIN
120 cc clear glass bottle with white cap & label. C.M.V. $5.00

1972 AMBER AFTER SHAVE – GERMANY, MEXICO
50 ml amber bottle came in Imperator, light blue label. Windjammer, dark blue label and Oland, tan label. Spicy in brown lable, Blue Blazer in blue, Wild country in black label, Deep Woods, orange label, Windjammer in light blue label with black cap. All other caps are silver. C.M.V. $7.50 each M.B.

1972 ORIGINAL AFTER SHAVE - SPAIN
118 cc bottle, red cap, white label. C.M.V. $8.00 M.B.
1973 OLOF COLOGNE - SPAIN
120 cc bottle with brown cap with silver O on top. C.M.V. $7.00 M.B.

1973 AFTER SHAVE - SPAIN
60 cc blue labels & silver caps. Blue Blazer, Windjammer, Excalibur & Wild Country. C.M.V. $4.00 ea. M.B.
1973 AVON STEEL AFTER SHAVE
EUROPE - 90 cc blue glass bottle, silver cap. C.M.V. $5.00 in box.

1970'S CARTE BLANCHE - CANADA
6 oz. After Shave, silver cap, clear glass. C.M.V. $6.00
5 oz. Soap On A Rope, C.M.V. $4.00
2 oz. Gentlemens Selection, silver cap, clear glass. C.M.V. $4.00

CANADA 1973 - FOUNDATION FOAM
Pink can, C.M.V. $1.00
1973 TRIBUTE AEROSOL DEODORANT FOR MEN - Blue & silver can. C.M.V. $2.00
1973 TRIBUTE CREAM HAIR DRESS
Blue & silver tube. C.M.V. $2.00
1973 ISLAND LIME AEROSOL DEODORANT
Green & yellow can. C.M.V. $2.00

1973-76 ELECTRIC PRE-SHAVE - FOREIGN
4 oz. bottle, clear glass, black cap, England. White cap, Australian. C.M.V. $6.00 M.B. ea.

1975 TODAYS MAN – EUROPE
Shaving bowl refill, in box. C.M.V. $4.00 M.B. Shaving Bown. Box holds black & gray plastic soap bowl in box. C.M.V. $7.00 M.B.

1973 TODAYS MAN - EUROPE
Mens Products came in spray deodorant C.M.V. $6.00
CLEAR HAIR DRESS - C.M.V. $5.00
HAIR GROOM SPRAY - C.M.V. $6.00
FOAM SHAVE CREAM - C.M.V. $5.00
LATHER SHAVE CREAM - C.M.V. $5.00
ELECTRIC PRE-SHAVE LOTION - C.M.V. $10.00 -
SHAVING BRUSH (not shown) C.M.V. $5.00

LEFT TO RIGHT
1977 TODAYS MAN HAIR TONIC – JAPAN
117 ml clear plastic bottle, black cap. C.M.V. $6.00
1977 TODAYS MAN DEODORANTE – MEIXCO
60 ml clear glass bottle, black cap. C.M.V. $3.00
1977 TODAYS MAN ROLL ON DEODORANT EUROPE
60 ml white plastic bottle, black cap. C.M.V. $4.00
1977 TODAYS MAN SHAVING BRUSH – EUROPE
Black and white plastic handle. C.M.V. $4.00
1977 TODAYS MAN SHAMPOO SHOWER SOAP ON A ROPE – AUSTRALIA
White soap and rope. C.M.V. $6.00

LEFT TO RIGHT
1976 IMPERATOR PRODUCTS – EUROPE
ELECTRIC PRE SHAVE - 180 ml. silver top, blue 4A cap. C.M.V. $8.00
COLOGNE AFTER SHAVE - both 120 ml blue decal labels and 4A caps. C.M.V. $6.00 ea.
SOAP SET FOR MEN
Blue and silver box holds 2 white bars with 4A embossed centers. C.M.V. $12.00 M.B.

LEFT TO RIGHT
1977 HUD – FOREIGN
After Shave in 15 ml size C.M.V. $5.00
After Shave in 100 ml size C.M.V. $8.00
Talc - grey and white 100 g size C.M.V. $4.00

1976 NEW WORLD – EUROPE
180 ml. size clear glass. Silver cap. Blue letters on cap. After shave. C.M.V. $4.00 M.B.
1976 HAWK – EUROPE
150 ml. size clear glass, gold cap. After shave. C.M.V. $10.00 M.B.
1980 HAWK - JAPAN
Same size & shape as Europe Hawk only has Japanese writing on bottle. CMV $15.00 MB.

LEFT TO RIGHT
1976 NEW WORLD AFTER SHAVE – MEXICO
After shave with light blue cap and cologne in light blue cap. Both clear glass. C.M.V. $5.00 each.
1977 NEW WORLD SPRAY TALC – AUSTRALIA
Blue metal can. C.M.V. $3.50
1977 NEW WORLD SHOWER SOAP – AUSTRALIA
Blue bar on blue rope. C.M.V. $6.00
1977 NEW WORLD AFTER SHAVE – AUSTRALIA
175 ml clear glass, silver cap. C.M.V. $8.00.

LEFT 1975 NEW WORLD TALC FOREIGN
White plastic container with blue paper label. C.M.V. $4.00
CENTER 1975 NEW WORLD TALC FOREIGN
Blue metal can, white cap. CMV $6.00
RIGHT 1977 PYRENEES COLOGNIA SPAIN
150 ml. clear glass, blue cap. CMV $7.00 MB.

LEFT TO RIGHT
1976 WINDJAMMER RUBDOWN COOLER – CANADA
10 oz. plastic bottle, blue and gold cap. C.M.V. $3.00
1977 WINDJAMMER AFTER SHAVE – EUROPE
120 ml light blue glass, blue paper front label. Indented all blue cap. C.M.V. $8.00
1978 EVEREST AFTER SHAVE – CANADA
4.9 oz. plastic bottle, blue cap. Painted white label in French and English. C.M.V. $3.00
1978 ENDEAVOUR SOAP ON A ROPE – EUROPE
Blue soap on a white rope. C.M.V. $5.00 M.B.
1978 ENDEAVOUR AFTER SHAVE – EUROPE
150 ml clear glass, blue cap. C.M.V. $6.00

1975 WINDJAMMER – MEXICO
Colonia Para Caballeros, dark purple glass, painted label. C.M.V. $25.00
WINDJAMMER COLOGNE
Left - Mexico - light blue glass, painted label. C.M.V. $10.00
Right - Canadian - painted label (address on front) C.M.V. $4.00

1978 TODAYS MAN PRODUCTS – JAPAN
Each is brown and cream color plastic in After Shave 120 ml. bottle, 1/5 g tube of Hair Gel, 115 gr tube of Hair Dress, 115 tube Skin Conditioner, 180 ml bottle Hair Tonic, 180 ml bottle Hair Liquid, 120 ml milky Lotion, C.M.V. $4.50 each.
1977 CARTE BLANCHE – CANADA
Spray Talc - metal can, green paper label and cap. C.M.V. $2.50
Carte Blanche After Shave Balm Tube - 3 oz. green and white tube. C.M.V. $1.50

1976 WINDJAMMER – AUSTRALIA
Shower Soap On A Rope, in blue box. C.M.V. $8.00 M.B.
AEROSOL SPRAY DEODORANT
4 oz. blue metal can and cap. C.M.V. $5.00

1976 HAIR TONIC SPICY – JAPAN
118 ml size, real dark green glass, black cap. Japanese label on back. C.M.V. $10.00 M.B.
1976 SUMMER LOTION – JAPAN
130 ml. clear plastic bottle, white cap. Japanese label on back. C.M.V. $6.00 M.B.

LEFT TO RIGHT
1977 SPICY AFTER SHAVE LOTION – EUROPE
120 ml clear glass, black cap. C.M.V. $4.50
1978 SPICY AFTER SHAVE LOTION – CANADA
4 oz. clear glass, black cap. C.M.V. $2.50
1978 SPICY AFTER SHAVE – CANADA
150 ml frosted plastic, black cap. C.M.V. $2.00

1973 EAU DE PARFUME – ENGLAND
15 ml glass bottle, gold flat cap as shown. Reissued in 1976 with gold flat top cap. CMV $8.00 each MB.

1976 SPICY — FOREIGN
Talc - Canada 2.75 oz. metal can.
C.M.V. $1.00
Spray Deodorant — Europe 81cc white plastic bottle, brown cap. C.M.V. $2.00
Savon Sur Corde Soap on a Rope - Canada
Tan soap, white rope. C.M.V. $4.00

1978 SPICY AFTER SHAVE — JAPAN
120 ml light amber glass, black cap.
C.M.V. $10.00
1978 SPICY COLOGNE — JAPAN
120 ml light amber glass, black cap.
C.M.V. $10.00
1978 SPICY AFTER SHAVE LOTION — MEXICO
117 ml dark amber glass, black cap, brown and black label. C.M.V. $6.00
1978 SPICY COLOGNE — MEXICO
117 ml dark amber glass, black cap.
Gold and black label. C.M.V. $6.00

COLOGNES - FOREIGN
½ oz. clear glass bottles, Canadian on left, English center two (gold & black caps) Canadian on right. C.M.V. $5.00 ea. M.B.

HAWAIIAN WHITE GINGER - MEXICO - C.M.V. $6.00
ELEGANTE COLOGNE - MEXICO
C.M.V. $6.00

1973 EAU DE COLOGNE - ENGLAND
15 m/l size, clear glass, gold cap. C.M.V. $6.00 MB.

1979 BUBBLE BATH, TRIAL SIZE - CANADA
40 ml pink plastic, white cap. CMV $1.00 full.
1979 SKIN SO SOFT TRIAL SIZE - CANADA
40 ml clear plastic, turquoise cap.
CMV $1.00 full.

1980 LIPSLICKER, EYESLICKER COMPACTS - EUROPE
Came in blue or pink plastic. CMV $6.00 MB
1980 FASHION MAKE-UP GROUP - JAPAN
White plastic compacts in Creamy Cake or Creamy color. CMV $6.00 MB.

1980 SAMPLES - JAPAN
COLOGNE SAMPLES
Package of 5. CMV $5.00
LIQUID MAKE-UP
Package of 7. CMV $8.00
ACCOLADE
Night cream. CMV $5.00 MB
NIGHT CREAM
Box of 5 packets. CMV $5.00

1979 COLORSTICK CASE - JAPAN
Brown vinyl. CMV $5.00
1979 SKIN SILK PADS - JAPAN
Box of cotton pads. CMV $4.00
1979 SHOWER CAP - JAPAN
Pink plastic shower cap with Avon printe on it. CMV $4.00

1980 SKIN FRESHENER - JAPAN
180 ml clear glass with gold top. CMV $10.00 MB
1980 SKIN FRESHENER - JAPAN
180 ml clear glass with silver top. CMV $10.00 MB
1980 SKIN SILK - JAPAN
180 ml clear glass with gold top. CMV $12.00 MB.
1980 SUMMER LOTION - JAPAN
180 ml clear glass with clear plastic top.
CMV $10.00 MB.
1980 VANITY JAR - JAPAN
140 g clear glass with gold cap. CMV $10.00 MB. Also issued in Europe. Same jar with silver cap. CMV $10.00 MB.

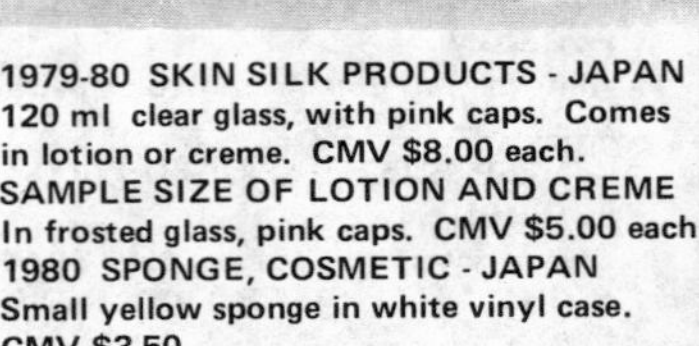

1979-80 SKIN SILK PRODUCTS - JAPAN
120 ml clear glass, with pink caps. Comes in lotion or creme. CMV $8.00 each.
SAMPLE SIZE OF LOTION AND CREME
In frosted glass, pink caps. CMV $5.00 each
1980 SPONGE, COSMETIC - JAPAN
Small yellow sponge in white vinyl case.
CMV $3.50

1979-80 CARE DEEPLY SET - JAPAN
Green box holds 2 white tubes hand cream. CMV $7.00 MB
1979-80 BEAUTY DUST - JAPAN
Brown turtle shell, plastic with gold trim. CMV $22.00 MB
1979-80 PURSE SPRAY COLOGNE - JAPAN
12 ml gold container. CMV $10.00 MB
1979-80 CHIC ULTRA PURSE SPRAY - JAPAN
12 ml black & gold case. CMV $10.00 MB
1979-80 MAKE-UP SPONGE - JAPAN
Beige top, burgundy plastic base. CMV $15.00 MB.

LEFT TO RIGHT
1969 COLOGNE – FOREIGN
Ribbed glass bottles with 4A insignia on plastic cap. C.M.V' $15.00
1970 LOCION CREAM – MEXICO
Embossed rose bottle, gold cap. C.M.V' $7.00
1972 COLOGNE SPRAY – MEXICO
Clear glass, silver cap with 4A on top. C.M.V. $6.00

1978 COLOGNES – MEXICO
Each is 58 ml size. Charisma, red paint over clear glass. Moonwind in cobalt blue, C.M.V. $6.50 each. All rest are clear glass in Somewhere, Raining Violets, Sweet Honesty, C.M.V. $5.00 each. To A Wild Rose and Sonnet C.M.V. $6.50 each.
1978 TO A WILD ROSE LOCION CREAM – MEXICO
White glass, pink cap. C.M.V. $5.00

1973 LOTION LUXURY - ENGLAND
Clear glass bottle, gold cap. C.M.V. $7.00 M.B.
1973 BUD VASE EAU DE COLOGNE ENGLAND - Clear glass bottle & cap. Holds 150 m/l cologne. C.M.V. $9.00 M.B.

LEFT TO RIGHT
1977 HAIR CREME - MEXICO
57 g. size red plastic. CMV $4.00
1977 HAIR LOTION - MEXICO
Clear glass, CMV $5.00
1980 CREME SILICONE LOTION - MEXICO
120 g. size green plastic. CMV $3.50
1980 SWEET HONESTY COLOGNE - MEXICO
57 ml. size clear glass, pink cap. CMV $6.00
1980 SPRING PROMISE COLOGNE - MEXICO
58 ml size clear glass with lavender cap. CMV $6.50
1980 COLOGNE SPRAY - EUROPE
27 g. clear glass, gold cap, different color neckbands for different fregrances. CMV $7.00
1980 COOL EAU DE AVON - EUROPE
50 ml size blue glass, silver cap. CMV $7.00
1980 COLOGNE SPRAY - JAPAN
70 ml. clear glass, gold cap, different color neckbands for different fragrances. CMV $9.00
1980 PERFUME ROLLETTE - JAPAN
10 ml size clear glass, gold cap, different color neckband for each fragrance. CMV $5.00

LEFT TO RIGHT
1978 COLOGNES – MEXICO
Roses Roses, 58 ml frosted glass, tall gold cap. C.M.V. $6.50
Roses Roses, 58 mo. clear glass, tall off white cap. C.M.V. $5.50
All rest are 57 or 58 ml clear glass in Rapture, Here's My Heart - C.M.V. $6.50 or Bird of Paradise, Unforgettable - C.M.V. $5.00 each.

1976 COLOGNES – FOREIGN
1/2 oz. each. Left to right - black cap, white cap and silver cap. 2 on left are from Canada and right is Europe.
C.M.V. $3.00 Canada, $3.00 Europe.

LEFT TO RIGHT
1976 DEVOTEE CREAM LOTION – MEXICO
59 g clear glass, gold cap. C.M.V. $5.00
1977 COLOGNE – JAPAN
59 ml clear glass, gold pointed cap. C.M.V. $8.00
1978 ARISTECRATICO COLOGNE – MEXICO
43 ml clear glass, clear plastic cap. C.M.V. $5.00
1976 LOCION CAPILAR – MEXICO
120 ml. clear glass, red cap and label. C.M.V' $8.00
1978 COLOGNE SPRAY – JAPAN
70 ml clear glass, red painted band around gold cap. C.M.V. $10.00
1978 COLOGNE SPRAY – EUROPE
57 g clear glass, gold cap. C.M.V. $6.00
1978 PERFUME CONCENTRATE SPRAY – JAPAN
12 ml black and gold metal container. C.M.V. $8.00

1980 SAMPLES - JAPAN
TUBE SAMPLES - CMV $2.00 each
AFTER SHAVE SAMPLES - CMV $5.00 each
CREAM SAMPLES - assorted. CMV $4.00 each

Left to Right - PICTURESQUE COLOGNE GERMAN - 20 cc swirl glass bottle with gold cap. C.M.V. $10.00 M.B.
DIAMOND COLOGNE - GERMAN
25 cc ribbed glass bottle, gold cap. C.M.V. $10.00 M.B.
BEAUTEMP COLOGNE - GERMAN
15 m/l bottle with gold cap. C.M.V. $5.00 M.B.
1972 EUROPEAN BELL - GERMAN
15 m/l bottle, tall gold cap. C.M.V. $10.00 M.B.

LEFT TO RIGHT
1978 COLOGNE – AUSTRALIA
15 ml gold tall cap. C.M.V. $4.00
1976 TEARDROP COLOGNE – AUSTRALIA
15 ml tall round gold cap. C.M.V. $4.00
1977 COLOGNE – JAPAN
15 ml short bottle, gold cap. C.M.V. $8.00
1977 EAU DE COLOGNE – EUROPE, JAPAN
30 ml square glass bottle, flat top, gold round cap. C.M.V. $6.00 Europe - $8.00 Japan. Europe label on bottom, Japan on back.
1977 CORONET COLOGNE – AUSTRALIA
30 ml. clear glass, round gold cap. C.M.V. $6.00
1975-78 PETITE COLOGNE – EUROPE
15 ml clear glass, silver or gold cap. C.M.V. $4.00

1977 COLOGNE MIST – FOREIGN
12 different pictured from Canada, Europe, and Australia. C.M.V. $3.00 each from Canada, $5.00 each on rest.
1978 CREAM SACHET – CANADA
19 g. ribbed glass bottom. Different colored tops with gold bands in 9 different fregrences. C.M.V. $2.50 ea.

LEFT TO RIGHT
1978 SPLASH COLOGNE
2 on left are Europe, 60 ml clear glass and 2 different size gold caps. C.M.V. $5.00 each. Center, 70 ml from Japan C.M.V. $8.00. 4th is Australia in 60 ml size, C.M.V. $4.00. Right is Canada, black cap, 57 ml size. C.M.V. $2.50. Gold caps on all but Canada.

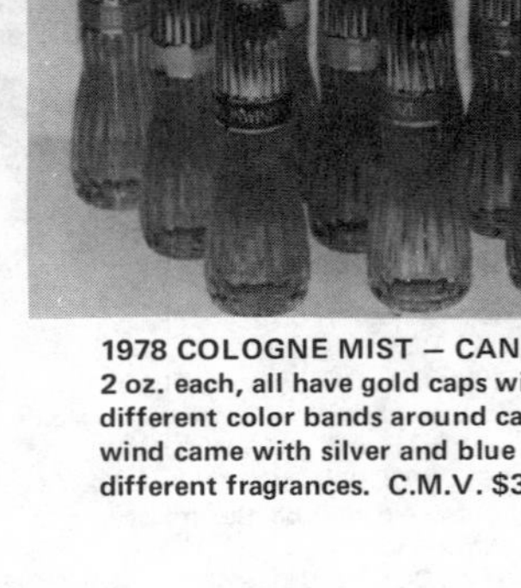

1978 COLOGNE MIST – CANADA
2 oz. each, all have gold caps with 11 different color bands around cap. Moonwind came with silver and blue cap. 11 different fragrances. C.M.V. $3.50 each.

1977 PERFUME ROLLETTE'S – FOREIGN
19 different pictured from Europe, Mexico and Canada, Australia. All are glass. C.M.V. $3.00

1974 FRAGRANCED SKIN SO SOFT – EUROPE
60 cc, blue and white front label, gold cap. C.M.V. $5.00
1977 IMPERIAL BOOT – MEXICO
54 ml clear glass boot, gold cap. Side buttons are small than U.S. issue. Came in cologne. C.M.V. $5.00
1976 TOQUE DE AMOR CREAM LOTION – BRAZIL
100 cm clear glass, white painted label and white beaded cap. Same as old Here's My Heart U.S. bottles. C.M.V. $10.00
1960's NOTION DE ESTRELAS COLOGNE – BRAZIL
Same as old U.S. Bright Night bottle. Clear gold speckeled cap different from U.S. issue. Spanish neck tag on gold string. C.M.V. $15.00

1974 BRAZIL COLOGNES
Left to Right
Octagonal Cologne – Clear glass, gold cap. 55 ml. C.M.V. $10.00
Charisma Cologne – Red paint over clear glass. Red and gold cap. 55 ml. C.M.V. $
Moonwind Cologne – Blue glass, silver cap. 55 ml. C.M.V. $5.00
Cold Eau D'Avon – Clear glass, silver cap. 55 ml. C.M.V. $8.00
Rosa Silvestre Cologne – White paint over clear glass, pink cap. 55 ml. C.M.V. $7.00

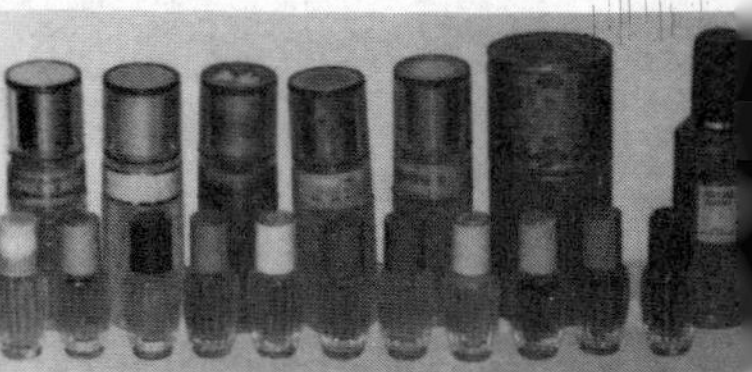

LEFT TO RIGHT
1978 COLOGNE MIST
5 on left are from Mexico in Here's My Heart, blue band; Sweet Honesty, light pink band; Rapture, dark blue; Somewher dark pink; Unforgettable in orange. C.M.V. $5.00 each.
1978 ELEGANCE SPRAY COLOGNE – EUROPE (far right)
80 ml clear glass painted green, green and gold cap. C.M.V. $7.00
1973 BROCADE SPRAY COLOGNE – EUROPE
Sandy brown plastic coated base, gold brocade cap. C.M.V. $8.00
1978 PERFUME ROLLETTE – CANADA
9 ml clear ribbed bottles. Each has different color cap. 12 different fragrances C.M.V. $2.50 each.

1972 COLONIA IMPERIO - MEXICO
Ribbed glass bottle, gold ribbed cap. CMV $6.00 each.
KAVON TOPAZE CREAM BODY LOTION - GERMAN CMV $22.50

73 YOUNG ROMANTICS - EUROPE
0 cc white plastic bottle, lavender cap.
olds bath oil. C.M.V. $10.00; 118 cc clear
ass bottle, lavender cap, holds cologne.
.M.V. $10.00

74 CANADA — BIRD OF PARADISE
AY - Turquoise plastic with gold band.
.V. $5.00
RFUMED SOAP - 3 oz. bar. C.M.V. $2.00
RFUMED TALC - 2.75 oz. turquoise metal
& blue cap. C.M.V. $2.00
FT NOTES - 15 sheets 5¾ x 8" with 18
ls. Sealed in plastic, C.M.V. $4.00

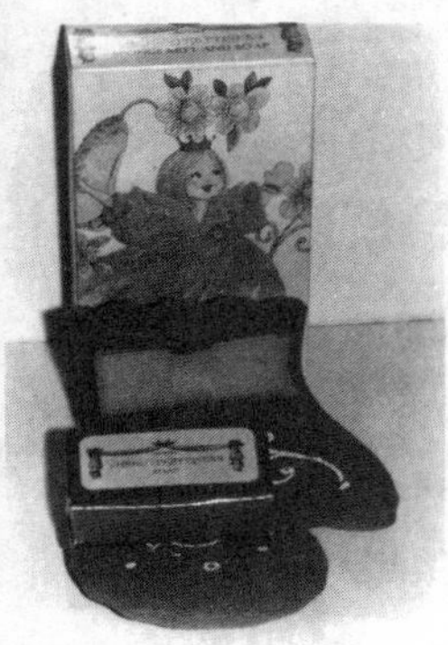

972 HER PRETTINESS SPONGE MITT
SOAP - CANADA - Pink & yellow sponge
bar of soap. C.M.V. $7.00 M.B.

1974 FIELD FLOWERS — CANADA
TRAY - Light green plastic tray with gold
edge & Field Flowers decal in center. C.M.V.
$5.00
PERFUMED TALC - 2.75 oz. metal can with
green cap. C.M.V. $2.00
GIFT NOTES - 15 sheets 5¾ x 8" with 18
seals, sealed in plastic. C.M.V. $4.00

1972-73 SMALL WORLD HAND CREAM
CANADA - 2.25 oz. green & white tube,
pink cap. O.S.P. $1.10 C.M.V. $5.00 M.B.
1975-76 FLOWER TALK HAND CREAM
CANADA - 60 ml (2.25 oz) white flowered
tube & cap. Canada. O.S.P. $2.00 C.M.V.
$1.50 M.B.

1975 HAWAIIAN WHITE GINGER —
CANADA PERFUMED TALC - 2.75 oz.
can, pink cap. C.M.V. $2.00
1975 PERFUMED SOAPS - Box holds 3
bars. C.M.V. $5.00

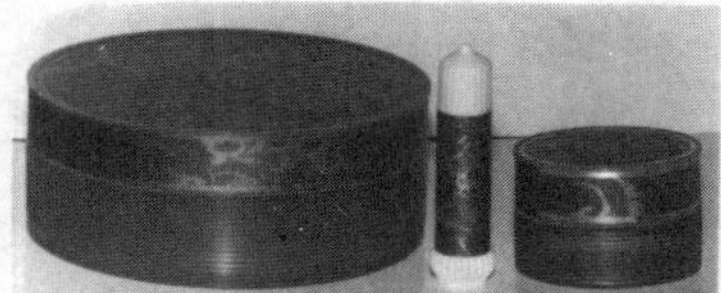

1973 BROCADE - ENGLAND
BEAUTY DUST - C.M.V. $10.00
DEMI STICK - C.M.V. $3.00
CREAM SACHET - C.M.V. $5.00

1972 BLUE PETAL - ENGLAND
Perfumed Talc in paper container.
C.M.V. $4.00 M.B.
CREAM SACHET - Lavender frosted glass
& lid. C.M.V. $5.00 M.B.

1974 REGENCE — CANADA
PERFUMED TALC - 2.75 oz. green metal
can, gold cap. C.M.V. $2.00
SAVON PERFUMED SOAP - Box holds 3
green bars. C.M.V. $5.00
PERFUMED SOAP - 3 oz. plain wrapper.
3 oz. green floral wrapper C.M.V. $2.00

1974 MOONWIND — CANADA
HAND & BODY CREAM LOTION - 8 oz.
blue plastic bottle, blue cap. C.M.V. $4.00
PERFUMED TALC - 2.75 oz. blue metal can,
blue cap. C.M.V. $2.00
MOONWIND TRAY - Blue plastic with silver
band & center design. CMV $12.50 MB.

1976 LEMON VELVET — CANADA
2.75 oz. Perfumed Talc, yellow metal
can, green cap. C.M.V. $2.00
1976 HAND CREAM — CANADA
3 oz. yellow tube, green cap. C.M.V.
$2.00
1975 PERFUMED TALC — AUSTRALIA
3½ oz. yellow & green cardboard
container with plastic shaker top.
C.M.V. $4.00

1975 ROSE GERANIO PERFUMED TALC
MEXICO - Pink metal shaker can. C.M.V.
$4.00
CREAM SACHET - Rose frosted jar with
gold cap. C.M.V. $4.00 M.B.

1974 HANA GASA — CANADA
PERFUMED TALC - 2.75 oz. yellow can and cap. C.M.V. $2.00
1974 PERFUMED SOAP - Single wrapped bar. C.M.V. $2.00
1974 GIFT NOTES - 15 yellow sheets 5¾ x 8" with 18 seals wrapped in plastic. C.M.V. $4.00.

1960 KAVON HERE'S MY HEART PERFUMED TALC — EUROPE
Kavon Cosmetics — Blue tin powder can. Early name used by Avon Cosmetics in Europe. RARE. Kavon name was used only a short time. C.M.V. $20.00
1960 KAVON PERSIAN WOOD EAU DE COLOGNE — EUROPE
4 oz. glass bottle, gold cap. RARE. Kavon name used only a short time, then changed to Avon Cosmetics. C.M.V. $20.00

1977 FLOWER TALK — CANADA
All are white with flower design.
Cream Sachet C.M.V. $1.50
Hand Cream C.M.V. $2.00
Perfumed Talc C.M.V. $2.00
Soap on a Rope - pink soap and white rope C.M.V. $5.00 M.B.

1979-80 CHIC PRODUCTS - EUROPE
Same as Candid in U.S. Foaming Shower Gel, Perfumed Talc, Purse Spray, 2 different colognes, Body Satin, Luxury Foam Bath. All products. CMV $3.50 MB, vanity mirror CMV $6.00 MB.

1980 FIRST FLOWERS PRODUCTS - EUROPE
Green and white flower daisy design, on all products. 60 ml Eau De Cologne, CMV $4.00 MB. Hair brush, CMV $4.00 MB, Perfume Glace, white & yellow plastic, CMV $5.00 MB. Soap, 3 white daisy bars CMV $6.50 MB. Perfumed Talc, CMV $3.50 MB. Hand Cream, CMV $2.00 MB

1979-80 CANDID PRODUCTS - JAPAN
Scarf, signed S.M. Kent CMV $6.00
Face Paper & Tissue Paper, vinyl case CMV $8.00 Pressed Powder Compact, plastic CMV $6.00

1980 REGENCE PRODUCTS - JAPAN
Elegant packaging, all have gold caps. White plastic Avon tray. CMV $12.00
Cleansing Cream, plastic; Toning Freshener, glass; Skin Lotion, glass; Milky Lotion, glass; Massage Cream, glass; Peal Off Pack, Plastic. All products CMV $10.00 MB.

1980 DELICATE DAISIES SET - AUSTRALIA
Green & white daisy flower design. Box holds 50 ml clear glass cologne with painted on daisies, and 100 g perfumed talc. CMV $10.00 MB
1980 DAISIES PERFUME ROLLETTE MEXICO
8.5 g clear glass with green and white daisy design plastic top. CMV $3.50 MB
1980 DAISIES HAND CREAM - MEXIC
43 g green & white plastic daisy design tube. CMV $2.00 MB.

1980 STYLE PRODUCTS - EUROPE
Left to Right. Same as U.S. Tempo.
COLOGNE 30 ml size. CMV $6.50 MB
PERFUMED TALC 100 g. CMV $3.00 MB
SOLID PERFUME 5.5 g. CMV $4.50 MB
ROLLETTE 10 ml. CMV $4.00 MB.

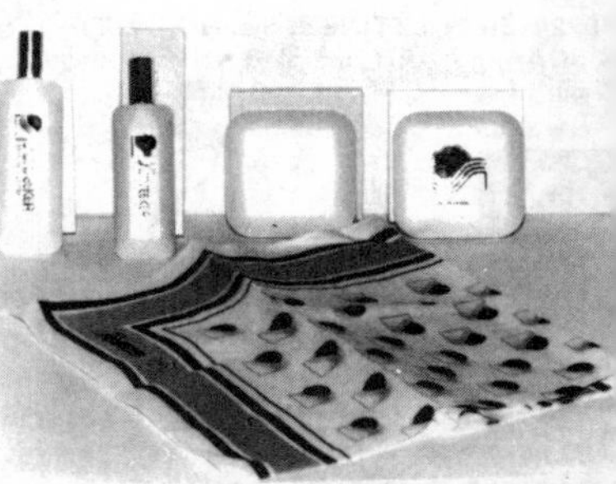

1980 SUNSEEKER PRODUCTS - JAPAN
Sunseeker scarf, orange, grey & white. CMV $8.00
Makeup Creme, white plastic; Foundation, blue plastic; Cake foundation, blue plastic compact; Color Control Cake, white pearl compact. All products CMV $6.00 MB.

EFT TO RIGHT
75 LAVENDER COLOGNE – SPAIN
cc white milk glass, purple painted owers, white cap. Came without neck bon. C.M.V. $5.00 M.B.
75 LAVENDER PERFUMED SOAPS – AIN
x of 3 long lavender bars. C.M.V. $10.00 B.
74 LAVENDER DUO SET – EUROPE
x holds 1 lavender bar of soap and 50 milk glass lavender cologne with neck bon. C.M.V. $12.00
76 LAVENDER PERFUMED SOAPS – JSTRALIA
x holds 3 square lavender soaps. M.V. $8.00 M.B.

72-75 CLASSIC COLLECTION - ANADA
oz. Perfumed Powder Mist. CMV 50c
eam Sachet. CMV $2.50 MB
logne Mist. CMV $4.00 MB
auty Dust. CMV $7.50 MB
aming Bath Oil. CMV $2.00 MB
rfumed Talc. CMV 50c.

EFT TO RIGHT
77 PURSE PERFUME SPRAY – JROPE
ue plastic coated over clear glass, gold and flower paper front decal. M.V. $6.00
77 PERFUME ON ROLLETTE – ROPE
ml white milk glass, painted flower sign, gold cap. C.M.V. $6.00
74 PATTERNS PERFUME ON ROLLETTE – ROPE
ite milk glass, black cap and painted sign. Gold band around neck. C.M.V. 00.
74 PATTERNS CREAM SACHET – ROPE
ite milk glass, black cap and painted sign. C.M.V. $5.00
78 PERFUME ROLLETTE – MEXICO
arisma is red paint over clear glass and onwind in cobalt blue glass. C.M.V. 50 each.

1978 GENESIS PRODUCTS – AUSTRALIA
Same design as U.S. Timeless.
Perfumette – 9 ml amber glass, gold cap. C.M.V. $4.00
Cologne Spray – amber glass, gold cap. C.M.V. $8.00
Perfumed Powder Mist – 200 g metal can. C.M.V. $5.00
Perfumed Soaps – Box of 3 tan bars. C.M.V. $7.00
Foaming Bath Oil – 200 ml plastic. C.M.V. $5.00
Ultra Cream Perfume – 19 g amber glass, gold cap. C.M.V. $5.00

1978 SPRING PROMISE PRODUCTS – CANADA
All are pink and white labels are French and English.
Fragrance Sample - 10 in a box. C.M.V. $1.00 box.
Perfumed Powder Mist - C.M.V. $3.50
Perfumed Skin Softener - Plastic C.M.V. $3.50
Shadow Collection Compact - C.M.V. $6.00
Cream Sachet - C.M.V. $2.50
Perfume Rollette - C.M.V. $3.00

LEFT TO RIGHT
1975 NILE BLUE BATH URN – EUROPE
180 ml deep cobalt blue glass. Holds perfumed bath oil. C.M.V. $12.00
1977 AGUA DE COLONIA (After Bath Freshener) – SPAIN
Large 470 ml frosted glass, white painted on label and design. white cap. C.M.V. $8.00
1978 SPRING PROMISE PRODUCTS – MEXICO
Talc in pink metal can - C.M.V. $4.00
Cologne, 58 ml, pink cap - C.M.V. $5.00
Perfume Rollette, pink cap - C.M.V. $3.00

1978 DAISIES – MEXICO
Cream Lotion – 118 ml size, turquoise plastic, white cap. C.M.V. $4.00
Cologne – 2 oz. clear glass, smaller than U.S. size. C.M.V. $4.00
Talc – 100 g size, green metal can. C.M.V. $4.00
Perfume Glace – White with yellow center. C.M.V. $4.50

1978 TIMELESS – MEXICO
All are clear glass, gold caps. U.S. issue is amber glass.
Ultra Perfume Rollette – C.M.V. $4.00
Ultra Cologne Splash – 58 ml size C.M.V. $6.00
Ultra Cologne Spray – 57 ml size C.M.V. $8.00
Ultra Cream Perfume – C.M.V. $4.50

1976 PROMISE OF HEAVEN – EUROPE
Soap – Blue box of 3 bars. C.M.V. $6.00
Perfumed Talc – 200 g size, blue can. C.M.V. $6.00
Perfumed Talc – 100 g size, blue can. C.M.V. $4.00
Perfumed Skin Softener – 150 g size blue plastic jar. C.M.V. $2.50
Foaming Bath oil – 150 ml size plastic bottle. C.M.V. $2.50
Perfumed Soap – 1 bar in blue box. C.M.V. $3.00
Cream Sachet – 19 g size blue glass. C.M.V. $4.00
Cologne Mist – 85 g size. C.M.V. $8.00

1973 PERFUMED BODY POWDERS – EUROPE
Somewhere - pink, Elegence - green, Rapture - blue, Occur! - black, Unforgettable - orange, Topaze - yellow, all are plastic bottles. C.M.V. $7.00 each.

LEFT TO RIGHT
1973 HONEYSUCKLE BODY POWDER – EUROPE
Yellow plastic, orange cap. C.M.V. $7.00
1973 HAWAIIAN WHITE GINGER BODY POWDER – EUROPE
Turquoise plastic, white cap. C.M.V. $7.00
1973 TOPAZE BATH OIL – EUROPE
Yellow plastic and cap. C.M.V. $7.00
1973 WISHING CREAM BODY LOTION – EUROPE
4.1 oz. white plastic, gold string and whisbone. C.M.V. $7.00
1973 WISHING SPRAY EAU DE COLOGNE – EUROPE
White plastic coated bottle. Came with 4 leaf clover around neck. C.M.V. $10.00
1978 CREAM LOTION – MEXICO
75 g pink plastic bottle, white cap. C.M.V. $3.00
1978 HAND CREAM – MEXICO
Light orange and white tube. C.M.V. $2.00

1977 GOLDEN NILE – EUROPE
Cream sachet, gold cap.
C.M.V. $2.00 M.B.
Perfumed talc, gold can.
C.M.V. $3.00 M.B.
1976 LAVENDER EAU DE COLOGNE EUROPE
120 ml. size clear glass, black cap.
C.M.V. $5.00 M.B.

1976 GOLDEN NILE – EUROPE
COLOGNE MIST 85 g size C.M.V. $8.00
PERFUMED SOAPS 3 bars. C.M.V. $6.00

1978 ELEGANTE – MEXICO
In the Topaze containers used in U.S.
Left to right is cream sachet C.M.V. $4.00
Perfumed Skin Softener. C.M.V. $4.00
1972 CREAM LOTION
C.M.V. $8.00
1978 COLOGNE MIST
C.M.V. $8.00
All are yellow containers.

Left to Right - CREAM BODY LOTION EUROPE 120 m/l plastic bottle, white cap. Came in all fragrances. C.M.V. $3.00 M.B.
1972 - HAND LOTION - EUROPE
120 cc pink plastic bottle & cap.
C.M.V. $2.50 in box.
1973 - DEW KISS - EUROPE
45 cc clear glass bottle, pink neck tag & cap. C.M.V. $5.00 in box.

1972 RING FLING - EUROPE
Lipsticks & matching rings. Green, yellow, white, orange, pink, turquoise. C.M.V. set in box $4.00 ea. M.B.

1976 FOLIGERE – GERMANY
150 cc green plastic bottle. C.M.V. $4.00
1976 FOLIGERE SOAP – GERMANY
Green box holds green soap. C.M.V. $5.00 M.B.

1977 BABY BRUSH & COMB SET – CANADA
Blue box holds small white plastic comb & brush with Avon on both.
C.M.V. $5.00
1977 NON TEAR SHAMPOO – CANADA
8 oz. clear plastic bottle, white cap.
C.M.V. $2.00
1977 BABY POWDER – CANADA
5 oz. white metal can, blue cap.
C.M.V. $2.00.

1973 VITA MOIST HAND COSMETIC ENGLAND
100 cc white & green plastic bottle, gold cap with Avon on lid. C.M.V. $5.00.

1974 PETTI-PAT – GERMANY
Perfume Glace - C.M.V. $10.00 M.B.
Lipstick-C.M.V. $3.00 M.B. Both are gold and black with pink flowers.

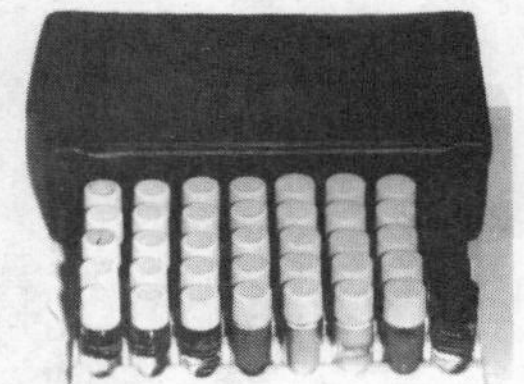

1976 CANADIAN SAMPLE CASE
Dark blue plastic case holds 40 sample bottles. C.M.V. $12.50.

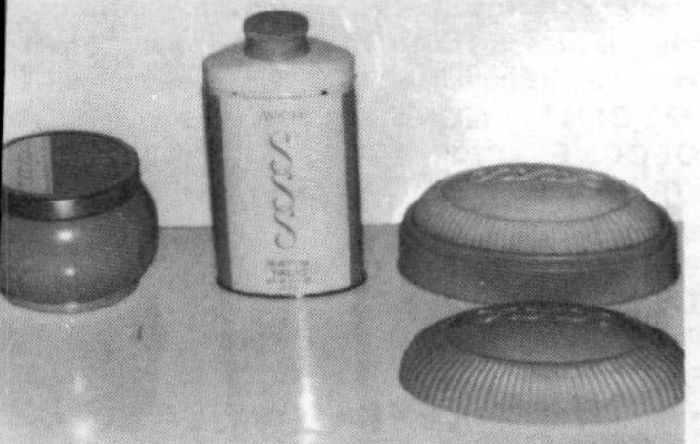

1978 SKIN SO SOFT – FOREIGN
SMOOTHING CREAM
C.M.V. $4.00.
SATIN TALC
2.75 oz. can. C.M.V. $3.00.
SOAP DISH & SOAP
Turquoise soap dish & bar of soap. C.M.V. $6.00 mint.

1973 SKIN SO SOFT BATH CAPSULES
GERMAN - Blue box holds glass jar of gold bath capsules blue neck tag on gold cord. C.M.V. $15.00 M.B.
1968 CREAM BODY LOTION – EUROPE
177 cc bottle with gold cap. Same as U.S. 1964 Skin So Soft. C.M.V. $12.00, $15.00 M.B.

1977 SKIN SO SOFT – EUROPE
120 cc plastic bottle, turquoise cap holds bath oil. C.M.V. $2.00. Turquoise & white metal can holds Satin Talc. C.M.V. $5.00 M.B.

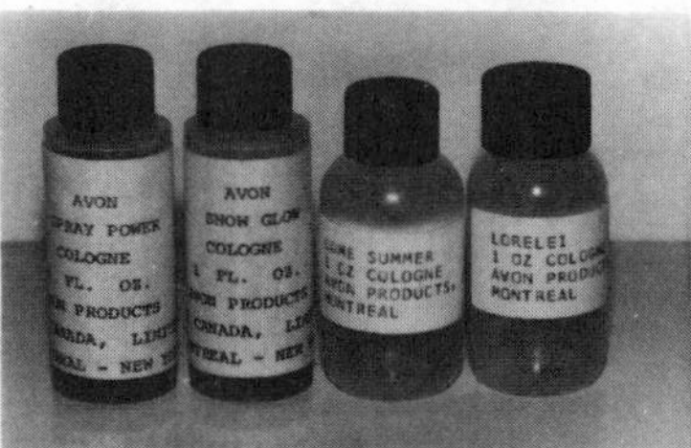

1972 COLOGNES SAMPLES – CANADA
1 oz plastic bottle of cologne test samples, black caps, paper labels. C.M.V. $4.00 each.

1975 BEAUTY DUST – CANADA
5 oz. white plastic, gold base band. C.M.V. $5.00.
CREAM SACHET
.66 oz. white glass bottom with white plastic top & gold band. C.M.V. $2.50.
COLOGNE MIST
3 oz. white plastic coated bottle, white plastic cap, gold band. C.M.V. $7.00.

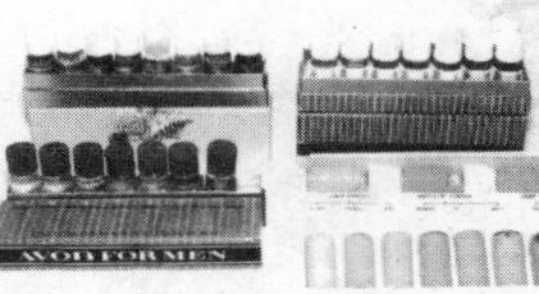

1970's AVON SAMPLES – EUROPE
T.L. AVON FRAGRANCES - SPAIN
Pink & gold box. 8 small bottles, white caps. C.M.V. $7.00.
T.R. AVON FRAGRANCE - GERMAN
Blue & gold box holds 14 small bottles, white caps. C.M.V. $7.00.
B.L. AVON FOR MEN - GERMAN
Red & black box holds 8 small bottles, red caps. C.M.V. $7.00.
B.R. MADE-UP DEMO - GERMAN
Pink box, clear plastic lid holds 11 white cap bottles. C.M.V. $7.00.

1978 EMPRESS DELUXE COMPACT – FOREIGN - White plastic flower design case. C.M.V. $6.00 M.B.
1977 PERFUME GLACE
White plastic flower designed case. C.M.V. $5.00 M.B.
1975 NOBLESSE COLOGNE
Box holds ½ oz. bottle same as U.S. 1966 ½ oz. cologne. Came in all fragrances. C.M.V. $5.00 M.B.
1975 CLEAN BOWLED SOAP ON A ROPE
AUSTRALIA - Red soap, white rope. C.M.V. $12.00 M.B.

LEFT TO RIGHT
1978 BABY SHAMPOO – AUSTRALIA
175 ml blue plastic, white cap. C.M.V. $2.00
1978 BABY OIL – AUSTRALIA
175 ml white plastic, blue cap. C.M.V. $2.00
1975 HARD WORK POWDERED HAND CLEANER – SPAIN
250 g blue and white plastic, C.M.V. $3.00
1974 BLUE LOTUS – BRAZIL
180 cm clear glass, lavender cap. C.M.V. $3.00
1970 WISHING TALC – BRAZIL
C.M.V. $5.00
1970 BALLAD TALC – BRAZIL
C.M.V. $6.00
1970 ROSA SILVESTRE TALC – BRAZIL
C.M.V. $5.00

LEFT TO RIGHT
1978 AGUA DE COLONIA – MEXICO
300 and 180 ml size plastic bottles, blue green caps. C.M.V. $5.00 big; $4.00 small.
1978 GLYCERINE HAND LOTION WITH SILICONE – AUSTRALIA
250 ml green plastic bottle, white cap. C.M.V: $4.00
1978 GLYCERINE HAND CREAM – AUSTRALIA
115 g green and white tube. C.M.V. $3.00
1978 SILICONE CREAM LOTION – MEXICO
120 g green plastic bottle, white cap. C.M.V. $3.00
1976 SONNET EMOLLIENT FRESHENER CANADA
6 oz. white plastic, gold cap. C.M.V. $3.00

LEFT 1978 DEMI STICKS – FOREIGN
Colored centers with white caps. Each different from U.S. issues. C.M.V. $2.50 each.
RIGHT 1977 PERFECT BEAUTY SAMPLES – EUROPE
Small beige color plastic bottle 2" high. Came in daytime moisturizer and cleansing lotion, skin freshener. Used as samples only for Avon Reps in Europe. C.M.V. $5.00 each.

1976 BUBBLE BATH – CANADA
8 oz. plastic, pink cap. C.M.V. $2.00
1976 PERFUMED BATH OILS – EUROPE, AUSTRALIA
All are plastic with different color caps. Some are 106 ml. and some 115 ml. size. Came in Violets - 115 ml, Lily of the Valley, 106 ml., Lilac 115 ml, Honey Suckle 106 and 115 ml. size. Carnation 115 ml. C.M.V. $3.00 each.
1976 CARNATION FOAMING BATH OIL – CANADA
8 oz. plastic, red letters and cap. C.M.V. $2.00
1974 ROSA GERANIO BATH FRESHENER – MEXICO
8 oz. clear glass bottle, pink cap. Also came in Madreselva with yellow cap. C.M.V. $4.00.

LEFT TO RIGHT
1978 BLUE BAY BUBBLE BATH – EUROPE
Blue plastic bottle, white caps in 200 ml and 480 ml size. C.M.V. $3.00 small. $4.00 large.
1978 SETTING LOTION – EUROPE
180 ml plastic bottles in Firm Hold, yellow bottle and Normal Hold, blue bottle. C.M.V. $3.00 each.
1977 INVIGORATE BATH GEL – AUSTRALIA
Came in 200 ml blue and white plastic bottle C.M.V. $3.00 and 100 g blue and white plastic tube. C.M.V. $2.00
1978 RICH MOISTURE HAND LOTION – EUROPE
120 ml blue green, white cap. C.M.V. $2.00

1972 SKIN SO SOFT BODY LOTION GERMANY
180 cc frosted glass bottle with pink cap. C.M.V. $5.00 M.B.
1972 SKIN SILK DAY CREAM
66 cc frosted glass jar with pink lid. C.M.V. $4.00 M.B.

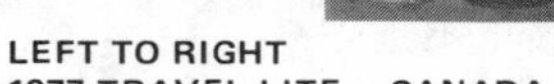

LEFT TO RIGHT
1977 TRAVEL LITE – CANADA
Beige plastic bottles, brown caps in deodorant, after shave, and shampoo shower soap. Labels French and English. C.M.V. $2.00
1972 GENTLEMEN'S SELECTION COLOGNE – CANADA
1.76 oz. black caps. Also came in after shave. C.M.V. $5.00
1977 SPECIAL PRESENTATION COLOGNE FOR MEN – MEXICO
48 ml. clear glass, silver cap. C.M.V. $4.50
1977 CREAM SACHET – MEXICO
Frosted glass base, gold edge cap with different color tops in Rosa Geranio, Jasmin, Hawaiian White Ginger. C.M.V. $4.00 ea.
1972 CHARISMA CREAM SACHET – EUROPE
Red paint over clear glass, red and gold cap. C.M.V. $4.50
1977 SONNET PERFUME ROLLETTE – MEXICO
White dull paint over clear glass, gold and white cap. C.M.V. $5.00

LEFT TO RIGHT
1976 THE CREAMERY – CANADA
6 oz. frosted glass, gold cap. label in French and English. C.M.V. $4.00
1978 FIJAPELO PARA NINOS (Hair Cream) – MEXICO
177 ml. white plastic, green cap. Deer on label. CMV $3.00
1978 SHAMPOO – MEXICO
177 ml white plastic, pink cap. Rabbit on front. C.M.V. $3.00
1978 BABY ACEITE – MEXICO
170 ml white plastic, blue cap. C.M.V. $3.00
1978 BABY TALCO – MEXICO
230 g white metal can, blue cap. C.M.V. $6.00
1978 BABY SHAMPOO – MEXICO
177 g white plastic, blue cap. C.M.V. $3.00
1978 BABY UNGUENTO – MEXICO
58 g white tube, blue cap. C.M.V. $2.00

1969 SKIN SO SOFT — FOREIGN
C.M.V. $7.00

1964 SKIN SO SOFT BATH CAPSULES - CANADA - Tall glass jar, green red & yellow capsules. C.M.V. $20.00 M.B.

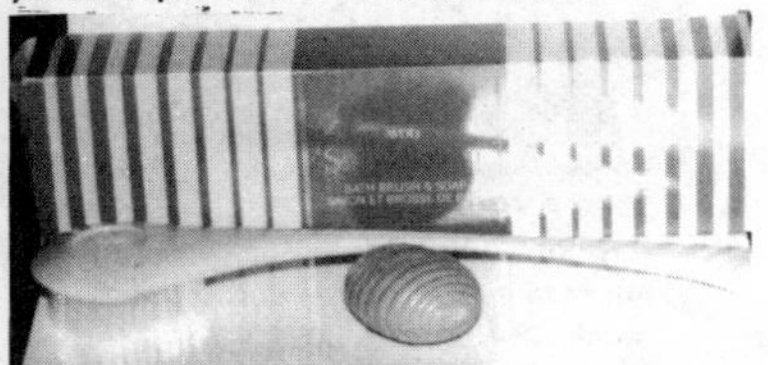

1974 SILK & HONEY BATH BRUSH & SOAP SET — CANADA
Box holds long brush, has Avon on handle. 1 bar of soap. C.M.V. $9.00

1974 SKIN SO SOFT — CANADA PERFUMED BATH OIL
2 oz. bottle, gold cap, bottom label only. C.M.V. $4.00.
BEAUTY DUST
5 oz. white plastic base with turquoise top. C.M.V. $7.00.
PERFUMED SOAP SET
Box holds 3 white bars. C.M.V. $5.00.

1975 NAIL POLISH & STAND — GERMANY, MEXICO
White plastic stand holds nail polish. Gold box issued in Australia in white, pink, or blue plastic base. CMV $5.00 each.
CREAM MASCARA - SPAIN
Pink box holds small pink tube & brush in white plastic case. C.M.V. $4.00 M.B.

CREAM LOTION - CANADA
5¼ oz. clear glass bottle with gold cap. C.M.V. $10.00
SKIN SO SOFT BATH CAPSULES CANADA - Blue glass jar & lid. Made in Belgium in bottom of jar. Blue & silver neck label. C.M.V. $12.00
SKIN SO SOFT DECANTER - CANADA
6 oz. clear glass bottle holds bath oil. Silver top fits over white cap. C.M.V. $10.00

LEFT 1977 BUBBLE BATH SAMPLE CANADA
40 ml. pink plastic bottle, white cap. C.M.V. $1.00
CENTER 1977 SKIN-SO-SOFT BATH OIL SAMPLE — CANADA
40 ml. clear plastic bottle. Turquoise cap. C.M.V. $1.00
RIGHT 1973 HAPPY JUNGLE TALC CANADA
2.75 oz. metal can green and orange, orange cap. C.M.V. $2.00

1975 EMERALD ELEGANCE CANADA
Box holds 6 oz. green glass jar and lid with Mineral Springs bath crystals. C.M.V. $5.00 M.B.

LEFT TO RIGHT
1977 MIRROR MIRROR — AUSTRALIA
Bright plastic double mirror and base came in orange, red, blue or lime green plastic. C.M.V. $5.00 each M.B.
1977 MINI BRUSH
To match each mirror. C.M.V. $2.00 each. M.B.
1977 PURSE POMANDER — EUROPE
Blue plastic in blue box. Came with white string. C.M.V. $4.00 M.B.
1975 OWL POMANDER — EUROPE
Blue plastic, white string. C.M.V. $5.00

LEFT TO RIGHT
1976 HIGHWAY BRUSH & COMB — AUSTRALIA
Brown plastic, C.M.V. $5.00 M.B.
1976 AUSSIE BEAR — AUSTRALIA
Red, white and blue brush and white comb. C.M.V. $5.00 M.B.
1976 VALET BRUSH & COMB — CANADA
Brown plastic, gold leaf on top. C.M.V. $3.50 M.B.
1977 FOREST LORD BRUSH & COMB — AUSTRALIA
Brown and gold plastic. C.M.V. $3.50 M.B.

LEFT TO RIGHT ALL FROM JAPAN
1978 DEEP CLEAN
177 ml plastic bottle in cleansing lotion in pink, wash off cleanser for oily skin, beige for normal skin blue and white. C.M.V. $5.00
1978 HAIR TONIC FOR WOMEN
180 ml green plastic bottle. C.M.V. $5.00
1978 RINSE 300 ml pink plastic for dry hair and green for normal hair. C.M.V. $5.00 each.
1978 SKIN FRESHENER
118 ml clear glass, blue cap on for normal skin and pink cap on for dry skin. C.M.V. $5.00 each.
1978 ASTRINGENT FRESHENER FOR OILY SKIN
118 ml clear glass, peach cap. C.M.V. $5.00

1978 SKIN SILK DAY CREAM – AUSTRALIA
175 g pink plastic jars and lid. C.M.V. $3.00
In 2¼ oz. frosted glass jar, pink lid. C.M.V. $4.00

1978 SKIN SILK MILD SKIN FRESHENER – AUSTRALIA
175 ml pink frosted plastic bottle and cap. C.M.V. $4.50

1978 SKIN CARE PRODUCTS – JAPAN
3 different products in 120 ml. 2 are clear glass and 1 frosted. Pink caps. C.M.V. $8.00 each.

1978 SKIN SILK DAY CREAM – JAPAN
64 g frosted glass jar, pink cap. C.M.V. $8.00

1977 SKIN BEAUTY DAY CREAM – CANADA
60 ml pink plastic jar and lid. C.M.V. $2.00
Also in 2.25 oz. frosted glass jar, pink lid with label on lid. C.M.V. $3.00

1977 HORMONE CREAM – CANADA
60 ml white plastic jar and lid. Label on lid. C.M.V. $2.00

1976 STRAWBERRY COOLER – SPAIN

1972 SKIN BEAUTY DAY CREAM – EUROPE
Frosted glass jar, pink cap with no writing on lid. C.M.V. $4.00

1972 PERFUMED PAIR - EUROPE
Matching Talc & Soap, all fragrances. C.M.V. $10.00 M.B.

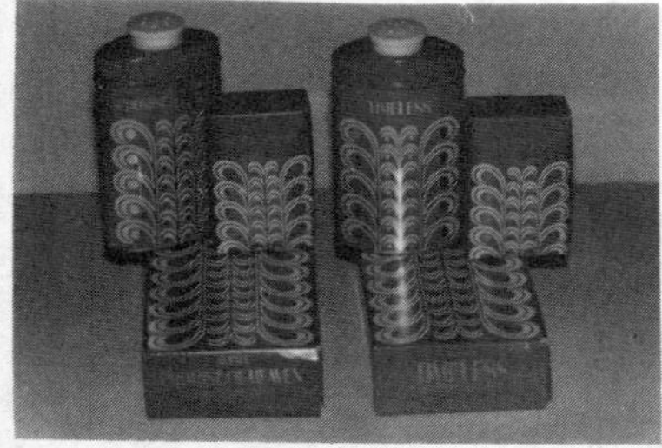

1976 PERFUMED PAIR SET – EUROPE
Different color boxes hold matching perfumed talc can and soap. C.M.V. $10.00 ea. set.

LEFT TO RIGHT

1974 PERFUMED PAIR – EUROPE
Came in 4 fragrances with different color on each one. Box holds bar of soap and perfumed talc in metal can. C.M.V. $11.00 each, M.B.

1975 PERFUMED PAIR – EUROPE
4 different fragrances in different colors with matching talc and bar of soap. C.M.V. $10.00 each, M.B.

1977 PERFUMED PAIR – EUROPE
4 different fragrances in different colors with matching metal talc and bar of soap. C.M.V. $9.00 each, M.B.

1975 PERFUMED PAIR – CANADA
Box holds can of perfumed talc and bar of matching soap. Came in all fragrances. C.M.V. $6.00 M.B.

1977 STATIONARY PERFUMED – AUSTRALIA
Folders on boxes came with sachet, envelopes and writing paper. Choice of Unspoken (C.M.V. $6.00 M.B.), Petal of Roses, Petal of Violets and Whispers of Lavender. C.M.V. $5.00 each.

1976 COLOR BOOKS – CANADA
Issued in 4th quarter 1976 in Canada. 1 printed in English and one in French. Given free to customers. C.M.V. $2.50 ea.

1974 AVON CARD GAME – EUROPE
Envelope holds 2 fold our sheets. Punch out card games. Given at Christmas wit purchase. C.M.V. $5.00

1970 AVON DICE GAME – EUROPE
2 page paper game given at Christmas, 1970 with purchase. C.M.V. $5.00

1971 COLOR BOOK - AVON – EUROP
Red cover. Given with purchase at Christmas, 1971. C.M.V. $5.00

CENTER 1977 SAVONS PERFUMED SOAPS – CANADA
Matching boxes came with 3 bars of Lavender, Lily of The Valley, green, Honeysuckle, yellow, and Apple Blossom in pink. C.M.V. $4.00 each set.
LEFT 1975 BUTTERFLY SOAP SET – SPAIN
Box holds 4 bars in yellow, orange, turquoise, and Lavender butterflys. C.M.V. $12.00 M.B.
RIGHT 1976 BUTTERFLY SOAPS – CANADA
Box holds 3 yellow bars. CMV $6.50 MB M.B.

LEFT TO RIGHT
1977 SKIN SO SOFT SOAPS – CANADA
Gray box holds 3 SSS white bars. C.M.V. $3.00 M.B.
1976 SKIN SO SOFT SOAPS – CANADA
Winter scent box holds 3 white bars of SSS soap. C.M.V. $4.00 M.B.
1976 PINE TREE GIFT SOAPS – CANADA
Green box holds 3 green tree soaps. C.M.V. $5.00 M.B.

1973 BOUTIQUE SOAP SET - EUROPE - Box holds 2 green bars & 2 lavender bars. C.M.V. $7.00 M.B.
1973 ROSE BLOSSOMS SOAP EUROPE, SPAIN - Box, pink, holds 4 flower embossed bars. C.M.V. $7.00 M.B.

1974 LOVE SOAPS – MEXICO
Love box holds 4 yellow bars. C.M.V. $20.00 M.B.

1975 GIFT OF THE SEA CANADA
Peralessen soap dish and 4 pink sea shell soaps. C.M.V. $7.00 M.B.

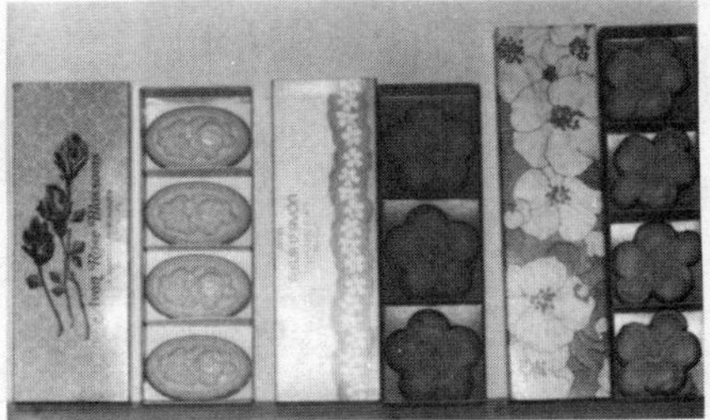

1975 ROSE BLOSSOMS SOAPS – MEXICO
Pink box holds 4 white bars C.M.V. $10.00 M.B.
1975 FLEUR D'AVON – SPAIN
Pink, white and green box holds 3 flower soaps. C.M.V. $12.00 M.B.
1976 PERFUMED FLOWER SOAPS – MEXICO
Green box holds 4 grey flower soaps. C.M.V. $12.50 M.B.

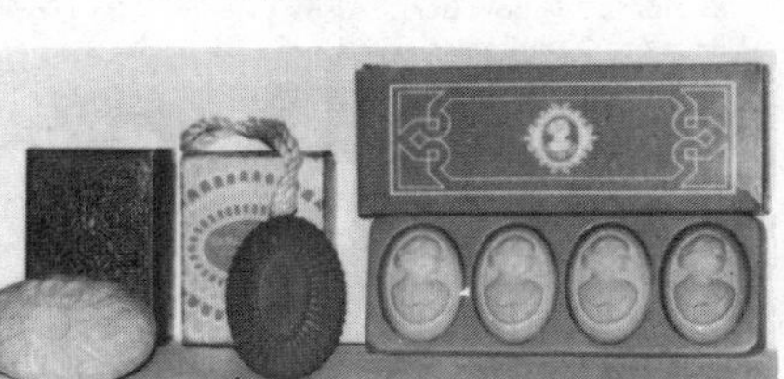

LEFT 1972 DECORATOR SOAP
Gold box holds 5 oz. white bar. C.M.V. $4.00 M.B.
CENTER 1976 SKIN SO SOFT SOAP ON A ROPE – CANADA
Turquoise soap with white rope C.M.V. $5.00 M.B.
RIGHT 1975 CAMEO SOAP SET
Blue box holds 4 white cameo soaps. CMV $4.50 MB. Also came in white box with blue trim. CMV $10.00

1978 COUNTRY PEACH SOAPS – EUROPE
Box holds 3 long bars. Also came in strawberry. C.M.V. $6.00 each, M.B.
1977 COUNTRY CUPBOARD SOAPS – AUSTRALIA
Box holds 3 square bars in peach - pink, or strawberry in red, soaps. C.M.V. $7.00 each, M.B.
1976 COUNTRY CUPBOARD SOAPS – CANADA
Box holds 3 long bars. Came in strawberry and peach. C.M.V. $7.00 M.B.

1978 PERFUMED SOAPS – JAPAN
3 different colored bars in own box in Bird of Paradise, Charisma and Unforgettable. C.M.V. $6.00 each.

1975 APPLE BLOSSOMS SOAP SET – CANADA
Green and white box holds 4 flower shaped soaps. C.M.V. $5.00 M.B.
1975 HOSTESS SOAP SET – CANADA
Green and pink box holds 2 pink bars, and 2 green bars. C.M.V. $4.00 M.B.

1978 SONNET SOAP – JAPAN
White box holds 6 pink soaps. C.M.V. $14.00 M.B. Also came in Moonwind, 6 to a box. C.M.V. $14.00 M.B.

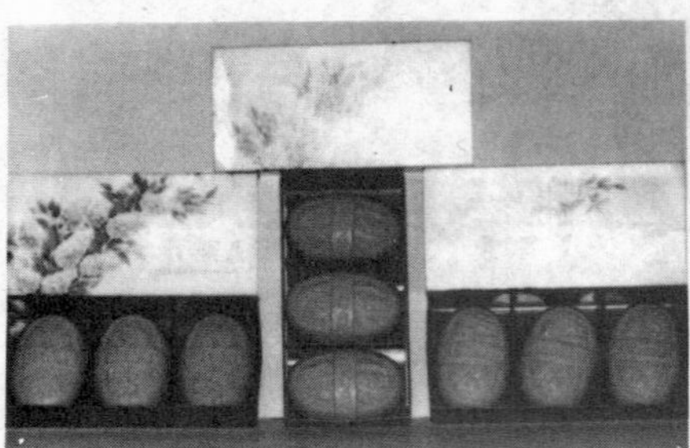

1975 PERFUMED SOAPS – SPAIN
Flowered boxes came with 3 bars in Lilac, Hyacinth, Magnolia. C.M.V. $10.00 each, M.B.

1974 TOUCH OF BEAUTY SOAPS – SPAIN
Gold and pink box holds 2 white bars. C.M.V. $10.00 M.B.
1974 FOUR SEASONS SOAP SET – EUROPE
Box holds 4 bars of orange, blue, yellow, and green soap. C.M.V. $10.00 M.B.
1974 ELEGANTE PERFUMED SOAPS – EUROPE
Green box holds 3 embossed aqua bars. C.M.V. $12.00 M.B.

1976 LAVENDER SOAPS – EUROPE
Red Christmas box holds 3 lavender soaps. C.M.V. $10.00 M.B.
1975 OCCUR! SOAPS – SPAIN
Black box holds 3 yucky colored bars. C.M.V. $10.00 M.B.
1975 AVONSHIRE BLUE SOAPS – AUSTRALIA
Blue box holds 3 bars , blue, in angel shape. C.M.V. $10.00 M.B.

LEFT TO RIGHT
1976 HONEYSUCKLE PERFUMED SOAPS – AUSTRALIA
Box holds 3 yellow bars. Also came in Lilac with 3 pink bars. C.M.V. $7.00 each M.B.
1978 TOPAZE SOAP – AUSTRALIA
Yellow box holds 3 topaze yellow bars. C.M.V. $7.00 M.B.
1975 TOPAZE SOAP COLUMN – SPAIN
Yellow box holds 3 yellow column bars in plastic holder. C.M.V. $12.00 M.B.

SOAPS SINGLE BARS
FROM EUROPE – Aqua soap, Elegance, Nearness and Dr. Zabriskies soap. C.M.V. $2.50 each bar.
FROM CANADA – Clear Skin, Regence, Moonwind, Scent of Roses, Hawaiian White Ginger, Charisma, Rich Moisture Soap and Blue Lotus. C.M.V. $2.00 each bar.
FROM SPAIN – Perfumed Deodorant Soap, Deluxe Toilette Soap, Charisma, Topaze, Regence in Brocade package. C.M.V. $3.00 each bar.
FROM AUSTRALIA – Occur!. C.M.V. $3.00

1975 UNFORGETTABLE SOAPS – SPAIN
Orange box holds 3 orange bars. 4A design embossed in center of soaps. C.M.V. $10.00 M.B.
1977 CHRISTMAS ORNAMENT – MEXICO
Pink and green hang-up card holds eye shadow wand. C.M.V. $10.00 mint.
1974 CHRISTMAS ORNAMENT – EUROPE

Small diamond shaped bottle, gold cap. Came in green and gold hang-on holder. C.M.V. $10.00 M.B.

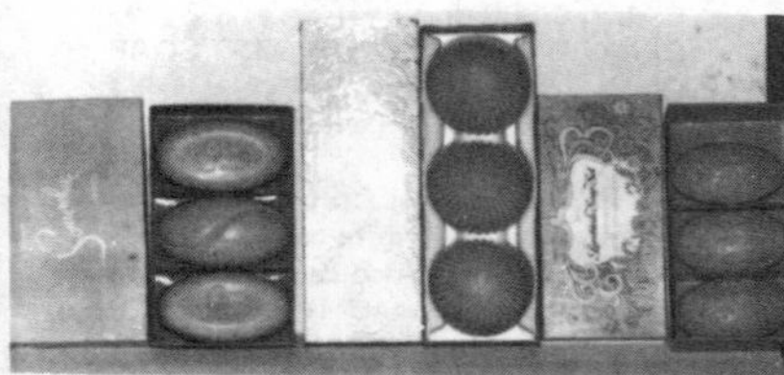

1975 SOMEWHERE SOAP – SPAIN
Box holds 3 pink S soaps. C.M.V. $10.00 M.B.
1975 NEARNESS PERFUMED SOAPS – SPAIN
White and gold box holds 3 pink ribbed soaps. C.M.V. $10.00 M.B.
1977 LOVEBIRDS SOAP SET – AUSTRALIA
Box holds 3 pink bird embossed soaps. C.M.V. $8.00 M.B.

LEFT TO RIGHT
1975 PERFUMED PAIR – CANADA
Box holds perfumed soap and metal talc in choice of fragrances. C.M.V. $6.00 M.B.
1977 BOUQUET OF PANSIES SOAP – AUSTRALIA
Blue box holds white bar with flowered decal. C.M.V: $4.50 M.B.
1978 PERFUMED SOAP BARS – EUROPE
Large bars in Lavender, Lilac and Lily of The Valley. C.M.V. $4.00 each, mint.

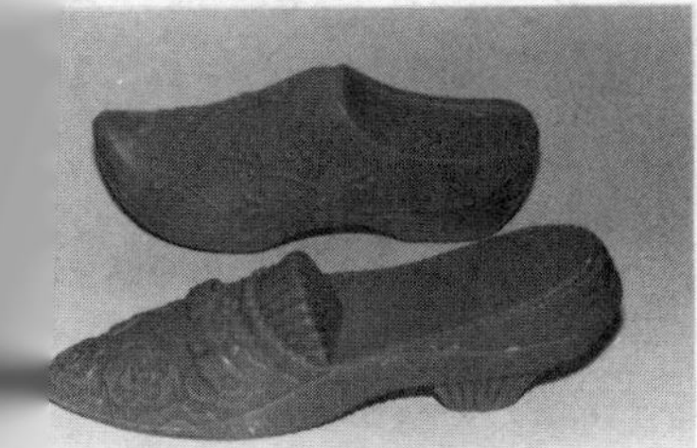

1974 DUTCH SHOE SOAP — SPAIN
Blue soap & box. C.M.V. $10.00 M.B. $8.00 soap only. Also sold Canada.

1974 LADY SLIPPER SOAP — SPAIN ENGLAND - Lavender soap & box. C.M.V. $10.00 M.B. $8.00 soap only.

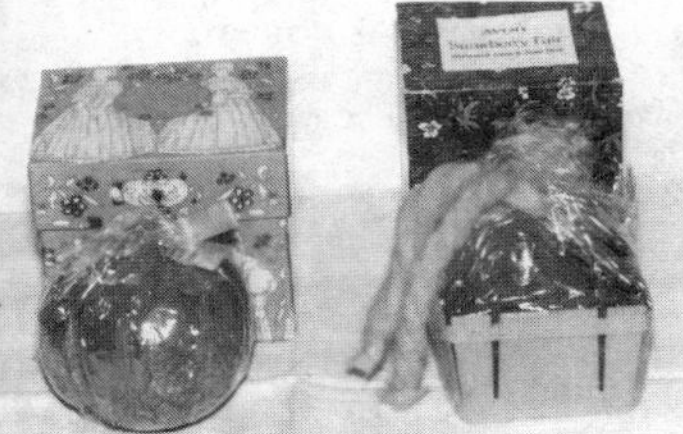

1972 LILAC SOAP - EUROPE
Blue box holds lilac soap with blue ribbon. C.M.V. $9.00 M.B.

1972 STRAWBERRY FAIR SOAP - EUROPE - Strawberry soap in yellow basket & ribbon. C.M.V. $8.00 M.B.

1974 AVON SOAP GEMS — FOREIGN
Orange, yellow & green soaps. C.M.V. $10.00 M.B.

1973 MINERAL ISLES SOAP ON A ROPE - ENGLAND
C.M.V. $5.00. M.B.

1973 MINERAL ISLES SAMPLES - ENGLAND - Box holds 5 sample packets of bath crystals. C.M.V. $1.00 per packet.

1973 FASHION BOOT HOSTESS SOAP ENGLAND
Soap is blue with lavender bow. C.M.V. $8.00 M.B.
CANADA soap is same only no bow. Boxes are different labels. C.M.V. $6.00 M.B.

1972 DECORATOR SOAP EGGS — CANADA - 6 eggs shaped soaps, 2 blue, 2 yellow, 2 pink. C.M.V. $5.00 M.B.

1973 HAWAIIAN WHITE GINGER SOAP CANADA - 3 white soaps. C.M.V. $4.00 M.B.

1972 SOAPS - EUROPE
Came in all fragrances. C.M.V. $5.00 ea. M.B.

1972-73 CAMEO SOAP ON A ROPE CANADA
Pink soap, white rope. C.M.V. $4.00 M.B.

1973 MINERAL SPRINGS SOAP ON A ROPE - CANADA
Beige soap, white rope. C.M.V. $4.00 M.B.

1972 JUMBO SOAP SET - EUROPE
Blue, tan & pink elephant soap. C.M.V. $10.00 M.B.

1972 TOP DOG SOAP - EUROPE
Tan colored soap on white rope. C.M.V. $10.00 M.B.

1975 CAMEO SOAP SET - CANADA
Brown box, 3 bars. C.M.V. $5.00 M.B.

1975 TOUCH OF ROSES SOAP ON A ROPE - Pink rose soap, white rope. C.M.V. $5.00 M.B.

1969 WHITE GINGER SOAP FOREIGN
Beige soap came in fancy box. C.M.V. $10.00 M.B.

1974 CHEEKY CHAPPIE SOAP - ON A ROPE - EUROPE
Light green soap on white rope. CMV $10.00 MB. Reissued 1979 - Australia - under name of Cheeky Charlie. CMV $6.00 MB.

AVON

1972 MOLLY MOUSE SOAP - EUROPE - Blue mouse soap on white rope. C.M.V. $10.00 M.B.
1972 MR. FROG SOAP - EUROPE
Green soap on pink or white rope. C.M.V.$10.00 M.B.

1975 ST. BERNARD SOAP – EUROPE
White soap. Blue & green box. C.M.V. $10.00 M.B. $8.00 soap only.
1975 BO BO SOAP – EUROPE
Yellow elephant soap. Blue & yellow soap. C.M.V. $10.00 M.B. $8.00 soap only.
1975 HIGH FLYER SOAP ON A ROPE - EUROPE - Yellow soap. White rope. Yellow soap & box. C.M.V. $10.00 M.B. $8.00 soap only.
1975 PERSIAN KITTEN SOAP – EUROPE; CANADA
White cat soap, blue box. C.M.V. $10.00 M.B. $8.00 soap only, Europe, Canada - C.M.V. $4.00 M.B.

1969-70 SOAPS ON A ROPE - FOREIGN
Each yellow soap, left to right.
HARRY THE HOUND
HAPPY COW
RUFUS THE SQUIRREL
CMV $15.00 each MB.

1977 PERSIAN KITTEN SOAP – CANADA
White soap in purple box. O.S.P. $4.00 C.M.V. $3.00

1975 FRAGRANCE BELL SOAP – EUROPE
Dark pink soap and box. C.M.V. $10.00 M.B.
1975 LITTLE GIRL BLUE SOAP – EUROPE
Blue soap, white and blue box. C.M.V. $10.00 M.B.
1975 KNIGHT IN ARMOR – EUROPE
White soap, black and yellow box. C.M.V. $17.00 M.B.

LEFT TO RIGHT
1976 SOCCER FOOTBALL SOAP ON A ROPE – EUROPE
White soap and rope. C.M.V. $6.00 M.B.
1977 HARVEY THE RABBIT SOAP ON A ROPE – EUROPE
Yellow rabbit soap, white rope. CIM.V. $6.00 M.B.
1978 BIG SHOT SOAP ON A ROPE – EUROPE, AUSTRALIA
Brownish gray soap on white rope. C.M.V. $6.00 M.B.
1978 HAPPY HIPPO SOAP ON A ROPE – CANADA
Hippo on white rope. C.M.V. $.4.00 M.B.
1978 LORD LEO SOAP ON A ROPE – EUROPE, AUSTRALIA
Tanish grey lion soap on white rope. C.M.V. $6.00 M.B.

LEFT TO RIGHT
1976 ERIC THE BRAVE SOAP EUROPE
Blue soap C.M.V. $8.00
1976 HUGGY BEAR SOAP – EUROPE
Tan color soap. C.M.V. $8.00 M.B.
1976 WINTER RIDE SOAP – EUROPE
Pink soap. C.M.V. $8.00 M.B.
RIGHT 1976 PIG IN A BONNET SOAP EUROPE
4.9 oz. pink pig soap. C.M.V. $8.00 M.B.

LEFT TO RIGHT
1977 PEEK A BOO SOAP – EUROPE
Yellow chick soap. C.M.V. $6.00 M.B.
1978 FRAGRANCE BELL SOAP – FOREI(
Pink bell soap from Canada - C.M.V. $4.00 M
Red bell soap from Europe - C.M.V. $6.00 M
1977 CHILDREN'S NOVELTY WALRUS SOAP – EUROPE
Green walrus soap. C.M.V. $6.00 M.B.
1977 CHEERFULL CHIMPY SOAP – EUROPE
Orange monkey soap. C.M.V. $6.00 M.B.
1977 GOLDEN CARRIAGE SOAP – EUROPE
Yellow carriage soap. C.M.V. $6.00 M.B.

LEFT TO RIGHT
1976 OLAND SOAP ON A ROPE – AUSTRALIA
Tan soap on white rope. C.M.V. $6.00 M.B.
1974 IMPERIAL GARDENS SOAP ON A ROPE – CANADA
White soap on orange rope. C.M.V. $5.00 M.B.
1976 SURE WINNER SKI BOOT SOAP ON A ROPE – CANADA
Blue soap, white rope. C.M.V. $6.00 M.B.
1977 PARISIENNE BELL SOAP – SPAIN
Pink lady bust soap. C.M.V. $8.00 M.B.

1976 WYNKEN, BLYNKEN, & NOD SOAP – CANADA
Box holds pink, yellow and blue soaps. C.M.V. $3.50 M.B.

1979-80 WINTER SONG SOAPS - EUROPE & CANADA
Cardinal box holds 2 white bird decal bars. CMV $6.00 MB Europe, CMV $4.00 MB Canada.
1979-80 LADY SLIPPER SOAPS - EUROPE
Box holds 2 white, 2 pink slipper bars. CMV $8.00 MB.

1979 A TOKEN OF LOVE SOAP - AUSTRALIA
White bar with pink center. CMV $6.50 MB
1979 ORCHARD FLOWERS SOAPS - EUROPE
Grey box holds 3 yellow flower embossed soaps. CMV $7.00 MB
1979 PIRATE PETE SOAP ON A ROPE - EUROPE
Yellow soap with orange rope. CMV $5.00 MB

1979 SOUTH SEAS SOAPS - EUROPE
Box holds 3 green fish shaped soaps. CMV $6.00 MB
1979 LEMON SOAP TRIO - EUROPE
Holds 3 yellow lemon shaped soaps. CMV $5.00 MB.

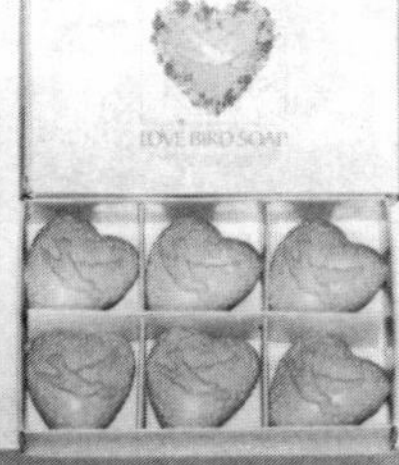

1979 PANSY SOAP SET - JAPAN
Blue box holds 3 decaled bars. CMV $18.00 MB
1979 LOVE BIRD SOAPS - JAPAN
Pink & white box holds 6 pink heart shaped bars. CMV $18.00 MB.

1979 FIELD FLOWERS SOAPS - JAPAN
Green box holds 2 pink, 2 green, & 2 yellow soaps. CMV $18.00 MB.
1979-80 TOUCH OF ROSES SOAPS - JAPAN
Red box holds 6 pink rose shaped bars. CMV $18.00 MB

1977 GARDEN GIRL SOAP CANADA
4 oz. bar. Garden Girl - 1 was light yellow in Field Flowers and one was Lilac and lavendar in color. C.M.V. $4.00 ea, M.B.

1975 TUBBY TIGERS SOAP SET CANADA
2 small orange tiger soaps. C.M.V. $5.00 M.B.

1976 OSIDOS BEAR SOAPS - MEXICO
Box holds 3 yellow bears. CMV $12.50 MB
1978 TEDDY BEAR COLOGNE - BRAZIL
20 cm dark amber glass, gold ring around neck. CMV $20.00 MB.

1972-73 LITTLE PRO SOAP & SPONGE CANADA
Left hand sponge light orange & white ball soap. Green box from Canada. OSP $4.00 CMV $9.00 MB.

1979 NATURE BEAUTIFUL SOAPS - CANADA
Box holds 2 bars with fruit decals only. CMV $5.00 MB
1979 NATURE BOUNTIFUL SOAP - CANADA
Holds 1 decal soap. CMV $3.00 MB
1979 WINTER SCAPE SOAP - CANADA
Holds 1 Currier & Ives decal soap. CMV $3.00 MB.

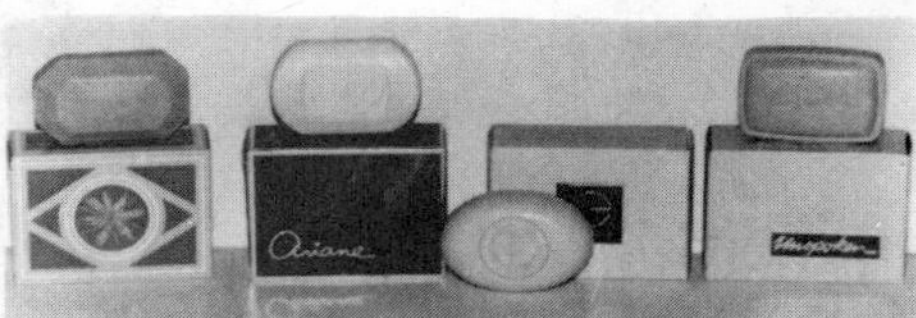

1980 PERFUMED SOAPS - EUROPE
Single bars, boxed. Came in Timeless, Ariane, Emprise, and Unspoken. CMV $3.00 each MB.

1979 SUMMER BUTTERFLIES SOAPS - JAPAN
Holds 3 butterfly bars. CMV $18.00 MB
1979 TOUCH OF BEAUTY SOAPS - JAPAN
Holds 2 pink flower embossed bars. CMV $10.00 MB

1975 GRAND TOURER SOAPS - EUROPE
Silver & black box in 2 different sizes holds 2 car embossed bars of the same size. CMV $12.00 MB each set.

1978 ORCHARD FLOWERS SOAPS – EUROPE
Yellow and gray box holds 3 yellow soaps. C.M.V. $7.00 M.B.
1973 JUMBO SOAP TRIO – CANADA
3 blue elephant soaps. C.M.V. $8.00 M.B.

1976 HIGH BUTTON SHOE SOAP ENGLAND & EUROPE
Pink boot soap. C.M.V. $10.00 M.B.

1974 PHINIAS T. FROG SOAP & SPONGE – CANADA
Green frog sponge and yellow-green an orange wrapped soap. C.M.V. $6.00 M.

1973 SNOWBIRDS SOAPS – CANADA
3 blue soaps. C.M.V. $6.00 M.B.

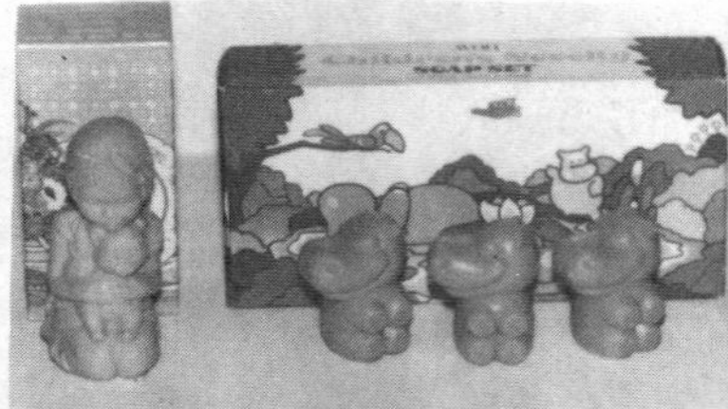

LEFT 1975 RECOLLECTIONS SOAP EUROPE
Yellow girl soap in green box. C.M.V. $5.00 M.B.
RIGHT 1976 CHILDRENS NOVELTY SOAP SET – EUROPE
Box holds 3 small hippo soaps in green, pink, and orange. C.M.V. $5.00 M.B.

1969 BATH FLOWER SOAP & SPONGE ENGLAND - Box holds bar of soap & flowered sponge. C.M.V. $20.00 M.B.

1973 TIMOTHY TIGER – GERMANY
Yellow plastic soap dish. CMV $12.00 MB

1974 STERLING SIX SOAP – MEXICO
Box holds 2 yellow car embossed bars. CMV $14.00 MB

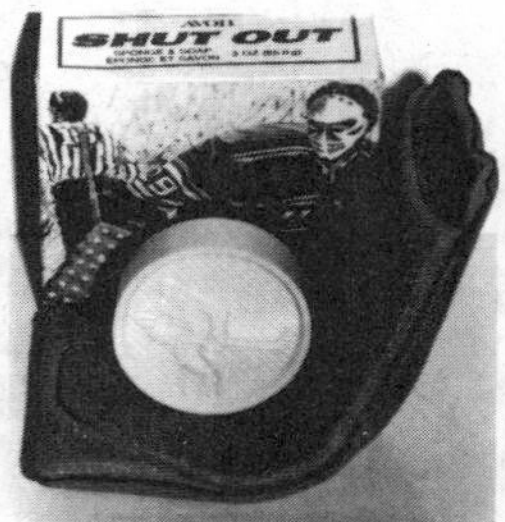

1975 SHUT OUT SOAP & SPONGE CANADA - Box holds orange Avon spon & white hockey puck soap. CMV $6.50

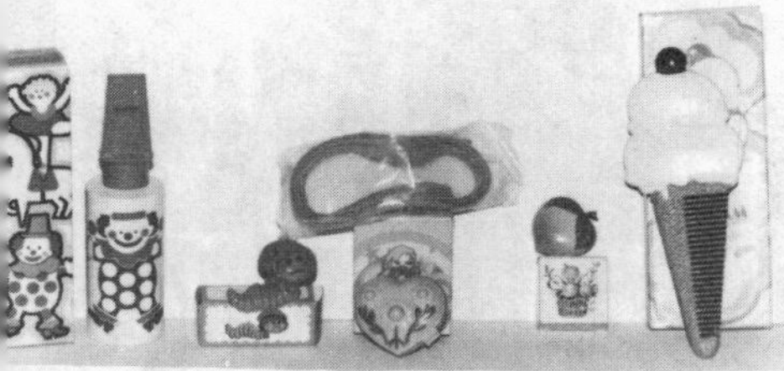

1979-80 SHAMPOO FOR CHILDREN - MEXICO
90 ml white, orange, and red plastic with orange whistle top. CMV $5.00 MB
1979-80 MADAME GUS PERFUME GLACE - MEXICO
.7 g green & purple plastic pin & perfume glace. CMV $4.50 MB.
1979-80 LOVE LOCKETT - MEXICO
Green, yellow & pink plastic. Solid perfume container. Comes with pink necklace. CMV $5.00 MB
1979-80 PRETTY PEACH SOLID PERFUME - MEXICO
.7 g peach & green colored plastic solid perfume container. CMV $5.00 MB
1979-80 ICE CREAM COMB FOR CHILDREN - MEXICO
Tan plastic with vanilla colored ice cream & red cherry. CMV $4.00 MB.

1970 ANDY CAPP - ENGLAND
Black & white plastic with green hat. Holds body powder. CMV $125.00 BO mint, $175.00 MB.

LEFT TO RIGHT
1975 MR. BUNNY – EUROPE
90 ml white plastic, blue hat. C.M.V. $5.00. It has an orange and green carrot.
1976 MR. BUNNY – SPAIN
90 cc size, all white plastic, blue hat. C.M.V. $6.00
1977 PINK ELEPHANT – EUROPE
150 ml pink plastic, dark pink cap. C.M.V. $5.00
1976 ELFY THE ELEPHANT – MEXICO
150 g pink plastic and cap. C.M.V. $6.00

1976 PACKY THE ELEPHANT – MEXICO
90 ml yellow plastic white cap. C.M.V. $5.00
1975 PIGS – EUROPE
150 ml pink plastic bottle and cap. C.M.V. $6.00
1978 LEO THE LION – MEXICO
290 ml yellow plastic, pink hat. C.M.V. $5.50.

LEFT 1976 RABBIT – MEXICO
68 g size. White plastic green hat, lotion. C.M.V. $4.00 M.B.
RIGHT 1976 PERFUMED TALC MEXICO
Tin can, gold and white C.M.V. $4.00.

1975 QUACK A. DOODLE – CANADA
Bar of soap with white and orange rubber duck. C.M.V. $5.00 M.B.

1976 WORLD BANK – EUROPE
300 ml size blue plastic globe with stick-on colored countries. It is larger than the U.S. issue on right. C.M.V. $8.00 M.B.

1972 THE RACER SPORTS TALC EUROPE
Orange plastic bottle, white cap. C.M.V. $7.00 M.B.

1973 CANADA - LITTLE PIGGY NON TEAR SHAMPOO - 150 cc pink plastic. C.M.V. $4.00
1973 CANADA - MAZE GAME - AMAZING CLOWN - 6 oz. green plastic, pink lid. Clown on face. C.M.V. $4.00

LEFT 1973 WILD COUNTRY AFTER SHAVE – BRAZIL
105 cm. Red plastic, green cap. C.M.V. $10.00
CENTER 1976 ELEPHANT IN A TUB
Box holds pink elephant soap and blue plastic tub brush. C.M.V. $5.00 M.B.
RIGHT 1974 FOOTBALL BOOT BRAZIL
85 cm. Black and white plastic boot after shave. C.M.V. $10.00

1977 CHESHIRE CAT SOAP AND SPONGE – AUSTRALIA
Cat soap and sponge in pink and white. C.M.V. $6.00 M.B.

1974 TUB TALK – AUSTRALIA
Yellow box holds red plastic telephone with light blue base and cap. Holds shampoo for children. CMV $7.00 MB. Reissued 1979 in yellow bottle with blue cap & handle. CMV $6.00 MB.

1979 RING RING PHONE - MEXICO
Same as Tub Talk only in blue plastic with yellow cap, & holder. CMV $5.00 MB.

1977 RULER COMB - EUROPE
Yellow plastic comb in metrics. CMV $3.50 MB.

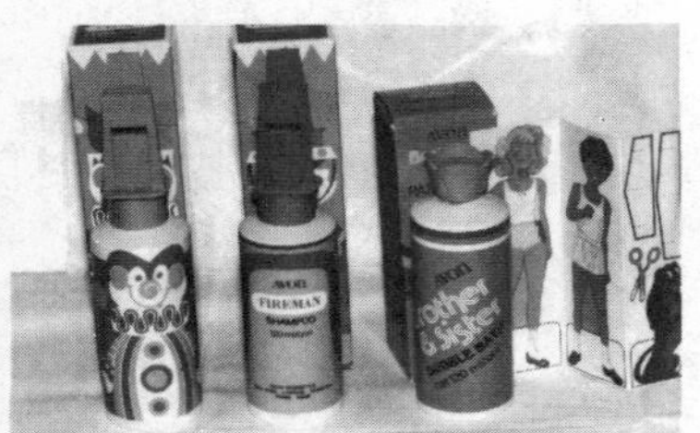

1972 CLOWN BUBBLE BATH - EUROPE
120 m/l plastic bottles, pink whistle cap. C.M.V. $6.00 M.B.

1972 FIREMAN SHAMPOO - EUROPE
120 m/l plastic bottles, orange whistle cap. C.M.V. $6.00 M.B.

1972 BROTHER & SISTER BUBBLE BATH - EUROPE - 120 m/l plastic bottle with blue flower cap & came with paper doll cut-outs & color booklet. C.M.V. $6.00 M.B.

1978 TALCS FROM MEXICO
All metal cans in Timeless, childrens talc, with white or blue top, Moonwind, Charisma, and Sweet Honesty on top row.
Bottom row left to right – 1974 Regence and Charisma in bright colored cans. C.M.V. $6.00 each. 1978 issue in Jasmin, Raining Violets, Blue Lotus, Bird of Paradise, Dia Fresco, and Nearness. C.M.V. $4.00 each on all 1978 talcs.

1976 MEXICO TALCS
All metal cans, plastic tops. Talco Desodorante, Bravo Talco, Desodorante Para, Caballeros. To a Wild Rose Talco Perfumado, Rapture Talco Perfumado, Occur Talco Perfumado. C.M.V. $4.00 ea.

CANADA - PERFUMED TALC
In Brocade, Elusive, Charisma, Somewhere. C.M.V. ea, $2.00
PERFUMED SOAPS - In Brocade, Elusive, Charisma, Somewhere. C.M.V. ea. $2.00

1976 CANADA - PERFUMED TALC
2.75 oz. each in Honeysuckle, Cotillion, Rapture, To A Wild Rose, Wishing. C.MV. $2.00
1976 PERFUMED SOAP - Single wrapped bars in To A Wild Rose, Topaze, Here's My Heart. Also came in other fragrances. C.M.V. $2.00

1976 CANADA – ANTISEPTIC POWDER
2.75 oz. metal can, white cap. C.M.V. $2.00

1975 SPICY TALC FOR MEN
2.75 oz. metal can, black cap. C.M.V. $2.00

1975 BLUE LOTUS PERFUMED TALC
2.75 oz. metal can, lavender cap. C.M.V. $2.00

1978 TALCS – CANADA
Two on top left are Christmas issues in Foliger (red) and Hawaiian White Ginger. C.M.V. $3.00 ea. Regular issues are Sonnet, Unspoken, Come Summer, Foliger (green), Sweet Honesty, Flower Talk, Apple Blossom, Topaze, Roses Roses, Imperial Garden, Emprise. 5 mens talcs are 2.75 oz. with cardboard sides, paper labels, plastic tops. C.M.V. $2.00 each.

1976 TALCS FROM CANADA
2.75 oz. metal cans. Mens came in Tai Winds, Deep Woods, Oland, Wild Country. Womens came in Lilac, Silk & Honey, Happy Jungle Talc, Roses Roses, Charisma, Here's My Heart, Topaze, Unforgettable. C.M.V. $3.00 each.

PERFUMED TALCS – EUROPE
Each is 100 g size.
1974 issued metal can, plastic top. C.M.V. $5.00 each.
1976 issued cardboard sides, plastic top and bottom. C.M.V. $4.00 each.
1978 issued in all plastic with painted label sides. C.M.V. $3.00 each. Came in Lily of The Valley, Honeysuckle, Her World, Nearness, Lavender, Lilac.

AWARDS - FOREIGN

1977 PERFUMED TALCS — EUROPE
200 g. metal cans. Came in Roses Roses, Charisma, Timeless, Moonwind, Foligere, Lilac, Lily of The Valley, Honeysuckle, Unspoken, Promise of Heaven. C.M.V. $5.00 each.

1978 PERFUMED TALCS — EUROPE
100 g metal cans in Nearness, Timeless, Sweet Honesty, Roses Roses, Charisma, Moonwind, Promise of Heaven, Country Peach, Country Strawberry, Come Summer. C.M.V. $3.00 each.
1975 PERFUMED TALCS — EUROPE
100 g metal can in Elegance (green) and Brocade in gold. C.M.V. $4.00 each.

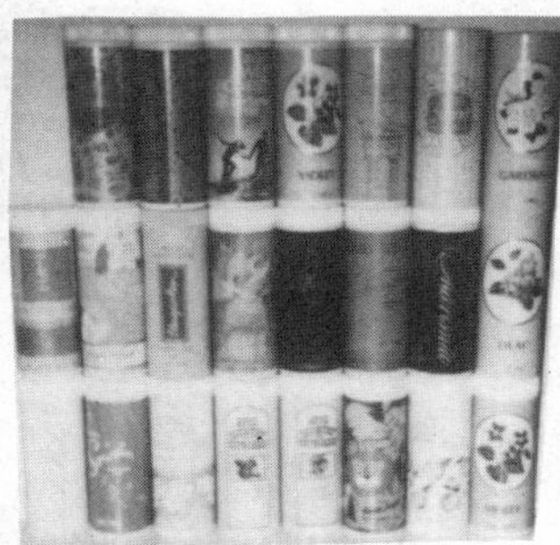

1978 PERFUMED TALCS — AUSTRALIA
100 g white plastic with paper band labels. Came in Bird of Paradise, Honeysuckle, Sweet Honesty, Violet, Topaze, Elusive, Lemon Velvet, Unspoken, Bouquet of Roses, Occur!, Unforgettable, Charisma, SSS Satin Talc, Somewhere, Sweet Violets, Country Cupboard Peach, Country Cupboard Strawberry, Happy Jungle, Pretty Peach. C.M.V. $3.00 each.
1976 & older talcs are 100 g cardboard as is pictured in Sonnet. All came this way. C.M.V. $4.00 each.
1978 PERFUMED TALCS — JAPAN
100 g cardboard or plastic sides. 3 on right are from Japan. Gardenia, Violet, Lilac. Came in all fragrances. C.M.V. $6.00 each.

LEFT 1978 AVON SMILE ORDER BOOK COVER - CANADA
White plastic & French & English order book in side. CMV $3.00
RIGHT 1977 CURRIER & IVES AWARD PLATE - CANADA
Given to reps for sales. Back side is printed in French & English. CMV $8.00

1970 ANNIVERSARY AWARD PLATE CANADA
Made of Aluminum, given to Reps. in C-9 1970 C.M.V. $25.00.

1972 PRESIDENT'S CLUB PLATE - CANADA
Given all President Club members. C.M.V. $22.50

1967 PRESIDENTS AWARD PLATE - CANADA
Metal plate, 13¼ inches. C.M.V. $75.

1977 COMMEMORATIVE PLATE ENGLAND
In celebrating the 25th anniversary of Queen Elizabeth. Given to Reps for selling 33 pounds (about $50.00 U.S.) of Avon products in C7-77. CMV $65.00 MB

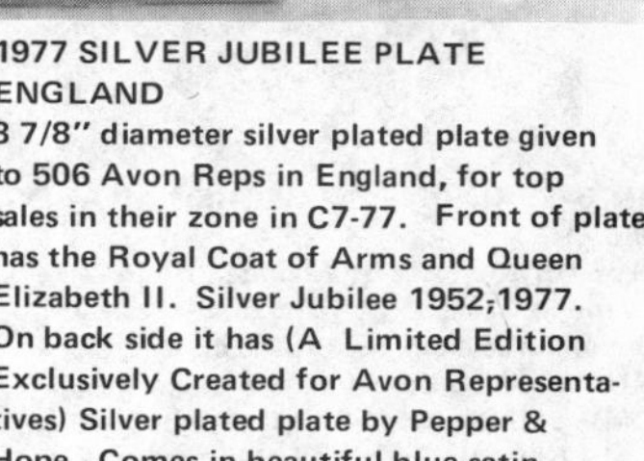

1977 SILVER JUBILEE PLATE ENGLAND
8 7/8" diameter silver plated plate given to 506 Avon Reps in England, for top sales in their zone in C7-77. Front of plate has the Royal Coat of Arms and Queen Elizabeth II. Silver Jubilee 1952;1977. On back side it has (A Limited Edition Exclusively Created for Avon Representatives) Silver plated plate by Pepper & Hope. Comes in beautiful blue satin lined box. RARE. C.M.V. $150.00 M.B.

1976 PONTESA DISHES AWARD SPAIN
Set of 4 bowls about 5 inches across, made by Pontesa and given to Reps in Spain for top sales. Dark pink in color. C.M.V. $15.00 M.B.
Also came set of 5 bowls and large matching serving bowl for meeting higher sales goals. C.M.V. $30.00 set M.B. Gold

1976-77-78 GENI CHRISTMAS PLATES CANADA
Each is 9" size. Front of plates are same as Avon plates only back is marked Geni Products. CMV $20.00 each.

1978 SPRING PROMISE DISH AWARDS - MEXICO
Won for top sales by Mexican Avon reps. Came in 4 steps. Step 1: gravy boat, salt & pepper shaker, toothpick holder; CMV $15.00. Step 2: creamer & sugar holder; CMV $15.00. Step 3: plate & butterdish; CMV $20.00. Step 4: bowl, coffee pot & bud vase; CMV $25.00. Made of ceramic by Munoz. All items complete set, CMV $100.00.

1979 10TH ANNIVERSARY HEART OF AVON AWARD - JAPAN
Box holds white porcelain heart with flower design, bottom says "Heart of Avon Exclusively made for Avon Lady" CMV $45.00 MB

1979 BELL CHRISTMAS GIFT - ENGLAND
White porcelain bell with Currier & Ives design, not marked Avon. White and blue box says "Happy Christmas from Avon" CMV $30.00 MB

1979 CURRIER & IVES AWARDS - EUROPE
Collection made in Bavaria for Avon.
Step 1 — Sweets plate, bowl, sugar bowl, cream jug set, cup & saucer. Choice of 1 item for 100 points on above. CMV $30.00 each piece.
Step 2 — Choice of 1 for 200 points. Milk jug, biscuit plate or butterdish. CMV $35.00 each item.
Step 3 — Choice of 1 for 400 points in sales. Cake stand, coffee pot & tea pot. CMV $40.00 each item.

BELL GIFT
Given to reps at Christmas 1979. CMV $20.00 MB

POSY VASE
Given to reps for placing an order in C1 and C2-79. CMV $20.00

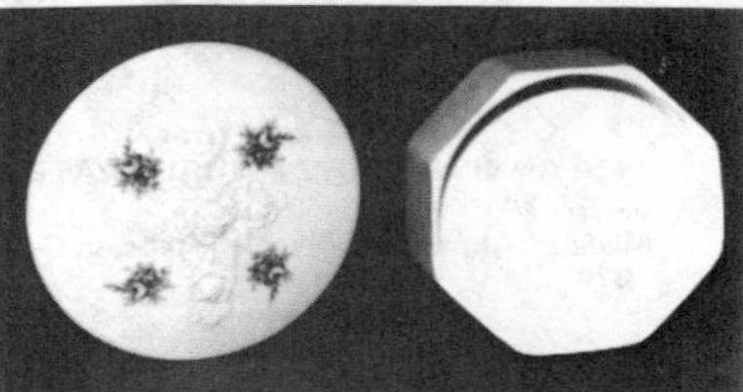

1977 CANDY DISH AWARD - GERMANY
White porcelain with pink flowers. Bottom Avon label made only for Avon. Given to German Avon reps. CMV $25.00

1979 SMILE COFFEE CUP AWARD - CANADA
Set of 6 given to reps for signing up new reps in Canada. Came in plain cardboard box. CMV $30.00 set of 6 MB, CMV $5.00 each cup.

1978 ALBEE AWARD - ENGLAND
Blue & pink figurine of 1st CPC Avon sales lady of 1886. Given to top 10 reps in each district in England. Bottom says "Florence Albee created exclusively for Avon 1886-1978 Made in England" CMV $250.00 MB

1979 TEDDY BEAR TEAM LEADER - CANADA
Stuffed teddy bear with French & English Avon tag. Given to Canada Team Leaders. CMV $35.00

1979 AUSTRALIAN AWARDS
ARIANE NOTE PAD
Red velvet. CMV $15.00
ARIANE INCH
In black bag. CMV $10.00
SERENITY CLOCK AWARD
Small white plastic clock made in Germany by Jerger. Has blue serenity flowers on face. CMV $25.00
PRESIDENTS CLUB SILVER PLATED COVERED DISH
Top flips open, glass dish inside. Given to reps. "Avon Presidents Club" inscribed on top. CMV $50.00

1979 CHRISTMAS PLATE TEAM LEADER GIFT - CANADA
Blue green pottery plate given to Team Leaders at Christmas 1979. Came with card shown from Avon. CMV $75.00

1974 PROMISE OF HEAVEN TEA SET AWARD – ENGLAND
21 piece fine English Bone China made only for Avon. Given to top Rep in each zone. C.M.V. $150.00 complete set.

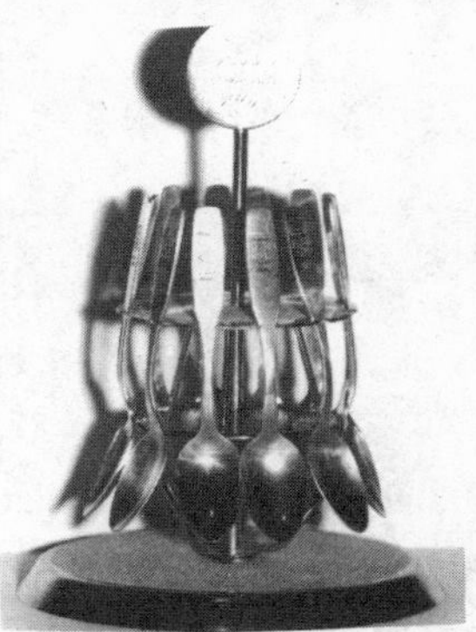

1967 PRESIDENTS AWARD SPOON HOLDER – CANADA
Gold and turquoise spoon holder. Holds 12 spoons from Oneida Silver with crest of each province on each spoon and 1 for Canada crest. Top says 1867-1967 on one side and Avon Presidents Award 1967 on other side. Awarded to Presidents Club Reps only. C.M.V. $125.00 complete, mint.

1979 FOUR SEASONS AWARD DOLLS - CANADA
4 ceramic dolls of each season in white blue & beige. Won by reps for sale achievement. Made only for Avon but does not say Avon on bottom. "Rex Made in Spain" on bottom. Plain cardboard box. CMV $75.00 set of 4.

1974 PROMISE OF HEAVEN AWARDS ENGLAND
1st step for selling 7 cream sachets won the 9" high white porcelain vase. C.M.V. $20.00
2nd step for selling 15 cream sachets won the white clock 3½" high x 3¼" wide. C.M.V. $20.00
3rd step for selling 25 cream sachets won the blue, white and gold electric lamp. C.M.V. $40.00

1974 PROMISE OF HEAVEN ORDER BOOK – ENGLAND
White plastic order book cover used by Avon reps. CMV $10.00
Each piece is decorated in Promise of Heaven design.

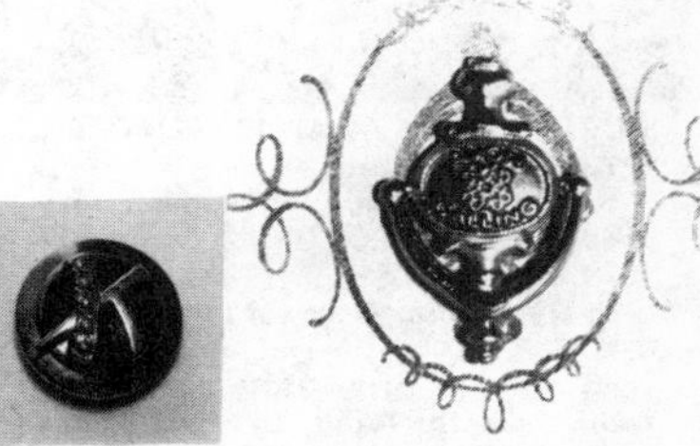

SILVER DOOR KNOCKER PIN - EUROPE
Silver Door Knocker pin with black center. 4A design. Came on turquoise Avon card. C.M.V. $20.00 on card.

1959-61 KVON I.D. PIN - GERMAN (On Left)
Used 3 years only & name was changed to Avon. Gold & black with 5 pearls. Very rare. C.M.V. $75.00

1979 SILK ROSE PRESIDENTS CLUB GIFT - CANADA
Blown glass vial 7" high with red silk rose given to all Presidents Club Reps in Canada. Came in gold box. Came with card from R. J. Fairholm, Avon Products. CMV $15.00

1975 X-MAS GIFT COLOGNE CANADA
Given to all Reps in Canada at X-Mas 1975. Box has outside sleeve that says in English and French "Especially for you from Avon". C.M.V. $15.00 as shown with sleeve. M.B.

1974 X-MAS GIFT COLOGNE CANADA
3 oz. bottle of cologne never sold to public, given to all Reps at X-Mas 1974 in Canada. Red lined gold box. Outside sleeve says in French and English - "A Gift to You from Avon". C.M.V. $20.00 M.B. as shown.

1979 PRESIDENTS CLUB CHRISTMAS GIFT - CANADA
Plastic tree ornament with Noel scene, gold sticker on bottom says Avon's Presidents Club Gift, 1979. CMV $15.00 MB.
1979 CHRISTMAS GIFT FOR REPS - CANADA
Fostoria nut bowl with 4A design on bottom in red & pink Noel box. Came with card from W. E. Griffin, Jr. President of Avon, Canada. CMV $10.00 MB.

1971 MOONWIND AWARDS - CANADA
Blue glass, silver over lay candy dish. C.M.V. $15. Cream & sugar & tray. C.M.V. $25. Jam set, C.M.V. $25.

1976 PEWTER GOBLETS AWARDS ENGLAND
Silver pewter goblets came in 3 sizes and were given to Reps for reaching sales goals in 3 steps. Small-C.M.V.$25.00 M.B. middle size - C.M.V.$40.00 M.B., large C.M.V. $60.00 M.B. Each came in blue and silver box. 4A design on side of each goblet. They are about 3-4-5 inches in height.

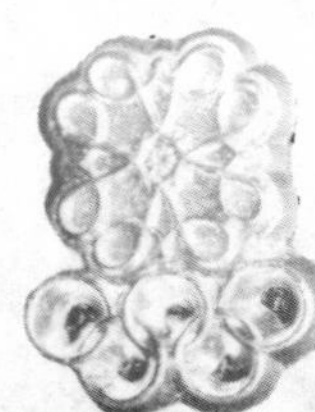

1972 4A OLYMPIC ID PIN - GERMANY
Gold color tin stick pin given to German Avon reps during Olympics in 1972. CMV $20.00 mint.

SILVER CIRCLE AWARDS - EUROPE
1979 CANDY DISH
With silver plated base. 1979 in bottom of glass. CMV $35.00
1978 CANDY DISH
Lead crystal dish. Does not say Avon. CMV $25.00
1979 COFFEE CUP - GERMANY (Left)
White china with 4A design on cup. Used by employees at Avon plant. CMV $25.00

1971 XMAS GIFT - GERMANY
Blue & silver box holds ribbed glass perfume rollette silver cap in Moonwind. Given to Avon reps. at Xmas.1971 C.M.V. $20.00 M.B.

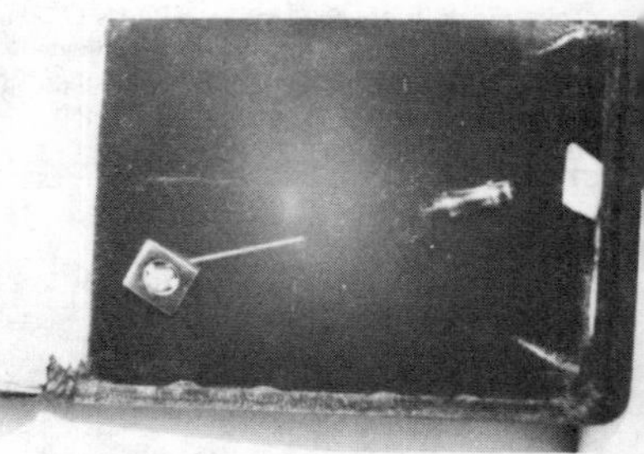

1978 DIAMOND STICK PIN - CANADA
Gold pin with .07 point diamond given to reps for selling $5000 in Avon in 6 months. Came in brown velvet box. CMV $75.00 MB

1976 ROSE STEMWARE — CANADA
Given to Reps for meeting sales goals. Each has Avon rose in design. Set consist of - Step 1 - 4-5 oz. wine glasses, C.M.V. $15.00 set. Step 2 - 4-6 oz. long stem parfait glasses with parfait spoons. Spoons say stainless Korea on back, C.M.V. $25.00 set. Presidents Club - Step 2 - 4-20 oz. long stem gobblets. C.M.V. $35.00 set. C.M.V. complete set $75.00

1978 PRESIDENTS CLUB KEY CHAIN - CANADA
Clear plastic on gold ring. 4A design. Given to each Presidents Club rep. CMV $10.00
1976 MANAGERS 90TH ANNIVERSARY PIN - CANADA
Sterling silver with 90th on front. Given to Avon managers. CMV $25.00

1973 CREAM & SUGAR AWARD — ENGLAND
White porcelain with green, pink, blue flowers on side. Given to reps in England. Does not say Avon. Came in plain box. CMV $10.00 set.

1978 PRESIDENTS CLUB WATCH - CANADA
Gruen watch in black case & box with Presidents Club on face of watch & 4A design. Won for $5000 in sales in 9 campaigns. CMV $100.00 MB.

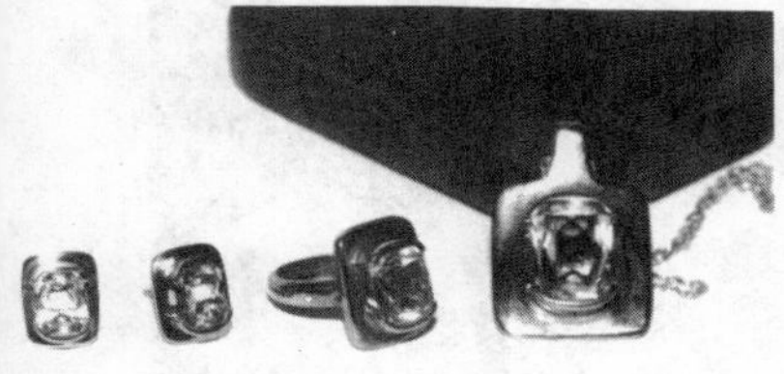

1977 UNSPOKEN AWARD JEWELRY - AUSTRALIA
Sterling silver with blue synthetic aqua marine stones. Earrings, ring & necklace. Each came in blue Avon boxes. CMV $75.00 set MB.

1979 GEMEM'S AWARDS - AUSTRALIA
Necklace with amber color stone. Goldtone. Avon on back. Given to reps. CMV $20.00 MB
Ring - goldtone, amber color stone. Came in tan felt box. CMV $25.00 MB.

1978 ARIANE NECKLACE PENDANT - CANADA
Given to all reps in Canada. Dated 1978. CMV $8.00

1978 WATCH AVON AWARD - GERMANY
17 jewel date watch with 4A design on face. Leather strap. Given to Avon reps in Germany. Avon on back. CMV $75.00 mint.

1970'S AWARD PINS - CANADA
LEFT MOONWIND PIN
Sterling silver. CMV $20.00
RIGHT 1978 CANDID PIN
Brass. CMV $10.00
CENTER 1977 A KEY PIN
Goldtone key pin. CMV $10.00
Each of these pins were given to Avon reps in Canada.

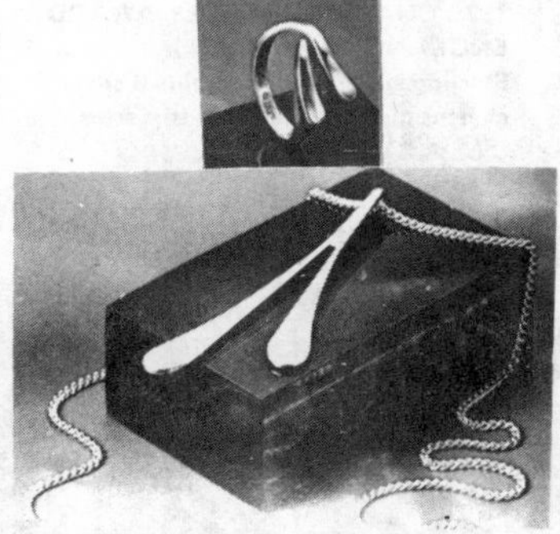

1977 RING AWARD - GERMANY
Sterling silver ring given to top selling reps in Germany. CMV not established.
1977 NECKLACE WISHBONE AWARD - GERMANY
Sterling silver wishbone necklace given to top selling reps in Germany. CMV not established.

1980 HEART LOCKET MANAGERS AWARD - CANADA
Goldtone locket with tiny diamond chip. Backside inscribed "You're the Heart of Avon" Given to managers only. CMV $35.00 MB.
1980 AVON PIN MANAGERS - CANADA
Goldtone Avon pin with red enamel center of heart shaped O. Given to managers only. CMV $25.00 MB.

1977 CHARM BRACELET AWARD - GERMANY
Sterling silver bracelet with possible 8 charms awarded to top selling reps. in Germany. CMV not established.

1978 CUSTOMER COUNT DOOR KNOCKER PIN AWARDS - CANADA
Given to reps for calling on customers. Door-knocker design. Pins came with 50, 75 & 100 on pins. 3 different. CMV 50 - $15.00, 75 - $20.00, 100 - $25.00

AWARDS – GERMANY
1978 BRACELET
Goldtone marked Avon. Red & black enamel. For high sales. CMV $15.00
1979 WATCH KEY AWARD
Goldtone watch & chain. Given to reps for getting new reps. Avon on back of case. CMV $50.00
1979 DOORKNOCKER
Goldtone, small 4A design in center. CMV $10.00
1978 4A PIN
Silvertone metal. 4A pin given to reps. CMV $15.00
1978 CHARM BRACELET
Gold chain & 3 charms with pearl, sapphire & diamond in center. Given for top sales. CMV not established.

1972 4A PIN – EUROPE
Sterling silver pin with blue stone in center. Given to Avon Reps in Europe. C.M.V. $15.00 pin only. $25.00 M.B.

1977 NO. 1 PENDANT AWARD CANADA
Gold No. 1 given to all Reps in the win district of each division for top sales in their division. C.M.V. $10.00 M.B.

1977 A-KEY PIN – CANADA
Small gold in color pin given to Reps for customer list. Blue box. C.M.V. $10.00 M.B.

1969 PRESIDENTS CAMPAIGN TEAM AWARD – CANADA
Sterling silver pendant on 18" silver chain. Back side says "President 1969" and front has 4A design. Given to all Re on winning team for top sales.
C.M.V. $20.00 M.B.

1978 DIAMOND "A" PENDANT NECK - LACE – CANADA
10 K gold "A" pin with small diamond. Given to 10 top reps in each division. Came in Keyes brown & gold box. CMV $75.00 MB

1975 CHARM BRACELET AWARD ENGLAND
Sterling silver bracelet holds 6 silver charms given to Reps for top sales.
C.M.V. $150.00

1972 BIRD OF PARADISE AWARD PIN - CANADA
Gift to representatives for meeting sales goal of Bird of Paradise products. C.M.V. $18.00 M.B.

LEFT 1973 AWARD BRACELET - FOREIGN
Gold chain, first charm with pearl, second charm rose with ruby set. Charms are size of U.S. dime. Awarded for sales goals.
C.M.V. $35.00 each.
RIGHT 1972 MANAGERS KEY CHAIN - GERMANY - Made of sterling silver. Has 4A design on front side. Only 60 were given to Avon managers in Germany for year end conference. CMV $160.00

1969 PRESIDENTS CAMPAIGN NATIONAL WINNER LOCKET AWARD – CANADA
Sterling silver locket 1" x 3/4" size on 18" silver chain. Given to winning team in each division for top sales. 4A design on front. C.M.V. $35.00 M.B.

1977 EMPRISE PENDANT AWARD - CANADA
10K gold and black "e" pendant given eps to reps selling most Emprise products in her district. CMV $40.00 MB.

1975 CAPUCCI SCARF
Brown and rust color silk scarf given to Reps in Germany for sales. Came in color matching envelope.
C.M.V. $10.00

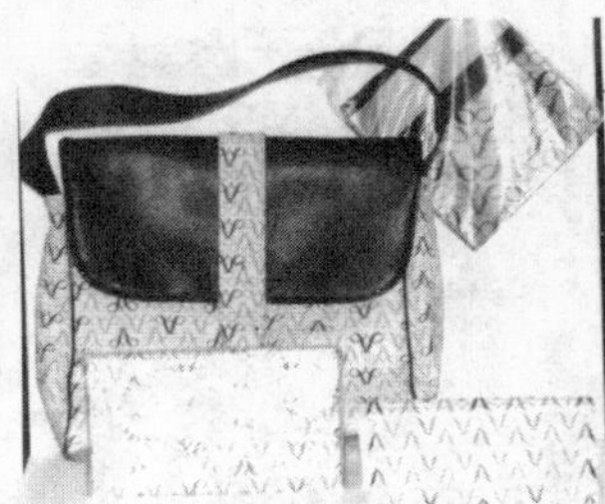

1976 SIGNATURE COLLECTION AWARDS – CANADA
Scarf, clutch purse, hand bag and large tote bag not shown, size 16½"x 14½". Each is brown and tan canvas. C.M.V. complete set is $45.00. 1976 Order Book also shown. Inside cover says Avon's 90th Anniversary Sales Achievement Award.
C.M.V. $4.00

1975 TIMELESS AWARDS – CANADA
Earrings. Gold color, brown center stone. Avon on back. Given to Reps for top sales. C.M.V. $10.00 M.B.
TIMELESS NECKLACE
Same as earrings. On a long chain.
C.M.V. $10.00 M.B.

1972 JEWELRY CASE AWARDS CANADA
Given to Presidents Club members only for sales goals on introduction of Avon Jewelry in Canada. 1st level award was Travel case. C.M.V. $15.00. 2nd level award was Deluxe Jewelry Case. On bottom of picture. C.M.V. $20.00 Avon rose inside of lid.

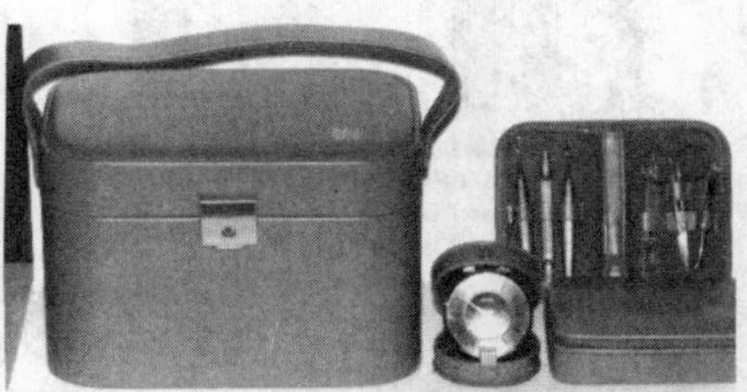

1976 TIMELESS AWARD SET – SPAIN
Set given to Reps in Spain for selling Timeless cologne mist. Set consists of leather overnight case, leather manicure set, travel clock made by Blessing and Avon on face, in leather case, and leather jewelry case. C.M.V. $80.00 complete set.

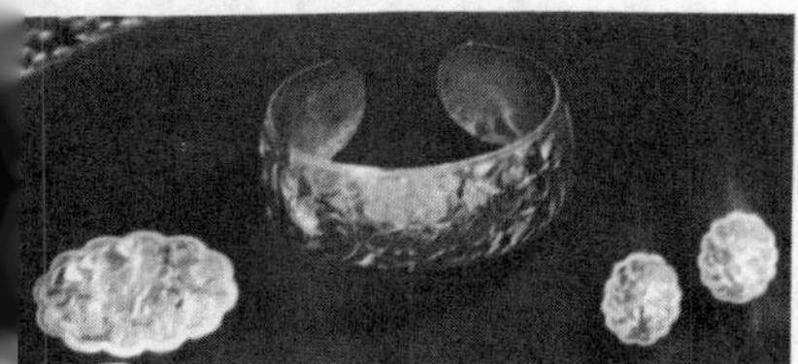

1969 PRESIDENTS CAMPAIGN AWARD – CANADA
Sterling silver earrings, broach, and bracelet given to Reps for reaching higher sales goals. 4A design on each piece. C.M.V. Earrings $5.00 M.B., C.M.V. Broach, $5.00 M.B., C.M.V. Bracelet $8.00 M.B.

1972 JEWELRY CASE AWARDS CANADA
Given to Reps on meeting sales goals on introduction of Avon Jewelry in Canada Avon Rose inside lid on both. 1st level is ring case, C.M.V. $10.00. 2nd level is Jewel case, C.M.V. $15.00.

1973 MOONWIND CLOCK AWARD GERMANY
Given to German Avon Reps for top sales. Blue and silver. Moonwind on clock face. C.M.V. $35.00
1967 DESK PEN SET AWARD CANADA
Black pen. Clear plastic base with 4A design and British Columbia crest on base with 0
with 50¢ Canadian coin inside clear base. Only 1 per district given to Reps only.
C.M.V. $25.00

1973 87th ANNIVERSARY AWARD CLOCK - CANADA
White plastic with roses. Made by Phinney Walker - Germany. C.M.V. $10.00
PRESIDENT'S CLUB ORDER BOOK COVER - CANADA
Winter scene on front. CMV $5.00

FIELD FLOWERS DESK SET - CANADA
Given to reps. C.M.V. $20.00 M.B.

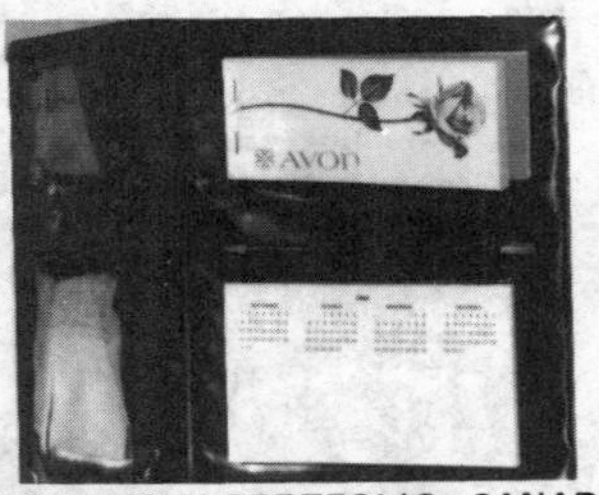

1968 CHARISMA PORTFOLIO - CANADA
Avon Xmas Award on Cover Order Book, pencil. Date pads. C.M.V. $8.00

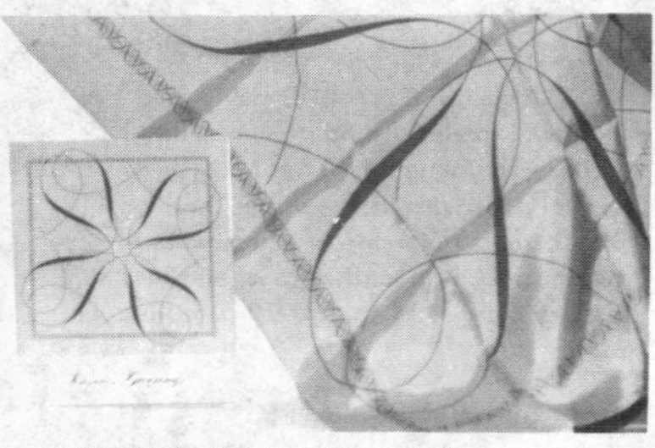

1973 REP CHRISTMAS GIFT CANADA
Tan and white card holds tan silk A scarf given to all Canada Reps at Christmas. C.M.V. $20.00 mint in card. Scarf only, $12.00

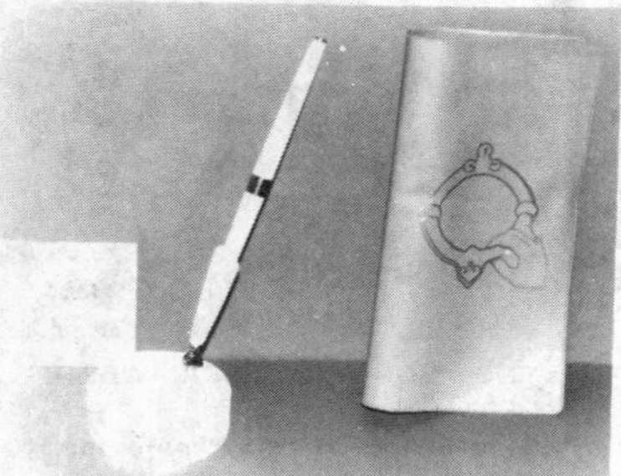

1980 PEN SET PRESIDENTS CLUB - CANADA
Clear & white plastic. 80 4A pin embedded in plastic base. "Presidents Club 1980" on pen. Came in green & gold box & Avon card. CMV $25.00 MB.
1977 TERRITORY RECORD COVER - CANADA
Blue plastic with gold door knocker. CMV $2.00

1979 SMILE BEACH BALL - ENGLAND
Given to reps in England. Orange & white plastic. CMV $5.00

1979 COLOGNE TEST SET - ENGLAND
White box has 5 samples. CMV $15.00
1979 AWARD BAG - ENGLAND
Suede hand tote bag. Avon tag. CMV $10.00

1978 SMILE PEN AWARD - CANADA
White & black pen with black silk ribbon. Given to reps for selling $400 in Avon in C6-C7 in 1978. Came in white Avon box. CMV $10.00 MB.

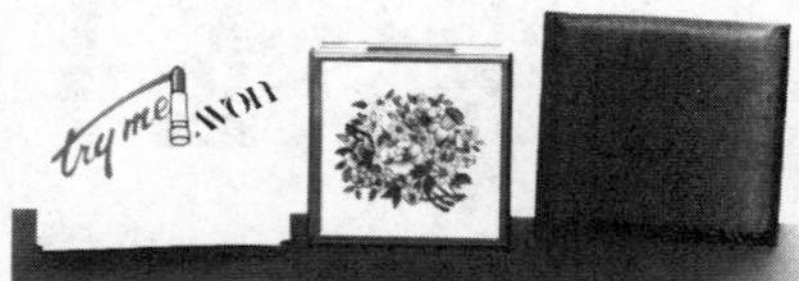

1980 TRY ME MIRROR AWARD - JAPAN
Goldtone mirror case in brown felt sleeve. White box. Given to reps in Japan. CMV $15.00 MB.

1979 SMILE UMBRELLA, TEAM LEAD CANADA
White nylon umbrella, red plastic handle. Avon in red. Given to Team Leaders in Canada. CMV $30.00 mint.

1978-79 4A TOWEL AWARDS - CANA
Reps could win 1st level 4A face cloth, ($5.00 MB; 2nd hand towels, CMV $7.00 3rd bath towels, CMV $10.00 MB each; bath sheet, CMV $20.00 MB each. Each in white or brown. Each had 4A design towel & came in Avon box. Boxes have French on one side & English on other.

1978 TRAVEL BAG AWARD - CANAD.
Beige canvas, navy trim bag given to winn team reps for sales in C14-78. CMV $5.0

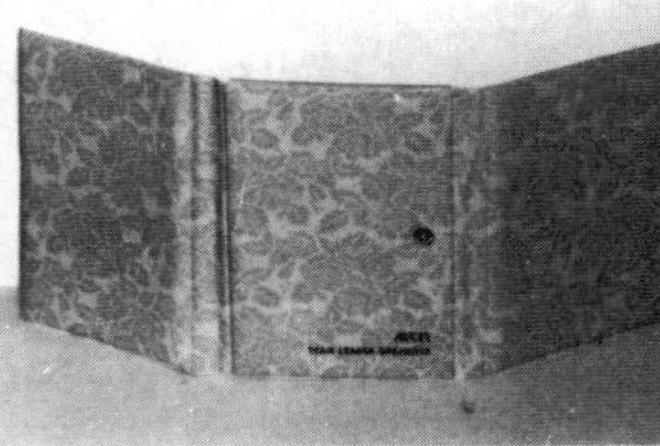

1978 TEAM LEADER ORGANIZER CANADA
Blue plastic, for reps in Canada. CMV $5.00

978 CANDID AWARD BAG - MEXICO
Given to Mexican Avon reps for top sales. CMV $15.00

1979 SHOPPING BAGS - JAPAN
Plastic coated paper bags. Came in blue pink & green. CMV $5.00 as a set.

1979 CARD, CHRISTMAS, & WRAPPING PAPER - EUROPE
Card CMV $3.00, Wrapping paper, CMV $4.00

SMILE PRODUCTS - ENGLAND
1979 SMILE TOTE BAG
Plastic coated cloth bag. Smile on back-side. CMV $7.50
SMILE BALLOONS
CMV 50c
1979 SMILE WITH AVON BUTTON
CMV $2.00
1979 OPERATION SMILE TAPE & FILM SET
Cassette & film used by managers at sales meeting. CMV $10.00 MB.

1979 JAPANESE AVON CALENDAR
Shows makeup products & described in Japanese. CMV $8.00

1979 CALENDAR - JAPAN
CMV $5.00
1980 CALENDAR - JAPAN
CMV $5.00

1979 CATALOG FOLDER - MEXICO
Blue vinyl folder used by reps. CMV $5.00
1980 CALENDAR - EUROPE
Foldout Avon calendar. CMV $4.00

1976 CHRISTMAS CARD GIFT - CANADA
Brown & beige card, 1st issue from Avon. Given to all reps at Christmas. 4A design on white card. Winter scene on inside. CMV $5.00

1979 DIARY, JEWEL PIN CLUB - JAPAN
Vinyl covered Avon diary given to Japanese reps. CMV $15.00
1979 CIRCLE OF EXCELLENCE ORDER BOOK COVER - MEXICO
Vinyl covered order book. Name on front Circulo de Distincion. CMV $5.00

1978 RECORD CHRISTMAS GIFT - CANADA
Record album given to all Canadian Avon reps at Christmas. Record is marked "Avon Presents A Christmas Concert by Boston Pops" CMV $8.00 mint.

1977 TIMELESS GIFT SET AWARD - CANADA
Gold box given to Avon reps in Canada for sales of Timeless products. Outside sleeve came in English & French. CMV $20.00

1977 CHRISTMAS CARD GIFT - CANADA
2nd issue gold fold out large card with Sugar Bush scene inside. 4A design on outside of card & envelope. Given to all reps at Christmas. CMV $4.00

1976 SALES BAG - EUROPE
Gray bag, brown A design. Used by Avon reps in Germany for deliveries. CMV $20.00

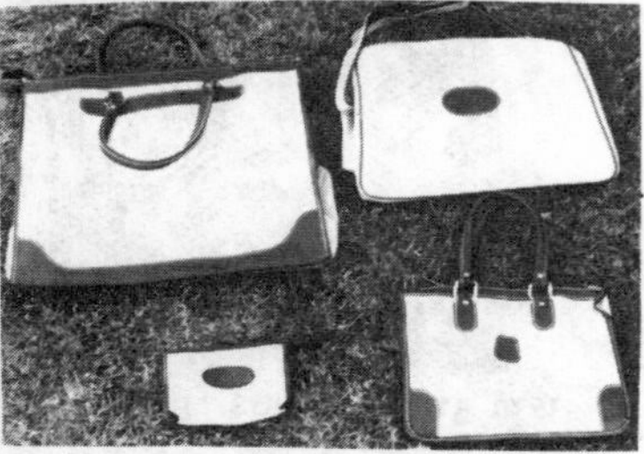

1977 SALES ACHIEVEMENT AWARD BAGS - CANADA
Tan canvas with brown leather trim. Given to reps for top sales. Clutch, handbag, medium tote and large tote. All 4 as set CMV $45.00

1979 SMILE NECK SCARF - CANADA
Red & white, black letters, Made in Canada. Given to managers only. CMV $25.00

1978 CRUISING HAT - CANADA
White & black hat. Given to each team leader in Canada. CMV $5.00
1979 SMILE HAT - CANADA
White, red & black hat given to team leaders in Canada. CMV $5.00

1979 PRESIDENTS CLUB BATHROOM SET AWARD - CANADA
Beige plastic set consists of trinket box, cotton box, tissue box, & beauty box with mirror. Given for best increase in sales. Designed by M. H. in Italy. CMV $60.00 set MB.

1978 CANDID AWARDS - CANADA
Candid Scarf, Step 1. CMV $5.00
Candid Scarf Clip, Step 2, CMV $8.00
Candid Umbrella, Step 3. CMV $20.00

1978 TOWEL AWARDS - GERMANY
Rust & beige color towels with doves on towels. Tag says "Made in Belgium by Santens for Avon" Large & small towel. CMV $10.00 small, CMV $15.00 large.

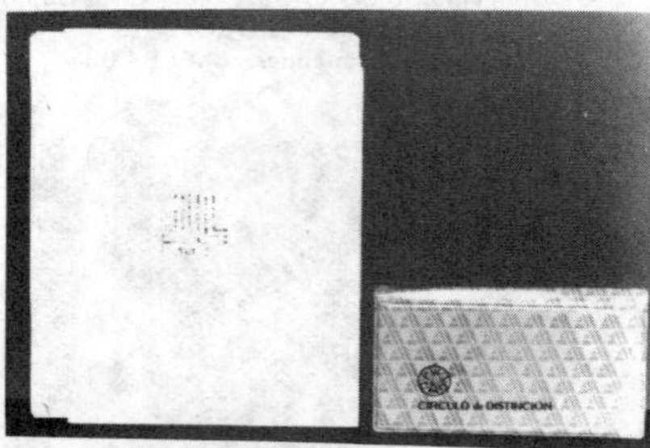

1979 MAKE-UP BINDER - JAPAN
White plastic 2 ring binder marked Avon. CMV $10.00
1979 CIRCLE OF DISTINCTIION ORDER BOOK COVER - MEXICO
Tan plastic cover. Same as our Presidents Club in U.S. CMV $10.00

1977 AWARDS – GERMANY CLUTCH
Gray & brown, A all over it. Came w calculator. CMV $30.00 with calculat
1978 ARIANE INCH
Silver tone dated 1978, has red plastic dabber. In red bag. CMV $15.00
1977 SCARF & PURSE
Brown & tan. CMV $10.00 scarf, CM $20.00 purse.

1977 RECOMMENDATION PRIZE - GERMANY
Terrycloth, plastic lined bags. Green or pink with 4A design. CMV $5.00 each.

1979 LIVE, LAUGH, LOVE TEMPO AWARDS - CANADA
Beige & red design. Level 1 – terry ha CMF $5.00. Level 2 – Lounger, CMV $20.00. Level 3 – terry warm up, CM $30.00.

1974 PEN & PENCIL SET - CANADA
Black & red Papermate pen box holds pens with 4A inscribed. Given to Presidents Club reps. CMV $35.00 set MB.

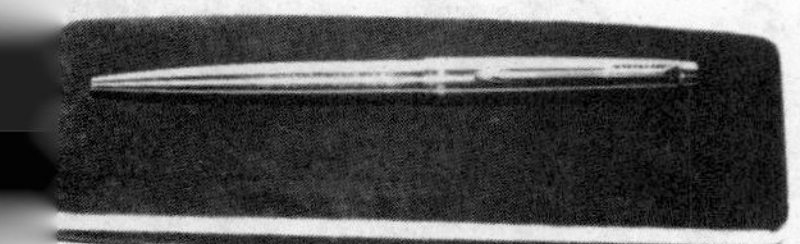

1979 PARKER PEN PRESIDENTS CLUB CANADA
Blue & gold box holds Parker 75 Pen inscribed on side (Presidents Club 1979) CMV $25.00 MB.

1972 AVON CALENDAR - GERMAN
Cloth roll up calendar, says Avon on bottom. C.M.V. $10.00
1973 AVON CALENDAR - GERMAN
Cloth roll up calendar, does not say Avon on it. C.M.V. $8.00 Both were given to reps. for sending in orders in C-1.

1972 ADVENT AVON CALENDAR - GERMAN
Given to reps. for getting a new rep. for Avon. C.M.V. $4.00

1972 REP CHRISTMAS GIFT CANADA
Green box holds Christmas card with black and red rose print on inside to be cut out and put in small gold picture frame. "Made in Austria" on back. Inside card says "from Avon" and signed by Avon President from Canada. Given to all Canada Avon Reps at Christmas. C.M.V. $20.00 M.B.

1978 CHRISTMAS AVON CARD - GERMANY
Gray card, Avon 78 on inside. CMV $2.00 in envelope.

1975 AVON CHRISTMAS CARDS GERMANY
Avon on inside and 4A design on front. C.M.V. $2.00

1971 REPS CHRISTMAS GIFT CANADA
Green Seasons Greetings envelope holds 4 8"x10" size pictures to frame with a letter from Canada's Avon President. Given to all Reps at Christmas. C,M.V. $20.00 complete, mint.

1975 CARD FILE - CANADA
For Avon ladies, green & gold. Field Flowers. C.M.V. $5.00.

TUBES - MISC.

All Tubes must be in original shape to be mint. Collapsed tubes - deduct at least 70% CMV.

1964 HAND CREAM X-MAS PACKAGING
Special X-Mas boxes in pink, blue and white, came with choice of green tube of 3 oz. hand cream, 4 oz. white plastic bottle of hand lotion, pink and white 3¾ oz. tube of moisturized hand cream and 2¼ oz. turquoise and white tube of Silicone Glove. O.S.P. 79¢ or 2 for $1.29. C.M.V. $3.00 each M.B.

1943 HAND CREAM NEW YEAR BOX
Regular issue tube of hand cream. Came in special short issue Flower designed box. RARE. O.S.P. 15¢ C.M.V. $16.00 M.B. as shown.

1941 HAND CREAM SPECIAL ISSUE BOX
Special issue flowered box holds regular issue tube of hand cream. Sold for 10¢ with regular order. C.M.V. $14.00 M.B. as shown.

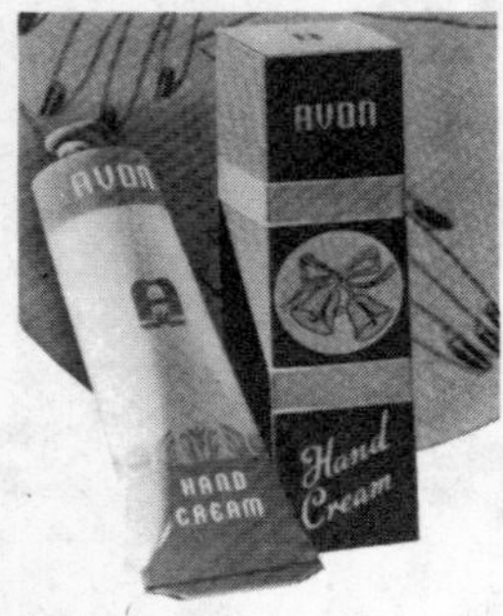

1938 HAND CREAM
10¢ with each order, Feb. 1938
Bells on Box C.M.V. in Box shown only $15.00.

1937 TOOTH PASTE SPECIAL ISSUE BOX
Regular issue tooth paste came in special issue box for 10¢ with regular order.
C.M.V. $16.00 M.B.

1942 HAND CREAM SPECIAL ISSUE BOX
Special issue box with flower design
Holds regular issue tube of hand crea
O.S.P. 10¢ C.M.V. $14.00 M.B. as sho

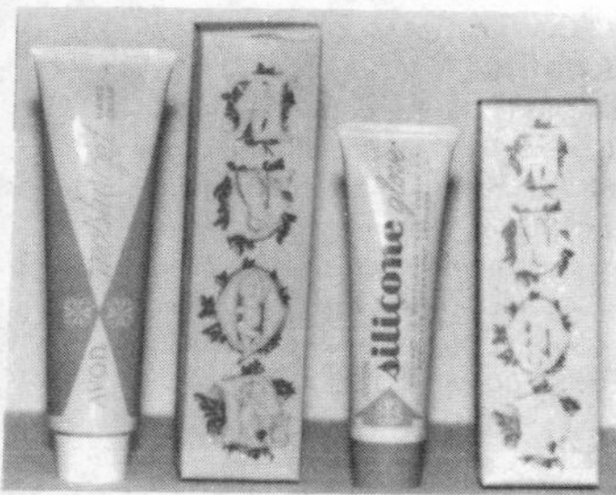

LEFT 1963 ONLY - MOISTURIZED HAND CREAM X-MAS BOX
3¾ oz. pink and white tube pictured with special issue Christmas box. O.S.P. 89¢ C.M.V. $2.00 M.B. Tube only sold 1957-67. C.M.V. tube only $1.00
RIGHT 1963 ONLY - SILICONE GLOVE X-MAS BOX
2¼ oz. turquoise and white tube in special issue Christmas box. O.S.P. 79¢ C.M.V. $2.00 M.B. Tube only sold 1960-69. C.M.V. Tube only $1.00

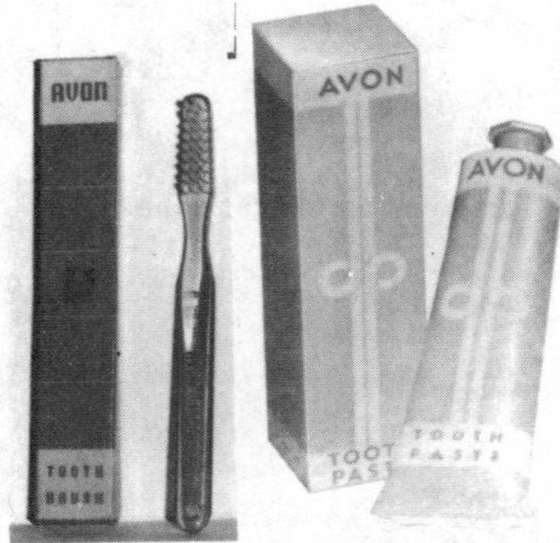

1940's - 50's TOOTH BRUSH
Turquoise and white box with Tulip A holds 1 Avon tooth brush. O.S.P. 50¢. C.M.V. $3.50 M.B.
1935-36 TOOTHPASTE
Red, white and green tube. O.S.P. 23¢ C.M.V. $15.00 in box. Tube only mint $12.00

1940 HAND CREAM SPECIAL ISSUE BOX
Special issue box is rose and white col
Has hand and flower on box with tulip
A in flower. Sold for 10¢. Holds regu
issue hand cream tube. C.M.V. $16.0
M.B. as shown.

1939 HAND CREAM SPECIAL ISSUE BOX
Short issue box came with regular issue tube of hand cream for 10¢ with regular order. C.M.V. $16.00 M.B. as shown.

1934-36 HAND CREAM
Blue & silver tube. O.S.P. 52¢
C.MV. $16.00 M.B. $12.00 tube only mint.

1938 TOOTH PASTE SPECIAL ISSUE BOX
Short issue box holds regular issue too
paste. Cost 10¢ with regular order.
C.M.V. $16.00 M.B. as shown.

1935 HAND CREAM CHRISTMAS BOX
Silver tube of hand cream came in special issue Christmas box for 10¢ with regular order. C.M.V. $16.00 M.B. as shown.

1953 67th ANNIVERSARY HAND CREAM DUO
Box holds two 2½ oz. tubes of hand cream. O.S.P. $1.10, C.M.V. $18.00 M.B.

1953 HAND CREAM DUO
Box holds 2 tubes 2½ oz. size of hand cream. Turquoise & white O.S.P. $1.18 C.M.V. $17.00 M.B.

1956 HAIR BEAUTY
Blue box holds two 2.4 oz. tubes creme shampoo. O.S.P. $1.29 C.M.V. $16.00 M.B.

1936-39 PORE CREAM (Left)
Turquoise & white tube. O.S.P. 78¢ C.M.V. $12.00 in box $8.00 tube only mint.
1930-36 PORE CREAM (Right)
Silver & blue tube. O.S.P. 78¢ C.M.V. in box $16.00, $12.00 tube only mint.

1953 Only-MERRY CHRISTMAS HAND CREAM DUO
2 turquoise & white metal tubes of hand cream in Merry Christmas box. O.S.P. $1.10, C.M.V. $18.00 M.B.

1956 Only - FOR BEAUTIFUL HANDS
Blue flowered box holds 2 tubes of 2¾ oz hand cream. O.S.P. $1.10 C.M.V. $15.00 M.B.

1954 FOR BEAUTIFUL HANDS
2½ oz. turquoise and white tubes with hand cream, turquoise caps. One tube with "Lanolin added" other regular issue. Box bouquet red roses. O.S.P. $1.10 C.M.V. $17.00 M.B.
In 1955 same box came with 2 tubes of hand cream like in the 1954 Merry Christmas Hand Cream Duo. C.M.V. $17.00 M.B.

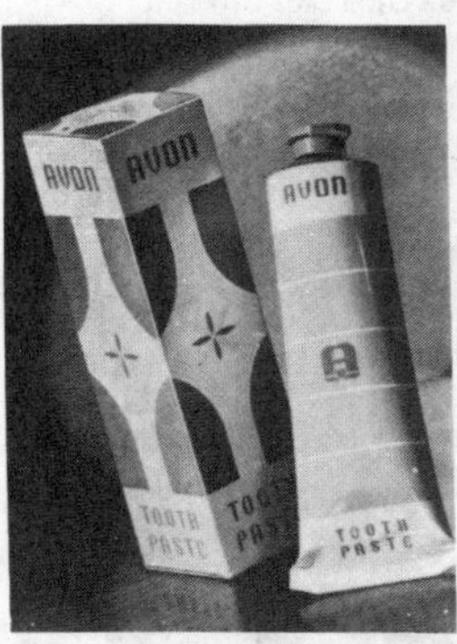

1939 TOOTHPASTE - SPECIAL BOX
O.S.P. 10¢ with good order October 1939 C.M.V. in box only $ 16.00 mint.

1974 CARE DEEPLY HAND CREAM
2 tubes 4 oz. in pink, blue, orange & purple box. O.S.P. $2.00 C.M.V. $2.00 M.B.

1954 DOUBLY YOURS
Rose box holds 2 tubes of Avon Hand Cream. O.S.P. $1.18 C.M.V. $17.00 M.B.

1931-34 DEPILATORY
Silver tube. O.S.P. 75¢ C.M.V. $16.00 in box, $12.00 tube only mint.
1948-53 DENTAL CREAM
Red cap, red, white & blue tube. O.S.P. 43¢ C.M.V. in box $6.00, tube only mint $4.00.

1958-59 MERRY CHRISTMAS GIFT BOXES
Special issue gift box came with choice of
Moisturized Hand Cream - pink and white tube. O.S.P. 79¢
Avon Hand Cream - Turquoise tube O.S.P. 59¢
Silicone Formula Hand Cream - white tube O.S.P. 98¢ C.M.V. $10.00 M.B. as shown each.

1949-55 AMMONIATED TOOTHPA
Green & white tube. O.S .P. 49¢ C.M.V. in box $8.00. $5.00 tube only mint.
1936-44 DENTAL CREAM
Turquoise & white tube. O.S.P. 26¢ C.M.V. $10.00 M.B. $7.00 tube only mint.

1954 MERRY CHRISTMAS HAND CREAM DUO
Red & white box holds two green tubes of Avon Hand Cream. O.S.P. $1.10 C.M.V. $17.00 M.B.

LEFT 1933-36 DENTAL CREAM
Green tube. O.S.P. 25¢ C.M.V. $15.00 M.B.
CENTER 1936-48 TOOTHPASTE NO. 2
Turquoise and white tube. O.S.P. 23¢ C.M.V. in box $8.00, tube only mint $6.00.
RIGHT 1936-48 TOOTHPASTE
Turquoise and white tube. O.S.P. 23¢ C.M.V. $10.00 M.B. Tube only mint $6.00

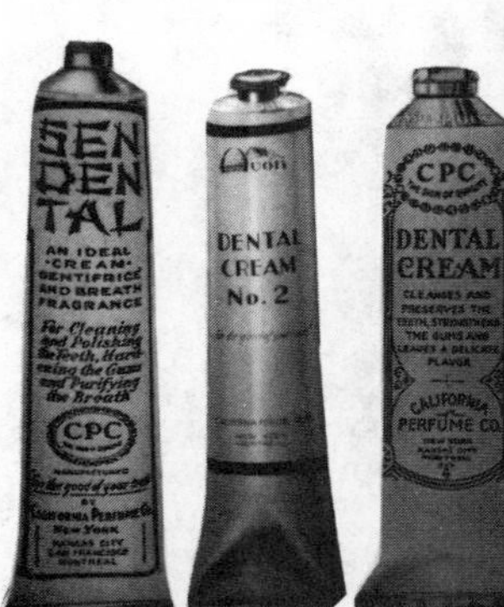

1923-33 SEN-DEN-TAL
Yellow tube. O.S.P. 47¢ C.M.V. $25.00 in box. $20.00 tube only mi
1933-36 DENTAL CREAM NO. 2
Green tube. O.S.P. 35¢ C.M.V. $15.0 M.B. Tube only mint $10.00.
1915-33 DENTAL CREAM
O.S.P. 23¢ 1915-23 tube was pink, 1923-33 tube was light blue. C.M.V pink tube mint $25.00, blue tube mint $20.00. Add $5.-- for box.

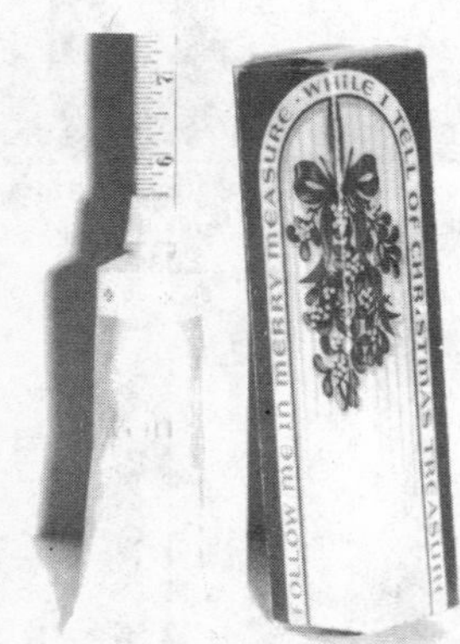

1960 ONLY - CHRISTMAS TREASURE BOX
Red and green box holds turquoise tube of hand cream. O.S.P. 69¢ C.M.V. $7.00 M.B. as shown. Tube only $2.00 mint.

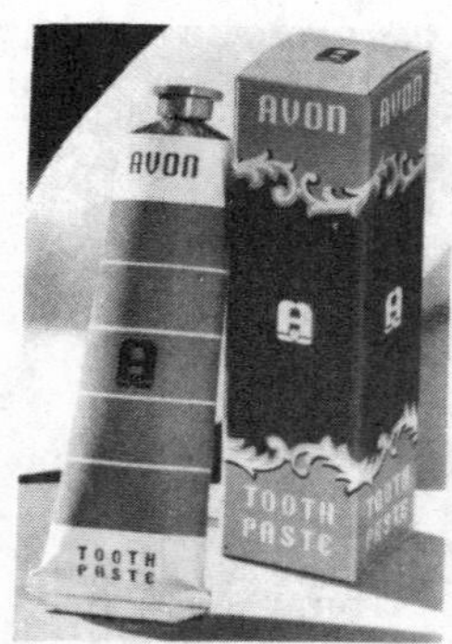

1940 TOOTHPASTE
Special Box, O.S.P. 10¢ with good order from Rep. in Sept 1940. C.M.V. in box only $16.00 mint.

1956 Only- MERRY CHRISTM
TWIN FAVORITES
Green & red box holds 2 tubes o Hand Cream. O.S.P. $1.18 C.M. $18.00 M.B.

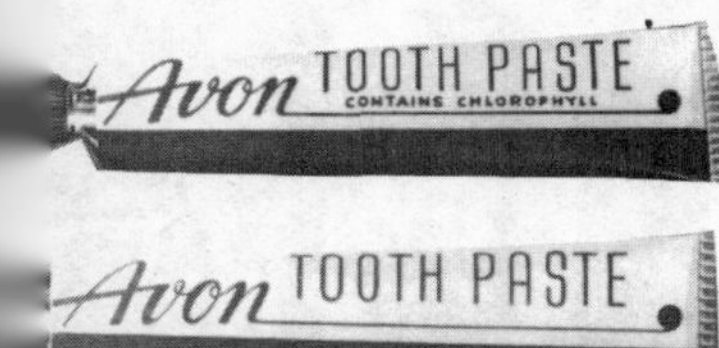

53-56 CHLOROPHYL TOOTHPASTE
en & white tube, green cap. O.S.P. C.M.V. in box $8.00 tube only mint $5.00.

1953-56 TOOTHPASTE
Blue & white tube, white cap. O.S.P. 49¢. C.M.V. in box $8.00, tube only mint $5.00.
Also came in ¾ oz. sample tube. C.M.V. $2.00 mint.

1923 BAYBERRY SHAVING CREAM
Green tube, came in Gentlemens Shaving Set C.M.V. $22.50 mint, $25.00 M.B.

1923 STYPTIC PENCIL
White pencil. O.S.P. 10¢ C.M.V. $5.00, $8.00 M.B.

1936-49 BRUSHLESS SHAVING CREAM
Maroon & ivory tube. O.S.P. 41¢ C.M.V. $12.00 M.B. $8.00 tube only mint.

1923 BAYBERRY SHAVE CREAM
Green tube. O.S.P. 33¢, C.M.V. $25.00 in box $20.00 tube only mint.

1923 SHAMPOO CREAM
Yellow tube, O.S.P. 48¢, C.M.V. $25.00 in box. $20.00 tube only mint.

1936-49 SHAVING CREAM
Maroon & ivory tube. O.S.P. 36¢ C.M.V. in box $10.00 Tube only mint $8.00.

1914 ALMOND CREAM BALM
Tube came in 2 sizes. O.S.P. 25¢ & 50¢ C.M.V. $35.00 in box, $30.00 tube only mint.

1923 COLD CREAM TUBE
Large & small tube. O.S.P. 23¢ & 45¢ C.M.V. $20.00 tube only mint. $25.00 M.B.

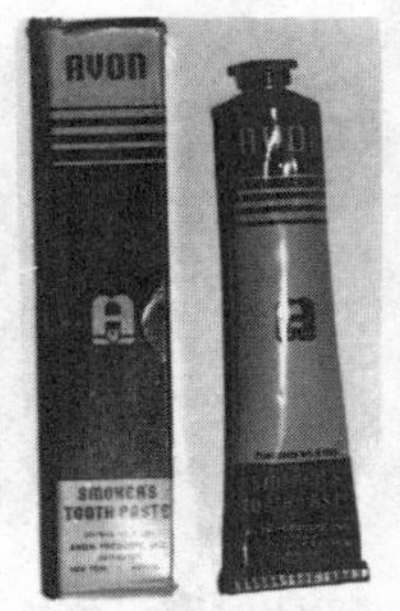

1941-50 SMOKER'S TOOTHPASTE
Maroon & cream colored tube.
O.S.P. 39¢ C.M.V. in box $10.00 M.B. $6.00 tube only mint.

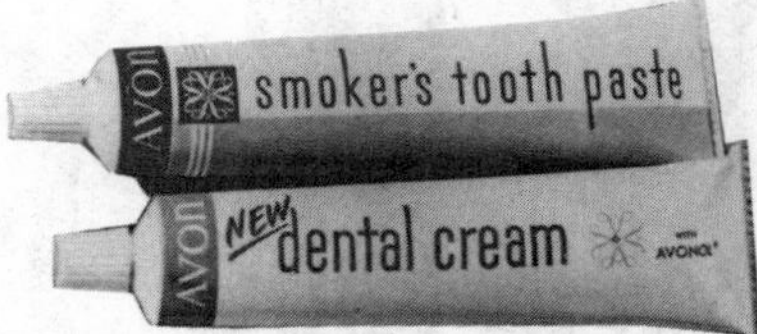

1957-67 SMOKER'S TOOTHPASTE
Red & white & grey tube. White cap. O.S.P. 50¢, C.M.V. $2.00 in box, $1.00 tube only mint.

1957-63 DENTAL CREAM WITH AVONOL
Red, white & gray tube, white cap. O.S.P. 50¢ C.M.V. in box $3.00 tube only $1.00.

1890 WITCH HAZEL CREAM
O.S.P. 2 oz. tube 25¢, 6 oz tube 50¢, C.M.V. $40.00 in box , $35.00 tube only.

1890 ALMOND CREAM BALM
O.S.P. 2 oz. tube 25¢ 6 oz. tube 50¢ C.M.V. $40.00 in box, $35.00 tube only.

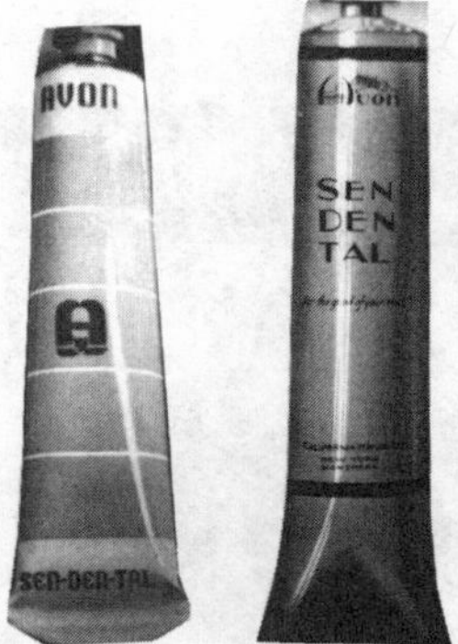

1936-42 SEN-DEN-TAL
Turquoise & white tube. O.S.P. 36¢ C.M.V. in box $15.00. Tube only mint $10.00.

1933-36 SEN-DEN-TAL
Green tube of tooth paste. O.S.P. 35¢ C.M.V. $16.00 in box, $12.00 tube only mint.

1930-36 BAYBERRY SHAVING CREAM
Green tube. O. S.P. 35¢ C.M.V. $17.00 in box $12.50 tube only - mint.

1935-36 BRUSHLESS SHAVING CREAM
Green & black tube. O.S.P. 51¢ C.M.V. $17.00 in box. $12.00 tube only mint.

1914 MENTHOL WITCH HAZEL
O.S.P. 25¢ C.M.V. $35.00 in box. $30.00 tube only mint.
1914 WITCH HAZEL CREAM
Small & large tube. O.S.P. 25¢ & 50¢ C.M.V. $35.00 in box, $30.00 tube only mint.

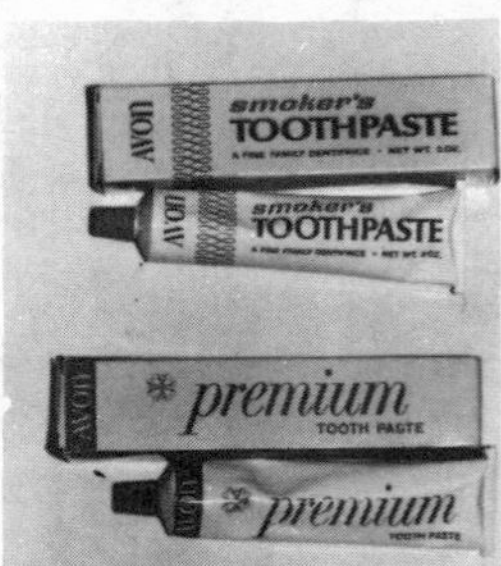

1964-67 SMOKERS TOOTHPASTE
5 oz. white tube, blue cap. O.S.P. 79¢ C.M.V. $1.50 M.B.
1964-66 PREMIUM TOOTHPASTE
5 oz. white tube, red cap. O.S.P. 89¢ C.M.V. $1.50 M.B.

1930-36 MENTHOL WITCH HAZEL CREAM
Green & black tube. O.S.P. 50¢ C.M.V. $15.00 in box. $10.00 tube only mint.
1930-36 WITCH HAZEL CREAM
Green & black tube O.S.P. 75¢ C.M.V. $15.00 in box, $10.00 tube only mint.

1908 WITCH HAZEL CREAM
2 & 6 oz. size tubes. O.S.P. 25¢ & 50¢ C.M.V. $35.00 ea. in box $30.00 tube only mint.
1908 ALMOND CREAM BALM
2 & 6 oz. size tubes O.S.P. 25¢ & 50¢, C.M.V. $35.00 ea. in box. $30.00 tube only.

1923 WITCH HAZEL CREAM
Large & small green tube. O.S.P. 30¢ & 59¢ C.M.V. $25.00 M.B. $20.00 tube only mint.

1936-44 WITCH HAZEL CREAM
Turquoise & white tube O.S.P. 52¢ C.M.V. in box $10.00 tube only mint $7.00.
1936-44 MENTHOL WITCH HAZEL CREAM
Maroon & ivory colored tube. O.S.P. 37¢ C.M.V. in box $10.00 tube only, mint $8.00.

1948-50 AMBER CREAM SHAMPOO OR AMBER GEL
Turquoise & white tube with blue cap. O.S.P. 59¢ C.M.V. $8.00 in box. $4.00 tube only.
1955-60 CREME SHAMPOO
Green and white tube
Humidor Set. CMV $10.00 MB

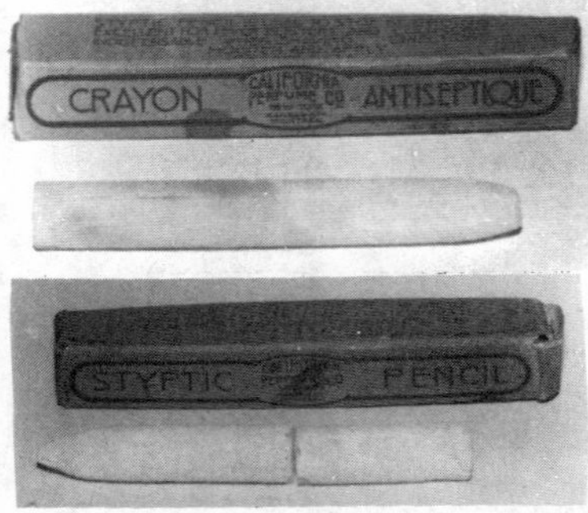

1925 STYPTIC PENCIL
White stick in CPC box. Came in Humidor Set. CMV $10.00 MB

1931-36 ROSE COLD CREAM SAMPLE
Small silver and blue sample tube, black cap. C.M.V. $5.00 mint.

23 MENTHOL WITCH HAZEL CREAM
een tube. O.S.P. 33¢ C.M.V.
5.00 M.B. Tube only mint $20.00.

TOP 1949-58 CREME SHAMPOO
Green tube with blue or white cap. OSP 59c, CMV mint tube only $5.00 in box $8.00

BOTTOM 1954-55 CREME SHAMPOO
Green tube with white cap.
O.S.P. 59¢ C.M.V. $8.00 M.B. Mint tube only $6.00.

1947 FLUFFY CLEANSING CREAM
1947 LIQUIFYING CLEANSING CREAM
Both tubes are pink 2¼ oz. Came in 1947 Cleansing Cream Demo Kit only. Was never sold to public. Very rare. CMV $12.50 each.

1960-62 CREME SHAMPOO WITH LANOLIN - Green & white box holds yellow tube with turquoise cap.
O.S.P. 69¢ C.M.V. $4.00 M.B.

1925 WITCH HAZEL CREAM SAMPLE
Green tube, says on back "Not for Sale Sample" C.M.V. $35.00, in box, $25.00 tube only.

1963-69 HAND CREAM
3 oz. Turquoise tube, white caps center tube older, bottom tube newer (1970-73) two different labels. O.S.P. 69¢ C.M.V. $1.00 (1963-69) and 50¢ (1970-73)

1980 TAKE ALONG HAND CREAM
1 oz. tube in Vita Moist red design, or Rich Moisture blue design. SSP 88c CMV 50c each.

1959 CREME SHAMPOO
2.4 oz. yellow tube & turquoise cap. Yellow & blue box. OSP 69c CMV $4.00 MB.

LEFT 1931-36 HAIR DRESS
Silver tube, O.S.P. 37¢ C.M.V. $15.00 in box, $10.00 tube only mint.

CENTER 1936-49 HAIR DRESS
Maroon & ivory colored tube. O.S.P. 37¢ C.M.V. $12.00 M.B. Tube only $8.00 mint.

RIGHT 1962-65 CREAM HAIR DRESS
4 oz. white tube. Red cap. Stage coach on tube, O.S.P. 89¢ C.M.V. $4.00, $6.00 M.B.

1954 Only - HAND CREAM WITH LANOLIN - 2½ oz. tube. O.S.P. 59¢ C.M.V. $12.00 M.B. $10.00 tube only mint.

1940-43 SPECIAL FORMULA CREAM
Turquoise & white tube. O.S.P. 78¢ C.M.V. $12.00 M.B. tube only mint $9.00.

1968-75 RICH MOISTURE HAND CREAM
3.75 oz. or 6 oz. pink and white with pink cap. O.S.P. 3.75 oz. $1.00 C.M.V. 25¢.
O.S.P. 6 oz. $2.00 C.M.V. 25¢
1976-78 Color changed to aqua same design.

1970-78 SILICONE GLOVE
4.5 oz or 2.25 oz. white & aqua tube with aqua cap. O.S.P. 2.25 oz. $1.00 C.M.V. 25¢ O.S.P. 4.5 oz $2.00 C.M.V. 25¢

LEFT TO RIGHT (CHECK ALL DATES)
1969 SATIN SUPREME CREME FOUNDATION
1 1/8 oz. lavender tube & cap. Came in 8 shades. OSP $1.50 CMV $1.00
1968-69 HIDE 'N' LITE
.75 oz. tube, beige cap. 1968 came with gold cap. OSP $1.50 CMV $1.00
1965 TONE 'N' TINT
2 oz. tube, rose color cap. OSP $1.50 CMV $2.00 MB
1970 SATIN SUPREME
1 1/8 oz. tube, white or lavender cap. CMV $1.00
1968-69 ULTRA COVER
2.1 oz. tube, blue cap. Came in 8 shades OSP $1.75 CMV $1.00
1968-69 TONE 'N' TINT
Pink tube & cap. 2 oz. Came in 8 shades OSP $1.50 CMV $1.00

1955-62 HAND CREAM (left)
Turquoise tube and cap. Flat cap sold 1955-57 2½ oz. tube. Tall cap sold 1957-62 2.65 oz. O.S.P. 59¢ C.M.V. $3.00 in box flat cap. Tube only $2.00 flat cap mint $1.00 less on tall cap tube.
1937-54 HAND CREAM (right)
2½ oz. turquoise and white tube. O.S.P. 52¢ C.M.V. $7.00 in box, tube only mint $4.00.

1964-66 FOUNDATION SUPREME
1½ oz. white tube, gold cap. O.S.P. $1.35 C.M.V. $1.00 mint.
1969-75 LOOK BRONZE
2 oz. brown & white tube with bronze cap. O.S.P. $2.00 C.M.V. 25¢

1966-68 HAND CREAM FOR MEN DOUBLE PAK
Box holds 2 black & orange tubes. O.S.P. $2.50 C.M.V. Tubes $2.00 ea. Set $7.00 M.B.

LEFT 1936 CLEANSING CREAM SAMPLE
¼ oz. tube, black or turquoise cap. C.M.V. $6.00. C.P.C. label add $4.00.
CENTER 1962-71 ROSEMINT FACIAL MASK
3 oz. pink and white tube. O.S.P. $1.00 C.M.V. $1.00 M.B.
RIGHT 1957 CLEANSING CREAM
2½ oz. white tube with gray band, turquoise lettering. O.S.P. 59¢, C.M.V. $3.00.

1969-74 DEEP CLEAN CREAM
4 oz white tube blue cap. O.S.P. $1.00 C.M.V. 25¢
1969-76 FASHION LEGS
6 oz white tube brown or white cap. O.S.P. $2.00 C.M.V. 25¢.
1970's FASHION LEGS SAMPLE
1 oz. white tube brown cap O.S.P. 49¢ C.M.V. 25¢.
1974-78 VITA MOIST HAND CREAM
6 oz yellow & white tube, white cap. O.S.P. $1.00 C.M.V. 25¢.

LEFT TO RIGHT
1977-78 BATH GELEE
4 oz. tube came in Roses, Roses, Honeysuckle, Apple Blossom or Strawberry. O.S.P. $3.50 C.M.V. 25¢
1977-78 FRESH STRAWBERRY PEEL OFF FACIAL MASK
3 oz. tube, white cap. O. S.P. $3.00 C.M.V. 25¢
1977-78 LEMON FACIAL MASK
3 oz. plastic tube. O.S.P. $3.00 C.M.V. 25¢
1976-78 CUCUMBER COOLER FACIAL MASK
3 oz. plastic tube O.S.P. $3.00 C.M.V. 25¢
1977-78 NATURAL EARTH FACIAL MASK
3 oz. plastic tube O.S.P. $3.00 C.M.V. 25¢
1977-78 MOISTURE WORKS FACIAL MASK
3 oz. plastic tube O.S.P. $3.00 C.M.V. 25¢

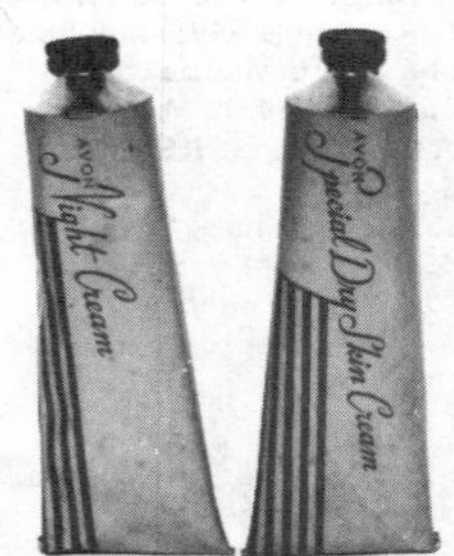

1948 NIGHT CREAM
1948 SPECIAL DRY SKIN CREAM
Both tubes are blue 2¼ oz. size. Came ir 1948 Skin Care Demo Kit. Was never sold to public. Very rare. CMV each $12.50 mint full.

1957-61 SILICONE FORMULA CREA
White tube, small turquoise cap. O.S.P. 98¢ C.M.V. in box $2.00 mint tube only $1.00.
1957-67 MOISTURIZED HAND CREA
Pink & white tube, small white cap. O.S.P. 79¢ C.M.V. in box $2.00 mint. tube only $1.00 mint.

?78-79 KEEP CLEAR ANTI-DANDRUFF ?REAM SHAMPOO
?oz. tube, white & blue, blue cap. SSP ?.69 CMV 25c
?979-80 RIPE AVOCADO CONDITIONING ?ASK
?oz. yellow & green tube. SSP $1.50 CMV 25c

LEFT 1956-59 CHAP CHECK
Small white plastic tube, red cap.
O.S.P. 25¢ C.M.V. $2.00 mint
CENTER 1960-73 CHAP CHECK
is same color as above only longer tube.
O.S.P. 39¢ C.M.V. 50¢
RIGHT 1951-55 CHAP CHECK
Small turquoise and white plastic tube.
1/10 oz. size. O.S.P. 25¢ C.M.V. $3.00 mint.

1977 CUTICLE CONDITIONER & CUTICLE REMOVER COMP TUBES
Hand painted tubes for Avon to photo for brochures. Given to NAAC with letter from Avon on 1 of a kind. RARE.
C.M.V. $30.00 each with letter from Avon.
1965-67 FOUNDATION SUPREME FOR EXTRA DRY SKIN
1½ oz. plastic tube, came in 11 shades.
O.S.P. $1.50 C.M.V. $1.00

Left to Right
1970's PROTEM LOTION SHAMPOO SAMPLE
1 oz. pink tube O.S.P. 49¢C.M.V. 25¢
1970's PROTEM HAIR CONDITIONER SAMPLE
1 oz. pink tube. O.S.P. 49¢ C.M.V. 25¢
1967-72 SHEEN HAIR DRESSING
2 oz. pink , white & gold with white cap O.S.P. $1.00 C.M.V. 25¢
1975-77 HI LIGHT DANDRUFF SHAMPOO
4 oz. blue & white plastic tube, white cap O.S.P. $1.00 C.M.V. 25¢
1975-78 HI LIGHT 60 SECOND HAIR CONDITIONER
6 oz yellow plastic, white cap. O.S.P. $1.00 C.M.V. 25¢
1975-77 HI LIGHT HAIR SETTING GEL
6 oz pink & white, white cap.
O.S.P. $1.00 C.M.V. 25¢
1970-75 DANDRUFF GEL SHAMPOO
3 oz clear plastic white cap O.S.P. $1.00 C.M.V. 25¢

Left to Right
1968-77 CUTICLE REMOVER
O.S.P. $1.00 C.M.V. 25¢
1968-77 CUTICLE CONDITIONER
O.S.P. $1.00 C.M.V. 25¢
1973-76 NAIL BUFFING CREAM
.25 oz. tube white and red. O.S.P. $1.00 C.M.V. 25¢
1955-60 NAIL BEAUTY
1 oz tube white & red cap.
O.S.P. 59¢C.M.V. $3.00 Mint.

1962-68 CUTICLE REMOVER
1 oz. white plastic tube, red cap.
O.S.P. 69¢ C.M.V. $2.00.
1962-68 NAIL BEAUTY
1 oz white plastic tube, red cap.
O.S.P. 69¢ C.M.V. $2.00

1957-60 ANTISEPTIC CREAM
1¾ oz. tube white & red & grey with red cap. O.S.P. 69¢
C.M.V. $3.00 mint.

1973 RESILENT CREME RINSE FOR ADDED BODY - SAMPLE
1 oz. yellow plastic tube.
C.M.V. $1.00.
1973 ESSENCE OF BALSAM HAIR CONDITIONER SAMPLE
1 oz. yellow plastic tube. C.M.V. $1.00.

1971-74 BRONZE GLORY TANNING GEL- 3 oz. brown plastic tube yellow cap O.S.P $1.00 C.M.V. 25¢
1965-76 SUN SAFE
4 oz. white, yellow with peach cap.
O.S.P. $1.00 C.M.V. 25¢
1975-78 BRONZE GLORY KWICK TAN - 5.5 oz. brown plastic, brown cap. O.S.P. $1.00 C.M.V. 25¢
1975-78 BRONZE GLORY SUN SAFE
5.5 oz. white plastic with white cap.
O.S.P. $1.00 C.M.V. 25¢

1975 THE GLISTENERS
Cheek color-pink tube & cap.
Lip color-red tube & cap.
Eye color-blue tube & cap.
O.S.P. $1.00 C.M.V. 25¢
1974-77 SOFTSHINE LIP COLOR
.2 oz. pink, red & white with white cap. O.S.P. $1.00 C.M.V. 25¢
1976-78 REAL ROUGE CREME FLUFF
.25 oz. pink and red, with red cap.
O.S.P. $1.00 C.M.V. 25¢

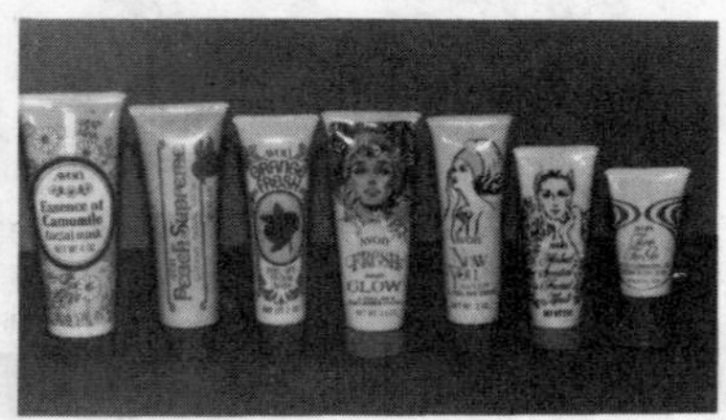

1975-76 ESSENCE OF CAMOMILE
4 oz white tube, green cap. O.S.P. $1.00 C.M.V. 25¢
1973-76 PEACH SUPREME
3 oz white tube with orange cap O.S.P. $1.00 C.M.V. 25¢
1974-76 ORANGE FRESH
2 oz white tube orange cap. O.S.P. $1.00 C.M.V. 25¢
1968-77 FRESH AND GLOW
3½ oz. white tube, red cap. O.S.P. $1.00 C.M.V. 25¢
1967-74 NEW YOU MASQUE
2 oz. white tube, red cap. O.S.P. $1.00 C.M.V. 25¢
1973-76 HERBAL SCENTED MASK
2 oz. white tube, green cap. O.S.P. $1.00 C.M.V. 25¢
1975 TWO TO-GO FOUNDATION & BLUSH
Pink and white. O.S.P. $2.00 C.M.V. 25¢

1975-78 MAKING EYES CREAM EYE SHADOW
.25 oz. light blue with turquoise lettering. O.S.P. $1.00 C.M.V. 25¢
1964-76 NATURAL RADIANCE
.25 oz. clear plastic tube gold cap. O.S.P. $2.00 C.M.V. 25¢
1970-73 FLOWING CREAM EYE SHADOW - .25 oz clear plastic tube, gold cap. O.S.P. $1.00 C.M.V. 25¢
1973-75 FLOWING CREAM EYE SHADOW
.25 oz. white plastic tube with gold cap. O.S.P. $1.00 C.M.V. 25¢

TOOTH TABLETS

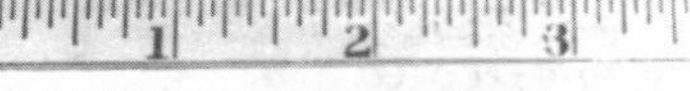

1887-1896 CALIFORNIA TOOTH TABLET
Blue and white painted metal lid. California Perfume Co., New York. Clear glass bottom has embossed California Tooth Tablet, Most Perfect Dentifrice. O.S.P. 25¢ C.M.V.$85.00 mint.

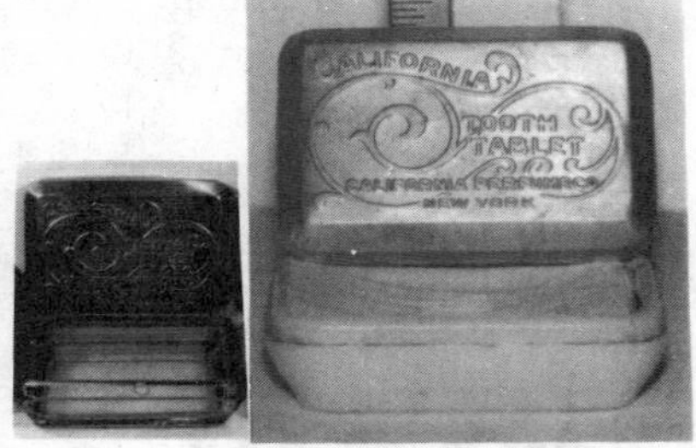

1921-23 TOOTH TABLET (Left)
Aluminum lid & clear glass bottom. O.S.P. 25¢ C.M.V. $60.00 mint.
Right **1923-34 TOOTH TABLET**
Aluminum lid with white glass bottom. O.S.P. 36¢ C.M.V. $55.00 mint. Both have same lid, different bottoms.

1896 TOOTH TABLET
Painted metal top with clear glass bottom embossed with Calif. Tooth Tablet in glass. 2 different boxes. 1906 to 1921 lid is painted just under New York with Food & Drug Act 1906. OSP 25c, CMV $70.00 mint, $90.00 MB each.

Left **1936-40 TOOTH TABLET**
Aluminum lid on white glass bottom. O.S.P. 36¢, C.M.V. $55.00 mint.
Right **1934-36 TOOTH TABLET**
Aluminum lid on white glass bottom. O.S.P. 36¢, C.M.V. $60.00 mint.

FRAGRANCE JARS

1948-57 ROSE FRAGRANCE JAR SET
Box contains one 6 oz. fragrance jar liquid. One 3 oz. fragrance jar cubes. One 8 oz. empty fragrance jar. CMV $80.00 set MB. set M.B.

1923 AMERICAN BEAUTY FRAGRANCE JAR CUBES - 4 oz. can. O.S.P. 48¢ C.M.V. $45.00 mint. Front & back view shown.

1943-49 FRAGRANCE JAR CUB
3 oz. jar. O.S.P. 85¢ C.M.V. $25.0
$35.00 M.B.

23-33 AMERICAN BEAUTY FRAGRANCE R (Left) - Clear glass jar & lid. Red ribbon ound neck. O.S.P. $2.95 C.M.V. $100.00
14-23 LAVENDER FRAGRANCE JAR lifferent sizes.
ft - 5½" high 3" wide base
nter - 5 7/8" high, 3" wide base
ght - 7" high, 3 9/16" wide base
also came 5 3/8" high & 3" wide base.
SP $2.50 each, CMV $125.00 each size.
0.00 clear stopper, $20.00 with frosted opper. Add $10.00 MB each.

1948 ROSE FRAGRANCE JAR TEST
Dark amber glass. Was not sold. Test bottle at factory. CMV $100.00

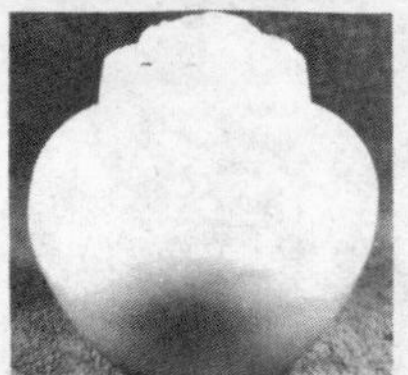

1946 FRAGRANCE JAR
made of pink ceramic, white flower on pink lid. Very short issue. Does not say "Avon" on it. Also came with white, blue & green flowers on lid. O.S.P. $2.75 C.M.V. $80.00 M.B. Jar only mint $60.00

1948-57 ROSE FRAGRANCE JAR
6 oz. First issue came out with clear rose shaped glass stopper. 1949 issue had frosted rose glass stopper. Both had red silk neck ribbon. OSP $3.50 CMV $30.00 clear stopper, $20.00 with frosted stopper. Add $10.00 MB each.

1934-36 FRAGRANCE JAR LIQUID
6 oz. bottle, aluminum cap. Silver & blue label. O.S.P. $1.75 C.M.V. $40.00 mint $45.00 M.B.

1955-57 FRAGRANCE JAR LIQUID
7 oz. white cap, gray label. O.S.P. $1.39 C.M.V. $15.00 - $20.00 M.B.

1921 FRAGRANCE JAR LIQUID
4 oz. cork stopper, brown label.
O.S.P. 96¢ C.M.V. $100.00

1925 AMERICAN BEAUTY FRAGRANCE JAR LIQUID - 4 oz. bottle, brown label, metal cap. O.S.P. 96¢ C.M.V. in box $80.00 Bottle only $65.00

1934-43 AMERICAN BEAUTY FRAGRANCE JAR - 6 oz. glass jar & stopper. Red tassel around neck. O.S.P. $2.75 C.M.V. $40.00 jar only mint. $55.00 with tassel M.B.

1936-54 FRAGRANCE JAR LIQUID
6 oz. green cap & label. O.S.P. $1.39 C.M.V. $25.00 in box. $20.00 jar only.

AMERICAN IDEAL

ALL CPC'S MUST BE NEW MINT CONDITION FOR CMV

1941 AMERICAN IDEAL
1/8 oz. clear glass bottle, gold cap, gold & blue label. O.S.P. 75¢ C.M.V. $35.00 BO, $55.00 MB

1908 AMERICAN IDEAL PERFUME
Glass stoppered bottle came in 1 & 2 oz. size. Velvet lined wood box. Neck ribbon on bottle, gold front & neck label. O.S.P. $2.00 & $3.75 C.M.V. $200.00 in box, bottle only $150.00

1922 AMERICAN IDEAL FACE POWDER
Green box holds green and gold paper container. OSP 96c, CMV $35.00 $45.00 MB.

1908 AMERICAN IDEAL SACHET
Glass bottle with metal cap. 2 piece gold label. OSP 50c, CMV $105.00 BO mint, $125.00 MB

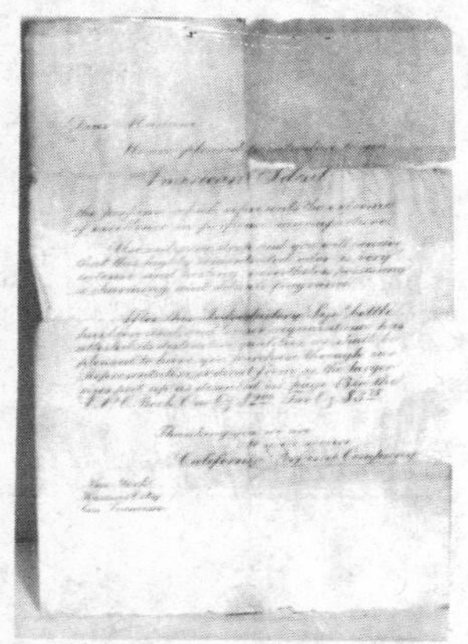

1914 AMERICAN IDEAL INTRODUCTION LETTER
Given to customers on trial size bottle of perfume. C.M.V. $20.00

1925 AMERICAN IDEAL PERFUME
1 oz. bottle with wide flat glass stopper. Green neck ribbon & gold & green label. O.S.P. $2.40 C.M.V. $150.00 M.B. $125.00 B.O. mint.

1911 AMERICAN IDEAL PERFUME
1 & 2 oz. size bottles, glass stopper Ladies face on paper label in green box. O.S.P. $2.50 & $4.75. C.M.V. in box $150.00. Bottle only $125.00 mint ea.

1911 AMERICAN IDEAL PERFUMES
Introductory size glass stoppered bottle with green neck ribbon & pink paper label with ladies face, in green box. O.S.P. 60¢ C.M.V. in box $150.00. Bottle only $100.00 mint.

1910 AMERICAN IDEAL PERFUME
Wood case with dark velvet lining holds 1 oz. glass stoppered bottle with gold label with ladies face. Neck ribbon matches inside of box. O.S.P. $2.00. C.M.V. $200.00 in box, bottle only $150.00 mint.

1917 AMERICAN IDEAL PERFUME INTRODUCTORY SIZE
Glass stopper in wood box, gold label with picture of lady on label. O.S.P. 75c, CMV bottle only $100.00
Bottle in wood box $225.00 mint.
1913 Only - AMERICAN IDEAL PERFUME (Right) - Introductory size octaginal shaped glass stoppered bottle fits in wood box with screw on wood lid, paper label with ladies face. O.S.P. 75¢ C.M.V. bottle only $100. mint. In wood box $225. Both came with neck ribbons.

1925 AMERICAN IDEAL TOILET SOAP
Green box holds 2 bars. O.S.P. 96¢ C.M.V. $60.00 M.B.

1917 AMERICAN IDEAL PERFUME
Glass stoppered bottle came in green box. 1 & 2 oz. size, gold neck & front label. Green neck ribbon. O.S.P. $2.50 & $4.75. C.M.V. $175.00 in box, $135.00 bottle only.
1917 AMERICAN IDEAL PERFUME
½ oz. Glass stoppered bottle, green box, gold label on front & neck. Green neck ribbon. O.S.P. 75¢ C.M.V. in box $125.00. Bottle only $100.00 mint.

941 Only - AMERICAN IDEAL PERFUME
dram glass stopper, paper neck tag. Name was
ıanged to Apple Blossom in 1941. O.S.P. $2.25
.M.V. bottle only $115.00. In box $140.00

923 AMERICAN IDEAL POWDER
ACHET - Glass bottle, brass cap, green
ıbel. OSP $1.20, CMV $95.00 BO,
ıint, $115.00 MB

1911 AMERICAN IDEAL TOILET SOAP
Pink & gold metal can holds 1 bar of soap wrapped in same design as can. OSP 50c CMV can only $60.00, with wrapped soap $85.00 mint.

1911 AMERICAN IDEAL POWDER SACHET
Large size sachet bottle with brass cap & lady on paper label. OSP $1.00, CMV $90.00 BO mint, $110.00 MB

1930-33 AMERICAN IDEAL PERFUME
1 oz. clear glass bottle with frosted glass stopper. In silver box. Label on top of bottle. OSP $2.40 CMV $130.00 MB, $100.00 BO

1928 AMERICAN IDEAL PERFUME
Flaconette size embossed bottle with brass cap over long dabber glass stopper. OSP $1.10 CMV $90.00 BO, $110.00 MB

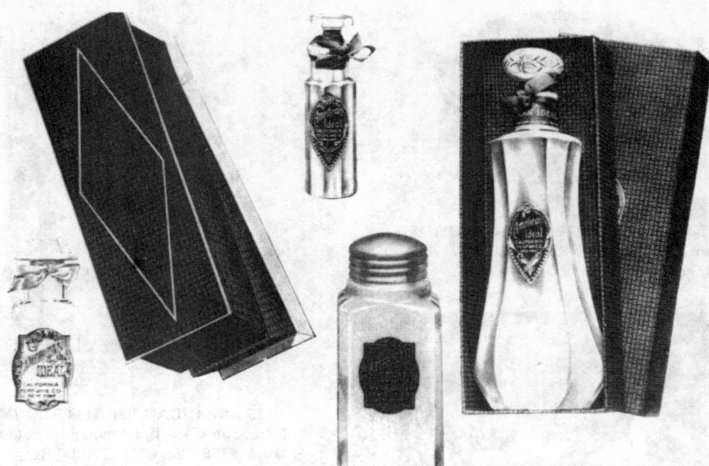

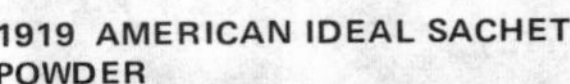

Left to Right - 1919 AMERICAN IDEAL PERFUME - 1 & 2 oz. glass bottle with glass stopper, green & gold label, green box, green neck ribbon. O.S.P. $2.40 & $4.65 C.M.V. $150.00 in box, bottle only $125.00

1923 AMERICAN IDEAL PERFUME
Introductory size bottle. Glass bottle & stopper. Green label & neck ribbon. O.S.P. 75¢ C.M.V. in green box $125.00 Bottle only $100.00 mint. Also came with octaginal glass stopper set in cork with long glass dabber. Same C.M.V.

1919 AMERICAN IDEAL SACHET POWDER
Glass bottle with brass cap, green label. OSP $1.20 CMV $90.00 BO, $110.00 MB

1923 AMERICAN IDEAL TOILET WATER
2 & 4 oz. glass stoppered bottle with green front & neck label & neck ribbon. Green box. OSP $1.50 & $2.85, CMV $130.00 MB, $105.00 BO mint.

1920 AMERICAN IDEAL TOILET SOAP
White box, green label. O.S.P. 48¢ CMV $55.00 MB

1920 AMERICAN IDEAL COMPACT
Contains face powder or rouge. Brass container with mirror on lid. O.S.P. 59¢ CMV in box $40.00, compact only $25.00 mint.

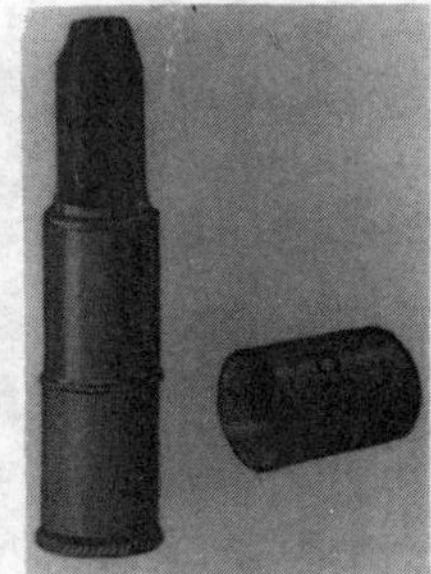

1929 AMERICAN IDEAL LIPSTICK
CPC on green metal tube. O.S.P. $1.00 CMV $10.00 tube only, $20.00 MB

1911 AMERICAN IDEAL TALCUM
Pink can with gold top. O.S.P. 35¢ C.M.V. $75.00. $90.00 M.B.

1915 AMERICAN IDEAL FACE POWDER
Green & gold box. O.S.P. 75¢ C.M.V. $50.00 M.B. Powder box only $35.00 mint.

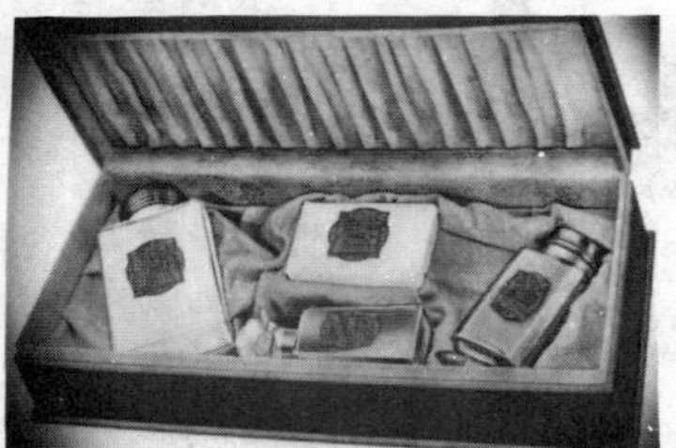

1919 AMERICAN IDEAL SET
Green silk lined box holds 1 oz. glass stoppered American Ideal Perfume, Powder Sachet, bottle of Talcum Powder & Toilet Soap. All have green labels. O.S.P. set $5.50 C.M.V. $350.00 M.B.

1917 AMERICAN IDEAL TALCUM POWDER
3½ oz. glass jar, gold metal lid & gold label. OSP 75c, CMV $90.00 BO, mint $110.00 MB.

1911 AMERICAN IDEAL BOX C SET
Flip top box holds glass stoppered perfume & powder sachet. O.S.P. 50¢ C.MV. $250.00 M.B.

1923 AMERICAN IDEAL TALCUM
3½ oz. glass jar, brass cap, gold & green label. OSP 72c, CMV $90.00 BO mint $110.00 MB.

1923 AMERICAN IDEAL SOAP
One bar toilet soap in white paper with gold label. OSP 48c, CMV $50.00 mint.

1923 AMERICAN IDEAL FACE POWDER
Green & gold box with green & gold label. O.S.P. 96¢ C.M.V. $40.00 in box. $35.00 powder box only mint.

1929 AMERICAN IDEAL TALCUM
Frosted glass bottle with brass lid, gold & green label. O.S.P. 75¢ C.M.V. $75.00 M.B. $70.00 bottle only mint.

1925 AMERICAN IDEAL FACE POWDER
Green & gold box. O.S.P. 96¢ C.M.V. $35.00 mint.

1923 AMERICAN IDEAL CREAM DELUXE
White glass jar with CPC on metal lid. Gold & green label. OSP 96c CMV $50.00 in box. $40.00 jar only mint.

1929 AMERICAN IDEAL PERFUME
1 oz. glass stoppered bottle in green satin lined box. Paper label on top of bottle. OSP $2.40, CMV $130.00 MB. $100.00 BO mint.

1911 AMERICAN IDEAL SET
Large fancy box with green lining holds American Ideal Talcum Powder, Powder Sachet, 1 oz. glass stoppered perfume & bar of toilet soap in pink soap can. O.S.P. $4.00 C.M.V. $400.00 mint.

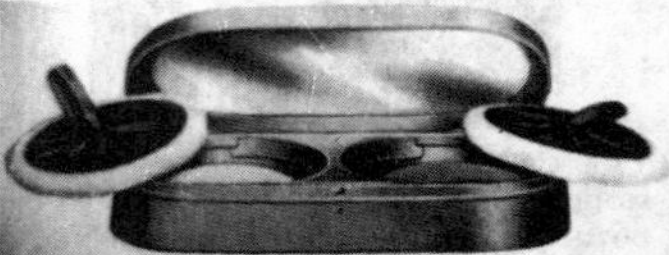

1921 AMERICAN IDEAL DOUBLE COMPACT - Contains face powder & rouge. Made of solid brass. O.S.P. $1.17 CMV in box $50.00. Compact only $35.00 mint.

3 AMERICAN IDEAL THREESOME
en box contains 2 oz. Toilet Water, bottle achet & glass bottle of Talc. Green & gold l. O.S.P. $3.95 C.M.V. $300.00 M.B.

925 AMERICAN IDEAL FOURSOME ET - Green box holds 1 oz. bottle with glass topper of perfume, glass bottle of talcum, reen box of face powder & white jar of anishing cream. O.S.P. $6.50 C.M.V. 325.00 M.B.

RIGHT – 1930 ARIEL PERFUME
1 oz. glass stoppered bottle with small silver label. Silver box. CMV $105.00 BO, $135.00 MB, OSP $2.50.
LEFT – 1930 ARIEL PERFUME FALCONETTE
Brass cap over glass stoppered embossed bottle. OSP 84c, CMV $85.00, BO, mint $105.00 MB.

1930-35 ARIEL TOILET WATER
2 oz. glass stoppered bottle, small label on top of bottle. Came in silver & blue box. O.S.P. $1.75 C.M.V. $100.00 bottle only $130.00 MB.

ARIEL

1930 ARIEL PERFUME
1 oz. glass stoppered bottle, large silver & blue label. Came in silver box. O.S.P. $2.50 CMV $105.00 BO, mint. $135.00 MB.

1933-37 ARIEL BATH SALTS SAMPLE
Small ribbed glass bottle with dark blue or black octaginal shaped cap. Silver label. C.M.V. $60.00 mint.

LEFT 1933-36 ARIEL PERFUM "RIBBED"
½ oz. ribbed glass bottle with black octaginal cap and gold label. Came in gold box set. C.M.V. $45.00 mint.
RIGHT 1933-36 ARIEL PERFUME
Small six sided octagonal shapped bottle with black octagonal cap. Came in Little Folks set and Handkerchief set. Has silver label. C.M.V. $45.00 mint.

1929-30 ARIEL BATH SALTS
10 oz. clear glass with chrome cap, silver and blue label. CMV $60.00 mint.

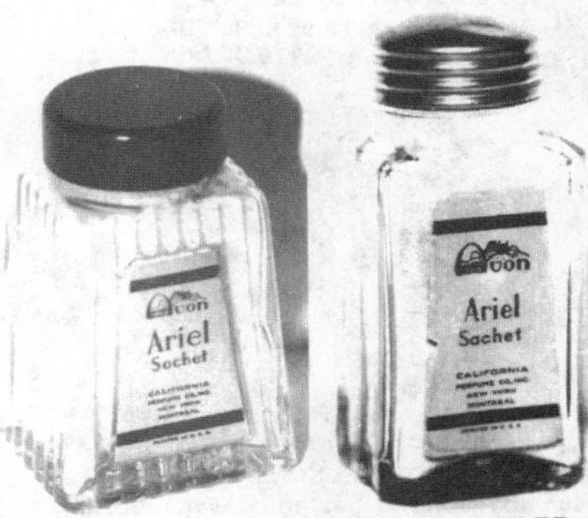

LEFT – 1934-36 ARIEL POWDER SACHET
1¼ oz. ribbed glass. Dark blue cap, OSP 78c, CMV $28.00, $33.00 MB.
RIGHT – 1930-34 ARIEL SACHET
Metal cap, silver and blue label. OSP 78c, CMV $60.00 mint, $70.00 MB

1931-33 ARIEL SET NO. 2
Silver & blue box holds silver & blue fan compact & silver box of Ariel face powder. O.S.P. $2.50 C.M.V. $60.00 MB.

1932-33 ARIEL THREESOME
Blue & silver compact, blue & silver Avon face powder & Ariel Flaconette with brass cap. In silver & blue box. OSP $3.12, CMV $115.00 MB.

DAPHNE

1920 DAPHNE POWDER SACHET
Brass cap & gold label. O.S.P. 96¢
CMV $90.00 mint, $110.00 MB.

1923 DAPHNE THREESOME
Green box contains 2 oz. toilet water, bottle of sachet & can of talc. O.S.P. $3.20 C.M.V. $250.00 M.B.

1925 DAPHNE PERFUME
1 and 2 oz. glass bottle with flat glass stopper. Bottle and top of stopper have embossed flowers. Came in green and gold box, gold label and green neck ribbons. OSP $1.35 and $3.45, CMV bottle only $125.00, $150.00 MB

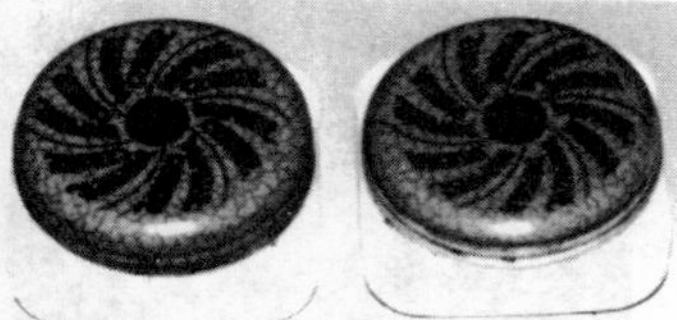

1925 DAPHNE DERMA CREAM
White glass jar ½" thick green lid. Came in Septette Gift box. C.M.V. $40.00 mint.

1925 DAPHNE CERATE
½" thick white glass jar, green lid. Came in Septette gift box. C.M.V. $40.00 mint.

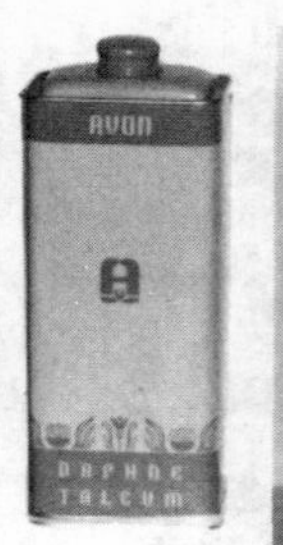

1936-43 then 1946-50 DAPHNE TALCUM
2.75 oz. turquoise & white can, turquoise cap. O.S.P. 37¢ C.M.V. $12.00. M.B. $15.00

1936-43 then 1946-50 DAPHNE TALCUM
14.5 Turquoise and white can, turquoise cap. O.S.P. $1.19 C.M.V. $20.00 M.B. $25.00.

FROM THE ONSTOT COLLECTION

1922 DAPHNE POWDER SACHET
Brass cap, green and gold square label. OSP 96c, CMV $90.00 BO mint, $110.00 MB.

1925-30 DAPHNE PERFUME
Clear glass, brass cap, box is brown, yellow & green. Came in Jack & Jill Jungle Jinks Set. CMV $70.00 MB.

1940 ONLY DAPHNE TALC MAY POLE BOX
Yellow box with dancing girls around May Pole holds regular issue 2.75 oz. Daphne Talc can. Sold in May 1940 for 10¢ with regular order from Avon lady. C.M.V. $30.00 M.B. as shown.

1916 DAPHNE PERFUME
1 & 2 oz. bottles shown with frosted glass stoppers. Also came in ½ oz. size. Each ca in green box. O.S.P. $1.00, $1.90 & $3.50 C.M.V. $125.00 in box. $100.00 bottle only.

1925 DAPHNE GLYCERINE SOAP
Green box & wrapping with gold labels. Two bars of soap. O.S.P. 72¢ C.M.V. $60.00 M.B.

1923 DAPHNE TOILET WATER
Green box holds 2 or 4 oz. size bottle with frosted glass stopper, gold front & neck label green neck ribbon. O.S P. $1.20 & $2.25 C.M.V. $100.00 bottle only. $125.00 M.B. Came with 2 different glass stoppers set in cork as pictured.

1918 DAPHNE SET
Green box holds Daphne Perfume in 1 oz. glass stoppered bottle, green box of Daphne Face Powder & green box of Daphne rouge. OSP $3.50 CMV, $200.00 MB.

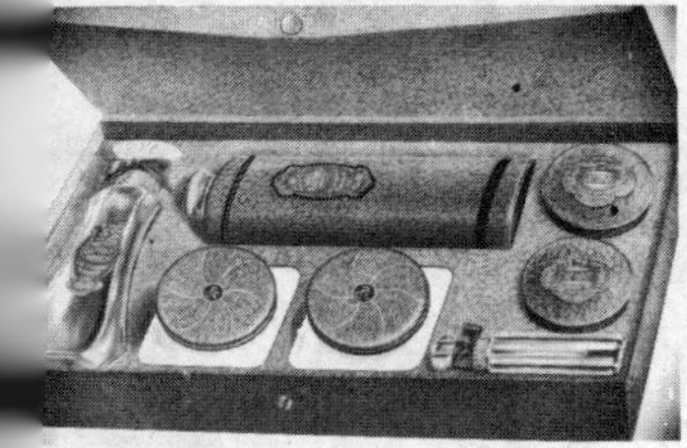

25 DAPHNE SEPTETTE GIFT BOX
een box holds jar of Derma Cream, jar of rate, green box of face powder, rouge mpact, can of talcum, 1 oz. bottle of let water & falconette of perfume. All in phne fragrance. O.S.P. $2.95 C.M.V. 00.00 M.B.

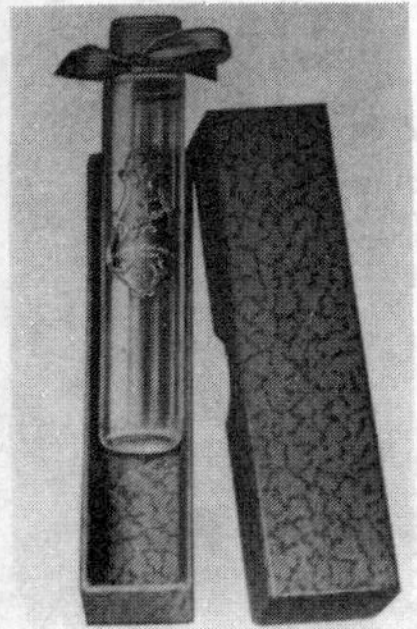

22 DAPHNE PERFUME
oz. vial given to customers for each .00 order in March 1922. C.M.V. in x $130.00 MB, $105.00 BO mint.

931-36 DAPHNE TALCUM
ilver and blue can with blue cap. OSP 35c, MV $25.00, $30.00 MB. Same can in old color. CMV $35.00. Silver and blue an in large 1 ob. family size, OSP $1.00 MV $30.00 can only. $40.00 MB.

1917 DAPHNE FACE POWDER VANITY COMPACT
Green box, came in white, pink and brunette tints, OSP 75c, CMV $40.00 MB. Same box also came in Daphne Rouge. Same CMV, $30.00 compact only mint.

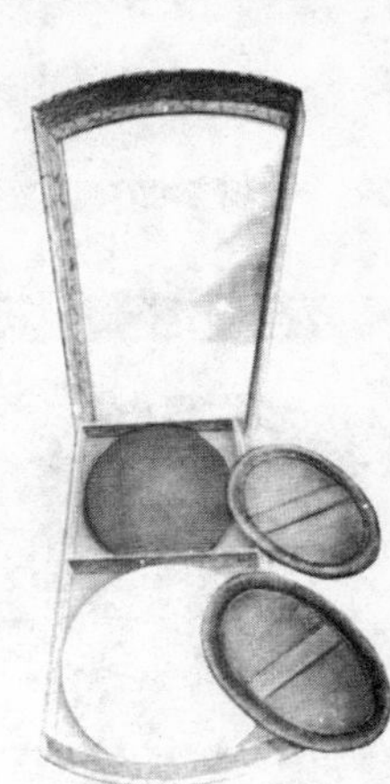

1938 Only - DAPHNE TALC 52nd ANNIVERSARY - Turquoise & white can in special box sold for 10¢ during 52nd anniversary campaign. CMV $30.00 in box shown.

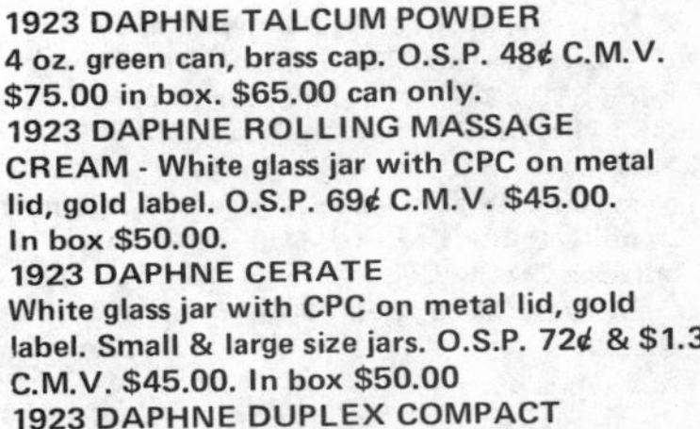

1923 DAPHNE TALCUM POWDER
4 oz. green can, brass cap. O.S.P. 48¢ C.M.V. $75.00 in box. $65.00 can only.
1923 DAPHNE ROLLING MASSAGE CREAM - White glass jar with CPC on metal lid, gold label. O.S.P. 69¢ C.M.V. $45.00. In box $50.00.
1923 DAPHNE CERATE
White glass jar with CPC on metal lid, gold label. Small & large size jars. O.S.P. 72¢ & $1.35. C.M.V. $45.00. In box $50.00
1923 DAPHNE DUPLEX COMPACT
Green compact & puffs, mirror on lid. O.S.P. 98¢ CMV $35.00, $45.00 MB.

1926 DAPHNE CERATE
½'' thick white glass jar, solid green lid says Daphne CPC Cerate on top. Also came in Daphne Derma Cream. Came in Septette gift box set. C.M.V. $35.00 ea. mint.

1929 DAPHNE CREAMS
Square white glass jars with ribbed sides & CPC on aluminum lids & gold labels. Came in Daphne Cerate, Daphne Derma Cream & Daphne Rolling Massage Cream. O.S.P. 75¢ C.M.V. $45.00 ea. in box. $40.00 jar only.
1925 DAPHNE BATH SALTS
Ribbed glass jar with brass lid, gold label. O.S.P. 98¢ C.M.V. $75.00 in box. $65.00 jar only.

1937 Only - 51st ANNIVERSARY DAPHNE TALCUM - Special box was given to Avon customers with any purchase. C.M.V. in box $30.00

1925 DAPHNE LIPSTICK & EYEBROW PENCIL
2 1/8 metal lipstick has embossed name & CPC on side. O.S.P. 39¢ C.M.V. $15.00 mint. $20.00 M.B. Gold Eyebrow pencil OSP 29c, CMV $15.00 mint, $20.00 MB
1925 DAPHNE CREAMS - Large & small size glass jars with gold labels & green lids. Came in Daphne Derma Cream & Daphne Rolling Massage Cream. Came in large size jars only. O.S.P. 72¢ C.M.V. $50.00 ea. in box. $45.00 jar only.

LEFT 1933-36 DAPHNE TALCUM
Metal can came in sets only. C.M.V. $35.00 mint.
RIGHT 1943-46 DAPHNE TALCUM
Turquoise & white paper box. Family size. O.S.P. $1.19 C.M.V. $30.00 M.B.

1940-41 DAPHNE TALCUM CHRISTMAS PACKAGE
Outer sleeve fits over short issue blue Christmas box with white Christmas tre Holds large size 14.5 oz. metal talc turquoise and white can of Daphne Talcum. Can only sold 1936-50.
OSP 89c, CMV $40.00 MB as shown.

1943 DAPHNE TALCUM CHRISTMAS BOX
Pale blue and pink outer box issued only at Christmas 1943 with cardboard large size talc. OSP 98c, CMV $40.00 MB. as shown. Talc only $30.00 mint.

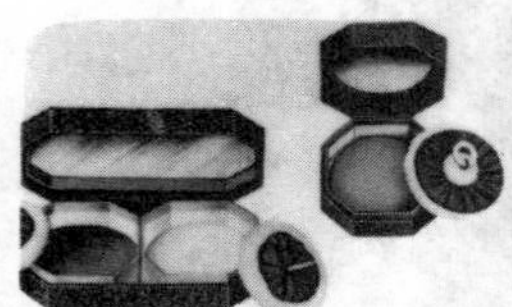

1917 DAPHNE DOUBLE VANITY COMPA
Contained face powder & rouge. Green com with mirror on lid. OSP $1.00, CMV $45.00, $35.00 compact only mint.
1917 DAPHNE VANITY COMPACT
Face powder, came in white, pink & brunet Green compact with mirror on lid. O.S.P. 5 CMV $40.00 MB, $30.00 compact only mint.

1944-46 DAPHNE TALCUM
Turquoise and white paper container. Plastic cap. O.S.P. 39¢ C.M.V. $20.00 mint.

DAPHNE TALCUM
Silver can in 2 special boxes. 49 Year box on left 1935 & 50th Year box on right 1936. O.S.P. 20¢ C.M.V. mint & boxed only in either box $50.00 each. Also came in gold can in 50th year box. CMV $60.00 MB.

MISSION GARDEN

FROM THE ONSTOT COLLECTION
1922-25 MISSION GARDEN PERFUME
1½ oz. bohemian glass bottle with frosted sides & frosted glass stopper. Satin lined tan box. O.S.P. $4.95 C.M.V. $200.00 in box. $150.00 bottle only mint.

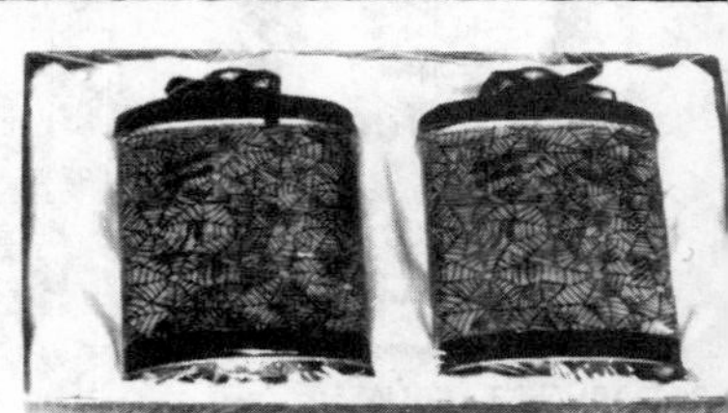

FROM THE ONSTOT COLLECTION
1923 MISSION GARDEN TALC SET
2 cans of Mission Garden Talc was a gift set to CPC employees. Red and gold silk lines box. CMV $200.00 MB.

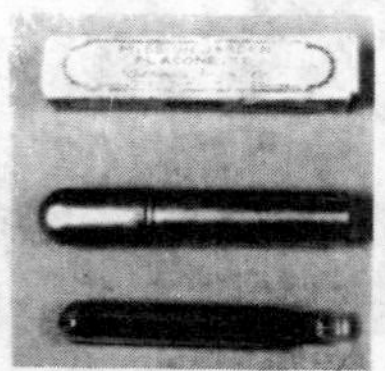

1922 MISSION GARDEN FLACONET
Glass tube of perfume in brass case. OS 98c, CMV $85.00 in box. Tube in case only $70.00.

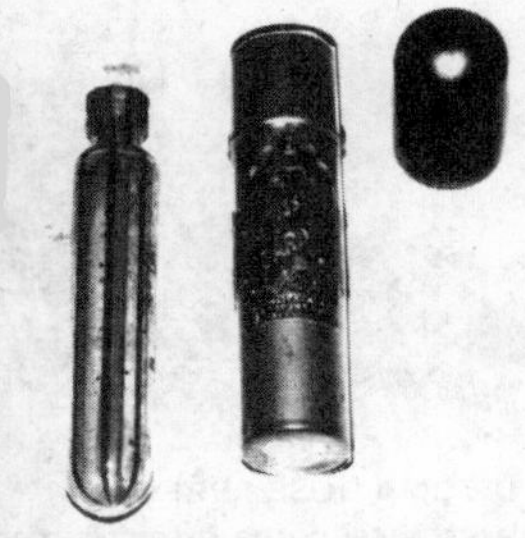

2 MISSION GARDEN FLACONETTE
ss tubes and cap with gold lavel on the
e. Holds clear glass vial with blue stripes
steel cap, glass stopper. OSP 98c,
V $85.00 mint as shown.

1922 MISSION GARDEN SACHET POWDER
Glass bottle with brass cap & gold label. O.S.P. $1.75 CMV $90.00 BO mint $110.00 MB.

1925 MISSION GARDEN THREESOME
Satin lined gold box holds 1 oz. Mission Garden Perfume, Talc & gold compact. OSP $7.00, CMV $265.00 MB.

25 MISSION GARDEN TALC
oz. red & gold can, brass cap. Came in
ssion Garden Threesome Set only.
M.V. $75.00 mint.

1925 MISSION GARDEN PERFUME
Flaconette size, gold box, embossed glass bottle with glass stopper. Brass cap over stopper. OSP $1.20, CMV $95.00 BO. $115.00 MB.

1925 MISSION GARDEN PERFUME
1 oz. glass bottle, flat embossed glass stopper. Satin lined gold box. OSP $2.85, CMV $110.00 BO $140.00 MB. Also came in 2 oz. size, $150.00 MB.

1925 MISSION GARDEN COMPACT
Mission Garden CPC on edge of compact. Embossed brass case in single or double compact. O.S.P. 98¢ & $1.48 C.M.V. $45.00 each in box, $30.00 compact only.

1922 MISSION GARDEN TOILET WATER - 2 & 4 oz. glass bottle with frosted glass stopper. Gold label on front & neck. O.S.P. $2.25 & $4.35. C.M.V. bottle only $125.00. In box $150.00

1922 MISSION GARDEN DOUBLE COMPACT - Contains face powder & rouge. Made of solid brass. O.S.P. $1.45 CMV $35.00, $45.00 MB.

NARCISSUS

1929-30 NARCISSUS PERFUME
1 oz. glass stoppered bottle. Came in silver, blue & gold box. Blue label on top of bottle. OSP $2.20 CMV $100.00 bottle only. $150.00 in box.

1931-34 NARCISSUS PERFUME
1 oz. glass stoppered bottle came in silver & blue box, label on top of bottle. Same as 1929 perfume only box is changed. O.S.P. $2.25 C.M.V. $100. bottle only. $135. in box.

1925 NARCISSUS PERFUME FLACONET FLACONETTE
Embossed bottle with glass stopper with long glass dobber under brass cap. O.S.P. .84¢ CMV $95.00 BO mint $115.00 MB.

1925 NARCISSUS PERFUME
1 oz. glass bottle with frosted embossed glass stopper. Bottle in blue & gold box, blue label & neck ribbon. O.S.P. $2.19 CMV $110.00 BO mint bottle in box $150.00.

1915 NATOMA ROSE PERFUME
1 oz, glass stopper bottle, green front and neck label. Green neck ribbon in green felt box. OSP 40c, CMV $105.00 BO mint, $130.00 MB.

NATOMA

1913 NATOMA ROSE ART OF MASSAGE BOOKLET
10 page booklet on giving a massage with Natoma Massage Cream. CMV $12.00

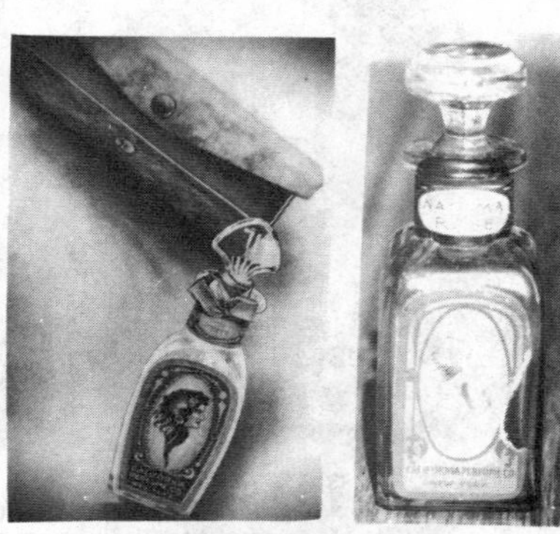

1916 NATOMA ROSE PERFUME
½ oz. glass stoppered bottle, green ribbon on neck, green neck & front label. Green box. OSP 40c, CMV $105.00 BO mint, $130.00 MB.

1914-21 NATOMA ROSE PERFUME
1 oz. clear glass, glass stopper, green label. O.S.P. $1.40 C.M.V. $150.00 M.B. $125.00 B.O. Mint.

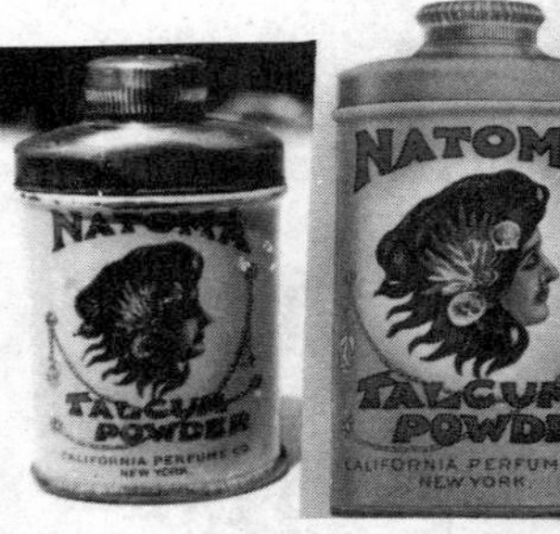

1915 NATOMA TALCUM POWDER
2" tall. Brass top. Came in 1915 Juvenile Set only. C.M.V. $150.00 Also came 3½ regular size. O.S.P. 33¢ C.M.V. $100.00 M

1914 NATOMA TALCUM POWDER
3½ oz. metal can. Brass cap. Label a cap a little different from 1915.issue. OSP 25c, CMV $125.00 MB as showr Can only mint, $100.00.

1915 NATOMA ROSE PERFUME
1 oz. bottle, glass stopper, front and neck label. OSP 60c, CMV $105.00 BO mint, $130.00 MB.

1914-21 NATOMA ROSE TALCUM
4 oz. green can with pink roses, brass cap. 3 different. 1 has green sifter cap, one brass cap and one has flowers painted on top of can and brass cap. CMV flower top can $85.00, $100.00 MB. OSP 25c, CMV $75.00 $75.00, mint $90.00 MB.

1914-17 NATOMA ROLLING MASSAGE CREAM
Glass stoppered jar with front & neck labe O.S.P. 50¢ C.M.V. $150.00 Mint $175.00

TRAILING ARBUTUS

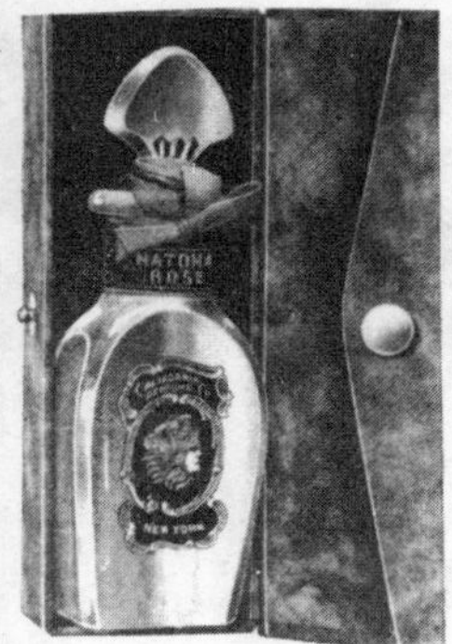

14-15 NATOMA ROSE PERFUME
oz. glass stoppered bottle with front & ck label. Green ribbon, green snap shut x. O.S.P. 40¢ C.M.V. $150. in box, bottle ly $125.00.

914-21 NATOMA ROSE PERFUME
Green box, holds 1, 2 or 4 oz. size glass stoppered bottle with green front & neck label with green neck ribbon. O.S.P. $1.40, $2.75 & $5.25. CMV $175.00 in box, $150.00 bottle only.

1918-21 NATOMA ROLLING MASSAGE CREAM
Metal screw on lid, green paper label. O.S.P. 75¢ C.M.V. $100.00, $125.00 M.B.

1928-29 TRAILING ARBUTUS PERFUME
Came in 1 & 2 oz. glass stoppered bottle with blue label. Blue box. O.S.P. $1.20 & $2.10 C.M.V. in box $150. Bottle only $115. mint.

1915 TRAILING ARBUTUS PERFUME
Fancy embossed box holds glass stoppered bottle with front & neck label. Came in 1, 2 & 4 oz. size. O.S.P. $1.10, $2.10 & $4.00 C.M.V. $175. M.B. $125. B.O. Mint.

1914 TRAILING ARBUTUS TALCUM POWDER
4 oz. blue can. 1914-17 can had brass sifter cap with grooved edge. CMV $85.00 in box $70.00 can only. 1917-29 can came with removable brass cap. OSP 33c, CMV $75.00 in box, $60.00 can only. Both came with 'The Story of Italian Talc' in box. 2 different labels on can.

1925 TRAILING ARBUTUS BATH POWDER
1 lb. size ble can with brass cap. OSP 89c CMV $80.00 in box, $70.00 can only mint

1940-42 TRAILING ARBUTUS PERFUME
3/8 oz. bottle, gold octaginal cap. Gold speckled box. O.S.P. $1.50 C.M.V. $60.00 B.O. mint, $80.00 M.B.

1930 TRAILING ARBUTUS PERFUME
½ oz. bottle with frosted glass stopper, silver label. CMV $95.00 mint.

1941-45 TRAILING ARBUTUS PERFUME
1/8 oz. bottle, white paper label, brass cap. O.S.P. $1.00 C.M.V. $35.00 B.O. Mint $40.00 M.B.

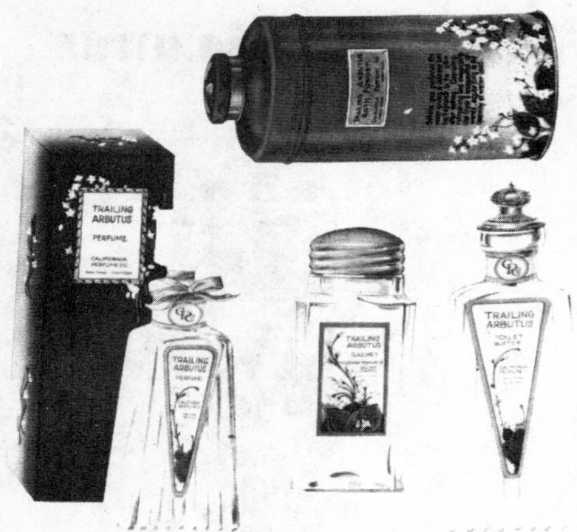

1925 TRAILING ARBUTUS PERFUME
1 and 2 oz. sizes. Ribbed bottle with glass stopper. Came in blue box. Front and neck label. OSP $1.17, and $2.10. CMV $115.00 BO, $140.00 MB.

1925 TRAILING ARBUTUS POWDER SACHET
Brass cap and blue label. OSP 72c, CMV $90.00 BO mint, $100.00 MB.

1925 TRAILING ARBUTUS TOILET WATER
2 and 4 oz. sizes. Ribbed bottle with metal and cork cap. OSP 59c, and $1.08, CMV $80.00 BO, $100.00 MB.

1925-29 TRAILING ARBUTUS BATH POWDER
4¾ oz. blue can and cap. OSP 35c, CMV $75.00 in box. $60.00 can only mint.

1925 TRAILING ARBUTUS BATH POWDER
1 lb. size blue can with brass cap. OSP 89c, 2 different labels on front and top of can. CMV $80.00 inbox, $70.00 can only mint.

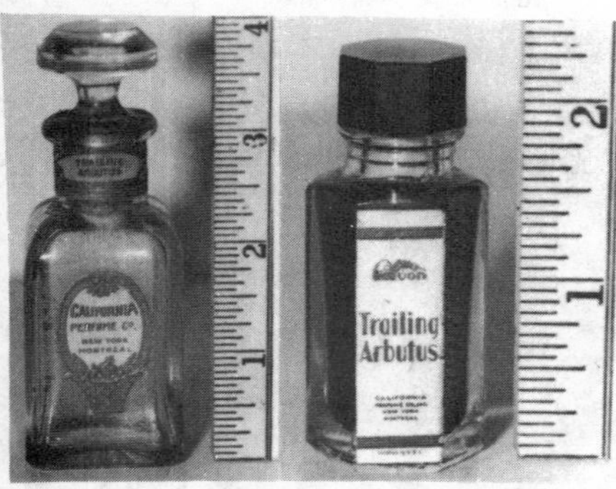

LEFT 1923 TRAILING ARBUTUS PERFUME
2 oz. glass stoppered bottle. Basket design front label and neck label. O.S.P. $2.10, C.M.V. $125.00 B.O. mint, $150.00 M.B.

RIGHT 1933-36 TRAILING ARBUTUS PERFUME
Small 6 sided octagonal bottle and black cap came in Little Folks Set and Handkerchief set. Silver label, came with CPC or CPC Avon Products, Inc. division label. CMV $45.00 mint.

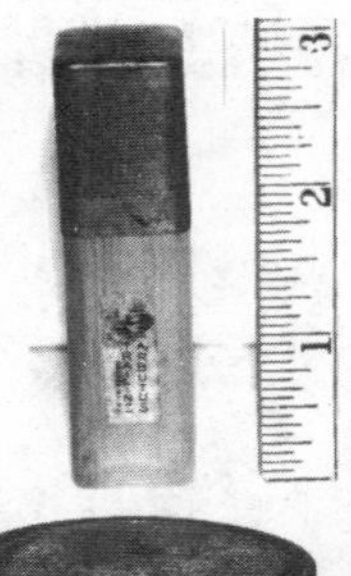

1925 TRAILING ARBUTUS PERFUME FLACON
Frosted ribbed glass with long glass stopper under CPC embossed brass cap. Front paper label. OSP 59c, CMV $90.00 mint with brass cap and label, $110.00 MB.

1918 TRAILING ARBUTUS TALCUM REFILL CAN
1 lb metal can with brass finish. Front paper label. CMV $75.00 mint in new condition.

1920 TRAILING ARBUTUS TALCUM POWDER
16 oz. Blue can, brass cap. O.S.P. 89¢ C.M.V. $80 in box. $70 can only mint.

1925 TRAILING ARBUTUS VEGETABLE OIL SOAP
Blue box holds 3 embossed soap bars. OSP 39c, CMV $75.00 MB.

1925-30 TRAILING ARBUTUS COLD CREAM CAN
Came in Jack & Jill Jungle Set, gold can with blue & pink lid. Box is brown, yellow and green. Also came in plain brown CPC box. CMV $40.00 MB.

1914 TRAILING ARBUTUS TALCUM POWDER SAMPLE
Small bue sample can, gold cap. Front box in English and back side in French. CMV $85.00 mint, $105.00 MB.

1925 TRAILING ARBUTUS CREAMS
Large and small white glass jars of Cold Cream and Vanishing Cream. CPC on blue or plain aluminum metal lids. OSP 33c and 59c, CMV in box $55.00 ea Jar only $45.00 mint.

1925 TRAILING ARBUTUS COLD CRE TUBE
Large and small size. Blue tubes. OSP 23 and 45c, CMV in box $25.00. Tube only $20.00 mint.

)33-34 TRAILING ARBUTUS TOILET ATER
oz. ribbed glass, black cap. Silver label. .S.P. 75¢, C.M.V. $50.00 B.O. mint. 60.00 M.B.

1915 TRAILING ARBUTUS TOILET WATER
2 oz. clear glass bottle with blue & gold front & neck label. Metal crown stopper set in cork. OSP 35c, CMV $125.00 BO mint.

1928-29 TRAILING ARBUTUS SEXTETTE GIFT BOX
Blue box holds 2 bars Vegetable Oil Soap, Cold Cream jar & Vanishing Cream jar, box of Face Powder & can of Talcum Powder. All are trimmed in blue & have Trailing Arbutus labels. OSP $1.60, CMV $250.00 MB

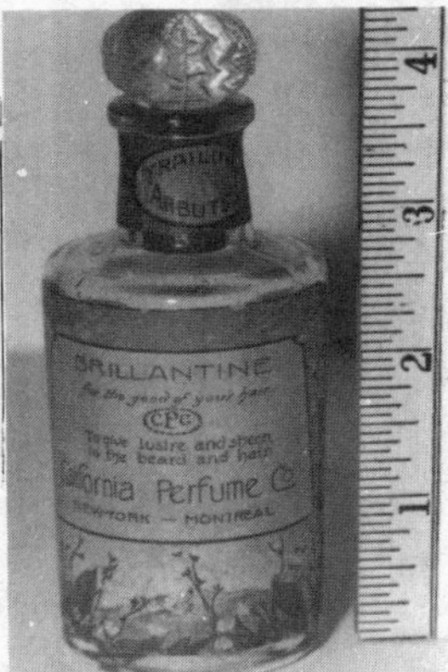

1928-29 TRAILING ARBUTUS CREAMS
Large & small round white glass jars with CPC on blue lids. Came in cold cream & vanishing cream. O.S.P. 33¢ & 59¢ C.M.V. in box $55.00. Jar only $45.00 each.

1923 BRILLANTINE
A hair dressing with Trailing Arbutus perfume scent. Glass bottle with frosted glass stopper. Blue front & neck label. O.S.P. 39¢ CMV $105.00 BO mint, $130.00 MB.

1915 TRAILING ARBUTUS SACHET
Brass cap, flowered label, clear glass, 2 different labels. OSP 60c, CMV $90.00 BO mint each, $110.00 MB.

1915 TRAILING ARBUTUS GIFT BOX
Red, green & pink box contains Trailing Arbutus talcum can, powder sachet & 4 oz. toilet water. O.S.P. $1.25 C.M.V. $275.

1925 TRAILING ARBUTUS SEXTETTE SET
Large blue box holds white glass jar of Trailing Arbutus Cold Cream & Vanishing Cream. Both have blue lids. Blue can of Talcum Powder, blue box of Face Powder & 2 bars of Vegetable Oil Soap. O.S.P. $1.59 CMV $250.00 MB.

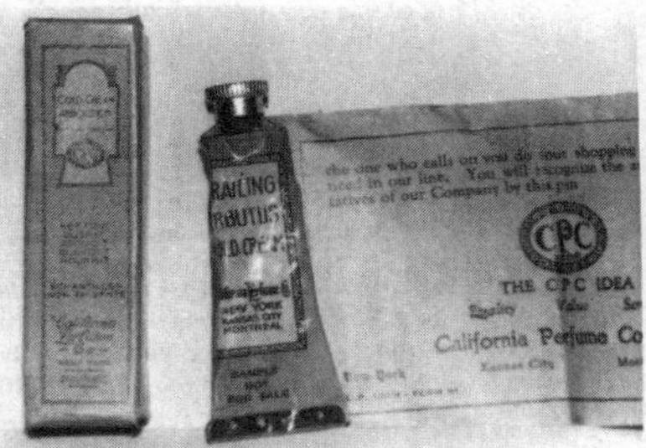

1925 TRAILING ARBUTUS COLD CREAM SAMPLE
Small sample tube in box marked sample. Came with CPC instruction sheet. C.M.V. $60.00 M.B. $50.00 tube only mint.

1925 TRAILING ARBUTUS SEXTETTE BOX
Box only showing label in center of box. C.M.V. box only $20.00 mint.

1925 TRAILING ARBUTUS FACE POWDER
Blue box. OSP 33c, CMV $40.00 MB, $30.00 powder box only, mint.

1928-29 TRAILING ARBUTUS ROUGE
Blue box. O.S.P. 40¢ C.M.V. $25. in box. Rouge only $20 mint.

1928-29 TRAILING ARBUTUS FACE POWDER
Blue & pink box. O.S.P. 35¢ C.M.V. $35. in box. $25 powder box only mint.

1923 TRAILING ARBUTUS THREESOME
Blue box contains 2 oz. bottle of toilet water, 4 oz. can of talcum & bottle of sachet powder. O.S.P. $1.85 C.MV. $250 M.B.

1927 VERNAFLEUR BATH SALTS
Clear glass, brass cap. Sent to Representatives to give to each customer that orders $2.00 worth of merchandise. Representative must attain $45.00 in customer sales on January 1927 order. Offer expired Jan. 31, 1927. (Not a Sample) Rare. CMV $150.00 mint. $175.00 MB as shown with paper.

1933 ATOMIZER GIFT SET
Blue box with green & red holly leaves holds 1 oz. bottle of Vernafleur perfume & 1 oz. red glass bottle with spray atomizer. OSP $2.86, CMV $175.00 MB

VERNAFLEUR

ALL CPC'S MUST BE NEW MINT CONDITION FOR CMV

1928 ATOMIZER PERFUME
2 oz., 5¾" tall. Green frosted bottle with gold plated top. Came in Vernafleur Perfume. Is not marked Avon or C.P.C. OSP $2.50, CMV $80.00 BO mint, $100.00 MB.

1928 VERNAFLEUR PERFUME
1 oz. ribbed clear glass bottle, frosted glass stopper, front label, neck ribbon. O.S.P. $1.17 CMV $105.00 BO mint, $130.00 MB.

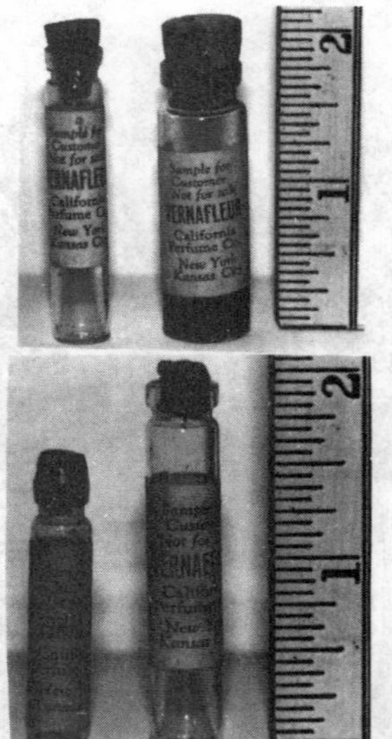

1946 VERNAFLEUR BATH SALTS
9 oz. jar, turquoise lid. Short issue. Special blue & white label. O.S.P. 63¢ C.M.V. $40. $55.00 MB. See Bath Salts Misc. section for regular issue.

1925 VERNAFLEUR NUTRI-CREME SAMPLE
Multi-colored tube, says on back side "Not for Sale Sample". C.M.V. $40.00 in box, $30.00 tube.

1925 VERNAFLEUR FACE POWDER SAMPLE
1½" small paper box used as sample. C.M.V. $35.00 mint

1931-33 VERNAFLEUR PERFUME
1 oz. bottle with plastic sealed cork stopper, silver and blue label. Silver box. CMV $70.00 BO mint, $100.00 MB.

FROM THE ONSTOT COLLECTION
1923 VERNAFLEUR SAMPLES
3 different small glass vials with cork stoppers. One is 1½" the other is 2" high & the fat one is 1¾" high. Not for sale on label. CMV $75.00 each mint.

33-36 VERNAFLEUR PERFUME
...all six sided bottle with black octogonal ... Silver label. Came in sets, only. CMV ...5.00 mint.

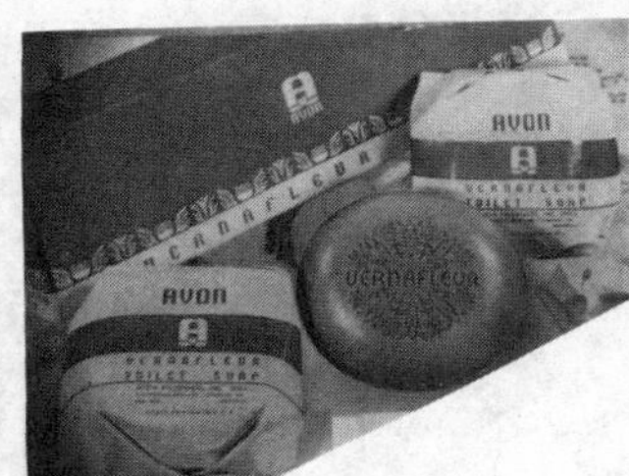

1936-39 VERNAFLEUR TOILET SOAP
Turquoise & white box & wrapping holds 3 violet colored bars. OSP 77c, CMV $50.00 MB..

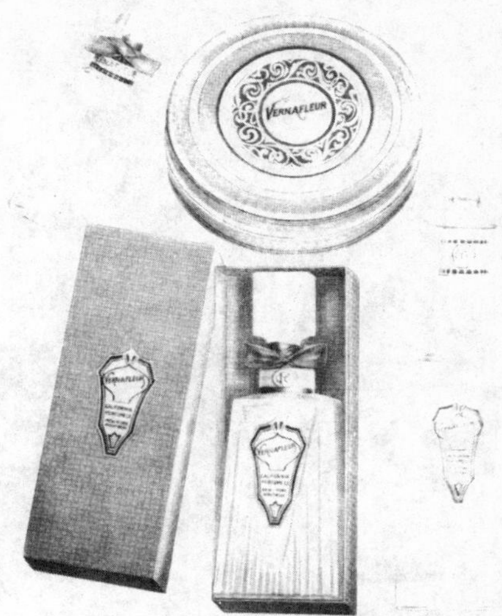

1923 VERNAFLEUR PERFUME EXTRACT
¼ oz. glass bottle with glass stopper. Neck label & ribbon. O.S.P. 48¢ C.M.V. $90. in box. $80 bottle only mint.
1923 VERNAFLEUR ADHERENT POWDER
Gray metal can. OSP 48c, CMV $45.00 MB, $35.00 can only.
1923 VERNAFLEUR PERFUME
Gray box holds 1 oz. ribbed glass bottle with frosted glass stopper. Front & neck label. Green ribbon on neck. OSP 1 oz. size $1.44, 2 oz. size $2.70, CMV $110.00 BO, $135.00 MB
1923 VERNAFLEUR TOILET WATER
2 & 4 oz. glass bottle with metal & cork shaker cap. OSP 74c & $1.35, CMV $100.00 MB. $85.00 BO mint.

1925 VERNAFLEUR TOILET WATER
2 & 4 oz. Ribbed glass bottle with metal & cork cap. OSP 74c & $1.35, CMV $85.00 BO, $100.00 MB.
1923 VERNATALC
4 oz. can of Talc Powder. Gray. O.S.P. 39¢ C.M.V. in box $60. Can only $50.
1923 VERNAFLEUR TISSUE CREAM
White glass jar with ribs on sides. CPC on metal lid. Large & small size jars. O.S.P. 48¢ & 89¢C.M.V. in box $45. Jar only $35.
1923 VERNAFLEUR NUTRI CREAM
Large & small white glass jar with ribs on sides. CPC on metal lid. O.S.P. 48¢ & 89¢ C.M. C.M.V. $45 in box, $35 jar only.

1931-36 VERNAFLEUR TOILET SOAP
Lavender in color, in white wrapper. Box of 3 bars. OSP 75c, CMV $55.00 MB

1928 VERNA TALC
4 oz. multi colored can, brass cap. OSP $1.15, CMV $75.00 mint, $90.00 MB
1928 VERNAFLEUR NUTRI CREME
Large & small white glass jar with ribbed sides. CPC on aluminum lid. OSP 50c & 90c, CMV $50.00 MB, $40.00 jar only mint.

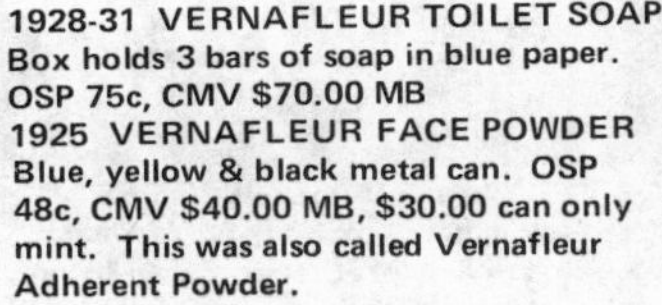

1928-31 VERNAFLEUR TOILET SOAP
Box holds 3 bars of soap in blue paper. OSP 75c, CMV $70.00 MB
1925 VERNAFLEUR FACE POWDER
Blue, yellow & black metal can. OSP 48c, CMV $40.00 MB, $30.00 can only mint. This was also called Vernafleur Adherent Powder.

1928 VERNAFLEUR BATH SALTS
10 oz. glass bottle with brass lid, ribbed glass sides. OSP 75c, CMV $80.00 MB, $70.00 jar only, mint.

1925 VERNAFLEUR PERFUME FLACON
Flaconette size frosted ribbed bottle with glass stopper, brass cap over stopper. Small front label. CPC on cap. Comes in yellow & green box. OSP 70c, CMV $90.00 with cap, $110.00 MB

1928 VERNAFLEUR TISSUE CREAM
Small & large size white glass jar with ribbed sides. CPC on aluminum lid. OSP 50c & 90c, CMV $50.00 MB, $40.00 jar only.

1928 VERNAFLEUR PERFUME
1 oz. glass stoppered bottle, blue, yellow & black box. OSP $1.45, CMV $150.00 MB in box, $110.00 BO mint.

1928 VERNAFLEUR COMPACT
Silver compact with Vernafleur on lid. Single & double compact. OSP $1.00 & $1.50, CMV $40.00, $30.00 compact only mint.

1929 CHRISTMAS CHEER
Red, white & blue boxes of Vernafleur Sachet Powder. Came in sets of 4 boxes. OSP $1.20, CMV $25.00 each box.

1925-28 VERNAFLEUR TOILET SOAP
Gray box & wrapping holds 3 bars. O.S.P. 69c, CMV $70.00 MB.

1929 VERNAFLEUR BATH SET
Black & gold box holds bottle of Vernafleur Bath Salts, Dusting Powder in gold & black striped can & 1 bar of Vernafleur Toilet Soap. OSP $3.50, CMV $200.00 MB.

1929 VERNAFLEUR QUINETTE SET
Blue, black & gold box holds Vernafleur Tissue Cream & Nutri Cream, Face Powder, Talc & Falconette of Perfume. O.S.P. $2.25 CMV $300.00 MB.

1928 VERNAFLEUR THREESOME GIFT BOX
Gray box holds 2 oz. bottle of Vernafleur Toilet Water, jar of Vanishing Cream & can of Face Powder. OSP $2.10, CMV $165.00 MB.

VIOLET

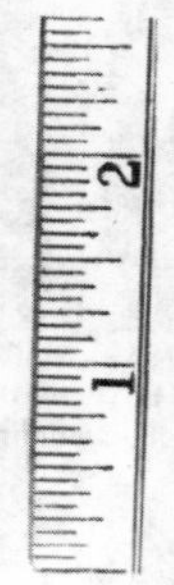

FROM THE ONSTOT COLLECTION

1915 VOILET TOILET WATER
2 oz. bottle, metal crown stopper in cork, front & neck label. OSP 35c, CMV $95.00 BO mint, $115.00 MB.

1915 VOILET TOILET WATER
¼ oz. clear glass, cork stopper. Came only in 1915 Juvenile Set. Rare. CMV $125.00 mint.

1915 VOILET PERFUME
Front & neck label, glass crown stopper in cork. OSP 50c, CMV $175.00 mint.

1923 VIOLET THREESOME SET
Contains 2 oz. bottle of Toilet Water, 3 & 1/3 oz. can of Talcum & bottle of Sachet Powder in violet colored box. O.S.P. $1.40 CMV $275.00 MB.

1915 VIOLET GIFT SET H
Green, white & purple box contains bottle of Violet Talcum, 1 oz. Perfume bottle with cork stopper & Atomizer, Violet Powder Sachet. OSP $1.35, CMV $350.00 MB.

1916 VIOLET TOILET WATER
2 oz. bottle with metal crown pour cap in cork. Colorful front and neck label. O.S.P. 35¢ C.M.V. $115.00 MB, $95.00 BO mint.

1923 VIOLET ALMOND MEAL
4 oz. sifter top metal can. 2 different labels. OSP 48c, CMV $50.00, $65.00 MB

1908 VIOLET ALMOND MEAL
8 oz. Glass jar with metal lid. O.S.P. 50¢ CMV $100.00 jar only mint, $120.00 MB

1915 VIOLET PERFUME
1 oz. size, cork stopper. Used with spray atomizer. Came in 1915 Violet Gift Box H set only. C.M.V. $100 mint.

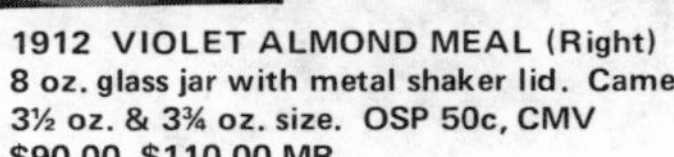

1912 VIOLET ALMOND MEAL (Right)
8 oz. glass jar with metal shaker lid. Came 3½ oz. & 3¾ oz. size. OSP 50c, CMV $90.00, $110.00 MB.

1923 VIOLET TALCUM
3 1/3 oz. Violet & green colored can, brass cap. O.S.P. 23¢ C.M.V. $75 mint, $85 M.B.

1915 VIOLET TALCUM POWDER
3½ oz. Glass jar. O.S.P. 25¢ C.M.V. $100 in box. $85 jar only mint.
1893 VIOLET TALCUM POWDER (Right)
3½ oz. Glass jar with metal cap. O.S.P. 25¢ CMV $110.00 jar only mint, $135.00 MB.

1893 VIOLET ALMOND MEAL
8 oz. glass jar with metal lid. O.S.P. 50¢ CMV $120.00 MB, $100.00 jar only mint.

C.P.C. BABY ITEMS

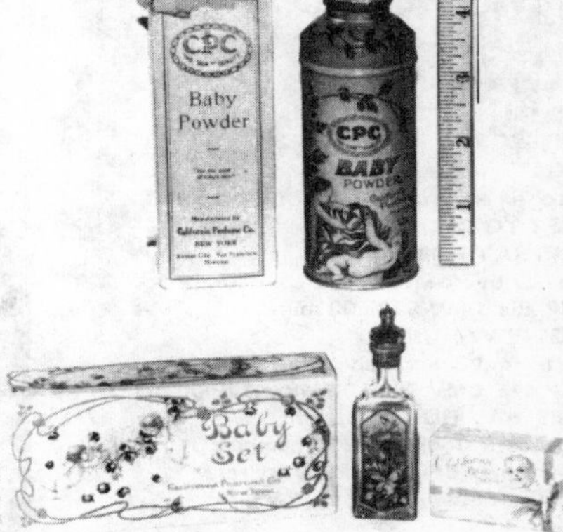

1916 BABY POWDER
Blue & pink can. OSP 25c, CMV $70.00 MB, $55.00 can only, mint.
1916 BABY SET
Baby set box holds can of Baby Powder as pictured above, without box, bar of Baby Soap & 2 oz. bottle of Violet Toilet Water. OSP 75c, CMV $225.00 MB

1893 BABY POWDER
Metal can. Eureka Trade Mark on label.
OSP 25c, CMV $110.00 mint, $130.00 MB

1923 BABY SET
Yellow box contains 2 oz. bottle of Toilet Water, bar of Baby Soap & can of Baby Powder. OSP 99c, CMV $160.00 MB, CMV Toilet water only $80.00 mint.

1925 BABY SET
Yellow box holds 4 oz. bottle of Supreme Olive Oil, 4 oz. yellow can of Baby Powder, yellow box of Boric Acid & 5 oz. yellow cake of genuine imported Castile Coap. O.S.P. $1.78 C.M.V. $175.00 M.B.
1925 SUPREME OLIVE OIL FOR BABY'S
4 oz. bottle with yellow label & cork stopper. Came in Baby Set only. C.M.V. $75.00 mint.
1925 CASTILE SOAP FOR BABY'S
5 oz. cake wrapped in yellow paper. Came in Baby Set only. C.M.V. $30.
1925 BORIC ACID FOR BABY
Yellow Box with soldiers on top. O.S.P. 33¢ C.M.V. $25.
1923 BABY POWDER
4 oz. Yellow can. O.S.P. 29¢ C.M.V. $45. in box, can only $35.

LEFT 1908 BABY POWDER
Metal can. OSP 25c, CMV $105.00, $125.00 MB
RIGHT 1912-16 BABY POWDER
Metal can. OSP 25c, CMV $65.00 mint $80.00 MB

BAY RUM

ALSO SEE AVON BAY RUM SECTION
ALL BOTTLES PRICED MINT
SEE PAGE 5 & 14 FOR GRADING

1908 BAY RUM (Left)
4 oz. glass stoppered bottle. O.S.P. 40¢ C.M.V. $125. Also came in ½ & 1 pint glass stoppered bottles. C.M.V. $125.00 ea. mint.
1912 BAY RUM
4 oz. glass stoppered bottle. Also came in ½ & 1 pint glass stoppered bottles. O.S.P. 40¢ C.M.V. $125.00 ea. mint.

1929 BAY RUM (Left)
16 oz. size with metal cap. O.S.P. $1.44 C.M.V. $85. Mint.
1923 BAY RUM (Right)
4 oz. bottle, metal shaker cap in cork. O.S.P. 47¢ C.M.V. $85. in box, $75. bottle only. Also came in 8 oz. O.S.P. 84¢, 32 oz. $2.40 C.M.V. ea. $85. mint.

FROM THE ONSTOT COLLECTION
LEFT TO RIGHT
1915 BAY RUM
4 oz. with crown metal & cork stopper. OSP 25c, CMV $125.00 mint.
1921 BAY RUM
4 oz. front & neck label. Cork stopper. OSP 47c, CMV $175.00 MB, $125.00 BO
1888 BAY RUM
4 oz. cork stopper. 126 Chambers St. on label where CPC started. Very rare. CMV not established.

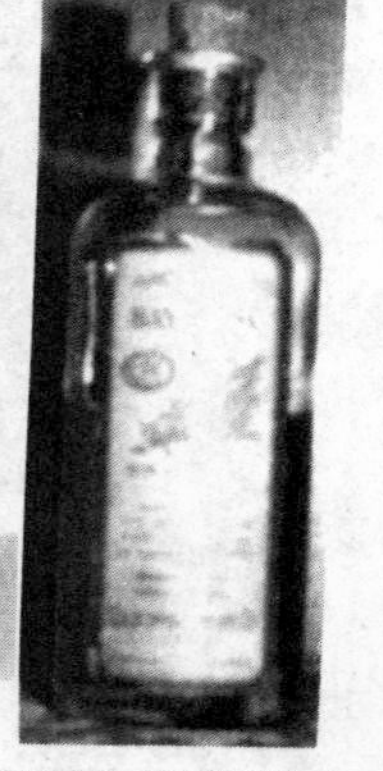

1927 BAY RUM
4 oz. metal & cork CPC embossed stopper. Front & neck label. Also came in 8 (shown on right) & 16 oz. size with cork stopper. OSP 50c, CMV $90.00 BO 4 oz., $100.00 8 & 16 oz. Add $20.00 for box, mint.

1930-36 BAY RUM
8 oz. clear glass bottle, black cap, green & black label. OSP 89c, CMV $35.00 BO mint, $45.00 MB

1920 BAY RUM
4 oz. clear glass bottle, glass stopper.
C.M.V. $100.00 mint, $125.00 M.B.

1912 BAY RUM
16 oz. clear glass, cork stopper. RARE.
C.M.V. $150.00

1930-36 BAY RUM
4 oz. Ribbed glass bottle with black cap & green label. O.S.P. 50¢ C.M.V. $50 in box, $45 bottle only. Also came in 16 oz. size O.S.P. 89¢ C.M.V. $50.

1896 BAY RUM
4 oz. glass stoppered bottle. O.S.P. 40¢ C.M.V. $150.00. Also came in 8 & 16 oz. size with glass stoppers. O.S.P. 75¢ & $1.25 C.M.V. $150.00 each.

1905 BAY RUM
16 oz. size glass stopper. O.S.P. $1.25 CMV $150.00 mint

C.P.C. BOTTLES - MISC.

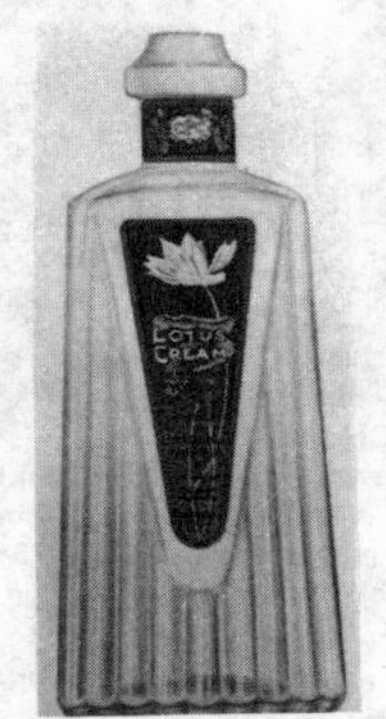

1925 LOTUS CREAM
4 oz. ribbed bottle with cork stopper, front & neck label. OSP 48c, CMV $65.00 BO mint, $80.00 MB

1917 LOTUS CREAM
12 oz. bottle has glass stopper. O.S.P. $1.23 C.M.V. $150. 4 oz. bottle has cork stopper O.S.P. 48¢ C.M.V. $100. Both have front & neck labels. Add $20.00 MB each.

LEFT 1920 WITCH HAZEL
16 oz. clear glass, cork stopper, front label. Rare. OSP 75c, CMV $125.00 mint

RIGHT 1930 Only WITCH HAZEL
4 oz. ribbed glass bottle, black cap, green label. Rare. CMV $65.00

LEFT 1923 ROSE WATER, GLYCERINE & BENZOIN
6 oz. clear glass bottle. Glass stopper set in cork. Print front & neck label. OSP 60c, CMV $85.00 mint.

RIGHT 1924-25 ROSE WATER, GLYCERINE & BENZOIN
6 oz. bottle with cork stopper. Front and neck label. This was a very short issue bottle. OSP 60c, CMV $90.00 MB, $75.00 BO mint.

LEFT 1929 Only ROSE WATER, GLYCERINE & BENZOIN
4 oz. clear glass ribbed bottle with black cap. Bottle came from Avon with small sample pink label marked not for resale. Bottle with this label rare. CMV $100.00 mint BO

RIGHT 1925 ROSE WATER, GLYCERINE & BENZOIN
4 oz. ribbed bottle with cork stopper, front & neck label. OSP 50c, CMV $60.00 mint, $75.00 MB.

1924 ROSE WATER,GLYCERINE & BENZOIN SAMPLE
Glass bottle, cork stopper. C.M.V. $70.00 M.B. $55.00 B.O. mint.

1917 LOTUS CREAM SAMPLE
Blue and white box holds ½ oz. sample bottle with cork stopper. Blue label. C.M.V. $75.00 M.B., $60.00 B.O. mint.

LEFT 1915 WITCH HAZEL
4 oz. glass bottle with cork stopper. O.S.P. 25¢ C.M.V. $90. 8 & 16 oz. size with glass stopper. O.S.P. 45¢ & 75¢ C.M.V. $125.00 ea. mint.
RIGHT 1924 WITCH HAZEL
4 oz. clear glass bottle, cork stopper. Front and neck label. O.S.P. 39¢ C.M.V. $75.00 B.O. mint, $85.00 M.B.

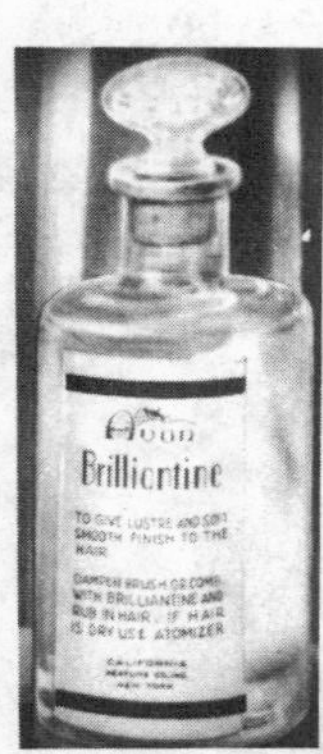

1930 Only - BRILLANTINE
2 oz. bottle with frosted glass stopper in cork. Silver label. O.S.P. 50¢ C.M.V. $75. mint.
1930 Only - DEODORANT
2 oz. bottle with corked frosted glass stopper. O.S.P. 50¢ C.M.V. $75 mint.

1896 WITCH HAZEL
4 & 8 oz. bottles came with sprinkler top. O.S.P. 25¢ & 45¢ C.M.V. $100. Pint bottle came with glass stopper. O.S.P. 75¢ C.M.V. $150. mint.
1905 WITCH HAZEL
16 oz. size, glass stopper. O.S.P. 75¢ C.MV. $150.00 Mint.

1923 WITCH HAZEL
4 oz. bottle with cork stopper, green front & neck label. O.S.P. 39¢ C.M.V. $75. Also came in 8, 16 & 32 oz. size. O.S.P. 69¢, $1.20 & $2.25. C.M.V. ea. $75. mint.
1925 WITCH HAZEL
4 oz. bottle with cork stopper, green label on front & neck. O.S.P. 39¢ C.M.V. $65. Also came in 8 & 16 oz. size. O.S.P. 69¢ & $1.20 C.M.V. ea. $75 mint.

LEFT 1908 WITCH HAZEL
16 oz. size glass stopper. O.S.P. 75¢ C.M.V. $150.00 Mint.
RIGHT 1908 WITCH HAZEL
Came in 4, 8 & 16 oz. bottles with glass stopper. Eureka Trade Mark on label. O.S.P. 25¢, 45¢ & 75¢ C.M.V. $150. Mint.

1931-36 HAIR TONIC EAU DE QUINI
Ribbed glass bottle with black cap & sil label. O.S.P. 90¢ C.M.V. $40.00 bottle only. $45.00 in box. Also came in 16 oz size. O.S.P. $1.75 C.M.V. $50.00 B.O. mint. $55.00 M.B.
1928 NULODOR
Bottle has frosted glass stopper, front & neck label. OSP 35c, CMV $85.00 mint

1896 EAU DE QUININE
6 oz. bottle with sprinkler top. O.S.P. 65¢ C.M.V. $100.00, $125.00 M.B.
1908 EAU DE QUININE
Glass bottle has cork stopper with metal c Front & neck label. Label has Eureka CP Trade Mark. OSP 65c, CMV $100.00 mint, $125.00 MB

1929 Only - GERTRUDE RECORDON' PEACH LOTION
Clear glass. Box states "This merchandis sent free for demonstration purposes or personal use. It must not be sold." C.M.V. $75.00 M.B.

1915 EAU DE QUININE
6 oz. glass bottle with metal crown & cork cap. O.S.P. 65¢ C.M.V. $100. in box. $85 bottle only.

1923 EAU DE QUININE
6 oz. glass bottle, metal shaker cap in cork. O.S.P. 69¢ C.M.V. $90.00 in box. $75.00 bottle only.

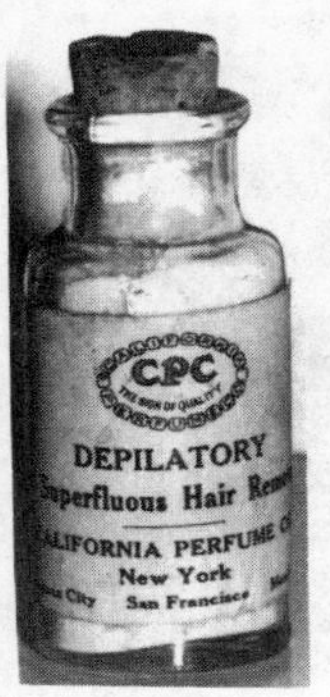

1912 NAIL BLEACH
1 oz. bottle, cork stopper. O.S.P. 25¢ C.M.V. $100.00 mint.

1915 DEPILATORY
1 oz. bottle with cork stopper. O.S.P. 50¢ C.M.V. $90.00 mint.

1918 FACE LOTION
6 oz. glass bottle has cork stopper, green front & neck label. Came with small sponge tied to neck. O.S.P. $1.00 C.M.V. $75.00 mint.

1923 FACE LOTION
6 oz. glass bottle, blue label, cork stopper. O.S.P. 97¢ C.M.V. $75.00 mint.

1896 FACE LOTION
Glass bottle with cork stopper. O.S.P. $1.00 C.M.V. $100.00 mint.

1908 FACE LOTION
Glass bottle, cork stopper, front & neck label. O.S.P. $1.00 C.M.V. $100.00 mint.

1923 LIQUID SHAMPOO
6 oz. front & neck label. Metal shaker cap in cork. O.S.P. 48¢ C.M.V. $75.00. In box $90.00

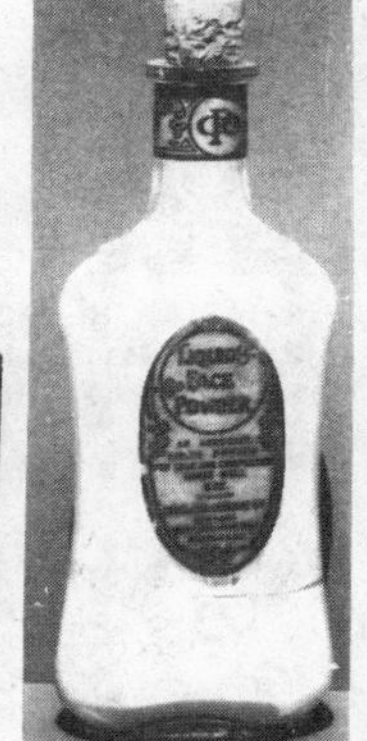

1929-30 CUTICLE REMOVER OR SOFTENER - ½ oz. bottle with brown label & cork stopper with glass dabber. Also came in Boudoir Set. O.S.P. 35¢ C.M.V. $60.00 BO, $75.00 MB.

1925 CUTRANE
Glass bottle with cork stopper with camel hair brush on stopper. Gold & black label. OSP 30c, CMV $60.00 BO mint, $75.00 MB

1920 LIQUID FACE POWDER
6 oz. clear glass, cork stopper. Has green front & neck label. OSP 97c, CMV $75.00 mint BO, $100.00 MB

LEFT 1912 FACE LOTION
6 oz. clear glass bottle, cork stopper. Front & neck label. Came in white & pink shades. OSP $1.00, CMV $85.00 BO, $105.00 MB

RIGHT 1915 LIQUID SHAMPOO
6 oz. glass bottle with metal cap. O.S.P. 35¢ C.M.V. $85.00 mint. $95.00 M.B.

LEFT 1908 TOOTH WASH
Glass bottle has cork stopper with metal crown top. Eureka Trade Mark on neck label. O.S.P. 25¢ C.M.V. $125.00 in box. Bottle only $100.00 mint.

RIGHT 1915 TOOTH WASH
Glass bottle with metal & cork cap. Back side of bottle is embossed California Tooth Wash. O.S.P. 25¢ C.M.V. $100.00 with label mint. Embossed bottle only $25.00

1908 ROUGE
Rouge powder can. C.M.V. $35.00
Liquid Rouge bottle C.M.V. $100.00
O.S.P. ea. 25¢. Eureka Trade Mark on both labels.

1893 SHAVING SOAP
1 bar of soap. O.S.P. 20¢ C.M.V. $50.00 in wrapper, mint.

1923 BAYBERRY SHAVING STICK
Three piece nickel metal container holds shaving soap. O.S.P. 33¢ C.M.V. $45.00 mint.

1914 NAIL BLEACH
2 oz. bottle with glass stopper, front paper label. 2 different labels shown. O.S.P. 25¢ C.M.V. $90.00 B.O. mint. $100.00 M.B. each.

1915 SHAVING CREAM STICK
Metal can. Came in soap stick, CPC on lid. O.S.P. 25¢ C.M.V. $50.00 M.B. $40.00 can only mint.

1916 ROUGE
Rouge O.S.P. 25¢ C.M.V. $35.00

1916 LIQUID ROUGE - Glass bottle, cork stopper. O.S.P. 25¢ C.M.V. $90.00 in box. $80.00 bottle only mint.

1921 TOOTH WASH
2 oz. glass bottle, brass & cork stopper. O.S.P. 25¢ C.M.V. $85.00 B.O. mint. $100.00 M.B.

1923 TOOTH WASH
2 oz. glass bottle, metal & cork cap. Front & neck label. O.S.P. 33¢ C.M.V. $85.00 mint.

1915 BENZOIN LOTION
2 oz. size, metal crown stopper in cork. Flowered label. OSP 75c. Also came in 4 oz. size at $1.50, CMV $100.00 each mint, $120.00 MB

1923 BENZOIN LOTION
2 oz. bottle with metal & cork stopper. OSP 59c, CMV $70.00, $90.00 MB.

1925 BENZOIN LOTION
2 oz. ribbed glass bottle with metal & cork stopper, blue & gold label. O.S.P. 59¢ CMV $65.00 BO, $80.00 MB

1896 LAIT VIRGINAL
2 oz. size, ribbed glass bottle has ribbed glass stopper set in cork. O.S.P. 65¢ CMV $150.00 mint, $175.00 MB.

C.P.C. JARS

1925 COLD CREAM
White glass jar with CPC on aluminum lid. OSP 63c, CMV $45.00 mint, $55.00 MB

1920-23 DERMOL MASSAGE CREAM
Glass jar with metal screw on lid. O.S.P. 96¢ C.M.V. $50.00 mint.

1908 CALIFORNIA COLD CREAM
2 oz. white glass jar with metal lid. OSP 25c, CMV $95.00 MB, $80.00 jar only mint.

1912 CPC COLD CREAM
Large white glass jar with metal lid. O.S.P. 45¢ C.M.V. $60.00 jar only. $75.00 M.B.

1896 COLD CREAM
White glass jar with metal lid. Eureka Trade Mark on label. O.S.P. 25¢ C.M.V. $90.00 mint.

1908 BANDOLINE
2 oz. glass bottle, cork stopper. O.S.P. 25¢ C.M.V. $100.00 in box. $85.00 bottle only mint.

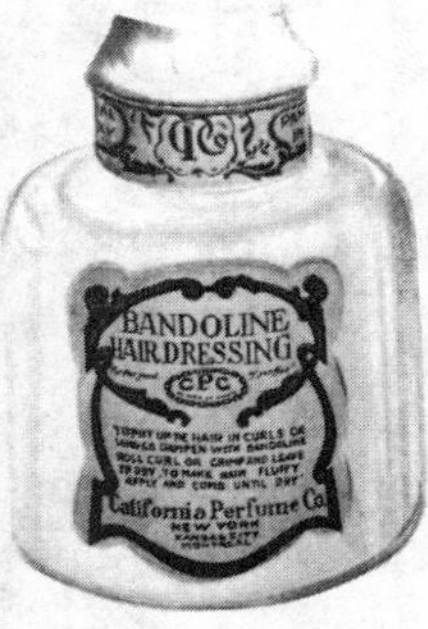

LEFT 1923-30 BANDOLINE HAIR DRESSING
2 oz. Yellow label & cork stopper, clear glass jar. O.S.P. 24¢ C.M.V. $60.00 mint. $70.00 M.B.
RIGHT 1923-30 BANDOLINE HAIR DRESSING
4 oz. size. Glass bottle, cork stopper, front & neck label. O.S.P. 45¢ C.M.V. $75.00 in box. $65.00 bottle only.

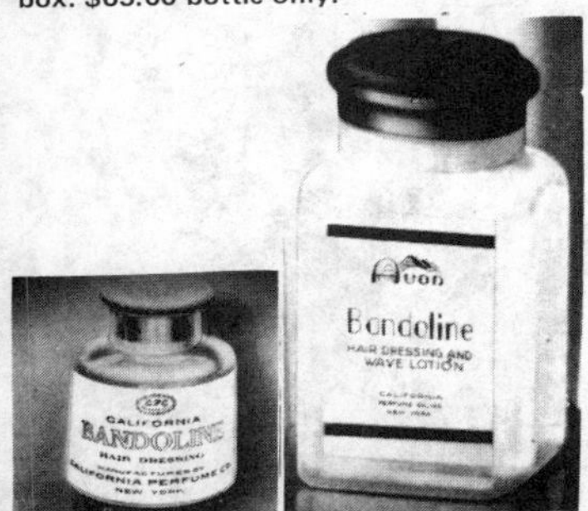

LEFT 1915 BANDOLINE
Glass bottle with cork stopper. OSP 25c, CMV $75.00 mint.
RIGHT 1930-35 BANDOLINE
Frosted glass bottle with blue wrapped cork stopper. OSP 37c, CMV $55.00 BO $65.00 MB.

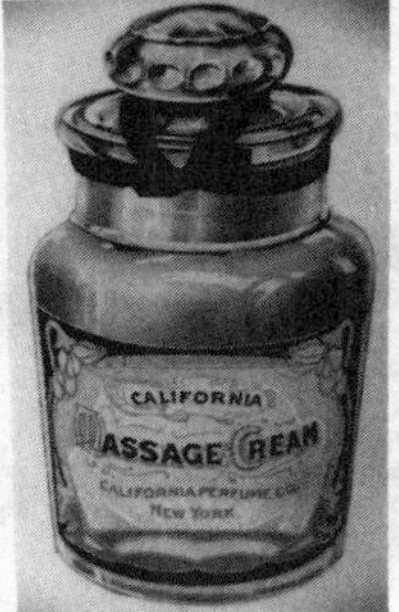

1916 MASSAGE CREAM
Glass jar has glass stopper, green ribbon on neck. OSP 50c, CMV $110.00 mint, $130.00 MB

1915 COLD CREAMS
Large & small white glass jars with CPC on metal lid. OSP 25c, & 45c, CMV $75.00 MB each, $60.00 jar only, mint.

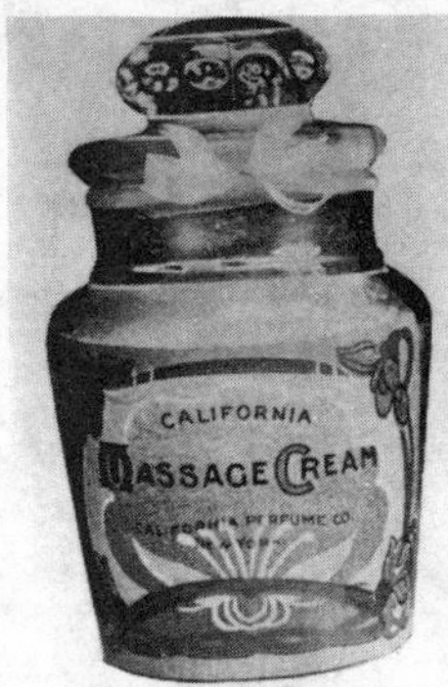

1896 MASSAGE CREAM
Glass jar with glass stopper. O.S.P. 75¢ CMV $125.00 mint, $150.00 MB

1915 SHAMPOO CREAM
4 oz. white glass jar, metal lid. O.S.P. 35¢ CMV $70.00 in box, $60.00 jar only mint.

1896 SHAMPOO CREAM
4 oz. white glass jar, metal lid. O.S.P. 35¢ C.M.V. $100.00 in box. $85.00 jar only mint.

1905 SHAMPOO CREAM
4 oz. white glass jar. O.S.P. 35¢ C.M.V. $85.00 M.B. $65.00 jar only mint.

1908 SHAMPOO CREAM
4 oz. white glass jar with metal lid. O.S.P. 35¢ C.M.V. $90.00 in box. $75.00 jar only.

1928-30 LEMONOL CLEANSING CREAM - Frosted glass jar with brass lid. OSP 50c, CMV $65.00 in box, $55.00 jar only.

1923 LAVENDER SALTS
Glass stoppered bottle, front & neck label. O.S.P. 49¢ C.M.V. $100.00 mint. $125.00 M.B.

LEFT 1893 LAVENDER SALTS
Emerald green glass bottle with green glass stopper with leather liner. O.S.P. 35¢ C.M.V. $200.00 mint.

RIGHT 1915 LAVENDER SALTS
Glass stoppered bottle. O.S.P. 35¢ C.M.V. $100.00 mint.

1923 DERMOL MASSAGE CREAM
White glass jar with ribbed sides. CPC on metal lid. O.S.P. 96¢ C.M.V. $50.00 - $60.00 M.B.

1925 VIOLET NUTRI-CREME
White glass jar with flowered label. O.S.P. 89¢ C.M.V. $50.00 - $60.00 M.B.

FROM THE ONSTOT COLLECTION
1910 LAVENDER SALTS
Emerald green glass. Same label only 1 bottle is 1/8" bigger than the other. Green glass stoppers set in rubber. OSP 35c, CMV $250.00 each mint.

LEFT 1912 LAVENDER SALTS
Glass stoppered bottle. O.S.P. 35¢ C.M.V. $100.00 mint.

RIGHT 1908 LAVENDER SALTS
Green glass bottle has green glass stopper with rubber base. O.S.P. 35¢ C.M.V. $150.00 mint.

LEFT 1915 VIOLET NUTRI-CREME
Small & large size white glass jars with aluminum lid. O.S.P. 50¢ & 90¢ C.M.V. $55.00 ea. in box. $45.00 jar only mint.

RIGHT 1923 VIOLET NUTRI-CREME
Large & small white glass jars with CPC on metal lid. OSP 49c, & 89c, CMV $45.00 each, $55.00

FROM THE ONSTOT COLLECTION
1888 LAVENDER SALTS
Teal green glass, octagonal shaped bottle. Ground glass stopper. Rare. OSP 35c, CMV not established.

1888 LAVENDER SALTS - METAL TOP
Emerald green glass, glass stopper with screw on metal top. Rare. OSP 35c, CMV not established.

1908 TOOTH POWDER
White glass bottle with metal cap. O.S.P. 25¢ C.M.V. $100.00 mint.

1915 SHAMPOO CREAM SAMPLE
Small 1" size aluminum round bottom container. Rare. CMV $50.00 mint.

C.P.C. PERFUME - MISC.

1896 TO 1914 PERFUMES

The following list of perfumes were sold by CPC from 1896 to 1914. Use this list to identify misc. perfumes.

The regular line of CP Floral extracts consists of thirty odors, in the following range of prices and sizes:

Roses, Lily of the Valley, White Rose, Violet, White Lilac, Sweet Peas, Hyacinth, Heliotrope, Carnation, Bouquet Marie, New Mown Hay, Marie Stewart, Rose Geranium, Stephanotis, Ylang Ylang, Jack Rose, Tube Rose, Treffle, California Bouquet

1 ounce bottle	*$ .60*
2 ounce bottle	*1.10*
4 ounce bottle	*2.00*
½ pint bottle	*3.75*
1 pint bottle	*7.00*

Crab Apple Blossom, Trailing Arbutus, Frangipanni, May Blossom, Jockey Club, White Heliotrope

1 ounce bottle	*$ .75*
2 ounce bottle	*1.40*
4 ounce bottle	*2.75*
½ pint bottle	*5.25*
1 pint bottle	*10.00*

Lou Lillie, Musk, Golf Club, Venetian Carnation, Golf Violet

1 ounce bottle	*$ .50*
2 ounce bottle	*.90*
4 ounce bottle	*1.75*
½ pint bottle	*3.25*
1 pint bottle	*6.00*

1915 TO 1921 PERFUMES

The very extensive CPC line gives a wide range of selection, and among the 27 different odors there is sure to be one or more to satisfy the most fastidious and exacting.

The prices are according to the cost of production and the value of the goods offered. All perfumes are in attractive bottles, put up in beautiful lithographed boxes, as illustrated.

Concentrated Floral Odors Triple Extracts

Violet, White Rose, Carnation, Heliotrope, Lily of the Valley, White Lilac, Hyacinth, California Bouquet, Roses, New Mown Hay, Sweet Pea, Treffle, Rose Geranium, Jack Rose

1 ounce bottle	*.50*
2 ounce bottle	*.90*
4 ounce bottle	*1.75*
½ pint bottle	*3.25*
1 pint bottle	*6.00*

Quadruple Extracts

Crab Apple Blossom, Trailing Arbutus, Jockey Club, Honeysuckle, White Heliotrope

1 ounce bottle	*$ .60*
2 ounce bottle	*1.10*
4 ounce bottle	*2.00*
½ pint bottle	*3.75*
1 pint bottle	*7.00*

Extra Concentrated Odors

Natoma Rose, Venetian Carnation, Golf Violet, Musk

1 ounce bottle	*.75*
2 ounce bottle	*1.40*
4 ounce bottle	*2.75*
½ pint bottle	*5.25*
1 pint bottle	*10.00*

1923 PERFUME FLACONETTE
Octagonal shaped bottle with long glass stopper, neck label. Came with & without brass cap with CPC on cap. Came in Daphne, Crab Apple, Vernafleur, Trailing Arbutus, White Rose, Carnation, Violet, White Lilac, Heliotrope, Roses, Lily of the Valley. O.S.P. 49¢ C.M.V. with brass cap $90.00 without cap $75.00

1896-1910 TRAVELER'S PERFUME
½ oz. size. Metal cap over glass stopper. Gold label. Bottle is octagonally shaped. Came in all fragrances of 1896-1908. Red flowered box. O.S.P. 50¢ C.M.V. $125.00 B.O. mint. $150.00 M.B.

1925 PERFUME FLACONETTE
Flaconette size embossed glass bottle with glass stopper. Brass cap over stopper. Came in Mission Garden, American Ideal, Narcissus, Daphne, Jardin D' Amour. OSP $1.10, CMV $90.00 bottle only, mint with brass cap. In box $110.00. The cap has fragrance on it.

LEFT 1896 EXTRACT PERFUMES
2 oz. round glass stopper. New York, Chicago, San Francisco on label. Came in all fragrances in 1908. O.S.P. 90¢ to $1.40. C.M.V. bottle only $150.00. In box $200.00.

RIGHT 1896-1908 FRENCH PERFUME
½ oz. bottle with glass stopper. Eureka Trade Mark in center of label. Came in Le Perfume des Roses, Peau d'Espagne, L'Odeur de Violette. O.S.P. 55¢ C.M.V. $150.00 bottle only. $200.00 in box.

1896 PERFUME
1 oz. octagonal shaped bottle, front & neck label with Eureka Trade Mark. Came in Atomizer Perfume Set with cork stopper. Came in all fragrances of 1896. C.M.V. $150.00

1887 EXTRACT ROSE GERANIUM PERFUME - 1 oz. glass stopper, paper label. O.S.P. 40¢ C.M.V. $200.00 mint.

1890 PERFUMES
1 oz. size, glass stopper, neck ribbons. White Rose, Lily of the Valley, Violet, Heliotrope. All different labels. O.S.P. 25¢ C.M.V. $100.00 each mint.

1925 PERFUME FLACONETTE
Frosted ribbed glass bottle with long glass stopper. Small paper label on front. Came with brass cap with CPC on cap. Came in Crab Apple, Daphne, Trailing Arbutus, Vernafleur, American Ideal, Carnation, Heliotrope, White Rose, Violet, Lily of the Valley. OSP 59c, CMV with brass cap $85.00, $70.00 BO, $100.00 MB

FROM THE ONSTOT COLLECTION
1928 PERFUME SPRAY ATOMIZER
1 is green opaque over clear glass & 1 is green painted over clear, gold plated top. CMV $85.00 each.

1890 FRENCH PERFUMES (Left)
¼ oz. bottle with glass stopper. Came in Le Perfume Des Roses, L'Odeur de Violette, Peau d'Espagne. O.S.P. 25¢ C.M.V. $125.00 bottle only. $150.00 M.B.

1896 FRENCH PERFUMES (Right)
¼ oz. glass bottle, cork stopper. Came in Le Perfume Des Roses, L'Odeur de Violette, Peau d'Espagne. O.S.P. 25¢ C.M.V. $125.00 mint - $150.00 M.B.

1896 PEAU D' ESPAGNE PERFUME
4" high flaconette size, cork stopper. CPC French perfume. OSP 25c, CMV $160.00 mint.

1910 CRAB APPLE BLOSSOM PERFUME
1 oz. glass stopper, front & neck label. CPC on label. CMV $100.00 mint, $135.00 MB

FROM THE ONSTOT COLLECTION
1896 WHITE ROSE PERFUME
1 oz. glass stopper. Bottom part of label is missing on bottle shown. OSP 40c, CMV $175.00 mint.

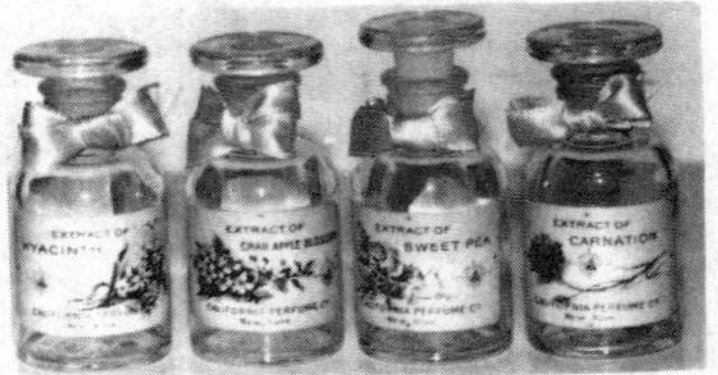

1890 PERFUMES
1 oz. size, glass stopper, neck ribbons. Hyacinth, Crab Apple Blossom, Sweet Pea, Carnation. All different labels. O.S.P. 25¢ C.M.V. $100.00 ea. mint.

1908 FRENCH PERFUME
Glass stoppered bottle came in ¼, ½, 1, 3 & 4 oz. sizes in these fragrances: Le Perfume des Roses, L'Odeur de Violette, & Peau d'Espagne. 1 oz. size pictured. O.S.P. 25¢ to $3.75. C.M.V. $150.00 bottle only. $200.00 in box.

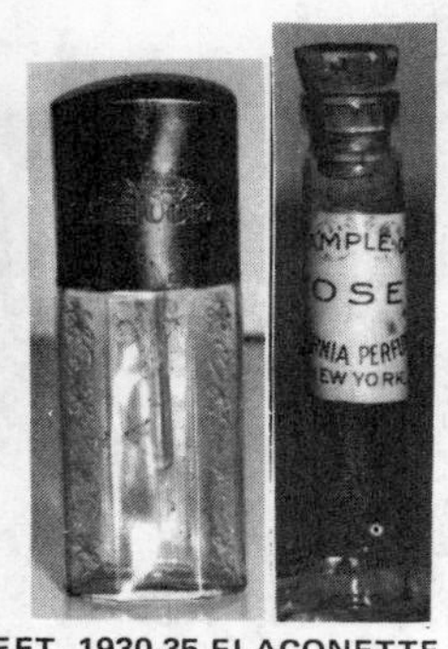

LEFT 1930-35 FLACONETTE
Embossed clear glass stopper, brass cap over glass stopper. Avon on cap. Came in all perfumes of 1930-35. OSP $1.10 CMV $90.00 each mint, $110.00 MB

RIGHT 1900 ROSE PERFUME SAMPLE
½ oz. size, cork stopper. Came in all fragrances of 1900. C.M.V. $125.00 mint.

1908 1 OZ. PERFUMES
1 oz. glass stoppered bottle. Eureka Trade Mark on label. In gray flowered box. Came in all fragrances of 1908. O.S.P. 50¢ to 75¢ C.M.V. ea. $200.00 in box. Bottle only $150.00 Each fragrance came with different flower on label. Heliotrope on left and Crab Apple Blossom on right.

1922 CPC PERFUME SAMPLE SET
Black carrying case with "California Perfume Co." on front. 4 glass flaconette with gold cap & fits into gold case. CMV $350.00 in box, $70.00 each flaconette.

1923 CPC PERFUME SAMPLE SET
Black box holds 4 glass stoppered perfume samples. Box has California Perfume Co. on front, 3 dram size. Each has neck labels. Labels read Daphne, Vernafleur, American Ideal, Trailing Arbutus. C.M.V. $75.00 ea. bottle. $325.00 set in box.

1915-20 CUT GLASS PERFUME
2 oz. bottle with cut glass stopper. 2 different labels in embossed gold. Leatherette box. Came in Trailing Arbutus & Crab Apple Blossom. OSP $2.25, CMV bottle only $175.00, in box $200.00 Octagonal label on right is 1911 issue. Same CMV.

The Proper Way to Demonstrate Perfumes

CALIFORNIA PERFUME COMPANY, Inc.

FROM THE ONSTOT COLLECTION

1925 PERFUME SAMPLE SET
Four 3 dram ribbed & frosted glass bottles with clear ribbed stoppers. Black carrying case case. Came in Daphne, Trailing Arbutus, Vernafleur, American Ideal, Crab Apple, Carnation, Heliotrope, White Rose, Violet & Lily of the Valley. CMV set $300.00 mint. Came with card on proper way to demonstrate perfumes. Add $10.00 for card.

1930 PERFUME SAMPLE SET
Same CPC black case & bottles as 1925 set only has very rare silver & blue labels on bottles. CMV $400.00 set, mint.

1918 PERFUME & ATOMIZER
1 oz. bottle with atomizer came in black box. Bottle has cork stopper & green front & neck label. Came in all fragrances of 1918, including American Ideal & Daphne. O.S.P. $1.50 C.M.V. $110.00 in box with atomizer. $90.00 bottle only.

LEFT 1918 CPC PERFUME
½ oz. glass & cork stopper. Came in 1918 Gift Box A Set. CMV $90.00 mint.

RIGHT 1919 ½ OZ. PERFUME
½ oz. glass crowned shaped stopper in cork. Came in all 1919 fragrances. OSP 75c, CMV $90.00 mint, $110.00 MB.

1916 CPC PERFUME
2 different glass stoppers shown. O.S.P. 50¢ C.M.V. $125.00 bottle only mint. $175.00 M.B.

FROM THE ONSTOT COLLECTION
1918 PERFUME
½ oz. bottle with crown glass stopper set in cork. Front & neck label. Came in all fragrances of 1918. OSP 50c, CMV $95.00 BO mint, $110.00 MB

1908 EXTRACT PERFUMES
1 oz. glass stopper, white paper label. Came in all fragrances of 1896. O.S.P. 50¢ C.M.V. in box $200.00. Bottle only $175.00

LEFT 1909 CHRISTMAS BOX NO. 5 PERFUME
White leather covered box holds 3 oz. glass stoppered perfume. OSP $1.50 CMV $200.00 MB. Bottle only $150.00 mint.
RIGHT 1896 MUSK PERFUME
1 oz. size, glass stoppered. Came in all fragrances. CMV $100.00 mint. $125.00 MB.

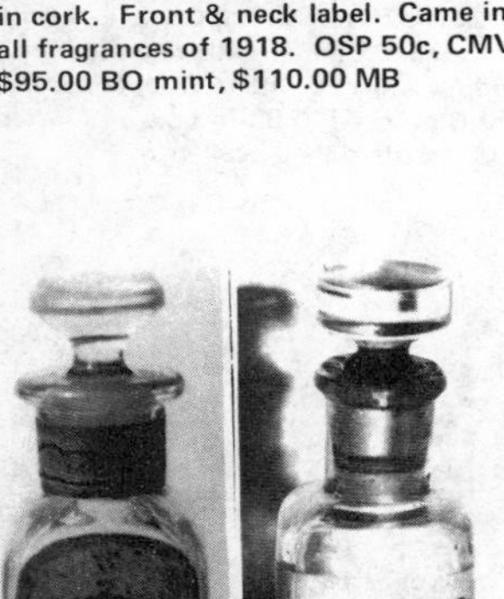

LEFT 1915 MUSK PERFUME
1 oz. clear glass bottle with glass stopper. Came in all 1915 fragrances. O.S.P. 75¢ C.M.V. $150.00 mint.

RIGHT 1908 CRAB APPLE BLOSSOM
1 oz. clear glass bottle, glass stopper, label has CPC Eureka Trade Mark. Came in all 1908 fragrances: Bottle came with different shaped stopper also. O.S.P. 50¢ - 75¢ C.M.V. $150.00 bottle only. $200.00 in box.

1907 CHRISTMAS PERFUME
2 oz. glass stopper perfume. OSP 75c CMV $175.00 MB. Bottle only $125.00 mint.

1916 2 OZ. PERFUME
2 oz. glass stopper either faceted or round. Front & neck label. Came in all fragrances of 1915. O.S.P. $1.10 C.M.V. in box $175.0 Bottle only $135.00

1906 CPC PERFUME
1 oz. perfume, gold front & neck label. Came in all 1906 perfumes. C.M.V. $200.00 M.B. $150.00 bottle only.

1906 PERFUMES
1 oz. round bottles came in Atomizer Perfume Set with cork stopper. Came in all fragrances of 1908. C.M.V. $100.00 ea. mint.

1908 PERFUME "FLORAL EXTRACTS"
1 oz. glass stoppered bottle with Eureka CP Trade Mark on label. Came in all 1908 perfumes. O.S.P. 50¢ C.M.V. $150.00 bottle only. $200.00 in box. Also came in 2, 4, 8 & 16 oz. bottles. C.M.V. same as 1 oz. size.

LEFT 1908 PERFUME
1 oz. glass stopper, gold label. Eureka Trade Mark on label. Came in all fragrances of 190 C.M.V. $150.00. Also came in several differe glass stoppers.
RIGHT 1908-1918 PERFUME
4 oz. glass stoppered bottle, gold embossed front & neck label. Came in all perfumes of the period. See list on front of this section. O.S.P. $2.75 C.M.V. $150.00 bottle only. $200.00 in box.

23 PERFUMES
oz. bottle with crown glass stopper set cork. Front & neck label. Crab Apple ossom, White Rose, Trailing Arbutus, oses, Carnation, Heliotrope, Violet, hite Lilac, & Lily of the Valley. Came red box. O.S.P. 59¢ C.M.V. $100.00 ottle only. $125.00 in box.

FROM THE ONSTOT COLLECTION
1890'S FRENCH PERFUMES
Trial size ¼ oz. on left. 2 oz. size on right. Cork stoppers. CMV $120.00 trial size mint, CMV $200.00 2 oz. size mint.

1916 FRENCH PERFUMES
2 different embossed glass bottles. Cork stoppers. Trial size. OSP 25c, CMV $120.00 BO mint, $145.00 MB.

1923 PERFUMES
1 & 2 oz. bottle in same shape & design with glass stopper. Front & neck label with gold basket design. Beige box. Came in Carnation, Roses, Heliotrope, Violet, White, Lilac, Lily of the Valley, Crab Apple Blossom, Trailing Arbutus, White Rose. O.S.P. $1.17 & $2.10. C.M.V. $125.00 bottle only. $150.00 in box. Also came in 4 oz. size.

Left - 1908 ATOMIZER PERFUME
1 oz. 6 sided bottle with cork stopper. Green neck & front label. Came in all fragrances of 1908. Came only in CPC Atomizer Sets. Used with Spray Atomizer. O.S.P. 50¢ C.M.V. $100.00 mint.

Right - 1918 ATOMIZER PERFUME
1 oz. bottle with green & gold front & neck label, cork stopper. Came in 1918 Atomizer Box Set only. Used with Spray Atomizer. Came in all 1918 perfumes. O.S.P. 50¢ C.M.V. $90.00 mint.

1916 FRENCH PERFUMES
Bottle on left is 1 oz., center is ¼ oz. trial size, right is ½ oz. size. Each has glass stopper. Came in L'Odeur De Violette, Le Parfume Des Roses & Peau De' Espagne.

Also came in 2 & 4 oz. size. OSP 25c, 55c, $1.00, $1.90 & $3.75. CMV bottle ½ oz. size to 4 oz. $135.00 each, ¼ oz. size $120.00. Add $25.00 for box.

LEFT 1915 ½ OZ. PERFUME
½ oz. bottle with glass stopper set in cork. Front & neck label. Came in Violet, White Rose, Carnation, White Lilac, Heliotrope, Lily of the Valley. O.S.P. 25¢ C.M.V. $100.00

RIGHT 1 OZ. EXTRA CONCENTRATED PERFUMES - 1 oz. size, front & neck label. Came in Golf Violet, Musk, Crab Apple Blossom, Natoma, Rose, Venetian Carnation. O.S.P. 75¢ C.M.V. in box $175.00. Bottle only $125.00

1908 LITTLE FOLKS PERFUMES
2" high small bottles with cork stoppers came in early 1900's Little Folks gift sets. Came in Heliotrope, Rose, Carnation, and Violet. Front labels and neck ribbons. C.M.V. $75.00 each mint.

1925-32 LITTLE FOLKS PERFUME (Left)
½ oz. bottle with brass screw on cap. Came in 1925 Little Folks Set only. Came in Violet, Carnation, Heliotrope, White Lilac, Daphne, Vernafleur, Trailing Arbutus. C.M.V. $65.00 ea. mint.

1896 LITTLE FOLKS PERFUME (Right)
2" high. Came in 1896 & 1906 Little Folks Set only in Rose, or White Rose, Heliotrope, Violet, & Carnation. Cork stopper. C.M.V. $75.00 ea. mint.

1915 LITTLE FOLKS PERFUME (Left)
Small gem size bottle with front label & ribbon on neck. Cork stopper. Came in 1915 Little Folks Set only. Came in Carnation, Violet, White Rose, Heliotrope. C.M.V. $75.00 ea. mint.

1912 LITTLE FOLKS PERFUME (Right)
2" high, cork stopper. Came in Little Folks Set only from 1912 to 1915. Both bottles pictured came in same fragrances. C.M.V. $75.00 mint.

1915 8 OZ. PERFUMES (Left)
8 oz. glass stoppered bottle. Came in Califor Bouquet. shown, Violet, White Rose, Carnat Heliotrope, Lily of the Valley, White Lilac, Hyacinth, Roses, New Mown Hay, Sweet Pea Treffle, Rose Geranium, Jack Rose, front paper label and also came with neck label. O.S.P. $3.25 ea. C.M.V. $175.00 ea. $225.00 in box.

1925 PERFUME (Right)
1 oz. glass stoppered bottle is ribbed. Came i Carnation, Crab Apple Blossom, Heliotrope, Lily of the Valley, Violet & White Rose. Fro & neck label. O.S.P. $1.17 C.M.V. $100.00 bottle only. $125.00 in box.

1916 PERFUMES
The above 6 glass stoppered 1 oz. bottles shown came in California Bouquet, Carnation, Heliotrope, Hyacinth, Lily of the Valley, New Mown Hay, Rose Geranium, Sweet Pea, Treffle, Violet, White Lilac, & White Rose. O.S.P. 50¢ C.M.V. $125.00 bottle only. $150.00 in box.

C.P.C. TOILET WATER

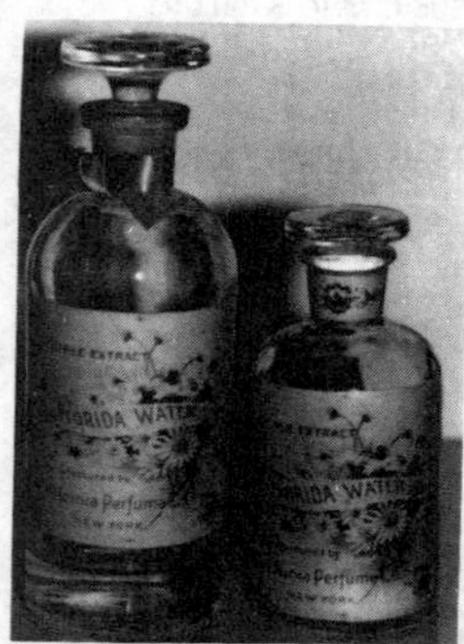

1887 FLORIDA WATER
2 & 4 oz. size, glass stopper, front & neck labels. C.M.V. $100.00 ea. mint.

1916 TOILET WATER
4 oz. bottle with metal & cork stopper. Came in red & gold box. Came in California Sweet Cologne, Carnation, Eau de Cologne, Florida Water, Lavender Water, Trailing Arbutus, Violet, White Lilac, White Rose. O.S.P. 65¢ C.M.V. $100.00 BO mint, $120.00 MB.

1922-25 TOILET WATERS - Came in
2, 4, & 8 oz. sizes in Violet, Vernafleur, Lavender, White Lilac, Lily of the Valley, Carnation, White Rose, Trailing Arbutus, Crab Apple Blossom, & Eau de Cologne. 2 & 4 oz. size same as pictured. Front & neck labels. Metal crown stopper in cork. OSP 59c, $1.08 & $1.95, CMV$80.00 MB each, $95.00 MB

1916 TOILET WATER
2 oz. bottle with metal pour cap in cork. California Sweet Cologne, Lait Virgital, Eau de Cologne, Trailing Arbutus, White Rose, Violet, White Lilac, Lavender Water, Florida Water, Crab Apple Blossom, & Carnation. Front & neck label, in 2 styles. OSP 35c, CMV $115.00 MB, $100.00 BO mint. Also came with brass crown and cork stopper.

1906 TOILET WATERS (Left)
2 oz. clear ribbed glass bottle & glass corked stopper. Pure food act 1906 on label. Came in Violet Water, White Rose, Lavender Water, Florida Water & California Sweet Cologne, Eau de Cologne. O.S,P. 35¢ C.M.V. $175.00 mint.
1896 TOILET WATERS (Right)
2 oz. ribbed glass bottle, glass stopper in cork. Front & neck label has Eureka Trade Mark. Came in California Sweet Cologne, Violet Water, White Rose, Lavender Water, & Florida Water. O.S.P. 35¢ C.M.V. $175.00

LEFT 1890 EAU DE COLOGNE
4 oz. size, glass stopper. Came in all Toilet Waters of 1890. O.S.P. 65¢ C,M.V. $100.00 mint.
CENTER 1890 PERFUME
1 oz. size, glass stopper, neck ribbon. Came in all fragrances of 1890. O.S.P. 25¢ C.M.V. $100.00 mint.
RIGHT 1890 CPC TOILET WATER
2 & 4 oz. size, glass stopper. Came in all fragrances of 1890. Front & neck labels. O.S.P. 65¢ C.M.V. $100.00 mint.

FROM THE ONSTOT COLLECTION
1905 FLORIDA WATER
1½ oz. size, glass crown & cork stopper. OSP 35c, CMV $175.00 mint.

1896 EAU DE COLOGNE FOR THE TOILET
2 oz. ribbed glass bottle. Front & neck label with Eureka trade mark. Glass stopper in cork. OSP 35c, CMV $175.00 mint.

1905 SWEET COLOGNE
2 & 4 oz. size, front & neck labels, cork stopper. O.S.P. 35¢ & 65¢. C.M.V. $150.00 ea. M.B. Bottle only $125.00 ea. mint.

1908 TOILET WATERS (Left)
2, 4, 8 & 16 oz. sizes. Glass stoppered bottle. Came in Violet, White Rose, Lavender, Florida, California Sweet Cologne & Eau De Cologne. Bottle shown in 2 oz. size. O.S.P. ea. 35¢ & 65¢, $1.25 & $2.00. C.M.V. ea. $150.00 bottle only. $200.00 in box.
1910 LAVENDER WATER (Right)
2 oz. glass stoppered bottle with Eureka Trade Mark on label. Also came in Violet, White Rose, Florida Water, California Sweet Cologne & Eau De Cologne. Also came in 4 & 8 oz. & 1 pint sizes with glass stopper. O.S.P. 35¢ C.M.V. $150.00 mint.

1910 TOILET WATER
8 oz. bottle with glass stopper. Front & neck label. Came in all fragrances of 1916 in Toilet Waters. O.S.P. $1.25 C.M.V. $150.00 bottle only mint. $175.00 M.B.

1916 TOILET WATER
2 oz. size with metal crown cork stopper. Came in either of 2 labels shown in Carnation, Florida Water, Trailing Arbutus, White Lilac, White Rose, Violet, Lavender Water, Eau de Cologne, California Sweet Cologne. O.S.P. 35c, CMV $100.00 each BO, $120.00 MB

LEFT
1896 TRIPLE EXTRACT TOILET WATER
4 oz. glass stopper, label has Eureka Trade Mark. Came in Violet Water, White Rose, Lavender Water, Florida Water, Eau De Cologne, California Sweet Cologne, O.S.P. ea. 65¢ C.M.V. $200.00 in box. $150.00 bottle only mint.

RIGHT 1900 FLORIDA WATER
2 oz. bottle, glass stopper. O.S.P. 35¢ C.M.V. $175.00 mint.

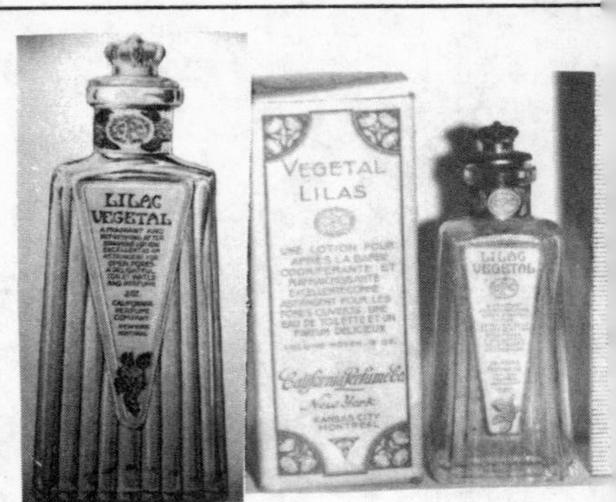

1928-29 LILAC VEGETAL (Left)
2 oz. ribbed glass bottle with crown metal top in cork. Pink front & neck label. This bottle with CPC on front label came in Humidor Shaving Set only. C.M.V. $80.00, $90.00 MB

1925-30 LILAC VEGETAL (Right)
2 oz. ribbed glass bottle with metal stopper in cork. Pink front & neck label. OSP 59c, CMV $80.00 BO $90.00 MB. Also came in 4 oz. size. OSP $1.08, CMV same as 2 oz. size.

LEFT 1923-29 TOILET WATERS
2 oz. metal crown cork stopper, ribbed bottle, front & neck label. Came in Lily of the Valley, Violet, White Rose, Carnation, Crab Apple Blossom. O.S.P. 59¢ C.M.V. $75.00 each mint, $90.00 MB

RIGHT 1923 BABY TOILET WATER
2 & 4 oz. size bottles. Red soldier on front label, blue neck label. Brass & cork stopper. OSP 48c & 89c, CMV $90.00 MB, $80.00 BO.

C.P.C. POWDERS

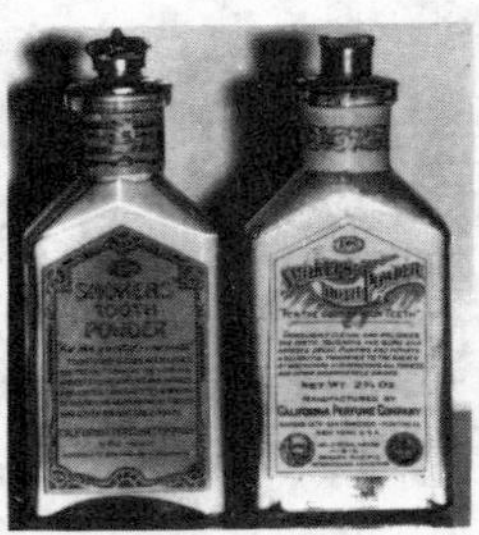

Left - 1918 SMOKERS TOOTH POWDER
2¾ oz. bottle with metal & cork stopper also comes with metal crown stopper. OSP 50c, CMV bottle only $100.00 mint. $125.00 in box.

Right - 1920 SMOKERS TOOTH POWDER
2¾ oz. metal & cork stopper. O.S.P. 50¢ C.M.V. bottle only $100.00. In box $125.0[illegible]

1925 PYROX TOOTH POWDER
Blue metal can. O.S.P. 24¢ C.M.V. $35.00 in box. $25.00 can only mint.

1923 CALIFORNIA ROSE TALCUM
4 oz. pink can with brass cap. O.S.P. 33¢ C.M.V. $75.00 in box. $65.00 can only mint.

1921 CALIFORNIA ROSE TALCUM
3½ oz. glass jar with brass cap. O.S.P. 33c, CMV $85.00 jar only, $100.00 MB M.B.

FROM THE ONSTOT COLLECTION

1925-33 SMOKERS TOOTH POWDER
4 oz. cream colored can. Label in French & English. OSP 50c, CMV $60.00 MB, $50.00 can only mint.

1906 ROSE TALCUM POWDER ANTISEPTIC - Metal can with brass sifter cap. O.S.P. 25¢ C.M.V. $75.00 mint.

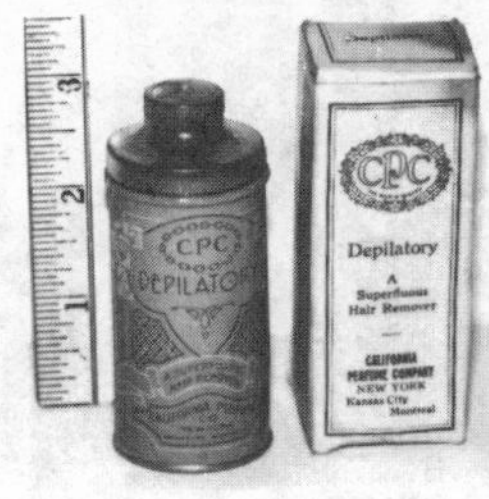

1914 DEPILATORY
A metal can of hair remover. OSP 50c, CMV $60.00 MB, $50.00 CO mint. Came with brass sifter cap or brass lift off cap.

1928-29 RADIANT NAIL POWDER
Small gold & black can. All 3 pieces came in 1928 Manicure Set. C.M.V. $35.00
1928-29 CUTI CREME OR NAIL CREAM
Small gold & black can. C.M.V. $20.00
1928-29 NAIL WHITE
Small gold & black can. C.M.V. $20.00

1919 WHITE LILAC TALCUM (left)
4 oz. blue metal can, blue sifter cap. O.S.P. 24¢ C.M.V. $65.00 can only mint. $75.00 M.B.
1917 WHITE LILAC TALCUM (right)
4 oz. paper box, purple in color. O.S.P. 25¢ C.M.V. $50.00 mint. $60.00 in box.

1928-29 CPC BODY POWDER
Yellow, black & rust colored metal can. CPC New York, Montreal on bottom. Came in Trailing Arbutus, Daphne & Baby Powder. O.S.P. $1.19 C.M.V. $60.00 mint.

1912 ELITE POWDER
Glass jar with aluminum lid.
OSP 25c, CMV $80.00 mint, $90.00 MB
1923 ELITE POWDER
Blue metal can with sifter cap. O.S.P. 24¢ C.M.V. $55.00 in box. $45.00 can only mint.

1915 Only - TOOTH POWDER (Left)
Small metal can came in 1915 Juvenile Set. CMV $75.00 mint
1915 TOOTH POWDER (Right)
Metal can. OSP 25c, CMV $60.00 MB $50.00 can only mint.

1906 HYGIENE FACE POWDER
Leatherette box trimmed in gold.
OSP 50c, CMV $60.00 mint.

1915 ELITE POWDER
Glass jar, metal sifter lid in CPC box.
OSP 25c, CMV $80.00 BO mint
$90.00 MB

FROM THE ONSTOT COLLECTION
1897 POWDER BOXES
2 different design aluminum powder cans with puffs. Does not say CPC on them but shown is old CPC literature. CMV not established.

1890-1915 SWEET SIXTEEN FACE POWDER
Paper box. OSP 25c, CMV $55.00 mint
1915 HYGIENE FACE POWDER
Green paper box. OSP 50c, CMV $50.00 mint.

1916 SWEET SIXTEEN FACE POWDER
Yellow, pink & green box. OSP 25c
CMV $45.00 mint.

1916 CALIFORNIA NAIL POWDER
Paper sides. OSP 25c, CMV $35.00 mint.

1923 ELITE POWDER
1 lb. blue can with English & French label. 2 different brass caps & narrow & wide blue band around top. OSP 89c, CMV $55.00 each, $65.00 MB

1923 ELITE POWDER REGULAR ISSUE
Pictured for size comparison on right.
FROM THE ONSTOT COLLECTION

1916 FACE POWDER LEAVES
Small book of 72 sheets of scented paper. Came in Rose , White, Rachel. O.S.P. 20¢ CMV $25.00 Mint.

1918 HYGIENE FACE POWDER
Green, gold & red powder box. O.S.P. 50c, CMV $55.00 mint.

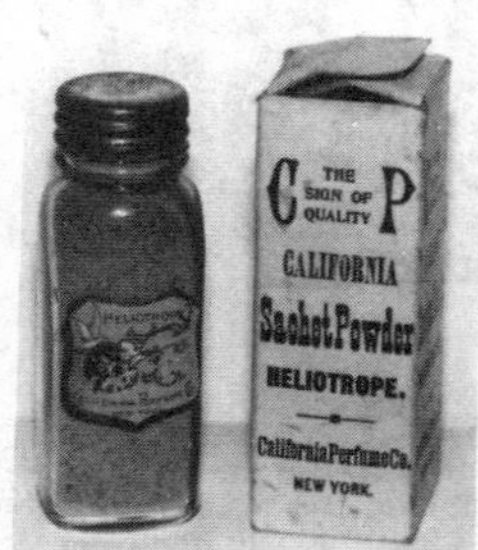

FROM THE ONSTOT COLLECTION

1888 SACHET POWDER
Heliotrope sachet in box. Metal cap. OSP 25c, CMV $100.00 MB, $90.00 BO mint.

LEFT 1915 CALIFORNIA BATH POWDER
Gold, white and green can. Came with sifter cap and take off cap. O.S.P. 25¢ C.M.V. $65.00, $80.00 MB

LEFT 1923 RADIANT NAIL POWDER
Blue & pink can. O.S.P. 24¢ C.M.V. $45.00 mint.

RIGHT 1915 SHAVING POWDER
2 oz. metal can. O.S.P. 25¢ C.M.V. $50.00 mint.

LEFT 1923 RADIANT NAIL POWDER
Blue & pink can. 2 different labels. OSP 24c, CMV $45.00 mint.

1 LB POWDER CAN
Gold tone can. Came in several fragrances as a refill. CMV $75.00 in new condition.

1920 WHITE LILAC TALCUM
4 oz. blue metal can with brass take off cap. Box came with paper on the Story of Italian Talc. O.S.P. 24¢ C.M.V. $65.00 can only mint, $80.00 MB as shown.

POWDER SACHETS - MISC.

ALL CPC'S MUST BE NEW MINT CONDITION FOR CMV

1915 POWDER SACHET
Gold cap, paper label on glass bottle. Came in Carnation, White Rose, Violet, White Lilac & Heliotrope. 2 different labels as shown. O.S.P. 25¢ C.M.V. $85.00 mint.

1908 SACHET POWDER ENVELOPES
Came in Violet, White Rose, & Heliotrope. O.S.P. 25¢ C.M.V. $30.00 mint.

LEFT 1923 POWDER SACHET
Brass cap, dark flowered label. This bottle came in CPC sets only. C.M.V. $90.00 BO - 10
RIGHT 1919 HELIOTROPE POWDER SACHET
Clear glass bottle, gold cap, label yellow with lavender flowers and green leaves. Came in other fragrances. Rare. C.M.V. $100.00 BO, $115.00 MB. Both bottles came in Carnation, Heliotrope, White Rose, Violet, White Lilac.

1890 CPC POWDER SACHET (Left)
Round glass bottle, aluminum lid. Came in Violet, Lilac, Rose, White Rose & Heliotrope. OSP 25c, CMV $110.00 MB, $90.00 BO mint. Also came with same label and cap in square glass bottle. Same CMV.
1886-1912 POWDER SACHET (Right)
Clear glass, gold cap, front label. Came in French Odors of Le Parfume de Roses, L'Odour de Violette, Peau D'Espagne. OSP 25c, CMV $110.00 MB, $90.00 BO mint.

1886-1912 POWDER SACHET - Silver or gold cap on glass bottle with front label. Came in Lilac, Rose, White Rose, Violet, Heliotrope. OSP 25c, CMV $110.00 MB, $90.00 BO mint. Each one has different label.

1887-1908 SACHET POWDER ENVELOPE - Eureka Trade Mark on label. Envelope contains powder in Violet, White Rose, Heliotrope. O.S.P. 25¢ C.M.V. $35.00 per envelope mint.

1922-25 POWDER SACHET
Large & small bottles with brass caps. Came in Carnation, Heliotrope, Violet, White Rose & Trailing Arbutus. OSP 49c, & 72c, CMV $90.00 BO, $110.00 MB each size.

C.P.C. SAMPLE CASES

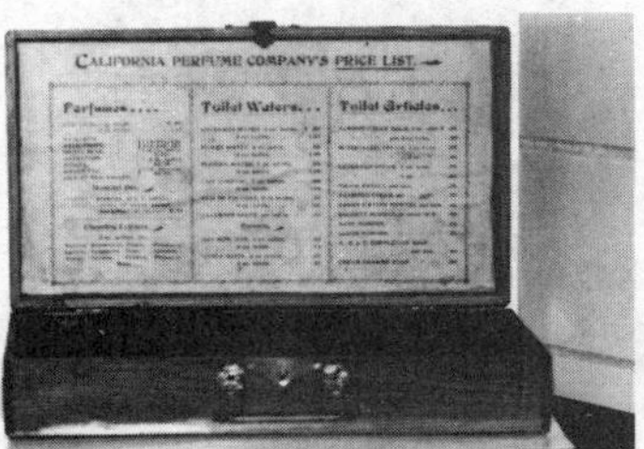

EARLY 1900's SAMPLE CASE
Plain wood box with brass handle.
C.M.V. $75.00 mint with CPC price list.
Case was used by CPC Reps to sell Products.

EARLY 1900's SAMPLE CASE
Plain wood box with leather handle. Red felt lining, printed paper price list inside lid. C.M.V. $75.00 mint with list.

1900 SAMPLE CASE
Black leather covered case with leather strap. Case came with CPC list of all products glued inside lid of case. Case was carried by CPC Reps to show products. C.M.V. Case mint full of products, $1,500.00 Case only mint $75.00 with list.

1920 CPC SALES CASE
Black case with red velvet lining. California Perfume Co. on chrome handle. Used by reps to show products. Case measures 14½" long x 8" wide, x 3½" high. CMV $75.00

C.P.C. SETS

WARNING!! Grading condition is paramount on sets.
CMV can vary 50% on grade.
Refer to page 5 on Grading.

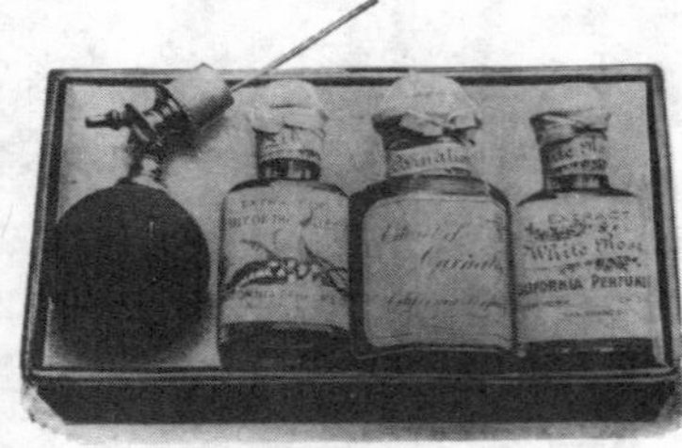

1896 ATOMIZER SET
Box holds atomizer & three 1 oz. bottles with cork stoppers. 2 bottles are round & center bottle is octagonal shape. Each has front & neck labels. O.S.P. $1.35 C.M.V. $400. M.B. complete set. Came in all fragrances of 1896.

1929 CPC ATOMIZER SET
Black box with green liner & gold tone lid holds green glass, lift off lid jar & 2 green glass spray atomizer bottle. Both have gold tone lids. Does not say CPC on it or box. CMV not established.

1909 CHRISTMAS BOX SET NO. 2
Babies on box, 2 glass stoppered perfumes. Gold labels. OSP 50c, CMV $275.00 MB.

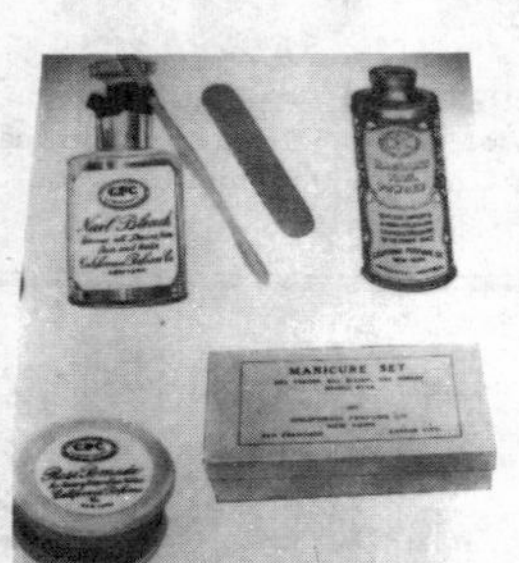

1923 MANICURE SET
White box holds can of Radiant Nail Powder, bottle of Nail Bleach with glass stopper, orange wood stick & jar of Rose Pomade. OSP 72c, CMV $200.00 MB

1900 MANICURE SET
Box holds bottle of Nail Bleach with glass stopper, C.M.V. $100. White jar of Rose Pomade, C.M.V. $50. & paper box of Nail Powder, C.M.V. $35. O.S.P. ea. 25¢ O.S.P. complete set 65c, CMV set $225.00 MB

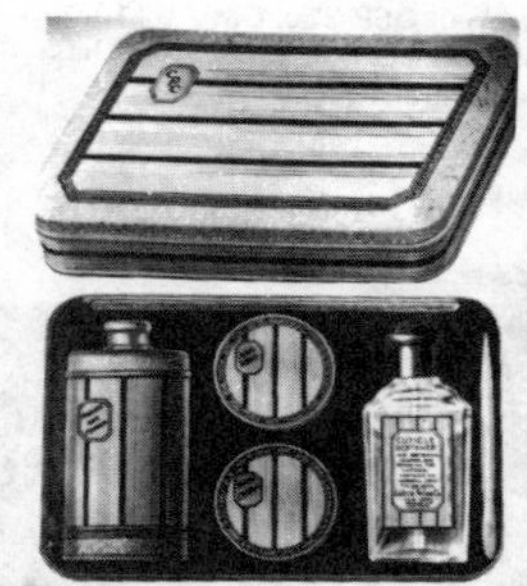

1925-28 MANICURE SET
Gold & black striped metal can holds gold & black can of Radiant Nail Powder, 1 can each of Nail White & Cuti-Cream & bottle of Cutrain with cork stopper. O.S.P. $1.20 CMV $165.00 MB

1929-30 BOUDOIR MANICURE SET
Same set as 1925 Manicure Set with name changed and has bottle of Cuticle Softener & small can of Nail Cream, Nail White & Radiant Nail Powder. All in same design. OSP $1.20, CMV $165.00 MB Set came with Lovely Hands Booklet.

1909 ATOMIZER BOX SET
Three 1 oz. bottles with cork stoppers & atomizer. Came in all fragrances of 1915. Green box. Each bottle has green front & neck labels. OSP $1.50, CMV $300.00 MB complete set.

1915 MANICURE SET
Black box contains buffer, scissors, file, Nail Bleach, Nail Powder & Rose Pomade. OSP $3.00, CMV $225.00 MB.

1916 MANICURE SET
Box holds glass stoppered bottle of Nail Bleach, jar of Rose Pomade and paper container of Nail Powder. O.S.P. 65¢ CMV complete set $200.00 MB

1914 NAIL POWDER
Paper box. O.S.P. 25¢ C.M.V. $35.00 mint.

1914 ROSE POMADE
White jar, glass. O.S.P. 25¢ C.M.V. $50.

1908 ATOMIZER SET
Box holds three 1 oz. bottles of perfume with cork stoppers & atomizer. Came in all fragrances of 1908. O.S.P. $1.50 C.M.V. $350.00 MB

1925-30 MANICURE SET BOX
Gold and black stripped metal can. C.M.V. $25.00, metal box only, mint.

1925-30 LOVELY HANDS BOOKLET
Came in Manicure Set shown. C.M.V. $10.00 booklet only mint.

1922 GIFT BOX NO. 2
½ oz. bottle of perfume & bottle of sachet. Came in Violet, White Rose, Carnation, Heliotrope & White Lilac. O.S.P. 97¢ CMV $200.00 MB.

1925-30 JACK & JILL JUNGLE JINKS SET
Brown decorated box holds 1 can Superite Trailing Arbutus Talcum, 1 bottle of Daphne Perfume, 1 cake of Apple Blossom soap, 1 can Trailing Arbutus Cold Cream, 1 tube Sen-Den-Tal Cream, 1 imported juvenile size tooth brush. O.S.P. $1.50, CMV $275.00 MB metal box only $65.00 mint.

1929 Only - GERTRUDE RECORDON'S FACIAL TREATMENT SET
4 oz. bottle of astringent with cork stopper, $75. 4 oz. bottle of peach lotion with cork stopper, $75. Ribbed white glass jar with CPC on metal lid each in cleansing cream & skin food. Each jar $45 O.S.P. $4. CMV complete set $275.00 MB

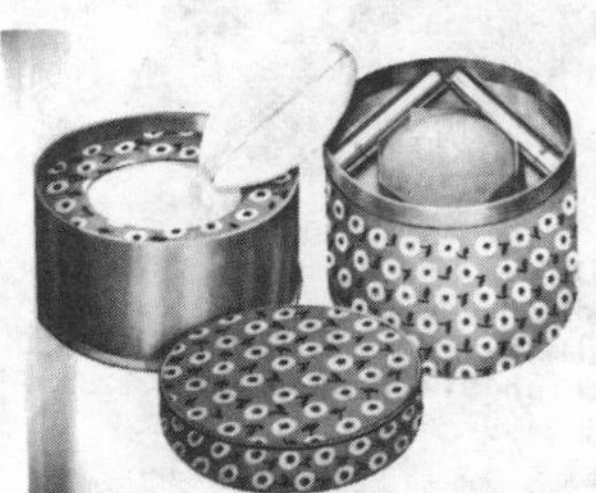

1929-30 DRESSING TABLE VANITY
Orange & gold two-section box has brass lipstick & eyebrow pencil & rouge compact in top half of box & bottom half is full of Jardin D'Amour or Ariel Face Powder. OSP $2.25, CMV $110.00 MB 3.

1909 CHRISTMAS BOX SET NO. 3
Roses on box, 2 perfumes, glass stoppered. OSP 65c, CMV $300.00 MB

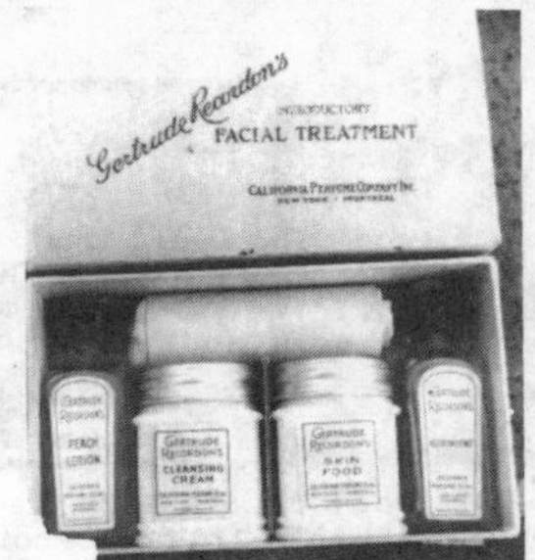

1929 Only - GERTRUDE RECORDON'S FACIAL TREATMENT SET
Box holds white jars of Gertrude Recordon's cleansing cream & skin food. C.M.V. ea. jar $50. 2 bottles with cork stoppers of peach lotion & astringent. C.M.V. ea. bottle $50. & roll of facial tissues. C.M.V. set mint in box. $275.00

1909 BOX A SET
Holly green, red & gold box holds 2, ½ oz. perfumes with glass stoppers. OSP 50c, CMV $275.00 MB

1915 GIFT BOX NO. 2
Yellow & purple box holds ½ oz. perfume & powder sachet. Choice of Carnation, Heliotrope, White Lilac, Violet & White Rose. O.S.P. 50¢ per set. Set $250.00 M.B.

1909 MEMORIES THAT LINGER SET
3 glass stoppered perfumes in book shaped box. Violet, White Rose & Carnation Perfume. OSP $2.00, CMV $400.00 MB.

1910 HOLLY SET
Holly design box holds 2 half ounce bottles with glass & cork stoppers. Gold front & neck labels. Choice of Violet, White Rose, White Lilac, Carnation, Heliotrope, Lily of the Valley perfume. O.S.P. 50¢ C.M.V. $250.00 M.B.

1915 HOLLY PATTERN BOX A
Set has two ½ oz. glass & cork stoppered perfume bottles. Came in Carnation, Lily of the Valley, Violet, White Rose, White Lilac & Heliotrope. O.S.P. 50¢ C.M.V. $250.00 set M.B.

FROM THE ONSTOT COLLECTION
1915 Only - JUVENILE SET
Box holds miniature size cans of Natoma Talcum Powder, Tooth Powder, small bottle of Violet Water with cork stopper & small cake of Savona Bouquet Soap. Each item is about 2" high. O.S.P. 50¢ C.M.V. $400.00 M.B.

1915 GIFT BOX NO. 2
Box holds ½ oz. perfume with glass & cork stopper & powder sachet in Carnation, White Lilac, Heliotrope, Violet & White Rose. O.S.P. 50¢ C.M.V. $225.00 M.B.

1915 GIFT BOX A
Same pattern as Holly Pattern set. Green & red holly box. Two ½ oz. glass stoppered perfumes in choice of Violet, White Rose, Carnation, White Lilac, Heliotrope & Lily of the Valley. O.S.P. 50¢ C.M.V. $250.

1918 GIFT BOX NO. 3
Box holds 2 half ounce bottles of perfume. Crown glass stopper set in cork. Came in all fragrances of 1917-18 period. CMV $250 MB.

1909 CHRISTMAS BOX SET NO. 4
Box holds Hygiene Face Powder, Savona soap & glass stoppered perfume. OSP $1.00, CMV $275.00 MB

LITTLE FOLKS SETS

ALL CPC'S MUST BE NEW MINT CONDITION FOR CMV

1932 Only - LITTLE FOLKS SET
Same box as 1923-32 Little Folks Set. Holds 4 octagonal shaped bottles. Silver labels, black caps. Came in Ariel, Bolero, Gardenia, & Trailing Arbutus. OSP 90c, CMV $250.00 set MB.

1932-36 LITTLE FOLKS SET
Four small bottles of Ariel, Verna Fleur, 391 & Trailing Arbutus perfumes with black caps. O.S.P. 90¢ C.M.V. $175.00 set mint. $35.00 ea. bottle.

1937-39 LITTLE FOLKS SET
Fancy box has four bottles of perfume in Gardenia, Cotillion, Narcissus & Trailing Arbutus, 2 dram size. O.S.P. 94¢ C.M.V. $125.00 M.B. Each bottle $25.00.

1905-1908 LITTLE FOLKS SET
4 small bottles of Violet, Carnation, White Rose or Rose & Heliotrope perfumes. Birds & kids on lid & edge of box. OSP 40c, CMV $350.00 MB.

08-1915 LITTLE FOLKS SET
our gem sized bottles of perfume came in iolet, Carnation, Rose & Heliotrope. Cork oppers. Same bottles & labels as 1896 ittle Folks Set. O.S.P. 50¢ C.M.V. $75.00 . bottle or $350.00 for set, mint.

1905-1908 LITTLE FOLKS SET
4 small bottles of Violet, Carnation, White Rose & Heliotrope perfumes. Birds & kids on lid. O.S.P. 40¢ C.M.V. $350.00 M.B.

1915-23 LITTLE FOLKS SET
Contains 4 gem bottles of perfume with Violet, Carnation, White Rose & Heliotrope. O.S.P. 50¢ C.M.V. $75.00 ea. bottle or $350.00 for set, M.B.

1896-1905 LITTLE FOLKS SET
Boy & girl with dog inside lid of box. 4 gem sized perfume bottles of Violet, Carnation, White Rose & Heliotrope. Bottles had cork stoppers & ribbons on neck. Flower on labels. Box size is 5½" x 3¼". O.S.P. 40¢ C.M.V. $400.00 for set, mint, or $75.00 ea. bottle.

1923-32 LITTLE FOLKS SET
Blue box contains four gem size bottles of Floral perfumes in Daphne, Verna Fleur, Trailing Arbutus & Carnation, Violet, Heliotrope or White Lilac. All have brass caps. O.S.P. 69¢ C.M.V. $300.00 for set, mint. $65.00 ea. bottle.

C.P.C. MEN'S SETS

1917 GENTLEMEN'S SHAVING SET
Brown box holds Cream Shaving Stick, Menthol Witch Hazel Cream tube, 50-sheet Shaving Pad, 2 oz. bottle of White Lilac Toilet Water, styptic pencil, 4 oz. bottle of genuine Bay Rum with glass stopper & box of White Lilac Talcum or jar of Violet Talcum. O.S.P. $1.50 C.M.V. $350. complete set.

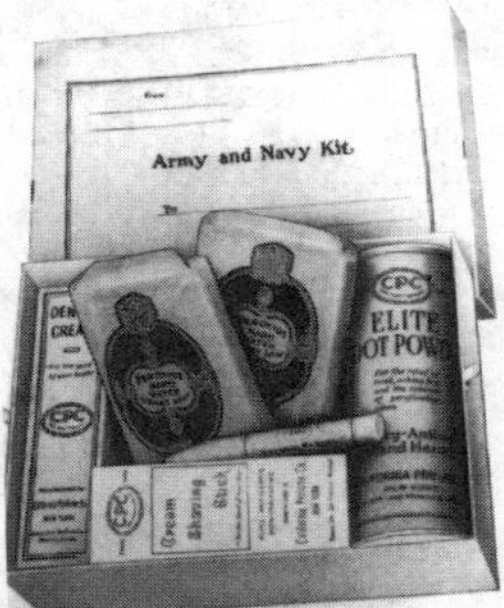

1918 ARMY & NAVY KIT
Heavy cardboard box holds 2 bars of Peroxide Toilet Soap, styptic pencil, Elite Foot Powder, Cream Shaving Stick, Dental Cream. O.S.P. $1.25 C.M.V. $150.

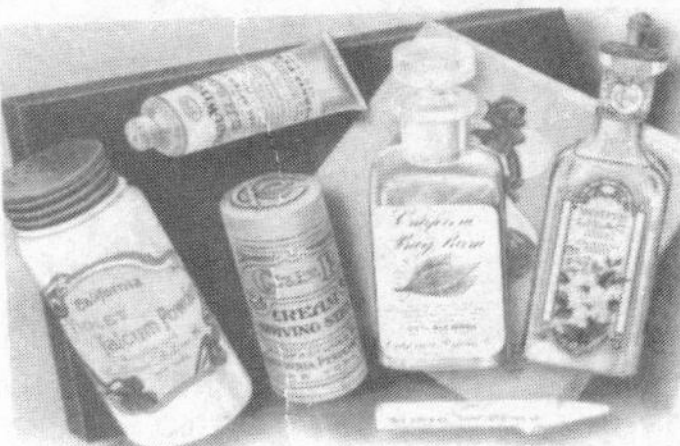

1915 GENTLEMANS SHAVING SET
Box holds glass bottle of Violet Talcum Powder, can of Cream Shaving Stick, tub of Menthol Witch Hazel Cream, Styptic Pencil, 4 oz. glass stoppered bottle of Bay Rum, 2 oz. White Lilac Toilet Water and 50 sheet shaving pad. OSP $1.50, CMV $400.00

1928-30 HUMIDOR SHAVING SET BOX
Metal gold striped box only. Measures 9¼" wide x 5¾" x 3" deep. Does not say CPC on box. Picture of ship on lid. CMV box only mint. $35.00

1925-29 HUMIDOR SHAVING SET BOX
Maroon & gold metal box only. Measures 9¼" wide x 5¾" x 3" deep. Bottom says Metal Packaging Corp. of New York. CMV box only mint. $35.00.

1919 GENTLEMANS SHAVING SET
Box contains blue can of White Lilac Talcum, green tube of Menthol Witch Hazel Cream, can ov Cream Shaving Stick, 4 oz. Bay Rum with cork stopper, Styptic Pencil, 2 oz. bottle of White Lilac Toilet Water and 50 sheet shaving pad, OSP $2.25, CMV $400.00 MB.

1923 GENTLEMEN'S SHAVING SET
Box contains Bayberry Shave Cream tube, White Lilac Talcum, White Lilac Toilet Water, styptic pencil, Bay Rum, Menthol Witch Hazel & Shaving Pad. O.S.P. $1.95 C.M.V. $275.00

1925-28 HUMIDOR SHAVING SET
Wood grained box trimmed in gold & black holds 2 oz. bottle of Lilac Vegetal, 4 oz. bottle of Bay Rum, blue can of White Lilac Talcum, Trailing Arbutus Cold Cream, tube of Menthol Witch Hazel Cream, Bayberry Shave Cream tube & styptic pencil. O.S.P. $1.95, CMV $275.00 MB

1928-29 HUMIDOR SHAVING SET
Gold & black metal box holds 4 oz. bottle Bay Rum, 2 oz. bottle Lilac Vegetal, styptic pencil, green tube Menthol Witch Hazel Cream, green tube Bayberry Shave Cream & can of either White Lilac Talcum or Avon Talc for Men. OSP $2.25, CMV $300.00 complete set MB.

1930 Only - HUMIDOR SHAVING SET
Gold & black metal box holds 4 oz. ribbed bottle of Bay Rum, 2 oz. bottle of Lilac Vegetal, Styptic pencil, green tubes of Menthol Witch Hazel cream & Bayberry Shaving cream & green can of Talc for Men. O.S.P. $2.50, CMV $250.00 MB

AWARDS & REPRESENTATIVES GIFTS

SEE WOMEN'S FRAGRANCE LINES FOR ADDITIONAL AWARDS

For additional information on Avon Awards and Gifts you may purchase an excellent book by Dee Schneider for $6.95 from Avon Research, Box 9321, Glendale, CA 91206.

Avon Research is not affiliated with Avon Products Inc. Bud Hastin highly recommends this book for the Awards Collector. (See Women's Fragrance lines for additional awards.)

WARNING: All Avon Awards with gold or silver content should be bought and sold with caution.

Unless it is marked 10K, 12K, 14K or marked "Solid Gold", it is described as gold for color only. For it to be real gold, it must be marked 10K, 12K, or 14K ONLY.

For it to be real silver, it must be marked Sterling or Solid Silver. Trays and goblets must be marked Sterling to be of any real metal value. Silver plate is of very little value in silver content.

If you have real solid gold or sterling silver awards, it would be best to ask someone who is buying the metal what they would pay for it. This is the true value of the metal. A jewelers appraisal is not worth the paper it is written on. It is a quote below what he would sell it for and the real value is the wholesale price of what he will pay for it.

With the exploding up and down prices on gold, silver and diamonds, we suggest you check on the value before you buy or sell such items. Prices can change from day to day. All prices quoted reflect the collectors value plus the gold price of $500.00 per ounce.

1968 MANAGERS DIAMOND RING
¼ carat art carved 58 faceted diamond set in a gold 4A design mounting. Given to managers for achievement of sales goals for several quarters. CMV $450.00 mint.

1971 CIRCLE OF EXCELLENCE RING
Same as pin only ring. CMV $250.00 mint.

1969 CIRCLE OF EXCELLENCE PIN
4A gold pin circled with pearls & diamonds in center. Managers only pin has a logo on back and can also be worn as a pendant. CMV $250.00

1961 MANAGERS DIAMOND 4A PIN
4A diamond pin with diamond crown guard. Given to managers reaching a special quota. in 1961. CMV $175.00.

1961 MANAGERS DIAMOND PIN
Gold 4A pin same as representatives except has an "M" made of 11 diamonds. C.M.V. $125.00 M.B.

1961-76 DIAMOND 4A PIN
Larger than other 4A pins; set with diamond Given for selling $3,000 at customer price in an 18 campaign period. In 1974-76 you had to sell $4,500.00 in 13 campaigns. C.M.V. $50.00 MB

1963-76 SAPPHIRE 4A PIN
Same as pearl pin ¾" dia. set with a genuine sapphire. Awarded for reaching $2,000 in customer sales price in a 9 campaign period. In 1974-76 you had to sell $3,500.00 in 13 campaigns. C.M.V. $30.00 M.B.

1963-70 PEARL 4A PIN
10 kt. gold in a 4A design with pearl in center. Awarded for reaching $1,000 in customer price sales in a 9 campaign period. 5/8" diameter. C.M.V. $20.00.

1973-76 RUBY 4A PIN
10 kt. gold with ruby in center. Awarded for selling $2,500 in customer price sales in 6 month period to become eligible for President's Club Membership. C.M.V. $15.00

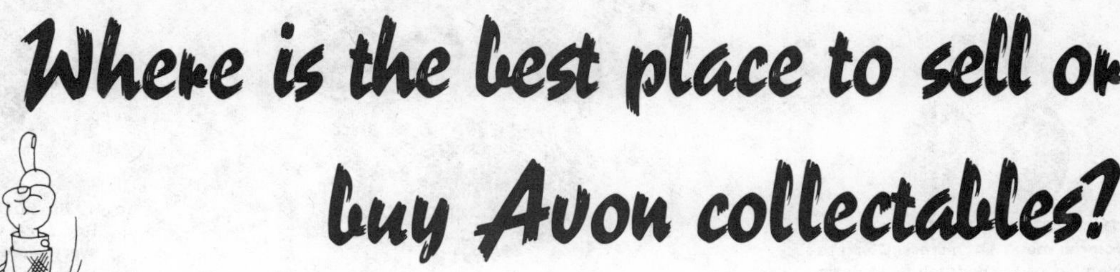

The #1 spot in the nation is through an ad in the AVON TIMES. A monthly publication of the Bud Hastin's National Avon Club. This is the world's largest Avon Collectors Club. Thousands of "Hard Core Avon Collectors" read the large want ad section of AVON TIMES each month. Avons advertised in AVON TIMES bring top prices.

Join the 1,000's of other Avon Collectors who know by experience it's a must to receive the Avon Times if you buy, sell or trade Avons.

Tell your friends about the AVON TIMES. It costs 15c per word to run a (quick results) ad in the AVON TIMES. Or you may join the Bud Hastin National Avon Club for $11.00 per year ($11.00 in Canada, U.S. money orders only), and receive 3 free ad coupons worth $22.50 in free advertising. Plus you get 12 monthly issues of AVON TIMES bringing you the latest on Avon collecting. It tells you where Avon Bottle Shows are held around the nation. It features monthly articles on different trends in Avon collecting, bringing you the news first when a "rare" or "odd" Avon is discovered so you will know what to look for. Plus the largest Avon advertising section in the United States. You get first hand information on buying Avon Club Bottles that double in value the first year. Club bottles issued in 1972 are now selling for $600.00 and only cost $11.95 seven years ago.

Don't miss the NEW LOOK of the AVON TIMES NOW professionally typeset and printed.

YOU CAN'T AFFORD NOT TO BELONG TO BUD HASTIN'S NATIONAL AVON CLUB AND GET THE AVON TIMES WITH $22.50 WORTH OF FREE ADS, DISCOUNT'S ON THE AVON ENCYCLOPEDIA. DON'T DELAY - TELL YOUR FRIENDS - JOIN TODAY!

It Doesn't Cost You—It Pays You To Belong

JOIN BUD'S BUNCH

Send 15c per word for ads or send $11.00 for 1 year (Canada - $11.00 for 1 year, U.S. money orders only) membership with $22.50 worth of free ad coupons.

Send Order To:

BUD HASTIN
P. O. Box 8400, Ft. Lauderdale, FL 33310

MEMBERSHIP AND AD RATES SUBJECT TO CHANGE WITHOUT NOTICE

1964 QUEENS AWARD PIN
gold colored metal 1¼" across. Given to each member of the winning team during the 78th Anniversary for top sales. C.M.V. $15.00

1938-45 IDENTIFICATION PIN
Silver with aqua enamel. Given to all representatives for identification. "Avon Products, Inc., Avon" on face of pin. CMV $30.00 mint

1938-45 HONOR I.D. PIN "GOLD"
Gold plated with aqua enamel. Given for $250.00 in sales. "Avon Products, Inc., Avon Honor" on face of pin. CMV $35.00 mint.

TOP — 1929-38 CPC AVON I.D. PIN
Given to all reps to show they work for Avon and the CPC. Silver pin with blue enamel. "California Perfume Co., INC., "Avon" on face of pin. This pin is larger in size than the 1938-45 I.D. pins. This pin came in 2 different ways. The A and V on Avon is close together on one and wide apart on the others. CMV $45.00 mint.

BOTTOM — 1929-38 I.D. HONOR AWARD PIN
Gold filled with dark blue enamel. Given to reps for $250.00 in sales. "CPC — AVON — HONOR" on face of pin. CMV $55.00 mint.

1936 - 50TH ANNIVERSARY PIN
Red circle with gold feather. Given every representative who made a ho to house sales trip of her area. CMV $55.00 mint.

1938-45 I.D. HONOR PIN - "SILVER" AND CASE
Silver with aqua enamel. Given to all representatives for identification. "Avon Products, Inc., Avon Honor" on face of pin. Black leatherette presentation case. "Avon highest honor" on case. CMV $30.00 pin only. Add $10.00 for case. Case also came in navy blue or a black case with no letters on it. Same CMV for plain case.

1910-25 CPC IDENTIFICATION PIN
Given to all representatives to identify them as official company representatives. Says CPC 1886 on face. CMV $90.00 mint.

1910-15 CPC IDENTIFICATION HONOR PIN
Given to representatives for selling $250.00 in merchandise. CMV $90.00 mint. Both pins are sold gold.

1956-61 JEWELED PIN - DIAMOND
Same as pearl jeweled pin except has diamonds instead of pearls. Came wit black & gold star guard also containir 5 diamonds. This was the top award a was given after attaining the 4 diamo star guard. A minimum of $25,000 in sales were required for this award. C.M.V. $135.00 mint.

1945-61 FIELD MANAGER'S I D PIN & GUARD - Same design as the jeweled pin but has no printing. The "M" guard is smooth gold. C.MV. $50.00.

1945-61 JEWELED PIN PEARL — HIGHEST HONOR
10K gold with black enamel background. 5 oriental pearls are set in the A. Came in black highest award case above. Add $15.00 for mint box. Given for sales of $1,000. CMV $30.00

1945-51 IDENTIFICATION PIN
Gold pin with black background. "A" has scroll design rather than jewels. Edges are plain, no writing. Given to representatives for $1,000 in sales. CMV $20.00

1945-61 JEWELED PIN - PEARL
10kt. gold with black enamel backgroun 5 oriental pearls are set in the A. Given f sales of $1,000.00 C.M.V. $30.00

1956-61 STAR GUARDS
Raised star on round gold metal pin. Give for each $5,000.00 in sales in any 12 mo period. Four guards could be won, each an additional diamond. Made to wear wi the jeweled pin. C.M.V. $15.00 one diamond. Add $12.50 for each additiona diamond.

1900 CPC I.D. PIN
Solid gold I.D. pin given to early day reps to show they worked for the CPC company. This is the 1st I.D. pin ever given by the CPC. CMV $150.00

1945-61 CITY MANAGERS I D PIN & PEARL GUARD - Given to all City Managers. Pin has 5 pearls. Guard is set with 11 seed pearls. C.M.V. $75.00 mint.

AN OPEN LETTER TO ALL AVON REPS.

Do you want to increase the number of Avon collectors in the world? This would greatly increase your sales, too, you know! Try to find out your customer's various interests and those of her children and husband, too! For example:

Mrs. Smith loves animals - bring every animal decanter to her attention as they appear on the market. Sell her the first one and she'll likely buy more, or all, that come! Mr. Smith is a sports fan! Point out what a smart collection he could have on a neat shelf in his den. Young Johnny would love the majestic elephant, or that dinosaur decanter and teenager Sue really "digs" the "Fried Egg" or "Hamburger" compacts.

All these people have a good chance of ending up being a collector! So what does that really mean? Well it means that your collectables will maintain their value and the market will grow steadily. Avon Reps. will have good steady sales. Collectors will have a wider and wider circle of ever growing and interested folk to swap and shop with.

Show your own collection to friends, help to stir the interest of others. Believe me, it will pay off in the end!!

Most important of all, don't forget to carry a copy of the Avon Encyclopedia to show your customers. Show them the color pages on "How collectors display their Avons." By showing this book to your customers, you can help create new collectors and you will profit 10 fold, as collectors will buy many more Avon products from you. Be sure to point out information on the Bud Hastin Avon Club which they can enjoy right from their own living room. Tell them about the free advertising to over 4000 members to buy, sell or trade Avons. Remember, if you help educate your customers on Avon Collecting you will profit greatly in bigger future sales.

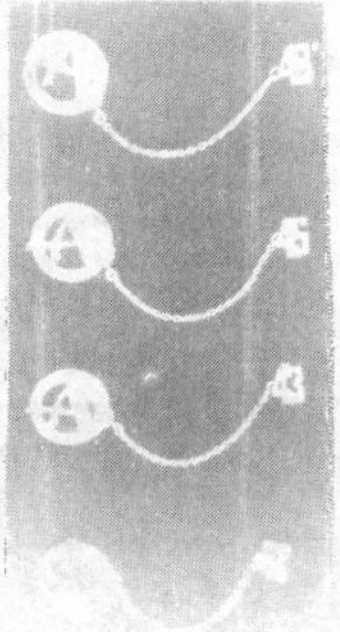

1945-56 JEWEL PIN NUMERAL GUARDS
Smooth gold numerals given for additional sales in multiples of $1,000 starting with No. 2. There was no No. 1. These are made to attach to the jewel pin. Highest numeral known is 115. The higher the number the more valuable. C.M.V. $8.00 on numbers 2 to 10. $12.00 on 11 to 20. $14.00 on 21 to 30 $18.00 on 31 to 40 $20.00 on 41 to 75 $25.00 ea. on 76 up.

1965 GOLDEN CIRCLE CHARM BRACELET AWARD
22 kt. gold finish double-link bracelet with safety chain and 5 gold charms. Each charm given for progressively higher sales. C.M.V. $7.00 each charm, plus bracelet $7.00. Came in an Avon box.

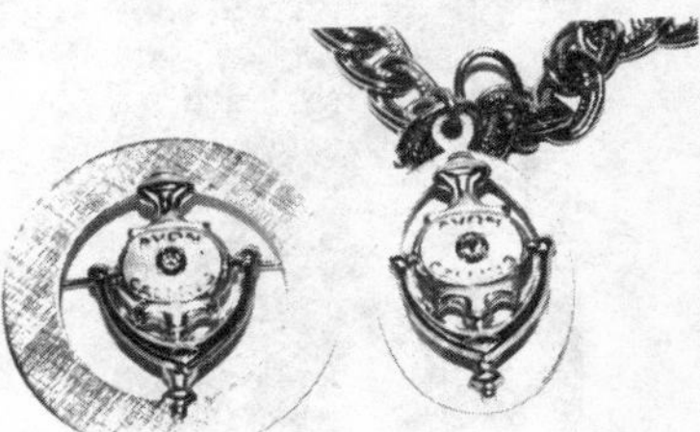

1974 MANAGERS ACHIEVEMENT AWARD PIN & CHARM BRACELET
1 given to top sales manager in each division. Brush sterling silver with blue sapphire in center of Avon Door Knocker. CMV $50.00 each.

1972-79 CIRCLE OF EXCELLENCE CHARM BRACELET
10K gold bracelet & gold charm with 3 diamonds & 4A design. Black & gold Avon box. Green inside. Given to managers only. CMV $150.00 MB Also same charm with 4 diamonds last charm. Value is high & not established because of gold & diamond value.

1959 SILVER CHARM BRACLET
Only 2 districts won in each branch. This was a test bracelet & very few were given for sales achievement. C.M.V. $175.00 mint with all 6 charms.

The Gold Medal

1931 THE GOLD STAR MEDAL
Highest honor given to representatives that achieved the goal of $1,000.00 in sales from January to January. If goal reached second year a second gold star is engraved, and so on. C.M.V. $200.00. M.B.

1969-70 TEAM CAPTAIN PIN (Bottom)
Torch pin says T C -69-70. CMV $15.00
1963 - 1500 PIN (Top)
Given to reps. for $1,500.00 in sales in one campaign. CMV $17.00.

1963-65 MANAGERS CHARM BRACELET
One charm was given each quarter for 3 years making a total of 12 charms possible. These were won by attaining certain sales increases which increased with each quarter making the later charms very difficult to get. For this reason charms past the eighth quarter are very hard to find. The bracelet & charms are 10 kt. gold. Only four bracelets were won with all 12 charms. A total of 6191 individual charms were given to 1445 managers. The last four charms are like the one pictured in center of bracelet. No. 9 has Rubys, No. 10 Saphire, No. 11, Emerald & No. 12 Diamond. Each one had 4 stones. C.M.V. 1st 8 charms $45.00 ea, plus bracelet. No. 9 & 10 $60.00 ea. No. 11, 12, $75.00 ea. C.M.V. all 12 charms $800.00 mint.

1964 SILVER DOOR KNOCKER PIN
Given to all managers in conjunction with the door knocker award program. C.M.V. $25.00 - $30.00 M.B.
1964-79 GOLD DOORKNOCKER PIN
Came on green or white cards. CMV $10.00 on card. CMV pin only $7.00

1960 ANNIVERSARY PRINCESS BRACELET
Awarded for increased sales. Bracelet with diamond. Bracelet with emerald, Bracelet with rubt or topaze. 14K gold. CMV $250.00 each

1971-76 GOLDEN ACHIEVEMENT AWARD - Bracelet & 1st charm awarded for $5,500.00 total sales in 6 month period. Each succeeding charm awarded for $5,500.00 within each subsequent 6 month period. First charm 2 joined 4A design with green stone. Second charm - Avon Rose with red stone. Third charm - The First Lady with a genuine topaze. Fourth charm - The "World of Avon" set with a genuine aquamarine. Fifth charm - The Doorknocker" with a genuine amethyst. Sixth charm - jeweled "A" with a genuine sapphire. Seventh charm - the "Key" with a genuine garnet. Eighth charm - Great Oak. (Above order of charms correct) CMV $35.00 each charm. Charm No. 8, $50.00

15 YEAR LOYAL SERVICE AWARD
Solid 10K gold. 4A emblem on front. Avon 15 years loyal service on back. Given to employees of Avon. Came on 10K gold wrist chain. CMV $150.00.

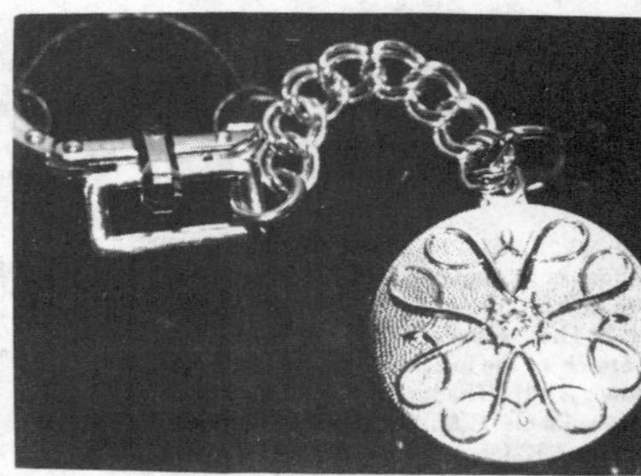

1976-77 SALES ACHIEVEMENT KEY CHAIN
Silver tone key chain. 4A emblem on front & back marked "Avon Sales Achievement Award C/23/76 C/9/77." In special Sales Achievement Award Avon box. CMV $10.00 MB.

1979 KEY CHAIN "THANKS AMERICA" AWARD
Team leader white box holds silver tone heart key chain "Thanks America for making us number one" Back side says "Avon loves team leaders." CMV $12.50 MB.

1978 "KEY CHAIN" DISTRICT MANAGER SAFE DRIVER AWARD
Large brass key chain has "4A" on one side & "Avon District Manager Safe Driver Award 1978" on other side. Came in white & green box. 4A on box lid. Came also with Avon card shown. CMV $10.00 MB.

WHAT IS AVON COLLECTING?

by Connie Clark, Kansas City, MO

Many of you readers may well be familiar with this "strange" hobby, or they may think, as many do, that Avon collectors only collect the cars, the figurines or any of the "pretty" containers. This is true, but only partially.

Avon collecting began in 1968-69 for most. This is when Avon began to promote what is referred to as "figural bottles", in other words, they depict a real object. Such as a duck, a car, a roll of money.

What is surprising is that Avon collecting covers many phases, somewhere, someone, an Avon collector, is trying to find an old metal tube, an old cardboard lipstick or any number of other items, not restricted to "pretty" things.

Avon was originally known as The California Perfume Company which had its beginnings in 1886 (they changed to Avon Products, Inc. in 1929). Collectors, and again we're not talking about all collectors, savor a "CPC" item. You must realize that these items were from the very early days and are very much sought after by collectors - and some of the most expensive. These items very rarely find their way to a garage sale, but many collectors have some very good "fish" tales to tell about their CPC's. The CPC items are attractive, but do not depict an object. They are simply old, and collectors try and find them in the best condition possible.

Avon begins, much like other companies, at the Corporate level. They offer service awards for continued service; this could be a string of pearls for the ladies, cuff-links for the men. Next we have the District Managers who are charged with a certain number of Representatives. They are given sales goals for their districts and when these goals are attained, they are rewarded with awards. The Representatives who make up the district are also given sales goals, and when they are met, they are rewarded with awards. They are also given the opportunity to receive prizes (we call them prizes, because they are not marked with the word Avon). The awards are usually marked in some manner.

As you are probably beginning to wonder or say, "So what?" — well, these are phases of Avon collecting that people do not generally think about . . . but collectors do try and obtain CPC's and Awards. These awards could consist of jewelry, silverware, desk sets, porcelain and many other items. From these Employees, District Managers and Representatives, collectors have added many very fine items to their collections.

We now have seen two phases of Avon collecting. There are still many, many other phases for the Avon collectors; magazine advertising, literature of all kinds, children's toys, fragrance lines, soaps and the list goes on. It must be said that at this point, many collectors have become more selective in their collecting and are beginning to specialize.

It is apparent, or has become so, to many collectors that to collect everything the California Perfume Co. and Avon Products, Inc. ever produced is absolutely non-attainable. Not only is the attainability a deterrent, but also space limitations and monetary considerations. After seeing the many products available, and considering the length of time in existance, it is understandable why collectors are beginning to specialize.

What do we mean by specializing? At a certain point in time, a collector realizes he is running out of space to display his collection, or he tires of certain items and wants to devote his entire collecting energy to one certain phase. This one phase is then the one and only item the collector seeks. However, we do know some collectors who have begun to specialize in several phases.

Let us then take a brief look at what some specialties are, and we'll look at the items that most people do not think of as Avon collectables! These specialties may not be bottles or even produced by Avon and there are several ways collectors will specialize. It could be by collecting everything in one category or in only one category up to a certain period of time. Along with the CPC's and Awards, comes the category of Literature.

Literature is not sold by the Avon Representative or is not particularly "pretty", but it is a desirable collectable to some. Literature is found at most all levels of the Avon organization. The employees have an "in-house" publication, the District Managers have a magazine or booklet printed just for them, and the Representative has the Avon Calling. There are the Outlooks (which are the counterpart of Avon Calling - in past years), the sales brochures, and any other printed or written material such as the sales order books, call back pads, prize catalogs and letterheads/envelopes.

All of these items, depending on the collector who wants them are valuable as a collectable. By valuable, I don't necessarily mean in dollars, but as an Avon item. Don't get me wrong, an old CPC Outlook or early stationery might command a high price, if there is someone willing to pay for it. A lot of collectors use this material for valuable reference material.

Another seldom thought of Avon collectable is the magazine advertising. Avon uses this method of promoting their products. They have been advertising since the very early days and there are collectors who seek this advertising in any shape or form (including T.V. films). Again, this is something Avon does not sell.

Continued on following page . . .

We call collectors who treasure literature paper collectors - and they may very well collect other specialties.

There is one other area of collectables that are not sold to the public, but are sold to Representatives, or given to them for sales aides. These are Samples. The Representatives use these samples to promote their products . . . and some collectors want these for their collections. Some of the older samples are very elaborate and are very much sought after.

The items we have discussed thus far are not items most people bring to mind when speaking of Avon collecting. There are the more common items: cars, figurals, soaps, children's toys, children's soaps, sets, fragrance lines and candles.

As I said above, "common" items. However, in each one of these categories, there are certain items that are not common! Let us, very briefly, look at some of these different categories.

When you speak about Cars and Figurals, you're speaking in the same category. They are items reproduced to look like an object. There are the animals, modes of all kinds of transportation, sports related items, and others. Each of these could be broken down into a specialty. Let us not forget there are also women's figurals . . . the same rule applies here.

Next, we have soaps - does a collector collect only children's soaps, women's soaps or men's soaps? They could collect all three . . . soaps in general. Of course, you have soaps with sponges and soaps with dishes, sets of soaps and only bars of soap.

Mention children's items to some and you're talking about a very hard-to-find specialty. Children have the habit of using these products and toys . . . some of the very old products are almost impossible to find in any kind of good condition.

Throughout the earlier days and especially in the 1930's, 1940's and 1950's, packaging was a great asset to Avon's sales. This is where the gift-set specialty gets into the act. Many collectors like to try and find these gift sets, and the better the condition, the better the price and the more they want them. These gift sets are very attractive and usually contain several items, even if it was only a lipstick and nail polish, the packaging was beautiful. Although they made many sets like the one mentioned above, there were even fancier ones . . . colored net or satin cloth background, with the products laying on top. Take a look at current boxes; they are a work of art in themselves . . . and these older boxes were certainly that!

When we speak of fragrance lines, we're talking about fragrance. Each time a fragrance was introduced, it was distinctive in its looks. For instance, Here's My Heart was blue in color and most of the items were shaped like a heart. Elegante was indeed elegant as it was bright red and had a satin appearance on the boxes. Some collectors like to try and find everything in these different fragrances . . . the specially packaged items. These fragrances were still bottled and sold in many, many other containers - not specially packaged, and that's were we get the various miscellaneous items. Some might try and obtain these miscellaneous items to go with their specially packaged items. And some may try and specialize in several of these old fragrances, cutting back at a certain date.

The glow of a candle is irresistable to some, and here you have candle collectors. Candles in every shape, size and color. Many of them are figurals and many of them can be used for candy after they are holders, most are refillable, some are not.

I am sure I've probably left out someone's very favorite collectable, but this does give you an idea of that Avon collecting consists of. There are still dyed-in-the-wood collectors who will purchase anything with the name Avon on it. They collect, display and are proud of their accomplishments, as all collectors are.

Avon collectors just like to collect . . . but, they also like to share their hobby. This is how Avon clubs came in existence. Yes, there are Avon clubs all over the United States and Canada. These clubs meet each month, and right now, as you read this, there more than likely is an Avon club meeting in progress. Different clubs enjoy different ideas, and one might be playing bingo, another might be presenting a program on awards, still another might be having a giant auction for the members to buy and sell their extra merchandise . . . for we've almost never met a collector who did not need to support his hobby.

From these clubs, in all different locations, sprang a national organization called the National Association of Avon Clubs. It consists, just like the name implies, of Avon clubs. A club may pay their dues, conform to certain criteria set out by the Association, and participate in whatever this Association has to offer. Which is quite a lot: annual conventions (held all over the United States), a chance to purchase unique collectables and the opportunity to join with other collectors to learn and talk about the hobby.

We have just begun to tell you what Avon collecting is all about. There is much more. Intangibles make up a large part of Avon collecting . . . knowledge, friendship, travel, hospitality, competition and challenges. It is truly through these 'intangibles' that Avon collecting has become a major hobby, one that might not be particularly well-known or publicized, but that is gaining momentum day by day, week by week and year by year; as more collectors join the ranks of a very determined hobby and people who make up the hobby.

In summary, there are many, many ways to collect Avon. And there are some we have not mentioned. But, these are the basics and it really doesn't make any difference how an Avon collector collects, or what they collect . . . that it's enjoyed, displayed and shared . . . is the major factor.

1976 CHARM "DAY TO REMEMBER" AWARD
Small gold tone charm marked "A Day to Remember - C21-76" Came in blue Avon box. CMV $15.00 MB.

1979 DREAM CHARM MANAGERS NECKLACE
Gold tone necklace & 3 charms of orchid, butterfly & sea shell. Given to Avon managers at 1979 Dream Conference. Does not say Avon on charms. Came in maroon satin bag with pink tie string. CMV $25.00 mint in bag.

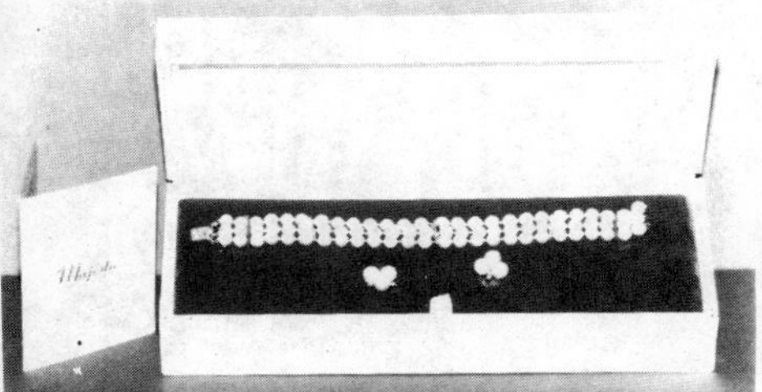

1960 MANAGERS CHRISTMAS GIFT
Pearl bracelet with small diamonds & matching earrings. Given to Avon managers at Christmas about 1960. Does not say Avon. Made by Majestic. CMV $300.00 MB

1968 ANNIVERSARY CAMPAIGN HONOR AWARD KEY CHAIN
White Avon box holds gold & silver double key ring. Made by Swank. C.M.V. $17.50 M.B.

1978 "YOU'RE PRECIOUS TO US" PENDANT MANAGERS GIFT
14K gold filled with real pearl & small diamond. Gold box says "You're Precious to Us" on lid. Given to Avon managers. Must be in box as described. Came with card signed by S. M. Kent. CMV $50.00 MB.

1973-75 4A KEY RING AWARD
Gold lucite key ring in green or red lined box. CMV $7.00 MB each.

1975 BOCA OR BUST MANAGERS KEY CHAIN - Silver 4A design. C.M.V. $12.50 M.B.

1967 DISTINGUISHED MANAGEMENT AWARD - Sterling silver key chain with raised 4A design set in brushed finish area. Given to top manager in each division. C.M.V. $32.50 M.B. $27.50 chain only.

LEFT - AVON STAR PIN
C.M.V. $55.00. If you have any information on what year or what this pin was given for, please write Bud Hastin and tell him.
RIGHT 1938 SERVICE AWARD
Bronze medallion hangs from aqua colored bar with Avon in gold. Given to representatives for outstanding improvement in sales. C.M.V. $45.00 mint.

1969 CHARM BRACLET AWARD
22 kt. gold finish double-link bracelet with safety chain & 5 charms. Each charm given for progressively higher sales. C.M.V. $7.00 ea. charm, plus bracelet.
1976-78 A PIN AWARD
Given to Reps. for selling $1,500.00 in Avon in a 13 campaign peroid. Came in blue lined box. C.M.V. $4.00 M.B. or red lined box C.M.V. $6.00 M.B.

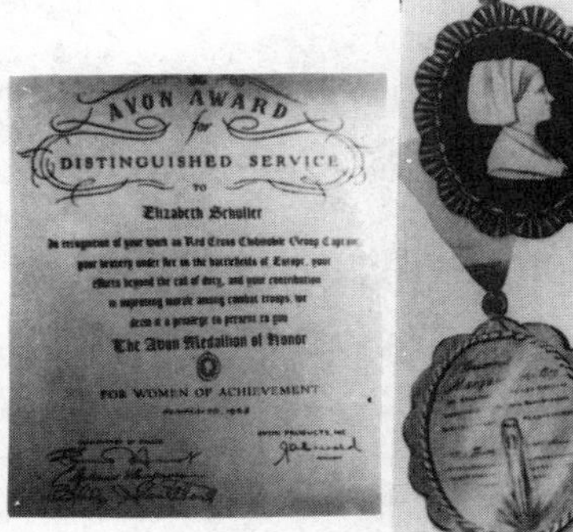

1945 MEDALLION OF HONOR
Made of solid gold, it is 1 7/8 inches long & 1 3/8 inches wide. Woman on the front is raised. Back side is engraved to person & date. Came with award scroll. Medal can be worn on a ribbon or brooch. This medal was given to women only in 1945 during world war II both military & civilian for service to their country above and beyond the call of duty. Very few medals were given out. C.M.V. medal $400.00, Scroll $50.00.

1930-38 STAR REPRESENTATIVE GOLD MEDALLION - 10 kt. gold filled medal. Given to representatives for selling $1,000.00 worth of Avon in any 12 month period. C.M.V. $100.00 - $115.00 M.B.

1937-45 STAR REPRESENTATIVE GOLD MEDALLION - 10 kt. gold filled medal, given to representatives for selling $1000.00 worth of Avon in any 12 month period. C.M.V. $45.00 mint.

LEFT 1968 ANNIVERSARY CAMPAIGN KEY CHAIN
Silver charm and key chain. C.M.V. $22.50

RIGHT 1972 CIRCLE OF EXCELLENCE KEY CHAIN
Silver charm and chain with 4A design on one side and Mexico 1972. This was given by Mexico Avon branch to Circle of Excellence Award winning managers for the year 1971. Trip was made in 1972 for the approximately 185 winning managers. C.M.V. $50.00 mint.

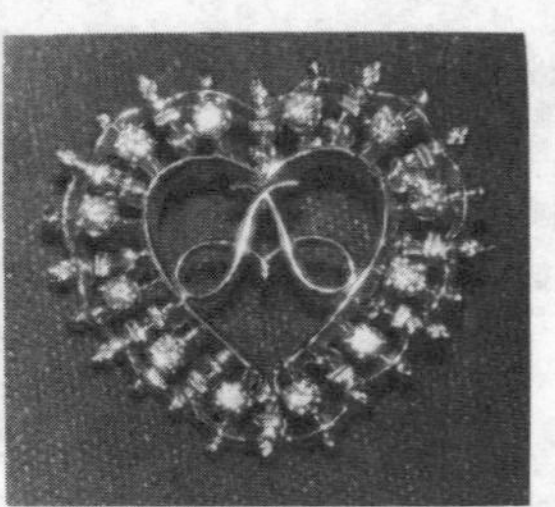

1977 HEART DIAMOND A PIN
14K gold heart shape pin with 12 small diamonds. Can also be used as pendant on chain. Came in gray felt box with white outer box. Only 1 given in each division for top rep. Rare. CMV $400.00 mint.

1979 MONEY CLIP TEAM LEADER AWARD
Green & white lined black & brass box holds 12K gold filled money clip with solid 10K gold emblem with 2 small diamonds on top. Awarded to male team leaders. Rare. "Team Leader 1979" on back. CMV $125.00 MB.

1979 CHRISTMAS GIFT - REPS.
Sterling silver goldtone chain with 10K gold charm with 2 small diamonds. Came in black felt box. Back is marked District managers 1979 - CMV $65.00, Team Leaders 1979 - CMV $50.00

1978 EARRINGS - TEAM LEADER CHRISTMAS GIFT
10K solid gold with small diamond chip Given to team leaders at Christmas, 197 Came in Avon box. CMV $40.00 MB.

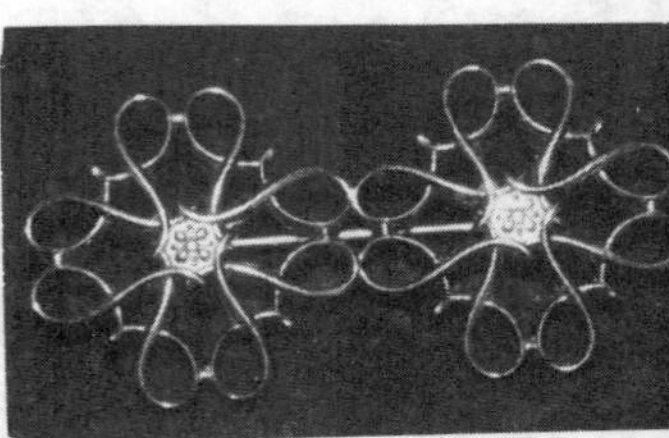

1960'S - 1970'S 4A DOUBLE STICK PI AWARD
10K gold double 4A stick pin. We have n information on what it is. Please contact Bud Hastin if you know. Comes in Avon box. CMV $75.00 MB.

1978 KEY RING 5 YEAR SERVICE AWARD
1/10 10K gold 4A symbol key ring give to Avon plant employees for 5 years service. Started in 1978. CMV $15.00

1978 - 4A BLUE ENAMEL PIN
Gold tone & blue enamel pin. Comes in Avon box. No information on wha it is for. CMV $10.00 MB.

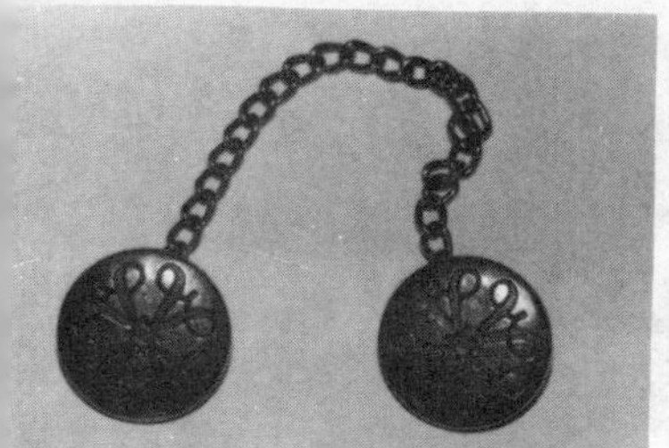

966 TOUR GUIDE JACKET GUARDS
ilver color aluminum with 4A design. Used y Avon plant tour guides. CMV $30.00

1979 AVON PIN - DIVISION MANAGER
Gold tone pin with red enamel filled heart shaped O given to division managers only. CMV $25.00 MB

1979 AVON PIN - REPS
Gold tone pin same as above only does not have red heart. CMV $10.00 MB

1979 AVON PIN - DISTRICT MANAGERS
Same gold tone pin as reps above only DM inscribed on back. CMV $15.00 MB

1974 TEAM LEADER BOOK MARK
Gold & red Book Mark. For Avon reps. use. C.M.V. $5.00

1978 VALENTINE HEART PENDANT AWARD
14K gold heart. Does not say Avon. Only 2500 were given to reps at sales meetings. Must have C3-78 brochure with heart to prove its from Avon. CMV $25.00 with brochure.

1979 FLAG PIN AWARD
Gold tone red, white & blue enamel lapel pin. Given to Circle of Excellence winners in Paris trip. Came in red velvet Avon ring box. CMV $50.00 MB

1976 MANAGERS PANELIST PIN
Gold tone name pin. Marked "Nat. District Managers Panelist" CMV $15.00. Given each year.

1968 SWEATER GUARD AWARD
6" gold chain with 4A design clips on each end. Given as general managers honor award to each representative of the winning team in each district. C.M.V. $25.00 - $30.00 M.B.

1962 SERVICE AWARD CHARM
22 kt. gold finish slightly larger than a quarter, given to all representatives who sold 50 or more customers during campaign 6. C.M.V. $18.00.

1969 PRESIDENTS COURT CHARM
22 kt. gold finish charm. Given to all representatives of the team in each district C.M.V. $15.00.

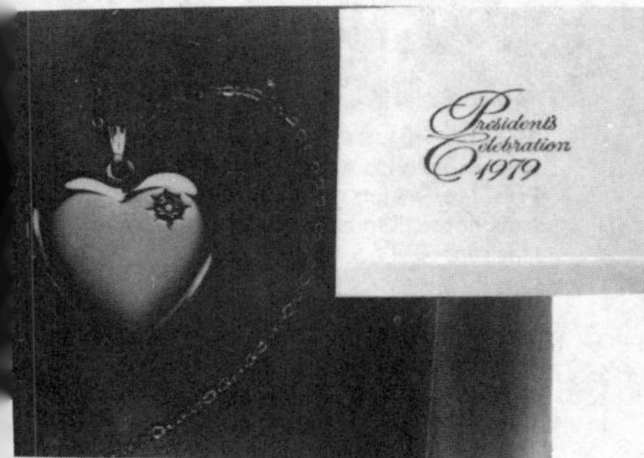

1979 PRESIDENT'S CELEBRATION DIAMOND HEART LOCKET AWARD
Given to top 20 reps in each district during President's Celebration. Inscribed on back "President's Club 1979" CMV $20.00 MB Same given to district managers only has DM inscribed on back also. CMV $30.00 MB

1977 TOP FIFTY PIN AWARD
Gold tone pin has top 50 & 4A design with red background. Given to top 50 reps in division for sales. CMV $15.00

1978 TOP FIFTY PIN AWARD
Same as 1977 pin only has red rose with green leaves. CMV $10.00

1961 BELL BRACELET AWARD
Silver bracelet & bell that rings. Avon not on bell. C.M.V. $20.00

1980 SHOOTING STAR PIN - MANAGERS
Gold tone pin in brown box with outer sleeve. Given to managers. CMV $30.00 MB

1979 EIFFEL TOWER MANAGERS PIN
Small gold tone tie tack type pin given to managers on Paris trip. Does not say Avon. In plain blue box. Pin is 1 1/8" high. CMV $15.00

1955 RED ROBIN PIN
Sterling silver pins made by Cora Company. Does not say Avon on it. Given in pairs for getting 12 new customers. C.M.V. $25.00

1976 - 90th ANNIVERSARY BICENTENNIAL PENDANT AWARD - Brass coin & chain given to reps. for selling $285.00 worth of Avon in 2 campaigns. Front & back view shown. C.M.V. $15.00 M.B.

1970 - 5 YEAR SERVICE PIN
For Avon plant employees, not reps. Gold circle with 4A emblem & blue stone. C.M.V. $25.00 M.B. $20.00 pin only.

1962 KEY PIN AWARD (Top)
Gold key, surprise gift for activity. CMV $8.00

1961 AWARD EARRINGS (Bottom)
Gold star design. Avon is not on them CMV $12.00 pair.

1966 4A MENS CUFF LINKS
Silver links with 4A design. Given to plant & office employees only. C.M.V. $35.00 pr.

1973 TOUR GUIDE JACKET GUARDS
Gold metal with pressed flower in center of 4A. Used by Avon plant tour guides. C.M.V. $25.00.

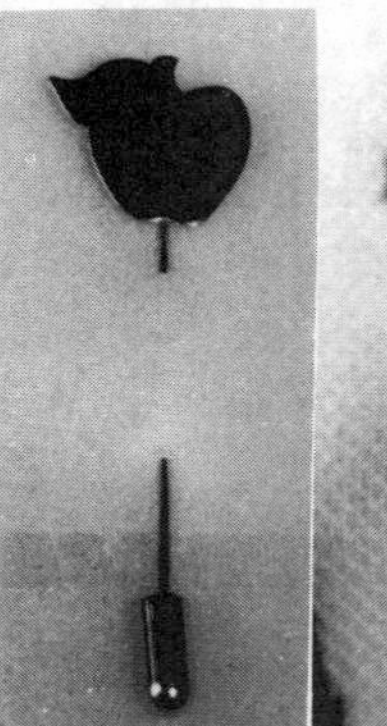

1977 APPLE STICK PIN
Red apple with 4A design 1977 & P.C. for President's Club on green leaf. Pin is gold tone color. We have no information on this pin. CMV $15.00

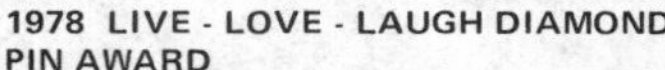

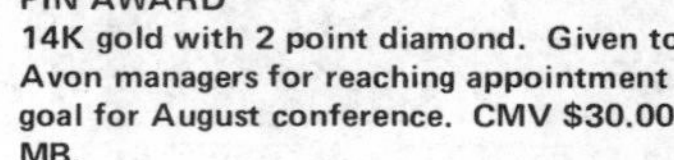

1978 LIVE - LOVE - LAUGH DIAMOND PIN AWARD
14K gold with 2 point diamond. Given to Avon managers for reaching appointment goal for August conference. CMV $30.00 MB.

1964 HAPPY ANNIVERSARY NECKLACE - For 38 years as a representative. October 1964. C.M.V. $30.00

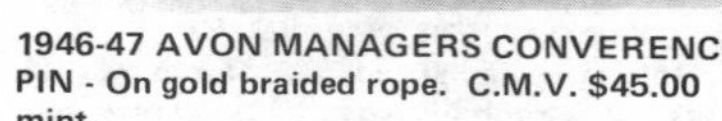

1946-47 AVON MANAGERS CONVERENCE PIN - On gold braided rope. C.M.V. $45.00 mint.

1975 SUNNY STAR AWARD NECKLACE
Given to managers on introduction to Sunny Star necklace. This is the same one that sold only it has Aug. 1975 engraved on it. It can easily be duplicated so a price above the cost from Avon should not be paid. Brass star & chain. C.M.V. $9.00 M.B.

1967 RETIREMENT PIN
Gold disk with raised 4A design hanging from a golden bow. Given to retiring representatives with 10 years or more of service. C.M.V. $50.00

1978 PRESIDENT'S CELEBRATION "A" PIN AWARD
White box holds "A" sterling silver pin given to President's Club reps only. CMV $10.00 MB

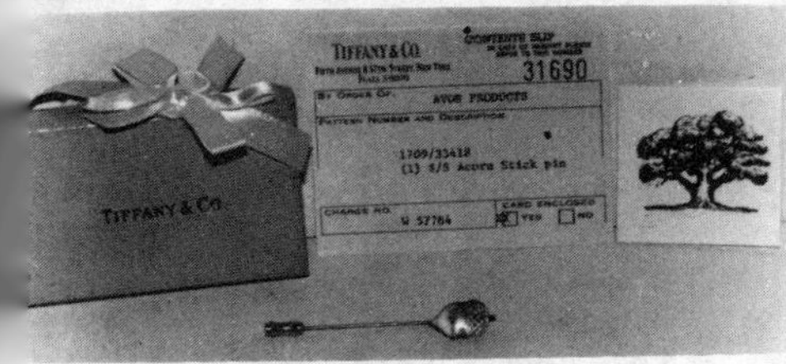

1979 ACORN STICK PIN AWARD
Sterling silver acorn pin from Tiffany & Co. given to managers. Came with small card with great oak & Tiffany card for Avon products. CMV $30.00 MB

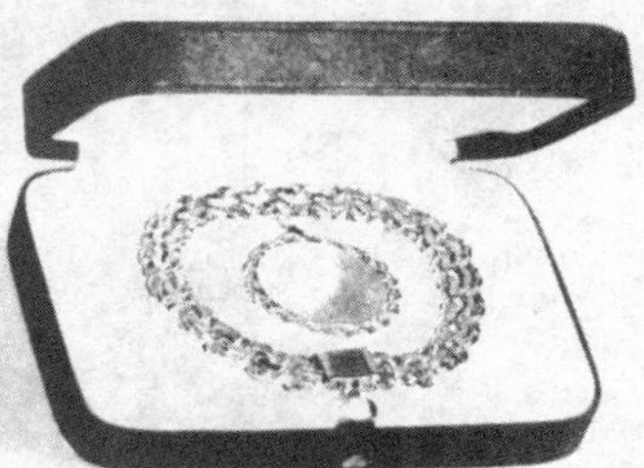

1956 MANAGERS BRACELET
Bracelet given to top selling city & district managers during presidents campaign 1956. C.M.V. $60.00 M.B.

1968 "G" CLEF MANAGERS PIN
Gold in color. Awarded to managers. C.M.V. $15.00 pin only. $20.00 M.B.

1978 HEART STICK PIN AWARD
Sterling silver heart pin made by Tiffany & Co. with Avon products slip. Given to managers only, during President's Celebration. Does not say Avon. Must be in box with Tiffany & Co. Avon card. CMV $20.00 MB.

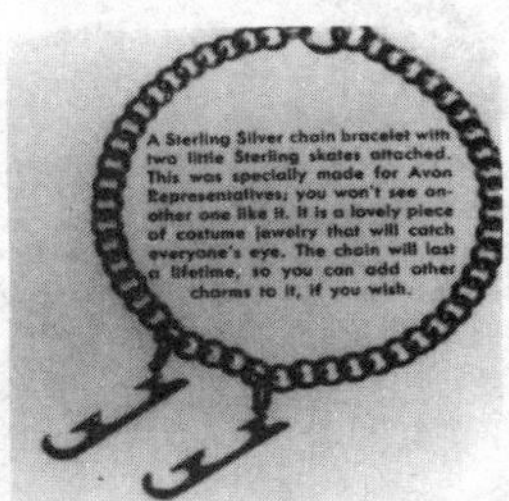

1951 FIGURE 8 CHARM BRACELET
Sterling silver bracelet with 2 skates attached. Given to representatives for interviewing 120 Avon customers during the figure 8 campaign 3-1951. Made only for Avon. C.M.V. $45.00

1969 SALES ACHIEVEMENT AWARD
Large gold Charisma design pin came in black Avon box. C.M.V. $20.00 M.B.

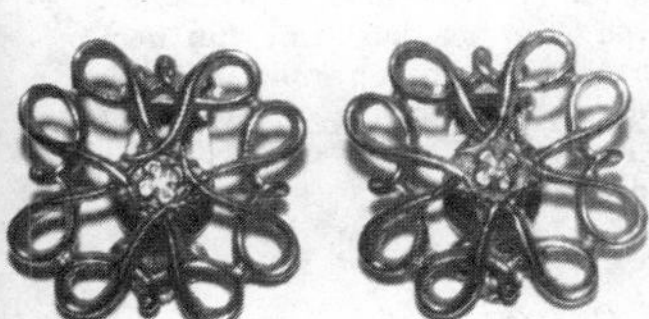

1965-68 DISTINGUISHED MANAGE–MENT AWARD EARRINGS - 4A design clip-on earrings. C.M.V. $35.00 pair M.B.

1964 BELL AWARDS
Gold bell earrings. Christmas sales award. C.M.V. $15.00
Gold bell charm bracelet. Christmas sales award. C.M.V. $25.00

1965 AWARD PIN
White plastic on blue background with silver or gold frame. CMV $25.00 in box. $15.00 pin only.

1953 AWARD BRACELET
1953 on back of silver heart shaped charm. C.M.V. $15.00
1969-70 AVON ATTENDANCE CHARM - 1969 AD on one charm & 1970 AD on the other. Both gold & chain. C.M.V. $12.50

1968 ANNIVERSARY AWARD ROSE PIN - Victory luncheon July 9, 1968. Gold rose pin with ruby stone in Avon box. C.M.V. $25.00 M.B. only.

1974 TEAM LEADER PIN (Right)
Gold raised letters & rim. Given to team leaders. CMV $7.00
1975 TEAM LEADER PIN (Left)
Gold with indented letters. Given to team leaders. CMV $5.00

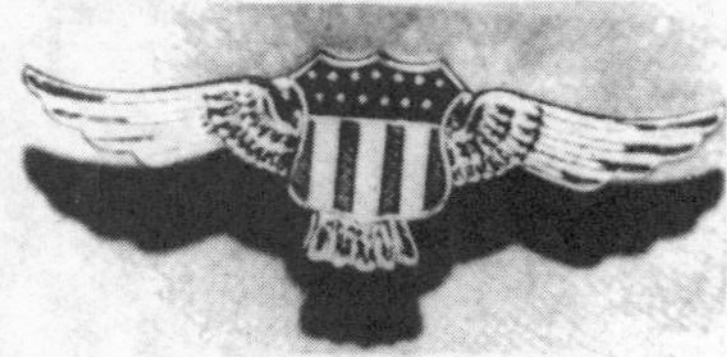

1942 VICTORY PIN AWARD
Sterling silver wing pin with red, white & blue center. Given to representatives during Acres of Diamonds campaign 1942 for getting new customers.
CMV $60.00

1943 MANAGERS AWARD PIN
Gold plated lapel pin with hand set stones, cost Avon $25.00 in 1943. Only 2 were given to the 2 top selling managers in U.S. during loyality campaign, March 2-22, 1943.
C.M.V. $125.00

LEFT 1968 SHELL JEWELRY
Given for recommending someone as a representative. For each name representatives could choose either the pin or earrings. For 2 or more names you got the set. C.M.V. $10.00
RIGHT 1955 NEARNESS MANAGERS PIN
Gold shell pin with pearl. C.M.V. $35.00

1966 DOOR KNOCKER EARRINGS
Gold earrings. Avon Calling on them.
C.M.V. $30.00 pr. M.B.

1944 Only - AWARD PIN
Hand made sterling silver pin with roses & lilies, given to reps. for selling $300.00 to $400.00 during Xmas campaign. C.M.V. $45.00

1951 CLOVER TIME PIN
Given to representatives for calling on 120 customers in one campaign. Pin is outlined with imitation seed pearls & dotted with aquamarine stones for color. Does not say Avon. Came with certificate from Avon.
CMV $25.00

1942 BOWKNOT AWARD PIN
Gold pin with sequins shaped like bow. Given to representatives for selling $100.00 to $150.00 in one campaign. C.M.V. $30.00

1971 - 85th ANNIVERSARY PINS
22 kt. gold plated sterling silver pin with diamond. Small pin for representative not in president club, representatives only. Given for meeting sales goal in C-12-71. C.M.V. small pin $15.00, Large pin $20.00

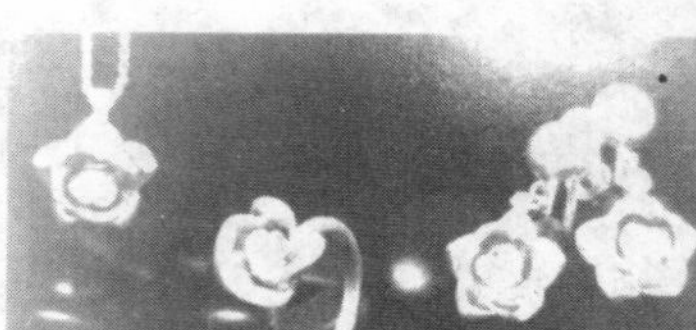

1971 - 85th ANNIVERSARY AWARD JEWELRY - 22 kt. gold plated sterling silver necklace, ring & earrings. Each shaped like a rose with diamond in center. Necklace was for representatives not in the presidents club, and the earrings for the presidents club members only. Two diamond rings were given in each district by a drawing. One was given to a presidents club member the other to a non-member. Ring also available in prize catalog for 2400 points. CMV necklace $30.00, Ring $75.00, Earrings $30.00

1974 PRESIDENTS CELEBRATION AWARD
14 kt. gold necklace with 3 point diamond. Given to 10 top representatives in each of the 81 winning districts for outstanding sales during this presidents celebration.
CMV $60.00 MB

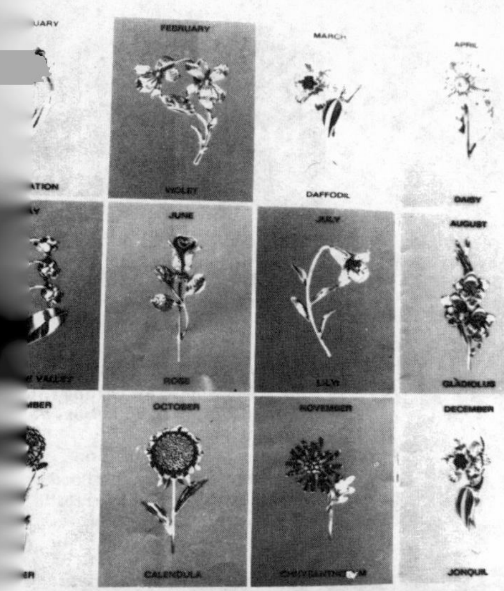

1967 - 81st ANNIVERSARY PINS
Sterling silver pins came in 12 different flowers. Representatives who met their personal prize goal for this anniversary campaign had their choice of one of these 12 flowers. Carnation, Violet, Daffodil, Daisy, Lily of the Valley, Rose, Lily, Gladiolus, Aster, Calendula, Chrysanthemum, and Jonquil. CMV Rose $15.00, $25.00 MB; Calendula $30.00, $40.00 MB; all others $20.00, $30.00 MB

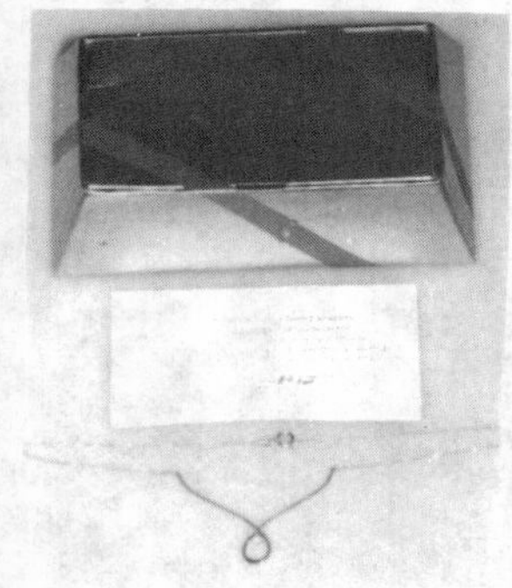

1977 MANAGERS GIFT DIAMOND LOOP
Diamond Loop necklace given to managers in special gold bar type box., on introduction of Avons new 14K gold filled jewelry. CMV $30.00 MB as pictured.

1975 FIRST AVON LADY PENDANT AWARD - Silver toned with scroll 'A' design around glass insert. On the presentation card it starts "Congratulations! We're happy to present you with this exclusive award. Designed especially for you. It's symbolic of the personal service upon which Avon was founded and which has guided us throughout the years" C.M.V. $20.00 M.B.

1964 LUCKY 7 PIN
Gold pin with simulated pearl in center. Given to each representative who sent in a certain size order. C.M.V. $10.00
1966 GOOD LUCK BRACELET
Gold double link bracelet with gold charm. Good luck & four leaf clover on the front. Back is plain. Not marked Avon. C.M.V. $12.00

1978 AVON SMILE PENDANT AWARD
Red and gold pendent given to all Avon Team Leaders. Back side says Avon, Team Leader, March 1978. C.M.V. $10.00 M.B. Also given to District Managers with D.M. on back. C.M.V. $15.00. Both came in red box with Avon Sleeve.

1977 TLC NECKLACE AWARD
Given to Team Leaders. 14K gold. CMV $25.00

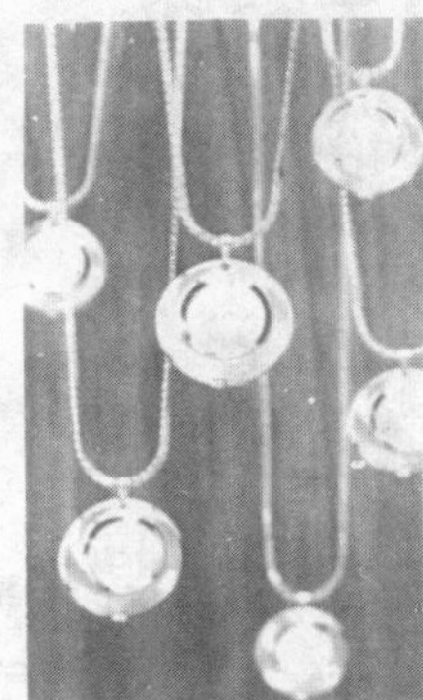

1970 PENDENT WATCH AWARD
Gold tone watch on neck chain given to 6 Reps in each district for top sales. Made by Sheffield. Also sold in stores. 9000 watches given by Avon. C.M.V. $20.00

1966 HONOR AWARD CAMEO PERFUME GLACE NECKLACE - Blue & white set trimmed in gold. C.M.V. $18.00

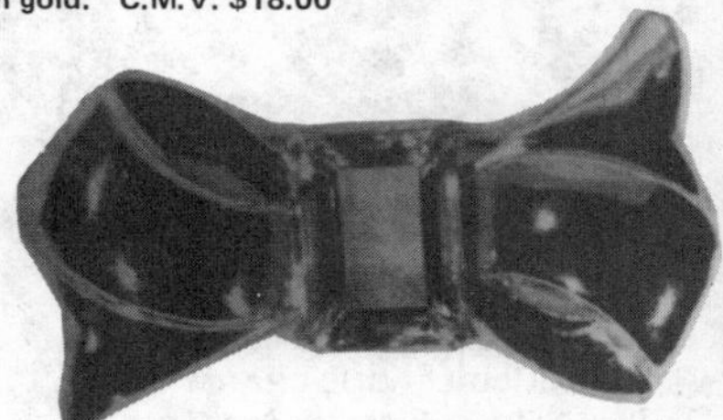

1944 BOW PIN AWARD
Lapel pin is gold plate with center stone of synthetic aquamarine. Given to Reps. for selling over $300.00 in 1 campaign. C.M.V. $25.00

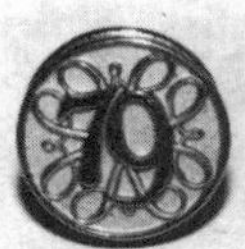

1979-80 PRESIDENT'S CLUB MEN'S PIN AWARD
Gold tone 4A design & 79 on one & 80 on the other. Given to all male President's Club members. Smaller than lady's pin. CMV $15.00 MB 79 pin, CMV $10.00 MB 80 pin.

1980-81 PRESIDENT'S CLUB MEN'S TIE TACK
Small gold tone 4A - 81 on face. Given to male President's Club members. CMV $15.00 MB

1978 SMOKY QUARTZ RING - MANAGERS
Smoky quartz stone, 14K gold mounting marked Avon. Given to managers in C26-78 for best activity event in Atlanta branch. CMV not established.

1977 PRESIDENT'S CELEBRATION STAR AWARD
Sterling silver star & chain with small diamond made by Tiffany. Was given to winning district manager in division. CMV not established.

1967 PRESIDENTS CAMPAIGN GLACE AWARD - Managers is in script writing with white lined box. C.M.V. $22.50 in box. $18.50 compact only.
Representatives is in block writing on Presidents Campaign with blue felt lined box. C.M.V. $10.00. $12.00 in box. Both came in Hawaiian White Ginger box.

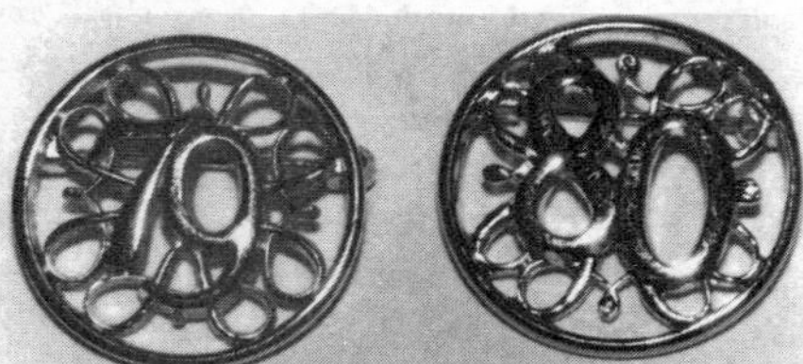

1979-80 PRESIDENT'S CLUB LADY'S PINS
Gold colored 4A pin - 79 in middle is 1st of an annual 4A year pin given to President's Club reps for meeting sales goal for that year. CMV $10.00 each year.

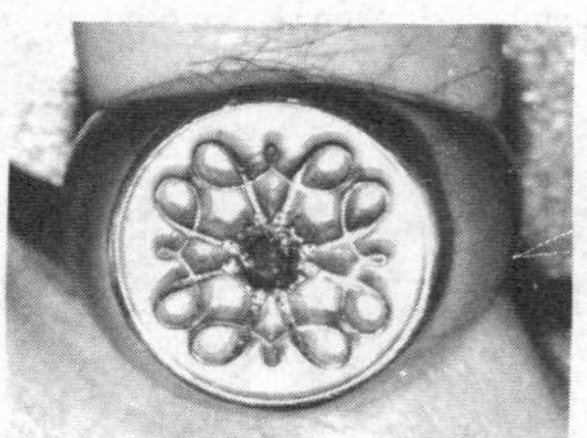

1978 PRESIDENT'S CLUB RING FOR MEN
Gold plated sterling silver 4A ring with ruby stone. Given to male Avon reps for selling $6000 worth of Avon in 1 year period. Came in plain blue velvet ring box. CMV $200.00 MB

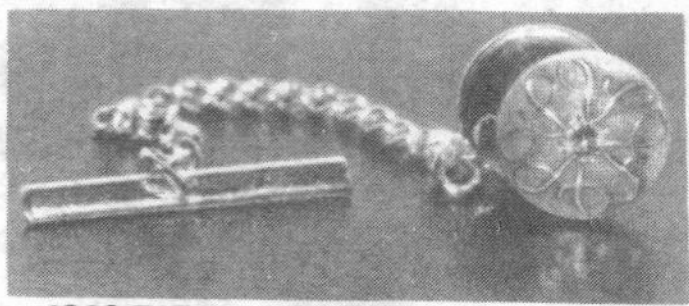

1969 TIE TAC AWARD
Small gold tie tac given to Avon Male Executive with blue sapphire in center. Came in Avon box. C.M.V. $50.00 M.B.

1968 FIELD OPERATIONS AWARD
Solid brass, Avon 4A emblem on front. Field operations seminar on back. Given to managers in Pasadena branch in Better Way program. CMV $55.00

1960 GOLD LEAGUE CHARM
1960 on back. Front has Avon League with 4A design & golfer. Solid brass. Given to Avon plant employees, Pasadena branch, for playing in golf tournament. CMV $40.00

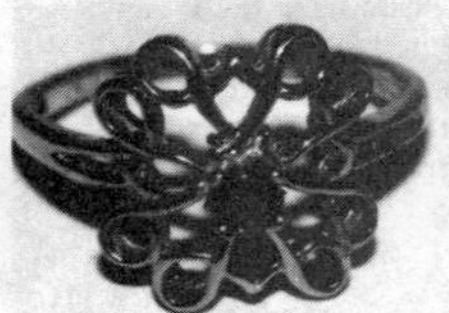

LEFT 1978 PRESIDENT'S CLUB RING "LADY'S"
Gold plated sterling 4A ring with red simulated ruby. Stone comes in several different shades. Given to all female President's Club reps. CMV $35.00 MB

RIGHT 1978 MANAGERS 4A RING
Silver 4A ring with high grade ruby stone given to 4 managers in Atlanta branch for best planning. CMV price not established.

1977 SALES ACHIEVEMENT AWARD PENDENT
1" gold pendent with 18" chain. Says 1977 Avon Sales Achievement Award & 4A design on other side. Came in white Avon box. Given to top 10% of sales Reps. in each division. C.M.V. $15.00 M.B.

1977 PRESIDENT'S CELEBRATION DIAMOND RING AWARD
14K gold ring with 8 small diamonds in center. Given to managers in Pasadena branch for largest increase in sales. Only 20 rings given in this branch. Does not say Avon. CMV not established.

1980 RECOMMENDATION CASIO PRIZE
Casio LC 315 calculator in 4A design black case. CMV $25.00

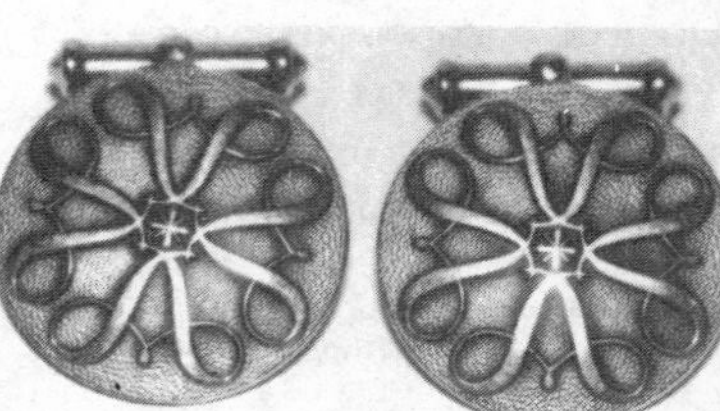

15 YEAR SERVICE CUFF LINKS
4A design on face and Avon 15 Years Loyal Service on back with persons initials. Given to Avon male executives after 15 years service with Avon. Made of solid 10K gold. CMV $300.00 pair, mint.

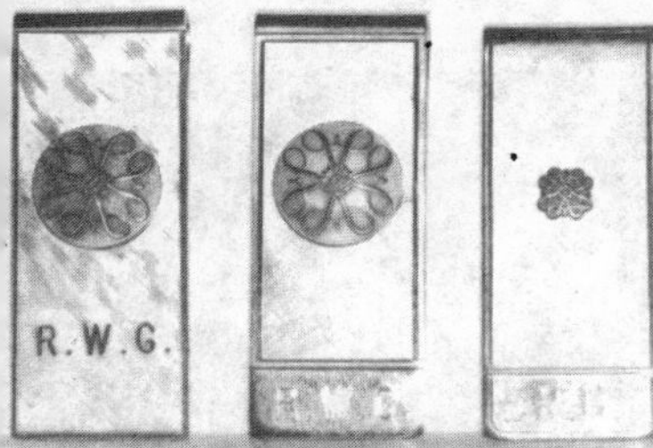

LEFT 1963 MONEY CLIP
10K gold filled. Back says Pathways of Achievement 1963. 4A design on front and initials. C.M.V. $75.00 M.B.
CENTER 1969 MONEY CLIP
Black and gold box holds 10K gold filled 4A design on front with initials. Back says Management Conference Atlanta, Georgia November 1969. C.M.V. $50.00 M.B.
RIGHT 1960 MONEY CLIP
10K gold filled. small 4A design on face and initials. Nothing on back. C.M.V.$40.00

1967 DISTINGUISHED MANAGEMENT AWARD - Glass plate with 4A design on bottom. Came in white box lined in red velvet. C.M.V. $40.00 plate only. $50.00 M.B.

1971 EMPLOYEES GIFT KEY CHAIN
Blue box with gray flannel bag holds gold horse shoe with Avon on one side and You're in Demand on back side of charm. C.M.V. $20.00 M.B.

975 TOP SALES MEDALIAN
Gold colored metal medalian. Avon ady carrying case. Italy at bottom of oot. No Avon on it. Given to Avon Reps. or top sales and touring Springdale plant. C.M.C. $15.00

1965 AVON HAWAIIAN HOLIDAY CHARM AWARD
14K gold given to 7 avon managers in Hawaii in 1965. Each manager had their initials put on back. C.M.V. $150.00

1975 AVON SALES ACHIEVEMENT AWARD BRACELET
Given for sales. Avon on one side and sales achievement on the other. Sterling. C.M.V. $10.00

1978 FOSTORIA LEAD CRYSTAL PLATES AWARD
Given for top sales. 1st four plates won by reps: Jeweled A, 1st representative, Door Knocker, great oak tree. CMV $30.00 set of 4 or $7.00 each.
Presidents Club reps & District Managers could win 1st 4 plus 4 more: 4A, Avon Key Key, World of Avon Globe, Avon Rose Last. Presidents Club set had P.C. marked on Rose plate & D.M. marked Jeweled A plate for managers set. CMV $100.00 D.M. set of 8, CMV $75.00 P.C. set of 8.

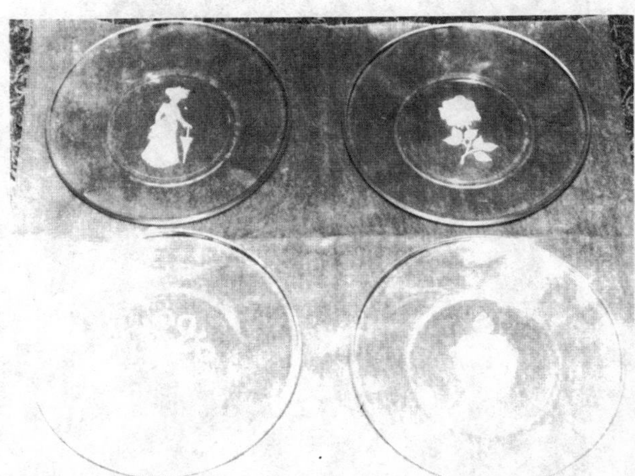

1971 CHRISTMAS GIFT PLATE
Sent to reps. at Christmas. Clear glass with frosted First Avon Lady. C.M.V. $17.00 M.B. $12.00 no box.

1972 CHRISTMAS GIFT PLATE
Sent to every rep. at Christmas. Clear glass frosted rose. C.M.V. $15.00 M.B. $10.00 no box.

1973 CHRISTMAS GIFT PLATE
Sent to reps. who had been with company less than 2 years. Clear glass frosted 4A. C.M.V. $15.00 M.B. $10.00 no box.

1974 CHRISTMAS GIFT PLATE
Sent to reps. at Christmas. Clear glass with frosted Door Knocker. C.M.V. $12.00 M.B. $8.00 no box.

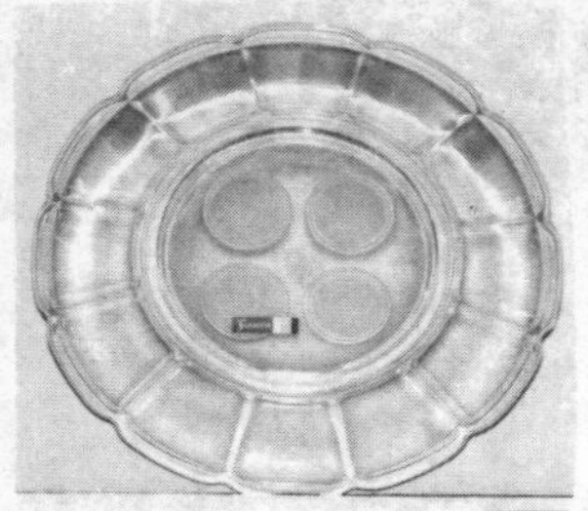

1970 FOSTORIA COIN PLATE AWARD
Does not say Avon. Must be in Avon box. CMV $12.00 MB.

1973 RECOMMENDATION GIFT SNACK SET
Fostoria lead crystal dish & bowl. Came in set of 4 each. Given to Avon reps for signing up new Avon ladies. CMV $15.00 each setting, $60.00 for all 8 pieces.

1973 REPRESENTATIVES AWARD PLATES - Awarded for years of service. First 5, white with colored decals. Two years - Door Knockers. C.M.V. $12.00. Five years - Oak Tree C.M.V. $18.00 Ten years - California Perfume Co. C.M.V. $24.00. Fifteen years - Rose C.M.V. $30.00. Twenty years - First Avon Lady C.M.V. $40.00. Twenty-five years - Sterling silver with message from Avon President. CMV $125.00 All prices are mint & boxed. CMV complete set $250.00 MB.

1975 BIRD PLATE AWARDS
Campaign 10, 1975 - available to reps. for meeting product goals; serving specified number of customers & meeting goals at suggested customer prices. Bluebird was lowest goal, Yellow Breasted Chat second & Baltimore Oriole last. If total goals attained rep. received all three plates. C.M.V. Bluebird $20.00 M.B. Yellow Breasted Chat $20.00 M.B. Baltimore Oriole $30.00 M.B.

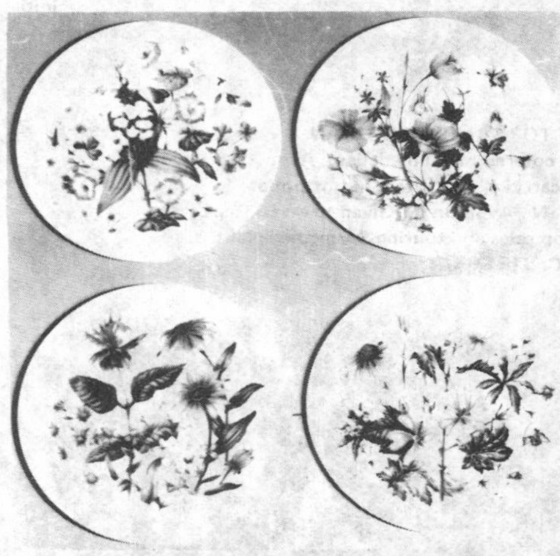

1976-78 WILD FLOWERS AWARD PLATES
Each is 8¾". Southern Wild Flower plate for $195.00 in sales. Southern & Eastern given for $245.00 in sales, & Southern, Eastern, Northern & Western flower plates for $330.00 in sales. C-11-1976. C.M.V. Southern $10.00 M.B. Eastern $15.00 M.B. All 4 plates M.B. $60.00 set. Northern & Western $20.00 each M.B. These same plates were reissued by Geni Products, a division of Avon in March, 78, as awards to their sales reps.

1978 PRESIDENT'S CELEBRATION TRAY AWARD
12" silver plated tray marked "Awarded Exclusively to Avon Representatives" on back side. Given to 1 winning team reps in each division. CMV $35.00 MB

1975 DIVISIONS SALES WINNER TRAY AWARD
17¾" long x 13" wide silver tray. Inscribed in center "Awarded to (name of manager) President's Program 1975 Division Sales Winner with Best Wishes, David S. Mitchell. Given to top district managers in sales. Came in blue felt bag & white box. CMV $150.00 MB in bag.

1977 EL CAMINO DIVISION SUGAR & CREAMER SET AWARD
Silver plated creamer & sugar bowl. Tray is engraved "Top 10 Sales - El Camino Division Campaigns 10-22-1977." Made by Sheridan. CMV $35.00 set mint.

1976 BICENTENNIAL PLATES
Blue & white. Given to representatives that sent in order for campaign 1, 2, 3 totaling $100.00 or more. Left - Independence Hall, on right Liberty Bell. Made in England. Has inscription on back. C.M.V. $20.00 Independence Hall; $30.00 Liberty Bell.

1974 TENDERNESS COMMEMORATIVE AWARD PLATE
9" diameter ceramic plate, pastel blue and greens. Awarded to representatives for sending in orders for campaign 1, 2, and 3, 1974. Inscription on back in blue letters "Tenderness Commemorative Plate, Special Edition, Awarded to Representatives in January, 1974". Plate is made by Pontessa Ironstone of Spain. Award plate has Pontessa in red letters. Regular issue Pontessa in blue letters. Plate also sold with no inscription on back. CMV $15.00, $17.50 MB. Red letter plate only.

1909 CPC SALES MANAGERS GIFT
4" x 4" size, pressed crystal glass jar with Rogers Silver Plate lid. Given to each rep. selling $50.00 in sales in December 1909. The silver lid has an embossed floral design. CMV $200.00 mint.

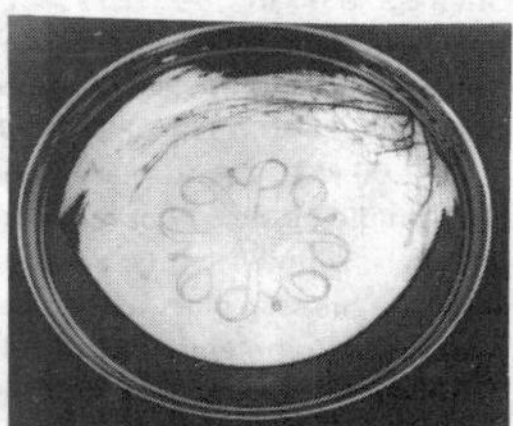

1964 SILVER SERVER
9" dia. Same as 1963 server except no 12" bowls given & all are gold lined on the inside. C.M.V. $40.00

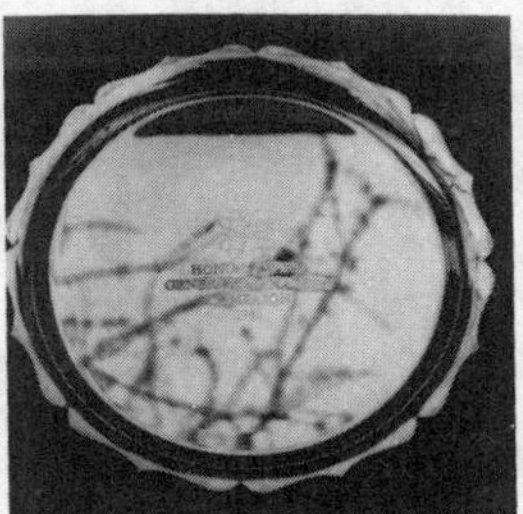

1965 SILVER TRAY
9 7/8" x 1" given to each representative from the winning group in each branch during the General Manager's Campaign, engraved "Honor Award - General Manager's Campaign 1965". C.M.V. $35.00

1956 REPRESENTATIVE AWARD BOWL - Sterling silver Paul Revere Bowl was given to each representative in the top selling district in each division during Presidents Campaign 1956. CMV $45.00

1966 NATIONAL CHAMPION AWARD
Glass bowl with 4A design on bottom. C.M.V. $50.00 M.B.

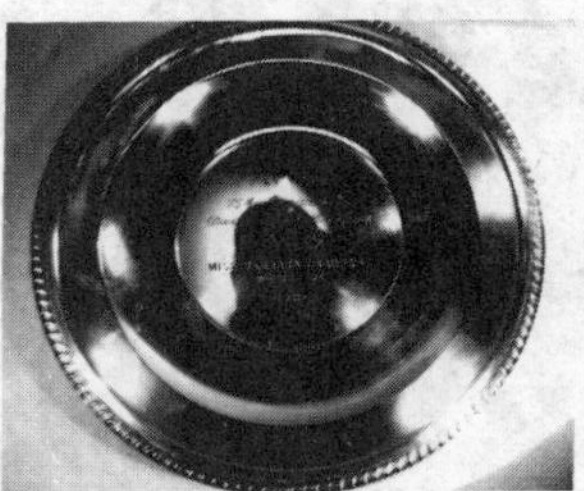

1961 - 75th ANNIVERSARY SALES CHAMPION SILVER TRAY - Awarded to the top Avon District Managers for best sales in campaign 9 & 10, 1961. C.M.V. $40.00

1963 SILVER SERVER AWARD
12 5/16"x2" given to the top 4 established representatives in each district for sales improvement over the previous year. 4A design engraved in the bottom. Small 9" servers were given to 3 newer representatives for highest sale & 3 for outstanding sales ability. C.M.V. 9" $40.00 - 12" $45.00

1961 ACHIEVEMENT AWARD SILVER TRAY
4A design in center of silver tray.
CMV $30.00

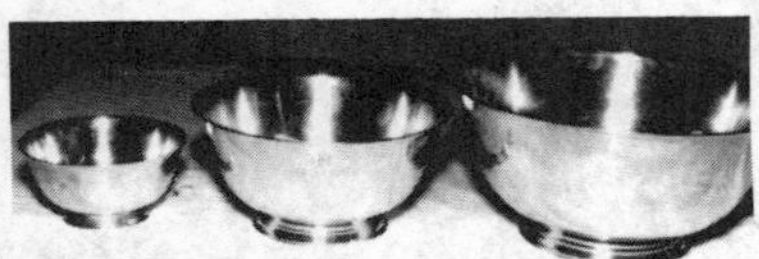

1962 PRESIDENTS AWARD SILVER BOWLS - 3 sizes silver bowls. 4A emblem & writing on outside. C.M.V. $25.00 - $30.00 - $35.00

1961-72 COIN GLASS
Coin glass in Avon boxes only are collectable. The same pieces are available in local stores with both 1886 & 1887 at low prices so get the box. Many pieces available at many different prices starting at $5.00 up to $35.00 in box. 1st issue 1961.

1964 - 78TH ANNIVERSARY FOSTORIA AWARD SET
Box marked Avon Cosmetics holds Fostoria salt & pepper, cruet & glass holding tray. Given to reps. CMV $35.00 in Avon box.

1960'S CAKE PLATE FOSTORIA COIN GLASS AWARD
Fostoria glass cake plate given to reps for sales award. Comes in Avon box. Same piece was sold in local stores. Must be in Avon box as shown. CMV $100.00 MB

1977 91st ANNIVERSARY COIN GLASS AWARDS
Footed compote on right won by Reps for selling $270.00 in C8-9-1977. C.M.V. $7.00 M.B. Footed compote centerpiece bowl and footed compote won for selling $540.00 in C8-9-1977. C.M.V. $12.00 M.B. Centerpiece bowl A pair of candle holders won by Presidents Club members only with P.C. embossed on bottom. This coin glass was made only for Avon, using Avon emblems in coins & 1886-1977 and the name Avon. Came with card on each piece from Avon and in Avon box. C.M.V. $17.00 Candle holders, M.B. District managers received a full set of Coin Glass with D.M. embossed in center of each piece. C.M.V. $75.00 M.B. for complete D.M.Set.

1971 ANTIQUE CAR GLASSES
Eight different glasses picturing Stanly Steamer, Silver Duesenberg, Gold Cadillac Sterling Six, Electric Charger, Packard Roadster, Touring T & Straight Eight. Selling 10 Avon cars won a set of 4 glasses. Selling 15 Avon cars won a set of 8 glasses. C.M.V. set of 4 $12.00. Set of 8 $24.00 boxed.

1971 ANTIQUE CAR PITCHER
Representatives won this by having one person they recommended as representativ appointed. Also available in prize catalog for 1400 points. 2 different pitchers. Rare one has silver Duesenberg & Stanley Steamer on it. CMV $35.00 Most of them have Straight Eight & Packard Roadster decal on it. CMV $25.00

1971 FRONT PAGE TUMBLERS
14 oz. tumblers with representatives name printed on "front page" of glass. Given for having a person recommended as a representative appointed. C.M.V. $12.00.

1963 - 77th ANNIVERSARY QUEEN AWARD - Awarded to 10 representatives in each district that had greatest dollar increase in sales, were crowned Queen & also received Fostoria Crystal serving dish with Avon 4 A in bottom. Tiara not marked Avon. Came with Avon Queen certificate - 2 different certificates were given. Also came with 1963 Queen Ribbon. 11¼" bowl. C.M.V. Bowl only $50.00 C.MV. Tiara with certificate & ribbon $50.00. C.M.V. complete set M.B. $100.00

1975 AVON LADY STEMWARE GLASSES AWARDS - C-20-75 Set of 6, 10oz. & 6, 6 oz. glasses with 1st. Avon Lady design. 1 set given to all reps. in the winning district for top sales. C.M.V. set $50.00.

1970 FOSTORIA SUGAR & CREAM SET AWARD
From Fostoria glass, box says Avon Cosmetics. Given to reps for sales achievement. Design is from the Henry Ford Collection. C.M.V. $27.50 M.B.only

1969 CHRISTMAS CUP
White glass mug. Avon on bottom. Given to District Managers for Christmas. C.M.V. $30.00

1977 - 1ST DIVISION - GLASS AWARD
Lead crystal champagne glass given to No. 1 division Avon managers. CMV $30.00
1975 WINE GLASS FOR MANAGERS
Yellow painted letters say "Avon Espana 1975" Came in 1975 Osborne Cream Sherry Managers Gift Set on trip to Spain. CMV $37.50.

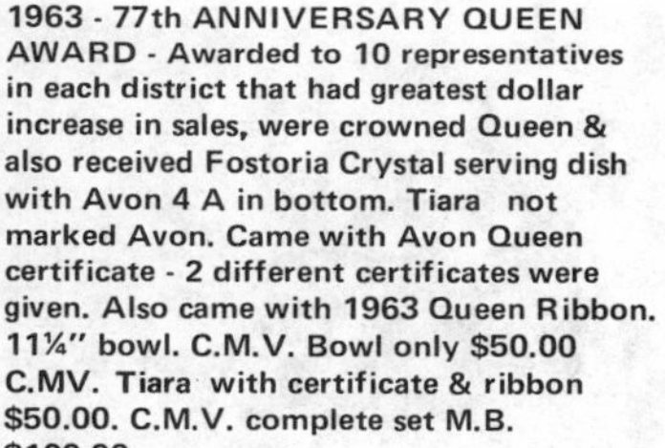

1970 INITIAL GLASS AWARD
Campaign 12 & 13, 1970. Representatives won the glasses and President's club members won the goblets with initial of their choice for reaching sales goals in each campaign. The coasters were won by both for reaching sales goals both campaigns. C.M.V. on coasters $3.00, glasses $3.00, goblets $4.00 each.

1977 MERRY CHRISTMAS MUG
Short glass mug with green lettering on front. CMV $5.00
1970'S CIRCLE OF EXCELLENCE MUG
Pewter mug inscribed Circle of Excellence Avon on front. CMV $20.00

1975 OSBORNE CREAM SHERRY MANAGERS GIFT SET
Wine cask on box lid. Box holds 2 wine glasses with "Avon Espana 1975" painted in yellow, bottle of Osborne Cream Sherry with special label "Specially bottled for the 1974 members of the Circle of Excellence" This set was given to each manager on their C of E trip to Madrid, Spain. Only 200 sets given out. CMV $125.00 set mint full.

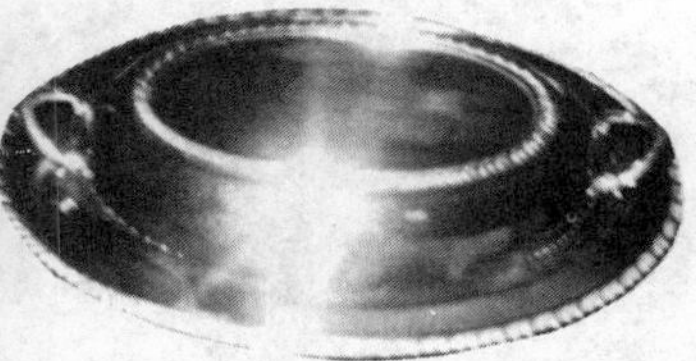

1950'S SILVER SERVER AWARD
11¾" x 8¾" silver plated tray & cover. Marked Avon Wm. Rogers on bottom. No information on why it was given to reps. CMV $45.00 in mint.

1977 SALES ACHIEVEMENT MUG AWARD
Pink rose on side & Sales Achievement 4th Qt. 1977 on other side. CMV $10.00

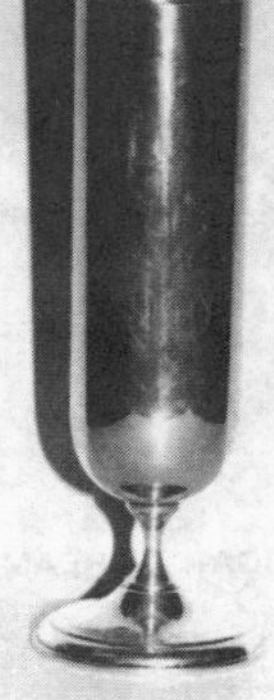

1975 GOBLET - CIRCLE OF EXCELLENCE AWARD
7½" high sterling silver goblet. Given to Circle of Excellence managers who went to Madrid Spain 1975. Base says "Circle of Excellence, Madrid 1975" CMV $60.00

1976 TEAM LEADER MUG - AWARD
White glass mug. CMV $15.00

1979 LENOX CHINA PRESIDENT'S CLUB BOWL AWARD
White box with gold trim & burgundy inside holds 4A inscribed china bowl. Bottom inscribed "For Avon's Very Best" given to all President's Club members for 1980. Box has Avon outer sleeve. CMV $40.00 MB, bowl only $30.00

1966 AWARD COMPACT
Sterling silver compact. Engraved on back "National Champion, President's Campaig 1966." C.M.V. $15.00

1960 AVON SUGAR BOWL CLUB
Awarded to sales ladies for getting new customers. C.M.V. $60.00

1972 SALAD SET GIFT
Given to reps as gift. Does not say Avon & was not made only for Avon. Can be bought in stores. Came in plain box with Avon mailing label. Set has large salad bowl & 4 small ones & silver plated spoon & fork. CMV $35.00 in Avon box.

1971 AVON XMAS GLASS
Given to reps. at special Christmas Meeting. Glass tumbler with red printing. C.M.V. $10.00

1971 ANTIQUE RENAULT CAR CLASS
Some sets come with this Renault Car in set. Very rare. C.M.V. $15.00.

1977 PROSPECT COFFEE JAR & CUP AWARD
Clear glass jar with green painted design on front says 1886 - Avon 1977. Filled with coffee beans. CMV $20.00 jar only
Coffee Cup - Came with jar in white box as set. Has Avon district manager 1977 on cup & other writings. CMV $15.00 cup only. Both given to Avon managers only.

1972 SILVER CANDLELIGHT SET GIFT
Given to reps as a gift. Does not say Avon on set & was not made only for Avon. Can be bought in stores. Set has punch bowl & 2 goblets with silver rim. Box has Avon mailing label. CMV $35.00 set in Avon box.

1974 PASADENA BRANCH WINE GLASS
No 1 in sales. 429 given. 19 Avon 74 Pasadena Branch on glasses. C.M.V. $15.00

1974 CIRCLE OF EXCELLENCE GLASS
Pasadena Branch No.1 in sales in Circle of Excellence. Made by Fostoria, very thin glass. Only 30 given to managers. C of E 1974 on side of glass. C.M.V. $60.00.

Same glass also came in 1973. Same CMV.

1950 SILVER TRAY AWARD
Silver tray 13½" long "Avon — Williams Rogers" on bottom. Awarded to Avon ladies in 1950's. Write to Bud Hastin if y have any info on this award. C.M.V. $30

976 HIGHEST SALES AWARD BOWL
ilver plated fruit bowl was awarded to
0 different Reps for highest sales in their
atagory. Each bowl is engraved different
rom the other. This one is engraved
ith "4A" design. "Highest Percentage
ncrease Christmas 1976".C.M.V.$25.00
Not awarded in all branches.

1977 TEAM ACHIEVEMENT AWARD
Goblet given in 1st and 3rd quarters to top team in each district. Came in white embossed Avon box. C.M.V. $20.00 each quarter. M.B.

1977 PRESIDENTS CELEBRATION AWARD BOWL
Over 40,000 were given as awards. 6 7/8" silver plated bowl given to Avon reps in 2 winning districts in each division for top sales, Inscription in center of bowl (Presidents Celebration 1977) on bottom of bowl. (Awarded exclusively to Avon Representatives) F.B. Rogers. Came in white box as shown. Red silk rose also given at same time with name tag. C.M.V. Rose only with tag. $5.00 CMV bowl $25.00 MB. Bowl did not come with rose.

1970 GIVE N GAIN PRIZE
10¾" high, 4" in diameter. a rose butterfly and lady bug are etched in glass. Given to Avon ladies as prize. This was also sold in stores to public. Came in plain box with Avon stamped on it. Made by Abilities. C.M.V. $25.00 M.B.

1973 TIC TAC TOE APPLE SALAD SET AWARD
3 piece set, 10" clear glass apple bowl with William Rogers silver plated fork and spoon. Won for prize goal. Must be in Avon box with card. C.M.V. $10.00 M.B.

1973 DIVIDED APPLE RELISH SET
3 piece set, 6" divided clear glass bowl with William Rogers silver plated fork and spoon. This bowl won by Presidents Club members only for prize goal. These items must be in the box with outlook and card, as they were not made only for Avon. C.M.V. $15.00 M.B.

1972 MIKASA CHINA SET
Candle holders and sugar/creamer set for reaching first prize goal. C.M.V. $5.00 ea. M.B. Beverage server for reaching second goal. C.M.V. $10.00 M.B. Eight cups and saucers for reaching third goal (to be won by President Club members only) C.M.V. $4.00. For each cup and saucer set. These items must be in Avon boxes with card or outlook as this set was not made just for Avon.

1978 SILVER FLOWER BASKET AUGUST CONFERENCE AWARD
Sterling silver basket made by Cartier, hand made. "August Conference 1978" on top of handle. Yellow silk flowers, green leaves. Given to managers only. CMV $100.00 mint.

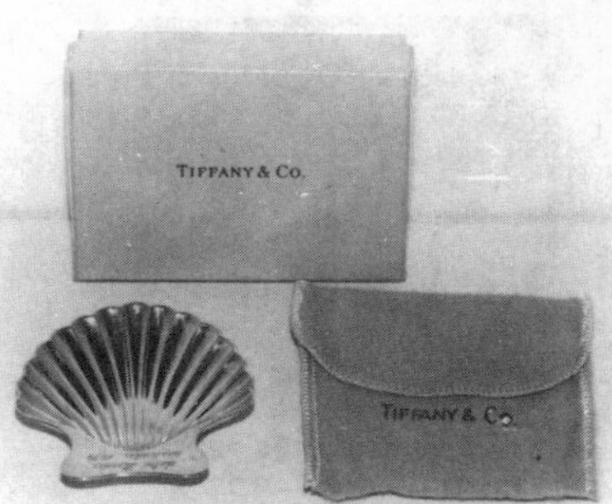

1979 SHELL SALES LEADER AWARD
Sterling silver shell comes in Tiffany felt bag & box. Given to managers. CMV $125.00 MB

1978 MILLION DOLLAR INCREASE GOBLET
Silver plated goblet given to all managers in top division for 1 million dollar increase in sales. CMV $25.00

1977 PORT O' CALL CANDY DISH & BAR
China dish by Ilmoges - France & bar of french candy given to managers for meeting appointment goal. Box has gold label "Meet me at the lamp post, Port O' Call Pasadena" CMV $10.00 MB

1930'S COVERED DISH AWARD
White ceramic bowl &lid. Gold trim with green & pink flowers. Bottom is stamped CPCo. Avon under glazing. Given to Avon reps for sales. CMV $100.00 mint.

1972 PEOPLE WHO LIKE PEOPLE PRIZE PROGRAM AWARDS
1st level prize. Walnut base with silver handle holds 3 crystal with silver trim 6 oz. bowls. Won by Reps for meeting sales goals. Was not made only for Avon. C.M.V. $12.00 M.B.

1969 SILVER AWARD BOWL
Silver plate bowl by Fina. Has 4A symbol and Avon in center of bowl. 2¾" high and 5" wide at top. Awarded to Avon Reps. C.M.V. $18.00.

1977 SALES EXCELLENCE AWARD
Paul Revere, Jostens Pewter 5" bowl C26-76 – C9-77 Awarded to top sales Reps. C.M.V. $20.00 M.B.

1974 88th ANNIVERSARY AWARD BOWL
6" across and 3" high silver plated by Oneida. Paul Revere Silver. Given to top 5 sales Reps in each district. C.M.V. $20.00 Same bowl given to top 5 presidents club sales Reps and their award bowl says Presidents Club over 4A ensignia. C.M.V. $20.00.

1977-78 CURRIER & IVES COLLECTION AWARDS
Made only for Avon & stamped on bottom. Given to Avon Reps for meeting sales goals. 1st step - Dinner Bell C.M V. $5.00 M.B. 2nd step - Butter Dish C.M.V. $10.00 M.B. 3rd Step - Water Pitcher 6½" high C.M.V. $15.00 M.B. 4th step Cake Plate 9½" diam. C.M.V. $30.00 M.B. Add $10.00 each piece for bottom writing printed backwards.

1977–78 CURRIER & IVES TEA SET
Set consists of plate, tea pot, sugar bowl and creamer. Avon Products, Inc. on bottom of each piece. Awarded to Avon Reps for Distinguished Sales Achievement 1977. Plate - 1st step. C.M.V. $5.00 Sugar bowl & creamer 2nd step. C.M.V. $10.00 Tea Pot, 3rd step. CMV $15.00 Cup & Saucer, 4th step. Saucer 1st issue marked 1977 on bottom. 1978 issue has no date. Add $2.00 each piece for 1977 date. CMV $30.00 set of 4. Add $10.00 if writing on bottom is printed backwards for each piece.

1977 SALES EXCELLENCE AWAR CUP
6½" high pewter cup. "4A design, A Sales Excellence Award 1977" of sid cup. Given to top 2% of sales Reps i each division C.M.V. $40.00 M.B.

1971 SCALLOPED SERVING DISH & SPOON PRIZE
Pressed glasss nut dish given to Reps fo meeting sales goals. Also available in local stores. C.M.V. $7.00 M.B.

1976 50 YEAR SERVICE PLATE
Gold plated plate given to Mrs. Bessie O'Neal on July 27, 1976 by David Mitchell President of Avon Products fo 50 continuous years as an Avon lady. is 86 years old and still selling Avon. A letter from Avon and Mr. Mitchell cam with the plate. The plate is 1 of a kind and priceless. The plate is made by Dirilyte. No value established.

72 PEOPLE WHO LIKE PEOPLE RIZE PROGRAM AWARDS
d level prize is a set of 8 10 oz. crystal d silver glasses. Won by Reps for meeting d level sales goals. Was not made only r Avon. C.M.V. $25.00 set M.B.

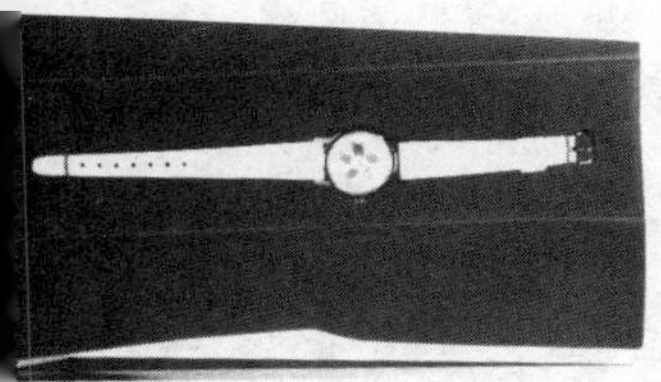

79 COLOR UP WATCH AWARD
Jour Time Co. watch in gold tone case, hite strap. Back side says "For the most lorful time of your life." Came in white x, sleeve & blue felt wrap. Given to ps for customers served. CMV $35.00 MB.

77 OUTSTANDING SALES ANAGEMENT CLOCK AWARD
elide 15 jewel Swiss solid brass clock. scribed on top "In Recognition Of Out-tanding Sales Management — Third uarter 1977" Given to No. 1 Avon anager in each division. CMV $75.00

977 LIBERTY CLOCK AWARD
iven to managers for 1 million dollar les increase. Gold tone clock by Bulova. nside slide clock cover says "To A Million ollar Baby (name of manager) Division 1,000,000 Sales Increase 1977" Came Bulova Americana Collection. CMV 125.00

1979 WATCH STICK PIN - MANAGERS
Gold tone 4A design on face. Given to managers. CMV $75.00

1978 FIELD SUPPORT PENDANT AWARD
1/20 12K gold filled. Back is dated "1978 Field Support Manager" Given to managers. CMV $30.00

1978 NAT. DISTRICT MANAGER PANELIST PIN
Gold tone. Given to managers. CMV $10.00

1972 PEOPLE WHO LIKE PEOPLE PRIZE PROGRAM AWARDS
4th level prize is a 9" diameter and 6" high silver base and trim crystal footed fruit bowl. Won by Reps for meeting 4th & final level sales goals. Was not made only for Avon. C.M.V. $25.00 M.B.

1972 PEOPLE WHO LIKE PEOPLE PRIZE PROGRAM AWARDS
2nd level prize is a 12¾" chip n dip serving set of crystal and silver trimmed. It comes with a 5" matching dip bowl in the center Won by Reps for meeting 2nd level sales goals. Was not made only for Avon. C.M.V. $15.00 M.B.

1973 AMERICAN HERITAGE AWARDS
Set of glass crystal edged with silver. Given to Reps in C-11-73 Consists of 10 7/8" relish dish. C.M.V. $20.00 M.B. Fruit bowl 7 1/8" high and 7 7/8" across C.M.V. $20.00 MB. Water Pitcher C.M.V. $20.00 M.B. Products were not made only for Avon.

1978 YOU MAKE ME SMILE GLASSES AWARDS
Set of 6 glasses made only for Avon given to Avon Reps. for signing up a new Avon lady. C.M.V. $10.00 set M.B.

1977 SEASONS GREETINGS AVON REPS.
5½" high vase marked on bottom Seasons Greetings Avon 1977 and has the 4A symbol. Given to all Avon Representatives at X-mas 1977 in special box. C.M.V. $12.00 M.B.

1978 ACHIEVEMENT AWARD MUG
"1st Quarter, 1978" on white ceramic mug given to team getting most new Avon ladies to sign up. C.M.V. $10.00

1974 PRESIDENTS CLUB MEMBERS WATCH - Awarded to club members. Gold watch & hands with black strap. Box blue & white. CMV $40.00 MB

1969 DIVISION MANAGERS AWARD CLOCK - Sterling silver Seth Thomas electric clock. 4" square face, bottom says "Divisional Managers Tribute 1969" CMV $75.00 mint.

1968 "AVON MANAGERS ACHIEVEMENT" Clock set in top of brushed gold hour glass enscribed on bottom "1968 Avon Manager Achievement". CMV $100.00 MB

1979 DOOR BELL - DOOR KNOCKER AWARDS
Redwood box with brass Avon Calling door knocker on front, door bell on back side. Given to 5 managers in each division. CMV $75.00

1968 DIARY CLOCK
Made by Seth Thomas. Gold, back opens & says "Avon Award". CMV $35.00

1977 TEAM LEADER WATCH
Given to all Avon Team Leaders for Christmas 1977. 2 different. Left is for Women and right is for men. The cases are different and the difference in size of winding stem. Very few of the mens watches given. C.M.V. for Womens $40.00 M.B. C.M.V. for Mens $100.00 M.B.

1977 MANAGERS WATCH
Avon watch same as team leader watch only face says Avon in place of Team Leader & 4A symbol that rotates instead of Avon. Came in male & female size watch as above. CMV $75.00 MB

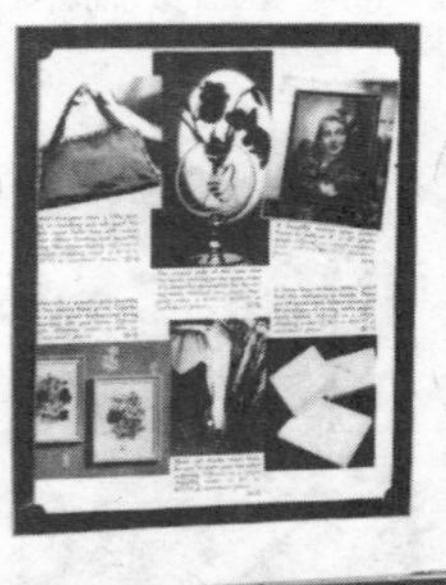

1943 PICTURE GLASS FRAME PRIZE
Etched glass frame holds 8 x 10 size picture Given to reps for selling over $75.00 during campaign. CMV $150.00

1980 PRESIDENT'S CLUB 1981 WATCH WOMEN'S
Gold tone 17 jewel watch on chain. Back says President's Club 81. CMV $50.00 MB

1980 PRESIDENTS CLUB 1981 MEN'S WATCH
Gold tone pocket watch on chain given to male President's Club reps. Inscribed on back "President's Club 1981" CMV $125.00 MB.

1979 CIRCLE OF EXCELLENCE AWARDS
Each item given to managers on Circle trip to Paris 1979.

TRAVEL ALARM CLOCK
Plaque on top says "Circle of Excellence 1979" CMV $25.00

TOTE BAG
Dark navy blue. Circle of Excellence on front. CMV $15.00

CIRCLE OF EXCELLENCE YEAR BOOK
Blue & gold cover shows all Circle of Excellence winners. CMV $10.00

FRAGRANCE & FASHION BINDER
White plastic. CMV $25.00 with contents.

1978 TED E. BEAR TEAM LEADER GI
Tan teddy bear with red shirt was given to all team leaders at end of year party Nov. 1978. Fold out Teddy Bear card was on e table at party. CMV $2.00 card, CMV $1 bear mint.

1968 JEWELRY BOX AWARD
10" long x 5" wide brocade & brass music box. Red lined. Given to reps for top sales Does not say Avon. CMV $60.00 mint.

1979 TEDDY AWARD
Black base with plaque. Brown top & bear has red shirt with Avon in white. Given to one Team Leader for recommendation support in each district. CMV $25.00

1979 TEDDY BEAR COOKIE JAR AWARD
Tan & red ceramic bear cookie jar. Given to Team Leaders at Christmas. CMV $35.00

1922 DESK VALET - CPC AWARD
Solid bronze. Marked CPC 1922. Awarded to CPC reps. CMV $90.00

1976 PRESIDENTS CELEBRATION AWARD CLOCK
Gold plastic and metal Westclock. 4 red roses on face. Was not made only for Avon. C.M.V. $12.00

1966 SOUNDS OF SEASONS MUSIC BOX - Given to managers only. Box holds green & gold Xmas Tree Pin, gold Key & Bell. Came from Cartier in New York. C.M.V. box only $65.00. Complete set $85.00 M.B.

1974 PRESIDENTS CELEBRATION SILVER CHEST - Silver plated, red lined. Embossed rose on lid. C.M.V. $45.00 MB.

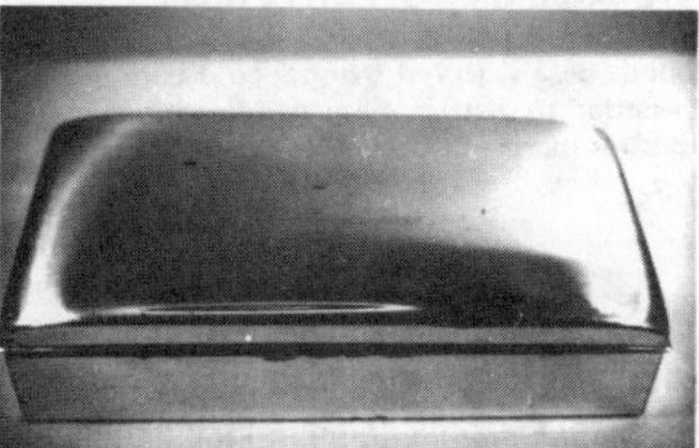

1961 REPRESENTATIVE GIFT CIGARETTE CASE - Silver colored metal case. 4A design & Christmas 1961 on lid. C.M.V. $40.00

1926 ROSE PERFUME LAMP AWARD
Rose colored frosted glass rose shaped electric lamp with antique green metal base. Top of rose had a small hole to put perfume to scent the air when lamp was burning. Given to only 8 Reps for top sales. C.M.V. $150.00

1973 CHINA BELL REP. GIFT
Christmas present to all representatives that had been with Avon over 2 years. White China with pink roses. C.M.V. $12.50 M.B.

1953 QUEEN ELIZABETH CUP & SAUCER
Avon 67th anniversary celebration coincided with Queen Elizabeth Cornation. Awarded at a banquet for top organization. C.M.V. $80.00 mint.

1962 SALES AWARD SACHET
Cream sachet in blue glass with blue, gold & white lid. Gold metal stand $12.00 jar only. $15.00 in box.

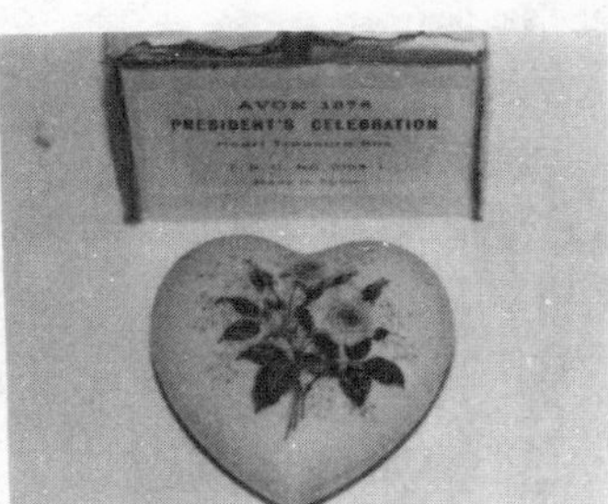

1976 HEART TREASURE BOX AWARD
Top sales teams in 252 winning districts won ceramic heart shaped box given in Presidents Celebration of 1976. Bottom says "Avon Presidents Celebration 1976" Made in Spain. C.M.V. $30.00 M.B.

1976 POSSET POT AWARD
9 inch high stoneware. Bottom reads (Made in Brazil Exclusively for Avon Products, Inc.) C.M.V. $20.00

1975-77 PITCHER & BOWL RECOMMENDATION PRIZE
Given for recommending someone, if appointed as a representative. Has Avon on bottom of both pieces. C.M.V. $25.00 set.

1949 PRESIDENTS CUP AWARD
Sterling silver trophy engraved with top selling team in city & district in each division during Presidents Campaign during the late 40's & early 50's. Given to managers. C.M.V. $165.00 mint.

1977 DECORATORS CHOICE PITCHER & BOWL PRIZE
Ceramic pitcher 10" high and bowl 15¼" across. Made only for Avon. Given to Reps for signing up 1 new Avon Rep. C.M.V. $25.00

1978 TEAM LEADER PICTURE FRAME AWARD
Chrome picture frame marked on top of frame "Made Exclusively for Avon Team Leaders" Given for meeting sales goals. CMV $10.00 mint.

1979 TEAM LEADER PLAQUE AWARD
Given to team leaders in Circle of Excellence winning division. CMV $30.00

1978 MILLION DOLLAR CLUB PLAQUE PASADENA BRANCH
Walnut base with red front & gold trim. Presented to district managers for outstanding sales increase. CMV $75.00

1977 DISTINGUISHED SALES MANAGEMENT PLAQUE AWARD
Solid walnut base holds white ceramic tile center plaque & brass name tag on bottom. Given to top 10 managers in each division. CMV $30.00

1963 MANAGERS DIPLOMA
Certificate given to new Avon managers during the 1960's. Did not come in frame. CMV $10.00

1971 - 3 YEAR WINNER TROPHY
Small wood base, brass plaque that says "Avon 3 year winner" Given to reps. CMV $15.00

1978 KEY TO SUCCESS TROPHY AWARD
Trophy floated to each winning manage in division till final winning manager wo & kept it. CMV $60.00

1978 ANNIVERSARY QUEEN TROPHY
Marble base. Given to top rep in each division for top sales. CMV $15.00
1978 QUEEN'S TIARA
Came with Queen's Trophy. Is not marke Avon. No price established.

1977 PRESIDENT'S CELEBRATION PLAQUE
Engraved wood plaque with Cape Cod Water Goblet attached. Given to Team Leaders with highest sales. CMV $15.00 mint.

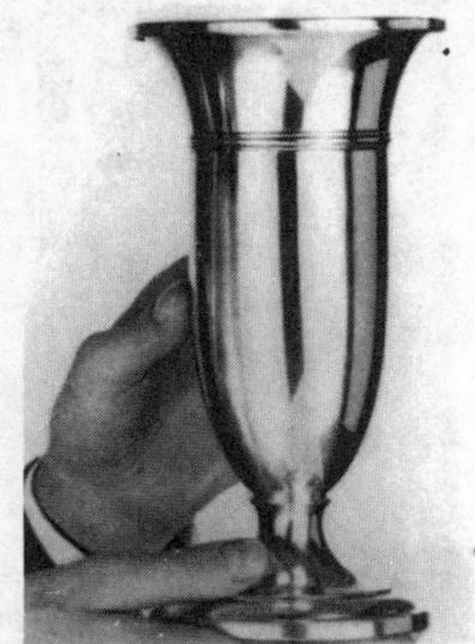

1959-60 PRESIDENTS TROPHY
Sterling silver trophy given to managers in top selling district in each division. Given late 50's to early 60's. Trophy is inscribed with winning team & year. C.M.V. $100.00

1965 BEST SUPPORTING PERFORMANCE TROPHY - This type trophy should not get too high in price as you can still buy the trophys & have a brass name plate put on them. C.M.V. $15.00

1958-59 ACHIEVEMENT AWARD TROPHY
This type has Avon in raised letters on the base of the metal figure. These cannot be purchased & should be worth more. C.M.V. $25.00

1950 ACHIEVEMENT AWARD
Pink & white with gold. Given for high sales during 64th Anniversary Celebration. This was celebrating new packaging & re-design of Cotillion. This matches packaging for this era. Approx. 10x14 inches. C.M.V. $25.00

1954 BUD VASE AWARD
8" tall sterling silver vase awarded to each representative in winning district during President's Campaign. C.M.V. $40.00

1954-56 PRESIDENTS TROPHY
13 5/8" high, sterling silver trophy was given to top selling city & district managers in each division during Presidents Campaign each year. Trophy sits on black base. C.M.V. $100.00

LEFT 1966 TOP SALES TROPHY
Small 5" high gold trophy, wood base. C-11-13-1966. CMV $15.00

RIGHT 1954 ACHIEVEMENT AWARD TROPHY
Avon in raised letters on the base of the metal figure. Given to top representatives in each district. C.M.V. $27.50

1966 DIVISION MANAGERS TROPHY
Large pewter trophy given to winning manager in each division. C.M.V. $135.00

1969 KANSAS CITY BRANCH TROPHY
"Number One" national sales increase. C.M.V. $17.00

1961 LOVING CUP TROPHY
Gold cup on white base. C.M.V. $20.00

1960'S WALL PLAQUE
Used at sales meetings. Blue & gold cardboard. CMV $25.00

1964 PAUL GREGORY PLAQUE
Silver plaque on black wood. Given to each manager in the winning division. C.M.V. $35.00

1960's HONORABLE MENTION PLAQUE - Green pearlessence plastic base with wood and brass plaque. C.M.V. $12.50.

1970 STAR SPANGLED MANAGER PLAQUE - Avon-Star Spangled Manager Summer 1970 on face plate. C.M.V. $14.00.

1977 TOP 10 DIVISION TROPHY
4½" high 4A design inside lucite top on wood base and brass plaque. Given to top 10 sales Reps in each division. Came in plain white box. C.M.V. $50.00

1977 JUBILEE ANNIVERSARY QUEEN TROPHY
Small wood base, gold top for Division Manager. C.M.V. $10.00

1974 NATIONAL DISTRICT PANEL PLAQUE - Picture frame plaque - Sara Fleming. Gold & brown. C.M.V. $15.00

LEFT 1975-76 HOOSIER CUSTOMER SERVICE TROPHY
Given to managers for most customers served. CMV $22.50
RIGHT 1978 PRESIDENT'S CELEBRATION TROPHY
Marble base. CMV $15.00

1971 OUTSTANDING MANAGERS PLAQUE - Wood base with gold plaque. Outstanding managers first quarter. C.M.V. $20.00

1960's 4A WALL PLAQUE
Used at sales meetings. Large size. C.M.V. $20.00

1972 TRAVELING TROPHY
Gold 4A with first Avon Lady over emblem on walnut base with engraved plate Team Honor Award. C.M.V. $30.00

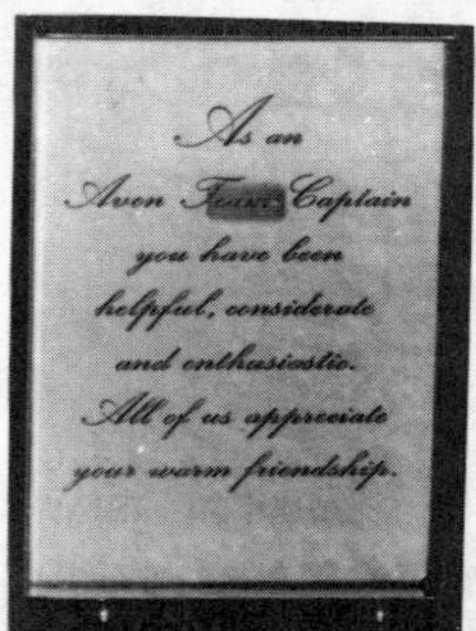

1972 TEAM CAPTAIN AWARD
Awarded to all Tean Captains in each district. Thick plastic over lettering with gold frame. C.M.V. $10.00

1965 DIVISION CHAMPION PLAQUE
Given for highest sales during general managers campaign 1965. C.M.V. $30.00

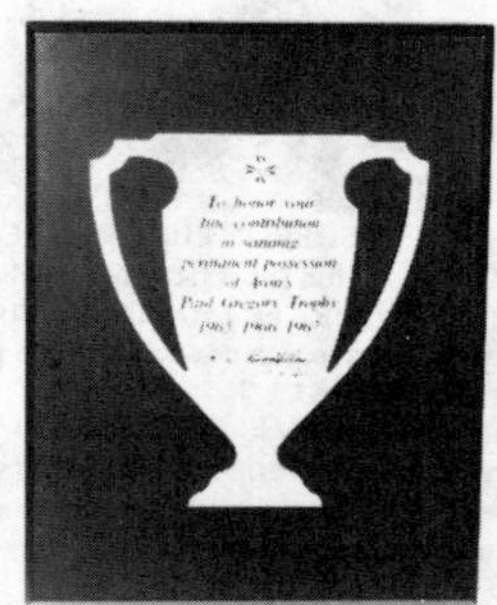

1965-67 PAUL GREGORY PLAQUE
Black & silver plaque given to winning division of Avons Paul Gregory Trophy. C.M.V. $30.00

1954-56 DIVISIONAL SALES CAMPAIGN AWARD - Only 20 black plaques with sterling silver rose, were given each year to managers in top selling district in each of the 20 divisions in U.S. C.M.V. $100.00.

1971 AWARD PLAQUE
Presented in campaign 1-26, 1971 for increased sales. C.M.V. $7.00.

1980 PRECIOUS MOMENTS AWARD
Rabbit figurine marked on bottom President's Club Luncheon 1980. Given to reps at President's Club Luncheon only CMV $20.00 MB

1976 FIRST LADY PORCELAIN FIGURINE
Blue, white & pink porcelain made in Spain. Given to Presidents Club members only for outstanding sales in 90th Anniversary celebration. CMV $45.00 MB

LEFT 1979 ALBEE AWARD NO. 1
Porcelain figurine 8½" high in honor of the 1st Avon lady of 1886, Mrs. P. F. E. Albee. Given to top reps in sales in each district. Pink umbrella is also porcelain. CMV $125.00 MB
RIGHT 1979 ALBEE AWARD NO. 2
Hand painted porcelain figurine of the 1st Avon rep of 1886. 2nd in a series. Given to President's Club reps for outstanding sales. Colors are blue & pink. CMV $100.00 MB
1979 ALBEE AWARD – CANADA
Is the same as 1978 Albee issued in U.S. only the bottom printing is in French & English & dated 1979. CMV $125.00 mint.

1980 PRECIOUS MOMENTS AWARD SET
Set of 3 rabbit figurines given to reps for top sales. No. 1 is "Ready for an Avon day" CMV $20.00 No. 2 is "My first call" CMV $30.00 No. 3 is 'Which shade do you prefer" CMV $60.00 Set of 3 CMV $110.00 Made in Japan only for Avon.

1973 AVON FIGURINE AWARD
Awarded to each representative in district with greatest total sales increase. Made by Hummel, numbered & says "Made for Avon" on bottom. Figurine 8" sits on white marble base with glass dome. CMV $200.00 MB

1961 WOMEN OF ACHIEVEMENT AWARD - Painted ceramic figure of 1886 sales lady. One given in each district for highest sales. Came with stained walnut base & gold plaque inscribed "Avon Woman of Achievement Award". Printed on bottom of figure "Imported Expressly for Avon Products, Inc. Made in West Germany" CMV $275.00, $300.00 MB
1969 WOMEN OF ACHIEVEMENT AWARD - White ceramic figure much the same as 1961 model. Base is tall & of white wood with gold trim. Only one given in each division for outstanding performance. Printed on bottom of figure "Imported Expressly for Avon Products, Inc. Made in Western Germany Dresden Art" CMV $250.00, $300.00 MB

RIGHT 1961 LADY OF ACHIEVEMENT TEST
Pictured on right is smaller size original artwork test figurine for 1961 Lady of Achievement Award. Stands 7" high. Rare. Was not sold or given out by Avon. No price established. Used by factory only.

1963 CHRISTMAS GIFT PERFUME
Given to Avon sales ladies for Christmas. The bottle at left is same as the one sealed in gold plastic container with green tassel & red ribbon. 4-10 oz. Christmas gift given to all representatives submitting an order in Dec. 1963. CMV $40.00 complete. Bottle only $15.00

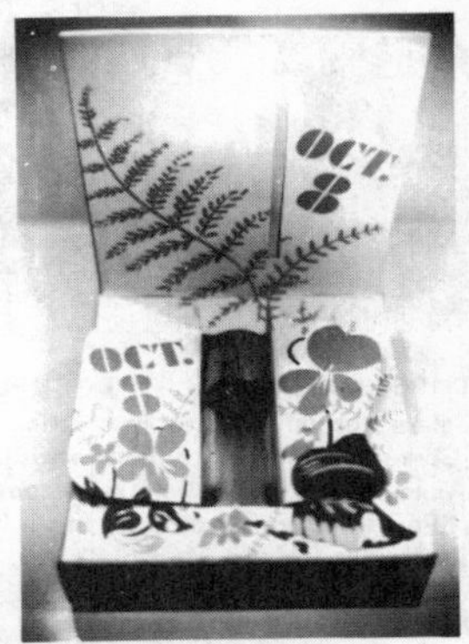

1951 OCTOBER 8 AWARD
1 dram Forever Spring Perfume, smooth gold cap & bottle. Given to each representative sending an order in campaign 12, 1951. C.M.V. $40.00 M.B.

1975 REPRESENTATIVE CHRISTMAS GIFT - Clear glass in blue box. Reproduction of Trailing Arbutus Powder Sachet. C.M.V. $12.00 M.B.

1948 PURSE OF GOLD AWARD
Cardboard tube contained 8 samples of Golden Promise. Came in packages shown. Given to each representative sending in an order at the close of campaign 3. C.M.V. $30.00

1979 PRESIDENT'S CELEBRATION HEART AWARD
Lucite heart marked "You're our number one - Avon 1979 President's Celebration" Made in Taiwan. Comes in white Avon box. CMV $20.00 MB
RIGHT 1979 MANAGERS HEART "YOU'RE NO. 1"
Clear lucite, has smaller hole on top & heart is about ¼" smaller. Came in red velvet bag. This one was given to managers only. CMV $30.00 mint in bag.

1963 PRESIDENTS AWARD PERFUME
Clear glass with glass stopper, silver 4A tag & string. Given to national winners in each division for Presidents Campaign, - 1963. Box silver & white base with clear plastic lid. Bottom label on bottle says (Occur! Perfume Avon Products, Inc., N.Y., N.Y. contains 1 fl. oz.) C.M.V. $200.00 bottle only. $250.00 M.B. with label and tag. Also came in ½ oz. size with gold neck 4A tag. Please write Bud Hastin if you know when and what the ½ oz. size was given for.

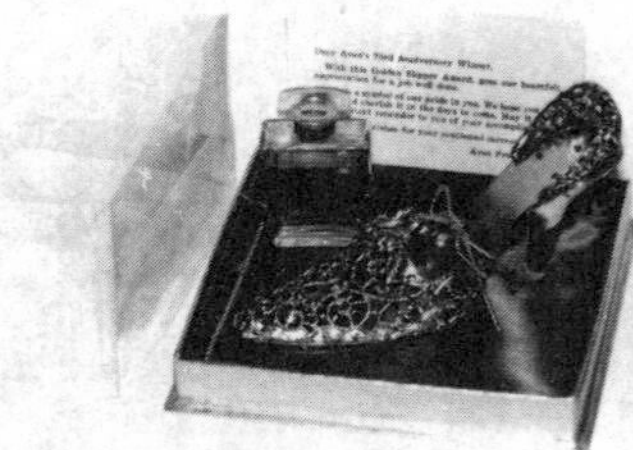

1959 GOLDEN SLIPPER AWARD
All gold metal slipper with red stone in toe & clear plastic heel. ½ oz. glass stoppered perfume bottle fits in slipper toe. No Avon name on shoe but has paper label on bottom of bottle saying "73rd Anniversary. Avon Products. Inc." Given to each representative in the winning group of each branch for top sales. C.M.V. $200.00 slipper & bottle with label. $250.00 M.B.

1978 APPLE PAPER WEIGHT AWARD
Given to managers for top sales. Clear crystal glass apple is engraved "You Made New York Smile" Avon March 1978 on front side. CMV $80.00

LEFT 1950 MANAGERS GIFT PERFUME
½ oz. glass stoppered bottle in plastic case. Given to managers to help introduce To A Wild Rose. Paper label on bottom reads "Perfume Avon Products, Inc., Distributor, New York, Montreal, Vol. ½ oz." Came with neck tassel. C.M.V. $250.00 mint, in plastic case.
RIGHT 1955 PRESIDENT'S AWARD CELEGRATION PERFUME
½ oz. perfume, glass stopper. Given to the winning team members for top sales. C.M.V. $100.00 B.O. mint. $140.00 in box.

1924 FRAGRANCE JAR AWARD
American Beauty fragrance jar hand painted design in blue & gold. Pink & green flowers on lid. Pink ribbon. Given to reps for top sales. CMV $350.00

1979 OBELISK COMMUNITY SERVICE AWARD
8¼" clear lucite. 1 given to managers in each division. Has 4A design & message of Ralph Waldo Emerson in center. CMV $50.00

1978 PERFUME – CIRCLE OF EXCELLENCE
1 oz. glass stopper bottle, made in France. Paper neck tag says "Made Exclusively for you. Circle of Excellence 1978" CMV $100.00 mint.

1979 REPRESENTATIVE CHRISTMAS GIFT
Ceramic tile picture frame made in Japan. Box says Happy Holidays Avon 1979. Given to all Avon reps at Christmas. CMV $10.00 MB

1979 "PICTURE FRAME" DREAM AWARD – SEPTEMBER CONFERENCE
Ceramic picture frame. White, pink & green flowers with white doves. Center is pink, says "Hold fast to your dreams, For if you do. . . Tomorrow you'll see More dreams can come true." CMV $15.00

1978 HUDSON MANOR BUD VASE - GIFT
Avon silver plated bud vase & red rose in silver box. Bottom says "Team Leader Aug. 78" Made in Italy. Same as regular issue only regular issue does not say Team Leader 78 on bottom. CMV $25.00 MB
1978 MANAGERS BUD VASE - GIFT
Same as above only says "August Conference 78" on bottom instead of Team Leader. CMV $35.00 MB

1971 CHRISTMAS BELLS - MANAGERS GIFT
Red strap with 5 bells given to Avon managers at Christmas. Came with card with bells on it & "for you from Avon" Must have Avon card. CMV $10.00 MB

LEFT 1977 MANAGERS CHRISTMAS TREE GIFT
Hand blown glass Christmas tree in clear, green, red & yellow. Given to Avon managers at Christmas 1977. Does not say Avon. CMV $25.00
RIGHT 1978 MANAGERS CHRISTMAS TREE GIFT
Brass Christmas tree ornament signed by "Bi Jan" on back. Given to Avon managers at Christmas 1978. Came in green box. CMV $20.00 MB

1979 VALENTINE TEAM LEADER GIFT
3½" across crystal heart shaped glass dish given to all team leaders for Valentines. CMV $10.00 MB

1966 PRESIDENT'S CAMPAIGN COMPACT AWARD
Case marked sterling & back marked "Branch champions President's Campaign 1966" Came in white & gold Avon box in felt bag. CMV $20.00 MB

1978 ADDITION'S AWARD
Black & clear plastic picture cube for recruiting new reps. CMV $25.00 MB

1978 REP CHRISTMAS GIFT BOWL
Fostoria bowl with 4A design & 1978 on bottom. Given to all Avon reps for Christmas 1979. Box shown with red ribbon & gold tag & white & gold plastic bell given to managers. CMV $10.00 reps, MB, CMV $15.00 managers with ribbon.

1979 MANAGERS FLOWER BASKET
Basket of silk flowers with Avon tag to managers. In Avon box. CMV $25.00 MB with tag.
1979 TEAM LEADER FLOWER BASKET
Same flower basket only different box & different tag given to team leaders. CMV $15.00 MB

1977 POLLY PROSPECTING BIRD AWARD
Stuffed toy by Possem Trot. Tag has Avon Products on it. Given to Avon managers for recruiting new reps. Came with 2 large cards as shown. CMV $25.00 with Avon tag. Add $1.00 each card. Came in Avon mailer tube & letter. CMV $35.00 MB all.

1950's AVON CALLING DOOR BELL
Used at Avon meetings. Has button on back to ring door bell. CMV $65.00 mint.

1962 PERFUME CREME ROLLETTE CHRISTMAS GIFT
.33 oz. gold cap, 4A embossed bottle and box. Given to reps. at Christmas, 1962. Came in Here's My Heart, Persian Wood, To A Wild Rose, Topaze, Somewhere, Cotillion. C.M.V. $12.00 in box shown.

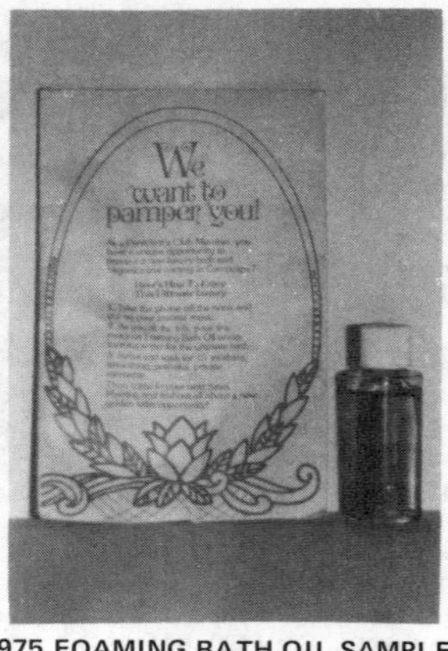

1975 FOAMING BATH OIL SAMPLE
Given to Presidents Club members. 1/2 oz. bottle, white cap. Presidents Club label on bottom. Came in introductory envelope. C.M.V. $3.50 in envelope.

1944 58th ANNIVERSARY GIFT BOX
Holds heart shaped sachet pillow. Given to all representatives on Avon's 58th anniversary. CMV $90.00 MB

a

1948 AVON APRON
Aqua in color with white center. Avon in center & pictures of Avon products of 1948 Given to Managers only for sales demo. C.M.V. $50.00 mint.

1960 SURPRISE GIFT
Silver & gold foil box contained one Deluxe Lipstick. Given as a Christmas gift to all representatives. C.M.V. $22.50 M.B.

1939 EMPLOYEE GIFT
Blue box with Avon's Suffern Plant on box. Holds Tulip label and gold cap of Cotillion Toilet water. CPC label & Cotillion powder sachet. Rare. CMV $95.00 MB

1942 ANNIVERSARY ALBUM AWARD SET
Book type box opens to show 2 satin pillowettes with 56th Anniversary on back of each. One is blue & one pink. Given during Anniversary campaign. C.M.V. $125.00

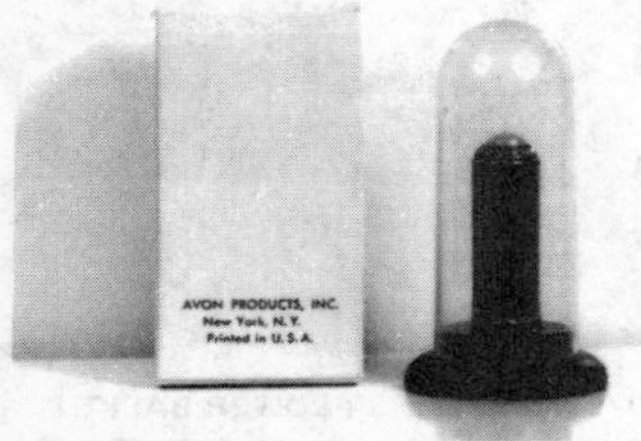

1961 LIPSTICK DEMONSTRATOR
A demonstrator piece sold to representatives for $1.35. Black plastic base with clear lucite dome. Came with silver deluxe lipstick with 4A on top. (Wrong lipstick shown in case.) C.M.V. $22.00 M.B.

1959 CHRISTMAS CAROL CANDLE SET
Red velvet box with green lining holds 4 red and white angel candles with blue eyes and blond hair. Candles made by Gurley Novelty Co., label on bottom. Outside of box says An Avon Christmas Carol. Given to Avon Managers at X-mas 1959. CMV $125.00 MB

1941 BETSY ROSS RED GIFT SET
Set given to employees of Avon's Suffern Plant as anniversary campaign gift. RARE. Came with hand written gift card. CMV $85.00 MB

1942 56th ANNIVERSARY AWARD
Satin Sachet pillows given to each Rep. who worked her territory for 56 hours during the Anniversary Campaign. Came 2 to a box, in blue and pink. C.M.V. $30.00 mint.

1978 PRESIDENT'S CLUB LUNCHEON BANNER
White canvas, red & gold letters. CMV $20.00

1976 AVON X-MAS CARD
White Avon embossed box holds hand screened fold our glass X-mas card given to all Avon Reps in 1976. C.M.V. $10.00 M.B.

MERRY MOODS OF CHRISTMAS ORNAMENT - Dark blue ornament for managers only. Other side says Avon Presents with 4A design. C.M.V. $35.00 mint.

1974 CHRISTMAS ORNAMENTS MUSICAL GIFT SET
Given to reps for getting new reps. Red & gold bell & green & gold ball. Both have music boxes inside. Made by Heinz Deichett, West Germany. Both came in red box as set. CMV $20.00 each no box, $50.00 set MB.

1976 MANAGERS BANNER
White silk banner about 8 ft. long, gold braid, pink letters. Used by managers to encourage Reps to call on new customers. C.M.V. $10.00

1952 CANDLESTICK AWARDS
Sterling silver candle sticks 2½" tall and 2¾" wide at the base. They were given to Reps for calling on 120 customers during the 66th Avon Anniversary campaign, 1952. Came in nice gift box. The candle sticks were not made just for Avon. Must be in box with Avon card as shown. C.M.V. $50.00 M.B.

1951-52 PRESIDENTS AWARD PENNANT
Royal blue pennant with gold trim & letters. Given to top selling city & district division managers during early 50's. C.M.V. $45.00

1966 OUR BANNER YEAR
Used during district sales meetings. C.M.V. $20.00. There are many different banners of this type. C.M.V. will range $15.00 to $20.00 on most.

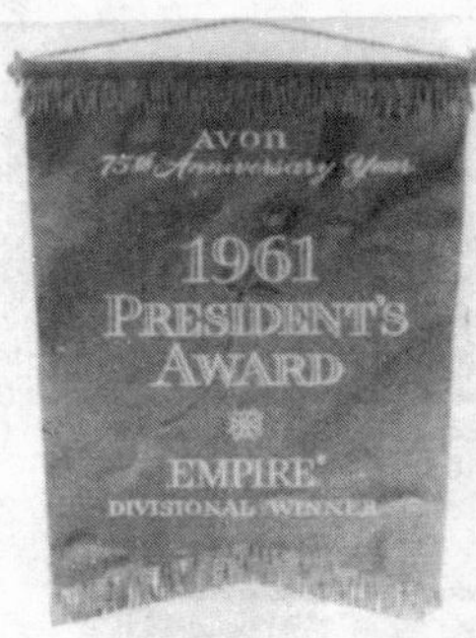

1961 PRESIDENTS AWARD BANNER
Small banner given to top sales team in each division. Each winning division had their name on banner. C.M.V. $25.00

1977 AVON CHRISTMAS TABLE CLOTH
4 x 4 ft. blue satin, white letters, used at Christmas dinner 1977 for Avon Reps. in Atlanta branch. C.M.V. $10.00.

1974 PRESIDENTS CELEBRATION BANNER
Small dark blue felt banner about 18" long yellow letters and cord. Used by managers. C.M.V. $10.00

LEFT 1979 SPOON - PRESIDENT'S CLUB AWARD
Silver plated serving spoon marked Avon President's Club 1979. Came in Avon box. CMV $10.00 MB

RIGHT 1978 CAKE SERVER AWARD
Silver plated serving spatula - Avon 92nd Anniversary - President's Club 1978 on spoon. Given to all President's Club members. Special box & card. CMV $10.00 MB

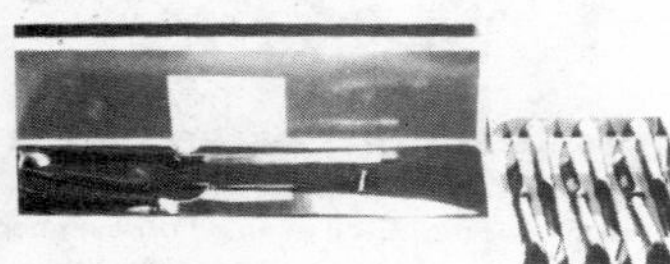

1972 STEAK KNIFE & CARVING SET
C-12-1972. In Avon box. C.M.V. $15.00 ea. set M.B.

1971 JUNE 15 BUTTON PIN
Bright green to remind customers June 15 was Fathers Day. C.M.V. $3.00.

1970 HELLO 1970 BUTTON PIN
Black background with red, yellow & blue letters & numbers. Given to all representatives to tell the world she welcomes successful seventies. C.M.V. $3.00.

1970 MOONWIND MANAGERS DISPLAY
Silver and blue card board display. C.M.V. $10.00

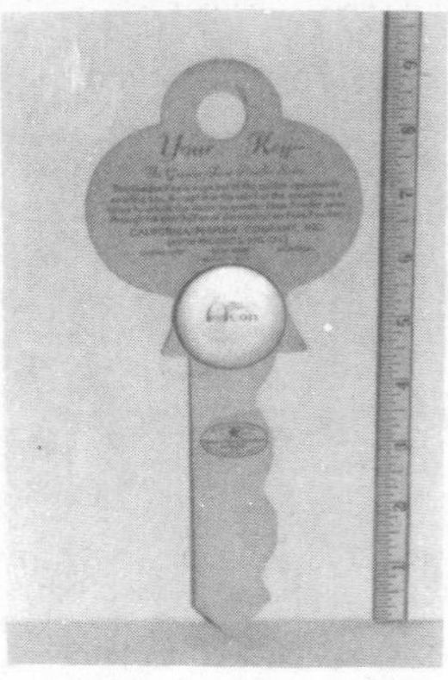

1936 FACE POWDER GOLD KEY
9½" long key is gold on one side with large tulip A & Avon. Back side holds silver face powder sample. CPC label. Given to Reps only. C.M.V. $20.00 mint as shown.

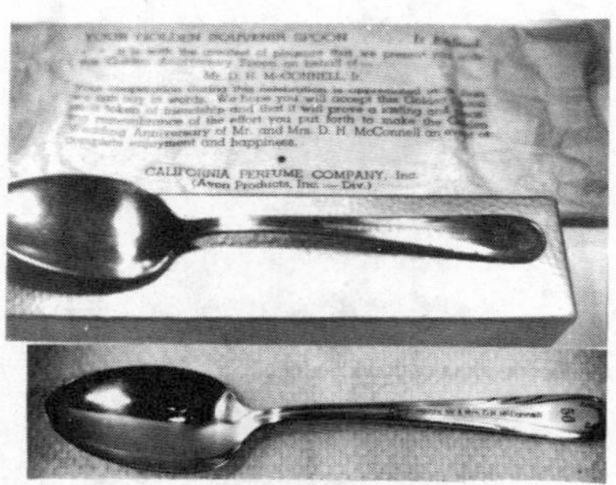

1936 - 50th ANNIVERSARY SPOON
Gold spoon engraved "Compliments Mr. & Mrs. D.H. McConnell - Anniversary 50" The gold on these spoons does not stay very well so many are found silver. C.M.V. in box gold spoon $100.00 mint. Silver $50.00 spoon only. Spoon with gold, mint $75.00

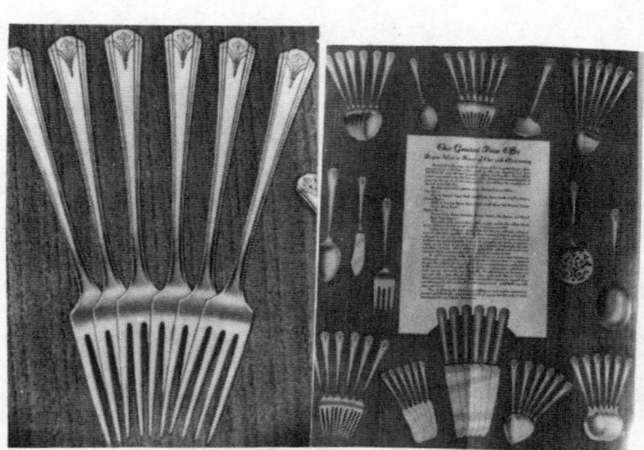

1938 SILVEWARE AWARD
Made only for Avon. Each piece marked on back Simeon L. & George H. Rogers Co. Ltd. X-Tra. Given for meeting sales goal during Avon's 50th Anniversary. 55 piece set. C.M.V. set in box. $125.00 mint.

1915 CPC SPOON "STERLING SILVER"
Sold as a souvenir at the CPC exhibit at the Panama-Pacific International Exposition. Front reads "Palace of Liberal Arts - Panama-Pacific Exposition - Tower of Jewels" Back of spoon reads "CPC 1915 Court of Four Seasons" CMV $100.00 in envelope, $75.00 spoon only. Was also given to reps for selling 12 CPC talcum powders, 1 free for each 12 talcs.

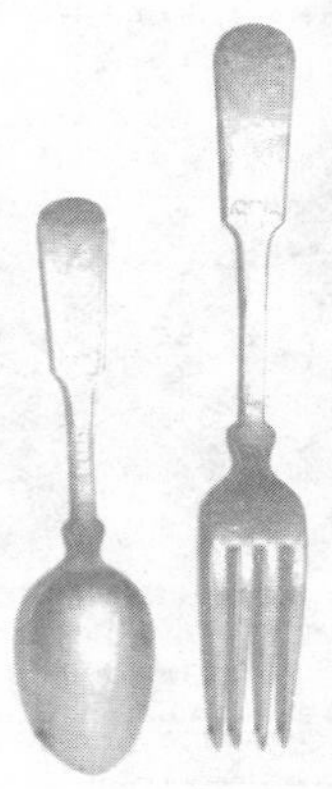

1920-30s CPC SILVERWARE
Used in CPC factorys for employee eating areas. CPC stamped on back of knife, fork and spoons. C.M.V. $3.00 each piece.

1969 AVON AWARD SPOONS
6 silver plated demitasse spoons. Each engraved with a design signifying a different fragrance: Occur, Rapture, Unforgettable, Regence, Brocade and Charisma. Each spoon was given in this order for progressively higher sales. A seventh spoon was given to each representative in the winning district of each branch. It was engraved 1886-1969 and had a picture of the 1886 Sales Lady. CMV $45.00 set MB with sleeve or $5.00 each spoon, 7th spoon $10.00

1975 MOISTURE SECRET PRESIDENT'S CLUB GIFT - Sent to President's Club members to introduce Moisture Secret. C.M.V. $6.00 M.B.

1975 I KNOW A SECRET PIN
For President's Club members. Pink pin. C.M.V. $1.00.

1974 I'M THE HEART PIN
Given to reps as being the heart of Avon. CMV $2.00

1979 ZANY BUTTON
Given to Avon reps on introduction of Zany products. CMV $1.00

1979 TEAM LEADER BUTTON
Given to Avon reps. CMV $1.00

1970's Early TEAM LEADER RIBBON BADGE
Yellow badge and ribbon used by Team Leaders at sales meetings. CMV $5.00

1978 I GOT IT PIN
Gray and white pin given to Reps at Avon sales meetings. Measures 2¼", CMV $1.00

1977 AVON 91ST BUTTON & RIBBON
Red & white button. CMV $1.00, Button & ribbon, $2.00

1979 "ASK ME ABOUT THE LOVE OF MY LIFE" BUTTON
White & red button. CMV $1.00

1977 LUGGAGE TAG
Round white plastic, back side says "The Magic of Avon" CMV $2.00

1968 Green felt board with 6 tin painted flowers pins. Managers gave a pin to each representative for recommending a new Avon representative. $35.00 complete card mint. Each Pin $4.00.

1960 4A NAME PIN
Used by Avon Reps at meetings. 2½" in diamater. C.M.V. $3.00

1977 COLOR WORKS MAKEUP BUTTONS
Given to Reps for sales meeting attendance. CMV $1.00

BUTTON – PINS
1978 Top Horizon 50 pin. CMV $2.00
1976 Say Yes Yes To No No's. CMV $1.00
1978 The Smile Starts Here. CMV $1.00

1978 POSTCARD GREATEST HOME–COMING
CMV 50c

1978 GREATEST HOMECOMING PIN
CMV $1.00
Both are yellow & blue. Used for President's Celebration.

1971 DAISY CHAIN JEWELRY & PIN
White & gold earrings 2 different pins or a daisy topped pen could be chosen by a representative for each person recommended as a representative. Only one gift for each name. C.M.V. $6.00 each. Daisy display card $7.00.

1972 RAIN HAT
Plastic rain hat in pink & white case. Given at Beauty Salons only. C.M.V. $2.00

1974 DING-DONG AVON CALLING PEN
Given at Christmas. Black and white pen. C.M.V. $3.00

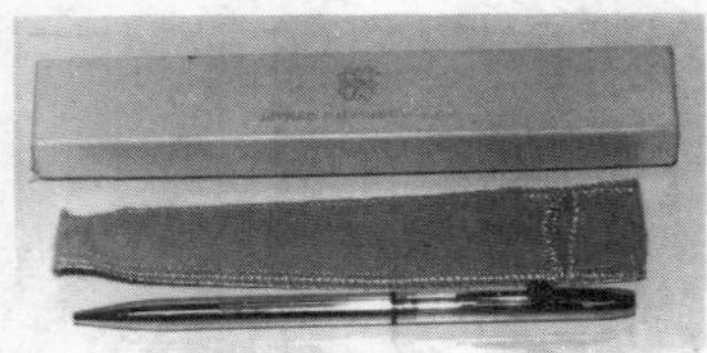

1969 DIVISION MANAGERS TRIBUTE PEN - Silver pen with 4A on clip. Came in blue flannel sleeve & white box. C.M.V. $27.50 M.B.

1960's AVON CHRISTMAS MAGIC PENCIL - White pencils from Avon. C.M.V. $1.00 ea.

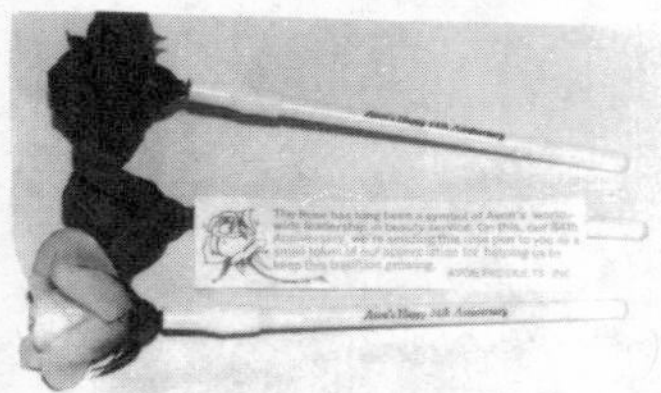

1970 84th ANNIVERSARY FLOWER PENS
Given for sending in an order C-12 84th anniversary. White barrel with red printing, with yellow, pink, red, orange or white rose. CMV $2.00 each, $3.00 in cellophane wrapper with card.

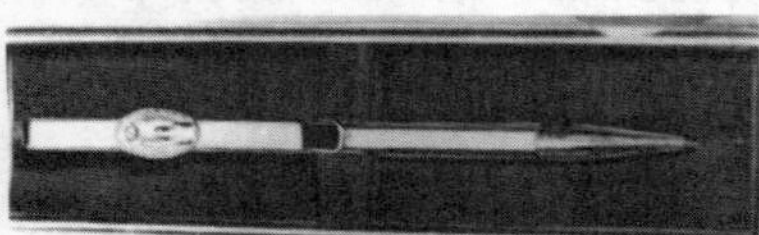

1950 AWARD PENCIL
Deluxe Eversharp, gold color. Given to representatives for writing 50 or more orders in campaign 2, 1950. 5 inches long with Avon Woman of Achievement on pencil. C.M.V. $25.00 pen only, $30.00 M.B.

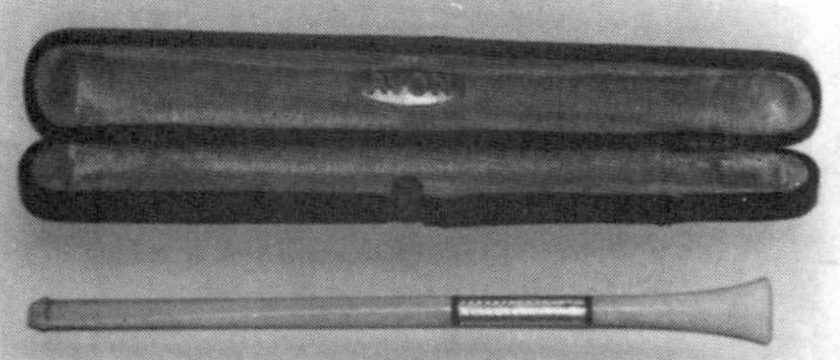

1934 CIGARETTE HOLDER AWARD
Made of solid ivory in velvet lined custom made blue & gold box marked Avon inside lid. Green & silver center band. CMV $75.00 MB

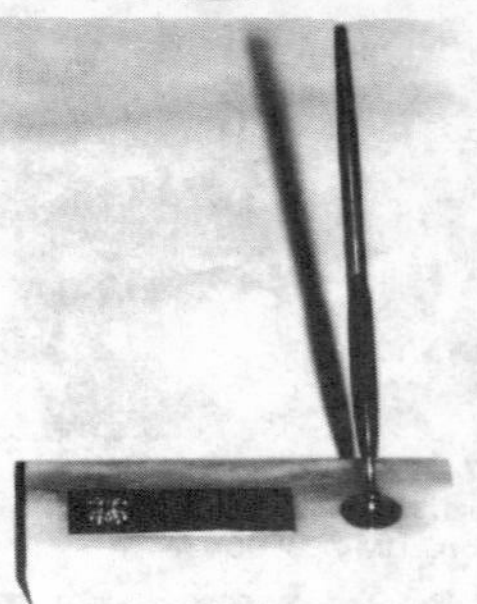

1972 MANAGER DESK SET AWARD
Has 4A emblem, marble base. C.M.V. $20.00

1973'S AVON DESK SET PRIZE
Brown plastic came with paper and pen. Given to Reps for meeting sales goals. C.M.V. $5.00.

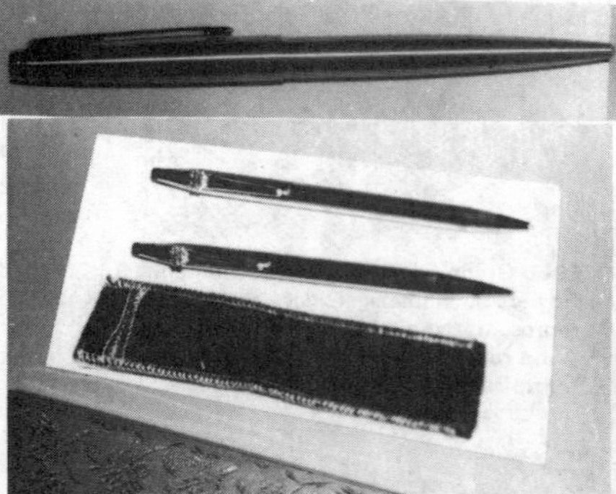

1979 PRESIDENT'S CLUB PEN AWARD
Parker 75 silver & gold pen. Inscribed on side "President's Club 1979" Comes in blue felt Parker case. CMV $20.00

1969 DIVISION MANAGERS PEN & PENCIL SET AWARD
Sterling silver pens. 4A emblem on pens. Came in blue brocade Cross pen box. Given to managers only. CMV $50.00 set MB, each pen only $20.00

1969 PEN FOR LEADERSHIP
Silver, black top with olive leaf on top. Garland Pen. Given to Avon reps. C.M.V. $5.00

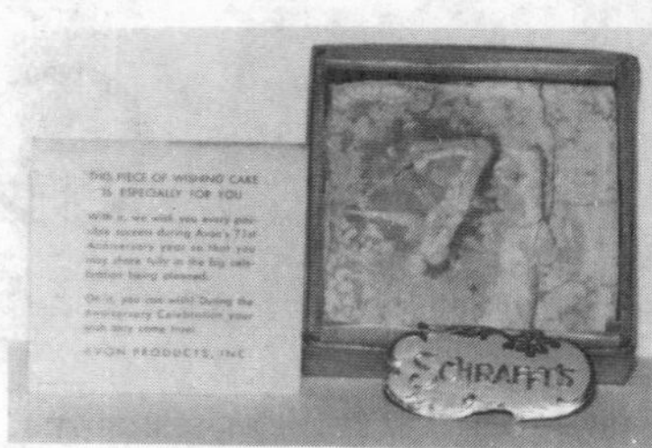

1957 - 71ST ANNIVERSARY CAKE
A real cake with 71 on top with Avon card given to managers. Made by Schraffts. CMV $50.00

1979 TEDDY BEAR PEN AWARD
Cross chrome pen with small bear marked TL for Team Leader. Avon bear sleeve fits over box. CMV $27.50 MB.

1970 WORLD OF CHRISTMAS - FLOWER PEN AWARD
Small white pen with red, yellow & green holly flower on cap. Given to Avon reps. CMV $2.50 mint.

1979 STERLING CLOCK PEN AWARD
Sterling silver pen with digital clock & calendar inside. Inscribed "Number 1 in $ Inc." plus name of division. Given to managers only. CMV $125.00 MB

1975 LETTER OPENER MANAGER AWARD
Red & black box holds wood handle letter opener. Brass Avon lady insignia & K.C. No. 1 1975 on handle. CMV $20.00 MB

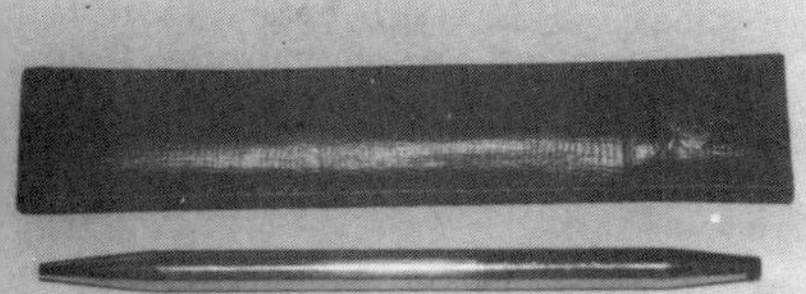

1976 AVON PEN
Gold color. Avon Calling on side of pen. in red leather case. Rose design in gold. Given to Reps for recommendation prize. Made by Cross. 5¼" long pen. C.M'V. $10.00 in case.

1977 INKWELL & PEN SET AWARD
Blue & gold display box holds wood base with old glass ink well & 3 feather quill pens and plastic bottle of ink. Avon card about pen set. Avon brass plaque on base. Given for recruiting new reps. CMV $25.00 MB

1974 88th ANNIVERSARY DESK SET
White marble base. Black pen. Turquoise and silver 4A says Avon 88th Anniversary. Given to Reps for selling $125.00 worth of Avon. C.M.V. $10.00

1976 CIRCLE OF EXCELLENCE LETTER OPENER
Given in Indiana only to Circle of Excellence Reps. Only 25 were given. Brass plaque and door knocker pin is embedded in black plastic handle. C.M.V. $40.00

LEFT 1976 AVON CALLING PEN
14K gold filled. Made by Cross. In grey bag and red leather pen holder. Given to Reps. C.M.V. $6.00
RIGHT 1977 TOP 6 TEAM LEADER TROPHY
Given for Top 6 Sales in Anniversary Celebration 1977. White marble base, gold statue. Blue plaque. C.M.V. $10.00

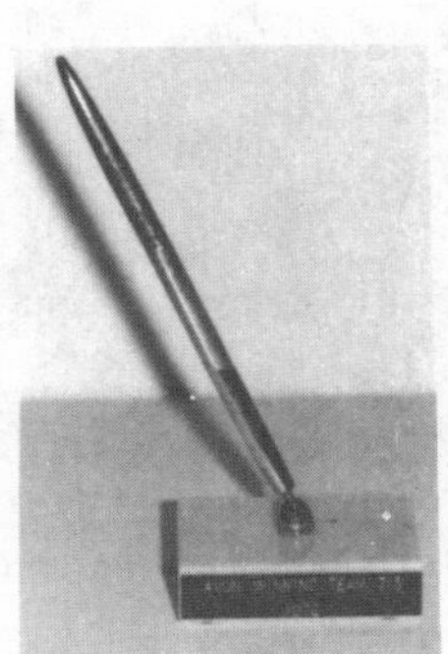

1976 WINNING TEAM DESK SET AWARD
Given for best sales team in district in 1976. White marble base, silver color pen. C.M.V. $5.00

1970 PICTURE YOURSELF MIRROR
Two sided mirror with antiqued gold. Awarded for selling 7 body lotions during campaing 7. C.M.V. $6.00.

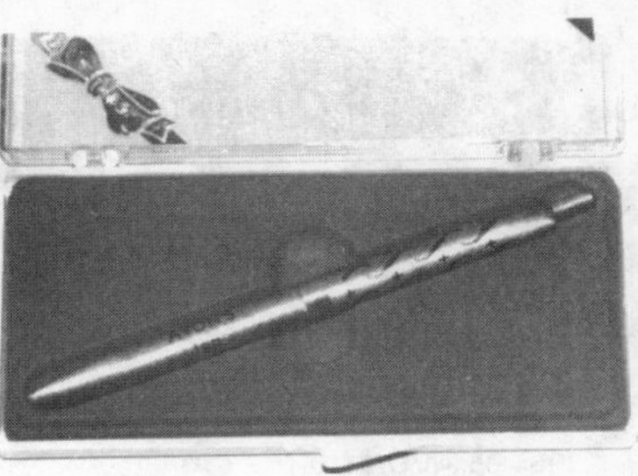

1975 AVON TOP REPRESENTATIVE PEN GIFT
Brass and black design ball point pen. Small size. Came in red velvet lined, plastic display box and gold sleeve. Given for meeting sales goals. C.M.V. $10.00 M.B. as shown. Pen only $5.00

1971 AVON KEY CASE
Blue case with large 4A design. C.M.V. $10.00.

1970 KEY CASE FLASHLIGHT
Red key case with flashlight inside. Not marked Avon. Made only for Avon. Given to representatives for meeting sales goals. C.M.V. $5.00 mint.

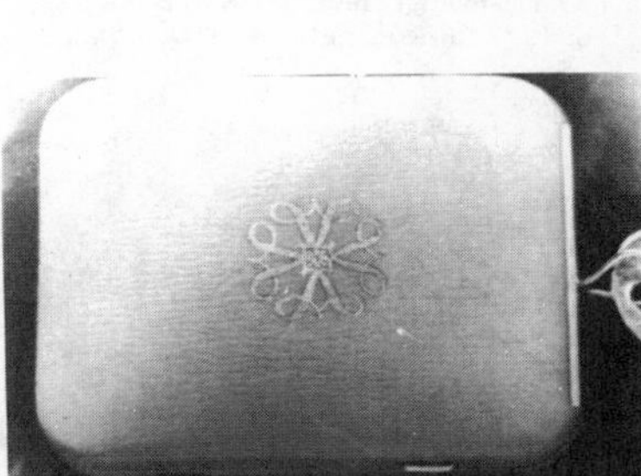

1967 AVON KEY CASE AWARD
Blue case with gold 4A emblem. Given to representatives for reaching sales goal in campaign 12. C.M.V. $10.00.

1964-65 AVON DUNCE CAPS
Came in several different colors of plastic used at sales meetings. 4A design on top. and bottom. C.M.V. $10.00 each.

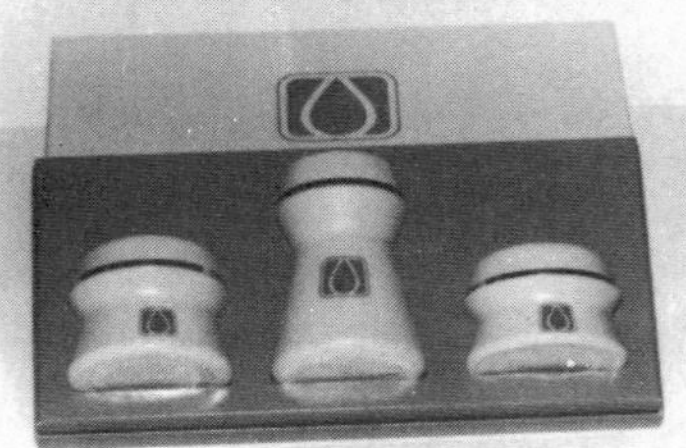

1975 MOISTURE SECRET MANAGERS GIFT SET - Pink box holds pink plastic jars of cremegel 4 oz., enriched freshener 5 oz., and night concentrate 3 oz. C-8-75. C.M.V. $15.00 set M.B.

1974 SPIRIT OF 76 CROCK SET AWARDS
MULTIPURPOSE PITCHER - earned for $150.00 in sales. C.M.V. $7.00 M.B.
BEAN POT CASSEROLE - Earned for $200.00 in sales. C.M.V. $14.00 M.B.
GOODIES JAR - Earned for $300.00 in sales. C.M.V. $18.00 M.B.

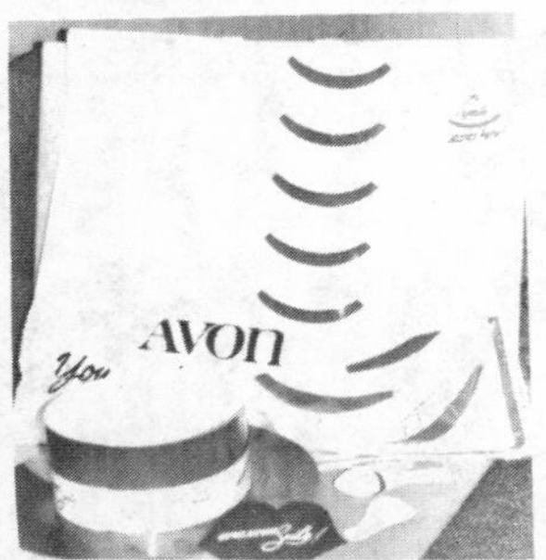

1978 AVON SMILE SALES PROMOTION ITEMS
Are all red and white.
SILK SCARF - $5.00
BALLOONS 2 different - 25¢ each.
HAT paper - $1.00
THE SMILE STARTS HERE button - $2.00
SALES BAG plastic, large size - $1.00
OPERATION SMILE LIPS red paper lips 50¢
RECORD Avon Smile, red, small record $2.00

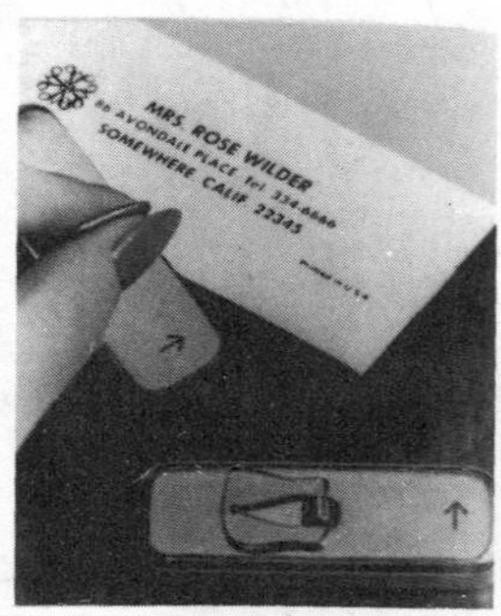

1967 AVON NAME STAMP
Won by representatives for reaching sales goal in campaign 12. Metal stamp has Avon 4A design on stamp. C.M.V. $7.00.

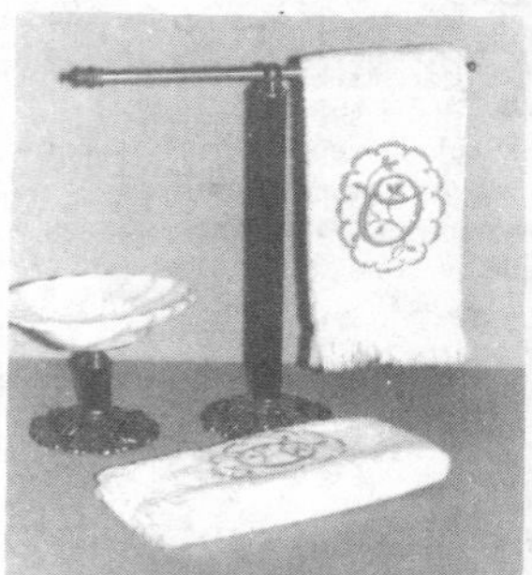

1972 TOWEL RACK PRIZE AND MILK GLASS SOAP DISH
An exclusive Avon prize. C.M.V. rack, $5.00. Soap dish $10.00. White glass dish, 2 white hand towels, gold initials black & brass stand.

1970 LUGGAGE TAG FOR MANAGERS
Black plastic, gold letters and 4A design. Given to Avon Managers. C.M.V. $6.00.
1977 CURRIER & IVES MATCH BOOK
Silk screen Cruuier & Ives winger scene. Inside says "Merry Christmas and Best Wishes for a Happy New Year. The Atlanta Management Team" Given to Avon Reps. at 1977 Christmas dinner. C.M.V. $5.00

1972 NAME STAMP
Two-toned blue with name & address. Awarded for entry into President's Club. C.M.V. $4.00.

1978 SWEET PICKLES BAG - GIFT
Green canvas bag given to district managers on introduction of Sweet Pickle products. CMV $12.50 bag only.

1974 WHATS COOKING — AVON GIFT
5 yellow plastic scoop, strainer, funnel, egg seperator, measurer. Given to Reps for Sales Meeting Attendance. Made by Geni, a div. of Avon. C.M.V. $2.00 ea.

AVON RECORDS
Christmas Records, given to reps. at Christmas. C.M.V. $7.50
Campaign 21, 1974 Sales meeting record. C.M.V. $3.00.
1970 AVON CHRISTMAS RECORD
33 1/3 RPM record in blue holder with letter from Avon president Fred Fusse. C.M.V. $7.50

1972 AVON SCARF
All silk pink, orange & white scarf with "A" on it. Avon in corner. Made in Italy. Came in silver box. CMV $10.00 mint.

960's MANAGERS CONFERENCE ORSAGE
reen and gold with red holly has Avon dollar bill attached. Bill says United tates of Avon. Given to Managers. .M.V. $20.00

1960'S AWARD PURSE
Avon marked box holds beige vinyl clutch purse trimmed in brass. Made by St. Thomas. Given to reps during President's Campaign. Purse does not say Avon. CMV $8.00 mint in Avon box.

1961 ANNIVERSARY CAMPAIGN AWARD PURSE
Same purse with deluxe lipstick & compact as Champagne Mood Set. In Avon award box. CMV $20.00 MB

979 PRESIDENT'S CLUB APRON
eige & red canvas apron says "I'd rather e selling Avon" Given to all President's lub reps. Modeled by Grace Powers. MV $10.00

1951 PURSE AWARD
Egg shell off white purse with clear plastic closure. Given to Avon reps for best sales. Came in Avon box. Purse not marked Avon. Must be in Avon box. CMV $25.00 mint.

1976 CIRCLE OF EXCELLENCE TOTE BAG
Tan & brown tote bag with C of E on front. Given to Avon managers on Hawaii C of E trip. CMV $15.00

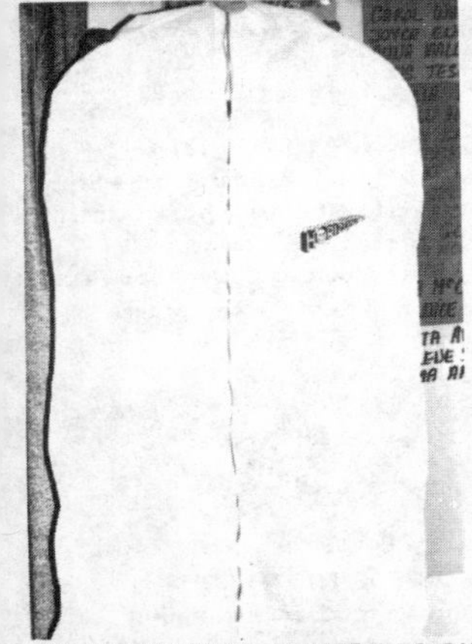

1977 HORIZONS CLOTHES BAG GIFT
Given to Avon managers. White plastic bag. CMV $15.00

1978 YOU MAKE ME SMILE LUGGAGE TAG
White plastic. CMV $3.00
1978 AVON CHAMPIONSHIP TENNIS HAT
White hat, red letters. CMV $7.00

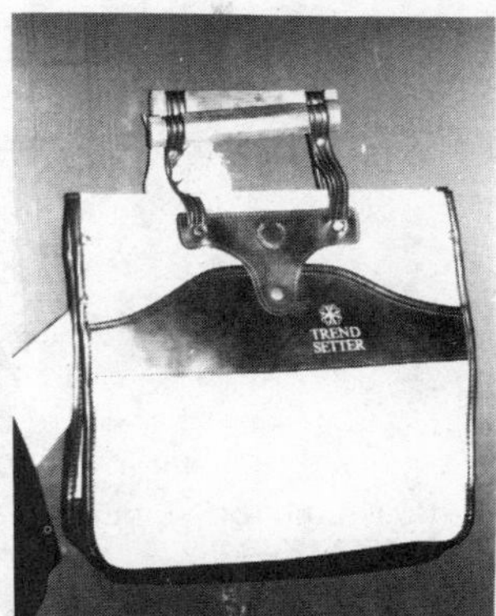

1975 TRENDSETTER CARRY ALL BAG
Made of tan burlap & brown leatherette. Given to managers only. CMV $45.00

1978 TIME OF YOUR LIFE BAG - AWARD
Beige canvas bag with red letters given to reps on trip to New York. CMV $5.00

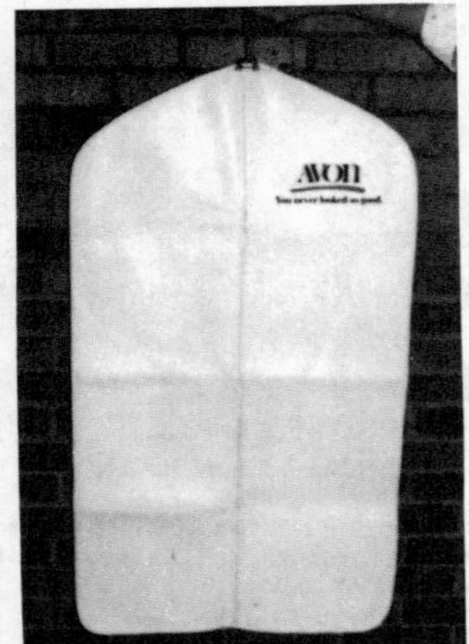

1978 TRAVEL BAG - CIRCLE OF EXCELLENCE
White leatherette bag given to 250 district managers. CMV $50.00

1979 HARD HAT - CIRCLE OF EXCELLENCE
White plastic hard hat with decal on front saying "Circle of Excellence" Given to managers in Pasadena branch. Hat was not made just for Avon. CMV $10.00

1979 T-SHIRT — AVON RUNNING
Red t-shirt given to each runner in Avon marathon race. CMV $10.00

1976 CIRCLE OF EXCELLENCE BEACH TOWEL
White & brown towel given to managers on Circle of Excellence Hawaii trip. CMV $20.00 mint.

1972 CIRCLE OF EXCELLENCE TOTE BAG
About 18" across black plastic. For trip to Mexico. Aztec calendar design. Given to Circle of Excellence managers on Mexico trip. CMV $30.00

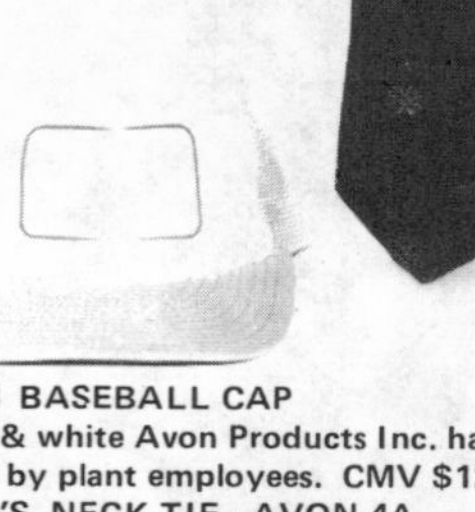

1978 BASEBALL CAP
Blue & white Avon Products Inc. hat. Used by plant employees. CMV $12.50

1970'S NECK TIE - AVON 4A
Used by Avon management. Tie has 4A design & is dark blue. Made of Dacron Polyester. CMV $12.50

1965 CAMEO VANITY SET PRIZE
Made by Syroco only for Avon. Set consists of Cameo brush, 2 combs, vanity mirror, and hand mirror. Given to Reps for selling 40 cameo lipstick or compacts for brush and comb. C.M.V. $7.00
76 total for vanity mirror C.M.V. $13.00
100 for hand mirror C.M.V. $15.00

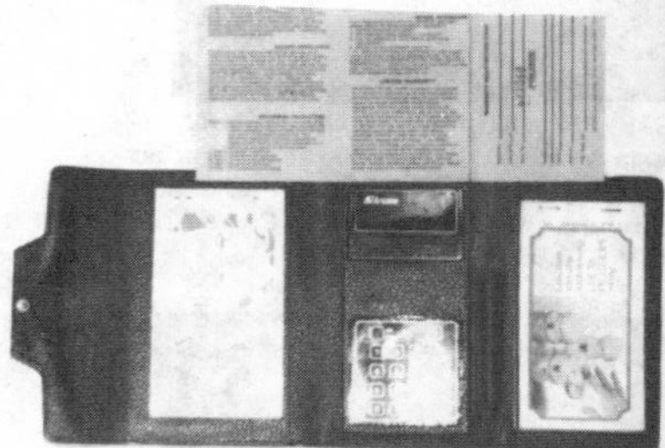

1976 RECOMENDATION PRIZE
Blue plastic case holds 2 order books and a Avon book calculator made by Arizona. Warranty card says made for Avon. Given to Reps for getting 2 new Avon Reps. C.M.V. $25.00 mint in working order.

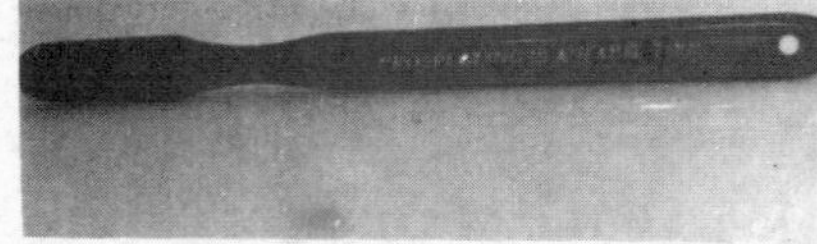

1976 MANAGERS TOOTH BRUSH
Given to managers. Came in different colors. (Avon) on one side (Prospecting is a habit too) on other side. C.M.V. $2.00

LEFT 1976 APRIL SHOWERS UMBRELLA - GIFT
Beige canvas, wood handle. Avon in blue letters. Given as recommendation prize. CMV $25.00

CENTER 1977 PRESIDENT'S CELEBRATION UMBRELLA
Marked New York. Given to winning teams. CMV $30.00

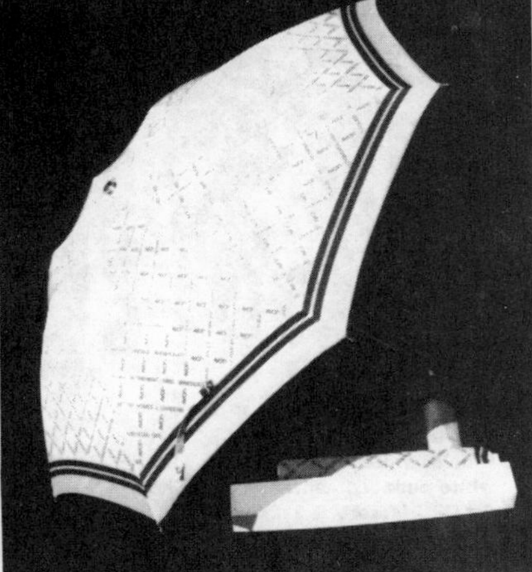

RIGHT 1978 ADVERTISING UMBRELLA
Avon stamped all over. Given to managers CMV $25.00

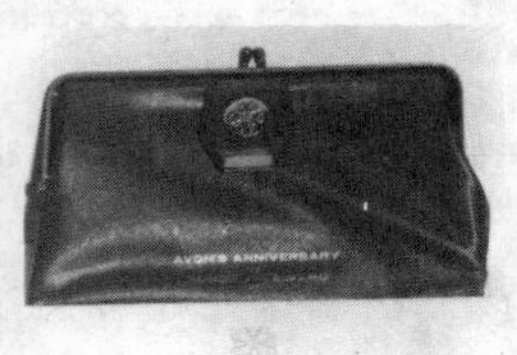

1966 ANNIVERSARY HONOR AWARD PURSE - Red leatherette purse given to representatives for high sales. 4A design on snap & Avon Anniversary Honor Award in gold letters on purse. Came in Avon box. C.M.V. $15.00 purse only. $18.00 M.B.

1978 MUSIC BOX TEAM AWARD
Red painted wood music box made in Japan only for Avon. Brass plate on lid says "You Made Avon Smile". Given to winning team for selling most lipsticks. CMV $30.00

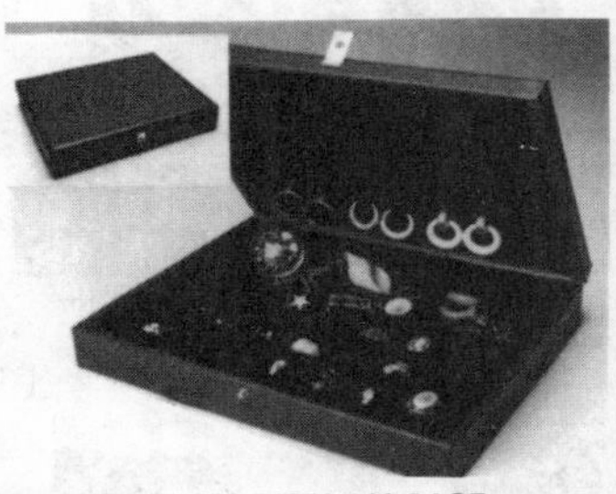

1975-78 JEWELRY DISPLAY CASE
Blue case won by Avon Reps. for meeting sales achievement goal. Avon on case. Was also sold for $4.00 to Reps for demo case. Case came empty. Measures 10½ x 8½ x 2 inches. Avon on lid and outer sleeve. C.M.V. $4.00 in sleeve.

LEFT 1976 AVON DELIVERY BAG
Blue brocade bag used by Avon Reps to make delivery of Avon products. C.M.V. $3.00
RIGHT 1976 BEAUTY SHOWCASE DEMO BAG
Used by Avon Reps to carry Avon Demonstrations products. Mathing blue brocade. C.M.V. $3.00

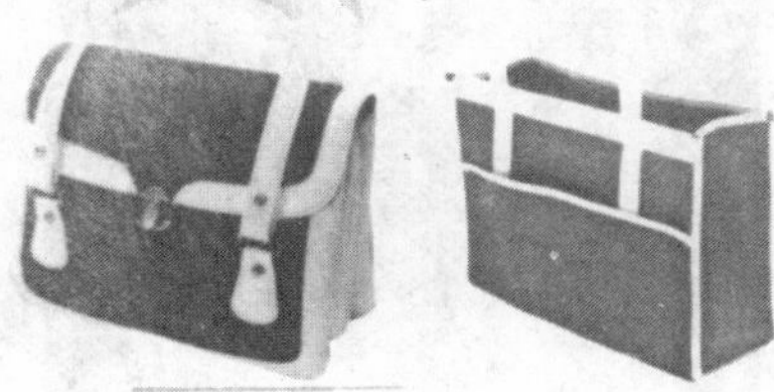

1974 FASHION PRIZES
Given to Reps for meeting sales goals. Blue and white in color. Made only for Avon. Bottom - Christian Dior Scarf 14"x 44" C.M.V. $8.00, top right - Sport Tote Bag 10" high 14" wide C.M.V. $10.00, Top left - Kadin Hand Bag, blue sail cloth with white vinyl trim. Given to Presidents Club members only 8" high, 10" wide. C.M.V. $12.00

1971 4A QUILT
Reversible, ruffled edged, cotton filled comforter in gold, avocado or blue. Given for having a person recommended as a representative appointed. C.M.V. $35.00
1969 4A QUILT
Pink quilt with white 4A design. C.M.V. $40.00

1941 FOUNDERS CAMPAIGN ACHIEVEMENT AWARD SCARF
Blue & white folder holds blue border, white pink & green silk scarf. Shows 1st CPC factory & 1st Avon lady with "The doorway to loveliness" marked under her. Given to reps in 1941. Very rare. CMV $75.00 in folder mint, $50.00 scarf only mint.

1952 SYMPHONY SCARF
Blue background with pink rose & parts of letters in French. Pure silk. Purchased fron store in New York & awarded for selling 36 products in the Prelude to Spring campaign. C.M.V. $30.00 mint.

1977 CHARGE CARD MACHINE
Red plastic, marked Avon. Used by Reps to take charge cards for Avon Sales. Used only for a short period. C.M.V. $5.00

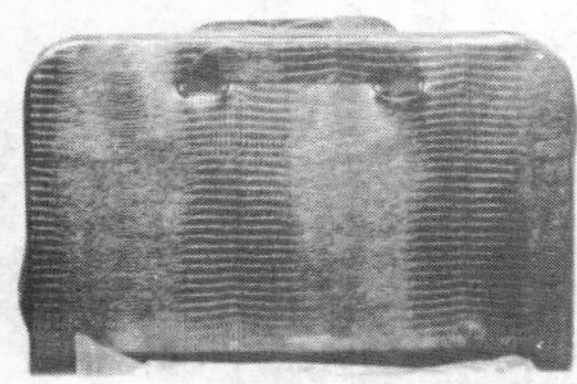

1976-78 SUNNY MAKE UP CASE
Blue vinyl reptile grain case with Avon zipper tag. Inside has clear vinyl pockets to hold make up samples. Won by Reps for signing up a new Avon Rep. and also sold to Reps. C.M.V. $5.00

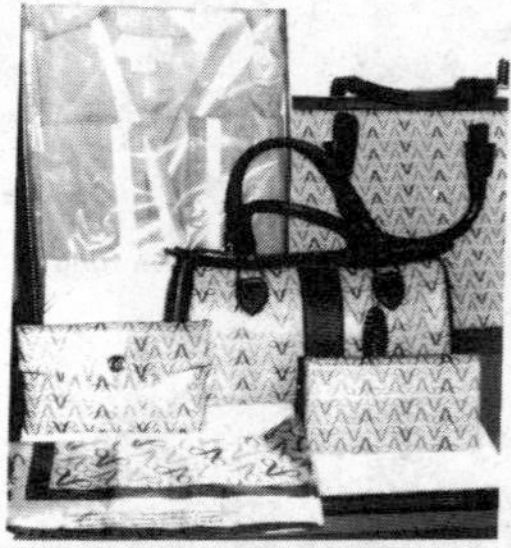

1975 S.M. KENT COLLECTION AWARDS - Given to representatives for reaching 4 different levels of selling certain amounts. Robe & handbag were for only Presidents Club members to win. The scarf was awarded for finding a "hidden customer" in territory. All items have brown or beige A's & signed by S.M. Kent (designer for Avon) C.M.V. clutch $10.00 Robe C.M.V. $20.00, C.M.V. purse $15.00, C.M.V. tote $12.00, C.M.V. cosmetic $8.00, CMV scarf $7.00, Order Book Cover $5.00

1970 AVON SILK SCARF
Beige & brown silk scarf. 4A design. Given to Avon reps. C.M.V. $20.00

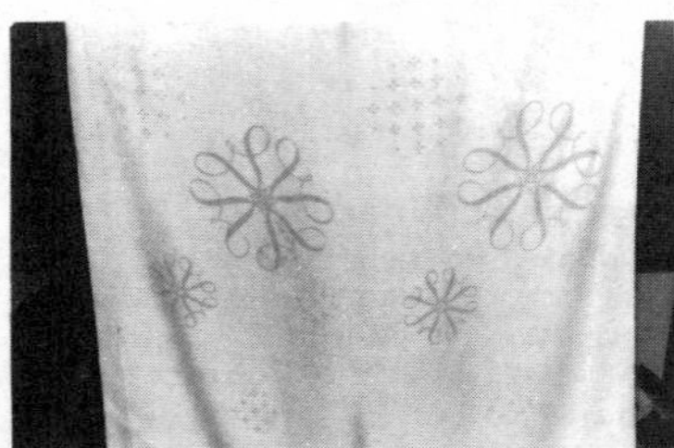

1960's AVON CURTAINS
Used to decorate in offices & Avon Plant. C.M.V. $20.00

1978 SALES MATES PRIZES
Will be awarded in 1978 for top sales goals. All are tan vinyl with Avon "A" design. Order book cover and pen C.M.V. $3.00, Tote bag, C.M.V. $7.00, Sample kit, C.M.V. $6.00, Fragrance Demonstrator, C.M.V. $4.00

1977 EMPRISE T SHIRT
Black T Shirt given to Avon managers to introduce Emprise line. C.M.V. $15.00

1978 JEWELRY DEMONSTRATOR PRIZE
Tan vinyl with A design given to Reps for selling $600.00 worth of Avon in 3 campaigns. Measures 13" long and 8" wide. C.M.V. $7.00

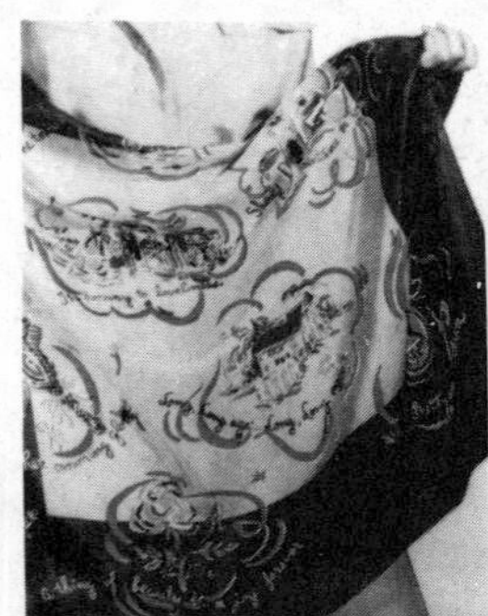

1950 - 64th ANNIVERSARY SCARF
Silk scarf was made only for Avon. Given to representatives for selling 64 pieces of Avon in campaign 9, 1950. Silk scarf has blue border white center with sketches in turquoise & rose. Some words on scarf say "Long, long ago" "A thing of beauty is a joy forever" "The doorway to loveliness" C.M.V. $50.00

1978 SALES MATES PRIZES PRESIDENTS CLUB
All are tan and beige in color, covered with "A" design. Umbrella, Beauty Showcase handbag and jewelry demonstrator given to President Club Reps for selling $975.00 worth of Avon in C4-5-6-1978.
C.M.V. Umbrella $20.00
C.M.V. Jewelry Demo Case $7.00
C.M.V. Handbag $7.00

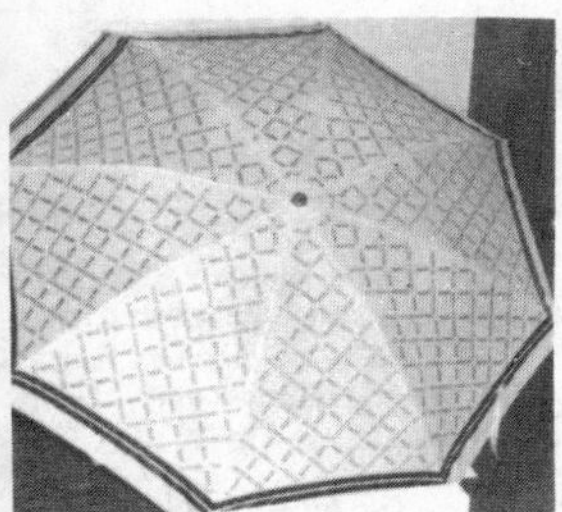

1977 ADVERTISING UMBRELLA
White Avon box holds brown plastic handle umbrella. Has the names of magazines and TV shows Avon advertises on. Given to District Managers. CMV $25.00 MB.

1953 PORTFOLIO SHOULDER BAG
Light color linen covered shoulder bag to carry Avon order book and samples. Won by Reps for placing a $100.00 order. C.M.V. $15.00 mint.

1965 PRESIDENTS CAMPAIGN AWARD PURSE
Bone beige coin and bill purse with 4A design on flap. Given to each Rep in 2 top sales teams in each branch for greatest sales increase over year before period. C.M.V. $15.00

1963 PRESIDENTS SERVICE AWARD PURSE
Given to all Reps who called on 35 or more customers during Presidents Campaign 1963. Egg shell color vinyl coin purse with 4A design on snap. Box says Avon Fashion First. CMV $20.00 MB

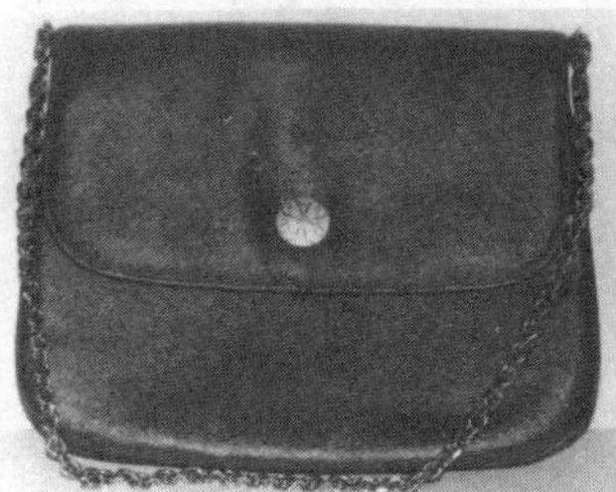

1970 PURSE – AVON PLANT TOUR GUIDE
Gray plastic purse with heavy silver chain. 4A silver button on purse. Used by tour guides at Avon Plants. C.M.V. $20.00

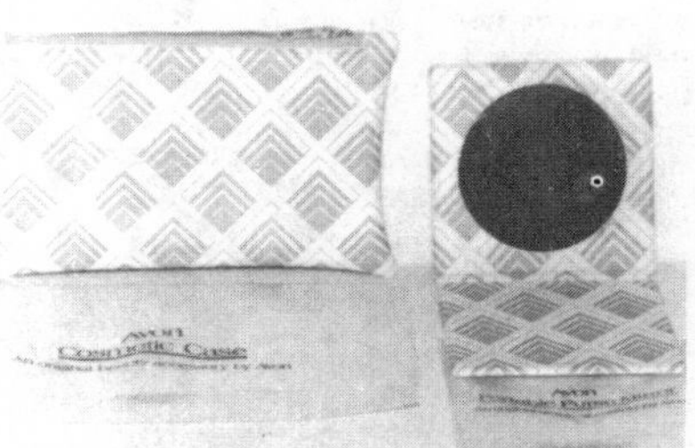

1977 COSMETIC CASE AWARD
Tan and white plastic zipper purse.
1977 PORTABLE PURSE MIRROR AWARD
Matches purse with mirror. Both given to Reps by Avon. Both came in plastic bags with Avon on them. C.M.V. $3.00 each. Mint in bag only.

1966 DISTINGUISHED MANAGEMENT AWARD LUGGAGE TAG
Plastic name tag for luggage on white strap. C.M.V. $7.50
1966 POCKET ADDRESS MEMORANDUM
2" x 3" white w/gold lettering. C.M.V. $7.00

1977 WHATS COOKING APRON
Blue apron was won by Reps at sales meeting in drawing for getting new Avon ladies. C.M.V. $6.00

1977 CANDID BLAZER & TIE
Off white blazer with CA on left pocket. Given to Division Managers only. Came in both male and female sizes. Tie is Candid color with CA on it. Very few of these blazers around. Modeled by Dwight Young. C.M.V. Blazer $75.00
C.M.V. Tie $10.00

1977 BLAZER JACKET
Blue blazer with 4A design buttons. Inside label says "Made exclusively for the Avon Representative by Family Fashions". Sold to Avon Reps. Red Avon sewn on patch for pocket. C.M.V. $35.00

1977 ITS NOT YOUR MOTHERS MAKEUP APRON
Light khaki color and orange plastic apron. Used by Avon managers at sales meetings to introduce colorworks. C.M.V. $5.00

1977 TOTE BAG
White canvas with black nylon straps. Came from Avon in New York. Was not issued to Reps. in U.S. C.M.V. $25.00

LEFT 1976 TREND SETTERS ORDER BOOK AWARD
Yellow plastic with 4A design and Avon Trend Setters on front. Given to Avon Trend Setters Reps. C.M.V. $5.00
RIGHT 1977 TEAM LEADER MIRROR GIFT
Mirror in red plastic, holder with white star and letters. Given to Avon Team leaders at Avon luncheon, Dec. 1977. C.M.V. $4.00.

1976 VALENTINE GIFT TO REPRESENTATIVES - Whitman Sampler sent to all reps. with Avon card. C.M.V. $3.00 with card only.

1978 VALENTINE CANDY
Red and gold heart box. Holds 4½ oz. of chocolates by Bartons. Back of box says "This candy heart selected by Avon and packaged especially for you. C.M.V. $5.00M.B.

1977 SUEDE ORDER BOOK COVER AWARD
Brown plastic suede order book cover holds 4 Avon order books. Given to Avon Reps. for reaching sales goals. 1886 Avon lady embossed on front. Was not awarded in all branches. CMV $10.00

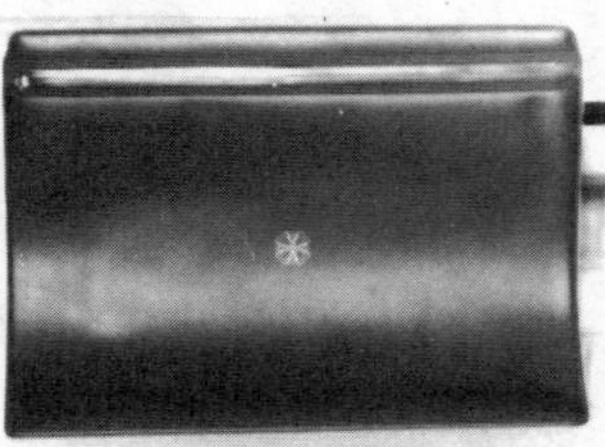

1974 AVON PORTFOLIO
Red plastic, 4A design for Avon Reps. C.M.V. $3.00

1970 REPRESENTATIVE CASES
Miscellaneous representatives portfolio cases, plastic. C.M.V. $4.00 each.

1971 LADY DESK FOLIO
Pink cover holds calender to be used as a plan guide for sending orders and making appointments. Given for sending a $75.00 or larger order in. C-1-71 C.M.V. $7.50

1971 DESIGNERS DREAM SWEEPSTAKES AWARD - C-7-1971 White lace hankerchief with note from Avon for sales accomplishments. C.M.V. $4.00
1961 FILE BOX
Turquoise cardboard file box with 4A design on lid. C.M.V. $5.00.

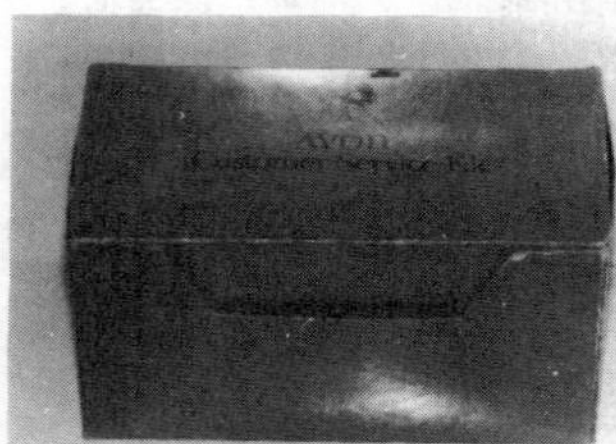

1969 CUSTOMERS SERVICE FILE
Turquoise paper box holds file envelopes for Avon lady sales. C.M.V. $5.00.

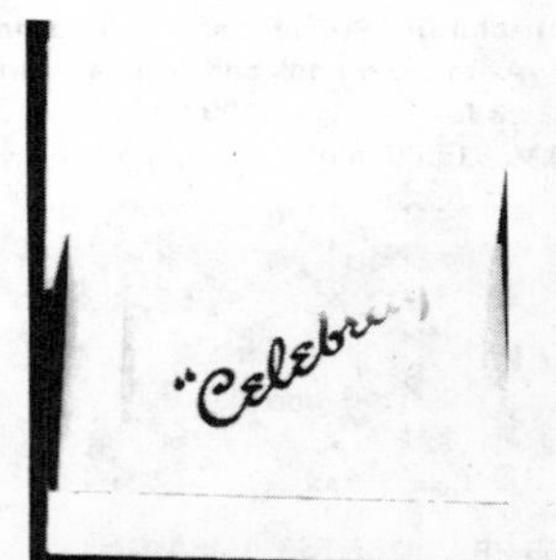

1965 CELEBRITY AUTOGRAPH BOOK
Not marked Avon. Only in box. C.M.V. $5.00.

961 MANAGERS SALES MEETING NOTE BOOK - Campaign,15, 16, 17, 18 sales meeting plans. Inside front cover says # so & so of a limited edition for the Management Staff Only". Cover is red satin 12" x 20", comes in white box. For you from Avon on cover. CMV $75.00 mint.

957 PRESIDENTIAL WINNERS AWARD Blue felt booklet given to winning district Avon representatives upon touring district Avon plant. C.M.V. $30.00.

1952 MANAGER-REPRESENTATIVE INTRODUCTION BOOK Turquoise & silver booklet. Used by managers to train new Avon reps. CMV $10.00

1976 NOTE PAD TRENDSETTERS
Clear plastic, Avon on top holder. Trendsetter note pads. Given to managers only. CMV $20.00

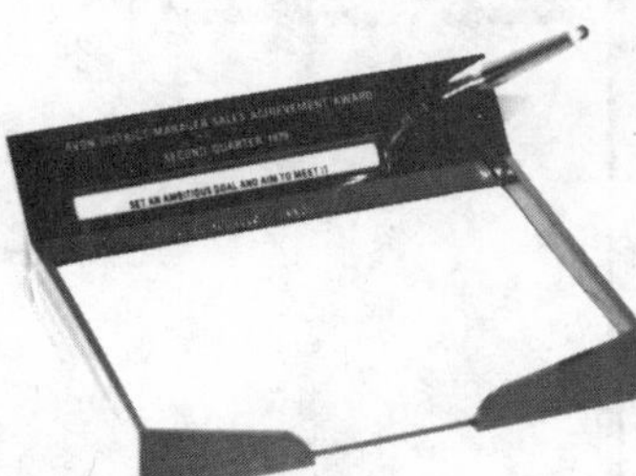

1979 "DESK SET" ACHIEVEMENT AWARD
Black plastic note pad & pen. Given to district managers for sales achievement. CMV $12.00

1980 RECORD - HAPPY BIRTHDAY
It's a most unusual day on cover. Given to President's Club reps on their birthday. CMV $5.00 mint.

1969-80 CIRCLE OF EXCELLENCE PASSPORT HOLDERS
Given each year. Each marked Circle of Excellence. Given to top managers only for annual C of E trip. Different color each year. CMV $5.00 each
CIRCLE OF EXCELLENCE PROGRAM
Given to C of E managers at annual C of E celebration. CMV $5.00 each year.

1970'S AVON COSMETICS MARKETING HIGHLIGHT BINDER BOOKLET
Used by managers. CMV $5.00

1980 NICE KRISPIES BOX
Small size cereal box given to team leaders. CMV $5.00

1979 MATCHES - PRESIDENT'S CELEBRATION
Blue foil top box. CMV $2.00
1970'S LUGGAGE TAG
White plastic with gold 4A emblem & The Better Way. CMV $5.00

1975 PRESIDENT'S CLUB ORDER BOOK COVER
Blue plastic. CMV $3.00

1979 KEY CHAIN "RECORD BREAKER"
Pink plastic. Has 4A design & says "I'm An Avon Record Breaker" Given to reps for getting new reps. CMV $5.00

1960-70 DIAMOND DECADE HONOR ROLL AWARD
Silver with blue 4A booklet. Given to managers for outstanding service. CMV $10.00

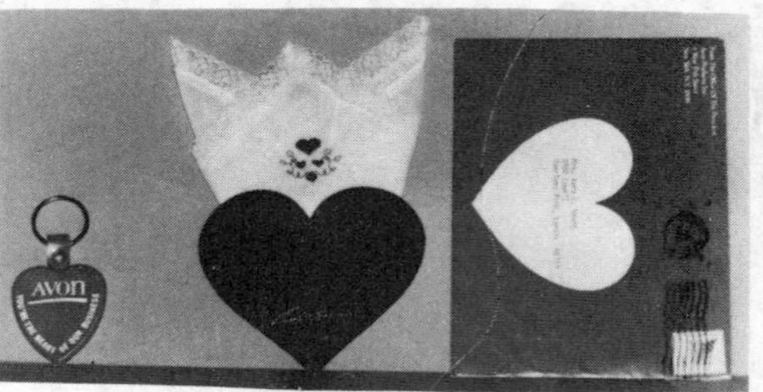

1980 VALENTINE - PRESIDENT'S CLUB
Given to President's Club reps. Red valentine & white, red & green lace handkerchief. CMV $2.00
1978 KEY CHAIN HEART
Red plastic heart given to managers. CMV $2.00

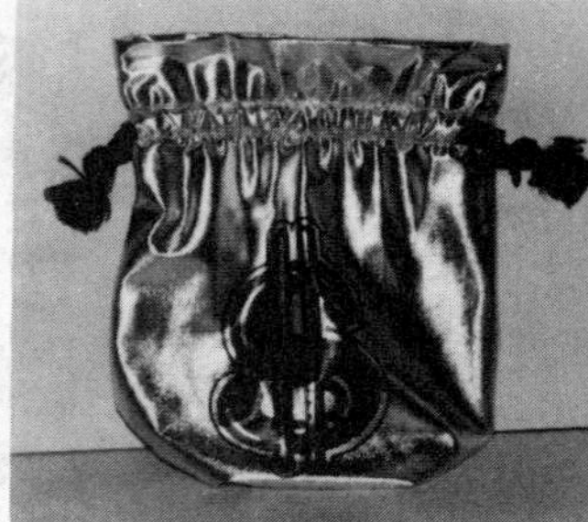

1980 WACKY MONEY BAG
Silver tone bag with red tie string & red $ design. Used at sales meetings. Does not say Avon. CMV $15.00

1978 PARIS PICTURE GIFT
French print scene by Bernard Picture Co. given to each manager with French printed Avon Circle of Excellence card & ribbon. CMV $7.50 Must have Avon card as shown.

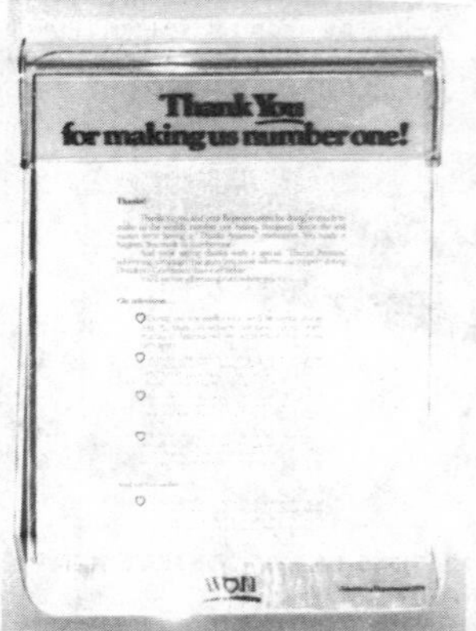

1979 LUCITE CLIP BOARD MANAGERS GIFT
Front says "Thank you for making us number one." Avon on bottom. Given to managers only. CMV $10.00

LEFT 1979 CALCULATOR - COLOR UP AMERICA AWARD
Avon color never looked so good on face of calculator. Came in Avon leatherette case & matching box. Given to reps for sales award. CMV $22.50 MB
RIGHT 1979 COME COLOR WITH US ANNOUNCEMENT
Inside has crayola & invitation to meeting. CMV $1.00

1978 TEAM LEADER CARDS
4 different cards given to team leaders, with bears on them. CMV 50c each.

1978 AUGUST CONFERENCE PICTURE HOLDER
Tan cover. Given to managers at August conference. CMV $15.00

1979 DATE BOOK
Rust color date book given out by Avon managers. Inside cover says "A gift from your Avon manager" CMV $2.00
PENCILS - AVON
1979 Blue Marking Pen - fine point. CMV $1.00
1979 Color Up America - red pencil. CMV $1.00

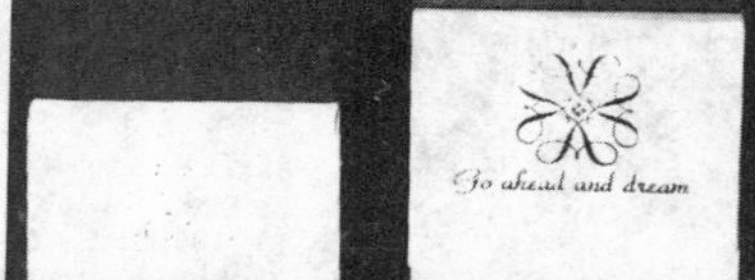

1979 CIRCLE OF EXCELLENCE MATCHES
Given to managers on trip to Paris 1979. White, gold letters. Matches are gold heads. CMV $5.00
1979 GO AHEAD & DREAM MATCHES
White, red letters. Given to managers at September conference. CMV $2.00 mint.

1979 CALENDAR - PRESIDENT'S CLUB GIFT
Red felt cover calendar with pages of Avon history on inside. Given to President's Club reps only. CMV $4.00 Also pictured is President's Club luncheon invitation card. Red. CMV 50c

78 COOK BOOK FOR TEAM LEADERS
ed cover 96 page book given to Team aders July 1978. CMV $10.00 mint.

979 MENU PRESIDENT'S CELEBRATION
iven to President's Club members at their ncheon celebration. CMV $2.00

978 STEPPIN' OUT KNEE HIGHS OR PANTY HOSE
Knee socks or panty hose given to reps for $200 in sales in C14-78. CMV $3.00 in package.
1978 STEPPIN' OUT ORDER BOOK
Used by reps in C14-78. CMV $1.00

LEFT 1963 RING THE BELL - MANAGERS GIFT
6½" tall brass bell, black handle. Used by Avon managers at sales meetings. Came with red ribbon & 7 bell shaped cards with Avon on each one. Must have Avon bell cards for value. CMV $60.00
RIGHT 1976 WALLET & KEY CASE - MANAGERS GIFT
Leather wallet & key case given to Avon managers with Avon card on top of box. CMV $15.00

1971 AVON CALLING PHONE INDEX
Given for sending in order of $75.00 or more. C-1-71. C.M.V. $5.00.

1979 PRESIDENT'S CLUB THANK YOU NOTES
White box with outer sleeve. Both has "President's Club, Avon's Very Best" on lid. Holds 25 thank you notes. Given to President's Club reps only. CMV $5.00 MB complete set.

LEFT 1960's ACHIEVMENT AWARD ORDER BOOK COVER Light blue cover. CMV $7.00.

RIGHT 1977 ORDER BOOK - CANADA
Dark blue plastic. Used by reps in Canada. Came with blue and gold pen and order book. CMV $5.00;

1961 - 75 YEAR HONOR AWARD ORDER BOOK
Red with gold letters. CMV $8.00 mint.

1973 ORDER BOOK COVER
Blue and green design matches delivery bag. Has turquoise and gold pen. Earned for prize points. C.M.V. $5.00

1978 AVONOPOLY
Game used by managers at Avon rep sales meeting C12-78. Also came with Avon play money of 25 & 50 green notes. CMV set $10.00

1960 PRESIDENT'S CLUB ORDER BOOK COVER - C.M.V. $7.00

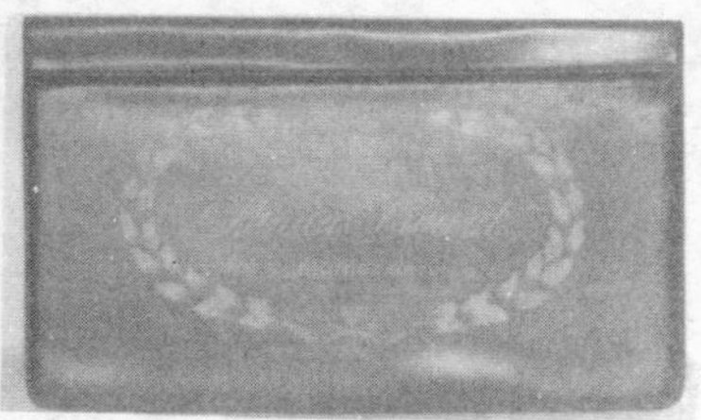

1960 GENERAL MANAGERS HONOR AWARD
Order book cover in blue. CMV $8.00 mint.

1970's VINYL CARD CASES AWARDS
President's Club. Pink & turquoise. C.M.V. $2.50. Top one Foreign. C.M.V. $5.00.

1964 PRESIDENTS HONOR AWARD ORDER BOOK COVER
Blue plastic with gold trim. C.M.V. $7.00.
1966 REGENCE ORDER BOOK HONOR AWARD
Green plastic with gold trim to match Regence packaging. C.M.V. $5.00.

1973 CHECK COVERS
Red & green plastic check book covers given to Reps. C.M.V. $2.00 ea.

1967 BROCADE HONOR AWARD ORDER BOOK COVER
Given to Reps for calling on customers during introduction of Brocade. Came with Avon pen also. C.M.V. $4.00

1976-77 ORDER BOOK COVER & PEN
Given to only new Avon Reps. Blue plastic cover and blue and gold pen. C.M.V. $3.00

LEFT 1959 HONOR AWARD ORDER BOOK COVER
Red plastic with gold trim, also had gold pen. CMV $10.00
RIGHT 1965 GENERAL MANAGERS HONOR AWARD ORDER BOOK COVER
Given to general managers. CMV $8.00

1975 WHAT'S COOKING RECIPE BOX
Given to Reps for drawing their name at sales meetings. Avon on the bottom. C.M.V. $5.00
LATE 1970's NAME TAGS
3 different stick on name tags used by reps. C.M.V. 50¢

1976 TERRITORY DIRECTORY
Blue plastic 2 ring binder used by Reps for customers in their territory. C.M.V. $1.00
1970's AVON BOOK MATCHES
Gold matches with red Avon rose. Inside says (Welcome your Avon Rep. when she calls). C.M.V. 25¢

1977 ARIANE MEMO BOOK
Red cover Memo Book given to Avon team leaders when Ariane came out. C.M.V. $7.00

1977 WHO'S WHO OF AVON DISTRICT MANAGERS
Red cover book with all Circle of Excellence 1976 winners. 72 pages. C.M.V. $10.00

1978 CUSTOMER SERVICE AWARD
Given to Reps for calling on 60 customers "Red cover" C.M.V. $4.00 or 100 customers "gold cover" C.M.V. $6.00. 2 ring binders were used to put Avon customer addresses in.

974 GROW WITH AVON
von card with 2 wooden stakes. one says
veet Basil and the other says Tomato.
M.V. $3.00

1976 AVON FUN DOLLARS
Small green paper play five dollar bill. Used by Reps at meetings. C.M.V. 50¢

1900 CPC SCRATCH PAD
5" square paper pad with 50 sheets. OSP 15c, CMV $50.00 mint.

1978 SPRING GARDEN CLUB FLOWER SEED
7 different flower seed packets made up for Avon, given to Reps at sales meeting. Packaged by James Vick's Seeds. C.M.V. $1.00 per pack.

1967 CARD CARRYING CASE PRIZE
Blue plastic with 4A design and says Avon Cosmetics. Given to Reps for selling $30.00 over their sales goals. C.M.V. $3.00

1977 PRESIDENTS CELEBRATION ORDER BOOK COVER
Red plastic C.M.V. $3.00

1976 PERSONAL POCKET DIARY
Blue plastic cover with Avon pocket diary and calendar inside. C.M.V.$3.00

1977 CURRIER & IVES COASTERS
Pack of 6 given to Team Leaders at Christmas. Also given to Reps for recommendation prize. Marked Avon. C.M.V. $8.00 pack of 6.

1973 AVON NOTE PAD PRIZE
Gold plastic with 4A design on front. Has 1973 calendar pad and pen inside. Used by Reps. C.M.V. $2.00

1970 LUCKY WAGON SWEEPSTAKES GIFT
2 white handkerchiefs with monogram in corner with choice of letters. Given for mens car decanter sales C11-70. In dark blue folder with card. C.M.V. $4.00

1970 LINEN TOWEL CALENDAR
Given to all Reps for sending in an order in C1-1970. Made only for Avon. Measures 15½"x 28½". C.M.V. $5.00

1965 HANDKERCHIEF GIFT
Pink and white card says "Thank you". Holds white with green and pink design handkerchief given to Reps for recomendation. C.M.V. $5.00 mint.

1966 PICTURE ALBUM AWARD
White Avon box holds large and small picture album and picture frame in brown and gold. Cover says For you, from Avon. C.M.V. $45.00 M.B.

1976 AVON CHRISTMAS CARD
Green & gold Christmas card. Inside says "From your Avon Representative". Box of 75 cards given to Avon Reps for recommendation of new Avon lady. C.M.V. $15.00 box of 75 mint. or 25¢ each card mint.

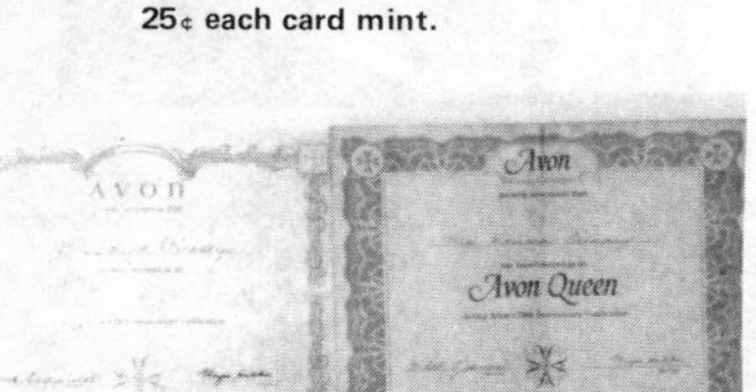

1964-65 AVON QUEEN CERTIFICATE
78th & 79th Anniversary Award Certificates. One red and others blue border. Given to top selling Reps only. C.M.V.$5.00 ea.

1945 MANAGERS INTRODUCTION BOOK
Blue cover, 28 page book, used by Avon Managers to sign up new Avon Reps. 11"x 14" size. Came with clear plastic cover. C.M.V. $35.00 mint.

1966 PLACE MAT AWARD
Plastic place mat showing Avon Daily Need Products. Given to Reps for meeting sales. C.M.V. $3.00.

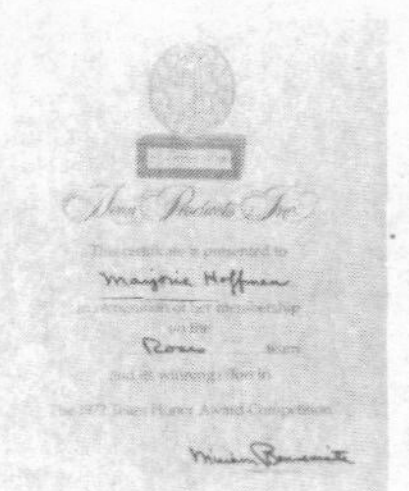

1972 TEAM HONOR AWARD CERTIFICATE
Given to Reps on winning teams for sales. C.M.V. $4.00

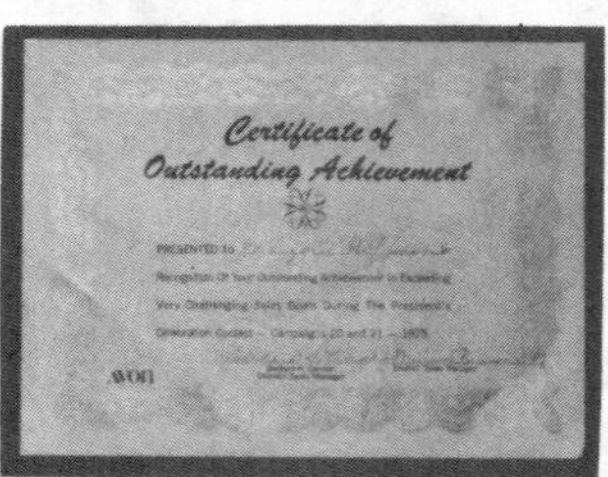

1975 OUTSTANDING ACHIEVEMENT CERTIFICATE
Given to Reps for top sales in C-20-21 1975. C.M.V. $4.00

1976 CIRCLE OF EXCELLENCE SCROLL
Given to managers each year with all the circle of excellence winners. C.M.V. $3.00

1947 PASADENA BRANCH DEDICATION BOOKLET
Gold spiral bound booklet given at opening of Pasadena Branch Sept. 22-27, 1947. Front says Avon Serves the Golden West. C.M.V. $25.00

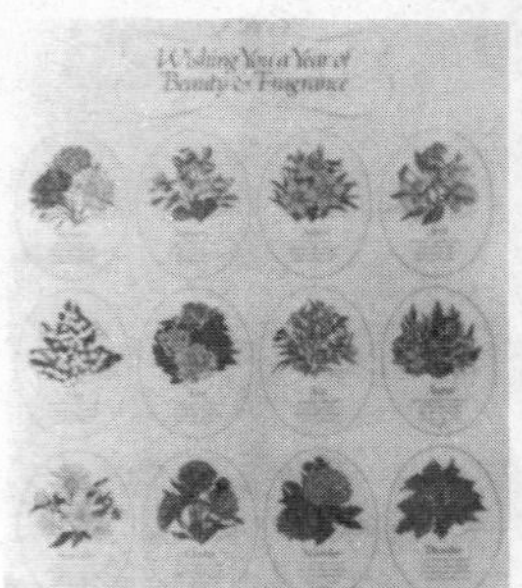

1978 BEAUTY & FRAGRANCE CALENDAR
Punch out calendar given to speci good customers in C24-77 by Avo reps. Made only for Avon. CMV $5.00 Only given in several states for test marketing.

1979 TASHA GO AHEAD AND DREA MANAGERS GIFT
1.8 oz. clear glass, silver neck band. Go Ahead & Dream in gold letters on front of bottle. Bottom label. Given to Avon managers at Christmas conference. CMV $25.00 MB

1979 TASHA - TEAM LEADER COLO SPRAY
1.8 oz. clear glass. This bottle given to A team leaders. Front of bottle has "Team Leader 1979" in gold letters. CMV $12.5

1979 LIVE - LAUGH - LOVE AWARDS
Given to reps on cruise to Caribbean Feb. 79. Silver & Red Menu, CMV $5.00 Tem Leather Luggage Tag, CMV $5.00 Napkin CMV 50c Tempo Leather Wallet for Ladi CMV $10.00

1980 TASHA UMBRELLA "I'M NUMBER ONE"
Tan silk umbrella given reps on Flight to Fantasy trip to Monte Carlo. CMV $30.00

1971 MOONWIND AWARD PIN
Sterling silver pin given to reps for meeting sales goals. CMV $22.50

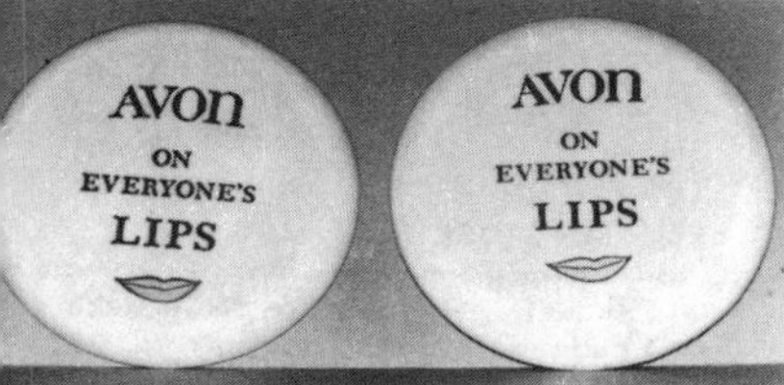

1976 FRISBEES - GIFT TO REPS
White plastic with red letters. CMV $3.00
White with red & green letters. CMV $5.00

1979 FLIGHT TO FANTASY RECORD
Given to reps in C20-79 to introduce Fantasy fragrance. CMV $3.00 record & cover mint.

TRAINING RECORDS - FILM STRIPS
Used by managers to show new products at sales meetings. Box came with record & 1 film strip for each record. Have been used for many years by Avon. No price established because of so many different varieties. CMV record only $2.00

1977 ARIANE NECKLACE & BOUQUET
Wood basket & plastic flowers holds sterling silver necklace with August Conference 77 on side. Given to Avon managers at August conference banquet. Necklace holds sample vial of Ariane perfume. CMV $60.00 mint.

LEFT 1978 TEMPO MANAGERS GIFT
.33 oz. silver over clear glass. Given to district sales managers at August Conference 1978. Came with red felt belt. Splash cologne. Came in beige felt bag & beige string. CMV $12.50 in bag.
1978 TEMPO SPRAY ATOMIZER GIFT
Given to Avon reps for advanced orders of Tempo fragrance. Silver color container red letters. "Tempo Fall 1978" printed on bottom of case. Came in beige velvet bag, red pull string in special issue box. CMV $5.00 MB

1979 COLOR UP AWARDS
Blue & Red Backdrop - used at sales meetings "Color Up America" CMV $5.00
Color Up Plastic Bag - CMV 50c
Color Sale Paper Bag - CMV 25c
Color Never Looked So Good On Glasses - Set of 6. CMV $10.00 set of 6.
Color Up Scarf - CMV $2.00
Clutch Bag - CMV $3.00
Make Up Bag - CMV $6.00
File Folder - CMV $6.00
Colors are red, white & blue striped.

1979 LIVE - LAUGH - LOVE TEMPO AWARDS
Given to reps on cruise to Caribbean.
Red T-Shirt — CMV $15.00
1978 Picture Cube — Says "New York - Bermuda - Circle of Excellence" CMV $15.00
Bahamas Stick Pin — In brown felt bag given to reps on cruise. Does not say Avon. CMV $2.00
1979 Cruise Program — Feb 2-5, 1979 CMV $2.00

1980 TASHA STOWAWAY BAG
Purple shoulder bag given to reps. Avon tag inside. CMV $15.00 Managers also got the same bag without the brass snap on the outside. CMV $20.00

1980 TASHA AWARDS
Monte Carlo scarf, CMV $20.00
Tasha picture of Princess Grace of Monte Carlo with Tasha card, CMV $15.00
Tasha matches - box & book matches, CMV $1.00 each
Items were won by reps on Avon trip to Monte Carlo.

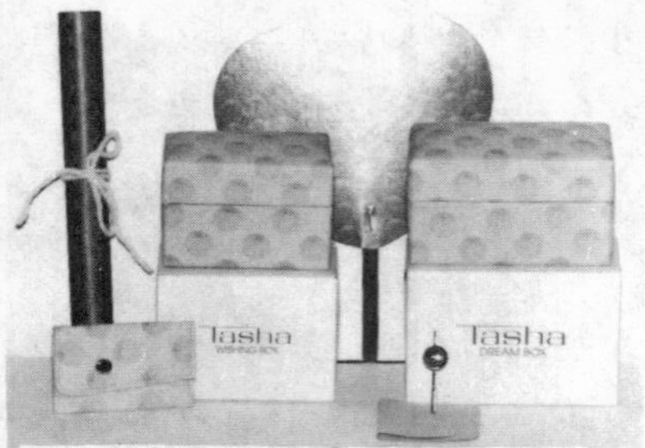

1979 TASHA AWARDS
All are pink & purple.
Wishing Box given to managers. CMV $15.00 MB
Dream Box with Tasha pin & tray inside. CMV $10.00 MB
Key Chain. CMV $2.00
Fan. CMV 50c
Scroll Dream Test. CMV $1.00
All were given to reps except wishing box.

1958 STOCKHOLDERS GIFT
Satin lined box with large ribbon across and stockholders card. Holds Here's My Heart Beauty dust, sachet lotion & Top Style lipstick. C.M.V. $60.00 M.B.

1976 CANDID SCARF GIFT
Silk scarf designed by S. M. Kent in Candid folder. Given to Avon President's Club members. CMV $5.00

1980 TASHA FLIGHT TO FANTASY VASE
White porcelain vase given to reps on Monte Carlo trip. CMV $40.00
1980 TASHA PASSPORT HOLDER
Given to reps on Monte Carlo trip, held luggage tag & misc. Tasha paper items, programs etc. CMV $20.00 for all.

1962 STOCKHOLDERS GIFT
Flip open box with Avon printed all over Holds Bay Rum jug after shave & skin so bud vase. With stockholders card. C.M.V. $60.00 M.B.

STOCKHOLDER'S GIFTS

1957 - 1973 STOCKHOLDERS XMAS GIFTS - Stockholders gifts were special packaged Avon items sent to each share holder of Avon Stock at Christmas each year. A special stockholders greeting card was sent with each gift & a stockholders gift is not mint or complete without this card. They were first sent in 1957 & discontinued at Christmas 1973. They are considered quite hard to find.

There are only 2 years of stockholders gifts not shown. If you have any of the following 2 complete sets with card, please contact Bud Hastin. 1957 set had Persian Wood Perfume Mist & Beauty Dust. 1959 set had Topaze Spray Perfume & Cologne Mist. Also listed is After Shower for Men. This could be 1 complete set or 2 different. 1 for men & 1 for women. Also listed for 1960 is 8 oz. Spice After Shave Lotion. This again sounds like 2 different items for 1960. All the other years are pictured & priced.

1979 BON APPETIT COOK BOOK
Given to managers on Circle of Excellence trip to Paris. Avon on front. CMV $5.00.

1960 TOPAZE TREASURE STOCKHOLDERS GIFT
Yellow & gold satin lined box holds Topaze Beauty Dust & 2 oz. cologne. Came with stockholders card. This was a general issue gift that was also sold. CMV $40.00 MB $50.00 MB with stockholders card.

'71 STOCKHOLDERS GIFT
ite foam box with blue felt band. ntains Moonwind Cologne Mist. C.M.V. 2.00 MB..

1970 STOCKHOLDERS GIFT
Bird of Paradise Cologne Mist in foam box. Gold band around box. Came with card from Avon as Xmas gift to stockholders. CMV $18.00 MB with card only.

1961 STOCKHOLDERS GIFT
Box with stockholders Xmas card, holds Cotillion Beauty Dust, cream sachet & cologne mist. This set is same as 1961-62 Cotillion Debut, only with special card. CMV $55.00 MB

967 STOCKHOLDERS GIFT
rown brocade design box holds 1st dition Book After Shave & Brocade 4 oz. ologne. CMV $35.00 MB

1964 STOCKHOLDERS GIFT
White flip open box with 4A design on both side of lid, holds 4A after shave and Rapture 2 oz. cologne. With stockholders card. C.M.V. $55.00 M.B.

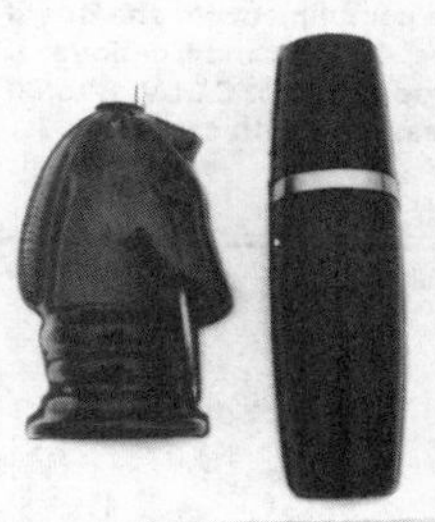

1968 STOCKHOLDERS GIFT
A special gift given to Avon stockholders. Short pony in Windjammer & Charisma Cologne Mist, set in white foam. set $30.00 M.B.

66 REGENCE STOCKHOLDERS GIFT
ite, green & gold box, given to representa-es on introudction of Regence. Says "Your troduction to a Fragrance Masterpiece by on. This same set was used as a stock-lders gift at Xmas 1966. Came with stock-lders card. C.M.V. $20.00 M.B., $25.00 B. with card.

1969 STOCKHOLDERS GIFT
Pink foam box holds Elusive Cologne Mist & Perfume Rollette, ribbon around box. CMV $22.00 MB

1963 STOCKHOLDERS GIFT
Box opens in center with double lid to show 3 oz. Occur cologne mist & Tribute After shave. Stockholders card. C.M.V. $45.00 M.B.

72 DEEP WOODS STOCKHOLDERS FT
own foam box shaped like a log, card on p, with brown gorgrain ribbon & gold cker, contains Deep Woods Cologne. M.V. $20.00 M.B.

1973 IMPERIAL GARDEN'S STOCK-HOLDERS GIFT
Cream sachet in white styrofoam with orange & gold ribbon. Also has card. C.M.V. $15.00 MB

1965 STOCKHOLDERS GIFT
Box with stockholders card & Just Two set. C.M.V. $80.00 M.B.

STOCKHOLDERS MEETING GIFTS
A special wrapped Avon product is given to each stockholder attending the Annual Avon Stockholders Meeting. Each gift comes with a special card which states - With the compliments of the Board of Directors, Officers and Employees of Avon Products, Inc. C.M.V. $15.00 to $20.00 ea. mint with card only.

1972 1ST ANNUAL NAAC AVON CLUB BOTTLE "1ST AVON LADY"
7" high, hand painted porcelain bottle. Made for Avon Club members only belonging to the National Association of Avon Clubs. 1st NAAC Club bottle issued. Made in image of first CPC sales-lady. Each bottle is numbered. Released in June 1972. Total issue was 2870. Bottle made and issued by National Association of Avon Clubs. OSP $11.95, CMV $200.00. 18 made with red hair and green purse. CMV $650.00 for a red head. No registration certificates were issued with the '72 Club Bottle. 4 bottles had blue lettering on bottle. Red had black letters. CMV blue letter bottom $650.00. Bud Hastin knows the numbers on all red head and blue bottoms. Check before buying. 1972 factory sample of 1st lady sold by mistake. Same as above only no lettering on bottom & neck is flush where cork fits top of bottle. No raised lip for cork as regular production was. Bottle has letter from Bud Hastin as 1 of a kind sample. CMV $400.00

AVON CLUB BOTTLES & N.A.A.C. COLLECTABLES

SOLD ONLY TO MEMBERS OF N.A.A.C. CLUBS

CLUB BOTTLES

What are they? Where do you get them? Club bottles are made for Avon collectors and are sold thru any of the more than 140 Avon Collectors Clubs throughout the United States and Canada. These clubs are all members of the National Association of Avon Clubs. Club bottles or plates are usually sold for a period of 60 days only and only the amount sold in that time is made. At the end of the sale period, the order is placed with the factory. It usually takes around 4 months to get them made and shipped to the collector. During the time it takes to make them, many new collectors want to buy them but it's too late so they have to pay a higher price from someone who bought extras for resale. The resale value of these low issue bottles or plates usually doubles by the time you get them from the factory. Each bottle is numbered with the quantity made. All club bottles are hand painted porcelain of the finest quality. The Avon club bottles are the best bottle investment around today for future value increase. If you do not have an Avon Club in your area belonging to the N.A.A.C. we invite you to join the Bud Hastin's Avon Club to be eligible to purchase all club bottles as they come out at the lowest possible price. $11.00 yearly dues ($11.00 for Canada, U.S. funds money orders only). Send to: Bud Hastin, P.O. Box 9868, Kansas City, Missouri 64134.

1973 2nd NAAC McCONNELL CLUB BC
2nd annual Club Bottle issued by the NA Clubs in honor of Mr. & Mrs. D.H. Mc Connel founders of Avon. The bottle ot is pictured with the registration certificat which goes with the bottle. 5604 bottles were sold & numbered. The mold was destroyed at the '73 NAAC Convention in Scramento, Calif. in June of 1973. C.M.V. $75.00 O.S.P. $11.95

1975 4th ANNUAL NAAC CLUB BOTT
The modern day Avon Lady is the 1975 Club bottle from the NAAC. Blue hand painted porcelain. Each bottle is number on bottom & came with registration card 6232 were made. OSP $12.45 CMV $35.

1976 5th ANNUAL NAAC AVON CLUB BOTTLE
In the image of the 1896 CPC Avon lad Blue dress, black bag, and blue feather hat. Black hair. 5622 were made. Can with registration card and numbered on bottom. O.S.P. $12.95. C.M.V. $40.0
1976 BLOND AVON LADY
Of the 5622 regular issue 1896 lady, 12 had blond hair. C.M.V. $200.00 on blo Rare.

77 NAAC CLUB BOTTLE
06 AVON LADY
h annual club bottle issues by the ational Association of Avon Clubs. ade of porcelain and hand painted in e image of the 1906 Avon Lady. She ands 7½" high with yellow dress, brown at and carrying the CPC Avon sales case the period. Only 5517 were made & ld for $12.95 each. Came with NAAC gistration certificate and is numbered n the bottom. C.M.V. $35.00 M.B. 00 sample bottles were given to each AAC Club and are the same only they re numbered and marked Club Sample n bottom. C.M.V. $100.00 Sample Bottle

1979 NAAC CLUB BOTTLE "1926 AVON LADY"
8th annual club bottle. Purple & black. Brown hat & shoes. 4749 were made & numbered on bottom. Came with certificate that says 4725. Actual count is 4749. OSP $14.95, CMV $30.00. 150 club samples were issued to NAAC clubs Bottom is marked club sample. CMV sample $100.00

1980'S NAAC CONVENTION BOTTLES
A series of 11 different Avon ladies dressed in their Sunday best of the 1890's style. To be issued 1 each year & sold only to members of NAAC Avon Collectors Clubs. All are hand painted porcelain, 7½" high & very limited editions. Each bottle will have the total number sold on the bottom. You can be eligible to buy this beautiful set of bottles by joining the Bud Hastin Avon Club or any of the more than 150 NAAC clubs throughout the U.S. & Canada. Their value is sure to increase fast.

LEFT 1978 NAAC MINI McCONNEL & CPC FACTORY
Miniature size figurines of the 1886 CPC Factory and Mr. & Mrs. McConnel, the founders of Avon. Issued by National Association of Avon Clubs. Only 1200 sets were sold. OSP $16.95 set. Original set came with McConnel & factory in center. Factory was too large so issued a second smaller factory on left. 1200 small factories made. CMV set with 1 factory & McConnel $30.00, CMV with both factories on left $45.00
RIGHT 1974 NAAC CPC FACTORY CLUB BOTTLE
3rd annual Club Bottle issued by the NAAC Clubs in honor of the 1st California Perfume Co. Factory in 1886. Came with a registration card. 4691 bottles were made the mold was broke at 3rd annual NAAC. Convention June 22, 1974 in Kansas City. OSP $11.95, CMV $50.00

1978 NAAC CLUB BOTTLE
7th Annual Club Bottle made in the image of the 1916 CPC Avon lady. She stands 7½" high with a rust colored coat and hat. Brown hair. Only 5022 were made. The bottle is numbered on the bottom and comes with a registration certificate. Made of hand painted porcelain. OSP $13.95, CMV $30.00 Club Sample was marked on the bottom of 125 club bottles given to each club in the NAAC. Sample bottles are same as regular issue only marked club sample. CMV $100.00

LEFT 1980 NAAC 1ST CONVENTION BOTTLE
Sold only NAAC club members. 1st in an annual series of NAAC Convention bottles to commemorate the annual NAAC convention in Spokane, Washington in 1980. 7½" high, lavender dress of 1890's style. Hand painted porcelain. This bottle is the only one in the series that the cork is in the head. The rest of the series will have a cork in the bottom to present a prettier bottle. Only 3593 were made & sold. OSP $14.95, CMV $30.00
RIGHT 1981 NAAC 2ND CONVENTION BOTTLE
2nd in an annual series of 11 bottles in 1890's style dress to commemorate the annual NAAC Avon convention in Anaheim, California. She is 7½" high with a yellow & green dress. Only the amount sold will be made & total number sold stamped on bottom. Sold only to members of NAAC clubs. Will be sold fall of 1980.
1981 CONVENTION CLUB SAMPLE
140 club sample bottles were made for NAAC clubs. Each marked club sample on bottom & numbered 140 edition. CMV $100.00 club sample

1980 PRESIDENTS GOLD SET
Set of six different president's busts, 22K gold plated. Will be issued by Bud Hastin & offered only to the members of Bud Hastin Avon Club late in 1980. Only 250 sets will be made & sold. Choice of 22K gold plate or antique brush gold finish sets.

1976 BUD HASTIN NATIONAL AVON CLUB BOTTLE
2nd issue. Hand painted porcelain made in the image of Mr. Dale Robinson, past director of National Association of Avon Clubs. 1000 bottles made & numbered. OSP $14.95, CMV $35.00

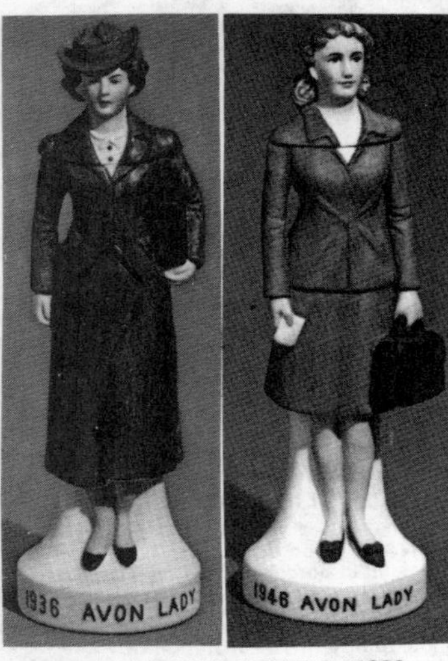

1980 NAAC CLUB BOTTLE "1936 AVON LADY"
9th annual club bottle. Purple dress, black bag. 7½" high. 4479 were made & sold, & numbered on the bottom as total sold. Did not come with certificate. OSP $14.95, CMV $25.00 Same bottle came with blue bag & marked club sample on bottom. 155 club samples were made & given to NAAC clubs. CMV $100.00 blue bag club sample.

1981 NAAC CLUB BOTTLE "1946 AVON LADY" 10th
Annual club bottle will be sold through the NAAC clubs January and February 1981. Only the amount sold will be made. Green dress, black bag. Club sample bottle. 140 Sample club bottles made and marked CLUB SAMPLE on bottom. CMV $100.00.

1976 BICENTENNIAL MINI AVON LADY SET No. 1
10 exact replicas in 3" high miniature figurines of the larger NAAC Club bottles. Issued by the Bud Hastin National Avon Club. 1775 sets were made and come with a numbered registration certificate. O.S.P. $60.00 for set of 10. C.M.V. $125.00 set M.B.

1974 BUD HASTIN NATIONAL AVON CLUB BOTTLE
1st issue Club Bottle by Bud Hastin Avon Club is a 3 piece Avon Family Scene. 3 separate bottles showing the Man, Child & Woman Avon Collectors. 1091 sets sold. OSP $45.00 per set. Sold in sets only. CMV $130.00 set.

1977 AVON LADY MINI SET No. 2
1265 sets of 11 miniature Avon ladies of the 1886-1900 period. Issued by the Bud Hastin National Avon Club in 1977. Set came in special display box. Came with numbered registration certificate. Sold only to Bud Hastins National Avon Club members. OSP $60.00 set, CMV $125.00 MB

Small World Display by Darlene Faulkner

CPC Display from the Onstot Collection

Special Limited Edition Avon Club Bottles

Special Limited Edition Avon Club Bottles

977 MINI RED HEAD SET
65 sets of Something Old - Something ew made. Issued by Bud Hastins ational Avon Club with registration ard. 3½" high, 1886 Avon lady on ft has green purse and red hair. 1975 von lady on right has red hair & Avon alling is misspelled on base of figurine. .S.P. $12.00 set. Sold as set only. .M.V. $25.00

974 GOLD COAST CLUB BOTTLE
ssued in honor of Mr. Bud Hastin for his contribution to the field of Avon collecting. st in an annual series. Only 2340 bottles were made. Bottle is 8½" high, white pants, naroon coat, black turtle neck shirt, black hoes. Few were made with white shirt. Rare. O.S.P. $11.95 C.M.V. black shirt 50.00 C.M.V. white shirt $110.00.

1976 GOLD COAST MINIS
A set of 3 miniature figurines 3½" high in the image of Bud Hastin, Jo Olsen, and Ron Price. The set sold 914 sets at $18.00 per set. C.M.V. $35.00 per set.

1975 WORLD WIDE JO OLSEN AVON CLUB BOTTLE
(Left) Light blue dress, black hair. 1102 bottles sold. Made in the image of Jo Olsen for her contribution to Avon collecting.
O.S.P. $12.95. C.M.V. $35.00.
1975 GOLD COAST RON PRICE CLUB BOTTLE
Green suit, brown hair and shoes. Holding book "Testing 1-2-3". 1096 bottles sold. Made in the image of Mr. Ron Price for his contribution to the field of Avon collecting. Mr. Ron Price was a member of Board of Directors of the NAAC. Mr. Price passed away in 1977. O.S.P. $12.95. C.M.V. $40.00.

1977 CLINT GOLD COAST CLUB BOTTLE
7 5/8" tall. Blue pants, shirt, jacket. Black shoes. Brown hair. 1264 made and numbered on the bottom. Also came with registration card. 4th Annual Club Bottle. O.S.P. $13.95 C.M.V. 27.50

1978 PRESIDENTS
A set of 6 3" high bust figurines of the 1st five presidents of the United States, plus Lincoln. Only 1050 sets made. Hand painted porcelain and came with a numbered registration card. Sold only to members of the the Bud Hastin National Avon Club. OSP for set of 6 $40.00, CMV $75.00
1978 PRESIDENTS "ALL WHITE"
Same set as painted presidents above only all white porcelain. Only 150 sets made. OSP $40.00, CMV $150.00 MB

1976 BETSY ROSS NAAC CONVENTION SOUVENIR
Given by Avon Products to all collectors touring Avon plant in Springdale, Ohio June 24, 1976. Special NAAC label on bottom. CMV $15.00 with special label.

1976 BETSY ROSS MOLD
Very rare steel mold given to Avon Collectors at 1976 NAAC Convention. Mold was cut into 5 pieces. Must have a letter from Avon Products stating it is 1 of a kind. CMV $500.00 with letter.

1975 THE KING II "FOR MEN"
Special label reads "Souvenir, June 19, 1975 NAAC Tour Monrovia Avon Plant" Given to each male taking the Avon plant tour at NAAC Convention. Monrovia, California. Only 150 bottles have this label. CMV $15.00
1975 SKIP A ROPE "FOR LADIES"
Same special label given to all ladies on same tour. CMV $15.00

1975 CALIFORNIA PERFUME ANNIVERSARY KEEPSAKE MOLD
This is the actual steel mold Avon used to make the 1975 Anniversary Keepsake bottle. Mr. Art Goodwin from Avon Products, Inc. New York presented this mold cut into 5 separate pieces to the National Association of Avon Clubs at the 4th annual NAAC Convention banquet at Anaheim, Calif. June 19, 1975. The mold was auctioned off bringing several hundred dollars on each piece. This is the 1st time a Avon mold has been destroyed & given to the general public. Very Rare. C.M.V. $600.00 each piece.

1976 ANNIVERSARY KEEPSAKE MOLD BASE
Steel base of Avons anniversary keepsake mold given to National Association of Avon Clubs by Avon Products and auctioned off to Avon collectors. The numbers (17) and 5215 on bottom. C.M.V. $500.00

1975-76 NAAC AVON CHESS BOARD
21½" square plastic chess board made for the Avon chess pieces. Silver & brown checker top with black rim border & back NAAC logo in center, silver over black. 105 were made for sample to each NAAC club with center gold logo over black. 1500 are numbered & last 1000 are not numbered on back. CMV gold logo $200.00 MB, CMV regular issue silver logo with number $70.00 MB black border no number, $50.00 MB, OSP $19.95 MB Also came brown border with large black logo in center. CMV $40.00 MB Last one to be issued had brown border & 4 small logos in center, brown back. CMV $40.00

1976-80 NAAC CONVENTION GOBLETS
Different color goblet sold each year at NAAC Convention. 1st year, red, 1976, 276 made. CMV $60.00. 1977, blue, 560 made. CMV $30.00. 1978, smoke, 560 made. CMV $20.00. 1979, clear, 576 made. CMV $15.00 1980, purple, 576 made. CMV $10.00. OSP was $4.00 to $6.00 each. 1978-79 a special marked goblet given to each NAAC delegate. CMV $25.00 Less than 100 delegate goblets made each year. Special marked goblets were made for each 7 NAAC board members. CMV no price established for board member goblet.

1975 PLATE - NAAC BOARD MEMBER
2" wide gold edge marked board member. Only 7 were issued. This was general issue plate. CMV $125.00
1975 PLATE - NAAC BOARD MEMBER
White plate with small gold edge marked board member. Only 7 were made. This plate was never issued to public. CMV $125.00

1979 NAAC PLATE "1896 AVON LADY"
Limited edition of 5000. Made by Avon Products exclusively for the NAAC. Came with gold edge & numbered on the back. CMV $35.00, and silver edge & no number. CMV $25.00. OSP $14.95 Sold only by NAAC clubs.

1980 NAAC PLATE "1916 AVON LAD
Limited edition of 4000. Came with gol edge & number on the back. 2060 made CMV not established yet. Or silver edg 1940 made, & no number. CMV not established. Made by Avon Products exclusively for the NAAC. OSP $14.95

1977 NAAC 6 YEAR PLATE
1886 Avon lady on plate. Made by Avo Products for the National Association of Avon Clubs. A beautiful china plate. To of 5000 were made with 1500 gold rimm and numbered. CMV $60.00 MB. 3500 were silver rimmed and not numbered. CMV $30.00 MB

1978 NAAC 7 YEAR PLATE
Made by Avon Products for the National Association of Avon Clubs. A beautiful china plate with a decal of t 1906 Avon Sales Lady. Only 5000 we made. OSP $14.95. 2310 were gold rimmed plates, CMV $40.00, and 2690 are silver rimmed plates, CMV $30.00

1976 3rd ANNUAL NAAC 5 YEAR AVON COLLECTORS PLATE
9 3/8" porcelain plate showing the 1st 4 NAAC club bottles. This plate is in beautiful colors and sure to be a real collectors item. 1755 were made. O.S.P. $13.95. C.M.V. $25.00 M.B.

1974 NAAC PLATE
1st in an annual series of plates. Clear crystal thumb print plate with blue & red background. Only 790 plates were made. O.S.P. $12.95. C.M.V. $50.00.
1974 NAAC BOARD MEMBER PLATE
Same as regular issue only have Board Member on plate. C.M.V. $100.00.

1973 CENTRAL VALLEY NAAC CONVENTION PLATE
Clear glass, frosted lettering. 124 were made and sold for 2nd annual NAAC convention at Sacremento, Calif. This plate was not made until 1975. O.S.P. $12.95 C.M.V. $25.00

1974 MID AMERICAN NAAC CONVENTION PLATE
Crystal plate with frosted inscription made in honor of the 3rd NAAC Convention by Mid America Club. 225 were made. O.S.P. $12.95 C.M.V. $30.00

NAAC CONVENTION PLATES
Made by Mid America Avon Club as the official NAAC Convention souvenir plate each year. Very low issue on each. All are etched clear glass & signed by the artist. OSP was $12.95 each. 1975 Orange County, CA - CMV $25.00
1977 Hollywood, FL - CMV $25.00
1978 Houston, TX - CMV $25.00
1979 ST. Louis, MO - CMV $25.00

1976 QUEEN CITY NAAC CONVENTION PLATE
Clear glass with frosted letters. O.S.P. $12.95 C.M.V. $20.00

1972 MID AMERICA NAAC CONVENTION PLATE
Clear glass with frosted lettering, 134 were made for the 1st annual NAAC convention in Kansas City, Kansas, June, 1972. This plate was not made until 1975. O.S.P. $12.95 C.M.V. $25.00

1975 NAAC CONVENTION PLATE
Only 250 made for 4th annual NAAC Convention, Anaheim, Calif. O.S.P. $12.95 C.M.V. $25.00

1975 NAAC PLATE
(Left) Sample plate never issued to general public. 84 were made and sent to each Avon Collectors Club in NAAC, numbered on the back. C.M.V. $100.00 each.
2nd ANNUAL 1975 NAAC PLATE
(Right) General issue plate Mr. & Mrs. McConnell founders of Avon in center, gold 2 inch band around edge. O.S.P. $12.95. C.M.V. $25.00
1975 NAAC BOARD MEMBER PLATE
Same as regular issue only has Board Member on front. only 7 were made. C.M.V. $100.00.

1977 NAAC CONVENTION DELIGATE PLATE
White china plate with the date & place of 6 NAAC Annual Conventions. Given to each NAAC Club deligate attending the convention "85 plates" CMV $50.00
7 board member plates were made the same only marked board member. CMV $75.00

1976 NAAC FREEDOM DOCUMENTS
Souvenir booklet sold by NAAC at Cincinnati, Ohio June 20-27 1976. CMV $5.00 mint

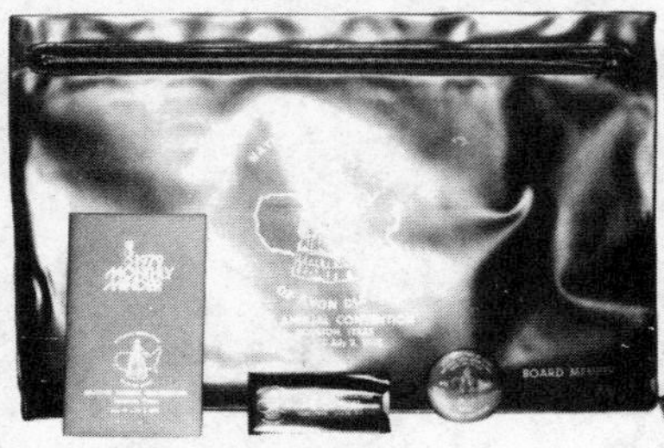

1978 NAAC CONVENTION SOUVENIRS
Convention Packet - green plastic. CMV $8.00
Monthly Minder 1979 - CMV $5.00
Magnifying Glass - CMV $1.00
All items given or sold at Houston, Texas 1978 NAAC Convention.

1979 NAAC CONVENTION SOUVENIRS
Each item was sold or given to collectors at annual St. Louis NAAC Convention. Most are very limited & hard to find.
Luggage Tag - CMV $2.00
Pen, brass - CMV $2.00
Monthly Minder Christmas 1980 - CMV $5.00
Matches NAAC - CMV 50c

1974-75 AVON ENCYCLOPEDIA HARD BOUND COLLECTOR'S EDITION
Only 1000 special limited collectors edition was printed. Blue hard bound cover with gold stamped letters on front. Eash is signed and numbered by Bud Hasti
O.S.P. $20.00 C.M.V. $32.50 mint.
1976-77 AVON ENCYCLOPEDIA HARD BOUND 2nd COLLECTORS EDITION
Only 500 special limited collectors edition were printed. Maroon hard bound cover with gold stamped letters on front. Each book is numbered and signed by Bud Hast
OSP $20.00, CMV $30.00 mint.
6 hard bounds were found with all pages upside down. Each was signed by Bud Hastin as 1 of 6 rare upside down books. Very rare. C.M.V. $40.00
1979 AVON ENCYCLOPEDIA HARD BOUND 3rd COLLECTORS EDITION
Only 350 special limited hard bound editions were printed. Blue hard bound covers with gold letters on front. Each bc will be signed and numbered by Bud Hasti
OSP $22.50, CMV $30.00

1974-75 NAAC STATIONARY
Blue box with NAAC logo on top. Back of box is signed by all board members of N.A.A.C. Only 214 boxes of stationary made & each is numbered. O.S.P. $7.00 C.M.V. $15.00 M.B.

LEFT 1976 NAAC CONVENTION BANQUET MIRROR
5th annual Avon collectors convention mirror in white with blue letters. Held in Cincinnati, Ohio June 25-27, 1976. Mirror on back. C.M.V. $10.00
1977 NAAC CONVENTION BANQUET MIRROR
6th annual Avon collectors convention mirror in blue with yellow letters. Mirror on back. Hollywood, Florida, June, 1977. C.M.V. $10.00

1974 NAAC CONVENTION SOUVENIER PIN
C.M.V. $2.00 Each year the mold for the annual NAAC club bottle is broken at the NAAC banquet and distributed to each person attending.
1974 Piece of mold and card for NAAC club bottle. Distributed at convention banquet. Overland Park, Kansas June 22, 1974. C.M.V. $10.00
1975 Piece of mold and card for NAAC club bottle. Distributed at convention banquet Anaheim, Calif. June 21, 1975. C.M.V. $10.00

1976 AVON ENCYCLOPEDIA COVER SHEET REJECTS
30,000 covers for the 1976 Avon Encyclopedia were printed with the word Encyclopedia spelled Encylopedia. The covers were never used but about 200 sheets were given to collectors with 4 covers and backs printed on a sheet. These sheets are rare. The rest of the covers were destroyed. C.M.V. $5.00 each sheet.

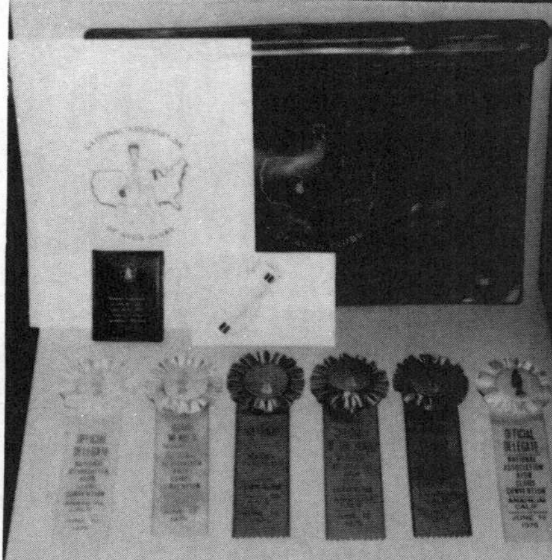

1975 NAAC CONVENTION SOUVENIERS
Given to each delegate and board member at NAAC Convention in Anaheim, Calif. June 19, 1975. Blue engraved plastic packet holds package of NAAC Stationery, Memo pad-blue (250 made C.M.V. $5.00), perfume nips on engraved card (250 made - C.M.V. $5.00) and yellow Delegate ribbon, Board Member nominee - grey ribbon, National Director - red ribbon, Chairman - purple ribbon, Board Member - green ribbon, Historian - white ribbon. C.M.V. $10.00 ea. ribbon

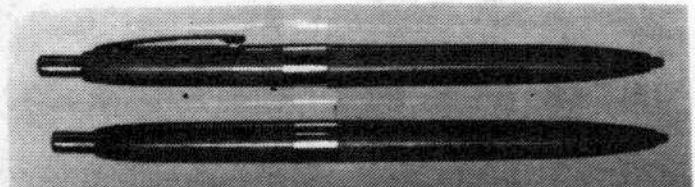

1973 NAAC CONVENTION SOUVENIERS
A few souvenier items were sold at the convention they are: matchbook, black letters on yellow cover: C.M.V. $1.00; a yellow ball point pen, with black lettering: C.M.V. $1.00; a green pennant with yellow letters that read "N.A.A.C. Convention 73": C.M.V. $1.50.

1977 NAAC CONVENTION SOUVENIERS
Each year at the annual NAAC Avon Collectors Convention a ribbon is given to each club deligate and each board member and alternate deligate. 1976 Cincinnati, Ohio ribbon has the 1896 Avon lady on the rosette. 1977 ribbon for Hollywood, Florida has the 1906 Avon lady. Also issued at the convention were book marks in white, green, blue, red; glass ash trays; pocket knife; NAAC in pin; Blue daily reminder book. We are not going to price these items as very few are around and you can only get them by attending the annual Collectors Convention. Prices will be set by public trading. A marble paper weight given by the Gold Coast Host Club is C.M.V. $15.00. .Piece of 1906 Avon lady club bottle mold & registration card was given. C.M.V. $10.00. NAAC plastic brief case with logo.

1979 ST. LOUIE BLUE PERFUME
Small glass bottle, white cap. Special perfume made & given by Mid America Avon Club at NAAC Convention in St. Louis, June 1979. 231 bottles with registration card & envelope. CMV $20.00 mint & about 120 bottles only given without envelope & card. CMV $10.00 BO

1972 N.A.A.C. CONVENTION MIRROR
Only 300 made, given at banquet, also some were made with pins instead of mirrors. These were dealers badges. C.M.V. $25.00 ea.

1974 N.A.A.C. CONVENTION BANQUET MIRROR
Yellow and black, mirror on backside. Convention held in Kansas City, Mo. June 22, 1974. C.M.V. $15.00
1975 N.A.A.C. CONVENTION BANQUET MIRROR
Blue and black, mirror on back. Convention held in Anaheim, Calif. June 21, 1975. C.M.V. $10.00 Both were given to each person attending the annual N.A.A.C. Avon Convention Banquet.

1973 CONVENTION, DELEGATES RIBBON
A red ribbon with a red rosette was given to all delegates. The rosette has a white button in the center with the McConnell bottle outlined in gold. The gold printing on the ribbon reads "Official Delegate National Association Avon Clubs Convention Sacremento, California, June 22, 1973. C.M.V. $8.00
1973 CONVENTION BOARD MEMBER RIBBON
Same as the delegate ribbon only in blue instead of red. Board member replaced the Official Delegate on the ribbon. C.M.V. $15.00
1973 CONVENTION NATIONAL CHAIRMAN RIBBON
Same as the Delegate ribbon only in maroon instead of red. National Chairman eplaced the Official Delegate on the ribbon. Only one of these ribbons was made. It is owned by Mr. Bud Hastin. No value established.
1972 NAAC CONVENTION SOUVENIER BADGE
Round, light blue background with FIRST CPC Lady in center. Has pin back. C.M.V. $10.00
1973 NAAC CONVENTION SOUVENIER BADGE
(Not shown) Same except has photo of Mr. & Mrs. McConnell. C.M.V. $5.00

1978 NAAC CONVENTION BANQUET MIRROR
Purple with mirror on back. Given to over 500 who attended the Avon Collectors Convention Banquet in Houston, Texas June 1978. CMV $10.00
1979 NAAC CONVENTION BANQUET MIRROR
White & red, mirror on back. Given to over 500 people attending the annual Avon Collectors Convention Banquet in St. Louis, MO June 1979. CMV $10.00

QUICK REFERENCE INDEX

AN AID TO FINDING CATEGORIES QUICKLY

ALPHABETICAL INDEX

If you cannot find the items you are looking for in this alphabetical index, check the Quick Reference Index in which it falls.

— A —

— B —

— C —

— D —

— E —

— F —

— I —

— J —

— K —

— L —

— P —

— T —

— U —

— V —

— W —

NOTES

NOTES

NOTES

NOTES

NOTES

ORDER FORM

POSTPAID FOURTH CLASS MAIL — 1981 Avon Encyclopedia of 11,000 Avons. Add $4.50 for First Class Postage in U.S. per book, Canada, add $4.75 postage for First Class per book. (First Class Mail - Money Order Only)

Money Orders — Your order is filled immediately. Personal Checks — Order is held till check has cleared your bank. SORRY NO C.O.D.'S OR CHARGES.

☐ **Quantity Ordered**

$18.95 U.S.A.

$19.95 Canada — U.S. Funds Money Orders Only

☐ 1 year's membership in Bud Hastin's National Avon Club $11.00 (U.S.) $11.00 (Canada). U.S. funds Money Orders only.

☐ Send me a 1981 Avon Encyclopedia and enroll me for 1 year in the National Avon Club for $26.00, a $3.95 savings. Canada $27.00.

PLEASE MAIL TO:

NAME ______________________

ADDRESS ______________________

CITY ______________ STATE ______________

ZIP ______________

DISCOUNT TABLE

The following discounts are for Avon Ladies, book and bottle dealers, Avon Clubs, and anyone else who feels he or she can sell my books to other collectors.

AVON ENCYCLOPEDIA	U.S.A.	CANADA
1 - 5	$18.95 ea.	$19.95 ea
6 - 11	14.00ea.	.15.00 ea
12 to 107	12.00ea.	.13.00 ea
108 up	10.50 (U.S. orders only on 100 or more.)	

Please Add 4% Sales Tax

ORDER NOW—

from BUD HASTIN
P.O. Box 8400, Ft. Lauderdale, FL 33310

All books postpaid Fourth Class Mail
Master Charge & Visa Accepted
(send card number and expiration date)

ALL PRICES SUBJECT TO CHANGE WITHOUT NOTICE — ALL SALES FINAL

* PLEASE NOTE NEW FLORIDA ADDRESS *

Books sent immediately when ordered by Visa, Master Charge, or Money Order. Orders paid by check will be held up to 40 days for bank clearance before shipping.

(Allow 6 weeks on checks for deliveries.)

NO ORDERS SHIPPED TILL CHECKS CLEAR!

ORDER FORM

POSTPAID FOURTH CLASS MAIL — 1981 Avon Encyclopedia of 11,000 Avons. Add $4.50 for First Class Postage in U.S. per book, Canada, add $4.75 postage for First Class per book. (First Class Mail - Money Order Only)

Money Orders — Your order is filled immediately. Personal Checks — Order is held till check has cleared your bank. SORRY NO C.O.D.'S OR CHARGES.

☐ **Quantity Ordered**

$18.95 U.S.A.

$19.95 Canada — U.S. Funds Money Orders Only

☐ 1 year's membership in Bud Hastin's National Avon Club $11.00 (U.S.) $11.00 (Canada). U.S. funds Money Orders only.

☐ Send me a 1981 Avon Encyclopedia and enroll me for 1 year in the National Avon Club for $26.00, a $3.95 savings. Canada $27.00.

PLEASE MAIL TO:

NAME ______________________

ADDRESS ______________________

CITY ______________ STATE ______________

ZIP ______________

DISCOUNT TABLE

The following discounts are for Avon Ladies, book and bottle dealers, Avon Clubs, and anyone else who feels he or she can sell my books to other collectors.

AVON ENCYCLOPEDIA	U.S.A.	CANADA
1 - 5	$18.95 ea.	$19.95 ea
6 - 11	14.00ea.	.15.00 ea
12 to 107	12.00ea.	.13.00 ea
108 up	10.50 (U.S. orders only on 100 or more.)	

Please Add 4% Sales Tax

ORDER NOW—

from BUD HASTIN
P.O. Box 8400, Ft. Lauderdale, FL 33310

All books postpaid Fourth Class Mail
Master Charge & Visa Accepted
(send card number and expiration date)

ALL PRICES SUBJECT TO CHANGE WITHOUT NOTICE — ALL SALES FINAL

ORDER FORM

POSTPAID FOURTH CLASS MAIL — 1981 Avon Encyclopedia of 11,000 Avons. Add $4.50 for First Class Postage in U.S. per book, Canada, add $4.75 postage for First Class per book. (First Class Mail - Money Order Only)

Money Orders — Your order is filled immediately. Personal Checks — Order is held till check has cleared your bank. SORRY NO C.O.D.'S OR CHARGES.

☐ **Quantity Ordered**

$18.95 **U.S.A.**

$19.95 **Canada** **U.S. Funds Money Orders Only**

☐ 1 year's membership in Bud Hastin's National Avon Club $11.00 (U.S.) $11.00 (Canada). U.S. funds Money Orders only.

☐ Send me a 1981 Avon Encyclopedia and enroll me for 1 year in the National Avon Club for $26.00, a $3.95 savings. Canada $27.00.

PLEASE MAIL TO:

NAME ____________________

ADDRESS ____________________

CITY ____________ STATE ____________

ZIP ____________

DISCOUNT TABLE

The following discounts are for Avon Ladies, book and bottle dealers, Avon Clubs, and anyone else who feels he or she can sell my books to other collectors.

AVON ENCYCLOPEDIA	U.S.A.	CANADA
1 - 5	$18.95 ea.	$19.95 ea
6 - 11	14.00ea.	.15.00 ea
12 to 107	12.00ea.	.13.00 ea
108 up	10.50 (U.S. orders only on 100 or more.)	

Please Add 4% Sales Tax

ORDER NOW

from BUD HASTIN
P.O. Box 8400, Ft. Lauderdale, FL 33310

All books postpaid Fourth Class Mail
Master Charge & Visa Accepted
(send card number and expiration date)

ALL PRICES SUBJECT TO CHANGE WITHOUT NOTICE — ALL SALES FINAL

* PLEASE NOTE NEW FLORIDA ADDRESS *

Books sent immediately when ordered by Visa, Master Charge, or Money Order. Orders paid by check will be held up to 40 days for bank clearance before shipping.

(Allow 6 weeks on checks for deliveries.)

NO ORDERS SHIPPED TILL CHECKS CLEAR!

ORDER FORM

POSTPAID FOURTH CLASS MAIL — 1981 Avon Encyclopedia of 11,000 Avons. Add $4.50 for First Class Postage in U.S. per book, Canada, add $4.75 postage for First Class per book. (First Class Mail - Money Order Only)

Money Orders — Your order is filled immediately. Personal Checks — Order is held till check has cleared your bank. SORRY NO C.O.D.'S OR CHARGES.

☐ **Quantity Ordered**

$18.95 **U.S.A.**

$19.95 **Canada** **U.S. Funds Money Orders Only**

☐ 1 year's membership in Bud Hastin's National Avon Club $11.00 (U.S.) $11.00 (Canada). U.S. funds Money Orders only.

☐ Send me a 1981 Avon Encyclopedia and enroll me for 1 year in the National Avon Club for $26.00, a $3.95 savings. Canada $27.00.

PLEASE MAIL TO:

NAME ____________________

ADDRESS ____________________

CITY ____________ STATE ____________

ZIP ____________

DISCOUNT TABLE

The following discounts are for Avon Ladies, book and bottle dealers, Avon Clubs, and anyone else who feels he or she can sell my books to other collectors.

AVON ENCYCLOPEDIA	U.S.A.	CANADA
1 - 5	$18.95 ea.	$19.95 ea
6 - 11	14.00ea.	.15.00 ea
12 to 107	12.00ea.	.13.00 ea
108 up	10.50 (U.S. orders only on 100 or more.)	

Please Add 4% Sales Tax

ORDER NOW

from BUD HASTIN
P.O. Box 8400, Ft. Lauderdale, FL 33310

All books postpaid Fourth Class Mail
Master Charge & Visa Accepted
(send card number and expiration date)

ALL PRICES SUBJECT TO CHANGE WITHOUT NOTICE — ALL SALES FINAL

Avon Times

MEMBER NATIONAL ASSOCIATION OF AVON CLUBS

Publisher, Bud Hastin — Shirley Rhoads, Editor

Vol. 9 - No. 3 — JUNE 1980

Mt. St. Helens Or Bust!

Spokane, Here We Come!

Bud & Vickie

AVONS FROM AROUND ...

Classified Advertising

Type or print clearly all Ad Copy; we are not responsible for errors in ads due to handwritten copy.

Advertising Abbreviations

Avon Times

MEMBER NATIONAL ASSOCIATION OF AVON CLUBS

Publisher, Bud Hastin — Shirley Rhoads, Editor

Vol. 9 - No. 2 — MAY 1980

"Avon Calling"– Hong Kong Style

By Bud Hastin

Ruth Shang, Avon District Sales Manager ... product testing area

Free Bonus Advertising Offer

Dear Avoners

With the 1981 edition of Bud Hastin's Avon Encyclopedia, you now own the finest book ever published on Avon Collectibles.

Even more information is available to you through the "Avon Times". This is the world's largest publication on Avon collecting, published monthly by the Bud Hastin National Avon Club.

We would like to offer you this chance to advertise in a 30 word maximum "FREE" ad; to buy, sell, or trade your Avon collectibles in the "Times".

You must send this coupon (a $4.50 value) from this book, along with $1.00 to cover postage and handling to: Bud Hastin, P.O. Box 8400, Ft. Lauderdale, FL 33310.

We will also mail you a free sample copy of the "Avon Times" in which your ad appears. All ads over 30 words, please send 15c per word.

Your subscription to "Avon Times" would be welcomed. The rates are $11.00 for 12 issues sent First Class mail. Subscribe today, and see why we are the world's largest Avon Club. You will receive $22.50 worth of "Free Ad Coupons" with each subscription.

CUT ALONG LINE

CUT ALONG LINE

Here is my 30 word "Free Ad" to run in your next issue of "Avon Times". Enclosed is $1.00 to cover the postage and handling to mail me an issue in which my "Free Ad" appears.

PLEASE PRINT PLAINLY

____

____

____

____

____

Name __________________________________

Address ________________________________

City ________________ State ______ Zip ________

This offer subject to change or revocation without notice. No Free Ads will be accepted that are not on this order form. Send to:

BUD HASTIN

P.O. Box 8400 **Ft. Lauderdale, FL 33310**